D1074281

COMPILER
DESIGN
IN
C

COMPILER DESIGN IN C

Allen I. Holub

Prentice Hall Software Series
Brian W. Kernighan, Editor

PRENTICE HALL
Englewood Cliffs, New Jersey 07632

Library of Congress Cataloging-in-Publication Data

Holub, Allen I.
    Compiler design in C / Allen I. Holub.
        p.   cm. -- (Prentice-Hall software series)
    Includes bibliographical references.
    ISBN 0-13-155045-4
    1. Compilers (Computer programs) 2. C (Computer program language)
I. Title. II. Series.
QA76.76.C65H65 1990
005.4'53--dc20   89-38733
                                                                     CIP

Editorial/Production supervision: Kathleen Schiaparelli
Cover design: Allen I. Holub and Lundgren Graphics Ltd.
Manufacturing buyer: Margaret Rizzi

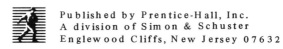

Published by Prentice-Hall, Inc.
A division of Simon & Schuster
Englewood Cliffs, New Jersey 07632

Trademark Acknowledgments: TEX is a Trademark of the American Mathematical Society. L^{E}X, because it is a visual pun on TEX is used with the kind permission of Donald Knuth. There is no other connection between either Dr. Knuth or the AMS and the programs or text in this book. L^{E}X, **occs, LLama, autopic,** and **arachne** are all trademarks of Allen I. Holub. UNIX is a trademark of Bell Laboratories. MS-DOS, Microsoft, and QuickC are trademarks of Microsoft, Inc. Turbo-C is a trademark of Borland, Inc. PostScript is a trademark of Adobe Systems. AutoCad and AutoSketch are trademarks of AutoDesk, Inc. EROFF is a trademark of the Elan Computer Group. DEC, PDP, and VAX are trademarks of Digital Equipment Corporation. **Macintosh** is a trademark of Apple Computer, Inc.

LIMITS OF LIABILITY AND DISCLAIMER OF WARRANTY: The author and publisher have used their best efforts in preparing this book. These efforts include the development, research, and testing of the theories and programs to determine their effectiveness. The author and publisher make no warranty of any kind, expressed or implied, with regard to these programs or the documentation contained in this book. The author and publisher shall not be liable in any event for incidental or consequential damages in connection with, or arising out of, the furnishing, performance, or use of these programs.

Printed in the United States of America

10 9 8 7 6 5 4 3 2 1

ISBN 0-13-155045-4

Prentice-Hall International (UK) Limited, *London*
Prentice-Hall of Australia Pty. Limited, *Sydney*
Prentice-Hall Canada Inc., *Toronto*
Prentice-Hall Hispanoamericana, S.A., *Mexico*
Prentice-Hall of India Private Limited, *New Delhi*
Prentice-Hall of Japan, Inc., *Tokyo*
Simon & Schuster Asia Pte. Ltd., *Singapore*
Editora Prentice-Hall do Brasil, Ltda, *Rio de Janeiro*

For Deirdre

Contents

Preface

This book presents the subject of Compiler Design in a way that's understandable to a programmer, rather than a mathematician. My basic premise is that the best way to learn how to write a compiler is to look at one in depth; the best way to understand the theory is to build tools that use that theory for practical ends. So, this book is built around working code that provides immediate practical examples of how given theories are applied. I have deliberately avoided mathematical notation, foreign to many programmers, in favor of English descriptions of the theory and using the code itself to explain a process. If a theoretical discussion isn't clear, you can look at the code that implements the theory. I make no claims that the code presented here is the only (or the best) implementation of the concepts presented. I've found, however, that looking at an implementation—at any implementation—can be a very useful adjunct to understanding the theory, and the reader is well able to adapt the concepts presented here to alternate implementations.

The disadvantage of my approach is that there is, by necessity, a tremendous amount of low-level detail in this book. It is my belief, however, that this detail is both critically important to understanding how to actually build a real compiler, and is missing from virtually every other book on the subject. Similarly, a lot of the low-level details are more related to program implementation in general than to compilers in particular. One of the secondary reasons for learning how to build a compiler, however, is to learn how to put together a large and complex program, and presenting complete programs, rather than just the directly compiler-related portions of those programs, furthers this end. I've resolved the too-many-details problem, to some extent, by isolating the theoretical materials into their own sections, all marked with asterisks in the table of contents and in the header on the top of the page. If you aren't interested in the nuts and bolts, you can just skip over the sections that discuss code.

In general, I've opted for clarity in the code rather than cleverness or theoretical efficiency. That is, since the main purpose of this book is to teach compiler-design concepts, it seemed reasonable always to go with a more understandable algorithm rather than an efficient but opaque algorithm. For example, I've used Thompson's Construction to make DFA's in L^{E}X rather than the more direct approach recommended in Aho's book, because Thompson's construction is more understandable (it also introduces certain key concepts [like closure], in a relatively easy-to-understand context). My method for computing LALR(1) lookaheads is also less efficient than it could be, but the algorithm is understandable and fast enough. I usually point the reader to the source for the more efficient algorithms, should he or she want to implement them.

In a sense, this book is really an in-depth presentation of several, very well documented programs: the complete sources for three compiler-generation tools are presented, as is a complete C compiler. (A lexical-analyzer generator modeled after the UNIX **lex** utility is presented along with two **yacc**-like compiler compilers.) As such, it is more of a compiler-engineering book than are most texts—a strong emphasis is placed on teaching you how to write a real compiler. On the other hand, a lot of theory is covered on the way to understanding the practice, and this theory is central to the discussion. Though I've presented complete implementations of the programs as an aid to understanding, the implementation details aren't nearly as important as the processes that are used by those programs to do what they do. It's important that you be able to apply these processes to your own programs.

The utilities are designed to be used as a learning aid. For example, **LLama** and **occs** (the two compiler compilers) can create an interactive window-oriented debugging environment, incorporating a "visible parser" that lets you watch the parse process in action. (One window shows the state and value stacks, others show the input, output, and a running commentary of what the parser's doing.) You can see the parse stack grow and shrink, watch attributes being inherited and synthesized, set breakpoints on certain conditions (a token being input, reduction by a particular production, a certain symbol on the top of stack, and so forth), and if necessary, log the entire parse (including snapshots of the stack) to a file. I've found that actually watching a bottom-up parse in action helps considerably in understanding how the parse process works, and I regularly use this visible parser in the classroom to good effect.

The C Compiler presented in Chapter Six implements an ANSI-compatible subset of C—I've left out a few things like floating point which would make the chapter even larger than it is without adding any significant value. I have tried to cover all of the hard implementation details that are usually omitted from books such as the present one. For example, the complete declaration syntax of C is supported, including structures and declarations of arbitrary complexity. Similarly, block nesting of declarations and the more complex control structures, such as switches, are also covered.

All the source code presented here is ANSI C, and is all portable to UNIX as well. For example, window management is done on the IBM-PC by emulating a standard UNIX window-management package (curses). The complete source code for the emulator is provided. All of the software is available electronically—versions are available for the UNIX, MS-DOS, and Macintosh environments.

I'm assuming throughout this book that you will actually read the code as well as the prose descriptions of the code. I don't waste space in the text discussing implementation details that are described adequately by the code itself. I do, however, use a lot of space describing the nonobvious parts of the programs.

Prerequisites

The primary prerequisite for using this book is a thorough knowledge of ANSI C in particular and programming in general. You should be familiar both with the language itself and with the standard library functions described in the ANSI standard.

I've used structured programming techniques throughout the book, and have made heavy use of data abstraction and similar techniques, but I haven't described what these techniques are or why I'm using them. The more complicated data structures are explained thoroughly in the text, but a previous knowledge of basic data structures like stacks and binary trees is assumed throughout. Similarly, a knowledge of basic set theory and a familiarity with graphs is also useful. Finally, familiarity with assembly-language concepts (like how a subroutine-call works) is mandatory, but an in-depth knowledge of a specific assembly language is not required (because I've used a C subset for generated code rather than assembly language).

Though a knowledge of C is mandatory, a knowledge of UNIX or MS-DOS is not. This book is UNIX oriented only in that several UNIX tools are constructed. The tools were all developed on an IBM-PC and run nicely in that environment. By the same token, several MS-DOS implementation details and portability concerns are discussed in depth here, but I've been careful to make the code itself as portable as possible. The only potential confusion for non-UNIX users is in Appendixes D and E, where differences between my own programs and the UNIX versions are occasionally mentioned in footnotes. Just ignore these notes if you're not going to use the UNIX tools.

The book is organized so that you can use it in two ways. If you have no interest in theory and just want to build a compiler, an overview of compiler design in general is presented in Chapter One, instructions for using the compiler construction tools (LEX and **occs**) are in Appendixes D and E, and code generation is discussed in Chapter Six. With these chapters behind you, you can get to the business of writing a compiler immediately, and go back later and absorb the theory.

Organization

A more rigorous approach goes through the book sequentially. You don't have to read every word of every chapter—if you're not interested in the nuts-and-bolts, just skip past those sections that describe the programs' inner workings. I'd strongly suggest reading the code, however, and reading Appendixes D and E before leaping into the text that describes these programs.

Various support functions that are used internally by the programs are concentrated in Appendix A. Covered functions do set manipulation, window management, and so forth. I've put them in one place so that the rest of the book isn't cluttered with function descriptions that aren't germane to the discussion at hand. This appendix shouldn't be viewed as an adjunct, however. The functions described in it are used heavily throughout the rest of the book, and you should be familiar with them—or at least with their calling syntax—before trying to read any of the other code.

One major organizational issue is the positioning of the theoretical and practical parts of the book. It's tempting to put all the theoretical material together at the head of each chapter so that you can skip past implementation details if you're not interested. I've opted, however, to intermix theoretical material with actual code because an examination of the code can often clarify things on the theoretical side. As I mentioned earlier, I've resolved the problem, somewhat, by isolating the theoretical material into individual sections. I often discuss the theory in one section and put a practical implementation in the following section. The theoretical sections in chapters that mix theoretical and practical material are marked with asterisks in the table of contents. This way you can skip past the implementation-related material with little difficulty, should you desire to do so.

A few compiler-related subjects are not covered here. Optimization is not discussed beyond the overview presented in Chapter Seven—I discuss how various optimizations move the code around, but I don't discuss the mechanics of optimization itself beyond a few, simple examples. Similarly, only the most common parse strategies are discussed (operator-precedence parsing is not mentioned, for example). All the material usually covered in an upper-division, undergraduate compiler-design course is covered here.

All the code in this book is written in ANSI C (I've used the Microsoft C compiler, version 5.1, for development purposes). For the most part, the MS-DOS code can be converted to the UNIX compiler by changing a few **#define**s before compiling. The disk that contains the code (see below) is shipped with the source of a small UNIX preprocessor that handles other conversion details (it does string concatenation, token pasting, etc.), and the output of this preprocessor can be submitted directly to UNIX **cc**. I'm assuming that the UNIX compiler supports those ANSI features that are implemented in most UNIX systems (like structure assignment).

Source Code and Portability

If you intend to use the code directly (without UNIX preprocessing), you'll need an ANSI-compatible compiler that supports function prototypes, and so forth. In particular:

- *<stdarg.h>* is used for variable-argument lists.
- white space around the **#** in a preprocessor directive must be permitted.
- structure assignment is used.
- **unsigned char** must be supported.
- function prototypes are used heavily.
- isdigit(), etc., may not have side effects.
- string concatenation is used in a few places.
- 16-character names must be permitted.

My only deviation from strict ANSI is in name lengths. In theory ANSI allows only six characters in an external name but I'm assuming that 16 are supported. I am also using the old, Kernighan & Ritchie style, subroutine-declaration syntax:

```
lorenzo( arg1, arg2 )
char    *arg1;
double  *arg2;
```

rather than:

```
lorenzo( char *arg1, double *arg2 )
```

I've done this because many compilers do not yet support the new syntax, and the old syntax is still legal in the standard (even though it's declared obsolescent).

I've deliberately avoided using special features of the Microsoft compiler: I've ignored things like the existence of the **far** keyword and **huge** pointers in favor of using the compact model even though the foregoing would make some of the code more efficient. By the same token, I haven't used **register** variables because the Microsoft compiler does a better job of assigning registers than I can do myself.

Unfortunately, the 8086 has an architecture that forces you to worry about the underlying machine on a regular basis, so the code has a certain amount of 8086-specific details. All of these details are isolated into macros, however, so that it's easy to port the code to a different environment by changing the macros and recompiling. I do discuss the foibles of the 8086 here and there; just skip over this material if you're not interested.

Getting the Code

All of the source code in this book—along with executable versions of L^{E}X, **LLama**, and **occs**—is available on disk from:

Software Engineering Consultants
P.O. Box 5679
Berkeley, California 94705
(415) 540-7954

The software is available right now for the IBM-PC and UNIX. (The UNIX version is shipped on an IBM-PC, 5-1/4 disk, however. You'll have to upload it using KERMIT or some other file-transfer protocol. It has been tested under UNIX System V, BSD 4.3—I can't vouch for any other UNIX variant.) The cost is $60.00 by a check or money order drawn on a U.S. bank. Please specify the disk size (5¼" or 3½"). California residents must add local sales tax. No credit cards (sorry). A Macintosh version will be available eventually. Binary site licenses are available for educational institutions.

Bug Reports and Electronic Mail

The code in this book is bound to have a few bugs in it, though I've done my best to test it as thoroughly as possible. The version distributed on disk will always be the most recent. If you find a bug, please report it to me, either at the above address, or electronically via Internet or UUCP (my electronic address is *holub@violet.berkeley.edu* or *...!ucbvax!violet!holub*).

The UNIX USENET network is the official channel for bug fixes and general discussion of the material in this book. The *comp.compilers* newsgroup should be used for this purpose. USENET messages have a way of filtering over to other networks, like BIX, but the best way to get up-to-date information is via USENET itself. Most universities are connected to this network, and you can get access to it by getting an account on a machine at a local university. (Most schools have a mechanism for people in the community to get such accounts.) I'd prefer for all postings to be sent to me—I'll digest them and post them to *comp.compilers* via its moderator. If you want to make a submission to *comp.compilers* directly, you have to mail it to the moderator, who will post it to the network. Type *help bboard usenet moderators* to get his or her name.

Acknowledgments

This book was written largely because my students found the "standard" text— Alfred Aho, Ravi Sethi, and Jeffrey Ullman's excellent, but at times abstruse *Compilers: Principles, Techniques, and Tools*—to be too theoretically oriented. The current volume owes a lot to Aho et al, however. I've used many of their algorithms, and their insights into the compiler-design practice are invaluable. I'm also indebted to Mike Lesk, Eric Schmidt, and Steve Johnson, the creators of UNIX's **lex** and **yacc** utilities, after which the programs in this book are modeled. My neighbor, Bill Wong, provided invaluable comments on the early drafts of this book, as did many of my students. Finally, I'm grateful to Brian Kernighan, Johnson M. Hart, Andrew Appel, Norman C. Hutchinson, and N.H. Madhavji (of Bell Labs, Boston University, Princeton University, The University of Arizona, and McGill University respectively) all of whom reviewed this book before it went to press. Their comments and suggestions have made this a much better book. I am particularly indebted to Brian Kernighan, whose careful scrutiny of the entire book—both the text and the code—caught many errors that otherwise would have made it into print.

Allen Holub
Berkeley, California

Typesetting Notes

This book was typeset on an IBM PC/AT using EROFF™, a version of the UNIX **troff** typesetter ported to MS-DOS by the Elan Computer Group. PostScript Times Roman and Italic were used for the text, Helvetica for chapter headings, and Courier, Courier Bold, and Courier Italic for the listings. Page proofs were generated using an Apple Laser-Writer, and the final typesetting was done on a Linotronic phototypesetter using EROFF-generated PostScript. The following command line was used throughout:

```
arachne file... | autopic | tbl | troff -mm
```

The arachne preprocessor is a version of Knuth's WEB documentation system that's tailored for C and **troff** (rather than Pascal and TEX). It runs under MS-DOS on an IBM-PC. With it, you can put the code and documentation together in a single input file. Used one way, it extracts the code and writes it out to the correct files for compilation. In a second mode it processes the code for **troff**, performing the necessary font changes, and so forth, needed to "pretty print" the code. It also automatically generates index entries for subroutine declarations. It adds line numbers to the listings and lets you reference these line numbers symbolically from the text (that is, you can add lines to the listings and the line numbers in the text automatically adjust themselves). Finally, it lets you discuss global variables and so forth where they're used, because it automatically moves them to the top of the output C program.

The second preprocessor, **autopic**, translates drawings generated by two commercially available drafting programs (AutoCad™ and AutoSketch™) into **troff** graphics primitives. It is much more useful that **pic** in that you have both a WYSIWYG capability and a much more powerful drawing system at your disposal. Since **troff** commands are generated as **autopic** output, the drawings are readily portable to any **troff** system.

Autopic and **arachne** are both compilers, and as such serve as an example of how you can apply the techniques presented in this book to applications other than writing compilers for standard programming languages. MS-DOS versions of **autopic** and **arachne** are available from Software Engineering at the address given earlier. Write for details.

1

Basic Concepts

This chapter introduces the basic concepts of compiler design. I'll discuss the internal organization of a compiler, introduce formal grammars and parse trees, and build a small recursive-descent expression compiler. Before leaping into the text, however, a word of encouragement, both about this chapter and the book in general, seems in order. Compilers are not particularly difficult programs to understand once you're familiar with the structure of a compiler in a general sort of way. The main problem is not that any one part of a compiler is hard to understand; but, rather, that there are so many parts— and you need to have absorbed most of these parts before any of them make sense. For now, my advice is to forge ahead without trying to figure out how it all ties together. You'll find that you will eventually reach a "click point" where the system as a whole suddenly makes sense.

1.1 The Parts of a Compiler

Compilers are complex programs. As a consequence, they're often broken into several distinct chunks, called *passes*, that communicate with one another via temporary files. The passes themselves are only part of the compilation process, however. The process of creating an executable image from a source-code file can involve several stages other than compilation (preprocessing, assembly, linking, and so forth). In fact, some operating systems (such as Microsoft's OS/2) can delay the final creation of an executable image until a program is actually loaded at run-time. The situation is muddled further by driver programs like UNIX's **cc** or Microsoft C's **cl**, which hide a good deal of the compilation process from you. These driver programs act as executives, controlling the various component programs that make up the compiler in such a way that you don't know that the components are being used. For the purposes of this book, I'll define a compiler as a program or group of programs that translates one language into another— in this case the source code of a high-level computer language is translated into assembly language. The assembler, linker, and so forth are not considered to be part of the compiler.

The structure of a typical four-pass compiler is shown in Figure 1.1. The preprocessor is the first pass. Preprocessors typically do macro substitutions, strip comments from the source code, and handle various housekeeping tasks with which you don't want to

Compiler passes.

'Compiler' defined.

Structure of a four-pass compiler.

1

Figure 1.1. Structure of a Typical Four-Pass Compiler

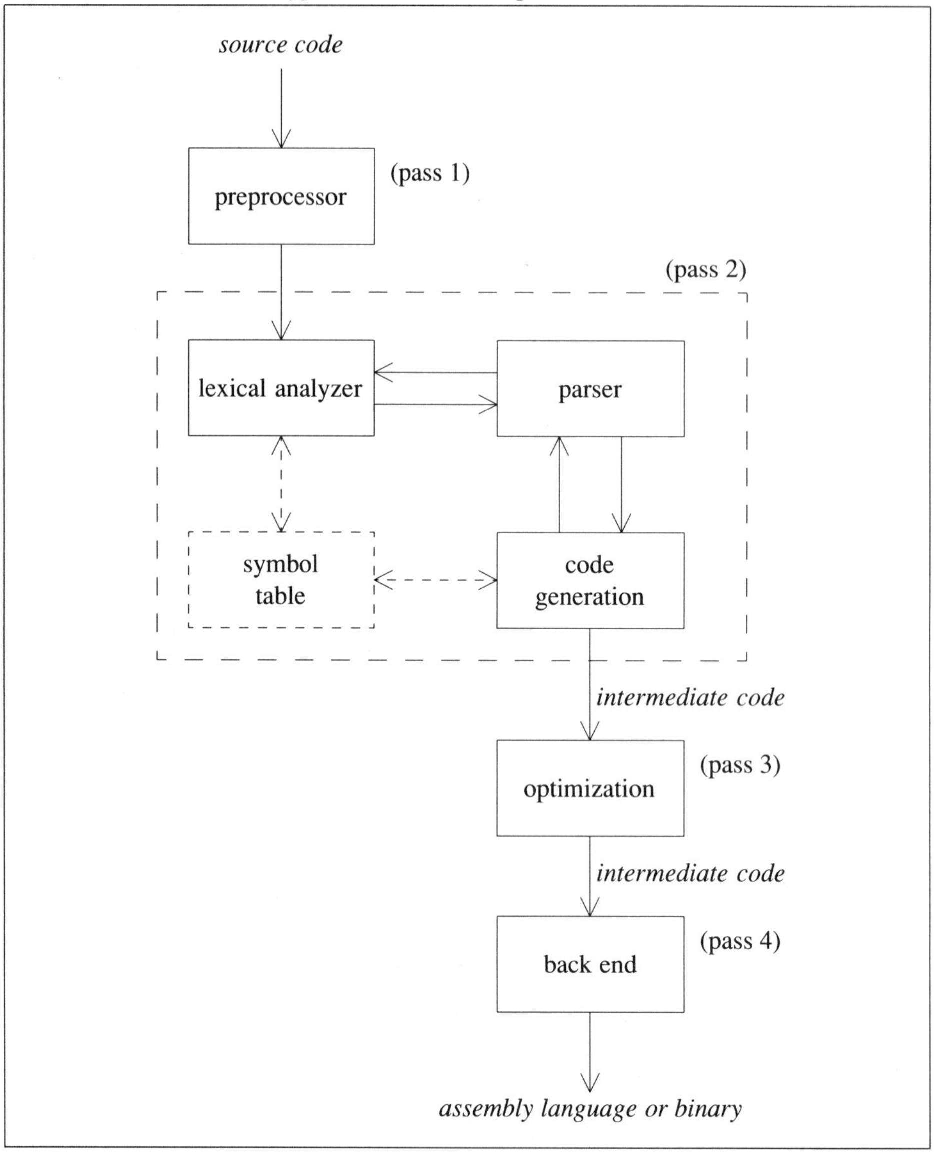

burden the compiler proper. The second pass is the heart of the compiler. It is made up of a lexical analyzer, parser, and code generator, and it translates the source code into an intermediate language that is much like assembly language. The third pass is the optimizer, which improves the quality of the generated intermediate code, and the fourth pass, the *back end*, translates the optimized code to real assembly language or some form of binary, executable code. Of course, there are many variations to this structure. Many compilers don't have preprocessors; others generate assembly language in the second pass, optimize the assembly language directly, and don't have a fourth pass; still others generate binary instructions directly, without going through an ASCII intermediate language like assembler.

The back end.

This book concentrates on the second pass of our model. There are several operations here too, but they interact in more complicated ways than the higher-level passes, and they share data structures (such as the symbol table) as well.

1.1.1 The Lexical Analyzer

A *phase* is an independent task used in the compilation process. Typically, several phases are combined into a single pass. The *lexical analyzer* phase of a compiler (often called a *scanner* or *tokenizer*) translates the input into a form that's more useable by the rest of the compiler. The lexical analyzer looks at the input stream as a collection of basic language elements called *tokens*. That is, a token is an indivisible lexical unit. In C, keywords like **while** or **for** are tokens (you can't say wh ile), symbols like >, >=, >>, and >>= are tokens, names and numbers are tokens, and so forth. The original string that comprises the token is called a *lexeme*. Note that there is not a one-to-one relation-ship between lexemes and tokens. A **name** or **number** token, for example, can have many possible lexemes associated with it; a **while** token always matches a single lexeme. The situation is complicated by tokens that overlap (such as the >, >=, >>, and >>=, used earlier). In general, a lexical analyzer recognizes the token that matches the longest lexeme—many languages build this behavior into the language specification itself. Given the input >>, a **shift** token is recognized rather than two **greater-than** tokens.

Phases.

Scanner, tokenizer.

Tokens.

Lexemes.

A lexical analyzer translates lexemes into tokens. The tokens are typically represented internally as unique integers or an enumerated type. Both components are always required—the token itself and the lexeme, which is needed in this example to differentiate the various **name** or **number** tokens from one another.

Lexemes are translated to tokens.

One of the early design decisions that can affect the structure of the entire compiler is the choice of a token set. You can have a token for every input symbol, or several sym-bols can be merged into a single token—for example, the >, >=, >>, and >>=, can be treated either as four tokens, or as a single **comparison-operator** token—the lexeme is used to disambiguate the tokens. The former approach can sometimes make code gen-eration easier to do. Too many tokens, however, can make the parser larger than neces-sary and difficult to write. There's no hard-and-fast rule as to which is better, but by the time you've worked through this book, you'll understand the design considerations and will be able to make intelligent choices. In general, arithmetic operators with the same precedence and associativity can be grouped together, type-declaration keywords (like **int** and **char**) can be combined, and so forth.

Choosing a token set.

The lexical analyzer is typically a self-contained unit that interfaces with the rest of the compiler via a small number (typically one or two) of subroutines and global vari-ables. The parser calls the lexical-analyzer every time it needs a new token, and the analyzer returns that token and the associated lexeme. Since the actual input mechanism is hidden from the parser, you can modify or replace the lexical analyzer without affecting the rest of the compiler.

Scanner is self-contained unit.

1.1.2 The Parser

Compilers are language translators—they translate a high-level language like C into a low-level language like 8086 assembler. Consequently, a good deal of the theoretical side of the subject is borrowed from linguistics. One such concept is the idea of parsing. To *parse* an English sentence is to break it up into its component parts in order to analyze it grammatically. For example, a sentence like this:

Parse, defined.

Jane sees Spot run.

is broken up into a subject ("Jane") and a predicate ("sees Spot run"). The predicate is in turn broken up into a verb ("sees"), a direct object ("Spot"), and a participle that modifies the direct object ("run"). Figure 1.2 shows how the sentence is represented by a conventional sentence diagram like the ones you learned to make in the sixth grade.

A compiler performs this same process (of decomposing a sentence into its com-ponent parts) in the *parser* phase, though it usually represents the parsed sentence in a

The parser phase.

Figure 1.2. A Sentence Diagram for *Jane Sees Spot Run*

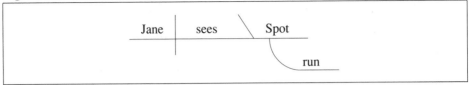

tree form rather than as sentence diagram. (In this case, the *sentence* is an entire program.)

Syntax diagrams and
trees.

Syntax trees.

Parse trees.

　　The sentence diagram itself shows the syntactic relationships between the parts of
the sentence, so this kind of graph is formally called a *syntax diagram* (or, if it's in tree
form, a *syntax tree*). You can expand the syntax tree, however, to show the grammatical
structure as well as the syntactic structure. This second representation is called a *parse
tree*. A parse tree for our earlier sentence diagram is shown in Figure 1.3. Syntax and
parse trees for the expression A*B+C*D are shown in Figure 1.4. A tree structure is used
here primarily because it's easy to represent in a computer program, unlike a sentence
diagram.

Figure 1.3. A Parse Tree for *Jane Sees Spot Run*

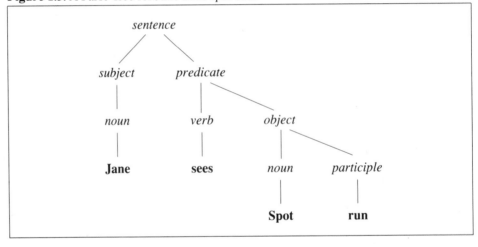

Sentence: formal
definition.

　　A *sentence*, by the way, is also a technical term, though it means the same thing as it
does in English. It's a collection of tokens that follow a well-defined grammatical structure. In the case of a compiler, the sentence is typically an entire computer program.
The analogy is evident in a language like Pascal, which mirrors English punctuation as
well as its grammar. A Pascal program ends with a period, just like an English sentence.
Similarly, a semicolon is used as punctuation to separate two complete ideas, just as it
separates two independent clauses in English.

　　To summarize: A parser is a group of subroutines that converts a token stream into a
parse tree, and a parse tree is a structural representation of the sentence being parsed.
Looked at another way, the parse tree represents the sentence in a hierarchical fashion,
moving from a general description of the sentence (at the root of the tree) down to the
specific sentence being parsed (the actual tokens) at the leaves. Some compilers create a
physical parse tree, made up of structures, pointers, and so forth, but most represent the

Figure 1.4. Syntax and Parse Trees for A*B + C*D

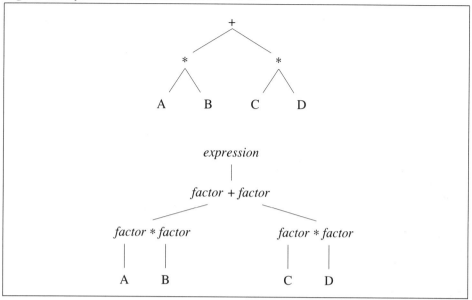

parse tree implicitly.[1] Other parse methods just keep track of where they are in the tree, without creating a physical tree (we'll see how this works shortly). The parse tree itself is a very useful concept, however, for understanding how the parse process works.

1.1.3 The Code Generator

The last part of the compiler proper is the code generator. It's somewhat misleading to represent this phase as a separate component from the parser proper, because most compilers generate code as the parse progresses. That is, the code is generated by the same subroutines that are parsing the input stream. It is possible, however, for the parser to create a parse tree for the entire input file, which is then traversed by a distinct code generator, and some compilers work in this way. A third possibility is for the parser to create an intermediate-language representation of the input from which a syntax tree can be reconstructed by an optimization pass. Some optimizations are easier to perform on a syntax tree than on a linear instruction stream. A final, code-generation pass can traverse the optimizer-modified syntax tree to generate code.

Though compilers can generate object code directly, they often defer code generation to a second program. Instead of generating machine language directly, they create a program in an *intermediate language* that is translated by the compiler's *back end* into actual machine language. You can look at an intermediate language as a sort-of super assembly language that's designed for performing specific tasks (such as optimization). As you might expect, there are many flavors of intermediate languages, each useful in different applications.

Intermediate languages, back ends.

There are advantages and disadvantages to an intermediate-language approach to compiler writing. The main disadvantage is lack of speed. A parser that goes straight from tokens to binary object code will be very fast, since an extra stage to process the intermediate code can often double the compile time. The advantages, however, are

Advantages and disadvantages of intermediate languages.

---

1. A physical parse tree is useful for some kinds of optimizations, discussed further in Chapter Seven.

usually enough to justify the loss of speed. These are, in a nutshell, optimization and flexibility. A few optimizations, such as simple constant folding—the evaluation of constant expressions at compile time rather than run time—can be done in the parser. Most optimizations, however, are difficult, if not impossible, for a parser to perform. Consequently, parsers for optimizing compilers output an intermediate language that's easy for a second pass to optimize.

Intermediate languages give you flexibility as well. A single lexical-analyzer/parser front end can be used to generate code for several different machines by providing separate back ends that translate a common intermediate language to a machine-specific assembly language. Conversely, you can write several front ends that parse several different high-level languages, but which all output the same intermediate language. This way, compilers for several languages can share a single optimizer and back end.

Interpreters.

A final use of an intermediate language is found in incremental compilers or interpreters. These programs shorten the development cycle by executing intermediate code directly, rather than translating it to binary first, thereby saving the time necessary for assembling and linking a real program. An interpreter can also give you an improved debugging environment because it can check for things like out-of-bounds array indexing at run time.

C Code: The intermediate language used in this book.

The compiler developed in Chapter Six uses an intermediate language for the output code. The language itself is described in depth in that chapter, but some mention of it is necessary here, because I'll be using the language informally for code-generation examples throughout this book. Put simply, the intermediate language is a subset of C in which most instructions translate directly to a small number of assembly-language instructions on a typical machine (usually one or two). For example, an expression like x=a+b*c+d is translated into something like this:

```
t0 =  _a ;
t1 =  _b ;
t1 *= _c ;
t0 += t1 ;
t0 += _d ;
```

Anonymous temporaries.

The t0 and t1 in the foregoing code are temporary variables that the compiler allocates to hold the result of the partially-evaluated expression. These are called *anonymous temporaries* (often shortened to just *temporaries*) and are discussed in greater depth below. The underscores are added to the names of declared variables by the compiler so that they won't be confused with variables generated by the compiler itself, such as t0, and t1 (which don't have underscores in their names).

Since the intermediate language is so C like, I'm going to just use it for now without a formal language definition. Remember, though, that the intermediate language is not C (there would be little point in a compiler that translated good C into bad C)—it is really an assembly language with a C-like syntax.

1.2 Representing Computer Languages

A compiler is like every other program in that some sort of design abstraction is useful when constructing the code. Flow charts, Warnier-Orr diagrams, and structure charts are examples of a design abstraction. In compiler applications, the best abstraction is one that describes the language being compiled in a way that reflects the internal structure of the compiler itself.

1.2.1 Grammars and Parse Trees

The most common method used to describe a programming language in a formal way is also borrowed from linguistics. This method is a formal grammar, originally developed by M.I.T.'s Noam Chomsky and applied to computer programs by J.W. Backus for the first FORTRAN compilers.

Formal grammars are most often represented in a modified *Backus-Naur Form* (also called *Backus-Normal Form*), BNF for short. A strict BNF representation starts with a set of tokens, called *terminal* symbols, and a set of definitions, called *nonterminal* symbols. The definitions create a system in which every legal structure in the language can be represented. One operator is supported, the ::= operator, translated by the phrase "is defined as" or "goes to." For example, the following BNF rule might start a grammar for an English sentence:

sentence ::= subject predicate

A *sentence* is defined as a *subject* followed by a *predicate*. You can also say "a sentence *goes to* a subject followed by a predicate." Each rule of this type is called a *production*. The nonterminal to the left of the ::= is the *left-hand side* and everything to the right of the ::= is the *right-hand side* of the production. In the grammars used in this book, the left-hand side of a production always consists of a single, nonterminal symbol, and every nonterminal that's used on a right-hand side must also appear on a left-hand side. All symbols that don't appear on a left-hand side, such as the tokens in the input language, are terminal symbols.

A real grammar continues with further definitions until all the terminal symbols are accounted for. For example, the grammar could continue with:

subject　　::=　　*noun*
noun　　::=　　**JANE**

where **JANE** is a terminal symbol (a token that matches the string "Jane" in the input).

The strict BNF is usually modified to make a grammar easier to type, and I'll use a modified BNF in this book. The first modification is the addition of an OR operator, represented by a vertical bar (I). For example,

noun　　::=　　**JANE**
noun　　::=　　**DICK**
noun　　::=　　**SPOT**

is represented as follows:

noun ::= **DICK | JANE | SPOT**

Similarly, a → is often substituted for the ::= as in:

noun → **DICK | JANE**

I use the → in most of this book. I also consistently use italics for nonterminal symbols and boldface for terminals (symbols such as + and * are also always terminals—they'll also be in boldface but sometimes it's hard to tell.)

There's one other important concept. Grammars must be as flexible as possible, and one of the ways to get that flexibility is to make the application of certain rules optional. A rule like this:

article → **THE**

says that **THE** is an *article*, and you can use that production like this:

Backus-Naur Form (BNF).

Terminal and nonterminal symbols.

The ::= and → operators.

Productions.
Left-hand and right-hand sides (LHS and RHS).

Modified BNF: the | operator.

→ used for ::=

Terminals=**boldface**.
nonterminals=*italic*.

Optional rules and ε.

object → article noun

Epsilon (ε) productions.

In English, an *object* is an *article* followed by a *noun*. A rule like the foregoing requires that <u>all</u> nouns that comprise an object be preceded by a participle. But what if you want the *article* to be optional? You can do this by saying that an *article* can either be the noun "the" or an empty string. The following is used to do this:

article → **THE** | ε

The ε (pronounced "epsilon") represents an empty string. If the **THE** token is present in the input, then the

article → **THE**

production is used. If it is not there, however, then the *article* matches an empty string, and

article → ε

is used. So, the parser determines which of the two productions to apply by examining the next input symbol.

A grammar that recognizes a limited set of English sentences is shown below:

sentence	→	*subject predicate*
subject	→	*noun*
predicate	→	*verb object*
object	→	*noun opt_participle*
opt_participle	→	*participle*	ε
noun	→	**SPOT**	**JANE**	**DICK**
participle	→	**RUN**
verb	→	**SEES**

Recognizing a sentence using the grammar.

An input sentence can be recognized using this grammar, with a series of replacements, as follows:

(1) Start out with the topmost symbol in the grammar, the goal symbol.
(2) Replace that symbol with one of its right-hand sides.
(3) Continue replacing nonterminals, always replacing the leftmost nonterminal with its right-hand side, until there are no more nonterminals to replace.

For example, the grammar can be used to recognize "Jane sees Spot run" as follows:

sentence	apply *sentence→subject predicate* to get:
subject predicate	apply *subject→noun* to get:
noun predicate	apply *noun→***JANE** to get:
JANE *predicate*	apply *predicate→verb object* to get:
JANE *verb object*	apply *predicate→verb object* to get:
JANE *verb object*	apply *verb→***SEES** to get:
JANE SEES *object*	apply *object→***noun op_participle** to get:
JANE SEES *noun opt_participle*	apply *noun→***SPOT** to get:
JANE SEES SPOT *opt_participle*	apply *opt_participle→participle* to get:
JANE SEES SPOT *participle*	apply *participle→***RUN** to get:
JANE SEES SPOT RUN	done—there are no more nonterminals to replace

These replacements can be used to build the parse tree. For example, replacing *sentence* with *subject predicate* is represented in tree form like this:

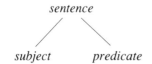

The second replacement, of *subject* with *noun,* would modify the tree like this:

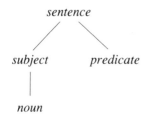

and so forth. The evolution of the entire parse tree is pictured in Figure 1.5.

A glance at the parse tree tells you where the terms terminal and nonterminal come from. Terminal symbols are always leaves in the tree (they're at the end of a branch), and nonterminal symbols are always interior nodes.

Terminals are leaf nodes. Nonterminals are interior nodes.

1.2.2 An Expression Grammar

Table 1.1 shows a grammar that recognizes a list of one or more statements, each of which is an arithmetic expression followed by a semicolon. *Statements* are made up of a series of semicolon-delimited expressions, each comprising a series of numbers separated either by asterisks (for multiplication) or plus signs (for addition).

Note that the grammar is recursive. For example, Production 2 has *statements* on both the left- and right-hand sides. There's also third-order recursion in Production 8, since it contains an *expression*, but the only way to get to it is through Production 3, which has an expression on its left-hand side. This last recursion is made clear if you make a few algebraic substitutions in the grammar. You can substitute the right-hand side of Production 6 in place of the reference to *term* in Production 4, yielding

Recursion in grammar.

$$expression \rightarrow factor$$

and then substitute the right-hand side of Production 8 in place of the *factor:*

$$expression \rightarrow (\ expression \ )$$

Since the grammar itself is recursive, it stands to reason that recursion can also be used to parse the grammar—I'll show how in a moment. The recursion is also important from a structural perspective—it is the recursion that makes it possible for a finite grammar to recognize an infinite number of sentences.

The strength of the foregoing grammar is that it is intuitive—its structure directly reflects the way that an expression goes together. It has a major problem, however. The leftmost symbol on the right-hand side of several of the productions is the same symbol that appears on the left-hand side. In Production 3, for example, *expression* appears both on the left-hand side and at the far left of the right-hand side. The property is called *left recursion*, and certain parsers (such as the recursive-descent parser that I'll discuss in a moment) can't handle left-recursive productions. They just loop forever, repetitively replacing the leftmost symbol in the right-hand side with the entire right-hand side.

Left recursion.

You can understand the problem by considering how the parser decides to apply a particular production when it is replacing a nonterminal that has more than one right-hand side. The simple case is evident in Productions 7 and 8. The parser can choose which production to apply when it's expanding a *factor* by looking at the next input symbol. If this symbol is a **number**, then the compiler applies Production 7 and replaces the

Why left recursion causes problems—an example.

Figure 1.5. Evolution of a Parse Tree

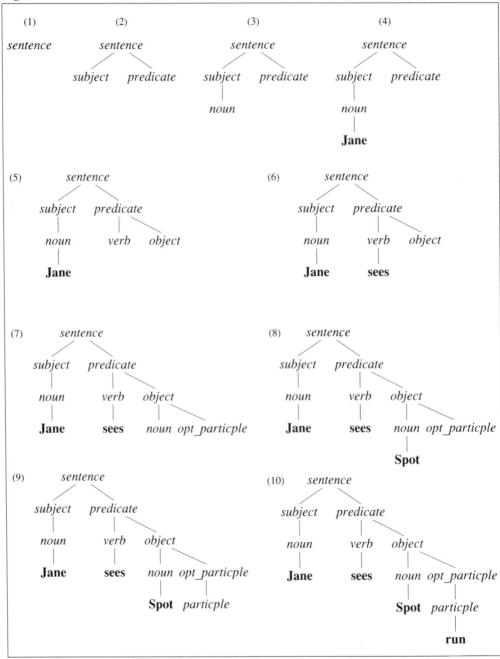

factor with a **number**. If the next input symbol was an open parenthesis, the parser would use Production 8. The choice between Productions 5 and 6 cannot be solved in this way, however. In the case of Production 6, the right-hand side of *term* starts with a *factor* which, in turn, starts with either a **number** or left parenthesis. Consequently, the parser would like to apply Production 6 when a *term* is being replaced and the next input symbol is a **number** or left parenthesis. Production 5—the other right-hand side—starts with a *term*, which can start with a *factor*, which can start with a **number** or left parenthesis, and these are the same symbols that were used to choose Production 6. To

Table 1.1. A Simple Expression Grammar

1.	statements	→	expression ;
2.		|	expression ; statements
3.	expression	→	expression + term
4.		|	term
5.	term	→	term * factor
6.		|	factor
7.	factor	→	**number**
8.		|	(expression)

summarize, the parser must be able to choose between one of several right-hand sides by looking at the next input symbol. It could make this decision in Productions 7 and 8, but it cannot make this decision in Productions 5 and 6, because both of the latter productions can start with the same set of terminal symbols.

The previous situation, where the parser can't decide which production to apply, is called a *conflict*, and one of the more difficult tasks of a compiler designer is creating a grammar that has no conflicts in it. The next input symbol is called the *lookahead symbol* because the parser looks ahead at it to resolve a conflict.

Conflicts and look-aheads.

Unfortunately, for reasons that are discussed in Chapter Four, you can't get rid of the recursion by swapping the first and last production element, like this:

Modified expression grammar.

expression→term + expression

so the grammar must be modified in a very counterintuitive way in order to build a recursive-descent parser for it. Several techniques can be used to modify grammars so that a parser can handle them, and all of these are discussed in depth in Chapter Four. I'll use one of them now, however, without any real explanation of why it works. Take it on faith that the grammar in Table 1.2 recognizes the same input as the one we've been using. (I'll discuss the ⊢ and ε that appear in the grammar momentarily.) The modified grammar is obviously an inferior grammar in terms of self-documentation—it is difficult to look at it and see the language that's represented. On the other hand, it works with a recursive-descent parser, and the previous grammar doesn't.

Table 1.2. Modified Simple-Expression Grammar

1.	statements	→	⊢
2.		|	expression ; statements
3.	expression	→	term expression′
4.	expression′	→	+ term expression′
5.		|	ε
6.	term	→	factor term′
7.	term′	→	* factor term′
8.		|	ε
9.	factor	→	**number**
10.		|	(expression)

The ⊢ symbol is an end-of-input marker. For the purposes of parsing, end of file is treated as an input token, and ⊢ represents end of input in the grammar. In this grammar, Production 1 is expanded if the current input symbol is end of input, otherwise Production 2 is used. Note that an explicit end-of-input marker is often omitted from a

End-of-input symbol (⊢).

grammar, in which case ⊢ is implied as the rightmost symbol of the starting production (the production whose left-hand side appears at the apex of the parse tree). Since eliminating the ⊢ symbol removes the entire right-hand side in the current grammar, you can use the following as an alternate starting production:

statements → ε | *expression* **;** *statements*

In English: *statements* can go to an empty string followed by an implied end-of-input marker.

Applying ε.   The replacement of the left-hand side by ε (the empty string) occurs whenever the current input symbol doesn't match a legal lookahead symbol. In the current grammar, a *term'* is replaced with the right-hand side **factor term'* if the lookahead symbol (the next input symbol) is a *. The *term'* is replaced with ε if the next input symbol isn't a *. The process is demonstrated in Figure 1.6, which shows a parse of 1+2 using the modified grammar in Table 1.2. The ε production stops things from going on forever.

Figure 1.6. A Parse of 1+2

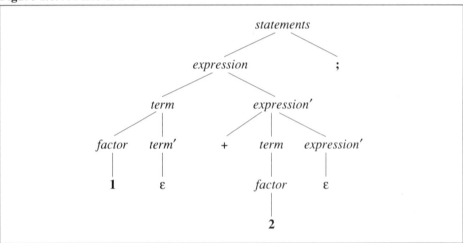

ε is a terminal, but not a token.   Note that ε is a terminal symbol that is not a token. It always appears at the end of a branch in the parse tree, so it is a terminal, but it does not represent a corresponding token in the input stream (just the opposite in fact—it represents the absence of a particular token in the input stream).

1.2.3 Syntax Diagrams

You can prove to yourself that the grammar in Table 1.2 works as expected by representing it in a different way—as a syntax diagram. We saw earlier that a syntax diagram can represent the entire syntactic structure of a parse, but you can also use it in a more limited sense to represent the syntax of a single production. Syntax diagrams are useful in writing recursive-descent compilers because they translate directly into flow charts (that's the main reason we're looking at them now). You can use them as a map that describes the structure of the parser (more on this in a moment). They are also somewhat more intuitive to an uninitiated reader, so they often make better documentation than does a formal grammar.

Translating grammars to syntax diagrams.   I'll translate our grammar into a syntax diagram in two steps. First, several of the productions can be merged together into a single diagram. Figure 1.7 represents Productions 3, 4, and 5 of the grammar in Table 1.2 on page 11. The ε production is represented by the uninterrupted line that doesn't go through a box. You can combine these two graphs by substituting the bottom graph for the reference to it in the top graph, and the same process can be applied to Productions 6, 7, and 8.

Figure 1.7. Syntax Diagram for Productions 3, 4, and 5

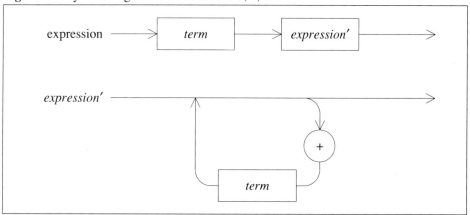

The entire grammar in Table 1.2 is represented as a syntax diagram in Figure 1.8. The topmost diagram, for example, defines a *statement* as a list of one or more semicolon-delimited *expressions*. The same thing is accomplished by

$$
\begin{aligned}
statements \quad &\rightarrow \quad expression\ ; \\
&| \quad expression\ ;\ statements
\end{aligned}
$$

but the BNF form is harder to understand.

The merged diagram also demonstrates graphically how the modified grammar works. Just look at it like a flow chart, where each box is a subroutine, and each circle or ellipse is the symbol that must be in the input when the subroutine returns. Passing through the circled symbol removes a terminal from the input stream, and passing through a box represents a subroutine call that evaluates a nonterminal.

Diagram shows how modified grammar works.

1.3 A Recursive-Descent Expression Compiler

We now know enough to build a small compiler, using the expression grammar we've been looking at (in Table 1.2 on page 11). Our goal is to take simple arithmetic expressions as input and generate code that evaluates those expressions at run time. An expression like a+b*c+d is translated to the following intermediate code:

```
t0  =  _a ;
t1  =  _b ;
t1 *=  _c ;
t0 += t1 ;
t0 +=  _d ;
```

1.3.1 The Lexical Analyzer

The first order of business is defining a token set. With the exception of numbers and identifiers, all the lexemes are single characters. (Remember, a *token* is an input symbol taken as a unit, a *lexeme* is the string that represents that symbol.) A **NUM_OR_ID** token is used both for numbers and identifiers; so, they are made up of a series of contiguous characters in the range ′0′−′9′, ′a′−′z′, or ′A′−′Z′. The tokens themselves are defined with the macros at the top of *lex.h*, Listing 1.1. The lexical analyzer translates a semicolon into a **SEMI** token, a series of digits into a **NUM_OR_ID** token,

Expression token set.

NUM_OR_ID

Figure 1.8. A Syntax Diagram

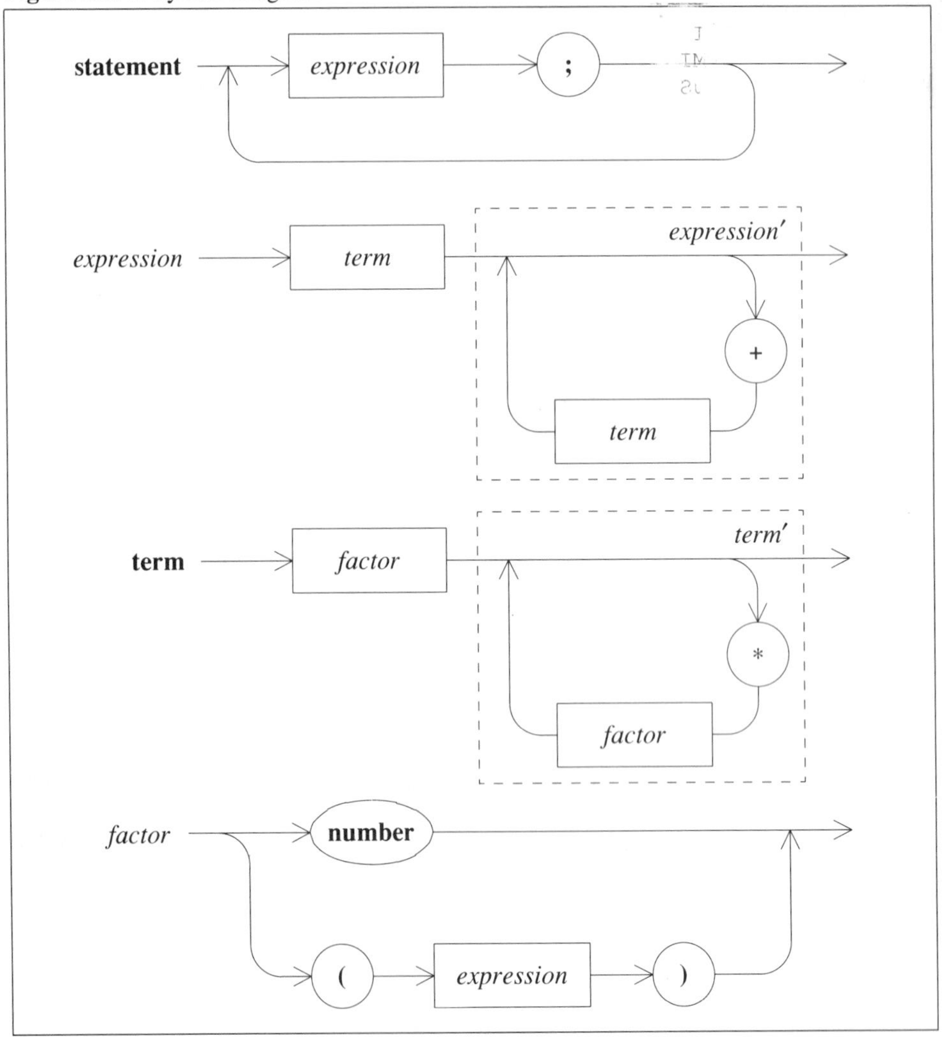

yytext, yyleng.

and so on. The three external variables at the bottom of *lex.h* are used by the lexical analyzer to pass information to the parser. yytext points at the current lexeme, which is not '\0' terminated; yyleng is the number of characters in the lexeme; and yylineno is the current input line number. (I've used these somewhat strange names because both **lex** and LEX use the same names. Usually, I try to make global-variable names begin with an upper-case letter and macro names are all caps. This way you can distinguish these names from local-variable names, which are always made up of lower-case letters only. It seemed best to retain UNIX compatibility in the current situation, however.)

Simple, buffered, input system.

The lexical analyzer itself starts on line nine of *lex.c*, Listing 1.2. It uses a simple, buffered, input system, getting characters a line at a time from standard input, and then isolating tokens, one at a time, from the line. Another input line is fetched only when the entire line is exhausted. There are two main advantages to a buffered system (neither of which are really exercised here, though the situation is different in the more sophisticated input system discussed in Chapter Two). These are speed and speed. Computers like to read data in large chunks. Generally, the larger the chunk the faster the throughput. Though a 128-byte buffer isn't really a large enough chunk to make a

Listing 1.1. *lex.h—* Token Definitions and **extern** statements

```
 1   #define EOI        0          /*   end of input            */
 2   #define SEMI       1          /*      ;                    */
 3   #define PLUS       2          /*      +                    */
 4   #define TIMES      3          /*      *                    */
 5   #define LP         4          /*      (                    */
 6   #define RP         5          /*      )                    */
 7   #define NUM_OR_ID  6          /* decimal number or identifier */
 8
 9   extern char  *yytext;         /* in lex.c                  */
10   extern int   yyleng;
11   extern int   yylineno;
```

difference, once the buffer size gets above the size of a disk cluster, the changes are more noticeable, especially if you can use the unbuffered I/O functions to do your reading and writing. The second speed issue has to do with *lookahead* and *pushback*. Lexical analyzers often have to know what the next input character is going to be without actually reading past it. They must *look ahead* by some number of characters. Similarly, they often need to read past the end of a lexeme in order to recognize it, and then *push back* the unnecessary characters onto the input stream. Consequently, there are often extra characters that must be handled specially. This special handling is both difficult and slow when you're using single-character input. Going backwards in a buffer, however, is simply a matter of moving a pointer.

Lookahead and push-back.

Listing 1.2. *lex.c—* A Simple Lexical Analyzer

```
 1   #include "lex.h"
 2   #include <stdio.h>
 3   #include <ctype.h>
 4
 5   char      *yytext   = "";   /* Lexeme (not '\0' terminated)  */
 6   int       yyleng    = 0;    /* Lexeme length.                */
 7   int       yylineno  = 0;    /* Input line number             */
 8
 9   lex()
10   {
11       static char input_buffer[128];
12       char        *current;
13
14       current = yytext + yyleng;          /* Skip current lexeme  */
15
16       while( 1 )                          /* Get the next one     */
17       {
18           while( !*current )
19           {
20               /* Get new lines, skipping any leading white space on the line,
21                * until a nonblank line is found.
22                */
23
24               current = input_buffer;
25               if( !gets( input_buffer ) )
26               {
27                   *current = '\0' ;
28                   return EOI;
29               }
30
```

Listing 1.2. continued...

```
31                ++yylineno;
32
33              while( isspace(*current) )
34                  ++current;
35          }
36
37      for( ; *current ; ++current )
38      {
39          /* Get the next token */
40
41          yytext = current;
42          yyleng = 1;
43
44          switch( *current )
45          {
46          case EOF: return EOI    ;
47          case ';': return SEMI   ;
48          case '+': return PLUS   ;
49          case '*': return TIMES  ;
50          case '(': return LP     ;
51          case ')': return RP     ;
52
53          case '\n':
54          case '\t':
55          case ' ' : break;
56
57          default:
58              if( !isalnum(*current) )
59                  fprintf(stderr, "Ignoring illegal input <%c>\n", *current);
60              else
61              {
62                  while( isalnum(*current) )
63                      ++current;
64
65                  yyleng = current - yytext;
66                  return NUM_OR_ID;
67              }
68
69              break;
70          }
71      }
72  }
73  }
```

Reading characters:
`input_buffer`,
`current`.

The input buffer used by `lex()` is declared on line 11 of Listing 1.2. `current` (on line 12) points at the current position in the buffer. On the first call, the increment on line 14 initializes `current` to point at an empty string (`yyleng` is 0 at this juncture, and `yytext` points at an empty string because of the initializer on line five). The **while** statement on line 18 tests true as a consequence. This **while** loop has two purposes. It gets lines (and increments the line number), and it skips past all blank lines (including lines that contain only white space). The loop doesn't terminate until `input_buffer` holds a nonblank line, and `current` will point at the first nonwhite character on that line.

Tokenization.

The **for** loop starting on line 37 does the actual tokenization. Single-character lexemes are recognized on lines 46–51, white space is ignored by the cases on lines 53–55, and the multiple-character NUM_OR_ID token is handled in the **else** clause on lines

60–67. An error message is printed if an illegal character is found. When the loop terminates, `yytext` points at the first character of the lexeme, and `yyleng` holds its length.

The next time `lex()` is called, the code on line 14 adjusts the current pointer to point past the previous lexeme, and then, if the input buffer hasn't been exhausted, the **while** test on line 18 fails and you go straight to the token-isolation code. `lex()` won't get another input line until it reaches the end of the line—`*current` is `'\0'` in this case.

The remainder of *lex.c* (in Listing 1.3) addresses the problem of *lookahead*. The parser must look at the next input token without actually reading it. Though a read/pushback scheme similar to `getc()`/`ungetc()` could be used for this purpose, it's generally a good idea to avoid going backwards in the input, especially if you have to push back entire lexemes rather than single characters. The problem is solved by using two subroutines: `match(token)` evaluates to true if the next token in the input stream matches its argument—it "looks ahead" at the next input symbol without reading it. `advance()` discards the current token and advances to the next one. This strategy eliminates the necessity of a push-back subroutine such as `ungetc()`.

The `Lookahead` variable (on line 74) holds the *lookahead* token. It's initialized to −1, which is not used for any of the input tokens. It's modified to hold a real token the first time `match()` is called. Thereafter, the test on line 81 will become inoperative and `match()` simply returns true if `Lookahead` matches its argument. This approach is relatively foolproof—though the fool in this case is myself. I know that I'll regularly forget to call an initialization routine before calling `match()`, so I'll let `match()` initialize itself the first time it's called. The `advance()` function just calls `lex()` to assign a new value to `Lookahead`.

Solving the lookahead problem.

`match()`, `advance()`.

Lookahead.

Listing 1.3. *lex.c*— Match and Advance Functions

```
74    static int Lookahead = -1;        /* Lookahead token   */
75
76    int match( token )
77    int token;
78    {
79        /* Return true if "token" matches the current lookahead symbol. */
80
81        if( Lookahead == -1 )
82            Lookahead = lex();
83
84        return token == Lookahead;
85    }
86
87    void advance()
88    {
89        /* Advance the lookahead to the next input symbol.  */
90
91        Lookahead = lex();
92    }
```

1.3.2 The Basic Parser

Moving on to the parser, since I'm planning to start with a naive implementation and refine it, I've isolated `main()` into a small file (Listing 1.4) that I can compile once and then link with the parser proper. The parser itself is called `statements()`.

The most naive parser for our grammar is shown in Listing 1.5. I've reproduced the grammar here for convenience:

`statements()`.

Listing 1.4. main.c

```
1   main()
2   {
3       statements();
4   }
```

1.	*statements*	$\rightarrow$	⊢
2.		|	*expression* **;** *statement*
3.	*expression*	$\rightarrow$	*term expression′*
4.	*expression′*	$\rightarrow$	*+ term expression′*
5.		|	ε
6.	*term*	$\rightarrow$	*factor term′*
7.	*term′*	$\rightarrow$	*∗ factor term′*
8.		|	ε
9.	*factor*	$\rightarrow$	**num_or_id**
10.		|	*(expression)*

Subroutines correspond to left-hand sides, implement right-hand sides.

The parser generates no code, it just parses the input. Each subroutine corresponds to the left-hand side in the original grammar that bears the same name. Similarly, the structure of each subroutine exactly matches the grammar. For example, the production

expression → *term expression′*

is implemented by the following subroutine (on line 23 of Listing 1.5):

```
expression()
{
    term();
    expr_prime();
}
```

ε recognized.

The ε production in

expression′ → **PLUS** *term expression′* | ε

Subroutines advance past recognized tokens.

is implemented implicitly when the test on line 37 fails (if it's not a **PLUS**, it's an ε). Note that each subroutine is responsible for advancing past any tokens that are on the equivalent production's right-hand side.

Listing 1.5. *plain.c*— A Naive Recursive-Descent Expression Parser

```
 1   /* Basic parser, shows the structure but there's no code generation */
 2
 3   #include <stdio.h>
 4   #include "lex.h"
 5
 6   statements()
 7   {
 8       /*  statements -> expression SEMI
 9        *             |  expression SEMI statements
10        */
11
12       expression();
13
14       if( match( SEMI ) )
15           advance();
```

Listing 1.5. continued...

```
16          else
17              fprintf( stderr, "%d: Inserting missing semicolon\n", yylineno );
18
19          if( !match(EOI) )
20              statements();                        /* Do another statement. */
21      }
22
23  expression()
24  {
25      /* expression -> term expression' */
26
27      term();
28      expr_prime();
29  }
30
31  expr_prime()
32  {
33      /* expression' -> PLUS term expression'
34       *             | epsilon
35       */
36
37      if( match( PLUS ) )
38      {
39          advance();
40          term();
41          expr_prime();
42      }
43  }
44
45  term()
46  {
47      /* term -> factor term' */
48
49      factor();
50      term_prime();
51  }
52
53  term_prime()
54  {
55      /* term' -> TIMES factor term'
56       *        | epsilon
57       */
58
59      if( match( TIMES ) )
60      {
61          advance();
62          factor();
63          term_prime();
64      }
65  }
66
67  factor()
68  {
69      /* factor   ->   NUM_OR_ID
70       *          |    LP expression RP
71       */
72
```

➡

Listing 1.5. continued. . .

```
73          if( match(NUM_OR_ID) )
74              advance();
75
76          else if( match(LP) )
77          {
78              advance();
79              expression();
80              if( match(RP) )
81                  advance();
82              else
83                  fprintf( stderr, "%d: Mismatched parenthesis\n", yylineno);
84          }
85          else
86              fprintf( stderr, "%d Number or identifier expected\n", yylineno );
87      }
```

The recursion in a
recursive-descent parser.

You can now see why a production like

expression → expression + term

can't be used by a recursive-descent parser. You can implement the foregoing as follows:

```
expression()
{
    expression();

    if( !match( PLUS ) )
      error();
    else
      advance();

    term();
}
```

But the first thing that `expression()` does is call itself, the recursion never stops, and
the program never terminates—at least not until it runs out of stack space and is abnormally terminated by the operating system.

At this point I'd suggest doing an exercise. Using a pencil and paper, trace what happens as the expression 1+2 is evaluated by the parser in Listing 1.5. Every time a subroutine is called, draw a downward pointing arrow and write the name of the called subroutine under the arrow; every time the subroutine returns, draw an arrow at the other
end of the same line. As the parser advances past tokens, write them down under the
name of the current subroutine. A partial subroutine trace for this expression is shown in
Figure 1.9. The diagram shows the condition of the parser when it is in subroutine
`expr_prime()` just before the `term()` call on line 40. It's advanced past the 1 and
the current lookahead token is the plus sign. If you finish this diagram, an interesting

Subroutine calling se-
quence mirrors the parse
tree.

fact emerges. The subroutine trace is identical to the parse tree for the same expression
in Figure 1.6 on page 12. So, even though no physical parse tree is created, a parse tree
is implicit in the subroutine-calling sequence.

Figure 1.9. A Partial Subroutine Trace for 1+2

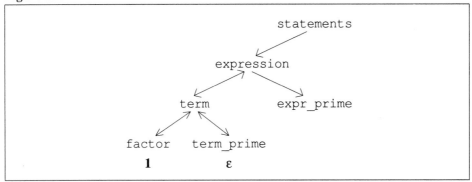

1.3.3 Improving the Parser

The naive parser discussed in the previous section is useful for explaining things, but is not much use in practice. The main difficulty is the tremendous amount of unnecessary recursion. Glancing at the syntax diagram for our grammar (in Figure 1.8 on page 14), two changes come to mind immediately. First, all the right recursion—productions in which the left-hand side also appears at the far right of the right-hand side—can be replaced by loops: If the last thing that a subroutine does is call itself, then that recursive call can be replaced by a loop. Right recursion is often called *tail* recursion.

Eliminate right recursion.

The second obvious improvement is that the same merging together of productions that was done to make the second and third graphs in Figure 1.8 can be applied to the subroutines that implement these productions. Both of these changes are made in Listing 1.6.

Merging productions into a single subroutine.

Listing 1.6. *improved.c*— An Improved Parser

```
1   /* Revised parser   */
2
3   #include <stdio.h>
4   #include "lex.h"
5
6   void    factor      ( void );
7   void    term        ( void );
8   void    expression  ( void );
9
10  statements()
11  {
12      /*  statements -> expression SEMI |  expression SEMI statements */
13
14      while( !match(EOI) )
15      {
16          expression();
17
18          if( match( SEMI ) )
19              advance();
20          else
21              fprintf( stderr, "%d: Inserting missing semicolon\n", yylineno );
22      }
23  }
24
```

Listing 1.6. continued...

```
25  void    expression()
26  {
27      /* expression  -> term expression'
28       * expression' -> PLUS term expression' |  epsilon
29       */
30
31      if( !legal_lookahead( NUM_OR_ID, LP, 0 ) )
32          return;
33
34      term();
35      while( match( PLUS ) )
36      {
37          advance();
38          term();
39      }
40  }
41
42  void    term()
43  {
44      if( !legal_lookahead( NUM_OR_ID, LP, 0 ) )
45          return;
46
47      factor();
48      while( match( TIMES ) )
49      {
50          advance();
51          factor();
52      }
53  }
54
55  void    factor()
56  {
57      if( !legal_lookahead( NUM_OR_ID, LP, 0 ) )
58          return;
59
60      if( match(NUM_OR_ID) )
61          advance();
62
63      else if( match(LP) )
64      {
65          advance();
66          expression();
67          if( match(RP) )
68              advance();
69          else
70              fprintf( stderr, "%d: Mismatched parenthesis\n", yylineno );
71      }
72      else
73          fprintf( stderr, "%d: Number or identifier expected\n", yylineno );
74  }
```

Error recognition, FIRST
sets.

I've made one additional change here as well. I've introduced a little error recovery by adding code to each subroutine that examines the current lookahead token before doing anything else. It's an error if that token cannot legitimately occur in the input. For example, expressions all have to start with either a **NUM_OR_ID** or an **LP**. If the lookahead character is a PLUS at the top of expression(), then something's wrong. This set of legitimate leading tokens is called a FIRST set, and every nonterminal symbol has its own FIRST set. FIRST sets are discussed in depth in Chapter Three—the informal definition will do for now, though.

The `legal_lookahead()` subroutine in Listing 1.7 checks these FIRST sets, and if the next input symbol is not legitimate, tries to recover from the error by discarding all input symbols up to the first token that matches one of the arguments. The subroutine takes a variable number of arguments, the last one of which must be zero. I've used the ANSI variable-argument mechanism here, so the routine can take any number of arguments as parameters, but the last one must be a 0. (This mechanism, and the *<stdarg.h>* file, is described in Appendix A if you're not already familiar with it.)

Error recovery:
`legal_lookahead()`.

One final C style note is needed to head off the inevitable criticism of the **goto** statement on line 118 of Listing 1.7. Though many programmers contend with almost religious fervor that the **goto** should be obliterated from all structured programs, I strongly feel that there are a few situations where a judiciously used **goto** makes for better code. Here, the **goto** branch to a single label is vastly preferable to multiple **return** statements. A subroutine that has a single exit point is much more maintainable than one with several exit points. You can put a single breakpoint or debugging diagnostic at the end of the subroutine instead of having to sprinkle them all over the place. You also minimize the possibility of accidentally falling off the bottom of the subroutine without returning a valid value. My rules of thumb about **goto**s are as follows:

Style note: the **goto**.

- Goto's are appropriate in two situations: (1) to eliminate multiple return statements and (2) to break out of nested loops. You can also do (2) with a flag of some sort (**while** (!done)), but flags tend to make the code both larger and harder to read, so should be avoided.
- Don't use a **goto** unless it is the only solution to the problem. You can often eliminate the need for a **goto** by reorganizing the code.
- A subroutine should have at most one label.
- All **goto** branches should be in a downwards direction to that single label.
- The target of a **goto** branch should be in the same block or at a higher (more outer) nesting level than the **goto** itself. Don't do this:

```
{
    goto label;
}
 ...
{
    label:
}
```

Listing 1.7. *improved.c*— Error Recovery for the Improved Parser

```
75    #include <stdarg.h>
76
77    #define MAXFIRST 16
78    #define SYNCH    SEMI
79
80    int     legal_lookahead( first_arg )
81    int     first_arg;
82    {
83        /* Simple error detection and recovery. Arguments are a 0-terminated list of
84         * those tokens that can legitimately come next in the input. If the list is
85         * empty, the end of file must come next. Print an error message if
86         * necessary. Error recovery is performed by discarding all input symbols
87         * until one that's in the input list is found
88         *
89         * Return true if there's no error or if we recovered from the error,
90         * false if we can't recover.
```

Listing 1.7. continued...

```
 91         */
 92
 93        va_list      args;
 94        int          tok;
 95        int          lookaheads[MAXFIRST], *p = lookaheads, *current;
 96        int          error_printed = 0;
 97        int          rval         = 0;
 98
 99        va_start( args, first_arg );
100
101        if( !first_arg )
102        {
103            if( match(EOI) )
104                rval = 1;
105        }
106        else
107        {
108            *p++ = first_arg;
109            while( (tok = va_arg(args, int)) && p < &lookaheads[MAXFIRST] )
110                *++p = tok;
111
112            while( !match( SYNCH ) )
113            {
114                for( current = lookaheads; current < p ; ++current )
115                    if( match( *current ) )
116                    {
117                        rval = 1;
118                        goto exit;
119                    }
120
121                if( !error_printed )
122                {
123                    fprintf( stderr, "Line %d: Syntax error\n", yylineno );
124                    error_printed = 1;
125                }
126
127                advance();
128            }
129        }
130
131  exit:
132      va_end( args )
133      return rval;
134  }
```

1.3.4 Code Generation

Recognizers.

    The parsers that we just looked at are, strictly speaking, *recognizer* programs in that, if they terminate without an error, the input sentence is a legal sentence in the grammar. All they do is recognize legal input sentences. Our goal is to build a compiler, however, and to do this, you need to add code generation to the bare-bones recognizer. Given the input

```
1 + 2 * 3 + 4
```

a typical compiler generates the following code:

```
t0 =   1
t1 =   2
t2 =   3
t1 *= t2
t0 += t1
t1 =   4
t0 += t1
```

An optimizer will clean up the unnecessary assignments. It's useful, for now, to look at the raw output, however. The temporary variables (t0, and so forth) are maintained internally by the compiler. A real compiler typically uses registers or the run-time stack for temporaries. Here, they're just global variables. The expression is evaluated operator by operator, with each temporary holding the result of evaluating the current subexpression. Sometimes (as is the case in this example) several temporaries must exist simultaneously in order to defer application of an operator because of precedence or associativity problems. Here, t0 holds the left operand of the addition operator until the higher-precedence multiply is performed. Temporary variables at run time.

You can also look at the temporary-variable assignments in terms of a syntax tree. The syntax tree for 1+2*3+4 is shown in Figure 1.10. The nodes are marked with the names of the temporaries that hold the evaluated subexpression represented by the subtree. Temporaries on the syntax tree.

Figure 1.10. Syntax Tree for 1+2*3+4

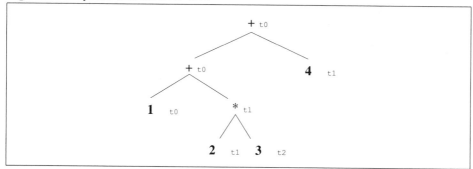

The first thing you need to generate code is a mechanism for allocating temporaries. Ideally, they should be recycled—the temporaries should be reused after they are no longer needed in the current subexpression. A simple, but effective, mechanism to do this is shown in Listing 1.8. (We'll look at a more elaborate system in Chapter Six.) A stack of temporary-variable names is declared on line one. When a new name is required, newname() pops one off the stack. When the temporary is no longer needed, a freename() call pushes it back. Compile-time, temporary-variable management.

newname(), freename().

The next code-generation problem is determining the name of the temporary that holds the partially-evaluated expression at any given moment. This information is passed around between the subroutines in the normal way, using arguments and return values. Using return values in parser.

To demonstrate the differences between the two methods, I'll show two parsers, one that uses return values exclusively, and another that uses arguments exclusively. The subroutine-calling tree for a parse of 1+2*3+4; (using the improved parser) is in Figure 1.11. The subroutines that generated this tree (and the earlier code) are in Listing 1.9. The arrows are marked to show the flow of temporary-variable names during the parse. Control flow goes counterclockwise around the drawing (the nodes are subscripted to show the order in which they're visited).

Listing 1.8. *name.c*— Temporary-Variable Allocation Routines

```
1    char   *Names[] = { "t0", "t1", "t2", "t3", "t4", "t5", "t6", "t7" };
2    char   **Namep  = Names;
3
4    char   *newname()
5    {
6        if( Namep >= &Names[ sizeof(Names)/sizeof(*Names) ] )
7        {
8            fprintf( stderr, "%d: Expression too complex\n", yylineno );
9            exit( 1 );
10       }
11
12       return( *Namep++ );
13   }
14
15   freename(s)
16   char    *s;
17   {
18       if( Namep > Names )
19           *--Namep = s;
20       else
21           fprintf(stderr, "%d: (Internal error) Name stack underflow\n",
22                                                            yylineno );
23   }
```

Figure 1.11. A Subroutine Trace of 1+2 (Improved Parser)

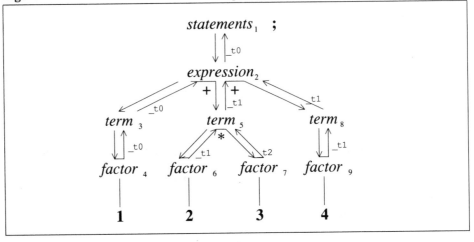

Listing 1.9. *retval.c*— Code Generation Using Return Values

```
 1  #include <stdio.h>
 2  #include "lex.h"
 3
 4  char    *factor      ( void );
 5  char    *term        ( void );
 6  char    *expression ( void );
 7
 8  extern char *newname( void      );
 9  extern void freename( char *name );
10
11  statements()
12  {
13      /*  statements -> expression SEMI  |  expression SEMI statements  */
14
15      char *tempvar;
16
17      while( !match(EOI) )
18      {
19          temporary = expression();
20
21          if( match( SEMI ) )
22              advance();
23          else
24              fprintf( stderr, "%d: Inserting missing semicolon\n", yylineno );
25
26          freename( temporary );
27      }
28  }
29
30  char    *expression()
31  {
32      /* expression -> term expression'
33       * expression' -> PLUS term expression' |  epsilon
34       */
35
36      char  *tempvar, *tempvar2;
37
38      tempvar = term();
39      while( match( PLUS ) )
40      {
41          advance();
42          temporary2 = term();
43          printf("    %s += %s\n", tempvar, tempvar2 );
44          freename( tempvar2 );
45      }
46
47      return tempvar;
48  }
49
50  char    *term()
51  {
52      char  *tempvar, *tempvar2 ;
53
54      tempvar = factor();
55      while( match( TIMES ) )
56      {
57          advance();
58          tempvar2 = factor();
59          printf("    %s *= %s\n", tempvar, tempvar2 );
```

Listing 1.9. continued...

```
60                freename( tempvar2 );
61          }
62
63          return tempvar;
64     }
65
66     char     *factor()
67     {
68          char *tempvar;
69
70          if( match(NUM_OR_ID) )
71          {
72              /* Print the assignment instruction. The %0.*s conversion is a form of
73               * %X.Ys, where X is the field width and Y is the maximum number of
74               * characters that will be printed (even if the string is longer). I'm
75               * using the %0.*s to print the string because it's not \0 terminated.
76               * The field has a default width of 0, but it will grow the size needed
77               * to print the string. The ".*" tells printf() to take the maximum-
78               * number-of-characters count from the next argument (yyleng).
79               */
80
81              printf("    %s = %0.*s\n", tempvar = newname(), yyleng, yytext );
82              advance();
83          }
84          else if( match(LP) )
85          {
86              advance();
87              tempvar = expression();
88              if( match(RP) )
89                  advance();
90              else
91                  fprintf(stderr, "%d: Mismatched parenthesis\n", yylineno );
92          }
93          else
94              fprintf( stderr, "%d: Number or identifier expected\n", yylineno );
95
96          return tempvar;
97     }
```

Generate t0=1.

Generate arithmetic instructions.

A likely place to generate instructions of the form t0=1 is in factor(), the subroutine that reads the 1. factor() calls newname() to get an anonymous-temporary name, generates the code to copy the input number into the temporary, and then returns the name to its parent. Similarly, the best place to generate multiplication instructions is the place where the times signs are read: in term(). After the two factor() calls, tempvar and tempvar2 hold the names of the two temporaries. Code is generated to do the multiplication, one of the temporaries is freed, and the other (which holds the result of the multiply) passed back up to the parent. So, this temporary, the one that holds the result of the subexpression evaluation, is used in the next step. Addition is handled the same way in expression().

Just to make sure that you understand the process, I suggest taking a moment to run through a parse of 1*(2+3)*4 by hand, creating a subroutine-calling graph as in the previous example and watching how the code is generated.

Using subroutine arguments to pass information.

Listing 1.10 shows the parser, modified once more to use subroutine arguments rather than return values. Here, instead of allocating the names when the instructions are generated, the temporary variables are allocated high up in the tree. Each subroutine passes to its child the name of the temporary in which it wants the subexpression result. That is, the high level routine is saying: "Do what you must to evaluate any subexpressions, but by the time you're finished, I want the result to be in the temporary variable whose name I'm passing to you." Recursive-descent compilers often use both of the methods just discussed—neither is more or less desirable. The code can be easier to understand if you restrict yourself to one or the other, though that's not always possible.

Listing 1.10. *args.c*— Code Generation Using Subroutine Arguments

```
1   #include <stdio.h>
2   #include "lex.h"
3
4   void    factor      ( char *tempvar );
5   void    term        ( char *tempvar );
6   void    expression ( char *tempvar );
7
8   extern char *newname( void      );
9   extern void freename( char *name );
10
11  statements()
12  {
13      /*  statements -> expression SEMI  |  expression SEMI statements    */
14
15      char *tempvar;
16
17      while( !match(EOI) )
18      {
19          expression( tempvar = newname() );
20          freename( tempvar );
21
22          if( match( SEMI ) )
23              advance();
24          else
25              fprintf( stderr, "%d: Inserting missing semicolon\n", yylineno );
26      }
27  }
28
29  void    expression( tempvar )
30  char    *tempvar;
31  {
32      /* expression  -> term expression'
33       * expression' -> PLUS term expression'  |  epsilon
34       */
35
36      char  *tempvar2;
37
38      term( tempvar );
39      while( match( PLUS ) )
40      {
41          advance();
42
43          term( tempvar2 = newname() );
44
45          printf("    %s += %s\n", tempvar, tempvar2 );
46          freename( tempvar2 );
47      }
48  }
49
```

→

Listing 1.10. continued...

```
50   void     term( tempvar )
51   char     *tempvar;
52   {
53       char   *tempvar2 ;
54
55       factor( tempvar );
56       while( match( TIMES ) )
57       {
58           advance();
59
60           factor( tempvar2 = newname() );
61
62           printf("    %s *= %s\n", tempvar, tempvar2 );
63           freename( tempvar2 );
64       }
65   }
66
67   void     factor( tempvar )
68   char     *tempvar;
69   {
70       if( match(NUM_OR_ID) )
71       {
72           printf("    %s = %0.*s\n", tempvar, yyleng, yytext );
73           advance();
74       }
75       else if( match(LP) )
76       {
77           advance();
78           expression( tempvar );
79           if( match(RP) )
80               advance();
81           else
82               fprintf( stderr, "%d: Mismatched parenthesis\n", yylineno );
83       }
84       else
85           fprintf( stderr, "%d: Number or identifier expected\n", yylineno );
86   }
```

1.4 Exercises

1.1.   Write a grammar that recognizes a C variable declaration made up of the following keywords:

   **int   char   long float double signed unsigned short
   const   volatile**

and a variable name.

1.2.   Write a grammar that recognizes a C variable declaration made up only of <u>legal</u> combinations of the following keywords:

   **int   char   long float double signed unsigned short
   const   volatile**

and a variable name. The grammar should be able to accept all such legal declarations. For example, all the following should be accepted:

```
volatile unsigned long int x;
unsigned long volatile int x;
long unsigned volatile int x;
long volatile unsigned int x;
        ...
```

but something like

```
unsigned signed short long x;
```

should not be accepted. Remember that the **int** keyword is optional in a declaration.

1.3. Modify your solution to the previous exercise so that declarations for arrays, pointers, pointers to arrays, arrays of pointers, arrays of pointers to arrays, and so on, are also recognized. That is, all legal combination of stars, brackets, parentheses, and names should be recognized.

1.4. Write a grammar (and a recursive-descent compiler for that grammar) that translates an English description of a C variable into a C-style variable declaration. For example, the input:

```
x is a pointer to an array of 10 pointers to functions that return int.
y is an array of 10 floats.
z is a pointer to a struct of type a_struct.
```

should be translated to:

```
int     (*(*x)[10])();
float   y[10];
struct a_struct *z;
```

1.5. Modify either of the expression compilers (in Figures 1.11 or 1.10) so that the C ++ and -- operators are supported.

1.6. LISP uses a prefix notation for arithmetic expressions. For example, 1+2 is represented as (+ 1 2), and 1+2*3 is (+ 1 (* 2 3)). Modify the expression compiler so that it translates infix expressions to prefix.

1.7. Write a LISP-to-infix translator.

1.8. Modify the expression compiler so that it translates expressions into postfix notation, such as that used by a Hewlett-Packard calculator. For example, the expression (1+2)*(3+4) should be translated to:

```
1 2 + 3 4 + *
```

1.9. Modify the expression compiler so that it prints the parse tree created by its input. I suggest creating a physical parse tree (with structures and so forth) and then printing the tree by traversing the physical parse tree.

1.10. (This is a very difficult problem.)
      a. Try to write a context-free grammar that correctly parses both "time flies like an arrow" and "fruit flies like a banana."
      b. One of the things that defines context-free grammars is that the left-hand side always consists of a single nonterminal symbol. How would the foregoing work if you were permitted to use more than one terminal or nonterminal symbol on a left-hand side? Try to write a parser for this sort of grammar.

2

Input and Lexical Analysis

This chapter looks at input strategies and at lexical analysis. I'll discuss a set of buffered input routines and construct L^{F}X, a program modeled after the UNIX **lex** utility, that translates regular expressions into a lexical analyzer. It's worth understanding how L^{F}X works, even if you're not going to build a version of your own. Various theoretical concepts such as finite automata and ε closure will crop up again when I discuss how programs like **occs** and **yacc** generate bottom-up parse tables, and you need to be able to understand how these tables are created in order to use these programs effectively. The concepts are easier to understand in the context of L^{F}X, however, so the theoretical material in this chapter is actually an introduction to the concepts that you'll need later. I'm using a bootstrap approach in that L^{F}X itself uses a hard-coded lexical analyzer and a recursive-descent parser to do its work. As such, it's a good example of a compiler built by hand, without special tools.

The techniques used for lexical analysis are useful in many programming applications other than compilers. Efficient I/O is a concern in virtually every computer program. Similarly, lexical analyzers are pattern-recognition engines—the concepts discussed here can be applied to many programs that need to recognize patterns: editors, bibliographic data-base programs, and so forth. You can extend the techniques to do things like assembly-line quality control and network-protocol processing.

If you intend to read the implementation parts of this chapter rather than just the theory, you should read Appendix D, which contains a user's manual for L^{F}X, before proceeding. Also many of the support routines used by L^{F}X are presented in Appendix A (the set routines are used heavily in the code that follows, and the hash functions are used as well).

2.1 The Lexical Analyzer as Part of a Compiler*

The main purpose of a lexical analyzer in a compiler application is to translate the

---

* An asterisk appended to a section heading is used throughout this and subsequent chapters to indicate theoretical material. Implementation-oriented sections are not so marked.

input stream into a form that is more manageable by the parser. It translates input strings or *lexemes*, into *tokens*—arbitrary integer values that represent the lexemes. A token can Lexemes, tokens. have a one-to-one relationship with a lexeme. For example, the keyword **while** is associated with a single token. More generic tokens such as identifiers or numbers have several lexemes associated with them. Lexical analyzers often have auxiliary functions as well. For example, a lexical analyzer can discard comments and skip over white space. Isolating this housekeeping from the parser can simplify the parser design (and the grammar of the language). The analyzer can keep track of the current line number so that intelligent error messages can be output by the parser. Program listings that show the source code intermixed with error messages are usually created by the lexical analyzer.

The lexical analyzer is an independent compilation phase that communicates with Interface to parser. the parser over a well-defined and simple interface. The relationship is pictured in Figure 2.1. The parser calls a single lexical-analyzer subroutine every time it needs a new token, and that subroutine returns the token and associated lexeme.

Figure 2.1. Interaction Between the Lexical Analyzer and Parser

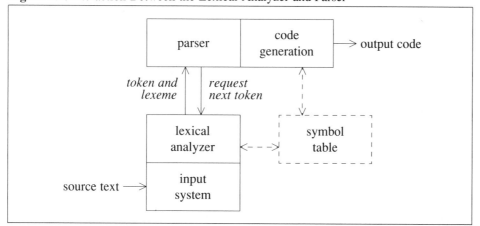

This organization has several things going for it. Since it's an independent phase, the Advantages of independent lexical analyzers. lexical analyzer is easy to maintain because changes to the analyzer do not affect the compiler as a whole, provided that the interface is not changed. Moreover, much of the code that comprises the lexical analyzer is the same for every compiler, regardless of the input language, so you can recycle much of the lexical analyzer's code. The only things that change from language to language in the table-driven lexical analyzers described later in this chapter are the tables themselves. Other advantages include speed—an independent lexical analyzer can optimize character-read times because it can read large amounts of data at once, and portability—the peculiarities of reading the source code under a particular operating system are all confined to the lexical analyzer itself. Notice that the actual input system in Figure 2.1 is isolated completely from the parser, even though it's closely linked to the lexical analyzer.

Sometimes a more complex interaction between lexical analyzer and parser is Shared symbol table. required. For example, the **typedef** statement in C effectively creates new keywords in the language. After the parser has processed the statement:

```
typedef int   alphonso;
```

the lexical analyzer must treat the input string *alphonso* as if it were a **type** token rather than as an **identifier** token. This sort of high-level communication is usually done through a shared data structure such as the symbol table. In this case, the parser can enter *alphonso* into the symbol table, identifying it as a **typedef** name, and the lexical analyzer can check the symbol table to determine if a string is a **type** or **identifier** token.

A lexical analyzer can also do work other than simple pattern recognition. For example, when it reads a numeric constant, it can translate that constant into the associated number [in a manner similar to `atoi()`] and return that number along with the token and lexeme. When an identifier is read, the analyzer can look up the identifier in the symbol table and return a pointer to a symbol-table entry along with the token. **Attributes.** These additional values associated with individual tokens are called *attributes*. (Note that the lexeme is also an attribute of the token, because it's a quantum of information that is associated with the token.) In general, it's best to restrict the lexical analyzer to simple pattern-recognition tasks in order to make it easier to maintain. If the analyzer is an independent module that performs only one task (pattern recognition), it's a simple matter to replace it if necessary.

There's one final point to make. Lexical analysis is often complicated if a language is not designed with ease-of-compilation in mind. For example,[1] PL/1 keywords are not reserved—you can use them as identifiers—and the lexical analyzer has to determine what it's looking at based on surrounding context. You can say something like this in PL/1:

```
if then then then = else; else else = then;
```

Separating the keyword `then` from the identifier `then` can be quite difficult.

2.2 Error Recovery in Lexical Analysis*

It's possible, of course, for errors to occur in the lexical-analysis as well as the parsing phase. For example, the at sign (@) and backquote (`) are both illegal outside of a string in a C program. The lexical analyzer can recover from these errors in several **Discarding characters.** ways, the simplest of which just discards the offending character and prints an appropriate error message. Even here, there are some choices that are driven by the application, however. If the last character of a multiple-character lexeme is incorrect, the analyzer can discard the entire malformed lexeme or it can discard only the first character of the lexeme and then try to rescan. Similarly, the lexical analyzer could try to correct the error. Some operating systems have a "do what I mean" feature that works along these lines. When faced with an error, the operating system's command-line interpreter (which is a compiler) tries to determine what the user meant to type and proceeds accordingly. If a word has only one misspelled letter, it's not too difficult to correct the problem by simple inspection.[2]

---

1. This example (and the other PL/1 example, below) is borrowed from [Aho], p. 87 and p. 90.

2. There are other, more sophisticated techniques that can be used to determine the similarity of two words. The most common technique is the "soundex" algorithm developed by Margaret Odell and Robert Russel, and described in [Knuth], vol. 3, pp. 391–392. Also of interest is the Ratcliff/Obershelp algorithm, described in [Ratcliff], and Allen Bickel's algorithm, described in [Bickel] and implemented in C in [Howell].

2.3 Input Systems*

Since the input system is usually an independent module, and since the concerns here are divorced from the mechanics of recognizing tokens, I'll look at input systems in depth before moving on to the issues of lexical analysis per se.

The lowest-level layer of the lexical analyzer is the input system—the group of functions that actually read data from the operating system. For the same reason that the analyzer should be a distinct module, it's useful for the input system itself to be an independent module that communicates with the analyzer via well-defined function calls. Since the analyzer itself can be isolated from the input mechanics, the resulting code is more portable. Most of the system-dependent operations of the analyzer are concentrated into the input layer.

The input system is an independent module.

Issues of optimization aside, most compilers spend a good portion of their time in the lexical analysis phase. Consequently, it's worthwhile to optimize lexical analysis for speed. The standard C buffered input system is actually a poor choice for several reasons. First, most buffered systems copy the input characters at least three times before your program can use them: from the disk to a buffer maintained by the operating system, from that buffer to a second buffer that's part of the `FILE` structure, and finally from the `FILE` buffer to the string that holds the lexeme. All this copying takes both time and buffer space. Moreover, the buffer size is not optimal. The more you can read from the disk at one time, the faster your input routines tend to be (though this is operating-system dependent—there's not much advantage under UNIX in reading more than one block at a time; MS-DOS, however, performs much better with very large reads).

Optimizing for speed.

The other issue is lookahead and pushback. The lexical analyzer may have to look ahead several characters in the input to distinguish one token from another, and then it must push the extra characters back into the input. Consider the earlier PL/1 expression:

Lookahead, pushback.

```
if then then then = else; else else = then;
```

The lexical analyzer can distinguish the **else** keyword from the `else` identifier by looking at the characters that follow the lexeme. The `else` must be an identifier if it is followed by an equal sign, for example. Another example is a PL/1 **declare** statement like this:

```
declare ( arg1, arg2, ..., argN )
```

The lexical analyzer can't distinguish the **declare** keyword from an identifier (a subroutine name in this case) until it has read past the rightmost parenthesis. It must read several characters past the end of the lexeme, and then push the extra characters back into the input stream once a decision has been made, and this lookahead and pushback must be done as efficiently as possible.

A final, admittedly contrived, example demonstrates that pushback is necessary even in recognizing individual tokens. If a language has the three tokens *xxyy*, *xx*, and *y*, and the lexical analyzer is given the input *xxy* it should return an *xx* token followed by a *y* token. In order to distinguish, however, it must read at least four characters (to see if *xxyy* is present) and then push the two *y*'s back into the input stream.

Most programming languages are designed so that problems such as the foregoing are not issues. If the tokens don't overlap, you can get by with only one character of pushback. LEX however, can't make assumptions about the structure of the lexemes, so must assume the worst.

The pushback problem means that you can't use the normal buffered input functions because `ungetc()` gives you only one character of pushback. You can add a layer around `getc()` that gives you more pushback by using a stack, as is demonstrated in Listing 2.1. Push back a character by pushing it onto the stack, and get the next input

`ungetc()` inappropriate. Stack-based pushback.

character either from the stack (if it's not empty) or from the real input stream (if it is). UNIX **lex** uses this method. A better method is described in the remainder of this section.

Listing 2.1. Using a Stack for Multiple-Character Pushback

```
 1   #include <stdio.h>
 2   #define   SIZE 128                    /* Maximum number of pushed-back characters  */
 3
 4   /* Pbackbuf is the push-back stack.
 5    * Pbackp   is the stack pointer. The stack grows down, so a push is:
 6    *           *--Pbackp=c   and a pop is:   c=*Pbackp++
 7    * get()    evaluates to the next input character, either popping it off the
 8    *          stack (if it's not empty) or by calling getc().
 9    * unget(c) pushes c back. It evaluates to c if successful, or to -1 if the
10    *          pushback stack was full.
11    */
12
13   int Pbackbuf[SIZE];
14   int *Pbackp = &Pbackbuf[SIZE];
15
16   #define get(stream) (Pbackp < &Pbackbuf[SIZE] ? *Pbackp++ : getc(stream) )
17   #define unget(c)     (Pbackp <= Pbackbuf      ? -1        : *--Pbackp=(c))
18
19   void    ungets( start, n )
20   char    *start;
21   int     n;
22   {
23       /* Push back the last n characters of the string by working backwards
24        * through the string.
25        */
26
27       char *p = start + strlen(start);    /* Find the end of the string. */
28
29       while( --p >= start && --n >= 0 )
30           if( unget(*p) == -1 )
31               fprintf( stderr, "Pushback-stack overflow\n" );
32   }
```

2.3.1 An Example Input System*

This section describes the input system used by a LEX-generated lexical analyzer (though not by LEX itself). This input system has many of the qualities that are desirable in a compiler's input system, and as such can be taken as characteristic. There are, of course, other solutions to the input problem,[3] but the current one has proven quite workable and provides a good example of the sorts of problems that come up. Several design criteria must be met:

Input-system design criteria.

- The routines should be as fast as possible, with little or no copying of the input strings.
- Several characters of pushback and lookahead must be available.
- Lexemes of a reasonable length must be supported.
- Both the current and previous lexeme must be available.

---

3. A system that's more appropriate in a Pascal environment is described in [Aho] pp. 88–92.

- Disk access should be efficient.

To meet the last criterion, consider how a disk is accessed by most operating systems. All disks are organized into *sectors* which must be read as a unit. Disk reads must be performed in sector-sized chunks. If your disk has 512-byte sectors, then you must read 512 bytes at a time. This limitation is imposed by the hardware. If you request one byte from the disk, the operating system will read an entire sector into a buffer, and then return a single byte from the buffer. Subsequent reads get characters from the buffer until it is exhausted, and only then is a new sector read. Some operating systems (MS-DOS is a case in point) impose further constraints in that a group of several sectors (called a *cluster* or *block*) is the smallest possible unit that can be accessed directly, so Clusters, blocks. you have to read an entire cluster at once. The minimum number of bytes that can be read is called an *allocation unit,* and, for the sake of efficiency, all reads must be done in Allocation units. terms of allocation units. That is, the number of bytes read from the disk at any one time should be a multiple of the allocation unit. Typically, the larger the buffer, the shorter the read time. Many operating systems reward you for doing block-sized transfers by not buffering the input themselves, as would be the case when an odd-sized block was requested from a low-level read call. The operating system transfers the data directly from the disk into your own buffer, thereby eliminating one level of copying and decreasing the read time. For example, MS-DOS read and write times improve dramatically when you read 32K bytes at a time.

The other design criteria are met by using a single input buffer and several pointers. Input system organization: buffers and pointers. My system is pictured in Figure 2.2. The drawing on the top shows the condition of the buffer just after it is loaded the first time. BUFSIZE is the actual buffer size. MAXLEX is Buffer pointers, BUF-SIZE, MAXLEX, END, Start_buf, End_buf. the maximum lexeme length, and the disk reads are always in multiples of this number. Start_buf marks the physical start of the buffer, and END marks the physical end of the buffer. End_buf points at the logical end of buffer. (Since reads are in multiples of MAXLEX, and since the buffer itself isn't an even multiple of MAXLEX in length, there is usually a scrap of wasted space at the end of the buffer. End_buf points just past the last valid character in the buffer.) Finally, Next points at the next input character. (I'll discuss DANGER and MAXLOOK momentarily.)

The middle picture in Figure 2.2 shows the buffer in its normal state, after the lexical analyzer has processed several tokens. Various pointers have been set to mark the boundaries of various lexemes: pMark points at the beginning of the previous lexeme, Lexeme markers, pMark, sMark, eMark. sMark points at the beginning of the current lexeme, and eMark points at the end of the current lexeme. The lexical analyzer has scanned several characters past the end of the current lexeme (Next is to the right of eMark). If the lexical analyzer finds a longer lexeme than the current one, all it need do is move the eMark to the current input position. If, on the other hand, it finds that it has read too far in the input, it can push back all the extra characters by setting Next back to the eMark.

Returning to MAXLOOK , this constant is the number of lookahead characters that are MAXLOOK, DANGER. supported. The DANGER marker tells the input routines when the Next pointer is getting too close to the end of the buffer (there must be at least MAXLOOK characters to the right of Next). When Next crosses the DANGER point, a buffer flush is triggered, giving us the Buffer flush. situation shown in the bottom picture in Figure 2.2. All characters between the pMark and the last valid character (pointed to by End_buf) have been shifted to the far left of the buffer. The input routines fill the remainder of the buffer from the disk, reading in as many MAXLEX-sized chunks as will fit. The End_buf pointer is adjusted to mark the new end of the buffer, and DANGER scales automatically: it's positioned relative to the new end of buffer. This may seem like a lot of copying, but in practice the lexemes are not that large, especially in comparison to the buffer size. Consequently, flushes don't happen very often, and only a few characters are copied when they do happen.

Figure 2.2. The Input Buffer

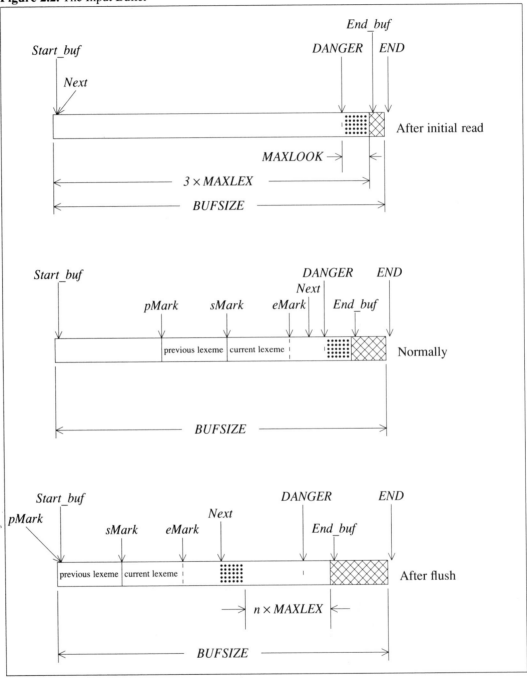

This approach has many advantages, the main one being a lack of copying. The lexical analyzer can just return the `sMark` as the pointer to the next lexeme, without having to copy it anywhere. Similarly a pushback is a single assignment (`Next=eMark`) rather than a series of pushes and pops. Finally, the disk reads themselves are reasonably efficient because they're done in block-sized chunks.

2.3.2 An Example Input System—Implementation

The foregoing is all implemented by the variables and macros declared at the top of *input.c*, in Listing 2.2. At this point we've looked at most of them, the others are discussed as they're used in the code. The macro definitions on lines 15 to 19 take care of a few system dependencies—COPY() is mapped to memmove() for the Microsoft C compiler [because Microsoft's memcpy() doesn't support overlapping strings].

Portability problems: COPY().

Listing 2.2. *input.c*— Macros and Data Structures

```
1    #include <stdio.h>
2    #include <stdlib.h>
3    #include <fcntl.h>
4    #include <tools/debug.h>
5
6    #include <tools/l.h>      /* Needed only for prototypes */
7    #include <string.h>       /* " */
8
9    /*------------------------------------------------------------------
10   * INPUT.C:    The input system used by LeX-generated lexical analyzers.
11   *------------------------------------------------------------------
12   * System-dependent defines.
13   */
14
15   #ifdef MSDOS
16   #        define COPY(d,s,a) memmove(d,s,a)
17   #else
18   #        define COPY(d,s,a) memcpy(d,s,a)
19   #endif
20
21   #define STDIN    0                              /* standard input */
22
23   /*----------------------------------------------------------------*/
24
25   #define MAXLOOK    16                   /* Maximum amount of lookahead */
26   #define MAXLEX     1024                 /* Maximum lexeme sizes.       */
27
28   #define BUFSIZE  ( (MAXLEX * 3) + (2 * MAXLOOK) )   /* Change the 3 only */
29
30   #define DANGER    ( End_buf - MAXLOOK )    /* Flush buffer when Next    */
31                                             /* passes this address       */
32
33   #define END      (&Start_buf[BUFSIZE])     /* Just past last char in buf */
34
35   #define NO_MORE_CHARS() ( Eof_read && Next >= End_buf )
36
37   typedef unsigned char    uchar;
38
39   PRIVATE    uchar   Start_buf[BUFSIZE]; /* Input buffer              */
40   PRIVATE    uchar   *End_buf = END;     /* Just past last character  */
41   PRIVATE    uchar   *Next    = END;     /* Next input character      */
42   PRIVATE    uchar   *sMark   = END;     /* Start of current lexeme   */
43   PRIVATE    uchar   *eMark   = END;     /* End of current lexeme     */
44   PRIVATE    uchar   *pMark   = NULL;    /* Start of previous lexeme  */
45   PRIVATE    int     pLineno  = 0;       /* Line # of previous lexeme */
46   PRIVATE    int     pLength  = 0;       /* Length of previous lexeme */
47
48   PRIVATE    int     Inp_file = STDIN;   /* Input file handle         */
49   PRIVATE    int     Lineno   = 1 ;      /* Current line number       */
50   PRIVATE    int     Mline    = 1 ;      /* Line # when mark_end() called */
51   PRIVATE    int     Termchar = 0;       /* Holds the character that was */
```

Listing 2.2. continued...

```
52                                          /* overwritten by a \0 when we    */
53                                          /* null terminated the last       */
54                                          /* lexeme.                         */
55    PRIVATE   int     Eof_read  = 0;      /* End of file has been read.      */
56                                          /* It's possible for this to be    */
57                                          /* true and for characters to      */
58                                          /* still be in the input buffer.   */
59
60    extern int open(), close(), read();
61
62    PRIVATE int   (*Openp)()  = open  ;   /* Pointer to open function        */
63    PRIVATE int   (*Closep)() = close ;   /* Pointer to close function       */
64    PRIVATE int   (*Readp)()  = read  ;   /* Pointer to read function        */
```

Change low-level input routines, `ii_io()`.

The actual code starts in Listing 2.3 with two initialization functions. The first, `ii_io()` on line 65 of Listing 2.3, is used to change the low-level input functions that are used to open files and fill the buffer. You may want to do this if you're getting input directly from the hardware, from a string, or doing something else that circumvents the normal input mechanism. This way you can use a LEX-generated lexical analyzer in an unusual situation without having to rewrite the input system.

Open new input file, `ii_newfile()`.

The `ii_newfile()` routine on line 81 of Listing 2.3 is the normal mechanism for opening a new input file. It is passed the file name and returns the file descriptor (not the `FILE` pointer) for the opened file, or −1 if the file couldn't be opened. The previous input file is closed unless it was standard input. `ii_newfile()` does not actually read the first buffer; rather, it sets up the various pointers so that the buffer is loaded the first time a character is requested. This way, programs that never call `ii_newfile()` will work successfully, getting input from standard input. The problem with this approach is that you must read at least one character before you can look ahead in the input (otherwise the buffer won't be initialized). If you need to look ahead before advancing, use:

```
ii_advance();   /* Read first bufferfull of input  */
ii_pushback(1); /* but put back the first character */
```

Reassigning standard input.

The default input stream [used if `ii_newfile()` is never called] is standard input. You can reassign the input to standard input (say, after you get input from a file) by calling:

```
ii_newfile(NULL);
```

It's also okay to do a `ii_newfile("/dev/tty")` (in both MS-DOS and UNIX), but input is actually taken from the physical console in this case. Redirection won't work. An `ii_newfile(NULL)` allows for redirected input, however.

Binary (untranslated) input.

Note that the indirect `open()` call on line 103 of Listing 2.3 uses the `O_BINARY` input mode in MS-DOS systems (it's mapped to zero in UNIX systems). A CR-LF (carriage-return, linefeed) pair is not translated into a single `'\n'` when binary-mode input is active. This behavior is desirable in most LEX applications, which treat both CR and LF as white space. There's no point wasting time doing the translation. The lack of translation might cause problems if you're looking for an explicit `'\n'` in the input, though.

First read is delayed until first advance.

Note that the input buffer is not read by `ii_newfile()`; rather, the various pointers are initialized to point at the <u>end</u> of the buffer on lines 111 to 114 of Listing 2.3. The actual input routine (`advance()`, discussed below) treats this situation the same as it would the `Next` pointer crossing the `DANGER` point. It shifts the buffer's tail all the way to the left (in this case the tail is empty so no characters are shifted, but the pointers are

Listing 2.3. *input.c*— Initialization Routines

```
65   void     ii_io( open_funct, close_funct, read_funct )
66   int      (*open_funct)();
67   int      (*close_funct)();
68   int      (*read_funct)();
69   {
70       /* This function lets you modify the open(), close(), and read() functions
71        * used by the i/o system. Your own routines must work like the real open,
72        * close, and read (at least in terms of the external interface. Open should
73        * return a number that can't be confused with standard input (not 0).
74        */
75
76       Openp  = open_funct;
77       Closep = close_funct;
78       Readp  = read_funct;
79   }
80   /*-------------------------------------------------------------------*/
81   int      ii_newfile( name )
82   char     *name;
83   {
84       /* Prepare a new input file for reading. If newfile() isn't called before
85        * input() or input_line() then stdin is used. The current input file is
86        * closed after successfully  opening the new one (but stdin isn't closed).
87        *
88        * Return -1 if the file can't be opened; otherwise, return the file
89        * descriptor returned from open(). Note that the old input file won't be
90        * closed unless the new file is opened successfully. The error code (errno)
91        * generated by the bad open() will still be valid, so you can call perror()
92        * to find out what went wrong if you like. At least one free file
93        * descriptor must be available when newfile() is called. Note in the open
94        * call that O_BINARY, which is needed in MS-DOS applications, is mapped
95        * to 0 under UNIX (with a define in <tools/debug.h>).
96        */
97
98       int fd;                         /* File descriptor */
99
100      MS(  if( strcmp(name, "/dev/tty") == 0 )    )
101      MS(         name = "CON" ;                  )
102
103      if( (fd = !name ? STDIN : (*Openp)(name, O_RDONLY|O_BINARY))  != -1 )
104      {
105          if( Inp_file != STDIN )
106              (*Closep)( Inp_file );
107
108          Inp_file = fd;
109          Eof_read = 0;
110
111          Next     = END;
112          sMark    = END;
113          eMark    = END;
114          End_buf  = END;
115          Lineno   = 1;
116          Mline    = 1;
117      }
118      return fd;
119  }
```

moved), and then loads the buffer from the disk. I've taken this approach because it's sometimes convenient to open a default input file at the top of a program, which is then overridden by a command-line switch or the equivalent later on in the same program. There's no point in reading from a file that's not going to be used, so the initial read is delayed until a character is requested.

Access functions.

The *input.c* file continues in Listing 2.4 with several small *access* functions. For maintenance reasons, it is desirable to limit external access of global variables, because the linker assumes that two global variables with the same name are the same variable. If you inadvertently declare two variables with the same name, one of them will seem to magically change its value when a subroutine that accesses the other is called. You can avoid this problem by declaring the variables **static**, thereby limiting their scope to the current file. PRIVATE is mapped to **static** in *debug.h*, discussed in Appendix A.

Limiting scope,
PRIVATE.

It's still necessary for external subroutines to access these variables however, and the safest way to do so is through the small routines in Listing 2.4. These subroutines are used for maintenance reasons only—two subroutines with the same name will result in an error message from the linker, unlike two variables with the same name, which are silently merged.

Functions to access lexemes: ii_text(), ii_length(), ii_lineno(), ii_ptext(), ii_plength(), ii_plineno().

The ii_text(), ii_length(), and ii_lineno() routines (lines 120 to 122 of Listing 2.4) return a pointer to the current lexeme, the lexeme's length, and the line number for the last character in the lexeme. The ii_ptext(), ii_plength(), and ii_plineno() routines (lines 123 to 125) do the same thing, but for the previous lexeme. The ii_mark_start() routine (line 127) moves the sMark to the current input position (pointed to by Next). It also makes sure that the end-of-lexeme marker (eMark) is not to the left of the start marker. ii_mark_end() (line 134) does the same for the end marker (eMark). It also saves the current line number in Mline, because the lexical analyzer might sweep past a newline when it scans forward looking for a new lexeme. The input line number must be restored to the condition it was in before the extra newline was scanned when the analyzer returns to the previous end marker.

Functions to mark lexeme boundaries,
ii_mark_start(),
ii_mark_end().

Move start marker,
ii_move_start().

The ii_move_start() routine on line 140 of Listing 2.4 lets you move the start marker one space to the right. It returns the new start marker on success, NULL if you tried to move past the end marker (sMark is not modified in this last case). ii_to_mark() (line 148) restores the input pointer to the last end mark. Finally, ii_mark_prev() modifies the previous-lexeme marker to reference the same lexeme as the current-lexeme marker. Typically, ii_mark_prev() is called by the lexical analyzer just before calling ii_mark_start() (that is, just before it begins to search for the next lexeme).

Restore pointer to previous mark,
ii_to_mark().
Mark previous lexeme,
ii_mark_prev().

Advance input pointer,
ii_advance().

The next group of subroutines, in Listings 2.5 and 2.6, comprise the advance and buffer-flush functions. ii_advance(), on line 168 of Listing 2.5, returns the next input character and advances past it. The code on lines 180 to 191 is provided for those situations where you want an extra newline appended to the beginning of a file. L^{E}X needs this capability for processing the start-of-line anchor—a mechanism for recognizing strings only if they appear at the far left of a line. Such strings must be preceded by a newline, so an extra newline has to be appended in front of the first line of the file; otherwise, the anchored expression wouldn't be recognized on the first line.[4]

---

4. L^{E}X Usage Note: This pushback could conceivably cause problems if there is no regular expression in the L^{E}X input file to absorb the newline, and YYBADINP is also #defined (You'll get an error message in this case). A regular expression that absorbs white space is usually present, however.

Listing 2.4. *input.c*— Small Access Routines and Marker Movement

```
120    PUBLIC char *ii_text      () { return( sMark         ); }
121    PUBLIC int   ii_length    () { return( eMark - sMark ); }
122    PUBLIC int   ii_lineno    () { return( Lineno        ); }
123    PUBLIC char *ii_ptext     () { return( pMark         ); }
124    PUBLIC int   ii_plength   () { return( pLength       ); }
125    PUBLIC int   ii_plineno   () { return( pLineno       ); }
126
127    char *ii_mark_start()
128    {
129        Mline = Lineno;
130        eMark = sMark = Next;
131        return( sMark );
132    }
133
134    PUBLIC char *ii_mark_end()
135    {
136        Mline = Lineno ;
137        return( eMark = Next );
138    }
139
140    PUBLIC char *ii_move_start()
141    {
142        if ( sMark >= eMark )
143            return NULL;
144        else
145            return ++sMark ;
146    }
147
148    PUBLIC char *ii_to_mark()
149    {
150        Lineno = Mline  ;
151        return( Next  = eMark );
152    }
153
154    char *ii_mark_prev()
155    {
156        /* Set the pMark. Be careful with this routine. A buffer flush won't go past
157         * pMark so, once you've set it, you must move it every time you move sMark.
158         * I'm not doing this automatically because I might want to remember the
159         * token before last rather than the last one. If ii_mark_prev() is never
160         * called, pMark is just ignored and you don't have to worry about it.
161         */
162
163        pMark   = sMark;
164        pLineno = Lineno;
165        pLength = eMark - sMark;
166        return( pMark );
167    }
```

The NO_MORE_CHARS() macro is used on line 193 to detect end of file. It was defined in the header as follows

Detect end of file, NO_MORE_CHARS().

#define NO_MORE_CHARS() (Eof_read && Next >= End_buf)

Eof_read is set to true when end of file is encountered. You must use both Eof_read and Next to detect end of input because EOF might have been read while the lexical analyzer was looking ahead. In this case, characters may have been pushed back after

Eof_read.

reading the EOF. You have to see both if end of file has been encountered and if the buffer is empty. This is a case where *end of input* and *end of file* are different things, because there still may be characters in the input buffer long after end of file has been read. The ii_flush() call on line 196 flushes the buffer if necessary, and the line number is advanced on line 199. The next input character is returned normally, 0 is returned on end of file, and −1 is returned if the buffer couldn't be flushed for some reason.

Listing 2.5. *input.c*— The Advance Function

```
168   int       ii_advance()
169   {
170         /* ii_advance() is the real input function. It returns the next character
171          * from input and advances past it. The buffer is flushed if the current
172          * character is within MAXLOOK characters of the end of the buffer. 0 is
173          * returned at end of file. -1 is returned if the buffer can't be flushed
174          * because it's too full. In this case you can call ii_flush(1) to do a
175          * buffer flush but you'll loose the current lexeme as a consequence.
176          */
177
178         static int been_called = 0;
179
180         if( !been_called )
181         {
182               /*  Push a newline into the empty buffer so that the LeX start-of-line
183                *  anchor will work on the first input line.
184                */
185
186               Next = sMark = eMark = END - 1;
187               *Next = '\n';
188               --Lineno ;
189               --Mline  ;
190               been_called = 1;
191         }
192
193         if( NO_MORE_CHARS() )
194               return 0;
195
196         if( !Eof_read  && ii_flush(0) < 0 )
197               return -1;
198
199         if( *Next == '\n' )
200               Lineno++;
201
202         return( *Next++ );
203   }
```

The actual buffer flush is done by ii_flush(), which starts at the top of Listing 2.6. The test on line 248 checks to see that there will be enough room after the move to load a new MAXLEX-sized bufferfull of characters—there might not be if the buffer contains two abnormally long lexemes. The test evaluates true if there isn't enough room. Normally, the routine returns −1 if there's no room, and 1 is returned if everything is okay. If the force argument is true, however, the buffer is flushed even if there's no room, and 1 is returned. The flush is forced by setting the start marker to the current input position and the left_edge of the character to be shifted to the Next pointer, effectively destroying the current lexeme. The code on lines 259 and 246 figures out how many characters have to be copied (`copy_amt`) and the distance that they have to be moved (`shift_amt`). The shift is done on line 260, and a new buffer is loaded by the `ii_fillbuf()` call on line 262. COPY was defined earlier (on line 16 of Listing 2.2) to map to either `memmove()` or `memcpy()`, depending on the compilation environment. The rest of the routine adjusts the various markers to compensate for the move.

`copy_amt, shift_amt.`

Listing 2.6. *input.c*— Buffer Flushing

```
204     int     ii_flush( force )
205     int     force;
206     {
207         /* Flush the input buffer. Do nothing if the current input character isn't
208          * in the danger zone, otherwise move all unread characters to the left end
209          * of the buffer and fill the remainder of the buffer. Note that input()
210          * flushes the buffer willy-nilly if you read past the end of buffer.
211          * Similarly, input_line() flushes the buffer at the beginning of each line.
212          *
213          *                                      pMark      DANGER
214          *                                       |          |
215          *        Start_buf                     sMark eMark |Next   End_buf
216          *        |                              ||    |    ||      |
217          *        V                              VV    V    VV      V
218          *        +------------------------------+-----------------+-------+
219          *        | this is already read         | to be done yet  | waste |
220          *        +------------------------------+-----------------+-------+
221          *        |                              |                 |       |
222          *        |<----- shift_amt ----->|<-- copy_amt -->|       |
223          *        |                              |                 |       |
224          *        |<----------------- BUFSIZE ------------------>|
225          *        *
226          * Either the pMark or sMark (whichever is smaller) is used as the leftmost
227          * edge of the buffer. None of the text to the right of the mark will be
228          * lost. Return 1 if everything's ok, -1 if the buffer is so full that it
229          * can't be flushed. 0 if we're at end of file. If "force" is true, a buffer
230          * flush is forced and the characters already in it are discarded. Don't
231          * call this function on a buffer that's been terminated by ii_term().
232          */

234         int     copy_amt, shift_amt ;
235         uchar *left_edge;

237         if( NO_MORE_CHARS() )
238             return 0;

240         if( Eof_read )                      /* nothing more to read */
241             return 1;

243         if( Next >= DANGER  ||  force )
244         {
245             left_edge = pMark ? min(sMark, pMark) : sMark;
246             shift_amt = left_edge - Start_buf ;

248             if( shift_amt < MAXLEX )                /* if(not enough room) */
249             {
250                 if( !force )
251                     return -1;

253                 left_edge = ii_mark_start();  /* Reset start to current character */
254                 ii_mark_prev();
255
```
➡

Listing 2.6. continued...

```
256                    shift_amt = left_edge - Start_buf ;
257                }
258
259            copy_amt = End_buf - left_edge;
260            COPY( Start_buf, left_edge, copy_amt );
261
262            if( !ii_fillbuf( Start_buf + copy_amt) )
263                ferr("INTERNAL ERROR, ii_flush: Buffer full, can't read.\n");
264
265            if( pMark )
266                pMark -= shift_amt;
267
268            sMark -= shift_amt;
269            eMark -= shift_amt;
270            Next  -= shift_amt;
271        }
272
273        return 1;
274    }
275
276    /*----------------------------------------------------------------------*/
277
278    PRIVATE  int    ii_fillbuf( starting_at )
279    unsigned char    *starting_at;
280    {
281        /* Fill the input buffer from starting_at to the end of the buffer.
282         * The input file is not closed when EOF is reached. Buffers are read
283         * in units of MAXLEX characters; it's an error if that many characters
284         * cannot be read (0 is returned in this case). For example, if MAXLEX
285         * is 1024, then 1024 characters will be read at a time. The number of
286         * characters read is returned. Eof_read is true as soon as the last
287         * buffer is read.
288         *
289         * PORTABILITY NOTE:  I'm assuming that the read function actually returns
290         *                    the number of characters loaded into the buffer, and
291         * that that number will be < need only when the last chunk of the file is
292         * read. It's possible for read() to always return fewer than the number of
293         * requested characters in MS-DOS untranslated-input mode, however (if the
294         * file is opened without the O_BINARY flag). That's not a problem here
295         * because the file is opened in binary mode, but it could cause problems
296         * if you change from binary to text mode at some point.
297         */
298
299        register unsigned need,    /* Number of bytes required from input. */
300                          got;     /* Number of bytes actually read.       */
301
302        need = ((END - starting_at) / MAXLEX) * MAXLEX ;
303
304        D( printf( "Reading %d bytes\n", need );   )
305
306        if( need < 0 )
307            ferr("INTERNAL ERROR (ii_fillbuf): Bad read-request starting addr.\n");
308
309        if( need == 0 )
310            return 0;
311
312        if( (got = (*Readp)(Inp_file, starting_at, need)) == -1 )
313            ferr("Can't read input file\n");
314
```

```
Listing 2.6. continued...
315        End_buf = starting_at + got ;
316
317        if( got < need )
318            Eof_read = 1;              /* At end of file */
319
320        return got;
321    }
```

The final routine in Listing 2.6 is `ii_fillbuf()`, starting on line 278 . It is passed a base address, and loads as many MAXLEX-sized chunks into the buffer as will fit. The `need` variable, initialized on line 302, is the amount needed. The logical-end-of-buffer marker is adjusted on line 315. Note that a single `read()` call does the actual read on line 312. (Readp is initialized to point at `read()` when it is declared up at the top of the file.) This can cause problems when a lexeme can span a line, and input is fetched from a line-buffered input device (such as the console). You'll have to use `ii_io()` to supply an alternate read function, in this case.

Listing 2.7 shows the lookahead function, `ii_look()`. It returns the character at the offset from the current character that's specified in its argument. An `ii_look(0)` returns the character that was returned by the most recent `ii_advance()` call, `ii_look(1)` is the following character, `ii_look(-1)` is the character that precedes the current one. MAXLOOK characters of lookahead are guaranteed, though fewer might be available if you're close to end of file. Similarly, lookback (with a negative offset) is only guaranteed as far as the start of the buffer (the pMark or sMark, whichever is smaller). Zero is returned if you try to look past end or start of the buffer, EOF if you try to look past end of file.

> Load input buffer, `ii_fillbuf()`.
>
> need.
>
> Lookahead, `ii_look()`.

Listing 2.7. *input.c*— Lookahead

```
322    int      ii_look( n )
323    {
324        /* Return the nth character of lookahead, EOF if you try to look past
325         * end of file, or 0 if you try to look past either end of the buffer.
326         */
327
328        uchar       *p;
329
330        p = Next + (n-1) ;
331
332        if( Eof_read && p >= End_buf )
333            return EOF;
334
335        return( p < Start_buf || p >= End_buf ) ?  0  : *p ;
336    }
```

Listing 2.8 contains the pushback function, `ii_pushback(n)`. It is passed the number of characters to push back. For example, `ii_pushback(5)` pushes back the five most recently read characters. If you try to push past the sMark, only the characters as far as the sMark are pushed and 0 is returned (1 is returned on a successful push). If you push past the eMark, the eMark is moved back to match the current character. Unlike `ungetc()`, you can indeed push back characters after EOF has been reached.

The remainder of `input.c`, in Listing 2.9, provides support for `'\0'`-terminated strings. These routines are not—strictly speaking—necessary, because the lexeme

> `ii_pushback(n)`.
>
> \0-terminated-string support.

Listing 2.8. *input.c*— Pushback

```
337   int      ii_pushback( n )
338   {
339       /* Push n characters back into the input. You can't push past the current
340        * sMark. You can, however, push back characters after end of file has
341        * been encountered.
342        */
343
344       while( --n >= 0  &&  Next > sMark )
345       {
346           if( *--Next == '\n'  ||  !*Next )
347               --Lineno;
348       }
349
350       if( Next < eMark )
351       {
352           eMark = Next;
353           Mline = Lineno;
354       }
355
356       return( Next > sMark );
357   }
```

length is always available. It's occasionally useful to have a terminator on the string, however. Note that these functions should be used exclusively after the string has been terminated—the other input functions will not work properly in this case.

The termination is done with a call to ii_term() (on line 358). It saves the character pointed to by Next in a variable called Termchar, and then overwrites the character with a '\0'. The ii_unterm() function (on line 366) puts everything back.

Terminate/unterminate current lexeme, ii_term(), ii_unterm().

Listing 2.9. *input.c*— Support for '\0'-terminated Strings

```
358   void    ii_term()
359   {
360       Termchar = *Next ;
361       *Next     = '\0' ;
362   }
363
364   /* - - - - - - - - - - - - - - - - - - - - - - - - - - - - -*/
365
366   void    ii_unterm()
367   {
368       if( Termchar )
369       {
370           *Next = Termchar;
371           Termchar = 0;
372       }
373   }
374
375   /* - - - - - - - - - - - - - - - - - - - - - - - - - - - - -*/
376
377   int     ii_input()
378   {
379
380       int rval;
381
```

→

Listing 2.9. continued...

```
382        if( Termchar )
383        {
384            ii_unterm();
385            rval = ii_advance();
386            ii_mark_end();
387            ii_term();
388        }
389        else
390        {
391            rval = ii_advance();
392            ii_mark_end();
393        }
394
395        return rval;
396    }
397
398    /* - - - - - - - - - - - - - - - - - - - - - - - - - - - - - -*/
399
400    void    ii_unput( c )
401    {
402        if( Termchar )
403        {
404            ii_unterm();
405            if( ii_pushback(1) )
406                *Next = c;
407            ii_term();
408        }
409        else
410        {
411            if( ii_pushback(1) )
412                *Next = c;
413        }
414    }
415
416    /* - - - - - - - - - - - - - - - - - - - - - - - - - - - - - -*/
417
418    int     ii_lookahead( n )
419    {
420        return (n == 1 && Termchar) ? Termchar : ii_look(n) ;
421    }
422
423    /* - - - - - - - - - - - - - - - - - - - - - - - - - - - - - -*/
424
425    int     ii_flushbuf()
426    {
427        if( Termchar )
428            ii_unterm();
429
430        return ii_flush(1);
431    }
```

This approach is better than putting the `ii_unterm()` code into `ii_advance()`, because the latter approach slows down all `ii_advance()` calls. On the other hand, you have to remember to call `ii_unterm()` before calling `ii_advance()`. For this reason, an `ii_input()` function has been provided (on line 377) to make sure that the lexeme is unterminated and then reterminated correctly. That is, `ii_input()` is a well-behaved input function meant to be used directly by the user. The function also moves the end marker, making the lexeme one character longer (moving the null terminator if necessary), and it returns the new input character, or 0 at end of file. −1 is returned if another character couldn't be read because the buffer was full.

`ii_unput()`.

`ii_unput()` (on line 400) is a reverse-input function. It backs up the input one notch and then overwrites the character at that position with its argument. `ii_unput()` works correctly on both terminated and unterminated buffers, unlike `ii_pushback()`, which can't handle the terminator.

`ii_lookahead()`.

The `ii_lookahead()` function bears the same relation to `ii_look()` that `ii_input()` bears to `ii_advance()`. That is, `ii_lookahead(1)` functions correctly for strings that have been terminated with `ii_term()` calls, `ii_look()` does not. Similarly, `ii_flushbuf()` flushes a terminated buffer by unterminating it before calling `ii_flush()`.

Ring buffers.

One final note on strategy. The buffer-flush approach that I've used here allows me to take advantage of C's pointer mechanism when scanning the input. This approach isn't appropriate in a language like FORTRAN, where arrays must be referenced using an index. Here, you're better off using a *circular array* or *ring buffer*. For example, the input buffer would be declared with

```
char input_buf[ SIZE ];
```

and the next character would be accessed with

```
x = input_buf[ current_character % SIZE ];
```

You would load a new chunk from the disk into the far left of the array when `current_character` was greater than or equal to SIZE, being careful not to overwrite the current lexeme in the process.

Why ring buffers are inappropriate here.

The problem here is that a lexeme can span the buffer. That is, a situation may arise where the first half of a lexeme is far right of `input_buf` and the other half is at the far left. As long as you're accessing all the characters with an array index modulus the array size, this is not a problem. C, however, wants its strings in contiguous memory so that it can scan through them using a pointer. Moreover, the array index and modulus operation needed to access every character is inherently less efficient than a simple pointer access; more inefficient, even, than the moves that are part of a buffer flush. Consequently, a ring buffer isn't particularly appropriate in a C implementation.

2.4 Lexical Analysis*

Now that we've developed a set of input routines, we need to apply them in a lexical-analysis application. There are two approaches to lexical analysis, both useful. First, you can hard code the analyzer, recognizing lexemes with nested **if/else** statements, switches, and so forth. If the lexemes aren't too long one effective approach uses a series of lookup tables to recognize tokens. (Lookup tables tend to be faster than **switch**s or **if/else** statements.) Listing 2.10 shows such a system for recognizing the following tokens:

Lookup tables in hard-coded scanners.

```
>   >=   <   <=   ==   !=
```

The basic strategy is to vector from one table to another until a complete lexeme is identified.

Hard-coded scanners: advantages and disadvantages.

The hard-coded approach has its advantages—hard-coded lexical analyzers tend to be very efficient, but hard-coded analyzers are difficult to maintain. When you're developing a new language, it's handy to be able to add new tokens to the language or take some away without too much work. This problem is solved by programs like **lex**

Listing 2.10. Using Lookup Tables for Character Recognition

```
 1   #define LESS_THAN                  1
 2   #define GREATER_THAN               2
 3   #define EQUAL                      3
 4   #define NOT                        4
 5   #define LESS_THAN_OR_EQUAL         5
 6   #define GREATER_THAN_OR_EQUAL      6
 7   #define NOT_OR_EQUAL               7
 8   #define ASSIGN                     8
 9
10   #define ERROR                      -1
11   #define CONTINUE                   0
12
13   #define SIZE_OF_CHARACTER_SET      128
14
15   char first [ SIZE_OF_CHARACTER_SET ];
16   char second[ SIZE_OF_CHARACTER_SET ];
17   int  s, f;
18   ...
19   memset( first,  -1, SIZE_OF_CHARACTER_SET ); /* Initialize to error token.   */
20   memset( second, -1, SIZE_OF_CHARACTER_SET ); /* Note that there's an implicit */
21                                                /* conversion of -1 to 255 here  */
22   ...                                          /* (signed int to unsigend char).*/
23   first [ '>' ] = GREATER_THAN;
24   first [ '<' ] = LESS_THAN;
25   first [ '!' ] = NOT;
26   first [ '=' ] = ASSIGN;
27   second[ '=' ] = EQUAL;
28
29   c = getchar();
30
31   if( (f = first[c]) == ERROR )            /* discard bad character */
32       return ERROR;
33
34   if( (s = second[c]) == ERROR )           /* 1-character lexeme     */
35   {
36       ungetchar();
37       return( f );
38   }
39   else                                     /* 2-character lexeme */
40   {
41       if( s == EQUAL )
42           switch( f )
43           {
44           case ASSIGN:            return EQUAL ;
45           case LESS_THAN:         return LESS_THAN_OR_EQUAL ;
46           case GREATER_THAN:      return GREATER_THAN_OR_EQUAL ;
47           case NOT:               return NOT_EQUAL ;
48           }
49
50       return ERROR;                        /* discard both characters */
51   }
```

and L^EX, which translate a description of a token set into a table-driven lexical analyzer. (Hereafter, when I say L^EX, I'm actually referring to both programs). L^EX itself just creates the tables, the remainder of the analyzer is the same for all L^EX-generated source code. The fact that a L^EX-generated analyzer is typically slower than a hard-coded one is, more often than not, a small price to pay for faster development time. Once the language is stable, you can always go back and hard code a lexical analyzer if it's really necessary to speed up the front end.

2.4.1 Languages*

Before looking at LEX itself, we'll need a little theory. First some definitions. An *alphabet* is any finite set of symbols. For example, the ASCII character set is an alphabet; the set {'0','1'} is a more-restricted, binary alphabet. A *string* or *word* is a sequence of alphabetic symbols. In practical terms, a string is an array of characters. There is also the special case of an empty string, represented by the symbol ε (pronounced epsilon). In C, the '\0' is <u>not</u> part of the input alphabet. As a consequence, it can be used as an end-of-string marker because it cannot be confused with any of the characters in the string itself, all of which <u>are</u> part of the input alphabet. An empty string in C can then be represented by an array containing a single '\0' character. Note, here, that there's an important difference between ε, an empty string, and a *null* string. The former is an array containing the end-of-string marker. The latter is represented by a NULL pointer—a pointer that doesn't point anywhere. In other words, there is no array associated with a null string.

A *language* is a set of strings that can be formed from the input alphabet. A *sentence* is a sequence of the strings that comprise a language. A language can be as small as one string and still be useful. (Zero-element languages are possible, but not of much utility.) The ordering of strings within the sentence is defined by a collection of syntactic rules called a *grammar*. Note that this definition does not attribute meaning to any of the strings and this limitation has important practical consequences. The lexical analyzer doesn't understand meaning. It has to distinguish tokens solely on the basis of surrounding context—by looking at the characters that surround the current word, without regard to the syntactic or semantic structure of the input sentence (the tokens that precede and follow the current token). [Aho] introduces several other useful terms and definitions, paraphrased here:[5]

prefix	A *prefix* is a string composed of the characters remaining after zero or more symbols have been deleted from the end of a string: "in" is a prefix of "inconsequential". Officially, ε is a prefix of every string.
suffix	A *suffix* is a string formed by deleting zero or more symbols from the front of a string. "ible" is a suffix of "incomprehensible". The suffix is what's left after you've removed a prefix. ε is a suffix of every string.
substring	A *substring* is what's left when you remove both a suffix and prefix: "age" is a substring of "unmanageable". Note that suffixes and prefixes are substrings (but not the other way around). Also ε, the empty string, is a substring of every string.
proper X	A *proper prefix*, *suffix*, or *substring* of the string x has at least one element and it is not the same as x. That is, it can't be ε, and it can't be identical to the original string.
sub-sequence	A *sub-sequence* of a string is formed by deleting zero or more symbols from the string. The symbols don't have to be contiguous, so "iiii" and "ssss" are both sub-sequences of "Mississippi".

Margin notes:
Alphabets, strings, words.

ε, the empty string.

Empty versus null strings

Languages, sentences, grammars.

---

5. [Aho], p. 93.

Several useful operations can be performed on strings. The *concatenation* of two strings is formed by appending all characters of one string to the end of another string. The concatenation of "fire" and "water" is "firewater". The empty string, ε, can be concatenated to any other string without modifying it. (In set theory, ε is the *identity element* for the concatenation operation. An arithmetic analogy is found in multiplication: 1 is the identity element for multiplication because $x \equiv x \times 1$.) The concatenation operation is sometimes specified with an operator (typically a × or ·), so you can say that

String concatenation.

ε is the identity element.

fire · water ≡ firewater

If you look at concatenation as a sort of multiplication, then exponentiation makes sense. An expression like x^n represents *x*, repeated *n* times. You could define a language consisting of the eight legal octal digits with the following:

String exponentiation.

L(octal) = { 0, 1, 2, 3, 4, 5, 6, 7 }

and then you could specify a three-digit octal number with *L(octal)*³.

The exponentiation process can be generalized into the *closure* operations. If *L* is a language, then the *Kleene closure* of *L* is *L* repeated zero or more times. This operation is usually represented as *L*∗. In the case of a language comprised of a single character, *L*∗ is that character repeated zero or more times. If the language elements are strings rather than single characters, *L*∗ are the strings repeated zero or more times. For example, *L(octal)*∗ is zero or more octal digits. If *L(v1)* is a language comprised of the string *Va* and *L(v2)* is a language comprised of the string *Voom*, then

Kleene Closure (∗).

L(v1)∗ · *L(v2)*

describes all of the following strings:

Voom   VaVoom   VaVaVoom   VaVaVaVoom   etc.

The *positive closure* of *L* is *L* repeated one or more times, usually denoted *L*+. It's otherwise just like Kleene closure.

Positive closure (+).

Since languages are sets of symbols, most of the standard set operations can be applied to them. The most useful of these is union, denoted with the ∪ operator. For example, if *letters* is a language containing all 26 letters [denoted by *L(letters)*] and *digits* is a set containing all 10 digits [denoted by *L(digits)*], then {*L(letters)*∪*L(digits)*} is the set of alphanumeric characters. Union is the equivalent of a logical OR operator. (If *x* is an element of A∪B, then it is a member of either A OR B.) Other set operations (like intersection) are, of course possible, but have less practical application.

Set operations on languages, union (∪).

The foregoing can all be applied to build a language from an alphabet and to define large languages (such as token sets) in terms of smaller languages (letters, digits, and so forth). For example

L(digit) = { 1, 2, 3, 4, 5, 6, 7, 8, 9 }
L(alpha) = { a, b, c, . . . , z }

you can say:

L(digit)+	is a decimal constant in C (one or more digits).
L(digit)∗	is an optional decimal constant (zero or more digits).
L(alpha) ∪ *L(digit)*	is the set of alphanumeric characters.
(*L(alpha)* ∪ *L(digit)*)∗	is any number of alphanumeric characters.
L(alpha) · (*L(alpha)* ∪ *L(digit)*)∗	is a C identifier.

2.4.2 Regular Expressions*

Programs like LEX use the foregoing language theory to specify a token set for a lexical analyzer. The possible lexemes that correspond to individual tokens are all defined using a series of set operations applied to previously defined languages, with a base alphabet of the ASCII character set. The programs then translate that language specification into the C source code for a computer program that recognizes strings in the language.

Forming regular expressions. Metacharacters.

Both programs use a notation called *regular expressions* for this purpose. Strictly speaking, a regular expression is any well-formed formula over union, concatenation and Kleene closure—as was the case with the examples in the previous section. A practical implementation of regular expressions usually add other operations, however, to make them easier to use. I'll examine an extended regular-expression syntax in the current section.

The simplest regular expression is just a series of letters that match a sequence of the same letters in the input. Several special characters, called *metacharacters*, can be used to describe more complex strings. Though there are variations in the notation used for regular expressions, the following rules are used by LEX to form a regular expression and can be taken as characteristic:[6]

c	*A single character that is not a metacharacter is a regular expression.* The character c forms a regular expression that matches the single character c.

Regular expression concatenation.

ee	*Two regular expressions concatenated form a regular expression that recognizes a match of the first expression followed by a match of the second.* If a, n, and d are regular expressions recognizing the characters a, n, and d, they can be concatenated to form the expression and which matches the pattern and in the input. Note that there's no explicit concatenation operator here, the two strings are just placed next to each other.

Wildcard character.

.	*A period (pronounced* dot*) matches any character except a newline.* For example, the expression a.y matches any, amy, and the agy in magyar.

Start-of-line anchor.

^	*An up arrow anchors the pattern to the start of the line.* The pattern ^and matches the string and only if it comprises the first three characters on the line (no preceding white space). Note that any newline character that precedes the and is not matched. That is, the newline is not part of the lexeme, even though its presence (or a start-of-file marker) is required for a successful match.

End-of-line anchor.

$	*A dollar sign anchors the pattern to end of line.* The pattern and$ matches the string only if it is the last three characters on the line (no following white space). Again, the newline character is not part of the lexeme. The pattern ^and$ matches the word only if it's the only thing on a line.

Character classes.

[...] [^...]	*Brackets match any of the characters enclosed in the brackets.* The [and] metacharacter form a *character class* which matches any of the characters listed. For example, [0123456789] matches any single decimal digit. Ranges of characters can be abbreviated using a dash, so [0-9] also matches a single decimal digit. [0-9A-Fa-f] matches a hexadecimal digit. [a-zA-Z] matches an alphabetic character. If the first character following the bracket is an up arrow (^), a *negative character class* (which matches any character except the ones specified) is formed. [^a-z]

---

6. Other UNIX utilities, like **grep**, **vi**, and **sed**, use a subset of these rules.

matches any character except a lower-case, alphabetic character. Only seven characters have special meaning inside a character class:

{	Start of macro name.
}	End of macro name.
]	End of character class.
–	Range of characters.
ˆ	Indicates negative character class.
"	Takes away special meaning of characters up to next quote mark.
\	Takes away special meaning of next character.

Use \], \-, \\, and so forth, to put these into a class. Since other metacharacters such as *, ?, and + are not special here, the expression [*?+] matches a star, question mark, or plus sign. Also, a negative character class does not match a newline character. That is, [ˆa-z] actually matches anything except a lower-case character or newline. Note that a negative character class must match a character. That is, [ˆa-z]$ does not match an empty line. The line must have at least one character, though it may not end in a nonalphabetic character.

* + ?   *A regular expression followed by a * (pronounced star) matches that expression repeated zero or more times; a + matches one or more repetitions, a ? matches zero or one repetitions.* These three metacharacters represent *closure* operations. They are higher precedence than concatenation. ll?ama matches two strings: llama and lama. The expression l+ama matches lama, llama, and llllllllllllama. The expression l*ama matches all of the above, but also matches ama. The expression – 0[xX][0-9a-fA-f]+ matches a hexadecimal number in C syntax; [0-7][0-7]? matches one or two octal digits.   *Closure operators.*

e{n,m}   *Matches* n *to* m *repetitions of the expression* e. This operator is recognized by **lex**, but not L^EX.   *Multiple matches.*

e|e   *Two regular expressions separated by a vertical bar recognize a match of the first expression OR a match of the second.* OR is lower precedence than concatenation. The expression either|or matches either either or or.   *The OR operator.*

(e)   *Parentheses are used for grouping.* The expression: *Grouping .*

    (frank|·john)ie

matches both frankie, and johnie. The expression

    (frank|john)(ie)?

matches frank and john as well. You can add a newline to the characters recognized by a negative character class with something like this: *Add '0 to negative character class.*

    ([ˆa-z]|\en)

Surrounding a string that contains metacharacters with double quotes ("*") or preceding a single metacharacter with a backslash (*) takes away its special meaning. (A character preceded by a backslash is said to be *escaped*.) The operator precedence is summarized in the Table 2.1. All operators associate left to right.   *Escaping metacharacters, quotes marks.*

Note that regular expressions can only define sequences of characters. They cannot do things like recognize any number of properly nested parentheses, something that can be recognized grammatically (by the parser). This is one of the main reasons that the lexical analyzer and parser are separate modules. The lexical analyzer is in charge of recognizing simple sequences of characters, and the parser recognizes more complex combinations.   *Limitations of regular expressions.*

Table 2.1. Regular-Expression Operator Precedence

operator	description	level
( )	parentheses for grouping	1 (highest)
[ ]	character classes	2
* + ?	closure: 0 or more, 1 or more, 0 or 1	3
cc	concatenation	4
|	OR	5
^ $	anchors to beginning and end of line	6 (lowest)

2.4.3 Regular Definitions*

There is an alternate way of describing a language's token set that takes a more grammatical approach, and which is used in many language specifications. A *regular definition* builds up a language specification using a combination of regular-expression operators and production-like specifiers. For example:

keyword	$\rightarrow$	**long | int | double | while | . . .**
digit	$\rightarrow$	**0 | 1 | 2 | . . . | 9**
digit_sequence	$\rightarrow$	*digit* +
sign	$\rightarrow$	+ | −
exponent_part	$\rightarrow$	**e** *sign? digit_sequence*
	|	**E** *sign? digit_sequence*
floating_constant	$\rightarrow$	*digit_sequence* **.** *digit_sequence? exponent_part?*
	|	*digit_sequence?* **.** *digit_sequence exponent_part?*
	|	*digit_sequence exponent_part*

Element$_{opt}$.

Occasionally you see an *opt* subscript used to denote an optional element, such as *digit$_{opt}$* rather than *digit?*. This grammatical approach to languages is discussed in greater depth in the next chapter.

2.4.4 Finite Automata*

Recognizers.

A *recognizer* program, such as a lexical analyzer, reads a string as input and outputs *yes* if the string is a sentence in a language, *no* if it isn't. A lexical analyzer has to do more than say yes or no to be useful, so an extra layer is usually added around the recognizer itself. When a certain string is recognized, the second layer performs an action associated with that string. LEX takes an input file comprised of regular expressions and associated actions (code). It then builds a recognizer program that executes the code in the actions when a string is recognized. LEX builds the recognizer component of the analyzer by translating regular expressions that represent the lexemes into a *finite automaton* or *finite state machine* (usually abbreviated to "state machine" or "FSM").

Finite automata, state machines.

Strictly speaking, an FSM consists of the following:

States.
- A finite set of *states*.

Transitions.
- A set of *transitions* (or moves) from one state to another. Each transition is labeled with a character from the input alphabet.

Start state.
- A special *start* state.

Accepting states.
- A set of final or *accepting* states.

Transition diagram.

State machines are best understood by looking at one. Figure 2.3 is a *transition diagram* for a state machine that recognizes the four strings "he", "she", "his", and "hers".

Figure 2.3. A State Machine

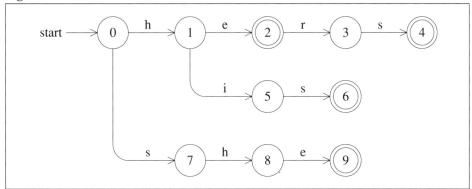

The circles are individual states, marked with the state number—an arbitrary number that identifies the state. State 0 is the *start state*, and the machine is initially in this state. The lines connecting the states represent the transitions, these lines are called *edges* and the label on an edge represents characters that cause the transition from one state to another (in the direction of the arrow). From the start state, reading an h from the input causes a transition to State 1; from State 1, an e gets the machine to State 3, and an i causes a transition to State 5; and so on. A transition from State *N* to state *M* on the character *c* is often represented with the notation: *next(N,c)=M*. This function is called the *move* function by some authors, [Aho] among them, but I feel that *next* better describes what the function is doing.

The states with double circles are called *accepting states*. Entering an accepting state signifies recognition of a particular input string, and there is usually some sort of action associated with the accepting state (in lexical-analyzer applications, a token is returned). Unmarked edges (for example, there are no outgoing edges marked with an *i*, *s*, *r*, or *e* from State 0) are all implied transitions to a special implicit *error state*.

State machines such as the foregoing can be modeled with two data structures: a single variable holding the current state number and a two-dimensional array for computing the next state. One axis is indexed by the input character, the other by the current state, and the array holds the next state. For example, the previous machine can be represented by the arrays in Table 2.2. Two arrays are used, one to hold the state transitions and another to tell you whether a state is accepting or not. (You could also use a single, two-dimensional array of structures, one element of which was the next state and the other of which was the accepting-state marker, but that would waste space.) The next state is determined from the current state and input character, by looking it up in the table as follows:

```
next_state = Transition_table[ input_character ][ current_state ];

if( Accepting[ next_state ] == 1 )
    do_an_accepting_action( next_state );
```

This input character is usually called the *lookahead* character because it's not removed from the input until the next-state transition is made. The machine derives the next state from the current state and lookahead character. If the next state is not the error state, then set the current state to that state and advance past the lookahead character (typically by reading, and discarding, it).

The machine we just looked at is called a *deterministic finite automaton* or *DFA*. A DFA is "deterministic" in that the next state can always be determined by knowing the current state and the current lookahead character. To be more specific, a DFA is a state

Table 2.2. Representing the State Machine

		Transition Table					Accepting
		Lookahead Character					
		e	h	i	r	s	
cur-rent state	0	–	1	–	–	7	0
	1	2	–	5	–	–	0
	2	–	–	–	3	–	1
	3	–	–	–	–	4	0
	4	–	–	–	–	–	1
	5	–	–	–	–	6	0
	6	–	–	–	–	–	1
	7	–	8	–	–	–	0
	8	9	–	–	–	–	0
	9	–	–	–	–	–	1

Nondeterministic finite automaton (NFA).

ε transitions match empty string.

machine in which all outgoing edges are labeled with an input character, and no two edges leaving a given state have the same label. There is also a second, more general type of state machine called a *nondeterministic finite automaton* or *NFA*, which is more useful in many applications, including the current one. (All DFAs are also NFAs, but not the other way around.) An NFA has no limitations on the number and type of edges: Two outgoing edges can have the same label, and edges can be labeled with the empty string, ε. This last type of edge is called an *epsilon edge* or *epsilon transition*. Since an ε transition matches an empty string, it is taken without advancing the input and is always taken—regardless of the input character. For example, how can the regular expression *(and|any)* be represented as a state machine? A DFA for this expression looks like this:

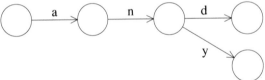

Unfortunately, DFA's are difficult to construct directly from regular expressions[7]— NFA's are easy to construct. Two possibilities are:

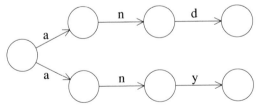

and

---

7. It is possible to construct a DFA directly from a regular expression, though I won't discuss how to do it here. See both [McNaughton] and [Aho] pp. 135–141.

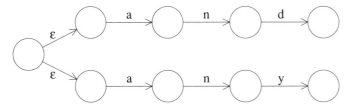

The second machine is preferable because it's easier to represent in a computer program (we'll see how in a moment). As you can see, the NFA can be an awkward data structure to use. It can have many more states than the equivalent DFA, and it's difficult to write a state-machine driver (a program that uses the state machine to do something, such as recognize tokens) that can use it directly.[8] LEX solves the problem by creating the state machine in a two-step process. It first makes an NFA representing the input regular expressions, and it then converts that NFA to a DFA, which it in turn outputs. I'll discuss how LEX performs this feat later in this chapter.

State-machine driver.

The state-machine representations we've been looking at are, of course, just one of many ways to represent them. You can generalize the definitions for NFAs and DFAs. A *nondeterministic finite automaton*, or NFA, is a mathematical model consisting of:

NFA: formal definition.

(1) A set of states, S.
(2) A special state in S called the *start* state. The machine is initially in this state.
(3) A set of states in S called *accepting* states, entry into which denotes recognition of a string. Some sort of action is usually associated with each of the accepting states.
(4) A set of input symbols (an input alphabet).
(5) A *next* function that, when given a state and an input symbol, returns the set of states to which control is transferred on that symbol from the indicated state. I'll describe this *next* function in greater detail in a moment—note, however, that the *next* function returns a <u>set</u> of states. The main implementation difference between an NFA and a DFA is this *next* function. The *next* function for a DFA always yields a single next state. The equivalent NFA function can yield several next states.

A *deterministic finite automaton* or DFA is an NFA with the following restrictions:

DFA: formal definition.

(1) No state can have an outgoing ε transition (an edge labeled with ε, the empty string).
(2) There may be no more than one outgoing transition from any state that is labeled with the same character.

In practical terms, the foregoing definition describes only the data structures (the set of states and the way that the transitions are represented) and the *next* function that determines the next state from the current one. In other words, it tells us how to make a transition matrix. There is no information here about how the state machine is used; and automata can, in fact, be used in different ways depending on the application. The state machine is itself distinct from the *driver* program—the program that uses that machine.

The state machine and driver are distinct.

State-machine driver.

---

8. In fact, a theoretical NFA often has fewer states than an equivalent DFA because it can have more edges leaving a single state than the DFA has. Nonetheless, this sort of NFA is difficult to represent in a computer program because it has an indeterminate number of outgoing edges. The NFA's discussed in the current chapter all have more states than the equivalent DFA's because the extra states help smooth over these difficulties. I'll show how in a moment.

2.4.5 State-Machine-Driven Lexical Analyzers*

Using state machines for
lexical analysis.
This section demonstrates how state machines are used for lexical analysis by look-ing, at a high level, at the method used by a LEX-generated lexical analyzer. I'll describe a simple table-driven lexical analyzer that recognizes decimal and floating-point con-stants. The following regular expressions describe these constants:

```
[0-9]+                                                        return ICON;
([0-9]+|[0-9]*\.[0-9]+|[0-9]+\.[0-9]*)(e[0-9]+)?   return FCON;
```

The code to the right of the regular expression is executed by the lexical analyzer when an input string that matches that expression is recognized. The first expression recog-nizes a simple sequence of one or more digits. The second expression recognizes a floating-point constant. The (e[0-9]+)? at the end of the second regular expression is the optional engineering notation at the end of the number. I've simplified by not allow-ing the usual + or − to follow the e, and only a lower-case e is recognized. The

```
([0-9]+    |    [0-9]*\.[0-9]+    |    [0-9]+\.[0-9]*)
```

recognizes one of three patterns (I've added the spaces to clarify what's going on—they're not really there): The [0-9]+ is a simple sequence of decimal digits. It's for numbers like 10e3. Because of the way that LEX works, the [0-9]+ on the previous line of the input specification takes precedence over the current one—an **ICON** is returned if a number does not have a trailing e, otherwise an **FCON** is returned. The [0-9]*\.[0-9]+ recognizes numbers with at least one digit to the right of the decimal point, the [0-9]+\.[0-9]* recognizes numbers with at least one digit to the left. You can't use [0-9]*\.[0-9]* because that pattern would accept a decimal point without numbers on either side. All of the following numbers are accepted:

    1.2   1.   .1   1.2e3   2e3   1

and, of these, the last is an ICON and the others are FCONs.

LEX uses a state-machine approach to recognize regular expressions, and a DFA that recognizes the previous expressions is shown in Figure 2.4. The same machine is represented as an array in Table 2.3. The next state is computed using that array with:

```
next_state = array[ current_state ][ input ]
```

Transition matrix.
A dash indicates a failure transition (no legal outgoing transition on the current input character from the current state). This array is typically called a *transition matrix* or *transition table*. There are three accepting states (states from which a token is recog-nized) in the machine: 1, 2, and 4. State 1 accepts an integer constant, and the other two recognize floating-point constants. The accepting states are recognized in an auxiliary array that is also indexed by state number, and which indicates whether or not a state is accepting.

As I mentioned earlier, the state machine itself and the driver program that uses that machine are distinct from one another. Two algorithms are commonly used in lexical analysis applications, and the same state machine (transition matrix) is used by both
The greedy algorithm
(matches longest string).
algorithms. A *greedy* algorithm, shown in Table 2.4, is used by LEX (because that's what's required by most programming-language specifications). This algorithm finds the longest possible sequence of input characters that can form a token. The algorithm can be stated informally as follows: If there's an outgoing transition from the current state, take it. If the new state is an accepting state, remember it along with the input position. If there's no outgoing transition (the table has a a dash in it), do the action associated with the most-recently seen accepting state. If there is no such state, then an error has occurred (LEX just ignores the partially-collected lexeme and starts over from State 0, in this situation).

Figure 2.4. State Machine That Recognizes Floating-Point Constants

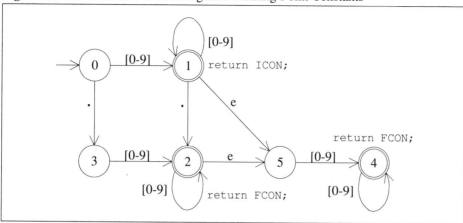

Table 2.3. State Machine in Figure 2.3 Represented as an Array

		lookahead character			accepting action
		.	0–9	e	
	0	3	1	–	–
	1	2	1	5	return ICON;
current	2	–	2	5	return FCON;
state	3	–	2	–	–
	4	–	4	–	return FCON
	5	–	4	–	–

I'll do two examples to show the workings of the machine, the first with the input *1.2e4*. LEX starts in State 0. The 1 causes a transition to State 1 and the input is advanced. Since State 1 is a potential accepting state, the current input position and state number is remembered. The dot now gets us to State 2 (and the input is advanced again). Since State 2 is also an accepting state, the previously remembered input position and state number are overwritten by the current ones. The next input character (the *2)* causes us to go from State 2 to itself. State 2 is still an accepting state, so the current input position overwrites the previously saved one. The *e* now gets us to State 5, which isn't an accepting state, so no other action is performed; and the final *4* causes a transition to State 4, which is an accepting state, so the current input position overwrites the previous one. The next input character is the end-of-input marker. There is no legal transition out of State 4 on end of input, so the machine enters the failure state. Here, the action associated with the most-recently seen accepting state (4) is performed and the machine returns FCON. The next time the subroutine is called, it returns zero immediately, because the lookahead character is end of input.

Example: 1.2e4.

The second example looks at the incorrect input *1.2e*, with no number following the *e*. This input causes a failure transition from State 5, because there's no legal outgoing transition on end of input from State 5. When the failure occurs, the most recently seen accepting state is State 2, so the input is backed up to the condition it was in in State 2 (the next input character is an *e*) and an FCON is returned. The next time the algorithm is entered, there will be a failure transition from the start state, because an *e* can't occur at the beginning of the number. The *e* is discarded, and the algorithm goes to State 0 (and terminates).

Bad-input example: 1.2e.

Table 2.4. Algorithm Used by the L^EX State-Machine Driver

```
current_state = 0;
previously_seen_accepting_state = none_seen;

if( lookahead character is end-of-input )
    return 0;

while( lookahead character is not end-of-input )
{
    if( there is a transition from the current state on the current lookahead character)
    {
        current_state = that state;
        advance the input;

        if( the current state is an accepting state )
        {
            remember the current position in the input
            and the action associated with the current state;
        }
    }
    else
    {
        if( no accepting state has been seen )
        {
            There's an error:
                Discard the current lexeme and input character.
                Current_state = 0;
        }
        else
        {
            back up the input to the position it was in when it saw the last accepting state
            perform the action associated with that accepting state;
        }
    }
}
```

Disadvantages of greedy algorithm.

Note that the greedy algorithm does have its disadvantages: It's tricky to implement and tends to be relatively slow. It can also cause the recognizer to behave in sometimes unexpected ways. (The L^EX input expression (\n|.)* tries to absorb the entire input file, for example.) It is nonetheless the best (and sometimes the only) choice in most real lexical-analysis applications.

The nongreedy algorithm (matches first string).

The second type of algorithm (the *nongreedy* algorithm) is much simpler. Here, the shortest possible input string is recognized, and the machine just accepts as soon as an accepting state is entered. A nongreedy recognizer program is much simpler to implement than a greedy one, and is much faster as well. Nonetheless, this algorithm can be

Terminal nodes.

used only when all the accepting states in the machine are terminal nodes—when they have no outgoing transitions.

2.4.6 Implementing a State-Machine-Driven Lexical Analyzer

This section shows how the machine in the previous section is implemented by analyzing a LEX output file in depth. You may want to skip over this section if you're not interested in this level of detail. You should read Appendixes A and D, in which various support functions and LEX itself are described, before continuing. A LEX input file that recognizes the floating-point constants we've been looking at is shown in Listing 2.11

LEX input file for floating-point constants.

Listing 2.11. *numbers.lex*— A LEX Input File to Recognize Floating-Point Constants

```
1    %{
2          #define FCON  1;
3          #define ICON  2;
4    %}
5    D         [0-9]                            /* a single decimal digit */
6    %%
7    {D}+                                       return  ICON;
8    ({D}+|{D}*\.{D}+|{D}+\.{D}*)(e{D}+)?       return  FCON;
9    %%
```

The lex output file—*lexyy.c*—begins in Listing 2.12.[9] The first two lines are from the header portion of the original LEX input file. They are followed by a comment that describes the state machine that LEX created. If a state is an accepting state, the first few characters of the equivalent code are printed (tabs are mapped to \t), along with the input line number. The goto transitions are shown along with the characters that cause the transitions. If several edges (outgoing transitions) all go to the same state, they are represented like this:

State-machine description in LEX output file.

```
goto  2 on 0123456789
```

The state goes to State 2 if the input character is a digit. The entire comment is surrounded with an **#ifdef** _ _NEVER_ _ in case a */ should accidentally come up in one of these lists of transition characters.

_ _NEVER_ _.

The next part of the LEX output file is copied directly from the template file (*/lib/lex.par* by default, but a different file can be specified with the *-m* command-line switch). This template file is separated into three parts by formfeed (Ctrl-L) characters. Everything from the beginning of the file up to the first formfeed is copied into the output file at this juncture. The relevant code is shown in Listing 2.13.

Template-file organization, lex.par

The **#ifndef** directive on line 35 of Listing 2.13 lets you define YYPRIVATE in the LEX-input-file header, without having to **#undef** it first. Most of the global variables in the file are declared as YYPRIVATE, which normally translates to the keyword **static**. Redefining this macro to an empty string makes these variables true globals, which can be accessed from outside the current file. I'm using the definition of NULL on line 39 to determine if *<stdio.h>* was included previously, and including it if not. Finally, if YYDEBUG is defined, various debugging diagnostics are activated. These are printed only if the variable yydebug is also true, thus the if statement on line 45. It's best to

YYPRIVATE.

YY_D, yydebug, YYDEBUG

---

9. Note that there are two kinds of text in *lexyy.c*: (1) text copied verbatim from the template file *lex.par* and (2) text generated by LEX itself. The listings that describe those parts of *lexyy.c* that are copied from the template file are labeled *lex.par* in the following discussion. LEX-generated text is in listings labeled *lexyy.c*. Line numbers carry over from one listing to another because there's really only a single output file.

Listing 2.12. *lexyy.c*— State-Machine Description

```
 1          #define FCON  1
 2          #define ICON  2
 3
 4    #ifdef __NEVER__
 5    /*---------------------------------------------
 6     * DFA (start state is 0) is:
 7     *
 8     * State 0 [nonaccepting]
 9     *      goto   3 on .
10     *      goto   1 on 0123456789
11     * State 1 [accepting, line 7 <return  ICON;>]
12     *      goto   2 on .
13     *      goto   1 on 0123456789
14     *      goto   5 on e
15     * State 2 [accepting, line 8 <return\tFCON;>]
16     *      goto   2 on 0123456789
17     *      goto   5 on e
18     * State 3 [nonaccepting]
19     *      goto   2 on 0123456789
20     * State 4 [accepting, line 8 <return\tFCON;>]
21     *      goto   4 on 0123456789
22     * State 5 [nonaccepting]
23     *      goto   4 on 0123456789
24     */
25
26    #endif
```

see how the macro works by looking at an example; if YYDEBUG is defined, then a debugging diagnostic like:

```
    YY_D( printf("aaaaaghhhh!!!") );
```

is expanded to:

```
    if( yydebug ){ printf("aaaaaghhhh!!!"); } else;
```

Note that the semicolon following the **else** comes from the original macro invocation and the semicolon following the printf() follows the x in the macro definition. That trailing **else** is important in order to make something like the following work correctly:

*Trailing **else** in multiple-statement macro.*

```
    if( something )
        YY_D(printf("aaaaaghhhh!!!") );
    else
        something_else();
```

The foregoing expands to:

```
    if( something )
        if( yydebug )
        {
            printf("aaaaaghhhh!!!");
        }
        else
                ;
    else
        something_else();
```

If the **else** weren't present in the macro definition, then the **else** something_else() clause in the original code would incorrectly bind to the

Listing 2.13. *lex.par*— Various Definitions Copied Into *lexyy.c*

```
27   /* YY_TTYPE is used for the DFA transition table: Yy_nxt[], declared below.
28    * YYF marks failure transitions in the DFA transition table. There's no failure
29    * state in the table itself, these transitions must be handled by the driver
30    * program. The DFA start state is State 0. YYPRIVATE is only defined here only
31    * if it hasn't be #defined earlier. I'm assuming that if NULL is undefined,
32    * <stdio.h> hasn't been included.
33    */
34
35   #ifndef YYPRIVATE
36   #       define YYPRIVATE static
37   #endif
38
39   #ifndef NULL
40   #       include <stdio.h>
41   #endif
42
43   #ifdef YYDEBUG
44           int     yydebug = 0;
45   #       define YY_D(x) if( yydebug ){ x; }else
46   #else
47   #       define YY_D(x)
48   #endif
49
50   typedef unsigned char   YY_TTYPE;
51   #define YYF                     (( YY_TTYPE ) (-1))
52
53   unsigned char    *ii_text();
```

if(yydebug) rather than the **if**(something). If YYDEBUG isn't defined in the header, then the argument to YY_D effectively disappears from the input (the macro expands to an empty string). In this case, the printf() statements go away.

The code on lines 50 and 51 of Listing 2.13 are used to declare and access the transition-matrix array. YY_TYPE is the type of one array element, and YY_F marks failure transitions in the array. This latter value cannot be used as a state number. Note that the cast to **unsigned char** effectively translates −1 to 255. Similarly, −1's in the tables are all silently converted to 255 as part of the initialization.

> YY_TYPE, YYF.

The next part of the LEX output file is the state-machine transition matrix. It is used to compute the next state from the current state and lookahead symbols. This array can take three forms. The first, uncompressed form is shown in in Figure 2.5 and Listing 2.14. I've simplified the picture by leaving all the error transitions blank. (They're initialized to −1 in Listing 2.14.) An uncompressed array is generated by specifying a *-f* (for fast) switch on the LEX command line. The next state is computed with:

> Transition matrix representations.

> Uncompressed transition matrix.

```
Yy_nxt[ current_state] ][ lookahead_character ]
```

This operation is encapsulated into the yy_next(state,c) macro on line 147 of Listing 2.14.

Notice that several columns in the uncompressed array are identical. All columns not associated with a period, *e*, or digit are the same—they're all error transitions. All the columns for the digits are the same. By the same token, the rows associated with States 4 and 5 are the same. (The states aren't equivalent because one is an accepting state and the other isn't.) This situation holds with most state machines that recognize real token sets. Taking C as a case in point, all the control characters and the space character are ignored, so the columns for these are identical. With a few exceptions like *L*

> Compressed transition matrix. Redundant row and column elimination.

Figure 2.5. The Uncompressed Transition Table

Yy_nxt[][]	.	0123456789	e	
0	3	1111111111		
1	2	1111111111	5	return ICON
2		2222222222	5	return FCON
3		2222222222		
4		4444444444		
5		4444444444		return FCON

Listing 2.14. *lexyy.c*— The Uncompressed Transition Table

```
54   YYPRIVATE YY_TTYPE  Yy_nxt[ 6 ][ 128 ] =
55   {
56   /* 00 */  {   -1,  -1,  -1,  -1,  -1,  -1,  -1,  -1,  -1,  -1,
57                 -1,  -1,  -1,  -1,  -1,  -1,  -1,  -1,  -1,  -1,
58                 -1,  -1,  -1,  -1,  -1,  -1,  -1,  -1,  -1,  -1,
59                 -1,  -1,  -1,  -1,  -1,  -1,  -1,  -1,  -1,  -1,
60                 -1,  -1,  -1,  -1,  -1,  -1,   3,  -1,   1,   1,
61                  1,   1,   1,   1,   1,   1,   1,   1,  -1,  -1,
62                 -1,  -1,  -1,  -1,  -1,  -1,  -1,  -1,  -1,  -1,
63                 -1,  -1,  -1,  -1,  -1,  -1,  -1,  -1,  -1,  -1,
64                 -1,  -1,  -1,  -1,  -1,  -1,  -1,  -1,  -1,  -1,
65                 -1,  -1,  -1,  -1,  -1,  -1,  -1,  -1,  -1,  -1,
66                 -1,  -1,  -1,  -1,  -1,  -1,  -1,  -1,  -1,  -1,
67                 -1,  -1,  -1,  -1,  -1,  -1,  -1,  -1,  -1,  -1,
68                 -1,  -1,  -1,  -1,  -1,  -1,  -1,  -1
69            },
70   /* 01 */  {   -1,  -1,  -1,  -1,  -1,  -1,  -1,  -1,  -1,  -1,
71                 -1,  -1,  -1,  -1,  -1,  -1,  -1,  -1,  -1,  -1,
72                 -1,  -1,  -1,  -1,  -1,  -1,  -1,  -1,  -1,  -1,
73                 -1,  -1,  -1,  -1,  -1,  -1,  -1,  -1,  -1,  -1,
74                 -1,  -1,  -1,  -1,  -1,  -1,   2,  -1,   1,   1,
75                  1,   1,   1,   1,   1,   1,   1,   1,  -1,  -1,
76                 -1,  -1,  -1,  -1,  -1,  -1,  -1,  -1,  -1,  -1,
77                 -1,  -1,  -1,  -1,  -1,  -1,  -1,  -1,  -1,  -1,
78                 -1,  -1,  -1,  -1,  -1,  -1,  -1,  -1,  -1,  -1,
79                 -1,  -1,  -1,  -1,  -1,  -1,  -1,  -1,  -1,  -1,
80                 -1,   5,  -1,  -1,  -1,  -1,  -1,  -1,  -1,  -1,
81                 -1,  -1,  -1,  -1,  -1,  -1,  -1,  -1,  -1,  -1,
82                 -1,  -1,  -1,  -1,  -1,  -1,  -1,  -1
83            },
84   /* 02 */  {   -1,  -1,  -1,  -1,  -1,  -1,  -1,  -1,  -1,  -1,
85                 -1,  -1,  -1,  -1,  -1,  -1,  -1,  -1,  -1,  -1,
86                 -1,  -1,  -1,  -1,  -1,  -1,  -1,  -1,  -1,  -1,
87                 -1,  -1,  -1,  -1,  -1,  -1,  -1,  -1,  -1,  -1,
88                 -1,  -1,  -1,  -1,  -1,  -1,  -1,  -1,   2,   2,
89                  2,   2,   2,   2,   2,   2,   2,   2,  -1,  -1,
90                 -1,  -1,  -1,  -1,  -1,  -1,  -1,  -1,  -1,  -1,
91                 -1,  -1,  -1,  -1,  -1,  -1,  -1,  -1,  -1,  -1,
92                 -1,  -1,  -1,  -1,  -1,  -1,  -1,  -1,  -1,  -1,
93                 -1,  -1,  -1,  -1,  -1,  -1,  -1,  -1,  -1,  -1,
94                 -1,   5,  -1,  -1,  -1,  -1,  -1,  -1,  -1,  -1,
95                 -1,  -1,  -1,  -1,  -1,  -1,  -1,  -1,  -1,  -1,
96                 -1,  -1,  -1,  -1,  -1,  -1,  -1,  -1
```

```
Listing 2.14. continued...
97                         },
98     /* 03 */  {  -1,   -1,   -1,   -1,   -1,   -1,   -1,   -1,   -1,   -1,
99                      -1,   -1,   -1,   -1,   -1,   -1,   -1,   -1,   -1,   -1,
100                     -1,   -1,   -1,   -1,   -1,   -1,   -1,   -1,   -1,   -1,
101                     -1,   -1,   -1,   -1,   -1,   -1,   -1,   -1,   -1,   -1,
102                     -1,   -1,   -1,   -1,   -1,   -1,   -1,   -1,    2,    2,
103                      2,    2,    2,    2,    2,    2,    2,    2,   -1,   -1,
104                     -1,   -1,   -1,   -1,   -1,   -1,   -1,   -1,   -1,   -1,
105                     -1,   -1,   -1,   -1,   -1,   -1,   -1,   -1,   -1,   -1,
106                     -1,   -1,   -1,   -1,   -1,   -1,   -1,   -1,   -1,   -1,
107                     -1,   -1,   -1,   -1,   -1,   -1,   -1,   -1,   -1,   -1,
108                     -1,   -1,   -1,   -1,   -1,   -1,   -1,   -1,   -1,   -1,
109                     -1,   -1,   -1,   -1,   -1,   -1,   -1,   -1,   -1,   -1,
110                     -1,   -1,   -1,   -1,   -1,   -1,   -1,   -1
111                        },
112    /* 04 */  {  -1,   -1,   -1,   -1,   -1,   -1,   -1,   -1,   -1,   -1,
113                     -1,   -1,   -1,   -1,   -1,   -1,   -1,   -1,   -1,   -1,
114                     -1,   -1,   -1,   -1,   -1,   -1,   -1,   -1,   -1,   -1,
115                     -1,   -1,   -1,   -1,   -1,   -1,   -1,   -1,   -1,   -1,
116                     -1,   -1,   -1,   -1,   -1,   -1,   -1,   -1,    4,    4,
117                      4,    4,    4,    4,    4,    4,    4,    4,   -1,   -1,
118                     -1,   -1,   -1,   -1,   -1,   -1,   -1,   -1,   -1,   -1,
119                     -1,   -1,   -1,   -1,   -1,   -1,   -1,   -1,   -1,   -1,
120                     -1,   -1,   -1,   -1,   -1,   -1,   -1,   -1,   -1,   -1,
121                     -1,   -1,   -1,   -1,   -1,   -1,   -1,   -1,   -1,   -1,
122                     -1,   -1,   -1,   -1,   -1,   -1,   -1,   -1,   -1,   -1,
123                     -1,   -1,   -1,   -1,   -1,   -1,   -1,   -1,   -1,   -1,
124                     -1,   -1,   -1,   -1,   -1,   -1,   -1,   -1
125                        },
126    /* 05 */  {  -1,   -1,   -1,   -1,   -1,   -1,   -1,   -1,   -1,   -1,
127                     -1,   -1,   -1,   -1,   -1,   -1,   -1,   -1,   -1,   -1,
128                     -1,   -1,   -1,   -1,   -1,   -1,   -1,   -1,   -1,   -1,
129                     -1,   -1,   -1,   -1,   -1,   -1,   -1,   -1,   -1,   -1,
130                     -1,   -1,   -1,   -1,   -1,   -1,   -1,   -1,    4,    4,
131                      4,    4,    4,    4,    4,    4,    4,    4,   -1,   -1,
132                     -1,   -1,   -1,   -1,   -1,   -1,   -1,   -1,   -1,   -1,
133                     -1,   -1,   -1,   -1,   -1,   -1,   -1,   -1,   -1,   -1,
134                     -1,   -1,   -1,   -1,   -1,   -1,   -1,   -1,   -1,   -1,
135                     -1,   -1,   -1,   -1,   -1,   -1,   -1,   -1,   -1,   -1,
136                     -1,   -1,   -1,   -1,   -1,   -1,   -1,   -1,   -1,   -1,
137                     -1,   -1,   -1,   -1,   -1,   -1,   -1,   -1,   -1,   -1,
138                     -1,   -1,   -1,   -1,   -1,   -1,   -1,   -1
139                        }
140    };
141
142    /*------------------------------------------
143     * yy_next(state,c) is given the current state and input
144     * character and evaluates to the next state.
145     */
146
147    #define yy_next(state, c)  Yy_nxt[ state ][ c ]
```

and x, all the columns for the letters are identical, as are most of the digit's columns. Moreover, at least half of the states in a typical machine have no legal outgoing transitions, so the rows associated with these states are identical—every cell holds −1.

LEX's default compression technique takes advantage of this situation and eliminates the redundant rows and columns by creating two supplemental arrays. The compressed

Figure 2.6. Transition Table With Redundant Rows and Columns Eliminated

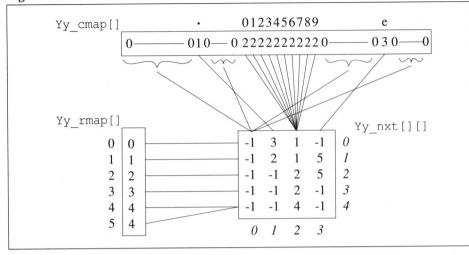

`Yy_cmap[]`, `Yy_nxt[]`

`Yy_rmap[]`.

table is shown in Figure 2.7 and in Listing 2.16. The `Yy_cmap[]` array is indexed by lookahead character and holds the index of one of the columns in the `Yy_nxt[]` array. When several columns in the original array are equivalent, the matching entries in `Yy_cmap[]` hold the index of a single column in `Yy_nxt[]`. For example, the columns associated with digits in the original table are all identical. Only one of these columns is present in the compressed array (at `Yy_nxt[x][2]`), and all columns corresponding to digits in `Yy_cmap` hold a `2`. The rows are compressed in the same way using `Yy_rmap[]`. Since rows 4 and 5 are identical in the uncompressed array, `Yy_rmap[4]` and `Yy_rmap[5]` both hold a 4, and `Yy_nxt[4][x]` holds the original row from the uncompressed table.

An array element is accessed using:

```
Yy_nxt[ Yy_rmap[current_state] ][ Yy_cmap[lookahead_character] ]
```

rather than the

```
Yy_nxt[ current_state] ][ lookahead_character ]
```

that's used for the uncompressed table. The `yy_next` macro for this type of table is defined on line 102 of Listing 2.15.

Compression ratio.

Redundant-row-and-column elimination is usually the best practical compression technique. The access time is fast, and the compression ratio is usually quite good. (In this example, the ratio is about 4:1 — 154 bytes, as compared to 640 bytes. The C lexical analyzer presented in Appendix D does even better, with a compression ratio of about 7:1 — 1,514 bytes versus 10,062 bytes.)

Pair-compressed transition matrix.

A second compression method yields better compression if the transition matrix is particularly sparse, though the access time is slower. The rows are split into distinct one-dimensional arrays, accessed indirectly through an array of pointers (see Figure 2.7).

`Yy_nxtN`, `Yy_nxt[]`.

The rows are all named `Yy_nxtN`, where *N* is the original row index in the uncompressed table (row 5 is in `Yy_nxt5[]`), and the array of pointers is called `Yy_nxt[]`. The current tables are compressed in this way in Listing 2.16.

If the first cell of the `Yy_nxtN` array is zero, then the remainder of the array is identical to the original row, and can be accessed directly using the lookahead character. To simplify a little:

Listing 2.15. *lexyy.c*— Transition Table With Redundant Rows and Columns Eliminated

```
 54   /*------------------------------------------
 55    * The Yy_cmap[] and Yy_rmap arrays are used as follows:
 56    *
 57    *   next_state= Yy_nxt[ Yy_rmap[current_state] ][ Yy_cmap[input_char] ];
 58    *
 59    * Character positions in the Yy_cmap array are:
 60    *
 61    *     ^@   ^A   ^B   ^C   ^D   ^E   ^F   ^G   ^H   ^I   ^J   ^K   ^L   ^M   ^N   ^O
 62    *     ^P   ^Q   ^R   ^S   ^T   ^U   ^V   ^W   ^X   ^Y   ^Z   ^[   ^\   ^]   ^^   ^_
 63    *          !    "    #    $    %    &    '    (    )    *    +    ,    -    .    /
 64    *     0    1    2    3    4    5    6    7    8    9    :    ;    <    =    >    ?
 65    *     @    A    B    C    D    E    F    G    H    I    J    K    L    M    N    O
 66    *     P    Q    R    S    T    U    V    W    X    Y    Z    [    \    ]    ^    _
 67    *     `    a    b    c    d    e    f    g    h    i    j    k    l    m    n    o
 68    *     p    q    r    s    t    u    v    w    x    y    z    {    |    }    ~    DEL
 69    */
 70
 71   YYPRIVATE YY_TTYPE  Yy_cmap[128] =
 72   {
 73         0,   0,   0,   0,   0,   0,   0,   0,   0,   0,   0,   0,   0,   0,   0,   0,
 74         0,   0,   0,   0,   0,   0,   0,   0,   0,   0,   0,   0,   0,   0,   0,   0,
 75         0,   0,   0,   0,   0,   0,   0,   0,   0,   0,   0,   0,   0,   0,   1,   0,
 76         2,   2,   2,   2,   2,   2,   2,   2,   2,   2,   0,   0,   0,   0,   0,   0,
 77         0,   0,   0,   0,   0,   0,   0,   0,   0,   0,   0,   0,   0,   0,   0,   0,
 78         0,   0,   0,   0,   0,   0,   0,   0,   0,   0,   0,   0,   0,   0,   0,   0,
 79         0,   0,   0,   0,   0,   3,   0,   0,   0,   0,   0,   0,   0,   0,   0,   0,
 80         0,   0,   0,   0,   0,   0,   0,   0,   0,   0,   0,   0,   0,   0,   0,   0
 81   };
 82
 83   YYPRIVATE YY_TTYPE  Yy_rmap[6] =
 84   {
 85         0,   1,   2,   3,   4,   4
 86   };
 87
 88   YYPRIVATE YY_TTYPE  Yy_nxt[ 5 ][ 4 ]=
 89   {
 90   /* 00 */  { -1,    3,    1,   -1 },
 91   /* 01 */  { -1,    2,    1,    5 },
 92   /* 02 */  { -1,   -1,    2,    5 },
 93   /* 03 */  { -1,   -1,    2,   -1 },
 94   /* 04 */  { -1,   -1,    4,   -1 }
 95   };
 96
 97   /*------------------------------------------
 98    * yy_next(state,c) is given the current state number and input
 99    * character and evaluates to the next state.
100    */
101
102   #define yy_next(state,c) (Yy_nxt[ Yy_rmap[state] ][ Yy_cmap[c] ])
```

```
YY_TTYPE *row;
row = Yy_nxt[ current_state ];

if( *row == 0 )
    next_state = (row + 1)[ lookahead_character ];
```

If the first cell of the Yy_nxt*N* array is nonzero, then the array holds a sequence of character/next-state pairs and the first cell holds the number of pairs. For example,

Figure 2.7. Pair-Compressed Transition Table

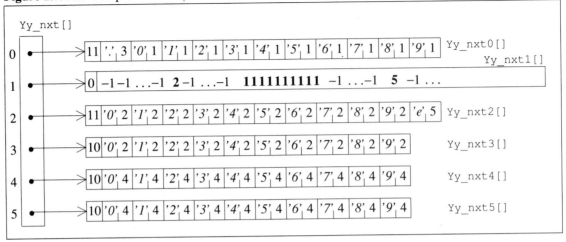

Listing 2.16. *lexyy.c*— Pair-Compressed Transition Table

```
54   YYPRIVATE YY_TTYPE  Yy_nxt0 [] = { 11,
55              '.',3, '0',1, '1',1, '2',1, '3',1,
56              '4',1, '5',1, '6',1, '7',1, '8',1,
57              '9',1};
58   YYPRIVATE YY_TTYPE  Yy_nxt1 [] = { 0,
59              -1,   -1,   -1,   -1,   -1,   -1,   -1,   -1,   -1,   -1,
60              -1,   -1,   -1,   -1,   -1,   -1,   -1,   -1,   -1,   -1,
61              -1,   -1,   -1,   -1,   -1,   -1,   -1,   -1,   -1,   -1,
62              -1,   -1,   -1,   -1,   -1,   -1,   -1,   -1,   -1,   -1,
63              -1,   -1,   -1,   -1,   -1,   -1,    2,   -1,    1,    1,
64               1,    1,    1,    1,    1,    1,    1,    1,   -1,   -1,
65              -1,   -1,   -1,   -1,   -1,   -1,   -1,   -1,   -1,   -1,
66              -1,   -1,   -1,   -1,   -1,   -1,   -1,   -1,   -1,   -1,
67              -1,   -1,   -1,   -1,   -1,   -1,   -1,   -1,   -1,   -1,
68              -1,   -1,   -1,   -1,   -1,   -1,   -1,   -1,   -1,   -1,
69              -1,    5,   -1,   -1,   -1,   -1,   -1,   -1,   -1,   -1,
70              -1,   -1,   -1,   -1,   -1,   -1,   -1,   -1,   -1,   -1,
71              -1,   -1,   -1,   -1,   -1,   -1,   -1,   -1};
72   YYPRIVATE YY_TTYPE  Yy_nxt2 [] = { 11,
73              '0',2, '1',2, '2',2, '3',2, '4',2,
74              '5',2, '6',2, '7',2, '8',2, '9',2,
75              'e',5};
76   YYPRIVATE YY_TTYPE  Yy_nxt3 [] = { 10,
77              '0',2, '1',2, '2',2, '3',2, '4',2,
78              '5',2, '6',2, '7',2, '8',2, '9',2
79              };
80   YYPRIVATE YY_TTYPE  Yy_nxt4 [] = { 10,
81              '0',4, '1',4, '2',4, '3',4, '4',4,
82              '5',4, '6',4, '7',4, '8',4, '9',4
83              };
84   YYPRIVATE YY_TTYPE  Yy_nxt5 [] = { 10,
85              '0',4, '1',4, '2',4, '3',4, '4',4,
86              '5',4, '6',4, '7',4, '8',4, '9',4
87              };
88
89   YYPRIVATE YY_TTYPE  *Yy_nxt[ 6 ] =
90   {
91       Yy_nxt0 , Yy_nxt1 , Yy_nxt2 , Yy_nxt3 , Yy_nxt4 , Yy_nxt5
```

```
    Listing 2.16. continued...
 92    };
 93
 94    /*------------------------------------------------------*/
 95
 96    YYPRIVATE YY_TTYPE  yy_next( cur_state, c )
 97    unsigned int    c ;
 98    int         cur_state ;
 99    {
100        /* Given the current state and the current input character
101         * return the next state.
102         */
103
104        YY_TTYPE   *p = Yy_nxt[ cur_state ] ;
105        register int i;
106
107        if( p )                            /* there are transitions */
108        {
109            if( (i = *p++)  == 0 )         /* row is uncompressed   */
110                return  p[ c ];
111
112            for( ; --i >= 0 ; p += 2 )     /* row is in in pairs    */
113                if( c == p[0] )
114                    return p[1];
115        }
116        return   YYF;
117    }
```

Yy_nxt0[] in Figure 2.7 contains 11 pairs (because 11 is in the first cell). The first pair
is ['.',3], which means that if the next input character is a dot, then the next state is
State 3. The next pair is ['0',1]— if the lookahead character is a '0', go to State 1, and
so forth. If you get to the end of the list without finding the current lookahead character,
there is a failure transition on that character. Again, simplifying a little:

```
YY_TTYPE *row;
row = Yy_nxt[ current_state ];

if( *row != 0 )
{
    for( num_pairs = *row++ ; --num_pairs >= 0 ; row += 2 )
      if( row[0] == lookahead_character )
      {
          next_state = row[1];
          break;
      }
}
```

The foregoing is implemented by the code on line 112 of Listing 2.16.

A third situation, unfortunately not illustrated in this example, occurs when a state
has no legal outgoing transitions. In this case, Yy_nxt[state] is set to NULL, so:

```
if( Yy_nxt[current_state] == NULL )
    next_state = FAILURE ;
```

This transition is activated when the test on line 107 of Listing 2.16 fails.

Note that further compression can be achieved at the expense of error recovery by
providing a default state other than the error state. Hitherto, an error was indicated when
you got to the end of the pair list. You can use the most common nonerror transition
instead of the error transition in this case, however. For example, Yy_nxt2 contains

Using a default transition.

these pairs:

['0',2]   ['1',2]   ['2',2]   ['3',2]   ['4',2]
['5',2]   ['6',2]   ['7',2]   ['8',2]   ['9',2]

All but one of the transitions are to State 2, so if you use the transition to State 2 as the default (rather than a transition to the error state), the row could be compressed as follows

```
YYPRIVATE YY_TTYPE   Yy_nxt2 [] = { 1, 2,   'e',5 };
```

The first number (1) is the pair count, as before. The second number (2) is the default next-state transition. If the *next* function gets through the entire list of pairs without finding a match, it will go to this default next state. The remainder of the array is the one pair that doesn't go to the default state. This extreme compression isn't very useful in a lexical-analyzer application because you can't really afford to discard all the error information, but it's sometimes useful in parser applications. The UNIX **yacc** utility uses a variation on this method to compress its tables.[10] Of course, if there are more transitions to an explicit state than to the error state, you can put the error transitions into the pair list and use the explicit state as the default state. This way you won't loose any information.

Setting pair-compression threshold in L^EX.

Pair compression is activated in L^EX with a *-cN* command-line switch. *N* is the threshold beyond which pairs are abandoned in favor of a simple array indexed by lookahead character. The example we've been looking at had the threshold set at 11, so any state with more than 11 outgoing transitions is handled with a simple array, and states with 11 or fewer outgoing transitions are represented with character/next-state pairs. The default threshold—used when no *N* is given on the command line—is four.

Pair compression, compression ratio.

The compression ratio here tends not to be as good as with redundant-row-and-column elimination in programming-language applications. The current example uses 247 bytes, versus 154 for the other method. The C lexical analyzer uses 3,272 bytes for the pair-compressed tables, versus 1,514 for the default method. It does do better when the data in the matrix is both sparse and randomly distributed, however. The *-v* command-line switch to L^EX causes the final table sizes to be printed, so you can judge which method is more appropriate for a given application.

You'll note that the redundant-row-and-column elimination could be combined with the pair-compression technique. For example, since the last two rows in the table shown in Figure 2.7 are the same, you really need to store only one of them and keep two pointers to it. I haven't implemented this combined method.

Accepting-state array, Yyaccept[].

The next part of `lexyy.c` is the accepting-state array, `Yyaccept[]`, shown in Listing 2.17. The array is indexed by state number. It evaluates to 0 if the state is not an accepting state. Other values set the conditions under which the lexeme is accepted. It holds 1 if the string is anchored to the start of the line (a ˆ was the leftmost symbol in the original regular expression—an extra newline will be at the far left of the lexeme in this case). It holds 2 if the string is anchored to the end of the line (a $ was the rightmost symbol in the original regular expression—an extra newline will be at the far right of the lexeme in this case). It holds 3 if the lexeme is anchored both to the beginning and the end of the line, and 4 if the lexeme is always accepted—no anchors were present in the original regular expression.

---

10. The method is described in [Aho], pp. 144–146. They use separate arrays for the pairs and the default transitions, but the rationale is the same.

Listing 2.17. *lexyy.c*— Accepting-State Identification Array

```
118   /*-----------------------------------------
119    * The Yyaccept array has two purposes. If Yyaccept[i] is 0 then state
120    * i is nonaccepting. If it's nonzero then the number determines whether
121    * the string is anchored, 1=anchored at start of line, 2=at end of
122    * line, 3=both, 4=line not anchored
123    */
124
125   YYPRIVATE YY_TTYPE   Yyaccept[] =
126   {
127           0 ,      /* State 0    */
128           4 ,      /* State 1    */
129           4 ,      /* State 2    */
130           0 ,      /* State 3    */
131           4 ,      /* State 4    */
132           0        /* State 5    */
133   };
```

The remainder of *lexyy.c* file is the actual state-machine driver, shown in Listing 2.18. The first and last part of this listing are the second and third parts of the Ctrl-L-delimited template file discussed earlier. The case statements in the middle (on lines 287 to 295 of Listing 2.18) correspond to the original code attached to the regular expressions in the input file and are generated by L^EX itself.

L^EX state-machine driver.

The various global variables that communicate with the parser are declared on lines 138 to 141. Note that `yyout` is provided for UNIX compatibility, but you shouldn't use it if you're using **occs** (because it will mess up the windows in the debugging system). Same goes for the `output()` and `ECHO` macros on lines 147 and 148. UNIX supports them but they shouldn't be used in an **occs** environment. It's best to use the actual output functions, or to supply similarly-named replacement functions that you can use to debug your lexical analyzer (assuming that the functions you supply will eventually be replaced by the **occs** versions). These replacement functions are shown in *lex_io.c* (Listing 2.18). Link this file to the lexical analyzer when you're debugging a lex output file without a parser. Use the versions of the routines that are in *l.lib*, and which support the **occs** debugging environment, when you're using an **occs**-generated parser.

yyout, output(), ECHO.

The `YYERROR()` macro on line 271 of Listing 2.19 prints internal error messages. There's no UNIX equivalent because **lex** doesn't print error messages. In the **occs** environment, you should redefine `YYERROR()` to use `yyerror()` rather than `fprintf()`. (Do it in a '%{ %}' block in the definitions section.)

YYERROR().

The `yymore()` macro on line 154 of Listing 2.19 just sets a flag to true. It forces the driver to continue processing the current lexeme, ignoring the current accepting action. `unput()` and `yyless()` (on lines 156 and 157) are the two pushback functions. They unterminate the current lexeme, push back any requested characters, and then reterminate the lexeme. I've made extensive use of the comma operator here in order to squeeze several instructions into a single macro. The comma operator just executes the comma-delimited statements in sequence. It evaluates to the rightmost statement in the list, but neither of these macros take advantage of this behavior—they'd be declared **void** if they were functions. Braces can't be used here because of the binding problems discussed earlier. Note that the conditional on line 158 sets 'yyleng' to zero if the `ii_pushback()` call fails, as it will if you try to push back too many characters; otherwise, 'yyleng' is just reduced by the number of pushed-back characters.

yymore(), yyless(), unput().

The `input()` function on line 162 of Listing 2.19 is complicated enough to be a subroutine. It has to return a value, and the contortions necessary to do this with a

input().

Listing 2.18. *lex_io.c*— Debugging Output Routines for LEX-Generated Analyzer

```
1    #include <stdio.h>
2    #include <stdarg.h>
3
4    /* This file contains two output routines that replace the ones in yydebug.c,
5     * found in l.lib and used by occs for output. Link this file to a LeX-
6     * generated lexical analyzer when an occs-generated parser is not present.
7     * Then use yycomment() for messages to stdout, yyerror() for messages to
8     * stderr.
9     */
10
11   PUBLIC  void yycomment( fmt, ... )
12   char    *fmt;
13   {
14       /* Works like printf(). */
15
16       va_list        args;
17       va_start( args, fmt );
18       vfprintf( stdout, fmt, args );
19       va_end  ( args );
20   }
21
22   PUBLIC void yyerror( fmt, ... )
23   char    *fmt;
24   {
25       /* Works like printf() but prints an error message along with the
26        * current line number and lexeme.
27        */
28
29       va_list        args;
30       va_start( args, fmt );
31
32       fprintf ( stderr, "ERROR on line %d, near <%s>\n", yylineno, yytext );
33       vfprintf( stderr, fmt, args );
34       va_end  ( args );
35   }
```

yylex(), yystate.

comma operator are not worth the effort.

The lexical analyzer itself, yylex() starts on line 177 of Listing 2.19. The current state is held in yystate, which initially set to −1—a value that's not used as a state number. The code on lines 187 to 192 is executed only once because yystate is set to −1 only the first time the subroutine is called. The

```
ii_advance();
ii_pushback(1);
```

forces an initial buffer load so that ii_look() can be used later on.

Control-flow in yylex().

The actual control flow through the program is unusual in that one branch of the main loop exits the subroutine entirely and reenters the loop from the top. In other words, if an action in the original input file contains a **return** statement, then control passes out of the loop at that point, and passes back into the loop on the next call. A normal path through the loop is also available when no such **return** is executed. The situation is illustrated in Figure 2.8. The initializations can't be done at the top of the loop because they're performed only on accepting a lexeme, not on every iteration of the loop.

Figure 2.8. Flow of Control Within `yylex()`

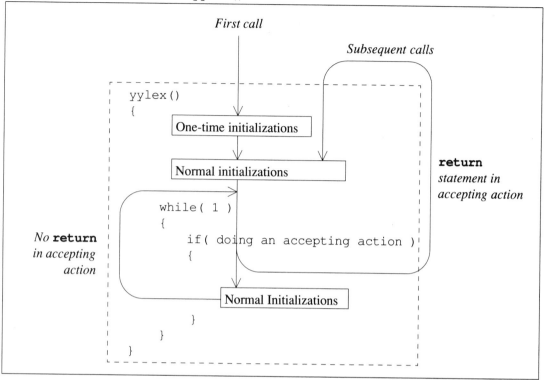

The initializations on lines 194 to 198 of Listing 2.19 are executed every time the loop is entered from the top, and these initializations are duplicated on lines 303 to 315 for those situations where an accepting action does not contain a **return** statement. This code unterminates the previous lexeme (`ii_unterm()`), sets the start marker for the current lexeme (`ii_mark_start()`), and sets `yylastaccept` to zero to signify that no accepting state has been seen (the start state, which is always State 0, cannot be an accepting state). The `ii_unterm()` call does nothing if the string is not `'\0'` terminated, as is initially the case.

Listing 2.19. *lex.par*— State-Machine Driver Copied to *lexyy.c*

```
134     /*------------------------------------------------------------
135      * Global variables used by the parser.
136      */
137
138     char    *yytext;            /* Pointer to lexeme.        */
139     int     yyleng;            /* Length of lexeme.         */
140     int     yylineno;          /* Input line number.        */
141     FILE    *yyout = stdout;
142
143     /*------------------------------------------------------------
144      * Macros that duplicate functions in UNIX lex:
145      */
146
147     #define output(c)    putc(c,yyout)
148     #define ECHO         fprintf(yyout, "%s", yytext )
149
```

➡

Listing 2.19. continued. . .

```
150   #ifndef YYERROR
151   #     define YYERROR(t)  fprintf(stderr,"%s", t  )
152   #endif
153
154   #define yymore()    yymoreflg = 1
155
156   #define unput(c)   (ii_unput(c), --yyleng )
157   #define yyless(n) (    ii_unterm(), \
158                       ( yyleng -= ii_pushback(n) ? n : yyleng ), \
159                       ii_term() \
160                   )
161
162   int   input()                          /* This is a macro in UNIX lex */
163   {
164       int c;
165
166       if( c = ii_input() )
167       {
168           yytext  = ii_text();
169           yylineno = ii_lineno();
170           ++yyleng;
171       }
172       return c;
173   }
174
175   /*------------------------------------------------------------------*/
176
177   yylex()
178   {
179       int         yymoreflg;         /* Set when yymore() is executed     */
180       static int yystate   = -1;     /* Current state.                    */
181       int         yylastaccept;      /* Most recently seen accept state    */
182       int         yyprev;            /* State before yylastaccept          */
183       int         yynstate;          /* Next state, given lookahead.       */
184       int         yylook;            /* Lookahead character                */
185       int         yyanchor;          /* Anchor point for most recently seen */
186                                      /* accepting state.                   */
187       if( yystate == -1 )
188       {
189           yy_init_lex();             /* One-time initializations */
190           ii_advance();
191           ii_pushback(1);
192       }
193
194       yystate      = 0;              /* Top-of-loop initializations */
195       yylastaccept = 0;
196       yymoreflg    = 0;
197       ii_unterm();
198       ii_mark_start();
199
200       while( 1 )
201       {
202           /* Check end of file. If there's an unprocessed accepting state,
203            * yylastaccept will be nonzero. In this case, ignore EOF for now so
204            * that you can do the accepting action; otherwise, try to open another
205            * file and return if you can't.
206            */
207
```

➡

Listing 2.19. continued...

```
208            while( 1 )
209            {
210                if( (yylook=ii_look(1)) != EOF )
211                {
212                    yynstate = yy_next( yystate, yylook );
213                    break;
214                }
215                else
216                {
217                    if( yylastaccept )              /* still something to do */
218                    {
219                        yynstate = YYF;
220                        break;
221                    }
222                    else if( yywrap() )             /* another file?  */
223                    {                               /* no             */
224                        yytext = "";
225                        yyleng = 0;
226                        return 0;
227                    }
228                    else
229                    {
230                        ii_advance();               /* load a new buffer */
231                        ii_pushback(1);
232                    }
233                }
234            }
235
236
237            if( yynstate != YYF )
238            {
239                YY_D( printf("    Transition from state %d", yystate )     );
240                YY_D( printf(" to state %d on <%c>\n",   yynstate, yylook) );
241
242                if( ii_advance() < 0 )                          /* Buffer full */
243                {
244                    YYERROR( "Lexeme too long, discarding characters\n" );
245                    ii_flush(1);
246                }
247
248                if(yyanchor = Yyaccept[ yynstate ])    /* saw an accept state */
249                {
250                    yyprev       = yystate ;
251                    yylastaccept = yynstate ;
252                    ii_mark_end();          /* Mark input at current character. */
253                                            /* A subsequent ii_to_mark()        */
254                                            /* returns us to this position.     */
255                }
256
257                yystate = yynstate;
258            }
259            else
260            {
261                if( !yylastaccept )                          /* illegal input */
262                {
263 #ifdef YYBADINP
264                    YYERROR( "Ignoring bad input\n" );
265 #endif
266                    ii_advance();           /* Skip char that caused failure.  */
267                }
```

Listing 2.19. continued...

```
268                  else
269                  {
270                      ii_to_mark();           /* Back up to previous accept state */
271                      if( yyanchor & 2 )      /* If end anchor is active        */
272                          ii_pushback(1);     /* push back the CR or LF         */
273
274                      if( yyanchor & 1 )              /* if start anchor is active */
275                          ii_move_start();            /* skip the leading newline  */
276
277                      ii_term();                      /* Null-terminate the string */
278                      yyleng   = ii_length ();
279                      yytext   = ii_text   ();
280                      yylineno = ii_lineno ();
281
282                      YY_D( printf("Accepting state %d, ", yylastaccept )    );
283                      YY_D( printf("line %d: <%s>\n",      yylineno, yytext ) );
284
285                      switch( yylastaccept )
286                      {
287                      case 1:                                 /* State 1   */
288                          return   ICON;
289                          break;
290                      case 2:                                 /* State 2   */
291                          return       FCON;
292                          break;
293                      case 4:                                 /* State 4   */
294                          return       FCON;
295                          break;
296
297                      default:
298                              YYERROR( "INTERNAL ERROR, yylex\n" );
299                              break;
300                      }
301                  }
302
303              ii_unterm();
304              yylastaccept = 0;
305
306              if( !yymoreflg )
307              {
308                  yystate = 0;
309                  ii_mark_start();
310              }
311              else
312              {
313                  yystate   = yyprev;     /* Back up */
314                  yymoreflg = 0;
315              }
316          }
317      }
318  }
```

yymoreflg.   The yymoreflg that is tested on line 306 of Listing 2.19 is set true by yymore().
If yymoreflg is false, the machine behaves normally: the next state is State 0 and the
start-of-lexeme marker is reset so that the machine can collect a new lexeme (on lines
308 and 309). If yymoreflg is true, the machine backs up one state rather than going to
State 0, and the start-of-lexeme marker isn't modified, so additional characters are added

to the end of the current lexeme. The only use of `yyprev` is to remember the last state so that the machine can back up.

yyprev

Generally, backing up is the correct action to take for `yymore()`. For example, the naive string-processing algorithm discussed in Chapter Two looked like this:

Problems with
yymore().

```
\"[^\"]*\"    if( yytext[yyleng-2] == '\\' )
                  yymore();
              else
                  return STRING;
```

This expression creates the following machine:

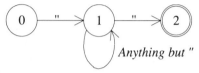

Anything but "

The problem is that the machine is in State 2 after the close quote is recognized. In order to continue processing the string, it needs to back up to State 1 (so that another close quote can get it back to State 2). The back up that's initiated by `yymore()` can cause problems (not very often, but, as Shiva says, to be four-armed is to be forewarned). One of my original attempts to handle the escape-sequence-in-a-string problem looked like this:

```
\"[^\"\\]*  if( ii_lookahead(1) == '\\' )
            {
                input();    /* Skip the backslash             */
                input();    /* and the character that follows. */
                yymore();
            }
            else                    /* it's a " */
            {
                input();            /* Get the close quote  */
                return STRING;
            }
```

The idea was to break out of the regular expression if either a backslash or quote was encountered, look ahead to see which of the two possible characters were there, and then absorb the escape sequence with `input()` calls. The state machine looks like this:

*Anything but " or *

The problem arises when you try to handle a string like:

```
"\""
```

The machine starts out in State 0, the quote puts it into State 1, and then the machine terminates because there's no outgoing transition from State 1 on a backslash. The code is now activated and the `if` statement tests true. The two `input()` calls absorb the backslash and the second quote, and `yymore()` backs us up to the previous state—State 0. Now the third quote is encountered, but the machine treats it as a start-of-string character, not as an end-of-string character. The code associated with State 1 won't be executed until a fourth quote or another backslash is encountered. The best solution to this problem prevents the backup by using:

```
yyprev = yystate;
yymore();
```

rather than a simple `yymore()` invocation. To see what's happening here, consider that `yyprev` holds the number of the state to back up to—the previous state; `yystate` holds the current state number. The assignment of the current state to the previous state means that the machine will back up to the current state when `yymore()` is invoked. That is, it won't back up at all.

Alternately, you could use the following:

```
ii_unterm();
continue;
```

instead of `yymore`, but I think that this latter solution is more confusing. (Look at the code to see what a **continue** will do here.) You don't want to **break** out of the loop because the existing lexeme is discarded in this case.

Returning to Listing 2.19, the **while** loop on lines 208 to 234 (page 77) gets the next input character and puts it into `yylook`—the input is not advanced by `ii_look()`. The normal situation of not being at end of file is handled on line 212, where the next state is computed. The **else** clause deals with end of file. If `yylastaccept` is true on line 217, then the machine hasn't executed the accepting action for the last lexeme in the file, so end-of-file processing is delayed until the action is done. If it's false, then `yywrap()` is called to open a new input file. This user-supplied subroutine can be used to chain together several input files. The default, library version just returns zero. If you have several input files, you can replace the default version with one that opens the next input file (and returns 1 until there are no more files to open). So, if `yywrap()` returns false, it's not time to wrap up and the code loops back up to line 208. The next state is then recomputed using the first character in the new file (as if the EOF had not been encountered). The code loops until a nonempty file is opened. There's some potential confusion here in that `yywrap()` returns true if the program should terminate, even though a false return value would be more intuitive in this situation. Remember, the name `yywrap()` stands for "go ahead and wrap up."[11]

When the loop terminates, `yylook` holds the current lookahead character, and the potential next state is figured on line 212. The machine has not changed state yet because `yystate` hasn't been modified. The machine is looking ahead at what the next state is going to be, given the current lookahead character.

If the next state is not a failure transition, the input is advanced (on line 242) and the machine looks to see if the new state is an accepting state (on line 248). If so, the accepting state is remembered in `yylastaccept`, and the state preceding the accepting state is also remembered for `yymore()` processing. Finally, the driver switches to a new state by modifying `yystate` on line 257.

The **else** clause that starts on line 259 handles failure transitions. In this case you want to perform the accepting action associated with the most recently seen accepting state (which you just remembered in `yylastaccept`). If `yylastaccept` is zero, then no such accepting state was encountered and you're looking at a bad lexeme (one that is not described by any regular expression in the input file). An error message is printed if `YYBADINP` is true and `ii_advance()` is called to skip the offending character.

If an accepting state had been encountered, the input is restored to the condition it was in at that time by the `ii_to_mark()` call on line 270. The test on line 271 checks for an end-of-line anchor, in which case the newline (which is part of the lexeme at this point) must be pushed back into the input (in case it is needed to match a start-of-line anchor in the next lexeme). The lexeme is terminated, and the global variables that communicate with the parser are initialized on lines 277 to 280. The **if** clause on the next

Finding the next state.

End-of-file processing, `yywrap()`.

Failure transitions in `yylex()`, `yylastaccept`.

YYBADINP

---

11. I've, perhaps wrongly, perpetuated the problem in order to keep UNIX compatibility.

line removes a newline that's at the start of the lexeme as the result of a beginning-of-line anchor.

The **switch** on line 285 contains all the accepting actions that were part of the original input file. The **case** statements are all generated by L⁴X itself—the **case** values are the state numbers of the associated accepting state. The **default** case on line 297 should never be executed. It's here as insurance, in case an unknown bug in L⁴X generates a bad state number in the **switch**.

Accepting actions in `yylex()`.

2.5 L⁴X—A Lexical-Analyzer Generator*

The remainder of this chapter presents the complete source code for L⁴X, along with the underlying theory. You must read Appendix A if you intend to look at the implementation details. The set routines presented there are used heavily in this chapter, and a familiarity with the calling conventions for these routines will be useful.

2.5.1 Thompson's Construction: From a Regular Expression to an NFA*

L⁴X constructs NFA's from regular expressions using a system called Thompson's Construction, developed by Ken Thompson at Bell Labs for the QED editor. It works as follows:

The simplest possible regular expression is a single character, and this expression can be represented by a correspondingly simple NFA. For example, a machine that matches an *a* is shown below:

Simple expressions.

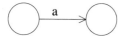

The concatenation of two regular expressions is also straightforward. The following machine represents the expression *ab* by constructing individual machines for each subexpression (the *a* and *b*), and then connecting the machines with an ε edge:

Concatenation.

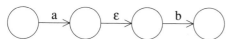

This method needlessly wastes states, however. A better solution merges the ending state of the first machine with the start state of the second one, like this:

There are two situations in a L⁴X application where an OR of two regular expressions is required. The first is the input specification itself. That is, the L⁴X input contains many regular expressions, but a single machine must be output that recognizes all of these expressions. This means that all the input expressions are effectively ORed together to create the output DFA. L⁴X does this high-level OR using the system shown in Figure 2.9. Each of the boxes is an NFA that represents an entire regular expression, and all of these are connected together using several dummy states and ε edges.

Logical OR at the top level.

The second OR situation is the OR operator (the vertical bar) which can appear in the regular expression itself (as in *a|b*). L⁴X processes the OR operator by constructing the machine shown in Figure 2.10. Again, the seemingly empty boxes in the pictures represent machines for entire subexpressions. Figure 2.11 shows how the expression *((a|b)|cd)* would be represented. L⁴X starts out by making two machines to recognize the *a* and *b*, and connects the two using the OR construction shown in Figure 2.10. L⁴X then creates two more machines to recognize the *c* and *d*, concatenating them together by merging the end state of the first machine with the start state of the second. Finally, it

OR operator (|).

Figure 2.9. Connecting the Regular Expressions in a LEX Input File

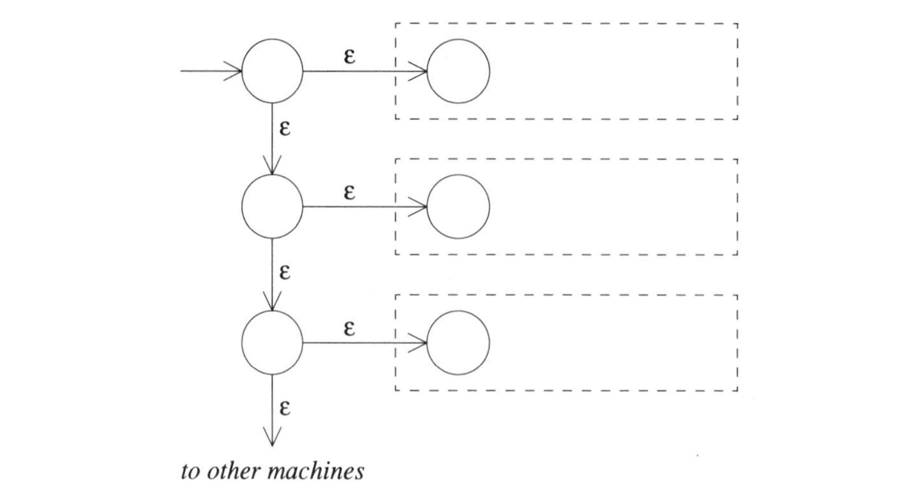

processes the second OR operator, applying the same construction that it used earlier, but this time using the machines representing the more-complicated subexpressions *(a/b)* and *cd* in place of the boxes in Figure 2.10.

Figure 2.10. Generic NFA for the OR operator

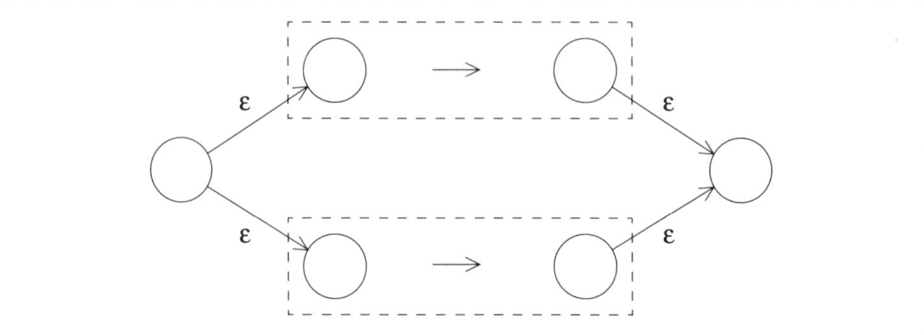

Closure operators: * + ?

The machines to recognize the three closure operators are a little more complicated looking. They are shown in Figure 2.12. Note that the machines that recognize + and ? are special cases of the machine for the * operator.

Evolution of a complex regular expression.

Figure 2.13 shows the evolution of a machine that recognizes a subset of the floating-point constants discussed earlier. The expression used is `(D*\.D|D\.D*)`. It recognizes numbers with one digit to the right of the point and zero or more digits preceding it and it also recognizes the inverse—one digit to the left of the decimal point and zero or more digits following the decimal point. LEX starts out constructing an expression for the first `D` in the expression [in Figure 2.13(a)]. It then reads the leftmost * and substitutes the first machine into the closure machine, yielding Figure 2.13(b). It then reads the dot, and tacks it on to the right edge of the partially constructed machine [Figure 2.13(c)], and it does the same for the next `D` [Figure 2.13(d)]. Encountering the | operator, LEX holds onto the previously constructed expression for a moment, and then constructs a second machine for the next subexpression `(D\.D*)`, not shown in the figure. Finally, it connects the two machines for the subexpressions together, using the OR construction [Figure 2.13(e)].

Figure 2.11. An NFA That Recognizes *((a|b)|cd)*

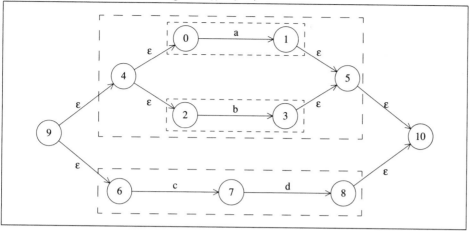

Figure 2.12. Representing the Closure Operators

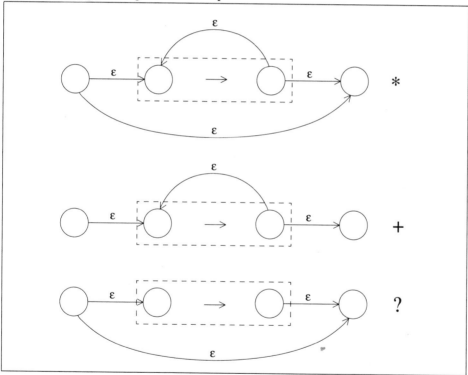

2.5.2 Implementing Thompson's Construction

This section presents a low-level implementation of the theory in the previous section. Skip forward to Section 2.5.3 if you're not interested in this level of detail.

2.5.2.1 Data Structures.

A machine built with Thompson's construction has several useful characteristics:

Characteristics of a Thompson machine

- All the machines that recognize subexpressions—no matter how complicated—have a single start state and a single end state.
- No state has more than two outgoing edges.

Figure 2.13. Constructing an NFA for (D*\.D|D\.D*)

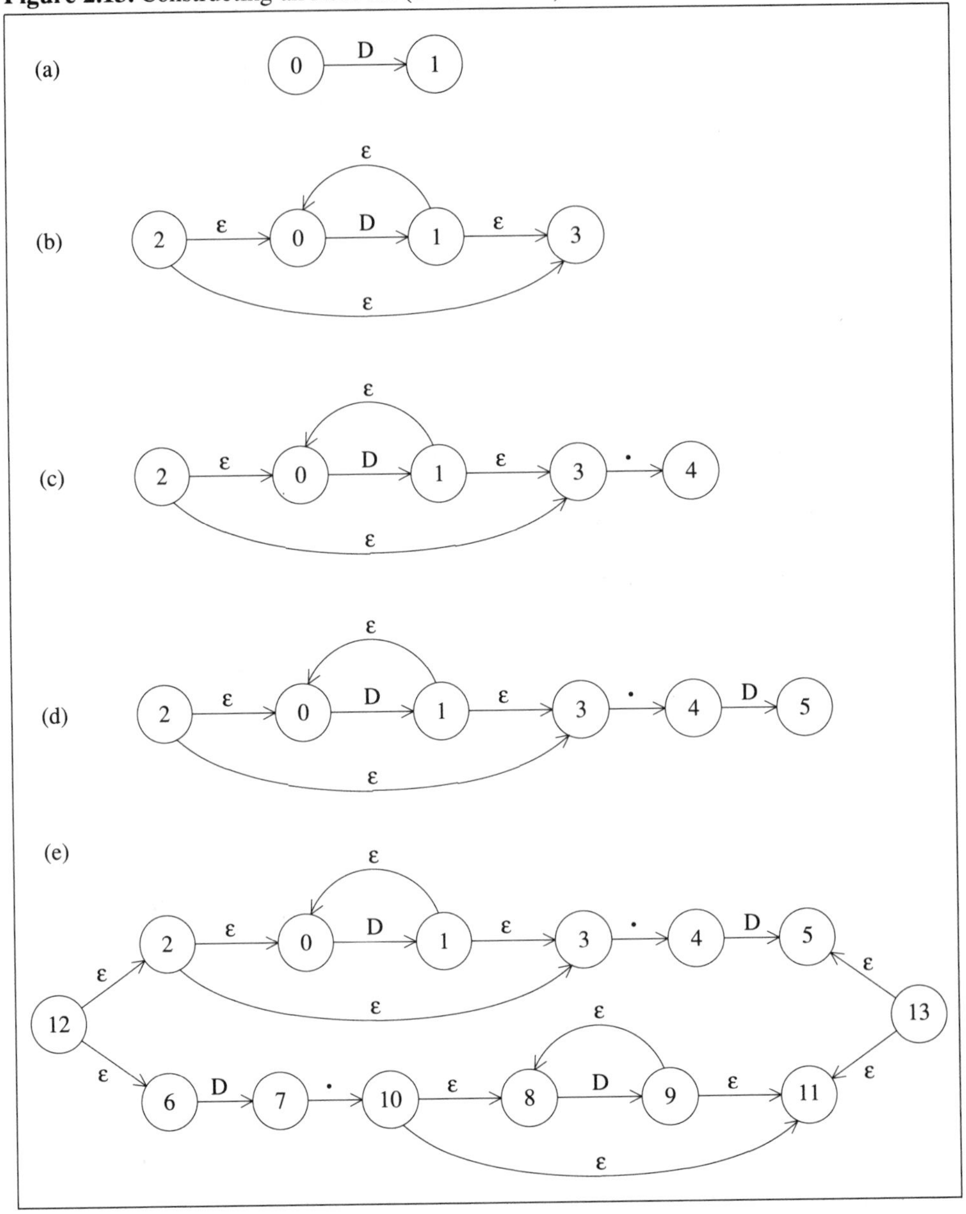

- There are only three possibilities for the labels on the edges: (1) there is only one outgoing edge labeled with a single input character, (2) there is only one outgoing edge labeled with ε, and (3) there are two outgoing edges labeled with ε. There are never two outgoing edges labeled with input characters, and there are never two edges, one of which is labeled with an input character and the other of which is labeled with ε.

The NFA data structure in Listing 2.20 uses these characteristics to implement an NFA state. The `next` field either points at the next state, or is set to NULL if there are no outgoing edges. The `next2` field is used only for states with two outgoing ε edges. It is set to NULL if there's only one such transition. The `edge` field holds one of four values that determine what the label looks like:

The NFA structure.

next, next2, and edge
fields of an NFA.

- If there is a single outgoing edge labeled with an input character, edge holds that character. — Single, non-ε edge.

- If the state has an outgoing ε edge, then edge is set to EPSILON. — ε edges, EPSILON.

- If a transition is made on a character class, all characters in the class are elements of the SET pointed to by bitset, and edge holds the value CCL. The set elements are just the ASCII values of the characters. For example, if an ASCII '0', which has the value 48_{10}, is in the character class, the number 48 will be in the set. — Character classes, CCL, bitset.

- If the state has no outgoing transitions, edge is set to EMPTY. — Terminal states, EMPTY.

Listing 2.20. *nfa.h*— Data Structures and Macros

```
 1   /*-------------------------------------------------------------
 2    * Nfa state:
 3    */
 4
 5   typedef struct nfa
 6   {
 7       int         edge;       /* Label for edge: character, CCL, EMPTY, or */
 8                               /* EPSILON.                                 */
 9       SET         *bitset;    /* Set to store character classes.          */
10       struct nfa  *next;      /* Next state (or NULL if none)             */
11       struct nfa  *next2;     /* Another next state if edge==EPSILON      */
12                               /* NULL of this state isn't used            */
13       char        *accept;    /* NULL if not an accepting state, else     */
14                               /* a pointer to the action string           */
15       int         anchor;     /* Says whether pattern is anchored and, if */
16                               /* so, where (uses #defines above).         */
17   } NFA;
18
19   #define EPSILON  -1                  /* Non-character values of NFA.edge    */
20   #define CCL      -2
21   #define EMPTY    -3
22
23                                        /* Values of the anchor field:  */
24   #define NONE     0                   /*    Not anchored              */
25   #define START    1                   /*    Anchored at start of line */
26   #define END      2                   /*    Anchored at end of line   */
27   #define BOTH     ( START | END )     /*    Anchored in both places   */
```

The accept field in the NFA structure is NULL for nonaccepting states; otherwise, it points at a string holding the action part of the original input rule—the code to be executed when that state is accepted. The string itself is of variable length. The first int's worth of characters hold the line number and the remainder of the array holds the string. For example, in a machine with a 16-bit int. The first two bytes of the string are the line number (in binary) and the remainder of the string is the actual input text. The pointer to the actual string is stored. — Storing accepting strings, accept.

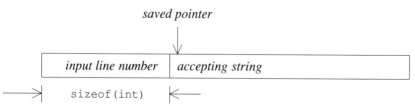

If p is a pointer to an NFA structure, the actual string is accessed with p->accept, and the line number can be accessed by casting accept into a pointer to **int** and backing up one notch—like this:

```
((int*)( p->accept ))[-1]
```

Because of various alignment problems, some care has to be taken to integrate the line number into the string in this fashion—the mechanics are discussed shortly. The technique is useful, not only in the current application, but also for doing things like attaching a precomputed string length to a string. The string can still be handled in the normal way, but the count is there when you need it.

The anchor field.

The macros on lines 24 to 27 of Listing 2.20 are possible values of the anchor field. They describe whether a ^, $, or both were present in the regular expression.

NFA_MAX, STR_MAX

The reminder of *nfa.h*, in Listing 2.21, holds other definitions needed to make the machine. NFA_MAX is the maximum number of NFA states that can be in the machine, and STR_MAX is the total space available for all the accepting actions combined. The rest of the file is just prototypes for the externally-accessible functions discussed below.

Listing 2.21. *nfa.h*— Other Definitions and Prototypes

```
28   #define NFA_MAX 512              /* Maximum number of NFA states in a      */
29                                    /* single machine. NFA_MAX * sizeof(NFA)  */
30                                    /* can't exceed 64K.                      */
31   #define STR_MAX (10 * 1024)      /* Total space that can be used by the    */
32                                    /* accept strings.                        */
33
34   void     new_macro( char *definition );          /* these three are in nfa.c */
35   void     printmacs( void );
36   NFA      *thompson( char *(*input_funct)(), int *max_state, NFA **start_state);
37   void     print_nfa( NFA *nfa, int len, NFA *start );          /* in printnfa.c */
```

Global-variable definitions: globals.h

The other file you need to look at before starting is *globals.h*, in Listing 2.22. This file holds definitions for all the true global variables in the program (globals that are shared between modules). All other globals are declared **static**, so their scope is limited to the file in which they are declared. For maintenance reasons, it's desirable that both the definition and declaration of a variable be in a single file. That way you don't have to worry about maintaining two files, one in which space is allocated and the other containing **extern** statements describing the variables. The problem is solved in *globals.h* using the CLASS and I(x) macros defined on lines three to seven of Listing 2.22. The following two lines are found in only one file [typically in the same file that contains main()]:

CLASS and I(x) macros, ALLOC.

```
#define  ALLOC
#include "globals.h"
```

All other files include *globals.h* without the previous ALLOC definition. When ALLOC exists, CLASS evaluates to an empty string and I(x) evaluates to its argument. So, the input line:

```
CLASS char *Template  I(="lex.par");
```

expands to

```
char *Template  ="lex.par";
```

If ALLOC doesn't exist, then CLASS expands to **extern** and I(x) expands to an empty string. The earlier input line expands to:

```
extern char *Template;
```

The variables on lines 11 to 15 of globals.h are set by command-line switches; the ones on lines 16 to 22 are used by the input routines to communicate with one another.

Listing 2.22. *globals.h*— Global-Variable Definitions

```
 1  /*                      GLOBALS.H: Global variables shared between modules */
 2  #ifdef ALLOC
 3  #       define CLASS
 4  #       define I(x) x
 5  #else
 6  #       define CLASS extern
 7  #       define I(x)
 8  #endif
 9  #define MAXINP  2048                     /* Maximum rule size              */
10
11  CLASS int  Verbose          I( = 0 );    /* Print statistics               */
12  CLASS int  No_lines         I( = 0 );    /* Suppress #line directives      */
13  CLASS int  Unix             I( = 0 );    /* Use UNIX-style newlines        */
14  CLASS int  Public           I( = 0 );    /* Make static symbols public     */
15  CLASS char *Template        I(="lex.par"); /* State-machine driver template */
16  CLASS int  Actual_lineno    I( = 1 );    /* Current input line number      */
17  CLASS int  Lineno           I( = 1 );    /* Line number of first line of   */
18                                           /* a multiple-line rule.          */
19  CLASS char Input_buf[MAXINP];            /* Line buffer for input          */
20  CLASS char *Input_file_name;             /* Input file name (for #line)    */
21  CLASS FILE *Ifile;                       /* Input stream.                  */
22  CLASS FILE *Ofile;                       /* Output stream.                 */
23  #undef CLASS
24  #undef I
```

2.5.2.2 A Regular-Expression Grammar.
The code in nfa.c, which starts in Listing 2.23, reads a regular expression and converts it to an NFA using Thompson's construction. The file is really a small compiler, comprising a lexical analyzer, parser, and code generator (though in this case, the generated code is a state-machine description, not assembly language). The grammar used to recognize a LEX input specification is summarized in Table 2.5. This is an informal grammar—it describes the input syntax in a general sort of way. Clarity is more important here than strict accuracy. I'll fudge a bit in the implementation in order to get the grammar to work. Precedence and associativity are built into the grammar (the mechanics are described in depth in the next chapter). Concatenation is higher precedence than |; closure is higher precedence still; everything associates left to right. The various left-recursive productions have not yet been translated into an acceptable form, as was discussed in Chapter One—I'll do that as I implement them.

2.5.2.3 File Header.
The header portion of *nfa.c* is in Listing 2.23. The ENTER and LEAVE macros on lines 21 to 28 are for debugging. They expand to empty strings when DEBUG is not defined. When debugging, they print the current subroutine name (which is passed in as an argument), the current lexeme and what's left of the current input line. An ENTER invocation is placed at the top of every subroutine of interest, and a LEAVE macro is put at the bottom. The text is indented by an amount proportional to the subroutine-nesting level—Lev is incremented by every ENTER invocation, and decremented by every LEAVE. Lev×4 spaces are printed to the left of every string using the printf()s * field-width capability. To simplify, the following printf() statement

Debugging: ENTER, LEAVE.

Table 2.5. A Grammar for LEX

Productions			Notes
machine	→	*rule machine*	A list of rules
	|	*rule* **END_OF_INPUT**	
rule	→	*expr* **EOS** *action*	A single regular expression followed by an accepting action.
	|	^ *expr* **EOS** *action*	Expression anchored to start of line.
	|	*expr* **$** **EOS** *action*	Expression anchored to end of line.
action	→	*white_space string*	An optional accepting action.
	|	*white_space*	
	|	ε	
expr	→	*expr | cat_expr*	A list of expressions delimited by vertical bars.
	|	*cat_expr*	
cat_expr	→	*cat_expr factor*	A list of concatenated expressions.
	|	*factor*	
factor	→	*term* *	A subexpression followed by a *.
	|	*term* +	A subexpression followed by a +.
	|	*term* ?	A subexpression followed by a ?.
	|	*term*	
term	→	[*string*]	A character class.
	|	[^ *string*]	A negative character class.
	|	[]	(nonstandard) Matches white space.
	|	[^]	(nonstandard) Matches everything but white space.
	|	.	Matches any character except newline.
	|	*character*	A single character.
	|	(*expr*)	A parenthesized subexpression.
white_space	→	*one or more tabs or spaces*	
character	→	*any single ASCII character except white_space*	
string	→	*one or more ASCII characters*	

outputs Lev spaces by printing an empty string in a field whose width is controlled by Lev.

```
printf( "%*s", Lev, "" );
```

Error messages:
Errmsgs,
parse_err().

2.5.2.4 Error-Message Processing. The next part of *nfa.c* is the error-message routines in Listing 2.24. I've borrowed the method used by the C buffered I/O system: possible error codes are defined in the enumerated type on lines 35 to 51, and a global variable is set to one of these values when an error occurs. The Errmsgs array on lines 53 to 68 is indexed by error code and evaluates to an appropriate error message. Finally, the parse_err() subroutine on line 70 is passed an error code and prints an appropriate message. The **while** loop on line 76 tries to highlight the point at which the error occurred with a string like this:

The up arrow will (hopefully) be close to the point of error. parse_err() does not return.

Managing NFA structures.

new(), discard().

2.5.2.5 Memory Management. Listing 2.25 contains the memory-management routines that allocate and free the NFA structures used for the states. Two routines are used for this purpose: new(), on line 105, allocates a new node and discard(), on line 131, frees the node. I'm not using malloc() and free() because they're too slow; rather, a large array (pointed to by Nfa_states) is allocated the first time new() is called (on line 112 — the entire **if** statement is executed only once, during the first call).

Stack strategy,
Nfa_states[].

A simple stack strategy is used for memory management: discard() pushes a pointer to the discarded node onto a stack, and new() uses a node from the stack if one

Listing 2.23. *nfa.c*— File Header

```
1    /* NFA.C---Make an NFA from a LeX input file using Thompson's construction */
2
3    #include <stdio.h>
4    #ifdef MSDOS
5    #      include <stdlib.h>
6    #else
7    #      include <malloc.h>
8    #endif
9
10   #include <ctype.h>
11   #include <string.h>
12   #include <tools/debug.h>
13   #include <tools/set.h>
14   #include <tools/hash.h>
15   #include <tools/compiler.h>
16   #include <tools/stack.h>
17   #include "nfa.h"                      /* defines for NFA, EPSILON, CCL */
18   #include "globals.h"                  /* externs for Verbose, etc.    */
19
20   #ifdef DEBUG
21   #      int     Lev = 0;
22   #      define ENTER(f) printf("%*senter %s [%c][%1.10s] \n",            \
23                                  Lev++ * 4, "", f, Lexeme, Input)
24   #      define LEAVE(f) printf("%*sleave %s [%c][%1.10s]\n",             \
25                                  --Lev * 4, "", f, Lexeme, Input)
26   #else
27   #      define ENTER(f)
28   #      define LEAVE(f)
29   #endif
```

is available, otherwise it gets a new node from the Nfa_states[] array (on line 124). new() prints an error message and terminates the program if it can't get the node. The new node is initialized with NULL pointers [the memory is actually cleared in dis-card() with the memset() call on line 136] and the edge field is set to EPSILON on line 125. The stack pointer (Sp) is initialized at run time on line 116 because of a bug in the Microsoft C compact model that's discussed in Appendix A.

edge initialized to EPSILON.

There's an added advantage to the memory-management strategy used here. It's convenient when constructing the NFA to create a physical machine with one node per state and actual pointers to the next state. Later on, it will be convenient to have the NFA represented as an array because you can use the array index as the state number. The stack gives you both representations in a single data structure. The only disadvantage is that any nodes that are still on the stack when the NFA construction is complete will be holes in the array. It turns out that there is at most one hole, but there's no way to know in advance where it's going to be.

The same data objects form both an array and a graph.

The other memory-management function in *nfa.c* is the string-management function, save(), also in Listing 2.25. This function is passed a pointer to a string, and returns a pointer to a copy—in static memory—of that string. The pointer is preceded in memory by an **int**-sized line number, as was discussed earlier on page 85. The array pointer (Strings, on line 100) is declared as a pointer to **int** for portability reasons. Many machines require **int**s to be aligned at more restrictive addresses than **char**s. For example, an **int** might have to be at an address that is an even multiple of four, but a **char** could be at any address. A run-time error would happen if you tried to put an **int** into an illegal address (one that was not an even multiple of four). Making Strings an

String management: save().

Alignment problems caused by leading line number in string.

Listing 2.24. *nfa.c*— Error-Processing Routines

```
30   /*------------------------------------------------------------
31    *      Error processing stuff. Note that all errors are fatal.
32    *------------------------------------------------------------
33    */
34
35   typedef enum _err_num_
36   {
37        E_MEM,         /* Out of memory                             */
38        E_BADEXPR,     /* Malformed regular expression              */
39        E_PAREN,       /* Missing close parenthesis                 */
40        E_STACK,       /* Internal error: Discard stack full        */
41        E_LENGTH,      /* Too many regular expressions              */
42        E_BRACKET,     /* Missing [ in character class              */
43        E_BOL,         /* ^ must be at start of expr or ccl         */
44        E_CLOSE,       /* + ? or * must follow expression           */
45        E_STRINGS,     /* Too many characters in accept actions     */
46        E_NEWLINE,     /* Newline in quoted string                  */
47        E_BADMAC,      /* Missing } in macro expansion              */
48        E_NOMAC,       /* Macro doesn't exist                       */
49        E_MACDEPTH     /* Macro expansions nested too deeply.       */
50
51   } ERR_NUM;
52
53   PRIVATE char    *Errmsgs[] =                    /* Indexed by ERR_NUM */
54   {
55        "Not enough memory for NFA",
56        "Malformed regular expression",
57        "Missing close parenthesis",
58        "Internal error: Discard stack full",
59        "Too many regular expressions or expression too long",
60        "Missing [ in character class",
61        "^ must be at start of expression or after [",
62        "+ ? or * must follow an expression or subexpression",
63        "Too many characters in accept actions",
64        "Newline in quoted string, use \\n to get newline into expression",
65        "Missing } in macro expansion",
66        "Macro doesn't exist",
67        "Macro expansions nested too deeply"
68   };
69
70   PRIVATE void    parse_err( type )
71   ERR_NUM type;
72   {
73        fprintf(stderr, "ERROR (line %d) %s\n%s\n", Actual_lineno,
74                                        Errmsgs[(int)type], S_input);
75
76        while( ++S_input <= Input )
77                putc('_', stderr);
78
79        fprintf( stderr, "^\n" );
80        exit( 1 );
81   }
```

int pointer takes care of the alignment problem at the cost of a little wasted space—the size of the region used to store the string itself must be rounded up to an even multiple of the **int** size. I'm assuming that a **char** will have less restrictive alignment rules than an **int**—a pretty safe assumption.

A single large array that will hold all the strings is allocated the first time save() is called on line 155 of Listing 2.25, thereby avoiding multiple inefficient malloc() calls every time a new string is required. The line number is put into the string on line 164, the pointer is incremented past the number, and the string itself is copied by the loop on line 166. A **char** pointer (textp) is used for the purpose of copying the string component. The test on line 161 is for lines starting with a vertical bar, which say that the action for the next line should be used for the current rule. No strings are copied in this situation—the same pointer is returned here as will be returned by the next save() call. That is, when the input string is a " | ", several pointers to the same accepting string are returned by consecutive save() calls. A pointer to the string itself (as compared to the line number) is returned on line 182 in order to facilitate debugging—this way you can examine the string directly without having to skip past the line number. The line number can be accessed later on, using an expression like the following:

Getting the line number from the left of the string.

```
char   *str = save("string");
line_number  = ( (int *)str )[-1];
```

Listing 2.25. *nfa.c*— Memory Management—States and String

```
82    PRIVATE NFA    *Nfa_states  ;       /* State-machine array              */
83    PRIVATE int    Nstates = 0  ;       /* # of NFA states in machine    .  */
84    PRIVATE int    Next_alloc;          /* Index of next element of the array */
85
86    #define SSIZE   32
87
88    PRIVATE NFA    *Sstack[ SSIZE ];     /* Stack used by new()              */
89    PRIVATE NFA    **Sp = &Sstack[ -1 ]; /* Stack pointer                    */
90
91    #define STACK_OK()     ( INBOUNDS(Sstack, Sp) )    /* true if stack not  */
92                                                       /* full or empty      */
93    #define STACK_USED()   ( (Sp-Stack) + 1      )  /* slots used           */
94    #define CLEAR_STACK()  ( Sp = Sstack - 1     )  /* reset the stack      */
95    #define PUSH(x)        ( *++Sp = (x)         )  /* put x on stack       */
96    #define POP()          ( *Sp--               )  /* get x from stack     */
97
98    /*----------------------------------------------------------------*/
99
100   PRIVATE int  *Strings;          /* Place to save accepting strings    */
101   PRIVATE int  *Savep;            /* Current position in Strings array.  */
102
103   /*----------------------------------------------------------------*/
104
105   PRIVATE NFA  *new()                      /* NFA management functions */
106   {
107       NFA *p;
108       static int first_time = 1;
109
110       if( first_time )
111       {
112           if( !( Nfa_states = (NFA *) calloc(NFA_MAX, sizeof(NFA)) ))
113               parse_err( E_MEM );
114
```

➡

Listing 2.25. continued...

```
115              first_time = 0;
116              Sp = &Sstack[ -1 ];
117          }
118
119      if( ++Nstates >= NFA_MAX )
120              parse_err( E_LENGTH );
121
122      /* If the stack is not ok, it's empty */
123
124      p = !STACK_OK() ? &Nfa_states[Next_alloc++] : POP();
125      p->edge = EPSILON;
126      return p;
127  }
128
129  /*- - - - - - - - - - - - - - - - - - - - - - - - - - - - - - - - */
130
131  PRIVATE void    discard( nfa_to_discard )
132  NFA     *nfa_to_discard;
133  {
134      --Nstates;
135
136      memset( nfa_to_discard, 0, sizeof(NFA) );
137      nfa_to_discard->edge = EMPTY ;
138      PUSH( nfa_to_discard );
139
140      if( !STACK_OK() )
141          parse_err( E_STACK );
142  }
143
144  /*----------------------------------------------------------------*/
145
146  PRIVATE char    *save( str )                /* String-management function. */
147  char    *str;
148  {
149      char        *textp, *startp;
150      int         len;
151      static int  first_time = 1;
152
153      if( first_time )
154      {
155          if( !(Savep = Strings = (int *) malloc( STR_MAX )) )
156              parse_err( E_MEM );
157
158          first_time = 0;
159      }
160
161      if( *str == '|' )
162          return (char *)( Savep + 1 );
163
164      *Savep++ = Lineno;
165
166      for( textp = (char *)Savep ; *str ; *textp++ = *str++ )
167          if( textp >= (char *)(Strings + (STR_MAX-1)) )
168              parse_err( E_STRINGS );
169
170      *textp++ = '\0' ;
171
172      /* Increment Savep past the text. "len" is initialized to the string length.
173       * The "len/sizeof(int)" truncates the size down to an even multiple of the
174       * current int size. The "+(len % sizeof(int) != 0)" adds 1 to the truncated
```

→

```
      Listing 2.25. continued...
175          * size if the string length isn't an even multiple of the int size (the !=
176          * operator evaluates to 1 or 0). Return a pointer to the string itself.
177          */
178
179          startp  = (char *)Savep;
180          len     = textp - startp;
181          Savep  += (len / sizeof(int)) + (len % sizeof(int) != 0);
182          return startp;
183     }
```

2.5.2.6 Macro Support. The next code segment (in Listing 2.26) comprises the macro-support routines. new_macro() (on line 202) is passed a pointer to a line that contains a macro definition and it files the macro in a small symbol table. The expand_macro(char **namep) routine on line 264 is passed a pointer to a character pointer, which in turn points at a macro invocation. The routine advances *namep past the invocation, and returns a string holding the macro's contents. The print-macs() subroutine on line 300 of Listing 2.26 prints the macros. The various hash routines and the HASH_TAB structure that are used here are discussed in Appendix A.

Macro substitution:
new_macro(),
expand_macro().

printmacs()

Listing 2.26. *nfa.c*— Macro Support

```
184     /*------------------------------------------------------------
185      * MACRO support:
186      */
187
188     #define MAC_NAME_MAX   34          /* Maximum name length            */
189     #define MAC_TEXT_MAX   80          /* Maximum amount of expansion text */
190
191     typedef struct
192     {
193         char name[ MAC_NAME_MAX ];
194         char text[ MAC_TEXT_MAX ];
195
196     } MACRO;
197
198     PRIVATE HASH_TAB *Macros; /* Symbol table for macro definitions */
199
200     /*----------------------------------------------------------*/
201
202     PUBLIC  void    new_macro( def )
203     char    *def;
204     {
205         /* Add a new macro to the table. If two macros have the same name, the
206          * second one takes precedence. A definition takes the form:
207          *          name <whitespace> text [<whitespace>]
208          * whitespace at the end of the line is ignored.
209          */
210
211         unsigned hash_add();
212
213         char   *name;              /* Name component of macro definition  */
214         char   *text;              /* text part of macro definition       */
215         char   *edef;              /* pointer to end of text part         */
216         MACRO *p;
217         static int first_time = 1;
218
```

Listing 2.26. continued...

```
219        if( first_time )
220        {
221            first_time = 0;
222            Macros = maketab( 31, hash_add, strcmp );
223        }
224
225        for( name = def; *def && !isspace(*def) ; def++ )        /* Isolate name */
226            ;
227        if( *def )
228            *def++ = '\0' ;
229
230        /* Isolate the definition text. This process is complicated because you need
231         * to discard any trailing whitespace on the line. The first while loop
232         * skips the preceding whitespace. The for loop is looking for end of
233         * string. If you find a white character (and the \n at the end of string
234         * is white), remember the position as a potential end of string.
235         */
236
237        while( isspace( *def ) )           /* skip up to macro body            */
238            ++def;
239
240        text = def;                        /* Remember start of replacement text */
241
242        edef = NULL;                       /* strip trailing white space         */
243        while(  *def  )
244        {
245            if( !isspace(*def) )
246                ++def;
247            else
248                for(edef = def++; isspace(*def) ; ++def )
249                    ;
250        }
251
252        if( edef )
253            *edef = '\0';
254                                           /* Add the macro to the symbol table  */
255
256        p  = (MACRO *) newsym( sizeof(MACRO) );
257        strncpy( p->name, name, MAC_NAME_MAX );
258        strncpy( p->text, text, MAC_TEXT_MAX );
259        addsym( Macros, p );
260    }
261
262    /* - - - - - - - - - - - - - - - - - - - - - - - - - - - - - - - - -*/
263
264    PRIVATE char    *expand_macro( namep )
265    char    **namep;
266    {
267        /* Return a pointer to the contents of a macro having the indicated
268         * name. Abort with a message if no macro exists. The macro name includes
269         * the brackets, which are destroyed by the expansion process. *namep
270         * is modified to point past the close brace.
271         */
272
273        char    *p;
274        MACRO   *mac;
275
```

➡

Listing 2.26. continued...

```
276        if( !(p = strchr( ++(*namep), '}')) )        /* skip { and find } */
277            parse_err( E_BADMAC );                    /* print msg & abort */
278        else
279        {
280            *p++    = '\0';                           /* Overwrite close brace. */
281
282            if( !(mac = (MACRO *) findsym( Macros, *namep )) )
283                parse_err( E_NOMAC );
284
285            *namep = p ;                              /* Update name pointer.   */
286            return mac->text;
287        }
288
289        return "ERROR";                               /* If you get here, it's a bug */
290    }
291
292    /* - - - - - - - - - - - - - - - - - - - - - - - - - - - - - -*/
293
294    PRIVATE print_a_macro( mac )                      /* Workhorse function needed by     */
295    MACRO   *mac;                                     /* ptab() call in printmacs(), below */
296    {
297        printf( "%-16s--[%s]--\n", mac->name, mac->text );
298    }
299
300    PUBLIC void printmacs()                           /* Print all the macros to stdout */
301    {
302        if( !Macros )
303            printf("\tThere are no macros\n");
304        else
305        {
306            printf("\nMACROS:\n");
307            ptab( Macros, print_a_macro, NULL, 1 );
308        }
309    }
```

2.5.2.7 LEX's Lexical Analyzer.

The lowest-level input functions are in *input.c*, Listing 2.27. get_expr() on line eight is the actual input function. It gets an entire rule—both the regular expression and any following code—from the input file (pointed to by Ifile) and puts it into Input_buf[]. Multiple-line rules are handled here in that lines that start with white space are concatenated to the previous line. Two line-number variables are modified in this routine. They are Lineno, which holds the input line number of the first line of the rule, and Actual_lineno, which holds the current input line number. get_expr() normally returns a pointer to the input string (in Input_buf[]). It returns NULL either at end of file or when a line starting with a %% is encountered. Since %% is treated as an end of file, the third part of the input file, which contains C source code that is passed directly to the output, is ignored by the parser.

get_expr()

Input buffers: Ifile, Input_buffer.

Multiple-line actions: Lineno, Actual_lineno.

Listing 2.28 holds the lexical analyzer itself. The token set is defined in the enumerated type on lines 310 to 330. The **L** token (*L* for literal) is used for all characters that aren't represented by explicitly defined tokens. Escaped characters and characters within quoted strings are also returned as **L** tokens, even if the lexeme would normally be an explicit token. The **EOS** token is returned at end of the regular expression, but the input buffer holds the entire rule, including a multiple-line accepting action. The parser uses this fact to pick up the accepting action when an **EOS** is encountered. Note that end of input is also treated as a token.

LEX's lexical analyzer.

Literal characters: the L token, EOS.

Listing 2.27. *input.c*— Low-Level Input Functions

```
 1   #include <stdio.h>
 2   #include <ctype.h>
 3   #include <tools/debug.h>
 4   #include "globals.h"
 5
 6   /* INPUT.C        Lowest-level input functions.  */
 7
 8   PUBLIC char      *get_expr()
 9   {
10       /* Input routine for nfa(). Gets a regular expression and the associated
11        * string from the input stream. Returns a pointer to the input string
12        * normally. Returns NULL on end of file or if a line beginning with % is
13        * encountered. All blank lines are discarded and all lines that start with
14        * whitespace are concatenated to the previous line. The global variable
15        * Lineno is set to the line number of the top line of a multiple-line
16        * block. Actual_lineno holds the real line number.
17        */
18
19       static  int lookahead = 0;
20       int         space_left;
21       char        *p;
22
23       p          = Input_buf;
24       space_left = MAXINP;
25       if( Verbose > 1 )
26           printf( "b%d: ", Actual_lineno );
27
28       if( lookahead == '%' )        /* next line starts with a % sign       */
29           return NULL;              /* return End-of-input marker           */
30
31       Lineno = Actual_lineno ;
32
33       while( (lookahead = getline(&p, space_left-1, Ifile)) != EOF )
34       {
35           if( lookahead == 0 )
36               lerror(1, "Rule too long\n");
37
38           Actual_lineno++;
39
40           if( !Input_buf[0] )                        /* Ignore blank lines */
41               continue;
42
43           space_left = MAXINP - (p-Input_buf);
44
45           if( !isspace(lookahead) )
46               break;
47
48           *p++ = '\n' ;
49       }
50
51       if( Verbose > 1 )
52           printf( "%s\n", lookahead ? Input_buf : "--EOF--" );
53
54       return lookahead ? Input_buf : NULL ;
55   }
56
57   /*-------------------------------------------------------------------*/
58
```

Listing 2.27. continued...

```
59    PRIVATE int getline( stringp, n, stream )
60    char     **stringp;
61    FILE     *stream;
62    {
63        /* Gets a line of input. Gets at most n-1 characters. Updates *stringp
64         * to point at the '\0' at the end of the string. Return a lookahead
65         * character (the character that follows the \n in the input). The '\n'
66         * is not put into the string.
67         *
68         * Return the character following the \n normally,
69         *        EOF   at end of file,
70         *        0     if the line is too long.
71         */
72
73        static int  lookahead  = 0;
74        char        *str, *startstr;
75
76        startstr = str = *stringp;
77
78        if( lookahead == 0 )                            /* initialize */
79            lookahead = getc( stream );
80
81        if( n > 0  && lookahead != EOF )
82        {
83            while( --n > 0 )
84            {
85                *str      = lookahead ;
86                lookahead = getc(stream);
87
88                if( *str == '\n' || *str == EOF )
89                    break;
90                ++str;
91            }
92            *str      = '\0';
93            *stringp = str ;
94        }
95        return (n <= 0) ? 0 : lookahead ;
96    }
```

Listing 2.28. *nfa.c*— L^{E}X's own Lexical Analyzer

```
310    typedef enum token
311    {
312        EOS = 1,              /*   end of string     */
313        ANY,                 /*   .                 */
314        AT_BOL,              /*   ^                 */
315        AT_EOL,              /*   $                 */
316        CCL_END,             /*   ]                 */
317        CCL_START,           /*   [                 */
318        CLOSE_CURLY,         /*   }                 */
319        CLOSE_PAREN,         /*   )                 */
320        CLOSURE,             /*   *                 */
321        DASH,                /*   -                 */
322        END_OF_INPUT,        /*   EOF               */
323        L,                   /*   literal character */
324        OPEN_CURLY,          /*   {                 */
325        OPEN_PAREN,          /*   (                 */
```

```
Listing 2.28. continued...
326        OPTIONAL,              /*   ?                   */
327        OR,                    /*   |                   */
328        PLUS_CLOSE             /*   +                   */
329
330    } TOKEN;
331
332    PRIVATE TOKEN   Tokmap[] =
333    {
334    /*    ^@   ^A   ^B   ^C   ^D   ^E   ^F   ^G   ^H   ^I   ^J   ^K   ^L   ^M   ^N  */
335        L,   L,   L,   L,   L,   L,   L,   L,   L,   L,   L,   L,   L,   L,   L,
336
337    /*    ^O   ^P   ^Q   ^R   ^S   ^T   ^U   ^V   ^W   ^X   ^Y   ^Z   ^[   ^\   ^]  */
338        L,   L,   L,   L,   L,   L,   L,   L,   L,   L,   L,   L,   L,   L,
339
340    /*    ^^   ^_   SPACE   !    "    #     $          %    &    '          */
341        L,   L,   L,      L,   L,   L,    AT_EOL,   L,   L,   L,
342
343    /*    (              )              *          +          ,    -     .   */
344        OPEN_PAREN,  CLOSE_PAREN, CLOSURE, PLUS_CLOSE, L, DASH, ANY,
345
346    /*    /    0    1    2    3    4    5    6    7    8    9    :    ;    <    =   */
347        L,   L,   L,   L,   L,   L,   L,   L,   L,   L,   L,   L,   L,   L,   L,
348
349    /*    >              ?                                              */
350        L,           OPTIONAL,
351
352    /*    @    A    B    C    D    E    F    G    H    I    J    K    L    M    N   */
353        L,   L,   L,   L,   L,   L,   L,   L,   L,   L,   L,   L,   L,   L,   L,
354
355    /*    O    P    Q    R    S    T    U    V    W    X    Y    Z              */
356        L,   L,   L,   L,   L,   L,   L,   L,   L,   L,   L,   L,
357
358    /*    [              \              ]              ^              */
359        CCL_START,   L,           CCL_END,         AT_BOL,
360
361    /*    _    '    a    b    c    d    e    f    g    h    i    j    k    l    m   */
362        L,   L,   L,   L,   L,   L,   L,   L,   L,   L,   L,   L,   L,   L,   L,
363
364    /*    n    o    p    q    r    s    t    u    v    w    x    y    z          */
365        L,   L,   L,   L,   L,   L,   L,   L,   L,   L,   L,   L,   L,
366
367    /*    {              |    }              DEL                        */
368        OPEN_CURLY,  OR,  CLOSE_CURLY, L
369    };
370
371    PRIVATE char   *(*Ifunct)() ;            /* Input function pointer          */
372    PRIVATE char   *Input = "" ;             /* Current position in input string */
373    PRIVATE char   *S_input   ;              /* Beginning of input string       */
374    PRIVATE TOKEN Current_tok ;              /* Current token                   */
375    PRIVATE int    Lexeme     ;              /* Value associated with LITERAL   */
376
377    #define MATCH(t)    (Current_tok == (t))
378
379    /*-------------------------------------------------------------
380     * Lexical analyzer:
381     *
382     * Lexical analysis is trivial because all lexemes are single-character values.
383     * The only complications are escape sequences and quoted strings, both
384     * of which are handled by advance(), below. This routine advances past the
385     * current token, putting the new token into Current_tok and the equivalent
```

```
     Listing 2.28. continued...
386       * lexeme into Lexeme. If the character was escaped, Lexeme holds the actual
387       * value. For example, if a "\s" is encountered, Lexeme will hold a space
388       * character.  The MATCH(x) macro returns true if x matches the current token.
389       * Advance both modifies Current_tok to the current token and returns it.
390       */
391
392      PRIVATE int      advance()
393      {
394          static int    inquote = 0;            /* Processing quoted string     */
395          int           saw_esc;                /* Saw a backslash              */
396          static char   *stack[ SSIZE ],        /* Input-source stack           */
397                        **sp = NULL;            /* and stack pointer.           */
398
399          if( !sp )                             /* Initialize sp.               */
400              sp = stack - 1;                   /* Necessary for large model    */
401
402          if( Current_tok == EOS )              /* Get another line             */
403          {
404              if( inquote )
405                  parse_err( E_NEWLINE );
406              do
407              {
408                  if( !(Input = (*Ifunct)()) )            /* End of file  */
409                  {
410                      Current_tok = END_OF_INPUT;
411                      goto exit;
412                  }
413                  while( isspace( *Input ) )          /* Ignore leading        */
414                      Input++;                        /* white space...        */
415
416              } while ( !*Input );                    /* and blank lines.      */
417
418              S_input = Input;                        /* Remember start of line */
419          }                                           /* for error messages.    */
420
421          while( *Input == '\0' )
422          {
423              if( INBOUNDS(stack, sp) )          /* Restore previous input source */
424              {
425                  Input = *sp-- ;
426                  continue;
427              }
428
429              Current_tok = EOS;                 /* No more input sources to restore */
430              Lexeme = '\0';                     /* ie. you're at the real end of    */
431              goto exit;                         /* string.                          */
432          }
433
434          if( !inquote )
435          {
436              while( *Input == '{' )             /* Macro expansion required      }*/
437              {
438                  *++sp = Input ;                /* Stack current input string    */
439                  Input = expand_macro( sp );    /* and replace it with the macro */
440                                                 /* body.                         */
441                  if( TOOHIGH(stack,sp) )
442                      parse_err(E_MACDEPTH);     /* Stack overflow */
443              }
444          }
445
```

```
Listing 2.28. continued...
446        if( *Input == '"' )
447        {                              /* At either start and end of a quoted    */
448            inquote = ~inquote;         /* string. All characters are treated  as */
449            if( !*++Input )             /* literals while inquote is true).        */
450            {
451                Current_tok = EOS ;
452                Lexeme = '\0';
453                goto exit;
454            }
455        }
456
457        saw_esc = (*Input == '\\');
458
459        if( !inquote )
460        {
461            if( isspace(*Input) )
462            {
463                Current_tok = EOS ;
464                Lexeme = '\0';
465                goto exit;
466            }
467            Lexeme = esc( &Input );
468        }
469        else
470        {
471            if( saw_esc && Input[1] == '"' )
472            {
473                Input += 2;
474                Lexeme = '"';
475            }
476            else
477                Lexeme = *Input++ ;
478        }
479
480        Current_tok = (inquote || saw_esc) ? L : Tokmap[Lexeme] ;
481    exit:
482        return Current_tok;
483    }
```

The translation problem is simplified by the fact that all lexemes are single characters. ([^, which starts a negative character class, is treated as a **CCL_START/AT_BOL**
pair). The Tokmap[] array on lines 332 to 369 is used to translate these single-
character lexemes into tokens. It is indexed by ASCII character, and evaluates to the
token value associated with that character.

Various other variables are needed by the lexical analyzer, all declared on lines 371
to 375 of Listing 2.28. Ifunct points at the current input function, which should work
like gets(), returning either the next input line or NULL at end of file. Input points at
the current input line, and S_input is the current position on that line. Current_tok
holds the current token, and Lexeme holds the associated lexeme (which is only needed
for **L** tokens). The MATCH(t) macro on line 377 of Listing 2.29 evaluates true if t is the
current lookahead token.

The advance() function on lines 392 to 483 of Listing 2.28 advances the input by
one character, modifying Current_tok and Lexeme as appropriate, and also returning
the current token. An **END_OF_INPUT** token is returned at end of file. This subroutine
is probably the most complicated routine in the parser, and is also a little long for my
taste, but it seemed best to keep the whole lexical analysis phase in a single subroutine

Ifunct, Input,
S_input, Current_tok,
Lexeme

MATCH(t)

advance()

for maintenance reasons. A new line is fetched on lines 402 to 419 only if the end of the previous line has been reached (Current_tok is **EOS**).

Lines 421 to 444 of Listing 2.28 handle macro expansion. Macros are delimited by braces, and they are recognized in the **while** loop on line 436, which finds the leading brace. It's a loop because macro definitions might be nested—if the first character of the macro body is also an open brace, the loop will expand this inner macro as well as the current one. Nested macros are handled with a stack. When an inner macro is encountered, the current input buffer is pushed onto a stack, and Input is modified to point at the macro-replacement text. The loop on line 421 is activated when you get to the end of the replacement text. The previous input string is restored at the top of the loop by popping it off the stack. The code on lines 429 to 431 is activated only if the stack is empty and no more characters are found in the current input source, in which case end of string has been reached. The **goto** statement on line 431 is functioning as a **return** statement here. I generally shun multiple **return** statements in favor of multiple **goto** branches to a label that precedes a single **return** statement. This way, the subroutine has only a single exit point so it's easier to set up breakpoints and debugging diagnostics.

Quotes are recognized on line 446, and inquote is set to true when processing a quoted string. Similarly, saw_escape is set to true on line 457 when a backslash is encountered. The clause on lines 461 to 467 handles normal text. **EOS**, which marks the end of the regular expression, is returned if any white space is encountered, and escape sequences are expanded by the esc() call on line 467. The following **else** clause handles quoted strings. The test on line 471 is looking for a ", which must be treated as a literal quote mark. All other characters, including white space, are considered to be part of the regular expression and are just returned in the normal way. Finally, the current token is put into Current_tok on line 480. If you're in a quoted string or if the current character is preceded by a backslash, then the current character is treated literally and an **L** token is returned; otherwise, the character is translated to a token by looking it up in Tokmap[].

2.5.2.8 Parsing. LEX's parser begins in Listing 2.29. The prototypes at the top of the listing are necessary, both for debugging and because the parser itself is highly recursive—there is no way to arrange the subroutines to avoid all forward references. The parser is a straightforward implementation of the grammar presented earlier. The topmost routine, machine() on line 508 of Listing 2.29, collects a series of rules and chains them together using ε transitions and dummy states (as was pictured in Figure 2.9 on page 82). The rule() calls on lines 516 and 522 return pointers to NFA's that represent each regular expression on the input line.

The rule() subroutine on line 531 of Listing 2.29 gets a single regular expression and associated action. Most of the work is done by expr(), called on lines 554 and 557. The routine is passed two pointers to NFA pointers. When expr() returns, these two pointers will have been modified to point at the first and last nodes in the machine (there will be only one of each). That is, synthesized attributes are used here (and throughout the rest of the parser), but I can't use the actual return value (the argument to a **return** statement) because there are two attributes. Consequently, I'm passing pointers to variables to be modified. (Put another way, I'm doing a call by reference here—passing pointers to the object to be modified).

Beginning- and end-of-line anchors are processed directly in rule() on lines 550 to 554 of Listing 2.29. An extra node is created with an outgoing transition on a newline so that the ˆ is treated as if it were a regular expression that matched a newline. The anchor field is modified on line 552 to remember that this newline is there as the result of an anchor, as compared to a specific match of a \n. The newline has to be discarded in the former case; it remains in the lexeme if a specific match was requested, however.

Macro expansion.

Quotes in regular expressions.

machine()

rule()

expr()

Anchor processing.

Listing 2.29. *nfa.c*— Parser, Part 1: `machine()` and `rule()`

```
484    PRIVATE int      advance          ( void           );
485    PRIVATE void     cat_expr         ( NFA**, NFA**   );
486    PRIVATE void     discard          ( NFA*           );
487    PRIVATE void     dodash           ( SET*           );
488    PRIVATE void     expr             ( NFA**, NFA**   );
489    PRIVATE void     factor           ( NFA**, NFA**   );
490    PRIVATE int      first_in_cat     ( TOKEN          );
491    PRIVATE NFA      *machine         ( void           );
492    PRIVATE NFA      *new             ( void           );
493    PRIVATE void     parse_err        ( ERR_NUM        );
494    PRIVATE NFA      *rule            ( void           );
495    PRIVATE char     *save            ( char*          );
496    PRIVATE void     term             ( NFA**, NFA**   );
497
498    /*-------------------------------------------------------------
499     * The Parser:
500     *      A simple recursive descent parser that creates a Thompson NFA for
501     *      a regular expression. The access routine [thompson()] is at the
502     *      bottom. The NFA is created as a directed graph, with each node
503     *      containing pointer's to the next node. Since the structures are
504     *      allocated from an array, the machine can also be considered
505     *      as an array where the state number is the array index.
506     */
507
508    PRIVATE  NFA     *machine()
509    {
510        NFA *start;
511        NFA *p;
512
513        ENTER("machine");
514
515        p = start = new();
516        p->next   = rule();
517
518        while( !MATCH(END_OF_INPUT) )
519        {
520            p->next2 = new();
521            p        = p->next2;
522            p->next  = rule();
523        }
524
525        LEAVE("machine");
526        return start;
527    }
528
529    /* - - - - - - - - - - - - - - - - - - - - - - - - - - - - - -*/
530
531    PRIVATE NFA  *rule()
532    {
533        /*  rule      --> expr  EOS action
534         *                ^expr EOS action
535         *                expr$ EOS action
536         *
537         *  action  --> <tabs> <string of characters>
538         *              epsilon
539         */
540
```

```
       ┌─────────────────────────────────────────────────────────────────────┐
       │ Listing 2.29. continued...                                           │
  541  │        NFA *p;                                                        │
  542  │        NFA *start = NULL;                                             │
  543  │        NFA *end   = NULL;                                             │
  544  │        int anchor = NONE;                                             │
  545  │                                                                       │
  546  │        ENTER("rule");                                                 │
  547  │                                                                       │
  548  │        if( MATCH( AT_BOL ) )                                          │
  549  │        {                                                              │
  550  │            start        =  new() ;                                    │
  551  │            start->edge =  '\n'  ;                                      │
  552  │            anchor        |= START ;                                    │
  553  │            advance();                                                 │
  554  │            expr( &start->next, &end );                                │
  555  │        }                                                              │
  556  │        else                                                           │
  557  │            expr( &start, &end );                                      │
  558  │                                                                       │
  559  │                                                                       │
  560  │        if( MATCH( AT_EOL ) )                                          │
  561  │        {                                                              │
  562  │            /*  pattern followed by a carriage-return or linefeed (use a│
  563  │             *  character class).                                      │
  564  │             */                                                        │
  565  │                                                                       │
  566  │            advance();                                                 │
  567  │            end->next =  new()      ;                                  │
  568  │            end->edge =  CCL        ;                                  │
  569  │                                                                       │
  570  │            if( !( end->bitset = newset()) )                           │
  571  │                parse_err( E_MEM );                                    │
  572  │                                                                       │
  573  │            ADD( end->bitset, '\n' );                                  │
  574  │                                                                       │
  575  │            if( !Unix )                                                │
  576  │                ADD( end->bitset, '\r' );                              │
  577  │                                                                       │
  578  │            end        =  end->next ;                                  │
  579  │            anchor     |= END       ;                                  │
  580  │        }                                                              │
  581  │                                                                       │
  582  │        while( isspace(*Input) )                                       │
  583  │            Input++ ;                                                   │
  584  │                                                                       │
  585  │        end->accept = save( Input );                                   │
  586  │        end->anchor = anchor;                                          │
  587  │        advance();                              /* skip past EOS */     │
  588  │                                                                       │
  589  │        LEAVE("rule");                                                 │
  590  │        return start;                                                  │
  591  │    }                                                                  │
       └─────────────────────────────────────────────────────────────────────┘
```

This information is eventually output as a table that will be used by the LEX-generated driver when it processes the newline at run time. The end-of-line anchor is handled in a similar way on lines 566 to 579 of Listing 2.29, though the extra node is put at the end of the machine rather than at the beginning.

MS-DOS, end-of-line prob-
lems in anchors.

Anchors are recognized with a character class that matches either a carriage return or linefeed (as compared to a literal match of a ′\n′ character). You must recognize both characters in MS-DOS "binary-mode" input, because all input lines are terminated with a CR-LF pair (in that order). Lines are terminated by a single newline only in "translated" mode. Since I don't want to worry about which of the two input modes are used, I'm testing for both possibilities. When expr() returns, the input is positioned at the start of the accepting action, which is saved on line 585 (remember, an entire multiple-line action is collected into the input string).

OR and concatenation:
expr(), cat_expr().

Subroutines expr() and cat_expr() are in Listing 2.30. These routines handle the binary operations: | (OR) and concatenation. I'll show how expr() works by watching it process the expression The cat_expr() call on line 621 creates a machine that recognizes the A:

```
   0  --A-->  1
```

*startp and *endp are modified to point at Nodes 0 and 1, and the input is advanced to the **OR** operator. The MATCH on line 623 succeeds and the OR is skipped by the subsequent advance() call. The second cat_expr() call (on line 625) creates a machine that recognizes the B:

```
   2  --B-->  3
```

and modifies e2_start and e2_end to point at nodes representing States 2 and 3. The two machines are then joined together to create the following machine:

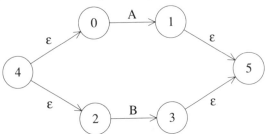

Node 4 is created on lines 628 to 630 and *startp is modified to point at Node 4 on line 631. Node 5 is set up in a similar way on the next four lines.

Listing 2.30. *nfa.c*— Parser, Part 2: Binary Operators

```
592    PRIVATE void expr( startp,  endp )
593    NFA      **startp, **endp ;
594    {
595        /* Because a recursive descent compiler can't handle left recursion,
596         * the productions:
597         *
598         *   expr     -> expr OR cat_expr
599         *        |  cat_expr
600         *
601         * must be translated into:
602         *
603         *   expr     -> cat_expr expr'
604         *   expr'    -> OR cat_expr expr'
605         *             epsilon
606         *
607         * which can be implemented with this loop:
608         *
609         *   cat_expr
```

Listing 2.30. continued...

```
610          *   while( match(OR) )
611          *           cat_expr
612          *           do the OR
613          */
614
615         NFA *e2_start = NULL; /* expression to right of | */
616         NFA *e2_end   = NULL;
617         NFA *p;
618
619         ENTER("expr");
620
621         cat_expr( startp, endp );
622
623         while( MATCH( OR ) )
624         {
625             advance();
626             cat_expr( &e2_start, &e2_end );
627
628             p = new();
629             p->next2 = e2_start ;
630             p->next  = *startp  ;
631             *startp  = p;
632
633             p = new();
634             (*endp)->next = p;
635             e2_end ->next = p;
636             *endp = p;
637         }
638         LEAVE("expr");
639     }
640
641  /* - - - - - - - - - - - - - - - - - - - - - - - - - - - - - - -*/
642
643  PRIVATE void cat_expr( startp,  endp )
644  NFA      **startp, **endp ;
645  {
646      /* The same translations that were needed in the expr rules are needed again
647       * here:
648       *
649       *   cat_expr  -> cat_expr | factor
650       *               factor
651       *
652       * is translated to:
653       *
654       *   cat_expr  -> factor cat_expr'
655       *   cat_expr' -> | factor cat_expr'
656       *               epsilon
657       */
658
659      NFA  *e2_start, *e2_end;
660
661      ENTER("cat_expr");
662
663      if( first_in_cat( Current_tok ) )
664          factor( startp, endp );
665
666      while(  first_in_cat( Current_tok )  )
667      {
668          factor( &e2_start, &e2_end );
669
```

➡

Listing 2.30. continued...

```
670              memcpy( *endp, e2_start, sizeof(NFA));
671              discard( e2_start );
672
673              *endp = e2_end;
674          }
675
676      LEAVE("cat_expr");
677  }
678
679  /* - - - - - - - - - - - - - - - - - - - - - - - - - - -*/
680
681  PRIVATE int      first_in_cat( tok )
682  TOKEN    tok;
683  {
684      switch( tok )
685      {
686      case CLOSE_PAREN:
687      case AT_EOL:
688      case OR:
689      case EOS:                return 0;
690
691      case CLOSURE:
692      case PLUS_CLOSE:
693      case OPTIONAL:       parse_err( E_CLOSE   ); return 0;
694
695      case CCL_END:        parse_err( E_BRACKET ); return 0;
696      case AT_BOL:         parse_err( E_BOL     ); return 0;
697      }
698
699      return 1;
700  }
```

Problems with implicit concatenation operator, first_in_cat().

Concatenation is a somewhat harder problem because there's no operator to look for. The problem is solved by first_in_cat() on line 681 of Listing 2.30, which looks to see if the next input token can reasonably be concatenated to the current one. That is, there is a set of tokens that can not just be concatenated—such as the parenthesis that terminates a parenthesized subexpression or an **OR** token—and the loop must terminate when one of these is encountered. These symbols are identified by the **case** statements on lines 686 to 689. The other cases test for obvious error conditions such as a close bracket (**CCL_END**) without a preceding open bracket or one of the closure operators without anything in front of it.

Concatenation.

Concatenation is performed in a manner similar to OR. The first operand is fetched with the factor() call on line 664 (which returns with *startp and *endp modified to point at the endpoints of a machine that recognizes the operand). The second and subsequent operands are fetched by the factor() call on line 668, and the two are concatenated by overwriting the contents of the end node of the first operand with the contents of the starting node of the second operand (with the memcpy() call on the next line). The now redundant start node of the second operand is then discarded.

As an example of the process, if the input expression is D*\.D, the first factor() call processes the D*, modifying *startp and *endp to point at nodes representing States 2 and 3 of the following machine:

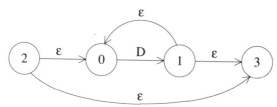

The second call modifies e2_start and e2_end to point at Nodes 4 and 5 of the following machine:

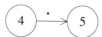

They are concatenated together by overwriting Node 3 with Node 4, yielding:

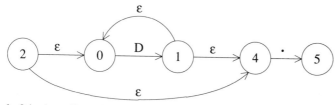

Node 3 is then discarded. The factor() call in the next iteration of the loop modifies e2_start and e2_end to point at the ends of:

(The discarded Node 3 is picked up again here because it will be at the top of the push-back stack.) This new machine is concatenated to the previous one by overwriting Node 5 with the contents of Node 3.

The unary closure operators are all handled by factor(), in Listing 2.31. It behaves just like the earlier routines, except that it builds a closure machine like the ones shown in Figure 2.12 on page 83. The code is simplified because the machines for + and ? are subsets of the one for *. The same number of extra nodes is created in all three situations. The backwards-pointing ε edge is created only if a '*' or a '+' is being processed; the forward-pointing edge is created only for a '*' or a '?'.

Closure operators: factor().

Single-character matches and parenthesized subexpressions are handled by term(), in Listing 2.32. The actual NFA structures are allocated and connected to each other on lines 761 and 762. The edge field is then initialized to the character or CCL, as appropriate. A dot is treated as a character class that matches everything but a newline. Normal character classes are assembled by dodash()[12] on line 811 of Listing 2.32. This routine converts the input tokens representing the class into a SET. A set can have one element ([x]) or several elements—[a-zA-Z] and the following large character class are equivalent:

Single characters and parenthesized subexpressions: term().

Character classes, dodash().

[abcdefghijklmnopqrstuvwxyzABCDEFGHIJKLMNOPQRSTUVWXYZ]

Note that the dash notation is expanded as sequential numbers. Since your machine probably uses the ASCII character set, this means that [A-z] contains the entire alphabet plus the following symbols:

---

12. Camptown ladies sing this song, dodash(), dodash(), Camptown race track five miles long ...

Listing 2.31. *nfa.c*— Parser, Part 3: Unary Operators (Closure)

```
701    PRIVATE void factor( startp, endp )
702    NFA       **startp, **endp;
703    {
704          /*              factor  --> term*  | term+  | term?
705          */
706
707        NFA *start, *end;
708
709        ENTER("factor");
710
711        term( startp, endp );
712
713        if( MATCH(CLOSURE) || MATCH(PLUS_CLOSE) || MATCH(OPTIONAL) )
714        {
715            start       = new()   ;
716            end         = new()   ;
717            start->next    = *startp ;
718            (*endp)->next = end     ;
719
720            if( MATCH(CLOSURE)  || MATCH(OPTIONAL) )          /*    * or ?   */
721                start->next2 = end;
722
723            if( MATCH(CLOSURE)  || MATCH(PLUS_CLOSE) )        /*    * or +   */
724                (*endp)->next2 = *startp;
725
726            *startp  = start ;
727            *endp    = end   ;
728            advance();
729        }
730
731        LEAVE("factor");
732    }
```

                          [\ ]   ^   _   .   `

You can get a dash into a character class with a \-, as in [_\-], which recognizes either a dash or an underscore. Note that the only metacharacters recognized as such in a character class are a ^ that immediately follows the bracket, a dash, and a close bracket (]); so [*?.] recognizes a star, question mark, or dot. The " and { that trigger a macro expansion are also active in a character class, but they are handled by the input routines. You can use \] to get a] into a class: [[\]] recognizes either an open or close bracket.

Listing 2.32. *nfa.c*— Parser, Part 4: Single Character Matches

```
733    PRIVATE void term( startp, endp )
734    NFA       **startp, **endp;
735    {
736        /* Process the term productions:
737         *
738         * term --> [...]  |  [^...]  |  []  |  [^]  |  .  | (expr) | <character>
739         *
740         * The [] is nonstandard. It matches a space, tab, formfeed, or newline,
741         * but not a carriage return (\r). All of these are single nodes in the
742         * NFA.
743         */
744
```
                                                                                    ➔

Listing 2.32. continued...

```
745        NFA *start;
746        int c;
747
748        ENTER("term");
749
750        if( MATCH( OPEN_PAREN ) )
751        {
752            advance();
753            expr( startp, endp );
754            if( MATCH( CLOSE_PAREN ) )
755                advance();
756            else
757                parse_err( E_PAREN );
758        }
759        else
760        {
761            *startp = start            = new();
762            *endp   = start->next = new();
763
764            if( !( MATCH( ANY ) || MATCH( CCL_START) ))
765            {
766                start->edge = Lexeme;
767                advance();
768            }
769            else
770            {
771                start->edge = CCL;
772
773                if( !( start->bitset = newset()) )
774                    parse_err( E_MEM );
775
776                if( MATCH( ANY ) )                    /*      dot (.)              */
777                {
778                    ADD( start->bitset, '\n' );
779                    if( !Unix )
780                        ADD( start->bitset, '\r' );
781
782                    COMPLEMENT( start->bitset );
783                }
784                else
785                {
786                    advance();
787                    if( MATCH( AT_BOL ) )            /* Negative character class */
788                    {
789                        advance();
790
791                        ADD( start->bitset, '\n' ); /* Don't include \n in class */
792                        if( !Unix )
793                            ADD( start->bitset, '\r' );
794
795                        COMPLEMENT( start->bitset );
796                    }
797                    if( ! MATCH( CCL_END ) )
798                        dodash( start->bitset );
799                    else                              /*      [] or [^]            */
800                        for( c = 0; c <= ' '; ++c )
801                            ADD( start->bitset, c );
802                }
803                advance();
804            }
```

Listing 2.32. continued...

```
805          }
806          LEAVE("term");
807      }
808
809      /* - - - - - - - - - - - - - - - - - - - - - - - - - - - - - - */
810
811      PRIVATE void      dodash( set )
812      SET      *set;                          /* Pointer to ccl character set */
813      {
814          register int           first;
815
816          for(; !MATCH( EOS )  &&  !MATCH( CCL_END ) ; advance() )
817          {
818              if( ! MATCH( DASH ) )
819              {
820                  first = Lexeme;
821                  ADD( set, Lexeme );
822              }
823              else
824              {
825                  advance();
826                  for(; first <= Lexeme ; first++ )
827                      ADD( set, first );
828              }
829          }
830      }
```

The final workhorse function is `printnfa()`, starting on line 57 of Listing 2.33, which is for debugging. It prints out the entire machine in human-readable form, showing the various pointers, and so forth.

Access routine: `thompson()`.

Nfa.c finishes up with a high-level access routine, `thompson()`, in Listing 2.34. (Everything else was declared `PRIVATE`, so was inaccessible from outside the current file). It is passed a pointer to an input function, and it returns two things: a pointer to an array of NFA structures that represents the state machine and the size of that array (the number of states in use).

Listing 2.33. *printnfa.c*— Print NFA to Standard Output

```
 1   #include <stdio.h>
 2   #include <tools/debug.h>
 3   #include <tools/set.h>
 4   #include <tools/hash.h>
 5   #include <tools/compiler.h>
 6   #include "nfa.h"
 7
 8   PRIVATE   void    printccl      ( SET* );
 9   PRIVATE   char    *plab         ( NFA*, NFA* );
10   PUBLIC    void    print_nfa     ( NFA*, int, NFA* );
11
12   /*-------------------------------------------------------------
13    *  PRINTNFA.C  Routine to print out a NFA structure in human-readable form.
14    */
15
16   PRIVATE void      printccl( set )
17   SET      *set;
18   {
19       static int  i;
```

Listing 2.33. continued...

```
20
21          putchar('[');
22          for( i = 0 ; i <= 0x7f; i++ )
23          {
24              if( TEST(set, i) )
25              {
26                  if( i < ' ' )
27                      printf( "^%c", i + '@' );
28                  else
29                      printf( "%c", i );
30              }
31          }
32
33          putchar(']');
34  }
35
36  /*----------------------------------------------------------*/
37
38  PRIVATE  char   *plab( nfa, state )
39  NFA      *nfa, *state ;
40  {
41      /* Return a pointer to a buffer containing the state number. The buffer is
42       * overwritten on each call so don't put more than one plab() call in an
43       * argument to printf().
44       */
45
46      static char buf[ 32 ];
47
48      if( !nfa || !state )
49              return("--");
50
51      sprintf( buf, "%2d", state - nfa );
52      return ( buf );
53  }
54
55  /*----------------------------------------------------------*/
56
57  PUBLIC  void    print_nfa( nfa, len, start )
58  NFA      *nfa, *start;
59  int      len;
60  {
61      NFA *s = nfa ;
62
63      printf( "\n---------------- NFA --------------\n" );
64
65      for(; --len >= 0 ; nfa++ )
66      {
67          printf( "NFA state %s: ", plab(s,nfa) );
68
69          if( !nfa->next )
70              printf("(TERMINAL)");
71          else
72          {
73              printf( "--> %s ",  plab(s, nfa->next ) );
74              printf( "(%s) on ", plab(s, nfa->next2) );
75
76              switch( nfa->edge )
77              {
```

Listing 2.33. continued...

```
78                case CCL:      printccl( nfa->bitset           );      break;
79                case EPSILON: printf  ( "EPSILON "             );      break;
80                default:       pchar   ( nfa->edge, stdout     );      break;
81                }
82            }
83
84        if( nfa == start )
85            printf(" (START STATE)");
86
87        if( nfa->accept )
88            printf(" accepting %s<%s>%s", nfa->anchor & START ? "^" : "",
89                                          nfa->accept,
90                                          nfa->anchor & END   ? "$" : "" );
91        printf( "\n" );
92        }
93    printf( "\n--------------------------------------\n" );
94 }
```

Listing 2.34. *nfa.c*— The High-Level Access Function

```
831    PUBLIC  NFA     *thompson( input_function, max_state, start_state )
832    char    *(*input_function)();
833    int     *max_state;
834    NFA     **start_state;
835    {
836       /* Access routine to this module. Return a pointer to a NFA transition
837        * table that represents the regular expression pointed to by expr or
838        * NULL if there's not enough memory. Modify *max_state to reflect the
839        * largest state number used. This number will probably be a larger
840        * number than the total number of states. Modify *start_state to point
841        * to the start state. This pointer is garbage if thompson() returned 0.
842        * The memory for the table is fetched from malloc(); use free() to
843        * discard it.
844        */
845
846       CLEAR_STACK();
847
848       Ifunct = input_function;
849
850       Current_tok = EOS;            /* Load first token      */
851       advance();
852
853       Nstates     = 0;
854       Next_alloc = 0;
855
856       *start_state = machine();   /* Manufacture the NFA   */
857       *max_state   = Next_alloc ; /* Max state # in NFA    */
858
859       if( Verbose > 1 )
860           print_nfa( Nfa_states, *max_state, *start_state );
861
862       if( Verbose )
863       {
864           printf("%d/%d NFA states used.\n", *max_state, NFA_MAX );
865           printf("%d/%d bytes used for accept strings.\n\n", Savep - Strings,
866                                                                    STR_MAX );
867       }
```

Listing 2.34. continued...

```
868        return Nfa_states;
869    }
```

2.5.3 Interpreting an NFA—Theory*

Now that we've constructed an NFA, we need to turn it into a DFA. The method used here is called *subset construction*; it is developed over the next few sections. First, let's look at how an NFA can be used directly to recognize a string. (Note that interpreting an NFA directly can make more sense in some applications, such as editors, in which the time required to manufacture the DFA from the NFA can be greater than the search time.)

Using an NFA to recognize strings.

The basic strategy makes use of the fact that, from any state, you are, for all practical purposes, also in every state that can be made by traversing ε edges from the current state. I'll demonstrate with a concrete example. The NFA for

ε edges effectively merge states.

```
(D*\.D|D\.D*)
```

is reproduced in Figure 2.14, and I'll recognize the string `1.2.` using this NFA.

Figure 2.14. NFA for (D*\.D|D\.D*)

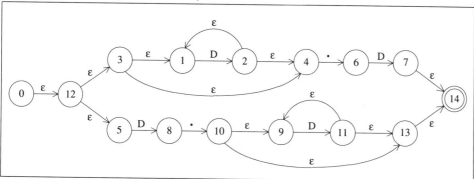

The terminal states (the ones with no outgoing edges) are all accepting states. Starting in the start state (State 0), you can take all ε transitions, regardless of the input character, and without reading any input. If the machine is in State 0, it is, for all practical purposes, simultaneously in States 1, 3, 4, 5, and 12 as well. (These states are all at the end of ε edges that start in State 0. For example, State 4 is there by traversing three edges, from State 0 to State 12 to State 3 to State 4.) This set of states—the ones that can be reached by making ε transitions from a given set of start states—is called the ε-*closure* set. This set also includes the start state—there's an implied ε transition from every state to itself. In this case, the set of start states has only one element: {0}, and you can make transitions to a set of five states: {1, 3, 4, 5, 12}. So:

ε-closure({0}) = {0, 1, 3, 4, 5, 12}.

Reading the `1` from the input, the next state is determined by looking at all transitions that can legitimately be made on a **D** from any of the states in the ε-closure set that was just created. There is a transition from State 1 to 2 on a **D**, and another from State 5 to 8; so from the states in the set {0, 1, 3, 4, 5, 12}, you can make transitions to states in the set {2, 8} on a **D**. This set of states is called the *move* set by [Aho], and it's created by a *move( )* function.[13] More formally, *move(S,c)*—where *S* is a <u>set</u> of states and *c* is an input character—is the set of states that can be reached by making transitions on *c* from any of the states in *S*. In this case:

move({0, 1, 3, 4, 5, 12}, **D**) = {2, 8}.

From States 2 and 8 the machine is also in all states that can be reached by making ε transitions out of States 2 and 8. There are ε transitions from State 2 to States 1 and 4, but there are no ε transitions out of State 8. So:

ε-closure({2, 8}) = {1, 2, 4, 8}

(Remember, the ε-closure set includes the original states.) Now get another input character, this time the dot, and look for outgoing transitions from the previously-computed ε-closure set. There is a transition from State 8 to 10 on a dot, and another from State 4 to 6:

move({1, 2, 4, 8}, .) = {6, 10}.

Continuing the process:

ε-closure({6, 10}) = {6, 9, 10, 13, 14}

State 14 is an accepting state, and the machine can accept if any of the states in the ε-closure set are accepting states. So the machine can accept at this point. Since there's more input, however, more processing is required—the same greedy algorithm that's used by the LEX-generated analyzer is used here. Reading the 2 :

move({6, 9, 10, 13, 14}, **D**) = {7, 11}

and:

ε-closure({7, 11}) = {7, 9, 11, 13, 14}.

This represents an accepting state because State 14 is present. Reading the end-of-input marker,

move({7, 9, 11, 13, 14}, **END_OF_INPUT**) = ∅

The resulting set is empty—there's nowhere to go. This situation is the equivalent of a failure transition, so the machine executes the most recently seen accepting action and accepts State 14.

The algorithm is stated more formally in Tables 2.6 and 2.7. The first of these algorithms is a *greedy* algorithm. It recognizes the longest possible string that matches a regular expression. The second algorithm is nongreedy. It accepts the first string that matches a regular expression. The main difference between these algorithms is that the greedy algorithm doesn't accept an input string until a failure transition out of some state occurs, whereupon it accepts the string associated with the most recently seen accepting state (which could be the current state if the machine fails out of an accepting state). The non-greedy algorithm just accepts as soon as it enters *any* accepting state.

Greedy and nongreedy algorithms.

---

13. The *move()* function is the same thing as the *next()* function that we've been using to find the next state in a DFA.

Table 2.6. Greedy NFA Interpretation (Terminates on Failure)

current	is the set of NFA states that represents the current position in the machine.
c	is the current input character.
accept	if the most recently computed ε-closure set includes an accepting state, this is the state number, otherwise it's false (0).

```
last_accept = FALSE;
current = ε-closure( state_state );
while( c = nextchar( ) )
{
        if( ε-closure( move(current, c) ) ≠ ∅ )
        {
                if( accept )
                        last_accept = accept ;
                current = next;
        }
        else if( last_accept )
        {
                ACCEPT( last_accept );
                last_accept = FALSE;
                current = ε-closure( state_state );
        }
        else
                ERROR;
}
```

Table 2.7. Non-Greedy NFA Interpretation (Terminates on First Accepting State)

current	is the set of NFA states that represents the current position in the machine.
c	is the current input character.
accept	if the most recently computed ε-closure set includes an accepting state, this is the state number, otherwise it's false (0).

```
current = ε-closure( state_state );
while( c = nextchar( ) )
{
        if( ε-closure( move(current, c) ) is not ∅ )
        {
                if( accept )
                {
                        ACCEPT( accept );
                        current = ε-closure( state_state );
                }
                else
                        current = next;
        }
}
```

2.5.4 Interpreting an NFA—Implementation

The foregoing theory is all implemented by the code in *terp.c*, which starts in Listing 2.35. The LARGEST_INT macro on line 19 evaluates to the largest positive integer that can be represented in an int. It is portable—the actual size of an int is immaterial. It

Computing largest positive integer:
LARGEST_INT

Nfa,Nfa_states,nfa()

works by shifting a number that contains all 1's to the right by one bit, shifting a 0 into the high bit. The cast to **unsigned** defeats sign extension on the right shift. Nfa is a pointer to the NFA that represents the regular expression, and Nfa_states is the number of states in that NFA. The nfa() subroutine on line 26 is passed a pointer to an input routine. It creates an NFA using the routines developed earlier, and returns the state number of the start state (its index in the array). The free_nfa() routine on line 43 discards the NFA created with the previous nfa() call.

free_nfa()

Listing 2.35. *terp.c*— File Header

```
1    #include <stdio.h>
2    #include <ctype.h>
3    #include <tools/debug.h>
4    #include <tools/set.h>
5    #include <tools/compiler.h>
6    #include "nfa.h"                             /* defines for NFA, EPSILON, CCL */
7
8    /*------------------------------------------------------------------
9     * Prototypes for subroutines in this file
10    */
11
12   PUBLIC int      nfa         ( char *(*)()        );
13   PUBLIC void     free_nfa    ( void               );
14   PUBLIC SET      *e_closure  ( SET*, char**, int* );
15   PUBLIC SET      *move       ( SET*, int          );
16
17   /*-----------------------------------------------------------------*/
18
19   #define LARGEST_INT   (int)(((unsigned)(~0)) >> 1)
20
21   PRIVATE NFA   *Nfa;                           /* Base address of NFA array   */
22   PRIVATE int   Nfa_states;                     /* Number of states in NFA     */
23
24   /*-----------------------------------------------------------------*/
25
26   PUBLIC int nfa( input_routine )
27   char     *(*input_routine)();
28   {
29       /* Compile the NFA and initialize the various global variables used by
30        * move() and e_closure(). Return the state number (index) of the NFA start
31        * state. This routine must be called before either e_closure() or move()
32        * are called. The memory used for the nfa can be freed with free_nfa()
33        * (in thompson.c).
34        */
35
36       NFA *sstate;
37       Nfa = thompson(input_routine, &Nfa_states, &sstate);
38       return( sstate - Nfa );
39   }
40
41   /*-----------------------------------------------------------------*/
42
43   PUBLIC void free_nfa()
44   {
45       free( Nfa );
46   }
```

The ε-closure set is computed by e_closure(), in Listing 2.36. It uses the NFA created by a previous nfa() call. It is passed a pointer to a set of states (input) and returns the ε-closure set, which is empty if either the input set or the ε-closure set is empty. If the ε-closure set contains an accepting state, it returns two additional values indirectly through pointers—*accept is modified to point at the string that holds the action code, and *anchor is modified to hold the value of the NFA structure's anchor field. *accept is set to NULL if there is no accepting state in the closure set. Since all members of the original set are also in the closure set, the output set is created by modifying the input set. That is, e_closure() returns its own first argument, but the set is modified to contain the elements of the closure set in addition to the initial elements.

Computing ε closure: e_closure()

If the ε-closure set contains more than one accepting state, the accepting action that has the lowest NFA state number is used. This way, conflicting states that are higher in the input file take precedence over the ones that occur later. The accept_num variable declared on line 69 of Listing 2.36 holds the state number of the last-assigned accepting state. If the current state has a lower number, the other state is overwritten. It is initialized to the largest positive integer. The algorithm in Table 2.8 is used.[14] The numbers in the algorithm reference comments in the code.

Resolving ambiguous accepting actions. Higher actions, higher precedence

Table 2.8. Algorithm for Computing ε-Closure

input	set of input states.
i	the current NFA state being examined.
N	state number of a next state that can be reached from State *i*.

1:	Push all states in the input set onto a stack.
2:	while(the stack is not empty)
	{
3:	Pop the top element into *i*.
	if(State *i* is an accepting state)
	*accept = the accept string;
4:	if(there's an ε transition from State *i* to State *N*)
	{
5:	if(*N* isn't in the closure set)
	{
6:	Add *N* to the closure set.
7:	Push *N* onto the stack.
	}
	}
	}

The *move* set is figured with the move() subroutine in Listing 2.37. It returns either the set of states that can be reached by making transitions on a specified input character from a specified set of states, or NULL if there are no such transitions.

Computing the move set: move().

The **for** loop on lines 129 to 143 does the work. The **if** statement at the top of the loop evaluates true for every element of the input set, and any next states are added to the output set on line 140. Note that the output set is not created unless there's something to put into it.

---

14. It is derived from the one in [Aho] p. 119.

Listing 2.36. *terp.c*— The ε-Closure Function

```
47    PUBLIC   SET   *e_closure( input, accept, anchor )
48    SET      *input  ;
49    char     **accept ;
50    int      *anchor  ;
51    {
52        /* input     is the set of start states to examine.
53         * *accept  is modified to point at the string associated with an accepting
54         *           state (or to NULL if the state isn't an accepting state).
55         * *anchor  is modified to hold the anchor point, if any.
56         *
57         * Computes the epsilon closure set for the input states. The output set
58         * will contain all states that can be reached by making epsilon transitions
59         * from all NFA states in the input set. Returns an empty set if the input
60         * set or the closure set is empty, modifies *accept to point at the
61         * accepting string if one of the elements of the output state is an
62         * accepting state.
63         */
64
65        int   stack[ NFA_MAX ];              /* Stack of untested states    */
66        int   *tos;                          /* Stack pointer               */
67        NFA   *p;                            /* NFA state being examined    */
68        int   i;                             /* State number of "           */
69        int   accept_num = LARGEST_INT ;
70
71        if( !input )
72                goto abort;
73
74        *accept = NULL;                                      /* Reference to algorithm: */
75        tos     = & stack[-1];                                       /* 1 */
76
77        for( next_member(NULL); (i = next_member(input)) >= 0 ;)
78            *++tos = i;
79
80        while( INBOUNDS(stack,tos) )                              /* 2 */
81        {
82            i = *tos-- ;                                          /* 3 */
83            p = & Nfa[ i ];
84            if( p->accept && (i < accept_num) )
85            {
86                accept_num = i ;
87                *accept     = p->accept ;
88                *anchor     = p->anchor ;
89            }
90
91            if( p->edge == EPSILON )                              /* 4 */
92            {
93                if( p->next )
94                {
95                    i = p->next - Nfa;
96                    if( !MEMBER(input, i) )                       /* 5  */
97                    {
98                        ADD( input, i );                         /* 6  */
99                        *++tos = i;                              /* 7  */
100                   }
101               }
102               if( p->next2 )
103               {
104                   i = p->next2 - Nfa;
```

Listing 2.36. continued...

```
105                      if( !MEMBER(input, i) )                      /* 5 */
106                      {
107                          ADD( input, i );                         /* 6 */
108                          *++tos = i;                              /* 7 */
109                      }
110                  }
111              }
112          }
113  abort:
114      return input;
115  }
```

Listing 2.37. *terp.c*— The *Move* Function

```
116  PUBLIC   SET *move( inp_set, c )
117  SET      *inp_set;                        /* input set               */
118  int      c;                               /* transition on this character */
119  {
120      /* Return a set that contains all NFA states that can be reached by making
121       * transitions on "c" from any NFA state in "inp_set." Returns NULL if
122       * there are no such transitions. The inp_set is not modified.
123       */
124
125      int  i;
126      NFA  *p;                               /* current NFA state       */
127      SET  *outset = NULL;                   /* output set              */
128
129      for( i = Nfa_states; --i >= 0; )
130      {
131          if( MEMBER(inp_set, i) )
132          {
133              p = &Nfa[i];
134
135              if( p->edge==c || (p->edge==CCL && TEST(p->bitset, c)))
136              {
137                  if( !outset )
138                      outset = newset();
139
140                  ADD( outset, p->next - Nfa );
141              }
142          }
143      }
144      return( outset );
145  }
```

Listing 2.38 uses the previous subroutines to build a small **egrep**-like program that copies standard input to standard output, printing only those lines that contain a match of a regular expression passed into the program on the command line. The next_char() subroutine on line 156 of Listing 2.38 gets the next input character. It buffers entire lines because **terp** must print the entire line when a match is found [otherwise getc() could be used]. getline() on line 177 is the input function passed to nfa(). It just passes along the regular expression that was on the command line. (Expr is initialized on line 215.) The remainder of the subroutine is a straightforward implementation of the non-greedy algorithm discussed in the previous section.

Listing 2.38. *terp.c*— A Simplified Egrep

```
146   #ifdef MAIN
147   #define ALLOCATE
148   #include "globals.h"     /* externs for Verbose */
149
150   #define BSIZE    256
151
152   PRIVATE char     Buf[ BSIZE ];   /* input buffer                    */
153   PRIVATE char     *Pbuf = Buf;    /* current position in input buffer   */
154   PRIVATE char     *Expr;          /* regular expression from command line */
155
156   int     nextchar()
157   {
158       if( !*Pbuf )
159       {
160           if( !fgets(Buf, BSIZE, stdin) )
161               return NULL;
162           Pbuf = Buf;
163       }
164       return *Pbuf++;
165   }
166
167   /*- - - - - - - - - - - - - - - - - - - - - - - - - - - - - - */
168
169   PRIVATE void    printbuf()
170   {
171       fputs(Buf, stdout);           /* Print the buffer and force a read  */
172       *Pbuf = 0;                    /* on the next call to nextchar().    */
173   }
174
175   /*------------------------------------------------------------*/
176
177   PRIVATE char    *getline()
178   {
179       static int  first_time_called = 1;
180
181       if( !first_time_called )
182           return NULL;
183
184       first_time_called = 0;
185       return Expr;
186   }
187
188   /*------------------------------------------------------------*/
189
190   main( argc, argv )
191   char **argv;
192   {
193       int sstate;              /* Starting NFA state          */
194       SET *start_dfastate; /* Set of starting nfa states  */
195       SET *current;        /* current DFA state           */
196       SET *next;
197       int accept;              /* cur. DFA state is an accept */
198       int c;                   /* current input character     */
199       int anchor;
200
201       if( argc == 2 )
202           fprintf(stderr,"expression is %s\n", argv[1] );
```

→

Listing 2.38. continued...

```
203          else
204          {
205              fprintf(stderr,"usage: terp pattern <input\n");
206              exit(1);
207          }
208
209          /*  1: Compile the NFA; initialize move() & e_closure().
210           *  2: Create the initial state, the set of all NFA states that can
211           *     be reached by making epsilon transitions from the NFA start state.
212           *  3: Initialize the current state to the start state.
213           */
214
215          Expr   = argv[1];                              /* 1 */
216          sstate = nfa( getline );
217
218          next = newset();                               /* 2 */
219          ADD( next, sstate );
220          if( !(start_dfastate = e_closure(next, &accept, &anchor)) )
221          {
222              fprintf(stderr, "Internal error: State machine is empty\n");
223              exit(1);
224          }
225
226          current = newset();                            /* 3 */
227          assign( current, start_dfastate );
228
229          /* Now interpret the NFA: The next state is the set of all NFA states that
230           * can be reached after we've made a transition on the current input
231           * character from any of the NFA states in the current state. The current
232           * input line is printed every time an accept state is encountered.
233           * The machine is reset to the initial state when a failure transition is
234           * encountered.
235           */
236
237          while( c = nextchar() )
238          {
239              if( next = e_closure( move(current, c), &accept, &anchor) )
240              {
241                  if( accept )
242                      printbuf();                         /* accept      */
243                  else
244                  {                                       /* keep looking */
245                      delset( current );
246                      current = next;
247                      continue;
248                  }
249              }
250
251              delset( next );                             /* reset       */
252              assign( current, start_dfastate );
253          }
254      }
255  #endif
```

2.5.5 Subset Construction: Converting an NFA to a DFA—Theory*

You can apply the foregoing procedure to translate NFA's to DFA's by computing the ε-closure and move sets for every possible input character. This generalized method, called *subset construction*, takes advantage of the fact that all NFA states connected with ε edges are effectively the same state. A single DFA state represents all NFA states that are connected in this manner. The outgoing edges from the DFA state are just the sum of the outgoing edges from all states in the ε-closure set. I'll demonstrate with an example. Using the NFA in Figure 2.14 on page 113, the starting DFA state consists of the ε-closure of the starting NFA state:

Subset construction: an example.

$$\varepsilon\text{-closure}(\{12\}) = \{0, 1, 3, 4, 5, 12\} \quad \text{(new DFA State 0)}$$

The next states in the DFA are then computed by figuring *move(current_state, c)*, for every possible input character. The input *alphabet* (the set of all possible input characters) contains only two elements: **D** and dot (.), so DFA States 1 and 2 are computed as follows:

$$move(\{0, 1, 3, 4, 5, 12\}, \mathbf{D}) = \{2, 8\} \quad \text{(new DFA State 1)}$$
$$move(\{0, 1, 3, 4, 5, 12\}, .) = \{6\} \quad \text{(new DFA State 2)}$$

This procedure is then applied to the two new states. Starting with State 2:

```
DFA State 2 = {6}
ε-closure({6})        = {6}
move({6}, .)          = ∅
move({6}, D)          = {7}              (new DFA State 3)


DFA State 1 = {2,8}
ε-closure({2,8})      = {1, 2, 4, 8}
move({1, 2, 4, 8}, D) = {2}             (new DFA State 4)
move({1, 2, 4, 8}, .) = {6, 10}         (new DFA State 5)
```

If the move operation results in an empty set—as is the case with move({6}, .), above—then there are no outgoing transitions from that state. Applying the procedure again to the three new DFA States:

```
DFA State 3 = {7}
ε-closure({7})           = {7, 13, 14}
move({7, 13, 14}, .)     = ∅
move({7, 13, 14}, D)     = ∅


DFA State 4 = {2}
ε-closure({2})           = {1, 2, 4}          (existing DFA State 4)
move({1, 2, 4}, .)       = {6}                (existing DFA State 2)
move({1, 2, 4}, D)       = {2}                (existing DFA State 4)


DFA State 5 = {6, 10}
ε-closure({6, 10})           = {6, 9, 10, 13, 14}
move({6, 9, 10, 13, 14}, .)  = ∅
move({6, 9, 10, 13, 14}, D)  = {7, 11}        (new DFA State 6)
```

DFA States 3 and 5 are accepting states because their ε-closure sets all contain an accepting state (NFA State 14). This last expansion introduced only one new state, which is now expanded:

DFA State 6 = {7, 11}
ε-closure({7, 11})   = {7, 9, 11, 13, 14}
move({7, 9, 11, 13, 14}, .)   = ∅
move({7, 9, 11, 13, 14}, **D**)   = {11}   (new DFA State 7)

And then this new state is expanded in turn:

DFA State 7 = {11}
ε-closure({7, 11})   = {9, 11, 13, 14}
move({9, 11, 13, 14}, .)   = ∅
move({9, 11, 13, 14}, **D**)   = {11}   (existing DFA State 7)

DFA States 6 and 7 are accepting states because they contain NFA accepting State 14. The process is summarized in Table 2.9, and the complete DFA is pictured in Figure 2.15. The procedure is formalized with the algorithm in Table 2.10.[15] Note that the state machine that this algorithm generates is not optimal. It has several more states than necessary. I'll look at how to remove these extra states in a moment.

Table 2.9. Converting NFA in Figure 2.14 (page 113) to a DFA

DFA State	NFA State	ε-closure	move(D)		move(.)		Accepting
			NFA	DFA	NFA	DFA	
0	{0}	{0,1,3,4,5,12}	{2,8}	1	{6}	2	no
1	{2,8}	{1,2,4,8}	{2}	4	{6, 10}	5	no
2	{6}	{6}	{7}	3	∅	–	no
3	{7}	{7,13,14}	∅	–	∅	–	yes
4	{2}	{1,2,4}	{2}	4	{6}	2	no
5	{6, 10}	{6,9,10,13,14}	{7,11}	6	∅	–	yes
6	{7, 11}	{7,9,11,13,14}	{11}	7	∅	–	yes
7	{11}	{9,11,13,14}	{11}	7	∅	–	yes

Figure 2.15. DFA for NFA in Figure 2.14

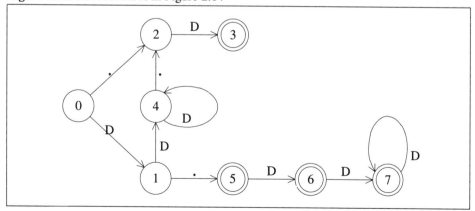

---

15. Adapted from [Aho], p. 118.

Table 2.10. Algorithm to Convert an NFA to a DFA

Dstates	is an array of DFA states. Each state is represented by a <u>set</u> of NFA states and a Boolean *mark* field.
Dtran	is the DFA transition matrix, an array as wide as the input character set and as deep as the maximum number of states. Dtran[current_state][input_character] ≡ the next state
i	is the index in Dtran of the current state.
nstates	is the index in Dtran of the place where a new state will be inserted.
S	is a set of NFA states that defines a DFA state.
c	is a possible input symbol.

Initially:	*Dstates*[0].set = ε-closure of NFA start state
	Dstates[0] is not marked.
	Nstates = 1.
	i = 0.
	S is empty.
	Dtran is initialized to all failure transitions.

```
while( there is an unmarked state at Dstates[i] )
{
        Dstates[i].mark = TRUE ;
        for( each input symbol c )
        {
                S = ε-closure( move( Dstate[i].set, c ) );
                if( S is not ∅ )
                {
                        if( a state with set≡S isn't in Dstates )
                                add a new unmarked state at Dstates[Nstates], with set=S
                                Dtran[i][c] = Nstates++
                        else
                                Dtran[i][c] = index of exiting state in Dstates
                }
        }
}
```

2.5.6 Subset Construction: Converting an NFA to a DFA—Implementation

This section shows how L^{E}X applies the theory in the previous section to make the output DFA. It uses the `e_closure()` and `move()` functions to build a complete DFA transition matrix from a previously constructed NFA. As before, you need to start with some constant and data-structure definitions, found in *dfa.h*, Listing 2.39.

The maximum number of DFA states is defined on line seven of Listing 2.40 to be 254. This number is more than adequate for most applications and has the added advantage of fitting into an **unsigned char**. The tables used for the transition matrix can be smaller as a consequence. You can make the number larger if you wish, but you'll have to change the driver discussed at the beginning of this chapter to compensate for the change in type. The `TTYPE` definition on line 12 is the type of the <u>output</u> tables—it must match the declared type of the tables in the state-machine driver. The internal versions of the same tables are all arrays of **int**. The F macro, defined on line 18, marks failure transitions in the internal tables. It must be −1, but hiding the −1 in a macro makes the code a little more readable. The ROW type on line 21 is one row of the DFA transition matrix. Declaring a row as a distinct type helps you use pointers to traverse individual

Output-table type: `TTYPE`

Failure transitions: `F`

The `ROW` type.

Listing 2.39. *dfa.h*— Definitions for a DFA

```
 1    /*-------------------------------------------------------------
 2     * DFA.H: The following definitions are used in dfa.c and in
 3     * minimize.c to represent DFA's.
 4     *-------------------------------------------------------------
 5     */
 6
 7    #define DFA_MAX      254            /* Maximum number of DFA states. If this
 8                                        * number >= 255, you'll have to change the
 9                                        * output routines and driver. States are
10                                        * numbered from 0 to DFA_MAX-1
11                                        */
12    typedef unsigned char TTYPE;       /* This is the type of the output DFA    */
13                                       /* transition table (the internal one is */
14                                       /* an array of int). It is used only to  */
15                                       /* figure the various table sizes printed */
16                                       /* by -V.                                 */
17
18    #define F            -1            /* Marks failure states in the table.    */
19    #define MAX_CHARS    128           /* Maximum width of dfa transition table. */
20
21    typedef int ROW[ MAX_CHARS ];      /* One full row of Dtran, which is itself */
22                                       /* an array, DFA_MAX elements long, of    */
23                                       /* ROWs.                                  */
24    /*-------------------------------------------------------------*/
25
26    typedef struct accept
27    {
28        char  *string;       /* Accepting string; NULL if nonaccepting.         */
29        int   anchor;        /* Anchor point, if any. Values are defined in NFA.H. */
30
31    } ACCEPT;
32
33    /*-------------------------------------------------------------
34     * External subroutines:
35     */
36
37    SET   *e_closure    (SET*,  char **, int *            ); /* terp.c     */
38    void  free_nfa      (void                             ); /* terp.c     */
39    SET   *move         (SET*,  int                       ); /* terp.c     */
40    int   nfa           (char *(*)()                      ); /* terp.c     */
41    int   dfa           (char *(*)(), ROW*[], ACCEPT**    ); /* dfa.c      */
42    int   min_dfa       (char *(*)(), ROW*[], ACCEPT**    ); /* minimize.c */
43    int   ttypesize     (int                              ); /* printdfa.c */
44    void  pdefines      (FILE*, int                       ); /* pdefines.c */
45    int   columns       (FILE*, ROW*,  int, int, char*    ); /* columns.c  */
46    void  cnext         (FILE*, char*                     ); /* columns.c  */
47
48    void  pheader(FILE *fp,    ROW dtran[], int nrows, ACCEPT *accept); /* print.c */
49    void  pdriver(FILE *output,             int nrows, ACCEPT *accept); /* print.c */
```

columns, because incrementing a pointer to an entire row will skip as many array elements as are in the row, effectively moving you down to the next element of the current column. For example, the following code allocates a NUM_ROWS element array (a two-dimensional array of size MAX_CHARS × NUM_ROWS) and then prints the sixth column. It initializes the column pointer (p) to the head of the sixth column, and moves the pointer to the next element of the same column with a simple increment on each iteration of the loop. Note that two stars are needed to get an array element in the `printf()` statement.[16]

```
#define NUM_ROWS 10

static ROW   Array[ NUM_ROWS ];
ROW          *p;
int          i;
     . . .
p = (ROW *)( &Array[0][6] );   /* Initialize p to head */
                               /* of column 6.        */

for( i = NUM_ROWS; --i >= 0; printf("%d ", **p++) )
    ;
```

ACCEPT structures

Returning to Listing 2.39, the ACCEPT structure on line 26 keeps track of the accepting strings, which are copied to an array of ACCEPT structures so that the memory used for the NFA can be discarded once it is translated into a DFA. The remainder of the file is just function prototypes.

DFA_STATE: accept, group, anchor, set fields

The actual conversion routines start in Listing 2.40 with a few more definitions. The DFA_STATE structure, **typedef**ed on lines 23 to 31, represents a single state in the DFA. The group field is used for minimization, discussed in the next section. The accept and anchor fields are the accepting string and anchor point copied from the NFA state in the case of an accepting state; set is the set of NFA states that comprise the current DFA state. Dstates, an array of DFA structures, is defined on line 33. The DFA state number is the array index. The actual transition matrix Dtran is declared on line 36, and the number of states Nstates is declared on the next line.

The transition matrix: Dtran, Nstates

Create a DFA: dfa().

The routines that create the DFA are all local to *dfa.c* and are accessed via the dfa() routine, also in Listing 2.40(on It is passed an input function, and returns the number of states in the transition matrix, the matrix itself, and an array holding the accepting string (the last two are returned indirectly through pointers). For the most part, this function is just allocating memory for the new tables and discarding memory for other tables once they're no longer needed. The NFA is constructed on line 69; it's converted to a DFA on line 81; the accepting strings are copied to the target array on line 91; and if verbose mode is active, a diagnostic message is printed on lines 101 to 114 of Listing 2.40.

---

16. C note: You need two stars because p points at a two-dimensional array. To see why, in C the square brackets can always be interpreted with the following identity: $p[i] \equiv *(p+i)$. If *i* is 0, then $p[0]\equiv*p$. Applying this identity to a two-dimensional array: $p[0][0]\equiv(*p)[0]\equiv**p$. Looked at another way, if p is a pointer to an array, then *p must be the array itself. But arrays are always represented in C by a pointer to the first element. Consequently, if p is a pointer to an array of **int**, then *p must be an array of **int**, which is represented by a pointer to the first element—a pointer to an **int**. Both p and *p will hold the same address, but p is of type "pointer to array of **int**" and *p is of type "pointer to **int**."

Using a pointer here is much more efficient than something like this:
```
for( i = 0; i < NUM_ROWS; i++ )
    printf("%d ", Array[i][6] )
```
because the array index forces the compiler to multiply *i* by the size of a row at every iteration of the loop. The following is better, but still not as good as the original version:
```
ROW *p;
for( p=Array, i=NUM_ROWS; --i >= 0; printf("%d ", (*p++)[6] )
    ;
```

Listing 2.40. *dfa.c*— NFA to DFA Conversion: File Header and Access Function

```
1   #include <stdio.h>
2   #ifdef MSDOS
3   #     include <stdlib.h>
4   #else
5   #     include <malloc.h>
6   #endif
7   #include <tools/debug.h>
8   #include <tools/set.h>
9   #include <tools/compiler.h>
10  #include "dfa.h"
11  #include "globals.h"                 /* externs for Verbose, etc. */
12
13  /*-----------------------------------------------------------------
14   * DFA.C   Make a DFA transition table from an NFA created with
15   *                 Thompson's construction.
16   *-----------------------------------------------------------------
17   * Dtran is the deterministic transition table. It is indexed by state number
18   * along the major axis and by input character along the minor axis. Dstates
19   * is a list of deterministic states represented as sets of NFA states.
20   * Nstates is the number of valid entries in Dtran.
21   */
22
23  typedef struct dfa_state
24  {
25      unsigned group  : 8;        /* Group id, used by minimize()        */
26      unsigned mark   : 1;        /* Mark used by make_dtran()            */
27      char     *accept;           /* accept action if accept state       */
28      int      anchor;            /* Anchor point if an accept state     */
29      SET      *set;              /* Set of NFA states represented by     */
30
31  } DFA_STATE;                    /* this DFA state                      */
32
33  PRIVATE DFA_STATE  *Dstates ;   /* DFA states table                    */
34  /*-----------------------------------------------------------------*/
35
36  PRIVATE ROW        *Dtran   ;   /* DFA transition table                */
37  PRIVATE int        Nstates  ;   /* Number of DFA states                */
38  PRIVATE DFA_STATE  *Last_marked;/* Most-recently marked DFA state in Dtran */
39
40  extern   char      *bin_to_ascii ( int, int );   /* in compiler.lib */
41
42  /*-----------------------------------------------------------------
43   * Prototypes for subroutines in this file:
44   */
45
46  PRIVATE DFA_STATE *get_unmarked ( void                    );
47  PRIVATE int       in_dstates    ( SET*                    );
48  PRIVATE void      free_sets     ( void                    );
49  PRIVATE void      make_dtran    ( int                     );
50  PUBLIC  int       dfa           ( char *(*)(), ROW*[], ACCEPT** );
51  /*-----------------------------------------------------------------*/
52
53  int     dfa( ifunct, dfap, acceptp )
54  char    *( *ifunct ) ();
55  ROW     *(  dfap[] );
56  ACCEPT  *(  *acceptp );
57  {
```

Listing 2.40. continued...

```
58          /* Turns an NFA with the indicated start state (sstate) into a DFA and
59           * returns the number of states in the DFA transition table. *dfap is
60           * modified to point at that transition table and *acceptp is modified
61           * to point at an array of accepting states (indexed by state number).
62           * dfa() discards all the memory used for the initial NFA.
63           */
64
65          ACCEPT      *accept_states;
66          int         i;
67          int         start;
68
69          start       = nfa( ifunct );                    /* make the nfa */
70          Nstates     = 0;
71          Dstates     = (DFA_STATE *) calloc( DFA_MAX, sizeof(DFA_STATE) );
72          Dtran       = (ROW *     ) calloc( DFA_MAX, sizeof(ROW)       );
73          Last_marked = Dstates;
74
75          if( Verbose )
76              fputs("making DFA: ", stdout);
77
78          if( !Dstates || !Dtran )
79              ferr( "Out of memory!" );
80
81          make_dtran( start );           /* convert the NFA to a DFA           */
82          free_nfa();                    /* Free the memory used for the nfa   */
83                                         /* itself (but not the accept strings). */
84
85          Dtran        = (ROW   *) realloc( Dtran, Nstates * sizeof(ROW)   );
86          accept_states = (ACCEPT*) malloc (        Nstates * sizeof(ACCEPT));
87
88          if( !accept_states || !Dtran )
89              ferr( "Out of memory!!" );
90
91          for( i = Nstates ; --i >= 0 ; )
92          {
93              accept_states[i].string = Dstates[i].accept;
94              accept_states[i].anchor = Dstates[i].anchor;
95          }
96
97          free( Dstates );
98          *dfap    = Dtran;
99          *acceptp = accept_states;
100
101         if( Verbose )
102         {
103             printf("\n%d out of %d DFA states in initial machine.\n",
104                                                  Nstates, DFA_MAX);
105
106             printf("%d bytes required for uncompressed tables.\n\n",
107                     Nstates * MAX_CHARS * sizeof(TTYPE)        /* dtran  */
108                     + Nstates           * sizeof(TTYPE) );     /* accept */
109
110             if( Verbose > 1 )
111             {
112                 printf("The un-minimized DFA looks like this:\n\n");
113                 pheader(stdout, Dtran, Nstates, accept_states);
114             }
115         }
116
```

→

```
Listing 2.40. continued...
117        return Nstates ;
118    }
```

Several support functions are needed to do the work, all in Listing 2.40. The
`add_to_dstates()` function on line 23 adds a new DFA state to the Dstates array and   add_to_dstates()
increments the number-of-states counter, `Nstates`. It returns the state number (the
index in `Dstates`) of the newly added state. `in_dstates()` on line 31 is passed a set   in_dstates()
of NFA states, and returns the state number of an existing state that uses the same set (or
−1 if there is no such state). The routine just does a linear search, which is probably not
the best strategy here. Something like a binary tree would be better.

Listing 2.41. *dfa.c*— NFA to DFA Conversion: Support Functions

```
119    int add_to_dstates( NFA_set, accepting_string, anchor )
120    SET     *NFA_set;
121    char    *accepting_string;
122    int     anchor;
123    {
124         int nextstate;
125
126         if( Nstates > (DFA_MAX-1) )
127             ferr("Too many DFA states\n");
128
129         nextstate = Nstates++ ;
130         Dstates[ nextstate ].set    = NFA_set;
131         Dstates[ nextstate ].accept = accepting_string;
132         Dstates[ nextstate ].anchor = anchor;
133
134         return nextstate;
135    }
136
137    /*- - - - - - - - - - - - - - - - - - - - - - - - - - - - - - - - - */
138
139    PRIVATE  int    in_dstates( NFA_set )
140    SET     *NFA_set;
141    {
142        /* If there's a set in Dstates that is identical to NFA_set, return the
143         * index of the Dstate entry, else return -1.
144         */
145
146        DFA_STATE *p;
147
148        for( p = &Dstates[Nstates]; --p >= Dstates ; )
149            if( IS_EQUIVALENT( NFA_set, p->set ) )
150                return( p - Dstates );
151
152        return( -1 );
153    }
154
155    /*- - - - - - - - - - - - - - - - - - - - - - - - - - - - - - - - - */
156
157    PRIVATE DFA_STATE       *get_unmarked()
158    {
159        /* Return a pointer to an unmarked state in Dstates. If no such state
160         * exists, return NULL. Print an asterisk for each state to tell the
161         * user that the program hasn't died while the table is being constructed.
162         */
```

Listing 2.41. continued...

```
163
164        for(; Last_marked < &Dstates[Nstates] ; ++Last_marked )
165        {
166            if( !Last_marked->mark )
167            {
168                putc   ( '*', stderr );
169                fflush ( stderr        );
170
171                if( Verbose > 1 )
172                {
173                    fputs("----------------\n", stdout );
174                    printf("working on DFA state %d = NFA states: ",
175                                                    Last_marked-Dstates);
176                    pset( Last_marked->set, fprintf, stdout );
177                    putchar('\n');
178                }
179
180                return Last_marked;
181            }
182        }
183        return NULL;
184    }
185                                                                  */
186    /*- - - - - - - - - - - - - - - - - - - - - - - - - - - - - -
187
188    PRIVATE void    free_sets()
189    {
190        /* Free the memory used for the NFA sets in all Dstate entries.  */
191
192        DFA_STATE *p;
193
194        for( p = &Dstates[Nstates]; --p >= Dstates ; )
195            delset( p->set );
196    }
```

get_unmarked()   A pointer to the next unmarked state is returned by get_unmarked(), declared on line 157. The Last_marked variable was initialized by dfa() on line 38 of Listing 2.40. Since new states are always added to the end of the table, everything above Last_marked will have been marked with a previous expansion, so these states don't have to be examined now. The asterisk that's printed on line 168 of Listing 2.41 actually has two purposes. It tells the user that the program hasn't hung (it takes a while to make the tables), and it lets the user terminate the program with a Ctrl-Break (a SIGINT under UNIX). It's needed because MS-DOS ignores Ctrl-Breaks until a system call of some sort is made by a program. No such call is made while creating the tables, but a system call is required to print the asterisks.

free_sets()   Finally, free_sets() on line 188 of Listing 2.41 goes through the entire Dstates array, deallocating the memory used for the sets of NFA states.

NFA to DFA Conversion: The actual NFA to DFA conversion is done by make_dtran(), in Listing 2.42. It is make_dtran().   a straightforward implementation of the algorithm in Table 2.10 on page 124.

Listing 2.42. *dfa.c*— NFA to DFA Conversion: Conversion Function

```
197   PRIVATE void      make_dtran( sstate )
198   int       sstate;                           /* Starting NFA state.            */
199   {
200       SET           *NFA_set;                 /* Set of NFA states that define  */
201                                                /* the next DFA state.            */
202       DFA_STATE     *current;                 /* State currently being expanded. */
203       int           nextstate;                /* Goto DFA state for current char. */
204       char          *isaccept;                /* Current DFA state is an accept  */
205                                                /* (this is the accepting string). */
206       int           anchor;                   /* Anchor point, if any.           */
207       int           c;                        /* Current input character.        */
208
209       /* Initially Dstates contains a single, unmarked, start state formed by
210        * taking the epsilon closure of the NFA start state. So, Dstates[0]
211        * (and Dtran[0]) is the DFA start state.
212        */
213
214       NFA_set = newset() ;
215       ADD( NFA_set, sstate );
216
217       Nstates          = 1;
218       Dstates[0].set   = e_closure(NFA_set,&Dstates[0].accept,&Dstates[0].anchor);
219       Dstates[0].mark = 0;
220
221       while( current = get_unmarked() )                        /* Make the table */
222       {
223           current->mark = 1;
224
225           for( c = MAX_CHARS ; --c >= 0 ; )
226           {
227               if( NFA_set = move(current->set, c) )
228                   NFA_set = e_closure( NFA_set, &isaccept, &anchor );
229
230               if( !NFA_set )                          /* no outgoing transitions */
231                   nextstate = F;
232
233               else if( (nextstate = in_dstates(NFA_set)) != -1 )
234                   delset( NFA_set );
235
236               else
237                   nextstate = add_to_dstates( NFA_set, isaccept, anchor );
238
239               Dtran[ current-Dstates ][ c ] = nextstate ;
240           }
241       }
242
243       putc( '\n', stderr );          /* Terminate string of *'s printed in
244                                        * get_unmarked();
245                                        */
246
247       free_sets();      /* Free the memory used for the DFA_STATE sets */
248   }
```

2.5.7 DFA Minimization—Theory*

The DFA created earlier (in Figure 2.15 on page 123) is not an optimal DFA. Only six of the eight states are actually required. A somewhat simplified version of the transition matrix for the original machine is reproduced in Table 2.11. A quick inspection of this table shows that States 6 and 7 are equivalent because they have identical next-state transitions and they're both accepting states. If all transitions into State 6 were replaced with transitions to State 7, the machine would still accept the same strings as before. One additional state can be eliminated, however, and simple inspection is not good enough for finding this extra state. I'll discuss how to find the extra state in this section.

Table 2.11. DFA Transition Matrix for DFA in Figure 2.15

		Lookahead		Accepting
		D	.	
	0	1	2	no
	1	4	5	no
	2	3	–	no
	3	–	–	yes
Current state	4	4	2	no
	5	6	–	yes
	6	7	–	yes
	7	7	–	yes

Finding equivalent states.

You find equivalent states by systematically eliminating those states that can't be equivalent—partitioning the initial array into potentially equivalent states, and then gradually partitioning the partitions. When you're done, states that share a partition are equivalent. Initially, you partition the matrix into two parts, one for accepting states and another for nonaccepting states:

	D	.	
0	1	2	
1	4	5	0
2	3	–	
4	4	2	
3	–	–	
5	6	–	1
6	7	–	
7	7	–	

Implicit failure state.

(The partition number is on the right.) The implicit failure state is alone in a special, unnumbered partition that's not shown in the foregoing table. The next step in the minimization process creates a set of new partitions by looking at the **goto** transitions for each state and eliminating states that are not equivalent. If the outgoing transitions from two states go to different partitions, then the states are not equivalent. You do the elimination on a column-by-column basis. Starting with the *D* column, States 0, 1, and 4 all go to a state in Partition 0 on a *D*, but State 2 goes to Partition 1 on a *D*. Consequently, State 2 must be removed from Partition 0. Formally, you say that State 4 *is distinguished* from the other states in the partition by a *D*. Continuing in this manner, State

'...is distinguished...'

3 is also distinguished from States 5, 6, and 7 by a *D* because State 3 goes to the failure state on a *D*, but the other states go to a state in Partition 1. The failure state is not in Partition 1, so State 3 is distinguished by a *D*.

	D	.	
0	1	2	
1	4	5	0
4	4	2	
2	3	–	2
3	–	–	3
5	6	–	
6	7	–	1
7	7	–	

Now you go down the dot (.) column. The dot distinguishes State 1 from States 0 and 4 because State 1 goes to a state in Partition 1 on a dot, but States 0 and 4 both go to States in Partition 2. The new partitions are:

	D	.	
0	1	2	0
4	4	2	
1	4	5	4
2	3	–	2
3	–	–	3
5	6	–	
6	7	–	1
7	7	–	

Next, you go through the array a second time, column by column. Now, D distinguishes State 0 from State 4 because State 0 goes to a state in Partition 4 on a D, but State 4 goes to a state in Partition 0 on a D. No other states can be distinguished from each other, so we're done. The final partitions look like this:

	D	.	
0	1	2	0
4	4	2	5
1	4	5	4
2	3	–	2
3	–	–	3
5	6	–	
6	7	–	1
7	7	–	

The next step is to build a new transition matrix. Each partition is a single state in the minimized DFA, and all next states in the original table are replaced by the number of the partition in which the state is found. For example, since States 5, 6, and 7 are all in Partition 1, all references to one of these states in the original table are replaced by a reference to the new State 1. The new table looks like this:

D

0	4	2
1	1	–
2	3	–
3	–	–
4	5	1
5	5	2

The algorithm is formalized in Table 2.12. The transition diagram for the new state machine is in Figure 2.16.

Table 2.12. DFA-Minimization Algorithm

c	A character in the alphabet used by the DFA.
group	A set of potentially equivalent states (a partition of the original transition matrix).
groups	A collection of *groups*.
new	The set of states that have been distinguished from other states in the current group.
first	First state in a *group*.
next	One of the other states in a *group*, FALSE if there is no such state.
goto_first	A transition on *c* out of the *first* state comes here.
goto_next	A transition on *c* out of the *next* state comes here.

Initially:	Partition the original states into a series of *groups*. All nonaccepting states are in a single group, and accepting states that have the same accepting string are grouped together. A one-element group containing a single accepting state is permissible.

Repeat the following until no new groups are added to *groups*:

```
for( each group in groups )
{
        new = Ø
        first = the first state in the current group.
        next = the next  state of the current group or FALSE if none.
        while( next )
        {
                for( each character c )
                {
                        goto_first = state reached by making a transition on c out of first.
                        goto_next = state reached by making a transition on c out of next.

                        if( goto_first is not in the same group as goto_next )
                                move next from the current group into new
                }
                next = the next state in the current group or FALSE if none.
        }
        if( new is not empty )
                add it to groups
}
```

Figure 2.16. Minimized DFA for (D*\. D|D\. D*)

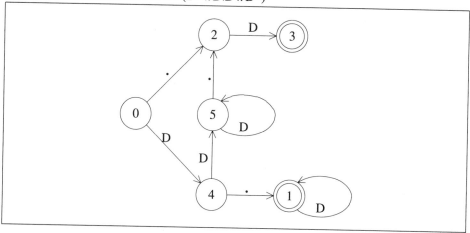

2.5.8 DFA Minimization—Implementation

The algorithm in the previous section is implemented by the code starting in Listing 2.43. The Groups[] array on line 16 is the collection of partitions. The array index is used as the partition number, and each group is a SET of NFA state numbers. Numgroups, on line 17, is the number of groups currently in the array. Ingroup[], on line 18, is the inverse of Groups[]. It is indexed by state number and evaluates to the group in which the state is found. All three of these are initialized to zeros by the access function min_dfa() (on lines 43 to 45). The DFA is created by the dfa() call on line 47, and it's minimized by the subroutine minimize(), called on the next line.

The Groups[] and Ingroup[] arrays are initialized in init_groups(), at the top of Listing 2.44. The program decides which group to place a state in by looking at the accepting-string pointer for that state. Since all nonaccepting states have NULL accepting strings, they'll all end up in a single group—Group 0 because DFA State 0 is always nonaccepting. The other groups in the initial partitioning contain accepting states. If two such states have the same accepting string, they are considered equivalent and are put into the same group. Note that since the starting state (0) always goes into Group 0, and since the minimization algorithm never moves the first element of the group to another partition, the starting state is still 0 after the minimization is complete.

The **goto** statement on line 78 of Listing 2.44 is necessary because it has to break out of a doubly nested loop in order to avoid forming a new group. The same thing could probably be done with a Boolean flag of some sort, but the **goto** seems cleaner.

The actual minimization is done by minimize() starting on line 104 of Listing 2.44. It is passed the number of states in the DFA transition table, a pointer to the DFA table itself, and a pointer to the accepting-state table. Note that there's an extra level of indirection in both of these last two parameters. That is, addresses of pointers to the two tables are passed to minimize(). I've done this because entirely new tables are created to replace the existing ones—*dfap and *accept are modified to point at the new tables. The memory used for the old tables is discarded automatically by minimize().

The routine is a straightforward implementation of the algorithm in Table 2.12 on page 134. It terminates when an entire pass is made through the set of groups without adding a new group. The test on lines 143 to 146 is complicated by the failure transitions, which have no explicit existence. There is no physical group that holds the failure state, so I have to test here to make sure that neither of the two next states are failure

The partitions:
Groups[], Ingroup[], Numgroups

Access function:
min_dfa()

Group initialization:
init_groups().

Minimization: minimize()

Listing 2.43. *minimize.c*— Data Structures and Access Function

```
1   #include <stdio.h>
2   #ifdef MSDOS
3   #     include <stdlib.h>
4   #else
5   #     include <malloc.h>
6   #endif
7   #include <tools/debug.h>
8   #include <tools/set.h>
9   #include <tools/hash.h>
10  #include <tools/compiler.h>
11  #include "dfa.h"
12  #include "globals.h"      /* externs for Verbose */
13
14  /* MINIMIZE.C:  Make a minimal DFA by eliminating equivalent states.   */
15
16  PRIVATE SET   *Groups [ DFA_MAX ];  /* Groups of equivalent states in Dtran */
17  PRIVATE int   Numgroups;            /* Number of groups in Groups          */
18  PRIVATE int   Ingroup [ DFA_MAX ];  /* the Inverse of Group                */
19
20  /*-------------------------------------------------------------------
21   * Prototypes for subroutines in this file:
22   */
23
24  PRIVATE void    fix_dtran      ( ROW*[],       ACCEPT**          );
25  PRIVATE void    init_groups    ( int,          ACCEPT*           );
26  PUBLIC  int     min_dfa        ( char *(*)(), ROW*[],   ACCEPT** );
27  PRIVATE void    minimize       ( int,          ROW*[],   ACCEPT** );
28  PRIVATE void    pgroups        ( int                             );
29
30  /*-----------------------------------------------------------------------*/
31
32  PUBLIC  int min_dfa( ifunct, dfap, acceptp )
33  char    *( *ifunct  )();
34  ROW     *( dfap[]   );
35  ACCEPT  *( *acceptp );
36  {
37      /* Make a minimal DFA, eliminating equivalent states. Return the number of
38       * states in the minimized machine. *sstatep = the new start state.
39       */
40
41      int   nstates;                   /* Number of DFA states            */
42
43      memset( Groups,  0, sizeof(Groups)  );
44      memset( Ingroup, 0, sizeof(Ingroup) );
45      Numgroups = 0;
46
47      nstates = dfa( ifunct,  dfap, acceptp );
48      minimize      ( nstates, dfap, acceptp );
49
50      return Numgroups;
51  }
```

Removing redundant states: `fix_dtran()`

transitions before allowing an index into the `Ingroup[]` array.

The `fix_dtran()` routine on line 177 of Listing 2.44 uses the previously-computed `Groups[]` to remove redundant states from the table. It's difficult to do the compression in place because the original states are randomly distributed throughout the groups, so two new arrays are allocated on lines 199 and 200. The original arrays are freed on lines 218 and 219, and the array pointers are changed to point at the new arrays on the next couple of lines.

The remainder of *minimize.c* consists of a few debugging routines in Listing 2.45. pgroups() prints out all the existing groups and is used for very-verbose-mode (*-V*) diagnostics.

Print the groups:
pgroups()

Listing 2.44. *minimize.c*— Minimization Functions

```
52   PRIVATE  void  init_groups( nstates, accept )
53   ACCEPT   *accept;
54   {
55       SET   **last ;
56       int   i, j ;
57
58       last      = & Groups[0] ;
59       Numgroups = 0;
60
61       for( i = 0; i < nstates ; i++ )
62       {
63           for( j = i;   --j >= 0 ;)
64           {
65               /* Check to see if a group already exists that has the same
66                * accepting string as the current state. If so, add the current
67                * state to the already existing group and skip past the code that
68                * would create a new group. Note that since all nonaccepting states
69                * have NULL accept strings, this loop puts all of these together
70                * into a single group. Also note that the test in the for loop
71                * always fails for group 0, which can't be an accepting state.
72                */
73
74               if( accept[i].string == accept[j].string )
75               {
76                   ADD( Groups[ Ingroup[j] ], i );
77                   Ingroup[i] = Ingroup[j];
78                   goto match;
79               }
80           }
81
82           /* Create a new group and put the current state into it. Note that ADD()
83            * has side effects, so "last" can't be incremented in the ADD
84            * invocation.
85            */
86
87           *last = newset();
88           ADD( *last, i );
89           Ingroup[i] = Numgroups++;
90           ++last;
91
92   match:; /* Group already exists, keep going */
93       }
94
95       if( Verbose > 1 )
96       {
97           printf ( "Initial groupings:\n" );
98           pgroups ( nstates );
99       }
100  }
101
```

```
Listing 2.44. continued...
102     /*------------------------------------------------------------------------*/
103
104     PRIVATE void minimize( nstates, dfap, acceptp )
105     int        nstates;              /* number of states in dtran[]          */
106     ROW        *( dfap[]   );        /* DFA transition table to compress     */
107     ACCEPT     *( *acceptp );        /* Set of accept states                 */
108     {
109         int    old_numgroups;  /* Used to see if we did anything in this pass. */
110         int    c;              /* Current character.                           */
111         SET    **current;      /* Current group being processed.               */
112         SET    **new ;         /* New partition being created.                 */
113         int    first;          /* State # of first element of current group.   */
114         int    next;           /* State # of next element of current group.    */
115         int    goto_first;     /* target of transition from first[c].          */
116         int    goto_next;      /* other target of transition from first[c].    */
117
118         ROW    *dtran  = *dfap;
119         ACCEPT *accept = *acceptp;
120
121         init_groups( nstates, accept );
122         do
123         {
124             old_numgroups = Numgroups;
125             for( current = &Groups[0]; current < &Groups[Numgroups]; ++current )
126             {
127                 if( num_ele( *current ) <= 1 )
128                     continue;
129
130                 new = &Groups[ Numgroups ];
131                 *new = newset();
132
133                 next_member( NULL );
134                 first = next_member( *current );
135
136                 while( (next = next_member(*current))  >= 0 )
137                 {
138                     for( c = MAX_CHARS; --c >= 0 ;)
139                     {
140                         goto_first = dtran[ first ][ c ];
141                         goto_next  = dtran[ next  ][ c ];
142
143                         if( goto_first != goto_next
144                             && (    goto_first == F
145                                  || goto_next  == F
146                                  || Ingroup[goto_first] != Ingroup[goto_next]
147                                )
148                           )
149                         {
150                             REMOVE( *current, next );    /* Move the state to  */
151                             ADD   ( *new,     next );    /* the new partition  */
152                             Ingroup[ next ] = Numgroups ;
153                             break;
154                         }
155                     }
156                 }
157
158                 if( IS_EMPTY( *new ) )
159                     delset( *new );
```

```
     Listing 2.44. continued...
160                 else
161                     ++Numgroups;
162             }
163
164     } while( old_numgroups != Numgroups );
165
166     if( Verbose > 1 )
167     {
168         printf("\nStates grouped as follows after minimization:\n");
169         pgroups( nstates );
170     }
171
172     fix_dtran( dfap, acceptp );
173 }
174
175 /*------------------------------------------------------------------------*/
176
177 PRIVATE void fix_dtran( dfap, acceptp )
178 ROW     *( dfap[]  );
179 ACCEPT  *( *acceptp );
180 {
181     /*      Reduce the size of the dtran, using the group set made by  minimize().
182      * Return the state number of the start state. The original dtran and accept
183      * arrays are destroyed and replaced with the smaller versions.
184      *      Consider the first element of each group (current) to be a
185      * "representative" state. Copy that state to the new transition table,
186      * modifying all the transitions in the representative state so that they'll
187      * go to the group within which the old state is found.
188      */
189
190     SET    **current   ;
191     ROW     *newdtran  ;
192     ACCEPT *newaccept  ;
193     int     state      ;
194     int     i          ;
195     int     *src, *dest ;
196     ROW     *dtran  = *dfap;
197     ACCEPT *accept = *acceptp;
198
199     newdtran  = (ROW    *) calloc( Numgroups, sizeof(ROW    ) );
200     newaccept = (ACCEPT *) calloc( Numgroups, sizeof(ACCEPT) );
201
202     if( !newdtran || !newaccept )
203         ferr("Out of memory!!!");
204
205     next_member( NULL );
206     for( current = &Groups[Numgroups]; --current >= Groups; )
207     {
208         dest  = &newdtran[ current-Groups ][ 0 ];
209         state = next_member(*current) ;
210         src   = & dtran[ state ][ 0 ];                /* All groups have at */
211                                                       /* least one element. */
212         newaccept[ current-Groups ]=accept[state];   /* Struct. assignment */
213
214         for( i = MAX_CHARS; --i >= 0 ; src++, dest++ )
215             *dest = (*src == F) ? F : Ingroup[ *src ];
216     }
217
```

Listing 2.44. continued...

```
218         free( *dfap    );
219         free( *acceptp );
220         *dfap    = newdtran  ;
221         *acceptp = newaccept ;
222     }
```

Listing 2.45. *minimize.c*— Debugging Routines

```
223     PRIVATE void pgroups( nstates )
224     int        nstates ;
225     {
226         /* Print all the groups used for minimization.  */
227
228         SET **current;
229
230         for( current = &Groups[Numgroups] ; --current >= Groups ; )
231         {
232             printf( "\tgroup %d: {", current - Groups );
233             pset( *current, fprintf, stdout );
234             printf( "}\n" );
235         }
236         printf("\n");
237         while( --nstates >= 0 )
238             printf("\tstate %2d is in group %2d\n", nstates, Ingroup[nstates] );
239     }
```

There are actually two additional minimizations that could be done here and are not:
Dead states.
dead states—nonaccepting states that have no outgoing transitions other than ones that loop back into the current state—can be removed, as can *unreachable* states—states with
Unreachable states.
no incoming edges. In practice, both types of states are rare, so it didn't seem worth the effort to remove them. I'll leave this further minimization as an exercise.

2.5.9 Compressing and Printing the Tables

The remainder of this chapter describes the remainder of LEX—primarily housekeeping and table-printing functions. Skip to the next chapter if you're not following the implementation details.

This section discusses three table-output routines: one for uncompressed tables, one for pair-compressed tables, and a third routine that eliminates redundant rows and columns and prints the result. The first two of these are of sufficient general utility to be put in a library. The third routine is used only by LEX.

2.5.9.1 Uncompressed Tables. The uncompressed tables are printed by two sub-routines in two separate input files. The `defnext()` routine in Listing 2.46 prints the
Generate `yy_next()` function: `defnext()`
`yy_next()` macro definition—`yy_next()` figures the next state from the current state and input character. The array access is hidden in a macro so that the state-machine driver can call `yy_next()` for the next state, regardless of the compression method used. Each compression method supplies a different version of `yy_next()`.

Printing two-dimensional arrays: `print_array()`
The uncompressed two-dimensional array is output by `print_array()` in Listing 2.47. The routine is passed a `FILE` pointer for the output stream, a pointer to the array, and the two dimensions. It is configured to print an array of **int**s, but you can change

Listing 2.46. *defnext.c*— Print Next-State Macro: Uncompressed Table

```
1   #include <stdio.h>
2   #include <tools/debug.h>
3   #include <tools/compiler.h>        /* needed only for prototype */
4
5   PUBLIC    void      defnext(fp, name)
6   FILE      *fp;
7   char      *name;
8   {
9       /* Print the default yy_next(s,c) subroutine for an uncompressed table. */
10
11      static char  *comment_text[] =
12      {
13          "yy_next(state,c) is given the current state and input character and",
14          "evaluates to the next state.",
15          NULL
16      };
17
18      comment( fp, comment_text );
19      fprintf( fp, "#define yy_next(state, c)  %s[ state ][ c ]\n", name );
20  }
```

this type by modifying the **typedef** for ATYPE on line eight. The array is treated internally as a one-dimensional array having nrows × ncols cells. The main use of the row size (nrows) is to print the inner brackets on lines 28 and 43. NCOLS, defined on line nine, determines how many array elements are printed on each output line. It controls formatting only—not any of the actual array dimensions. print_array() just prints the initialization part of the declaration (and the terminating semicolon). It doesn't print the actual declaration. Use it like this:

(margin: ATYPE)

(margin: NCOLS)

```
printf("unsigned char Array[%d][%d]=\n", nrows, ncols );
print_array( stdout, array, nrows, ncols );
```

The declared type of the output array (**unsigned char** above) is immaterial, even though the input array must be **int**s. It's up to you to make sure that all values in the input array fit into the cells of the output array. In the current example, no cell in the input array can have a value greater than 255 or the number will effectively be truncated.

2.5.9.2 Pair-Compressed Tables. The next set of routines, in Listing 2.48, produce pair-compressed tables, as were pictured in Figure 2.7 on page 70. Various macros on lines 21 to 26 control the names and types used for both the input and output array. ATYPE and NCOLS are used as before: they are the declared type of the input array and the number of columns on one line of the output array. The other three definitions are used for the storage class of the array and the type of one array cell. The printed tables assume that the table type and storage class are defined somewhere—you have to put something like the following at the top of the file in which the tables are placed:

(margin: ATYPE, NCOLS)

```
typedef unsigned char YY_TTYPE;
#define YYPRIVATE static
```

Note that the yy_next(), which figures the next state, can be declared with a different storage class than the tables themselves (though it isn't in the current configuration). This way you can have a public decoding routine and **static** tables.

The table-generation routine, pairs(), starts on line 29 of Listing 2.48. It is passed three more arguments than print_array(). The name argument is the name used for the output arrays. The names for the arrays that represent rows are manufactured by

(margin: Printing pair-compressed tables: pairs())

Listing 2.47. *print_ar.c*— Print A Two Dimensional Array

```
 1    #include <stdio.h>
 2    #include <tools/debug.h>
 3    #include <tools/compiler.h>            /* for prototypes only */
 4    /*-------------------------------------------------------------------
 5     * PRINT_AR.C:  General-purpose subroutine to print out a 2-dimensional array.
 6     */
 7
 8    typedef int      ATYPE;
 9    #define NCOLS    10      /* Number of columns used to print arrays        */
10    /*-------------------------------------------------------------------*/
11
12    PUBLIC   void    print_array( fp, array, nrows, ncols )
13    FILE     *fp;                           /* DFA transition table          */
14    ATYPE    *array;                        /* Number of rows    in array[]  */
15    int      nrows;                         /* Number of columns in array[]  */
16    int      ncols;
17    {
18        /* Print the C source code to initialize the two-dimensional array pointed
19         * to by "array." Print only the initialization part of the declaration.
20         */
21
22        int      i;
23        int      col;     /* Output column          */
24
25        fprintf( fp, "{\n" );
26        for( i = 0; i < nrows ; i++ )
27        {
28            fprintf(fp, "/* %02d */  { ", i );
29
30            for( col = 0;   col < ncols; col++ )
31            {
32                fprintf(fp, "%3d" , *array++ );
33                if( col < ncols-1 )
34                        fprintf(fp, ", " );
35
36                if( (col % NCOLS) == NCOLS-1  &&  col != ncols-1 )
37                        fprintf(fp, "\n              ");
38            }
39
40            if( col > NCOLS )
41                fprintf( fp,  "\n           "  );
42
43            fprintf( fp, " }%c\n", i < nrows-1 ? ',' : ' ' );
44        }
45        fprintf(fp, "};\n");
46    }
```

threshold argument to
pairs()

putting a numeric suffix at the end of this string. The array of pointers to rows uses the string without modification. The threshold argument determines the point at which character/next-state pairs are abandoned in favor of a one-dimensional array. If the number of transitions in a row are less than or equal to threshold, then pairs are used, otherwise an array is used. Finally, numbers controls the output format of the character part of the pair. If it's true, a decimal number is used (an ASCII 'a', for example, is output as 97); if false, character constants are used (an 'a' is printed as an 'a').

The pairs() routine returns the number of cells used to store the row arrays. The number of bytes used by the entire table is:

$$(number\_of\_cells \times \mathbf{sizeof}(\text{TYPE})) + (\text{nrows} \times \mathbf{sizeof}(\text{TYPE*}))$$

The rows are printed in the loop that starts on line 52 of Listing 2.48. The loop on line nine counts the number of nonfailure transitions in the row, and the row is generated only if there are nonfailure transitions. The elements themselves are printed in the loop on line 75. The second half of the subroutine, on lines 110 to 129 prints out the array of pointers to the rows. The pnext() subroutine that starts on line 135 prints the next-state subroutine (it's too big to be a macro).

Listing 2.48. *pairs.c*— Pair Compression

```
 1   #include <stdio.h>
 2   #include <tools/debug.h>
 3   #include <tools/compiler.h>              /* for prototypes only */
 4
 5   /* PAIRS.C      This module contains the routines to compress a table
 6    *              horizontally (using char/next pairs) and then print the
 7    *              compressed table. The compressed array looks like this:
 8    *
 9    *  Yy_nxt:        Yy_nxtDD:
10    *  +------+       +-------+----------------------------------------+
11    *  |  *--|----->|   0   | Next state array, indexed by character  |
12    *  +------+       +-------+----------------------------------------+
13    *  |      |
14    *  +------+       +-------+----+----+----+----+-----+
15    *  |  *--|----->| count | c1 | s1 | c2 | s2 | ... |
16    *  +------+       +-------+----+----+----+----+-----+
17    *  | NULL |                    (there are no non-failure transitions if NULL)
18    *  +------+
19    */
20
21   typedef int     ATYPE;          /* Declared type of input tables          */
22
23   #define NCOLS   10              /* Number of columns used to print arrays  */
24   #define TYPE    "YY_TTYPE"     /* Declared type of output tables.        */
25   #define SCLASS  "YYPRIVATE"   /* Storage class of all the tables        */
26   #define D_SCLASS "YYPRIVATE"  /* Storage class of the decoding routine  */
27   /*-----------------------------------------------------------------------*/
28
29   PUBLIC  int  pairs( fp, array, nrows, ncols, name, threshold, numbers )
30
31   FILE    *fp;                            /* output file                    */
32   ATYPE   *array;                         /* DFA transition table           */
33   int     nrows;                          /* Number of rows in array[]      */
34   int     ncols;                          /* Number of columns in array[]   */
35   char    *name;                          /* Name used for output array.    */
36   int     threshold;                      /* Array vs. pairs threshold      */
37   int     numbers;                        /* Use numbers for char. part of pair */
38   {
39       /* Generate the C source code for a pair-compressed DTRAN. Returns the
40        * number of cells used for the YysDD arrays. The "numbers" argument
41        * determines the output format of the character part of a
42        * character/next-state pair. If numbers is true, then normal numbers
43        * are used, otherwise ASCII characters are used. For example: 'a',100
44        * as compared to: 97,100 ('a' == 0x61 == 97, decimal).
45        */
46
47       int     i, j, ntransitions, nprinted, ncommas;
48       int     num_cells = 0;                      /* cells used for rows */
49       ATYPE   *p;
```

Listing 2.48. continued...

```
 50          char      *bin_to_ascii();
 51
 52          for( i = 0;  i < nrows ;  i++ )
 53          {
 54              ntransitions = 0;
 55              for( p = array + (i * ncols), j = ncols;  --j >= 0;  p++ )
 56                  if( *p != -1 )
 57                      ++ntransitions ;
 58
 59              if( ntransitions > 0 )
 60              {
 61                  fprintf(fp, "%s %s %s%-2d[] = { ", SCLASS, TYPE, name, i );    /*}*/
 62                  ++num_cells;
 63                  if( ntransitions > threshold )                        /* array */
 64                      fprintf(fp, "0,\n                 ");
 65                  else                                                  /* pairs */
 66                  {
 67                      fprintf(fp, "%2d, ", ntransitions );
 68                      if( threshold > 5 )
 69                          fprintf(fp, "\n                " );
 70                  }
 71
 72                  nprinted = NCOLS;
 73                  ncommas  = ntransitions;
 74
 75                  for( p = array + (i * ncols),  j = 0;   j < ncols; j++, p++ )
 76                  {
 77                      if( ntransitions > threshold )                    /* array */
 78                      {
 79                          ++num_cells ;
 80                          --nprinted  ;
 81
 82                          fprintf(fp, "%3d" , *p );
 83                          if( j < ncols-1 )
 84                              fprintf(fp, ", ");
 85                      }
 86                      else if( *p != -1 )                               /* pairs */
 87                      {
 88                          num_cells += 2;
 89
 90                          if( numbers )
 91                              fprintf(fp, "%d,%d", j, *p );
 92                          else
 93                              fprintf(fp, "'%s',%d", bin_to_ascii(j,0), *p );
 94
 95                          nprinted -= 2;
 96                          if( --ncommas > 0 )
 97                              fprintf(fp, ", ");
 98                      }
 99
100                      if( nprinted <= 0 )
101                      {
102                          fprintf(fp, "\n                 ");
103                          nprinted = NCOLS;
104                      }
105                  }
106                  fprintf(fp, "};\n" );
107              }
108          }
109
```

→

```
Listing 2.48. continued...
110       fprintf(fp,"\n%s %s *%s[ %d ] =\n{\n     ", SCLASS, TYPE, name, nrows );
111
112       nprinted = 10;                          /* 10 elements on a line */
113       for( --nrows, i = 0; i < nrows ; i++ )
114       {
115           ntransitions = 0;
116           for( p = array + (i * ncols), j = ncols; --j >= 0; p++ )
117               if( *p != -1 )
118                   ++ntransitions ;
119
120           fprintf(fp, ntransitions ? "%s%-2d, " : "NULL,  ", name, i );
121
122           if( --nprinted <= 0 )
123           {
124               fprintf(fp,"\n     ");
125               nprinted = 10;
126           }
127       }
128
129       fprintf(fp, "%s%-2d\n};\n\n", name, i );
130       return num_cells;
131   }
132
133   /*----------------------------------------------------------------------*/
134
135   PUBLIC  void    pnext( fp, name )
136   char    *name;
137   FILE    *fp;
138   {
139       /* Print out a next(state,c) subroutine for a table compressed    */
140       /* into char/next-state pairs by the routines in pairs.c.         */
141
142       static char *toptext[]=
143       {
144         "unsigned int   c ;",
145         "int            cur_state ;",
146         "{",
147         "    /* Given the current state and the current input character, return",
148         "     * the next state.",
149         "     */",
150         "",
151         NULL
152       };
153       static char *boptext[]=
154       {
155         "    int i;",
156         "",
157         "    if( p )",
158         "    {",
159         "        if( (i = *p++)  == 0 )",
160         "            return  p[ c ];",
161         "",
162         "        for( ; --i >= 0 ; p += 2 )",
163         "            if( c == p[0] )",
164         "                return p[1];",
165         "    }",
166         "    return  YYF;",
167         "}",
168         NULL
169       };
```

```
Listing 2.48. continued...
170         fprintf (fp, "\n/*-------------------------------------------------*/\n");
171         fprintf (fp, "%s %s yy_next( cur_state, c )\n", D_SCLASS, TYPE          );
172         printv  (fp, toptext );
173         fprintf (fp, "    %s   *p = %s[ cur_state ] ;\n", TYPE, name );
174         printv  (fp, boptext );
175    }
```

2.5.9.3 Redundant-Row-and-Column-Compressed Tables. The routines to print the array with redundant row and columns removed are in Listing 2.49. Since these are used only in LEX, I've taken less pains to make them as flexible as possible. The subroutine goes through the array column by column using the algorithm in Table 2.13. The same algorithm is used to compress the rows. Note that the row compression creates a single row that contains nothing but failure transitions. This approach seems better than setting the map-array entries to a failure marker because it makes the array access both more consistent and faster at the cost of only a few bytes—you don't have to test for failure before indexing into the map array.

Table 2.13. Algorithm to Eliminate Redundant Columns

array	array to compress
map	the map array being created
save	is the set of columns that are not redundant
i, j	counters
Initially:	*save* is empty.

```
for( i = each column in array )
{
        while( i is a column that's already been marked as redundant )
                ++i;
        add i to save set;
        j = i+1 ;
        while( j < rightmost column )
                if( column i ≡ column j )
                {
                        column map[j] = i;
                        mark j as redundant;
                }
}
j = 0;
for( i = each element of save set )
{
        copy column i to column j;
        ++j;
}
```

Listing 2.49. *squash.c*— Redundant Row and Column Elimination

```
1    #include <stdio.h>
2    #include <ctype.h>
3    #ifdef MSDOS
4    #       include <stdlib.h>
5    #else
6    #       include <malloc.h>
7    #endif
8    #include <tools/debug.h>
9    #include <tools/set.h>
10   #include <tools/compiler.h>
11
12   #include "dfa.h"
13   #include "globals.h"
14
15   /* SQUASH.C -- This module contains the routines to compress a table
16    * horizontally and vertically by removing redundant columns and rows, and then
17    * print the compressed table. I haven't been as careful about making this
18    * routine general purpose because it's only useful to LeX. The pairs
19    * compression routines in pairs.c are used to compress the occs- and
20    * llama-generated tables so they're a little more complicated.
21    */
22
23   PRIVATE int      Col_map[ MAX_CHARS ];
24   PRIVATE int      Row_map[ DFA_MAX   ];
25
26   #define NCOLS    16
27   #define TYPE      "YY_TTYPE"  /* Declared type of output tables.      */
28   #define SCLASS    "YYPRIVATE" /* Storage class of all the tables      */
29
30   /*-------------------------------------------------------------------
31    * Subroutine in this file:
32    */
33
34   PRIVATE int  col_equiv          ( int*,  int*,  int                    );
35   PRIVATE void col_cpy            ( int*,  int*,  int , int , int        );
36   PRIVATE void reduce             ( ROW*,  int*,  int*                   );
37   PRIVATE void print_col_map      ( FILE*                                );
38   PRIVATE void print_row_map      ( FILE*, int                           );
39   PUBLIC  void pmap               ( FILE*, int*,  int                    );
40   PUBLIC  void cnext              ( FILE*, char*                         );
41   PUBLIC  int  squash             ( FILE*, ROW*,  int , int, char*       );
42
43   /*--------------------------------------------------------------------*/
44
45   #define ROW_EQUIV(r1,r2,ncols)  (memcmp( r1, r2, ncols * sizeof(int))==0 )
46   #define ROW_CPY(r1,r2,ncols)    (memcpy( r1, r2, ncols * sizeof(int))    )
47
48   /*--------------------------------------------------------------------*/
49
50   PUBLIC  int      squash( fp, dtran, nrows, ncols, name )
51   FILE     *fp;
52   ROW      *dtran;
53   char     *name;
54   {
55       /* Compress (and output) dtran using equivalent-column elimination.
56        * Return the number of bytes required for the compressed tables
57        * (including the map but not the accepting array).
58        */
59
```

→

Listing 2.49. continued…

```
60          int oncols = ncols;                           /* original column count */
61          int onrows = nrows;                           /* original row    count */
62
63          reduce( dtran, &nrows, &ncols );              /* Compress the tables   */
64
65          print_col_map ( fp );
66          print_row_map ( fp, onrows );
67
68          fprintf(fp, "%s %s %s[ %d ][ %d ]=\n", SCLASS, TYPE, name, nrows, ncols);
69          print_array( fp, (int *)dtran, nrows, ncols );
70
71          return(  ( nrows * ncols  * sizeof(TTYPE))             /* dtran   */
72                  +(         onrows * sizeof(TTYPE))             /* row map */
73                  +(         oncols * sizeof(TTYPE)) );          /* col map */
74      }
75
76      /*------------------------------------------------------------------*/
77
78      PRIVATE  int col_equiv( col1, col2, nrows )
79      int      *col1, *col2;
80      {
81          /* Return 1 if the two columns are equivalent, else return 0 */
82
83          while( --nrows >= 0  &&  *col1 == *col2 )
84          {
85              col1 += MAX_CHARS;          /* Advance to next cell in the column */
86              col2 += MAX_CHARS;
87          }
88
89          return( !(nrows >= 0) );
90      }
91
92      /*- - - - - - - - - - - - - - - - - - - - - - - - - - - - - - - - - */
93
94      PRIVATE void col_cpy( dest, src, nrows, n_src_cols, n_dest_cols )
95      int      *dest;          /* Top of destination column                */
96      int      *src;           /* Top of source column                     */
97      int      nrows;          /* Number of rows                           */
98      int      n_src_cols;     /* Number of columns in source array        */
99      int      n_dest_cols;    /* Number of columns in destination array   */
100     {
101         /* Copy a column from one array to another. Both arrays are nrows deep,
102          * the source array is n_src_cols wide and the destination array is
103          * n_dest_cols wide.
104          */
105
106         while( --nrows >= 0   )
107         {
108             *dest  = *src;
109              dest += n_dest_cols;
110              src  += n_src_cols;
111         }
112     }
113
114     /*- - - - - - - - - - - - - - - - - - - - - - - - - - - - - - - - - */
115
116     PRIVATE void     reduce( dtran, p_nrows, p_ncols )
117     ROW     *dtran;                          /* DFA transition table       */
118     int     *p_nrows;                        /* # of states in dtran       */
119     int     *p_ncols;                        /* Pointer to column count    */
```

```
Listing 2.49. continued...
120    {
121        /* Reduce dtran horizontally and vertically, filling the two map arrays
122         * with the character mapping to the final, reduced transition table.
123         * Return the number of columns in the reduced dtran table.
124         *
125         * Col_map is the x (character) axis, Row_map is the y (next state) axis.
126         */
127
128        int   ncols = *p_ncols;    /* number of columns in original machine    */
129        int   nrows = *p_nrows;    /* number of rows     in original machine   */
130        int   r_ncols;             /* number of columns in reduced machine     */
131        int   r_nrows;             /* number of rows     in reduced machine    */
132        SET   *save;               /* rows or columns that will remain in table */
133        int   *current;            /* first of several identical columns       */
134        int   *compressed;         /* pointer to compressed array              */
135        int   *p;
136        int   i, j;
137
138        /* ..............................................................
139         *  First do the columns.
140         */
141
142        memset( Col_map, -1, sizeof(Col_map) );
143        save = newset();
144
145        for( r_ncols = 0 ;; r_ncols++ )
146        {
147            /* Skip past any states in the Col_map that have already been
148             * processed. If the entire Col_map has been processed, break.
149             */
150
151            for(i = r_ncols;  Col_map[i] != -1  && i < ncols  ; i++ )
152                ;
153
154            if( i >= ncols )
155                break;
156
157            /* Add the current column to the save set. It eventually ends up
158             * in the reduced array as column "r_ncols" so modify the Col_map
159             * entry accordingly. Now, scan trough the array looking for
160             * duplicates of the current column (pointed to by current). If you
161             * find a duplicate, make the associated Col_map entry also point to
162             * "r_ncols."
163             */
164
165            ADD( save, i );
166            Col_map[i] = r_ncols;
167
168            current = &dtran[0][i];
169            p       = current + 1;
170
171            for( j = i; ++j < ncols ; p++ )
172                if( Col_map[j]==-1 && col_equiv(current, p, nrows) )
173                    Col_map[j] = r_ncols ;
174        }
175
176        /* Compress the array horizontally by removing all of the columns that
177         * aren't in the save set. We're doing this by moving all the columns
178         * that are in the save set to the proper position in a newly allocated
179         * array.  You can't do it in place because there's no guarantee that the
```

Listing 2.49. continued...

```
180          * equivalent rows are next to each other.
181          */
182
183          if( !(compressed = (int *) malloc(nrows * r_ncols * sizeof(int))) )
184              ferr("Out of memory");
185
186          p = compressed;
187          for( next_member(NULL); (i = next_member(save)) != -1; )
188              col_cpy( p++, &dtran[0][i], nrows, ncols, r_ncols );
189
190          /* ..........................................................
191           *  Eliminate equivalent rows, working on the reduced array
192           *  created in the previous step. The algorithm used is the
193           *  same.
194           */
195
196          memset( Row_map, -1, sizeof(Row_map) );
197          CLEAR( save );
198
199          for( r_nrows = 0 ;; r_nrows++ )
200          {
201              for( i = r_nrows; Row_map[i] != -1  && i < nrows; i++ )
202                      ;
203
204              if( i >= nrows )
205                      break;
206
207              ADD( save, i );
208              Row_map[i] = r_nrows;
209
210              current = compressed + ((i  ) * r_ncols );
211              p       = compressed + ((i+1) * r_ncols );
212
213              for( j = i; ++j < nrows ; p += r_ncols )
214                  if( Row_map[j]==-1 && ROW_EQUIV(current, p, r_ncols) )
215                          Row_map[j] = r_nrows ;
216          }
217
218          /*
219           * Actually compress rows, copying back into the original array space.
220           * Note that both dimensions of the array have been changed.
221           */
222
223          p = (int *)dtran;
224
225          for( next_member(NULL); (i = next_member(save)) != -1; )
226          {
227              ROW_CPY( p, compressed + (i * r_ncols) , r_ncols );
228              p += r_ncols;
229          }
230
231          delset ( save        );
232          free   ( compressed );
233
234          *p_ncols = r_ncols ;
235          *p_nrows = r_nrows ;
236      }
237
```

Listing 2.49. continued...

```
238     /*----------------------------------------------------------------------*/
239
240     PRIVATE void print_col_map( fp )
241     FILE    *fp;
242     {
243         static char *text[] =
244         {
245             "The Yy_cmap[] and Yy_rmap arrays are used as follows:",
246             "",
247             " next_state= Yydtran[ Yy_rmap[current_state] ][ Yy_cmap[input_char] ];",
248             "",
249             "Character positions in the Yy_cmap array are:",
250             "",
251             "    ^@  ^A  ^B  ^C  ^D  ^E  ^F  ^G  ^H  ^I  ^J  ^K  ^L  ^M  ^N  ^O",
252             "    ^P  ^Q  ^R  ^S  ^T  ^U  ^V  ^W  ^X  ^Y  ^Z  ^[  ^\\  ^]  ^^  ^_",
253             "        !   \"   #   $   %   &   '   (   )   *   +   ,   -   .   /",
254             "    0   1   2   3   4   5   6   7   8   9   :   ;   <   =   >   ?",
255             "    @   A   B   C   D   E   F   G   H   I   J   K   L   M   N   O",
256             "    P   Q   R   S   T   U   V   W   X   Y   Z   [   \\   ]   ^   _",
257             "    `   a   b   c   d   e   f   g   h   i   j   k   l   m   n   o",
258             "    p   q   r   s   t   u   v   w   x   y   z   {   |   }   ~   DEL",
259             NULL
260         };
261
262         comment(fp, text);
263         fprintf(fp, "%s %s  Yy_cmap[%d] =\n{\n    ", SCLASS, TYPE, MAX_CHARS );
264         pmap    (fp, Col_map, MAX_CHARS );
265     }
266
267
268     PRIVATE void print_row_map( fp, nrows )
269     FILE    *fp;
270     int     nrows;
271     {
272         fprintf(fp, "%s %s  Yy_rmap[%d] =\n{\n    ", SCLASS, TYPE, nrows );
273         pmap    (fp, Row_map, nrows );
274     }
275
276     PRIVATE void pmap( fp, p, n )                      /* output stream    */
277     FILE    *fp;                                       /* pointer to array */
278     int     *p;                                        /* array size       */
279     int     n;
280     {
281         /* Print a one-dimensional array.
282         */
283
284         int j;
285         for( j = 0; j < (n - 1); j++ )
286         {
287             fprintf(fp, "%3d," , *p++ );
288
289             if( (j % NCOLS) == NCOLS-1 )
290                 fprintf(fp, "\n    ");
291         }
292
293         fprintf( fp, "%3d\n};\n\n", *p );
294     }
295
```

```
Listing 2.49. continued...
296   /*------------------------------------------------------------------*/
297
298   PUBLIC   void      cnext( fp, name )
299   FILE     *fp;
300   char     *name;
301   {
302       /*   Print out a yy_next(state,c) subroutine for the compressed table.
303        */
304
305       static char   *text[] =
306       {
307           "yy_next(state,c) is given the current state number and input",
308           "character and evaluates to the next state.",
309           NULL
310       };
311
312       comment( fp, text );
313       fprintf( fp,
314           "#define yy_next(state,c) (%s[ Yy_rmap[state] ][ Yy_cmap[c] ])\n",
315           name
316       );
317   }
```

2.5.10 Tying It All Together

LᴱX is completed by the subroutines presented in this section. (in Listings 2.50, 2.51, 2.52, and 2.53). These listings are commented sufficiently that additional comments here would be tedious. Read the code if you're interested.

I should also add, at this point, that there are more efficient methods than the one I've just described for converting a regular expression to a finite automata. (See [Aho] pp. 134–141.) I've chosen the current method because it serves to introduce several concepts (like closure) that will be useful later on.

Listing 2.50. *signon.c*— Print Sign-on Message

```
1    #include <stdio.h>
2    #include <tools/debug.h>
3    #include "date.h"
4
5    signon()
6    {
7        /* Print the sign-on message. Since the console is opened explicitly, the
8         * message is printed even if both stdout and stderr are redirected.
9         */
10
11       FILE *screen;
12
13       UX( if( !(screen = fopen("/dev/tty", "w")) )          )
14       MS( if( !(screen = fopen("con:",      "w")) )          )
15               screen = stderr;
16
17       /* The ANSI __DATE__ macro yields a string of the form: "Sep 01 1989". */
18       /* The __DATE__+7 gets the year portion of that string.             */
19
```

```
Listing 2.50. continued...

20        fprintf(screen,"LeX 1.0 [%s]. (c) %s, Allen I. Holub. "
21                        "All rights reserved.\n", __DATE__, __DATE__+7 );
22
23        if( screen != stderr )
24            fclose(screen);
25    }
```

Listing 2.51. *print.c*— Print Remainder of Output File

```
1    #include <stdio.h>
2    #include <ctype.h>
3    #include <tools/debug.h>
4    #include <tools/set.h>
5    #include <tools/compiler.h>
6    #include "dfa.h"
7    #include "nfa.h"
8    #include "globals.h"
9
10   /*  PRINT.C:  This module contains miscellaneous print routines that do
11    *  everything except print the actual tables.
12    */
13
14   PUBLIC void pheader( FILE *fp,      ROW dtran[], int nrows, ACCEPT *accept);
15   PUBLIC void pdriver( FILE *output,              int nrows, ACCEPT *accept);
16   /*-----------------------------------------------------------*/
17
18   PUBLIC  void     pheader( fp, dtran, nrows, accept )
19   FILE    *fp;                    /* output stream                        */
20   ROW     dtran[];                /* DFA transition table                 */
21   int     nrows;                  /* Number of states in dtran[]          */
22   ACCEPT  *accept;                /* Set of accept states in dtran[]      */
23   {
24       /*  Print out a header comment that describes the uncompressed DFA. */
25
26       int        i, j;
27       int        last_transition ;
28       int        chars_printed;
29       char       *bin_to_ascii() ;
30
31       fprintf(fp, "#ifdef __NEVER__ \n" );
32       fprintf(fp, "/*--------------------------------------------------\n");
33       fprintf(fp, " * DFA (start state is 0) is:\n *\n" );
34
35       for( i = 0; i < nrows ; i++ )
36       {
37           if( !accept[i].string )
38               fprintf(fp, " * State %d [nonaccepting]", i );
39           else
40           {
41               fprintf(fp, " * State %d [accepting, line %d <",
42                                    i , ((int *)(accept[i].string))[-1] );
43
44               fputstr( accept[i].string, 20, fp );
45               fprintf(fp, ">]" );
46
```

```
Listing 2.51. continued...
47                   if( accept[i].anchor )
48                       fprintf( fp, " Anchor: %s%s",
49                                           accept[i].anchor & START ? "start " : "",
50                                           accept[i].anchor & END   ? "end"   : "" );
51           }
52
53           last_transition = -1;
54           for( j = 0; j < MAX_CHARS; j++ )
55           {
56               if( dtran[i][j] != F )
57               {
58                   if( dtran[i][j] != last_transition )
59                   {
60                       fprintf(fp, "\n *    goto %2d on ", dtran[i][j] );
61                       chars_printed = 0;
62                   }
63
64                   fprintf(fp, "%s", bin_to_ascii(j,1) );
65
66                   if( (chars_printed += strlen(bin_to_ascii(j,1))) > 56 )
67                   {
68                       fprintf(fp, "\n *                " );
69                       chars_printed = 0;
70                   }
71
72                   last_transition = dtran[i][j];
73               }
74           }
75           fprintf(fp, "\n");
76       }
77       fprintf(fp," */\n\n" );
78       fprintf(fp,"#endif\n" );
79  }
80
81  /*-------------------------------------------------------------*/
82
83  PUBLIC  void    pdriver( output, nrows, accept )
84  FILE    *output;
85  int     nrows;              /* Number of states in dtran[]        */
86  ACCEPT  *accept;            /* Set of accept states in dtran[]    */
87  {
88      /* Print the array of accepting states, the driver itself, and the case
89       * statements for the accepting strings.
90       */
91
92      int     i;
93      static  char   *text[] =
94      {
95          "The Yyaccept array has two purposes. If Yyaccept[i] is 0 then state",
96          "i is nonaccepting. If it's nonzero then the number determines whether",
97          "the string is anchored, 1=anchored at start of line, 2=at end of",
98          "line, 3=both, 4=line not anchored",
99          NULL
100     };
101
102     comment( output, text );
103     fprintf(output, "YYPRIVATE YY_TTYPE  Yyaccept[] =\n" );
104     fprintf(output, "{\n"                          );
105
```

```
      Listing 2.51. continued...
106       for( i = 0 ; i < nrows ; i++ )                              /* accepting array */
107       {
108           if( !accept[i].string )
109               fprintf( output, "\t0   " );
110           else
111               fprintf( output, "\t%-3d",accept[i].anchor ? accept[i].anchor :4);
112
113           fprintf(output, "%c    /* State %-3d */\n",
114                               i == (nrows -1) ? ' ' : ',' , i );
115       }
116       fprintf(output, "};\n\n" );
117
118       driver_2( output, !No_lines );                              /* code above cases */
119
120       for( i = 0 ; i < nrows ; i++ )                              /* case statements  */
121       {
122           if( accept[i].string )
123           {
124               fprintf(output, "\t\tcase %d:\t\t\t\t\t/* State %-3d */\n",i,i);
125               if( !No_lines )
126                   fprintf(output, "#line %d \"%s\"\n",
127                                       *( (int *)(accept[i].string) - 1),
128                                       Input_file_name );
129
130               fprintf(output, "\t\t    %s\n",    accept[i].string );
131               fprintf(output, "\t\t    break;\n"            );
132           }
133       }
134
135       driver_2( output, !No_lines );                      /* code below cases */
136   }
```

Listing 2.52. *lex.c*— `main()` and Other High-Level Functions (Part 1)

```
 1    #include <stdio.h>
 2    #include <ctype.h>
 3    #include <stdarg.h>                           /* For vprintf() */
 4    #include <tools/debug.h>
 5    #include <tools/set.h>
 6    #include <tools/hash.h>
 7    #include <tools/compiler.h>
 8    #include "dfa.h"
 9
10    #define ALLOCATE
11    #include "globals.h"
12
13    /*----------------------------------------------------------------------*/
14
15    PUBLIC  void  error    (int usage, char *fmt, ...);
16    PUBLIC  int   main     (int argc,  char **argv);
17    PRIVATE int   getline  (char **stringp, int n, FILE *stream);
18    PRIVATE void  do_file  (void);
19    PRIVATE void  tail     (void);
20    extern  char *get_expr (void);               /* in input.c */
21
```

```
     Listing 2.52. continued...
 22    /*-------------------------------------------------------------------*/
 23
 24    #define DTRAN_NAME   "Yy_nxt"      /* Name used for DFA transition table. Up to */
 25                                        /* 3 characters are appended to the end of  */
 26                                        /* this name in the row-compressed tables.  */
 27
 28    #define E(x)     fprintf(stderr,"%s\n", x)
 29
 30    PRIVATE int     Column_compress = 1;  /* Variables for command-line switches */
 31    PRIVATE int     No_compression  = 0;
 32    PRIVATE int     Threshold       = 4;
 33    PRIVATE int     No_header       = 0;
 34    PRIVATE int     Header_only     = 0;
 35
 36    extern int      Verbose;                    /* in globals.h */
 37    extern int      No_lines;                   /* in globals.h */
 38    extern int      Lineno;                     /* In globals.h, the line number  */
 39                                                /* used to print #line directives. */
 40
 41    /*-------------------------------------------------------------------*/
 42
 43    PRIVATE void    cmd_line_error( usage, fmt, ...)
 44    char      *fmt;
 45    {
 46        /* Print an error message and exit to the operating system. This routine is
 47         * used much like printf(), except that it has an extra first argument.
 48         * If "usage" is 0, an error message associated with the current value of
 49         * errno is printed after printing the format/arg string in the normal way.
 50         * If "usage" is nonzero, a list of legal command-line switches is printed.
 51         *
 52         * I'm using the ANSI conventions for a subroutine with a variable number of
 53         * arguments. These differ a little from the Unix V conventions. Look up
 54         * _doprnt() [it's in the "printf(3S)" entry] in the Unix Programmer's
 55         * Manual for details. A version of the <stdarg.h> macros used here is in
 56         * Appendix A.
 57         */
 58
 59        extern char *sys_errlist[];
 60        extern int  errno;
 61        va_list     args;
 62
 63        va_start(args, fmt);
 64        fprintf ( stderr, "lex: "   );
 65        vfprintf( stderr, fmt, args );
 66
 67        if( !usage )
 68            fprintf( stderr, "(%s)\n", sys_errlist[errno] );
 69        else
 70        {
 71            E("\n\nUsage is:    LeX [options] file"                        );
 72            E("-f  for (f)ast. Don't compress tables."                      );
 73            E("-h  suppress (h)eader comment that describes state machine." );
 74            E("-H  print the (H)eader only."                                );
 75            E("-l  Suppress #(l)ine directives in the output."             );
 76            E("-mS Use string S as template name rather than lex.par."     );
 77            E("-cN use pair (c)ompression, N = threshold (default 4)."     );
 78            E("-t  Send output to standard output instead of lexyy.c"      );
 79            E("-u  UNIX mode, newline is \\n, not \\n or \\r"              );
 80            E("-v  (v)erbose mode, print statistics."                      );
 81            E("-V  More (V)erbose, print internal diagnostics as lex runs." );
```
⟶

Listing 2.52. continued...

```
 82        }
 83        exit(1);
 84        va_end(args);
 85    }
 86
 87    /*-------------------------------------------------------------------------*/
 88
 89    PUBLIC  void     lerror( status, fmt, ...)
 90    char    *fmt;
 91    {
 92        /* Print an error message and input line number. Exit with
 93         * indicated status if "status" is nonzero.
 94         */
 95
 96        extern int  errno;
 97        va_list     args;
 98
 99        va_start(args, fmt);
100        fprintf  ( stderr, "lex, input line %d: ", Actual_lineno );
101        vfprintf ( stderr, fmt, args );
102        if( status )
103            exit( status );
104        va_end(args);
105    }
106
107    /*-------------------------------------------------------------------------*/
108
109    PUBLIC  main( argc, argv )
110    char    **argv;
111    {
112        static char         *p ;
113        static int  use_stdout = 0;
114
115        signon();
116
117        for( ++argv; argc && *(p = *argv) == '-'; ++argv, --argc )
118        {
119            while( *++p )
120            {
121                switch( *p )
122                {
123                case 'f':  No_compression  = 1;      break;
124                case 'h':  No_header       = 1;      break;
125                case 'H':  Header_only     = 1;      break;
126                case 'l':  No_lines        = 1;      break;
127                case 'm':  Template     = p + 1;     goto out;
128                case 'p':  Public          = 1;      break;
129                case 't':  use_stdout      = 1;      break;
130                case 'u':  Unix            = 1;      break;
131                case 'v':  Verbose         = 1;      break;
132                case 'V':  Verbose         = 2;      break;
133                case 'c':  Column_compress = 0;
134
135                        if( !isdigit(p[1]) )
136                            Threshold = 4;
137                        else
138                        {
139                            Threshold = atoi( ++p );
```

Listing 2.52. continued...

```
140                                      while( *p && isdigit( p[1] ) )
141                                          ++p;
142                                  }
143                              break;
144
145                    default:  cmd_line_error(1, "-%c illegal argument.", *p);
146                              break;
147                  }
148              }
149      out:;
150      }
151
152      if( argc > 1 )
153          cmd_line_error( 1, "Too many arguments. Only one file name permitted" );
154
155      else if( argc <= 0 )
156          cmd_line_error( 1, "File name required" );
157      else /* argc == 1 */
158      {
159          if( Ifile = fopen(*argv,"r") )
160              Input_file_name = *argv;
161          else
162              cmd_line_error( 0, "Can't open input file %s", *argv );
163      }
164
165      if( !use_stdout )
166          if( !(Ofile = fopen( Header_only ? "lexyy.h" : "lexyy.c", "w")))
167              cmd_line_error( 0, "Can't open output file lexyy.[ch]" );
168
169      do_file ();
170      fclose  ( Ofile );
171      fclose  ( Ifile );
172      exit    ( 0 );
173  }
174
175  /*----------------------------------------------------------------------*/
176
177  PRIVATE void do_file( )
178  {
179      int    nstates;           /* Number of DFA states       */
180      ROW    *dtran;            /* Transition table           */
181      ACCEPT *accept;           /* Set of accept states in dfa */
182      FILE   *input, *driver_1(); /* Template file for driver   */
183      int    i;
184
185      /* Process the input file */
186
187      head( Header_only );                      /* print everything up to first %% */
188
189      nstates = min_dfa( get_expr, &dtran, &accept );       /* make DFA */
190      if( Verbose )
191      {
192          printf("%d out of %d DFA states in minimized machine\n", nstates,
193                                                          DFA_MAX );
194          printf("%d bytes required for minimized tables\n\n",
195                  nstates * MAX_CHARS * sizeof(TTYPE)          /* dtran  */
196                + nstates *            sizeof(TTYPE) );        /* accept */
197      }
198
```

Listing 2.52. continued...

```
199        if( !No_header )
200              pheader( Ofile, dtran, nstates, accept );         /* print header */
201                                                                 /* comment.     */
202        if( !Header_only )
203        {
204
205                                                                 /* first part */
206          if( !(input = driver_1( Ofile, !No_lines, Template )) )  /* of driver. */
207          {
208              perror( Template );
209              exit(1);
210          }
211
212          if( No_compression )                                   /* compressed tables */
213          {
214              fprintf (Ofile ,"YYPRIVATE YY_TTYPE  %s[ %d ][ %d ] =\n",
215                                      DTRAN_NAME, nstates, MAX_CHARS);
216
217              print_array( Ofile, (int *)dtran, nstates, MAX_CHARS );
218              defnext    ( Ofile, DTRAN_NAME );
219          }
220          else if( Column_compress )                             /* column-compressed tables. */
221          {
222              i = squash ( Ofile, dtran, nstates, MAX_CHARS, DTRAN_NAME   );
223              cnext       ( Ofile, DTRAN_NAME                             );
224
225              if( Verbose )
226                  printf("%d bytes required for column-compressed tables\n\n",
227                          i                                      /* dtran      */
228                          + (nstates * sizeof(int)) );           /* Yy_accept  */
229          }
230          else                                                   /* pair-compressed tables */
231          {
232              i = pairs( Ofile, (int *)dtran, nstates,
233                              MAX_CHARS, DTRAN_NAME, Threshold, 0);
234              if( Verbose )
235              {
236                  /* Figure the space occupied for the various tables. The
237                   * Microsoft compiler uses roughly 100 bytes for the yy_next()
238                   * subroutine. Column compression does yy_next in line with a
239                   * macro so the overhead is negligible.
240                   */
241
242                  i =   (i        * sizeof(TTYPE ))   /* YysDD arrays   */
243                      + (nstates  * sizeof(TTYPE*))   /* Dtran[]        */
244                      + (nstates  * sizeof(TTYPE ))   /* Yy_accept[]    */
245                      + 100                        ;  /* yy_next()      */
246
247                  printf("%d bytes required for pair-compressed tables\n", i );
248              }
249
250              pnext( Ofile, DTRAN_NAME );
251          }
252
253          pdriver( Ofile, nstates, accept );        /* print rest of driver   */
254          tail();                                    /* and everything following */
255                                                     /* the second %%            */
256      }
257  }
258
```

Listing 2.52. continued...

```
259    /*---------------------------------------------------------------
260     * Head processes everything up to the first %%. Any lines that begin
261     * with white space or are surrounded by %{ and %} are passed to the
262     * output. All other lines are assumed to be macro definitions.
263     * A %% can not be concealed in a %{ %} but it must be anchored at start
264     * of line so a %% in a printf statement (for example) is passed to the
265     * output correctly. Similarly, a %{ and %} must be the first two characters
266     * on the line.
267     */
268
269    PRIVATE head( suppress_output )
270    int suppress_output;
271    {
272        int  transparent = 0;          /* True if in a %{ %} block */
273
274        if( !suppress_output  && Public )
275            fputs( "#define YYPRIVATE\n\n", Ofile );
276
277        if( !No_lines )
278            fprintf( Ofile, "#line 1 \"%s\"\n", Input_file_name);
279
280        while( fgets( Input_buf, MAXINP, Ifile) )
281        {
282            ++ Actual_lineno;
283
284            if( !transparent )                       /* Don't strip comments */
285                strip_comments( Input_buf );         /* from code blocks.     */
286
287            if( Verbose > 1 )
288                printf( "h%d: %s", Actual_lineno, Input_buf );
289
290            if( Input_buf[0] == '%' )
291            {
292                if( Input_buf[1] == '%' )
293                {
294                    if( !suppress_output )
295                        fputs( "\n", Ofile );
296                    break;
297                }
298                else
299                {
300                    if( Input_buf[1] == '{' )                        /*}{*/
301                        transparent = 1;
302
303                    else if( Input_buf[1] == '}' )
304                        transparent = 0;
305
306                    else
307                        lerror(0, "Ignoring illegal %%%c directive\n",
308                                                        Input_buf[1] );
309                }
310            }
311            else if( transparent || isspace(Input_buf[0]) )
312            {
313                if( !suppress_output )
314                    fputs( Input_buf, Ofile );
315            }
316            else
317            {
318                new_macro( Input_buf );
```

Listing 2.52. continued...

```
319                 if( !suppress_output )
320                     fputs( "\n", Ofile );    /* Replace macro def with a blank */
321                                               /* line so that the line numbers  */
322                                               /* won't get messed up.           */
323             }
324         }
325
326     if( Verbose > 1 )
327         printmacs();
328 }
329
330 /*-------------------------------------------------------------------*/
331
332 strip_comments( string )
333 char    *string;
334 {
335     /* Scan through the string, replacing C-like comments with space
336      * characters. Multiple-line comments are supported.
337      */
338
339     static int incomment = 0;
340
341     for(; *string ; ++string )
342     {
343         if( incomment )
344         {
345             if( string[0]=='*' && string[1]=='/' )
346             {
347                 incomment =  0 ;
348                 *string++ = ' ';
349             }
350
351             if( !isspace( *string ) )
352                 *string = ' ';
353         }
354         else
355         {
356             if( string[0]=='/' && string[1]=='*' )
357             {
358                 incomment =  1 ;
359                 *string++ = ' ';
360                 *string   = ' ';
361             }
362         }
363     }
364 }
365
366 /*-------------------------------------------------------------------*/
367
368 PRIVATE void    tail()
369 {
370     fgets(Input_buf, MAXINP, Ifile);    /* Throw away the line that */
371                                          /* had the %% on it.        */
372
373     if( !No_lines )
374         fprintf( Ofile, "#line %d \"%s\"\n",
375                         Actual_lineno + 1, Input_file_name);
376
```

```
Listing 2.52. continued...
377         while( fgets(Input_buf, MAXINP, Ifile) )
378         {
379             if( Verbose > 1 )
380                 printf( "t%d: %s", Actual_lineno++, Input_buf );
381
382             fputs(Input_buf, Ofile);
383         }
384     }
```

2.6 Exercises

2.1. Modify the simple expression grammar used in Chapter 1 so that COMMENT tokens can appear anywhere in the expression. This exercise demonstrates graphically why it's useful for a lexical analyzer to do things like remove comments from the input.

2.2. Write a lexical analyzer that processes the PL/1 statement

```
if then then then = else; else else = then;
```

correctly, distinguishing the keywords from the identifiers.

2.3. Write a regular expression that can recognize all possible integer constants in C. All of the following should be recognized:

```
0x89ab 0123 45 'z' '\t' '\xab' '\012'
```

2.4. Write a regular expression that recognizes a C identifier. Construct an NFA for this expression using Thompson's Construction, convert the NFA to a DFA using Subset Construction, and minimize the DFA.

2.5. Write a set of input functions that can handle interactive input from a human being more elegantly than the ones in *input.c*. (They should support command-line editing, and so forth). Your routines must work with the default driver generated by LEX (they must use the same interface as the default ones). The routines should be able to get input directly from the console, rather than from standard input.

2.6. Use LEX to rewrite its own lexical analyzer.

2.7. Write a set of regular expressions that can recognize C subroutine declarations. You can assume that the entire declaration is on one line. Declarations such as the following should be recognized:

```
TYPE            *doo( wha, ditty )
unsigned char   (*foo())[10]
int             ( *signal(signal, ptr) )()
```

but not the following

```
extern int   ( *signal(int signal, (*ptr)()) )();
sam( dave );
```

2.8. Use the regular expressions developed in the previous exercise to write a LEX program that inputs a list of C programs whose names are listed on the command line, and which outputs all subroutine declarations along with the name of the file in which they are found and their input line numbers.

2.9. Modify the previous exercise so that only the subroutine name is printed, rather than the entire declaration.

2.10. Various UNIX editors support the \(and \) operators, which bracket subexpressions in a regular expression. For example, an expression like this:

```
\(abc\)def\(ghi\)
```

recognizes the string `abcdefghi`, and the two substrings `abc` and `ghi` can be accessed later using the notation \1 and \2 respectively. Modify LEX to support a similar feature, but as follows:

A subexpression in a regular expression is indicated with parenthesis.

a. Modify LEX so that repeated subexpressions in the regular expressions themselves can be referenced using the notation \0, \1, and so forth. \0 references the first subexpression, \1 the next one, and so forth. A subexpression's number is derived by counting the number of open parentheses to the left of the one that starts that subexpression. For example, the following regular expression recognizes three, comma-delimited decimal numbers:

```
[0-9]+,[0-9]+,[0-9]+
```

You should be able to express the same thing as follows:

```
([0-9]+)(,)\0\1\0
```

The \0 in the regular expression tells LEX to duplicate the first subexpression `([0-9]+)`, the \1 duplicates the second `(,)`.
The double-quote character and double backslash should still work as expected. Both of the following expressions should recognize an input string like `"1234\1\2\1"`:

```
([0-9]+)(,)"\1\2\1"
([0-9]+)(,)\\1\\2\\1
```

The backslashes are treated as literal characters here.

b. Modify LEX so that the lexemes associated with the matched subexpression can be accessed in an action using an `argv`-like array of string pointers called `yyv`: `yyv[0]` holds the lexeme that matches the first subexpression, `yyv[1]` the second, and so on. An integer called `yyc` should hold the number of valid entries in `yyv`. For example, the expression in the following rule recognizes the input pattern `abcdefghi`:

```
((abc(def))(ghi))        while( --yyc >= 0 )
                             printf("%s\n", *yyv++ );
```

The associated action prints:

```
abcdefghi
abcdef
def
ghi
```

2.11. Modify LEX to support a unary NOT operator. It should be higher precedence than the closure operators and lower precedence than concatenation. It should precede its operand. For example, `!c` matches anything except the character `c`; the expression `a!(bc)` should match an *a* followed by any sequence of characters other than the two character sequence `bc`; `!(and|or)` should match any string except *and* or *or*; finally, `![a-z]` should work just like *[ˆa-z]*. Be careful of the newline, which should not be matched by any of the foregoing patterns.

2.12. Add the / lookahead operator to LEX. The expression *a/b*— where *a* and *b* are both regular expressions — matches *a*, but only if it is followed by *b*. The characters that match *b* should not be put into the lexeme. In fact, they should be pushed back into the input after being recognized. For example, the regular expression `abc/def` should match an *abc* only if it's followed by a *def*, and the *def* should be pushed back into the input for subsequent processing. You can simulate the *$* operator with `xxx/[\r\n]`. Similarly, the following pattern matches the string *if*, but only if the next nonwhite character isn't a semicolon, plus sign, minus sign, or asterisk:

```
if/[\s\t\n\r]*[^;+-*]`
```

By the same token, `if/[\s\t\n\r]*(` matches an *if* only if the next nonwhite character is an open parenthesis.

2.13. Add the `REJECT` directive to LEX. This directive selects the next alternative accepting action when regular expressions conflict. For example, the following recognizes the word *he*, even if it's imbedded in *she*:

```
int he=0, she=0;
%%
he        { ++he;  REJECT; }
she       { ++she; REJECT; }

(.|\n)   ; /* ignore */
%%
main()
{
    yylex();
    printf("Saw %d he's and %d she's\n", he, she );
}
```

It recognizes the `she` first, then the `REJECT` action causes it to execute the code associated with the *he* regular expressions too. Note that it's not doing anything special with the input, it's only executing all possible accepting actions for the expression. The program should print

```
Saw 2 he's and 1 she's
```

when given the input:

```
he she
```

2.14. Add the *X{a,b}* operator to LEX. This expression matches *X* repeated *a* to *b* times. For example `l{1,3}ama` recognizes *lama*, *llama*, and *lllama*.

2.15. Add left-context sensitivity to LEX. Do it like this: The statement

```
%START NAME
```

is placed in the first, definitions part of the LEX input file. It creates a class of regular expressions that are active only in certain situations (discussed below). NAME can be an arbitrary name having up to eight characters. All regular expressions that start with `<NAME>` are placed in the class. The angle brackets must be present, like this:

```
<NAME>(a|b)*     { some_code(); }
```

Activate all states in the class with the following line anywhere in the <u>code</u> part of a rule:

```
BEGIN NAME;
```

That is, the earlier regular expression, *(a|b)**, won't be recognized until a `BEGIN`

NAME has been executed in a code block. Use `BEGIN 0;` to disable all special regular expressions. An expression can be put into several classes like this:

```
<NAME1,NAME2,NAME3>expression    { some_code(); }
```

Once an expression is activated, the usual input-file precedence rules are also active. That is, if a special expression occurs earlier in the input file than a conflicting expression, the special one takes precedence once it's activated.

2.16. Modify L𝖤X to detect which of the two compression methods yields the smallest tables, and then use that method automatically.

2.17. Add a command-line switch to L𝖤X that causes the two compression methods to be combined: Pair compression should be applied first, then a map array should be used to compress the uncompressed rows in the pair-compressed tables. Only one copy of two or more identical rows should be kept, with several pointers in `Yy_nxt[]` addressing the single copy of the row.

2.18. Modify the minimization routines to remove dead states—nonaccepting states that have no outgoing transitions other than ones that loop back into the current state.

2.19. Modify the minimization routines to remove unreachable states—states that have no incoming edges.

2.20. Sometimes it's useful for a program's users to be able to modify the token set when they install a program. This way, they can customize a program's input syntax to fit their own preferences. Modify L𝖤X so that it produces a file containing binary representations of the state and auxiliary tables rather than C source code. Modify `yylex()` so that it reads the tables from this file into memory the first time it is called. This way, the user can change the L𝖤X input file and generate a new state table without having to recompile the program that is using that state table.

Note that the actions still have to be put into the compiled program—there's no way to read them from disk at run time. Consequently, though the regular expressions can be modified at installation time, the number of regular expressions must stay the same. The position of the regular expression from the top of the file determines the action to execute when that expression is recognized. That is, the second action in the original input file is executed when the second regular expression is matched, even if that expression is changed at installation time.

3

Context-Free Grammars

The discussion of formal grammars started in Chapter One continues here. I discuss the general, more theoretical aspects of grammars, but with emphasis on building real grammars, discussing precedence and associativity, list and expression grammars, and so forth. Attributed and augmented grammars are introduced as well, and they are put into the context of a recursive-descent parser. Grammars are discussed further in Chapter Four, where various grammatical transformations are presented.

3.1 Sentences, Phrases, and Context-Free Grammars

This section quickly summarizes the terms introduced in Chapters One and Two and extends these terms somewhat.

Alphabet.
String, word.
Token.

An *alphabet* is a collection of characters. The ASCII character set is a good example of an alphabet. A *string* or *word* is a specific sequence of symbols from an input *alphabet*. In compiler parlance, a word in the language is called a *token*—an indivisible lexical unit of the language.

Language, sentence.

A *language* is a set of words, and a *sentence* is a sequence of one or more of the words that comprise the language. Strictly speaking, there is no inherent ordering of the words within the sentence, and that's where a *grammar* comes into play. A formal *grammar* is a system of rules (called *productions*) that control the order in which words may occur in a sentence.

Grammar, production.

Syntax.

The *syntax* of a sentence determines the relationships between the words and phrases in a sentence. That is, the syntax of a language controls the <u>structure</u> of a sentence and nothing more. Taking English as an example, the syntax of English requires that the subject precede the verb, or that an adjective must precede the noun that it modifies. The syntax rules tell you nothing about what the sentence actually means, however.

Context-free grammar.

Informally, a *context-free grammar* is a system of definitions that can be used to break up a sentence into phrases solely on the basis of the sequence of strings in the input sentence. A context-free grammar is usually represented in *Backus-Naur* form (BNF), in which productions are represented as follows:

Backus-Naur Form, →,
::=.

$$part\_of\_speech \rightarrow definition$$

Left-hand side (LHS).

The → operator (often represented as ::=) is the "is defined as" or "goes to" operator.

166

The left-hand side of the production (often abbreviated to LHS), is the name of the syntactic unit within the language (noun, verb, prepositional phrase, and so forth). The right-hand side (or RHS) is a list of symbols that define the LHS. For example:

sentence → subject predicate **PERIOD**

A *sentence* is a *subject*, followed by a *predicate*, followed by a **PERIOD**. There are two types of symbols on the right-hand side: *Nonterminal* symbols are terms that have to be defined further somewhere in the grammar (they have to appear on a left-hand side), and *terminal* symbols such as tokens which need no further definition. The nonterminal nodes form interior nodes in the parse tree; the terminal nodes are all at the ends of branches. There are terminal symbols other than tokens, discussed below.

So, a context-free grammar is one in which all input sentences can be parsed strictly on the basis of syntax. Formally, a context-free grammar is composed of the following:

- A finite set of terminal symbols or tokens.
- A finite set of nonterminal symbols.
- A finite set of productions of the form $s{\rightarrow}\alpha$, where s is a nonterminal symbol, and α is a list of zero or more terminal and nonterminal symbols. s is called the *left-hand side* of the production and α is called the *right-hand side*. Every nonterminal symbol that appears in the right-hand side in some production must also appear on a left-hand side. No terminal symbols may appear on a left-hand side.
- A single *start* or *goal* symbol from which all the productions derive.

It's theoretically possible to have a "context-sensitive" grammar that does consider semantics when analyzing a sentence, but this type of grammar is beyond the scope of this book and won't be discussed further.

A grammar can also distinguish groups of words that are related syntactically. For example, in English, the syntax of the language helps separate a subject from a predicate, recognize prepositional phrases, and so forth. Each of these syntactically related lists of words are called *phrases*. In a computer language, a loop-control statement and associated body is a phrase, as is an entire subroutine declaration. Note that the phrases can be organized hierarchically—a sentence can contain a predicate, which can in turn contain a prepositional phrase. A grammatical phrase can be as short as a single word: in C, a single identifier can comprise a phrase. It can also be empty—I'll discuss this case below. A production is a rule that describes the syntax of a single phrase.

Syntactic rules are used to break a sentence into its component parts of speech and analyze the relationship of one part to another (this process is called *parsing* the sentence). The term is used in both linguistic and compiler theory. A *parser* is a computer program that uses a context-free grammar to parse an input sentence—to isolate the component parts of speech for subsequent processing. Most parser programs are also *recognizer* programs. They accept (returns *yes*) only if the input forms a syntactically correct sentence. The fact that a parser can also generate code is actually immaterial from a theoretical point of view.

The parser can analyze only the structure of the sentence. Even in English, the syntax of a sentence tells you nothing about what the sentence means. Meaning comes under the purview of *semantics*. A context-free grammar defines the structure of the sentence only. It tells you nothing about the semantics—the meanings of the words—except that you can sometimes infer meaning from the position of the word within a sentence. For example, a grammar could tell you that a variable declaration is comprised of a sequence of type-specification tokens (**int**, **long**, **short**, and so forth) followed by a single identifier, but it is just manipulating sequences of strings, it has no idea what the strings mean. In the case of a declaration, it knows nothing about the characteristics of the individual types—as far as the grammar is concerned, the following declarations are

Right-hand side (RHS).

Nonterminal and terminal symbols.

Context-free grammar: formal definition.

Phrase.

Parsing.

Recognizer programs.

Semantics and syntax.

all reasonable because they're all sequences of type specifiers followed by a single identifier:

```
long      john_silver;
short     stop;
long short muddle;
```

What the grammar *does* do is distinguish the specifiers from the identifiers. If a type specifier were redefined so that it could represent an **int** only, then the meaning of the specifier could be extrapolated from the syntax. That is, when the parser encountered a type specifier, it would know that the specifier was an **int**, because that was the only possibility. This sort of degenerate case is not much use in natural languages like English, but it can be used effectively in languages with limited syntactic and semantic scope, such as programming languages, which might have only a few verbs (**while, do, for**), and the same number of nouns (**int, float, double**).

Syntax-directed transla-
tion.

In *syntax-directed translation*, code is generated (the input language is translated to the output language) strictly on the basis of the syntax of a sentence—the meaning of a phrase or word is inferred from its position within the sentence. In practical terms, the parser performs certain code-generation actions as it traverses a parse tree which is created using syntactic rules. It performs a code-generation action every time a node on the tree is visited.

3.2 Derivations and Sentential Forms

Derivations.

A *derivation* is a way of showing how an input sentence can be recognized with a grammar. You can also look at it as a type of algebraic substitution using the grammar. As an example of the derivation process, you start a leftmost derivation with the topmost nonterminal in a grammar, called the *start* or *goal* symbol. You then replace this nonterminal with one of its right-hand sides. Continue in this manner—but replace the leftmost nonterminal created from the previous step with one of the right-hand sides of that nonterminal—until there are no more nonterminals to replace.

Start, goal symbol.

The following grammar recognizes a simple semicolon-terminated expression consisting of interspersed numbers and **PLUS** tokens:

1:	*stmt*	→	*expr* **SEMI**
2:	*expr*	→	*factor* **PLUS** *expr*
3:		|	*factor*
4:	*factor*	→	**NUMBER**

All you need do to prove that an input sentence (like `1+2;`) can be recognized for this grammar is come up with a derivation that can match the input sentence, token for token. The following derivation does just that (the ⇒ symbol means *derives),*

The ⇒ symbol.

stmt	⇒	*expr* **SEMI**	*by Production 1*
	⇒	*factor* **PLUS** *expr* **SEMI**	*by Production 2*
	⇒	**NUMBER PLUS** *expr* **SEMI**	*by Production 4*
	⇒	**NUMBER PLUS** *factor* **SEMI**	*by Production 3*
	⇒	**NUMBER PLUS NUMBER SEMI**	*by Production 4*

Leftmost derivation.

This process is called a *leftmost* derivation because you always replace the leftmost nonterminal in the partially-parsed sentence with the equivalent production's right-hand side. Start with the goal symbol (the topmost symbol in the grammar) and then replace the leftmost nonterminal at each step. The $\overset{L}{\Rightarrow}$ operator signifies a leftmost derivation. X$\overset{L}{\Rightarrow}$Y means "X derives Y by a leftmost derivation." You can say that expr **SEMI** $\overset{L}{\Rightarrow}$ factor **PLUS** expr **SEMI**

by substituting *expr* for its right-hand side. The foregoing derivation was created in a *top-down* fashion, starting with the topmost symbol in the grammar and working down to the tokens. This process is called a *top-down parse*.

Top-down parse.

Each of the steps in the earlier example (each partial derivation) is formally called a *viable prefix*. You can look at a viable prefix as a partially parsed sentence. Another useful term is a *handle*, which is the portion of the viable prefix that is replaced at each step in the derivation. The handle is always a contiguous sequence of zero or more symbols at the far right or far left of the viable prefix (depending on how the derivation is done).

Viable prefix, handle.

You can also have a *rightmost derivation* which starts with the goal symbol and replaces the rightmost nonterminal with each step. The $\overset{R}{\Rightarrow}$ operator can be used to indicate this kind of derivation. It's also possible to have a *bottom-up* parse—one that starts with the leaves of the tree and works its way up to the root. Bottom-up parsers use right-most derivations. They start with the input symbols and, when a *right-hand* side is encountered in a viable prefix, replaces the symbols that comprise the right-hand side with the equivalent left-hand side. You still go through the input from left to right, but you always replace the rightmost handle in the viable prefix. Using the same grammar and input as before, you can derive the goal symbol from the input symbols as follows:

Rightmost derivation.
Bottom-up parse.

	NUMBER PLUS NUMBER SEMI	*Start with the input.*
$\overset{R}{\Rightarrow}$	*factor* **PLUS NUMBER SEMI**	*Apply factor→***NUMBER**
$\overset{R}{\Rightarrow}$	*factor* **PLUS** *factor* **SEMI**	*Apply factor→***NUMBER**
$\overset{R}{\Rightarrow}$	*factor* **PLUS** *expr* **SEMI**	*Apply expr→factor*
$\overset{R}{\Rightarrow}$	*expr* **SEMI**	*Apply expr→factor* **PLUS** *expr*
$\overset{R}{\Rightarrow}$	*stmt*	*Apply stmt→expr* **SEMI**

The parser scans the viable prefix (the partially-parsed sentence) for a handle that matches the right-hand side of some production, and then replaces the handle with the left-hand side of that production. For example, **NUMBER** is the right-hand side of *factor*→**NUMBER**, and this production is applied in the first derivation, replacing the **NUMBER** with the *factor*. *factor* **PLUS** doesn't form a right hand side, so the parser moves to the next symbol, the second **NUMBER**, for the next replacement, and so forth. A practical bottom-up parser, which uses a rightmost derivation, is discussed in great detail in Chapter Five, so don't worry about it if the foregoing didn't sink in.

Note that top-down parsers that do rightmost derivations and bottom-up parsers that do leftmost derivations are theoretically possible, but they are difficult to implement. Similarly, you can go through the input from right to left rather than left to right, but again, the practice is not common.

In general, the $\Rightarrow$, $\overset{L}{\Rightarrow}$, and $\overset{R}{\Rightarrow}$ symbols mean that only one substitution has occurred between the left- and right-hand side of the equation. Several other forms of the $\Rightarrow$ symbol are commonly used: $\overset{*}{\Rightarrow}$ and $\overset{+}{\Rightarrow}$ means derives in zero or more and in one or more steps, respectively. The various forms can also be combined in reasonable ways: $\overset{L}{\underset{*}{\Rightarrow}}$ $\overset{L}{\underset{+}{\Rightarrow}}$ $\overset{R}{\underset{*}{\Rightarrow}}$ $\overset{R}{\underset{+}{\Rightarrow}}$.

We need one more term before continuing: if $S\overset{L}{\underset{*}{\Rightarrow}}\alpha$ (if there is a leftmost derivation of the viable prefix α from the nonterminal S), then α is sometimes called a *left-sentential* form of S. *Right-sentential form* is used for a rightmost derivation and a just plain *sentential form* is used when the type of derivation isn't known or doesn't matter. For example, **NUMBER PLUS** *expr* **SEMI** is a left-sentential form of *stmt* because *stmt*$\overset{L}{\underset{*}{\Rightarrow}}$**NUMBER PLUS** *expr* **SEMI**.

Sentential forms.

3.2.1 LL and LR Grammars

The concepts of left and right derivations apply directly to the two types of parsers that are discussed in Chapters Four and Five. In fact, the derivation closely follows the process that a parser uses to analyze the input sentence. Chapter Four discusses LL parsers, which go through the input stream from left to right (that's the first *L*), performing a leftmost derivation (that's the second *L*). Recursive-descent parsers, such as the ones examined in Chapter 1, are also LL parsers.

An LL grammar is a grammar that can be parsed by an LL parser. (There are many grammars that can't be so parsed.) An LL(1) grammar is a grammar that can be parsed by an LL parser with one symbol of lookahead. That is, if a nonterminal has more than one right-hand side, the parser can decide which one to apply by looking at the next input symbol.

It's possible to have an LL(k) grammar, where k is some number other than 1, and which requires k symbols of lookahead, but such grammars are not very practical. If the number is missing, 1 is assumed.

The other type of parser that we'll look at in this book is an LR parser which goes through the input from left to right, but does a bottom-up, rightmost derivation. The class of grammars that can be parsed by LR parsers are LR(k) grammars, and as before, we're interested primarily in LR(1) grammars, which require the parser to look ahead only one symbol to recognize a handle. LALR(k) grammars ("Look-Ahead" LR grammars), which are also discussed in depth in Chapter Five, are a special case of the more general LR(k) grammars.

3.3 Parse Trees and Semantic Difficulties

The grammar in Table 3.1 recognizes a very limited set of English sentences: A sentence is a subject and a predicate. Subjects are made up of nouns with an optional preceding article; predicates are either single verbs or a verb followed by a prepositional phrase; a prepositional phrase is a preposition followed by an object; and so on. A noun can be one of the tokens **time** or **arrow**.

You can use this grammar to parse the sentence: **Time flies like an arrow.** with the following leftmost derivation:

sentence	$\overset{L}{\Rightarrow}$	*subject predicate*	*by Production 1*
	$\overset{L}{\Rightarrow}$	*noun predicate*	*by Production 2*
	$\overset{L}{\Rightarrow}$	**time** *predicate*	*by Production 9*
	$\overset{L}{\Rightarrow}$	**time** *verb prep_phrase*	*by Production 5*
	$\overset{L}{\Rightarrow}$	**time flies** *prep_phrase*	*by Production 13*
	$\overset{L}{\Rightarrow}$	**time flies** *preposition object*	*by Production 6*
	$\overset{L}{\Rightarrow}$	**time flies like** *object*	*by Production 14*
	$\overset{L}{\Rightarrow}$	**time flies like** *article noun*	*by Production 8*
	$\overset{L}{\Rightarrow}$	**time flies like an** *noun*	*by Production 12*
	$\overset{L}{\Rightarrow}$	**time flies like an arrow**	*by Production 10*

The derivation process can be represented diagramatically as a *parse tree*, a graph in which the root node of each subtree is a nonterminal symbol in the language, and the subtree itself represents the right-hand side of a replaced symbol. The goal symbol is always at the apex of the parse tree. The parse tree for the previous derivation is in Figure 3.1.

Note that the parser would happily have applied *noun*→**time** in the last step of the derivation, even though *time flies like a time* is not a reasonable sentence, and this is an example of a *semantic* versus a *syntactic* problem—a meaning-related versus a structural

Table 3.1. A Grammar for an English Sentence

Production Number	Production Left-hand Side		Right-hand Side
1.	*sentence*	→	*subject predicate*
2.	*subject*	→	*noun*
3.		|	*article noun*
4.	*predicate*	→	*verb*
5.		|	*verb prep_phrase*
6.	*prep_phrase*	→	*preposition object*
7.	*object*	→	*noun*
8.		|	*article noun*
9.	*noun*	→	**time**
10.		|	**arrow**
11.	*article*	→	**a**
12.		|	**an**
13.	*verb*	→	**flies**
14.	*preposition*	→	**like**

problem. This situation often arises in computer-language implementations. The foregoing problem could probably be fixed grammatically, but it's not always possible to do so, and the resulting grammar will always be larger than necessary (the larger the grammar, the slower the parser). There's an even more serious problem that becomes clear when you add the following productions to the grammar:

noun → **time** | **banana**

The grammar now parses:

Fruit flies like a banana

without errors. Nonetheless, the sentence is actually parsed incorrectly because **flies** is being treated as a verb, not a noun. That is, you've just given bananas the capability of independent flight. You could try to rectify the situation by adding the following productions:

adjective	→	**fruit**
noun	→	**flies**

and modifying *subj* as follows:

subj → *noun* | *adjective noun*

But now, the grammar has become almost impossible to parse because the parser has to know the meanings of the various words in order to figure out which of the productions to apply. Making the wrong choice causes further errors (like the existence of a time fly, which can move forward or backwards in time to avoid being swatted). To parse both *time flies like an arrow* and *fruit flies like a banana* correctly, you'd have to know that there are no such things as time flies and that fruit can't fly, and it's very difficult (if not impossible) to build this semantic knowledge into a context-free grammar.

The foregoing example illustrates the limitations of context-free grammars, which can only specify syntax, not semantics. Though there are a few exceptions in artificial-intelligence applications, most real parsers are limited by the limitations of the grammar—they only know about syntax. Consequently, if semantic knowledge is

Figure 3.1. Evolution of a Parse Tree for *Time Flies Like An Arrow*

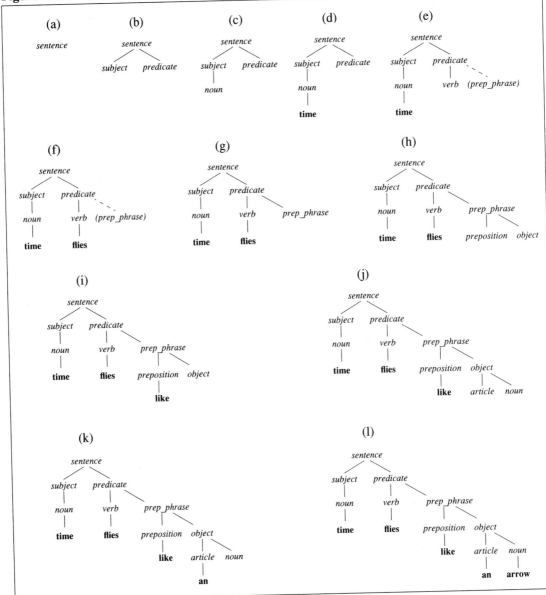

necessary to control the parse of a specific grammar, it becomes very difficult to build a computer program that can parse an input sentence. It's usually not possible to resolve all the semantic ambiguities of a computer language in the grammar. For example, the grammar itself can't tell you whether a variable is of the correct type when it's used in an expression, it can't recognize multiple declarations like **int** x, **long** x;, and so forth. To do the foregoing, you need to know something about meaning. Errors like the foregoing are best detected by the code-generation part of the compiler or by auxiliary code in the parser, not in the grammar itself.

3.4 ε Productions

I mentioned earlier that a grammatical phrase (a right-hand side) can be empty. More correctly, it's permitted for a right-hand side to match the empty string, ε. Productions of the form *s*→ε are called ε *productions* (pronounced "epsilon productions").

Consider the following grammar that recognizes compound statements:

1:	*compound_stmt*	→	**LEFT_CURLY** *stmt* **RIGHT_CURLY**
2:	*stmt*	→	**NUMBER**
3:		|	ε
...			

I've simplified by defining a statement as either a single number or an empty string. This grammar supports empty compound statements, as does C. First, note that an ε production can effectively disappear from a derivation. The input { } generates the following derivation:

compound_stmt $\overset{L}{\Rightarrow}$
$\overset{L}{\Rightarrow}$

The application of *expr*→ε effectively removes the nonterminal from the derivation by replacing it with an empty string. This disappearance is important when you consider how an LL parser decides which of several productions to apply when the nonterminal being replaced has several right-hand sides. There's no problem if all of the right-hand sides start with different terminal symbols; the parser can decide on the basis of the look-ahead symbol. If the current lookahead symbol matches one of the terminals, then the production whose right-hand side starts with that symbol is used. This kind of grammar—where the leftmost symbols of all the right-hand sides of any given nonterminal are different terminal symbols—is called an *S grammar*, and S grammars are among the simplest of the LL(1) grammars to recognize.

S grammars.

An ε production causes problems because the parser has to look beyond the current production to make its decision. The parser still decides whether or not a symbol matches an empty string by looking at the next input symbol, but it also has to look at the grammatical symbols that can <u>follow</u> the nonterminal that goes to ε. In the current example, if the next input symbol is a **NUMBER**, then the parser can apply *stmt*→**NUMBER**. It applies the ε production if the next input symbol is a **CLOSE_CURLY**. The reasoning here is that, if an empty string is matched, then the current nonterminal can effectively disappear from the derivation, and as a consequence, the next input symbol must be a symbol that can follow that nonterminal.

Since the parser can decide which production to apply in the current grammar by looking at a single lookahead character, then this is an LL(1) grammar. If a *stmt* could start with a **CLOSE_CURLY**, or if a **NUMBER** could follow a *stmt*, then the parser wouldn't be able to decide what to do, and the grammar would not be LL(1). The real situation is a little more complicated than the foregoing would indicate—I'll discuss the ins and outs of LL(1) grammars in depth in the next chapter. The current example serves to illustrate the sorts of problems that are involved, however.

3.5 The End-of-Input Marker

Another symbol that bears mentioning is the end-of-input marker, represented by ⊢. Strictly speaking, the end-of-input marker is treated as a token, and it always follows the rightmost symbol on the right-hand side of the start production—the one with the goal symbol on its left-hand side. An explicit ⊢ is often omitted from a grammar, however. The ⊢ is still there—it's just not shown. This omission doesn't present problems in many

The ⊢ symbol.

situations. Consider the case of a Pascal program that has to end in a period. The starting production in a Pascal grammar could look like this:

> *program* → *definitions* **PERIOD**

and the parser would just look for the period to detect the end of the input sentence. Any input that followed the period, including the ⊢, could be ignored in this situation. The situation is complicated in C, because the start production can look like this:

> *program* → *definitions* | ε

In this case, the parser has to look for an ⊢ marker, even though there's no explicit marker in the grammar. Just mentally tack a ⊢ to the end of all the right-hand sides of the start production. (Remember, ε is an identity element for string concatenation, so ε⊢ is the same thing as ⊢.)

3.6 Right-Linear Grammars

State machines and grammars.

This section moves away from a general discussion of grammars to the specifics of implementing them. Chapter Two described how state machines can be used for lexical analysis, and the notion of a regular definition, a grammatical representation of the input language, was also introduced. It turns out that all languages that can be represented as state machines can also be represented grammatically, and I'll use this similarity to demonstrate the relationships between the two systems here.

Right-linear grammars.

Grammars that can be translated to DFAs are called *right-linear* grammars. A grammar is right-linear if the right-hand side of each nonterminal has at most one nonterminal in it, and that nonterminal is at the far right of the right-hand side. (A *left-linear* grammar is the same, except that the nonterminal symbol must be at the far left.)

Translating a right-linear grammar to a DFA.

A right-linear grammar can be translated directly into a DFA if all productions in the grammar are either of the form $a{\rightarrow}ε$ or $a{\rightarrow}X\ b$. That is, the right-hand side must either be ε, or it must be made up of a single terminal symbol followed by a single nonterminal symbol. To make a DFA, you must add the further restriction that, if a production has more than one right-hand side, the right-hand sides must all start with different symbols. (If they don't, you have an NFA.) The state machine is created from the grammar as follows:

(1)   The set of terminal symbols in the grammar form the DFA's input alphabet.
(2)   The set of nonterminal symbols in the grammar form the states in the DFA. The start production is the DFA start state.
(3)   If a production takes the form $a{\rightarrow}ε$, then State a is an accepting state.
(4)   If a production takes the form $a{\rightarrow}X\ b$, then a transition is made from State a to State b on the character **X**.

Figure 3.2 shows both a state machine and grammar for recognizing a subset of the C floating-point constants (the regular expression `D*\.D|D\.D*` is recognized).

A parser for this sort of grammar is, of course, trivial to implement. In fact, that's what the L^EX-generated state-machine driver is—a parser for a right-linear grammar. State transitions are made based on the current state and input character, and an action is executed when an accepting state is entered. A right-linear grammar that doesn't have the properties discussed earlier can easily be modified to have the required properties using the transformation rules discussed in Chapter Four.

Figure 3.2. State-machine and Grammar That Recognizes `D*\.D|D\.D*`

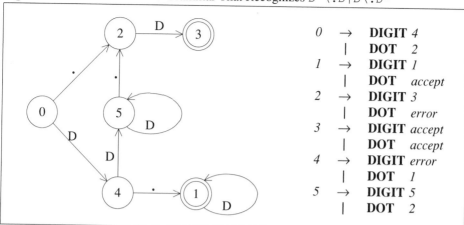

3.7 Lists, Recursion, and Associativity

Probably the most common grammatical structure is a list. Programs are lists of variable declarations and subroutines, subroutines are lists of statements, expressions are lists of identifiers and constants delimited by operators, and so forth. We've actually been using lists informally up until now, but it's worthwhile to look at them in depth.

3.7.1 Simple Lists

Lists are loops, and loops are implemented grammatically using recursion. You can see what's going on graphically by looking at the grammatical representations of States 1 and 5 in Figure 3.2 on page 175. The loops in these states recognize lists of digits, but you can use the same grammatical structure to recognize loops of any sort.

The recursion can be implemented in two ways. A *left-recursive* production is one *Left and right recursion.* where the left-hand side appears as the leftmost symbol on the right-hand side. A *right-recursive* production is the other way around, the left-hand side is duplicated at the far right. Note that a grammar can be right (or left) recursive and not be right (or left) linear because there can be more than one nonterminal on the right-hand side.

The following grammar provides an example of a simple, left-recursive list of statements:

$$stmt\_list \quad \rightarrow \quad stmt\_list \ \ stmt$$
$$| \quad stmt$$

If you also supply a simple definition of *stmt* as one of three terminal symbols:

$$stmt \quad \rightarrow \quad \textbf{A} \ | \ \textbf{B} \ | \ \textbf{C}$$

then the list ABC generates the parse tree in Figure 3.3.

A typical parser creates the parse tree from left to right as it reads the input, but it *Associativity and recursion.* does a left-to-right, depth-first traversal of the parse tree as it generates code. (The tree is traversed left-to-right, but the nodes further down on the tree are visited first.) The subscripts in Figure 3.3 show the order in which nodes are visited. Assuming that the code that processes a statement is executed when the *stmt_list* nodes are traversed, the list elements are processed from left to right. That is, the elements in the list associate from left to right. This is always the case. Left-recursive productions always associate from left to right.

Figure 3.3. Parse Tree for a Simple, Left-Recursive List

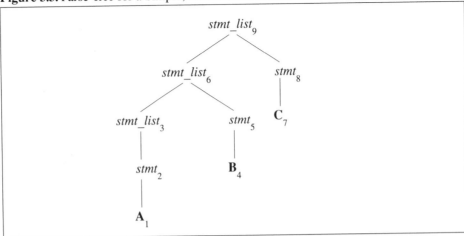

Changing the grammar to a right-recursive form illustrates the change to right associativity. The new grammar looks like this:

$$stmt\_list \quad \rightarrow \quad stmt \; stmt\_list \mid stmt$$
$$stmt \qquad\quad \rightarrow \quad \mathbf{A} \mid \mathbf{B} \mid \mathbf{C}$$

and the parse tree for ABC is shown in Figure 3.4. Again, a depth-first traversal causes the nodes to be visited in the indicated order, and the important thing is the order in which the *stmt_list* nodes are visited. The elements in this list are processed from right to left.

Figure 3.4. Parse Tree for a Simple, Right-Recursive List

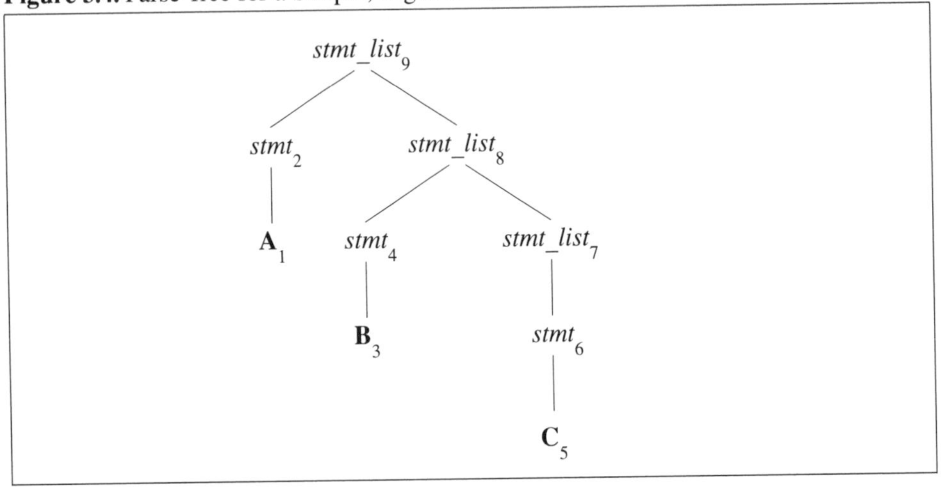

Fudging left associativity with a right-recursive grammar.

Recursive-descent parsers can cheat and generate code as the tree is built from the top down. This cheating can give surprising results, because a list can be processed from left to right, even though the grammar would indicate otherwise. For example, Listing 3.1 shows the list being processed from left to right, and Listing 3.2 processes the same input from right to left. The grammar is the same, right-recursive grammar in both listings, but the position of the `process_statement()` subroutine has been changed. In Listing 3.1, `process_statement()` is called before the recursive `stmt_list()` call, so the list element is processed before the subtree is built. In the second listing, the processing happens after the recursive call, so the subtree will have been traversed before the list element is processed.

Listing 3.1. Left Associativity with a Right-Recursive Grammar

```
1   stmt_list()
2   {
3       /* Code is generated as you create the tree, before the subtree is
4        * processed.
5        */
6
7       remember = stmt();
8
9       process_statement( remember );
10
11      if( not_at_end_of_input() )
12          stmt_list();
13  }
14
15  stmt()
16  {
17      return( read() );
18  }
```

Listing 3.2. Right Associativity with a Right-Recursive Grammar

```
1   stmt_list()
2   {
3       /* Code is generated as you create the tree, after the subtree is
4        * processed.
5        */
6
7       remember = stmt();
8
9       if( not_at_end_of_input() )
10          stmt_list();
11
12      process_stmt();
13  }
14
15  stmt()
16  {
17      return read();
18  }
```

Since you can't have left recursion in a recursive-descent parser, this technique is often useful, but it can also cause maintenance problems, because some code is generated as the tree is created, but other code must be generated as the tree is traversed. You can't apply this technique in processing expressions, for example. Consequently, it's usually best always to generate code after the call to a subroutine that visits a subtree, not before it. In Chapter Four, we'll look at a method for modifying grammars that can eliminate the left recursion but maintain the left associativity; in general, this is the best approach.

There is one maintainable way to get left associativity with a right-associative grammar, though this method can be used only occasionally. Looking again at Figure 3.4, you'll notice that the *stmt* nodes are processed from left to right, even though the *stmt_list* nodes go from right to left. Consequently, if the statements can be processed in *stmt* rather than in *stmt_list*, the associativity is effectively reversed.

Strictly speaking, the grammars we've been looking at are *self* left or right recursive. *Self recursive* productions are those where the left-hand side appears at one end or the other of the right-hand side. It's also possible for a grammar to have *indirect* recursion, however. Here, one or more steps have to be added to a derivation before the recursion becomes evident. For example, the following grammar has indirect left recursion in it:

1.	*s*	$\rightarrow$	*a* **AHH**
2.	*a*	$\rightarrow$	*c* **CHOO**
3.	*c*	$\rightarrow$	*s* **DOO_WOP**

because, all derivations that start with *s* ultimately end up with an *s* on the far left of the viable prefix (of the partial derivation):

$$s \quad \overset{L}{\Rightarrow} \quad a \text{ \textbf{AHH}} \qquad \qquad by\ Production\ 1$$
$$\overset{L}{\Rightarrow} \quad c \text{ \textbf{CHOO AHH}} \qquad by\ Production\ 2$$
$$\overset{L}{\Rightarrow} \quad s \text{ \textbf{DOO\_WOP CHOO AHH}} \qquad by\ Production\ 3$$

In general, indirect recursion is not desirable in a grammar because it masks the fact that the grammar is recursive.

3.7.2 The Number of Elements in a List

The grammar we just looked at creates a list with at least one element in it. It's possible for a list to be empty, however. The following productions recognize zero or more declarations:

$$decl\_list \quad \rightarrow \quad decl\_list \quad declaration$$
$$| \quad \varepsilon$$

Productions executed first or last.

Since a *decl_list* can go to ε, the list could be empty. Parse trees for left and right recursive lists of this type are shown in Figure 3.5. Notice here, that the *decl_list*→ε production is the first list-element that's processed in the the left-recursive list, and it's the last list-element processed in the right-recursive list. The same sort of thing was also true in the nonempty lists that we looked at in the last section—the *stmt_list*→*stmt* production was processed only once in both types of lists, and it was processed first in the left-recursive list and last in the right-recursive list. This fact comes in handy when you're doing code generation, because you can use the ε production to trigger initializations or clean-up actions. The technique is used heavily in Chapter Six.

It's also possible to specify a limited number of repetitions, using something like the following:

$$list \quad \rightarrow \quad element$$
$$| \quad element\ element$$
$$| \quad element\ element\ element$$

The method is cumbersome, but workable. Though this method is the only way to do it with a grammar, you can solve the limited-number-of-repetitions problem semantically rather than syntactically. Instead of building the counts into the grammar, you can use a more general-purpose list and have the parser keep track of how many times the list productions are applied, printing an error message if there are an incorrect number of repetitions.

Figure 3.5. Lists Terminated with ε Productions

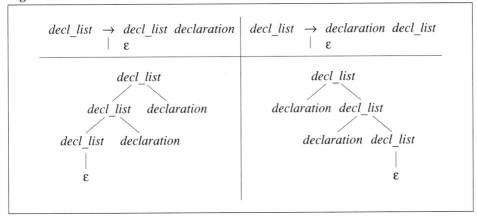

3.7.3 Lists with Delimiters

Most lists must incorporate delimiters of some sort into them, and the delimiters can be handled in two ways. In C, for example, a comma <u>separates</u> multiple names in a declaration, as in:

```
int x, y, z;
```

Semicolons <u>terminate</u> elements of a list of several declarations, however. Both types of lists are illustrated in the following grammar:

$$
\begin{array}{lll}
decl\_list & \rightarrow & decl\_list \quad declaration \\
           & | & \varepsilon \\
declaration & \rightarrow & declarator\_list \quad specifier\_list \quad \textbf{SEMICOLON} \\
declarator\_list & \rightarrow & \textbf{TYPE} \quad declarator \\
           & | & \varepsilon \\
specifier\_list & \rightarrow & specifier\_list \quad \textbf{COMMA} \quad \textbf{NAME} \\
           & | & \textbf{NAME}
\end{array}
$$

A *decl_list* is a list of zero or more declarations (it's left associative). The *declaration* production defines a single list element. It is made up of declarators followed by specifiers, and is terminated with a **SEMICOLON**. Since **SEMICOLON** is a terminator, it's at the far right of the production that describes the list element, rather than being in the list-production (the *decl_list*) itself. A *declarator_list* is a simple list of zero or more **TYPE** tokens. Finally, a *specifier_list* is a **COMMA**-separated list of identifiers. Here, the **COMMA**, since it is a separator, is part of the list-definition production itself.

The *specifier_list* is left recursive. A right-recursive version of the same thing could be done like this:

$$
\begin{array}{lll}
specifier\_list & \rightarrow & \textbf{NAME} \quad \textbf{COMMA} \quad specifier\_list \\
           & | & \textbf{NAME}
\end{array}
$$

The relative positions of the **COMMA** and **NAME** must also be reversed here. Common ways to do the various types of lists are all summarized in Table 3.2.

Table 3.2. List Grammars

	No Separator	
	Right associative	**Left associative**
At least one element	*list* → MEMBER *list* | MEMBER	*list* → *list* MEMBER | MEMBER
Zero elements okay	*list* → MEMBER *list* | ε	*list* → *list* MEMBER | ε
	Separator Between List Elements	
	Right associative	**Left associative**
At least one element	*list* → MEMBER **delim** *list* | MEMBER	*list* → *list* **delim** MEMBER | MEMBER
Zero elements okay	*list* → MEMBER *more list* | ε *more* → **delim** MEMBER *more* | ε	*list* → *list* MEMBER *more* | ε *more* → *more* **delim** MEMBER | ε

A MEMBER is a list element; it can be a terminal, a nonterminal, or a collection of terminals and nonterminals. If you want the list to be a list of terminated objects such as semicolon-terminated declarations, MEMBER should take the form: MEMBER→ α **TERMINATOR**, where α is a collection of one or more terminal or nonterminal symbols.

3.8 Expressions

One special form of a list is an expression. For example `1+2+3` is a plus-sign-delimited list of numbers. Table 3.3 shows a grammar that recognizes a list of one or more statements, each of which is an arithmetic expression followed by a semicolon. A *stmt* is made up of a series of semicolon-delimited expressions (*exprs*), each a series of numbers separated either by asterisks (for multiplication) or plus signs (for addition). This grammar has several properties that are worth discussing in depth.

Table 3.3. A Simple Expression Grammar

1.	*stmt*	→	*expr* **;**
2.		|	*expr* **;** *stmt*
3.	*expr*	→	*expr* **+** *term*
4.		|	*term*
5.	*term*	→	*term* ***** *factor*
6.		|	*factor*
7.	*factor*	→	**number**
8.		|	**(** *expr* **)**

Depth-first traversal.

Figure 3.6 shows the parse tree generated by the foregoing grammar when the input statement `1+2*(3+4)+5;` is processed. The code-generation pass does a *depth-first* traversal of the tree—the deeper nodes are always processed first. The subscripts in the figure show the order in which the nodes are visited. Assuming that code is generated only after an entire right-hand side has been processed, the depth-first traversal forces the `3+4` to be done first (because it's deepest in the tree and the *expr* associated with the subexpression `3+4` is processed before any of the other *exprs*); then, moving up the tree, the result of the previous addition is multiplied by the `2`; then `1` is added to the accumulated subexpression; and, finally, the `5` is added into the total.

Figure 3.6. A Parse Tree for `1+2*(3+4)+5;`

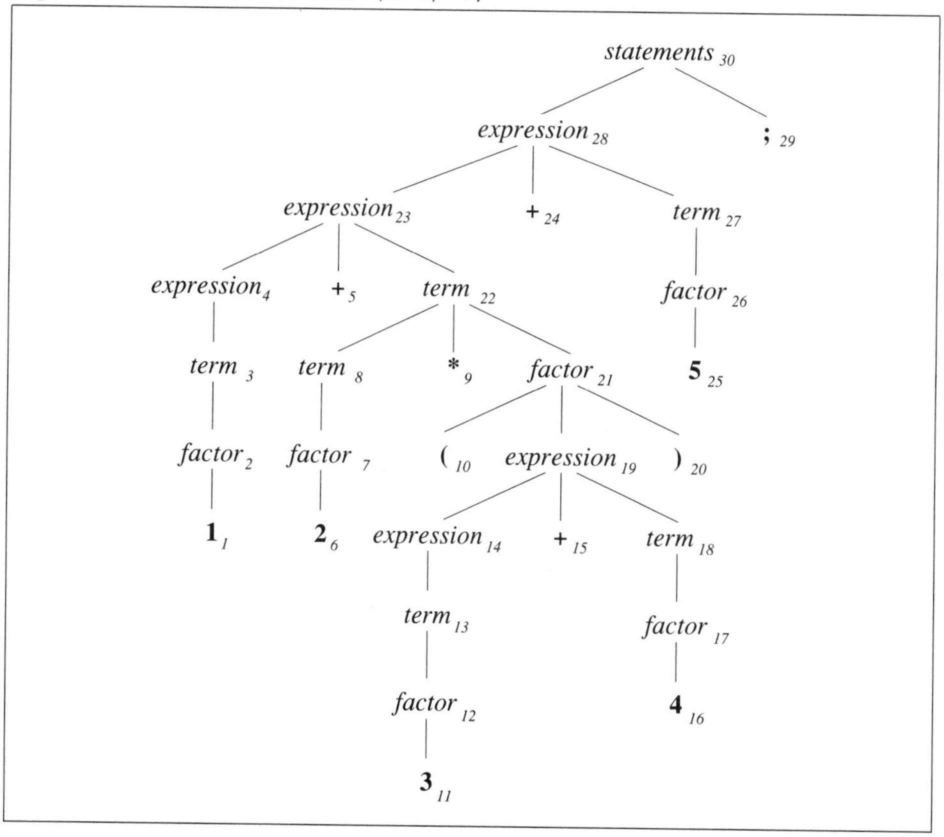

Note that the order of evaluation is what you would expect—assuming that multiplication is higher precedence than addition, that addition associates from left to right, and that parenthesized expressions are evaluated first. Since the parse tree in Figure 3.7 is the only possible one, given the grammar used, this means that associativity and precedence are actually side effects of the grammatical structure. In particular, subtrees that are lower down on the parse tree are always processed first, and positioning a production further down in the grammar guarantees a lower relative position in the parse tree. Higher-precedence operators should then be placed lower down in the grammar, as is the case in the grammar used here. (The only way to get to a *term* is through an *expr*, so multiplication is always further down the tree than addition.) Parentheses, since they are at the bottom of the grammar, have higher precedence than any operator. The associativity is still determined by left or right recursion, as is the case in a simple list.

Order of evaluation as controlled by grammar.

Unary operators tend to be lower in the grammar because they are usually higher precedence than the binary operators. You can add unary minus to the previous grammar by modifying the factor rules as follows:

Unary operators.

1.	*stmt*	→	*expr* ;
2.		|	*expr* ; *stmt*
3.	*expr*	→	*expr* + *term*
4.		|	*term*
5.	*term*	→	*term* * *unop*
6.		|	*unop*
7.	*unop*	→	− *factor*
8.		|	*factor*
9.	*factor*	→	**number**
10.		|	(expr)

The placement of the new productions insure that unary minus can be applied to parenthesized subexpressions as well as single operands.

Unary operators can sometimes be treated as lists. For example, the C pointer-dereference operators (*), can pile up to the left of the operand, like this: ***p. You can introduce a star into the previous grammar by adding the following list production:

factor → * *factor*

Note that the right recursion correctly forces right-to-left associativity for this operator.

3.9 Ambiguous Grammars

The expression grammar just discussed is a *unambiguous* grammar because only one possible parse tree can be created from any given input stream. The same parse tree is generated, regardless of the derivation used. It's possible to write an *ambiguous* grammar, however. For example, expressions could be represented as follows:

statement	→	*expr* ;
expr	→	*expr* + *expr*
	|	*expr* * *expr*
	|	(*expr*)
	|	*number*

A grammar is ambiguous when the same nonterminal appears twice on a right-hand side (because the order in which the nonterminals are evaluated is dependent on the derivation). Two of the possible parse trees that can be generated for A+B*C are shown in Figure 3.7.

Ambiguous grammars are generally to be avoided exactly because they're ambiguous. That is, because there are two possible parse trees, the expression can be evaluated in two different ways, and there's no way to predict which one of these ways will be used from the grammar itself. Precedence and associativity can't be controlled by the grammar alone. Ambiguous grammars do tend to be smaller, however, and easier to read. So, parser-generation programs like **yacc** and **occs** generally provide mechanisms for using them. These programs can force specific associativity or precedence by controlling the parse in predetermined ways when an ambiguous production is encountered. The technique is discussed in depth in Chapter Five.

Figure 3.7. Parse Trees Derived from an Ambiguous Grammar

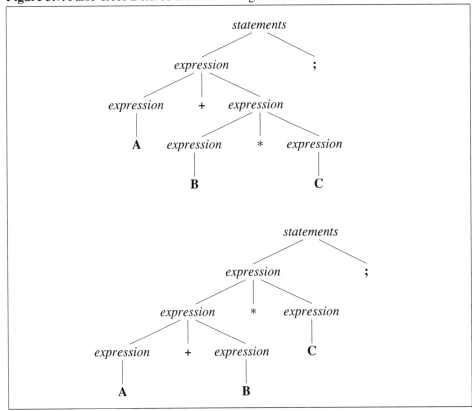

3.10 Syntax-Directed Translation

I mentioned earlier that if the syntactic scope of a language was sufficiently limited, you could derive semantic information from a formal grammar—from the position of particular symbols in the input sentence, and by extension in the grammar itself. This is how compilers, in fact, generate code—by executing code-generation actions at times that are controlled by the positions of various strings in the input sentence. We did this on an ad-hoc basis in Chapter One, first by building a parser for a grammar, and then by adding code-generation actions to the parser. The process is discussed in greater depth in this section.

3.10.1 Augmented Grammars

In an augmented grammar, code-generation actions are placed in the grammar itself, and the relative position of the action in the grammar determines when it is executed. For example, a production like this:

Augmentations.

$$expr!' \rightarrow + \text{ } term \text{ } \{ \texttt{op} (\text{ } '+' \text{ }) ; \} \text{ } expr'$$

could be coded in a recursive-descent parser as follows:

```
expr_prime()
{
    if( match( PLUS ) )
    {
        term();
        op('+');
        expr_prime();
    }
}
```

Generating code to evaluate expressions.

I'll demonstrate how an augmented grammar works by generating code to evaluate expressions. You need two subroutines for this purpose, both of which generate code. In addition, between the two of them, they manage a local stack of temporary-variable names. An expression of the form 1+2+3 generates the following code:

```
t0 = 1;
t1 = 2;
t0 += t1;
t1 = 3;
t0 += t1;
```

Anonymous temporaries.

The variables t0 and t1 are known as *anonymous temporaries* (or just plain *temporaries*) because the compiler makes up the names, not the programmer. The actual code is generated with the following sequence of actions (the numbers identify individual actions, several of which are repeated):

(1)   Read the 1.
(2)   Get a temporary-variable name (t0), and output t0 = 1.
(3)   Push the temporary-variable name onto a local stack.
(4)   Read the "+" and remember it.
(1)   Read the 2.
(2)   Get a temporary-variable name (t1), and output t1 = 2.
(3)   Push the temporary-variable name onto a local stack.
(5)   Pop two temporary-variable names off the stack and generate code to add them together: t0 += t1 [you're adding because you remembered it in (4)].
(6)   Push the name of the temporary that holds the result of the previous operation and discard the second one.
(4)   Read the "+" and remember it.
(1)   Read the 3.
(2)   Get a temporary-variable name (t1), and output t1 = 3.
(3)   Push the temporary name onto a local stack.
(5)   Pop two temporary-variable names off the stack and generate code to add them together: t0 += t1.
(6)   Push the name of the temporary that holds the result of the previous operation and discard the second one.

When you're done, the name of the anonymous temporary that holds the evaluated expression is at the top of the stack. Many of the previous actions are identical—the time that the action is executed is the important factor here.

The subroutines that do the work are in Listing 3.3. Temporary-variable names are allocated and freed with the newname() and freename() calls on lines nine and ten using the method described in Chapter One. You allocate a name by popping it off a stack (declared on line six), and free the name by pushing it back. I've removed the error-detection code to simplify things.

The rest of Listing 3.3 shows the code-generation actions. The create_tmp() subroutine (on line 14) does two things, it generates the code that copies the current lexeme

Listing 3.3. *expr.y*— Action Code for the Augmented Grammar

```
 1   #include <tools/stack.h>                    /* Described in Appendix A. */
 2
 3   stack_dcl(Temporaries, char*, 128);    /* Temporaries: stack of 128 char ptrs. */
 4   /*-----------------------------------------------------------------------*/
 5
 6   char   *Names[] = { "t0", "t1", "t2", "t3", "t4", "t5", "t6", "t7" };
 7   char   **Namep  = Names;
 8
 9   char   *newname()            { return( *Namep++ ); }
10   void   freename(s) char *s; { *--Namep = s;       }
11
12   /*-----------------------------------------------------------------------*/
13
14   create_tmp( str )        /* Create a temporary holding str and push its name. */
15   char *str;
16   {
17       char    *name = getname();
18       yy_code("    %s = %s;\n", name, str );
19       push( Temporaries, name );
20   }
21
22   op( what )
23   int what;
24   {
25       char *left, *right;
26
27       right = pop( Temporaries );
28       left  = tos( Temporaries );
29
30       yy_code("    %s %c= %s;\n", left, what, right );
31       freename(right);
32   }
```

into an anonymous temporary, and it pushes the name of that temporary onto the `Temporaries` stack. The `op()` subroutine on line 22 generates code to do the actual operation. It takes two temporary-variable names from the `Temporaries` and generates the code necessary to perform the required operation. Note that only one of the temporaries is actually popped. The other remains on the stack because it holds the result of the generated operation. The popped name is recycled for future use on line 31.

Now, armed with the proper tools, you can design the parser. The augmented grammar in Table 3.4 performs the actions described earlier in the correct order. The "remember it" action is implicit in the grammar itself (because, to get to the `op()` call in Production 4, for example, you must have passed a previous +). The order of evaluation is controlled, as usual, by the structure of the parse tree and the fact that you're doing a bottom-up traversal. Action symbols in the grammar are treated like other terminal symbols—they're just put onto the parse tree in the appropriate places and executed when that node is traversed. A parse tree for 1+2+3 is shown in Figure 3.8. The subscripts indicate the order in which nodes are visited.

Designing the parser.

An exercise is in order at this juncture. Take a pencil and piece of paper and draw both the parse tree and the contents of the `Temporaries` stack (which holds the temporary-variable names) as the expression 1+2*3 is parsed. Note how the `Temporaries` stack keeps track of the name of the variable that holds the 1 until after the higher-precedence multiplication operator is processed. The 2 is stored in the same way until the parenthesized subexpression can be handled. Also, note how the name at top of

Table 3.4. An Augmented Expression Grammar

1.	*stmt*	$\rightarrow$	ε
2.		|	*expr* **;** *stmt*
3.	*expr*	$\rightarrow$	*term expr'*
4.	*expr'*	$\rightarrow$	**+** *term* {op('+') ; } *expr'*
5.		|	ε
6.	*term*	$\rightarrow$	*factor term'*
7.	*term'*	$\rightarrow$	***** *factor* {op('*') ; } *term'*
8.		|	ε
9.	*factor*	$\rightarrow$	**number_or_id** {create_tmp(yytext); }
10.		|	**(** *expr* **)**

Figure 3.8. Augmented Parse Tree for 1+2+3

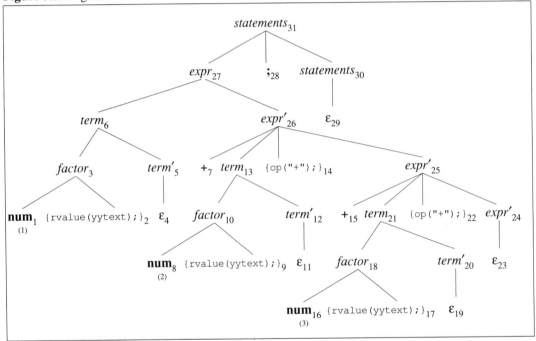

stack always holds the value of the most recently processed subexpression.

3.10.2 Attributed Grammars

Attributes.

So far, the concept of an *attribute* has been used in a limited, informal way. An attribute is a piece of information that is associated with a grammatical symbol. Tokens all have at least one attribute—the associated lexeme. They can have other attributes as well. For example a **NUMBER** token could have an integer attribute that was the number represented by the lexeme. A **NAME** token could have an attribute that was a pointer to a symbol-table entry for that name. Attributes of this type are usually represented with subscripts. For example, the two attributes attached to a **NUMBER** could be represented as follows:

NUMBER$_{("156", 156)}$

The first attribute is the lexeme, the second is the numeric value of the lexeme.

Nonterminal symbols can have attributes as well. Take, for example, a recursive-descent parser. You can look at the subroutines that implement nonterminals as symbols that represent the nonterminal, not the other way around. Looked at in this way, a subroutine's argument or return value represents a quantum of information that is attached to the grammatical symbol—to the nonterminal that the subroutine is implementing, so the subroutine arguments and return values can be viewed as the attributes of the associated nonterminal symbol.

Attributes for nonterminals.

There are two types of attributes that are attached to nonterminals, and these two types correspond to the two methods used to pass information around in the two parsers presented at the end of Chapter One. An *inherited* attribute is passed down the parse tree, from a parent to a child, so in a recursive-descent compiler, inherited attributes are subroutine arguments. A *synthesized* attribute goes in the other direction, up the tree from a child to a parent. In a recursive-descent compiler, synthesized attributes are return values.[1] The best way to keep track of which term is which is to think of the actual English usage of the two words. Children "inherit" something from their parents, not the other way around. So, an "inherited" attribute is one that's passed from the parent to the child in the parse tree. The code-generation in the previous section was done without the benefit of attributes. That is, all information was passed between code-generation actions using global variables rather than attaching the information to the grammatical elements themselves. Drawing an analogy to recursive-descent parsers, it's as if you didn't use subroutine arguments or return values anywhere in the parser.

Inherited and synthesized attributes.

The attribute mechanism can be extended to grammars in general and is very useful in designing a compiler. The attributes can help you specify code-generation actions in the grammar in greater detail than would be possible with an augmented grammar alone. A grammar to which attributes have been added in this way is called an *attributed grammar*. In a typical compiler design, you put attributes into the grammar in a manner similar to the augmentations used in the previous sections. That is, the first step in the design process is the creation of an augmented and *attributed* grammar. It's easier to understand the concepts, however, if you start with working code, so I'll demonstrate the process by going backwards from a working parser to an attributed, augmented grammar. The naive recursive-descent parser in Listing 3.4 implements the following grammar:

Attributed grammar.

1.	*stmt*	→	ε
2.		|	*expr* **;** *stmt*
3.	*expr*	→	*term expr′*
4.	*expr′*	→	**+** *term expr′*
5.		|	ε
6.	*term*	→	*factor term′*
7.	*term′*	→	***** *factor term′*
8.		|	ε
9.	*factor*	→	**number**
10.		|	**(** *expr* **)**

This parser is essentially the naive parser developed in Chapter One, where you'll find the `match()` and `advance()` subroutines that comprise the lexical analyzer, `newname()` and `freename()` were discussed earlier. The parser uses inherited

---

1. In ALGOL-like languages such as Pascal, an inherited attribute is a subroutine argument that's passed by value; a synthesized attribute is either passed by reference or is a function's return value.

attributes, which are passed down the parse tree from parent to child as subroutine arguments.

Listing 3.4. *naive.c*— Code Generation with Synthesized Attributes

```
 1   void     factor   ( char *t );          /* Prototypes to avoid  */
 2   void     term     ( char *t );          /* forward references   */
 3   void     expr     ( char *t );          /* in the code.         */
 4
 5   stmt()                          /*  stmt -> expr SEMI  |  expr SEMI stmt   */
 6   {
 7       char *t;
 8
 9       while( !match(EOI) )
10       {
11           expr( t = newname() );
12           freename( t );
13
14           if( match( SEMI ) )
15               advance();
16       }
17   }
18   /*------------------------------------------------------------------*/
19   void     expr( t )                          /* expr  -> term expr' */
20   char     *t;
21   {
22       term( t );
23       expr_prime( t );
24   }
25   /*------------------------------------------------------------------*/
26   expr_prime( t )                 /* expr' -> PLUS term expr'  |  epsilon */
27   char     *t;
28   {
29       char *t2;
30
31       if( match( PLUS ) )
32       {
33           advance();
34
35           term( t2 = newname() );
36
37           printf("    %s += %s\n", t, t2 );
38           freename( t2 );
39
40           expr_prime( t );
41       }
42   }
43   /*------------------------------------------------------------------*/
44   void     term( t )                          /* term  -> factor term' */
45   char     *t;
46   {
47       factor     ( t );
48       term_prime ( t );
49   }
50   /*------------------------------------------------------------------*/
51   term_prime( t )                 /* term' -> TIMES factor term'  |  epsilon */
52   char     *t;
53   {
54       char *t2 ;
55
```

Listing 3.4. continued...

```
56        if( match( TIMES ) )
57        {
58            advance();
59
60            factor( t2 = newname() );
61
62            printf("    %s *= %s\n", t, t2 );
63            freename( t2 );
64
65            term_prime( t );
66        }
67    }
68    /*------------------------------------------------------------------*/
69    void     factor( t )                    /* factor -> NUMBER_OR_ID | LP expr RP   */
70    char     *t;
71    {
72        if( match(NUMBER_OR_ID) )
73        {
74            printf("    %s = %0.*s\n", t, yyleng, yytext );
75            advance();
76        }
77        else if( match(LP) )
78        {
79            advance();
80
81            expr( t );
82
83            if( match(RP) )
84                advance();
85        }
86    }
```

Now, consider the flow of attributes (the temporary-variable names) through the parse tree as the expression `1+2*3` is processed. The parser generates the following output:

```
t0 = 1
t1 = 2
t2 = 3
t1 *= t2
t0 += t1
```

and the associated parse tree is shown in Figure 3.9. The flow of attributes is shown in this figure by labeling edges in the graph with the attribute's value. That is, the fact that `stmt()` passes `t0` to `expr()` is indicated by labeling the edge between the *stmt* and *expr* nodes with a `t0`. The attribute is in boldface when the calling function creates that attribute with a `newname()` call; otherwise, the attribute came into a function as an argument and was passed to a child function. You should trace through the first few subroutine calls in the parse to see what's happening. Remember, each child node in the tree represents a subroutine call made by the parent, and the attributes are subroutine arguments, so they flow down the tree from the parent to the child.

You can represent the flow of attributes by borrowing the notation used for arguments in a programming language. Each attribute has a name just like subroutine arguments have names. All attributes that are passed into a production are listed next to the name on the left-hand side of that production, like a formal argument list in a subroutine declaration. Those attributes can then be referenced by name by the symbols on the

Borrow attribute notation from subroutine-calling conventions.

Figure 3.9. The Flow of Inherited Attributes Through a Parse Tree for `1+2*3`

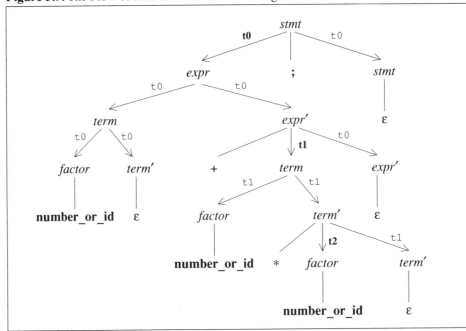

right-hand side of the production, as if they were used in the subroutine. For example, the fact that an attribute representing a temporary variable name is to an *expr* is represented like this in the subroutine representing the *expr*:

```
expr( t )
char  *t;
{
    . . .
}
```

and like this in the grammar:

$$expr_{(t)} \rightarrow \ldots$$

A *t* attribute would also be attached to every *expr* on a right-hand side, as if it were the argument to a recursive subroutine call:

$$stmt \rightarrow expr_{(t)} ; stmt$$

If the same attribute appears on both the left- and right-hand sides, then that attribute comes into the subroutine as an argument, and is passed down to a child subroutine, in turn. An attribute can also be used internally in an action, as if it were a variable.

Attributes can also be created within an action in a manner analogous to local variables, and that new attribute can be, in turn, passed to another grammatical symbol (to a subroutine) as an attribute (as an argument). Note that a leftmost derivation requires the flow of attributes to be from left-to-right across the production, just like the flow of control in a recursive-descent parser that implements the grammar. So, in an LL parser (which uses a leftmost derivation), inherited attributes can be passed from a left-hand side to a symbol on the right-hand side, and an attribute can be passed from a code-generation action to a symbol to its right. Synthesized attributes are used differently, and are discussed in depth in Chapter Five along with the bottom-up parsers that use this type of attribute.

An attributed version of our expression grammar is shown in Table 3.5. The attribute names are taken from the previous recursive-descent compiler. An attribute attached to a left-hand side is treated like a formal argument in a subroutine declaration—it's the attribute that is passed to the current production from its parent in the tree. An attribute on the right-hand side is treated like an argument in a subroutine call; it is passed down the tree to the indicated production.

Table 3.5. An Attributed Grammar

1.	*stmt*	$\rightarrow$	ε
2.		$\mid$	*expr*$_{(t)}$ **;** *stmt*
3.	*expr*$_{(t)}$	$\rightarrow$	*term*$_{(t)}$ *expr'*$_{(t)}$
4.	*expr'*$_{(t)}$	$\rightarrow$	**+** *term*$_{(t2)}$ *expr'*$_{(t)}$
5.		$\mid$	ε
6.	*term*$_{(t)}$	$\rightarrow$	*factor term'*
7.	*term'*$_{(t)}$	$\rightarrow$	***** *factor*$_{(t2)}$ *term'*$_{(t)}$
8.		$\mid$	ε
9.	*factor*$_{(t)}$	$\rightarrow$	**number_or_id**
10.		$\mid$	**(** *expr*$_{(t)}$ **)**

The attributes by themselves are not much use. You need to augment the grammar to show how the attributes are manipulated. Remember that the flow of control in a top-down parser is from left to right across the grammar, so an action can affect only those symbols to its right and can use only those symbols that are initialized to its left (or which appear as an attribute of the left-hand side). An augmented, attributed grammar is shown in Table 3.6. The code-generation actions are taken from the previous recursive-descent parser.

Augmented, attributed grammar.

Table 3.6. An Augmented, Attributed Grammar

1.	*stmt*	$\rightarrow$	ε
2.		$\mid$	`{t=newname();}` *expr*$_{(t)}$ **;** *stmt*
3.	*expr*$_{(t)}$	$\rightarrow$	*term*$_{(t)}$ *expr'*$_{(t)}$
4.	*expr'*$_{(t)}$	$\rightarrow$	**+** `{t2=newname();}` *term*$_{(t2)}$ `{printf("%s+=%s\n",t,t2); freename(t2);}` *expr'*$_{(t)}$
5.		$\mid$	ε
6.	*term*$_{(t)}$	$\rightarrow$	*factor term'*
7.	*term'*$_{(t)}$	$\rightarrow$	***** `{t2=newname();}` *factor*$_{(t2)}$ `{printf("%s+=%s\n",t,t2); freename(t2);}` *term'*$_{(t)}$
8.		$\mid$	ε
9.	*factor*$_{(t)}$	$\rightarrow$	**number_or_id** `{ printf("%s=%0.*s\n", t, yyleng, yytext); }`
10.		$\mid$	**(** *expr*$_{(t)}$ **)**

As I said at the beginning of this section, I've demonstrated the process in a topsy-turvey fashion. Generally, you would create the augmented, attributed grammar first, and then use that grammar as a specification when coding. The compiler-generation tools developed in the next two chapters take augmented, attributed grammars as their input, and output parsers for these grammars, thereby eliminating the necessity of coding a parser at all. You still have to write the grammar, however, and figure out how to generate code by adding actions to it in appropriate places.

One final note: It's possible for a single grammar to use both inherited and synthesized attributes, but it's not a good idea. In a recursive-descent parser—the only kind of parser in which combined attribute types are really practical—maintenance becomes a problem because it's more difficult to follow the flow of data as the parser executes. Other types of parsers, such as the one-pass, table driven ones discussed in the next two chapters, can handle only one type of attribute.

3.11 Representing Generic Grammars

As we discuss grammars in the remainder of this book, it will be handy, occasionally, to discuss generic productions. In these discussions, when I don't say otherwise the term *symbol*, without the word "terminal" or "nonterminal," is used for when something can be either a terminal or nonterminal. As usual, italics are used for nonterminals and boldface is used for terminals, but I'll use upper-case letters that look like this:

Generic symbols.

$$\mathcal{A\,B\,C\,D\,E\,F\,G\,H\,I\,J\,K\,L\,M\,N\,O\,P\,Q\,R\,S\,T\,U\,V\,W\,X\,Y\,Z}$$

to represent an unspecified symbol. A production like this:

$$s \rightarrow \mathcal{A}\ \mathcal{B}$$

has two symbols on its right-hand side, and these can be either terminals or nonterminals. The following production has three symbols on its right-hand side: the first is a nonterminal, the second is a terminal, and the third can be either a terminal or nonterminal:

$$s \rightarrow a\ \mathbf{T}\ \mathcal{A}$$

Greek letters represent sequence of symbols.

To confuse matters further, I'll use Greek letters to represent a sequence of symbols. For example, a generic production can be written like this:

$$s \rightarrow \alpha$$

s is a nonterminal because it's in italics, and α represents an arbitrary sequence of terminals and nonterminals. Unless I say otherwise, a Greek letter represents zero or more symbols, so something like this:

$$s \rightarrow \alpha\ \mathbf{A}\ \beta$$

represents all productions that have s on their left-hand side and an **A** somewhere on their right-hand side. The **A** can be preceded by zero or more symbols (terminals or nonterminals), and it can be followed by zero or more symbols. A sequence of symbols represented by a Greek letter can go to ε. That is, it can be replaced in the equation by an empty string, effectively disappearing from the production. For example, the production

$$s \rightarrow \mathbf{A}\ \alpha\ \mathbf{B}$$

has to start with an **A** and end with a **B**, but it can have any number of terminals and nonterminals (including zero) in between.

Multiple right-hand sides, α_n.

If a generic production has several right-hand sides, I'll represent these with subscripts. For example, in the following generic grammar, the nonterminal s has n <u>different</u> right-hand sides, one of which could be ε:

$$
\begin{array}{ccl}
s & \rightarrow & \alpha_1 \\
  & | & \alpha_2 \\
  & \cdots & \\
  & | & \alpha_n
\end{array}
$$

Multiple tokens, $\mathbf{T}_n$.

By the same token (so to speak), the following represents n <u>different</u> terminal symbols: $\mathbf{T}_1\ \mathbf{T}_2 \ldots \mathbf{T}_n$.

All the foregoing may seem abstruse, but it will sink in once you've used it a few times. I'll call out exactly what's going on if the generic production gets too complicated.

3.12 Exercises

3.1. Show a step-by-step leftmost derivation of the expression

```
1 + 2 * ((3+4) + 5) + 6;
```

using the following grammar:

1.	*statements*	→	ε
2.				*expr* ; *statements*
3.	*expr*	→	*term expr'*
4.	*expr'*	→	+ *term expr'*
5.				ε
6.	*term*	→	*factor term'*
7.	*term'*	→	* *factor term'*
8.				ε
9.	*factor*	→	**number**
10.				(*expr*)

3.2. Build a recursive-descent parser that implements the augmented grammar in Table 3.6 on page 191.

3.3. The following regular expression recognizes a series of binary digits, with the pattern **000** used to terminate the series:

(0|1)*000

Translate that expression into a right-linear grammar.

3.4. Assuming that each character in the ASCII character set forms a token, create a grammar that recognizes all C integer and character constants. All of the following should be recognized by your grammar:

```
0xabcd 0123 45 'a' '\t' '\x0a' '\123'
```

3.5. In LISP, a simple expression is formed as follows: (+ a b) represents *a+b*, (+ a (* b c)) represents *a+b*c*, and so forth. Write a grammar that recognizes all such LISP expressions, with an arbitrary level of parentheses nesting. The +, −, *, and / operators must be supported, + and − should be lower precedence than *, and /.

3.6. Write an expression grammar that supports variable names, an assignment operator, a plus operator and array references. Array references are done in a FORTRAN-like fashion: a three-dimensional array element can be accessed using the notation a[x,y,z]. x is the minor axis, so the list of array indexes should be processed from right to left. Similarly an expression like a = b[2] = c[1,2] should be recognized, and the assignment operator should associate right to left. Addition associates left to right, however. The order of precedence should be brackets (highest precedence), then addition, then assignment.

3.7. Write a grammar that recognizes Pascal subroutine declarations. Draw the parse tree that results from a top-down parse of the following declaration:

```
function subr( var arg1: string; x: integer; s: string):
                                        integer;
```

3.8.   Write a grammar for 8086 assembly language (or whatever assembly language that you know).

3.9.   Write a grammar that describes the input language used by your calculator. Every key on the calculator represents a token in the language.

3.10. Listing 3.5 shows a specification for a DFA transition matrix. The state statements define the rows of the matrix; each **goto** statement controls the contents of a column in that row. The accept statements say that the current state is an accepting state, and the code that follows is to be executed when the accepting action occurs. The outer braces are part of the accept statement itself, but the included code must also be able to have braces in it. Unspecified transitions are filled with the number specified in the error statement.

Listing 3.5. A State Machine Specification

```
1    rows 4;          /* Number of rows    in the table.              */
2    columns 128;     /* Number of columns in the table.             */
3    error -1;        /* Use this value for all unspecified table elements.   */
4
5    state 0
6    {
7        goto 0 on 'a';
8        goto 1 on 'b';
9        goto 2 on 'c';
10       goto 2 on 100;      /* = 0x64 = 'd'. */
11       loop on   0x65;     /* 0x65 = 'e', same as "goto <current state>." */
12       accept              /* Define an accepting action for this state.   */
13       {
14           execute_this_code();
15       }
16   }
17
18   state 1 { goto 2 on b; }              /* Not accepting. */
19   state 2 { goto 3 on c; }              /* Not accepting. */
20   state 3 { accept{ hi_there("BOO!"); } }
```

(a)   Write a grammar for the language just described.

(b)   Augment the grammar with sufficient code-generation actions and attributes that a parser could be coded that reads in a state-machine specification, and which outputs C source code, which, when compiled, implements those tables. Two array declarations and a subroutine should be output. The first array should be the transition matrix itself, the second array should be indexed by state number and should evaluate to 1 if that state is an accepting state. The subroutine should contain a **switch** statement which, when passed the state number of an accepting state, executes the associated code.

(c)   Implement the grammar developed in (b).

3.11. Modify your solution to the foregoing exercise so that you can give symbolic names to a state and then use those symbolic names in **goto** statements. Names are declared implicitly by using them instead of a number in a state statement. The compiler must assign state numbers in this case, and you should make sure that a state number supplied by the compiler doesn't conflict with one supplied in a state statement. Forward references should be permitted.

4

Top-Down Parsing

This chapter develops the idea of recursive-descent parsing by discussing ways to do the same thing in a more maintainable, table-driven fashion. The chapter includes a description of top-down parsing techniques and an in-depth discussion of LL grammars, including techniques for modifying grammars to be LL(1). A **yacc**-like utility called **LLama**—which translates an augmented, attributed LL(1) grammar into a parser—is constructed. If you intend to read the implementation parts of this chapter, you should read Appendix E, which contains a user's manual for **LLama** and **occs**, before continuing.

One thing I'm not doing here is presenting an extended example of how to use **LLama**. I've left this out because **LLama** is, in itself, not nearly as useful a tool as is **occs**. The main reason this chapter is here, in fact, is to present several concepts and procedures that are used later to construct **occs** (but in a somewhat simpler context than **occs** itself). That is, **LLama**, is just a step on the way to **occs**. I do present a short example of using **LLama** in that I use **LLama** to rewrite its own parser. Also, a significant part of the code used by **LLama** is also used by **occs**, and the common code is presented only in the current chapter.

4.1 Push-Down Automata*

We saw in Chapter Three that certain right-linear grammars can be converted directly to DFAs. If you can represent a programming language in this way, you can implement a parser for it as a state machine with a code-generation action associated with each state. Consider the following simple grammar that recognizes expressions of the form **number + number**.

Parsing with a state machine.

---

* As in Chapter Two, asterisks mark sections containing theoretical material.

$E \rightarrow$ **number** A
$A \rightarrow + B$
$B \rightarrow$ **number** C
$C \rightarrow \varepsilon$

This grammar satisfies the conditions necessary for implementation as a DFA: it's right linear, and every production is of the form $a \rightarrow \varepsilon$ or $b \rightarrow \mathbf{X}c$, where a, b, and c are nonterminals and $\mathbf{X}$ is a terminal. Consequently, you can represent this grammar with the state machine in Figure 4.1 and can parse that grammar using the state machine.

Figure 4.1. Using a State Machine for Parsing

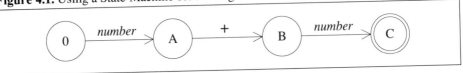

State machines can't count.

The problem with a straightforward state-machine implementation of a real grammar is that a simple state machine can't count; or to be more precise, it can count only by adding additional states. Of course, most grammars can't count beyond 1 either. For example, the only way to get one, two, or three of something is with:

$s \rightarrow$ *stooge* | *stooge stooge* | *stooge stooge stooge*

Nonetheless, a grammar *can* handle nested structures, such as parentheses, and keep track of the nesting level without difficulty, and a simple DFA cannot. For example, the following grammar recognizes properly nested lists of parentheses:

list $\rightarrow$ *plist* | *plist list*
plist $\rightarrow$ (*list*) | ε

The grammar accepts input like the following: (( ) (( ))), but it rejects expressions without properly-nested parentheses. This grammar can't be parsed with a state machine alone, precisely because the state machine can't count. A straightforward state machine that recognizes nested parentheses is shown in Figure 4.2.

Figure 4.2. A State Machine to Recognize Nested Parentheses

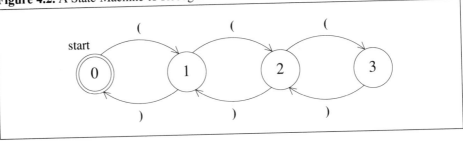

Push-down automata (PDA).

This machine works fine as long as you don't have more than three levels of nesting. Each additional nesting level requires an additional state tacked on to the right edge of the machine, however. You don't want to limit the nesting level in the grammar itself, and it's not a great idea to modify the state machine on the fly by adding extra states as open parentheses are encountered. Fortunately, the situation can be rectified by using a state machine augmented with a stack. This state-machine/stack combination is called a *push-down automaton* or *PDA*. Most table-driven parsers are push-down automata. They are driven by a state machine and use a stack to keep track of the progress of that state machine.

A push-down automaton that recognizes nested parentheses is shown in Figure 4.3. The associated state table is in Table 4.1. A PDA is different from a normal state machine in several ways. First of all, the stack is an integral part of the machine. The number at the top of stack is the current state number. Secondly, the contents of the state table are not next-state numbers; rather, they are actions to perform, given a current state (on the top of stack) and input symbol. Four types of actions are supported:

accept   A sentence in the input grammar has been recognized.
error   A syntax error has been detected in the input.
push N   Push N onto the stack, effectively changing the current state to N.
pop   Pop one item from the stack, changing the current state to whatever state number is uncovered by the pop. The input is advanced with each push or pop.

Figure 4.3. A Push-Down Automata to Recognize Nested Parentheses

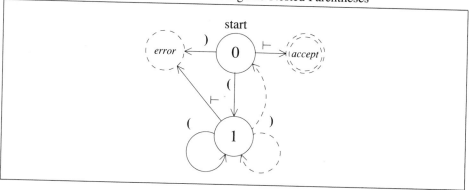

Table 4.1. State Table for PDA in Figure 4.3

		Input Symbol		
		(	)	⊢
State	0	push 1	error	accept
	1	push 1	pop	error

The following algorithm is used to parse an input sentence:

> Push the number of the start state.
> while((*action* = state_table[top_of_stack_symbol][input_symbol]) ≠ accept)
> {
>   if(*action* = error)
>   reject;
>   else
>   do the indicated action.
> }

Using a PDA to count parentheses.

The parse stack and input stream for a parse of (() (())) is summarized in Table 4.2. This PDA is using the stack as a counting device. The 0 marks the bottom of the stack, and the 1 is used as a nesting-level marker. The marker is pushed every time an open parenthesis is encountered and popped when the matching close parenthesis is found. The machine accepts an input string only if the start-state marker is on the stack when end of input is encountered.

Stack used for counting.

Table 4.2. A Parse of (( ) (( )))

Parse Stack	Input	Next Action
0	(( ) (( ))) ⊢	push 1 and advance
0 1	( ) (( ))) ⊢	push 1 and advance
0 1 1	) (( ))) ⊢	push 1 and advance
0 1	(( ))) ⊢	pop and advance
0 1 1	( ))) ⊢	push 1 and advance
0 1 1 1	))) ⊢	pop and advance
0 1 1	)) ⊢	pop and advance
0 1	) ⊢	pop and advance
0	⊢	accept

This machine has several advantages over the previous one. Not only can it handle any level parenthesis nesting (or, at least, the only limitation in that regard is the depth of the parse stack), but it has many fewer states than would a straight DFA for a reasonable nesting level. We'll look at how to use pushdown automata in more sophisticated ways in a moment.

4.1.1 Recursive-Descent Parsers as Push-Down Automata*

It's instructive to see how the foregoing applies to a recursive-descent parser. Most programming languages use a run-time stack to control subroutine calls and returns. The simplest possible situation is an assembly-language, subroutine-call instruction like JSR *addr*, which pushes the address of the instruction following the JSR onto the run-time stack, and then starts executing instructions at *addr*. A matching RET instruction pops an address off the stack and starts executing code at that address. In this simple case, the stack frame consists of nothing but the return address.

How recursive-descent parsers use the stack.

A programming language that supports recursion must use the stack more extensively. The actual details are discussed in depth in Chapter Six, but for now, suffice it to say that space for subroutine arguments and automatic local variables are allocated from the stack as part of the subroutine-call process. A C subroutine call, for example, usually involves the following sequence of operations:

(1) Push the arguments onto the stack.
(2) Call the subroutine.
(3) Allocate space for local variables by decrementing the stack pointer by some constant (I'm assuming that the stack grows towards low memory, as is usually the case).

Everything is done in reverse order when the subroutine returns, except that the arguments are discarded rather than being popped.

Stack frame.

This entire block (arguments, return address, and local variables) comprises the subroutine's *stack frame*. Figure 4.4 shows the various stack frames as they're created and destroyed as the naive recursive-descent parser in Chapter One processes the expression 1+2 using the grammar in Table 4.3. Each new stack frame represents a subroutine call, and when the stack frame disappears, the subroutine has returned. The input is shown on the right as it is gradually absorbed. In terms of compilers, the entire stack frame represents a nonterminal—the left-hand side of some production, and the local variables and argument components of the stack frame are the attributes associated with that nonterminal.

Table 4.3. An LL(1) Expression Grammar

1.	*stmt*	→	ε
2.		|	*expr* **;** *stmt*
3.	*expr*	→	*term expr'*
4.	*expr'*	→	*+ term expr'*
5.		|	ε
6.	*term*	→	*factor term'*
7.	*term'*	→	** factor term'*
8.		|	ε
9.	*factor*	→	**number_or_id**
10.		|	*(expr)*

Figure 4.4. The Parser's Stack Frames

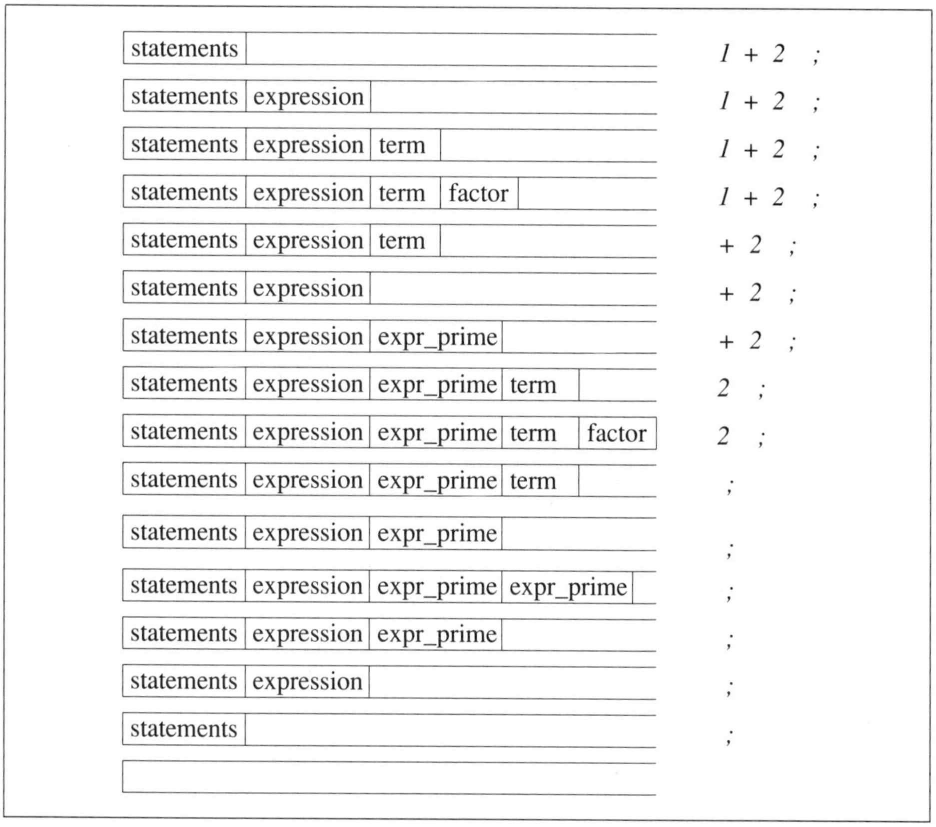

The question to ask is: what are these stack frames really doing as the parse progresses? They're doing two things. First, they're keeping track of the current position on the parse tree. The stack always holds the path from the root down to the current node on the tree. You can traverse up to a parent by popping one stack element. Second, the stack keeps track of attributes; since a stack frame represents a subroutine call, it also represents a nonterminal symbol in the parse tree. If you view a subroutine's arguments and local variables as attributes of the nonterminal, then the portion of the stack frame that holds these objects represents the attributes. The same nonterminal symbol can be on the stack in several places, but since each instance of the associated subroutine has its own stack frame (with its own local variables and arguments), each instance of the

Stack used to remember attributes and position on parse tree.

Recursive subroutines have unique stack frames, attributes.

associated nonterminal can have a unique set of attributes attached to it. For example, when `expr_prime()` calls itself recursively (in the fifth stack from the bottom of Figure 4.4), there are two stack frames, each with a unique set of local variables and arguments.

You can make the transition from recursive descent to a table-driven parser by realizing that neither the recursion nor the subroutines themselves are actually necessary, provided that you can simulate the recursive-descent parser's stack frames using a local stack. That is, instead of using the implicit, run-time stack to keep track of the attributes and the position in the parse, you can maintain an explicit stack that does the same thing. That explicit stack can then be controlled by a nonrecursive subroutine and a table. For example, a production like this:

Replace recursion with loop and explicit stack.

$$
\begin{array}{lcl}
factor & \rightarrow & MINUS\ unop \\
unop & \rightarrow & \textbf{NUMBER} \\
& | & \textbf{IDENTIFIER}
\end{array}
$$

can be implemented in a recursive-descent parser as follows:

```
factor()
{
    if( match( MINUS ) ) { advance(); unop(); }
    else                 { error();          }
}

unop()
{
    if    ( match( NUMBER     ) ) advance();
    else if( match( IDENTIFIER ) ) advance();
    else                          error();
}
```

And these subroutines can be simulated as follows:

```
#define factor 1
#define unop   2

push( factor );                   /* Push the goal symbol */
while( stack_not_empty() )
{
    switch( top_of_stack_symbol )
    {
    case factor: if( match(MINUS) ) { advance(); push( unop ); }
                 else               { error();                 }
                 pop();
                 break;

    case unop:   if    ( match( NUMBER     ) ) advance();
                 else if( match( IDENTIFIER ) ) advance();
                 else                          error();
                 pop();
                 break;
    }
}
```

Rather than calling a subroutine, a symbol representing that subroutine is pushed onto a local stack. The pops replace the **return** statements. Since the foregoing loop is, in effect, a DFA, you can translate it to a table with little difficulty.

4.2 Using a PDA for a Top-Down Parse*

A top-down parse can be implemented using a grammar, a stack, and the following algorithm. The parse stack is initialized by pushing the goal symbol (the topmost production in the grammar).

Rules for top-down parsing with a PDA.

(0)   If the parse stack is empty, the parse is complete.

(1)   If the item at top of stack is a nonterminal, replace it with its right-hand side, pushing the symbols in reverse order. For example, if you have a production: $a{\rightarrow}b\ c\ d$, and a is at the top of stack, pop the a and push the right-hand side in reverse order: first the d, then the c, and then the b. In the case of an ε production (a production with ε as its right-hand side), an item is popped, but nothing is pushed in its place. Goto (0).

(2)   Otherwise, if the item at top of stack is a terminal symbol, that symbol must also be the current lookahead symbol. If it's not, there's a syntax error, otherwise pop the terminal symbol and advance the input. Goto (0).

Note that step (2), above, requires certain symbols to be in the input at specific times because tokens at the top of stack must match the current input symbol. The parser is effectively predicting what the next input token will be. The parser just described is often called a *predictive* parser. Note that only certain classes of grammars (which I'll discuss shortly) can be parsed by predictive parsers. Table 4.4 shows the parse stack as `1+2;` is processed using the grammar in Table 4.3 on page 199 and a predictive parser.

Predictive parsers.

4.3 Error Recovery in a Top-Down Parser*

One of the advantages of top-down parsers is that effective error recovery is easy to implement. The basic strategy makes use of a set of tokens called a *synchronization set*. Symbols in this set are called *synchronization tokens*. Members of the synchronization set are typically symbols that can end blocks of code.

Synchronization set, tokens.

A syntax error occurs in a predictive parser when a token is at top of stack and that same token is not the current lookahead character. The synchronization set is used to recover from the error as follows:

(1)   Pop items off the parse stack until a member of the synchronization set is at top of stack. Error recovery is not possible if no such item is on the stack.

(2)   Read input symbols until the current lookahead symbol matches the symbol at top of stack or you reach end of input.

(3)   If you are at end of input, error recovery failed, otherwise you have recovered.

An alternate method, which is harder to implement but more robust, examines the parse stack and creates a list of those synchronization symbols that are on the stack when the error occurred. It then reads the input until any of these symbols are encountered, and pops items off the stack until the same symbol is at top of stack.

Synchronization-set stack.

Ideally, every production should have its own set of synchronization symbols, which are changed when the production is activated. To do this properly, you must have a stack of synchronization sets, and replacing a nonterminal with its right-hand side involves the following operations:

(1)   Push the associated synchronization set onto the synchronization-set stack.

(2)   Pop the nonterminal from the parse stack.

(3)   Push a special *pop* marker onto the parse stack.

(4)   Push the right-hand side of the nonterminal onto the parse stack in reverse order.

Table 4.4. A Top-Down Parse of `1+2;`

Parse Stack	Input	Comments
stmt	1+2;⊢	Apply *stmt→expr ; stmt*
—	1+2;⊢	
stmt	1+2;⊢	(This *stmt* is the one on the right of *stmt→expr ; stmt*)
stmt ;	1+2;⊢	
stmt ; expr	1+2;⊢	Apply *expr→term expr′*
stmt ;	1+2;⊢	
stmt ; expr′	1+2;⊢	
stmt ; expr′ term	1+2;⊢	Apply *term→factor term′*
stmt ; expr′	1+2;⊢	
stmt ; expr′ term′	1+2;⊢	
stmt ; expr′ term′ factor	1+2;⊢	Apply *factor→***num_or_id**
stmt ; expr′ term′	1+2;⊢	
stmt ; expr′ term′ **num_or_id**	1+2;⊢	TOS symbol matches lookahead, pop and advance
stmt ; expr′ term′	+2;⊢	Apply *term′→ε*
stmt ; expr′	+2;⊢	Apply *expr′→+ term expr′*
stmt ;	+2;⊢	
stmt ; expr′	+2;⊢	
stmt ; expr′ term	+2;⊢	
stmt ; expr′ term +	+2;⊢	TOS symbol matches lookahead, pop and advance
stmt ; expr′ term	2;⊢	Apply *term→factor term′*
stmt ; expr′	2;⊢	
stmt ; expr′ term′	2;⊢	
stmt ; expr′ term′ factor	2;⊢	Apply *factor→***num_or_id**
stmt ; expr′ term′	2;⊢	
stmt ; expr′ term′ **num_or_id**	2;⊢	TOS symbol matches lookahead, pop and advance
stmt ; expr′ term′	;⊢	Apply *term′→ε*
stmt ; expr′	;⊢	Apply *expr′→ε*
stmt ;	;⊢	TOS symbol matches lookahead, pop and advance
stmt	⊢	Apply *stmt→ε*
—	⊢	Done

When a *pop* marker is found on the parse stack, one set is popped from the synchronization-set stack. The set at the top of the synchronization-set stack is used when an error is encountered.

In practice, a synchronization-set stack is usually not worth the effort to implement because most synchronization sets have the same tokens in them. It's usually adequate to have one synchronization set that can work in most situations and is used universally whenever an error is encountered. Taking C as an example, a good choice of synchronization tokens would be a semicolon, comma, close-brace, and close parenthesis. In other words, symbols that end commonly occurring phrases in the input language are good choices.

4.4 Augmented Grammars and Table-Driven Parsers*

Though the parser just described is nice, it's not very useful because there's no provision for code generation. It's like the initial stab at a recursive-descent parser back in Chapter One, before the code generation had been added to the actions. Fortunately this omission is easy to rectify.

As was discussed in Chapter Three, an *augmented* grammar is one in which code-generation actions are inserted directly into the grammar. An augmented version of the previous grammar is shown in Table 4.5. (It's the augmented grammar from the last chapter.) The augmented grammar is parsed just like the unaugmented one. The actions are just pushed onto the parse stack along with other symbols. When an action is at the top of the stack, it's executed.

Top-down code generation using augmented grammar.

Actions executed as parse tree traversed.

Table 4.5. An Augmented LL(1) Expression Grammar

1.	*statements*	→	⊢
2.		|	*expression* **;** *statements*
3.	*expression*	→	*term expression'*
4.	*expression'*	→	**+** *term* { op (' + ') ; } *expression'*
5.		|	ε
6.	*term*	→	*factor term'*
7.	*term'*	→	***** *factor* { op (' * ') ; } *term'*
8.		|	ε
9.	*factor*	→	**number_or_id** { create_tmp (yytext) ; }
10.		|	**(** *expression* **)**

The action subroutines that do the code generation (op ( ) and create_tmp ( )) were discussed in Chapter Three, but to summarize:

- The create_tmp ( ) subroutine generates code to copy the operand into an anonymous temporary variable, and it pushes the name onto a local Temporaries stack.
- The op ( ) subroutine performs the operation on the two previously-generated temporary variables, popping their names off the stack, generating code to perform the operation, and then pushing the name of the temporary that holds the result.

A sample parse of 1+2 is shown in Table 4.6. Note that the op ( ) call follows the *term* in *expr'*→**+** *term* { op (' + ') ; } *expr'*. Since the temporaries are generated indirectly by the *terms*, two names will exist on the Temporaries stack when the op ( ) call is executed.

4.4.1 Implementing Attributed Grammars in a PDA*

The previous example generated code without benefit of attributes. It is possible to use attributes in a PDA, however. A top-down parser such as the one we're looking at uses inherited attributes (the equivalent of subroutine arguments) exclusively. It's very difficult to represent return values (synthesized attributes) in this kind of parser, though the situation is reversed in the bottom-up parsers discussed in the next chapter.

Inherited attributes in top-down parser.

We'll support attributes by introducing a second stack, called an *attribute* or *value* stack, which simulates that part of a subroutine's stack frame that holds the subroutine arguments. This stack is a stack of structures, one field of which is used to hold the attribute associated with a production's left-hand side, and the other element of which is used to hold a symbol's own attribute. Every time a symbol is pushed onto the normal parse stack as part of a replacement operation, the attribute attached to the left-hand side that's being replaced is pushed onto the value stack (it's copied to both fields of the structure).

Value, attribute stack.

An action is executed when it's at the top of the stack, and all symbols to the right of the action in the production are still on the parse stack when the execution occurs. For example, when the action ( ) in the following production is executed:

Table 4.6. A Top-Down Parse of `1+2;` Using the Augmented Grammar

Parse Stack	Input	Comments
stmt	1+2;⊢	Apply *stmt*→*expr* ; *stmt*
—	1+2;⊢	
stmt	1+2;⊢	
stmt ;	1+2;⊢	
stmt ; *expr*	1+2;⊢	Apply *expr*→*term expr'*
stmt ;	1+2;⊢	
stmt ; *expr'*	1+2;⊢	
stmt ; *expr' term*	1+2;⊢	Apply *term*→*factor term'*
stmt ; *expr'*	1+2;⊢	
stmt ; *expr' term'*	1+2;⊢	
stmt ; *expr' term' factor*	1+2;⊢	Apply *factor*→**n** {create_tmp(yytext);}
stmt ; *expr' term'*	1+2;⊢	
stmt ; *expr' term'* {create_tmp(yytext);}	1+2;⊢	
stmt ; *expr' term'* {create_tmp(yytext);} **n**	1+2;⊢	TOS symbol matches lookahead, pop and advance
stmt ; *expr' term'* {create_tmp(yytext);}	+2;⊢	Generate t0=1;
stmt ; *expr' term'*	+2;⊢	Apply *term'*→ε
stmt ; *expr'*	+2;⊢	Apply *expr'*→+ *term* {op('+');} *expr'*
stmt ;	+2;⊢	
stmt ; *expr'*	+2;⊢	
stmt ; *expr'* {op('+');}	+2;⊢	
stmt ; *expr'* {op('+');} *term*	+2;⊢	
stmt ; *expr'* {op('+');} *term* +	+2;⊢	TOS symbol matches lookahead, pop and advance
stmt ; *expr'* {op('+');} *term*	2;⊢	Apply *term*→*factor term'*
stmt ; *expr'* {op('+');}	2;⊢	
stmt ; *expr'* {op('+');} *term'*	2;⊢	
stmt ; *expr'* {op('+');} *term' factor*	2;⊢	Apply *factor*→**n** {create_tmp(yytext);}
stmt ; *expr'* {op('+');} *term'*	2;⊢	
stmt ; *expr'* {op('+');} *term'* {create_tmp(yytext);}	2;⊢	
stmt ; *expr'* {op('+');} *term'* {create_tmp(yytext);} **n**	2;⊢	TOS symbol matches lookahead, pop and advance
stmt ; *expr'* {op('+');} *term'* {create_tmp(yytext);}	;⊢	Generate t1=2;
stmt ; *expr'* {op('+');} *term'*	;⊢	Apply *term'*→ε
stmt ; *expr'* {op('+');}	;⊢	Generate t0+=t1;
stmt ; *expr'*	;⊢	Apply *expr'*→ε
stmt ;	;⊢	TOS symbol matches lookahead, pop and advance
stmt	⊢	Apply *stmt*→ε
—	⊢	Done

num_or_id is abbreviated as **n** so that the table can fit onto the page.

$$a \rightarrow b \text{ \{action();\} } c\, d$$

The action symbol itself is at the top of the stack, *c* is directly underneath it, and *d* is under the *c*. The attribute for a symbol can be modified from within an action by modifying the right-hand-side field of an attribute-stack structure. The distance from the top of stack to the required structure is the same as as the distance in the grammar from action to the required symbol. In the earlier example, *d* is two symbols to the right of the {action()} and its attributes are two symbols beneath the {action()}'s attributes on the value stack. If that action wants to modify the attribute for *d* it need only modify the attribute at offset 2 from the top of the attribute stack.[1] The value stack can be implemented using the modified top-down parse algorithm in Table 4.7.

---

1. It's also possible to keep track of attributes on the parse stack itself rather than on an auxiliary value stack. See [Lewis], pp. 311–337. This method is difficult to implement so is not discussed here.

Table 4.7. Top-Down Parse Algorithm with Attributes

Data Structures: A *parse stack* of **int**s.
A *value stack* of the following structures:

```
typedef struct
{
        YYSTYPE left;
        YYSTYPE right;
}
yyvstype;
```

YYSTYPE is an arbitrary type—it is a character pointer in the current example.
A variable, *lhs*, of type YYSTYPE.

Initially: Push the start symbol on the parse stack.
Push garbage onto the value stack.

---

(0) If the parse stack is empty, the parse is complete.

(1) If the item at the top of the parse stack is an action symbol: execute the associated code and pop the item.

(2) If the item at the top of the parse stack is a nonterminal:

    (a) *lhs* = the right field of the structure currently at the top of the value stack.

    (b) replace the symbol at the top of the parse stack with its right-hand side, pushing the symbols in reverse order. Every time an item is pushed onto the parse stack, push an item onto the value stack, initializing both fields to *lhs*.

    (c) Goto (0).

(3) Otherwise, if the item at the top of the parse stack is a terminal symbol, that symbol must also be the current lookahead symbol. If it's not, there's a syntax error, otherwise pop the terminal symbol and advance the input. Goto (0).

I'll give an example of how to use this attribute-passing mechanism in a moment. First, however, I need to introduce a new notation for attribute management. Attributes need only be referenced explicitly inside an action. Rather than giving attributes arbitrary names, all you need is a mechanism to reference them from the perspective of the action itself. The following notation, similar to the one used by **yacc**, does the job: The attribute associated with a left-hand side is always called $$, and attributes for symbols on the right-hand side are referenced by the notation $1, $2, and so forth, where the number represents the offset of the desired symbol to the right of the current action. Consider this production:

Attribute notation ($N).

    expr′ → +   `{$1=$2=newname();}`
                term   `{printf("%s+=%s\n",$$,$0); freename($0);}`
                 expr′

(That's one long production, split up into several lines to make it easier to read, not three right-hand sides.) The $1 in `{$1=$2=newname();}` attaches an attribute to the *term* because *term* is one symbol to the right of the action. When the parser replaces this *term* with its right-hand side, the symbols on that right-hand side can all use $$ to access the attribute associated with the *term*. In the current right-hand side, the `$$` in the `printf()` statement references an attribute that was attached to the *expr'* at some earlier point in the parse. The `$2` in `{$1=$2=newname();}` references the second action, which is two symbols to the right of `{$1=$2=newname();}`. The second action can get at this attribute using `$0`. That is, the value assigned to `$2` in the first action is accessed with `$0` in the second action.

LLama can translate the dollar notation directly into value-stack references when it outputs the **switch** statement that holds the action code. When an action is executed, `$$` is the left-hand-side field of the structure at the top of the value stack, `$0` is the right-hand-side field of the same structure, `$1` is the structure at offset one from the top of the stack, `$2` is at offset two, and so forth.

The entire grammar, modified to use our new notation, is shown in Table 4.8. You can see how all this works by looking at the parse of `1+2` that is shown in Table 4.9. Remember that the symbols on the right-hand side of a replaced nonterminal inherit the attributes in the nonterminal's `right` field—both the `left` and `right` fields of the attribute-stack structure are initialized to hold the `right` field of the parent nonterminal.

Table 4.8. An Augmented, Attributed Grammar Using the $ Notation

1.	*stmt*	→	ε
2.		|	`{$1=$2=newname();}` expr `{freename($0);}` ; stmt
3.	*expr*	→	*term expr'*
4.	*expr'*	→	+ `{$1=$2=newname();}` term `{printf("%s+=%s\n",$$,$0); freename($0);}` expr'
5.		|	ε
6.	*term*	→	*factor term'*
7.	*term'*	→	* `{$1=$2=newname();}` factor `{printf("%s*=%s\n",$$,$0); freename($0);}` term'
8.		|	ε
9.	*factor*	→	**number_or_id** `{printf("%s=%0.*s\n",$$,yyleng,yytext);}`
10.		|	(*expr*)

Table 4.9. A Parse of `1+2` Showing Value Stacks

Parse and Value Stacks								Notes
stmt [?,?]								stmt→expr ; stmt
stmt [?,?]	; [?,?]	{1} [?,?]	expr [?,?]	{0} [?,?]				$1=$2=newname(); $1 references expr, $2 references {1}
stmt [?,?]	; [?,?]	{1} [?,t0]	expr [?,t0]					expr→expr' term
stmt [?,?]	; [?,?]	{1} [?,t0]	expr' [t0,t0]	term [t0,t0]				term→term' factor
stmt [?,?]	; [?,?]	{1} [?,t0]	expr' [t0,t0]	term' [t0,t0]	factor [t0,t0]			factor→**num_or_id**
stmt [?,?]	; [?,?]	{1} [?,t0]	expr' [t0,t0]	term' [t0,t0]	{3} [t0,t0]	**n** [t0,t0]		**num_or_id** token matches 1 in input
stmt [?,?]	; [?,?]	{1} [?,t0]	expr' [t0,t0]	term' [t0,t0]	{3} [t0,t0]			`printf("%s=%0.*s\n",$$,yyleng,yytext);` outputs: t0=1
stmt [?,?]	; [?,?]	{1} [?,t0]	expr' [t0,t0]	term' [t0,t0]				term'→ε
stmt [?,?]	; [?,?]	{1} [?,t0]	expr' [t0,t0]					expr'→+ term expr'
stmt [?,?]	; [?,?]	{1} [?,t0]	expr' [t0,t0]	{2} [t0,t0]	term [t0,t0]	{0} [t0,t0]	+ [t0,t0]	+ token matches + in input
stmt [?,?]	; [?,?]	{1} [?,t0]	expr' [t0,t0]	{2} [t0,t1]	term [t0,t1]	{0} [t0,t0]		$1=$2=newname(); $1 references term, $2 references {2}
stmt [?,?]	; [?,?]	{1} [?,t0]	expr' [t0,t0]	{2} [t0,t1]	term [t0,t1]			term→factor term'
stmt [?,?]	; [?,?]	{1} [?,t0]	expr' [t0,t0]	{2} [t0,t1]	term' [t1,t1]	factor [t1,t1]		factor→**num_or_id**
stmt [?,?]	; [?,?]	{1} [?,t0]	expr' [t0,t0]	{2} [t0,t1]	term' [t1,t1]	{3} [t1,t1]	**n** [t1,t1]	**num_or_id** token matches 2 in input
stmt [?,?]	; [?,?]	{1} [?,t0]	expr' [t0,t0]	{2} [t0,t1]	term' [t1,t1]	{3} [t1,t1]		`printf("%s=%0.*s\n",$$,yyleng,yytext);` outputs: t1=2
stmt [?,?]	; [?,?]	{1} [?,t0]	expr' [t0,t0]	{2} [t0,t1]	term' [t1,t1]			term'→ε
stmt [?,?]	; [?,?]	{1} [?,t0]	expr' [t0,t0]	{2} [t0,t1]				`printf("%s+=%s\n",$$,$0);freename($0);` outputs: t0+=t1
stmt [?,?]	; [?,?]	{1} [?,t0]	expr' [t0,t0]					expr'→ε
stmt [?,?]	; [?,?]	{1} [?,t0]						`freename($0);`
stmt [?,?]	; [?,?]							; token matches ; in input
stmt [?,?]								stmt→ε

```
n      =  num_or_id
{0} = { $1 = $2 = newname(); }
{1} = { freename($0); }
{2} = { printf("%s+=%s\n",  $$, $0); freename($0);}
{3} = { printf("%s=%0.*s\n",$$, yyleng, yytext);   }
```

Value-stack elements are shown as `[left,right]` pairs; `[$$,$0]` in attribute notation.

4.5 Automating the Top-Down Parse Process*

Now that we have an algorithm, we need a way to automate the parse process. The solution is a push-down automata in which a state machine controls the activity on the stack. I'll start by looking at how a table-driven top-down parser works in a general way, and then I'll examine a **LLama** output file in depth by way of example. I'll discuss how **LLama** itself works, and how the tables are generated, in the next section.

4.5.1 Top-Down Parse Tables*

PDA's in top-down parsing, parse tables.

The tables for the push-down automata used by the parser are relatively straightforward. The basic strategy is to give a numeric value to all the symbols in the grammar, and then make tables of these numeric values. For example, the numeric values in Table 4.10 represent the symbols in the augmented grammar in Table 4.5 on page 203.

Table 4.10. Numeric and Symbolic Values For Symbols in Expression Grammar

Symbolic Value	Numeric Value	Notes
LP	5	Terminal Symbols
NUM_OR_ID	4	
PLUS	2	
RP	6	
SEMI	1	
TIMES	3	
EOI	0	(End of input marker, created by **LLama**)
expr	257	*Nonterminal Symbols*
expr'	259	
factor	260	
stmt	256	
term	258	
term'	261	
`{op('+');}`	512	*Actions*
`{op('*');}`	513	
`{create_tmp(yytext);}`	514	

Numeric values for symbols.

The various symbol types can be distinguished by their numeric value. The end-of-input marker is always 0, tokens are all in the range 1–6, nonterminals are in the range 256–261, and actions are in the range 512–514. The parse stack contains these numbers rather than the terminals, nonterminals, and actions that they represent. For example, every appearance of an *expr* in a stack picture corresponds to a 257 on the real stack. The earlier parse of 1+2 is shown in both symbolic and numeric form in Table 4.11. For clarity, I will continue to use the symbolic names rather than the numbers, but remember that the stack itself actually has the numeric, not the symbolic, values on it.

Executing actions.

The parser takes care of actions with a switch statement controlled by symbolic constants—like the one in Listing 4.1.[2] The **switch** is executed when a number representing an action is encountered at top of stack—that same number (`actnum`) is used as the argument to the **switch**, and there's a **case** for every action symbol.

The parse itself is accomplished using two tables, `Yy_pushtab` and `Yy_d`, shown in Figures 4.5 and 4.6. The algorithm is in Table 4.12. `Yy_pushtab` holds the right-hand

---

2. This **switch** statement could be made easier to read by using macros to convert the numbers to a more-readable string, but this mapping would make both **LLama** itself and the output code more complex, so I decided not to do it. The symbol table is available from **LLama** if you need to examine the output code.

Table 4.11. A Parse of `1+2` Showing Both Symbols and Numeric Equivalents

Stack (Symbols)	Stack (Numbers)					
stmt	256					
—	—					
stmt	256					
stmt ;	256	1				
stmt ; *expr*	256	1	257			
stmt ;	256	1				
stmt ; *expr′*	256	1	259			
stmt ; *expr′ term*	256	1	259	258		
stmt ; *expr′*	256	1	259			
stmt ; *expr′ term′*	256	1	259	261		
stmt ; *expr′ term′ factor*	256	1	259	261	260	
stmt ; *expr′ term′*	256	1	259	261		
stmt ; *expr′ term′* {2}	256	1	259	261	514	
stmt ; *expr′ term′* {2} **n**	256	1	259	261	514	4
stmt ; *expr′ term′* {2}	256	1	259	261	514	
stmt ; *expr′ term′*	256	1	259	261		
stmt ; *expr′*	256	1	259			
stmt ;	256	1				
stmt ; *expr′*	256	1	259			
stmt ; *expr′* {0}	256	1	259	512		
stmt ; *expr′* {0} *term*	256	1	259	512	258	
stmt ; *expr′* {0} *term* +	256	1	259	512	258	2
stmt ; *expr′* {0} *term*	256	1	259	512	258	
stmt ; *expr′* {0}	256	1	259	512		
stmt ; *expr′* {0} *term′*	256	1	259	512	261	
stmt ; *expr′* {0} *term′ factor*	256	1	259	512	261	260
stmt ; *expr′* {0} *term′*	256	1	259	512	261	
stmt ; *expr′* {0} *term′* {2}	256	1	259	512	261	514
stmt ; *expr′* {0} *term′* {2} **n**	256	1	259	512	261	514	4
stmt ; *expr′* {0} *term′* {2}	256	1	259	512	261	514
stmt ; *expr′* {0} *term′*	256	1	259	512	261	
stmt ; *expr′* {0}	256	1	259	512		
stmt ; *expr′*	256	1	259			
stmt ;	256	1				
stmt	256					
—	—					

{0} represents `$1=$2=newname();`
{2} represents `printf("%s+=%s\n",$$,$0);freename($0);`

Listing 4.1. Executing Actions from a **switch**

```
1    switch( actnum )
2    {
3    case 512: { op('+'); }                    break;
4    case 513: { op('*'); }                    break;
5    case 514: { create_tmp(yytext); }         break;
6
7    default:  printf("INTERNAL ERROR: Illegal action number\n");
8             break;
9    }
```

sides of the productions in reverse order (because you have to push them in reverse order when you do a replace operation). The index into the `Yy_pushtab` array is the production number—an arbitrary, but unique, number assigned to each production. Here, the topmost production in the grammar is Production 0, the next one is Production 1, and so forth.[3] The right-hand sides are represented by zero-terminated arrays of the earlier symbolic values. `Yy_d` is used to determine the actual replacement to perform. It is indexed by potential lookahead symbols along one axis, and nonterminals along the other, and is used with the parse algorithm in Table 4.12.

Figure 4.5. LLama Parse Tables: `Yy_pushtab[]`

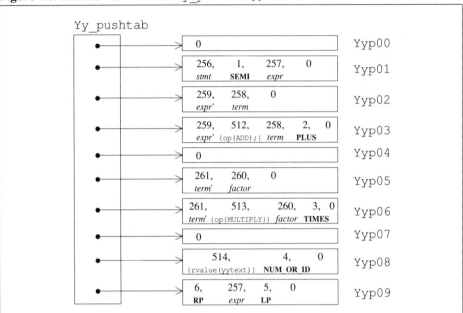

Figure 4.6. LLama Parse Tables: `Yy_d[]`

Yyd	⊢	SEMI	PLUS	TIMES	NUM_OR_ID	LP	RP
stmt	0	-1	-1	-1	1	1	-1
expr	-1	-1	-1	-1	2	2	-1
term	-1	-1	-1	-1	5	5	-1
expr'	-1	4	3	-1	-1	-1	4
factor	-1	-1	-1	-1	8	8	-1
term'	-1	7	7	6	-1	-1	7

At this point, I'd suggest running through the parse of `1+2` again, using the algorithm and tables just discussed.

---

3. Production numbers for **LLama**-generated parsers can be found by looking at the *llout.sym* file generated by **LLama**'s *-D, -S,* or *-s* switch.

Table 4.12. Top-Down Parse Algorithm, Final Version

parse stack	a stack of `int`s
value stack	a stack of `yyvstype` structures, with `left` and `right` fields, as described earlier. This stack is the same size as the parse stack.
`Yy_d`	one of the two tables in Figure 4.6.
`Yy_pushtab`	the other of the two tables in Figure 4.6.
Initially:	Push the numeric value of the goal symbol onto the parse stack. Push a meaningless place marker onto the value stack so that it is in phase with the parse stack.

```
while( the parse stack is not empty )
{
    if( the symbol at top of stack represents an action )
    {
        Execute the associated code and pop the action item.
    }
    else if( the symbol at top of stack represents a terminal )
    {
        if( that symbol doesn't match the input symbol )
            Syntax error.
        else
        {
            Pop one item off the parse stack.
            Advance.
        }
    }
    else                          /* top-of-stack symbol is a nonterminal */
    {
        what_to_do = Yyd[ top-of-stack symbol ] [ current lookahead symbol ];

        if( what_to_do == -1 )
            Syntax error.
        else
        {
            val = right field of item at top of value stack

            Pop one item off both the parse and value stacks.
            Push all the items listed in Yy_pushtab[ what_to_do ] onto the parse stack.
            Push the same number of items onto the value stack,
                                    initializing both fields to val.
        }
    }
}
```

4.6 LL(1) Grammars and Their Limitations*

The concept of an LL(1) grammar was introduced in Chapter Three. This class of grammar can be parsed by a parser that reads the input from left to right and does a left-most derivation of the parse tree. It needs at most one character of lookahead. There are LL(0) grammars, which require no lookahead, but they're too limited to be useful in a   LL(0) grammars. compiler—all that they can do is recognize finite strings. LL(0) grammars are a subset

of the right-linear grammars discussed in the last chapter—they can have no ε productions in them.

The main task of a program like **LLama** is to manufacture the parse tables from the
tokenized input grammar. The basic parse table (called Yyd in the previous section) is a
two-dimensional array, the rows are indexed by nonterminal symbols and columns by
terminal symbols. The array contains either an error indicator or the number of the production to apply when a specified nonterminal is at the top of the parse stack and a particular terminal is in the input stream. This parse table can only be created if the input
grammar is an LL(1) grammar.

An LL(1) grammar is limited in many ways, which are best explained by looking at
how the parser determines what productions to apply in a given situation, and by looking
at grammars that the parser can't use because it can't make this determination. Consider
the following production that recognizes simple expressions comprised of numbers,
parentheses and minus signs.

> *How a parser decides which productions to apply.*

1:	*expression*	→	**OPEN_PAREN** *expression* **CLOSE_PAREN**
2:		|	**NUMBER MINUS** *expression*

If an *expression* is on top of the parse stack, the parser must determine which of the two
possible productions to apply. It makes the decision by looking at the current lookahead
token. If this token is a **OPEN_PAREN**, the parser applies the top production; if it's a
NUMBER, the bottom production is applied. If any other symbol is the lookahead symbol, then an error has occurred. Note that if you were to add a production of the form

expression → **NUMBER PLUS** *expression*

to the foregoing grammar, you could no longer determine which of the two right-hand
sides that start with a **NUMBER** to apply when an *expression* was on top of the stack.
The grammar would not be LL(1) in this case.

The situation is complicated somewhat in the following grammar:

1:	*expression*	→	**OPEN_PAREN** *expression* **CLOSE_PAREN**
2:		|	*term* **MINUS** *expression*
3:	*term*	→	**NUMBER**
4:		|	**IDENTIFIER**

Here also, the top production is applied when an *expression* is on top of the stack and an
OPEN_PAREN is in the input. You need to look further than the actual production to
determine whether you can apply Production 2, however. Since the second production
starts with a nonterminal, you can't tell what to do by looking at Production 2 only. You
can resolve the problem by tracing down the grammar, looking at the symbols that can
occur at the beginning of the nonterminal. Since a *term* begins the second production,
and a *term* can start with either a **NUMBER** or **IDENTIFIER**, the parser can apply the
second production if an *expression* is on top the stack and the input symbol is a
NUMBER or **IDENTIFIER**. Note that problems would arise if you added a production
of the form

expression → **NUMBER**

in the previous grammar, because, if a **NUMBER** were the lookahead symbol, the parser
couldn't determine whether to apply Production 2 or the new production. If this situation existed, the grammar would not be LL(1).

Let's complicate the situation further with this grammar, which describes a simple
compound statement that can either contain another statement or be empty:

1:	*statement*	→	**OPEN_CURLY** *expression* **CLOSE_CURLY**
2:		|	*expression* **SEMICOLON**
3:	*expression*	→	**OPEN_PAREN** *expression* **CLOSE_PAREN**
4:		|	*term* **MINUS** *expression*
5:		|	ε
6:	*term*	→	**NUMBER**
7:		|	**IDENTIFIER**

Production 1 is applied if a *statement* is on top of the stack and the input symbol is an **OPEN_CURLY.** Similarly, Production 2 is applied when a *statement* is on top of the stack and the input symbol is an **OPEN_PAREN, NUMBER,** or **IDENTIFIER** (an **OPEN_PAREN** because an *expression* can start with an **OPEN_PAREN** by Production 3, a **NUMBER** or **IDENTIFIER** because an *expression* can start with a *term,* which can, in turn, start with a **NUMBER** or **IDENTIFIER.** The situation is complicated when an *expression* is on top of the stack, however. You can use the same rules as before to figure out whether to apply Productions 3 or 4, but what about the ε production (Production 5)? The situation is resolved by looking at the symbols that can <u>follow</u> an *expression* in the grammar. If *expression* goes to ε, it effectively disappears from the current derivation (from the parse tree)—it becomes transparent. So, if an *expression* is on top of the stack, apply Production 5 if the current lookahead symbol can <u>follow</u> an *expression* (if it is a **CLOSE_CURLY, CLOSE_PAREN,** or **SEMICOLON**). In this last situation, there would be serious problems if **CLOSE_CURLY** could also start an *expression.* The grammar would not be LL(1) were this the case.

4.7 Making the Parse Tables*

I'll now formalize the foregoing rules and show how to use these rules to make a top-down parse table such as the one in Figure 4.6 on page 210. This section discusses the theory; code that implements this theory is presented later on in the chapter.

4.7.1 FIRST Sets*

The set of terminal symbols that can appear at the far left of any parse tree derived from a particular nonterminal is that nonterminal's *FIRST* set. Informally, if you had a bunch of productions that all had *expression* on the left-hand side, FIRST(*expression*) (pronounced "first of expression") would comprise all terminals that can start an expression. In the case of the C language, this set would include numbers, open parentheses, minus signs, and so forth, but it would not include a close parenthesis, because that symbol can't start an expression. Note that ε is considered to be a terminal symbol, so it can appear in a FIRST set. First sets can be formed using the rules in Table 4.13. I'll demonstrate how to find FIRST sets with an example, using the grammar in table 4.13.

The FIRST sets are put together in a multiple-pass process, starting out with the easy ones. Initially, add those nonterminals that are at the far left of a right-hand side:

Computing FIRST sets, an example.

FIRST(*stmt*)	=	{ }
FIRST(*expr*)	=	{ }
FIRST(*expr'*)	=	{**PLUS**}
FIRST(*term*)	=	{ }
FIRST(*term'*)	=	{**TIMES**}

Table 4.13. Finding FIRST Sets

(1)	FIRST(**A**), where **A** is a terminal symbol, is {**A**}. If A is ε, then ε is put into the FIRST set.
(2)	Given a production of the form

$$s \rightarrow \mathbf{A}\, \alpha$$

where s is a nonterminal symbol, **A** is a terminal symbol, and α is a collection of zero or more terminals and nonterminals, **A** is a member of FIRST(s).

(3)   Given a production of the form

$$s \rightarrow b\, \alpha$$

where s and b is are single nonterminal symbols, and α is a collection of terminals and nonterminals, everything in FIRST(b) is also in FIRST(s).

This rule can be generalized. Given a production of the form:

$$s \rightarrow \alpha\, \mathcal{B}\, \beta$$

where s is a nonterminal symbol, α is a collection of zero or more <u>nullable</u> nonterminals,† $\mathcal{B}$ is a single terminal or nonterminal symbol, and β is a collection of terminals and nonterminals, then FIRST(s) includes the union of FIRST($\mathcal{B}$) and FIRST(α). For example, if α consists of the three nullable nonterminals x, y, and z, then FIRST(s) includes all the members of FIRST(x), FIRST(y), and FIRST(z), along with everything in FIRST($\mathcal{B}$).

† A nonterminal is nullable if it can go to ε by some derivation. ε is always a member of a nullable nonterminal's FIRST set.

Table 4.14. Yet Another Expression Grammar

1:	*stmt*	→	*expr* **SEMI**
2:	*expr*	→	*term* *expr*′
3:		|	ε
4:	*expr*′	→	**PLUS** *term* *expr*′
5:		|	ε
6:	*term*	→	*factor* *term*′
7:	*term*′	→	**TIMES** *factor* *term*′
8:		|	ε
9:	*factor*	→	**LEFT_PAREN** *expr* **RIGHT_PAREN**
10:		|	**NUMBER**

FIRST(*factor*)   =   {**LEFT_PAREN, NUMBER**}

Next, close the sets (perform a closure operation on the initial sets) using the foregoing rules. Everything in FIRST(*factor*) is also in FIRST(*term*) because *factor* is the leftmost symbol on the right-hand side of *term*. Similarly, everything in FIRST(*term*) is also in FIRST(*expr*), and everything in FIRST(*expr*) is also in FIRST(*stmt*). Finally, *expr* is a nullable nonterminal at the left of *stmt*'s right-hand side, so I'll add SEMI to FIRST(*stmt*). Applying these relationships yields the following first sets:

FIRST(*stmt*)   =   {**LEFT_PAREN, NUMBER, SEMI**}
FIRST(*expr*)   =   {**LEFT_PAREN, NUMBER**}

FIRST(*expr'*)	=	{**PLUS**}
FIRST(*term*)	=	{**LEFT_PAREN, NUMBER**}
FIRST(*term'*)	=	{**TIMES**}
FIRST(*factor*)	=	{**LEFT_PAREN, NUMBER**}

One final note: the FIRST notation is a little confusing because you see it used in three ways:

FIRST(**A**)   (**A** is a terminal) is **A**. Since ε is a terminal, then FIRST(ε) = {ε}.

FIRST(*x*)   (*x* is a nonterminal) is that nonterminal's FIRST set, described above.

FIRST(α)   (α is a collection of terminals and nonterminals) is the FIRST set computed using the procedure in Rule (3), above: FIRST(α) always includes the FIRST set of the leftmost symbol in α. If that symbol is nullable, then it is the union of the FIRST sets of the first two symbols, if both of these symbols are nullable, then it is the union of the first three symbols, and so forth. If all the symbols in α are nullable, then FIRST(α) includes ε.

A subroutine that computes FIRST sets is presented towards the end of the current chapter in Listing 4.27 on page 305.

4.7.2 FOLLOW Sets*

The other set of symbols that you need in order to make the parse tables are the *FOLLOW* sets. A terminal symbol is in a nonterminal's FOLLOW set if it can follow that nonterminal in some derivation. You can find a nonterminal's FOLLOW set with the rules in Table 4.15. To see how Rule 3 in Table 4.14 works, consider the following grammar:

1:	*compound_stmt*	→	**OPEN_CURLY** *stmt_list* **CLOSE_CURLY**
2:	*stmt_list*	→	*stmt_list stmt*
3:	*stmt*	→	*expr* **SEMI**

CLOSE_CURLY is in FOLLOW(*stmt_list*) because it follows *stmt_list* in Production 1. **CLOSE_CURLY** is also in FOLLOW(*stmt*) because of the second of the following derivations:

$$compound\_stmt \overset{L}{\Rightarrow} \textbf{OPEN\_CURLY } stmt\_list \textbf{ CLOSE\_CURLY}$$
$$\overset{L}{\Rightarrow} \textbf{OPEN\_CURLY } stmt\_list \ stmt \textbf{ CLOSE\_CURLY}$$
$$\overset{L}{\Rightarrow} \textbf{OPEN\_CURLY } stmt\_list \ expr \textbf{ SEMI CLOSE\_CURLY}$$

The *stmt_list* in the first sentential form was replaced by the right-hand side of Production 2 (*stmt_list stmt*), and in that derivation, a **CLOSE_CURLY** followed the *stmt*.

I'll demonstrate how to compute FOLLOW sets with the earlier grammar in Table 4.14 on page 214. In the initial pass, apply the first two rules for forming FOLLOW sets: **SEMI** and **RIGHT_PAREN** are added to FOLLOW(*expr*) because they actually follow it in Productions 1 and 9; **PLUS** is added to FOLLOW(*term*) because everything in FIRST(*expr'*) must be in FOLLOW(*term*) by Production 4; **TIMES** is added to FOLLOW(*factor*) because everything in FIRST(*term'*) must be in FOLLOW(*factor*) by Productions 6 and 7. The initial pass looks like this:

Computing FOLLOW sets, an example.

FOLLOW(*stmt*)	=	{⊢}
FOLLOW(*expr*)	=	{**SEMI, RIGHT_PAREN**}
FOLLOW(*expr'*)	=	{}

Table 4.15. Finding FOLLOW Sets

(1)	If s is the goal symbol, $\vdash$ (the end-of-input marker) is in FOLLOW(s);
(2)	Given a production of the form:

$$s \rightarrow \ldots a \, \mathcal{B} \ldots$$

where a is a nonterminal and $\mathcal{B}$ is either a terminal or nonterminal, FIRST($\mathcal{B}$) is in FOLLOW(a);

To generalize further, given a production of the form:

$$s \rightarrow \ldots a \, \alpha \, \mathcal{B} \ldots$$

where s and a are nonterminals, α is a collection of zero or more nullable nonterminals and $\mathcal{B}$ is either a terminal or nonterminal. FOLLOW(a) includes the union of FIRST(α) and FIRST($\mathcal{B}$).

(3)	Given a production of the form:

$$s \rightarrow \ldots a$$

where a is the rightmost nonterminal on the right-hand side of a production, everything in FOLLOW(s) is also in FOLLOW(a). (I'll describe how this works in a moment.) To generalize further, given a production of the form:

$$s \rightarrow \ldots a \, \alpha$$

where s and a are nonterminals, and α is a collection of zero or more nullable nonterminals, everything in FOLLOW(s) is also in FOLLOW(a).

$$
\begin{aligned}
\text{FOLLOW}(\textit{term}) &= \{\textbf{PLUS}\} \\
\text{FOLLOW}(\textit{term}') &= \{\} \\
\text{FOLLOW}(\textit{factor}) &= \{\textbf{TIMES}\}
\end{aligned}
$$

Now close the FOLLOW sets by making several passes through them, applying Rule 3 repetitively until nothing more is added to any FOLLOW set. The following holds:

- Everything in FOLLOW(*expr*) is also in FOLLOW(*expr'*) by Production 2.
- Everything in FOLLOW(*term*) is also in FOLLOW(*term'*) by Production 7.
- Since *expr'* is nullable, everything in FOLLOW(*expr'*) is also in FOLLOW(*term*) by Production 4.
- Since *term'* is nullable, everything in FOLLOW(*term'*) is also in FOLLOW(*factor*) by Production 7.

The first closure pass applies these identities to the original FOLLOW sets, yielding the following sets:

$$
\begin{aligned}
\text{FOLLOW}(\textit{stmt}) &= \{\vdash\} \\
\text{FOLLOW}(\textit{expr}) &= \{\textbf{SEMI, RIGHT\_PAREN}\} \\
\text{FOLLOW}(\textit{expr}') &= \{\textbf{SEMI, RIGHT\_PAREN}\} \\
\text{FOLLOW}(\textit{term}) &= \{\textbf{PLUS, SEMI, RIGHT\_PAREN}\} \\
\text{FOLLOW}(\textit{term}') &= \{\textbf{PLUS}\} \\
\text{FOLLOW}(\textit{factor}) &= \{\textbf{TIMES, PLUS}\}
\end{aligned}
$$

Another pass, using the same identities, adds a few more elements:

$$
\begin{aligned}
\text{FOLLOW}(\textit{stmt}) &= \{\vdash\} \\
\text{FOLLOW}(\textit{expr}) &= \{\textbf{SEMI, RIGHT\_PAREN}\}
\end{aligned}
$$

FOLLOW($expr'$)	=	{SEMI, RIGHT_PAREN}
FOLLOW($term$)	=	{PLUS, SEMI, RIGHT_PAREN}
FOLLOW($term'$)	=	{PLUS, SEMI, RIGHT_PAREN}
FOLLOW($factor$)	=	{TIMES, PLUS, SEMI, RIGHT_PAREN}

A third pass adds nothing to the FOLLOW sets, so you're done. A subroutine that computes FOLLOW sets is presented towards the end of the current chapter in Listing 4.28 on page 307.

4.7.3 LL(1) Selection Sets*

To review a bit, an LL(1) parse table looks like this:

input symbol

nonterminal | error marker or production number

The columns are indexed by input symbol, the rows by nonterminal symbol. The table holds either a marker that signifies a syntax error or the number of a production to apply, given the current top-of-stack and input symbols. Each production has a unique, but arbitrary, production number. Typically, the start production is Production 0, the next one is Production 1, and so forth.

The LL(1) *selection set* for a given production is the set of nonterminals for which there are legal entries in any given row of the parse table. For example, a grammar could have the following productions in it: LL(1) selection set.

1.	*terminal*	→	**PERKIN_ELMER** *pk*
2.		|	**ADM3** *adm*
3.		|	*dec_term*
4.	*dec_term*	→	**VT_52**
5.		|	**VT_100**

The parse table for this grammar looks like this:

	PERKIN_ELMER	**ADM3**	**VT_52**	**VT_100**
terminal	1	2	3	3
dec_term	error	error	4	5

The number 1 is in the **PERKIN_ELMER** column of the *terminal* row, because Production 1 is applied if a *term* is at top of stack and **PERKIN_ELMER** is the lookahead symbol, and so forth. The same relationships are indicated by these selection sets:

SELECT(1)	=	{ **PERKIN_ELMER** }
SELECT(2)	=	{ **ADM3** }
SELECT(3)	=	{ **VT_52, VT_100** }
SELECT(4)	=	{ **VT_52** }
SELECT(5)	=	{ **VT_100** }

SELECT(3) indicates that Production 3 is selected if the left-hand side of Production 3 is on the top of the stack, and the current lookahead symbol is **VT_52** or **VT_100**. In general, if you have both a production N (which takes the form $s{\to}\alpha$) and a token **T**, then **T** is in SELECT(N) if production N should be applied when s is on the top of the parse stack and **T** is the current lookahead symbol. Note that the selection sets are attached to the individual productions, not to the nonterminals. For a grammar to be LL(1), all productions that share a left-hand side must have unique selection sets, otherwise the parser wouldn't know what to do in a given situation. [This is the real definition of LL(1).] The

LL(1) selection sets are formed using the rules in Table 4.16.

Table 4.16. Finding LL(1) Selection Sets

(1)	A production is *nullable* if the entire right-hand side can go to ε. This is the case, both when the right-hand side consists only of ε, and when all symbols on the right-hand side can go to ε by some derivation.
(2)	**For nonnullable productions:** Given a production of the form $s \rightarrow \alpha\ \mathcal{B}$ where s is a nonterminal, α is a collection of one or more nullable nonterminals, and $\mathcal{B}$ is a terminal or a nonnullable nonterminal (one that can't go to ε), the LL(1) select set for that production is the union of FIRST(α) and FIRST($\mathcal{B}$). That is, it's the union of the FIRST sets for every nonterminal in α plus FIRST($\mathcal{B}$). If α doesn't exist (there are no nullable nonterminals to the left of B), then SELECT(s)={FIRST($\mathcal{B}$)}.
(3)	**For nullable productions:** Given a production of the form $s \rightarrow \alpha$ where s is a nonterminal, α is a collection of zero or more nullable nonterminals (it can be ε), the LL(1) select set for that production is the union of FIRST(α) and FOLLOW(s). In plain words: if a production is nullable, it can be transparent—it can disappear entirely in some derivation (be replaced by an empty string). Consequently, if the production is transparent, you have to look through it to the symbols that can follow it to determine whether it can be applied in a given situation.

Note that ε is used to compute the selection sets because s is nullable if FIRST(s) contains ε. Nonetheless, ε is not itself a member of any selection set. The selection sets can be translated into a parse table with the algorithm in Table 4.17.

Translating SELECT sets into an LL(1) parse table.

Table 4.17. Translating SELECT Sets into LL(1) Parse Tables.

```
Initialize the table to all error transitions;
for( each production, N, in the grammar )
{
        lhs = the left-hand side of production N;
        for( every token in SELECT(N) )
                parse_table[ lhs ][ token ] = N;
}
```

4.8 Modifying Grammars*

All top-down parsers, including recursive-descent parsers, must use LL(1) grammars, which are are quite limited. The main problem is that LL(1) grammars can't be left recursive. Since you can't just dispense with left associativity, LL(1) grammars would not be very useful unless some mechanism existed to translate left-recursive grammars into left associative, LL(1) grammars. This section looks at various ways that you can manipulate grammars algebraically to make them LL(1); the techniques are useful with other classes of grammars as well.

The following discussion uses the generic-grammar notation discussed at the end of Chapter Three without always calling out what everything means. Just remember that Greek letters represent collections of terminals and nonterminals, letters like $\mathcal{A}$ and $\mathcal{B}$ represent a single terminal or nonterminal, italics are used for single nonterminals, and boldface is used for single terminals.

4.8.1 Unreachable Productions*

An *unreachable* nonterminal is one that can't possibly appear in a parse tree rooted at the goal symbol. That is, there's no derivation from the goal symbol in which the unreachable nonterminal can appear in the viable prefix. For example, in the following grammar:

Unreachable nonterminal.

1.   *s*   →   *a*
2.   *a*   →   **TERM**
3.   *b*   →   **TERM_TWO**

Production 3 is clearly unreachable because *b* appears on no right-hand side. The situation is not always so cut and dried. Productions 3 and 4 are both unreachable in the following grammar, even though *b* and *c* both appear on right-hand sides:

1.   *s*   →   *a*
2.   *a*   →   **TERM**
3.   *b*   →   **TERM_TWO** *c*
4.   *c*   →   **TERM_TOO** *b*

Many of the transformation techniques discussed below create unreachable nonterminals and, since productions with these nonterminals on their left-hand sides have no useful function in the grammar, they should be removed. You can use the algorithm in Table 4.18.

4.8.2 Left Factoring*

A production like the following has two problems: It is clearly not LL(1) because the left-hand sides of both productions start with an **IF** token so they can't possibly have disjoint selection sets. Also, it is ambiguous because the same nonterminal appears twice on the right-hand side:

    statement   →   **IF** *test* **THEN** *statement* **ELSE** *statement*
               | **IF** *test* **THEN** *statement*

Note that this is also a pretty serious ambiguity because it controls the ways that **if** and **else** statements bind. Input like the following:

*Ambiguity in **if/else**, binding problems.*

```
if( expr ) then
    if( expr2 ) then
        statement();
    else
        statement();
```

can create either of the trees pictured in Figure 4.7. The top parse causes the **else** to bind to the closest preceding **if**—the behavior required by most programming languages. In the second parser, though, the **else** incorrectly binds to first **if**.

Both problems can be solved by a process known as *left factoring*, which isolates the common parts of two productions into a single production. Any production of the form:

Left factoring.

Table 4.18. Eliminating Unreachable Productions

Data structures:	A stack A list of reachable nonterminals.
Initially:	Both the stack and the list are empty.
(1)	Add the goal symbol to the set of reachable nonterminals and push the goal symbol onto the stack.

(2)	while(the stack is not empty)
	{
	    s = pop one item off the stack
	    for(each nonterminal, x, on a right-hand side of s)
	        if(x is not in the list of reachable nonterminals)
	        {
	            push x;
	            add x to the list of reachable nonterminals
	        }
	}

(3)	Remove from the grammar all productions whose left-hand sides are not in the list of reachable nonterminals.

Figure 4.7. Parse Trees of an Ambiguous IF/ELSE Grammar

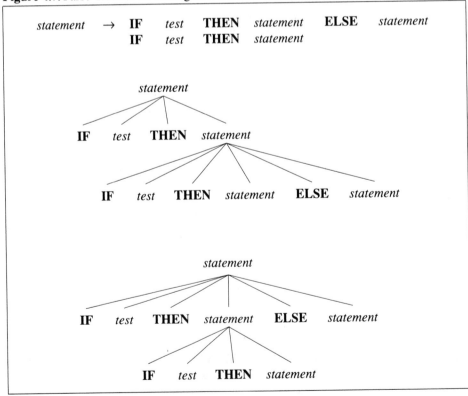

$$a \quad \rightarrow \quad \alpha\,\beta_1$$
$$\cdots$$
$$| \quad \alpha\,\beta_n$$

where α is a sequence of <u>one</u> or more symbols that appear at the start of every right-hand side, and β_1 to β_n are dissimilar collections of zero or more symbols, can be replaced by the following:

$$a \quad \rightarrow \quad \alpha\,a'$$
$$a' \quad \rightarrow \quad \beta_1$$
$$\cdots$$
$$| \quad \beta_n$$

The a' is just an arbitrary name for the new left-hand side. In the current example:

a	corresponds to	*statement*
α	corresponds to	**IF** *test* **THEN** *statement*
β_1	corresponds to	**ELSE** *statement*
β_2	corresponds to	ε

β_2 goes to ε because there's nothing in the second production that corresponds to the **ELSE** *statement* in the first production. You can plug the foregoing into our equation and replace the original productions with the following:

statement	$\rightarrow$	**IF** *test* **THEN** *statement* *opt_else_clause*
opt_else_clause	$\rightarrow$	**ELSE** *statement*
		ε

Note that this replacement has also eliminated the ambiguity, because only one parse tree can now be generated from the earlier input.

4.8.3 Corner Substitution*

In general, given a left-hand side with one or more right-hand sides:

$$p \quad \rightarrow \quad \alpha_1$$
$$| \quad \alpha_2$$
$$\cdots$$
$$| \quad \alpha_n$$

and given a production of the form:

$$s \quad \rightarrow \quad \beta\ p\ \gamma$$

this last production can be replaced with several productions of the form:

$$s \quad \rightarrow \quad \beta\ \alpha_1\ \gamma$$
$$| \quad \beta\ \alpha_2\ \gamma$$
$$\cdots$$
$$| \quad \beta\ \alpha_n\ \gamma$$

This process is called a *substitution*.   Substitution.

In a production of the form $a \rightarrow \mathcal{A}\,\alpha$, the leftmost symbol on the right-hand side ($\mathcal{A}$) is said to be a *corner* of a. An ε production doesn't have a corner. In a *corner substitution*   Corner. you replace one or more of the nonterminal corners in a grammar with that corner's right-hand sides.

For example, consider the following grammar, which recognizes a list of one or more **ATOM**s. The **ATOM**s can be single **ATOM**s, they can be followed by a bracketed number (**LB** and **RB** stand for left and right bracket), or they can be preceded by any number of **STAR**s.

1.	*atom_list*	$\rightarrow$	**ATOM**
2.		|	*list_ele atom_list*
3.	*list_ele*	$\rightarrow$	**ATOM LB NUMBER RB**
4.		|	**STAR** *list_ele*

This grammar is not LL(1) because, **ATOM** is in FIRST(*list_ele*) by Production 3, and as a consequence, is also in SELECT(2). A substitution of the *list_ele* corner of Production 2 can help fix this situation. First, you replace all instances of *list_ele* in Production 2 with the right-hand sides of the two *list_ele* productions (3 and 4), yielding:

1.	*atom_list*	$\rightarrow$	**ATOM**	
2a.		|	**ATOM LB NUMBER LB**	*atom_list*
2b.		|	**STAR** *list_ele*	*atom_list*
3.	*list_ele*	$\rightarrow$	**ATOM LB NUMBER RB**	
4.		|	**STAR** *list_ele*	

The grammar is still not LL(1) because Productions 1 and 2a both start with an **ATOM**, but that situation can be rectified by left factoring:

1.	*atom_list*	$\rightarrow$	**ATOM** *atom_list'*
2b.		|	**STAR** *list_ele atom_list*
1b.	*atom_list'*	$\rightarrow$	**LB NUMBER RB** *atom_list*
1c.		|	ε
3.	*list_ele*	$\rightarrow$	**ATOM LB NUMBER RB**
4.		|	**STAR** *list_ele*

Corner substitution preserves LL(1) properties.

Corner substitution preserves the LL(1) properties of a grammar—grammars that start out LL(1) are still LL(1) after the corner substitution is made. You can see why if you consider how FIRST sets are computed. If x is a corner of production s, then FIRST(s) includes FIRST(x), and FIRST(x) is computed by looking at the right-hand side of x. Substituting x for its right-hand side does not affect this computation.

Q Grammars.

One common use of corner substitution and left factoring takes advantage of this property by rearranging the grammar so that every right-hand side in the grammar either starts with a unique terminal symbol or is ε. That is, if a nonterminal has several right-hand sides, then all those right-hand sides will start with different terminal symbols or be ε. This particular type of grammar is called a Q grammar and is handy when you build recursive-descent parsers because it's very easy to code from a Q grammar. That is, given a Q grammar like the following:

p	$\rightarrow$	$\mathbf{T}_1\, \alpha_1$
	|	$\mathbf{T}_2\, \alpha_2$
$\cdots$		
	|	$\mathbf{T}_n\, \alpha_n$
	|	ε

where $\mathbf{T}_1 \ldots \mathbf{T}_n$ are unique terminal symbols, you can code it like this:

```
p()
{
    switch( lookahead_character )
    {
    case T₁:   advance(); α₁
    case T₂:   advance(); α₂
    ...
    case Tₙ:   advance(); αₙ

    default:           /* Handle the epsilon production */
    }
}
```

4.8.4 Singleton Substitution*

Generally, it's not productive to replace symbols that aren't corners—you shouldn't replace nonterminals that aren't at the far left of a right-hand side. The problem here is that the substitution usually creates several productions that have the same corner, and as a consequence the resulting grammar won't be LL(1). For example, substituting the *num_or_id* for its right-hand side in the following grammar:

Substitutions can create ambiguity.

1.	*expr*	→	*UNOP num_or_id*
2.	*num_or_id*	→	*NAME*
3.		|	*IDENTIFIER*

yields the following, non-LL(1) grammar:

1.	*expr*	→	*UNOP NAME*
1a.		|	*UNOP IDENTIFIER*

You've just done a reverse left factoring.

If a production has only one right-hand side, of course, the substitution is harmless. In fact, it can reduce the size of the grammar by eliminating productions and is often useful for this reason. This sort of production is called a *singleton*.

It's sometimes desirable to create singletons by breaking out a group of symbols from the middle of a production. That is, the following:

$$s \quad \rightarrow \quad \alpha \beta \gamma$$

can be changed into:

$$s \quad \rightarrow \quad \alpha s' \gamma$$
$$s' \quad \rightarrow \quad \beta$$

This technique is used primarily in bottom-up parsers, in which action symbols must be at the far right of the production. As a consequence, a production like this:

Singleton substitution used to isolate actions for bottom-up parser.

$$s \quad \rightarrow \quad tempest \ \{\texttt{act(1);}\} \ scene\_5$$

must be implemented like this:

$$s \quad \rightarrow \quad tempest \ s' \ scene\_5$$
$$s' \quad \rightarrow \quad \{\texttt{act(1);}\}$$

4.8.5 Eliminating Ambiguity*

Ambiguous productions are those that have more than one occurrence of a given nonterminal on their right-hand side. As we've seen, left factoring can be used to eliminate ambiguity, moving the rightmost of these nonterminals further down the parse tree by introducing a new production. In general given an ambiguous production of the form:

$$s \quad \rightarrow \quad \alpha\, p\, \beta\, p\, \gamma$$

you can eliminate the ambiguity by introducing a new production, as follows:

$$s \quad \rightarrow \quad \alpha\, p\, \beta\, s'$$
$$s' \quad \rightarrow \quad p\, \gamma$$

If the grammar has a production of the form:

$$p \quad \rightarrow \quad s$$

Controlling associativity when eliminating ambiguity.

this transformation makes the grammar left-associative, because there is now an indirect left recursion, demonstrated with the following derivation:

$$s' \Rightarrow p\, \gamma \Rightarrow s\, \gamma$$

If an ambiguous right-hand side is one of several, then all of these must move as part of the substitution. For example, given:

$$e \quad \rightarrow \quad e + e$$
$$\mid \quad \textbf{NUM}$$

you transform the grammar to be left-associative like this:

$$e \quad \rightarrow \quad e + t \mid t$$
$$t \quad \rightarrow \quad e$$
$$\mid \quad \textbf{NUM}$$

or right-associative like this:

$$e \quad \rightarrow \quad t + e \mid t$$
$$t \quad \rightarrow \quad e$$
$$\mid \quad \textbf{NUM}$$

Note that the foregoing transformation introduced a production of the form $e \rightarrow t$ into the grammar. You can use this production to modify the grammar again:

$$e \quad \rightarrow \quad t + e \mid t$$
$$t \quad \rightarrow \quad t$$
$$\mid \quad \textbf{NUM}$$

A production of the form $t \rightarrow t$ does nothing useful, so it can be eliminated:

$$e \quad \rightarrow \quad t + e \mid t$$
$$t \quad \rightarrow \quad \textbf{NUM}$$

To generalize, given grammars of the form:

$$s \quad \rightarrow \quad \alpha\, s\, \beta\, s\, \gamma \mid \alpha_1 \mid ... \mid \alpha_n$$

you can eliminate the ambiguity in favor of right associativity by replacing the foregoing with the following:

$$s \quad \rightarrow \quad \alpha\, s'\, \beta\, s\, \gamma \mid s'$$
$$s' \quad \rightarrow \quad s \mid \alpha_1 \mid ... \mid \alpha_n$$

Now, because a production of the form $s \rightarrow s'$ has been created you can substitute the s's for s''s in the new production, yielding:

$$s \quad \rightarrow \quad \alpha\, s'\, \beta\, s\, \gamma \quad | \quad s'$$
$$s' \quad \rightarrow \quad s' \quad | \quad \alpha_1 \quad |...| \quad \alpha_n$$

and since that production of the form $s' \rightarrow s'$ doesn't do anything useful, it can be eliminated, yielding:

$$s \quad \rightarrow \quad \alpha\, s'\, \beta\, s\, \gamma \quad | \quad s'$$
$$s' \quad \rightarrow \quad \alpha_1 \quad |...| \quad \alpha_n$$

The same applies in a left-associative situation. Productions of the form:

$$s \quad \rightarrow \quad \alpha\, s\, \beta\, s\, \gamma \mid \alpha_1 \mid...\mid \alpha_n$$

can be disambiguated in favor of left-associativity by replacing the right occurrence of s rather than the left one in the initial step.

If a grammar has several ambiguous productions, it can be modified by repetitive application of the previous transformation. Similarly, if the s in the earlier general example appears on more than one right-hand side, then it can be replaced with s' in all the right-hand sides. For example, starting with the following expression grammar:

1.	e	$\rightarrow$	$e + e$
2.		|	$e * e$
3.		|	**NUM**

I'll eliminate the ambiguity one production at a time. Note that the order in which the disambiguating rules are applied also affects operator precedence—the operators that are lower down in the grammar are of higher precedence. In an expression grammar like the current one, you want to start with the right-hand side that has the lowest-precedence operator, Production 1. Since addition must be left associative, the transformed production must also be left associative, so you must replace the <u>right</u> e in Production 1, yielding:

Controlling precedence when eliminating ambiguity.

1a.	e	$\rightarrow$	$e + e'$
1b.		|	e'
1c.	e'	$\rightarrow$	e
2.		|	$e * e$
3.		|	**NUM**

Now, since a production of the form $e \rightarrow e'$ exists, you can substitute e's for e''s in Productions 1c, and 2, yielding:

1a.	e	$\rightarrow$	$e + e'$
1b.		|	e'
1c.	e'	$\rightarrow$	e'
2.		|	$e' * e'$
3.		|	**NUM**

Production 1c now does nothing useful because the left- and right-hand sides are identical, so it can be removed from the grammar:

1a.	e	$\rightarrow$	$e + e'$
1b.		|	e'
2.	e'	$\rightarrow$	$e' * e'$
3.		|	**NUM**

You can now apply the same process to Production 2 to get the following grammar:

1a.	e	$\rightarrow$	$e + e'$
1b.		|	e'
2a.	e'	$\rightarrow$	$e' * e''$
2b.		|	e''
2c	e''	$\rightarrow$	e'
3.		|	**NUM**

and substituing the e' for e'' in Production 2c, you get:

1a.	e	$\rightarrow$	$e + e'$
1b.		|	e'
2a.	e'	$\rightarrow$	$e' * e''$
2b.		|	e''
2c.	e''	$\rightarrow$	e''
3.		|	**NUM**

Finally, removing the redundant production yields:

1a.	e	$\rightarrow$	$e + e'$
1b.		|	e'
2a.	e'	$\rightarrow$	$e' * e''$
2b.		|	e''
3.	e''	$\rightarrow$	**NUM**

This grammar is left associative, and + is lower precedence than *.

4.8.6 Eliminating Left Recursion*

LL(1) grammars cannot be left recursive.

LL(1) grammars cannot be left recursive. The basic proof of this statement is as follows:

(1) In all practical grammars, if any right-hand side of a production is left recursive, there must be at least one nonrecursive right-hand side for the same nonterminal. For example, if a grammar has a singleton production of the form $s \rightarrow s\ \alpha$, all derivations that use that production go on forever:

s	$\Rightarrow$	$s\ \alpha$
	$\Rightarrow$	$s\ \alpha\ \alpha$
	$\Rightarrow$	$s\ \alpha\ \alpha\ \alpha$
	$\cdots$	

You need to add a nonrecursive right-hand side of s for the derivation to terminate.

(2) If x is a left-recursive nonterminal, the selection sets for all productions with x on their left-hand side must contain FIRST(x), so, in all practical grammars, left-recursive productions must have selection-set conflicts.

Unfortunately, you need left recursion to get left associativity in a list. Fortunately, you can always eliminate left recursion from a grammar in such a way that the translated grammar recognizes the same input strings. The basic strategy looks at what left-recursive list grammars actually do. A list such as an expression (a list of operands separated by operators) is either a single operand or a single operand followed by one or more operator/operand pairs. You can express this structure with the following left-recursive grammar:

list	$\rightarrow$	*operand*
	|	*list operator operand*

The following nonrecursive grammar recognizes the same input strings, however:

> *list*   →   *operand list′*
> *list′*   →   *operator operand*
> | ε

So, our goal is to translate lists of the first form into lists of the second form. If a production is a self left recursive like the following:

> $s \rightarrow s\,\alpha\,|\,\beta$

(the left-hand side is duplicated as the first symbol on the right-hand side: *s* is a single nonterminal; α and β are collections of terminals and nonterminals), you can make it nonrecursive by shuffling the production around as follows:

> *s*   →   β *s′*
> *s′*   →   α *s′*
> | ε

Applying this translation rule to the following productions:

> *expr* → *expr* + *term* {act2} | *term* {act1}

the following relationships exist between the *s*, α, and β in the rule and the real productions:

> *s*   →   *s*   α | β
> *expr* → *expr* + *term* {act2} | *term* {act1}

s, which is a single nonterminal, corresponds to an *expression;* α, which is a collection of terminals and nonterminals, corresponds to the + *term*, and β, which is also a collection of terminals and nonterminals, corresponds to the second *term* (in this case, it's a collection of only one symbol). Productions like the foregoing can be shuffled around to look like this:

> *s*   →   β *s′*
> *s′*   →   α *s′*
> | ε

The *s′* is a new nonterminal. You could call it anything, but just adding a ′ is easiest. Applying the foregoing to the real productions yields:

> *s*   →   β   *s′*
> *expr* → *term* {act1}   *expr′*
>
> *s′*   →   α   *s′* | ε
> *expr′* → + *term* {act2}   *expr′* | ε

Figure 4.8 shows a parse for the input `1+2+3` for both the untranslated and translated grammars. The important thing to notice is that, even though the parse tree for the translated grammar is now right associative (as you would expect from looking at the grammar), the order in which the terminal nodes are processed is identical in both trees. That is, the actions are performed in the same sequence relative to the input in both grammars. So there is still left associativity from the point of view of code generation, even though the parse itself is right associative.

Order in which actions are executed with transformed grammar.

The foregoing substitution process can be generalized for more complex grammars as follows:

Figure 4.8. Parse Trees for Translated and Untranslated, Left-Associative Grammars

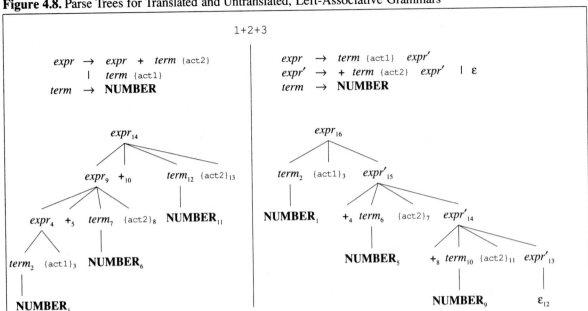

$$s \quad \rightarrow \quad s \ \alpha_1 \mid s \ \alpha_2 \mid \ldots \mid s$$
$$\alpha_n \mid \beta_1 \mid \beta_2 \mid \ldots \mid \beta_m$$

you can replace the foregoing with:

$$s \quad \rightarrow \quad \beta_1 \ s' \mid \beta_2 \ s' \mid \ldots \mid \beta_m \ s'$$
$$s' \quad \rightarrow \quad \alpha_1 \ s' \mid \alpha_2 \ s' \mid \ldots \mid \alpha_n \ s' \mid \varepsilon$$

Corner substitution translates indirect recursion to self recursion.
Though the method just described works only with self-recursive productions, it's an easy matter to use a corner substitution to make an indirectly recursive grammar self recursive. For example, in a grammar like this:

1.   *expr* $\rightarrow$ *ele_list*
2.   *ele_list* $\rightarrow$ *NUMBER*
3. | *expr PLUS NUMBER*

You can use a corner substitution to make the grammar self-recursive, replacing the *ele_list* corner in Production 1 with the right-hand sides of Productions 2 and 3 to yield the following:

1a.   *expr* $\rightarrow$ *NUMBER*
1b. | *expr PLUS NUMBER*

2.   *ele_list* $\rightarrow$ *NUMBER*
3. | *expr PLUS NUMBER*

Productions 2 and 3 are now unreachable, so can be eliminated from the grammar.

4.9 Implementing LL(1) Parsers

The remainder of this chapter discusses implementation details for the foregoing theory. Skip to the next chapter if you're not interested.

4.9.1 Top-Down, Table-Driven Parsing—The LLama Output File

First, an in-depth look at the **LLama** output file, in which the top-down parse algorithm is actually implemented, seems in order. A user's manual for **LLama** is presented in Appendix E, and you should read that appendix before continuing. This section examines the **LLama** output file created from the input file at the end of Appendix E. Listing 4.2 shows token definitions that are generated from the `%term` directives in the **LLama** input file. These are the same symbolic values that are used in the previous section.

Definitions generated from `%term`.

Listing 4.2. *llout.h*— Symbolic Values for Tokens

```
1   #define _EOI_      0
2   #define PLUS       1
3   #define TIMES      2
4   #define NUM_OR_ID  3
5   #define LP         4
6   #define RP         5
7   #define SEMI       6
```

The **LLama** C-source-code output file begins in Listing 4.3. Most of the file is copied from the template file *llama.par*, in a manner identical to the L^{E}X template file described in Chapter Three[4]. Lines three to 23 were copied from the input file, and the remainder of the listing was generated by **LLama**. Lines 28 to 33 define the boundaries of the numbers that represent terminals, nonterminals, and actions on the stack (as were described in the previous section). The minimums won't change, but the maximums will.

Numerical limits of tokenized input symbols.

The next part of *llout.c* (in Listing 4.4) is copied from the template file. *<stdarg.h>* is included on Line 42 only if it hasn't been included earlier. The *<tools/yystack.h>* file included on the next line contains various stack-manipulation macros, and is described in Appendix A. The macros on lines 45 to 47 determine what *x* is, using the earlier limits. The remainder of the listing is macros that define various parser limits described in Appendix E. These definitions are active only if you haven't defined the macros yourself in a `%{ %}` block at the top of the input file. `YY_TTYPE` (on line 34) is used to declare the tables.

Various stacks are declared on lines 89 to 108 of Listing 4.4. The *<yystack.h>* macros described in Appendix A are used for this purpose, and various *<yystack.h>* macros are customized on lines 90 to 94 for the current use—`yyerror()` works like `printf()` but doesn't mess up the windows when it's used. The parse stack is defined on line 98, and the value to stack is on lines 100 to 108. Note that the *<yystack.h>* macros can't be used here because the value stack is a stack of structures.

Parse- and value-stack declarations.

The next part of *llout.c* (in Listing 4.5) is generated by **LLama**. It contains the definitions for the parse tables discussed in the previous section. The tables in Listing

Parse-table declarations.

---

4. That's why some of the following listings are labeled *llama.par* and others are labeled *llout.c*. The tables (which are generated by **LLama**) are in listings labeled *llout.c*. I'm sorry if this is confusing, but it's the only way I can keep track of what's where.

Listing 4.3. *llout.c*— File Header—Numeric Limits

```
1    #include <stdio.h>
2    #define YYDEBUG
3        /*-------------------------------------------------------------
4         * Temporary-variable names are stored on a stack. name() pops a name off
5         * the stack and freename(x) puts it back. A real compiler would do some
6         * checking for stack overflow here, but there's no point in cluttering the
7         * code for now.
8         */
9
10       char        *Namepool[] =
11       {
12           "t0", "t1", "t2", "t3", "t4", "t5", "t6", "t7", "t8", "t9"
13       };
14
15       char **Namep = Namepool ;
16
17       char *newname()          { return(*Namep++);      }
18       char *freename( char *x)  { return(*--Namep = x); }
19
20       extern char *yytext;
21       extern int  yyleng;
22
23       #define YYSTYPE char*
24
25   /*-------------------------------------*/
26   #include "llout.h"
27
28   #define YY_MINTERM      1      /* Smallest terminal.                  */
29   #define YY_MAXTERM      6      /* Largest  terminal.                  */
30   #define YY_MINNONTERM   256    /* Smallest nonterminal.               */
31   #define YY_MAXNONTERM   261    /* Largest  nonterminal.               */
32   #define YY_START_STATE  256    /* Goal symbol (push to start parse).  */
33   #define YY_MINACT       512    /* Smallest action.                    */
```

Listing 4.4. *llama.par*— File Header—Macro Definitions

```
34   typedef unsigned char   YY_TTYPE;        /* Type used for tables.        */
35   #define YYF      (YY_TTYPE)( -1 )         /* Failure transition in table. */
36
37   /*-------------------------------------------------------------
38    *  Parser for llama-generated tables
39    */
40
41   #ifndef va_start
42   #include <stdarg.h>
43   #endif
44
45   #define YY_ISTERM(x)    (YY_MINTERM    <= (x) && (x) <= YY_MAXTERM    )
46   #define YY_ISNONTERM(x) (YY_MINNONTERM <= (x) && (x) <= YY_MAXNONTERM)
47   #define YY_ISACT(x)     (YY_MINACT     <= (x)                        )
48
49   #ifndef YYACCEPT
50   #    define YYACCEPT return(0)  /* Action taken when input is accepted.    */
51   #endif
52
```

→

Listing 4.4. continued...

```
53   #ifndef YYABORT
54   #    define YYABORT return(1)     /* Action taken when input is rejected.      */
55   #endif
56
57   #ifndef YYPRIVATE
58   #    define YYPRIVATE static      /* Define to a null string to make public.   */
59   #endif
60
61   #ifndef YYMAXERR
62   #    define YYMAXERR 25           /* Abort after this many errors.             */
63   #endif
64
65   #ifndef YYMAXDEPTH               /* Parse- and value-stack depth.             */
66   #    define YYMAXDEPTH 128
67   #endif
68
69   #ifndef YYSTYPE                  /* Used to declare fields in value stack. */
70   #    define YYSTYPE int
71   #endif
72
73   extern int       yylineno;                  /* Supplied by LeX.      */
74   extern int       yyleng;
75   extern char      *yytext;
76
77   extern int       ii_plineno()   ;           /* in l.lib::input.c.   */
78   extern char      *ii_ptext()    ;
79   extern int       ii_lineno()    ;
80   extern char      *ii_text()     ;
81   extern void      ii_mark_prev() ;
82
83   void    yyerror( char *fmt, ...);
84
85   /*----------------------------------------------------------------------
86    * Parse and value stacks:
87    */
88
89   #include <tools/yystack.h>
90   #undef   yystk_cls
91   #define  yystk_cls YYPRIVATE
92   #undef   yystk_err
93   #define  yystk_err(o)  ((o) ? (yyerror("Stack overflow\n" ),exit(1)) \
94                              : (yyerror("Stack underflow\n"),exit(1)) )
95
96   #define yytos(stk)  yystk_item( stk, 0 ) /* Evaluates to top-of-stack item. */
97
98   yystk_dcl( Yy_stack, int, YYMAXDEPTH );
99
100  typedef struct                  /* Typedef for value-stack elements. */
101  {
102      YYSTYPE  left;              /* Holds value of left-hand side attribute.    */
103      YYSTYPE  right;             /* Holds value of current-symbol's attribute. */
104
105  } yyvstype;
106
107  yyvstype Yy_vstack[ YYMAXDEPTH ];                /* Value stack.          */
108  yyvstype *Yy_vsp = Yy_vstack + YYMAXDEPTH;       /* Value-stack pointer. */
109
```

➡

Listing 4.4. continued. . .

```
110   @
111   @ Tables go here. LLama removes all lines that begin with @ when it copies
112   @                                          llama.par to the output file.
113   ^L
```

4.5 are identical in content to the ones pictured in Figure 4.6 on page 210. Note that the Yyd table on lines 179 to 184 is not compressed because this output file was generated with the –*f* switch active. Were –*f* not specified, the tables would be pair compressed, as is described in Chapter Two. The yy_act() subroutine on lines 199 to 234 contains the **switch** that holds the action code. Note that $ references have been translated to explicit value-stack references (Yy_vsp is the value-stack pointer). The Yy_synch array on lines 243 to 248 is a –1-terminated array of the synchronization tokens specified in the %synch directive.

Listing 4.5. *llout.c*— Parse Tables

```
114   /*-------------------------------------------------------
115    * The YypNN arrays hold the right-hand sides of the various productions, listed
116    * back to front (so that they will be pushed in reverse order), NN is the
117    * production number (to be found in the symbol-table listing output with a -s
118    * command-line switch).
119    *
120    * Yy_pushtab[] is indexed by production number and points to the appropriate
121    * right-hand-side (YypNN) array.
122    */
123
124   YYPRIVATE int Yyp07[]={ 0 };
125   YYPRIVATE int Yyp06[]={ 261, 517, 260, 516, 2, 0 };
126   YYPRIVATE int Yyp09[]={ 5, 257, 4, 0 };
127   YYPRIVATE int Yyp08[]={ 518, 3, 0 };
128   YYPRIVATE int Yyp04[]={ 0 };
129   YYPRIVATE int Yyp03[]={ 259, 515, 258, 514, 1, 0 };
130   YYPRIVATE int Yyp05[]={ 261, 260, 0 };
131   YYPRIVATE int Yyp02[]={ 259, 258, 0 };
132   YYPRIVATE int Yyp01[]={ 256, 6, 513, 257, 512, 0 };
133   YYPRIVATE int Yyp00[]={ 0 };
134
135   YYPRIVATE int  *Yy_pushtab[] =
136   {
137           Yyp00,
138           Yyp01,
139           Yyp02,
140           Yyp03,
141           Yyp04,
142           Yyp05,
143           Yyp06,
144           Yyp07,
145           Yyp08,
146           Yyp09
147   };
148
149   /*-------------------------------------------------------
150    * Yyd[][] is the DFA transition table for the parser. It is indexed
151    * as follows:
```

Listing 4.5. continued...

```
152      *                            Input symbol
153      *                  +----------------------+
154      *          L   |    Production number    |
155      *          H   |        or YYF           |
156      *          S   |                         |
157      *                  +----------------------+
158      *
159      * The production number is used as an index into Yy_pushtab, which
160      * looks like this:
161      *
162      *            Yy_pushtab          YypDD:
163      *            +-------+         +---------------+
164      *            |   *---|------>|                 |
165      *            +-------+         +---------------+
166      *            |   *---|---->
167      *            +-------+
168      *            |   *---|---->
169      *            +-------+
170      *
171      * YypDD is the tokenized right-hand side of the production.
172      * Generate a symbol table listing with llama's -l command-line
173      * switch to get both production numbers and the meanings of the
174      * YypDD string contents.
175      */
176
177      YYPRIVATE YY_TTYPE  Yyd[ 6 ][ 7 ] =
178      {
179      /* 00 */  {    0,   -1,   -1,    1,    1,   -1,   -1 },
180      /* 01 */  {   -1,   -1,   -1,    2,    2,   -1,   -1 },
181      /* 02 */  {   -1,   -1,   -1,    5,    5,   -1,   -1 },
182      /* 03 */  {   -1,    3,   -1,   -1,   -1,    4,    4 },
183      /* 04 */  {   -1,   -1,   -1,    8,    9,   -1,   -1 },
184      /* 05 */  {   -1,    7,    6,   -1,   -1,    7,    7 }
185      };
186
187      /*--------------------------------------------------------
188       * yy_next(state,c) is given the current state and input
189       * character and evaluates to the next state.
190       */
191
192      #define yy_next(state, c)   Yyd[ state ][ c ]
193
194      /*--------------------------------------------------------
195       * Yy_act() is the action subroutine. It is passed the tokenized value
196       * of an action and executes the corresponding code.
197       */
198
199      YYPRIVATE int yy_act( actnum )
200      {
201          /* The actions. Returns 0 normally but a nonzero error code can be returned
202           * if one of the acts causes the parser to terminate abnormally.
203           */
204
205          switch( actnum )
206          {
207              case 512:
208                      {(Yy_vsp[1].right)=(Yy_vsp[2].right)=newname();}
209                      break;
```

Listing 4.5. continued...

```
210            case 513:
211                        {freename((Yy_vsp[0].right));}
212                    break;
213            case 514:
214                        {(Yy_vsp[1].right)=(Yy_vsp[2].right)=newname();}
215                    break;
216            case 515:
217                        { yycode("%s+=%s\n",Yy_vsp->left,(Yy_vsp[0].right));
218                                            freename((Yy_vsp[0].right));}
219                    break;
220            case 516:
221                        {(Yy_vsp[1].right)=(Yy_vsp[2].right)=newname();}
222                    break;
223            case 517:
224                        {yycode("%s*=%s\n",Yy_vsp->left,(Yy_vsp[0].right));
225                                            freename((Yy_vsp[0].right));}
226                    break;
227            case 518:
228                        { yycode("%s=%0.*s\n",Yy_vsp->left,yyleng,yytext); }
229                    break;
230        default:  printf("INTERNAL ERROR: Illegal act number (%s)\n", actnum);
231                    break;
232        }
233        return 0;
234    }
235
236    /*-------------------------------------------------------
237     * Yy_synch[] is an array of synchronization tokens. When an error is
238     * detected, stack items are popped until one of the tokens in this
239     * array is encountered. The input is then read until the same item is
240     * found. Then parsing continues.
241     */
242
243    YYPRIVATE int  Yy_synch[] =
244    {
245            RP,
246            SEMI,
247            -1
248    };
249
250    /*-------------------------------------------------------
251     * Yy_stok[] is used for debugging and error messages. It is indexed
252     * by the internal value used for a token (as used for a column index in
253     * the transition matrix) and evaluates to a string naming that token.
254     */
255
256    char  *Yy_stok[] =
257    {
258            /*    0 */   "_EOI_",
259            /*    1 */   "PLUS",
260            /*    2 */   "TIMES",
261            /*    3 */   "NUM_OR_ID",
262            /*    4 */   "LP",
263            /*    5 */   "RP",
264            /*    6 */   "SEMI"
265    };
266
```

→

Listing 4.5. continued...

```
267
268     #ifdef YYDEBUG
269
270     /*-------------------------------------------------------
271      * Yy_snonterm[] is used only for debugging. It is indexed by the
272      * tokenized left-hand side (as used for a row index in Yyd[]) and
273      * evaluates to a string naming that left-hand side.
274      */
275
276     char *Yy_snonterm[] =
277     {
278             /* 256 */    "stmt",
279             /* 257 */    "expr",
280             /* 258 */    "term",
281             /* 259 */    "expr'",
282             /* 260 */    "factor",
283             /* 261 */    "term'"
284     };
285
286     /*-------------------------------------------------------
287      * Yy_sact[] is also used only for debugging. It is indexed by the
288      * internal value used for an action symbol and evaluates to a string
289      * naming that token symbol.
290      */
291
292     char *Yy_sact[] =
293     {
294             "{0}","{1}","{2}","{3}","{4}","{5}","{6}"
295     };
296
297     #endif
```

The arrays following line 256 provide human-readable diagnostics; they translate the various numeric values of the symbols into strings representing those symbols. Yy_stok, on lines 256 to 265, is indexed by token value and evaluates to a string representing the token's name. Similarly, Yy_snonterm[] on line 276 translates nonterminals, and Yy_sact[] on line 431 puts the actions in some sort of readable form. The {0}, and so forth, are mapped to the actual code in the *llout.sym* file, generated by giving **LLama** a *–s*, *–S*, or *–D* command-line switch.

Symbol-to-string conversion arrays: Yy_stok, Yy_snonterm, Yy_sact.

Listing 4.6 starts moving into the parser proper. The streams declared on lines 300 to 302 are used for output to the code, bss, and data segments respectively. They're all initialized to stdout, but you can change them with an fopen() call.

Output streams.

The remainder of Listing 4.6 provides alternate versions of functions and macros for debugging (YYDEBUG defined) production modes. The macros and subroutines on lines 306 to 431 are used if debug mode is active, otherwise the same macros and subroutines are redefined on lines 431 to 497 not to print diagnostics, and so forth.

Debugging functions and macros, YYDEBUG.

If YYDEBUG is defined, a second parse stack (Yy_dstack) is defined on line 308. This second, *symbol* stack exactly parallels the normal parse stack, but it holds strings representing the symbols, which are in turn represented by the numbers on the normal parse stack. For example, an *expr* is represented by the number 257 on the parse stack, and every time a 257 is pushed on the normal parse stack, the string "expr" is pushed onto the debugging stack. A string is popped (and discarded) from the symbol stack when a number is popped from the normal parse stack. This symbol stack is used in the debugging environment to make stack activity a little easier to follow.

Symbol stack, Yy_dstack.

Listing 4.6. *llama.par—* Macros for Parsing and Debugging Support

```
298    /*----------------------------------------------------------------*/
299
300    FILE   *yycodeout = stdout ;        /* Output stream for code.              */
301    FILE   *yybssout  = stdout ;        /* Output stream for initialized data.   */
302    FILE   *yydataout = stdout ;        /* Output stream for uninitialized data. */
303    int    yynerrs    = 0;              /* Error count.                          */
304
305    /*----------------------------------------------------------------*/
306    #ifdef YYDEBUG                                 /* Debugging parse stack. */
307
308    yystk_dcl( Yy_dstack, char *, YYMAXDEPTH );
309
310    YYPRIVATE char *yy_sym( sym )
311    {
312        /* Return a pointer to a string representing the symbol, using the
313         * appropriate table to map the symbol to a string.
314         */
315
316        return ( YY_ISTERM( sym ) || !sym ) ?   Yy_stok    [sym]:
317               ( YY_ISNONTERM( sym )       ) ?   Yy_snonterm [sym - YY_MINNONTERM]:
318               /* assume it's an act          */  Yy_sact    [sym - YY_MINACT] ;
319    }
320
321    /* Stack-maintenance. yy_push and yy_pop push and pop items from both the
322     * parse and symbol stacks simultaneously. The yycomment calls in both routines
323     * print a message to the comment window saying what just happened. The
324     * yy_pstack() call refreshes the stack window and also requests a new command
325     * from the user. That is, in most situations, yy_pstack() won't return until
326     * the user has typed another command (exceptions are go mode, and so forth).
327     * yy_pstack() also checks for break points and halts the parse if a breakpoint
328     * condition is met.
329     */
330
331    YYPRIVATE   yy_push(x, val)
332    int        x;                            /* Push this onto the state stack.*/
333    YYSTYPE    val;                          /* Push this onto the value stack.*/
334    {
335        yypush ( Yy_stack,  x              );
336        yypush_( Yy_dstack, yy_sym(x)      );
337
338        --Yy_vsp;                                    /* The push() macro checked */
339        Yy_vsp->left = Yy_vsp->right = val;          /* for overflow already.     */
340
341        yycomment( "push %s\n", yy_sym( x )  );
342        yy_pstack( 0, 1 );
343    }
344
345    YYPRIVATE   yy_pop()
346    {
347        int prev_tos = yypop( Yy_stack );
348        ++Yy_vsp;
349
350        yycomment( "pop %s\n", yypop_( Yy_dstack ) );
351        yy_pstack ( 0, 1 );
352
353        return prev_tos;
354    }
355
```

Listing 4.6. continued...

```
356   YYPRIVATE yy_say_whats_happening(tos_item, production)
357
358   int tos_item;            /* Item at top of stack                    */
359   int production;          /* production number we're about to apply */
360   {
361       /* Print a message in the comment window describing the replace operation
362        * about to be performed. The main problem is that you must assemble a
363        * string that represents the right-hand side of the indicated production.
364        * I do this using the appropriate Yy_pushtab element, but go through the
365        * array backwards (the Yy_pushtab arrays have been reversed to make the
366        * production-mode parse more efficient--you need to unreverse them here).
367        */
368
369       char   buf[80];       /* Assemble string representing right-hand side here.*/
370       int    count;         /* Maximum size of string representing RHS.        */
371       int    *start, *end;  /* Start and end of Yy_pushtab array that holds RHS. */
372
373       for( start = end = Yy_pushtab[ production ]; *end; end++ )    /* Find end.*/
374           ;
375
376       *buf = '\0';
377       for( count = sizeof(buf); --end >= start && count > 0 ;)    /* Assemble */
378       {                                                            /* string.  */
379           strncat( buf, yy_sym(*end), count );
380           if( (count -= strlen( yy_sym(*end) + 1)) < 1 )
381                   break;
382           strncat( buf, " ", --count );
383       }
384
385       yycomment( "Applying %s->%s\n", yy_sym(tos_item), buf );
386   }
387
388   /* Use the following routines just like printf() to create output. In debug
389    * mode, all three routines print to the output window (yy_output() is in
390    * yydebug.c). In production mode, equivalent routines print to the associated
391    * streams (yycodeout, yybssout, or yydataout). The first argument to
392    * yy_output() tells the routine which stream is being used. If the stream is
393    * still set to the default stdout, then the message is written only to the
394    * window. If the stream has been changed, however, the output is sent both
395    * to the window and the associated stream.
396    */
397
398   yycode( fmt )                        /* Write something to the code-segment stream. */
399   char    *fmt;
400   {
401       va_list       args;
402       va_start( args,  fmt );
403       yy_output( 0, fmt, args );
404   }
405
406   yydata( fmt )                        /* Write something to the data-segment stream. */
407   char    *fmt;
408   {
409       va_list       args;
410       va_start( args,  fmt );
411       yy_output( 1, fmt, args );
412   }
413
```

➡

```
Listing 4.6. continued...
414   yybss( fmt )                          /* Write something to the bss-segment stream.  */
415   char    *fmt;
416   {
417       va_list       args;
418       va_start( args,  fmt );
419       yy_output( 2, fmt, args );
420   }
421
422   /* Debugging versions of yycomment() and yy_error() are pulled out of yydebug.c
423    * when YYDEBUG is defined. Similarly, yy_break(), which halts the parse if a
424    * break-on-production-applied breakpoint has been triggered, is found in
425    * yydebug.c. It is eliminated from the production-mode output by defining it as
426    * an empty macro, below. Finally, yy_nextoken(), which evaluates to a yylex()
427    * call in production mode, and which is defined in yydebug.c, both gets the
428    * next token and prints it in the TOKEN window.
429    */
430
431   #else  /*- - - - - - - - - - - - - - - - - - - - - - - - - - - - - */
432
433   #    define   yy_push(x,v)       ( yypush(Yy_stack, x),                       \
434                                       --Yy_vsp, Yy_vsp->left=Yy_vsp->right=v )
435
436   #    define   yy_pop()           ( ++Yy_vsp, yypop(Yy_stack) )
437   #    define   yy_nextoken()      yylex()
438   #    define   yy_quit_debug()
439   #    define   yy_sym()
440   #    define   yy_say_whats_happening(tos_item,prod)
441   #    define   yy_redraw_stack()
442   #    define   yy_pstack(refresh,print_it)
443   #    define   yy_break(x)
444
445   #ifndef va_list
446   #    include <stdarg.h>
447   #else
448   #    ifdef va_dcl
449         MUST USE ANSI VARIABLE-ARGUMENT CONVENTIONS IN <stdarg.h>
450   #    endif
451   #endif
452
453   void    yycode( fmt, ... )
454   char    *fmt;
455   {
456           va_list   args;
457           va_start( args,    fmt );
458           vfprintf( yycodeout, fmt, args );
459   }
460
461   void    yydata( fmt, ... )
462   char    *fmt;
463   {
464           va_list           args;
465           va_start( args,  fmt );
466           vfprintf( yydataout, fmt, args );
467   }
468
469   void    yybss( fmt, ... )
470   char    *fmt;
471   {
472           va_list           args;
473           va_start( args,  fmt );
```

→

Listing 4.6. continued. . .

```
474                vfprintf( yybssout, fmt, args );
475    }
476
477    void     yycomment( fmt, ... )
478    char     *fmt;
479    {
480                va_list  args;
481                va_start( args,   fmt );
482                vfprintf( stdout, fmt, args );
483    }
484
485    void     yyerror( fmt, ... )
486    char     *fmt;
487    {
488                va_list   args;
489                extern char *yytext;
490                extern int  yylineno;
491
492                va_start( args, fmt );
493                fprintf ( stderr, "ERROR (line %d near %s): ", yylineno, yytext );
494                vfprintf( stderr, fmt, args );
495                fprintf ( stderr, "\n" );
496    }
497    #endif
```

The symbol stack is manipulated in the push() and pop() subroutines on lines 331 to 354. Stack boundary checking is done only on the actual parse stack because, since all stacks are the same size and they all run in parallel, additional checking is redundant. These subroutines are translated into macros on lines 433 to 436 if YYDEBUG isn't active. Most other details are called out in comments in the listing, to which you are referred. I'll look at *yydebug.c*, which holds all the debug-mode support routines, in a moment.

The rest of *llout.c* is the error-recovery code and the actual parser, in Listing 4.7. Error-recovery is done with two subroutines on lines 502 to 545. yy_in_synch() (on line 502) checks to see if the symbol passed to it is in the set of synchronization symbols given to the %synch directive and listed in the Yy_synch table. yy_synch() does the actual error recovery. The error-recovery algorithm is described in the comment on line 516.

Listing 4.7. *llama.par*— The Parser

```
498    /*-------------------------------------------------------------
499     *   ERROR RECOVERY:
500     */
501
502    YYPRIVATE yy_in_synch( sym )
503    {
504        /*  Return 1 if sym is in the synchronization set defined in Yy_synch. */
505
506        int *p ;
507
508        for( p = Yy_synch; *p  &&  *p > 0 ; p++ )
509            if( *p == sym )
510                return 1;
511        return 0;
512    }
```

Listing 4.7. continued...

```
513
514    YYPRIVATE yy_synch( lookahead )
515    {
516        /* Recover from an error by trying to synchronize the input stream and the
517         * stack. Return the next lookahead token or 0 if we can't recover. Yyparse()
518         * terminates if none of the synchronization symbols are on the stack. The
519         * following algorithm is used:
520         *
521         * (1) Pop symbols off the stack until you find one in the synchronization
522         *     set.
523         * (2) If no such symbol is found, you can't recover from the error. Return
524         *     an error condition.
525         * (3) Otherwise, advance the input symbol either until you find one that
526         *     matches the stack symbol uncovered in (1) or you reach end of file.
527         */
528
529        int     tok;
530
531        if( ++yynerrs > YYMAXERR )
532            return 0;
533
534        while( !yy_in_synch( tok = yytos( Yy_stack )) \
535                                && !yystk_empty( Yy_stack ))        /* 1 */
536            yy_pop();
537                                                                   /* 2 */
538        if( yystk_empty(Yy_stack) )
539            return 0;
540                                                                   /* 3 */
541        while( lookahead && lookahead != tok )
542            lookahead = yy_nextoken();
543
544        return lookahead;
545    }
546
547    /*-------------------------------------------------------------------
548     * The actual parser. Returns 0 normally, -1 if it can't synchronize after an
549     * error, otherwise returns a nonzero value returned by one of the actions.
550     */
551
552    int yyparse()
553    {
554        int      *p;              /* General-purpose pointer.                   */
555        YY_TTYPE prod;            /* Production being processed.                */
556        int      lookahead;       /* Lookahead token.                          */
557        int      errcode = 0;     /* Error code returned by an act.            */
558        int      tchar;           /* Holds terminal character in yytext.       */
559        int      actual_lineno;   /* Actual input line number.                 */
560        char     *actual_text;    /* Text of current lexeme.                   */
561        int      actual_leng;     /* Length of current lexeme.                 */
562        YYSTYPE  val;             /* Holds $$ value for replaced nonterm.      */
563
564 #      ifdef YYDEBUG
565            if( !yy_init_debug( Yy_stack,  &yystk_p(Yy_stack),
566                               Yy_dstack, &yystk_p(Yy_dstack),
567                               Yy_vstack, sizeof(yyvstype), YYMAXDEPTH) )
568                YYABORT;
569
```

Listing 4.7. continued...

```
570            yystk_clear(Yy_dstack);
571  #    endif
572
573      yystk_clear(Yy_stack);
574      Yy_vsp = Yy_vstack + YYMAXDEPTH;
575
576      yy_push( YY_START_STATE, (Yy_vsp-1)->left );   /* Push start state onto  */
577                                                     /* parse stack and junk   */
578                                                     /* onto the value stack.   */
579      yy_init_llama( Yy_vsp );                       /* User-supplied init.    */
580      lookahead = yy_nextoken();
581
582      while( !yystk_empty(Yy_stack) )
583      {
584          if( YY_ISACT( yytos(Yy_stack) ) )          /* if TOS is an action, do */
585          {                                          /* it and pop the action.  */
586              yylineno      = ii_plineno() ;
587              yytext        = ii_ptext()   ;
588              tchar         = yytext[ yyleng = ii_plength() ];
589              yytext[yyleng] = '\0' ;
590
591              if( errcode = yy_act( yytos(Yy_stack) ))
592                  return errcode;
593
594              yy_pop();
595              yy_redraw_stack();
596              yytext[ yyleng ] = tchar ;
597          }
598          else if( YY_ISTERM( yytos(Yy_stack) ))   /* Advance if it's a terminal.*/
599          {
600              if( yytos(Yy_stack) != lookahead )   /* ERROR if it's not there.   */
601              {
602                  yyerror( "%s expected\n", Yy_stok[ yytos(Yy_stack) ]);
603                  if( !(lookahead = yy_synch(lookahead)) )
604                      YYABORT;
605              }
606              else
607              {
608                  /* Pop the terminal symbol at top of stack. Mark the current
609                   * token as the previous one (we'll use the previous one as
610                   * yytext in subsequent actions), and advance.
611                   */
612
613                  yy_pop();
614                  ii_mark_prev();
615
616                  lookahead     = yy_nextoken();
617                  actual_lineno = yylineno;
618                  actual_text   = yytext ;
619                  actual_leng   = yyleng ;
620              }
621          }
622          else
623          {
624              /* Replace a nonterminal at top of stack with its right-hand side.
625               * First look up the production number in the table with the
626               * yy_next call. If prod==YYF, there was no legal transition and
627               * error-processing is activated. Otherwise the replace operation
628               * is done by popping the nonterminal, and pushing the right-hand
629               * side from the appropriate Yy_pushtab entry.
```

➡

Listing 4.7. continued...

```
630                         */
631
632               prod = yy_next( yytos(Yy_stack)-YY_MINNONTERM, lookahead );
633
634               if( prod == YYF )
635               {
636                   yyerror( "Unexpected %s\n", Yy_stok[ lookahead ] );
637                   if( !(lookahead = yy_synch(lookahead)) )
638                       YYABORT;
639               }
640               else
641               {
642                   yy_say_whats_happening( yytos(Yy_stack), prod );
643                   yy_break( prod );
644
645                   val = Yy_vsp->right ;
646                   yy_pop();
647
648                   for( p = Yy_pushtab[ prod ] ; *p ; ++p )
649                       yy_push( *p, val );
650               }
651           }
652       }
653
654       yylineno = actual_lineno ;    /* Make these hold reasonable values in case */
655       yytext   = actual_text   ;    /* the remainder of the input file must be   */
656       yyleng   = actual_leng   ;    /* processed further.                        */
657
658       yy_quit_debug();
659       YYACCEPT;
660   }
```

Top-down parser:
`yyparse()`.

Phase problems with
`yytext`.

The actual parser, `yyparse()`, starts on line 552 of Listing 4.7. For the most part, it is a straightforward implementation of the algorithm in Table 4.12 on page 211. The one difficulty not covered in the algorithm is the lexeme, `yytext`, which must be valid when the action is executed. The problem is that the match-and-advance operation that's triggered when a lexeme is on top of the stack overwrites `yytext` with the new lexeme. Consequently, you have to mark the current lexeme as the previous one before advancing, using the `ii_mark_prev()` call on line 614 (which was put into the input routines described in Chapter Three for this very purpose). When a subsequent action is actually performed (starting on line 586), `yytext` is modified to reference the previous lexeme, not the current one—it references the lexeme associated with the token that we just advanced past, not the lookahead token. The code on lines 588, 589, and 596 is just null terminating the lexeme.

The remainder of *llout.c* is just copied from the input file at the end of Appendix D. I won't reproduce it here.

4.9.2 Occs and LLama Debugging Support—*yydebug.c*

This section discusses the debug-mode support routines used by the **LLama**-generated parser in the previous section. The same routines are used by the **occs**-generated parser discussed in the next chapter. You should be familiar with interface to the *curses*, window-management functions described in Appendix A before continuing.

The debugging module, yydebug.c, starts in Listing 4.8 with various definitions, which you should read now (there are extensive comments that describe what the variables and definitions do—I'll discuss some of them a bit more in a moment).

Listing 4.8. *yydebug.c*— Definitions

```
 1   #include <stdio.h>
 2   #include <ctype.h>
 3   #include <sys/types.h>    /* ANSI/UNIX time functions.              */
 4   #include <sys/timeb.h>    /* ANSI/UNIX time functions.              */
 5   #include <curses.h>       /* Window functions.                      */
 6   #include <signal.h>       /* Needed by signal.                      */
 7   #include <stdarg.h>       /* ANSI variable-argument lists.          */
 8   #include <io.h>           /* Prototypes for access().               */
 9   #include <string.h>       /* Prototypes for string functions.       */
10   #include <stdlib.h>       /* Prototypes for other library functions. */
11   #include <tools/debug.h>  /* Various macros.                        */
12   #include <tools/l.h>      /* Prototypes for all of l.lib, including all */
13                            /* functions in the current file.         */
14   extern char *yytext;      /* Generated by LeX and lex.              */
15   extern int  yylineno;
16   extern int  yyleng;
17
18   /* If your system doesn't have an <stdarg.h>, use the following:
19    *
20    * typedef char *va_list;
21    * #define va_start(arg_ptr,first)  arg_ptr = (va_list)&first + sizeof(first)
22    * #define va_arg(arg_ptr,type)     ((type*)(arg_ptr += sizeof(type)))[-1]
23    * #define va_end()
24    *-------------------------------------------------------------------
25    * The following macros take care of system dependencies. They assume a 25-line
26    * screen on the IBM and a 24-line screen under Unix. Code put inside an MS()
27    * macro compiles only if MSDOS is #defined. Code in a UX() macro compiles only
28    * if MSDOS is not #defined. The NEWLINE define takes care of a bug in the UNIX
29    * curses package that isn't present in the DOS version presented in this book
30    * (it clears the bottom line after a scroll). box.h (in Appendix A) holds
31    * #defines for the IBM Box-drawing characters. #define NOT_IBM_PC to use the
32    * more portable defines in that file ('+' is used for corners, '|' for vertical
33    * lines, and '-' for horizontal ones) rather than the less-portable IBM
34    * graphics characters. fcntl() is also used only in UNIX mode.
35    */
36
37   #ifdef MSDOS
38   #        include <tools/box.h>
39   #        define SCRNSIZE 25
40   #        define NEWLINE(win) (Interactive ? waddch( win, '\n') :0)
41   #else
42   #        define NOT_IBM_PC
43   #        include <tools/box.h>
44   #        include <fcntl.h>
45   #        define SCRNSIZE 24
46   #        define NEWLINE(win) (Interactive ? (waddch( win, '\n'), wclrtoeol(win))\
47                                             : 0 )
48   #endif
49
50   /* -------------------------------------------------------------------
51    * Defines for the windows. STACK_TOP is the top line of the stack window.
52    * DEFSTACK is the default size of the text area of the stack window.
53    * STACK_WINSIZE is the height of the stack window, including the border. IO_TOP
54    * is the top line of both the I/O and comments windows, and IO_WINSIZE is the
55    * height of the text area of those windows. It should use the whole screen
```

Listing 4.8. continued...

```
56      * less the area used for the stack and prompt windows.
57      */
58
59     #define STACK_TOP          0
60     #define DEFSTACK           11                      /* Stacksize=DEFSTACK by default. */
61     #define STACK_WINSIZE      (Stacksize +2)
62     #define PROMPT_TOP         (SCRNSIZE - 3)
63     #define PROMPT_WINSIZE     3
64     #define IO_TOP             (STACK_WINSIZE-1)
65     #define IO_WINSIZE         ((SCRNSIZE - (STACK_WINSIZE + PROMPT_WINSIZE)) + 2)
66
67     #define TOKEN_WIDTH   22      /* Width of token window including border. */
68     #define PRINTWIDTH    79      /* Only this many characters are printed on each
69                                    * line by the write-screen (w) command. Extra
70                                    * characters are truncated.
71                                    */
72
73     #define ESC    0x1b          /* ASCII ESC character.                    */
74
75     /* ------------------------------------------------------------------
76      * Breakpoints. A breakpoint is set with a 'b' command. It causes automatic-mode
77      * operation to terminate immediately before applying a specific production or
78      * when a specified symbol is on the top of stack. P_breakpoint holds the
79      * production breakpoint; T_breakpoint holds the top-of-stack breakpoint;
80      * I_breakpoint is the input breakpoint. The former is an int because it's
81      * always a number. The latter two are strings because they can be symbolic
82      * names as well as numbers. The last variable, L_breakpoint, is the input-
83      * line breakpoint.
84      */
85
86     #define BRKLEN 33        /* Longest lexeme recognized in a breakpoint + 1. */
87
88     PRIVATE int    P_breakpoint            = -1 ;
89     PRIVATE int    L_breakpoint            = -1 ;
90     PRIVATE char   S_breakpoint[ BRKLEN ]  = { '\0' } ;
91     PRIVATE char   I_breakpoint[ BRKLEN ]  = { '\0' } ;
92
93     /*------------------------------------------------------------------
94      * I've attempted to isolate these routines as much as possible from the actual
95      * parser. They do need to know where all the stacks are, however. The following
96      * variables are initialized at run-time by an access routine [yy_init_debug()]
97      * and are used to access static variables in the parser itself. Note that the
98      * addresses of the stack pointers are stored, not the contents of the stack
99      * pointers.
100     */
101
102     PRIVATE int    Abort   ;             /* Force input routine to return EOI.   */
103     PRIVATE char   *Vstack ;             /* Base address of value stack (or NULL */
104                                          /* if called by llama-generated parser).*/
105     PRIVATE int    Vsize   ;             /* Size of one element of value stack.  */
106     PRIVATE char   **Dstack ;            /* Base address of debug (symbol) stack.*/
107     PRIVATE char   ***P_dsp ;            /* Pointer to debug-stack pointer.      */
108     PRIVATE int    *Sstack ;             /* Base address of state stack.         */
109     PRIVATE int    **P_sp ;              /* Pointer to state-stack pointer.      */
110     PRIVATE int    Depth   ;             /* Stack depth (all three stacks).      */
111
112     /*------------------------------------------------------------------
113      * The following variables are all used internally
114      */
115
```

Listing 4.8. continued...

```
116    PRIVATE WINDOW    *Stack_window    ;        /* Windows for the debugging screen.     */
117    PRIVATE WINDOW    *Prompt_window   ;
118    PRIVATE WINDOW    *Code_window     ;
119    PRIVATE WINDOW    *Comment_window  ;
120    PRIVATE WINDOW    *Token_window    ;
121    PRIVATE int        Stacksize = DEFSTACK;/* Number of active lines in the stack    */
122                                            /*      window (doesn't include border). */
123    PRIVATE int   Onumele     = 0;         /* Number of elements on the stack.       */
124    PRIVATE int   Interactive = 1;         /* Interactive mode (not n or N).         */
125    PRIVATE int   Singlestep  = 1;         /* Single step through parse if true.     */
126    PRIVATE long  Delay       = 0L;        /* Amount of time to wait after printing  */
127                                           /* each stack update when not single      */
128                                           /* stepping (milliseconds).               */
129    PRIVATE int   Inp_fm_file = 0;         /* 1 if input file is open.               */
130    PRIVATE FILE *Log         = NULL;      /* Pointer to   the log file if one is open.*/
131    PRIVATE int   No_comment_pix = 0;      /* 1 if no comment-window output is printed.*/
132    PRIVATE int   No_stack_pix  = 0;       /* 1 if no stack pictures are to be printed */
133                                           /*                      in the log file.*/
134    PRIVATE int Horiz_stack_pix = 0;       /* 1 if stack pictures are printed horiz-  */
135                                           /*                ontally in the log file. */
136    PRIVATE int Parse_pix;                 /* if(Horiz_stack_pix), print state stack.  */
137    PRIVATE int Sym_pix;                   /* if(Horiz_stack_pix), print symbol stack. */
138    PRIVATE int Attr_pix;                  /* if(Horiz_stack_pix), print attrib. stack.*/
139
140    #ifndef MSDOS  /*------------------ UNIX SYSTEM V ONLY ----------------------*/
141                                           /* Since MS-DOS has a system call that
142                                            * gives the keyboard status, detecting
143                                            * if a key has been pressed without
144                                            * reading the character is easy. In
145                                            * UNIX you must use SIGIO to set a
146                                            * flag (Char_avail). kbready() is the
147                                            * SIGIO exception handler.
148                                            */
149    PRIVATE int       Char_avail = 0;
150    #define kbhit() Char_avail
151
152    #else    /*-------------------DOS VERSION ONLY -----------------------*/
153
154    extern int    kbhit ( void );              /* Microsoft function. returns 1 if a */
155                                               /* character is waiting to be read    */
156                                               /* from the keyboard buffer. This     */
157                                               /* function is provided in most       */
158                                               /* MS-DOS compiler's libraries.       */
159
160    /* The Map[] array converts IBM box-drawing characters to something that's
161     * printable. The corners are converted to plus signs, horizontal lines go to
162     * dashes, and vertical lines map to vertical bars. The conv() subroutine is
163     * passed a character and returns a mapped character. It must be a subroutine
164     * because of the way that it's used below. It would have unacceptable
165     * side-effects if rewritten as a macro.
166     */
167
168    PRIVATE unsigned char Map[] =
169    {
170        '|', '+', '+', '+', '+', '+', '+', '|', '+', '+', '+', '+', '+', '+',
171        '+', '+', '+', '-', '+', '+', '+', '+', '+', '+', '+', '+', '=', '+',
172        '+', '+', '+', '+', '+', '+', '+', '+', '+', '+', '+', '+'
173    };
174
```

➡

```
Listing 4.8. continued...
175    PRIVATE int  conv(c)
176    {
177         return (VERT <= c && c <= UL) ?  Map[c - VERT] : c ;
178    }
179    #endif   /*----------------------------------------------------------*/
```

Initialize debugging:
`yy_init_debug()`.

The actual code starts in Listing 4.9. The `yy_init_debug()` function on line 180 initializes the debugging functions. It is passed pointers to various variables in the parser proper that it needs to draw the windows (things like the base addresses of the stacks). Note that pointers to the stack pointers are passed, rather than the contents of the stack pointers. This way the parser can push and pop stuff at will without having to tell the debugging routines every time it does a push or pop. The debugging routines can just examine the pointers themselves. The `vstack` argument is NULL if a **LLama**-generated parser is active (because **LLama** doesn't use a value stack). In this case, the value stack is not printed in the log file or the stack window.

Getting keyboard status under UNIX, SIGIO.

The `signal()` call on line 197 is used to determine keyboard status in UNIX systems. (The UX macro is defined in *debug.h*. It's discussed in Appendix A.) The SIGIO signal is generated every time a key is struck. Here, the signal activates the `kbready()` function (declared on line 257) which sets a global flag (`Char_avail`) to true. This flag can be examined when you're looking to see if a character is ready. The flag is explicitly set back to zero when the character is finally read. The `fcntl()` call on line 198 enables SIGIO (the signal is not generated otherwise).

Disable curses on abort.

The second `signal()` call on line 211 is used to disable curses when a Ctrl-Break (Ctrl-C or DEL in UNIX) comes along. Curses must be turned off explicitly in this case to prevent the screen from being left in an unknown state (with characters not echoing, and so forth). The handler is on line 263. Note that it disables SIGINT on line 265 so that another Ctrl-Break won't interrupt the shut-down process (this is not a problem on newer UNIX, versions, but it can't hurt). The *q* command to the debugger quits by raising the SIGINT signal, which will execute the handler. This way, any cleaning up of temporary files that is done by a signal handler in the compiler itself is also done when you quit the debugger. You can use the *a* command if you want to leave the debugger without cleaning up.

q command raises
SIGINT.

Input buffering and character echo is turned off on line 213 of Listing 4.9. Note that this is necessary in the BSD curses that runs on the UNIX system that I use, but may be contraindicated on other systems. Ask your system administrator if this is the correct thing to do with your implementation. The windows themselves are opened on the next few lines. The `boxwin()` function (defined on line 287) works much like a standard `newwin()` call. It opens up two windows: the outer one as a subwindow to `stdscr`, and the inner one as a subwindow to the outer one. The outer window holds the box and the inner window holds the text. This way, text written to the inner window won't overwrite the box. The window title is printed, centered, in the top line of the box.

Parsing command-line arguments:
`yy_get_args()`.

The final routine of interest in Listing 4.9 is the `yy_get_args()` function on line 320. This routine parses the command line for a stack size (specified with *-s*) and an input-file name. If you don't want to get this information from the command line, you can do the following:

```
floccinaucinihilipilification()
{
    static char *vects[] =      /* Simulate argv.                    */
    {
      "",                       /* Junk                              */
      "-s18",                   /* Stack-window size == 18 lines.    */
      "test"                    /* Input file name.                  */
    };

      yy_get_args( 3, vects );
}
```

Listing 4.9. *yydebug.c*— Initialization

```
180   PUBLIC   int yy_init_debug(sstack, p_sp, dstack, p_dsp, vstack, v_ele_size, depth)
181
182   int      *sstack;         /* Base address of state stack.                    */
183   int      **p_sp;          /* Address of state-stack pointer.                 */
184   char     **dstack;        /* Address of debug stack.                         */
185   char     ***p_dsp;        /* Address of debug-stack pointer.                 */
186   void     *vstack;         /* Base address of value stack or NULL for LLama.  */
187   int      v_ele_size;      /* Size of one element of value stack.             */
188   int      depth;           /* Number of elements in all three stacks.         */
189   {
190       /* Initialize for interactive I/O for curses. Return 1 on a successful
191        * initialization, 0 otherwise.
192        */
193
194       char buf[80];
195
196       UX( int flags;                                           )
197       UX( signal( SIGIO, kbready );                            )
198       UX( flags = fcntl( fileno(stdin), F_GETFL, 0 );          )
199       UX( fcntl( fileno(stdin), F_SETFL, flags | FASYNC ); )
200
201       Sstack = sstack;
202       Dstack = dstack;
203       Vstack = (char *) vstack;
204       Vsize  = v_ele_size;
205       P_sp   = p_sp;
206       P_dsp  = p_dsp;
207       Depth  = depth;
208       Abort  = 0;
209
210       initscr();
211       signal( SIGINT, die_a_horrible_death );
212
213       noecho();                /* Don't echo input characters automatically.     */
214       crmode();                /* Don't buffer input.                            */
215       MS( nosave(); )          /* Don't save region under windows (my curses only). */
216
217       Stack_window   = boxwin( STACK_WINSIZE, 80, STACK_TOP, 0, "[stack]"    );
218       Comment_window = boxwin( IO_WINSIZE,    40, IO_TOP,    0, "[comments]" );
219       Code_window    = boxwin( IO_WINSIZE,    41, IO_TOP,   39, "[output]"   );
220
221       Prompt_window  = boxwin(PROMPT_WINSIZE, (80 - TOKEN_WIDTH) + 1,
222                                               PROMPT_TOP,  0, "[prompts]"  );
223
224       Token_window   = boxwin(PROMPT_WINSIZE, TOKEN_WIDTH, PROMPT_TOP,
225                                               80 - TOKEN_WIDTH, "[lookahead]" );
226       scrollok( Stack_window,    TRUE  );
```

→

```
Listing 4.9. continued...
227        scrollok( Comment_window,  TRUE  );
228        scrollok( Code_window,     TRUE  );
229        scrollok( Prompt_window,   TRUE  );
230        scrollok( Token_window,    TRUE  );
231        wrapok  ( Token_window,    FALSE );
232
233        Onumele = 0;
234
235        while( !Inp_fm_file )
236        {
237            /* If you don't have an input file yet, get one. yyprompt() prints the
238             * prompt in the PROMPT window, and fills buf with the reply.
239             */
240
241            if( !yyprompt( "Input file name or ESC to exit: ", buf, 1 ) )
242            {
243                yy_quit_debug();
244                return 0;
245            }
246            new_input_file( buf );
247        }
248        delay();                     /* Wait for a command before proceeding.*/
249        return 1;
250    }
251
252    /*------------------------------------------------------------------
253     * Exception handlers:
254     */
255
256    #ifndef MSDOS
257    PRIVATE void    kbready()          /* Called when new character is available. */
258    {
259        Char_avail = 1;
260    }
261    #endif
262
263    PRIVATE void die_a_horrible_death()          /* Come here on a SIGINT */
264    {                                            /* or 'q' command.       */
265        signal( SIGINT, SIG_IGN );
266        yy_quit_debug();
267        exit( 0 );
268    }
269
270    PUBLIC  void yy_quit_debug()                        /* Normal termination. */
271    {
272        echo();                                    /* Turn echo and editing back on. */
273        nocrmode();
274        move( 24, 0 );                /* Put the cursor on the bottom of the screen. */
275        refresh();
276        endwin();                                       /* Turn off curses. */
277
278        if( Log )
279            fclose( Log );
280
281        stop_prnt();
282        signal( SIGINT, SIG_DFL );
283    }
284
```

Listing 4.9. continued...

```
285     /*------------------------------------------------------------------*/
286
287     PRIVATE WINDOW   *boxwin( lines, cols, y_start, x_start, title )
288     int      lines;
289     int      cols;
290     int      y_start;
291     int      x_start;
292     char     *title;
293     {
294         /* This routine works just like the newwin() except that the window has a
295          * box around it that won't be destroyed by writes to the window. It
296          * accomplishes this feat by creating two windows, one inside the other,
297          * with a box drawn in the outer one. It prints the optional title centered
298          * on the top line of the box. Set title to NULL (or "") if you don't want
299          * a title. Note that all windows are made subwindows of the default window
300          * to facilitate the print-screen command.
301          */
302
303         WINDOW *outer;
304
305         outer = subwin( stdscr, lines, cols, y_start, x_start);
306         box( outer, VERT, HORIZ );
307
308         if( title && *title )
309         {
310             wmove  ( outer, 0, (cols - strlen(title))/2 );
311             wprintw( outer, "%s", title );
312         }
313
314         wrefresh ( outer );
315         return subwin( outer, lines-2, cols-2, y_start+1, x_start+1 );
316     }
317
318     /*------------------------------------------------------------------*/
319
320     PUBLIC   int      yy_get_args( argc, argv )
321     char     **argv;
322     {
323         /* Scan argv arguments for the debugging options and remove the arguments
324          * from argv. Recognized arguments are:
325          *
326          * -sN       Set stack-window size to N lines. The size of the other windows
327          *           scale accordingly. The stack window is not permitted to get so
328          *           large that the other windows will disappear, however.
329          *
330          * The first argument that doesn't begin with a minus sign is taken to be
331          * the input file name. That name is not removed from argv. All other
332          * arguments are ignored and are not removed from argv, so you can process
333          * them in your own program. This routine prints an error message and
334          * terminates the program if it can't open the specified input file.
335          * Command-line processing stops immediately after the file name is
336          * processed. So, given the line:
337          *
338          *         program -x -s15 -y foo -s1 bar
339          *
340          * Argv is modified to:
341          *
342          *         program -x -y foo -s1 bar
343          *
344          * The file "foo" will have been opened for input and the stack window will
```

➡

Listing 4.9. continued...

```
345              * be 15 lines high. Return new value of argc that reflects the removed
346              * arguments;
347              */
348
349          char   **newargv;
350          char   **oldargv = argv;
351          char   *filename = NULL;
352          int    ssize     = DEFSTACK;
353
354          newargv  = ++argv;
355          for( --argc; --argc >= 0; ++argv )
356          {
357              if( argv[0][0] != '-' )
358              {
359                  filename = *newargv++ = *argv;
360                  break;
361              }
362              else if( argv[0][1] == 's' )                         /* -s */
363                  ssize = atoi( &argv[0][2] );      /* Don't copy to *newargv here. */
364              else                                                 /* -? */
365                  *newargv++ = *argv;
366          }
367
368          Stacksize = ( ssize < 1            )  ? DEFSTACK   :
369                      ( ssize > (SCRNSIZE-6) )  ? SCRNSIZE-6 :
370                      /* ssize is in bounds */    ssize      ;
371
372          if( filename )
373          {
374              /* Open input file if one was specified on the command line. */
375
376              if( ii_newfile(filename) != -1 )
377                  Inp_fm_file = 1;
378              else
379              {
380                  perror( filename );
381                  exit( 1 );
382              }
383          }
384          return newargv - oldargv;
385      }
```

Output functions: yyer-
ror().

The next listing (Listing 4.10) holds all the output functions. There is one such routine for each window. In addition, yyerror() (on line 510), writes to the comment window and simulates the standard yyerror() function by adding an input line number and token value to the error message. In addition to the standard output functions, display_file() (on line 558 of Listing 4.10) is used by the *f* command to print a file in the stack window, and write_screen() is used by the *w* command to save the current screen to a file. Note that, since everything's a subwindow to stdscr, the stdscr functions can be used on line 654 to read the entire screen (rather than doing it window by window).

Listing 4.10. *yydebug.c*— Window Output Functions

```
386    PRIVATE void      prnt_putc(c, win)
387    WINDOW *win;
388    {
389        /*     All output done through prnt_putc is suppressed in Go mode. Also note
390         * that the arguments are reversed from addch(). This reversal lets you use
391         * the prnt() subroutine (described in Appendix A), which expects a putc()-
392         * like output function. Newlines are suppressed here so that you can have
393         * more control over scrolling. Similarly, sequences of white space are
394         * replaced by a single space character to conserve space in the window.
395         *     Test_c is used to take care of the IBM graphics characters that form
396         * the vertical line separating the stream-identification column from the
397         * actual output. The c is mapped to a '|' if it's too large to be an ASCII
398         * character (so isspace() will work properly).
399         */

400
401        static WINDOW *last_win = NULL;
402        static int     last_c   = 0;
403        int            test_c;
404
405        if( Interactive && c != '\n' )
406        {
407            test_c = (c < 0x7f) ? c : '|';
408
409            if( !(win==last_win && isspace(test_c) && isspace(last_c)) )
410                waddch( win, isspace(test_c) ? ' ' : c );
411
412            last_win = win;
413            last_c   = test_c;
414        }
415    }
416
417    PRIVATE void refresh_win( win )
418    WINDOW *win;
419    {
420        /* Refresh the windows if you're not in go mode. (If you are, nothing will
421         * have been written, so there's not point in doing the refresh
422         */
423
424        if( Interactive )
425            wrefresh( win );
426    }
427
428    /*- - - - - - - - - - - - - - - - - - - - - - - - - - - - - - - - - - - - */
429
430    PUBLIC  void yy_output( where, fmt, args )              /* Generate code */
431    int     where;
432    char    *fmt;
433    va_list args;
434    {
435        /* Works like vprintf(), but sends output to the code window. In the window,
436         * it ignores any newlines in the string but prints a newline after every
437         * call. All code sent to yycode(), yydata(), and yybss() is funneled
438         * here. "where" should be one of the following:
439         *
440         *          0 : code
441         *          1 : data
442         *          2 : bss
443         *
444         * Note that if the three associated streams (yycodeout, yybssout, and
```

Listing 4.10. continued...

```
445          * yydataout--all declared in the parser output file) are not directed to
446          * stdout, output is sent to that stream TOO. Don't modify these to point
447          * at stderr (or any other stream that accesses the console: /dev/tty, con,
448          * etc.) or you'll mess up the screen.
449          *
450          * Note that the real yycode(), etc (ie. the ones supplied when YYDEBUG
451          * is not defined) don't do anything special with newlines. In particular,
452          * they are not inserted automatically at the end of the line. To make both
453          * sets of routines compatible, your output strings should all have exactly
454          * one newline, placed at the end of the string (don't imbed any in the
455          * middle).
456          */
457
458          extern FILE *yycodeout, *yydataout, *yybssout;
459
460          if( Log )
461          {
462              fprintf( Log,    where == 0  ?  "CODE->" :
463                               where == 1  ?  "DATA->" : "BSS-->" );
464              prnt ( fputc, Log, fmt, args );
465              fputc( '\n', Log );
466          }
467
468          NEWLINE( Code_window );
469
470          prnt_putc( where==0 ? 'C' : where==1 ? 'D' : 'B',   Code_window );
471          prnt_putc( VERT,                                    Code_window );
472
473          prnt( prnt_putc, Code_window, fmt, args );
474          refresh_win( Code_window );
475
476          if( where == 0 && yycodeout != stdout )
477              vfprintf( yycodeout, fmt, args );
478
479          if( where == 1 && yydataout != stdout )
480              vfprintf( yydataout, fmt, args );
481
482          if( where == 2 && yybssout != stdout )
483              vfprintf( yybssout, fmt, args );
484      }
485
486  /*- - - - - - - - - - - - - - - - - - - - - - - - - - - - - - - */
487
488  PUBLIC  void yycomment( fmt, ... )
489  char    *fmt;
490  {
491      /* Works like printf() except that it automatically prints a newline
492       * IN FRONT OF the string and ignores any \n's in the string itself. Writes
493       * into the comment window, and outputs a message to the log file if
494       * logging is enabled.
495       */
496
497      va_list      args;
498      va_start( args, fmt );
499
500      if( Log && !No_comment_pix )
501          prnt( fputc, Log, fmt, args );
502
```

➡

Listing 4.10. continued...

```
503        NEWLINE( Comment_window );
504        prnt( prnt_putc, Comment_window, fmt, args );
505        refresh_win( Comment_window );
506    }
507
508    /*- - - - - - - - - - - - - - - - - - - - - - - - - - - - - - - - - - */
509
510    PUBLIC  void yyerror( fmt, ... )
511    char    *fmt;
512    {
513        /* Debugging version of the error routine. Works just like the nondebugging
514         * version, but writes to the comment window. Note that yycomment() copies
515         * the error message to the Log file. Interactive mode is temporarily
516         * enabled to assure that error messages get printed.
517         */
518
519        int       old_interactive;
520        va_list  args;
521        va_start( args, fmt );
522
523        old_interactive = Interactive;
524        Interactive      = 1;
525
526        yycomment( "ERROR, line %d near <%s>\n", yylineno, yytext );
527
528        if( Log )
529            prnt( fputc, Log, fmt, args );
530
531        NEWLINE     ( Comment_window );
532        prnt        ( prnt_putc, Comment_window, fmt, args );
533        refresh_win ( Comment_window );
534
535        Interactive = old_interactive;
536        Singlestep  = 1;                        /* Force a breakpoint */
537        yy_pstack( 0, 1 );
538    }
539
540    /*- - - - - - - - - - - - - - - - - - - - - - - - - - - - - - - - - */
541
542    PRIVATE   void yy_input( fmt, ... )
543    char    *fmt;
544    {
545        /* This is not an input function; rather, it writes to the INPUT window.
546         * It works like printf(). Note that nothing is logged here. The logging
547         * is done in nextoken(). Ignores all \n's in the input string.
548         */
549
550        va_list        args;
551        va_start( args, fmt );
552        prnt( prnt_putc, Prompt_window, fmt, args );
553        refresh_win( Prompt_window );
554    }
555
556    /*----------------------------------------------------------------*/
557
558    PRIVATE  void display_file( name, buf_size, print_lines )
559    char    *name;                          /* Initially holds the file name, but */
560    int      buf_size;                      /*        recycled as an input buffer. */
561    int      print_lines;
562    {
```

Listing 4.10. continued...

```
563       /* Display an arbitrary file in the stack window, one page at a time.
564        * The stack window is not refreshed by this routine.
565        */
566
567       FILE   *fd;
568       int    i;
569       int    lineno = 0;
570
571       if( !(fd = fopen( name, "r")) )
572       {
573           NEWLINE   ( Prompt_window                         );
574           wprintw   ( Prompt_window, "Can't open %s",  name );
575           wrefresh  ( Prompt_window                         );
576           presskey ();
577       }
578       else                          /* Note that order of evaluation is important in  */
579       {                             /* the following while statement. You don't want   */
580                                     /* to get the line if i goes past 0.               */
581
582           for( i = Stacksize-1 ;; i = (*name == ' ') ? 1 : Stacksize - 2 )
583           {
584               while(  --i >= 0  &&  fgets(name, buf_size, fd) )
585               {
586                   if( print_lines )
587                       wprintw( Stack_window, "%3d:", ++lineno );
588
589                   wprintw ( Stack_window, "%s", name );
590                   wrefresh( Stack_window );
591               }
592
593               if( i > 0 )
594                   break;
595
596               if(!yyprompt("ESC quits. Space scrolls 1 line. Enter for screenful",
597                                                                   name, 0) )
598                   break;
599           }
600           yyprompt("*** End of file. Press any key to continue ***", name, 0 );
601           fclose( fd );
602       }
603   }
604
605   /*-------------------------------------------------------------------*/
606
607   PRIVATE void write_screen( filename )
608   char      *filename;
609   {
610       /* Print the current screen contents to the indicated file. Note that the
611        * right edge of the box isn't printed in order to let us have 79-character
612        * lines. Otherwise, the saved screen shows up as double-spaced on most
613        * printers. The screen image is appended to the end of the file. In MS-DOS,
614        * Use "prn:" as the file name if you want to go to the printer.
615        *
616        * Syserrlist and errno are both defined in <stdlib.h>
617        */
618
619       char      buf[2];
620       char      *mode = "a";
621       int       row, col, y, x;
622       FILE      *file;
```

→

```
Listing 4.10. continued...
623
624          if( access( filename, 0 ) == 0 )
625              if( !yyprompt("File exists, overwrite or append? (o/a): ", buf, 0) )
626              {
627                  NEWLINE ( Prompt_window          );
628                  yy_input( "Aborting command." );
629                  presskey();
630                  return;
631              }
632          else
633          {
634              if( toupper(*buf) == 'O' )
635                  mode = "w";
636          }
637
638          if( file = fopen( filename, mode) )
639              yy_input("...%s %s...",
640                          *mode=='w' ? "overwriting" : "appending to", filename );
641          else
642          {
643              yy_input( "Can't open %s: %s.", filename, sys_errlist[errno]);
644              presskey();
645              return;
646          }
647
648          getyx( Prompt_window, y, x );
649
650          for( row = 0; row < SCRNSIZE; row++ )
651          {
652              for( col = 0; col < PRINTWIDTH; col++ )
653              {
654                  UX( fputc(          mvinch(row,col)   , file ); )
655                  MS( fputc( conv( mvinch(row,col) ), file ); )
656              }
657
658              fputc( '\n', file );
659          }
660
661          fclose( file );
662          wmove( Prompt_window, y, x );
663      }
```

The routines in Listing 4.11 do the real work. yy_pstack() (on line 664) is called by the parser every time the stack is modified. The stack is printed to the log file, if necessary, on line 700 to 773. Interactive is false on line 775 if the debugger is in noninteractive mode (initiated with an *n* command), In this case, a speedometer readout that tells you that the program is actually doing something is updated (it can take a while to parse a big input file, even in noninteractive mode) and the routine returns. A Stack breakpoint is triggered on line 785 if necessary (the debugger is just thrown back into single-step mode if one is found).

The delay() call on line 874 does one of two things. If you're not single stepping, it just delays by zero or more seconds (you can modify the number with the *d* command). delay() gets and executes a command if you're single stepping or you hit a key during the delay. delay() doesn't exit until one of the commands that starts up the parse again (space to singlestep, *n* to enter noninteractive mode, or *g* to go) is executed. The delay() subroutine itself starts at the top of the following Listing (Listing 4.12). Note

Update stack window,
yy_pstack().

Stack breakpoint.

Main command loop,
delay().

that I'm using the UNIX/ANSI time ftime() function here to get the time in milliseconds. It loads the time_buf structure with the elapsed number of seconds since January 1, 1970 (time_buf.time) and the number of milliseconds as well (in time_buf.millitm). The Delay variable holds the desired delay (in milliseconds).

Listing 4.11. *yydebug.c*— Stack-Window Maintenance and the Control Loop

```
664    PUBLIC  void yy_pstack( do_refresh, print_it )
665
666    int     do_refresh;          /* redraw entire window rather than update  */
667    int     print_it;            /* if true, print the stack to the log file */
668    {
669        /* Print the state, debug, and value stacks.
670         *
671         * The library routine yypstk() (which returns an empty string by default)
672         * is called to print value stack items. It should return a pointer to a
673         * string that represents the value-stack contents. Just provide a similarly
674         * named routine to print your real value stack. The LLAMA parser passes
675         * garbage to yypstk(), so use the default routine in LLAMA. The OCCS parser
676         * passes yypstk() a pointer to a value-stack item and it should return a
677         * pointer to a string representing attributes of interest. The line should
678         * not contain any newlines and it should be at most 58 characters long.
679         * If do_refresh is true, the entire stack window is redrawn, otherwise
680         * only those parts of the window that have been changed are modified.
681         */
682
683        int          numele        ;  /* # of elements on the stack       */
684        int          *toss         ;  /* top of state stack               */
685        char         **tods        ;  /* top of debug stack               */
686        char         *tovs         ;  /* top of value stack               */
687        int          *state        ;  /* current state-stack pointer      */
688        char         **debug       ;  /* current debug-stack pointer      */
689        char         *value        ;  /* current value-stack pointer      */
690        int          width         ;  /* Width of column in horiz. stack  */
691        static int   times_called = -1 ;  /* # of times this subroutine called */
692        char         *p            ;
693        int          i             ;
694
695        state = *P_sp;
696        debug = *P_dsp;
697        numele = Depth - (state - Sstack);
698        value  = (Vstack + (Depth - numele) * Vsize);
699
700        if( Log && !No_stack_pix && print_it )
701        {
702            /* Print the stack contents out to the log file.  */
703
704            if( !Horiz_stack_pix )
705            {
706                fprintf(Log, "   +---+------------------+\n");
707                if( numele <= 0 )
708                    fprintf( Log," * | * |   ***********   |   Stack is empty.\n");
709                else
710                {
711                    toss = state;
712                    tods = debug;
713                    tovs = value;
714                    for(i = numele; --i >= 0; ++toss, ++tods, tovs += Vsize )
715                        fprintf( Log, "%3d|%3d| %16.16s | %1.52s\n",
716                                 toss - state, *toss, *tods, yypstk(tovs, *tods));
717                }
```

➡

Listing 4.11. continued...

```
718                    fprintf(Log, "    +---+------------------+\n");
719            }
720        else
721        {
722            if( state < Sstack )
723                fprintf( Log,"*** Stack empty ***\n");
724            else
725            {
726                /* Print horizontal stack pictures. Note that you have to go
727                 * through the stack from bottom to top to get the top-of-stack
728                 * element on the right.
729                 */
730
731                for( i = 0; i <= 2; ++i )
732                {
733                    if( !Parse_pix && i == 0 ) continue;
734                    if( !Sym_pix   && i == 1 ) continue;
735                    if( !Attr_pix  && i == 2 ) continue;
736
737                    switch( i )
738                    {
739                    case 0: fprintf( Log, "   PARSE  " ); break;
740                    case 1: fprintf( Log, "   SYMBOL " ); break;
741                    case 2: fprintf( Log, "   ATTRIB " ); break;
742                    }
743
744                    toss = Sstack +  (Depth - 1);
745                    tods = Dstack +  (Depth - 1);
746                    tovs = Vstack + ((Depth - 1) * Vsize);
747
748                    for(; toss >= state; --toss, --tods, tovs -= Vsize )
749                    {
750                        /* Find width of the column. I'm assuming that the
751                         * numbers on the state stack are at most 3 digits
752                         * long, if not, change the 3, below.
753                         */
754
755                        p     = yypstk( tovs, *tods );
756                        width = 3;
757
758                        if( Sym_pix  ) width = max( width, strlen(*tods) );
759                        if( Attr_pix ) width = max( width, strlen(p)     );
760
761                        switch( i )
762                        {
763                        case 0: fprintf( Log, "%-*d ", width, *toss ); break;
764                        case 1: fprintf( Log, "%-*s ", width, *tods ); break;
765                        case 2: fprintf( Log, "%-*s ", width, p     ); break;
766                        }
767                    }
768
769                    fputc( '\n', Log );
770                }
771            }
772        }
773    }
774
775    if( !Interactive )
776    {
```

Listing 4.11. continued...

```
777              if( ++times_called % 25 == 0 )
778              {
779                  wprintw ( Stack_window, "working: %d\r", times_called );
780                  wrefresh( Stack_window );
781              }
782              return;
783          }
784
785      if( *S_breakpoint  &&   state < Sstack + Depth )
786      {
787          /* Break if the breakpoint is a digit and the top-of-stack item has that
788           * value, or if the string matches the string currently at the top of
789           * the symbol stack.
790           */
791
792          if( isdigit(*S_breakpoint)  )
793          {
794              if( atoi(S_breakpoint) == *state )
795                  Singlestep = 1;
796          }
797          else if( !strcmp(S_breakpoint, *debug) )
798                  Singlestep = 1;
799      }
800
801      if( do_refresh )                                        /* Redraw entire stack */
802          yy_redraw_stack();
803
804      else if( numele > Onumele )
805      {
806          /* The stack has grown. Redraw only those parts of the stack that have
807           * changed. (I'm assuming only by one element.) The main difficulty
808           * here is that only the top few elements of a large stack are
809           * displayed. Consequently, the stack window may have to scroll up
810           * or down a line if the stack size is hovering around the window size.
811           * There's no portable way to scroll the window up under UNIX curses, so
812           * we have to redraw the stack to scroll up in this situation. We'll
813           * overwrite the top element with itself by the wprintw() call, but
814           * that's no big deal, and it simplifies the code.
815           */
816
817          if( numele > Stacksize )           /* scroll down, opening up top line */
818          {
819              MS( wscroll( Stack_window, -1 );      )
820              UX( yy_redraw_stack();                )
821
822              wmove( Stack_window, 0, 0 );
823          }
824          else
825              wmove( Stack_window, Stacksize - numele, 0 );
826
827          wprintw( Stack_window, "%3d%c %16.16s %c %1.52s",
828                              *state, VERT, *debug, VERT, yypstk(value, *debug) );
829          wrefresh( Stack_window );
830      }
831      else
832      {
833          /* The stack has shrunk, perhaps by several elements. Remove them one at
834           * a time. (It's too confusing if several elements disappear from the
835           * stack at once. It's best to watch them go one at a time.) If the
836           * number of elements on the stack (i) is greater than the window size,
```

Listing 4.11. continued...

```
837                 * you can pop an element by scrolling up and then writing in a new
838                 * bottom line, otherwise, just go to the correct line and erase it.
839                 * Do a refresh after each pop.
840                 */
841
842             for( i = Onumele; i > numele; --i )
843             {
844                 if( i > Stacksize )
845                 {
846                     /* Do a pop by scrolling up, the easiest way to scroll is to
847                      * move to the right edge of the bottom line and then issue
848                      * a newline. After the scroll, overwrite the now-blank bottom
849                      * line with the appropriate stack information. The involved
850                      * expression that is the first argument to yypstk is doing:
851                      *          (Vstack + Depth)[ -i + Stacksize ]
852                      * It must do the pointer arithmetic explicitly, however, by
853                      * multiplying by the size of one value-stack item (Vsize).
854                      */
855
856                     wmove    ( Stack_window, Stacksize-1, 77          );
857                     NEWLINE  ( Stack_window                           );
858                     wprintw  ( Stack_window, "%3d%c %16.16s %c %1.52s",
859                                (Sstack + Depth)[ -i + Stacksize ], VERT,
860                                (Dstack + Depth)[ -i + Stacksize ], VERT,
861                                yypstk( (Vstack + (Depth*Vsize)) +
862                                         ((-i + Stacksize) * Vsize),
863                                        (Dstack + Depth)[ -i + Stacksize ] )
864                             );
865                 }
866                 else
867                 {
868                     wmove    ( Stack_window, Stacksize - i, 0 );
869                     wclrtoeol( Stack_window                    );
870                 }
871                 wrefresh( Stack_window );
872             }
873         }
874     delay();
875     wrefresh( Stack_window );
876     Onumele = numele;
877 }
878
879 /*--------------------------------------------------------------------*/
880
881 PUBLIC   void yy_redraw_stack()
882 {
883     /* Redraw the entire stack screen by writing out the top Stacksize elements
884      * of the stack in the stack window. Note that scrolling is turned off so
885      * that the screen won't scroll when you print the last line. Unlike
886      * yy_pstack(), this routine won't pause for a command.
887      */
888
889     int  i;
890     int  numele;                        /* Number of elements on the stack */
891     int  *state = *P_sp;                /* Pointer to top of state stack    */
892     char **debug = *P_dsp;              /* Pointer to top of debug stack    */
893     char *value;                        /* Pointer to top of value stack    */
894
```

➡

Listing 4.11. continued...

```
895         werase   ( Stack_window );
896         scrollok ( Stack_window, FALSE );
897
898         numele =  Depth - (state - Sstack);
899         value  =  Vstack + ((Depth - numele) * Vsize);
900
901         wmove( Stack_window, numele <= Stacksize ? Stacksize - numele : 0, 0 );
902
903         for( i=min(Stacksize, numele); --i >= 0;  ++state, ++debug, value += Vsize )
904             wprintw( Stack_window, "%3d%c %16.16s %c %1.52s\n",
905                                                 *state, VERT,
906                                                 *debug, VERT, yypstk(value, *debug) );
907
908         scrollok( Stack_window, TRUE );
909     }
```

Listing 4.12. *yydebug.c*— Delay and Main Control Loop

```
910    PRIVATE void delay()
911    {
912        /* Print a prompt and wait for either a carriage return or another command.
913         * Note that the time returned by time() is the elapsed time, in seconds,
914         * from 00:00:00, January 1, 1970 GMT. Since there are roughly 31,557,600
915         * seconds in a year (365.25 * 24 * 60 * 60) and the largest (signed)
916         * 32-bit long int can hold 2,147,483,647, the time won't roll over until
917         * January 18, 2038 at 2:56:02 A.M. Don't use this program on January 18,
918         * 2038 at 2:56:02 A.M.
919         */
920
921        long          start, current;
922        char          buf[80];
923        int           print_lines;
924        struct timeb time_buf;                    /* defined in sys/timeb.h */
925
926        if( !Interactive )                         /* n command (noninteractive) issued */
927            return;
928
929        if( !Singlestep && kbhit() )
930        {
931            /* If we're not single stepping (a 'g' command has been issued) and
932             * there's a key pressed, stop single stepping and get the character.
933             */
934            input_char();
935            Singlestep = 1;
936        }
937
938        if( !Singlestep )
939        {
940            /* If we're still doing a go command (no key was found in the previous
941             * if statement), then delay for a while. Must use two if statements
942             * here because we don't want to delay if we've just stopped go-ing.
943             * If a key is hit while we're delaying, stop looping immediately and
944             * revert back to single-step mode.
945             */
946
```

→

Listing 4.12. continued...

```
947            ftime( &time_buf );
948            start   = (time_buf.time * 1000) + time_buf.millitm;
949
950            while( 1 )
951            {
952                ftime( &time_buf );
953                current = (time_buf.time * 1000) + time_buf.millitm;
954
955                if( current - start >= Delay )
956                    break;
957
958                if( kbhit() )                    /* If a key is hit, stop delaying */
959                {                                /* and revert back to single-step */
960                    input_char();                /* mode.                          */
961                    Singlestep = 1;
962                    break;
963                }
964            }
965            if( !Singlestep )            /* If we're still not single stepping, then  */
966                return;                  /* we're done (don't get a command),         */
967                                         /* otherwise, fall out of this block and     */
968                                         /* enter the command loop, below.            */
969        }
970
971        while( 1 )
972        {
973            yyprompt( "Enter command (space to continue, ? for list): ", buf, 0 );
974
975            switch( *buf )
976            {
977            case '\0' :
978            case ' '  :
979            case '\n' :                                /* singlestep  */
980                goto outside;
981
982            case '?' :                                 /* help        */
983                cmd_list();
984                NEWLINE ( Prompt_window );
985                presskey();
986                yy_redraw_stack();
987                break;
988
989            case 'a':                                  /* abort       */
990                Abort = 1;
991                Singlestep = 0;
992                goto outside;
993
994            case 'b':                                  /* breakpoints */
995                breakpoint();
996                yy_redraw_stack();
997                break;
998
999            case 'd':                                  /* set delay time */
1000
1001                if(yyprompt("Delay time (in seconds, CR=0, ESC cancels): ", buf,1))
1002                    Delay = (long)( atof(buf) * 1000.0 );
1003                break;
1004
```

```
Listing 4.12. continued...
                                                                            /* read file */
1005           case 'f':
1006
1007               if( !yyprompt( "Print line numbers? (y/n, CR=y, ESC cancels): ",
1008                                                                              buf, 0))
1009                   break;
1010
1011               print_lines = *buf != 'n';
1012               if( !yyprompt( "File name or ESC to cancel: ", buf, 1) )
1013                   break;
1014
1015               werase( Stack_window );
1016               display_file( buf, sizeof(buf), print_lines );
1017               yy_redraw_stack();
1018               break;
1019                                                                            /* go!  */
1020           case 'g':
1021               Singlestep = 0;
1022               goto outside;
1023
1024           case 'i':
1025               if( yyprompt( "Input file name or ESC to cancel: ", buf, 1 ) )
1026                   new_input_file( buf );
1027               break;
1028                                                                       /* enable logging */
1029           case 'l':
1030               to_log( buf );
1031               break;
1032                                                                   /* noninteractive w/o logging */
1033           case 'N':
1034               Log          = NULL;
1035               No_stack_pix = 1;
1036               Interactive  = 0;
1037               Singlestep   = 0;
1038               Delay        = 0L;
1039               werase( Stack_window );
1040               goto outside;
1041                                                                   /* noninteractive mode w/ log */
1042           case 'n':
1043               if( !Log  &&  !to_log(buf) )
1044                   break;
1045               Interactive = 0;
1046               Singlestep  = 0;
1047               Delay       = 0L;
1048               werase( Stack_window );
1049               goto outside;
1050                                                                   /* exit to operating system */
1051           case 'q':                                             /* as if Ctrl-C was entered */
1052               raise( SIGINT );
1053               exit(0);
1054                                                                   /* redraw the stack window */
1055           case 'r':
1056               yy_redraw_stack();
1057               break;
1058                                                                   /* write screen to file */
1059           case 'w':
1060               if( yyprompt( "Output file name or ESC to cancel: ", buf, 1) )
1061                   write_screen( buf );
1062               break;
1063
```

→

```
Listing 4.12. continued...
1064            case 'x':                                    /* show lexemes */
1065                yycomment( "current   [%0.*s]\n", yyleng,        yytext   );
1066                yycomment( "previous  [%0.*s]\n", ii_plength(), ii_ptext() );
1067            break;
1068
1069            case 0x01: yyhook_a(); break;    /* Ctrl-A debugger hook (see text) */
1070            case 0x02: yyhook_b(); break;    /* Ctrl-B                          */
1071
1072            default:
1073                yyprompt( "Illegal command, press any key to continue", buf, 0 );
1074            break;
1075        }
1076    }
1077 outside:
1078    werase  ( Prompt_window );
1079    wrefresh( Prompt_window );
1080 }
1081
1082 /*-------------------------------------------------------------------*/
1083
1084 PRIVATE void cmd_list()
1085 {
1086    /* Print a list of commands in the stack window & prompt for an action. */
1087
1088    werase  (Stack_window );
1089    wmove   (Stack_window, 0, 0 );
1090    wprintw (Stack_window, "a  (a)bort parse by reading EOI    \n");
1091    wprintw (Stack_window, "b  modify or examine (b)reakpoint  \n");
1092    wprintw (Stack_window, "d  set (d)elay time for go mode    \n");
1093    wprintw (Stack_window, "f  read (f)ile                     \n");
1094    wprintw (Stack_window, "g  (g)o (any key stops parse)      \n");
1095    wprintw (Stack_window, "i  change (i)nput file             \n");
1096    wmove   (Stack_window, 0, 39 );
1097    wprintw (Stack_window, "l  (l)og output to file");
1098    wmove   (Stack_window, 1, 39 );
1099    wprintw (Stack_window, "n  (n)oninteractive mode");
1100    wmove   (Stack_window, 2, 39 );
1101    wprintw (Stack_window, "q  (q)uit (exit to dos)");
1102    wmove   (Stack_window, 3, 39 );
1103    wprintw (Stack_window, "r  (r)efresh stack window");
1104    wmove   (Stack_window, 4, 39 );
1105    wprintw (Stack_window, "w  (w)rite screen to file or device\n");
1106    wmove   (Stack_window, 5, 39 );
1107    wprintw (Stack_window, "x  Show current and prev. le(X)eme\n");
1108    wmove   (Stack_window, 7, (78-29)/2 );
1109    wprintw (Stack_window, "Space or Enter to single step" );
1110    wrefresh (Stack_window );
1111 }
```

One point of note is the Ctrl-A and Ctrl-B commands, processed on lines 1069 and 1070 of Listing 4.12. These commands call the `yyhook_a()` and `yyhook_b()` subroutines (in Listings 4.13 and 4.14), which do nothing at all. Their purpose is twofold. First, if you are running the parser under your compiler's debugger, these commands give you a hook into that debugger. You can set a breakpoint at `yyhook_a()`, and then issue a Ctrl-A to transfer from the running parser to the debugger itself. These hooks also let you add commands to the parser without having to recompile it. Since `yyhook_a()` and `yyhook_b()` are alone in separate files, customized versions that you supply are

Debugger hooks for Ctrl-A, Ctrl-B: `yyhook_a()`, `yyhook_b()`.

linked rather than the default ones in the library. You can effectively add commands to the parser's debugging environment by providing your own version of one or both of these routines. For example, it's convenient to print the symbol table at various states of the compilation process so you can watch symbols being added. You can add this capability to the parser by writing a routine that prints the symbol table and calling that routine yyhook_a( ). Thereafter, you can print the symbol table by issuing a Ctrl-A at the parser's *command* prompt.

Listing 4.13. *yyhook_a.c*— Debugger Hook 1

```
1   void yyhook_a(){}              /* entered with a ^A command */
```

Listing 4.14. *yyhook_b.c*— Debugger Hook 2

```
1   void yyhook_b(){}              /* entered with a ^B command */
```

Production breakpoints.

Token input:
yy_nextoken() calls
yylex().

Listing 4.15 contains support for the input and production breakpoints. (Stack breakpoints were handled in yy_pstack()—the code of interest starts on line 785 of Listing 4.10, page 258). The yy_nextoken() function (starting on line 1112 of Listing 4.15) gets an input token from yylex(), though if Abort is true, then an *a* command has been issued, and the end-of-input marker (0) is used rather than the next token. The routine then echoes the new token to the input window, and triggers a breakpoint (on line 1142) if necessary, by setting Singlestep true. Singlestep causes delay() to wait for a command the next time it's called (after the next stack-window update). yy_break() (on line 1167) does the same thing, but for production breakpoints. It is called from the **LLama**-generated parser just before every production is applied (when a nonterminal on the stack is replaced by it's right-hand side). In **occs**, it's called just before a reduction takes place. breakpoint() (on line 1187 of Listing 4.15) takes care of setting the breakpoints, and so forth. It processes the *b* command.

The remainder of the file (in Listing 4.16) comprises little support functions which are adequately commented and don't require additional discussion here.

Listing 4.15. *yydebug.c*— Breakpoint Support

```
1112   PUBLIC  int yy_nextoken()
1113   {
1114       /* Input a token from yylex() and echo to both the token and comment
1115        * windows. Yy_comment() writes to the log file too. Break if the input
1116        * breakpoint is set and the required token has just been read. The token
1117        * name is centered in the token window if it's short enough. It's
1118        * truncated at TOKEN_WIDTH characters otherwise.
1119        */
1120
1121       static int   tok = -1;               /* current token */
1122       int          width;
1123       char         *str;
1124       char         *lexeme;
1125       char         buf[ TOKEN_WIDTH ];
1126       extern char  *Yy_stok[];             /* Generated by occs and llama */
1127
1128       if( tok >= 0 && (Interactive || Log) )
1129           yycomment( "Advance past %s\n", Yy_stok[tok] );
1130
```

Listing 4.15. continued...

```
1131            lexeme = ((tok = Abort ? 0 : yylex()) == 0) ? "" : yytext;
1132
1133        if( Interactive || Log )
1134            yycomment( "Read %s <%s>\n", str = Yy_stok[tok], lexeme );
1135
1136        if( Interactive )
1137        {
1138            NEWLINE( Token_window );
1139            concat( TOKEN_WIDTH, buf, str, " ", lexeme, NULL );
1140            wprintw( Token_window, "%0.*s", TOKEN_WIDTH - 2, buf );
1141
1142            if( L_breakpoint != -1  &&  L_breakpoint <= yylineno )
1143            {
1144                L_breakpoint = -1;
1145                Singlestep   = 1;
1146                yy_pstack( 0, 1 );
1147            }
1148            else if( ( *I_breakpoint &&
1149                         (   ( isdigit(*I_breakpoint) && tok == atoi(I_breakpoint) )
1150                          || !strcmp( lexeme,        I_breakpoint)
1151                          || !strcmp( Yy_stok[tok],  I_breakpoint)
1152                         )
1153                       )
1154                     )
1155            {
1156                Singlestep = 1;
1157                yy_pstack( 0, 1 );
1158            }
1159        }
1160
1161        delay();
1162        return tok;
1163    }
1164
1165    /*------------------------------------------------------------------*/
1166
1167    PUBLIC   void yy_break( production_number )
1168    int   production_number;
1169    {
1170        /*  Handles production-number breakpoints. If a break is required, start
1171         *  single stepping and print the stack. Stack breakpoints are handled in
1172         *  yy_pstack and input breakpoints are done in yy_nextoken().
1173         *
1174         *  If production_number == -1, a break is forced regardless of the value
1175         *  of P_breakpoint;
1176         */
1177
1178        if( production_number == P_breakpoint || production_number == -1 )
1179        {
1180            Singlestep = 1;
1181            yy_pstack( 0, 1 );
1182        }
1183    }
1184
1185    /*------------------------------------------------------------------*/
1186
1187    PRIVATE int breakpoint()
1188    {
```

Listing 4.15. continued...

```
1189        /* Set up a breakpoint by prompting the user for any required information.
1190         * Return true if we have to redraw the stack window because a help screen
1191         * was printed there.
1192         */
1193
1194        int         type;
1195        char        **p;
1196        char        buf[80];
1197        int         rval    = 0;
1198        static char *text[] =
1199        {
1200            "Select a breakpoint type (i,l,p,or s) or command (c or l):",
1201            "Type: Description:          Enter breakpoint as follows:",
1202            " i    input...................number for token value",
1203            "                             or string for lexeme or token name",
1204            " l    input line read..........line number",
1205            " p    reduce by production......number for production number",
1206            " s    top-of-stack symbol.......number for state-stack item",
1207            "                             or string for symbol-stack item",
1208            " c = clear all breakpoints",
1209            " d = display (list) all breakpoints",
1210            NULL
1211        };
1212
1213        if( !yyprompt("Enter type or command, ? for help, ESC aborts: ", buf,0) )
1214            return 1;
1215
1216        if( *buf == '?' )
1217        {
1218            rval = 1;
1219            werase   (Stack_window);
1220            wmove    (Stack_window, 0, 0);
1221
1222            for( p = text; *p; p )
1223                wprintw(Stack_window, "%s\n", *p++ );
1224
1225            wrefresh (Stack_window);
1226            if( !yyprompt("Enter breakpoint type or command, ESC aborts: ", buf,0))
1227                return rval;
1228        }
1229
1230        if( (type = *buf)  == 'p' )
1231        {
1232            if( yyprompt("Production number or ESC to cancel: ", buf, 1 ))
1233            {
1234                if( !isdigit( *buf ))
1235                    yyprompt("Must be a number, press any key to continue.", buf,0);
1236                else
1237                    P_breakpoint = atoi( buf );
1238            }
1239        }
1240        else if( type == 'l' )
1241        {
1242            if( yyprompt("Input line number or ESC to cancel: ", buf, 1 ))
1243                L_breakpoint = atoi( buf );
1244        }
1245        else if( type == 'i' || type == 's' )
1246        {
```

Listing 4.15. continued...

```
1247                if( yyprompt("Symbol value or ESC to cancel: ", buf, 1 ))
1248                    strncpy( type == 'i' ? I_breakpoint : S_breakpoint, buf, BRKLEN );
1249        }
1250        else
1251        {
1252            switch( type )
1253            {
1254            case 'c':
1255                    P_breakpoint  = -1;
1256                    L_breakpoint  = -1;
1257                    *S_breakpoint = 0;
1258                    *I_breakpoint = 0;
1259                    break;
1260
1261            case 'd':
1262                    rval = 1;
1263                    werase (Stack_window);
1264                    wmove  (Stack_window, 0, 0);
1265
1266                    wprintw(Stack_window,
1267                        P_breakpoint == -1 ? "Production = none\n"
1268                                           : "Production = %d\n", P_breakpoint);
1269
1270                    wprintw(Stack_window, "Stack      = %s\n",
1271                                           *S_breakpoint ? S_breakpoint : "none" );
1272
1273                    wprintw(Stack_window, "Input      = %s\n",
1274                                           *I_breakpoint ? I_breakpoint : "none" );
1275                    wprintw(Stack_window,
1276                        I_breakpoint == 0  ? "Input line = none\n"
1277                                           : "Input line = %d\n", I_breakpoint);
1278                    wrefresh(Stack_window);
1279                    NEWLINE (Prompt_window);
1280                    presskey();
1281                    break;
1282
1283            default:
1284                    yyprompt("Illegal command or type, Press any key.", buf, 0);
1285                    break;
1286            }
1287        }
1288
1289        return rval;
1290    }
```

Listing 4.16. *yydebug.c*— Input Routines

```
1291    PRIVATE int       new_input_file( buf )
1292    char      *buf;
1293    {
1294        /* Open up a new input file. Input must come from a file because the
1295         * keyboard is used to get commands. In theory, you can use both standard
1296         * input and the keyboard (by opening the console as another stream), but I
1297         * had difficulties doing this in a portable way, and eventually gave up.
1298         * It's not that big a deal to require that test input be in a file.
1299         */
1300
```

```
      Listing 4.16. continued...
1301          NEWLINE( Prompt_window );
1302          wrefresh( Prompt_window );
1303
1304          if( ii_newfile( buf ) != -1 )
1305              Inp_fm_file = 1;
1306          else
1307          {
1308              wprintw(Prompt_window, "Can't open %s.", buf );
1309              presskey();
1310          }
1311          return Inp_fm_file;
1312      }
1313
1314      /*----------------------------------------------------------------------*/
1315
1316      PRIVATE  FILE    *to_log( buf )
1317      char     *buf;
1318      {
1319          /* Set up everything to log output to a file (open the log file, etc.). */
1320
1321          if( !yyprompt("Log-file name (CR for \"log\", ESC cancels): ", buf,1) )
1322              return NULL;
1323
1324          if( !*buf )
1325              strcpy( buf, "log" );
1326
1327          if( !(Log = fopen( buf, "w")) )
1328          {
1329              NEWLINE(Prompt_window );
1330              wprintw(Prompt_window, "Can't open %s", buf );
1331              presskey();
1332              return NULL;
1333          }
1334
1335          if( !yyprompt("Log comment-window output? (y/n, CR=y): ", buf,0) )
1336              return NULL;
1337          else
1338              No_comment_pix = (*buf == 'n');
1339
1340          if( !yyprompt( "Print stack pictures in log file? (y/n, CR=y): ",buf,0) )
1341              return NULL;
1342
1343          if( !(No_stack_pix = (*buf == 'n')) )
1344          {
1345              if( !yyprompt( "Print stacks horizontally? (y/n, CR=y): ",buf,0) )
1346                  return NULL;
1347
1348              if( Horiz_stack_pix = (*buf != 'n') )
1349              {
1350                  if( !yyprompt("Print SYMBOL stack (y/n, CR=y): ",buf,0) )
1351                      return NULL;
1352                  Sym_pix = (*buf != 'n');
1353
1354                  if( !yyprompt("Print PARSE  stack (y/n, CR=y): ",buf,0) )
1355                      return NULL;
1356                  Parse_pix = (*buf != 'n');
1357
1358                  if( !yyprompt("Print VALUE  stack (y/n, CR=y): ",buf,0) )
1359                      return NULL;
1360                  Attr_pix = (*buf != 'n');
```

```
Listing 4.16. continued...
1361                    }
1362            }
1363        return Log;
1364    }
1365
1366    /*----------------------------------------------------------------------*/
1367
1368    PRIVATE int  input_char( void )
1369    {
1370        /* Get a character from the input window and echo it explicitly. If we've
1371         * compiled under Unix, reset the character-available flag.
1372         */
1373
1374        int c;
1375
1376        if( (c = wgetch(Prompt_window) & 0x7f) != ESC )
1377            waddch( Prompt_window, c );
1378
1379        UX( Char_avail = 0; )
1380        return c;
1381    }
1382
1383    /*----------------------------------------------------------------------*/
1384
1385    PUBLIC int yyprompt( prompt, buf, getstring )
1386    char *prompt, *buf;
1387    int  getstring;     /* get entire string (as compared to a single character */
1388    {
1389        /* Print a prompt and then wait for a reply, load the typed characters into
1390         * buf. ^H (destructive backspace) is supported. An ESC causes yyprompt()
1391         * to return 0 immediately, otherwise 1 is returned. The ESC is not put
1392         * into the buffer. If "getstring" is true, an entire string is fetched and
1393         * prompt returns when the newline is typed. If "getstring" is false, then
1394         * one character is fetched and yyprompt() returns immediately after getting
1395         * that character. Leading and trailing white space is stripped from the
1396         * line if getstring is true. (You can get a single space character if it's
1397         * false, however.)
1398         */
1399
1400        register int  c;
1401        int           y, x;
1402        char          *startbuf = buf;
1403
1404        NEWLINE ( Prompt_window                    );
1405        wprintw ( Prompt_window, "%s", prompt );
1406        wrefresh( Prompt_window                    );
1407
1408        if( !getstring )
1409            c = *buf++ = input_char();
1410        else
1411        {
1412            while( (c = input_char()) != '\n'  &&  c != ESC )
1413            {
1414                if( isspace(c) && buf==startbuf )
1415                    continue;                                /* skip leading white space */
1416
1417                if( c != '\b' )
1418                    *buf++ = c;
```

Listing 4.16. continued...

```
1419              else                                    /* handle destructive backspace */
1420              {
1421                  getyx( Prompt_window, y, x );
1422
1423                  if( buf <= startbuf )
1424                      wmove ( Prompt_window, y, x+1 );
1425                  else
1426                  {
1427                      waddch( Prompt_window, ' ' );
1428                      wmove ( Prompt_window, y, x );
1429                      --buf;
1430                  }
1431              }
1432              wrefresh( Prompt_window );
1433          }
1434
1435      while( isspace( buf[-1] )  &&  buf > startbuf )
1436          --buf;                      /* Strip trailing white space */
1437      }
1438      *buf = 0;
1439      return (c != ESC);
1440 }
1441
1442 /*--------------------------------------------------------------------*/
1443
1444 PRIVATE void presskey()
1445 {
1446      /* Ask for a key to be pressed and wait for it.  Note that this command
1447       * does a refresh, but it intentionally does not clear the window before
1448       * printing the prompt.
1449       */
1450
1451      wprintw ( Prompt_window, " Press any key: " );
1452      wrefresh( Prompt_window );
1453      input_char();
1454 }
```

4.10 LLama—Implementing an LL(1) Parser-Generator

The remainder of this chapter discusses how **LLama** works. Much of the following code is used by both **LLama** and **occs** (all the files whose names start with *ll* are used only by **LLama**, everything else is used jointly). As usual, I expect you to actually read the code (I've not repeated in the text those things that are adequately described in comments in the code itself). I also expect you to be familiar with the set and hash-table functions described in Appendix A.

4.10.1 LLama's Parser

Llama's own, recursive-descent parser.

This section describes **LLama**'s own parser. It provides a good example of a working recursive-descent compiler for a small programming language (**LLama** is itself a compiler, after all). It translates a very high-level language (a grammatical description of a programming language) to a high-level language (C).

I built **LLama** in a two-step process, initially developing yet another recursive-descent parser (the last one we'll look at in this book) that supports a bare-bones input language. I then used this recursive-descent version of **LLama** to rebuild its own parser, substituting the **LLama** output file for the recursive-descent parser when I linked the new version. This process is typical of how a language is brought up on a new machine. You first construct a simple compiler for a subset of the target language using the tools at hand—typically an assembler. The output of this compiler is typically the same assembly language that the compiler itself is written in. Using your subset language, you then write a compiler for a more complete version of the language.

Bootstrapping a compiler using language subsets.

For example, you could start writing a C compiler with a very small subset of C, written in assembly language—an adequate subset would support simple expressions (no fancy operators like conditionals), global variables of type **int** and **char** (but no local variables), one-dimensional arrays of **int** and **char**, simple control-flow statements (**while**, **if**, and **else** are adequate), and some sort of block structure. Note that, at this level, a compiler is little more than a macro translator. (See [Angermeyer], pp. 51–92, where all of the foregoing are implemented as macros using the Microsoft macro assembler, MASM.)

In the next step, you write a larger subset of C using the language defined in the previous step, and compile it using the subset-of-C compiler. Typically, this second level would add better typing (introducing structures, for example), support local variables and subroutine arguments, and so forth. Continuing in this manner, you can bootstrap yourself up to a full language implementation.

LLama, like most compilers, is easily divided into several distinct phases. The lexical analyzer is created with LᴇX. (The specification is in Listing 4.17 and the required token definitions are in Listing 4.18.) Note that white space (a comment is treated like white space) is ignored if the global variable `Ignore` (declared on line 27) is true, otherwise a `WHITESPACE` token is returned. The variable is modified using the access routines on lines 215 and 216. Also note how actions are processed on lines 73 to 153. The entire action is treated as a single token. LᴇX recognizes an initial open brace, and the associated code absorbs everything up to and including the matching close brace. That is, the code doesn't terminate until a close brace is found at nesting level 1, as defined by `nestlev`. Other close braces are absorbed into the lexeme.

Llama's lexical analyzer, tokens, LeX input specification.

Listing 4.17. *parser.lex*— LᴇX Input File for **occs/LLama** Lexical Analyzer

```
 1   %{
 2   #include <stdio.h>
 3   #include <tools/debug.h>
 4   #include <tools/hash.h>
 5   #include <tools/set.h>
 6   #include "llout.h"
 7
 8   #define CREATING_LLAMA_PARSER    /* Suppress various definitions in parser.h */
 9   #include "parser.h"              /* that conflict with LeX-generated defs.   */
10
11   /* --------------------------------------------------------------------
12    * Lexical analyzer for both llama and yacc. Note that llama doesn't support
13    * %left, %right, %noassoc, or %prec. They are recognized here so that we can
14    * print an error message when they're encountered. By the same token, yacc
15    * ignores the %synch directive. Though all legal llama input files can be
16    * processed by yacc, the reverse is not true.
17    *
18    * --------------------------------------------------------------------
19    * Whitespace, comments, and otherwise illegal characters must be handled
20    * specially. When we're processing code blocks, we need to get at
```

→

Listing 4.17. continued...

```
21      *   the characters so that they can be passed to the output, otherwise, the
22      *   characters should be ignored. The ws() and nows() subroutines (at the
23      *   bottom of the file) switch between these behaviors by changing the value
24      *   if Ignore. If Ignore is true, white space is ignored.
25      */
26
27      PRIVATE int    Ignore = 0;
28      PRIVATE int    Start_line;           /* starting line number  */
29
30      /* ---------------------------------------------------------------
31       *   Prototypes for functions at the bottom of this file:
32       */
33
34      void stripcr P(( char *src ));   /* Remove carriage returns (but not   */
35                                       /* linefeeds) from src.               */
36      void nows    P(( void ));        /* Ignore white space, etc            */
37      void ws      P(( void ));        /* Don't ignore white space, etc      */
38      %}
39
40      c_name    [A-Za-z_][A-Za-z_0-9]*
41      %%
42
43      "/*"                    {       /* Absorb a comment (treat it as WHITESPACE) */
44
45                              int i;
46                              int start = yylineno;
47
48                              while( i = input() )
49                              {
50                                  if( i < 0 )
51                                  {
52                                      ii_unterm();
53                                      ii_flush(1);
54                                      ii_term();
55                                      lerror(NONFATAL,"Comment starting on line %d " \
56                                                  "too long, truncating\n", start);
57                                  }
58                                  else if( i == '*'  &&  ii_lookahead(1) == '/' )
59                                  {
60                                      input();
61                                      stripcr( yytext );
62
63                                      if( Ignore ) goto end;
64                                      else            return WHITESPACE;
65                                  }
66                              }
67
68                              lerror(FATAL, "End of file encountered in comment\n");
69
70                          end:;
71                          }
72
73                          /* Suck up an entire action. Handle nested braces here.
74                           * This code won't work if the action is longer than the
75                           * buffer length used by the input functions. If this is a
76                           * problem, you have to allocate your own buffer and copy
77                           * the lexeme there as it's processed (in a manner similar to
78                           * the %{ processing, below). If space is really a problem,
79                           * the code blocks can be copied to a temporary file and the
80                           * offset to the start of the text (as returned by ftell()) ➡
```

Listing 4.17. continued...

```
81                           * can be stored rather than the string itself.
82                           */
83
84    \{                     {
85                               int  i;
86                               int  nestlev;              /* brace-nesting level     */
87                               int  lb1;                  /* previous character      */
88                               int  lb2;                  /* character before that   */
89                               int  in_string;           /* processing string constant */
90                               int  in_char_const;       /* processing char. constant */
91                               int  in_comment;          /* processing a comment      */
92
93                               lb1 = lb2     = 0;
94                               in_string     = 0;
95                               in_char_const = 0;
96                               in_comment    = 0;
97                               Start_line    = yylineno;
98
99                               for( nestlev=1; i=input(); lb2=lb1, lb1=i )
100                              {
101                                  if( lb2=='\n' && lb1=='%' && i=='%' )
102                                      lerror( FATAL,
103                                          "%%%% in code block starting on line %d\n",
104                                          Start_line );
105
106                                  if( i < 0 )            /* input-buffer overflow */
107                                  {
108                                    ii_unterm();
109                                    ii_flush(1);
110                                    ii_term();
111                                    lerror( FATAL,
112                                        "Code block starting on line %d too long.\n",
113                                                              Start_line);
114                                  }
115
116                                  /* Take care of \{, "{", '{', \}, "}", '}'  */
117
118                                  if( i == '\\' )
119                                  {
120                                      if( !(i = input()) )    /* discard backslash  */
121                                          break;
122                                      else
123                                          continue;          /* and following char */
124                                  }
125
126                                  if( i == '"' && !(in_char_const || in_comment) )
127                                      in_string = !in_string;
128
129                                  else if( i == '\'' && !(in_string || in_comment) )
130                                      in_char_const = !in_char_const;
131
132                                  else if( lb1 == '/' && i == '*' && !in_string )
133                                      in_comment = 1;
134
135                                  else if( lb1 == '*' && i == '/' && in_comment )
136                                      in_comment = 0;
137
```

➡

Listing 4.17. continued...

```
138                                      if( !(in_string || in_char_const || in_comment) )
139                                      {
140                                          if( i == '{' )
141                                              ++nestlev;
142
143                                          if( i == '}' && --nestlev <= 0 )
144                                          {
145                                              stripcr( yytext );
146                                              return ACTION;
147                                          }
148                                      }
149                                  }
150
151                                  lerror(FATAL, "EOF in code block starting on line %d\n",
152                                                                            Start_line );
153                              }
154
155      ^"%%"                   return SEPARATOR;               /* Must be anchored because  */
156                                                             /* it can appear in a printf */
157                                                             /* statement.                */
158      "%{"[\s\t]*             {
159                                  /* Copy a code block to the output file.  */
160
161                                  int c, looking_for_brace = 0;
162
163                                  #undef output              /* replace macro with function */
164                                                             /* in main.c                   */
165                                  if( !No_lines )
166                                      output( "\n#line %d \"%s\"\n",
167                                                          yylineno, Input_file_name );
168
169                                  while( c = input() )       /* while not at end of file   */
170                                  {
171                                      if( c == -1 )          /* buffer is full, flush it    */
172                                          ii_flushbuf();
173
174                                      else if( c != '\r' )
175                                      {
176                                          if( looking_for_brace ) /* last char was a %  */
177                                          {                                          /* { */
178                                              if( c == '}' ) break;
179                                              else           output( "%%%c", c );
180                                          }
181                                          else
182                                          {
183                                              if( c == '%' ) looking_for_brace = 1;
184                                              else           output( "%c", c );
185                                          }
186                                      }
187                                  }
188                                  return CODE_BLOCK;
189                              }
190
191      <{c_name}>             return FIELD;                  /* for occs only          */
192      "%union"              return PERCENT_UNION;          /* for occs only          */
193      "%token"              |
194      "%term"               return TERM_SPEC;
195      "%type"               return TYPE;                   /* for occs only          */
196      "%synch"              return SYNCH;                  /* for llama only         */
197      "%left"               return LEFT;                   /* for occs only          */
```

```
      Listing 4.17. continued...
198    "%right"              return RIGHT;              /* for occs only            */
199    "%nonassoc"           return NONASSOC;           /* for occs only            */
200    "%prec"               return PREC;               /* for occs only            */
201    "%start"              return START;              /* for error messages only */
202    ":"                   return COLON ;
203    "|"                   return OR    ;
204    ";"                   return SEMI  ;
205    "["                   return START_OPT ;
206    "]"                          |
207    "]*"                  return END_OPT;
208
209    [^\x00-\s%\{}[\]()*:|;,<>]+     return NAME;
210    \x0d                           ; /* discard carriage return (\r) */
211    [\x00-\x0c\x0e-\s]             if( !Ignore ) return WHITESPACE;
212    %%
213    /*-----------------------------------------------------------------*/
214
215    PUBLIC  void  nows() { Ignore = 1; }    /* Ignore white space, etc.      */
216    PUBLIC  void  ws  () { Ignore = 0; }    /* Don't ignore white space, etc. */
217
218    PUBLIC  int   start_action()    /* Return starting line number of most */
219    {                               /* recently read ACTION block          */
220        return Start_line;
221    }
222    /*-----------------------------------------------------------------*/
223
224    PRIVATE void stripcr( src )      /* Remove all \r's (but not \n's) from src. */
225    char    *src;
226    {
227        char        *dest;
228        for( dest = src ; *src ; src++ )
229            if( *src != '\r' )
230                *dest++ = *src;
231        *dest = '\0';
232    }
```

LLama's parser uses the LEX-generated lexical analyzer to parse the **LLama** input file, creating a symbol table with what it finds there. A *symbol table* is a large data structure, indexed by symbol name (the lexeme associated with the name in the input file). A good analogy is an array of structures, one field of which is a string holding the symbol name. The other fields in the structure hold things like the numeric value assigned to each symbol (the token value) and the symbols's type (in the current case, the type is *terminal*, *nonterminal*, or *action*, as compared to the more usual **int**, **long**, and so forth). **LLama**'s symbol also stores tokenized versions of the right-hand sides as elements of the symbol-table entry for each nonterminal. I'll discuss the details of this process in a moment. The **LLama** code-generation phase is passed the symbol table, which in this case serves as a representation of the entire input language, and outputs code—the parse tables needed to parse an input file in the target language. It also copies the output parser from the template file to the output file.

LLama's symbol-table.

The *parser.h* file, which starts in Listing 4.19, is **#include**d in most of the files that comprise both **LLama** and **occs**. It starts out on lines six to 12 with conditional-compilation macros that work like the D() macro in *<tools/debug.h>* (described in Appendix A). The argument to the LL() macro compiles only if you're making **LLama** (I usually define LLAMA on the compiler's command line with a *cc -DLLAMA*), the opposite applies to the OX() macro. The listing also contains a few predefined exit codes.

Conditional compilation macros: LL(), OX().

Listing 4.18. *llout.h—* **LLama** Token Definitions

```
 1  #define _EOI_           0
 2  #define ACTION          1
 3  #define CODE_BLOCK       2
 4  #define COLON           3
 5  #define END_OPT         4
 6  #define FIELD           5
 7  #define LEFT            6
 8  #define NAME            7
 9  #define NONASSOC        8
10  #define OR              9
11  #define OTHER          10
12  #define PREC           11
13  #define RIGHT          12
14  #define SEMI           13
15  #define SEPARATOR      14
16  #define START          15
17  #define START_OPT      16
18  #define SYNCH          17
19  #define TERM_SPEC      18
20  #define TYPE           19
21  #define PERCENT_UNION  20
22  #define WHITESPACE     21
```

Listing 4.19. *parser.h—* Compilation Directives and Exit Stati

```
 1  /*      PARSER.H        This file contains those #defines, etc., that
 2   *                      are used by both llama and yacc. There's also
 3   *                      a yacc.h file that's used only by the yacc code.
 4   */
 5
 6  #ifdef LLAMA
 7  #define LL(x)  x
 8  #define OX(x)
 9  #else
10  #define LL(x)
11  #define OX(x)  x
12  #endif
13
14  /*-----------------------------------------------------------------
15   * Various error exit stati. Note that other errors found while parsing cause
16   * llama to exit with a status equal to the number of errors (or zero if
17   * there are no errors).
18   */
19
20  #define EXIT_ILLEGAL_ARG    255    /* Illegal command-line switch      */
21  #define EXIT_TOO_MANY       254    /* Too many command-line args       */
22  #define EXIT_NO_DRIVER      253    /* Can't find llama.par             */
23  #define EXIT_OTHER          252    /* Other error (syntax error, etc.) */
24  #define EXIT_USR_ABRT       251    /* Ctrl-Break                       */
```

Token values: MINNON-
TERM, MINACT.

Parser.h continues in Listing 4.20 with the definitions of the numbers that represent terminals, nonterminals, and actions. You can change the values of MINNONTERM and MINACT (on lines 29 and 30), but they must always be in the same relative order. The following must hold:

$$(0 = \_EOI\_) < (MINTERM = 1) < MINNONTERM < MINACT$$

Zero is reserved for the end-of-input marker (_EOI_), and MINTERM must be 1. Also note that there must be at least one hole between the maximum terminal and minimum nonterminal values. This hole is generated with the -2 in the MAXNONTERM definition on line 41. It's required because the symbolic value used for ε is one more than the largest number actually used to represent a terminal symbol; the hole guarantees that there's enough space for the ε. (EPSILON is defined on line 65.) The listing finishes with a few miscellaneous definitions for various file names, and so forth.

Listing 4.20. *parser.h*— Numeric Limits for Token Values

```
25   #define MAXNAME      32   /* Maximum length of a terminal or nonterminal name   */
26   #define MAXPROD     512   /* Maximum number of productions in the input grammar */
27
28   #define MINTERM       1   /* Token values assigned to terminals start here      */
29   #define MINNONTERM  256   /* nonterminals start here                            */
30   #define MINACT      512   /* acts start here                                    */
31
32                             /* Maximum numeric values used for terminals
33                              * and nonterminals (MAXTERM and MINTERM), as
34                              * well as the maximum number of terminals and
35                              * nonterminals (NUMTERMS and NUMNONTERMS).
36                              * Finally, USED_TERMS and USED_NONTERMS are
37                              * the number of these actually in use (i.e.
38                              * were declared in the input file).
39                              */
40
41   #define MAXTERM      (MINNONTERM -2)
42   #define MAXNONTERM   (MINACT     -1)
43
44   #define NUMTERMS     ((MAXTERM-MINTERM) +1)
45   #define NUMNONTERMS  ((MAXNONTERM-MINNONTERM)+1)
46
47   #define USED_TERMS      ((Cur_term    - MINTERM)    +1)
48   #define USED_NONTERMS   ((Cur_nonterm - MINNONTERM) +1)
49
50                             /* These macros evaluate to true if x represents
51                              * a terminal (ISTERM), nonterminal (ISNONTERM)
52                              * or action (ISACT)
53                              */
54
55   #define ISTERM(x)    ((x) && (MINTERM    <= (x)->val && (x)->val <= MAXTERM    ))
56   #define ISNONTERM(x) ((x) && (MINNONTERM <= (x)->val && (x)->val <= MAXNONTERM))
57   #define ISACT(x)     ((x) && (MINACT     <= (x)->val                          ))
58
59                                /* Epsilon's value is one more than the largest
60                                 * terminal actually used. We can get away with
61                                 * this only because EPSILON is not used until
62                                 * after all the terminals have been entered
63                                 * into the symbol table.
64                                 */
65   #define EPSILON  (Cur_term+1)
66                                /* The following macros are used to adjust the
67                                 * nonterminal values so that the smallest
68                                 * nonterminal is zero. (You need to do this
69                                 * when you output the tables). ADJ_VAL does
70                                 * the adjustment, UNADJ_VAL translates the
```

```
Listing 4.20. continued...
71                                                   * adjust value back to the original value.
72                                                   */
73
74  #define ADJ_VAL(x)    ((x)-MINNONTERM )
75  #define UNADJ_VAL(x)  ((x)+MINNONTERM )
76
77  /*-----------------------------------------------------------------------*/
78
79  #define NONFATAL         0         /* Values to pass to error() and lerror(), */
80  #define FATAL            1         /* defined in main.c.                       */
81  #define WARNING          2
82
83  #define DOLLAR_DOLLAR    ((unsigned)~0 >>1)      /* Passed to do_dollar() to */
84                                                   /* indicate that $$ is to   */
85                                                   /* be processed.            */
86
87  /*-----------------------------------------------------------------------*/
88
89  #ifdef LLAMA                                      /* Various file names:              */
90  #     define TOKEN_FILE    "llout.h"     /* output file for token #defines    */
91  #     define PARSE_FILE    "llout.c"     /* output file for parser            */
92  #     define SYM_FILE      "llout.sym"   /* output file for symbol table      */
93  #     define DOC_FILE      "llout.doc"   /* LALR(1) State machine description */
94  #     define DEF_EXT       "lma"         /* foo.lma is default input extension */
95  #     define PAR_TEMPL     "llama.par"   /* template file for parser          */
96  #     define PROG_NAME     "llama"
97  #else
98  #     define TOKEN_FILE    "yyout.h"     /* output file for token #defines    */
99  #     define PARSE_FILE    "yyout.c"     /* output file for parser            */
100 #     define ACT_FILE      "yyact.c"     /* Used for output if -a specified   */
101 #     define TAB_FILE      "yyoutab.c"   /* output file for parser tables (-T)*/
102 #     define SYM_FILE      "yyout.sym"   /* output file for symbol table      */
103 #     define DOC_FILE      "yyout.doc"   /* LALR(1) State machine description */
104 #     define DEF_EXT       "ox"          /* foo.ox is default input extension */
105 #     define PAR_TEMPL     "occs.par"    /* template file for PARSE_FILE      */
106 #     define ACT_TEMPL     "occs-act.par" /* template file for ACT_FILE        */
107 #     define PROG_NAME     "occs"
108 #endif
```

Definitions for output functions, `YY_TTYPE`

Listing 4.21 shows several definitions used by the output functions. The **typedef**s for `YY_TTYPE` on lines 115 and 116 are used only to predict the size of the output transition tables. They should agree with the the YY_TTYPE definitions in the parser-template files.

Symbol-table data structures.

The next part of *parser.h*, the `SYMBOL` and `PRODUCTION` structures declared in Listing 4.22, are used for **LLama**'s symbol table. Symbol tables tend to be the most complex data structure in the compiler, and the **LLama** symbol table is no exception. Figure 4.9 shows a symbol table containing an entry for the following three productions:

$$expr \quad \rightarrow \quad term \ \textbf{PLUS} \ expr$$
$$\quad | \quad term$$
$$term \quad \rightarrow \quad \textbf{NUMBER} \ \{\texttt{create\_tmp(yytext);}\}$$

For clarity, I've left out unimportant fields, and `NULL` pointers are just left blank in the picture.

SYMBOL structure.

The symbol table itself is made up of `SYMBOL` structures, shown in the dashed box in Figure 4.9. This box is actually a hash table, put together with the functions described in

Listing 4.21. *parser.h*— Simple Types

```
109   /* The following are used to define types of the OUTPUT transition tables. The
110    * ifndef takes care of compiling the llama output file that will be used to
111    * recreate the llama input file. We must let the llama-generated definitions
112    * take precedence over the the default ones in parser.h in this case.
113    */
114   #ifndef CREATING_LLAMA_PARSER
115       LL( typedef unsigned char    YY_TTYPE ;        )
116       OX( typedef int              YY_TTYPE ;        )
117   #endif
```

Listing 4.22. *parser.h*— The SYMBOL and PRODUCTION Data Structures

```
118   /* SYMBOL structure (used for symbol table). Note that the name itself */
119   /* is kept by the symbol-table entry maintained by the hash function.  */
120
121   #define NAME_MAX 32                              /* Max name length + 1 */
122
123   typedef struct _symbol_
124   {
125       char            name  [ NAME_MAX ];         /* symbol name. Must be first */
126       char            field [ NAME_MAX ];         /* %type <field>              */
127       unsigned        val;                        /* numeric value of symbol    */
128       unsigned        used;                       /* symbol used on an rhs      */
129       unsigned        set;                        /* symbol defined             */
130       unsigned        lineno;                     /* input line num. of string  */
131       unsigned char   *string;                    /* code for actions.          */
132       struct   _prod_ *productions;               /* right-hand sides if nonterm*/
133       SET             *first;                     /* FIRST set                  */
134   LL( SET             *follow; )                  /* FOLLOW set                 */
135   } SYMBOL;
136
137   #define NULLABLE(sym) ( ISNONTERM(sym) && MEMBER((sym)->first, EPSILON) )
138   /*--------------------------------------------------------------------------*/
139   /* PRODUCTION Structure.  Represents right-hand sides.                    */
140
141   #define MAXRHS    31      /* Maximum number of objects on a right-hand side  */
142   #define RHSBITS   5       /* Number of bits required to hold MAXRHS           */
143
144   typedef struct _prod_
145   {
146       unsigned        num;                        /* production number          */
147       SYMBOL          *rhs[ MAXRHS + 1];          /* Tokenized right-hand side  */
148       SYMBOL          *lhs;                       /* Left-hand side             */
149       unsigned char rhs_len;                      /* # of elements in rhs[] array */
150       unsigned char non_acts;                     /*        " that are not actions */
151       SET             *select;                    /* LL(1) select set           */
152       struct _prod_ *next;                        /* pointer to next production */
153                                                   /*      for this left-hand side. */
154       OX( int         prec; )                     /* Relative precedence        */
155
156   } PRODUCTION;
```

Appendix A. A SYMBOL contains the name of the symbol (name) and the internal numeric value (val). If the symbol is an action, the string field points at a string that holds the code specified in the **LLama** input file. In the case of a nonterminal, the

Figure 4.9. Structure of the **LLama** Symbol Table

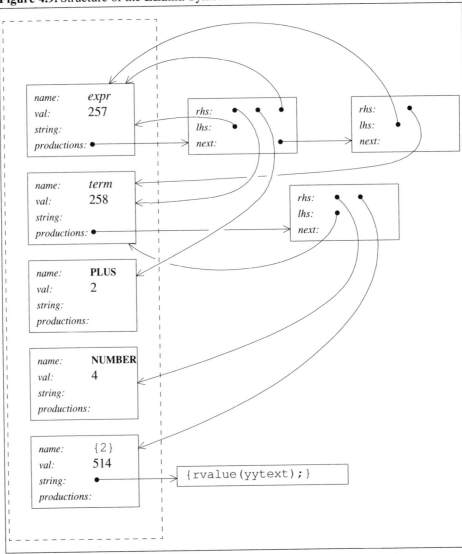

`productions` field points at the head of a linked list of PRODUCTION structures, one element of the list for each right-hand side. The right-hand side is represented within the PRODUCTION as an array of pointers to symbol-table entries for each element of the right-hand side. The size of this array obviously limits the size of the right-hand side. I opted for this approach rather than keeping an array of numeric values for the symbols, because the latter would require an additional table lookup every time I had to access a symbol on a right-hand side. Note that the PRODUCTIONs form a doubly linked list in that the `lhs` field of each PRODUCTION points back to the production's left-hand side. The `next` field is just the next element in the linked list.

Other fields in the PRODUCTION are the production number (num)—an arbitrary, but unique, number assigned to each production; `rhs_len` is the number of symbols in the `rhs[]` array; `non_acts` is the number of elements in `rhs[]` that are not actions; finally, `select` is the LL(1) select set. (I'll discuss exactly what this is in a moment.) The `prec` field holds the relative precedence level of the current production if you're compiling for **occs**. This number is usually the precedence level of the rightmost terminal on the right-hand side, but it can be changed with a %prec directive.

Other fields in the SYMBOL structure are: lineno—the input line number on which the symbol is defined; used is set true when a symbol is used on a right-hand side; and set is set true when a symbol is defined with a %term or by appearing as a left-hand side. It's a hard error for a symbol to be used without having been defined (set). It's just a warning if the symbol is defined but not used, however. Actions are set implicitly by being used. I'll discuss the first and follow fields in a moment.

The next data structure of interest is the PREC_TAB structure defined on lines 159 to 164 of Listing 4.23. This structure is used only by **occs**—it holds precedence and associativity information for the terminal symbols. An array of these (defined on line 200) is indexed by nonterminal value. This information could also be incorporated into the SYMBOL structure, but it's easier to keep it as a separate table. The remainder of *parser.h* comprises global-variable and subroutine declarations. Space is allocated for the variables if ALLOCATE is defined before *parser.h* is **#include**d.

Precision table:
PREC_TAB

Listing 4.23. *parser.h*— Declarations and Type Definitions

```
157    #ifdef OCCS
158
159    typedef struct _prectab_
160    {
161        unsigned char level;   /* Relative precedence, 0=none, 1=lowest       */
162        unsigned char assoc;   /* associativity: 'l'=left,'r'=right,'\0'=none */
163
164    } PREC_TAB;
165
166    #define DEF_FIELD "yy_def"      /* Field name for default field in a       */
167                                    /* %union.                                 */
168    #endif
169    #ifdef ALLOCATE                          /* If ALLOCATE is true, allocate space and */
170    #       define CLASS                     /* activate the initializer, otherwise the */
171    #       define I(x)  x                   /* storage class is extern and the         */
172    #else                                    /* initializer is gobbled up.              */
173    #       define CLASS extern
174    #       define I(x)
175    #endif                                            /* The following are set in      */
176                                                      /* main.c, mostly by command-    */
177                                                      /* line switches.                */
178    CLASS int  Debug             I( = 0         ); /* True for debug diagnostics    */
179    CLASS char *Input_file_name  I( = "console" ); /* Input file name               */
180    CLASS int  Make_actions      I( = 1         ); /* ==0 if -p on command line     */
181    CLASS int  Make_parser       I( = 1         ); /* ==0 if -a on command line     */
182    CLASS int  Make_yyoutab      I( = 0         ); /* ==1 if -T on command line     */
183    CLASS int  No_lines          I( = 0         ); /* Suppress #lines in output     */
184    CLASS int  No_warnings       I( = 0         ); /* Suppress warnings if true     */
185    CLASS FILE *Output           I( = stdout    ); /* Output stream.                */
186    CLASS int  Public            I( = 0         ); /* Make static symbols public    */
187    CLASS int  Symbols           I( = 0         ); /* Generate symbol table.        */
188    CLASS int  Threshold         I( = 4         ); /* Compression threshold         */
189    CLASS int  Uncompressed      I( = 0         ); /* Don't compress tables         */
190    CLASS int  Use_stdout        I( = 0         ); /* -t specified on command line  */
191    CLASS int  Verbose           I( = 0         ); /* Verbose-mode output (1 for    */
192                                                   /* -v and 2 for -V)              */
193
194    CLASS SYMBOL   *Terms[ MINACT ];       /* This array is indexed by terminal or
195                                            * nonterminal value and evaluates to a
196                                            * pointer to the equivalent symbol-table
197                                            * entry.
198                                            */
```

Listing 4.23. continued...

```
199
200   OX( CLASS PREC_TAB Precedence[ MINNONTERM ]; )   /* Used only by occs. Holds    */
201                                                    /* relative precedence and     */
202                                                    /* associativity information   */
203                                                    /* for both terminals and      */
204                                                    /* nonterminals.               */
205
206   LL( CLASS   SET   *Synch; )              /* Error-recovery synchronization */
207                                            /* set (specified with %synch).   */
208                                            /* Synch is initialized in acts.c */
209                                            /* It is used only by llama.       */
210   CLASS  char      *Template  I(=PAR_TEMPL);   /* Template file for the parser; */
211                                                /* can be modified in main.c     */
212   CLASS HASH_TAB   *Symtab;                /* The symbol table itself        */
213                                            /* (initialized in yyact.c)       */
214   CLASS SYMBOL     *Goal_symbol I(=NULL);  /* Pointer to symbol-table entry  */
215                                            /* for the start (goal) symbol    */
216                                                /* The following are used     */
217                                                /* by the acts [in llact.c]   */
218   CLASS int        Cur_term        I(= MINTERM-1   ); /* Current terminal      */
219   CLASS int        Cur_nonterm     I(= MINNONTERM-1); /*    "      nonterminal */
220   CLASS int        Cur_act         I(= MINACT-1    ); /*    "      action      */
221   CLASS int        Num_productions I( = 0          ); /* Number of productions */
222
223   #undef CLASS
224   #undef I
225   /*-------------------------------------------------------------------*/
226
227   #define  outc(c)  putc(c,Output);        /* Character routine to complement */
228                                            /* output() in main.c              */
```

LLama's parser does one thing: it loads the symbol table with the grammar represented by the input file. The process is analogous to creating a physical parse tree—the input language can be represented entirely by the symbol table, just as normal programming language can be represented by the parse tree.

LLama input language: recursive-descent grammar, LLama input file.

An augmented grammar for the simple, recursive-descent version of the **LLama** parser is shown in Table 4.19. The **LLama** input file in Listing 4.24 specifies the complete input grammar for both **LLama** and **occs**. I'll build a recursive-descent **LLama** first, and then build a more complete parser later, using the stripped-down version of **LLama** for this purpose.

Recursive-descent parser for LLama.

The recursive-descent parser for **LLama** is in Listing 4.24. It is a straightforward representation of the grammar in Table 4.18.

Table 4.19. LLama Grammar (Small Version)

Production			Implemented in this subroutine
spec	→	*definitions* {first_sym()} *body* stuff	yyparse()
definitions	→	**TERM_SPEC** *tnames definitions*	definitions()
	|	**CODE_BLOCK** *definitions*	definitions()
	|	**SYNCH** *snames definitions*	definitions()
	|	**SEPARATOR**	definitions()
	|	**_EOI_**	definitions()
snames	→	**NAME** {add_synch(yytext)} snames	definitions()
tnames	→	**NAME** {make_term(yytext)} tnames	definitions()
body	→	*rule body*	body()
	|	*rule* **SEPARATOR**	body()
	|	*rule* **_EOI_**	body()
rule	→	**NAME** {new_nonterm(yytext,1)} **COLON** right_sides	body()
	|	ε	body()
right_sides	→	{new_rhs()} rhs **OR** right_sides	right_sides()
	|	{new_rhs()} rhs **SEMI**	right_sides()
rhs	→	**NAME** {add_to_rhs(yytext,0)} rhs	rhs()
	|	**ACTION** {add_to_rhs(yytext,start_action())} rhs	rhs()

Listing 4.24. *parser.lma*— **LLama** Input Specification for Itself

```
1   %{
2   #include <stdarg.h>
3   #include <tools/debug.h>
4   #include <tools/hash.h>
5   #include <tools/set.h>
6
7   #define CREATING_LLAMA_PARSER   /* Suppress various definitions in parser.h */
8   #include "parser.h"             /* that conflict with llama-generated defs. */
9
10  /* This file is a llama input file that creates a parser for llama, like a snake
11   * eating its tail. The resulting yyparse.c file can be used in place of the
12   * recursive-descent parser in llpar.c. Note that, though this file is certainly
13   * easier to write than the recursive-descent version, the resulting code is
14   * about 1K larger. nows() should be called before firing up the parser.
15   * Most of the external subroutines called from this module are in acts.c.
16   * Exceptions are:
17   */
18
19  extern char    *yytext;        /* Generated by lex       */
20  extern int     yylineno;       /* Generated by lex       */
21  extern void    nows(), ws();   /* Declared in llama.lex. */
22
23  #define YYSTYPE  char*          /* Value-stack type.      */
24  %}
25
26  %token ACTION          /*      {str}      */
27  %token CODE_BLOCK      /*      %{ ... %}  */
28  %token COLON           /*      :          */
29  %token END_OPT         /*      ] ]*       */
30  %token FIELD           /*      <name>     */
31  %token LEFT            /*      %left      */
```

→

```
Listing 4.24. continued...
32   %token NAME                  /*        name         */
33   %token NONASSOC              /*        %nonassoc    */
34   %token OR                    /*        |            */
35   %token OTHER                 /*   anything else     */
36   %token PREC                  /*        %prec        */
37   %token RIGHT                 /*        %right       */
38   %token SEMI                  /*        ;            */
39   %token SEPARATOR             /*        %%           */
40   %token START                 /*        %start       */
41   %token START_OPT             /*        [            */
42   %token SYNCH                 /*        %synch       */
43   %token TERM_SPEC             /*  %term or %token    */
44   %token TYPE                  /*        %type        */
45   %token PERCENT_UNION         /*        %union       */
46   %token WHITESPACE            /*   0 <= c <= ' '     */
47
48   %synch SEMI OR
49   %%
50   spec            : defs SEPARATOR { first_sym(); } rules end
51                   ;
52   end             : {ws();} SEPARATOR
53                   | /* empty */
54                   ;
55   defs            : SYNCH snames defs
56                   | PERCENT_UNION ACTION  { union_def( yytext ); } defs
57                   | TYPE                         fnames {new_field("");} defs
58                   | TERM_SPEC { new_lev ( 0 ); } tnames {new_field("");} defs
59                   | LEFT      { new_lev ('l'); } pnames {new_field("");} defs
60                   | RIGHT     { new_lev ('r'); } pnames {new_field("");} defs
61                   | NONASSOC  { new_lev ('n'); } pnames {new_field("");} defs
62                   | CODE_BLOCK    /* the block is copied out by yylex */  defs
63                   | START
64                     {
65                         lerror( NONFATAL,
66                                 "%start not supported by occs. The first\n"
67                                 "\t\t\tproduction is the start production\n");
68                     }
69                     opt_names defs
70
71                   | /* empty */
72                   ;
73   fnames          : NAME  { new_nonterm (yytext,0); } fnames
74                   | FIELD { new_field    (yytext);   } fnames
75                   | /* empty */
76                   ;
77   tnames          : NAME  { make_term(yytext); } tnames
78                   | FIELD { new_field(yytext); } tnames
79                   | /* empty */
80                   ;
81   pnames          : NAME  { prec_list(yytext); } pnames
82                   | FIELD { new_field(yytext); } pnames
83                   | /* empty */
84                   ;
85   opt_names       : NAME opt_names
86                   | /* empty */
87                   ;
88   snames          : NAME { add_synch(yytext); } snames | /* empty */ ;
89   rules           : rule rules
90                   | /* empty */
91                   ;
```

Listing 4.24. continued...

```
 92    rule            : NAME  { new_nonterm(yytext,1); } COLON right_sides
 93                    | FIELD { new_nonterm(yytext,1); } COLON right_sides
 94                    ;
 95    right_sides     : { new_rhs(); } rhs end_rhs
 96                    ;
 97    end_rhs         : OR right_sides
 98                    | SEMI
 99                    ;
100    rhs             : NAME        { add_to_rhs(yytext, 0            ); } rhs
101                    | FIELD       { add_to_rhs(yytext, 0            ); } rhs
102                    | ACTION      { add_to_rhs(yytext, start_action()); } rhs
103                    | PREC NAME   { prec      (yytext              ); } rhs
104                    | START_OPT     { start_opt( yytext ); }
105                          rhs END_OPT { end_opt  ( yytext ); }
106                              rhs
107                    | /* empty */
108                    ;
109    %%
110    yy_init_llama( tovs )
111    yyvstype *tovs;
112    {
113        tovs->left = tovs->right = "" ;
114    }
115
116    char *yypstk(tovs, tods)
117    yyvstype *tovs;
118    char      *tods;
119    {
120        static char buf[128];
121
122        if( *tovs->left || *tovs->right )
123        {
124            sprintf(buf,"[%s,%s]", tovs->left, tovs->right);
125            return buf;
126        }
127        else
128            return "";
129    }
```

Listing 4.25. *llpar.c*— Recursive-Descent Parser for **LLama**

```
 1    #include <stdio.h>
 2    #include <stdarg.h>
 3    #include <tools/debug.h>
 4    #include <tools/set.h>
 5    #include <tools/hash.h>
 6    #include <tools/compiler.h>
 7    #include <tools/l.h>
 8
 9    #include "llout.h"
10    #include "parser.h"
11
12    /* LLPAR.C:      A recursive-descent parser for a very stripped down llama.
13     *               There's a llama input specification for a table-driven parser
14     *               in llama.lma.
15     */
16
```

```
Listing 4.25. continued...
17     void advance      P(( void                  ));      /* local */
18     void lookfor      P(( int first,...         ));
19     void definitions P(( void                   ));
20     void body         P(( void                  ));
21     void right_sides P(( void                   ));
22     void rhs          P(( void                  ));
23     int  yyparse      P(( void                  ));      /* public */
24     extern int        yylineno;                          /* Created by lex.*/
25     extern char       *yytext;
26     extern int        yylex();
27     /*------------------------------------------------------------------*/
28
29     PUBLIC  int yynerrs;              /* Total error count           */
30     PRIVATE int Lookahead;           /* Lookahead token             */
31
32     /*==================================================================
33      * Low-level support routines for parser:
34      */
35
36     #define match(x) ((x) == Lookahead)
37
38     PRIVATE void advance()
39     {
40         if( Lookahead != _EOI_ )
41             while( (Lookahead = yylex()) == WHITESPACE )
42                     ;
43     }
44
45     /*------------------------------------------------------------------*/
46
47     PRIVATE void    lookfor( first, ... )
48     int     first;
49     {
50         /* Read input until the current symbol is in the argument list. For example,
51          * lookfor(OR, SEMI, 0) terminates when the current Lookahead symbol is an
52          * OR or SEMI. Searching starts with the next (not the current) symbol.
53          */
54
55         int *obj;
56
57         for( advance() ;; advance() )
58         {
59             for( obj = &first;  *obj  &&  !match(*obj) ; obj++ )
60                 ;
61
62             if( *obj )
63                 break;                  /* Found a match */
64
65             else if( match(_EOI_) )
66                 lerror(FATAL, "Unexpected end of file\n");
67         }
68     }
69
70     /*==================================================================
71      * The Parser itself
72      */
73
74     PUBLIC  int yyparse()                /* spec : definitions body stuff      */
75     {
76             extern yylineno;
```

Listing 4.25. continued...

```
77              Lookahead = yylex();           /* Get first input symbol */
78              definitions();
79              first_sym();
80              body();
81      }
82
83      /*---------------------------------------------------------------------*/
84
85      PRIVATE void    definitions()
86      {
87          /*
88           * definitions  : TERM_SPEC tnames   definitions              implemented at:
89           *               | CODE_BLOCK          definitions              1
90           *               | SYNCH snames        definitions              2
91           *               | SEPARATOR                                    3
92           *               | _EOI_                                        4
93           * snames       : NAME {add_synch} snames                       4
94           * tnames       : NAME {make_term} tnames                       5
95           *                                                              6
96           * Note that LeX copies the CODE_BLOCK contents to the output file
97           * automatically on reading it.
98           */
99
100         while( !match(SEPARATOR) && !match(_EOI_) )                      /* 4 */
101         {
102             if( Lookahead == SYNCH )                                     /* 3 */
103             {
104                 for( advance(); match(NAME); advance() )                 /* 5 */
105                     add_synch( yytext );
106             }
107             else if( Lookahead == TERM_SPEC )                            /* 1 */
108             {
109                 for( advance(); match(NAME); advance() )                 /* 6 */
110                     make_term( yytext );
111             }
112             else if( Lookahead != CODE_BLOCK )                           /* 2 */
113             {
114                 lerror(NONFATAL,"Ignoring illegal <%s> in definitions\n", yytext );
115                 advance();
116             }
117         }
118
119         advance();                                      /* advance past the %% */
120     }
121
122     /*---------------------------------------------------------------------*/
123
124     PRIVATE void    body()
125     {
126         /*
127          * body    : rule body                                     implemented at:
128          *          | rule SEPARATOR                                       1
129          *          | rule _EOI_                                           1
130          * rule    : NAME {new_nonterm} COLON right_sides                  1
131          *          : <epsilon>                                            2
132          */                                                                3
133
134         while( !match(SEPARATOR)  &&  !match(_EOI_) )                    /* 1 */
135         {
```

Listing 4.25. continued...

```
136           if( match(NAME) )                                              /* 2 */
137           {
138               new_nonterm( yytext, 1 );
139               advance();
140           }                                                              /* 3 */
141           else
142           {
143               lerror(NONFATAL, "Illegal <%s>, nonterminal expected.\n", yytext);
144               lookfor( SEMI, SEPARATOR, 0 );
145               if( match(SEMI) )
146                   advance();
147               continue;
148           }
149
150           if( match( COLON ) )
151               advance();
152           else
153               lerror(NONFATAL, "Inserted missing ':'\n");
154
155           right_sides();
156       }
157       ws();                                           /* Enable white space (see parser.lex) */
158       if( match(SEPARATOR)  )
159           yylex();                                    /* Advance past %%                     */
160   }
161
162   /*------------------------------------------------------------------*/
163
164   PRIVATE void    right_sides()
165   {
166       /* right_sides      : {new_rhs} rhs OR right_sides                 1
167        *                   | {new_rhs} rhs SEMI                          2
168        */
169
170       new_rhs();
171       rhs();
172
173       while( match(OR) )                                              /* 1 */
174       {
175           advance();
176           new_rhs();
177           rhs();
178       }
179
180       if( match(SEMI) )                                               /* 2 */
181           advance();
182       else
183           lerror(NONFATAL, "Inserted missing semicolon\n");
184   }
185
186   /*------------------------------------------------------------------*/
187
188   PRIVATE void    rhs()
189   {
190       /* rhs      : NAME    {add_to_rhs} rhs  */
191       /*          | ACTION {add_to_rhs} rhs  */
192
193       while( match(NAME) || match(ACTION) )
194       {
195           add_to_rhs( yytext, match(ACTION) ? start_action() : 0 );
```

```
Listing 4.25. continued...
196              advance();
197          }
198
199      if( !match(OR) && !match(SEMI) )
200          {
201              lerror(NONFATAL, "illegal <%s>, ignoring rest of production\n", yytext);
202              lookfor( SEMI, SEPARATOR, OR, 0 );
203          }
204      }
```

The action subroutines, in Listings 4.26, 4.27, and 4.28. work as follows:

LLama actions:

add_synch(**char** *yytext)

Listing 4.28, lines 628 and 690.

Add the symbol named by yytext to the synchronization set used for error recovery.

add_to_rhs(**char** *yytext, **int** isact)

Listing 4.27, line 488.

Add the symbol named by yytext to the current right-hand side. The isact argument should be true if the symbol is an action.

end_opt(**char** *yytext)

Listing 4.28, line 596.

Mark the end of an optional production. This routine processes **occs**' [...], [...]* operators by adding extra elements to the production.

first_sym(**void**)

Listing 4.27, line 380.

This routine finds the goal symbol, which is the left-hand side of the first production that follows the first %% directive. The problem here is that, in **occs**, a nonterminal can be declared explicitly in a previous %type directive, so you can't assume that the first nonterminal that's declared is the goal symbol.

lerror(**int** error_type, **char** *format,...)

In main.c.

This routine prints an error message. The first argument should be FATAL, NON-FATAL, or WARNING (these are defined at the top of *parser.h*). If the error is FATAL, all files are closed and **LLama** is terminated, otherwise parsing continues. The input file name and line number is automatically appended to the front of the message. This routine works like fprintf() in other respects.

make_term(**char** *yytext)

Listing 4.27, line 335.

Make an entry for a terminal symbol.

new_field(**char** *yytext)

Listing 4.28, lines 675 and 793.

Change the name of the %union field to which subsequent input symbols are attached.

new_lev(**int** associativity)

Listing 4.28, lines 648 and 698.

Increment the precedence level by one notch (all subsequent arguments to a %left, %right, or %nonassoc use this new level). Also change the current associativity as specified. This argument should be 'l' for left , 'r' for right, 'n' for none, or 0 for unspecified.

Listing 4.27, line 391.	`new_nonterm(`**`char`** `*yytext,` **`int`** `is_lhs)`

Create a symbol-table entry for a nonterminal if one doesn't already exist. `yytext` is the symbol name. `is_lhs` tells the subroutine whether the nonterminal was created implicitly (whether it was used before appearing on the left-hand side of a production). `is_lhs` zero in this case. Return a pointer to the SYMBOL or NULL if an attempt is made to use a terminal symbol as a left-hand side.

Listing 4.27, line 460.	`new_rhs(`**`void`**`)`

Stop adding symbols to the current right-hand side, and start up a new (and empty) right-hand side.

In main.c.	`output(`**`char`** `*format,...)`

Works like `fprintf(Output,...);` sends the string to the current output stream, typically standard output but it can be changed from the command line.

Listing 4.28, lines 659 and 735.	`prec(`**`char`** `*yytext)`

Process the argument to a `%prec` directive. (Change the precedence level of the current right-hand side from the default level to the one indicated in `yytext`.)

Listing 4.28, lines 671 and 710.	`prec_list(`**`char`** `*yytext)`

Process an argument to `%left`, `%right`, or `%nonassoc`.

Listing 4.28, line 581.	`start_opt(`**`char`** `*yytext)`

Mark the start of an optional or repeating portion of a right-hand side [see `end_opt()`].

Listing 4.28, lines 665 and 762.	`union_def(`**`char`** `*yytext)`

Create a typedef for the **occs** value stack, using the `%union` definition in `yytext`.

Listing 4.26. *acts.c*— **LLama** Action Subroutines

```
 1    #include <stdio.h>
 2    #include <malloc.h>
 3    #include <ctype.h>
 4    #include <string.h>
 5    #include <tools/debug.h>
 6    #include <tools/set.h>
 7    #include <tools/hash.h>
 8    #include <tools/compiler.h>
 9    #include <tools/l.h>
10
11    #include <tools/stack.h>      /* stack-manipulation macros   */
12    #undef  stack_cls             /* Make all stacks static      */
13    #define stack_cls static
14
15    #include "parser.h"
16    #include "llout.h"
17
18    /*  ACTS.C      Action routines used by both llama and occs. These build
19     *              up the symbol table from the input specification.
20     */
21
```

```
Listing 4.26. continued...

22   void     find_problems  P(( SYMBOL *sym, void *junk        )); /* local */
23   int      c_identifier    P(( char *name                    ));
24   void     print_tok       P(( FILE *stream, char *format, int arg )); /* public */
25   void     pterm           P(( SYMBOL *sym,   FILE *stream    ));
26   void     pact            P(( SYMBOL *sym,   FILE *stream    ));
27   void     pnonterm        P(( SYMBOL *sym,   FILE *stream    ));
28   void     print_symbols   P(( FILE    *stream               ));
29   int      problems        P(( void                          ));
30   void     init_acts       P(( void                          ));
31   SYMBOL   *make_term      P(( char *name                    ));
32   void     first_sym       P(( void                          ));
33   SYMBOL   *new_nonterm    P(( char *name, int is_lhs        ));
34   void     new_rhs         P(( void                          ));
35   void     add_to_rhs      P(( char *object, int is_an_action ));
36   void     start_opt       P(( char *lex                     ));
37   void     end_opt         P(( char *lex                     ));
38   void     add_synch       P(( char *yytext                  ));
39   void     new_lev         P(( int how                       ));
40   void     prec_list       P(( char *name                    ));
41   void     prec            P(( char *name                    ));
42   void     union_def       P(( char *action                  ));
43   int      fields_active   P(( void                          ));
44   void     new_field       P(( char *field_name              ));
45
46   /*-------------------------------------------------------------------*/
47
48   extern int      yylineno;                 /* Input line number--created by LeX. */
49   PRIVATE int     Associativity;            /* Current associativity direction.   */
50   PRIVATE int     Prec_lev = 0;             /* Precedence level. Incremented       */
51                                             /* after finding %left, etc.,          */
52                                             /* but before the names are done.      */
53   PRIVATE char    Field_name[NAME_MAX];     /* Field name specified in <name>.     */
54   PRIVATE int     Fields_active = 0;        /* Fields are used in the input.       */
55                                             /* (If they're not, then automatic     */
56                                             /* field-name generation, as per        */
57                                             /* %union, is not activated.)           */
58   PRIVATE int     Goal_symbol_is_next =0;   /* If true, the next nonterminal is    */
59                                             /* the goal symbol.                    */
60
61   /*- - - - - - - - - - - - - - - - - - - - - - - - - - - - - - - - -
62    * The following stuff (that's a technical term) is used for processing nested
63    * optional (or repeating) productions defined with the occs [] and []*
64    * operators. A stack is kept and, every time you go down another layer of
65    * nesting, the current nonterminal is stacked and an new nonterminal is
66    * allocated. The previous state is restored when you're done with a level.
67    */
68
69   #define SSIZE    8                /* Max. optional-production nesting level */
70   typedef struct _cur_sym_
71   {
72       char         lhs_name[NAME_MAX]; /* Name associated with left-hand side. */
73       SYMBOL       *lhs;               /* Pointer to symbol-table entry for    */
74                                        /*          the current left-hand side. */
75       PRODUCTION   *rhs;               /* Pointer to current production.       */
76
77   } CUR_SYM;
78
79   CUR_SYM Stack[ SSIZE ],             /* Stack and                            */
80           *Sp = Stack + (SSIZE-1); /* stack pointer. It's inconvenient to use */
```

Listing 4.26. continued...

```
81                                       /* stack.h because stack is of structures. */
82
83     /*=======================================================================
84      * Support routines for actions
85      */
86
87     PUBLIC  void print_tok( stream, format, arg )
88     FILE    *stream;
89     char    *format;              /* not used here but supplied by pset() */
90     int     arg;
91     {
92         /* Print one nonterminal symbol to the specified stream.   */
93
94         if     ( arg == -1      ) fprintf(stream, "null "                        );
95         else if( arg == -2      ) fprintf(stream, "empty "                       );
96         else if( arg == _EOI_   ) fprintf(stream, "$ "                           );
97         else if( arg == EPSILON ) fprintf(stream, "<epsilon> "                   );
98         else                      fprintf(stream, "%s ", Terms[arg]->name        );
99     }
100
101    /*-------------------------------------------------------------------
102     * The following three routines print the symbol table. Pterm(), pact(), and
103     * pnonterm() are all called indirectly through ptab(), called in
104     * print_symbols(). They print the terminal, action, and nonterminal symbols
105     * from the symbol table, respectively.
106     */
107
108    PUBLIC  void pterm( sym, stream )
109    SYMBOL  *sym;
110    FILE    *stream;
111    {
112        int i;
113
114        if( !ISTERM(sym) )
115            return;
116
117        LL( fprintf( stream, "%-16.16s  %3d\n", sym->name, sym->val );        )
118        OX( fprintf( stream, "%-16.16s  %3d    %2d      %c      <%s>\n",\
119                                    sym->name,\
120                                    sym->val,\
121                                    Precedence[sym->val].level ,\
122                                    (i = Precedence[sym->val].assoc) ? i : '-',\
123                                    sym->field ); )
124    }
125
126    /*-------------------------------------------------------------------*/
127
128    PUBLIC  void pact( sym, stream )
129    SYMBOL  *sym;
130    FILE    *stream;
131    {
132        if( !ISACT(sym) )
133                return;
134
135        fprintf( stream, "%-5s %3d,",    sym->name, sym->val );
136        fprintf( stream, " line %-3d: ", sym->lineno    );
137        fputstr( sym->string, 55, stream );
138        fprintf( stream, "\n");
139    }
140
```

```
Listing 4.26. continued...
141    /*-------------------------------------------------------------------------*/
142
143    PUBLIC   char *production_str( prod )
144    PRODUCTION    *prod;
145    {
146        /* return a string representing the production */
147
148        int          i, nchars, avail;
149        static char buf[80];
150        char         *p;
151
152        nchars = sprintf(buf,"%s ->", prod->lhs->name );
153        p      = buf + nchars;
154        avail  = sizeof(buf) - nchars - 1;
155
156        if( !prod->rhs_len )
157            sprintf(p, " (epsilon)" );
158        else
159            for( i = 0; i < prod->rhs_len && avail > 0 ; ++i )
160            {
161                nchars = sprintf(p, " %0.*s", avail-2, prod->rhs[i]->name );
162                avail -= nchars;
163                p     += nchars;
164            }
165
166        return buf;
167    }
168
169    /*-------------------------------------------------------------------------*/
170
171    PUBLIC   void pnonterm( sym, stream )
172    SYMBOL   *sym;
173    FILE     *stream;
174    {
175        int          i;
176        char         *s;
177        PRODUCTION   *p;
178        int          chars_printed;
179
180        stack_dcl( pstack, PRODUCTION *, MAXPROD );
181
182        if( !ISNONTERM(sym) )
183            return;
184
185        fprintf( stream, "%s (%3d)   %s", sym->name, sym->val,
186                                     sym == Goal_symbol ? "(goal symbol)" : "" );
187
188        OX( fprintf( stream, " <%s>\n", sym->field );          )
189        LL( fprintf( stream, "\n" );                            )
190
191        if( Symbols > 1 )
192        {
193            /* Print first and follow sets only if you want really verbose output.*/
194
195            fprintf( stream, "   FIRST : " );
196            pset( sym->first, print_tok, stream );
197
198            LL(   fprintf(stream, "\n   FOLLOW: ");            )
199            LL(   pset( sym->follow, print_tok, stream );      )
200
```

Listing 4.26. continued...

```
201            fprintf(stream, "\n");
202        }
203
204        /* Productions are put into the SYMBOL in reverse order because it's easier
205         * to tack them on to the beginning of the linked list. It's better to print
206         * them in forward order, however, to make the symbol table more readable.
207         * Solve this problem by stacking all the productions and then popping
208         * elements to print them. Since the pstack has MAXPROD elements, it's not
209         * necessary to test for stack overflow on a push.
210         */
211
212        for( p = sym->productions ; p ; p = p->next )
213            push( pstack, p );
214
215        while( !stack_empty( pstack ) )
216        {
217            p = pop(pstack);
218
219            chars_printed = fprintf(stream, "   %3d: %s",
220                                            p->num, production_str( p ));
221
222     LL(  for( ; chars_printed <= 45; ++chars_printed )    )
223     LL(      putc( '.', stream );                         )
224     LL(  fprintf(stream, "SELECT: ");                     )
225     LL(  pset( p->select, print_tok, stream );            )
226
227     OX(  if( p->prec )                                    )
228     OX(  {                                                )
229     OX(      for( ; chars_printed <= 60; ++chars_printed )    )
230     OX(          putc( '.', stream );                     )
231     OX(      if( p->prec )                                )
232     OX(          fprintf(stream, "PREC %d", p->prec );    )
233     OX(  }                                                )
234
235            putc('\n', stream);
236        }
237
238        fprintf(stream, "\n");
239    }
240
241    /*------------------------------------------------------------------*/
242
243    PUBLIC  void print_symbols( stream )
244    FILE    *stream;
245    {
246        /* Print out the symbol table. Nonterminal symbols come first for the sake
247         * of the 's' option in yydebug(); symbols other than production numbers can
248         * be entered symbolically. ptab returns 0 if it can't print the symbols
249         * sorted (because there's no memory. If this is the case, try again but
250         * print the table unsorted).
251         */
252
253        putc( '\n', stream );
254
255        fprintf( stream, "---------------- Symbol table ----------------\n" );
256        fprintf( stream, "\nNONTERMINAL SYMBOLS:\n\n" );
257        if( ptab( Symtab, pnonterm, stream, 1 ) == 0 )
258            ptab( Symtab, pnonterm, stream, 0 );
259
```

                                                                                            →

Listing 4.26. continued...

```
260        fprintf( stream, "\nTERMINAL SYMBOLS:\n\n");
261        OX( fprintf( stream, "name                    value  prec  assoc   field\n"); )
262        LL( fprintf( stream, "name                    value\n");                       )
263
264        if( ptab( Symtab, pterm, stream, 1 ) == 0 )
265            ptab( Symtab, pterm, stream, 0 );
266
267        LL(  fprintf( stream, "\nACTION SYMBOLS:\n\n");                                 )
268        LL(  if( !ptab( Symtab, pact, stream, 1 ) )                                     )
269        LL(        ptab( Symtab, pact, stream, 0 );                                     )
270        LL(  fprintf( stream, "---------------------------------------\n" ); )
271    }
272
273    /*----------------------------------------------------------------------
274     * Problems() and find_problems work together to find unused symbols and
275     * symbols that are used but not defined.
276     */
277
278    PRIVATE void find_problems( sym, junk )
279    SYMBOL  *sym;
280    void    *junk;  /* not used */
281    {
282        if( !sym->used && sym!=Goal_symbol )
283            error( WARNING,  "<%s> not used (defined on line %d)\n",
284                                                    sym->name, sym->set );
285        if( !sym->set && !ISACT(sym) )
286            error( NONFATAL, "<%s> not defined (used on line %d)\n",
287                                                    sym->name, sym->used );
288    }
289
290    PUBLIC  int problems()
291    {
292        /* Find, and print an error message, for all symbols that are used but not
293         * defined, and for all symbols that are defined but not used. Return the
294         * number of errors after checking.
295         */
296
297        ptab( Symtab, find_problems, NULL, 0 );
298        return yynerrs;
299    }
300
301    /*----------------------------------------------------------------------*/
302
303    PRIVATE int hash_funct( p )
304    SYMBOL *p;
305    {
306        if( !*p->name )
307            lerror( FATAL, "Illegal empty symbol name\n" );
308
309        return hash_add( p->name );
310    }
311
312    PUBLIC  void init_acts()
313    {
314        /* Various initializations that can't be done at compile time. Call this
315         * routine before starting up the parser. The hash-table size (157) is
316         * an arbitrary prime number, roughly the number symbols expected in the
317         * table.
318         */
319
```

→

```
Listing 4.26. continued...
320        extern int      strcmp();
321        static SYMBOL    bogus_symbol;
322
323        strcpy( bogus_symbol.name, "End of Input" );
324
325        Terms[0]        = &bogus_symbol;
326        Symtab          = maketab( 157, hash_funct, strcmp );
327
328        strncpy( Sp->lhs_name, "garbage", NAME_MAX );
329
330        LL( Synch       = newset(); )
331    }
332                                                                          */
333    /*-----------------------------------------------------------------*/
334
335    PUBLIC  SYMBOL *make_term( name )                 /* Make a terminal symbol */
336    char    *name;
337    {
338        SYMBOL        *p;
339
340        if( !c_identifier(name) )
341            lerror(NONFATAL, "Token names must be legitimate C identifiers\n");
342
343        else if( p = findsym(Symtab, name) )
344            lerror(WARNING, "Terminal symbol <%s> already declared\n", name );
345        else
346        {
347            if( Cur_term >= MAXTERM )
348                lerror(FATAL, "Too many terminal symbols (%d max.).\n", MAXTERM );
349
350            p = (SYMBOL *) newsym( sizeof(SYMBOL) );
351            strncpy ( p->name,  name,        NAME_MAX );
352            strncpy ( p->field, Field_name, NAME_MAX );
353            addsym  ( Symtab, p );
354
355            p->val = ++Cur_term ;
356            p->set = yylineno;
357
358            Terms[Cur_term] = p;
359        }
360        return p;
361    }
362
363    /*-----------------------------------------------------------------*/
364
365    PRIVATE c_identifier( name )               /* Return true only if name is  */
366    char    *name;                             /* a legitimate C identifier.   */
367    {
368        if( isdigit( *name ) )
369            return 0;
370
371        for(; *name ; ++name )
372            if( !( isalnum(*name) || *name == '_' ))
373                return 0;
374
375        return 1;
376    }
377
```

Listing 4.26. continued...

```c
378    /*----------------------------------------------------------------------*/
379
380    PUBLIC void      first_sym()
381    {
382        /*  This routine is called just before the first rule following the
383         *  %%. It's used to point out the goal symbol;
384         */
385
386        Goal_symbol_is_next = 1;
387    }
388
389    /*----------------------------------------------------------------------*/
390
391    PUBLIC   SYMBOL  *new_nonterm( name, is_lhs )
392    char     *name;
393    int      is_lhs;
394    {
395        /* Create, and initialize, a new nonterminal. is_lhs is used to
396         * differentiate between implicit and explicit declarations. It's 0 if the
397         * nonterminal is added because it was found on a right-hand side. It's 1 if
398         * the nonterminal is on a left-hand side.
399         *
400         * Return a pointer to the new symbol or NULL if an attempt is made to use a
401         * terminal symbol on a left-hand side.
402         */
403
404        SYMBOL      *p;
405
406        if( p = (SYMBOL *) findsym( Symtab, name ) )
407        {
408            if( !ISNONTERM( p ) )
409            {
410                lerror(NONFATAL, "Symbol on left-hand side must be nonterminal\n");
411                p = NULL;
412            }
413        }
414        else if( Cur_nonterm >= MAXNONTERM )
415        {
416            lerror(FATAL, "Too many nonterminal symbols (%d max.).\n", MAXTERM );
417        }
418        else                                     /* Add new nonterminal to symbol table */
419        {
420            p = (SYMBOL *) newsym( sizeof(SYMBOL) );
421            strncpy ( p->name,  name,       NAME_MAX );
422            strncpy ( p->field, Field_name, NAME_MAX );
423
424            p->val = ++Cur_nonterm ;
425            Terms[Cur_nonterm] = p;
426
427            addsym  ( Symtab, p );
428        }
429
430        if( p )                                   /* (re)initialize new nonterminal */
431        {
432            if( Goal_symbol_is_next )
433            {
434                Goal_symbol = p;
435                Goal_symbol_is_next = 0;
436            }
437
```

Listing 4.26. continued...

```
438            if( !p->first )
439                p->first  = newset();
440
441  LL(      if( !p->follow )                    )
442  LL(          p->follow = newset();           )
443
444           p->lineno = yylineno ;
445
446           if( is_lhs )
447           {
448                strncpy( Sp->lhs_name, name, NAME_MAX );
449                Sp->lhs        = p ;
450                Sp->rhs        = NULL;
451                Sp->lhs->set = yylineno;
452           }
453       }
454
455      return p;
456  }
457
458  /*-----------------------------------------------------------------------*/
459
460  PUBLIC  void new_rhs()
461  {
462      /* Get a new PRODUCTION and link it to the head of the production chain.
463       * of the current nonterminal. Note that the start production MUST be
464       * production 0. As a consequence, the first rhs associated with the first
465       * nonterminal MUST be the start production. Num_productions is initialized
466       * to 0 when it's declared.
467       */
468
469      PRODUCTION  *p;
470
471      if( !(p = (PRODUCTION *) calloc(1, sizeof(PRODUCTION))) )
472          lerror(FATAL, "Out of memory\n");
473
474      p->next              = Sp->lhs->productions;
475      Sp->lhs->productions = p;
476
477      LL( p->select = newset(); )
478
479      if( (p->num = Num_productions++) >= MAXPROD )
480          lerror(FATAL, "Too many productions (%d max.)\n", MAXPROD );
481
482      p->lhs  = Sp->lhs;
483      Sp->rhs = p;
484  }
485
486  /*-----------------------------------------------------------------------*/
487
488  PUBLIC  void add_to_rhs( object, is_an_action )
489  char    *object;
490  int     is_an_action;   /* 0 of not an action, line number otherwise */
491  {
492      SYMBOL     *p;
493      PRODUCTION *prod;
494      int i;
495      char       buf[32];
496
```

Listing 4.26. continued...

```
497         /* Add a new element to the RHS currently at top of stack. First deal with
498          * forward references. If the item isn't in the table, add it. Note that,
499          * since terminal symbols must be declared with a %term directive, forward
500          * references always refer to nonterminals or action items. When we exit the
501          * if statement, p points at the symbol table entry for the current object.
502          */
503
504         if( !(p = (SYMBOL *) findsym( Symtab, object)) )   /* not in tab yet */
505         {
506             if( !is_an_action )
507             {
508                 if( !(p = new_nonterm( object, 0 )) )
509                 {
510                     /* Won't get here unless p is a terminal symbol */
511
512                     lerror(FATAL, "(internal) Unexpected terminal symbol\n");
513                     return;
514                 }
515             }
516             else
517             {
518                 /* Add an action. All actions are named "{DDD}" where DDD is the
519                  * action number. The curly brace in the name guarantees that this
520                  * name won't conflict with a normal name. I am assuming that calloc
521                  * is used to allocate memory for the new node (ie. that it's
522                  * initialized to zeros).
523                  */
524
525                 sprintf(buf, "{%d}", ++Cur_act - MINACT );
526
527                 p = (SYMBOL *) newsym( sizeof(SYMBOL) );
528                 strncpy ( p->name, buf, NAME_MAX );
529                 addsym ( Symtab, p );
530
531                 p->val    = Cur_act      ;
532                 p->lineno = is_an_action ;
533
534                 if( !(p->string = strsave(object)) )
535                     lerror(FATAL, "Insufficient memory to save action\n");
536             }
537         }
538
539         p->used = yylineno;
540
541         if( (i = Sp->rhs->rhs_len++)  >=  MAXRHS )
542             lerror(NONFATAL, "Right-hand side too long (%d max)\n", MAXRHS );
543         else
544         {
545             LL(  if( i == 0  &&  p == Sp->lhs )                                )
546             LL(       lerror(NONFATAL, "Illegal left recursion in production.\n");)
547             OX(  if( ISTERM( p ) )                                            )
548             OX(       Sp->rhs->prec = Precedence[ p->val ].level ;            )
549
550             Sp->rhs->rhs[ i     ] = p;
551             Sp->rhs->rhs[ i + 1 ] = NULL;                /* NULL terminate the array. */
552
553             if( !ISACT(p) )
554                 ++( Sp->rhs->non_acts );
555         }
556 }
```

Listing 4.26. continued...

```
557
558     /*-----------------------------------------------------------------
559      * The next two subroutines handle repeating or optional subexpressions. The
560      * following mappings are done, depending on the operator:
561      *
562      * S : A [B]  C ;          S   -> A 001 C
563      *                         001 -> B | epsilon
564      *
565      * S : A [B]* C ;          S   -> A 001 C                          (occs)
566      *                         001 -> 001 B | epsilon
567      *
568      * S : A [B]* C ;          S   -> A 001 C                          (llama)
569      *                         001 -> B 001 | epsilon
570      *
571      * In all situations, the right hand side that we've collected so far is
572      * pushed and a new right-hand side is started for the subexpression. Note that
573      * the first character of the created rhs name (001 in the previous examples)
574      * is a space, which is illegal in a user-supplied production name so we don't
575      * have to worry about conflicts. Subsequent symbols are added to this new
576      * right-hand side. When the ), ], or *) is found, we finish the new right-hand
577      * side, pop the stack and add the name of the new right-hand side to the
578      * previously collected left-hand side.
579      */
580
581     PUBLIC   void start_opt( lex )              /* Start an optional subexpression */
582     char    *lex;
583     {
584             char    name[32], *tname;
585             static int num = 0;
586
587             --Sp;                               /* Push current stack element    */
588             sprintf( name, " %06d", num++ );    /* Make name for new production */
589             new_nonterm( name, 1 );             /* Create a nonterminal for it. */
590             new_rhs();                          /* Create epsilon production.    */
591             new_rhs();                          /* and production for sub-prod. */
592     }
593
594     /*- - - - - - - - - - - - - - - - - - - - - - - - - - - - - - - - */
595
596     PUBLIC   void end_opt( lex )                /* end optional subexpression */
597     char    *lex;
598     {
599         char    *name = Sp->lhs_name ;
600         SYMBOL  *p;
601         int     i;
602
603         if( lex[1] == '*'  )                    /* Process a [...]*              */
604         {
605             add_to_rhs( name, 0 );              /* Add right-recursive reference.  */
606
607 #ifdef OCCS                                     /* If occs, must be left recursive.*/
608             i = Sp->rhs->rhs_len - 1;           /* Shuffle things around.        */
609             p = Sp->rhs->rhs[ i ];
610             memmove( &(Sp->rhs->rhs)[1], &(Sp->rhs->rhs)[0],
611                                         i * sizeof( (Sp->rhs->rhs)[1] ) );
612             Sp->rhs->rhs[ 0 ] = p ;
613 #endif
614         }
615
```

```
Listing 4.26. continued...
616        ++Sp;                                       /* discard top-of-stack element */
617        add_to_rhs( name, 0 );
618    }
619
620    /*========================================================================
621     * The following routines have alternate versions, one set for llama and another
622     * for occs. The routines corresponding to features that aren't supported in one
623     * or the other of these programs print error messages.
624     */
625
626    #ifdef LLAMA
627
628    PUBLIC  void add_synch( name )
629    char     *name;
630    {
631        /*  Add "name" to the set of synchronization tokens
632        */
633
634        SYMBOL       *p;
635
636        if( !(p = (SYMBOL *) findsym( Symtab, name )) )
637            lerror(NONFATAL,"%%synch: undeclared symbol <%s>.\n", name );
638
639        else if( !ISTERM(p) )
640            lerror(NONFATAL,"%%synch: <%s> not a terminal symbol\n", name );
641
642        else
643            ADD( Synch, p->val );
644    }
645
646    /* - - - - - - - - - - - - - - - - - - - - - - - - - - - - - - - - - - */
647
648    PUBLIC void new_lev( how )
649    {
650        switch( how )
651        {
652        case  0 : /* initialization: ignore it */                          break;
653        case 'l': lerror (NONFATAL, "%%left not recognized by LLAMA\n"     ); break;
654        case 'r': lerror (NONFATAL, "%%right not recognized by LLAMA\n"    ); break;
655        default : lerror (NONFATAL, "%%nonassoc not recognized by LLAMA\n"); break;
656        }
657    }
658
659    PUBLIC void prec( name )
660    char *name;
661    {
662        lerror( NONFATAL, "%%prec not recognized by LLAMA\n" );
663    }
664
665    PUBLIC void union_def( action )
666    char     *action;
667    {
668        lerror(NONFATAL,"%%union not recognized by LLAMA\n");
669    }
670
671    PUBLIC void prec_list( name ) char *name;
672    {
673    }
674
```

```
Listing 4.26. continued...
675    PUBLIC void new_field( field_name )
676    char     *field_name;
677    {
678        if( *field_name )
679            lerror(NONFATAL, "<name> not supported by LLAMA\n");
680    }
681
682    PUBLIC  make_nonterm(name)
683    char     *name;
684    {
685        lerror(NONFATAL, "%type not supported by LLAMA\n");
686    }
687
688    #else   /*==============================================================*/
689
690    PUBLIC void add_synch(yytext)
691    char *yytext;
692    {
693        lerror(NONFATAL, "%%synch not supported by OCCS\n");
694    }
695
696    /* - - - - - - - - - - - - - - - - - - - - - - - - - - - - - - - - - */
697
698    PUBLIC void new_lev( how )
699    {
700        /* Increment the current precedence level and modify "Associativity"
701         * to remember if we're going left, right, or neither.
702         */
703
704        if( Associativity = how )   /* 'l', 'r', 'n', (0 if unspecified)  */
705            ++Prec_lev;
706    }
707
708    /* - - - - - - - - - - - - - - - - - - - - - - - - - - - - - - - - - */
709
710    PUBLIC void prec_list( name )
711    char     *name;
712    {
713        /* Add current name (in yytext) to the precision list. "Associativity" is
714         * set to 'l', 'r', or 'n', depending on whether we're doing a %left,
715         * %right, or %nonassoc. Also make a nonterminal if it doesn't exist
716         * already.
717         */
718
719        SYMBOL *sym;
720
721        if( !(sym = findsym(Symtab,name)) )
722            sym = make_term( name );
723
724        if( !ISTERM(sym) )
725            lerror(NONFATAL, "%%left or %%right, %s must be a token\n", name );
726        else
727        {
728            Precedence[ sym->val ].level = Prec_lev ;
729            Precedence[ sym->val ].assoc = Associativity  ;
730        }
731    }
732
```

Listing 4.26. continued...

```
733    /* - - - - - - - - - - - - - - - - - - - - - - - - - - - - - - - - - - - */
734
735    PUBLIC void prec( name )
736    char *name;
737    {
738        /* Change the precedence level for the current right-hand side, using
739         * (1) an explicit number if one is specified, or (2) an element from the
740         * Precedence[] table otherwise.
741         */
742
743        SYMBOL      *sym;
744
745        if( isdigit(*name) )
746            Sp->rhs->prec = atoi(name);                                    /* (1) */
747        else
748        {
749            if( !(sym = findsym(Symtab,name)) )
750                lerror(NONFATAL, "%s (used in %%prec) undefined\n" );
751
752            else if( !ISTERM(sym) )
753                lerror(NONFATAL, "%s (used in %%prec) must be terminal symbol\n" );
754
755            else
756                Sp->rhs->prec = Precedence[ sym->val ].level;              /* (2) */
757        }
758    }
759
760    /* - - - - - - - - - - - - - - - - - - - - - - - - - - - - - - - - - - - */
761
762    PUBLIC void union_def( action )
763    char    *action;
764    {
765        /*  create a YYSTYPE definition for the union, using the fields specified
766         *  in the %union directive, and also appending a default integer-sized
767         *  field for those situation where no field is attached to the current
768         *  symbol.
769         */
770
771        while( *action && *action != '{' )  /* Get rid of everything up to the */
772            ++action;                       /* open brace                      */
773        if( *action )                       /* and the brace itself            */
774            ++action;
775
776        output( "typedef union\n" );
777        output( "{\n" );
778        output( "    int   %s;  /* Default field, used when no %%type found */",
779                                                        DEF_FIELD );
780        output( "%s\n",  action );
781        output( "yystype;\n\n"  );
782        output( "#define YYSTYPE yystype\n" );
783        Fields_active = 1;
784    }
785
786    PUBLIC  fields_active()
787    {
788        return Fields_active ;                   /* previous %union was specified */
789    }
790
```

→

Listing 4.26. continued...

```
791    /* - - - - - - - - - - - - - - - - - - - - - - - - - - - - - - */
792
793    PUBLIC  void new_field( field_name )
794    char     *field_name;
795    {
796        /* Change the name of the current <field> */
797
798        char        *p;
799
800        if( !*field_name )
801            *Field_name = '\0' ;
802        else
803        {
804            if( p = strchr(++field_name, '>') )
805                *p = '\0' ;
806
807            strncpy( Field_name, field_name, sizeof(Field_name) );
808        }
809    }
810    #endif
```

4.10.2 Creating The Tables

The next step is to create the parse tables from the grammar we just assembled, and the LL(1) select sets are needed to do this.

4.10.2.1 Computing FIRST, FOLLOW, and SELECT Sets. LLama starts by creating the FIRST sets, using the code in Listing 4.27, which implements the algorithm described earlier. The subroutine `first()`, on line 21, figures the FIRST sets for all the nonterminals in the symbol table. The `ptab()` call on line 30 traverses the table, calling `first_closure()` (on line 37) for every table element (`ptab()` is one of the hash functions described in Appendix A). Multiple passes are made through the table, until nothing is added to any symbol's FIRST set.

The `first_rhs()` subroutine on line 97 computes the first set for an entire right-hand side, represented as an array of SYMBOL pointers. (They're stored this way in a PRODUCTION structure). `first_rhs()` won't work if called before `first()`.

The subroutines in Listing 4.28 compute FOLLOW sets for all nonterminals in **LLama**'s symbol table, again using the procedure described earlier in this Chapter. Finally, **LLama** uses the FIRST and FOLLOW sets to create the LL(1) selection sets in Listing 4.29.

4.10.3 The Rest of LLama

The remainder of **LLama** is Listings 4.30. to 4.37. All that they do is print out the tables, and so forth. They are adequately commented and need no further description here.

Listing 4.27. *first.c*— Find FIRST Sets

```
1    #include <stdio.h>
2    #include <tools/debug.h>
3    #include <tools/set.h>
4    #include <tools/hash.h>
5    #include <tools/compiler.h>
6    #include <tools/l.h>
7    #include "parser.h"
8
9    /* FIRST.C        Compute FIRST sets for all productions in a symbol table.
10    *-------------------------------------------------------------------------
11    */
12
13   int     first_closure    P(( SYMBOL *lhs ));                   /* local */
14   void    first            P(( void ));                         /* public */
15   int     first_rhs        P(( SET *dest, SYMBOL **rhs, int len ));
16
17   PRIVATE int Did_something;
18
19   /*-------------------------------------------------------------------------*/
20
21   PUBLIC  void first( )
22   {
23       /* Construct FIRST sets for all nonterminal symbols in the symbol table. */
24
25       D( printf("Finding FIRST sets\n"); )
26
27       do
28       {
29           Did_something = 0;
30           ptab( Symtab, first_closure, NULL, 0 );
31
32       } while( Did_something );
33   }
34
35   /*-------------------------------------------------------------------------*/
36
37   PRIVATE first_closure( lhs )
38   SYMBOL  *lhs;                              /* Current left-hand side        */
39   {
40       /* Called for every element in the FIRST sets. Adds elements to the first
41        * sets. The following rules are used:
42        *
43        * 1) given lhs->...Y... where Y is a terminal symbol preceded by any number
44        *    (including 0) of nullable nonterminal symbols or actions, add Y to
45        *    FIRST(x).
46        *
47        * 2) given lhs->...y... where y is a nonterminal symbol preceded by any
48        *    number (including 0) of nullable nonterminal symbols or actions, add
49        *    FIRST(y) to FIRST(lhs).
50        */
51
52       PRODUCTION   *prod;           /* Pointer to one production side       */
53       SYMBOL       **y;             /* Pointer to one element of production */
54       static SET   *set = NULL;     /* Scratch-space set.                   */
55       int          i;
56
57       if( !ISNONTERM(lhs) )         /* Ignore entries for terminal symbols  */
58            return;
59
```

Listing 4.27. continued...

```
60       if( !set )                              /* Do this once. The set isn't free()d */
61           set = newset();
62
63       ASSIGN( set, lhs->first );
64
65       for( prod = lhs->productions; prod ; prod = prod->next )
66       {
67           if( prod->non_acts <= 0 )                    /* No non-action symbols   */
68           {                                            /* add epsilon to first set */
69               ADD( set, EPSILON );
70               continue;
71           }
72
73           for( y = prod->rhs, i = prod->rhs_len; --i >= 0; y++ )
74           {
75               if( ISACT( *y ) )                        /* pretend acts don't exist */
76                   continue;
77
78               if( ISTERM( *y ) )
79                   ADD( set, (*y)->val );
80
81               else if( *y )                            /* it's a nonterminal */
82                   UNION( set, (*y)->first );
83
84               if( !NULLABLE( *y ))            /* it's not a nullable nonterminal  */
85                   break;
86           }
87       }
88
89       if( !IS_EQUIVALENT(set, lhs->first) )
90       {
91           ASSIGN( lhs->first, set );
92           Did_something = 1;
93       }
94   }
95
96   /*------------------------------------------------------------------------*/
97   PUBLIC   int       first_rhs( dest, rhs, len )
98   SET               *dest;                     /* Target set          */
99   SYMBOL            **rhs;                      /* A right-hand side   */
100  int                len;                       /* # of objects in rhs */
101  {
102      /* Fill the destination set with FIRST(rhs) where rhs is the right-hand side
103       * of a production represented as an array of pointers to symbol-table
104       * elements. Return 1 if the entire right-hand side is nullable, otherwise
105       * return 0.
106       */
107
108      if( len <= 0 )
109      {
110          ADD( dest, EPSILON );
111          return 1;
112      }
113
114      for(; --len >= 0 ; ++rhs )
115      {
116          if( ISACT( rhs[0] ) )
117              continue;
118
```

Listing 4.27. continued...

```
119          if( ISTERM( rhs[0] )  )
120              ADD( dest, rhs[0]->val );
121          else
122              UNION( dest, rhs[0]->first );
123
124          if( !NULLABLE( rhs[0] ) )
125              break;
126      }
127
128      return( len < 0 );
129  }
```

Listing 4.28. *follow.c*— Find FOLLOW Sets

```
1    #include <stdio.h>
2    #include <tools/debug.h>
3    #include <tools/set.h>
4    #include <tools/hash.h>
5    #include <tools/compiler.h>
6    #include <tools/l.h>
7    #include "parser.h"
8    #include "llout.h"
9
10   /* FOLLOW.C          Compute FOLLOW sets for all productions in a
11    *                   symbol table. The FIRST sets must be computed
12    *                   before follow() is called.
13    */
14
15   int     follow_closure P(( SYMBOL *lhs ));              /* local */
16   int     remove_epsilon P(( SYMBOL *lhs ));
17   void    init           P(( SYMBOL *lhs ));
18   void    follow         P(( void        ));              /* public */
19
20   /*------------------------------------------------------------------*/
21
22   PRIVATE int     Did_something;
23
24   /*------------------------------------------------------------------*/
25
26   PUBLIC  void follow()
27   {
28       D( int pass = 0;                                    )
29       D( printf( "Initializing FOLLOW sets\n" ); )
30
31       ptab( Symtab, init, NULL, 0 );
32
33       do {
34           /* This loop makes several passes through the entire grammar, adding
35            * FOLLOW sets. The follow_closure() routine is called for each grammar
36            * symbol, and sets Did_something to true if it adds any elements to
37            * existing FOLLOW sets.
38            */
39
40           D(  printf( "Closure pass %d\n", ++pass ); )
41           D( fprintf( stderr, "%d\n",        pass ); )
42
```

Listing 4.28. continued...

```
43            Did_something = 0;
44            ptab( Symtab, follow_closure, NULL, 0 );
45
46        } while( Did_something );
47
48        /* This last pass is just for nicety and could probably be eliminated (may
49         * as well do it right though). Strictly speaking, FOLLOW sets shouldn't
50         * contain epsilon. Nonetheless, it was much easier to just add epsilon in
51         * the previous steps than try to filter it out there. This last pass just
52         * removes epsilon from all the FOLLOW sets.
53         */
54
55        ptab( Symtab, remove_epsilon, NULL, 0 );
56        D( printf("Follow set computation done\n"); )
57    }
58
59    /*------------------------------------------------------------------*/
60
61    PRIVATE void init( lhs )
62    SYMBOL *lhs;              /* Current left-hand side        */
63    {
64        /* Initialize the FOLLOW sets. This procedure adds to the initial follow set
65         * of each production those elements that won't change during the closure
66         * process. Note that in all the following cases, actions are just ignored.
67         *
68         * (1) FOLLOW(start) contains end of input ($).
69         *
70         * (2) Given s->...xY... where x is a nonterminal and Y is
71         *     a terminal, add Y to FOLLOW(x). x and Y can be separated
72         *     by any number (including 0) of nullable nonterminals or actions.
73         *
74         * (3) Given x->...xy... where x and y are both nonterminals,
75         *     add FIRST(y) to FOLLOW(x). Again, x and y can be separated
76         *     by any number of nullable nonterminals or actions.
77         */
78
79        PRODUCTION  *prod;   /* Pointer to one production            */
80        SYMBOL      **x;     /* Pointer to one element of production */
81        SYMBOL      **y;
82
83        D( printf("%s:\n", lhs->name); )
84
85        if( !ISNONTERM(lhs) )
86            return;
87
88        if( lhs == Goal_symbol )
89        {
90            D( printf( "\tAdding _EOI_ to FOLLOW(%s)\n", lhs->name ); )
91            ADD( lhs->follow, _EOI_ );
92        }
93
94        for( prod = lhs->productions; prod ; prod = prod->next )
95        {
96            for( x = prod->rhs ; *x ; x++ )
97            {
98                if( ISNONTERM(*x) )
99                {
100                    for( y = x + 1 ; *y ; ++y )
101                    {
```

Listing 4.28. continued...

```
102                        if( ISACT(*y) )
103                            continue;
104
105                        if( ISTERM(*y) )
106                        {
107                            D( printf("\tAdding %s ",      (*y)->name ); )
108                            D( printf("to FOLLOW(%s)\n", (*x)->name ); )
109
110                            ADD( (*x)->follow, (*y)->val );
111                            break;
112                        }
113                        else
114                        {
115                            UNION( (*x)->follow, (*y)->first );
116                            if( !NULLABLE(*y) )
117                                break;
118                        }
119                    }
120                }
121            }
122        }
123 }
124
125 /*------------------------------------------------------------------------*/
126
127 PRIVATE follow_closure( lhs )
128 SYMBOL  *lhs;              /* Current left-hand side      */
129 {
130     /* Adds elements to the FOLLOW sets using the following rule:
131      *
132      *   Given s->...x  or  s->...x... where all symbols following
133      *   x are nullable nonterminals or actions, add FOLLOW(s) to FOLLOW(x).
134      */
135
136     PRODUCTION  *prod;      /* Pointer to one production side       */
137     SYMBOL      **x, **y ; /* Pointer to one element of production */
138
139     D( printf("%s:\n", lhs->name ); )
140
141     if( ISACT(lhs) || ISTERM(lhs) )
142         return;
143
144     for( prod = lhs->productions; prod ; prod = prod->next )
145     {
146         for( x = prod->rhs + prod->rhs_len; --x >= prod->rhs ; )
147         {
148             if( ISACT(*x) )
149                 continue;
150
151             if( ISTERM(*x) )
152                 break;
153
154             if( !subset( (*x)->follow, lhs->follow ) )
155             {
156                 D( printf("\tAdding FOLLOW(%s) ", lhs->name  ); )
157                 D( printf("to FOLLOW(%s)\n",      (*x)->name ); )
158
159                 UNION( (*x)->follow, lhs->follow );
160                 Did_something = 1;
161             }
```

Listing 4.28. continued...

```
162
163                    if( ! NULLABLE(*x) )
164                        break;
165                }
166        }
167 }
168
169 /*----------------------------------------------------------------*/
170
171 PRIVATE remove_epsilon( lhs )
172 SYMBOL  *lhs;
173 {
174     /* Remove epsilon from the FOLLOW sets. The presence of epsilon is a
175      * side effect of adding FIRST sets to the FOLLOW sets willy nilly.
176      */
177
178     if( ISNONTERM(lhs) )
179         REMOVE( lhs->follow, EPSILON );
180 }
```

Listing 4.29. *llselect.c*— Find LL(1) Select Sets

```
 1   #include <stdio.h>
 2
 3   #include <tools/debug.h>
 4   #include <tools/set.h>
 5   #include <tools/hash.h>
 6   #include <tools/compiler.h>
 7   #include <tools/l.h>
 8   #include "parser.h"
 9
10   /* LLSELECT.C    Compute LL(1) select sets for all productions in a
11    *               symbol table. The FIRST and FOLLOW sets must be computed
12    *               before select() is called. These routines are not used
13    *               by occs.
14    */
15
16   /*----------------------------------------------------------------*/
17
18   void find_select_set    P(( SYMBOL *lhs ));     /* local  */
19   void select             P(( void       ));     /* public */
20
21   /*----------------------------------------------------------------*/
22
23   PRIVATE void    find_select_set( lhs )
24   SYMBOL  *lhs;                               /* left-hand side of production */
25   {
26       /* Find the LL(1) selection set for all productions attached to the
27        * indicated left-hand side (lhs). The first_rhs() call puts the FIRST sets
28        * for the initial symbols in prod->rhs into the select set. It returns true
29        * only if the entire right-hand side was nullable (EPSILON was an element
30        * of the FIRST set of every symbol on the right-hand side.
31        */
32
33       PRODUCTION  *prod;
34
```

➡

Listing 4.29. continued...

```
35          for( prod = lhs->productions; prod ; prod = prod->next )
36          {
37              if( first_rhs( prod->select, prod->rhs, prod->rhs_len ) )
38                  UNION( prod->select, lhs->follow );
39
40              REMOVE( prod->select, EPSILON );
41          }
42      }
43
44      /*-------------------------------------------------------------------*/
45
46      PUBLIC  void select( )
47      {
48          /* Compute LL(1) selection sets for all productions in the grammar */
49
50          if( Verbose )
51              printf("Finding LL(1) select sets\n");
52
53          ptab( Symtab, find_select_set, NULL, 0 );
54      }
```

Listing 4.30. *llcode.c*— Routines That Make the Parse Tables

```
1   #include <stdio.h>
2   #include <stdlib.h>
3   #include <ctype.h>
4
5   #include <tools/debug.h>
6   #include <tools/set.h>
7   #include <tools/hash.h>
8   #include <tools/compiler.h>
9   #include <tools/l.h>
10  #include "parser.h"
11
12  /*      LLCODE.C        Print the various tables needed for a llama-generated
13   *                      LL(1) parser. The generated tables are:
14   *
15   *      Yyd[][]         The parser state machine's DFA transition table. The
16   *                      horizontal axis is input symbol and the vertical axis is
17   *                      top-of-stack symbol. Only nonterminal TOS symbols are in
18   *                      the table. The table contains the production number of a
19   *                      production to apply or -1 if this is an error
20   *                      transition.
21   *
22   *      YydN[]          (N is 1-3 decimal digits). Used for compressed tables
23   *                      only. Holds the compressed rows.
24   *
25   *      Yy_pushtab[]    Indexed by production number, evaluates to a list of
26   *      YypDD[]         objects to push on the stack when that production is
27   *                      replaced. The YypDD arrays are the lists of objects
28   *                      and Yy_pushtab is an array of pointers to those lists.
29   *
30   *      Yy_snonterm[]   For debugging, indexed by nonterminal, evaluates to the
31   *                      name of the nonterminal.
32   *      Yy_sact[]       Same but for the acts.
33   *      Yy_synch[]      Array of synchronization tokens for error recovery.
34   *      yy_act()        Subroutine containing the actions.
```

→

Listing 4.30. continued...

```
35     *
36     * Yy_stok[] is make in stok.c. For the most part, the numbers in these tables
37     * are the same as those in the symbol table. The exceptions are the token
38     * values, which are shifted down so that the smallest token has the value 1
39     * (0 is used for EOI).
40     */
41
42     #define DTRAN              "Yyd"              /* Name of DFA transition table   */
43                                                  /* array in the PARSE_FILE.       */
44
45     /*-------------------------------------------------------------------*/
46
47     extern  void tables            P(( void ));                     /* public */
48
49     static  void fill_row          P(( SYMBOL *lhs, void *junk )); /* local */
50     static  void make_pushtab      P(( SYMBOL *lhs, void *junk ));
51     static  void make_yy_pushtab   P(( void ));
52     static  void make_yy_dtran     P(( void ));
53     static  void make_yy_synch     P(( void ));
54     static  void make_yy_snonterm  P(( void ));
55     static  void make_yy_sact      P(( void ));
56     static  void make_acts         P(( SYMBOL *lhs,void *junk ));
57     static  void make_yy_act       P(( void  ));
58
59     /*-------------------------------------------------------------------*/
60
61     PRIVATE int      *Dtran;            /* Internal representation of the parse table
62                                         */
63
64     /*-------------------------------------------------------------------*/
65
66     PUBLIC void      tables()
67     {
68             /* Print the various tables needed by the parser.  */
69
70             make_yy_pushtab();
71             make_yy_dtran();
72             make_yy_act();
73             make_yy_synch();
74             make_yy_stok();
75             make_token_file();
76
77             output( "\n#ifdef YYDEBUG\n");
78
79             make_yy_snonterm();
80             make_yy_sact();
81
82             output( "\n#endif\n" );
83     }
84
85     /*-------------------------------------------------------------------
86      * fill_row()
87      *
88      * Make one row of the parser's DFA transition table.
89      * Column 0 is used for the EOI condition; other columns
90      * are indexed by nonterminal (with the number normalized
91      * for the smallest nonterminal). That is, the terminal
92      * values in the symbol table are shifted downwards so that
93      * the smallest terminal value is 1 rather than MINTERM.
94      * The row indexes are adjusted in the same way (so that
```

Listing 4.30. continued...

```
 95      *   row 0 is used for MINNONTERM).
 96      *
 97      *   Note that the code assumes that Dtran consists of  byte-size
 98      *   cells.
 99      */
100
101     PRIVATE void     fill_row( lhs, junk )
102     SYMBOL  *lhs;                              /* Current left-hand side  */
103     void    *junk;
104     {
105         PRODUCTION  *prod;
106         int         *row;
107         int         i;
108         int         rowsize;
109
110         if( !ISNONTERM(lhs) )
111             return;
112
113         rowsize = USED_TERMS + 1;
114         row     = Dtran + ((i = ADJ_VAL(lhs->val)) * rowsize );
115
116         for( prod = lhs->productions; prod ; prod = prod->next )
117         {
118             next_member( NULL );
119             while( (i = next_member(prod->select)) >= 0 )
120             {
121                 if( row[i] == -1 )
122                     row[i] = prod->num;
123                 else
124                     error(NONFATAL, "Grammar not LL(1), select-set conflict in " \
125                                     "<%s>, line %d\n", lhs->name, lhs->lineno );
126             }
127         }
128     }
129
130     /*-----------------------------------------------------------------------*/
131
132     PRIVATE void     make_pushtab( lhs, junk )
133     SYMBOL  *lhs;
134     void    *junk;
135     {
136         /* Make the pushtab. The right-hand sides are output in reverse order
137          * (to make the pushing easier) by stacking them and then printing
138          * items off the stack.
139          */
140
141         register int  i ;
142         PRODUCTION    *prod ;
143         SYMBOL            **sym ;
144         SYMBOL            *stack[ MAXRHS ], **sp;
145
146         sp = &stack[-1] ;
147         for( prod = lhs->productions ; prod ; prod = prod->next )
148         {
149             output( "YYPRIVATE int Yyp%02d[]={ ", prod->num );
150
151             for( sym = prod->rhs, i = prod->rhs_len ; --i >= 0  ;)
152                 *++sp = *sym++ ;
153
```

```
Listing 4.30. continued...
154          for(; INBOUNDS(stack,sp) ; output ("%d, ", (*sp--)->val) )
155              ;
156
157          output (  "0 };\n", prod->rhs[0] );
158      }
159  }
160
161  /*- - - - - - - - - - - - - - - - - - - - - - - - - - - - - - - - - - - */
162
163  PRIVATE void    make_yy_pushtab()
164  {
165      /* Print out yy_pushtab. */
166
167      register int        i;
168      register int        maxprod = Num_productions - 1;
169      static      char    *text[] =
170      {
171          "The YypNN arrays hold the right-hand sides of the productions, listed",
172          "back to front (so that they are pushed in reverse order), NN is the",
173          "production number (to be found in the symbol-table listing output",
174          "with a -s command-line switch).",
175          "",
176          "Yy_pushtab[] is indexed by production number and points to the",
177          "appropriate right-hand side (YypNN) array.",
178          NULL
179      };
180
181      comment( Output, text );
182      ptab    ( Symtab, make_pushtab, NULL, 0 );
183
184      output (  "\nYYPRIVATE int  *Yy_pushtab[] =\n{\n");
185
186      for( i = 0; i < maxprod; i++ )
187              output (  "\tYyp%02d,\n", i );
188
189      output (  "\tYyp%02d\n};\n", maxprod );
190  }
191
192  /*-------------------------------------------------------------------*/
193
194  PRIVATE void    make_yy_dtran( )
195  {
196      /* Print the DFA transition table.   */
197
198      register int        i;
199      int         nterms, nnonterms;
200      static char *text[] =
201      {
202          "Yyd[][] is the DFA transition table for the parser. It is indexed",
203          "as follows:",
204          "",
205          "                    Input symbol",
206          "         +--------------------+",
207          "      L  |  Production number  |",
208          "      H  |      or YYF         |",
209          "      S  |                     |",
210          "         +--------------------+",
211          "",
212          "The production number is used as an index into Yy_pushtab, which",
213          "looks like this:",
```

Listing 4.30. continued...

```
214            "",
215            "          Yy_pushtab       YypDD:",
216            "          +-------+       +---------------+",
217            "          |   *---|------>|               |",
218            "          +-------+       +---------------+",
219            "          |   *---|---->",
220            "          +-------+",
221            "          |   *---|---->",
222            "          +-------+",
223            "",
224            "YypDD is the tokenized right-hand side of the production.",
225            "Generate a symbol table listing with llama's -l command-line",
226            "switch to get both production numbers and the meanings of the",
227            "YypDD string contents.",
228            NULL
229        };
230
231        nterms       = USED_TERMS + 1;      /* +1 for EOI */
232        nnonterms = USED_NONTERMS;
233
234        i = nterms * nnonterms * sizeof( *Dtran );
235
236        if( !(Dtran = (int *) malloc(i)) )
237            ferr("Out of memory\n");
238
239        memset( Dtran, -1, i );        /* Initialize Dtran to all failures */
240        ptab( Symtab, fill_row, NULL, 0 ); /* & fill nonfailure transitions   */
241
242        comment( Output , text );      /* Print header comment */
243
244        if( Uncompressed )
245        {
246            fprintf( Output,"YYPRIVATE YY_TTYPE  %s[ %d ][ %d ] =\n",
247                                            DTRAN, nnonterms, nterms );
248
249            print_array( Output, Dtran, nnonterms, nterms );
250            defnext     ( Output, DTRAN );
251
252            if( Verbose )
253                printf("%d bytes required for tables\n", i * sizeof(YY_TTYPE) );
254        }
255        else
256        {
257            i = pairs( Output, Dtran, nnonterms, nterms, DTRAN, Threshold, 1);
258            pnext( Output, DTRAN );
259
260            if( Verbose )
261                printf("%d bytes required for compressed tables\n",
262                    (i * sizeof(YY_TTYPE)) + (nnonterms * sizeof(YY_TTYPE*)));
263        }
264
265        output("\n\n");
266    }
267
268    /*----------------------------------------------------------------------*/
269
270    PRIVATE void    make_yy_synch()
271    {
272        int  mem ; /* current member of synch set  */
273        int  i;    /* number of members in set     */
```

```
     Listing 4.30. continued...
274
275      static char *text[] =
276      {
277          "Yy_synch[] is an array of synchronization tokens. When an error is",
278          "detected, stack items are popped until one of the tokens in this",
279          "array is encountered. The input is then read until the same item is",
280          "found. Then parsing continues.",
281          NULL
282      };
283
284      comment( Output, text );
285      output( "YYPRIVATE int   Yy_synch[] =\n{\n" );
286
287      i = 0;
288      for( next_member(NULL); (mem = next_member(Synch)) >= 0 ;)
289      {
290          output( "\t%s,\n", Terms[mem]->name );
291          ++i;
292      }
293
294      if( i == 0 )                    /* No members in synch set */
295          output( "\t_EOI_\n" );
296
297      output( "\t-1\n};\n" );
298      next_member( NULL );
299  }
300
301  /*-------------------------------------------------------------------*/
302
303  PRIVATE void    make_yy_snonterm()
304  {
305      register int  i;
306
307      static char *the_comment[] =
308      {
309          "Yy_snonterm[] is used only for debugging. It is indexed by the",
310          "tokenized left-hand side (as used for a row index in Yyd[]) and",
311          "evaluates to a string naming that left-hand side.",
312          NULL
313      };
314
315      comment( Output, the_comment );
316
317      output(  "char *Yy_snonterm[] =\n{\n");
318
319      for( i = MINNONTERM; i <= Cur_nonterm; i++ )
320      {
321          if( Terms[i] )
322              output(  "\t/* %3d */   \"%s\"", i, Terms[i]->name );
323
324          if( i != Cur_nonterm )
325                  outc( ',' )
326
327          outc( '\n' );
328      }
329
330      output(  "};\n\n" );
331  }
332
```

```
Listing 4.30. continued...
333    /*---------------------------------------------------------------------*/
334
335    PRIVATE void    make_yy_sact()
336    {
337        /* This subroutine generates the subroutine that implements the actions.  */
338
339        register int  i;
340        static char *the_comment[] =
341        {
342            "Yy_sact[] is also used only for debugging. It is indexed by the",
343            "internal value used for an action symbol and evaluates to a string",
344            "naming that token symbol.",
345            NULL
346        };
347
348        comment( Output, the_comment );
349        output("char *Yy_sact[] =\n{\n\t" );
350
351        if( Cur_act < MINACT )
352            output("NULL    /* There are no actions */");
353        else
354            for( i = MINACT; i <= Cur_act; i++ )
355            {
356                output( "\"{%d}\"%c", i - MINACT, i < Cur_act ? ',' : ' ' );
357                if( i % 10 == 9 )
358                    output("\n\t");
359            }
360
361        output("\n};\n");
362    }
363
364    /*---------------------------------------------------------------------*/
365
366    PRIVATE void    make_acts( lhs, junk )
367    SYMBOL  *lhs;                            /* Current left-hand side  */
368    void    *junk;
369    {
370        /* This subroutine is called indirectly from yy_act, through the subroutine
371         * ptab(). It prints the text associated with one of the acts.
372         */
373
374        char *p;
375        int  num;               /* The N in $N */
376        char *do_dollar();
377        char fname[80], *fp;
378        int  i;
379
380        if( !lhs->string )
381                return;
382
383        output( "        case %d:\n", lhs->val );
384
385        if ( No_lines )
386            output( "\t\t" );
387        else
388            output( "#line %d \"%s\"\n\t\t", lhs->lineno, Input_file_name );
389
390        for( p = lhs->string ; *p ; )
391        {
```

→

Listing 4.30. continued...

```
392            if( *p == '\r' )
393                continue;
394
395            if( *p != '$' )
396                output( "%c", *p++ );
397            else
398            {
399                /* Skip the attribute reference. The if statement handles $$ the
400                 * else clause handles the two forms: $N and $-N, where N is a
401                 * decimal number. When you hit the do_dollar call (in the output()
402                 * call), "num" holds the number associated with N, or DOLLAR_DOLLAR
403                 * in the case of $$.
404                 */
405
406                if( *++p != '<' )
407                    *fname = '\0';
408                else
409                {
410                    ++p;                    /* skip the < */
411                    fp = fname;
412
413                    for(i=sizeof(fname); --i>0  && *p && *p != '>'; *fp++ = *p++ )
414                        ;
415                    *fp = '\0';
416
417                    if( *p == '>' )
418                        ++p;
419                }
420
421                if( *p == '$' )
422                {
423                    num = DOLLAR_DOLLAR;
424                    ++p;
425                }
426                else
427                {
428                    num = atoi( p );
429                    if( *p == '-' )
430                        ++p ;
431                    while( isdigit(*p) )
432                        ++p ;
433                }
434
435                output( "%s", do_dollar(num, 0, 0, NULL, fname) );
436            }
437        }
438
439        output(  "\n                      break;\n" );
440    }
441
442    /*- - - - - - - - - - - - - - - - - - - - - - - - - - - - - - - - - - - */
443
444    PRIVATE void    make_yy_act()
445    {
446        /* Print all the acts inside a subroutine called yy_act() */
447
448        static char *comment_text[] =
449        {
450            "Yy_act() is the action subroutine. It is passed the tokenized value",
451            "of an action and executes the corresponding code.",
```

Listing 4.30. continued...

```
452             NULL
453         };
454
455     static char *top[] =
456         {
457             "YYPRIVATE int yy_act( actnum )",
458             "{",
459         "    /* The actions. Returns 0 normally but a nonzero error code can",
460         "     * be returned if one of the acts causes the parser to terminate",
461         "     * abnormally.",
462         "     */",
463         "",
464         "    switch( actnum )",
465         "    {",
466             NULL
467         };
468     static char *bottom[] =
469         {
470         "    default:  printf(\"INTERNAL ERROR: \"\
471                             "Illegal act number (%s)\\n\", actnum);",
472         "        break;",
473         "    }",
474         "    return 0;",
475         "}",
476             NULL
477         };
478
479     comment( Output, comment_text               );
480     printv ( Output, top                        );
481     ptab   ( Symtab, make_acts, NULL, 0         );
482     printv ( Output, bottom                     );
483     }
```

Listing 4.31. *lldriver.c*— Routines That Make Driver Subroutines

```
1    #include <stdio.h>
2    #include <stdlib.h>
3
4    #include <tools/debug.h>
5    #include <tools/set.h>
6    #include <tools/hash.h>
7    #include <tools/compiler.h>
8    #include <tools/l.h>
9    #include "parser.h"
10
11   /*----------------------------------------------------------------------*/
12
13   extern  void file_header        P(( void ));                    /* public */
14   extern  void code_header        P(( void ));
15   extern  void driver             P(( void ));
16
17   /*----------------------------------------------------------------------*/
18
19   PRIVATE FILE    *Driver_file = stderr ;
20
```

```
Listing 4.31. continued...
21    /*------------------------------------------------------------------------
22     * Routines in this file are llama specific. There's a different version
23     * of all these routines in yydriver.c.
24     *------------------------------------------------------------------------
25     */
26
27    PUBLIC  void file_header()
28    {
29        /* This header is printed at the top of the output file, before
30         * the definitions section is processed. Various #defines that
31         * you might want to modify are put here.
32         */
33
34        output( "#include <stdio.h>\n\n" );
35
36        if( Public )
37            output( "#define YYPRIVATE\n" );
38
39        if( Debug )
40            output( "#define YYDEBUG\n" );
41
42
43        output( "\n/*---------------------------------------------*/\n\n");
44
45    }
46
47    /*-------------------------------------------------------------------------*/
48
49    PUBLIC  void    code_header()
50    {
51        /* This header is output after the definitions section is processed,
52         * but before any tables or the driver is processed.
53         */
54
55        output( "\n\n/*---------------------------------------*/\n\n");
56        output( "#include \"%s\"\n\n",        TOKEN_FILE              );
57        output( "#define YY_MINTERM       1\n"                        );
58        output( "#define YY_MAXTERM       %d\n", Cur_term             );
59        output( "#define YY_MINNONTERM    %d\n", MINNONTERM           );
60        output( "#define YY_MAXNONTERM    %d\n", Cur_nonterm          );
61        output( "#define YY_START_STATE   %d\n", MINNONTERM           );
62        output( "#define YY_MINACT        %d\n", MINACT               );
63        output( "\n"                                                  );
64
65        if( !( Driver_file = driver_1(Output, !No_lines, Template) ))
66            error( NONFATAL, "%s not found--output file won't compile\n", Template);
67    }
68
69    /*-------------------------------------------------------------------------*/
70
71    PUBLIC  void    driver()
72    {
73        /* Print out the actual parser by copying the file llama.par
74         * to the output file.
75         */
76
77        driver_2( Output, !No_lines );
78        fclose( Driver_file );
79    }
```

Listing 4.32. *stok.c*— Routines to Make *yyout.h* and *yy_stok[]*

```c
1    #include <stdio.h>
2
3    #include <tools/debug.h>
4    #include <tools/set.h>
5    #include <tools/hash.h>
6    #include <tools/compiler.h>
7    #include <tools/l.h>
8    #include "parser.h"
9
10   /*----------------------------------------------------------------*/
11
12   extern   void make_yy_stok     P(( void ));                    /* public */
13   extern   void make_token_file P(( void ));
14
15   /*----------------------------------------------------------------*/
16
17   PUBLIC   void      make_yy_stok()
18   {
19       /* This subroutine generates the Yy_stok[] array that's
20        * indexed by token value and evaluates to a string
21        * representing the token name. Token values are adjusted
22        * so that the smallest token value is 1 (0 is reserved
23        * for end of input).
24        */
25
26       register int   i;
27
28       static char *the_comment[] =
29       {
30           "Yy_stok[] is used for debugging and error messages. It is indexed",
31           "by the internal value used for a token (as used for a column index in",
32           "the transition matrix) and evaluates to a string naming that token.",
33           NULL
34       };
35
36       comment( Output, the_comment );
37
38       output( "char  *Yy_stok[] =\n{\n" );
39       output( "\t/*   0 */   \"_EOI_\",\n" );
40
41       for( i = MINTERM; i <= Cur_term; i++ )
42       {
43           output( "\t/* %3d */   \"%s\"", (i-MINTERM)+1, Terms[i]->name );
44           if( i != Cur_term )
45               outc( ',' );
46
47           if( (i & 0x1) == 0  ||  i == Cur_term )      /* Newline for every */
48               outc( '\n' );                            /* other element    */
49       }
50
51       output( "};\n\n");
52   }
53
54   /*----------------------------------------------------------------*/
55
56   PUBLIC void      make_token_file()
57   {
```

Listing 4.32. continued...

```
58          /* This subroutine generates the yytokens.h file. Tokens have
59           * the same value as in make_yy_stok(). A special token
60           * named _EOI_ (with a value of 0) is also generated.
61           */
62
63          FILE    *tokfile;
64          int     i;
65
66          if( !(tokfile = fopen( TOKEN_FILE , "w") ))
67              error( FATAL, "Can't open %s\n", TOKEN_FILE );
68
69   D( else if( Verbose )                                    )
70   D(     printf("Generating %s\n", TOKEN_FILE );          )
71
72          fprintf( tokfile, "#define _EOI_        0\n");
73
74          for( i = MINTERM; i <= Cur_term; i++ )
75              fprintf( tokfile, "#define %-10s %d\n",
76                                          Terms[i]->name, (i-MINTERM)+1 );
77          fclose( tokfile );
78   }
```

Listing 4.33. *main.c*— Command-Line Parsing and `main()`

```
1    #include <stdio.h>
2    #include <ctype.h>
3    #include <stdarg.h>
4    #include <signal.h>
5    #include <malloc.h>
6    #include <errno.h>
7    #include <time.h>
8    #include <sys/types.h>
9    #include <sys/timeb.h>
10   #include <process.h>
11
12   #include "date.h"
13
14   #include <tools/debug.h>
15   #include <tools/set.h>
16   #include <tools/hash.h>
17   #include <tools/compiler.h>
18   #include <tools/l.h>
19
20   #ifdef LLAMA
21   #       define  ALLOCATE
22   #       include "parser.h"
23   #       undef   ALLOCATE
24   #else
25   #       define  ALLOCATE
26   #       include "parser.h"
27   #       undef   ALLOCATE
28   #endif
29
30   PRIVATE  int    Warn_exit     = 0;      /* Set to 1 if -W on command line */
31   PRIVATE  int    Num_warnings  = 0;      /* Total warnings printed         */
32   PRIVATE  char   *Output_fname = "????"; /* Name of the output file        */
33   PRIVATE  FILE *Doc_file       = NULL;   /* Error log & machine description */
```

→

Listing 4.33. continued...

```
34
35    #define VERBOSE(str)    if(Verbose){  printf( str ":\n" );  }else
36
37    /*-------------------------------------------------------------------------*/
38
39    void onintr        P(( void                    ));            /* local */
40    int  parse_args    P(( int argc,   char **argv  ));
41    int  do_file       P(( void                    ));
42    void symbols       P(( void                    ));
43    void statistics    P(( FILE *fp                ));
44    void tail          P(( void                    ));
45
46    int  main          P(( int argc,   char **argv  ));            /* public */
47    void output        P(( char *fmt, ...           ));
48    void lerror        P(( int fatal, char *fmt, ... ));
49    void error         P(( int fatal, char *fmt, ... ));
50    char *open_errmsg  P(( void                    ));
51    char *do_dollar    P(( int num, int rhs_size, int lineno, PRODUCTION *prod, \
52                                                    char *fname));
53
54    /*-------------------------------------------------------------------------
55     * There are two versions of the following subroutines--used in do_file(),
56     * depending on whether this is llama or occs.
57     * The occs versions is discussed in the next Chapter.
58     *
59     * subroutine:         llama version in:        occs version in:
60     *
61     * file_header()       lldriver.c               yydriver.c
62     * code_header()       lldriver.c               yydriver.c
63     * driver()            lldriver.c               yydriver.c
64     * tables()            llcode.c                 yycode.c
65     * patch()             -----                    yypatch.c
66     * select()            llselect.c               ------
67     * do_dollar()         lldollar.c               yydollar.c
68     *
69     * Also, several part of this file are compiled only for llama, others only for
70     * occs. The llama-specific parts are arguments to LL() macros, the occs-
71     * specific parts are in OX() macros. We'll look at what the occs-specific
72     * parts actually do in the next Chapter.
73     *-------------------------------------------------------------------------
74     */
75
76    PUBLIC  main( argc, argv )
77    char     **argv;
78    {
79        _amblksiz = 2048;              /* Declared in malloc.h                 */
80
81        signon();                      /* Print sign on message                */
82        signal( SIGINT, onintr );      /* Close output files on Ctrl-Break.    */
83        parse_args( argc, argv );
84
85        if( Debug && !Symbols )
86            Symbols = 1;
87
88        OX( if( Make_parser )                                            )
89        OX( {                                                            )
90        OX(     if( Verbose == 1 )                                       )
91        OX(     {                                                        )
92        OX(         if( !(Doc_file = fopen( DOC_FILE, "w") ) )           )
93        OX(             ferr( "Can't open log file %s\n", DOC_FILE );    )
```

Listing 4.33. continued...

```
 94        OX(        }                                                          )
 95        OX(        else if( Verbose > 1 )                                     )
 96        OX(            Doc_file = stderr;                                     )
 97        OX( }                                                                 )
 98
 99        if( Use_stdout )
100        {
101            Output_fname = "/dev/tty" ;
102            Output       = stdout;
103        }
104        else
105        {
106            OX( Output_fname = !Make_parser ? ACT_FILE : PARSE_FILE ; )
107            LL( Output_fname = PARSE_FILE;                           )
108
109            if( (Output = fopen( Output_fname, "w")) == NULL )
110                error( FATAL, "Can't open output file %s: %s\n",
111                                                Output_fname, open_errmsg() );
112        }
113
114        if( (yynerrs = do_file()) == 0 )        /* Do all the work  */
115        {
116            if( Symbols )
117                symbols();                      /* Print the symbol table        */
118
119            statistics( stdout );               /* And any closing-up statistics. */
120
121            if( Verbose && Doc_file )
122            {
123                OX(  statistics( Doc_file );    )
124            }
125        }
126        else
127        {
128            if( Output != stdout )
129            {
130                fclose( Output );
131                if( unlink( Output_fname ) == -1 )
132                    perror( Output_fname );
133            }
134        }
135
136        /* Exit with  the number of hard errors (or, if -W was specified, the sum
137         * of the hard errors and warnings) as an exit status. Doc_file and Output
138         * are closed implicitly by exit().
139         */
140
141        exit( yynerrs + (Warn_exit ? Num_warnings : 0) );
142    }
143
144    /*----------------------------------------------------------------------*/
145
146    PRIVATE void onintr()                       /* SIGABRT (Ctrl-Break, ^C) Handler */
147    {
148        if( Output != stdout )                  /* Destroy parse file so that a */
149        {                                       /* subsequent compile will fail */
150            fclose( Output );
151            unlink( Output_fname );
152        }
153
```

Listing 4.33. continued...

```
154         exit( EXIT_USR_ABRT );
155    }
156
157    /*------------------------------------------------------------------*/
158
159    PRIVATE parse_args( argc, argv )
160    int      argc;
161    char     **argv;
162    {
163         /* Parse the command line, setting global variables as appropriate */
164
165         char          *p;
166         static char   name_buf[80];              /* Use to assemble default file names */
167
168         static char *usage_msg[] =
169             {
170    #ifdef LLAMA
171             "Usage is: llama [-switch] file",
172             "Create an LL(1) parser from the specification in the",
173             "input file. Legal command-line switches are:",
174             "",
175             "-cN       use N as the pairs threshold when (C)ompressing",
176             "-D        enable (D)ebug mode in yyparse.c (implies -s)",
177             "-f        (F)ast, uncompressed, tables",
178    #else
179             "Usage is:  occs [-switch] file",
180             "",
181             "\tCreate an LALR(1) parser from the specification in the",
182             "\tinput file. Legal command-line switches are:",
183             "",
184             "-a        Output actions only (see -p)",
185             "-D        enable (D)ebug mode in yyparse.c (implies -s)",
186    #endif
187             "-g        make static symbols (G)lobal in yyparse.c",
188             "-l        suppress #(L)ine directives",
189             "-m<file>  use <file> for parser te(M)plate",
190             "-p        output parser only (can be used with -T also)",
191             "-s        make (s)ymbol table",
192             "-S        make more-complete (S)ymbol table",
193             "-t        print all (T)ables (and the parser) to standard output",
194             "-T        move large tables from yyout.c to yyoutab.c",
195             "-v        print (V)erbose diagnostics (including symbol table)",
196             "-V        more verbose than -v. Implies -t, & yyout.doc goes to stderr",
197             "-w        suppress all warning messages\n",
198             "-W        warnings (as well as errors) generate nonzero exit status",
199             NULL
200         };
201
202         /* Note that all global variables set by command-line switches are declared
203          * in parser.h. Space is allocated because a #define ALLOC is present at
204          * the top of the current file.
205          */
206
207         for( ++argv,--argc; argc && *(p = *argv) == '-'; ++argv, --argc )
208         {
209             while( *++p )
210             {
211                 switch( *p )
212                 {
213             OX( case 'a':  Make_parser  = 0;                          )
```

→

```
Listing 4.33. continued...

214          OX(             Template    = ACT_TEMPL;         )
215          OX(             break;                           )
216
217             case 'D':  Debug         = 1;          break;
218             case 'g':  Public        = 1;          break;
219      LL( case 'f':  Uncompressed = 1;          break;           )
220             case 'l':  No_lines      = 1;          break;
221             case 'm':  Template      = p + 1;      goto out;
222      OX( case 'p':  Make_actions = 0;          break;           )
223             case 's':  Symbols       = 1;          break;
224             case 'S':  Symbols       = 2;          break;
225             case 't':  Use_stdout    = 1;          break;
226             case 'T':  Make_yyoutab  = 1;          break;
227             case 'v':  Verbose       = 1;          break;
228             case 'V':  Verbose       = 2;          break;
229             case 'w':  No_warnings   = 1;          break;
230             case 'W':  Warn_exit     = 1;          break;
231      LL( case 'c':  Threshold = atoi( ++p );                 )
232      LL(             while( *p && isdigit( p[1] ) )           )
233      LL(                 ++p;                                 )
234      LL(             break;                                   )
235          default :
236                     fprintf(stderr, "<-%c>: illegal argument\n", *p);
237                     printv (stderr, usage_msg );
238                     exit( EXIT_ILLEGAL_ARG );
239             }
240         }
241  out: ;
242
243      }
244
245      if( Verbose > 1 )
246          Use_stdout = 1;
247
248      if( argc <= 0 )                          /* Input from standard input    */
249          No_lines = 1;
250
251      else if( argc > 1 )
252      {
253          fprintf( stderr, "Too many arguments.\n" );
254          printv ( stderr, usage_msg );
255          exit   ( EXIT_TOO_MANY );
256      }
257      else                                     /* argc == 1, input from file   */
258      {
259          if( ii_newfile( Input_file_name = *argv ) < 0 )
260          {
261              sprintf( name_buf, "%0.70s.%s", *argv, DEF_EXT );
262
263              if( ii_newfile( Input_file_name = name_buf ) < 0 )
264                  error( FATAL, "Can't open input file %s or %s: %s\n",
265                                              *argv, name_buf, open_errmsg());
266          }
267      }
268  }
269
270  /*-----------------------------------------------------------------------*/
271
```

```
Listing 4.33. continued...
272    PRIVATE int      do_file()
273    {
274        /* Process the input file. Return the number of errors.  */
275
276        struct timeb start_time, end_time ;
277        long          time;
278
279        ftime( &start_time );     /* Initialize times now so that the difference  */
280        end_time = start_time;    /* between times will be 0 if we don't build the */
281                                  /* tables. Note that I'm using structure assign- */
282                                  /* ment here.                                    */
283
284        init_acts  ();            /* Initialize the action code.                   */
285        file_header();            /* Output #defines that you might want to change */
286
287        VERBOSE( "parsing" );
288
289        nows       ();            /* Make lex ignore white space until ws() is called */
290        yyparse    ();            /* Parse the entire input file                   */
291
292        if( !( yynerrs || problems()) )      /* If no problems in the input file */
293        {
294            VERBOSE( "analyzing grammar" );
295
296              first ();               /* Find FIRST sets,                    */
297            LL( follow(); )             /* FOLLOW sets,                        */
298            LL( select(); )             /* and ll(1) select sets if this is llama */
299
300            code_header();          /* Print various #defines to output file  */
301            OX( patch(); )          /* Patch up the grammar (if this is occs) */
302                                    /* and output the actions.               */
303
304            ftime( &start_time );
305
306            if( Make_parser )
307            {
308                VERBOSE( "making tables" );
309                tables ();                              /* generate the tables, */
310            }
311
312            ftime  ( &end_time       );
313            VERBOSE( "copying driver" );
314
315            driver();                                   /* the parser, */
316
317            if( Make_actions )
318                tail();                     /* and the tail end of the source file. */
319        }
320
321        if( Verbose )
322        {
323            time = ( end_time.time * 1000) +  end_time.millitm ;
324            time -= (start_time.time * 1000) + start_time.millitm ;
325            printf( "time required to make tables: %ld.%-031d seconds\n",
326                                               (time/1000), (time%1000));
327        }
328
329        return yynerrs;
330    }
```

Listing 4.34. *main.c*— Error, Output, and Statistics Routines

```
331   PRIVATE void    symbols( void )                  /* Print the symbol table */
332   {
333       FILE  *fd;
334
335       if( !(fd = fopen( SYM_FILE, "w")) )
336           perror( SYM_FILE );
337       else
338       {
339           print_symbols ( fd );
340           fclose         ( fd );
341       }
342   }
343
344   /*-------------------------------------------------------------------*/
345
346   PRIVATE void    statistics( fp )
347   FILE    *fp;
348   {
349       /* Print various statistics
350        */
351
352       int conflicts;                   /* Number of parse-table conflicts */
353
354       if( Verbose )
355       {
356           fprintf (fp, "\n");
357           fprintf (fp, "%4d/%-4d terminals\n",    USED_TERMS,    NUMTERMS   );
358           fprintf (fp, "%4d/%-4d nonterminals\n", USED_NONTERMS, NUMNONTERMS);
359           fprintf (fp, "%4d/%-4d productions\n",  Num_productions, MAXPROD   );
360   LL(     fprintf (fp, "%4d     actions\n",      (Cur_act - MINACT) +1     );)
361   OX(     lr_stats(fp );                                                      )
362       }
363
364   LL( conflicts = 0;                       )
365   OX( conflicts = lr_conflicts(fp);    )
366
367       if( fp == stdout )
368           fp = stderr;
369
370       if( Num_warnings - conflicts > 0 )
371           fprintf(fp, "%4d     warnings\n", Num_warnings - conflicts);
372
373       if(yynerrs)
374           fprintf(fp, "%4d     hard errors\n", yynerrs   );
375   }
376
377   /*-------------------------------------------------------------------*/
378
379   PUBLIC  void output( fmt, ... )
380   char    *fmt;
381   {
382       /* Works like printf(), but writes to the output file. See also: the
383        * outc() macro in parser.h
384        */
385
386       va_list    args;
387       va_start( args,  fmt );
388       vfprintf( Output, fmt, args );
389   }
```

```
Listing 4.34. continued...
390
391    /*----------------------------------------------------------------------*/
392
393    PUBLIC   void document( fmt, ... )
394    char     *fmt;
395    {
396        /* Works like printf() but writes to yyout.doc (provided that the file
397         * is being created.
398         */
399
400        va_list   args;
401
402        if( Doc_file )
403        {
404            va_start( args,   fmt );
405            vfprintf( Doc_file, fmt, args );
406        }
407    }
408
409    document_to( fp )
410    FILE    *fp;
411    {
412        /* Change document-file output to the indicated stream, or to previous
413         * stream if fp=NULL.
414         */
415
416        static FILE *oldfp;
417
418        if( fp )
419        {
420            oldfp    = Doc_file;
421            Doc_file = fp;
422        }
423        else
424            Doc_file = oldfp;
425    }
426
427    /*----------------------------------------------------------------------*/
428
429    PUBLIC   void lerror( fatal, fmt, ... )
430    char     *fmt;
431    {
432        /* This error-processing routine automatically generates a line number for
433         * the error. If "fatal" is true, exit() is called.
434         */
435
436        va_list     args;
437        char        *type;
438        extern int  yylineno;
439
440        if( fatal == WARNING )
441        {
442            ++Num_warnings;
443            if( No_warnings )
444                return;
445            type = "WARNING: ";
446        }
447        else
448        {
449            type = "ERROR: ";
```

Listing 4.34. continued...

```
450              ++yynerrs;
451          }
452
453      va_start( args,   fmt);
454      fprintf ( stdout, "%s %s (%s, line %d): ", PROG_NAME, type,
455                                          Input_file_name, yylineno );
456      vfprintf( stdout, fmt, args );
457
458      OX( if( Verbose && Doc_file )                                    )
459      OX( {                                                           )
460      OX(      fprintf ( Doc_file, "%s (line %d) ", type, yylineno );  )
461      OX(      vfprintf( Doc_file, fmt, args );                        )
462      OX( }                                                           )
463
464      yynerrs += (fatal != WARNING);
465
466      if( fatal == FATAL )
467          exit( EXIT_OTHER );
468  }
469
470  PUBLIC  void error( fatal, fmt, ... )
471  char     *fmt;
472  {
473      /* This error routine works like lerror() except that no line number is
474       * generated. The global error count is still modified, however.
475       */
476
477      va_list  args;
478      char     *type;
479
480      if( fatal == WARNING )
481      {
482          ++Num_warnings;
483          if( No_warnings )
484              return;
485          type = "WARNING: ";
486      }
487      else
488      {
489          type = "ERROR: ";
490          ++yynerrs;
491      }
492
493      va_start ( args,   fmt  );
494      fprintf ( stdout, type );
495      vfprintf ( stdout, fmt, args );
496
497      OX( if( Verbose && Doc_file )                      )
498      OX( {                                              )
499      OX(      fprintf ( Doc_file, type );               )
500      OX(      vfprintf ( Doc_file, fmt, args );         )
501      OX( }                                              )
502
503      if( fatal == FATAL )
504          exit( EXIT_OTHER );
505  }
506
507  PUBLIC char     *open_errmsg()
508  {
```

Listing 4.34. continued...

```
509        /* Return an error message that makes sense for a bad open */
510
511        extern   errno;
512        switch( errno )
513        {
514        case EACCES:        return "File is read only or a directory";
515        case EEXIST:        return "File already exists";
516        case EMFILE:        return "Too many open files";
517        case ENOENT:        return "File not found";
518        default:            return "Reason unknown";
519        }
520    }
521
522    /*--------------------------------------------------------------------*/
523
524    PRIVATE void tail()
525    {
526        /* Copy the remainder of input file to standard output. Yyparse will have
527         * terminated with the input pointer just past the %%. Attribute mapping
528         * ($$ to Yyval, $N to a stack reference, etc.) is done by the do_dollar()
529         * call.
530         *
531         * On entry, the parser will have read one token too far, so the first
532         * thing to do is print the current line number and lexeme.
533         */
534
535        extern int   yylineno ;     /* LeX generated */
536        extern char *yytext  ;      /* LeX generated */
537        int          c, i, sign;
538        char         fname[80], *p; /* field name in $<...>n */
539
540        output( "%s", yytext);                  /* Output newline following %% */
541
542        if( !No_lines )
543            output( "\n#line %d \"%s\"\n", yylineno, Input_file_name );
544
545        ii_unterm();                            /* Lex will have terminated yytext */
546
547        while( (c = ii_advance()) != 0 )
548        {
549            if( c == -1 )
550            {
551                ii_flush(1);
552                continue;
553            }
554            else if( c == '$' )
555            {
556                ii_mark_start();
557
558                if( (c = ii_advance()) != '<' )
559                    *fname = '\0';
560                else                                    /* extract name in $<foo>1 */
561                {
562                    p = fname;
563                    for(i=sizeof(fname); --i > 0  &&  (c=ii_advance()) != '>';)
564                        *p++ = c;
565                    *p++ = '\0';
566
```

Listing 4.34. continued...

```
567                         if( c == '>' )                    /* truncate name if necessary */
568                             c = ii_advance();
569                     }
570
571                 if( c == '$' )
572                     output( do_dollar( DOLLAR_DOLLAR, -1, 0, NULL, fname ) );
573                 else
574                 {
575
576                     if( c != '-' )
577                         sign = 1 ;
578                     else
579                     {
580                         sign = -1;
581                         c = ii_advance();
582                     }
583
584                     for( i = 0; isdigit(c); c = ii_advance() )
585                         i = (i * 10) + (c - '0');
586
587                     ii_pushback(1);
588                     output( do_dollar(i * sign, -1, ii_lineno(), NULL, fname ) );
589                 }
590             }
591         else if( c != '\r' )
592             outc( c );
593     }
594 }
```

Listing 4.35. *lldollar.c*— $ Attribute Processing (**LLama** Version).

```
1  #include <stdio.h>
2  #include <tools/debug.h>
3  #include <tools/set.h>
4  #include <tools/hash.h>
5  #include "parser.h"
6
7  PUBLIC char *do_dollar( num, rhs_size, lineno, prod, field )
8  int        num;                                      /* the N in $N */
9  int        rhs_size;                                 /* not used    */
10 int        lineno;                                   /* not used    */
11 PRODUCTION *prod;                                    /* not used    */
12 char       *field;                                   /* not used    */
13 {
14     static char buf[32];
15
16     if( num == DOLLAR_DOLLAR )
17         return "Yy_vsp->left";
18     else
19     {
20         sprintf( buf, "(Yy_vsp[%d].right)",  num );   /* assuming that num */
21         return buf;                                   /* has < 16 digits   */
22     }
23 }
```

Listing 4.36. *signon.c*— Print Sign-on Message

```
1   #include <stdio.h>
2   #include <tools/debug.h>
3   #include <tools/hash.h>
4   #include <tools/set.h>
5   #include "parser.h"
6
7   PUBLIC void        signon()
8   {
9       /* Print the sign-on message. Note that since the console is opened
10       * explicitly, the message is printed even if both stdout and stderr are
11       * redirected. I'm using the ANSI __TIME__ and __DATE__ macros to get the
12       * time and date of compilation.
13       */
14
15      FILE *screen;
16
17      UX( if( !(screen = fopen("/dev/tty", "w")) )          )
18      MS( if( !(screen = fopen("con:",       "w")) )          )
19              screen = stderr;
20
21      LL( fprintf(screen, "LLAMA 1.0 [" __DATE__ " " __TIME__ "]\n" ); )
22      OX( fprintf(screen, "OCCS  1.0 [" __DATE__ " " __TIME__ "]\n" ); )
23
24      fprintf( screen,"(C) " __DATE__ ", Allen I. Holub. All rights reserved.\n");
25      if( screen != stderr )
26          fclose(screen);
27  }
```

4.11 Exercises

4.1.   A standard, recursive, in-order, binary-tree traversal routine looks like this:

```
typedef struct node
{
    int key;
    struct node *left, *right;
}
NODE;

traverse( root )
NODE    *root;
{
    if( !root )
        return;

    traverse( root->left );
    printf( "%d\n", root->key );
    traverse( root->right );
}
```

Write a nonrecursive binary-tree traversal function that uses a local stack to hold pointers to the parent of the current subtree rather than using the run-time stack, as is implicit in the recursive algorithm.

4.2.   A palindrome is a word or phrase that reads the same backwards as forwards, such as the Napoleonic palindrome: "Able was I ere I saw Elba."

a. Write a grammar that recognizes simple palindromes made up of digits. Each digit should appear exactly twice, and the center of the palindrome should be marked with a | character. For example, the input string *1234|4321* should be recognized.

b. Write a program that uses a push-down automata to recognize palindromes such as the foregoing.

c. Can you modify your grammar to recognize real palindromes, such as "able was I ere I saw Elba." If so, implement the grammar; if not, explain why.

4.3. Write a computer program that translates the right-linear grammars discussed in Chapter 3 into the state-machine grammars discussed in the same chapter.

4.4. Determine the FIRST and FOLLOW sets for all nonterminals in the first 10 productions in the grammar for C, presented in Appendix C. Is this grammar LL(1)? Why or why not?

4.5. Modify the following grammar so that it is not ambiguous and is LL(1):

$$
\begin{array}{rcl}
expr & \rightarrow & - \; expr \\
      & | & * \; expr \\
      & | & expr * expr \\
      & | & expr \, / \, expr \\
      & | & expr = expr \\
      & | & expr + expr \\
      & | & expr - expr \\
      & | & (\; expr \;)
\end{array}
$$

Operator precedence and associativity should be according to the following table (higher lines in the table are higher precedence operators).

Associativity	Operator	Description
left to right	( )	parentheses for grouping (highest precedence)
left to right	– *	unary minus and pointer dereference
left to right	* /	multiplication, division
left to right	+ –	addition, subtraction
right to left	=	assignment (lowest precedence)

4.6. Write an LL(1) grammar for the state-machine-description language presented as an exercise in the last chapter, and implement a table-driven, top-down parser for that language.

4.7. Is the following grammar LL(1)? Why or why not? If it isn't, convert it to LL(1).

$$
\begin{array}{rcl}
s & \rightarrow & symbol \; stuff \\
  & | & TOKEN \; TOKEN \; stuff \\
  & | & star\_list \; stuff \\
star\_list & \rightarrow & star\_list \; STAR \\
  & | & \varepsilon \\
symbol & \rightarrow & \textbf{TOKEN} \\
stuff & \rightarrow & \textbf{ANOTHER\_TOKEN}
\end{array}
$$

4.8. Design and implement a desk-calculator program using **LLama** and LᶠX. The program should take process an input file that contains various semicolon-terminated statements. Support C syntax and the following C operators:

```
+    -    /    %    *    ^    ~    >>    <<
+=   -=   /=   %=   *=   ^=   ~=   >>=   <<=
++   --
(    )
```

The − is both unary and binary minus. The * is a multiply. Your calculator should support a reasonable number of variables (say, 128) with arbitrary names. A variable is declared implicitly the first time it's used. In addition to the foregoing operators, your calculator should support the following pseudo subroutine:

```
printf ("` \I{format} `",...);
```

The `printf()` pseudo subroutine should work like the normal `printf()`, except that it needs to support only the `%d`, `%x`, `%o`, and `%f` conversions. It does not have to support field widths, left justification, and so forth.

4.9.   Modify the calculator built in the previous exercise so that it generates the assembly language necessary to evaluate the expression, rather than actually evaluating the expression at run time.

4.10. Modify **LLama** so that it automatically makes the following transformations in the input grammar. Productions of the form:

```
s : symbol stuff
  | symbol other stuff
  ;
```

should be transformed to:

```
s : symbol s'
  ;
s': stuff
  | other stuff
  ;
```

The transformations should be applied recursively for as long as the initial symbols on the right-hand side are the same. For example,

```
s : symbol other
  | symbol other stuff
  ;
```

should become:

```
s : symbol s'
  ;
s': other
  | other stuff
  ;
```

should become:

```
s   : symbol s'
    ;
s'  : other s''
    ;
s'' : stuff
    | /* empty */
    ;
```

4.11. Modify the interactive debugging environment in yydebug.c so that you can look at the actual code associated with an action. You can do this by storing all action code in a file rather than in internal buffers and keeping a pointer to the file position for the start of the code in the **occs** symbol table (rather than a string pointer). Normally, this intermediate file would be destroyed by **LLama**, but the file should remain in place if *–D* is specified on the command line. To make this file available from the debugger, **LLama** will need to output the source code for an array indexed by production number which evaluates to the correct file position. Finally, add two commands to yydebug.c: The first prompts for a production number and displays the associated code in the stack window. The second causes the code to be printed in the comments window every time a reduction occurs.

4.12. Several arrays output by **LLama** are used only for debugging, and these arrays take up unnecessary space in the executable image Modify **LLama** and *yydebug.c* so that this information is stored in binary in an auxiliary file that is read by the debugger at run time. Don't read the entire file into memory—use `lseek()` to find the required strings and transfer them directly to the screen.

4.13. The action code and the debugging-environment subroutines in *yydebug.c* could be overlays—code in an action doesn't call debugger subroutines and vice versa. Arrange for overlays to be used for the debugger to save space in the executable image.

5

Bottom-Up Parsing

The first part of this chapter looks at bottom-up parsing in general—at how the bottom-up parse process works, how it can be controlled by a state machine, and how the state machine itself, and the associated tables, are generated. The second part of the chapter looks at a practical implementation of the foregoing: The internals of **occs**, a **yacc**-like program that builds a bottom-up parser from a grammar, is discussed in depth, as is the **occs** output file that implements the parser. There is no extended example of how **occs** is used because Chapter Six, in which code generation is discussed, provides such an example.

Bottom-up parsers such as the ones created by **yacc** and **occs** work with a class of grammars called *LALR(1)* grammars, which are special cases of the more inclusive *LR(1)* class. As with the LL(1) notation, the *(1)* in LR(1) means that one token of lookahead is required to resolve conflicts in the parse. Similarly, the first L means that input is read left to right. The *R* means that a *rightmost* derivation is used to construct the parse tree—the rightmost nonterminal is always expanded instead of expanding the leftmost nonterminal, as was done in the previous chapter. The *LA* in LALR(1) stands for "look ahead"—information about certain lookahead characters is actually built into LALR(1) parse tables. I'll explain the exact characteristics of these grammars when I discuss how bottom-up parse tables are created, below. All LL(1) grammars are also LR(1) grammars, but not the other way around.

LALR(1) grammars.

Most LR grammars cannot be parsed with recursive-descent parsers, and LR and LALR grammars tend to be more useful than LL grammars because they are easier to write—there aren't so many restrictions placed on them. This grammatical flexibility is a real advantage when writing a compiler. LR parsers have many disadvantages, however. It is difficult to write an LR parser unless you have a tool, such as **occs** or **yacc**, to help you construct the tables used by the parser. Also, the tables are larger than LL parse tables and the parser tends to be slower. LR error recovery is difficult to do—error recovery in **yacc**-generated parsers is notoriously bad.

Advantages and disadvantages of LR parsers.

5.1 How Bottom-Up Parsing Works*

Bottom-up parsers use push-down automata to build the parse tree from the bottom up rather than from the top down. Instead of starting at the root, as is the case with a top-down parser, a bottom-up parser starts with the leaves and, when it's collected enough leaves, it connects them together with a common root. The process is best illustrated with an example. I'll use the following expression grammar:

0.	s	$\rightarrow$	e
1.	e	$\rightarrow$	$e+t$
2.		|	t
3.	t	$\rightarrow$	$t*f$
4.		|	f
5.	f	$\rightarrow$	(e)
6.		|	**NUM**

The nonterminals are e (for expression), t (for term), and f (for factor). The terminals are +, *, (,), and **NUM**. (**NUM** is a number—a collection of ASCII characters in the range ′0′ to ′9′). Multiplication is of higher precedence than addition: since the star is further down in the grammar, it will be lower on the parse tree than the plus unless parentheses force it to go otherwise. The special symbol s is called the *goal symbol*. A bottom-up grammar must have one unique goal symbol, and only one production can have that goal symbol on its left-hand side. Note that this grammar can't be parsed from the top down because it's left recursive.

A bottom-up parser is a push-down automaton; it needs a state machine to drive it and a stack to remember the current state. For now, we'll ignore the mechanics of the state machine and just watch the stack. The parse process works as follows:

(1) If the top few items on the stack form the right-hand side of a production, pop these items and replace them with the equivalent left-hand side. This procedure (popping the number of elements on a right-hand side and pushing the left-hand side) is known as a *reduce* operation.

(2) Otherwise, push the current input symbol onto the stack and advance the input. This operation is known as a *shift*.

(3) If the previous operation was a reduce that resulted in the goal symbol at the top of stack, *accept* the input—the parse is complete. Otherwise, go to 1.

Don't confuse shifting and reducing with pushing and popping. A *shift* always pushes a token, but it also advances the input. A *reduce* does zero or more pops followed by a push. (There are no pops on ε productions.) I'll illustrate the process with a parse of 1*(2+3). Initially, the stack (on the left, below) is empty and none of the input characters (on the right, below) have been read:

	1 * (2 + 3)

Since there's no legitimate right-hand side on the stack, apply rule two: shift a **NUM** and advance past it in the input.

NUM	* (2 + 3)

Note that the input character 1 has been translated to a **NUM** token as part of the input process. The right-hand side of Production 6 is now at top of stack, so reduce by $f\rightarrow$**NUM**. Pop the **NUM** and replace it with an f:

	* (2 + 3)
f	* (2 + 3)

Margin notes:
Goal symbol.

Bottom-up parsing with a PDA, basic algorithm.

Reduce.

Shift.

Accept.

Shift≠push, reduce≠pop.

The previous operation has put another right-hand side on the stack, this time for Production 4 ($t \rightarrow f$); reduce by popping the f and pushing a t to replace it:

	* (2 + 3)
t	* (2 + 3)

The t at top of stack also forms a right-hand side, but there's a problem here. You could apply Production 2 ($e \rightarrow t$), popping the t and replacing it with an e, but you don't want to do this because there's no production that has an e followed by a * (the next input symbol) on its right-hand side. There is, however, a production with a t followed by a * (Production 3: $t \rightarrow t*f$). So, by looking ahead at the next input symbol, the conflict is resolved in favor of the shift (rather than a reduction by Production 2) in the hope that another f will eventually get onto the stack to complete the right-hand side for Production 3. The stack now looks like this:

$t *$	(2 + 3)

There's still no reasonable right-hand side on the stack, so shift the next input symbol to the stack:

$t * ($	2 + 3)

and the 2 as well:

$t * ($ **NUM**	+ 3)

Now there is another legitimate right-hand side on the stack: the **NUM**. The parser can apply the same productions it used to process the earlier **NUM**:

$t * ($	+ 3)
$t * (f$	+ 3)
$t * ($	+ 3)
$t * (t$	+ 3)

The next input symbol is a plus sign. Since the grammar doesn't have any productions in which a plus follows a t, it applies Production 2 ($e \rightarrow t$) instead of shifting:

$t * ($	+ 3)
$t * (e$	+ 3)

Again, since there's still input, shift the next input symbol rather than reducing by Production 1.

$t * (e +$	3)

and the next one:

$t * (e +$ **NUM**	)

The number forms a legitimate right-hand side, so the parsers process it as before:

$t * (e +$	)
$t * (e + f$	)
$t * (e +$	)
$t * (e + t$	)

Another right-hand side has now appeared on the stack—$e+t$ is the right-hand side of Production 1—so the parser can apply this production, popping the entire right-hand side (three objects) and pushing the corresponding left-hand side:

$t * (e +$	)

$t * (e$	$)$

$t * ($	$)$

$t * (e$	$)$

As before, the parser defers the application of Production 0 because there's still input; it shifts the final input symbol onto the stack:

$t * (e)$

thereby creating another right-hand side—(e) is the right-hand side of Production 5, $f{\rightarrow}(e)$. Reduce by this production:

$t * (e$

$t * ($

$t *$

$t * f$

The three symbols now at top of stack form the right-hand side of Production 3 ($t{\rightarrow}t*f$); pop them and push the left-hand side:

$t *$

t

t

Reduce by Production 2:

e

Finally, since there's no more input, apply Production 0:

s

Since the goal symbol is at the top of stack, the machine accepts and the parse is complete. The entire process is summarized in Table 5.1. Figure 5.1 shows the parse tree as it's created by this parse. Notice that you can determine the state of the stack for any of the partially created trees by reading across the roots of the various subtrees. For example, the tops of the subtrees shown in Figure 5.1(m) are (from left to right) t, $*$, $($, e, $+$, and f, and these same symbols comprise the stack at the equivalent time in the parse. So, you can look at the stack as a mechanism for keeping track of the roots of the partially-collected subtrees.

Relationship between stack and parse tree.

5.2 Recursion in Bottom-Up Parsing*

Hitherto, left recursion has been something to avoid in a grammar, primarily because top-down parsers can't handle it. The situation is reversed in a bottom-up parser: Left recursion should always be used for those lists in which associativity is not an issue. Right recursion can be used for right-associative lists, but it should be used only when right associativity is required. The reason for this change can be seen by looking at how right- and left-recursive lists are parsed by a bottom-up parser. Consider a left-recursive grammar, such as the following list of numbers:

List processing in a bottom-up parser.

Table 5.1. A Bottom-Up Parse of 1*(2+3)

Stack	Input	Next action	See Fig. 5.1
	1 * (2 + 3)	Shift **NUM**	a
NUM	* (2 + 3)	Reduce by $f \rightarrow$ **NUM**	b
	* (2 + 3)		
f	* (2 + 3)	Reduce by $f \rightarrow t$	c
	* (2 + 3)		
t	* (2 + 3)	Shift *	d
t *	(2 + 3)	Shift (	e
t * (	2 + 3)	Shift **NUM**	f
t * (**NUM**	+ 3)	Reduce by $f \rightarrow$ **NUM**	g
t * (	+ 3)		
t * (f	+ 3)	Reduce by $t \rightarrow f$	h
t * (	+ 3)		
t * (t	+ 3)	Reduce by $e \rightarrow t$	i
t * (	+ 3)		
t * (e	+ 3)	Shift +	j
t * (e +	3)	Shift **NUM**	k
t * (e + **NUM**	)	Reduce by $f \rightarrow$ **NUM**	l
t * (e +	)		
t * (e + f	)	Reduce by $t \rightarrow f$	m
t * (e +	)		
t * (e + t	)	Reduce by $e \rightarrow e+t$	n
t * (	)		
t * (e	)	Shift)	o
t * (e)		Reduce by $f \rightarrow (e)$	p
t *			
t * f		Reduce oy $t \rightarrow t$* f	q
t		Reduce by $e \rightarrow t$	r
e		Reduce by $s \rightarrow e$	s
s		Accept	t

1. $list$ $\rightarrow$ $list$ **NUM**
2. | **NUM**

The input 1 2 3 generates the following bottom-up parse:

Stack	Input	Comments
—	1 2 3	
NUM	2 3	shift a **NUM**
$list$	2 3	reduce by $list \rightarrow$ **NUM**
$list$ **NUM**	3	shift a **NUM**
$list$	3	reduce by $list \rightarrow list$ **NUM**
$list$ **NUM**		shift a **NUM**
$list$		reduce by $list \rightarrow list$ **NUM**

The stack never grows by more than two elements because a reduction occurs every time that a new **NUM** is shifted. Note that the nonrecursive production, $list \rightarrow$ **NUM** is applied first because the parser must get a $list$ onto the stack in order to process the rest of the list elements. This is always the case in left-recursive lists such as the foregoing, and is

Nonrecursive list element reduced first.

Figure 5.1. Evolution of Parse Tree for `1*(2+3)`

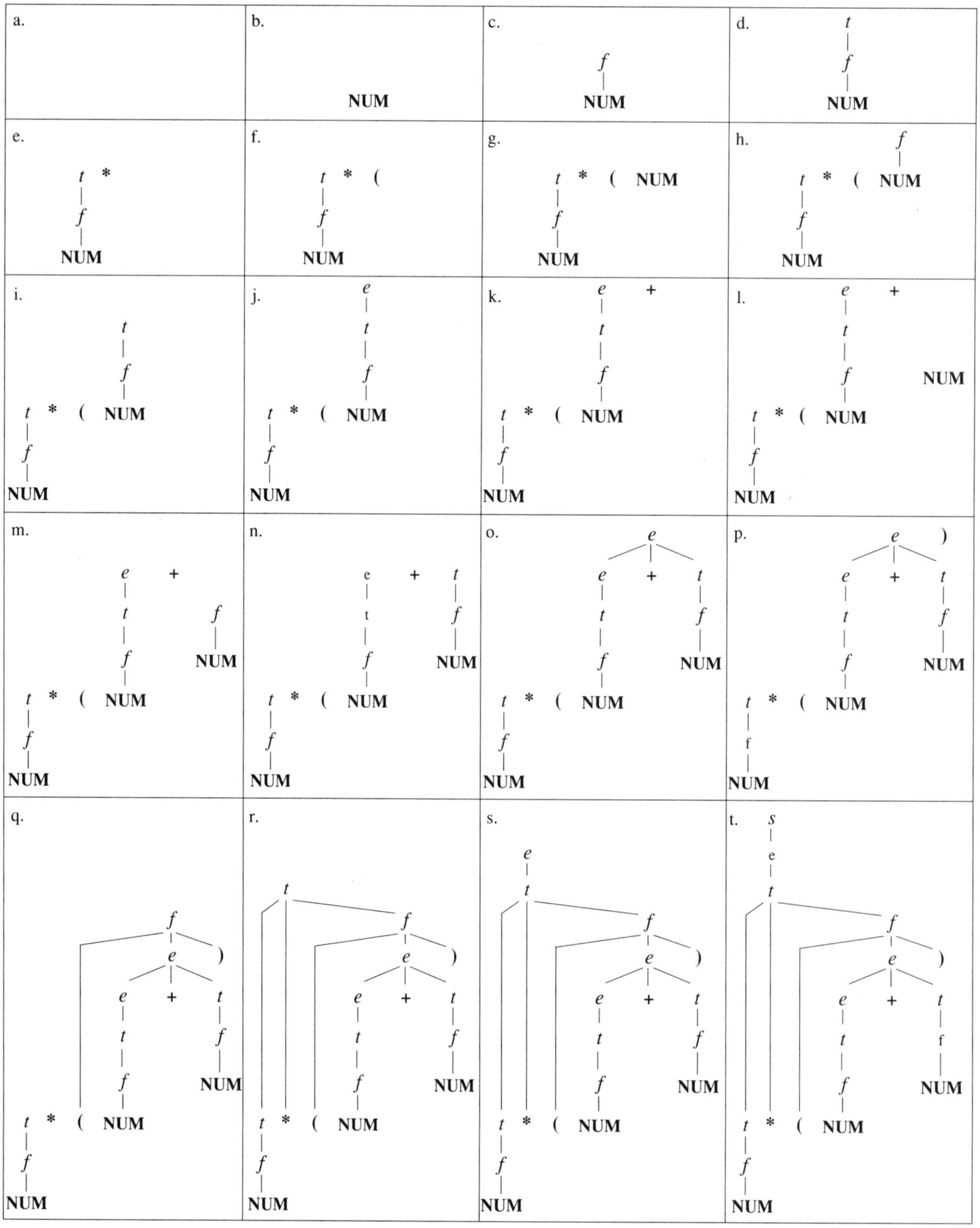

handy when doing code generation because it provides a hook for initialization actions. (More on this in the next chapter.)

Now consider a right-recursive list, such as the following:

1. *list* → **NUM** *list*
2. | **NUM**

Right-recursive lists use a lot of stack.

The input 1 2 3 now generates the following bottom-up parse:

Stack	Input	Comments
–	1 2 3	Shift a **NUM**
NUM	2 3	Shift a **NUM**
NUM NUM	3	Shift a **NUM**
NUM NUM NUM		Apply list→**NUM**
NUM NUM *list*		Apply list→**NUM** list
NUM *list*		Apply list→**NUM** list
list		Apply list→**NUM** list

Here, all of the list elements are pushed onto the stack <u>before</u> any of them are processed via a reduction. This behavior is always the case—right-recursive productions use a lot of stack because all the list elements must be pushed before a reduction can occur, so it's worth avoiding right associativity if at all possible. Of course, you can't do this in an expression grammar because certain operators just have to associate in certain ways. Lists, however, are another matter.

5.3 Implementing the Parser as a State Machine*

I need to introduce a few terms at this point. At the risk of repeating myself, a *shift* is the process of moving a token from the input stream to the stack—push the current token and advance the input. A *reduce* is the process of replacing a right-hand side on the stack with the matching left-hand side—pop as many items as there are on the right-hand side of a production and push the left-hand side. A *viable prefix* is a partially parsed expression—an incomplete derivation. In a bottom-up parser, the symbols on the parse stack from bottom to top, are identical to the viable prefix, read left to right.

Shift, reduce, viable prefix.

A *handle* is a right-hand side on the top few items of the stack. The parser scans the stack looking for a handle, which when found, triggers a reduce operation. Put another way, a reduce can be performed when the rightmost symbols of the viable prefix form a right-hand side. Strictly speaking, a handle is a right-hand side which, when found on the stack, triggers a reduction. The parser might defer a reduction even though a right-hand side is at the top of the stack—the associativity and precedence rules built into the grammar might require that more input symbols be read before any reductions occur. In this situation, a right-hand side does not form a handle because it doesn't trigger a reduction. In most situations, however, a reduction occurs as soon as the right-hand side appears on the stack.

Handle.

Not all right-hand sides in viable prefix form handles.

To automate a bottom-up parser, some mechanism is needed for recognizing handles as they appear on the stack. Of course, you could do this by brute force—scanning the stack and comparing what you find there to a list of right-hand sides—but this method is so inefficient as to be impractical. It's better to build a state machine that keeps track of all the push and pop operations. The condition of the stack can then be inferred from a knowledge of what items have been pushed or popped. The accepting states in the machine trigger a reduce operation. Nonaccepting states represent either a shift or the push of a left-hand side that is part of a reduce operation. The state machine in Figure 5.2. serves to illustrate some of the concepts involved. This machine implements the

Using a state machine to recognize handles.

following grammar, a subset of the one used in the previous example.

0.	s	$\rightarrow$	e
1.	e	$\rightarrow$	$e + t$
2.		$\mid$	t
3.	t	$\rightarrow$	**NUM**

This grammar recognizes expressions composed either of single numbers or of alternating numbers and plus signs. The expressions associate from left to right. The state machine can be viewed as a sort of super syntax diagram that reflects the syntactic structure of an entire language, not just of the individual productions. It's as if you formed an NFA by combining the syntax diagrams for all the productions in the grammar.

Figure 5.2. A Simple LR State Machine

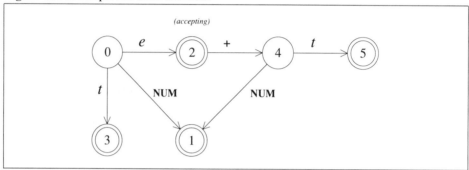

Stack remembers state transitions. Arrows indicate pushes.

The automaton's stack keeps track of state transitions. The current state is the one whose number is at top of stack. The direction of the arrows in the state diagram represents pushes. (The state number associated with the next state is pushed.) Pops cause us to retrace the initial series of pushes. That is, the stack serves as a record of the various state transitions that were made to get to the current state. You can retrace those transitions backwards by popping the states. For example, starting at State 0, a zero is at the top of the stack. Shifting a **NUM** results in a transition from State 0 to State 1, and a 1 is pushed to record this transition. Reducing by $t\rightarrow$**NUM** involves a pop (which causes a retrace from State 1 back to State 0) and a push of a 3 (which causes a transition from State 0 to State 3). The parser can retrace the original path through the machine because that information is on the stack—the state that you came from is at the top of the stack after the pop part of the reduction.

How terminals and nonterminals get onto stack.

It's important to notice here that the <u>only</u> way that a terminal symbol can get onto the stack is by the push that occurs in a shift operation, and the <u>only</u> way that a nonterminal symbol can get onto the stack is by the push that occurs during a reduction.

States and handles.

The purpose of the state machine is to detect handles. In this machine, States 1, 2, 3, and 5 represent the recognition of a handle. (A reduce from State 2 also terminates the parse successfully.) Entering one of these states usually triggers a reduce operation (depending on the next input character). For example, if the machine is in State 1, the parser must have just shifted a **NUM**, so it will reduce by $t\rightarrow$**NUM**. If the machine is in State 3, the parser must have just reduced by a production that had a t on its left-hand side, and it will do another reduce (by $e\rightarrow t$). If the machine's in State 2, the parser reduces by $s\rightarrow e$ only if the next input character is the end-of-input marker, otherwise it will shift to State 4. State 5 tells the parser that an e, plus, and t must have been pushed so the handle $e+t$ is recognized, and it reduces by $e\rightarrow e+t$. Since the state stack itself, along with a knowledge of what those states represent, is sufficient to see what's going on, there's no reason to keep a stack of actual symbols, as I did in the previous section.

LR parse tables: *Action* and *Goto* components.

The state machine from Figure 5.2. is represented in array form in Table 5.2—columns are possible input symbols (in the *Action* section) or nonterminal symbols (in the *Goto* section). The special symbol ⊢ in the *Action* table is an end-of-input marker. The rows represent possible states of the machine. The basic parsing algorithm is shown in Table 5.3.

Table 5.2. Array Representation of an LR State Machine

		Action			Goto	
		⊢	**NUM**	+	*e*	*t*
	0	–	s1	–	2	3
	1	r3	–	r3	–	–
Top	2	Accept	–	s4	–	–
of	3	r2	–	r2	–	–
Stack	4	–	s1	–	–	5
	5	r1	–	r1	–	–

I'll demonstrate the parse process by parsing the expression `1+2+3`. (The entire parse is summarized in Table 5.4—I'll do the parse step by step here, however.) The algorithm starts off by pushing 0, the state number of the start state.

Table-driven LR parse, an example.

| 0 | | `1 + 2 + 3 ⊢` |

Action[0][**NUM**] holds an *s1*, so shift a 1 onto the stack entering State 1. Advance the input as part of the shift operation:

| 0 1 | | `+ 2 + 3 ⊢` |

Now, since the new top-of-stack symbol is a 1, the parser looks at Action[1][+] and finds an r3 (reduce by production <u>3</u>). The algorithm in Figure 5.2 tells the parser to execute a code-generation action and pop one item off the stack (because there's one item on the right-hand side of *t*→**NUM**).

| 0 | | `+ 2 + 3 ⊢` |

The parser now has to figure the Goto transition. The left-hand side of Production 3 is a *t* and popping the 1 uncovered the 0, so the parser consults Goto[0][*t*], finding a 3, which it pushes onto the state stack:

| 0 3 | | `+ 2 + 3 ⊢` |

Spinning back up to the top of the `while` loop, Action[3][+] is an *r2*, a reduction by Production 2 (*e*→*t*). The parser pops one item and then pushes the contents of Goto[0][*e*], State 2:

| 0 | | `+ 2 + 3 ⊢` |

| 0 2 | | `+ 2 + 3 ⊢` |

Looping again, Action[2][+] is an *s4*—shift a 4, advancing the input:

| 0 2 4 | | `2 + 3 ⊢` |

Action[4][**NUM**] is an *s1* so we shift again:

| 0 2 4 1 | | `+ 3 ⊢` |

Action[1][+] is an *r3*.

| 0 2 4 | | `+ 3 ⊢` |

This time, however, the uncovered top-of-stack item is a 4, not a 0, as it was the first time the parser reduced by Production 3. Goto[4][*t*] is a 5, so the machine goes to State 5 by

Table 5.3. State-Machine-Driven LR Parser Algorithm

```
          push( 0 )
          while( Action[TOS][input] ≠ Accept )
          {
             if( Action[TOS][input] = − )
                  error( )
               else if ( Action[TOS][input] = sX )
                  push( X )
                  advance( )
               else if ( Action[TOS][input] = rX )
                  act( X )
                  pop( as many items as are in the RHS of Production X )
                  push( Goto[ uncovered TOS ][ LHS of Production X ] )
          }
          accept( );
```

	Definitions:
Action	Columns in the *Action* part of the state-machine array.
accept()	Return success status. An accept is actually a reduction by Production 0 on end of input.
act(X)	Perform the action associated with a reduction of Production X. This action usually generates code.
advance()	Discard current input symbol and get the next one.
error()	Print error message and do some sort of error recovery.
Goto	Columns in the *Goto* part of the state-machine array.
input	Current input symbol.
Stack	State stack.
push(*X*)	Push state *X* onto the stack.
pop(*N*)	Pop *N* items from the stack.
TOS	State number at the top of the stack.

pushing a 5 onto the stack:

```
0 2 4 5                          + 3 ⊢
```

Looping yet again, Action[5][+] is an r1, so an *e*, plus, and *t* must be on the stack, and the parser reduces by Production 1 ($e \rightarrow e + t$). Note that the current state (5) can only be reached by making transitions on an *e*, +, and *t*. Since each forward-going transition is a push, the stack must contain these three symbols. Since there are three items on the right-hand side of the production, pop three states:

```
0                                + 3 ⊢
```

and then push Goto[0][*e*] to replace them:

```
0 2                              + 3 ⊢
```

Next, since Action[2][+] is a s4, the parser goes to State 4 with a shift:

```
0 2 4                            3 ⊢
```

Action[4][**NUM**] is an s1 so it shifts to State 1:

```
0 2 4 1                          ⊢
```

Action[1][⊢] calls for a reduction by Production 3:

0 2 4	⊢
0 2 4 5	⊢

Action[5][⊢] is a reduction by Production 1:

0 2 4	⊢
0 2	⊢
0	⊢
0 2	⊢

Action[2][⊢] is an accept action, so the parse is finished. The tree implied by the previous parse is shown in Figure 5.3.

Table 5.4. A Bottom-Up Parse of 1+2+3 Using a State Machine

State Stack	Symbols	Input	Notes
0	$	1 + 2 + 3 ⊢	*Push start state*
0 1	$ **NUM**	+ 2 + 3 ⊢	*Shift* **NUM**
0	$	+ 2 + 3 ⊢	*Reduce by t→***NUM**
0 3	$ t	+ 2 + 3 ⊢	
0	$	+ 2 + 3 ⊢	*Reduce by e→t*
0 2	$ e	+ 2 + 3 ⊢	
0 2 4	$ e +	2 + 3 ⊢	*Shift +*
0 2 4 1	$ e + **NUM**	+ 3 ⊢	*Shift* **NUM**
0 2 4	$ e +	+ 3 ⊢	*Reduce by t→***NUM**
0 2 4 5	$ e + t	+ 3 ⊢	
0 2 4	$ e +	+ 3 ⊢	*Reduce by e→e + t*
0 2	$ e	+ 3 ⊢	
0	$	+ 3 ⊢	
0 2	$ e	+ 3 ⊢	
0 2 4	$ e +	3 ⊢	*Shift +*
0 2 4 1	$ e + **NUM**	⊢	*Shift* **NUM**
0 2 4	$ e +	⊢	*Reduce by t→***NUM**
0 2 4 5	$ e + t	⊢	
0 2 4	$ e +	⊢	*Reduce by e→e + t*
0 2	$ e	⊢	
0	$	⊢	
0 1	$ e	⊢	*Accept*

There is one difference between a symbol-oriented stack, as was discussed in the previous section, and a state stack: the latter requires an initial push of the start state that wasn't required on the symbol stack. I'm using a $ to hold the place of this extra stack item on the symbol stack. Also, note that the term *accept* is often used in two ways when PDA-based parsers are discussed. First of all, there are normal accepting states, in this case States 1, 2, 3, and 5. A transition into an accepting state signifies that a handle has been recognized. The action associated with these states is a reduce (and the associated code-generation actions, which are discussed below). You can also use the word *accept* to signify that a complete program has been parsed, however. If you look at the parser as a recognizer program, the machine as a whole *accepts* or *rejects* an input sentence. (A *sentence* in this context is a complete program, as represented by the grammar. A valid sentence in a grammar forms a complete parse tree.)

Difference between symbol and state stack.

Accept.

Reject.
Sentence.

Figure 5.3. A Parse Tree for 1+2+3

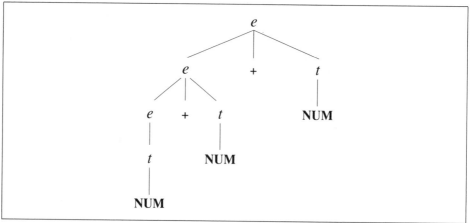

5.4 Error Recovery in an LR Parser*

Stack lacks lookahead information for error recovery.

Panic-mode error recovery.

Error recovery in a bottom-up parser is notoriously difficult. The problem is that, unlike a top-down parser's stack, the bottom-up parse stack contains no information about what symbols are expected in the input. The stack tells you only what's already been seen. One effective technique, called *panic-mode* error recovery, tries to get around this difficulty by using the parse tables themselves to find legal input symbols. It works as follows:

(0)   Error recovery is triggered when an error transition is read from the parse table entry for the current lookahead and top-of-stack symbols (when there's no legal outgoing transition from a state on the current input symbol).

(1)   Remember the current condition of the stack.

(2)   Discard the state at the top of stack.

(3)   Look in the parse table and see if there's a legal transition on the current input symbol and the uncovered stack item. If so, the parser has recovered and the parse is allowed to progress, using the modified stack. If there's no legal transition, and the stack is not empty, go to (2).

(4)   If all items on the stack are discarded, restore the stack to its original condition, discard an input symbol, and go to (2).

The algorithm continues either until it can start parsing again or until the complete input file is absorbed. Table 5.5 shows what happens when the incorrect input 1++2 is parsed using the simple LR state machine in Table 5.2 on page 345. Messages should be suppressed if a second error happens right on the tail of the first one in order to avoid cascading error messages. Nothing should be printed if an error happens within a limited number (four or five is a good choice) of parse cycles (shift or reduce operations) from the point of the previous error.

Avoid cascading error messages.

5.5 The Value Stack and Attribute Processing*

The next issue is how bottom-up parsers, such as the one generated by **occs**, handle attributes and use them to generate code. In a recursive-descent parser, attributes can be computed anywhere in the parse process, but they are only passed in two places: Inherited attributes are passed when a subroutine is called, and synthesized attributes are passed when the subroutine returns. Since a table-driven LR parser doesn't use

Attributes in recursive descent.

Table 5.5. Error Recovery for `1++2`

Stack				Input	Comments
− −				1 + + 2 ⊢	*Shift start state*
0 $				1 + + 2 ⊢	*Shift **NUM** (goto 1)*
0 $	1 **NUM**			+ + 2 ⊢	*Reduce by Production 3 (t→**NUM**)* *(Return to 0, goto 3)*
0 $	3 t			+ + 2 ⊢	*Reduce by Production 2 (e→t)* *(Return to 0, goto 2)*
0 $	2 e			+ + 2 ⊢	*Shift + (goto 4)*
0 $	2 e	4 +		+ 2 ⊢	*ERROR (no transition in table)* *Pop one state from stack*
0 $	2 e			+ 2 ⊢	*There is a transition from 2 on +* *Error recovery is successful*
0 $	2 e			+ 2 ⊢	*Shift + (goto 4)*
0 $	2 e	4 +		2 ⊢	*Shift **NUM** (goto 1)*
0 $	2 e	4 +	1 **NUM**	2 ⊢	*Shift **NUM** (goto 1)*
0 $	2 e	4 +	1 **NUM**	⊢	*Reduce by Production 3 (t→**NUM**)* *(Return to 4, goto 5)*
0 $	2 e	4 +	5 t	⊢	*Reduce by Production 1 (e→e+t)* *(Return to 0, goto 2)*
0 $	2 e			⊢	*Accept*

Bottom-up parser uses
synthesized attributes.

subroutine calls, another method is required to pass attributes and execute code-generation actions. To simplify matters, it's rarely necessary to use inherited attributes in a bottom-up parser; I'll concentrate on synthesized attributes only.

Reviewing the relationship between a bottom-up parse and the parse tree itself, a production like $e{\rightarrow}t{+}e$ generates the following tree:

In a bottom-up parse, the t is pushed onto the stack by means of a reduction by $t{\rightarrow}$**NUM**, the plus is just shifted, then there is a flurry of activity which terminates by the bottom e being pushed as part of a reduction by either $e{\rightarrow}e{+}t$ or $e{\rightarrow}t$. In any event, once the t, plus, and e are on the stack, a handle is recognized; all three symbols are popped, and an e (the left-hand side) is pushed. Synthesized attributes move up the parse tree—from the children to the parent, and they are passed during a reduce operation—when the handle is replaced with the left-hand side. The synthesized attribute is attached to the left-hand side that is pushed as part of a reduce. Inherited attributes, which go from a parent to a child, would be pushed as part of a shift operation. The situation is simplified by ignoring any inherited attributes, so attributes of interest are all passed during the reduce operation—when the parser moves up the tree. If you reexamine the LR parse algorithm presented in Table 5.3 on page 346, you'll notice that code generation occurs only on a reduce operation.

Value, attribute stack.

It turns out that the easiest place to store attributes is on the parse stack itself. In practical terms, you can do this in one of two ways, either make the state stack a stack of structures, one field of which is the state number and the rest of which is for attributes, or implement a second stack that runs parallel to the state stack. This second stack is called a *value* or *attribute* stack. Every push or pop on the state stack causes a corresponding push or pop on the value stack. All code-generation actions in a bottom-up parser are executed after the parser decides to reduce, but before the parser pops anything off the stack. So, you need to arrange for any attributes that are needed by a code-generation action to be on the value stack at the appropriate time. Similarly, the code-generation action needs to be able to put attributes onto the value stack for use by subsequent actions. I'll demonstrate with an example.

Bottom-up attribute passing, an example.

Figure 5.4 shows a parse of 1+2+3 with both the state and value stacks shown (the value stack is on the bottom). Emitted code is printed to the right of the value stack. The attributes that appear on the value stack are the names of the temporary variables used in expression evaluation. (I'll demonstrate how they get there shortly.) I've used □ to mark undefined value-stack entries.

Look, initially, at stack number two in Figure 5.4. Here, a **NUM** has been shifted onto the stack and the corresponding value-stack item is undefined. The next stage in the parse is a reduce by $t{\rightarrow}$**NUM**. Before the parser does the actual reduction, however, it executes some code. Two actions are performed: First, the t0=1 instruction is generated. (The 1 is the lexeme attached to the **NUM** token that is shifted onto Stack 2 in Figure 5.4.) Next, the code that outputs the instruction leaves a note for the parser saying that the attribute t0 should be placed on top of the value stack after the reduction is performed. When the left-hand side is pushed as the last step of a reduction, the parser must push a t0 in the corresponding place on the value stack.

The parser now does the actual reduction, popping the **NUM** from the state stack and replacing it with a *t*. It modifies the value stack too, popping one item and, instead of pushing garbage, it pushes a t0 onto the value stack. In other words, the attribute t0 on the value stack is now attached to the *t* on the state stack (because it's at the same relative position). The *t* has acquired the attribute t0.[1]

The next step in the parse process is application of $e{\rightarrow}t$. No code is generated here. There is an associated action, however. The *e* must acquire the attributes formerly associated with the *t*. So, again, the parser leaves a note for itself saying to push t0 onto the value stack as it pushes the new left-hand side onto the state stack.

The next transition of interest is the one from stack seven to eight. Here, the handle $e{+}t$ is recognized and the parser applies $e{\rightarrow}e{+}t$. Two actions are performed. A t0+=t1 instruction is generated, and the attribute t0 is acquired by the *e* (is passed to the *e*). The important thing to notice here is that the names of the two temporary variables are attributes of *e* and *t*. <u>The names of these variables are on the value stack.</u> The code that generates the add instruction can discover these names by examining the cells at offsets zero and two from the top of the value stack. Moreover, the position of these attributes on the

The names of the temporaries are on the value stack.

---

1. Note that it's a common, but incorrect, usage to say that the left-hand side inherits attributes from the right-hand side, probably because that's the way that control flows through the actual code (the child's code is executed first). I'd recommend against this usage because of the potential confusion involved. It's better to say that a parent *acquires* an attribute (or *is passed* an attribute) that's synthesized by the child.

Figure 5.4. The Value Stack and Code Generation

stack can be determined by examining the grammar. The handle on the stack comprises a right-hand side, so the position of the attribute on the stack corresponds to the position of the symbol on the right-hand side. The rightmost symbol is at top of stack. The e is two symbols away from the rightmost symbol in the production, so it's at offset two from the top of stack.

The synthesized attribute here is the name of the temporary variable that holds the result of the addition at run time; the `t0` that's attached to the e on stack eight is the name of the anonymous temporary that holds the result of the entire subexpression evaluation. It's just happenstance that the attribute is the same one that was attached to the e in in stack seven. The e in stack eight is not the same e as the one in stack seven—the one in stack eight is the one on the left-hand side of $e{\rightarrow}e{+}t$, the e in stack seven is on the right-hand side of the same production. If the code generator had decided to emit an instruction like `t3=t0+t1`, then the synthesized attribute would have been `t3`.

The next step in building a parser is to augment the earlier grammar to incorporate code-generation and attribute-passing rules. This augmentation is done in Table 5.6.

Augmented and attributed grammars for bottom-up parsing.

$$ represents left-hand side.

The actions are performed immediately before reducing by the associated production. The special symbol $$ is used to leave a note about what attribute to push. The value that's assigned to $$ in an action is, in turn, attached to the left-hand side that's pushed as part of the reduce operation. ($$ is pushed onto the value stack when the new left-hand side is pushed onto the parse stack.) The code assumes that the value stack is declared as an array of character pointers:

```
char    *Value_stack[128] ;
char    **Vsp = Value_stack + sizeof(Value_stack);
```

Vsp is the stack pointer. The stack grows towards low memory: *--Vsp=value is a push and value=*Vsp++ is a pop.[2] Consequently, Vsp[0] is the item at top of stack, Vsp[1] is the cell immediately below that, and so forth.

Table 5.6. Expression Grammar with Actions

	Grammar		Actions
0.	S	→ e	generate("answer = %s", Vsp[0]);
1.	e	→ e + t	generate("%s += %s", Vsp[2], Vsp[0]); free_name(Vsp[0]); $$ = Vsp[2];
2.	e	→ t	$$ = Vsp[0];
3.	t	→ **NUM**	name = new_name(); generate("%s = %s", name, yytext); $$ = name

Parser maintains value stack.

The value stack is maintained directly by the parser. A place marker that correspond to the terminal that's pushed onto the parse stack is pushed onto the value stack during a shift. In a reduce, as many objects as are removed from the parse stack are also popped off the value stack, then $$ is pushed to correspond with the push of the left-hand side.

generate(), new_name(), free_name().

The actions in Table 5.6 call three subroutines: generate() works like printf(), except that it puts a newline at the end of every line, new_name() returns a string that holds the name of a temporary variable, free_name() puts the name back into the name pool so that it can be reused by a subsequent new_name() call. The three routines are implemented in Listing 5.1. (Error detection has been removed for clarity.) The Names array is a stack of available temporary-variable names, initialized to hold eight names. Namep is the name-stack pointer. The new_name() subroutine pops a name and returns it; free_name() pushes the name to be freed.

---

2. Downward-growing stacks are required by ANSI C unless you want to waste one cell of the array. An ANSI pointer is assumed always to point into an array, though it can go one cell past the end of the array. It cannot point below the base address of the array, however. The following code demonstrates the problem:

```
int x[10];
p = & x[10];    /* this is valid       */
p = x;          /* this is valid       */
--p;            /* p is now undefined   */
```

The problem is a real one in an 8086-family machine. If x is at address 1000:0000, the --p in a compact- or large-model program usually evaluates to 1000:fffe rather than 0fff:fffe. Consequently p<x is always false because 1000:fffe is larger than 1000:0000.

Listing 5.1. *support.c*— Support Routines for Actions in Table 5.6

```c
1   #include <stdio.h>
2   #include <stdarg.h>
3
4   char *Names[] ={ "t0", "t1", "t2", "t3", "t4", "t5", "t6", "t7" };
5   char **Namep =Names;
6
7   void    generate( fmt, ... )
8   char    *fmt;
9   {
10      va_list             args;
11      va_start( args,   fmt );
12      vfprintf( stdout, fmt, args );
13      fputc   ( '\n', stdout );
14  }
15
16  char    *new_name()
17  {
18      if( Namep >= &Names[ sizeof(Names)/sizeof(*Names) ] )
19      {
20          printf("Expression too complex\n");
21          exit( 1 );
22      }
23
24      return( *Namep++ );
25  }
26
27  free_name(s)
28  char    *s;
29  {
30      *--Namep = s;
31  }
```

5.5.1 A Notation for Bottom-Up Attributes*

Though attributes are actually at specific offsets from the top of the value stack, it's inconvenient always to refer to them in terms of the stack pointer. **Yacc** and **occs** both use a notation for describing attributes that is sufficiently useful to merit mention here. (This notation is used heavily in the next chapter.) As before, $$ holds the value that is pushed as part of a reduction. Other attributes are indicated with the notation $1, $2, and so forth, where the number represents the position of the symbol on the right-hand side, for example:

Bottom-up attribute notation: $$, $1, $2, etc.

```
$$         $1   $2    $3    $4    ...
 s   →     A    B     C     D     ...
```

In addition, **yacc** and **occs** automatically provide a default action of $$ = $1 if no explicit assignment is made to $$. Don't confuse this notation with the similar notation used by **LLama**, in which the number in $n is the offset of a symbol to the right of an action. Here, *n* is the absolute position of the symbol on the right-hand side, not a relative position.

Default action: $$=$1.

Table 5.7 shows the augmented expression grammar we just looked at modified to use these conventions. The actions are all enclosed in curly braces to separate them from other symbols in the production. No explicit actions are now required in Production 2 because the default $$=$1 is used.

Table 5.7. Augmented Expression Grammar with Dollar Notation

0.	s	$\rightarrow$ e	`{ generate( "answer = %s", $1 ); }`
1.	e	$\rightarrow$ $e + t$	`{ generate( "%s += %s", $1, $3 );`
			`free_name( $3 ); }`
2.	e	$\rightarrow$ t	
3.	t	$\rightarrow$ **NUM**	`{ name = new_name();`
			`generate( "%s = %s", $$ = name, yytext ); }`

5.5.2 Imbedded Actions*

Note that the actions are not really grammatical symbols in a bottom-up parser, as they were in the top-down parser—the actions are not part of the viable prefix, they are just executed at appropriate times by the parser. In particular, an action is performed only when the parser performs a reduction. Hitherto, our actions have all been to the far right of the production to signify this fact. It's convenient sometimes to put an action in the middle of a production, however, as in the following production:

function_body→*arg_list* `{args_done();}` *compound_stmt* `{funct_done();}`

In order to process this sort of production, you must modify the grammar so that the middle action can be done as part of a reduction. The easiest way to do this is to provide a dummy ε production as follows:

function_body	$\rightarrow$	*arg_list* *dummy* *compound_stmt* `{funct_done();}`
dummy	$\rightarrow$	ε `{args_done();}`

Shift/reduce conflicts caused by imbedded actions.

Both **yacc** and **occs** do this transformation for you automatically, but the extra ε production can often create parsing problems called shift/reduce conflicts, discussed below in detail. You can often eliminate the unwanted shift/reduce conflict by inserting an imbedded action immediately to the right of a terminal symbol in the production, but it's generally better to avoid imbedded actions entirely. You could rearrange the previous grammar as follows without introducing an ε production:

function_body	$\rightarrow$	*formal_arg_list* *compound_stmt* `{funct_done();}`
formal_arg_list	$\rightarrow$	*arg_list* `{args_done();}`

5.6 Creating LR Parse Tables—Theory*

This section discusses how LR parse tables are created, and also discusses the LR-class grammars in depth.

5.6.1 LR(0) Grammars*

I'll start discussing LR-class grammars by considering two, more restrictive LR grammars and why they're too limited for most practical applications. These are LR(0) grammars—LR grammars that require no lookahead tokens—and SLR(1) grammars (*simple* LR(1) grammars). The expression grammar in Table 5.8 is used throughout the current section. The nonterminals are +, *, (,), and **NUM** (a number). Note that this grammar is not LL(1), so it can't be parsed with a top-down parser. The parse table for this grammar is represented as a graph in Figure 5.5 and in tabular form in Table 5.9.

Table 5.8. An Expression Grammar

0:	s	$\rightarrow$	e
1:	e	$\rightarrow$	$e + t$
2:	e	$\rightarrow$	t
3:	t	$\rightarrow$	$t * f$
4:	t	$\rightarrow$	f
5:	f	$\rightarrow$	(e)
6:	f	$\rightarrow$	**NUM**

Figure 5.5. LALR(1) State-Machine for Grammar in Listing 5.8

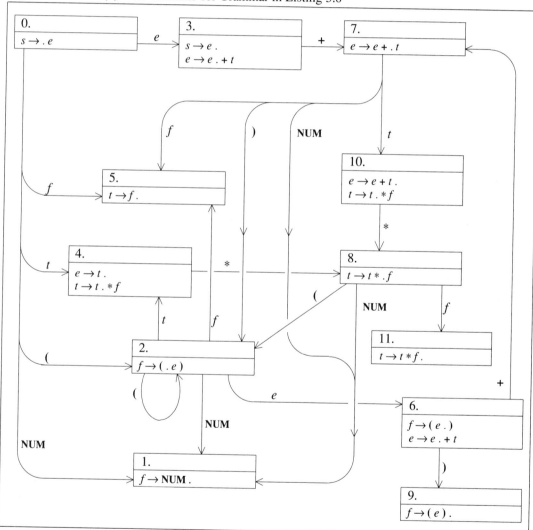

The table and graph relate to one another as follows:

- Each box is a state, and the state number is the row index in both the *action* and *goto* parts of the parse table.
- Outgoing edges labeled with nonterminal symbols represent the *goto* part of the parse table—a number representing the nonterminal is used as a column index and

How bottom-up parse table relates to state diagram.

Nonterminal edges are *goto* entries.

Table 5.9. State-Transition Table for Grammar in Table 5.8

		Shift/Reduce Table (Yy_action)					**Goto Table** (Yy_goto)			
	⊢	**NUM**	+	*	(	)	s	e	t	f
0	–	s1	–	–	s2	–	–	3	4	5
1	r6	–	r6	r6	–	r6	–	–	–	–
2	–	s1	–	–	s2	–	–	6	4	5
3	accept	–	s7	–	–	–	–	–	–	–
4	r2	–	r2	s8	–	r2	–	–	–	–
5	r4	–	r4	r4	–	r4	–	–	–	–
6	–	–	s7	–	–	s9	–	–	–	–
7	–	s1	–	–	s2	–	–	–	10	5
8	–	s1	–	–	s2	–	–	–	–	11
9	r5	–	r5	r5	–	r5	–	–	–	–
10	r1	–	r1	s8	–	r1	–	–	–	–
11	r3	–	r3	r3	–	r3	–	–	–	–

sN=shift to state N.   rN=reduce by production N.
Error transitions are marked with –.

Terminal edges are *shift* entries.

Reduce directives.

Error transitions.

LR(0) items: Dots in productions.

Dot movement.

the table holds the next-state number. Remember that this path represents the push part of a reduction.

- All outgoing edges that are labeled with terminal symbols become shift directives in the *action* part of the parse table. The token value is used as a column index, and the parser shifts from the current to the indicated state when it encounters that token.
- Reduce directives in the parse table are found by looking at the productions in each state. A reduction happens from a state when a production has a dot at its far right. A reduction by *f*→**NUM** can happen from State 1 because State 1 has the production *f*→**NUM.** in it. (Remember, the dot to the right of the **NUM** signifies that a **NUM** has already been read and shifted onto the stack.) I'll describe how **occs** decides in which column to put the reduce directives in a moment.
- Everything else in the table is an error transition.

The productions in the bottom part of each state are *LR(0) items*; an LR(0) item is different from a production in that it is augmented with a dot, which does two things. First, it keeps track of what's on the parse stack—in a given state, everything to the left of the dot is on the stack. When a dot moves to the far right of a production, the entire right-hand side is on the stack and the parser can reduce by that production. Second, the dot shows you how much input has been read so far—everything to the right of the dot in an item for a given state has not yet been input when the parser is in that state. Consequently, symbols to the right of the dot can be used as lookahead symbols.

When you move from one state to another, the dot moves from the left of the symbol with which the edge is labeled to the right of that symbol. In the case of a terminal symbol, the dot's movement means that the parser has read the token and shifted it onto the stack. In the case of a nonterminal, the parser will have read all the input symbols that comprise that nonterminal—in terms of parse trees, the parser will have processed the entire subtree rooted at that nonterminal, and will have read all the terminal symbols that form leaves in the subtree. In other words, the dot movement signifies that the parser has pushed a nonterminal onto the stack—something that can happen only as part of a reduction. When the parser reduces, it will have processed all of the input associated with the pushed nonterminal.

Now, I'll demonstrate how particular items get into particular states. First, notice that there are two classes of states: those that have incoming edges labeled with terminal symbols, and those with incoming edges labeled with nonterminal symbols. There are no states with both kinds of incoming edge—it's either one or the other. I'll look at the two classes of states separately.

Start by considering how the parse works. From State 0, a **NUM** token causes a shift to State 1, which in turn causes the dot to move past the **NUM**. Since the parser just shifted the **NUM** to the stack, it's at the top of the stack, and the dot is to its immediate right. Since all transitions into State 5 involve a shift of a **NUM**, all items in State 5 must have a **NUM** immediately preceding the dot. This is the case with all states that have incoming edges labeled with terminal symbols. The dot follows that nonterminal in every item in the state.

You must examine the reduce operation to see what's happening with the other states. All reductions are done in two steps. First, a previous state is restored by going backwards through the machine (against the direction of the arrows) by popping as many states as there are symbols on a right-hand side of the production. Next, the parser makes a transition to a new state by following an edge labeled with the left-hand side of the production by which you're reducing. These next states comprise the goto part of the parse table.

We're interested in the second of these steps, the outgoing edges that are labeled with left-hand sides. Looking at an example, since the dot is to the far right of the production in State 5, the parser reduces from State 1 by applying $f \rightarrow$**NUM**. The reduction involves a single pop, which uncovers State 0, followed by a push of the f, which moves us to State 5. Looking at the items in State 5, you'll notice that the dot follows the f. Since an f must be on top of the stack in this state, the dot must be to the immediate right of the f in all items in State 5. The next reduction is by $t \rightarrow f$ and gets us, first back to State 0, and then to State 4. Since a t must now be at top of stack, all items in State 4 have a dot to the immediate right of t. Let's look at it another way. State 0 contains the item $[e \rightarrow . e + t]$.[3] A reduction by some production that has an e on its left-hand side causes us to return to State 0 and then go to State 3. When the parser does this reduction, it has read past all input symbols that comprise the e, and the following item appears in State 3 to signify this fact: $[e \rightarrow e . + t]$. Given the foregoing, you can create the parse table with the following procedure:

(1) **Initialize:** State 0 is the start state. Initially, it contains a single LR(0) item consisting of the *start production* (the one with the goal symbol as its left-hand side), and a dot at the far left of the right-hand side. The initial set of items in this state (and all other states) is called the *kernel* or *seed* items. The set of kernel items for the start state looks like this:

0
$s \rightarrow . e$

(2) **Close the kernel items:** The kernel items for the next states are created with a *closure* operation, which creates a set of *closure items*. Closure is performed on those kernel items that have a nonterminal symbol to the right of a dot. (I'll call this nonterminal symbol the *closure symbol*.) Add to the closure set items for those

---

3. Items are usually differentiated from simple productions by surrounding them with brackets, as is done here.

productions which, when reduced, can return us to the current state.

(a) Initiate the closure process by adding to the closure set all productions that have the closure symbol on their left-hand side. Remember, if the dot is to the left of a nonterminal, there will be an outgoing transition from the current state (labeled with that nonterminal), and that transition represents the push part of a reduction. Consequently, productions with that nonterminal on their left-hand side could return us to the current state when a reduction by that production is performed.

The new item is formed by placing a dot at the far left of the right-hand side of the production. In the current grammar, since an *e* is to the right of the dot in all the kernel items, items containing all productions with an *e* on their left-hand side are added. The closure set looks like this so far:

0
$s \rightarrow . e$
$e \rightarrow . e + t$
$e \rightarrow . t$

(b) Repeat the closure process on the newly added items. If a newly added item has a nonterminal to the right of the dot, and closure has not yet been performed on that nonterminal, add to the closure set all productions that have that nonterminal as their left-hand side. In the current example, the second production has a *t* to the right of the dot, so I'll add all productions with *t* on their left-hand side, yielding the following:

0
$s \rightarrow . e$
$e \rightarrow . e + t$
$e \rightarrow . t$
$t \rightarrow . t * f$
$t \rightarrow . f$

(c) Repeat (b) until no more items can be added. A production with an *f* to the right of a dot was added in the previous step, so the closure set is extended to include all productions that have *f* on their left-hand sides, yielding:

0
$s \rightarrow . e$
$e \rightarrow . e + t$
$e \rightarrow . t$
$t \rightarrow . t * f$
$t \rightarrow . f$
$f \rightarrow . (e)$
$f \rightarrow . $ NUM

Since none of the new productions have dots to the left of a nonterminal, the procedure is complete.

(3) **Form the kernel items for the next states:**

(a) **Partition the items:** Group together all items in the current state (both kernel and closure items) that have the same symbol to the right of the dot. I'll call this symbol the *transition symbol*, and all items that share a transition symbol form a *partition*. The following picture shows the items partitioned by symbol to the right of the dot.

Transition symbols.

0.
$s \rightarrow . e$
$e \rightarrow . e + t$
$e \rightarrow . t$
$t \rightarrow . t * f$
$t \rightarrow . f$
$f \rightarrow . (e)$
$f \rightarrow .$ **NUM**

Partitions that have dots at the far right of the productions do not form new states because they represent reductions from the current state. (There will be, at most, one of these partitions, and all ε productions are part of this partition.) All other partitions form the kernels of the new states.

(b) **Form the kernel items for the next states:** Modify the items in those partitions that form the new states by moving the dot one notch to the right, and:

(c) **Add next-state transitions:** If a state already exists that has the same set of kernel items as the modified partition, add an edge labeled with the transition symbol that goes from the current state to the existing state. Otherwise, create a new state, using the group of modified items as the kernel items. Add an edge from the current state to the new one on the transition symbol.

(4) Repeat steps (2) and (3) on the kernel items of any new states until no more states can be added to the table.

Figure 5.6 shows a complete state machine built from our grammar using the foregoing procedure. The initial state is State 0, the first pass of the algorithm added States 1 to 5, and so on.

The issue of ε productions deserves further mention. ε productions are special only in one way. There are no outgoing edges from any state that are labeled ε; rather, if an ε production is added to a state as part of a closure operation, the machine reduces from the current state on that production. In other words, the right-hand side of an ε production effectively has the dot at its far right to begin with—the ε may as well not be there because it represents an empty string. Consider a grammar such as the following fragment:

$$s \quad \rightarrow \quad a\, b$$
$$b \quad \rightarrow \quad ε$$
$$\qquad | \quad \mathbf{X}$$

which generates the following states:

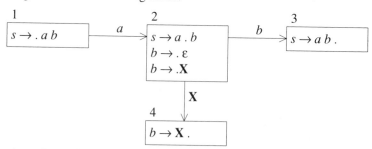

The item [$a{\rightarrow}a{\bullet}b$] adds the closure items [$b{\rightarrow}ε{\bullet}$] and [$b{\rightarrow}{\bullet}\mathbf{X}$], the latter of which appears as [$b{\rightarrow}\mathbf{X}{\bullet}$] in State 4. If b goes to ε in State 2, a reduction is performed from that state. Since there are no symbols on the right-hand-side, you won't pop anything off the state stack, so you won't change states in the first part of the reduce. Nonetheless, since b is the left-hand side of the production, you do want to go to State 2 in the goto part of

ε productions in bottom-up parse tables.

Figure 5.6. An LR(0) State Machine

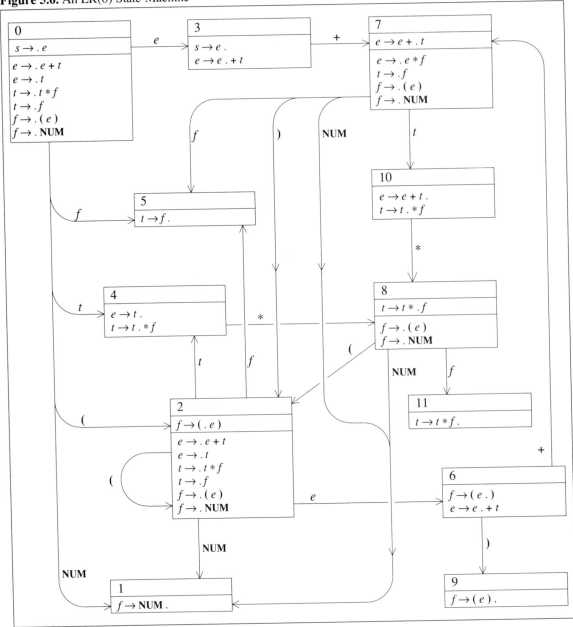

the reduce operation, so there's a transition on *b* from State 1.

Shift/reduce, reduce/reduce conflicts.

Unfortunately, LR(0) state machines have problems. As I said earlier, a reduction is performed from any given state if a dot is at the far right of an item, and a terminal symbol is shifted if the dot is to its immediate left. But consider a state like State 4 in Figure 5.6, where one of the items has a dot to the far right, and the other has a dot buried in the middle of the production. Should the parser shift or reduce? This situation is called a *shift/reduce conflict*. It's also possible for a state to have two items with different productions, both of which have dots at the far right. This situation is called a conflict—I'll look at one in a moment. States that contain shift/reduce or reduce/reduce conflicts are called *inadequate states*. A grammar is LR(0) if you can use the foregoing procedures to

Inadequate states.

create a state machine that has no inadequate states. Obviously, our current grammar is not LR(0).

5.6.2 SLR(1) Grammars*

There is a simple way to resolve some shift/reduce conflicts. Remember how the FOLLOW sets were used to form LL(1) select sets in the previous chapter. If a right-hand side was nullable, you could apply that production if the lookahead symbol was in the FOLLOW set of the left-hand side, because there could be a derivation in which all elements of the right-hand side could effectively disappear, and the symbol following the left-hand side would be the next input symbol in this case.

Use FOLLOW sets to resolve conflicts.

You can use similar reasoning to resolve shift/reduce conflicts. In order to do a reduction, the next input symbol must be in the FOLLOW set of the nonterminal on the left-hand side of the production by which we're reducing. Looking at State 3 in the LR(0) machine in Figure 5.6, you can reduce by $s{\rightarrow}e$ if the lookahead symbol is in FOLLOW(s). Similarly, you must shift if the lookahead symbol is a plus sign. As long as FOLLOW(s) doesn't contain a plus sign, the shift/reduce conflict in this state can be resolved by using the next input symbol. If all inadequate states in the LR(0) machine generated from a grammar can be resolved in this way, then you have an SLR(1) grammar.

The FOLLOW sets for our current grammar are in Table 5.10. Looking at the shift/reduce conflict in State 4, FOLLOW(e) does not contain a *, so the SLR(1) method works in this case. Similarly, in State 3, FOLLOW(s) doesn't contain a +, so everything's okay here as well. State 10 presents problems, however. FOLLOW(e) contains a *, and there is also an outgoing edge labeled with a *. So the FOLLOW set alone is not enough to resolve the shift/reduce conflict in State 10, and as a consequence, this is not an SLR(1) grammar either.

Table 5.10. FOLLOW Sets for the Expression Grammar

FOLLOW(s)	≡	{ ⊢ }
FOLLOW(e)	≡	{ ⊢) + }
FOLLOW(t)	≡	{ ⊢) + * }
FOLLOW(f)	≡	{ ⊢) + * }

5.6.3 LR(1) Grammars*

Continuing our quest for a way to resolve shift/reduce conflicts, a closer look at the machine yields some interesting facts. A nonterminal's FOLLOW set includes *all* symbols that can follow that nonterminal in every possible context. The state machine, however, is more limited. You don't really care which symbols can follow a nonterminal in every possible case; you care only about those symbols that can be in the input when we reduce by a production that has that nonterminal on its left-hand side. This set of relevant lookahead symbols is typically a subset of the complete FOLLOW set, and is called the *lookahead set*.

Some symbols in FOL-LOW set are not needed.

Lookahead set.

The lookahead set associated with a nonterminal is created by following a production as it moves through the state machine, looking at those terminal symbols that can actually follow the nonterminal just <u>after a reduction.</u> In the case of the inadequate State 10, there are two paths from State 0 to State 10 (0–3–7–10 and 0–2–6–7–10). For the purposes of collecting lookaheads, the only important terminals are those that follow nonterminal symbols preceded by dots. (We're looking for the sequence: dot-nonterminal-terminal.) Remember, here, that we're really figuring out which elements of the

Creating lookahead sets.

FOLLOW set tell us whether or not to reduce in a given situation. If a dot precedes a nonterminal, then that nonterminal can be pushed onto the parse stack as part of the reduction, and when the nonterminal is pushed, one of the terminals that follows it in the grammar better be in the input.

Look at State 0 in Figure 5.6. The parser can enter State 0 in the middle of a reduction by some production that has an *e* on its left-hand side, and it will exit State 0 by the *e* edge. This edge was created because a dot preceded an *e* in some item in that state. Looking at State 0 again, a plus can be in the input when the parser reduces by a production with *e* on its left-hand side because of the item:

$$[e \rightarrow . e + t]$$

If the parser enters State 0 in the middle of a reduction by a production with *e* on its left-hand side, then a + could reasonably be the next input symbol. Looked at another way, after all the tokens that comprise the *e* are read, + could be the next input symbol in this context. There's also an implied end-of-input marker in the start production, so

$$[s \rightarrow . e \vdash]$$

tells us to add $\vdash$ to the lookahead set. The item:

$$[f \rightarrow . (e)]$$

doesn't add anything to the lookahead set, even though it has an *e* in it, because this item isn't considered when a reduction is performed (the dot doesn't precede the *e*). Of the other states along the two paths from State 0 to State 10, the only other lookahead is added in State 4, because of the item:

$$[f \rightarrow (. e)]$$

If the parser enters State 4 in the middle of a reduction by some production with an *e* on its left-hand side, then a right parenthesis is also a possible input character. When you get to State 10, the only elements of FOLLOW(*e*) that can actually follow an *e* <u>in this context</u> are the elements that you've collected by looking at things that can actually follow an *e* in some state on the path from the start state to State 10. This set of lookaheads has only three elements: +,), and $\vdash$. A * is not part of this set, so a * cannot legally follow the *e* in this context, and the parser doesn't have to consider the * when it's deciding whether to reduce from State 10. It can safely reduce if the lookahead symbol is a +,), or $\vdash$, and shift on a *.

LR(1) items.

Formalizing the foregoing procedure, an *LR(1) item* is an LR(0) item augmented with a lookahead symbol. It has three parts (a production, a dot, and a lookahead) and is typically represented like this: $[s \rightarrow \alpha . \beta, \mathbf{D}]$, where $\mathbf{D}$ is the lookahead symbol. Note that the lookahead is part of the item; two items with the same production and dot position, but with different lookaheads, are different items.

Creating LR(1) state machines.

The process of creating an LR(1) state machine differs only from that used to make an LR(0) machine only in that LR(1) items are created in the closure operation rather than LR(0) items. The initial item consists of the start production with the dot at the far left and $\vdash$ as the lookahead character. In the grammar we've been using, it is:

$$[s \rightarrow . e, \vdash]$$

An LR(1) item is created from a kernel item as follows: Given an item and a production that take the following forms:

$$[s \quad \rightarrow \quad \alpha . x \beta, \mathbf{C}]$$
$$x \quad \rightarrow \quad . \gamma$$

(*s* and *x* are nonterminals, α, β, and γ are collections of any number of terminals and non- terminals ["any number" includes zero], and **C** is a terminal symbol) add:

$[x \rightarrow .\gamma, \text{FIRST}(\beta\ \mathbf{C})]$.

to the closure set. FIRST(β **C**) is computed like FIRST of a right-hand side. If β is not nullable, then FIRST(β **C**) is FIRST(β), otherwise it is the union of FIRST(β) and **C**.

$[s \rightarrow \alpha\ .\ x\ \beta,\ \mathbf{C}]$.

$[x \rightarrow .\gamma,\ \text{FIRST}(\beta\ \mathbf{C})]$.

Looking at a real situation, the start production relates to the previous formula as follows:

[	*s*	→	α	.	*x*	β,	**C**	]
[	*s*	→		.	*e*,		⊢	]

Note that both α and β match empty strings in this situation. Using the previous formula, there are two productions that have *e* on the left-hand side: *e→e+t* and *e→t*, so add the following to the closure set:

α and β can be empty.

[	*s*	→		.γ,	FIRST(β **C**)	]
[	*e*	→		. *e* + *t*,	FIRST(ε ⊢)	]
[	*e*	→		. *t*,	FIRST(ε ⊢)	]

I'm using ε here to signify that β in the original item matched an empty string. FIRST(ε⊢) is {⊢}. Continue the closure operation by closing both of the newly added items: The first one is:

[	*s*	→	α	.	*x*	β,	**C**	]
[	*e*	→		.	*e*	+ *t*,	⊢	]

so add:

[	*s*	→		.γ,	FIRST(β **C**)	]
[	*e*	→		. *e* + *t*,	FIRST(+ *t* ⊢)	]
[	*e*	→		. *t*,	FIRST(+ *t* ⊢)	]

Note that these items differ from the previous ones only in the lookahead sets. Since + is not nullable, FIRST(+ *t* ⊢) is +. The second production derived directly from the kernel item was:

[	*s*	→	α	.	*x*	β,	**C**	]
[	*e*	→		.	*t*	,	⊢	]

so add:

[	*s*	→		.γ,	FIRST(β **C**)	]
[	*t*	→		. *t* * *f*,	FIRST(ε ⊢)	]
[	*t*	→		. *f*,	FIRST(ε ⊢)	]

The process continues in this manner until no more new LR(1) items can be created. The next states are created as before, adding edges for all symbols to the right of the dot and moving the dots in the kernel items of the new machine. The entire LR(1) state machine for our grammar is shown in Figure 5.7. I've saved space in the Figure by merging together all items in a state that differ only in lookaheads. The lookaheads for all such items are shown on a single line in the right column of each state. Figure 5.8 shows how the other closure items in State 0 are derived. Derivations for items in States 2 and 14 of the machine are also shown.

The LR(1) lookaheads are the relevant parts of the FOLLOW sets that we looked at earlier. A reduction from a given state is indicated only if the dot is at the far right of a production and the current lookahead symbol is in the LR(1) lookahead set for the item

Figure 5.7. LR(1) State Machine

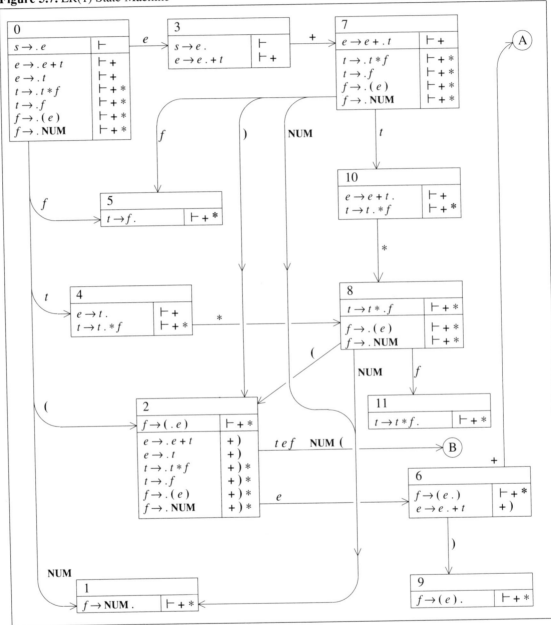

that contains that production. As before, a shift is indicated when the lookahead symbol matches a terminal label on an outgoing edge; outgoing edges marked with nonterminals are transitions in the goto part of the parse table. If there's a conflict between the lookahead sets and one of the outgoing edges, then the input grammar is not LR(1).

ε items.   ε items are special only in that they're a degraded case of a normal LR(1) item. In particular, ε items take the form $[s \rightarrow \varepsilon \cdot, \mathbf{C}]$, where the lookahead **C** was inherited from the item's parent in the derivation tree. An ε item is never a kernel item, so will never generate transitions to a next state. The action associated with an ε item is always a reduce on **C** from the current state.

Figure 5.7. continued. LR(1) State Machine

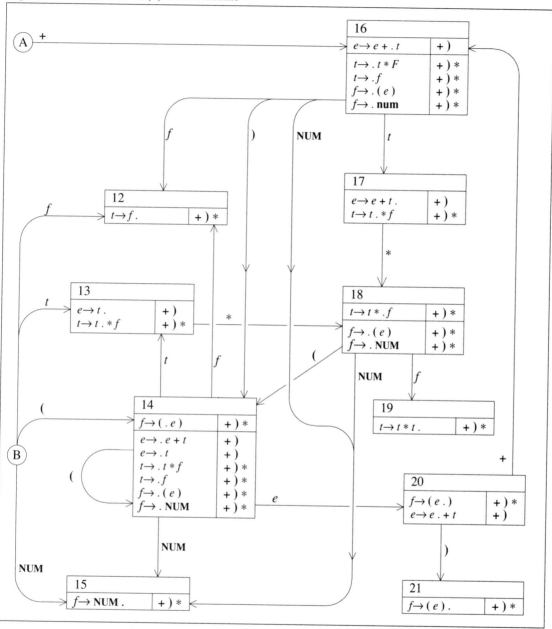

5.6.4 LALR(1) Grammars*

The main disadvantage of a LR(1) state machine is that it is typically twice the size of an equivalent LR(0) machine, which is pretty big to start out with [the C grammar used in the next chapter uses 287 LR(0) states]. Fortunately, it's possible to have the best of both worlds. Examining the LR(1) machine in Figure 5.8, you are immediately struck by the similarity between the two halves of the machine. A glance at the looka-heads tells you what's happening. A close parenthesis is a valid lookahead character only in a parenthesized subexpression—it can't appear in a lookahead set until after the open parenthesis has been processed. Similarly, the end-of-input marker is not a valid lookahead symbol inside a parenthesized expression because you must go past a close

Figure 5.8. Deriving Closure Items for LR(1) States 0, 2 and 14

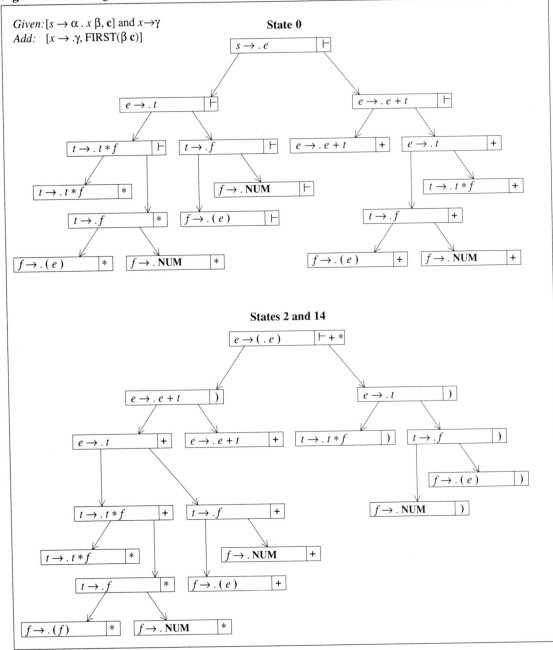

parenthesis first. The outer part of the machine (all of the left half of Figure 5.8 except States 6 and 9) handles unparenthesized expressions, and the inner part (States 6 and 9, and all of the right half of Figure 5.8) handles parenthesized subexpressions. The parser moves from one part to the other by reading an open parenthesis and entering State 2, which acts as a portal between the inner and outer machines. The parser moves back into the outer part of the machine by means of a reduction; it pops enough items so that the uncovered state number is in the outer machine.

You can take advantage of the similarity between the machines by merging them together. Two LR(1) states can be merged if the production and dot-position components of all kernel items are the same. The states are merged by combining the lookahead sets for the items that have the same production and dot position, and then modifying the next-state transitions to point at the merged state. For example, States 2 and 14 are identical in all respects but the lookaheads. You can merge them together, forming a new State 2/14, and then go through the machine changing all next-state transitions to either State 2 or State 14 to point at the new State 2/14. This merging process creates the machine pictured in Figure 5.9.

Figure 5.9. LALR(1) State Machine for the Expression Grammar

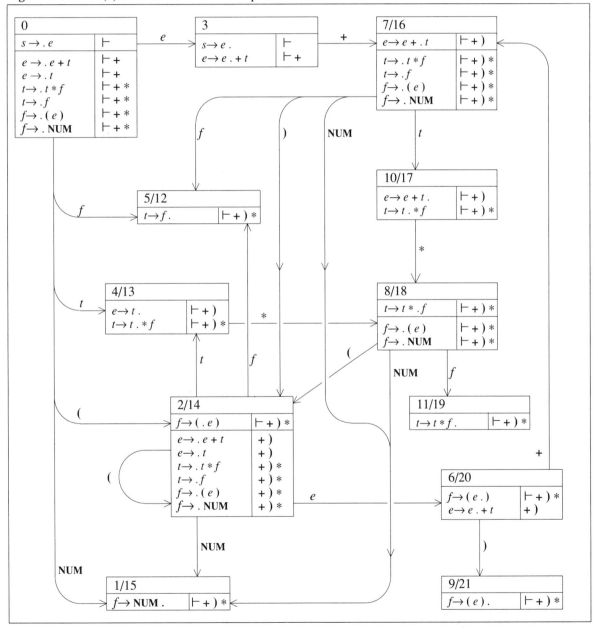

The merging process does not affect error detection in the grammar. It usually takes a little longer for the merged machine to detect an error, but the merged machine reads no more input than the unmerged one. There is one pitfall, however. The merging does,

Merging does not affect error recovery, might add inadequate states.

after all, add elements to the lookahead sets. Consequently, there might be inadequate states in the merged machine that are not present in the original LR(1) machine. (This is rare, but it can happen.) If no such conflicts are created by the merging process, the input grammar is said to be an LALR(1) grammar.

Manufacturing the tables.

If you compare the LALR(1) machine in Figure 5.9 with the LR(0) machine in Figure 5.6 on page 360 you'll notice that the machines are identical in all respects but the lookahead characters. This similarity is no accident, and the similarity of the machines can be exploited when making the tables; you can save space when making an LALR(1) machine by constructing an LR(0) machine directly and adding lookaheads to it, rather than creating the larger LR(1) machine and then merging equivalent states. You can do this in several ways—the method used by **occs** is the simplest. It proceeds as if it were making the LR(1) machine, except that before creating a new state, it checks to see if an equivalent LR(0) state (an LR(1) state with the same productions and dot positions in the kernel) already exists. If it finds such a state, **occs** adds lookaheads to the existing state rather than creating a new one. I'll look at this procedure in depth, below.

More efficient table-generation methods.

There are other, more efficient methods for creating LALR(1) machines directly from the grammar that I won't discuss here. An alternate method that is essentially the same as the foregoing, but which uses different data structures and is somewhat faster as a consequence, is suggested in [Aho], pp. 240–244. An LR(0) state machine is created and then lookaheads are added to it directly. You can see the basis of the method by looking at Figure 5.8 on page 366. Lookaheads appear on the tree in one of two ways, either they propagate down the tree from a parent to a child or they appear spontaneously. A lookahead character propagates from the item $[s\rightarrow\alpha.x\beta,\mathbf{c}]$ to its child when FIRST(β) is nullable. It appears spontaneously when FIRST(β) contains only terminal symbols. An even more efficient method is described in [DeRemer79] and [DeRemer82]; it is summarized in [Tremblay], pp. 375–383.

5.7 Representing LR State Tables

The LALR(1) state machine is easily represented by a two dimensional array of integers, where the value of the number represents the actions. The row index is typically the state number, and the columns are indexed by numbers representing the tokens and nonterminals. The LALR(1) state machine in Figure 5.9 is represented by the two-dimensional array in Table 5.11. (This is the same table as in Figure 5.9.) Shifts can be represented by positive numbers, and reductions can be represented with negative numbers. For example, a *s6* directive can be represented by the number 6, and an *r5* can be represented by a −5. A very large integer that's not likely to be a state number can be used to signify error transitions. The accept action, which is really a reduction by Production 0, can be represented by a zero.

Positive numbers=shift, Negative numbers=reduce, 0=accept.

LALR(1) parse-table size.

Though the table can be represented by a two-dimensional array, such a table is likely to be very large. Taking the C grammar that's used in the next chapter as characteristic, the grammar has 182 productions, 50 terminal symbols, and 75 nonterminal symbols. It generates 310 LALR(1) states. The resulting LALR(1) transition matrix has as many rows as there are states, and as many columns as there are terminal and nonterminal symbols (plus one for the end-of-input marker), so there are (50+75+1) = 125 columns and 310 rows, or 38,750 cells. Given a 2-byte int, that's 77,500 bytes. In most systems, it's worthwhile to minimize the size of the table.

Pair-compression in LALR(1) parse tables.

Only 3,837 cells (or 10%) of the 38,750 cells in the uncompressed table are nonerror transitions. As a consequence, you can get considerable compression by using the pair-compression method discussed in Chapter Two: Each row in the table is represented by an array, the first element of which is a count of the number of pairs in the array, and the

Table 5.11. Tabular Representation of Transition Diagram in Figure 5.9

	Shift/Reduce Table (`Yy_action`)						Goto Table (`Yy_goto`)			
	⊢	NUM	+	*	(	)	s	e	t	f
0	–	s1	–	–	s2	–	–	3	4	5
1	r6	–	r6	r6	–	r6	–	–	–	–
2	–	s1	–	–	s2	–	–	6	4	5
3	accept	–	s7	–	–	–	–	–	–	–
4	r2	–	r2	s8	–	r2	–	–	–	–
5	r4	–	r4	r4	–	r4	–	–	–	–
6	–	–	s7	–	–	s9	–	–	–	–
7	–	s1	–	–	s2	–	–	–	10	5
8	–	s1	–	–	s2	–	–	–	–	11
9	r5	–	r5	r5	–	r5	–	–	–	–
10	r1	–	r1	s8	–	r1	–	–	–	–
11	r3	–	r3	r3	–	r3	–	–	–	–
Error transitions are marked with –										

remainder of which is series of [nonterminal,action] pairs. For example, Row 4 of the transition matrix can be represented as follows:

```
state_4[] = { 4, [),r2], [+,r2], [⊢,r2], [*,s8] };
```

The initial 4 says that there are four pairs that follow, the first pair says to reduce by Production 2 if the input symbol is a close parentheses, and so forth. If the current input symbol is not attached to any pair, then an error transition is indicated.

Another array (call it the *index* array) is indexed by state number and each cell evaluates to a pointer to one of the pairs arrays. If an element of the index array is NULL, then there are no outgoing transitions from the indicated state. If several rows of the table are identical (as is the case in the current table), only a single copy of the row needs to be kept, and several pointers in the index array can point at the single row. The *goto* portion of the table is organized the same way, except that the row array contains [nonterminal, next state] pairs. Figure 5.10 shows how the table in Listing 5.11 is represented in an **occs** output file. The actual code is in Listing 5.2.

The `Yya` arrays on lines 20 to 28 of Listing 5.2 represent the rows, and `Yy_action` (on lines 30 to 34) is the index array; the pairs consist of tokenized input symbols and action descriptions, as described earlier. The values used for tokens are as follows:

*Yya*N **arrays,** `Yy_action`

Token	Value returned from lexical analyzer
⊢	0
NUM	1
+	2
*	3
(	4
)	5

Looking at row four of the table (`Yya004` on line 23), the pair [5,–2] is a reduction by Production 2 (–2) on a close parenthesis (5). [3,8] is a shift to State 8 (8) on a * (3), and so on. The tables can be decompressed using the `yy_next()` subroutine in Listing 5.3.

Parse-table decompression.

Figure 5.10. Actual Representation of Parse Tables for Grammar in Listing 5.8

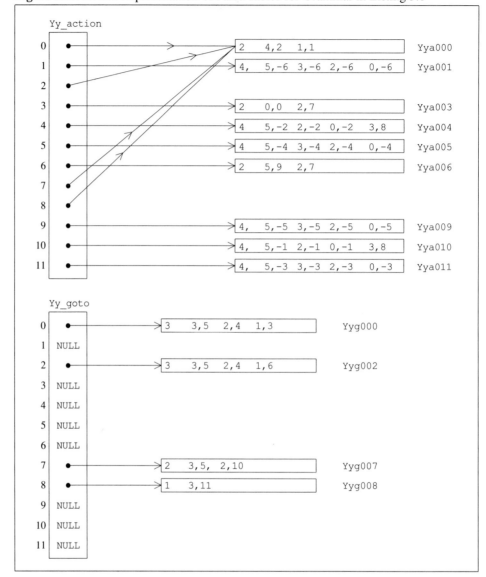

Listing 5.2. C Representation of the Parse Tables

```
 1    /*--------------------------------------------------------
 2     * The Yy_action table is action part of the LALR(1) transition
 3     * matrix. It's compressed and can be accessed using the yy_next()
 4     * subroutine, declared below.
 5     *
 6     *              Yya000[]={    3,     5,3    ,   2,2    ,   1,1   };
 7     *    state number---+           |     | |
 8     *    number of pairs in list-+        | |
 9     *    input symbol (terminal)------+   |
10     *    action-----------------------+
11     *
12     *    action = yy_next( Yy_action, cur_state, lookahead_symbol );
13     *
14     *        action <  0   -- Reduce by production n
```

Listing 5.2. continued. . .

```
15      *         action == 0   -- Accept (ie. reduce by production 0)
16      *         action >  0   -- Shift to state n
17      *         action == YYF -- error
18      */
19
20      int Yya000[]={ 2,   4,2   ,   1,1   };
21      int Yya001[]={ 4,   5,-6  ,   3,-6  ,   2,-6  ,   0,-6  };
22      int Yya003[]={ 2,   0,0   ,   2,7   };
23      int Yya004[]={ 4,   5,-2  ,   2,-2  ,   0,-2  ,   3,8   };
24      int Yya005[]={ 4,   5,-4  ,   3,-4  ,   2,-4  ,   0,-4  };
25      int Yya006[]={ 2,   5,9   ,   2,7   };
26      int Yya009[]={ 4,   5,-5  ,   3,-5  ,   2,-5  ,   0,-5  };
27      int Yya010[]={ 4,   5,-1  ,   2,-1  ,   0,-1  ,   3,8   };
28      int Yya011[]={ 4,   5,-3  ,   3,-3  ,   2,-3  ,   0,-3  };
29
30      int *Yy_action[12] =
31      {
32          Yya000, Yya001, Yya000, Yya003, Yya004, Yya005, Yya006, Yya000, Yya000,
33          Yya009, Yya010, Yya011
34      };
35
36      /*-------------------------------------------------------
37       * The Yy_goto table is goto part of the LALR(1) transition matrix. It's com-
38       * pressed and can be accessed using the yy_next() subroutine, declared below.
39       *
40       *   nonterminal = Yy_lhs[ production number by which we just reduced ]
41       *
42       *                 Yyg000[]={   3,    5,3   ,   2,2   ,   1,1   };
43       *    uncovered state-+             |    | |
44       *    number of pairs in list--+    | |
45       *    nonterminal------------------+ |
46       *    goto this state----------------+
47       *    goto_state = yy_next( Yy_goto, cur_state, nonterminal );
48       */
49
50      int Yyg000[]={ 3,   3,5   ,   2,4   ,   1,3   };
51      int Yyg002[]={ 3,   3,5   ,   2,4   ,   1,6   };
52      int Yyg007[]={ 2,   3,5   ,   2,10  };
53      int Yyg008[]={ 1,   3,11  };
54
55      int *Yy_goto[12] =
56      {
57          Yyg000, NULL  , Yyg002, NULL  , NULL  , NULL  , NULL  , Yyg007, Yyg008,
58          NULL  , NULL  , NULL
59      };
60
61      /*-------------------------------------------------------
62       * The Yy_lhs array is used for reductions. It is indexed by production
63       * number and holds the associated left-hand side adjusted so that the
64       * number can be used as an index into Yy_goto.
65       */
66
67      YYPRIVATE int Yy_lhs[7] =
68      {
69              /*   0 */        0,
70              /*   1 */        1,
71              /*   2 */        1,
```

Listing 5.2. continued...

```
72              /*    3 */        2,
73              /*    4 */        2,
74              /*    5 */        3,
75              /*    6 */        3
76    };
77
78    /*-----------------------------------------------------
79     * The Yy_reduce[] array is indexed by production number and holds
80     * the number of symbols on the right-hand side of the production.
81     */
82
83    YYPRIVATE int Yy_reduce[7] =
84    {
85              /*    0 */        1,
86              /*    1 */        3,
87              /*    2 */        1,
88              /*    3 */        3,
89              /*    4 */        1,
90              /*    5 */        3,
91              /*    6 */        1
92    };
```

Listing 5.3. *yynext.c*— Table Decompression

```
1    int   yy_next( table, cur_state, symbol )
2    int   **table;                                /* table to decompress  */
3    int   symbol;                                 /* column index         */
4    int   cur_state;                              /* row index            */
5    {
6        /* Given current state and input symbol, return next state. */
7
8        int    *p = table[ cur_state ] ;
9        int    i;
10
11       if( p )
12           for( i = (int) *p++; --i >= 0 ; p += 2 )
13               if( symbol == p[0] )
14                   return p[1];
15
16       return  YYF;                              /* error indicator */
17   }
```

Goto transitions. Yy_lhs, Yy_reduce.

The goto transitions are computed using two arrays. Yy_lhs (on line 67 of Listing 5.2) is indexed by production number and evaluates to an integer representing the symbol on the left-hand side of that production. That integer is, in turn, used to search the goto part of the array for the next-state transition. A second array, Yy_reduce on line 83 of Listing 5.2, is indexed by production number and evaluates to the number of symbols on the right-hand side of that production. A simplified version of the **occs** parser loop, which demonstrates how the tables are used, is shown in Listing 5.4.

Goto transitions could be compressed by column.

Since there tend to be fewer nonterminals than states, the Yy_goto array could be made somewhat smaller if it were compressed by column rather than by row. The Yy_goto array could be indexed by nonterminal symbol and could contain *[current_state, next_state]* pairs. **Occs** doesn't do this both because two table-decompression subroutines would be needed and because the parser would run more

Listing 5.4. Simplified Parser Loop Demonstrating Parse-Table Usage

```
1    push( 0 );                /* Push start state */
2    lookahead = yylex();      /* get first lookahead symbol */
3
4    while( 1 )
5    {
6        do_this = yy_next( Yy_action, state_at_top_of_stack(), yylookahead );
7
8        if( do_this == YYF  )
9        {
10           /* ERROR */
11       }
12       else if( do_this > 0 )                    /* Simple shift action  */
13       {
14           lookahead = yylex();                  /* advance              */
15           push( do_this );                      /* push new state       */
16       }
17       else                                      /* reduction            */
18       {
19           yy_act( -do_this );                   /* do code-generation action */
20
21           if( do_this == YYACCEPT )
22               break ;
23           else
24           {
25               production_number = -do_this;
26
27               rhs_length = Yy_reduce[ production_number ];
28
29               while( --rhs_len >= 0 )                    /* pop rhs_len items */
30                   pop();
31
32               next_state = yy_next( Yy_goto, state_at_top_of_stack(),
33                                          Yy_lhs[production_number] );
34               push( next_state );
35           }
36       }
37   }
```

slowly because the chain lengths would be a bit longer. You can also combine the two arrays, putting shift actions, reduce actions, and goto transitions together in a single row array; but again, it would take longer to decompress the table because of the extra chain lengths.

5.8 Eliminating Single-Reduction States*

Reexamining Table 5.11 on page 369, you'll notice that States 1, 5, 9, and 11 all consist of nothing but error transitions and reductions by a single production. For example, all the actions in State 1 are reductions by Production 6. These states, called *single-reduction* states, are typically caused by productions that are used only to add precedence rules to a grammar—they are created by productions with a single symbol on the right-hand side, such as the $e{\rightarrow}t$ and $t{\rightarrow}f$ in the grammar we've been using.

Single-reduction states.

You can see what these states are actually doing by looking at how one of the states is used as the parse progresses. If a **NUM** is found in State 0, for example, the parser shifts to State 6, where the only legal action is a reduce by Production 6 if the next input character is ⊢, +, * or close parenthesis. This reduction just gets us back to State 0, without having advanced the input. All this backing and forthing is really unnecessary because the parser could reduce by Production 6 directly from State 0 if the next input character is a **NUM** and the following character is a ⊢, +, * or close parenthesis. If something else is in the input, the error is caught the next time the parser tries to shift, so the error information is actually duplicated in the table.

Removing single-reduction states from parse table.

All single-reduction states can be removed from the table by introducing another class of action items. If a row of the table contains a shift to a single-reduction state, replace it with a directive of the form *dN*, where N is the number of the production by which the parser would reduce had it gone to the single-reduction state. In the current table, for example, all *s1* directives would be replaced by *d6* directives. The parser processes a *d* directive just like a normal reduce directive, except that it pops one fewer than the number of symbols on the right-hand side of the indicated production, because it didn't push the last of these symbols.

A similar substitution has to be made in the *goto* portion of the table—all transitions into single-reduction states must be replaced with equivalent *d* directives. This change forces a second modification to the parser because several code-generation actions might now have to be executed during a reduction if a *d* directive is encountered in the *goto* table. The earlier table is modified to eliminate single-reduction states in Table 5.12. A parser algorithm for the new table is in Table 5.13.

Table 5.12. Parse Table with Single-Reduction States Removed

	Shift/Reduce Table (Yy_action)						**Goto Table** (Yy_goto)			
	⊢	**NUM**	+	*	(	)	*s*	*e*	*t*	*f*
0	–	d6	–	–	s2	–	–	3	4	d4
2	–	d6	–	–	s2	–	–	6	4	d4
3	accept	–	s7	–	–	–	–	–	–	–
4	r2	–	r2	s8	–	r2	–	–	–	–
6	–	–	s7	–	–	d5	–	–	–	–
7	–	d6	–	–	s2	–	–	–	10	d4
8	–	d6	–	–	s2	–	–	–	–	d3
10	r1	–	r1	s8	–	r1	–	–	–	–
Error transitions are marked with –										

Can't remove single-reduction state if there is an action.

There's one final caveat. You cannot eliminate a single-reduction state if there is a code-generation action attached to the associated production because the stack will have one fewer items on it than it should when the action is performed—you you won't be able to access the attributes correctly. In practice, this limitation is enough of a problem that **occs** doesn't use the technique. In any event, the disambiguating rules discussed in the next section eliminate many of the single-reduction states because the productions that cause them are no longer necessary.

There is one thing that's easy to do that does not affect the grammar at all, however, and can significantly reduce the table sizes in a pair-compressed array. Since the error information associated with single-reduction states is redundant (because the error is caught with the next shift), you can replace the entire chain of pairs that represent the single-reduction state with a single, default, reduce action that is performed regardless of the input symbol. The UNIX **yacc** utility takes this idea even further by providing a default action for every row of the table that represents the most common action in that row. The problem here is the error recovery, which is now very difficult to do because it is difficult to determine legal lookahead characters while doing the recovery.

Table 5.13. LR Parser Algorithm for Single-Reduction-Minimized Tables

```
push( 0 );
while( Action[TOS][input] ≠ Accept )
{
    if( Action[TOS][input] = − )
        error( );
    else if ( Action[TOS][input] = sX )
    {
        push( X );
        advance( );
    }
    else if ( Action[TOS][input] = rX )
    {
        act( X );
        pop( as many items as are in the RHS of production X );
        while( (i = Goto[ uncovered TOS ][ LHS of production X ]) = dX )
        {
            act( X );
            pop( one fewer than the number of symbols in the RHS of production X );
        }
        push i;
    }
    else if ( Action[TOS][input] = dX )
    {
        act( X );
        pop( one fewer than the number of symbols in the RHS of production X )
        while( (i = Goto[ uncovered TOS ][ LHS of production X ]) = dX )
        {
            act( X );
            pop( one fewer than the number of symbols in the RHS of production X );
        }
        push i;
    }
}
accept( );
```

5.9 Using Ambiguous Grammars*

Even though LR(1) and LALR(1) grammars are more flexible than the SLR(1) and LR(0), they still can't be ambiguous, because, as you would expect, an ambiguous grammar yields an ambiguous parse. The ambiguity is reflected in the resulting state machine as a shift/reduce conflict. Ambiguous productions are, nonetheless, useful. They tend to make a grammar both smaller and easier to read. The two most common ambiguities are found in Productions 2, 4, and 5 of the following grammar:

1.	*stmt* →	*expr* **SEMI**
2.			**IF** *stmt* **ELSE** *stmt*
3.			**IF** *stmt*
4.	*expr* →	*expr* **PLUS** *expr*
5.			*expr* **TIMES** *expr*
6.			**ID**

ID is an identifier

This grammar creates the state machine pictured in Figure 5.11, and the ambiguities are reflected as shift/reduce conflicts in the States 5, 10, and 11. The LALR(1) lookaheads are shown in brackets next to those items that trigger reductions.

Resolving ambiguities when making parse tables.

Though the foregoing grammar is not LALR(1), it is nonetheless possible to use it to create a parser. The basic strategy examines the various shift/reduce conflicts in the machine, and makes decisions as to whether a shift or reduce is appropriate in that situation, basing the decision on the semantic rather than syntactic description of the language. In practical terms, you need to know the relative precedence and the associativity of those tokens that appear in ambiguous productions, and this information can be used to disambiguate the tables.

Precedence and associativity information is used to resolve ambiguities in arithmetic expressions as follows: State 10 contains the following items:

$$expr \quad \rightarrow \quad expr \,.\, + \, expr$$
$$expr \quad \rightarrow \quad expr + expr \,.\quad [; + *]$$
$$expr \quad \rightarrow \quad expr \,.\, * \, expr$$

The parser wants to reduce by

$$expr \rightarrow expr + expr$$

if the lookahead symbol is a semicolon, plus sign, or star; it also wants to shift on a plus sign or star. The semicolon poses no problem, but the arithmetic operators do.

Shift for right associativity. Reduce for left associativity.

Now, consider the parse caused by the input a+b+c. The stack and input looks like this after the a, +, and b are processed:

expr + *expr*	+ c ;

The parser now looks ahead and sees the plus, and it has a problem. If the plus operator is left associative, it will want to reduce immediately (before processing the next plus sign). A left-associative parse would continue as follows:

expr + *expr*	+ c ;
expr	+ c ;
expr +	c ;
expr + **ID**	;
expr + *expr*	;
expr	;
expr ;	
stmt	

This way the left subexpression would be processed before going on with the input. Right associativity is handled differently. Here the parser wants to put the whole expression onto the stack so that it can reduce from right to left, like this:

Figure 5.11. State Machine for an Ambiguous Grammar

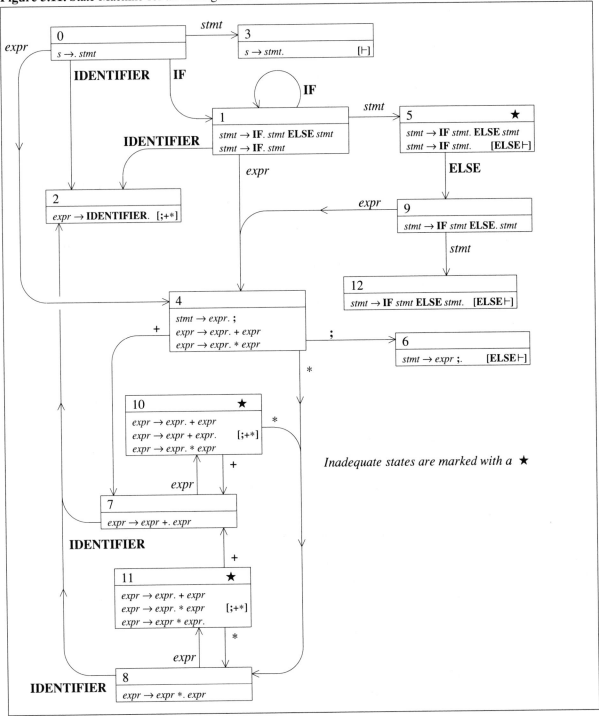

expr + *expr*	+ c ;
expr + *expr* +	c ;
expr + *expr* + **ID**	;
expr + *expr* + *expr*	;
expr + *expr*	;
expr	;
expr ;	
stmt	

So the decision of whether to shift or reduce here is based on the desired associativity of the plus operator. In this case, you get left associativity by resolving the conflict in favor of the reduce.

Shift for higher precedence, reduce for lower.

State 10 has one other problem—illustrated by the input a+b*c. Here, the star is higher precedence than the plus, so the multiplication must be done first. The conflict is active when the following stack condition exists:

expr + *expr*	* c ;

Reducing at this point would effectively ignore the relative precedence of + and *; the addition would be done first. Resolving in favor of the shift, however, correctly generates the following parse:

expr + *expr* *	c ;
expr + *expr* * **ID**	;
expr + *expr* * *expr*	;
expr + *expr*	;
expr	;
expr ;	
stmt	

and the multiplication is done before the addition. So, the conflict should be resolved in favor of the shift if the lookahead operator is higher in precedence than the token closest to the top of the stack.

Dangling else.

Precedence and associativity help only if a production implements an arithmetic expression, however. The sensible default for handling a shift/reduce conflict in nonarithmetic productions is to decide in favor of the shift. This decision takes care of the conflict in State 5, which contains the following items

IF *stmt* **. ELSE** *stmt*
IF *stmt* **.**   [⊢ **ELSE**]

Here, the machine wants both to shift and reduce when the lookahead token is an **ELSE**. The problem is exemplified by the following input:

```
IF
    ID ;
ELSE
    IF
        ID ;
    ELSE
        ID ;
```

Most programming languages require an ELSE to bind with the closest preceding IF. A partial parse of the foregoing generates the following stack:

IF *stmt*	ELSE IF ID ; ELSE ID ;

A shift is required in this situation, because an **ELSE** is present in the input. Were you to reduce **IF** *stmt* to *stmt*, the **ELSE** would be left dangling in the input. That is, since a *stmt* can't start with an **ELSE**, a syntax error would be created if the parser reduced.

Letting the parse continue—shifting on every conflict—you'll eventually get the following on the stack:

IF *stmt* **ELSE IF** *stmt* **ELSE** *stmt*

which can then be reduced to:

IF *stmt* **ELSE** *stmt*

and then to:

stmt

Since the rightmost statement is reduced first, the **ELSE** binds to the closest **IF**, as required. The foregoing rules can be summarized as follows:

(1) Assign precedence and associativity information to all terminal symbols and precedence information to productions.[4] If no precedence and associativity is assigned, a terminal symbol is assigned a precedence level of zero (very low) and is nonassociative. Productions are assigned the same precedence level as the rightmost terminal symbol in the production or zero if there are no terminal symbols on the right-hand side.[5]

Rules for resolving ambiguities in parse table.

(2) When a LALR(1) shift/reduce conflict is encountered, the precedence of the terminal symbol to be shifted is compared with the precedence of the production by which you want to reduce. If either the terminal or the production is of precedence zero, then resolve the conflict in favor of the shift. Otherwise, if the precedences are equal, resolve using the following table:

associativity of lookahead symbol	resolve in favor of
left	reduce
right	shift
nonassociative	shift

Otherwise, if the precedences are not equal, use the following table:

---

4. **Yacc** and **occs** do this with the `%left`, `%right` and `%nonassoc` directives.

5. **Yacc** and **occs** let you override this default with a `%prec TOKEN` directive where TOKEN is a terminal symbol that was declared with a previous `%left`, `%right`, or `%nonassoc`. The production is assigned the same precedence level as the token in the `%prec` directive. Note that the `%prec` directive must be to the left of the semicolon or vertical bar that terminates the production.

precedence	resolve in favor of
lookahead symbol < production	reduce
lookahead symbol > production	shift

There's another kind of conflict that can appear in your grammar—a *reduce/reduce* conflict. Consider the following grammar that implements one rule of Kernighan and Cherry's troff preprocessor, **eqn**:[6]

1.	*expr*	$\rightarrow$	*expr* **SUB** *expr* **SUP** *expr*
2.		|	*expr* **SUB** *expr*
3.		|	*expr* **SUP** *expr*
4.		|	*LB expr RB*
5.		|	**CONST**

Eqn typesets equations. The implemented grammar does the following:

Input	Typeset as follows:
X sub 1	X_1
X sup 2	X^2
X sub 1 sup 2	X_1^2

The last case has to be handled specially to prevent the subscript and superscript from getting out of line, like this:

X_1^2

The earlier grammar takes care of the special case by adding an extra production (Production 1) that takes care of a case that would actually be handled by the rest of the grammar were it not there—X sub 1 sup 2 would be parsed without difficulty if Production 1 wasn't in the grammar. It wouldn't be recognized as a special case, however. The grammar as presented yields a state with the following kernel items:

expr	$\rightarrow$	*expr* **SUB** *expr* **SUP** *expr* **.**	[⊢ **SUB SUP RB**]
expr	$\rightarrow$	*expr* **SUP** *expr* **.**	[⊢ **SUB SUP RB**]
expr	$\rightarrow$	*expr* **.** **SUB** *expr* **SUP** *expr*	
expr	$\rightarrow$	*expr* **.** **SUB** *expr*	
expr	$\rightarrow$	*expr* **.** **SUP** *expr*	

Here, the parser can't decide which of the two productions that have dots on the far right should be reduced. (This situation is a *reduce/reduce* conflict.) The sensible default is to resolve the conflict in favor of the production that is higher in the grammar.

Note that reduce/reduce conflicts should generally be avoided by modifying the grammar. More often than not, this type of conflict is caused by an error in the grammar, like this:

foo	$\rightarrow$	**TOKEN**
	...	
	|	**TOKEN**

6. This example is taken from [Aho], pp. 252–254. It's significant that neither I nor any of the other compiler programmers that I know could think of a real example of a valid reduce/reduce conflict other than the current one. Reduce/reduce conflicts are almost always caused by errors in the grammar.

They can also appear when you do seemingly reasonable things like this, however:

karamazov	$\rightarrow$	*dmitry*	*ivan*	*alyosha*

dmitry	$\rightarrow$	**NAME** *do_something*
ivan	$\rightarrow$	**NAME** *do_something_else*
alyosha	$\rightarrow$	**NAME** *do_yet_another_thing*

This second situation is essentially the same as the earlier example. Several of *karamazov*'s right-hand sides begin with the same terminal symbol. Here, however, the fact has been disguised by an intervening nonterminal. Because of the first-production-has-higher-precedence rule, *ivan* and *alyosha* are never executed.[7] The solution is to restructure the grammar as follows:

karamazov	$\rightarrow$	**NAME** *brother*
brother	$\rightarrow$	*dmitry*	*ivan*	*alyosha*
dmitry	$\rightarrow$	*do_something*
ivan	$\rightarrow$	*do_something_else*
alyosha	$\rightarrow$	*do_yet_another_thing*

or to go a step further:

karamazov	$\rightarrow$	**NAME** *brother*
brother	$\rightarrow$	*do_something*
	|	*do_something_else*
	|	*do_yet_another_thing*

5.10 Implementing an LALR(1) Parser—The Occs Output File

The remainder of this chapter discusses both the **occs** output file and how **occs** itself works; you can skip to the next chapter if you're not interested in this level of detail. In any event, you should read Appendix E, which contains a user's manual for **occs**, before continuing, because **occs** will be used in the next chapter.

Most of the code that comprises **occs** is taken directly from **LLama**, and was discussed in the last chapter. The two main differences are the parser itself and the parse-table generation routines. This section discusses the parser, using the output file created from the **occs** input file in Listing 5.5. (The associated lexical analyzer is defined by the L^{E}X input file in Listing 5.6.)

The grammar used here is not a particularly good use of **occs**, because I've built precedence and associativity information into the grammar itself, rather than using the %left and %right directives as I did with the expression grammar in Appendix E. I've done this because **occs** fudges the tables for ambiguous grammars, using the rules described in the previous section. For the purposes of discussion, however, it's better to work with a grammar that is a strict LALR(1) grammar. Note that I've extended the definition of the **NUM** token to recognize an identifier as well as a number (and renamed it to NUM_OR_ID as a consequence).

---

7. In **yacc** and **occs**, be careful of blithely using %prec to solve a problem like the foregoing without considering the consequences. The problem may well have been caused by a deficiency in the grammar and, though the %prec may eliminate the warning message, the problem will still exist.

Listing 5.5. *expr.y*— Occs Input File for an Expression Compiler

```
 1   %term  NUM_OR_ID          /*  a number or identifier               */
 2
 3   %left  PLUS               /*  +            (lowest precedence)      */
 4   %left  STAR               /*  *                                    */
 5   %left  LP RP              /*  ( )          (highest precedence)     */
 6
 7   %{
 8   #include <stdio.h>
 9   #include <ctype.h>
10   #include <malloc.h>
11   #include <tools/debug.h>
12   #include <tools/stack.h>
13
14   extern char *yytext;
15
16   stack_dcl( Namepool, char*, 10 );          /* Stack of 10 temporary-var names */
17   #define freename(x) push( Namepool, (x) )  /* Release a temporary variable    */
18   #define getname()   pop ( Namepool      )  /* Allocate an temporary variable  */
19
20   typedef char            *stype;        /* Value stack is stack of char pointers */
21   #define YYSTYPE         stype
22
23   #define YYSHIFTACT(tos) (*tos="")                    /* Shift a null string */
24   %}
25
26   %%
27   /* A small expression grammar that recognizes numbers, names, addition (+),
28    * multiplication (*), and parentheses. Expressions associate left to right
29    * unless parentheses force it to go otherwise. * is higher precedence than +.
30    */
31
32   s       : e ;
33
34   e       : e PLUS t    { yycode("%s += %s\n", $1, $3); freename($3); }
35           | t             /* $$ = $1   */
36           ;
37
38   t       : t STAR f    { yycode("%s *= %s\n", $1, $3); freename($3); }
39           | f             /* $$ = $1   */
40           ;
41
42   f       : LP e RP     { $$ = $2; }
43           | NUM_OR_ID   {
44                             /* Copy operand to a temporary. Note that I'm adding an
45                              * underscore to external names so that they can't con-
46                              * flict with the compiler-generated temporary names
47                              * (t0, t1, etc.).
48                              */
49
50                             yycode("%s = %s%s\n", $$ = getname(),
51                                                  isdigit(*yytext) ? "" : "_",
52                                                  yytext );
53                         }
54           ;
55   %%
56   /*--------------------------------------------------------------------*/
57
```

➡

```
     Listing 5.5. continued...
58   char    *yypstk( vptr, dptr )
59   char    **vptr;                  /* Value-stack pointer           */
60   char    *dptr;                   /* Symbol-stack pointer (not used) */
61   {
62       /* Yypstk is used by the debugging routines. It is passed a pointer to a
63        * value-stack item and should return a string representing that item. Since
64        * the current value stack is a stack of string pointers, all it has to do
65        * is dereference one level of indirection.
66        */
67
68       return *vptr ? *vptr : "-" ;
69   }
70
71   /*----------------------------------------------------------------------*/
72
73   yy_init_occs()
74   {
75       /* Called by yyparse just before it starts parsing. Initialize the
76        * temporary-variable-name stack and output declarations for the variables.
77        */
78
79       push( Namepool, "t9" ); push( Namepool, "t8" ); push( Namepool, "t7" );
80       push( Namepool, "t6" ); push( Namepool, "t5" ); push( Namepool, "t4" );
81       push( Namepool, "t3" ); push( Namepool, "t2" ); push( Namepool, "t1" );
82       push( Namepool, "t0" );
83
84       yycode( "public word t0, t1, t2, t3, t4;\n" );
85       yycode( "public word t5, t6, t7, t8, t9;\n" );
86   }
87
88   /*----------------------------------------------------------------------*/
89
90   main( argc, argv )
91   char    **argv;
92   {
93       yy_get_args( argc, argv );
94
95       if( argc < 2 )
96           ferr("Need file name\n");
97
98       else if( ii_newfile(argv[1]) < 0 )
99           ferr( "Can't open %s\n", argv[1] );
100
101      yyparse();
102      exit( 0 );
103  }
```

Occs generates several output files for these input files. A symbol-table dump is in Listing 5.7 (*yyout.sym*), and token definitions are in *yyout.h*, Listing 5.8. The symbol table shows the internal values used for other various symbols including the production numbers that are assigned by **occs** to the individual productions. These numbers are useful for deciphering the tables and debugging. The token-definitions file is typically **#include**d in the LEX input file so that the analyzer knows which values to return. The token names are taken directly from the %term and %left declarations in the **occs** input file.

Occs token definitions (*yyout.h*), symbol table (*yyout.sym*).

Listing 5.6. *expr.lex*— LeX Input File for an Expression Compiler

```
 1   %{
 2   #include "yyout.h"
 3   %}
 4   digit    [0-9]
 5   alpha    [a-zA-Z_]
 6   alnum    [0-9a-zA-Z_]
 7   %%
 8
 9   "+"              return PLUS;
10   "*"              return STAR;
11   "("              return LP;
12   ")"              return RP;
13   {digit}+            |
14   {alpha}{alnum}*  return NUM_OR_ID;
15   .                   ;
16   %%
```

Listing 5.7. *yyout.sym*— Symbol Table Generated from Input File in Listing 5.5

```
 1   --------------- Symbol table ------------------
 2
 3   NONTERMINAL SYMBOLS:
 4   e (257)   <>
 5      FIRST : NUM_OR_ID LP
 6        1: e -> e PLUS t ....................................PREC 1
 7        2: e -> t
 8
 9   f (259)   <>
10      FIRST : NUM_OR_ID LP
11        5: f -> LP e RP ...................................PREC 3
12        6: f -> NUM_OR_ID
13
14   s (256)  (goal symbol) <>
15      FIRST : NUM_OR_ID LP
16        0: s -> e
17
18   t (258)   <>
19      FIRST : NUM_OR_ID LP
20        3: t -> t STAR f .................................PREC 2
21        4: t -> f
22
23
24   TERMINAL SYMBOLS:
25
26   name            value  prec  assoc  field
27   LP                4     3     1      <>
28   NUM_OR_ID         1     0     -      <>
29   PLUS              2     1     1      <>
30   RP                5     3     1      <>
31   STAR              3     2     1      <>
```

Listing 5.8. *yyout.h*— Token Definitions Generated from Input File in Listing 5.5

```
1   #define _EOI_     0
2   #define NUM_OR_ID 1
3   #define PLUS      2
4   #define STAR      3
5   #define LP        4
6   #define RP        5
```

The **occs**-generated parser starts in Listing 5.9. As before, listings for those parts of the output file that are just copied from the template file are labeled *occs.par*. The **occs**-generated parts of the output file (tables, and so forth) are in listings labeled *yyout.c*. Since we are really looking at a single output file, however, line numbers carry from one listing to the other, regardless of the name. The output starts with the file header in Listing 5.9. Global variables likely to be used by yourself (such as the output streams) are defined here. Note that *<stdio.h>*, *<stdarg.h>*, and *<tools/yystk.h>*, are **#include**d on lines one to three. *<stdarg.h>* contains macros that implement the ANSI variable-argument mechanism and *<tools/yystk.h>* contains stack-maintenance macros. These last two files are both described in Appendix A. The remainder of the header, in Listing 5.10, is copied from the header portion of the input file.

Listing 5.9. *occs.par*— File Header

```
1   #include <stdio.h>
2   #include <stdarg.h>
3   #include <tools/yystack.h>
4
5   FILE   *yycodeout = stdout ;          /* Output stream (code). */
6   FILE   *yybssout  = stdout ;          /* Output stream (bss ). */
7   FILE   *yydataout = stdout ;          /* Output stream (data). */
8   int    yylookahead ;                  /* Lookahead token.      */
9
10  extern char *yytext;                  /* Declared by lex in lexyy.c */
11  extern int  yylineno;
12  extern int  yyleng;
13
14  extern char *ii_ptext()  ;            /* Lookback function used by lex  */
15  extern int  ii_plength() ;            /* in /src/compiler/lib/input.c.  */
16  extern int  ii_plineno() ;
17
18  #ifdef YYDEBUG                /* Define YYD here so that it can be used */
19  #   define YYD(x) x          /* in the user-supplied header.           */
20  #else
21  #   define YYD(x) /* empty */
22  #endif
23
24  /*-----------------------------------------------------------------*/
```

The output file continues in Listing 5.11 with various macro definitions. As was the case in the LEX output file, these macros are not redefined if you defined them in the header part of the input file. (That's what all the **#ifndef**s are for.) Note that `printf()` calls are mapped to `yycode()` calls on line 44 if debugging is enabled. I've done this because the standard `printf()` circumvents the window-output mechanism and messes up the screen. This way, all `printf()` calls in the **occs** input file, at least, will behave properly. Direct output to the screen in other files is still a problem,

Macro definitions.

`printf()` mapped to `yycode()`.

Listing 5.10. *yyout.c*— Code Taken from Input-Specification Header

```
25  #include <stdio.h>
26  #include <ctype.h>
27  #include <malloc.h>
28  #include <tools/debug.h>
29  #include <tools/stack.h>
30
31  extern char *yytext;
32
33  stk_dcl( Namepool, char*, 10 );          /* Stack of 10 temporary-var names */
34  #define freename(x) push( Namepool, (x) )  /* Release a temporary variable   */
35  #define getname()   pop ( Namepool     )   /* Allocate a temporary variable  */
36
37  typedef char            *stype;      /* Value stack is stack of char pointers */
38  #define YYSTYPE         stype
39
40  #define YYSHIFTACT(tos) (*tos="")                    /* Shift a null string */
```

Stack-macro customization.
    however. The stack macros, discussed in Appendix A and **#include**d on line three of Listing 5.9, are customized on line 87 of Listing 5.11. The redefinition of yystk_cls causes all the stacks declared with subsequent yystk_dcl() invocations to be **static**.

Listing 5.11. *occs.par*— Definitions

```
41  #undef YYD              /* Redefine YYD in case YYDEBUG was defined  */
42  #ifdef YYDEBUG          /* explicitly in the header rather than with  */
43  #   define YYD(x) x     /* a -D on the occs command line.             */
44  #   define printf  yycode  /* Make printf() calls go to output window  */
45  #else
46  #   define YYD(x) /* empty */
47  #endif
48
49  #ifndef YYACCEPT
50  #   define YYACCEPT return(0)   /* Action taken when input is accepted.    */
51  #endif
52
53  #ifndef YYABORT
54  #   define YYABORT return(1)    /* Action taken when input is rejected.    */
55  #endif
56
57  #ifndef YYPRIVATE
58  #   define YYPRIVATE static     /* define to a null string to make public   */
59  #endif
60
61  #ifndef YYMAXERR
62  #   define YYMAXERR 25          /* Abort after this many errors            */
63  #endif
64
65  #ifndef YYMAXDEPTH         /* State and value stack depth            */
66  #   define YYMAXDEPTH 128
67  #endif
68
69  #ifndef YYCASCADE         /* Suppress error msgs. for this many cycles */
70  #   define YYCASCADE 5
71  #endif
72
```
→

Listing 5.11. continued...

```
73   #ifndef YYSTYPE                       /* Default value stack type          */
74   #      define YYSTYPE int
75   #endif
76                                         /* Default shift action: inherit $$  */
77   #ifndef YYSHIFTACT
78   #      define YYSHIFTACT(tos)  ( (tos)[0] = yylval )
79   #endif
80
81   #ifdef YYVERBOSE
82   #      define YYV(x)  x
83   #else
84   #      define YYV(x)
85   #endif
86
87   #undef  yystk_cls                      /* redefine stack macros for local */
88   #define yystk_cls YYPRIVATE            /* use.                            */
89
90   /* -------------------------------------------------------------------
91    * #defines used in the tables. Note that the parsing algorithm assumes that
92    * the start state is State 0. Consequently, since the start state is shifted
93    * only once when we start up the parser, we can use 0 to signify an accept.
94    * This is handy in practice because an accept is, by definition, a reduction
95    * into the start state. Consequently, a YYR(0) in the parse table represents an
96    * accepting action and the table-generation code doesn't have to treat the
97    * accepting action any differently than a normal reduce.
98    *
99    * Note that if you change YY_TTYPE to something other than short, you can no
100   * longer use the -T command-line switch.
101   */
102
103   #define YY_IS_ACCEPT    0             /* Accepting action (reduce by 0) */
104   #define YY_IS_SHIFT(s)  ((s) > 0)     /* s is a shift action            */
105
106   typedef short    YY_TTYPE;
107   #define YYF      ((YY_TTYPE)( (unsigned)~0 >>1 ))
108
109   /*-------------------------------------------------------------------
110    * Various global variables used by the parser. They're here because they can
111    * be referenced by the user-supplied actions, which follow these definitions.
112    *
113    * If -p or -a was given to OCCS, make Yy_rhslen and Yy_val (the right-hand
114    * side length and the value used for $$) public, regardless of the value of
115    * YYPRIVATE (yylval is always public). Note that occs generates extern
116    * statements for these in yyacts.c (following the definitions section).
117    */
118
119   #if !defined(YYACTION) || !defined(YYPARSER)
120   #      define YYP /* nothing */
121   #else
122   #      define YYP    YYPRIVATE
123   #endif
124
125   YYPRIVATE int      yynerrs = 0;               /* Number of errors.        */
126
127   yystk_dcl( Yy_stack, int, YYMAXDEPTH );       /* State stack.             */
128
129       YYSTYPE yylval;                           /* Attribute for last token. */
130   YYP YYSTYPE Yy_val;                           /* Used to hold $$.         */
```

Listing 5.11. continued...

```
131    YYP YYSTYPE Yy_vstack[ YYMAXDEPTH ];      /* Value stack. Can't use    */
132    YYP YYSTYPE *Yy_vsp;                       /* yystack.h macros because  */
133                                               /* YYSTYPE could be a struct.*/
134    YYP int      Yy_rhslen;                    /* Number of nonterminals on */
135                                               /* right-hand side of the    */
136                                               /* production being reduced. */
```

YY_IS_SHIFT, YY_TTYPE.

The definitions on lines 103 to 107 of Listing 5.11 are used for the tables. Shift actions are represented as positive numbers (the number is the next state), reduce operations are negative numbers (the absolute value of the number is the production by which you're reducing) and zero represents an accept action (the input is complete when you reduce by Production 0). YY_IS_SHIFT on line 104 is used to differentiate between these. YY_TTYPE on the next line is the table type. You should probably change it to **short** if your machine uses a 16-bit **short** and 32-bit **int**. YY_TTYPE must be signed, and a **char** is usually too small because of the number of states in the machine.

Error marker: YYF.

YYF, on line 107 of Listing 5.11, represents failure transitions in the parse tables. (YYF is not stored in the compressed table, but is returned by the table-decompression subroutine, yy_act_next(), which I'll discuss in a moment.) It evaluates the largest positive integer. (I'm assuming two's complement numbers). Breaking the macro down: **(unsigned)** ~0 is an unsigned int with all its bits set. The **unsigned** suppresses sign extension on the right shift of one bit, which yields a number with all but the high bit set. The resulting quantity is cast back to a YY_TTYPE so that it will agree with other elements of the table. Note that this macro is not particularly portable, and might have to be changed if you change the YY_TTYPE definition on the previous line. Just be sure that YYF has a value that can't be confused with a normal shift or reduce directive.

YYP.

The final part of Listing 5.11 comprises declarations for parser-related variables that might be accessed in one of the actions. The state and value stacks are defined here (along with the stack pointers), as well as some house-keeping variables. Note that those variables of class YYP are made public if *-a* or *-p* is specified to **occs**. (In which case, YYACTION and YYPARSER are not both present—the definition is output by **occs** itself at the top of the file, and the test is on line 119).

Action subroutine, yy_act().

Listing 5.12 holds the action subroutine, which executes the code-generation actions from the **occs** input file. Various tables that **occs** generates from the input grammar are also in this listing. The actions imbedded in the input grammar are output as **case** statements in the **switch** in yy_act() (on lines 137 to 169 of Listing 5.12). As in **LLama**, the **case** values are the production numbers. Each production is assigned a unique but arbitrary number by **occs**; these numbers can be found in *yyout.sym* in Listing 5.7 on page 384, which is generated when **occs** finds a *-D*, *-s*, or *-S* command-line switch. The production numbers precede each production in the symbol-table output file. The start production is always Production 0, the next one in the input file is Production 1, and so forth.

Translated dollar attributes: $$, $1, etc.

Note that the dollar attributes have all been translated to references to the value stack at this juncture. For example, on line 164, the line:

```
t : t STAR f { yycode("%s *= %s\n", $1, $3); freename($3); }
  ;
```

has generated:

```
{ yycode("%s *= %s\n", yyvsp[2], yyvsp[0]); freename(yyvsp[0]); }
```

in the action subroutine. yyvsp is the value-stack pointer and a downward-growing stack is used. (A push is a *--yyvsp=x; a pop is a *yyvsp++.) The situation is

Listing 5.12. *yyout.c*— The Action Subroutine and Tables

```
137   yy_act( yy_production_number, yyvsp )
138   int       yy_production_number;
139   YYSTYPE *yyvsp;
140   {
141       /* This subroutine holds all the actions in the original input
142        * specification. It normally returns 0, but if any of your actions return a
143        * non-zero number, then the parser will halt immediately, returning that
144        * nonzero number to the calling subroutine. I've violated my usual naming
145        * conventions about local variables so that this routine can be put into a
146        * separate file by occs.
147        */
148
149       switch( yy_production_number )
150       {
151       case 1:
152           { yycode("%s += %s\n", yyvsp[2], yyvsp[0]); freename(yyvsp[0]); }
153           break;
154       case 6:
155           { yycode("%s = %s%s\n", Yy_val = getname(),
156                               isdigit(*yytext) ? "" : "_",
157                               yytext );
158           }
159           break;
160       case 5:
161           { Yy_val = yyvsp[1];      }
162           break;
163       case 3:
164           { yycode("%s *= %s\n", yyvsp[2], yyvsp[0]); freename(yyvsp[0]); }
165           break;
166       default: break;        /* In case there are no actions */
167       }
168       return 0;
169   }
170
171   /*-------------------------------------------------------
172    * Yy_stok[] is used for debugging and error messages. It is indexed
173    * by the internal value used for a token (as used for a column index in
174    * the transition matrix) and evaluates to a string naming that token.
175    */
176
177   char    *Yy_stok[] =
178   {
179           /*   0 */    "_EOI_",
180           /*   1 */    "NUM_OR_ID",
181           /*   2 */    "PLUS",
182           /*   3 */    "STAR",
183           /*   4 */    "LP",
184           /*   5 */    "RP"
185   };
186
187   /*-------------------------------------------------------
188    * The Yy_action table is action part of the LALR(1) transition matrix. It's
189    * compressed and can be accessed using the yy_next() subroutine, below.
190    *
191    *               Yya000[]={    3,    5,3   ,   2,2   ,   1,1   };
192    * state number---+          |    | |
193    * number of pairs in list-+    | |
194    * input symbol (terminal)------+ |
195    * action-----------------------+
```

Listing 5.12. continued...

```
196   *
197   *       action = yy_next( Yy_action, cur_state, lookahead_symbol );
198   *
199   *        action <  0    -- Reduce by production n
200   *        action == 0    -- Accept (ie. reduce by production 0)
201   *        action >  0    -- Shift to state n
202   *        action == YYF -- error
203   */
204
205   YYPRIVATE YY_TTYPE Yya000[]={ 2,   4,2    ,  1,1    };
206   YYPRIVATE YY_TTYPE Yya001[]={ 4,   5,-6   ,  3,-6   ,  2,-6   ,  0,-6  };
207   YYPRIVATE YY_TTYPE Yya003[]={ 2,   0,0    ,  2,7    };
208   YYPRIVATE YY_TTYPE Yya004[]={ 4,   5,-2   ,  2,-2   ,  0,-2   ,  3,8   };
209   YYPRIVATE YY_TTYPE Yya005[]={ 4,   5,-4   ,  3,-4   ,  2,-4   ,  0,-4  };
210   YYPRIVATE YY_TTYPE Yya006[]={ 2,   5,9    ,  2,7    };
211   YYPRIVATE YY_TTYPE Yya009[]={ 4,   5,-5   ,  3,-5   ,  2,-5   ,  0,-5  };
212   YYPRIVATE YY_TTYPE Yya010[]={ 4,   5,-1   ,  2,-1   ,  0,-1   ,  3,8   };
213   YYPRIVATE YY_TTYPE Yya011[]={ 4,   5,-3   ,  3,-3   ,  2,-3   ,  0,-3  };
214
215   YYPRIVATE YY_TTYPE *Yy_action[12] =
216   {
217       Yya000, Yya001, Yya000, Yya003, Yya004, Yya005, Yya006, Yya000, Yya000,
218       Yya009, Yya010, Yya011
219   };
220
221   /*--------------------------------------------------------
222    * The Yy_goto table is goto part of the LALR(1) transition matrix. It's com-
223    * pressed and can be accessed using the yy_next() subroutine, declared below.
224    *
225    *   nonterminal = Yy_lhs[ production number by which we just reduced ]
226    *
227    *                   Yyg000[]={   3,   5,3    ,  2,2    ,   1,1   };
228    *   uncovered state-+            |   |  |
229    *   number of pairs in list--+   |  |
230    *   nonterminal------------------+  |
231    *   goto this state-----------------+
232    *   goto_state = yy_next( Yy_goto, cur_state, nonterminal );
233    */
234
235   YYPRIVATE YY_TTYPE Yyg000[]={ 3,   3,5    ,  2,4    ,  1,3    };
236   YYPRIVATE YY_TTYPE Yyg002[]={ 3,   3,5    ,  2,4    ,  1,6    };
237   YYPRIVATE YY_TTYPE Yyg007[]={ 2,   3,5    ,  2,10   };
238   YYPRIVATE YY_TTYPE Yyg008[]={ 1,   3,11   };
239
240   YYPRIVATE YY_TTYPE *Yy_goto[12] =
241   {
242       Yyg000, NULL  , Yyg002, NULL  , NULL  , NULL  , NULL  , Yyg007, Yyg008,
243       NULL  , NULL  , NULL
244   };
245
246   /*--------------------------------------------------------
247    * The Yy_lhs array is used for reductions. It is indexed by production number
248    * and holds the associated left-hand side, adjusted so that the number can be
249    * used as an index into Yy_goto.
250    */
251
252   YYPRIVATE int Yy_lhs[7] =
253   {
```

```
      Listing 5.12. continued...

254              /*    0 */         0,
255              /*    1 */         1,
256              /*    2 */         1,
257              /*    3 */         2,
258              /*    4 */         2,
259              /*    5 */         3,
260              /*    6 */         3
261      };
262
263      /*-------------------------------------------------------
264       * The Yy_reduce[] array is indexed by production number and holds
265       * the number of symbols on the right hand side of the production.
266       */
267
268      YYPRIVATE int Yy_reduce[7] =
269      {
270              /*    0 */         1,
271              /*    1 */         3,
272              /*    2 */         1,
273              /*    3 */         3,
274              /*    4 */         1,
275              /*    5 */         3,
276              /*    6 */         1
277      };
278      #ifdef YYDEBUG
279
280      /*-------------------------------------------------------
281       * Yy_slhs[] is a debugging version of Yy_lhs[]. Indexed by production number,
282       * it evaluates to a string representing the left-hand side of the production.
283       */
284
285      YYPRIVATE char *Yy_slhs[7] =
286      {
287              /*    0 */         "s",
288              /*    1 */         "e",
289              /*    2 */         "e",
290              /*    3 */         "t",
291              /*    4 */         "t",
292              /*    5 */         "f",
293              /*    6 */         "f"
294      };
295
296      /*-------------------------------------------------------
297       * Yy_srhs[] is also used for debugging. It is indexed by production number
298       * and evaluates to a string representing the right-hand side of the production.
299       */
300
301      YYPRIVATE char *Yy_srhs[7] =
302      {
303              /*    0 */         "e",
304              /*    1 */         "e PLUS t",
305              /*    2 */         "t",
306              /*    3 */         "t STAR f",
307              /*    4 */         "f",
308              /*    5 */         "LP e RP",
309              /*    6 */         "NUM_OR_ID"
310      };
311      #endif
```

complicated by the fact that attributes are numbered from left to right, but the rightmost (not the leftmost) symbol is at the top of the parse stack. Consequently, the number that is part of the dollar attribute can't be used directly as an offset from the top of stack. You can use the size of the right-hand side to compute the correct offset, however. When a reduction is triggered, the symbols on the parse stack exactly match those on the right-hand side of the production. Given a production like $t{\rightarrow}t$ **STAR** f, f is at top of stack, **STAR** is just under the f, and t is under that. The situation is illustrated in Figure 5.12. yyvsp, the stack pointer, points at f, so $3 translates to yyvsp[0] in this case. Similarly, $2 translates to yyvsp[1], and $3 translates to yyvsp[2]. The stack offset for an attribute is the number of symbols on the right-hand side of the current production less the number that is part of the dollar attribute. $1 would be at yyvsp[3] if the right-hand side had four symbols in it.

Figure 5.12. Translating $N to Stack References

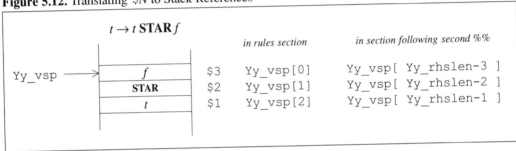

Figure 5.12 also shows how attributes are handled when they are found in the third part of the **occs** input file rather than imbedded in a production. The problem here is that the number of symbols on the right-hand side is available only when **occs** knows which production is being reduced (as is the case when an action in a production is being processed). Code in the third section of the input file is isolated from the actual production, so **occs** can't determine which production the attribute references. The parser solves the problem by setting a global variable, Yy_rhslen, to the number of symbols on the right-hand side of the production being reduced. Yy_rhslen is modified just before each reduction. This variable can then be used at run-time to get the correct value-stack item. Note that negative attribute numbers are also handled correctly by **occs**.[8] Figure 5.13 shows the value stack just before a reduction by $b{\rightarrow}d\ e\ f$ in the following grammar:

$$
\begin{aligned}
s &\rightarrow & a\ b\ c \\
b &\rightarrow & d\ e\ f\ \{\text{x=\$-1;}\}
\end{aligned}
$$

The $-1 in the second production references the a in the partially assembled first production.

Listing 5.12 continues on line 177 with a token-to-string translation table. It is indexed by token value (as found in *yyout.h*) and evaluates to a string naming that token. It's useful both for debugging and for printing error messages. The other conversion tables are used only for the debugging environment, so are **#ifdef**ed out when YYDEBUG is not defined. Yy_slhs[] on line 285 is indexed by production number and holds a string representing the left-hand side of that production. Yy_srhs[] on line 301 is

Attributes in code section of input file.

Right-hand-side length: Yy_rhslen.

Token-to-string conversion: Yy_stok[].

Yy_slhs[], Yy_srhs[].

---

8. They aren't accepted by **yacc**.

Figure 5.13. Translating $-N to Stack References

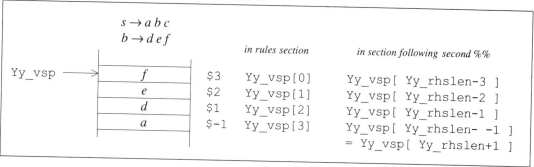

similar, but it holds strings representing the right-hand sides of the productions.

Lines 187 to 277 of Listing 5.12 hold the actual parse tables. The state machine for our current grammar was presented earlier (in Table 5.11 on page 369) and the compressed tables were discussed in that section as well. Single-reduction states have not been eliminated here. I'll demonstrate how the parse tables are used with an example parse of (1+2). The parser starts up by pushing the number of the start state, State 0, onto the state stack. It determines the next action by using the state number at the top of stack and the current input (lookahead) symbol. The input symbol is a left parenthesis (an **LP** token), which is defined in *yyout.h* to have a numeric value of 4. (It's also listed in *yyout.sym.*) The parser, then, looks in `Yy_action[0][4]`. Row 0 of the table is represented in `Yya000` (on Line 205 of Listing 5.12), and it's interested in the first pair: [4,2]. The 4 is the column number, and the 2 is the parser directive. Since 2 is positive, this is a shift action: 2 is pushed onto the parse stack and the input is advanced. Note that `Yya000` also represents rows 2, 6, and 7 of the table because all four rows have the same contents.

The next token is a number (a **NUM_OR_ID** token, defined as 1 in *yyout.h*). The parser now looks at `Yy_action[2][1]` (2 is the current state, 1 the input token). Row 2 is also represented by `Yya000` on line 205 of Listing 5.12, and Column 1 is represented by the second pair in the list: [1,1]. The action here is a shift to State 1, so a 1 is pushed and the input is advanced again.

A 1 is now on the top of the stack, and the input symbol is a **PLUS**, which has the value 2. `Yy_action[1][2]` holds a −6 (it's in the third pair in Yya000, on line 205), which is a reduce-by-Production-6 directive (reduce by *f*→**NUM_OR_ID**). The first thing the parser does is perform the associated action, with a `yy_act(6)` call. The actual reduction is done next. `Yy_reduce[6]` evaluates to the number of objects on the right-hand side of Production 6—in this case, 1. So, one object is popped, uncovering the previous-state number (2). Next, the goto component of the reduce operation is performed. The parser does this with two table lookups. First, it finds out which left-hand side is associated with Production 6 by looking it up in `Yy_lhs[6]` (it finds a 3 there). It then looks up the next state in `Yy_goto`. The machine is in State 2, so the row array is fetched from `Yy_goto[2]`, which holds a pointer to `Yyg002`. The parser then searches the pairs in `Yyg002` for the left-hand side that it just got from `Yy_lhs` (the 3), and it finds the pair [3,5]—the next state is State 5 (a 5 is pushed). The parse continues in this manner until a reduction by Production 0 occurs.

Listing 5.13 contains the table-decompression routine mentioned earlier (`yy_next()` on line one), and various output subroutines as well. Two versions of the output routines are presented at the end of the listing, one for debugging and another version for production mode. The output routines are mapped to window-output functions if debugging mode is enabled, as in **LLama**. Also of interest is a third, symbol stack

Using occs' compressed parse tables.

```
0                    (1+2)
```

```
0 2                  1+2)
```

```
0 2 1                +2)
```

```
0 2                  +2)
```

```
0 2 5                +2)
```

Table decompression: `yy_next()`.

Symbol stack: (Yy_dstack) defined on line 24. This stack is the one that's displayed in the middle of
Yy_dstack.   the debugging environment's *stack* window. It holds strings representing the symbols
                           that are on the parse stack.

Listing 5.13. *occs.par*— Table-Decompression and Output Subroutines

```
1    YYPRIVATE YY_TTYPE  yy_next( table, cur_state, inp )
2    YY_TTYPE  **table;
3    YY_TTYPE  cur_state;
4    int       inp;
5    {
6        /* Next-state routine for the compressed tables. Given current state and
7         * input symbol (inp), return next state.
8         */
9
10       YY_TTYPE   *p = table[ cur_state ] ;
11       int        i;
12
13       if( p )
14           for( i = (int) *p++; --i >= 0 ; p += 2 )
15               if( inp == p[0] )
16                   return p[1];
17
18       return  YYF;
19   }
20
21   /*--------------------------------------------------------------------*/
22   #ifdef YYDEBUG
23
24   yystk_dcl( Yy_dstack, char*, YYMAXDEPTH );                /* Symbol stack        */
25
26   yycode( fmt )
27   char    *fmt;
28   {
29       va_list        args;
30       va_start( args,  fmt );
31       yy_output( 0, fmt, args );
32   }
33
34   yydata( fmt )
35   char    *fmt;
36   {
37       va_list        args;
38       va_start( args,  fmt );
39       yy_output( 1, fmt, args );
40   }
41
42   yybss( fmt )
43   char    *fmt;
44   {
45       va_list        args;
46       va_start( args,  fmt );
47       yy_output( 2, fmt, args );
48   }
49
50   /* yycomment() and yyerror() are defined in yydebug.c */
51
52   #else   /*- - - - - - - - - - - - - - - - - - - - - - - - - - - - */
53
```

Listing 5.13. continued...

```
54    #       define yy_nextoken()        yylex()     /* when YYDEBUG isn't defined.    */
55    #       define yy_quit_debug()
56    #       define yy_init_debug()
57    #       define yy_pstack(x,y)
58    #       define yy_sym()
59
60    /* Use the following routines just like printf() to create output. The only
61     * differences are that yycode is sent to the stream called yycodeout, yydata
62     * goes to yydataout, and yybss goes to yybssout. All of these are initialized
63     * to stdout. It's up to you to close the streams after the parser terminates.
64     */
65
66    yycode( fmt )
67    char    *fmt;
68    {
69            va_list    args;
70            va_start( args,      fmt );
71            vfprintf( yycodeout, fmt, args );
72    }
73
74    yydata( fmt )
75    char    *fmt;
76    {
77            va_list         args;
78            va_start( args,  fmt );
79            vfprintf( yydataout, fmt, args );
80    }
81
82    yybss( fmt )
83    char    *fmt;
84    {
85            va_list         args;
86            va_start( args,  fmt );
87            vfprintf( yybssout, fmt, args );
88    }
89
90    void    yycomment( fmt )
91    char    *fmt;
92    {
93            va_list  args;
94            va_start( args,   fmt );
95            vfprintf( stdout, fmt, args );
96    }
97
98    void    yyerror( fmt, ... )
99    char    *fmt;
100   {
101           extern char *yytext;
102           extern int  yylineno;
103           va_list    args;
104
105           va_start( args, fmt );
106           fprintf ( stderr, "ERROR (line %d near %s): ", yylineno, yytext );
107           vfprintf( stderr, fmt, args );
108           fprintf ( stderr, "\n" );
109   }
110   #endif
```

          The parser itself starts in Listing 5.14. The shift and reduce operations have been
broken out into subroutines (on lines 111 and 128) in order to simplify the code in the
parser itself. A new state is pushed onto the state stack on line 115. Garbage is pushed
onto the value stack on line 116, but the user-supplied, default shift action [in the macro
`YYSHIFTACT()`] is performed on the next line. This macro is passed a pointer to the top
of the value stack (after the push)—the default action (defined on line 78 of Listing 5.11,
page 387) pushes the contents of `yylval` onto the stack, so you can push an attribute for
a nonterminal by modifying `yylval` from an accepting action in a LEX input file. (This
process is discussed in Appendix E.) The debugging stack is kept aligned with the other
stacks by pushing a string representing the shifted token on line 121. The
`yy_pstack()` call on the next line updates the stack window and waits for another
command if necessary. Breakpoints are also activated there.

Listing 5.14. *occs.par*— The Parser

```
111   YYPRIVATE    yy_shift( new_state, lookahead )      /* shift            */
112   int          new_state;                            /* push this state  */
113   int          lookahead;                            /* Current lookahead */
114   {
115       yypush( Yy_stack, new_state );
116       --Yy_vsp;                                       /* Push garbage onto value stack */
117       YYSHIFTACT( Yy_vsp );                           /* Then do default action        */
118
119   #ifdef YYDEBUG
120       yycomment( "Shift %0.16s (%d)\n", Yy_stok[ lookahead ], new_state);
121       yypush_( Yy_dstack, Yy_stok[lookahead] );
122       yy_pstack(0, 1);
123   #endif
124   }
125
126   /*-------------------------------------------------------------------*/
127
128   YYPRIVATE        yy_reduce( prod_num, amount )
129   int     prod_num;                       /* Reduce by this production              */
130   int     amount;                         /* # symbols on right-hand side of prod_num */
131   {
132       int next_state;
133
134       yypopn( Yy_stack,  amount );        /* Pop n items off the state stack */
135       Yy_vsp += amount;                   /* and the value stack.            */
136       *--Yy_vsp = Yy_val;                 /* Push $$ onto value stack        */
137
138       next_state = yy_next( Yy_goto, yystk_item(Yy_stack,0), Yy_lhs[prod_num] );
139
140   #ifndef YYDEBUG
141
142       yypush_ ( Yy_stack, next_state );
143
144   #else
145
146       yy_break( prod_num );                           /* activate production breakpoint */
147
148       yypopn_ ( Yy_dstack, amount );
149
150       YYV( yycomment("   pop %d item%s\n", amount, amount==1 ? "" : "s"); )
151       yy_pstack( 0, 0 );
152
```

→

```
     Listing 5.14. continued...
153          yypush_ ( Yy_stack, next_state            );
154          yypush_ ( Yy_dstack,  Yy_slhs[ prod_num ] );
155
156          YYV( yycomment("    push %0.16s (%d)", Yy_slhs[prod_num], next_state ); )
157
158          yy_pstack ( 0, 1 );
159
160      #endif
161      }
162
163      /*------------------------------------------------------------------*/
164
165      YYPRIVATE       void    yy_init_stack()          /* Initialize the stacks  */
166      {
167          yystk_clear( Yy_stack );
168          yypush_    ( Yy_stack,  0 );                 /* State stack = 0         */
169
170          Yy_vsp = Yy_vstack + (YYMAXDEPTH-1);         /* Value stack = garbage */
171
172      #   ifdef YYDEBUG
173          yystk_clear ( Yy_dstack );
174          yypush_     ( Yy_dstack, "$" );
175          yycomment   ( "Shift start state\n" );
176          yy_pstack   (0, 1);                          /* refresh stack window */
177      #   endif
178      }
179
180      /*------------------------------------------------------------------*/
181
182      YYPRIVATE        int yy_recover( tok, suppress )
183
184      int     tok;               /* token that caused the error      */
185      int     suppress;          /* No error message is printed if true  */
186      {
187          int         *old_sp  = yystk_p(Yy_stack);            /* State-stack pointer */
188          YYD( char   **old_dsp = yystk_p(Yy_dstack); )
189          YYD( char   *tos;                                    )
190
191          if( !suppress )
192          {
193              yyerror( "Unexpected %s\n", Yy_stok[tok] );
194              if( ++yynerrs > YYMAXERR )
195              {
196                  yyerror("Too many errors, aborting\n");
197                  return 0;
198              }
199          }
200
201          do {
202
203              while( !yystk_empty(Yy_stack)
204                        && yy_next( Yy_action, yystk_item(Yy_stack,0), tok) == YYF )
205              {
206                  yypop_ ( Yy_stack );
207
208                  YYD( tos = yypop_(Yy_dstack); )
209                  YYD( yycomment("Popping %d from state stack\n", tos); )
210                  YYD( yy_pstack(0, 1);                                   )
211              }
212
```

```
Listing 5.14. continued...
213            if( !yystk_empty(Yy_stack) )            /* Recovered successfully */
214            {
215                /* Align the value (and debug) stack to agree with the current
216                 * state-stack pointer.
217                 */
218
219                Yy_vsp = Yy_vstack + (yystk_ele(Yy_stack) - 1);
220
221                #ifdef YYDEBUG
222                    yystk_p(Yy_dstack) = Yy_dstack + (yystk_ele(Yy_stack) - 1);
223                    yycomment("Error recovery successful\n");
224                    yy_pstack(0, 1);
225                #endif
226
227                return tok;
228            }
229
230        yystk_p( Yy_stack ) = old_sp ;
231
232        YYD( yystk_p( Yy_dstack ) = old_dsp ;                      )
233        YYD( yycomment("Restoring state stack.");                  )
234        YYD( yy_pstack(1, 1);                                      )
235        YYD( yycomment("discarding %s\n", Yy_stok[tok]);     )
236
237    } while( ii_mark_prev(), tok = yy_nextoken() );
238
239    YYD( yycomment("Error recovery failed\n");  )
240    return 0;
241 }
242
243 /*----------------------------------------------------------------------*/
244
245 int      yyparse()
246 {
247     /* General-purpose LALR parser. Return 0 normally or -1 if the error
248      * recovery fails. Any other value is supplied by the user as a return
249      * statement in an action.
250      */
251
252     int act_num ;          /* Contents of current parse table entry     */
253     int errcode ;          /* Error code returned from yy_act()          */
254     int tchar   ;          /* Used to \0-terminate the lexeme            */
255     int suppress_err ;     /* Set to YYCASCADE after an error is found   */
256                            /* and decremented on each parse cycle. Error */
257                            /* messages aren't printed if it's true.      */
258
259 #ifdef YYDEBUG
260     if( !yy_init_debug( Yy_stack,  &yystk_p(Yy_stack ),
261                         Yy_dstack, &yystk_p(Yy_dstack),
262                         Yy_vstack, sizeof(YYSTYPE), YYMAXDEPTH) )
263         YYABORT;
264 #endif
265
266     yy_init_stack ();                              /* Initialize parse stack    */
267     yy_init_occs  ( Yy_vsp );
268
269     yylookahead  = yy_nextoken();                  /* Get first input symbol    */
270     suppress_err = 0;
271
```

Listing 5.14. continued...

```
272         while( 1 )
273         {
274             act_num = yy_next( Yy_action, yystk_item(Yy_stack,0), yylookahead );
275
276             if( suppress_err )
277                 --suppress_err;
278
279             if( act_num == YYF  )
280             {
281                 if( !(yylookahead = yy_recover( yylookahead, suppress_err )) )
282                     YYABORT;
283
284                 suppress_err = YYCASCADE;
285             }
286             else if( YY_IS_SHIFT(act_num) )                /* Simple shift action */
287             {
288                 /* Note that yytext and yyleng are undefined at this point because
289                  * they were modified in the else clause, below. You must use
290                  * ii_text(), etc., to put them into a reasonable condition if
291                  * you expect to access them in a YY_SHIFT action.
292                  */
293
294                 yy_shift( act_num, yylookahead );
295
296                 ii_mark_prev();
297                 yylookahead = yy_nextoken();
298             }
299             else
300             {
301                 /* Do a reduction by -act_num. The activity at 1, below, gives YACC
302                  * compatibility. It's just making the current lexeme available in
303                  * yytext and '\0' terminating the lexeme. The '\0' is removed at 2.
304                  * The problem is that you have to read the next lookahead symbol
305                  * before you can reduce by the production that had the previous
306                  * symbol at its far right. Note that, since Production 0 has the
307                  * goal symbol on its left-hand side, a reduce by 0 is an accept
308                  * action. Also note that ii_ptext()[ii_plength()] is used at (2)
309                  * rather than yytext[yyleng] because the user might have modified
310                  * yytext or yyleng in an action.
311                  *
312                  * Rather than pushing junk as the $$=$1 action on an epsilon
313                  * production, the old tos item is duplicated in this situation.
314                  */
315
316                 act_num   = -act_num ;
317                 Yy_rhslen = Yy_reduce[ act_num  ];
318                 Yy_val    = Yy_vsp[ Yy_rhslen ? Yy_rhslen-1 : 0 ];   /* $$ = $1 */
319
320                 yylineno        = ii_plineno() ;                      /* (1)     */
321                 yytext          = ii_ptext  () ;
322                 tchar           = yytext[ yyleng = ii_plength() ];
323                 yytext[yyleng] = '\0' ;
324
325                 YYD( yycomment("Reduce by (%d) %s->%s\n", act_num, \
326                                           Yy_slhs[act_num], Yy_srhs[act_num]); )
327
328                 if( errcode = yy_act( act_num, Yy_vsp ) )
329                     return errcode;
330
```

```
Listing 5.14. continued...
331              ii_ptext()[ ii_plength() ] = tchar;              /*  (2)     */
332
333              if( act_num == YY_IS_ACCEPT )
334                  break ;
335              else
336                  yy_reduce( act_num, Yy_rhslen );
337          }
338      }
339      YYD( yycomment( "Accept\n" );        )
340      YYD( yy_quit_debug();                )
341
342      YYACCEPT;
343  }
```

Reduce subroutine,
`yy_reduce()`.

Reductions are done in `yy_reduce()`, on line 128 of Listing 5.14. The subroutine pops as many stack items as are on the right-hand side of the production by which the parser's reducing on lines 134 to 136; the goto state is computed on line 138, and is pushed on line 142 (153 if debugging is enabled). Nothing is popped in the case of an ε production because `amount` is zero in this situation. `Yy_val` (which holds $$) is initialized to $1 before `yy_reduce` is called.[9] Similarly, the action code (in which `Yy_val` could be modified via $$) is executed after the initialization but before the `yy_reduce()` call. The code on lines 144 to 158 of Listing 5.14 is activated in debugging mode. The actions that I just described are performed here too, but they're done in several steps so that breakpoints and screen updates happen in reasonable places.

Stack initialization.

The stacks are all initialized in `yy_init_stack()` on line 165. This initialization must be done at run time because the parser might be called several times within a program (if, for example, it's being used to parse expressions in some large program rather than for a complete compiler). Initially, 0 is pushed onto the state stack, garbage onto the value stack, and the string "$" onto the debugging symbol stack.

Error recovery:
`yy_recover()`.

The next issue is error recovery, which is handled by `yy_recover()` on line 182 of Listing 5.15. This routine is passed the token that caused the error. It prints an error message if its second argument is false, and tries to recover from the error by manipulating the stack. The *panic-mode* error-recovery technique described earlier is used:

(1) Pop items off the stack until you enter a state that has a legitimate action on the current token (for which there is a nonerror transition on the current token). If you find such a state, you have recovered. Return the input token.

(2) Otherwise, if there are no such states on the stack, advance the input, restore the stack to its original condition (that is, to the condition it was in when the error occurred) and go to (1).

(3) If you get to the end of input, you can't recover from the error. Return 0 in this case.

The algorithm is represented in pseudocode in Table 5.14.

The parser itself:
`yyparse()`.

The actual parser, `yyparse()`, begins on line 245 of Listing 5.15. It is a straightforward implementation of the simplified, bottom-up parse algorithm in Listing 5.4 on page 373. The remainder of the output file is the third portion of the input file from Listing 5.5

---

9. **Yacc** hackers: Don't confuse this variable with `yylval`, discussed earlier. **Yacc** uses `yylval` both for $$ and for the default shift value—**occs** uses two different variables.

Table 5.14. Bottom-Up, Error-Recovery Algorithm

```
recover( tok )
{
    remember the_real_stack_pointer ;

    do {
        sp = the_real_stack_pointer ;

        while( stack not empty   && no_legal_transition( sp, tok ) )
            --sp;

        if( the stack is not empty )
        {
            the_real_stack_pointer = sp;
            return tok;
        }
    } while( (tok = advance( )) ≠   end_of_input );

    return 0;
}
```

on page 383. It is not reproduced here.

5.11 Implementing an LALR(1) Parser Generator— Occs Internals

This section discusses the source code for **occs**, a yacc-like program that translates an augmented, attributed grammar into the C source code for a parser. If you still haven't done it, you must read Appendix E, which is a user's manual for **occs**, before continuing. (I really mean it this time.)

5.11.1 Modifying the Symbol Table for LALR(1) Grammars

Most of the important differences between **LLama** and **occs** are in the do_file() subroutine (Listing 4.36, page 327, line 272). The OX() macros conditionally compile the code that is unique to **occs**. [LL() is used for **LLama**-specific code.] There are other trivial changes scattered throughout the program, but the important ones are in do_file().

The first order of business is modifying the grammar somewhat. **LLama**'s top-down parser can handle actions imbedded in the middle of a production because it just puts them onto the parse stack like any other symbol. The bottom-up parser used by **occs** has to do the actions as part of a reduction, however. Consequently, it has to handle actions differently. The patch() subroutine (on line 29 of Listing 5.15) modifies the grammar to be suitable for **occs**, and at the same time removes all actions from the PRODUCTIONs themselves. Actions are output as cases in the **switch** statement in the yy_act() subroutine (discussed earlier on page 388). The output **case** statements reference the production number with which the action is associated. The action code itself can safely be discarded once it is output because **occs** no longer needs it.

Modifying the grammar for occs: 'do_patch()'

Listing 5.15. *yypatch.c*— Modify Grammar for Use in **Occs**

```
 1   #include <stdio.h>
 2   #include <ctype.h>
 3   #include <malloc.h>
 4
 5   #include <tools/debug.h>
 6   #include <tools/set.h>
 7   #include <tools/hash.h>
 8   #include <tools/compiler.h>
 9   #include <tools/l.h>
10   #include "parser.h"
11
12   /*----------------------------------------------------------------*/
13
14   void patch          P(( void            ));                    /* public */
15
16   void dopatch        P(( SYMBOL *sym     ));                    /* local  */
17   void print_one_case P(( int case_val, unsigned char *action, \
18                      int rhs_size, int lineno, struct _prod_ *prod ));
19
20   /*----------------------------------------------------------------*/
21
22   PRIVATE int     Last_real_nonterm ;     /* This is the number of the last    */
23                                           /* nonterminal to appear in the input */
24                                           /* grammar [as compared to the ones   */
25                                           /* that patch() creates].             */
26
27   /*----------------------------------------------------------------*/
28
29   PUBLIC void patch()
30   {
31       /*   This subroutine does several things:
32        *
33        *       * It modifies the symbol table as described in the text.
34        *       * It prints the action subroutine and deletes the memory associated
35        *         with the actions.
36        *
37        * This is not a particularly good subroutine from a structured programming
38        * perspective because it does two very different things at the same time.
39        * You save a lot of code by combining operations, however.
40        */
41
42       void dopatch();
43
44       static char *top[] =
45       {
46           "",
47           "yy_act( yypnum, yyvsp )",
48           "int           yypnum;               /* production number   */",
49           "YYSTYPE       *yyvsp;               /* value-stack pointer */",
50           "{",
51           "     /* This subroutine holds all the actions in the original input",
52           "      * specification. It normally returns 0, but if any of your",
53           "      * actions return a non-zero number, then the parser halts",
54           "      * immediately, returning that nonzero number to the calling",
55           "      * subroutine.",
56           "      */",
57           "",
58           "     switch( yypnum )",
59           "     {",
```

Listing 5.15. continued...

```
60              NULL
61         };
62
63         static char *bot[] =
64         {
65              "",
66              "   #ifdef YYDEBUG",
67              "       default: yycomment(\"Production %d: no action\\n\", yypnum);",
68              "           break;",
69              "   #endif",
70              "       }",
71              "",
72              "   return 0;",
73         "}",
74              NULL
75         };
76
77         Last_real_nonterm = Cur_nonterm;
78
79         if( Make_actions )
80             printv( Output, top );
81
82         ptab( Symtab, dopatch, NULL, 0 );
83
84         if( Make_actions )
85             printv( Output, bot );
86     }
87
88  /*------------------------------------------------------------------------*/
89
90  PRIVATE void dopatch(sym)
91  SYMBOL   *sym;
92  {
93      PRODUCTION   *prod;      /* Current right-hand side of sym            */
94      SYMBOL       **p2 ;      /* General-purpose pointer                   */
95      SYMBOL       **pp ;      /* Pointer to one symbol on rhs              */
96      SYMBOL       *cur ;      /* Current element of right-hand side        */
97
98      if( !ISNONTERM(sym)  ||  sym->val > Last_real_nonterm )
99      {
100         /* If the current symbol isn't a nonterminal, or if it is a nonterminal
101          * that used to be an action (one that we just transformed), ignore it.
102          */
103         return;
104     }
105
106     for( prod = sym->productions; prod ; prod = prod->next )
107     {
108         if( prod->rhs_len == 0 )
109             continue;
110
111         pp  = prod->rhs + (prod->rhs_len - 1);
112         cur = *pp;
113
114         if( ISACT(cur) )                            /* Check rightmost symbol */
115         {
116             print_one_case(  prod->num, cur->string, --(prod->rhs_len),
117                                         cur->lineno, prod );
118
```

Listing 5.15. continued...

```
119                  delsym  ( (HASH_TAB*) Symtab, (BUCKET*) cur );
120                  free    ( cur->string );
121                  freesym ( cur );
122                  *pp-- = NULL;
123              }
124                              /* cur is no longer valid because of the --pp above. */
125                              /* Count the number of nonactions in the right-hand  */
126                              /* side.                                             */
127
128          for(; pp >= prod->rhs; --pp )
129          {
130              cur = *pp;
131
132              if( !ISACT(cur) )
133                  continue;
134
135              if( Cur_nonterm >= MAXNONTERM )
136                  error(1,"Too many nonterminals & actions (%d max)\n", MAXTERM);
137              else
138              {
139                  /* Transform the action into a nonterminal. */
140
141                  Terms[ cur->val = ++Cur_nonterm ] = cur ;
142
143                  cur->productions = (PRODUCTION*) malloc( sizeof(PRODUCTION) );
144                  if( !cur->productions )
145                      error(1, "INTERNAL [dopatch]: Out of memory\n");
146
147                  print_one_case( Num_productions,  /* Case value to use.       */
148                                  cur->string,      /* Source code.             */
149                                  pp - prod->rhs,   /* # symbols to left of act.*/
150                                  cur->lineno,      /* Input line # of code.    */
151                                  prod
152                              );
153
154                  /* Once the case is printed, the string argument can be freed.*/
155
156                  free( cur->string );
157                  cur->string             = NULL;
158                  cur->productions->num     = Num_productions++ ;
159                  cur->productions->lhs     = cur ;
160                  cur->productions->rhs_len = 0;
161                  cur->productions->rhs[0]  = NULL;
162                  cur->productions->next    = NULL;
163                  cur->productions->prec    = 0;
164
165                  /* Since the new production goes to epsilon and nothing else,
166                   * FIRST(new) == { epsilon }. Don't bother to refigure the
167                   * follow sets because they won't be used in the LALR(1) state-
168                   * machine routines [If you really want them, call follow()
169                   * again.]
170                   */
171
172                  cur->first = newset();
173                  ADD( cur->first, EPSILON );
174              }
175          }
176      }
177  }
178
```

Listing 5.15. continued...

```
179   PRIVATE void print_one_case( case_val, action, rhs_size, lineno, prod )
180   int            case_val;          /* Numeric value attached to case itself.*/
181   unsigned char  *action;           /* Source Code to execute in case.       */
182   int            rhs_size;          /* Number of symbols on right-hand side. */
183   int            lineno;            /* input line number (for #lines).       */
184   PRODUCTION     *prod;             /* Pointer to right-hand side.           */
185   {
186       /* Print out one action as a case statement. All $-specifiers are mapped
187        * to references to the value stack: $$ becomes Yy_vsp[0], $1 becomes
188        * Yy_vsp[-1], etc. The rhs_size argument is used for this purpose.
189        * [see do_dollar() in yydollar.c for details].
190        */
191
192       int        num, i;
193       char       *do_dollar();            /* source found in yydollar.c   */
194       extern char *production_str();      /* source found in acts.c       */
195       char       fname[40], *fp;          /* place to assemble $<fname>1  */
196
197       if( !Make_actions )
198           return;
199
200       output("\n    case %d: /*  %s  */\n\n\t", case_val, production_str(prod) );
201
202       if( !No_lines )
203           output("#line %d \"%s\"\n\t", lineno, Input_file_name );
204
205       while( *action )
206       {
207           if( *action != '$' )
208               output( "%c", *action++ );
209           else
210           {
211               /* Skip the attribute reference. The if statement handles $$ the
212                * else clause handles the two forms: $N and $-N, where N is a
213                * decimal number. When we hit the do_dollar call (in the output()
214                * call), "num" holds the number associated with N, or DOLLAR_DOLLAR
215                * in the case of $$.
216                */
217
218               if( *++action != '<' )
219                   *fname = '\0';
220               else
221               {
222                   ++action;        /* skip the < */
223                   fp = fname;
224
225                   for(i=sizeof(fname); --i>0 && *action && *action != '>'; )
226                       *fp++ = *action++;
227
228                   *fp = '\0';
229                   if( *action == '>' )
230                       ++action;
231               }
232
233               if( *action == '$' )
234               {
235                   num = DOLLAR_DOLLAR;
236                   ++action;
237               }
```

Listing 5.15. continued...

```
238                   else
239                   {
240                       num = atoi( action );
241                       if( *action == '-' )
242                               ++action ;
243                       while( isdigit(*action) )
244                               ++action ;
245                   }
246
247                   output( "%s", do_dollar( num, rhs_size, lineno, prod, fname ));
248               }
249           }
250       output ("\n            break;\n"              );
251   }
```

Those actions that are already at the far right of a production are just output with the production number as the case value (by the **if** statement in do_patch() on lines 114 to 123 of Listing 5.15). The action is effectively removed from the production with the *pp--=NULL on line 122. The **for** loop that starts on line 128 looks for imbedded actions, and, if any are found, modifies the grammar accordingly. Productions of the form:

Imbedded actions.

```
s   :   symbols {action();} symbols ;
```

are translated into:

```
s   :   symbols 001 symbols
        ;

001 :   { action(); }
        ;
```

The new nonterminal (named 001, above) is created on lines 141 to 145 (and initialized on lines 156 to 173) by transforming the existing SYMBOL structure (the one that represents the action) into a nonterminal that has an empty right-hand side. The new production number is assigned on line 141. Note that the production in which the action was imbedded doesn't need to be modified. The SYMBOL pointer that used to reference the action now references the nonterminal, but it's the same pointer in both situations.

The print_one_case() routine, which prints the code associated with the action, starts on line 179 of Listing 5.15. Dollar attributes ($$, $1, $-1, and so forth) are handled on lines 209 to 248. The actual work is done by do_dollar(), in Listing 5.16. It is passed the attribute number (the 1 in $1), the number of symbols on the right-hand side of the current production, the input line number (for error messages) and a pointer to the PRODUCTION. It evaluates to a string holding the code necessary to reference the desired attribute (using the translations discussed earlier on Page 388).

Dollar-attribute translation: do_dollar().

Fields that are attached to a %union are also handled here (on lines 25 to 36 and 57 to 75 of Listing 5.16). The code on lines 25 to 36 handles any fields associated with $$, the names of which are found in *prod->lhs->field. The code on lines 57 to 75 handles other attributes. Since num is the *N* in $*N*, (prod->rhs)[num-1]->field gets the field associated with the specified element of the right-hand side. Note that fields can't be used with negative attribute numbers (because **occs** has no way of knowing what right-hand side corresponds to that field). A warning is printed in this case.

%union fields.

Listing 5.16. *yydollar.c* — Process $ Attributes

```
1    #include <stdio.h>
2    #include <tools/debug.h>
3    #include <tools/set.h>
4    #include <tools/hash.h>
5    #include "parser.h"
6
7    PUBLIC char *do_dollar( num, rhs_size, lineno, prod, fname )
8    int        num;          /* The N in $N, DOLLAR_DOLLAR for $$ (DOLLAR_DOLLAR) */
9                             /* is defined in parser.h, discussed in Chapter Four. */
10   int        rhs_size;     /* Number of symbols on right-hand side, 0 for tail  */
11   int        lineno;       /* Input line number for error messages              */
12   PRODUCTION *prod;        /* Only used if rhs_size is >= 0                      */
13   char       *fname;       /* name in $<name>N                                  */
14   {
15       static char buf[ 128 ];
16       int i, len ;
17
18       if( num == DOLLAR_DOLLAR )                              /* Do $$ */
19       {
20           strcpy( buf, "Yy_val" );
21
22           if( *fname )                                        /* $<name>N */
23               sprintf( buf+6, ".%s", fname );
24
25           else if( fields_active() )
26           {
27               if( *prod->lhs->field )
28                   sprintf( buf+6, ".%s", prod->lhs->field );
29               else
30               {
31                   error( WARNING, "Line %d: No <field> assigned to $$, "
32                                   "using default int field\n",    lineno );
33
34                   sprintf( buf+6, ".%s", DEF_FIELD );
35               }
36           }
37       }
38       else
39       {
40           if( num < 0 )
41               ++num;
42
43           if( rhs_size < 0 )                                  /* $N is in tail */
44               sprintf( buf, "Yy_vsp[ Yy_rhslen-%d ]" , num );
45           else
46           {
47               if(  (i = rhs_size - num) < 0 )
48                   error( WARNING, "Line %d: Illegal $%d in production\n",
49                                                           lineno, num);
50               else
51               {
52                   len = sprintf( buf, "yyvsp[%d]", i );
53
54                   if( *fname )                                /* $<name>N */
55                       sprintf( buf + len, ".%s", fname );
56
57                   else if( fields_active() )
58                   {
```

→

Listing 5.16. continued...

```
59                              if( num <= 0 )
60                              {
61                                  error(NONFATAL, "Can't use %%union field with negative"
62                                                  " attributes. Use $<field>-N\n" );
63                              }
64                              else if( * (prod->rhs)[num-1]->field )
65                              {
66                                  sprintf( buf + len, ".%s", (prod->rhs)[num-1]->field );
67                              }
68                              else
69                              {
70                                  error( WARNING, "Line %d: No <field> assigned to $%d, "
71                                                  "using default int field\n",
72                                                                  lineno, num );
73                                  sprintf( buf + len, ".%s", DEF_FIELD );
74                              }
75                          }
76                      }
77                  }
78              }
79
80          return buf;
81      }
```

5.12 Parser-File Generation

The routines in Listing 5.17 and 5.18 handle the **occs** parser-file generation. They are much like the **LLama** routines with the same names. There are two possible template files, however. The one that we've been looking at (*occs.par*) is used in most situations. If *-a* is specified on the command line, however, the file *occs-act.par* (in Listing 5.19) is used instead. All that's needed here are external declarations that give us access to variables declared in the associated parser file (generated with a *-p* command-line switch).

Listing 5.17. *yycode.c*— Controller Routine for Table Generation

```
1   void      tables()
2   {
3       make_yy_stok();                          /* in stok.c   */
4       make_token_file();                       /* in stok.c   */
5       make_parse_tables();                     /* in yystate.c */
6   }
```

5.13 Generating LALR(1) Parse Tables

The only part of **occs** we've yet to explore is the table-generation subroutines, all concentrated into a single (somewhat large) module called *yystate.c*. The routines create an LR(1) parse table, but before creating a new LR(1) state, the code looks for an existing state with the same LR(0) kernel items as the new one. If such a state exists, lookaheads are added to the existing state rather than creating a new one.

Listing 5.18. *yydriver.c*— Routines to Create **Occs** Output File

```
 1   #include <stdio.h>
 2   #include <stdlib.h>
 3
 4   #include <tools/debug.h>
 5   #include <tools/set.h>
 6   #include <tools/hash.h>
 7   #include <tools/compiler.h>
 8   #include <tools/l.h>
 9   #include "parser.h"
10
11   /*-----------------------------------------------------------------*/
12
13   void file_header        P(( void ));              /* public */
14   void code_header        P(( void ));
15   void driver             P(( void ));
16
17   /*-----------------------------------------------------------------*/
18
19   PRIVATE FILE    *Driver_file = stderr ;
20
21   /*-----------------------------------------------------------------
22    * Routines in this file are occs specific. There's a different version of all
23    * these routines in lldriver.c. They MUST be called in the following order:
24    *                    file_header()
25    *                    code_header()
26    *                    driver()
27    *-----------------------------------------------------------------
28    */
29
30   PUBLIC  void file_header()
31   {
32       /* This header is printed at the top of the output file, before the
33        * definitions section is processed. Various #defines that you might want
34        * to modify are put here.
35        */
36
37       output( "#include \"%s\"\n\n",  TOKEN_FILE  );
38
39       if( Public )
40           output( "#define PRIVATE\n" );
41
42       if( Debug )
43           output( "#define YYDEBUG\n" );
44
45       if( Make_actions )
46           output( "#define YYACTION\n" );
47
48       if( Make_parser )
49           output( "#define YYPARSER\n" );
50
51       if( !( Driver_file = driver_1(Output, !No_lines, Template) ))
52           error( NONFATAL, "%s not found--output file won't compile\n", Template);
53   }
54
55   /*-----------------------------------------------------------------*/
56
57   PUBLIC  void    code_header()
58   {
```

→

Listing 5.18. continued...

```
59          /* This stuff is output after the definitions section is processed, but
60           * before any tables or the driver is processed.
61           */
62
63          driver_2( Output, !No_lines );
64      }
65
66      /*------------------------------------------------------------------*/
67
68      PUBLIC  void    driver()
69      {
70          /* Print out the actual parser by copying llama.par to the output file.
71           */
72
73          if( Make_parser )
74              driver_2( Output, !No_lines );
75
76          fclose( Driver_file );
77      }
```

Listing 5.19. *occs-act.par*— File Header for *-a* Output

```
1   #ifdef YYDEBUG
2   #    define YYD(x) x
3   #else
4   #    define YYD(x) /* empty */
5   #endif
6   ^L      /* User-supplied code from definitions section goes here */
7   #ifndef YYSTYPE                     /* Default value stack type      */
8   #    define YYSTYPE int
9   #endif
10
11  #undef YYD                          /* Redefine YYD in case YYDEBUG was defined  */
12  #ifdef YYDEBUG                      /* explicitly in the header rather than with */
13  #    define YYD(x) x                /* a -D on the occs command line.            */
14  #    define printf  yycode         /* Make printf() calls go to output window.  */
15  #else
16  #    define YYD(x) /* empty */
17  #endif
18
19  extern void yycode    ();
20  extern void yydata    ();
21  extern void yybss     ();
22  extern void yycomment ();
23
24  extern YYSTYPE *Yy_vsp;     /* Value-stack pointer                            */
25  extern YYSTYPE Yy_val;      /* Must hold $$ after act is performed            */
26  extern int     Yy_rhslen;   /* number of symbols on RHS of current production */
```

Representing LR(1)
items:, ITEM.

Though this process is straightforward, a lot of code and several data structures have to work in concert to implement it. These data structures start on line 25 of Listing 5.20 with an ITEM declaration, which represents an LR(1) item. There is a certain amount of redundancy here in order to speed up the table generation process. For example, the right_of_dot field points to the symbol to the right of the dot. (Remember, the PRO-DUCTION itself is stored as an array of SYMBOL pointers. It holds NULL if the dot is at the far right of the production.) **Occs** could extrapolate this information from the PRO-DUCTION and dot position (the offset to which is in dot_posn) every time it used the ITEM, but it's best, for speed reasons, to do the extrapolation only once since the dot position does not change within a given ITEM. Similarly, the production number could be derived from the PRODUCTION structure, but I've copied it here to avoid an extra level of indirection every time the production number is used. The RIGHT_OF_DOT macro on line 35 of Listing 5.20 gets the numeric, tokenized value of the SYMBOL to the right of the dot. It evaluates to zero (which isn't used for any of the input symbols) if the dot is at the far right of the production.

Listing 5.20. *yystate.c*— Universal Constants and LR(1) Items

```
 1   #include <stdio.h>
 2   #include <malloc.h>
 3
 4   #include <tools/debug.h>
 5   #include <tools/set.h>
 6   #include <tools/hash.h>
 7   #include <tools/compiler.h>
 8   #include <tools/l.h>
 9   #include "parser.h"
10   #include "lltok.h"                     /* For _EOI_ definition */
11
12   /*-------------------------------------------------------------*/
13                                          /* For statistics only:               */
14   PRIVATE int     Nitems       = 0;      /* number of LR(1) items              */
15   PRIVATE int     Npairs       = 0;      /* # of pairs in output tables        */
16   PRIVATE int     Ntab_entries = 0;      /* number of transitions in tables    */
17   PRIVATE int     Shift_reduce = 0;      /* number of shift/reduce conflicts   */
18   PRIVATE int     Reduce_reduce = 0;     /* number of reduce/reduce conflicts  */
19
20   #define MAXSTATE   512    /* Max # of LALR(1) states.                 */
21   #define MAXOBUF    256    /* Buffer size for various output routines  */
22
23   /*-------------------------------------------------------------*/
24
25   typedef struct _item_                  /* LR(1) item:                         */
26   {
27       int            prod_num;           /* production number                   */
28       PRODUCTION     *prod;              /* the production itself               */
29       SYMBOL         *right_of_dot;      /* symbol to the right of the dot      */
30       unsigned char  dot_posn;           /* offset of dot from start of production */
31       SET            *lookaheads;        /* set of lookahead symbols for this item */
32
33   } ITEM;
34
35   #define RIGHT_OF_DOT(p) ( (p)->right_of_dot ? (p)->right_of_dot->val : 0 )
```

The next data structure of interest represents an LR(1) state. The STATE structure is defined, along with a few related constants, in Listing 5.21. Most of the closure items don't have to be stored in the STATE because they can be derived from the kernel items if necessary. The exceptions are items that contain ε productions, because these items cause reductions from the current state, not a transition to a new state. The closure items with ε productions are effectively part of the kernel, at least from the perspective of the parse table. The set of ε items are in their own array because the table-creation code occasionally compares two STATE structures to see if they're equivalent. This equivalence can be determined by comparing the true kernel items only. There's no

Representing an LR(1) state: STATE.

point in also comparing the ε items too, because the same kernel items in both states generate the same closure items—including the ε items—in both states. The `kernel_items[]` array is kept sorted to facilitate `STATE` comparisons. The sort criteria is pretty much arbitrary, but the sorting serves to get the two sets of kernel items to appear in the same order in both `STATE`s. I'll discuss the comparison routine that's used for this purpose in a moment.

Listing 5.21. *yystate.c*— LR(1) States

```
36  #define MAXKERNEL   32     /* Maximum number of kernel items in a state.      */
37  #define MAXCLOSE    128    /* Maximum number of closure items in a state (less */
38                             /* the epsilon productions).                        */
39  #define MAXEPSILON 8       /* Maximum number of epsilon productions that can be */
40                             /* in a closure set for any given state.            */
41
42  typedef short STATENUM;
43
44  typedef struct _state_                  /* LR(1) state                          */
45  {
46      ITEM   *kernel_items  [MAXKERNEL ];  /* Set of kernel items.                */
47      ITEM   *epsilon_items [MAXEPSILON];  /* Set of epsilon items.               */
48
49      unsigned nkitems  : 7 ;              /* # items in kernel_items[].          */
50      unsigned neitems  : 7 ;              /* # items in epsilon_items[].         */
51      unsigned closed   : 1 ;              /* State has had closure performed.    */
52
53      STATENUM num;                        /* State number (0 is start state).    */
54
55  } STATE;
```

Internal representation of the parse table:
`Actions, ACT, Goto.`

The next listing (Listing 5.22) contains definitions used to build the internal representation of the actual parse tables. The mechanism used is essentially the same as that used by the output tables, but the transitions are stored as linked lists of structures rather than input-symbol/next-state pairs. The `Actions[]` array (on line 64) is indexed by current state. Each cell of `Actions[]` points at the head of a linked list of `ACT` structures, one element of which is an input symbol, and the other element of which is the action to take when that symbol is encountered from the current state. The `Goto[]` table (on line 68) is essentially the same.

Memory management:
`new().`

The table-generation code begins in Listing 5.23 with several routines to manage the parse table just discussed. The allocation routine, `new()` on line 73 allocates space for an `ACT` structure. Since the space used by these structures need never be freed, `malloc()`, which is both slow and expensive in terms of system resources, need not be called every time a new structure is required; rather, `new()` allocates an array of structures with a single `malloc()` call on line 84. CHUNK, **#define**d on line 71, determines the number of structures in the array. `new()` then returns pointers to structures in this array until all array elements have been allocated. Only then does it get another array of structures from `malloc()`. The remainder of the routines in the listing either put new elements in the table, or return pointers to existing elements.

CHUNK.

Listing 5.22. *yystate.c*— Internal Representation of the Parse Table

```
56   typedef struct act_or_goto
57   {
58       int sym;                      /* Given this input symbol,            */
59       int do_this;                  /* do this. >0 == shift, <0 == reduce  */
60       struct act_or_goto *next;     /* Pointer to next ACT in the linked list. */
61
62   } ACT;
63   typedef ACT GOTO;                 /* GOTO is an alias for ACT */
64   PRIVATE ACT *Actions[MAXSTATE];   /* Array of pointers to the head of the action
65                                      * chains. Indexed by state number.
66                                      * I'm counting on initialization to NULL here.
67                                      */
68   PRIVATE GOTO *Gotos[MAXSTATE];    /* Array of pointers to the head of the goto
69                                      * chains.
70                                      */
```

Listing 5.23. *yystate.c*— Parse-Table Memory Management

```
71   #define CHUNK      128                 /* New() gets this many structures at once */
72
73   PRIVATE void     *new()
74   {
75       /* Return an area of memory that can be used as either an ACT or GOTO.
76        * These objects cannot be freed.
77        */
78
79       static ACT  *eheap = (ACT *) 0;
80       static ACT  *heap  = (ACT *) 1;
81
82       if( heap >= eheap )
83       {
84           if( !(heap = (ACT *) malloc( sizeof(ACT) * CHUNK) ))
85               error( FATAL, "No memory for action or goto\n" );
86
87           eheap = heap + CHUNK ;
88       }
89       ++Ntab_entries ;
90       return heap++  ;
91   }
92
93   /* - - - - - - - - - - - - - - - - - - - - - - - - - - - - - - - - - - - -*/
94
95   PRIVATE ACT     *p_action( state, input_sym )
96   int state, input_sym;
97   {
98       /* Return a pointer to the existing ACT structure representing the indicated
99        * state and input symbol (or NULL if no such symbol exists).
100       */
101
102      ACT *p;
103
104      for( p = Actions[state]; p ; p = p->next )
105          if( p->sym == input_sym )
106              return p;
107
```

Listing 5.23. continued...

```
108         return NULL;
109    }
110
111    /* - - - - - - - - - - - - - - - - - - - - - - - - - - - - - - - - - - - -*/
112
113    PRIVATE void    add_action( state, input_sym, do_this )
114    int state, input_sym, do_this;
115    {
116         /* Add an element to the action part of the parse table. The cell is
117          * indexed by the state number and input symbol, and holds do_this.
118          */
119
120         ACT *p;
121
122         if( Verbose > 1 )
123             printf("Adding shift or reduce action from state %d:  %d on %s\n",
124                                      state, do_this, Terms[ input_sym ]->name);
125         p             = (ACT *) new();
126         p->sym        = input_sym ;
127         p->do_this    = do_this ;
128         p->next       = Actions[state];
129         Actions[state] = p;
130    }
131
132    /* - - - - - - - - - - - - - - - - - - - - - - - - - - - - - - - - - - - -*/
133
134    PRIVATE GOTO    *p_goto( state, nonterminal )
135    int state, nonterminal;
136    {
137         /* Return a pointer to the existing GOTO structure representing the
138          * indicated state and nonterminal (or NULL if no such symbol exists). The
139          * value used for the nonterminal is the one in the symbol table; it is
140          * adjusted down (so that the smallest nonterminal has the value 0)
141          * before doing the table look up, however.
142          */
143
144         GOTO   *p;
145
146         nonterminal = ADJ_VAL( nonterminal );
147
148         for( p = Gotos[ state ] ; p ; p = p->next )
149             if( p->sym == nonterminal )
150                 return p;
151
152         return NULL;
153    }
154
155    /* - - - - - - - - - - - - - - - - - - - - - - - - - - - - - - - - - - - -*/
156
157    PRIVATE void    add_goto( state, nonterminal, go_here )
158    int     state, nonterminal, go_here;
159    {
160         /* Add an element to the goto part of the parse table, the cell is indexed
161          * by current state number and nonterminal value, and holds go_here. Note
162          * that the input nonterminal value is the one that appears in the symbol
163          * table. It is adjusted downwards (so that the smallest nonterminal will
164          * have the value 0) before being inserted into the table, however.
165          */
166
```

```
Listing 5.23. continued. . .

167        GOTO          *p;
168        int           unadjusted;                    /* Original value of nonterminal   */
169
170        unadjusted  = nonterminal;
171        nonterminal = ADJ_VAL( nonterminal );
172
173        if( Verbose > 1 )
174                printf( "Adding goto from state %d to %d on %s\n",
175                                        state, go_here, Terms[unadjusted]->name );
176        p           = (GOTO *) new();
177        p->sym      = nonterminal;
178        p->do_this  = go_here;
179        p->next     = Gotos[state];
180        Gotos[state] = p;
181    }
```

The next listing (Listing 5.24) contains definitions for the data structures used to to   State management.
manage the LR(1) STATEs as the state machine is constructed. Before looking at the
actual code, consider the logic used to create the machine, summarized in Table 5.15.

Table 5.15. An Algorithm for Creating an LALR(1) State Machine

Data structures:
    A state data base.
    A list of unclosed states in the state data base.

Initially: Create the start state and put it into both the state data base and the unclosed-state list.

Create LALR(1) state machine:

a.   for(each *state* in the list of unclosed states)
      {
b.   Perform LR(1) closure on *state*, generating a set of new states and associated lookaheads.
c.   for(each *new_state* generated by the closure operation)
          {
d.   if(an *existing_state* with the same kernel items as the *new_state* already exists)
            {
e.   Merge appropriate next-state transitions from *state* with *existing_state*.
f.   Add lookaheads in *new_state* to the lookaheads in *existing_state*.
g.   if(the previous step added new symbols to the lookahead set AND
                   the existing state isn't already in the list of unclosed states)
h.   Add the existing state to the list of unclosed states.
            }
           else
           {
i.   Add appropriate next-state transitions from *state* to *new_state*.
j.   Add the *new_state* to the state data base.
k.   Add the *new_state* to the list of unclosed states.
           }
          }
      }

Two data structures are used by the algorithm to keep track of the states. The states   Finished-states list.
themselves must be stored in a data base of some sort because every time a new state is
created, you have to see if a state with the same set of kernel items already exists. (If it

Listing 5.24. *yystate.c*— LR-State Memory Management—Data Structures

```
182   PRIVATE HASH_TAB *States        = NULL;    /* LR(1) states                    */
183   PRIVATE int       Nstates       = 0;       /* Number of states.               */
184
185   #define MAX_UNFINISHED  128
186
187   typedef struct tnode
188   {
189       STATE          *state;
190       struct tnode *left, *right;
191
192   } TNODE;
193
194   PRIVATE TNODE     Heap[ MAX_UNFINISHED ]; /* Source of all TNODEs            */
195   PRIVATE TNODE     *Next_allocate = Heap ; /* Ptr to next node to allocate    */
196
197   PRIVATE TNODE     *Available = NULL;       /* Free list of available nodes    */
198                                             /* linked list of TNODES. p->left  */
199                                             /* is used as the link.            */
200   PRIVATE TNODE     *Unfinished = NULL;      /* Tree of unfinished states.      */
201
202   PRIVATE ITEM      **State_items;           /* Used to pass info to state_cmp  */
203   PRIVATE int       State_nitems;            /*             "                   */
204   PRIVATE int       Sort_by_number = 0;      /*             "                   */
205
206   #define NEW       0                         /* Possible return values from     */
207   #define UNCLOSED  1                         /* newstate().                     */
208   #define CLOSED    2
```

does exist, the next-state transitions go to the existing state rather than the newly created one.) An unsorted array is inappropriate for holding the list of existing states because the search time is too long. Fortunately, we already have a quite workable data-base manager in the guise of the hash-table functions that we've been using for symbol-table management, and I use those routines here to keep track of the existing states. The States pointer (declared on line 182 of Listing 5.24) points at a hash table of LR(1) states. The maketab() call that initializes the table is done in one of the higher-level routines discussed later in this section.

Unfinished-states list.

The next data structure keeps track of those states that are created in a closure operation, but have not, themselves, been closed. Since each closure operation creates several new states, a mechanism is needed to keep track of those states on which closure has not yet been performed. Look-up time is an issue here, as well, because step (g) of the algorithm must test to see if the state is already in the list of unclosed states before adding it to the list. Though a hash table could also be used here, I've opted for a binary tree because it's both easy to implement in this application and somewhat more efficient than the general-purpose hash-table functions. It's also easier, in the current application, to remove an arbitrary state from a binary tree than from the hash table—the removed state is always a leaf, here. So, the unclosed-state list is implemented as a binary tree of pointers to STATEs in the hash table. The TNODE structure used for the tree nodes is defined on lines 187 to 192 of Listing 5.24. The complete system is pictured in Figure 5.14.

TNODE.

Unfinished-state management: Available.

The Available list at the bottom of Figure 5.14 manages nodes in the tree that have been used at least once. Tree nodes are, initially, managed like the STATES. An array of several of them (called Heap) is defined on line 194 of Listing 5.24. Next_allocate (defined on the next line) is a pointer to the next available node in

Next_allocate, Heap.

Figure 5.14. The State Data Base and Unclosed-State List

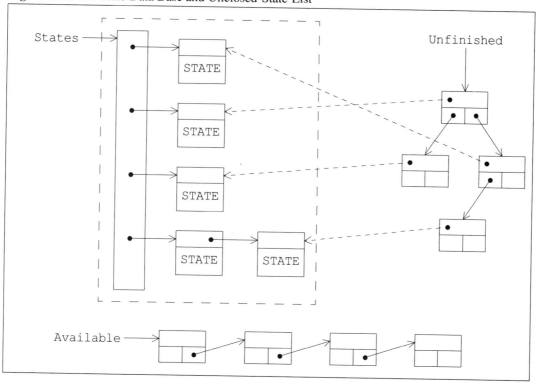

Heap[]. Initially, nodes are taken from the Heap[] by incrementing the Next_allocate pointer. When a node is removed from the unclosed-state tree, that node is added to the linked list pointed to by Available. New nodes are allocated from the linked list if it isn't empty, otherwise a new node is fetched from the Heap[]. This strategy is necessary because malloc() and free() are too slow.

New states are created and initialized by *newstate*, at the top of Listing 5.25. Note that you don't have to initialize the new node until after you've decided whether or not to put it into the tree. You can get away with this delay because the comparison function used to do the insertion is always called with: cmp(existing,new), where existing is the node already in the tree and new is the new one. The comparison function doesn't have to actually examine the new node to do the comparison, however. The ITEM pointer and count that's passed into newstate() can be copied into global variables, and the comparison function can look at those global variables instead of the actual contents of the new node. State_items and State_nitems, which were declared on lines 202 and 203 of Listing 5.24, are used for this purpose. The delayed initialization gives you a little more speed, because you don't have to do a true initialization unless it's absolutely necessary.

STATE allocation: new-state().

The add_unfinished() subroutine on line 267 of Listing 5.25 adds nodes to the unfinished list, but only if the node is not already there. As discussed earlier, a binary tree is used for the list. Note that this is not an ideal data structure because nodes are, at least initially, inserted in ascending order, yielding a worst-case linked list. Things improve once the lookaheads start being added because previously removed states are put back onto the list more or less randomly. This situation could be improved by using a unique random number as an identifier rather than the state number. But, it will most likely take longer to generate this number than it will to chase down the list. Alternately, you could keep the list as an array and do a binary-insertion sort to put in the new

Add to unfinished list: add_unfinished().

Listing 5.25. *yystate.c*— LR-State Memory Management—Subroutines

```
209    PRIVATE int      newstate( items, nitems, statep )
210    ITEM    **items;
211    int     nitems;
212    STATE   **statep;
213    {
214        STATE   *state;
215        STATE   *existing;
216        int     state_cmp() ;
217
218        if( nitems > MAXKERNEL )
219            error( FATAL, "Kernel of new state %d too large\n", Nstates );
220
221
222        State_items  = items;        /* set up parameters for state_cmp */
223        State_nitems = nitems;       /* and state_hash.                 */
224
225        if( existing = findsym( States, NULL ) )
226        {
227            /* State exists; by not setting "state" to NULL, we'll recycle  */
228            /* the newly allocated state on the next call.                  */
229
230            *statep = existing;
231            if( Verbose > 1 )
232            {
233                printf("Using existing state (%sclosed): ",
234                                                 existing->closed ? "" : "un" );
235                pstate_stdout( existing );
236            }
237            return existing->closed ? CLOSED : UNCLOSED ;
238        }
239        else
240        {
241            if( Nstates >= MAXSTATE )
242                error(FATAL, "Too many LALR(1) states\n");
243
244            if( !(state = (STATE *) newsym(sizeof(STATE)) ))
245                error( FATAL, "Insufficient memory for states\n" );
246
247            memcpy( state->kernel_items, items, nitems * sizeof(ITEM*) );
248            state->nkitems  = nitems;
249            state->neitems  = 0;
250            state->closed   = 0;
251            state->num      = Nstates++ ;
252            *statep         = state;
253            addsym( States, state );
254
255            if( Verbose > 1 )
256            {
257                printf("Forming new state:");
258                pstate_stdout( state );
259            }
260
261            return NEW;
262        }
263    }
264
265    /*-------------------------------------------------------------------*/
266
```

Listing 5.25. continued. . .

```
267     PRIVATE void    add_unfinished( state )
268     STATE    *state;
269     {
270         TNODE **parent, *root;
271         int    cmp;
272
273         parent = &Unfinished;
274         root   = Unfinished;
275         while( root )                          /* look for the node in the tree */
276         {
277             if( (cmp = state->num - root->state->num) == 0 )
278                 break;
279             else
280             {
281                 parent = (cmp < 0) ? &root->left : &root->right ;
282                 root   = (cmp < 0) ?  root->left :  root->right ;
283             }
284         }
285
286         if( !root )                            /* Node isn't in tree.       */
287         {
288             if( Available )                    /* Allocate a new node and   */
289             {                                  /* put it into the tree.     */
290                 *parent   = Available ;        /* Use node from Available   */
291                 Available = Available->left ;  /* list if possible, otherwise */
292             }                                  /* get the node from the Heap. */
293             else
294             {
295                 if( Next_allocate >= &Heap[ MAX_UNFINISHED ] )
296                     error(FATAL, "Internal: No memory for unfinished state\n");
297                 *parent = Next_allocate++;
298             }
299
300             (*parent)->state = state;                    /* initialize the node */
301             (*parent)->left  = (*parent)->right = NULL;
302         }
303     }
304
305     /*------------------------------------------------------------------------*/
306
307     PRIVATE STATE   *get_unfinished()
308     {
309         /* Returns a pointer to the next unfinished state and deletes that
310          * state from the unfinished tree. Returns NULL if the tree is empty.
311          */
312
313         TNODE        *root;
314         TNODE        **parent;
315
316         if( !Unfinished )
317             return NULL;
318
319         parent = &Unfinished;                   /* find leftmost node */
320         if( root = Unfinished )
321         {
322             while( root->left )
323             {
324                 parent = &root->left ;
325                 root   = root->left ;
326             }
```

```
┌──────────────────────────────────────────────────────────────────────────────┐
│ Listing 5.25. continued...                                                     │
│ 327        }                                                                   │
│ 328                                                                            │
│ 329        *parent     = root->right ;          /* Unlink node from the tree  */ │
│ 330        root->left  = Available;             /* Put it into the free list  */ │
│ 331        Available   = root;                                                 │
│ 332                                                                            │
│ 333        return root->state ;                                                │
│ 334    }                                                                       │
│ 335                                                                            │
└──────────────────────────────────────────────────────────────────────────────┘
```

elements. Again, the time required to move the tail end of the array is comparable to the time required to chase down the list. Another solution uses a SET of unfinished-state numbers. The problem here is that, towards the end of creating a big table (when things are slower anyway), almost all of the unfinished states will have large state numbers. If the smallest state number is 256 (for example) you'll have to look at 16 empty words in the bit map before finding one with a set bit. Empirical testing showed that using a SET slowed things down by about 5% (which translates to about 10 seconds on a big grammar, with **occs** running on my 8MHz IBM-PC/AT). The `get_unfinished()` subroutine on line 307 of Listing 5.25 gets a node from the unfinished list. It returns 0 when the list is empty.

STATE comparison, `state_cmp()`.

The next Listing (Listing 5.26) holds a comparison and a hash function that can be used to order the states. The comparison function, `state_cmp()` on line 336 of Listing 5.26, is needed to compare states when searching for a particular state in the array. States are equivalent if they have the same set of kernel items, and equivalence can be determined from the production numbers and dot positions only. The lookaheads don't matter because you're testing for equivalence only to see if the lookaheads for a new LR(1) state can be merged with those of an existing one. Similarly, the actual ordering of states is immaterial as long as the ordering is consistent, so you can do easy things for sort criteria. The rules are:

(1)   The STATE with the most items is larger.
(2)   If the STATEs have the same number of items, the two lists of items are compared. Remember, these lists are sorted, so you can do what amounts to a lexicographic comparison, here. The **for** loop on lines 360 to 367 of Listing 5.26 scans the list of items until it finds a mismatched item. If there are no mismatched items, the states are equivalent.
(3)   The items are compared using two criteria: The item with the largest production number is the largest (this test is on line 362). Otherwise, if both items have the same production number, the item with the dot further to the right is the larger (this test is on line 365).

STATE hashing, `state_hash()`.

The hash function on line 372 of Listing 5.26 is used to manage the finished-state list. It is much easier to implement than the sort-comparison function. It just sums together the production numbers and dot positions of the items.

ITEM management, `newitem()`, `free_item()`, `free_recycled_items()`. `movedot()`.

The next set of subroutines, in Listing 5.27 takes care of ITEM management. `newitem()` (on line 394) allocates space for (and initializes) a new item, `freeitem()` (on line 421) puts an item on a recycle heap for later allocation by `newitem()`. `free_recycled_items()` (on line 429) cleans up after all processing finishes—it frees memory used for the entire set of items. The `movedot()` function on line 442 moves the dot over one notch and updates associated fields in the ITEM structure.

ITEM comparison: `item_cmp()`.

The `item_cmp()` function on line 365 is used to sort the items within a STATE structure. The primary sort criterion is the numeric value that represents the symbol to

Listing 5.26. *yystate.c*— State Comparison Functions

```
336    PRIVATE int      state_cmp( new, tab_node )
337    STATE    *new ;                          /*  Pointer to new node (ignored */
338                                             /*  if Sort_by_number is false). */
339    STATE    *tab_node;                      /*  Pointer to existing node     */
340    {
341        /* Compare two states as described in the text. Return a number representing
342         * the relative weight of the states, or 0 of the states are equivalent.
343         */
344
345        ITEM  **tab_item ; /* Array of items for existing state   */
346        ITEM  **item      ; /* Array of items for new state        */
347        int    nitem      ; /* Size of "                           */
348        int    cmp        ;
349
350        if( Sort_by_number )
351            return( new->num - tab_node->num );
352
353        if( cmp = State_nitems - tab_node->nkitems )     /* state with largest */
354            return cmp;                                  /* number of items is */
355                                                         /* larger.            */
356        nitem    = State_nitems ;
357        item     = State_items  ;
358        tab_item = tab_node->kernel_items;
359
360        for(; --nitem >= 0 ; ++tab_item, ++item )
361        {
362            if( cmp = (*item)->prod_num - (*tab_item)->prod_num )
363                return cmp;
364
365            if( cmp = (*item)->dot_posn - (*tab_item)->dot_posn  )
366                return cmp;
367        }
368
369        return 0;                                        /* States are equivalent */
370    }
371
372    PRIVATE int state_hash( sym )
373    STATE    *sym;                            /* ignored */
374    {
375        /* Hash function for STATEs. Sum together production numbers and dot
376         * positions of the kernel items.
377         */
378
379        ITEM  **items  ;    /* Array of items for new state          */
380        int    nitems  ;    /* Size of "                             */
381        int    total   ;
382
383        items  = State_items  ;
384        nitems = State_nitems ;
385        total  = 0;
386
387        for(;  --nitems >= 0 ; ++items )
388            total += (*items)->prod_num  +  (*items)->dot_posn;
389
390        return total;
391    }
```

the right of the dot. This means that ε productions float to the top of the list, followed by productions with terminals to the right of the dot, followed by productions with nonterminals to the right of the dot. The ordering is handy when you're partitioning the closure items to create new state kernels. Items with the same symbol to the right of the dot will be adjacent in the sorted list. The second sort criteria (if the same symbol is to the right of the dot in both items) is the production number, and the ternary criteria is the dot position.

Listing 5.27. *yystate.c*— ITEM Management

```
392    ITEM      *Recycled_items = NULL;
393
394    PRIVATE ITEM      *newitem( production )
395    PRODUCTION        *production;
396    {
397        ITEM          *item;
398
399        if( Recycled_items )
400        {
401            item = Recycled_items ;
402            Recycled_items = (ITEM *) Recycled_items->prod;
403            CLEAR( item->lookaheads );
404        }
405        else
406        {
407            if( !(item = (ITEM *) malloc( sizeof(ITEM) )) )
408                error( FATAL, "Insufficient memory for all LR(1) items\n" );
409
410            item->lookaheads = newset() ;
411        }
412
413        ++Nitems;
414        item->prod        = production ;
415        item->prod_num    = production->num ;
416        item->dot_posn    = 0;
417        item->right_of_dot = production->rhs[0] ;
418        return item;
419    }
420
421    PRIVATE void    freeitem( item )
422    ITEM    *item;
423    {
424        --Nitems;
425        item->prod = (PRODUCTION *) Recycled_items ;
426        Recycled_items = item;
427    }
428
429    PRIVATE void    free_recycled_items()
430    {
431        /* empty the recycling heap, freeing all memory used by items there */
432
433        ITEM *p;
434
435        while( p = Recycled_items )
436        {
437            Recycled_items = (ITEM *) Recycled_items->prod ;
438            free(p);
439        }
440    }
441
```

➡

Listing 5.27. continued. . .

```
442  PRIVATE movedot( item )
443  ITEM    *item;
444  {
445      /* Moves the dot one position to the right and updates the right_of_dot
446       * symbol.
447       */
448
449      item->right_of_dot = ( item->prod->rhs )[ ++item->dot_posn ] ;
450  }
451
452  PRIVATE int    item_cmp( item1p,  item2p )
453  ITEM  **item1p, **item2p ;
454  {
455      /* Return the relative weight of two items, 0 if they're equivalent.  */
456
457      int rval;
458      ITEM *item1 = *item1p;
459      ITEM *item2 = *item2p;
460
461      if( !(rval = RIGHT_OF_DOT(item1) - RIGHT_OF_DOT(item2)) )
462          if( !(rval = item1->prod_num - item2->prod_num ) )
463              return item1->dot_posn - item2->dot_posn ;
464
465      return rval;
466  }
```

The next three listings contain subroutines that make the LR(1) parse table using the logic discussed previously on page 415. The remainder of the chapter is boring stuff that does things like print out the tables. Rather than discuss the routines here, I have commented them copiously so that you don't have to be flipping back and forth between the listing and the text.

Making the parse tables.

Listing 5.28. *yystate.c*— High-Level, Table-Generation Function

```
467  PUBLIC void      make_parse_tables()
468  {
469      /* Prints an LALR(1) transition matrix for the grammar currently
470       * represented in the symbol table.
471       */
472
473      ITEM         *item;
474      STATE        *state;
475      PRODUCTION   *start_prod;
476      void         mkstates();
477      int          state_cmp();
478      FILE         *fp, *old_output;
479
480      /* Make data structures used to produce the table, and create an initial
481       * LR(1) item containing the start production and the end-of-input marker
482       * as a lookahead symbol.
483       */
484
485      States = maketab( 257, state_hash, state_cmp );
486
487      if( !Goal_symbol )
488          error(FATAL, "No goal symbol.\n" );
489
```

➡

Listing 5.28. continued...

```
490        start_prod = Goal_symbol->productions ;
491
492        if( start_prod->next )
493            error(FATAL, "Start symbol must have only one right-hand side.\n" );
494
495        item = newitem( start_prod );            /* Make item for start production */
496        ADD( item->lookaheads, _EOI_ );          /* FOLLOW(S) = {$}              */
497
498        newstate( &item, 1, &state );
499
500        if( lr( state ) )                         /* Add shifts and gotos to the table */
501        {
502            if( Verbose )
503                printf("Adding reductions:\n");
504
505            reductions();                                   /* add the reductions */
506
507            if( Verbose )
508                printf("Creating tables:\n" );
509
510            if( !Make_yyoutab )                        /* Tables go in yyout.c */
511            {
512                print_tab( Actions, "Yya", "Yy_action", 1);
513                print_tab( Gotos  , "Yyg", "Yy_goto"  , 1);
514            }
515            else
516            {
517                if( !(fp = fopen(TAB_FILE, "w")) )
518                {
519                    error( NONFATAL, "Can't open " TAB_FILE ", ignoring -T\n");
520
521                    print_tab( Actions, "Yya", "Yy_action", 1);
522                    print_tab( Gotos  , "Yyg", "Yy_goto"  , 1);
523                }
524                else
525                {
526                    output ( "extern YY_TTYPE *Yy_action[]; /* in yyoutab.c */\n" );
527                    output ( "extern YY_TTYPE *Yy_goto[];   /* in yyoutab.c */\n" );
528
529                    old_output = Output;
530                    Output     = fp;
531
532                    fprintf(fp, "#include <stdio.h>\n" );
533                    fprintf(fp, "typedef short YY_TTYPE;\n" );
534                    fprintf(fp, "#define YYPRIVATE %s\n",
535                                        Public ? "/* empty */" : "static" );
536
537                    print_tab( Actions, "Yya", "Yy_action", 0 );
538                    print_tab( Gotos  , "Yyg", "Yy_goto"  , 0);
539
540                    fclose( fp );
541                    Output = old_output;
542                }
543            }
544            print_reductions();
545        }
546    }
```

Listing 5.29. *yystate.c*— Table-Generation Functions

```
547   PRIVATE int lr( cur_state )
548   STATE  *cur_state;
549   {
550       /* Make LALR(1) state machine. The shifts and gotos are done here, the
551        * reductions are done elsewhere. Return the number of states.
552        */
553
554       ITEM    **p;
555       ITEM    **first_item;
556       ITEM    *closure_items[ MAXCLOSE ];
557       STATE   *next;                    /* Next state.                         */
558       int     isnew;                    /* Next state is a new state.          */
559       int     nclose;                   /* Number of items in closure_items.   */
560       int     nitems;                   /* # items with same symbol to right of dot.*/
561       int     val;                      /* Value of symbol to right of dot.    */
562       SYMBOL  *sym;                     /* Actual symbol to right of dot.      */
563       int     nlr  = 0;                 /* Nstates + nlr == number of LR(1) states. */
564
565       add_unfinished( cur_state );
566
567       while( cur_state = get_unfinished() )
568       {
569           if( Verbose > 1 )
570                   printf( "Next pass...working on state %d\n", cur_state->num );
571
572           /* closure()   adds normal closure items to closure_items array.
573            * kclose()    adds to that set all items in the kernel that have
574            *             outgoing transitions (ie. whose dots aren't at the far
575            *             right).
576            * assort()    sorts the closure items by the symbol to the right
577            *             of the dot. Epsilon transitions will sort to the head of
578            *             the list, followed by transitions on nonterminals,
579            *             followed by transitions on terminals.
580            * move_eps() moves the epsilon transitions into the closure kernel set.
581            */
582
583           nclose = closure  (cur_state, closure_items, MAXCLOSE          );
584           nclose = kclosure (cur_state, closure_items, MAXCLOSE, nclose  );
585
586           assort( closure_items, nclose, sizeof(ITEM*), item_cmp );
587
588           nitems  = move_eps( cur_state, closure_items, nclose );
589           p       = closure_items + nitems;
590           nclose -= nitems ;
591
592           if( Verbose > 1 )
593               pclosure( cur_state, p, nclose );
594
595           /* All of the remaining items have at least one symbol to the   */
596           /* right of the dot.                                             */
597
598           while( nclose > 0 )
599           {
600               first_item = p ;
601               sym        = (*first_item)->right_of_dot ;
602               val        = sym->val ;
603
```

```
Listing 5.29. continued...
604                    /* Collect all items with the same symbol to the right of the dot.
605                     * On exiting the loop, nitems will hold the number of these items
606                     * and p will point at the first nonmatching item. Finally nclose is
607                     * decremented by nitems. items = 0 ;
608                     */
609
610                    nitems = 0 ;
611                    do
612                    {
613                        movedot( *p++ );
614                        ++nitems;
615
616                    } while( --nclose > 0  &&  RIGHT_OF_DOT(*p) == val );
617
618                    /* (1) newstate() gets the next state. It returns NEW if the state
619                     *     didn't exist previously, CLOSED if LR(0) closure has been
620                     *     performed on the state, UNCLOSED otherwise.
621                     * (2) add a transition from the current state to the next state.
622                     * (3) If it's a brand-new state, add it to the unfinished list.
623                     * (4) otherwise merge the lookaheads created by the current closure
624                     *     operation with the ones already in the state.
625                     * (5) If the merge operation added lookaheads to the existing set,
626                     *     add it to the unfinished list.
627                     */
628
629                    isnew = newstate( first_item, nitems, &next );            /* 1 */
630
631                    if( !cur_state->closed )
632                    {                                                         /* 2 */
633                        if( ISTERM( sym ) )
634                            add_action ( cur_state->num, val, next->num );
635                        else
636                            add_goto   ( cur_state->num, val, next->num );
637                    }
638
639                    if( isnew == NEW )
640                        add_unfinished( next );                               /* 3 */
641                    else                                                      /* 4 */
642                    {
643                        if( merge_lookaheads( next->kernel_items, first_item, nitems))
644                        {
645                            add_unfinished( next );                           /* 5 */
646                            ++nlr;
647                        }
648                        while( --nitems >= 0 )
649                            freeitem( *first_item++ );
650                    }
651
652                    fprintf( stderr, "\rLR:%-3d LALR:%-3d", Nstates + nlr, Nstates );
653            }
654            cur_state->closed = 1;
655    }
656
657    free_recycled_items();
658
659    if( Verbose )
660        fprintf(stderr, " states, %d items, %d shift and goto transitions\n",
661                                        Nitems, Ntab_entries );
662    return Nstates;
663 }
```

Listing 5.29. continued...

```
664
665     /*------------------------------------------------------------------*/
666
667     PRIVATE int     merge_lookaheads( dst_items, src_items, nitems )
668     ITEM    **src_items;
669     ITEM    **dst_items;
670     int     nitems;
671     {
672         /* This routine is called if newstate has determined that a state having the
673          * specified items already exists. If this is the case, the item list in the
674          * STATE and the current item list will be identical in all respects except
675          * lookaheads. This routine merges the lookaheads of the input items
676          * (src_items) to the items already in the state (dst_items). 0 is returned
677          * if nothing was done (all lookaheads in the new state are already in the
678          * existing state), 1 otherwise. It's an internal error if the items don't
679          * match.
680          */
681
682         int did_something = 0;
683
684         while( --nitems >= 0 )
685         {
686             if(      (*dst_items)->prod     != (*src_items)->prod
687                 ||  (*dst_items)->dot_posn != (*src_items)->dot_posn )
688             {
689                 error(FATAL, "INTERNAL [merge_lookaheads], item mismatch\n" );
690             }
691
692             if( !subset( (*dst_items)->lookaheads, (*src_items)->lookaheads ) )
693             {
694                 ++did_something;
695                 UNION( (*dst_items)->lookaheads, (*src_items)->lookaheads );
696             }
697
698             ++dst_items;
699             ++src_items;
700         }
701
702         return did_something;
703     }
704
705     /*------------------------------------------------------------------*/
706
707     PRIVATE int     move_eps( cur_state, closure_items, nclose )
708     STATE   *cur_state;
709     ITEM    **closure_items;
710     {
711         /* Move the epsilon items from the closure_items set to the kernel of the
712          * current state. If epsilon items already exist in the current state,
713          * just merge the lookaheads. Note that, because the closure items were
714          * sorted to partition them, the epsilon productions in the closure_items
715          * set will be in the same order as those already in the kernel. Return
716          * the number of items that were moved.
717          */
718
719         ITEM **eps_items, **p ;
720         int  nitems, moved ;
721
```

```
Listing 5.29. continued...
722        eps_items = cur_state->epsilon_items;
723        nitems    = cur_state->neitems ;
724        moved     = 0;
725
726        for( p = closure_items; (*p)->prod->rhs_len == 0 && --nclose >= 0; )
727        {
728            if( ++moved > MAXEPSILON )
729                error(FATAL, "Too many epsilon productions in state %d\n",
730                                                      cur_state->num );
731            if( nitems )
732                UNION( (*eps_items++)->lookaheads, (*p++)->lookaheads );
733            else
734                *eps_items++ = *p++ ;
735        }
736
737        if( moved )
738            cur_state->neitems = moved ;
739
740        return moved ;
741    }
742
743    /*-------------------------------------------------------------------*/
744
745    PRIVATE int    kclosure( kernel, closure_items, maxitems, nclose )
746    STATE *kernel;                      /* Kernel state to close.          */
747    ITEM  **closure_items;              /* Array into which closure items are put. */
748    int    maxitems;                    /* Size of the closure_items[] array.   */
749    int    nclose;                      /* # of items already in set.      */
750    {
751        /* Adds to the closure set those items from the kernel that will shift to
752         * new states (ie. the items with dots somewhere other than the far right).
753         */
754
755        int        nitems;
756        ITEM       *item, **itemp, *citem ;
757
758        closure_items += nclose;                        /* Correct for existing items */
759        maxitems      -= nclose;
760
761        itemp = kernel->kernel_items ;
762        nitems = kernel->nkitems ;
763
764        while( --nitems >= 0 )
765        {
766            item = *itemp++;
767
768            if( item->right_of_dot )
769            {
770                citem             = newitem( item->prod );
771                citem->prod       = item->prod ;
772                citem->dot_posn   = item->dot_posn ;
773                citem->right_of_dot = item->right_of_dot ;
774                citem->lookaheads = dupset( item->lookaheads );
775
776                if( --maxitems < 0 )
777                    error( FATAL, "Too many closure items in state %d\n",
778                                                      kernel->num );
779                *closure_items++ = citem;
780                ++nclose;
781        }
```

```
     Listing 5.29. continued...
782          }
783          return nclose;
784      }
785
786      /*-----------------------------------------------------------------------*/
787
788      PRIVATE int closure( kernel, closure_items, maxitems )
789      STATE *kernel;                    /* Kernel state to close.            */
790      ITEM  *closure_items[];           /* Array into which closure items are put */
791      int   maxitems;                   /* Size of the closure_items[] array.    */
792      {
793          /* Do LR(1) closure on the kernel items array in the input STATE. When
794           * finished, closure_items[] will hold the new items. The logic is:
795           *
796           * (1) for( each kernel item )
797           *         do LR(1) closure on that item.
798           * (2) while( items were added in the previous step or are added below )
799           *         do LR(1) closure on the items that were added.
800           */
801
802          int  i ;
803          int  nclose        = 0 ;              /* Number of closure items */
804          int  did_something = 0 ;
805          ITEM **p           = kernel->kernel_items ;
806
807          for( i = kernel->nkitems; --i >= 0 ;)                              /* (1) */
808          {
809              did_something |= do_close( *p++, closure_items, &nclose, &maxitems );
810          }
811
812          while( did_something )                                             /* (2) */
813          {
814              did_something = 0;
815              p = closure_items;
816              for( i = nclose ; --i >= 0 ; )
817                  did_something |= do_close( *p++, closure_items, &nclose, &maxitems);
818          }
819
820          return nclose;
821      }
822
823      /*- - - - - - - - - - - - - - - - - - - - - - - - - - - - - - - - - - */
824
825      PRIVATE int   do_close( item, closure_items, nitems, maxitems )
826      ITEM  *item;
827      ITEM  *closure_items[]; /* (output) Array of items added by closure process */
828      int   *nitems;          /* (input)  # of items currently in closure_items[] */
829                              /* (output) # of items in closure_items after       */
830                              /*                                     processing */
831      int   *maxitems;        /* (input)  max # of items that can be added        */
832                              /* (output) input adjusted for newly added items    */
833      {
834          /* Workhorse function used by closure(). Performs LR(1) closure on the
835           * input item ([A->b.Cd, e] add [C->x, FIRST(de)]). The new items are added
836           * to the closure_items[] array and *nitems and *maxitems are modified to
837           * reflect the number of items in the closure set. Return 1 if do_close()
838           * did anything, 0 if no items were added (as will be the case if the dot
839           * is at the far right of the production or the symbol to the right of the
840           * dot is a terminal).
841           */
```

Listing 5.29. continued...

```
842
843        int         did_something = 0;
844        int         rhs_is_nullable;
845        PRODUCTION  *prod;
846        ITEM        *close_item;
847        SET         *closure_set;
848        SYMBOL      **symp;
849
850        if( !item->right_of_dot )
851            return 0;
852
853        if( !ISNONTERM( item->right_of_dot ) )
854            return 0;
855
856    closure_set = newset();
857
858    /* The symbol to the right of the dot is a nonterminal. Do the following:
859     *
860     *(1)  for( every production attached to that nonterminal )
861     *(2)      if( the current production is not already in the set of
862     *                                              closure items)
863     *(3)          add it;
864     *(4)      if( the d in [A->b.Cd, e] doesn't exist )
865     *(5)          add e to the lookaheads in the closure production.
866     *          else
867     *(6)          The d in [A->b.Cd, e] does exist, compute FIRST(de) and add
868     *              it to the lookaheads for the current item if necessary.
869     */
870                                                                    /* (1) */
871
872    for( prod = item->right_of_dot->productions; prod ; prod = prod->next )
873    {                                                               /* (2) */
874
875        if( !(close_item = in_closure_items(prod, closure_items, *nitems)))
876        {
877            if( --(*maxitems) <= 0 )
878                error(FATAL, "LR(1) Closure set too large\n" );
879                                                                    /* (3) */
880            closure_items[ (*nitems)++ ] = close_item = newitem( prod );
881            ++did_something;
882        }
883
884        if( !*(symp = & ( item->prod->rhs [ item->dot_posn + 1 ]))) )   /* (4) */
885        {
886            did_something |= add_lookahead( close_item->lookaheads,    /* (5) */
887                                            item->lookaheads );
888        }
889        else
890        {                                                           /* (6) */
891            truncate( closure_set );
892
893            rhs_is_nullable = first_rhs( closure_set, symp,
894                                    item->prod->rhs_len - item->dot_posn - 1 );
895
896            REMOVE( closure_set, EPSILON );
897
898            if( rhs_is_nullable )
899                UNION( closure_set, item->lookaheads );
900
```

Listing 5.29. continued...

```
901                 did_something |= add_lookahead(close_item->lookaheads, closure_set);
902            }
903        }
904
905        delset( closure_set );
906        return did_something;
907    }
908
909    /*- - - - - - - - - - - - - - - - - - - - - - - - - - - - - - - - - - - */
910
911    PRIVATE ITEM      *in_closure_items(production, closure_item, nitems)
912    ITEM        **closure_item;
913    PRODUCTION *production;
914    {
915        /* If the indicated production is in the closure_items already, return a
916         * pointer to the existing item, otherwise return NULL.
917         */
918
919        for(; --nitems >= 0 ; ++closure_item )
920            if( (*closure_item)->prod == production )
921                return *closure_item;
922
923        return NULL;
924    }
925
926    /*- - - - - - - - - - - - - - - - - - - - - - - - - - - - - - - - - - - */
927
928    PRIVATE int      add_lookahead( dst, src )
929    SET     *dst, *src;
930    {
931        /* Merge the lookaheads in the src and dst sets. If the original src
932         * set was empty, or if it was already a subset of the destination set,
933         * return 0, otherwise return 1.
934         */
935
936        if( !IS_EMPTY( src ) && !subset( dst, src ) )
937        {
938            UNION( dst, src );
939            return 1;
940        }
941
942        return 0;
943    }
```

Listing 5.30. *yystate.c*— Adding Reductions to Tables

```
944    PRIVATE void      reductions()
945    {
946        /* Do the reductions. If there's memory, sort the table by state number */
947        /* first so that yyout.doc will look nice.                              */
948
949        void  addreductions();                                /* below */
950
951        Sort_by_number = 1;
952        if( !ptab( States, addreductions, NULL, 1 ) )
953            ptab( States, addreductions, NULL, 0 );
954    }
```

Listing 5.30. continued...

```
955
956    /*- - - - - - - - - - - - - - - - - - - - - - - - - - - - - - - - - - - */
957
958    PRIVATE void addreductions( state, junk )
959    STATE    *state;
960    void     *junk;
961    {
962        /* This routine is called for each state. It adds the reductions using the
963         * disambiguating rules described in the text, and then prints the state to
964         * yyout.doc if Verbose is true. I don't like the idea of doing two things
965         * at once, but it makes for nicer output because the error messages will
966         * be next to the state that caused the error.
967         */
968
969        int         i;
970        ITEM        **item_p;
971
972        for( i = state->nkitems, item_p = state->kernel_items;  --i>=0; ++item_p )
973            reduce_one_item( state, *item_p );
974
975        for( i = state->neitems, item_p = state->epsilon_items; --i>=0; ++item_p )
976            reduce_one_item( state, *item_p );
977
978        if( Verbose )
979        {
980            pstate( state );
981
982            if( state->num % 10 == 0 )
983                fprintf( stderr, "%d\r", state->num );
984        }
985    }
986
987    /*- - - - - - - - - - - - - - - - - - - - - - - - - - - - - - - - - - - */
988
989    PRIVATE void     reduce_one_item( state, item )
990    ITEM    *item;                          /* Reduce on this item   */
991    STATE   *state;                         /* from this state       */
992    {
993        int         token;                  /* Current lookahead                */
994        int         pprec;                  /* Precedence of production         */
995        int         tprec;                  /* Precedence of token              */
996        int         assoc;                  /* Associativity of token           */
997        int         reduce_by;
998        int         resolved;               /* True if conflict can be resolved */
999        ACT         *ap;
1000
1001       if( item->right_of_dot )            /* No reduction required */
1002               return;
1003
1004       pprec = item->prod->prec ;          /* precedence of entire production */
1005
1006       for( next_member(NULL); (token = next_member(item->lookaheads)) >= 0 ;)
1007       {
1008           tprec = Precedence[token].level ;       /* precedence of lookahead */
1009           assoc = Precedence[token].assoc ;       /* symbol.                 */
1010
1011           if( !(ap = p_action( state->num, token )) )    /* No conflicts */
1012           {
1013               add_action( state->num, token, -(item->prod_num) );
1014           }
```

Listing 5.30. continued...

```c
1015            else if( ap->do_this <= 0 )
1016            {
1017                /* Resolve a reduce/reduce conflict in favor of the production */
1018                /* with the smaller number. Print a warning.                    */
1019
1020                ++Reduce_reduce;
1021
1022                reduce_by   = min( -(ap->do_this), item->prod_num );
1023                ap->do_this = -reduce_by ;
1024
1025                error( WARNING, "State %2d: reduce/reduce conflict "
1026                            "%d/%d on %s (choose %d).\n",
1027                                    state->num,
1028                                    -(ap->do_this), item->prod_num ,
1029                                    token ? Terms[token]->name: "<_EOI_>",
1030                                    reduce_by                            );
1031            }
1032        else                               /* Shift/reduce conflict. */
1033        {
1034            if( resolved = (pprec && tprec) )
1035                if( tprec < pprec || (pprec == tprec && assoc != 'r')  )
1036                    ap->do_this = -( item->prod_num );
1037
1038            if( Verbose > 1 || !resolved )
1039            {
1040                ++Shift_reduce;
1041                error( WARNING, "State %2d: shift/reduce conflict %s/%d"
1042                            " (choose %s) %s\n",
1043                                state->num,
1044                                Terms[token]->name,
1045                                item->prod_num,
1046                                ap->do_this < 0 ? "reduce"     : "shift",
1047                                resolved          ? "(resolved)" : ""
1048                                );
1049            }
1050        }
1051    }
1052 }
```

Listing 5.31. *yystate.c*— Statistics Functions

```c
1053 PUBLIC void lr_stats( fp )
1054 FILE    *fp;
1055 {
1056     /* Print out various statistics about the table-making process */
1057
1058     fprintf(fp, "%4d     LALR(1) states\n",                    Nstates );
1059     fprintf(fp, "%4d     items\n",                             Nitems  );
1060     fprintf(fp, "%4d     nonerror transitions in tables\n", Ntab_entries  );
1061     fprintf(fp, "%4d/%-4d unfinished items\n", Next_allocate - Heap,
1062                                                    MAX_UNFINISHED);
1063     fprintf(fp, "%4d     bytes required for LALR(1) transition matrix\n",
1064                         (2 * sizeof(char*) * Nstates) /* index arrays */
1065                         + Nstates                     /* count fields */
1066                         + (Npairs * sizeof(short))    /* pairs        */
1067             );
1068     fprintf(fp, "\n");
```

```
        Listing 5.31. continued...
1069    }
1070
1071    /*------------------------------------------------------------------*/
1072
1073    PUBLIC int lr_conflicts( fp )
1074    FILE     *fp;
1075    {
1076        /* Print out statistics for the inadequate states and return the number of
1077         * conflicts.
1078         */
1079
1080        fprintf(fp, "%4d     shift/reduce  conflicts\n",  Shift_reduce  );
1081        fprintf(fp, "%4d     reduce/reduce conflicts\n",  Reduce_reduce );
1082        return Shift_reduce + Reduce_reduce ;
1083    }
```

Listing 5.32. *yystate.c*— Print Functions

```
1084    #define MAX_TOK_PER_LINE  10
1085    PRIVATE int Tokens_printed;        /* Controls number of lookaheads printed */
1086                                       /* on a single line of yyout.doc.        */
1087    PRIVATE void sprint_tok( bp, format, arg )
1088    char     **bp;
1089    char     *format;                  /* not used here, but supplied by pset() */
1090    int      arg;
1091    {
1092        /* Print one nonterminal symbol to a buffer maintained by the
1093         * calling routine and update the calling routine's pointer.
1094         */
1095
1096        if     ( arg == -1    ) *bp += sprintf( *bp, "null "          );
1097        else if( arg == -2    ) *bp += sprintf( *bp, "empty "         );
1098        else if( arg == _EOI_ ) *bp += sprintf( *bp, "$ "            );
1099        else if( arg == EPSILON) *bp += sprintf( *bp, ""             );
1100        else                     *bp += sprintf( *bp, "%s ", Terms[arg]->name );
1101
1102        if( ++Tokens_printed >= MAX_TOK_PER_LINE )
1103        {
1104            *bp += sprintf(*bp, "\n\t\t");
1105            Tokens_printed = 0;
1106        }
1107    }
1108
1109    PRIVATE  char  *stritem( item, lookaheads )
1110    ITEM    *item;
1111    int      lookaheads;
1112    {
1113        /* Return a pointer to a string that holds a representation of an item. The
1114         * lookaheads are printed too if "lookaheads" is true or Verbose is > 1
1115         * (-V was specified on the command line).
1116         */
1117
1118        static char buf[ MAXOBUF * 2 ];
1119        char      *bp;
1120        int       i;
1121
```

```
        Listing 5.32. continued...
1122        bp   = buf;
1123        bp += sprintf( bp, "%s->", item->prod->lhs->name );
1124
1125        if( item->prod->rhs_len <= 0 )
1126            bp += sprintf( bp, "<epsilon>. " );
1127        else
1128        {
1129            for( i = 0; i < item->prod->rhs_len ; ++i )
1130            {
1131                if( i == item->dot_posn )
1132                    *bp++  = '.' ;
1133
1134                bp += sprintf(bp, " %s", item->prod->rhs[i]->name );
1135            }
1136
1137            if( i == item->dot_posn )
1138                *bp++  = '.' ;
1139        }
1140
1141        if( lookaheads || Verbose >1 )
1142        {
1143            bp += sprintf( bp, " (production %d, precedence %d)\n\t\t[",
1144                                        item->prod->num, item->prod->prec );
1145            Tokens_printed = 0;
1146            pset( item->lookaheads, sprint_tok, &bp );
1147            *bp++ = ']'  ;
1148        }
1149
1150        if( bp - buf >= (MAXOBUF * 2) )
1151            error(FATAL, "Internal [stritem], buffer overflow\n" );
1152
1153        *bp = '\0' ;
1154        return buf;
1155    }
1156
1157    /*----------------------------------------------------------------------*/
1158
1159    PRIVATE void    pstate( state )
1160    STATE    *state;
1161    {
1162        /* Print one row of the parse table in human-readable form yyout.doc
1163         * (stderr if -V is specified).
1164         */
1165
1166        int         i;
1167        ITEM        **item;
1168        ACT         *p;
1169
1170        document( "State %d:\n", state->num );
1171
1172        /* - - - - - - - - - - - - - - - - - - - - - - - - - - - - - -*/
1173        /* Print the kernel and epsilon items for the current state.  */
1174
1175        for( i=state->nkitems, item=state->kernel_items  ; --i >= 0 ; ++item )
1176            document("     %s\n", stritem(*item, (*item)->right_of_dot==0 ));
1177
1178        for( i=state->neitems, item=state->epsilon_items ; --i >= 0 ; ++item )
1179            document( "     %s\n", stritem(*item, 1) );
1180
```

```
       Listing 5.32. continued...
1181        document( "\n" );
1182
1183        /* - - - - - - - - - - - - - - - - - - - - - - - - - - - - - - -*/
1184        /* Print out the next-state transitions, first the actions,    */
1185        /* then the gotos.                                             */
1186
1187        for( i = 0; i < MINTERM + USED_TERMS; ++i )
1188        {
1189            if( p = p_action( state->num, i ) )
1190            {
1191                if( p->do_this == 0 )
1192                {
1193                    if( p->sym == _EOI_ )
1194                        document( "    Accept on end of input\n" );
1195                    else
1196                        error( FATAL, "INTERNAL: state %d, Illegal accept",
1197                                                                   state->num);
1198                }
1199                else if( p->do_this < 0 )
1200                    document( "    Reduce by %d on %s\n", -(p->do_this),
1201                                                    Terms[p->sym]->name );
1202                else
1203                    document( "    Shift to %d on %s\n", p->do_this,
1204                                                    Terms[p->sym]->name );
1205            }
1206        }
1207
1208        for( i = MINNONTERM; i < MINNONTERM + USED_NONTERMS; i++ )
1209            if( p = p_goto(state->num, i) )
1210                document( "    Goto %d on %s\n", p->do_this,
1211                                                    Terms[i]->name );
1212        document("\n");
1213    }
1214
1215    PRIVATE void    pstate_stdout( state )
1216    STATE    *state;
1217    {
1218        document_to( stdout );
1219        pstate( state );
1220        document_to( NULL );
1221    }
1222
1223    /*-------------------------------------------------------------------*/
1224
1225    PRIVATE pclosure( kernel, closure_items, nitems )
1226    STATE    *kernel;
1227    ITEM     **closure_items;
1228    {
1229        printf( "\n%d items in Closure of ", nitems );
1230        pstate_stdout( kernel );
1231
1232        if( nitems > 0 )
1233        {
1234            printf( "    -----closure items:----\n" );
1235            while( --nitems >= 0 )
1236                printf( "   %s\n", stritem( *closure_items++, 0) );
1237        }
1238    }
```

Listing 5.33. *yystate.c*— Routines That Create Auxiliary Tables

```
1239   PRIVATE void      make_yy_lhs( prodtab )
1240   PRODUCTION         **prodtab;
1241   {
1242       static char *text[] =
1243       {
1244           "The Yy_lhs array is used for reductions. It is indexed by production",
1245           "number and holds the associated left-hand side adjusted so that the",
1246           "number can be used as an index into Yy_goto.",
1247           NULL
1248       };
1249       PRODUCTION *prod;
1250       int         i;
1251
1252       comment ( Output, text );
1253       output  ( "YYPRIVATE int Yy_lhs[%d] =\n{\n", Num_productions );
1254
1255       for( i = 0; i < Num_productions; ++i )
1256       {
1257           prod = *prodtab++;
1258           output("\t/* %3d */\t%d", prod->num, ADJ_VAL( prod->lhs->val ) );
1259
1260           if( i != Num_productions-1 )
1261               output(",");
1262
1263           if( i % 3 == 2 || i == Num_productions-1 )      /* use three columns */
1264               output( "\n" );
1265       }
1266       output("};\n");
1267   }
1268
1269   /*----------------------------------------------------------------------*/
1270
1271   PRIVATE void      make_yy_reduce( prodtab )
1272   PRODUCTION         **prodtab;
1273   {
1274       static char *text[] =
1275       {
1276           "The Yy_reduce[] array is indexed by production number and holds",
1277           "the number of symbols on the right-hand side of the production",
1278           NULL
1279       };
1280       PRODUCTION *prod;
1281       int         i;
1282
1283       comment ( Output, text );
1284       output  ( "YYPRIVATE int Yy_reduce[%d] =\n{\n", Num_productions );
1285
1286       for( i = 0; i < Num_productions; ++i )
1287       {
1288           prod = *prodtab++;
1289           output( "\t/* %3d */\t%d", prod->num, prod->rhs_len );
1290
1291           if( i != Num_productions-1 )
1292               output(",");
1293
1294           if( i % 3 == 2 || i == Num_productions-1 )      /* use three columns */
1295               output( "\n" );
1296       }
1297       output("};\n");
```

Listing 5.33. continued...

```
1298    }
1299
1300    /*------------------------------------------------------------------*/
1301
1302    PRIVATE make_yy_slhs( prodtab )
1303    PRODUCTION      **prodtab;
1304    {
1305        static char *text[] =
1306        {
1307            "Yy_slhs[] is a debugging version of Yy_lhs[]. It is indexed by",
1308            "production number and evaluates to a string representing the",
1309            "left-hand side of the production.",
1310            NULL
1311        };
1312
1313        PRODUCTION *prod;
1314        int        i;
1315
1316        comment ( Output, text );
1317        output  ( "YYPRIVATE char *Yy_slhs[%d] =\n{\n", Num_productions );
1318
1319        for( i = Num_productions; --i >= 0 ; )
1320        {
1321            prod = *prodtab++;
1322            output("\t/* %3d */\t\"%s\"", prod->num, prod->lhs->name );
1323            output ( i != 0 ? ",\n" : "\n" );
1324        }
1325        output("};\n");
1326    }
1327
1328    PRIVATE make_yy_srhs( prodtab )
1329    PRODUCTION      **prodtab;
1330    {
1331        static char *text[] =
1332        {
1333            "Yy_srhs[] is also used for debugging. It is indexed by production",
1334            "number and evaluates to a string representing the right-hand side of",
1335            "the production.",
1336            NULL
1337        };
1338
1339        PRODUCTION *prod;
1340        int        i, j;
1341
1342        comment ( Output, text );
1343        output  ( "YYPRIVATE char *Yy_srhs[%d] =\n{\n", Num_productions );
1344
1345        for( i = Num_productions; --i >= 0 ; )
1346        {
1347            prod = *prodtab++;
1348            output("\t/* %3d */\t\"",  prod->num );
1349
1350            for( j = 0; j < prod->rhs_len ; ++j )
1351            {
1352                output( "%s", prod->rhs[j]->name );
1353                if( j != prod->rhs_len - 1 )
1354                    outc( ' ' );
1355            }
1356
```

```
Listing 5.33. continued...
1357            output( i != 0 ? "\",\n" : "\"\n" );
1358        }
1359        output("};\n");
1360    }
1361
1362    /*------------------------------------------------------------------
1363     * The following routines generate compressed parse tables. There's currently
1364     * no way to do uncompressed tables. The default transition is the error
1365     * transition.
1366     */
1367
1368    PRIVATE void     print_reductions()
1369    {
1370        /* Output the various tables needed to do reductions */
1371
1372        PRODUCTION **prodtab;
1373
1374        if(!(prodtab= (PRODUCTION**) malloc(sizeof(PRODUCTION*) * Num_productions)))
1375            error(FATAL,"Not enough memory to output LALR(1) reduction tables\n");
1376        else
1377            ptab( Symtab, mkprod, prodtab, 0 );
1378
1379        make_yy_lhs    ( prodtab );
1380        make_yy_reduce ( prodtab );
1381
1382        output("#ifdef YYDEBUG\n");
1383
1384        make_yy_slhs   ( prodtab );
1385        make_yy_srhs   ( prodtab );
1386
1387        output("#endif\n");
1388        free( prodtab );
1389    }
1390
1391    /*------------------------------------------------------------------------*/
1392
1393    PRIVATE void     mkprod( sym, prodtab )
1394    SYMBOL          *sym;
1395    PRODUCTION      **prodtab;
1396    {
1397        PRODUCTION  *p;
1398
1399        if( ISNONTERM(sym) )
1400            for( p = sym->productions ; p ; p = p->next )
1401                prodtab[ p->num ] = p ;
1402    }
1403
1404    /*------------------------------------------------------------------------*/
1405
1406    PRIVATE void     print_tab( table, row_name, col_name, make_private )
1407    ACT     **table;
1408    char    *row_name;       /* Name to use for the row arrays              */
1409    char    *col_name;       /* Name to use for the row-pointers array      */
1410    int     make_private;    /* Make index table private (rows always private) */
1411    {
1412        /* Output the action or goto table. */
1413
1414        int         i, j;
1415        ACT         *ele, **elep; /* table element and pointer to same        */
1416        ACT         *e, **p;
```

Listing 5.33. continued...

```
1417        int         count;          /* # of transitions from this state, always >0 */
1418        int         column;
1419        SET         *redundant = newset();           /* Mark redundant rows */
1420
1421        static char *act_text[] =
1422        {
1423            "The Yy_action table is action part of the LALR(1) transition",
1424            "matrix. It's compressed and can be accessed using the yy_next()",
1425            "subroutine, declared below.",
1426            "",
1427            "           Yya000[]={   3,    5,3   ,   2,2   ,   1,1   };",
1428            "  state number---+         |    | |",
1429            "  number of pairs in list-+      | |",
1430            "  input symbol (terminal)------+ |",
1431            "  action----------------------+",
1432            "",
1433            "  action = yy_next( Yy_action, cur_state, lookahead_symbol );",
1434            "",
1435            "      action <  0   -- Reduce by production n",
1436            "      action == 0   -- Accept (ie. reduce by production 0)",
1437            "      action >  0   -- Shift to state n",
1438            "      action == YYF -- error",
1439            NULL
1440        };
1441        static char *goto_text[] =
1442        {
1443            "The Yy_goto table is goto part of the LALR(1) transition matrix",
1444            "It's compressed and can be accessed using the yy_next() subroutine,",
1445            "declared below."
1446            "",
1447            " nonterminal = Yy_lhs[ production number by which we just reduced ]",
1448            "",
1449            "           Yyg000[]={   3,    5,3   ,   2,2   ,   1,1   };",
1450            "  uncovered state-+         |    | |",
1451            "  number of pairs in list--+     | |",
1452            "  nonterminal------------------+ |",
1453            "  goto this state-------------+",
1454            ""
1455            " goto_state = yy_next( Yy_goto, cur_state, nonterminal );",
1456            NULL
1457        };
1458
1459        comment( Output, table == Actions ? act_text : goto_text );
1460
1461        /* - - - - - - - - - - - - - - - - - - - - - - - - - - - - -
1462         * Modify the matrix so that, if a duplicate rows exists, only one
1463         * copy of it is kept around. The extra rows are marked as such by setting
1464         * a bit in the "redundant" set. (The memory used for the chains is just
1465         * discarded.) The redundant table element is made to point at the row
1466         * that it duplicates.
1467         */
1468
1469        for( elep = table, i = 0; i < Nstates ; ++elep, ++i )
1470        {
1471            if( MEMBER( redundant,i ) )
1472                continue;
1473
1474            for( p=elep+1, j=i ; ++j < Nstates ; ++p )
1475            {
```

```
       Listing 5.33. continued...
1476                  if( MEMBER( redundant, j) )
1477                      continue;
1478
1479                  ele = *elep;        /* pointer to template chain        */
1480                  e   = *p;           /* chain to compare against template */
1481
1482                  if( !e || !ele )    /* either or both strings have no elements */
1483                      continue;
1484
1485                  for( ; ele && e ; ele=ele->next, e=e->next )
1486                      if( (ele->do_this != e->do_this) || (ele->sym != e->sym) )
1487                          break;
1488
1489                  if( !e && !ele )
1490                  {
1491                      /* Then the chains are the same. Mark the chain being compared
1492                       * as redundant, and modify table[j] to hold a pointer to the
1493                       * template pointer.
1494                       */
1495
1496                      ADD( redundant, j );
1497                      table[j] = (ACT *) elep;
1498                  }
1499              }
1500          }
1501
1502      /* - - - - - - - - - - - - - - - - - - - - - - - - - - - - - -
1503       * Output the row arrays
1504       */
1505
1506      for( elep = table, i = 0 ; i < Nstates ; ++elep, ++i )
1507      {
1508          if( !*elep || MEMBER(redundant, i) )
1509              continue;
1510                              /* Count the number of transitions from this state */
1511          count = 0;
1512          for( ele = *elep ; ele ; ele = ele->next )
1513              ++count;
1514
1515          output("YYPRIVATE YY_TTYPE %s%03d[]={%2d,",row_name, elep-table, count);
1516                                                                        /*}*/
1517
1518          column = 0;
1519          for( ele = *elep ; ele ; ele = ele->next )
1520          {
1521              ++Npairs;
1522              output( "%3d,%-4d", ele->sym, ele->do_this );
1523
1524              if( ++column != count )
1525                  outc( ',' );
1526
1527              if( column % 5 == 0  )
1528                  output("\n\t\t\t          ");
1529          }
1530                                                              /* { */
1531          output( "};\n" );
1532      }
1533
```

```
Listing 5.33. continued...
1534        /* - - - - - - - - - - - - - - - - - - - - - - - - - - - - - -
1535         * Output the index array
1536         */
1537
1538        if( make_private )
1539            output( "\nYYPRIVATE YY_TTYPE *%s[%d] =\n", col_name, Nstates );
1540        else
1541            output( "\nYY_TTYPE *%s[%d] =\n", col_name, Nstates );
1542
1543        output ( "{\n/*   0 */  " );                                        /* } */
1544
1545        for( elep = table, i = 0 ; i < Nstates ; ++i, ++elep )
1546        {
1547            if( MEMBER(redundant, i) )
1548                output( "%s%03d", row_name, (ACT **)(*elep) - table );
1549            else
1550                output( *elep ? "%s%03d" : "  NULL" , row_name, i );
1551
1552            if( i != Nstates-1 )
1553                output( ", " );
1554
1555            if( i==0  || (i % 8)==0 )
1556                output ("\n/* %3d */  ", i+1 );
1557        }
1558                                                                     /* { */
1559        delset( redundant );                  /* Mark redundant rows */
1560        output( "\n};\n");
1561    }
```

5.14 Exercises

5.1.   (a) Write an algorithm that creates a physical syntax tree from a postfix representation of an arithmetic expression. For example, the input ab*cd*+ should create the following tree:

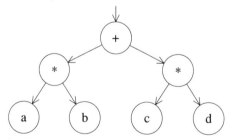

(b) Implement your algorithm.

5.2.   (a) Write an augmented, attributed grammar for a bottom-up parser that builds the syntax tree required for the previous exercise.

(b) Rewrite your grammar to support infix expressions as input rather than postfix. Parenthesized subexpressions must be supported.

(c) Implement both of the previous grammars using **occs**.

5.3.   Using the LR parse table in Table 5.11 on page 369, show the contents of the state and symbol stacks as the following input is processed:

```
1 + ( 2 * 3 ) * 4
```

5.4. Create bottom-up, LALR(1) parse tables for the following grammar:

1.	stmt	→	expr SEMI
2.		|	WHILE LP expr RP stmt
3.		|	LC stmt_list RC
4.	stmt_list	→	stmt_list stmt
5.		|	ε
6.	expr	→	expr PLUS term
7.		|	STAR expr
8.		|	term
9.		|	ε
10.	term	→	IDENTIFIER
11.		|	LP expr RP

This grammar produces one shift/reduce conflict, which should be resolved according to the following table:

Input symbol	Token	Precedence	Associativity
( )	LP RP	high	none
*	STAR	medium	right to left
+	PLUS	low	left to right
{ }	LC RC	none	left to right
;	SEMI	none	none

Hand in the tables and graphs showing both the LR and LALR state machines.

5.5. Modify the grammar in the previous exercise to include an assignment operator (x=y;) and an exponentiation operator (x^^y) is x to the yth power . Assignment should be the lowest precedence operator and exponentiation the highest. Make LALR(1) parse tables for this modified grammar.

5.6. Implement a parser that uses the parse tables created in Exercises 5.4 or 5.3.

5.7. Add code-generation actions to the grammar created in Exercises 5.4 or 5.3 . You may output either assembly language or C.

5.8. Add the code-generation actions from the previous exercise to the parser implementation created in Exercise 5.5.

5.9. Why are fewer shift/reduce conflicts generated when imbedded actions are inserted into a production immediately to the right of terminal symbols?

5.10. Think up a real-world situation where a reduce/reduce conflict is inevitable (other than the one presented earlier).

5.11. A more-efficient method for creating LALR(1) parse tables than the one presented in the current chapter is described in [Aho], pp. 240–244. An LR(0) state machine is created and then lookaheads are added to it directly. You can see the basis of the method by looking at Figure 5.8 on page 366. Lookaheads appear on the tree in one of two ways, either they propagate down the tree from a parent to a child or they appear spontaneously. A lookahead character propagates from the item [!s→α.xβ,c] to its child when FIRST(β) is nullable. It appears spontaneously when FIRST(!b) contains only terminal symbols. Modify **occs** to use this method rather than the one presented in the current chapter. Is the method in [Aho] actually more efficient once implementation details are considered? Why or why not?

5.12. An even more efficient method for creating LALR(1) parse tables, developed by DeRemer and Pennello, is described in [DeRemer79] and [DeRemer82]. It is summarized in [Tremblay], pp. 375–383. Modify **occs** to use this table-creation method.

5.13. **LLama** and **occs** currently supports optional and repeating productions, indicated with brackets:

```
s :   a [optional] b
  |   c [repeating zero or more times]* d
  ;
```

These are implemented in the `start_opt()` and `end_opt()` subroutine presented in Chapter 4 and the transformations involved are discussed in Appendix E. **Occs** uses left-recursive lists and **LLama** uses a right-recursive lists for these transformations.

(a) Add a + operator to **occs** and **LLama** that can be used in place of the star in a repeating production. It causes the enclosed sub-production to repeat one or more times.

(b) Add the operator `[...]`(a, b)`*` for a to b repetitions of the sub-production—a and b are decimal numbers.

(c) Add the `[...]*>` and `[...]+>` operators to **occs**. These should work just like `[...]*` and `[...]+`, but should use right-recursive rather than left-recursive list productions.

6

Code Generation

Having looked at how parsers are created, it's now time to look at the real heart of the compiler: the code generation phase. We've actually been looking at code generation in a backhanded way. L^{E}X, **LLama**, and **occs** are all compilers, after all, and they do generate code of sorts—the tables and drivers. This chapter looks at more conventional code generation and at the run-time environment by building a C compiler. I'm assuming that you can generalize from a description of a specific implementation once you understand the design issues. The grammar used here is summarized in Appendix C and is discussed piecemeal in the current chapter as it's used.

Because a production-quality, full ANSI compiler would both take up too much space and actually obscure some code-generation issues, I've implemented a proper subset of ANSI C. Most of the hard stuff is implemented, but I've omitted some functionality that you can add on your own if you're interested.[1] The modifications are left as exercises at the end of the chapter. Note that these limitations exist only at the semantic level. The grammar recognizes ANSI C, but the compiler ignores a few ANSI constructs when they are encountered. The compiler has the following limitations:

ANSI-C subset implemented.

- Floating point is not supported.
- The **auto**, **const**, **volatile**, and **register** keywords are ignored.
- Structures do not form lvalues. You can't pass or return them by value or assign to a structure.
- Compile-time initializations work only on nonaggregate global variables like this:

    int x = 5;

  Arrays, structures, and local variables of any sort may not be initialized at compile time.
- Strong type checking on enumerated types is not supported. An enumerated type is treated just like an **int**, and any integer value can be assigned to a variable of that type, even if the value was declared as part of a different enumerated type. The

---

1. Adding some of the missing stuff, like structure lvalues, floating point, and proper initializations, is a nontrivial enterprise. Other omissions, like bit fields, are easy.

elements of the enumeration list are treated just like a macro would be treated, it is just replaced by a **int** constant wherever it's found. The following declaration:

```
enum tag { Beaver, Wally, June, Ward; } Cleaver;
```

is treated like this:

```
#define Beaver 0
#define Wally  1
#define June   2
#define Ward   3

int Cleaver;
```

- Bit fields are ignored. The associated structure field is treated as if the bit field wasn't present in the input.
- Function prototypes are treated as simple **extern** declarations. The argument or type list is ignored. The new C++-style function-definition syntax is supported, however.
- One nonstandard escape sequence is supported in character constants: \^C (backslash-caret-letter) evaluates to the associated control character. It cannot be used in a string constant.

A simple, one-pass compiler is developed in this chapter: the compiler generates assembly language directly rather than creating a true intermediate language that is processed by a back end. I've taken this approach because it represents something of a worst-case scenario, and so makes a better example. The chapter starts out discussing the run-time environment and how a typical machine is used by the generated code. Intermediate languages are discussed briefly, and an output assembly language with a C-like syntax is developed. Internal data structures such as the symbol table are discussed, and then the compiler is developed.

One failing of the current chapter is that the recursive nature of the grammar precludes a strictly hierarchical discussion of the code-generation actions. As a consequence, there's a certain amount of skipping around in the grammar in the later sections. I've tried to minimize this as much as possible, but you may have to read the chapter more than once before the overall structure of the compiler becomes apparent. The entire grammar is listed hierarchically in Appendix C, and it will be worthwhile for you to study the grammar thoroughly before proceeding to the discussion of the code-generation issues.

As a final disclaimer, compilers are complicated programs and are notoriously difficult to debug. I don't expect the current compiler to be any different in this respect. The compiler has been tested as well as I am able, but there's nothing like having several thousand people reading your code to show up bugs that you never dreamed existed. The electronically distributed version will always be the most up-to-date, and bug fixes will be posted to USENET on a regular basis. Please notify me when you find a bug so I can tell everyone else about it (either c/o Software Engineering, or electronically; the addresses are in the Preface).

You must be thoroughly familiar with the bottom-up parse process described in the last chapter before continuing.

6.1 Intermediate Languages

Compilers often generate *intermediate languages* rather than translate an input file directly to binary. You can look at an intermediate language as a model assembly language, optimized for a nonexistent, but ideal, computer called a *virtual machine*. The

The virtual machine.

compiler's output can be tested by simulating this virtual machine with a computer program. There are several advantages to an intermediate-language approach. First, you can design an intermediate language with ease of optimization in mind, and thereby improve the resultant binary image because it can be more heavily optimized. Next, the intermediate-to-binary translation is usually done by a separate compilation pass called a *back end*, and you can provide several back ends for different target machines, all of which use the same parser and code generator (called the *front end*). By the same token, you can provide several front ends for different languages, all of which generate the same intermediate language and all of which share the same back end to generate real code.[2]

Back ends and front ends.

Virtual machines typically have many registers, very orthogonal instruction sets (all instructions can be performed on all registers, the syntax for register operations is the same as the memory-access syntax), and so forth. There are trade-offs, though. The ideal machine hardly every maps to a real machine in an efficient way, so the generated code is typically larger and less efficient than it would be if the parser knew about the actual target machine. The ability to mix and match front and back ends compensates to some extent for the inefficiencies.

Virtual machine characteristics.

Intermediate languages typically take one of three forms. These are *triples, quads* (short for quadruples), and *postfix* (reverse-Polish) notation.

Most real assembly languages are made up of *triples* which are made of of three parts: an *operator*, a *source*, and a *destination* or *target*. For example, the 68000 instruction ADD.W D0,D1 is a triple that adds the contents of the D0 and D1 registers and puts the result in D1. A C representation of a similar triple would be:

Triples (two-address instructions).

```
d += s;
```

and a typical mathematical representation is:

```
(+=, d, s)
```

Triples are sometimes called *triplets* or *3-tuples*. They are also sometimes called *two-address* instructions because the binary representation of most instructions comprise an operator and source and destination addresses.

Quads, also called *quadruples* or *three-address* instructions, have four parts. The following quad has two sources, an operand, and a destination:

Quads (three-address instructions).

```
d = s1 + s2;
```

A more mathematical representation of the same quad would be:

```
(+, d, s1, s2)
```

Note that, in spite of the name, some quads, such as an assignment quad, have only three parts, with an empty fourth field. This empty element is usually marked with a dash:

```
(=, d, s, -)
```

The first field defines the operation. Since it's never empty, a dash there signifies subtraction.

Not all quads and triples involve implicit assignments. The first of the following triples compares two numbers and remembers the result of the comparison internally. The

Quads and triples without explicit assignments.

---

2. For example, the Microsoft Pascal, FORTRAN, and C compilers all share the same back end.

second triple, which branches to a specific label, is executed only if the previous comparison was true. Neither instruction involves an assignment.

```
(LESS_THAN, a,        b)
(GOTO,      target, -)
```

Arithmetic operations may not involve assignment either. The following two triples execute A=B+C. The first one does the addition and stores the result in an internal register called the *accumulator*. The second assigns the result of the previous operation—the .−1—to *A*.

```
(+, B,  C )
(=, A,  .-1)
```

The dot represents the position of the current instruction: .−1 references the previous instruction, .−2 the instruction before that, and so on.

Advantages of quads versus triples.

Triples have one advantage over quads: they're very close in structure to many real assembly languages, so they can ease code generation for these assemblers. I'm using them in the compiler generated in this chapter for this reason. Quads have two advantages over triplets. They tend to be more compact; a quad like (+, d, s1, s2) requires two triplets to do the same work:

```
(=  d, s1 );
(+= d, s2 );
```

Also, certain optimizations are easier to do on quads because triples are more position dependent. In the previous example, the two triples must be treated as a single unit by any optimizations that move the code around, and the ordering of the two triples is important. Since it's self-contained, the quad can be moved more easily.

Postfix, Reverse-Polish Notation (RPN).

The third kind of common intermediate language is *postfix* or *Reverse-Polish Notation* (RPN.) Forth, PostScript, and Hewlett-Packard calculators are examples of postfix languages. This representation has several advantages. The first is that expressions can be evaluated with less work than usual: no parentheses are needed to represent them, and the compiler doesn't need to allocate temporary variables to evaluate postfix expressions—it uses a run-time stack instead. All operands are pushed onto the stack and all operators affect the top few stack elements. For example, an expression like this:

```
(1+2) * (3+4)
```

is represented in postfix as follows:

```
1 2 + 3 4 + *
```

and is evaluated as shown in Table 6.1.

Postfix languages often have various operators designed specifically for stack operations, such as a *dup* operator that duplicates and pushes the top of stack element—X^2 can be represented with:

```
X dup *
```

Another common stack operator is the *swap* operator, which swaps the two elements at the top of stack.

RPN has one other advantage: It's easy to reconstruct the original syntax tree from a postfix representation of the input language. (We'll look at this process further in Chapter Seven.) Since some optimizations require the production of a syntax tree, a postfix intermediate language is a convenient way to transfer a compiled program to the optimizer.

Table 6.1. Postfix Evaluation of `1 2 + 3 4 + *`

stack	input	comments
empty	`1 2 + 3 4 + *`	*push 1*
`1`	`2 + 3 4 + *`	*push 2*
`1 2`	`+ 3 4 + *`	*add the two items at top of stack and replace them with the result.*
`3`	`3 4 + *`	*push 3*
`3 3`	`4 + *`	*push 4*
`3 3 4`	`+ *`	*add the two items at top of stack and replace them with the result.*
`3 7`	`*`	*multiply the two items at top of stack and replace them with the result.*
`21`		*the result is at top of stack.*

6.2 C-code: An Intermediate Language and Virtual Machine[3]

The syntax of an intermediate language is pretty much arbitrary. Ideally it reflects the characteristics of the most likely target machines. For purposes of clarity, however, I've decided to use a C-like intermediate language in the compiler created later in this chapter. I've defined a C subset in which all instructions have direct analogs in most assembly languages—all the instructions translate directly into a small number of machine instructions (usually one). This way, the assembly-language syntax will be familiar to you, regardless of your background. In addition, you can use your C compiler and normal debugging tools to exercise the output from the compiler. The code is simple enough so that a translation to assembly language is very straightforward. I've dubbed this intermediate language *C-code*.

C-code is really more of an assembly language than a true intermediate language. The main problem is that it is very restrictive about things like word width, alignment, and storage classes. It forces the compiler itself to worry about details that are usually handled by the back end and, as a consequence, makes a back end harder to write because the back end must occasionally undo some of the things that the compiler has done (like add padding to local variables to get proper alignment).

The current section describes C-code in considerable depth. Though the description is, by necessity, full of specific implementation details, reading it should give you a good idea of the sorts of things that are required in a more general-purpose intermediate language. The current section also serves as a review of assembly-language concepts. The C-code description is pretty terse in places, and a previous familiarity with a real assembly language will help considerably in the following discussion. Finally, I've also used the current section as a vehicle for discussing the memory organization and subroutine-linkage procedures that are almost universal among C compilers, so you should read through it even if you're very familiar with assembler.

The C-code virtual machine—the hypothetical machine that would run C-code as its assembly language—is modeled by a series of macros in a file called *<tools/virtual.h>*,

<tools/virtual.h>

---

3. For convenience, all the C-code directives described in this section are also summarized in Appendix F.

which should be **#include**d at the top of every C-code file. This file contains definitions that allow you to compile and run the generated C-code, using your normal C compiler as an assembler. *Virtual.h* is described piecemeal as the various C-code language elements are discussed. Unfortunately, the code in *virtual.h* is not particularly portable. I've made all sorts of assumptions about the sizes of various data types, the ordering of bytes within a word, and so forth. You can compensate for these system-dependent problems by modifying the include file, however.

A typical development cycle looks like this:

```
vi file.c      Edit the C source-code file.
c  file.c      Run the source code through the compiler developed in the
               current chapter. The compiler generates a C-code output file
               called output.c.

cc output.c    "Assemble" the compiler's output, using your normal compiler
               as an assembler. You can debug the compiler's output using
               dbx, CodeView, or whatever debugger you normally use.
```

Table 6.2 shows how a C input file is translated into C-code by the compiler in the current chapter. The rightmost column demonstrates how the C-code relates to 8086 assembler. Table 6.2 is intended to demonstrate what's happening in a general way. Don't worry about the details—I'll discuss what's going on in great detail as the chapter progresses. For now, notice how similar the C-code is to the true assembly language. It's easy to translate from one to another. C-code is really an assembly language, regardless of the superficial similarities to C.

6.2.1 Names and White Space

White space.

As in C, white space is ignored in C-code except as needed to separate tokens. Comments delimited with /* . . . */ are treated as white space. Multiple-line comments are not permitted—the /* and */ must be on the same line.

Identifiers.

Identifiers can be made up of letters, digits, and underscores only. The first character in the name may not be a digit, and names are restricted to 31 characters. Names are truncated if they're longer. In addition to the standard C keywords, all of the C-code directives discussed below should be treated as keywords and may not be used for identifiers.

6.2.2 Basic Types

The primary design considerations in the virtual machine are controlled by the sizes of the variables that are manipulated by the machine. Four basic data types are supported: 8-bit bytes, 16-bit words, 32-bit long words, and generic pointers (nominally 32 bits). These types are declared with the byte, word, lword, and ptr keywords respectively. The array and record keywords can be used as a synonym for byte in order to provide some self-documentation when declaring a structure or array of structures. All but ptrs are signed quantities.

byte, word, lword, array, record.

Listing 6.1 shows the type definitions from *virtual.h*. I'm making nonportable assumptions about word widths here; you may have to change these definitions in your own system. The ptr type is a character pointer, as compared to a **void** pointer, so that it can be incremented if necessary.

<tools/c-code.h>

The *<tools/c-code.h>* file, which is **#include**d on line one of Listing 6.1, contains various definitions that control the widths of basic types. It is shown in Listing 6.2. This information has been split into a second header file because it is likely to be used by the compiler that is generating C-code, but is not much use in interpreting the C-code.

Table 6.2. Translating C to C-code to 8086 Assembly Language

C Input	C-Code Output	8086 Assembler

	```#include <tools/virtual.h>```
	```#define T(x)```
	```SEG(bss)```
	```#define L0 1 /* strcpy: locals */```
	```#define L1 2 /* strcpy: temps. */```
	```#undef T```
	```#define T(n) (fp-L0-(n*4))```
		```_BSS SEGMENT WORD PUBLIC```

	```SEG(code)```	```_BSS ENDS```
		```_TEXT SEGMENT WORD PUBLIC```
		``` ASSUME CS:_TEXT```

```strcpy(dst, src)```	```PROC(_strcpy,public)```	```PUBLIC _strcpy``` ```_strcpy PROC NEAR```
```char *dst, *src;```	```/* fp+4 = dst [argument] */``` ```/* fp+8 = src [argument] */```	```; [bp+2] = dst``` ```; [bp+4] = src```

```{```	```link(L0+L1);```	```push bp```
		```mov bp,sp```
		```sub sp,6```

``` char *start;```	```/* fp-4 = start [variable] */```	```; [bp-2] = start```
```start = dst;```	```BP(fp-4) = BP(fp+4);```	```mov ax,WORD PTR [bp+2]``` ```mov WORD PTR [bp-2],ax```

```while(*src)```
```{```
	```TST1:```
	``` EQ(*BP(fp+8),0) /* src */```
	``` goto EXIT1;```
		```TST1:```
		``` mov bx,WORD PTR [bp+4]```
		``` mov al,BYTE PTR [bx]```
		``` or al,al```
		``` jz EXIT1```

```*dst++ = *src++ ;```	```BP(T(1)) = BP(fp+4); /* t1=dst */```
	```BP(fp+4) += 1; /* dst++ */```
	```BP(T(2)) = BP(fp+8); /* t2=src */```
	```BP(fp+8) += 1; /* src++ */```
	```*BP(T(1)) = *BP(T(2)); /* *t1=t2 */```
		```mov si,WORD PTR [bp+2]```
		```inc WORD PTR [bp+2]```
		```mov di,WORD PTR [bp+4]```
		```inc WORD PTR [bp+4]```
		```mov bx,di```
		```mov al,BYTE PTR [bx]```
		```mov bx,si```
		```mov BYTE PTR [bx],al```

```}```	``` goto TST1;``` ```EXIT1:```	```jmp TST1``` ```EXIT1:```
```return start;```	```rF.pp = BP(fp-4);``` ```goto RET1;```	```mov bx,WORD PTR [bp-4]``` ```jmp RET1```

```}```	```RET1:```
	``` unlink();```
	``` ret();```
	```ENDP(_strcpy)```
		```RET1:```
		``` mov sp,bp```
		
		```_strcpy ENDP```
		```_TEXT ENDS```
		``` END```

6.2.3 The Virtual Machine: Registers, Stack, and Memory

The C-code virtual machine is pictured in Figure 6.1. The machine has a set of 16   *The register set.*
general-purpose *registers* named *r0, r1, r2*, and so forth. An entire 32-bit register can be
accessed from any instruction, as can either of the 16-bit words or any of four 8-bit bytes
that comprise the same register. These registers are memory locations that are physically
part of the CPU itself—they don't have addresses. Use the syntax shown in Table 6.3 to
access a register. The name must always be fully qualified; one of the forms shown in
Table 6.3 must always be used. The register name by itself (without the dot and type
reference) is illegal.

Listing 6.1. *virtual.h*— Basic Types

```
1   #include <tools/c-code.h>              /* Basic types           */
2                                          /* 8  bit                */
3   typedef char   byte;                   /* 16 bit                */
4   typedef short  word;                   /* 32 bit                */
5   typedef long   lword;                  /* Nominally 32 bit.     */
6   typedef char   *ptr;
7                                          /* Aliases for "byte."   */
8   typedef byte   array;
9   typedef byte   record;
```

Listing 6.2. *c-code.h*— Various Widths

```
1   #define  BYTE_WIDTH        1        /* Widths of the basic types.         */
2   #define  WORD_WIDTH        2
3   #define  LWORD_WIDTH       4
4   #define  PTR_WIDTH         4
5
6   #define  BYTE_HIGH_BIT   "0xff80"      /* High-bit mask. */
7   #define  WORD_HIGH_BIT   "0x8000"
8   #define  LWORD_HIGH_BIT  "0x80000000L"
```

The stack, fp, sp.

In addition to the register set, there is a 2048-element, 32-bit wide stack, and two special-purpose registers that point into the stack: the fp and sp registers—discussed in depth, below.

The instruction pointer, ip.

Finally, there is the *ip* or instruction-pointer register. This register holds the address (in the code segment) of the <u>next</u> instruction to execute, not of the current instruction. It is updated every time an instruction is processed, and is modified indirectly by various instructions. A call, for example, pushes the *ip* and then transfers control to somewhere else. A ret pops the address at top of stack into the *ip*. A goto modifies the *ip* directly. The instruction pointer is not used directly by the current compiler, and its value won't change if you just use your C compiler to assemble the C-code output. Access to it is occasionally useful, however, and the register is available in all real machines. It's included here for completeness' sake.

Virtual machine implementation.

The register set and stack are implemented in Listings 6.3 and 6.4. Note that the definition for reg on lines 21 to 28 of Listing 6.4 is <u>not</u> portable because I'm assuming that an 8086-style byte ordering is used—the least-significant byte is lowest in memory, and the most-significant byte is highest. Exactly the opposite holds in 68000-style machines. The LSB is highest in memory, so you'd have to redefine the _words and _bytes fields as follows for those machines:

```
struct _words  { word  high,  low;  };
struct _bytes  { byte b3, b2, b1, b0; };
```

The address of an object is the physical address of the least-significant byte in both the 8086 and 68000 family. Other machines may require even more shuffling.

Figure 6.1. The C-code Virtual Machine

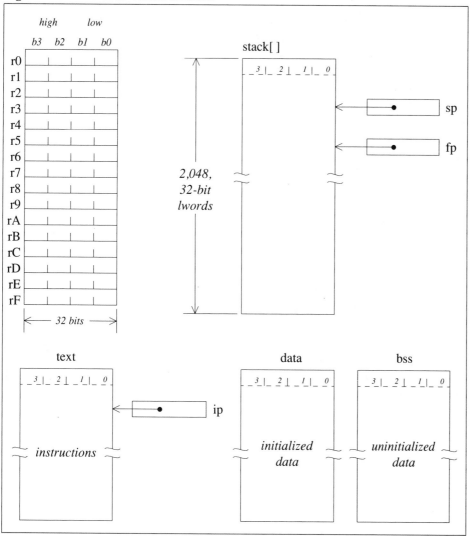

Table 6.3. The Virtual-Machine Register Set

r1 contains:	access syntax:			
pointer	r1.pp			
32-bit long word	r1.l			
two 16-bit words	r1.w.high	r1.w.low		
four 8-bit bytes (byte 0 is low)	r1.b.b3	r1.b.b2	r1.b.b1	r1.b.b0

Listing 6.3. *c-code.h*— Stack-size Definitions

```
 9   #define SWIDTH        LWORD_WIDTH   /* Stack width (in bytes).        */
10   #define SDEPTH        1024          /* Number of elements in stack.  */
```

Listing 6.4. *virtual.h*— The Register Set and Stack

```
10   #ifdef ALLOC
11   #     define I(x)   x
12   #     define CLASS /* empty */
13   #else
14   #     define I(x)   /* empty */
15   #     define CLASS extern
16   #endif
17
18   struct _words  { word   low, high;    };
19   struct _bytes  { byte   b0, b1, b2, b3; };        /* b0 is LSB, b3 is MSB */
20
21   typedef union reg
22   {
23       char            *pp;        /* pointer                */
24       lword           l;          /* long word              */
25       struct _words   w;          /* two 16-bit words       */
26       struct _bytes   b;          /* four 8-bit bytes       */
27   }
28   reg;
29
30   CLASS reg r0, r1, r2, r3, r4, r5, r6, r7 ;        /* Registers */
31   CLASS reg r8, r9, rA, rB, rC, rD, rE, rF ;
32
33   CLASS reg         stack[ SDEPTH ];                /* run-time stack */
34   CLASS reg         *__sp I(= &stack[ SDEPTH ]);    /* Stack pointer  */
35   CLASS reg         *__fp I(= &stack[ SDEPTH ]);    /* Frame pointer  */
36
37   #define fp        ((char *) __fp)
38   #define sp        ((char *) __sp)
```

Note that the stack itself is declared as an array of reg unions on line 33 of Listing 6.4, and the stack and frame pointers are reg pointers. The sp and fp registers are referenced in C-code directives using the macros on lines 37 and 38, however. The cast assures that pointer arithmetic is defeated in the based addressing modes discussed below.

The stack is deliberately made as wide as the worst-case basic type—if a 64-bit **double** were supported, I would have made the stack 64 bits wide. This way, all stack access can be done with a single instruction. I've done this in order to make the back end's life a little easier. It's a simple matter to translate single push and pop instructions into multiple instructions (if the target-machines stack is 16 bits wide, for example). It's difficult to go in the other direction, however—to translate multiple pushes and pops into single instructions.

Allocating space for the virtual-register set, AL-LOC.

You must put the following two lines into only one module of your program to actually allocate space for the stack and register set:

```
#define ALLOC
#include <tools/virtual.h>
```

You can create a two-line file, compile it, and link it to your other code if you like.

When `ALLOC` is defined, the definitions on lines 11 and 12 are activated. Here, `CLASS`   CLASS.
evaluates to an empty string, so all invocations of the `CLASS` macro effectively disappear
from the file. The `I()` macro evaluates to its argument, so an invocation like   The `I()` macro.

```
I(= &stack[SDEPTH]);
```

evaluates to

```
= &stack[SDEPTH];
```

The macro's argument is the entire string `=&stack[SDEPTH]`. When `ALLOC` is not
defined, the opposite situation holds, `CLASS` expands to the keyword **extern** and the
contents of the `I()` macro are discarded.

The run-time stack, stack pointer, and frame pointer registers are defined at the bottom of Listing 6.4. The stack is the same width as a register, and the stack pointer is initialized to point just above the top stack element. It grows towards low memory with the
first push.

6.2.4 Memory Organization: Segments

The stack represents only a portion of the memory that can be used by the running
program. This memory is partitioned into several *segments*, one of which is the *stack*   Segments.
segment. Figure 6.2 shows how the segments are usually arranged.

Figure 6.2. Segments

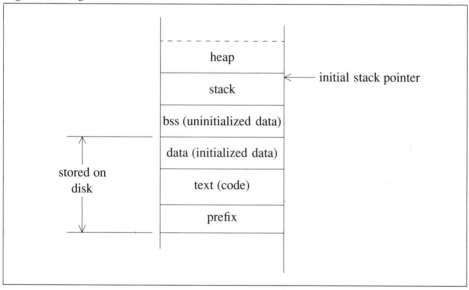
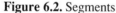

The rationale behind this partitioning is best understood by looking at how a program   The program-load process.
is loaded by the operating system. Initially, a contiguous region of memory is allocated
for the program to use. This region can be physical memory, as it is in most microcomputers, or can be virtual memory, as on a mainframe. In the later case, the physical
memory might not form a contiguous block, but it's convenient to look at it that way.

The *prefix* segment holds information that is used by the operating system to load the   The program prefix.
program. Typically, the sizes of the various segments are stored there, as are things like
the initial values of the program counter and stack pointer. Some operating systems (like
MS-DOS) read the prefix into memory, and it's available for the program to use at run
time. Other operating systems read the prefix to get the information that it contains, and
then overwrite the prefix with the other segments.

Executable image.
Text (or code) and (initialized) *data* segments.

Using the information in the prefix, the operating system then allocates a block of memory large enough to hold the remainder of the program, called the *executable image*. The *text* and *data* segments are then copied directly from the disk into memory. The *text* or *code* segment holds the executable code; the *data* segment holds <u>initialized</u> data, only. That's why an initialized **static** local variable comes up with an initial value, but once that value is changed it stays changed—the initial value is just read from the disk into the proper place in memory. Note that there are two types of initialized data: variables that have been given an initial value when declared, and initialized constants (like string constants) whose values are not expected to change. The constant data is sometimes stored in the *text* segment, along with the code, in order to make the operating system's life a little easier. It knows that the text segment is not modified, so it doesn't have to swap this region out to the disk if it needs the memory for another process.

One of two things can happen once the *text* and *data* segments are loaded, depending on the operating system. Either control can be transferred directly to the program, which must continue the initialization process, or the operating system itself initializes the other segments. In any event, the *bss*[4] segment, which holds all uninitialized data, is initialized to all zeros at load-time. (There's no point in storing masses of zeros on the disk.) The stack pointer is then initialized to point at the correct part of the *stack* segment, which holds the run-time stack used for subroutine calls, and so forth. Stacks grow down in most computers, so the stack pointer is typically initialized to the top of the stack segment. Various pointers that manipulate the *heap*, the region of memory used for dynamic storage, are also initialized. The heap is used, in C, by the memory-allocation subroutines `malloc()` and `free()`.[5] In some languages the heap is also used in code generated by the compiler itself. The C++ `new` operator allocates memory for an object; and a user-defined class might do memory allocation transparently when an object in that class is declared. Similarly, PL/1 supports dynamically allocable arrays—arrays whose size is not known until run time, and the PL/1 compiler uses the heap to allocate space for that array when the scope of that declaration is entered at run time (when the block that holds the declaration is entered). The compiler just translates a compile-time declaration into code that allocates space for the array and initializes a pointer to access the first element—it effectively calls `malloc()` when the subroutine is entered and `free()` at exit. The contents of the stack and heap segments are typically uninitialized at load time, so the contents of variables allocated from these regions are undefined. The heap is typically at the top of the image because it may have to grow larger as the program runs, in which case the memory-allocation functions request that the operating system enlarge the size of the executable image. The heap and stack segments are often combined, however. Since the stack pointer typically grows down, and the memory allocation from the heap can start in low memory and go up, the shared space can be allocated from both ends as needed, like this:

Bss segment.

Stack segment.

Heap segment.

Dynamic arrays.

Combined heap and stack.

---

4. *Bss* stands for "block starting with symbol," a term dating from the Mesozoic, at least.

5. The source code for a `malloc()` and `free()` implementation is in [K&R] pp. 185–189.

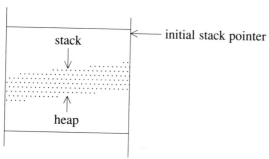

This way, if a program has an unusually large stack and unusually small heap or vice versa, space can be transferred from one area to the other with ease. It's difficult to expand the size of the heap after the top of heap runs into the stack, however, and such expansion almost always results in a fragmented heap. The virtual-memory manager could solve the fragmentation problem, but it might not.

Many compilers provide a mechanism for the program to determine the positions of various segments at run time. For example, the UNIX compiler automatically declares a variable at the end of the *bss* segment called `ebss`. All memory whose address is greater than `&ebss` must be in the stack or heap segments. Other variables (called `etext` and `edata`) are provided for the other segment boundaries. Similarly, many compilers generate code that checks the value of the stack pointer when every subroutine is entered and terminates the program if the stack pointer is not in the stack segment.

> Segment-end markers: `ebss`, `etext`, `edata`.

C-code lets you change from one segment to another by issuing a `SEG()` directive, which takes one of the following forms:

> The `SEG()` directive.

```
SEG( text )
SEG( data )
SEG( bss  )
```

Note that no semicolon is used here—this is the case for all C-code directives whose names are in all caps. Everything that follows a `SEG(text)` (up to the next `SEG()` directive or end of file) is in the text segment, and so forth. You can use `SEG(code)` instead of `SEG(text)`. There's no direct access to the *prefix, stack,* and *heap* segments because these exist only at run time, and the compiler uses other mechanisms to access them. You may not change segments in the middle of a subroutine. No `SEG` directives can appear between the `PROC` and `ENDP` directives, discussed below. The `SEG()` directive is defined as an empty macro in *virtual.h*. It's shown in Listing 6.5.

> No semicolon used with upper-case C-code directives.

Listing 6.5. *virtual.h*— The `SEG()` directive.

```
39   #define SEG(segment)    /* empty */
```

6.2.5 Variable Declarations: Storage Classes and Alignment

C-code supports global-level variable declarations only. All variables must be declared in the *data* or *bss* segments, depending on whether or not they are initialized. Four storage classes are available (they are related to C in Table 6.4):

`private`   Space is allocated for the variable, but the variable cannot be accessed from outside the current file. In C, this class is used for all **static** variables, be they local or global. Initialized variables go into the *data* segment, other variables go into the *bss* segment.

public   Space is allocated for the variable, and the variable can be accessed from any file in the current program. In C, this class is used for all initialized nonstatic global variables. It is illegal for two public variables in the same program to have the same name, even if they're declared in different files. Since public variables must be initialized when declared, they must be in the *data* segment.

common   Space for this variable is allocated by the linker. If a variable with a given name is declared common in one module and public in another, then the public definition takes precedence. If there are nothing but common definitions for a variable, then the linker allocates space for that variable in the *bss* segment. C uses this storage class for all uninitialized global variables.

external   Space for this variable is allocated elsewhere. If a label is external, an identical label must be declared common or public in some other module of the program. This storage class is not used for variables in the current application, all of which are common, public, or private. It is used for subroutines, though.

Table 6.4. Converting C Storage Classes to C-code Storage Classes

	static	not static	
	static	definition	declaration (**extern** or prototype)
Subroutine (in *text* segment).	private	public	external
Uninitialized variable (in *bss* segment).	private	common	
Initialized variable (in *data* segment).	private	public	

The following example shows how these classes are used in C:

```
int kookla = 1;    /* Public--it's initialized and not static. */
static int fran;   /* Private--it's static. Initialized to 0.  */
int ollie;         /* Common--it's declared without an extern. */
int ollie;         /* Not a redefinition because default class */
                   /* is extern. Both instances of ollie are   */
                   /* common.                                   */

void ronnie()
{
    static float george; /* Private--it's declared static.      */
    extern dan;          /* Common.                             */
    int    dick = 1;     /* No declaration is generated. (The   */
                         /* memory is allocated on the stack).  */
}
```

The four storage classes can be broken into two broad categories—classes that allocate space in the executable image (as stored on the disk) and classes that don't allocate space. I'll have to dip into real assembly language (8086 assembler) for a moment to show what's actually going on. The assembler actually builds a physical copy of the executable image in memory as it works, and it copies this image to the disk when assembly is complete. The assembler keeps track of the current position in the executable image that it's building with an internal variable called the *location counter*. A directive like the following allocates space for a variable:

Location counter.

```
_var : dw 10
```

This instruction tells the assembler to do the following:

- Create a symbol-table entry for _var and remember the current value of the location counter there.
- Fill the next two bytes with the number 10. Two bytes are allocated because of the dw—other codes are used for different sizes; db allocates one byte, for example. The 10 is taken from the dw directive.
- Increment the location counter by two bytes.

The allocated space (and the number 10, which is used here to fill that space) end up on the disk as part of the executable image. Instructions are processed in much the same way. For example, a

```
MOV ax,_var
```

instruction moves the contents of _var into the ax register. This instruction tells the assembler to do the following:

- Copy a binary code representing the "move into ax" operation into the place referenced by the current location counter. This binary code is called the *op code*.
- Copy the address of _var into the next two bytes. This address is the location-counter value that was remembered in the symbol table when space for _var was allocated.
- Increment the location counter by three.

op code.

From the assembler's perspective, code and data are the same thing. All it knows about is the current location counter. There is nothing preventing us from putting a MOV instruction into memory as follows:

```
db 0A0H      ; 0xA0 is the 8086 op code for "MOV into AX"
dw _var      ; address of _var
```

Applying the foregoing to C-code storage classes, public and private definitions are translated into dw directives in 8086 assembler. They cause the location counter to be moved, and some value is copied into the allocated space. This value ends up on the disk as part of the executable image. The external directive is at the other extreme. No space is allocated; the location counter is not modified. The assembler does create a symbol-table entry for the associated label, however. If that label is referenced in the code, place holders are put into the image instead of the actual addresses, which are not known by the compiler. The linker replaces all place holders with the correct addresses when it puts together the final program. The external directive must reference a region of memory allocated with a dw directive or equivalent somewhere else in the program. The unpatched binary image (with the place holders still in it) is usually called a *relocatable object module.*[6]

Relocatable object module.

The common storage class is somewhere in between external and public. If the name associated with the common is used elsewhere in a public or private declaration, then the common is treated just like an external. Things change when <u>all</u>

---

6. One common way to organize a relocatable module puts a symbol table into the object file. The table has one element for each unresolved reference—private symbols are not put into the table. The symbol-table elements hold the symbol's name and the offset from the start of the file to the first place holder that references that symbol. That place holder, in turn, holds the offset to the next place holder for the same symbol, in a manner similar to a linked list. The last element of the list is usually marked with zeros. Most 8086 relocatable-object-module formats derive from the specification described in [Intel] and in [Armbrust].

references to the variable are commons, however. Space is allocated for the variable at load time, not at compile time. Remember, the executable image on the disk represents only part of the space that is used when the program is running. Space for a common is always allocated in the *bss* segment, which is created when the program is loaded—it has no existence at compile time and won't be part of the binary image on the disk. The linker replaces the place holders in those instructions that use the common variable with references to the place at which the variable is found at run time, but no dw directive is generated. Space is allocated implicitly because the linker leaves a note in the executable image's file header that tells the loader the size of the *bss* region. Instead of incrementing the location counter at compile time, the assembler tells the loader to increment it at load time, by making the size of the executable image large enough to encompass the extra space.

Allocating variables.   Returning to C-code, all variables must be declared using a basic type (byte, word, lword, or ptr) and one of the foregoing storage classes (private, public, common, external). In addition, one-dimensional arrays can be declared using trailing brackets. Multi-dimensioned arrays are not permitted. The following declarations (only) are available;

```
class type name;               /* single variable */
class type name [ constant ];  /* array          */
```

A structure must be declared as a byte array, though the keyword record can be used as a synonym for byte for documentation purposes.

Public and private variables in the *data* segment may be initialized with an explicit C-style initializer. Character constants and implicit array sizes are both supported. For example:

```
SEG( data )
public  byte name    = 'z' ;
public  byte name[]  = 'a', 'b', 'c', 'd', '\0' ;
public  byte name[]  = "abcd";
private word name    = 10;
public  word name[3] = 10, 11, 12 ;
```

The double-quote syntax can be used only to initialize byte arrays. A C declaration such as the following:

```
kings[4] =
{
    "henry",
    "kong",
    "elvis"
    "balthazar"
};
```

must be declared as follows in C-code:

```
SEG( data );
private byte S1[]       = "henry\0"     ;
private byte S2[]       = "kong\0"      ;
private byte S3[]       = "elvis\0"     ;
private byte S4[]       = "balthazar\0" ;
public  ptr  kings[4] = { S1, S2, S3, S4 };
```

These declarations are all in the *data* segment because they're initialized. The anonymous string names must be private because the same labels may be used for other anonymous strings in other files. kings is public, because it wasn't declared **static**. The *virtual.h* definitions for the various storage classes are in Listing 6.6.

Listing 6.6. *virtual.h*— Storage Classes

```
40  #define public    /* empty */
41  #define common    /* empty */
42  #define private   static
43  #define external  extern
```

The C-code assembler assumes that memory is made up of of 32-bit wide cells, each of which occupies four addresses. The various basic types control the way that the four bytes can be accessed. In particular, the least significant byte of an object must also be at an address that is an even multiple of the object's size—a `byte` can be anywhere, a `word` must be at an even address, an `lword` and `ptr` must be at an address that's an even multiple of four. All objects are stored with the least-significant byte at the lowest physical address and the most-significant byte at the highest address. A pointer to an object holds the physical address of the least-significant byte. The system is pictured in Figure 6.3.

Alignment.

LSB is at the lowest address.

Figure 6.3. Memory Alignment

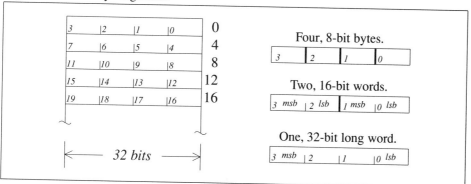

A good analogy for these restrictions is a book printed in a typeface that's half a page high. The typeface is also so wide that only two digits can fit on a line. The rules are that a two-digit number must be on a single line. A four-digit number, which requires two lines to print, must be on a single page. An eight-digit number, which requires four lines to print, must be on two facing pages.

These restrictions are called *alignment* restrictions. (You would say that words must be aligned at even addresses, and so forth.) Alignment restrictions are usually imposed by the hardware for efficiency's sake. If the data path from memory to the CPU is 32 bits wide, the machine would like to fetch all 32 bits at once, and this is difficult to do if the 32-bit word can be split across a multiple-of-four boundary.

The actual byte ordering is not critical in the present application provided that it's consistent, but the alignment restrictions are very important when doing something like allocating space for a structure. For example, the following structure requires 16 bytes rather than nine, because the 16-bit **int** must be aligned on an even boundary; the 32-bit **long** must start at an address that's an even multiple of four, and padding is required at the end to assure that the next object in memory is aligned properly, regardless of its type. A declaration like the following:

Structure-field allocation and alignment.

```
struct
{
    char  c1;
    int   i;
    char  c2;
    long  l;
    char  c3;
}
fred;
```

allocates fields placed in memory like this:

Though C guarantees that the ordering of structure members will be preserved, a clever compiler for another language might shuffle around the ordering of the fields to make the structure smaller. If c1 were moved next to c2, then four bytes would be saved. The three bytes of padding at the end of the structure are required in case you have an array of structures. A clever compiler could actually eliminate the padding in the current example, but nothing could be done if the first field of the structure was a **long**, which needs to be aligned on a multiple-of-four boundary.

ALIGN() directive.

C-code variable declarations automatically force proper alignment for that variable, so if you declare a byte-sized variable followed by a 16-bit word, one byte of memory is wasted because the word requires even alignment. There are occasional situations where alignment must be forced explicitly, and C-code provides the ALIGN (*type*) directive for this purpose. The assembler inserts sufficient padding to assure that the next declared variable is aligned as if it were of the indicated *type*. ALIGN is defined in *virtual.h* in Listing 6.7. The worst-case alignment boundary is declared for use by the compiler in *c-code.h* (Listing 6.8).

Listing 6.7. *virtual.h*— The ALIGN Directive

```
44   #define ALIGN(type)   /* empty */
```

Listing 6.8. *c-code.h*— Worst-case Alignment Restriction

```
11   #define ALIGN_WORST      LWORD_WIDTH       /* Long word is worst-case alignment. */
```

6.2.6 Addressing Modes

Constants and all variable and register names are referenced in instructions by means of various *addressing modes*, summarized in Table 6.5.

Immediate mode.

The *immediate* addressing mode is used for numbers. C-style hex, octal, decimal, and character constants are all recognized (0xabc 0377 123 'c'); lword (32-bit) constants should be indicated by a trailing L (0x12345678L). The immediate addressing mode is used in real assemblers to put a physical number into an instruction rather than an address. Many real assemblers require a special symbol like # to precede immediate data.

Direct mode.

The *direct* mode is used to fetch the contents of a variable. There is usually no special operator here; you just use the variable's name. Note, however, that array and function names cannot be accessed in direct mode—their name is always treated as the address of the first element or instructions.

The *effective-address* mode gets the address of an object. The operand of the & operator is usually a label (&x where x is a name in a previous declaration), but it can also be used in conjunction with one of the based addressing modes, discussed shortly. Note that the & should be omitted from a function or array name.

The *indirect* modes work only on objects of pointer type: a variable that was declared ptr, a register name followed by the .pp selector, or the sp or fp registers. You must do two things to access an object indirectly. You must surround the variable or register that holds the address with parentheses to indicate indirection, and you must tell the C-code assembler the kind of object that the pointer is referencing. You do the latter by preceding the parenthesis with one of the following one- or two-character modifiers:

Indirect modes.

Indirection indicated by parentheses.

Code	Points at object of this type.
B	byte
W	word
L	lword
P	ptr
BP	pointer to byte
WP	pointer to word
LP	pointer to lp
PP	pointer to ptr

For example, W(r0.pp) fetches the word whose address is in r0.pp. You can also access an object at a specified offset from a pointer with the following syntax:

W(*p*), W(*p+offset*)

W(*p* + *offset*)

The *offset* may be a number, a numeric register reference (as compared to a pointer reference), or a numeric variable. The following example references the word whose address is derived by adding together the contents of the fp register and r0.w.low:

W(fp + r0.w.low)

The following instruction references the long word at an offset of −16 (bytes) from the frame pointer:

L(fp-16)

If the fetched object is of type BP, WP, LP, or PP, a star may be added to fetch the object to which the pointer points. For example, WP(fp+6) fetches the word pointer at offset 6 from the frame pointer; *WP(fp+6) fetches the object pointed to by that word pointer. Note that these *double indirect* modes, though found on most big machines like VAX's, are missing from many machines. You would have to use two instructions to access the referenced object—like this:

WP(*p*), *WP(*p*)

```
r0.pp = WP(fp+6);
r1.w  = W(r0.pp);
```

The effective-address and indirect modes can be combined in various ways, summarized in Table 6.6. The alternate syntaxes are useful when doing code generation, because variables on the stack can be treated the same way as variables at fixed addresses. For example, the address of a word pointer that is stored at offset 8 from the frame pointer can be fetched with &WP(fp+6), and the address of a word pointer, _p, at a fixed address can be accessed with &WP(&_p). The convenience will become evident when code-generation for the arithmetic operators is discussed, below. You can look at

Combined effective-address and indirect modes. &WP(&*p*).

Table 6.5. Addressing Modes

Mode	Example	Notes
immediate	93	Decimal number. Use leading 0x for hex, 0 for octal.
direct	x, r0.1	Contents of variable or register.
indirect	B(p) W(p) L(p) P(p) BP(p) WP(p) LP(p) PP(p)	byte whose address is in p. word whose address is in p. lword whose address is in p. ptr whose address is in p. byte pointer whose address is in p. word pointer whose address is in p. lword pointer whose address is in p. ptr pointer whose address is in p.
double indirect	*BP(p) *WP(p) *LP(p) *PP(p)	byte pointed to by pointer whose address is in p. word pointed to by word pointer whose address is in p. lword pointed to by lword pointer whose address is in p. ptr pointed to by ptr whose address is in p.
based indirect	B(p+N) W(p+N) L(pN) . . .	byte at byte offset N from address in p. word at byte offset N from address in p. lword at byte offset N from address in p.
effective address	&name &W(p+N)	Address of variable or first element of array. Address of word at offset $+n$ from the pointer p (The effective-address modes can also be used with other indirect modes see below.)

A generic pointer, p, is a variable declared ptr or a pointer register: rN.pp, fp, sp. N is any integer: a number, a numeric register (r0.w.low), or a reference to a byte, word, or lword variable. The based indirect modes can take negative offsets as in B(p-8).

these alternate addressing modes as a way to specify an explicit type in the variable reference. An &W(&p) tells you that p points at a word, information that you would not have if p were used by itself.

Note that p may not be preceded by an ampersand if it references a register because registers don't have addresses. Also, the ampersand preceding the p in the examples in Table 6.6 is optional if p is the name of an array or function. Since some compilers print a warning if you use the ampersand in front of an array or function name, you should leave the ampersand off unless your compiler requires it.

Finally, note that C-style pointer arithmetic is used when a double-indirect directive tells the assembler the type of the referenced object.

```
ptr p;
p += 1          /* Adds 1 to p because the referenced */
                /*    object's type is unspecified.   */
BP(&p) += 1     /* Adds 1 (size of a  byte) to p.     */
WP(&p) += 1     /* Adds 2 (size of a  word) to p.     */
LP(&p) += 1     /* Adds 4 (size of a lword) to p.     */
```

The macros that implement the various type directives are in Listing 6.9. The prefixes themselves are declared, for the benefit of the compiler that's generating the C-code, in *c-code.h* and are shown in Listing 6.10.

Table 6.6. Combined Indirect and Effective-Address Modes

Syntax:	Evaluates to:
&p &W(&p) &WP(&p) &WP(fp+*n*)	address of the pointer
p &W(p) WP(&p) WP(fp+*n*)	contents of the pointer itself
W(p) *WP(&p) *WP(fp+*n*)	contents of the word whose address is in the pointer

Listing 6.9. *virtual.h*— Direct-Stack-Access Directives

```
45   #define W      * (word    *)
46   #define B      * (byte    *)
47   #define L      * (lword   *)
48   #define P      * (ptr     *)
49   #define WP     * (word   **)
50   #define BP     * (byte   **)
51   #define LP     * (lword  **)
52   #define PP     * (ptr    **)
```

Listing 6.10. *c-code.h*— Indirect-Mode Prefixes

```
12   #define BYTE_PREFIX      "B"       /* Indirect-mode prefixes. */
13   #define WORD_PREFIX      "W"
14   #define LWORD_PREFIX     "L"
15   #define PTR_PREFIX       "P"
16   #define BYTEPTR_PREFIX   "BP"
17   #define WORDPTR_PREFIX   "WP"
18   #define LWORDPTR_PREFIX  "LP"
19   #define PTRPTR_PREFIX    "PP"
```

6.2.7 Manipulating the Stack

Two C-code directives are provided to do explicit stack manipulation. These are: Push and pop directives.

push (*something*)

and

something = pop (*type*)

The push() macro pushes the indicated object, and the pop() macro pops an object of the indicated type. For example, if x were declared as an lword, you could say: x = pop(lword). The lword is the declared type of the target (of x). The target can also be a register, but the types on the two sides of the equal sign must agree:

```
r1.w.low = pop( word );
```

The stack is 32 bits wide, so part of the stack word is wasted when you push or pop small objects. For example:

```
r1.w.low = pop( word )
```

pops the bottom word of the current top-of-stack item into the low half of `r1`. The top half of the stack item is discarded, and the top half of `r1` is not modified. A `push` instruction modifies a 32-bit quantity, and the pushed object is right-adjusted in the 32-bit word. If `r1` holds 0x12345678, the following instruction:

```
push( r1.b.b3 )
```

pushes the number 0x??????12. The question marks represent undefined values. A

```
push( r1.w.low )
```

directive pushes 0x????5678,

```
push( r1.w.high )
```

pushes 0x????1234, and

```
push( r1.w.l )
```

pushes the entire number 0x12345678.

A simple `push(r1)` is not permitted. The register name must be fully qualified. Use `push(r1.l)` to push the entire register.

The two stack directives are defined in *virtual.h* in Listing 6.11.

Listing 6.11. *virtual.h*— Pushing and Popping

```
53   #define push(n)          (--sp)->l = (lword)(n)
54   #define pop(t)           (t)( (sp++)->l )
```

6.2.8 Subroutines

Subroutines must all be defined in the *text* segment. External-subroutine declarations should be output as follows:

```
external name();
```

No return value may be specified.

Subroutine definitions are created by surrounding the code that comprises the subroutine with `PROC(name, class)` and `ENDP(name)` directives. The `name` is the function name and the `class` is the storage class (either `public` or `private`). `private` functions cannot be accessed outside the current file. Invocations of `PROC()` and `ENDP()` <u>may not</u> be followed by semicolons.

A subroutine is called using a `call(name)` directive and control is passed back to the calling function with a `ret()` directive. For example:

```
SEG ( text )
PROC( _sylvester, public )
    call( _tweety );          /* Call subroutine tweety.   */
    ret();                    /* Return to calling function. */
ENDP( _sylvester )
```

The argument to `call()` can be either a subroutine name or a reference to a variable or register [like `call(r1.pp)`, which calls the subroutine whose address is in `r1.pp`].

Note that the compiler has inserted underscores in front of the variable names so that these names won't conflict with internally generated labels. A `ret()` statement is supplied if one is not already present immediately before the `ENDP`.

Leading underscores avoid name conflicts.

The *virtual.h* definitions for these macros are in Listing 6.12. The `call()` macro simulates an assembly-language call instruction which pushes the return address (the address of the instruction that follows the call) onto the stack and then transfers control to the address that is the call's argument. Here, the return-address push is simulated by pushing the "stringized" version of the subroutine name onto the stack, and then the subroutine is called.[7] An assembly-language return instruction pops the address at the top of stack into the instruction pointer. The `ret()` directive simulates this process by popping the name from the stack and returning.

Virtual.h implementation of `call()` and `ret()`.

Listing 6.12. *virtual.h*— Subroutine Definitions, Calls, and Returns

```
55   #define PROC(name,cls)    cls name(){
56   #define ENDP(name)        ret();}                        /* Name is ignored. */
57
58   #define call(name)        (--__sp)->pp = #name, (*(void (*)())(name))()
59
60   #define ret()             __sp++; return
```

The subroutine call on line 58 of Listing 6.12 is complicated by the fact that function pointers must be handled as well as explicit function names. The argument must first be cast into a pointer to a subroutine:

```
(void (*)()) (name)
```

and then can be called indirectly through the pointer. This cast does nothing if *name* is already a subroutine name, but it correctly converts register and variable references into indirect subroutine calls.

6.2.9 Stack Frames: Subroutine Arguments and Automatic Variables

Of the various memory segments, the stack segment is of particular importance to subroutines. The run-time stack is used to make subroutine calls in the normal way: The return address is pushed as part of the call and the return pops the address at top of stack into the instruction pointer. Languages like C, which support recursion, use the stack for other purposes as well. In particular, the stack is used to pass arguments to subroutines, and certain local variables, called *automatic* variables, are stored on the stack at run time. In C, all local variables that aren't declared **static** are automatic. The following sequence of events occurs when a subroutine is called:

Subroutine linkage.

Automatic variables.

Subroutine linkage: creating the stack frame.

(1) The arguments are pushed in reverse order.
(2) The subroutine is called, pushing the return address as part of the call.
(3) The called subroutine pushes a few housekeeping registers, including the frame pointer, discussed below.
(4) The subroutine advances the stack pointer so that room is freed on the stack for local, automatic variables and anonymous temporaries.

---

7. The **#** directive is new to ANSI C. It turns the associated macro argument into a string by surrounding the matching text with implicit quotation marks.

Stack frame (activation record).

Building a stack frame.

This entire area of the stack, extending from the first argument pushed to the upper-most local variable or temporary, is called an *activation record* or *stack frame*. The compiler uses the stack and stack-manipulation macros described earlier to translate the code in Listing 6.13 into the output code in Listing 6.14. The complete stack frame is pictured in Figure 6.4.

Listing 6.13. `call(of,the,wild)`: Compiler Input

```
1   int dog1, dog2, dog3;
2
3   static call( of, the, wild )
4   int of, the, wild;
5   {
6       int  buck, thornton;
7       long john_silver;
8       ...
9   }
10  spitz()
11  {
12      call( dog1, dog2, dog3 );
13  }
```

Listing 6.14. `call(of,the,wild)`: Compiler Output

```
1   SEG( bss )
2   int       _dog1;
3   int       _dog2;
4   int       _dog3;
5
6   SEG (text )
7   PROC(_call, private)
8           push( fp );              /* Save old frame pointer.                  */
9           fp  = sp;                /* Set up new frame pointer.                */
10          sp -= 8;                 /* Make room for local vars. & temporaries. */
11          call( chkstk );          /* Check for stack overflow.                */
12          ...                      /* Code goes here.                          */
13          sp = fp;                 /* Discard local variables and temporaries. */
14          fp = pop( ptr );         /* Restore previous subroutine's fp.        */
15          ret();
16  ENDP (_call)
17  PROC (_spitz, public)
18          push( fp );
19          fp = sp;                 /* No sp-=N because there're no local vars.  */
20          call( chkstk );
21          push( _dog3 );           /* call( dog1, dog2, dog3 );                 */
22          push( _dog2 );
23          push( _dog1 );
24          call( _call );
25          sp += 8;                 /* Discard the arguments to call().          */
26          sp = fp;                 /* Return from spitz(): discard local vars.  */
27          fp = pop( ptr );         /* Restore calling routine's frame pointer.  */
28          ret();
29  ENDP ( _spitz )
```

Local variables in the stack frame.

The `sp-=8` on line ten of Listing 6.14 decrements the stack pointer to make room both for local variables and for a small scratch space to use for the anonymous temporaries. (Note that the stack pointer must be decremented in even multiples of 4 [the stack width]

Figure 6.4. Stack Frame for `call(of,the,wild)`

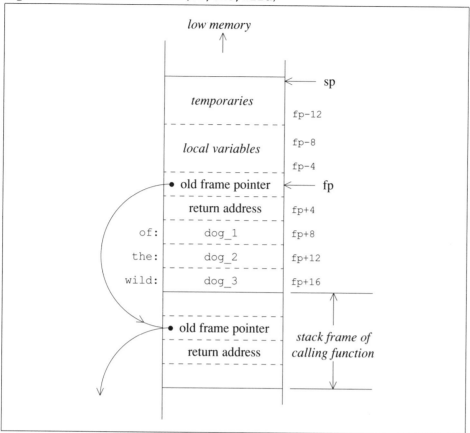

when you modify it explicitly, as compared to modifying it implicitly with a `push` or `pop`.) Unlike the arguments, the positions of local variables and temporaries within their area are arbitrary.[8] Don't be confused by the fact that part of the stack frame is created by the calling function and the other part is created by the called function. The stack frame is a single entity. Everybody is responsible for undoing what they did, so the calling function cleans the arguments off the stack, and the called function gets rid of everything else. Note that this organization of the stack frame, though characteristic, is not mandatory. Many compilers put the temporaries in different places or not on the stack at all. Sometimes, space on the stack frame is reserved to pass arguments to run-time library functions, to push registers used for **register** variables, and so on.

Figure 6.5 shows the local-variable and argument portion of the stack frame in greater detail. The *frame-pointer* register (`fp`) provides a fixed reference into the stack frame. It is used to access all the arguments and automatic variables. The argument `wild`—which contains `dog_3`—can be accessed using the indirect addressing mode as follows:

The frame pointer: arguments and automatic variables.

Accessing subroutine arguments.

---

8. The `chkstk()` subroutine, called on line 11, checks that the stack pointer hasn't crossed over into a different segment, as can happen if you allocate a large automatic array. It aborts the program if an error is discovered. This routine can also be used by a profiler subroutine to log the time at which the subroutine was entered. There would be a second subroutine call that logs the exit time at the bottom of the function.

```
W(fp+16)
```

The arguments are put onto the stack with push directives, and since an **int** is word sized, the high half of the 32-bit stack item is undefined. The actual, symbolic names of the argument do not appear in the output. All generated code that references wild uses W(fp+16) instead of the symbolic name, wild.

Figure 6.5. The Stack Frame, Magnified

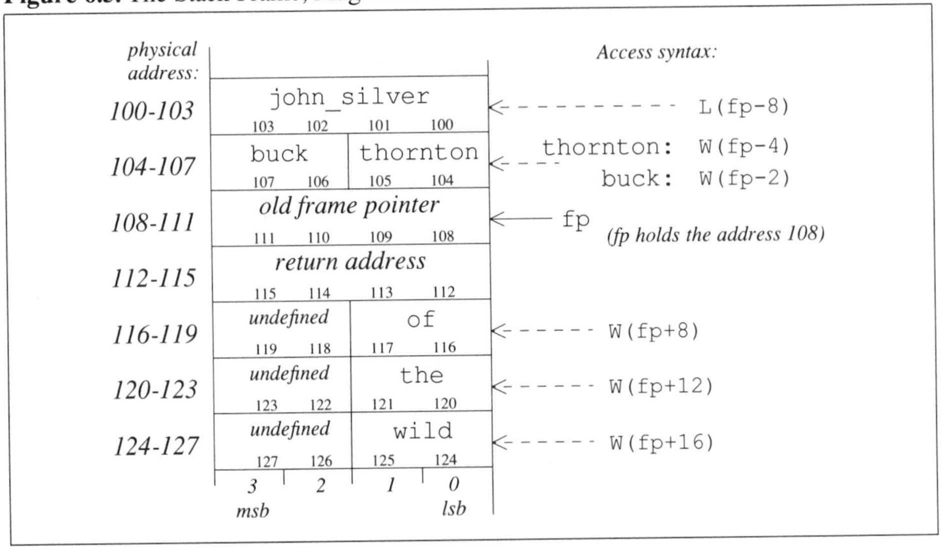

Accessing local auto-matic variables.

The local-variable region differs from the arguments in that the compiler treats a block of memory on the stack as a region of normal memory, and packs the local variables into that space as best it can. Again, the indirect modes are the best way to access these variables. For example, buck can be accessed using W(fp-2). (buck is at physical addresses 106 and 107, and the frame pointer holds physical address 108, so the byte offset from one to the other is −2.) The W(fp-2) directive causes a word-size object to be fetched from address 106. The low byte of buck can be accessed directly with B(fp-2) and the high byte with B(fp-1). Similarly, john_silver can be accessed with L(fp-8). (Remember that the object's address is the physical address of the least-significant byte, so the offset is −8 here.) A pointer-to-word variable can be fetched with WP(fp-N). The object to which it points can be fetched with *WP(fp-N).

Stack frame advantages: size,

recursion.

This use of the stack has two real advantages. First, the same relatively small area of memory (the stack) can be recycled from subroutine to subroutine, so less of the total memory area need be allocated for variables. Second, this organization makes recursive subroutines possible because each recursive instance of a subroutine has its own stack frame with its own set of local variables, and these variables are accessed relative to the current frame pointer. A recursive subroutine does not know that it's calling itself; it does the same thing for a recursive call that it would do for a nonrecursive call: push the arguments and transfer control to the top of the required subroutine. The called routine doesn't know that it has been called recursively, it just sets up the stack frame in the normal way. It doesn't matter if more than one stack frame for a given subroutine exists at once—only the top one is active.

Also note that the address of the leftmost argument is always (fp+8), regardless of the number of arguments or their type. This is one of the things that makes it possible to have a variable number of arguments in a C subroutine—you can always find the leftmost one.

The stack frame's organization has disadvantages, too. The problem is that the code that pushes the arguments is generated by the compiler when it processes the subroutine call, but the offsets are figured when the compiler processes the subroutine declaration. Since the call and declaration can be in different files, there's no way that the compiler can check for consistency unless you use a function prototype in a common header file. If you don't use the prototype, a particularly nasty bug, called a *phase error*, can appear at run time. Figure 6.6 shows the stack frames created, both by the earlier call(of,the,wild) and an incorrect call(), with no arguments. When the call() subroutine modifies wild, it just modifies the memory location at fp+4, and on the incorrect stack, ends up modifying the return address of the calling function. This means that call() could work correctly, as could the calling function, but the program would blow up when the calling function returned.

Stack frame disadvantages: phase errors.

Figure 6.6. A Phase Error

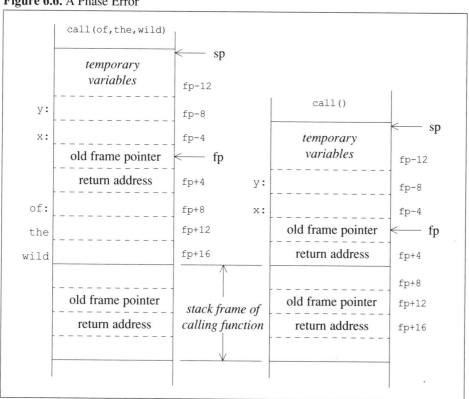

The sequence of instructions that set up a stack frame are so common that C-code provides two instructions for this purpose. The link(*N*) instruction does the following:

link and unlink instructions.

```
push( fp );
fp   = sp;
sp   -= N × stack_width;    /* Decrement by one stack element. */
```

and an unlink() directive does the following:

```
sp = fp;
fp = pop( ptr );
```

The earlier call(of, the, wild) is modified to use link() and unlink() in Listing 6.15. Listing 6.16 shows the link and unlink() implementations in *virtual.h*.

Listing 6.15. `call(of,the,wild)`: Compiler Output with `link()` and `unlink()`

```
 1    SEG( bss )
 2    int      _of;
 3    int      _the;
 4    int      _wild;
 5
 6    SEG (text )
 7    PROC(_call)
 8            link( 2 );          /* Create stack frame, 2 stack elements for locals. */
 9            ...
10            unlink();
11            ret();
12    ENDP(_call)
13
14    PROC(_spitz)
15            link( 0 );          /* No local variables so argument is zero.           */
16            push( _wild );  /* call( of, the, wild );                                */
17            push( _the  );
18            push( _of   );
19            call( _call );
20            unlink();
21            ret();
22    ENDP(_spitz)
```

Listing 6.16. *virtual.h*— Subroutine Linkage Directives

```
61    #define link(n)   ((--__sp)->pp = (char *)__fp) , (__fp = __sp) , (__sp -= (n))
62
63    #define unlink()  (__sp = (reg *)__fp) , (__fp = (reg *)((__sp++)->pp))
```

Dynamic, static links.

The stack frames can also be viewed as a linked list of data structures, each representing an active subroutine. It's possible (in an object-oriented programming environment, for example) for these structures to be allocated from discontinuous memory rather than from a stack. The frame pointer is sometimes called the *dynamic link* because it links together activation records.[9]

6.2.10 Subroutine Return Values

A function's return values should be placed into a register, according to Table 6.7.

---

9. Some languages require a second pointer, called the *static link*, discussed in Appendix B.

Table 6.7. Return Values: Register Usage

Type	Returned in:
char	rF.w.low (A **char** is always promoted to **int**.)
int	rF.w.low
long	rF.l
pointer	rF.pp

6.2.11 Operators

A very limited set of operators are supported in C-code. The following arithmetic operators (only) are available:

Arithmetic operators.

```
=   +=   -=   *=   /=   %=   ^=   &=   |=   <<=   >>=   =-   =~   lrs(x,n)
```

The ones that look like C operators work just like the equivalent C operators. $>>=$ is an arithmetic right shift (sign extension is assumed). Three special operators are supported. The $=-$ operator performs a two's complement operation, as in $x =- c$. The $=~$ operator does a one's complement, as in $x =~ c$. Both of these instructions are perfectly legitimate C. I'm assuming that the lexical analyzer breaks the foregoing into:

```
x = -c ;
x = ~c ;
```

Lint might print an "obsolete syntax" error message, though. You need binary operators here, because C-code is attempting to mimic real assembly language, and though most machines support a unary "negate" operator such as the 8086 NEG AX, which does a two's-complement negation of the AX register, you can't implement this operator without an equal sign in C. It seemed better to use a syntax consistent with the other operators than to bury the operation in an macro.

One additional operation is supported by means of a macro. A lrs(x,n) directive does a logical right shift rather than an arithmetic shift ($>>=$). It shifts x, n bits to the right, with zero fill in the high bits rather than sign extension. This directive is defined in *virtual.h* in Listing 6.17.

Listing 6.17. *virtual.h*— The Logical-Right-Shift Directive

```
64   #define lrs(x,n)    ((x) = ((unsigned long)(x) >> (n)))
```

All C-code expressions must contain exactly two operands and one operator. They must be semicolon terminated. Only one expression is permitted on a line, and the entire expression must be on a single line.

6.2.12 Type Conversions

No automatic type conversions are supported in C-code. Both operands in an expression must be of the same type, but if one of the operands is an explicit (immediate-mode) number, it is automatically converted to the type of the other operand.[10]

---

10. Note that, because of this restriction, most real assembly languages attach the type to the operator rather than the operand. You would move a 32-bit long word in 68000 assembler with a MOV.L d1,d0 instruction. In C-code you'd use r1.l = r0.l to do the same thing.

Sign extension.

Cast operators may not be used to do type conversion, but sign extension can be performed using one of the following directives:

`ext_low(reg)`	Duplicate high bit of `reg.b.b0` in all bits of `reg.b.b1`
`ext_high(reg)`	Duplicate high bit of `reg.b.b2` in all bits of `reg.b.b3`
`ext_word(reg)`	Duplicate high bit of `reg.w.low` in all bits of `reg.w.high`

An `ext_low(reg)` directive fills `reg.b.b1` with ones if the sign bit in `reg.b.b0` is set, otherwise it's filled with zeros. These directives only work in a register, so given input like this:

```
int   archy;
long mehitabel;
mehitabel = archy + 1;
```

the compiler should output something like the following:

```
public word  _archy;
public lword _mehitabel;

r0.w.low = _archy ;    /* Get archy.          */
r0.w.low += 1 ;        /* Add 1 to it.        */
ext_word( r0 );        /* Convert to long.    */
_mehitabel = r0.l ;    /* Do the assignment. */
```

The `ext_word()` directive effectively converts the `word` into an `lword`. If `archy` were unsigned, a `r0.w.high=0` would be used instead of `ext_word(r0)`. The definitions of the sign-extension directives are in Listing 6.18.

Listing 6.18. *virtual.h*— Sign-Extension Directives

```
65   #define ext_low(reg)    (reg.w.low  = (word )reg.b.b0   )
66   #define ext_high(reg)   (reg.w.high = (word )reg.b.b2   )
67   #define ext_word(reg)   (reg.l      = (lword)reg.w.low  )
```

6.2.13 Labels and Control Flow

Labels and the `goto`.

Labels in C-code are like normal C labels. They are defined as a name followed by a colon:

```
label:
```

The only control-flow statement is the `goto` branch, which is used in the normal way:

```
goto label;
```

The target of the **goto** branch must be in the same subroutine as the **goto** itself.

Test directives.

Conditional flow of control is performed using one of the test directives summarized in Table 6.8. These all compare two operands, and the instruction on the line following the test is executed only if the test evaluates true, otherwise the instruction on the next line is ignored. The following code executes the `goto` branch if `all` is equal to `things` (all things being equal).

```
    EQ( all, things )
        goto jail;
go:
    /* collect $200 */
jail:
```

All the addressing modes described earlier can be used in a test. The normal comparisons assume signed numbers, but the `U_LT()`, `U_LE()`, `U_GT()`, and `U_GE()` directives compare the two numbers as unsigned quantities. The instruction following the test may not be another test. The test directives are implemented with the macros in Listing 6.19.

Table 6.8. C-code Test Directives

Directive:	Execute following line if:	
EQ(a, b)	$a = b$	
NE(a, b)	$a \neq b$	
LT(a, b)	$a < b$	
LE(a, b)	$a \leq b$	
GT(a, b)	$a > b$	
GE(a, b)	$a \geq b$	
U_LT(a, b)	$a < b$	(unsigned comparison)
U_LE(a, b)	$a \leq b$	(unsigned comparison)
U_GT(a, b)	$a > b$	(unsigned comparison)
U_GE(a, b)	$a \geq b$	(unsigned comparison)
BIT(b, s)	bit b of s is set to 1	(bit 0 is the low bit).

Listing 6.19. *virtual.h*— Comparison Directives

```
68   #define EQ(a,b)        if( (long)(a) ==  (long)(b) )
69   #define NE(a,b)        if( (long)(a) !=  (long)(b) )
70   #define LT(a,b)        if( (long)(a) <   (long)(b) )
71   #define LE(a,b)        if( (long)(a) <=  (long)(b) )
72   #define GT(a,b)        if( (long)(a) >   (long)(b) )
73   #define GE(a,b)        if( (long)(a) >=  (long)(b) )
74
75   #define U_LT(a,b)      if( (unsigned long)(a) <   (unsigned long)(b) )
76   #define U_GT(a,b)      if( (unsigned long)(a) >   (unsigned long)(b) )
77   #define U_LE(a,b)      if( (unsigned long)(a) <=  (unsigned long)(b) )
78   #define U_GE(a,b)      if( (unsigned long)(a) >=  (unsigned long)(b) )
79
80   #define BIT(b,s)       if( (b) & (1 << (b)) )
```

6.2.14 Macros and Constant Expressions

Various C-preprocessor macros, summarized in Table 6.9, may be used in a C-code file. C-style, parameterized macros are supported, but the ANSI *defined( )* pseudo op, the concatenation operator (**##**), and the "stringizing" operator (**#**name) are not supported. Arithmetic expressions that involve nothing but constants and the following operators can appear in an **#if** directive and anywhere that a constant would appear in an operand:

```
    +  -  *  /  %  &  &&  |  ||  ==  !=  <  >  <=  >=  ~  !
```

The − is both unary and binary minus. The ∗ is multiplication. Multiple-operator expressions such as the following are legal:

```
#define L1 (-24)
WP(fp-4) = WP(fp-L1-6);    /* The L1-6 is a constant expression. */
```

Table 6.9. C-code Preprocessor Directives

#line *line-number "file"*
#define NAME *text*
#define NAME (args) *text*
#undef NAME
#ifdef NAME
#if *constant expression*
#endif
#else
#include *<file>*
#include *"file"*

Note that the constant expression must completely precede or follow a variable or register reference in an operand. For example, the following is not permitted because the register reference (fp) is imbedded in the middle of the expression:

```
WP(fp-4) = WP(6 + fp + 10);
```

6.2.15 File Organization

All variable and macro declarations must precede their use. Forward references are permitted with **goto** branches, however.

C-code files should, ideally, take the following form:

```
#include <tools/virtual.h>
SEG( data )
    initialized data declarations
SEG( bss )
    uninitialized data declarations
SEG( text )
    subroutines
```

Can't issue SEG() between PROC() and ENDP().

You can switch back and forth between the *data* and *bss* segments as much as you like, but you can't change segments in the middle of a subroutine definition bounded by a PROC() and ENDP() directive. **extern** declarations should be placed in the *bss* segment. Macro definitions can go anywhere in the file.

6.2.16 Miscellany

Translate _main() to main().

One other handy macro is in *virtual.h*. Since the point of C-code is to create a language that can be assembled with your C compiler rather than a real assembler, it's desirable to be able for a main() function in the source to really be main(). Unfortunately, the compiler puts a leading underscore in front of main when it outputs the PROC directive. The _main() macro on line 81 of Listing 6.20 takes care of this problem.

Print virtual-machine state, pm().

The last part of *virtual.h* (on lines 84 to 118 of Listing 6.20) is an actual function, created only if ALLOC is defined. pm() prints the top few stack elements and the contents of the virtual-machine registers to standard output as follows:

Listing 6.20. *virtual.h*— Run-time Trace Support

```
81   #define  _main  main
82
83   #ifdef ALLOC
84   pm()
85   {
86       reg *p;
87       int i;
88
89       /* Print the virtual machine (registers and top 16 stack elements). */
90
91       printf("r0= %08lx   r1= %08lx   r2= %08lx   r3= %08lx\n",
92                r0.l,       r1.l,       r2.l,       r3.l            );
93       printf("r4= %08lx   r5= %08lx   r6= %08lx   r7= %08lx\n",
94                r4.l,       r5.l,       r6.l,       r7.l            );
95       printf("r8= %08lx   r9= %08lx   rA= %08lx   rB= %08lx\n",
96                r8.l,       r9.l,       rA.l,       rB.l            );
97       printf("rC= %08lx   rD= %08lx   rE= %08lx   rF= %08lx\n",
98                rC.l,       rD.l,       rE.l,       rF.l            );
99
100      if( __sp >= &stack[SDEPTH] )
101          printf("Stack is empty\n");
102      else
103          printf("\nitem byte real addr   b3 b2 b1 b0      hi   lo            l\n");
104
105      for( p = __sp, i=16; p < &stack[SDEPTH]  &&  --i>=0; ++p )
106      {
107          printf("%04d %04d %9p  [%02x|%02x|%02x|%02x] = [%04x|%04x] = [%08lx]",
108              p-__sp,                (p-__sp)*4,       (void far *)p,
109              p->b.b3 & 0xff,     p->b.b2 & 0xff,   p->b.b1 & 0xff, p->b.b0 & 0xff,
110              p->w.high & 0xffff, p->w.low & 0xffff,
111              p->l
112          );
113
114          if( p == __sp ) printf("<-SP");
115          if( p == __fp ) printf("<-FP");
116          printf("\n");
117      }
118  }
119  #endif
```

```
r0= 00000000   r1= 00000000   r2= 00000000   r3= 00000000
r4= 00000000   r5= 00000000   r6= 00000000   r7= 00000000
r8= 00000000   r9= 00000000   rA= 00000000   rB= 00000000
rC= 00000000   rD= 00000000   rE= 00000000   rF= 00000000

item byte real addr   b3 b2 b1 b0      hi   lo            l
0000 0000 2C8F:1878  [00|00|00|00] = [0000|0000] = [00000000]<-SP
0001 0004 2C8F:187C  [00|00|00|00] = [0000|0000] = [00000000]
0002 0008 2C8F:1880  [00|00|18|8c] = [0000|188c] = [0000188c]<-FP
0003 0012 2C8F:1884  [00|00|04|f2] = [0000|04f2] = [000004f2]
0004 0016 2C8F:1888  [ab|cd|ef|12] = [abcd|ef12] = [abcdef12]
0005 0020 2C8F:188C  [00|00|18|90] = [0000|1890] = [00001890]
```

The stack is printed three times, broken up as bytes, words, and lwords. The leftmost, *item*, column is the offset in stack elements from the top of stack to the current element; the *byte* column is the byte offset to the least-significant byte of the stack item; and the *real addr* is the physical address of the stack element (it's in 8086 segment:offset form).

The position of the sp and fp register is indicated at the far right. pm() is used in the compiler to print a run-time trace as the output code executes. The compiler described below can be put in a mode where most instructions are output like this:

```
r0.l = r1.l;                    printf("r0.l = r1.l;\n"); pm();
```

so you can what the virtual machine is doing as the code executes.

6.2.17 Caveats

C-code is similar enough to assembly language that it's easy to forget it's really C, and make mistakes accordingly. The biggest problem is labels. Most assembly languages treat all labels the same, regardless of what they are used for: a label always evaluates to an address, and any label can be used in any instruction. C-code is different, however: Array names evaluate to addresses, most other labels evaluate to the contents of a variable, but labels that are followed by colons can only be used as targets of **goto** branches. These restrictions make C-code a little more difficult to write than real assembler. They also make some common assembly-language data structures impossible to implement. For example, most assemblers let you code a **switch** statement as follows:

C-code labels are different from assembly language.

Jump tables can't be implemented in C-code.

```
SEG( data )
switch_table: dw L1                        /* Array of four labels. */
              dw L2
              dw L3
              dw L4
SEG( text )

         t0 = /* evaluated argument to switch */
         goto switch_table[ t0 ]
L1:      code...
L2:      code...
L3:      code...
L4:      code...
```

This data structure, called a *jump table*, is not legal C-code—you can't have an array of labels and you can't use a variable as an argument to a **goto**.

6.3 The Symbol Table

Subroutine prefix, body, and suffix.

Like Gaul, most computer languages can be divided into three parts: declarations, expressions, and statements. Looking back at Table 6.2 on page 451, the output code is divided into three logical sections. Each section is generated from a separate part of the input file, and the code generation for each of these parts is controlled by distinct parts of the grammar. Every subroutine has a *prefix* portion that's generated when the declarations and argument list are processed. The *body* of the subroutine, which contains statements and expressions, comes next. Finally, code to clean up and return from a subroutine is generated at the end of the definition. This last section is called the *suffix*. I'll start by looking at the first of these sections, the subroutine-prefix and declaration processing.

6.3.1 Symbol-Table Requirements

The symbol table.

We need to examine the data structures that are used to process a declaration before looking at the actual code-generation actions. A compiler's declaration system centers around a set of data structures collectively called the *symbol table*. Strictly speaking, the symbol table is a database that contains information about subroutines, variables, and so forth. The database is indexed by a *key* field—here a subroutine or variable's name— Key, record. and each record (each entry in the database) contains information about that item such as the variable's type or subroutine's return value. A record is added to the database by the code that processes declarations, and it is deleted from the database when the scoping rules of the language determine that the object can no longer be referenced. C local variables, for example, are deleted when the compiler finishes the block in which they are declared.

Symbol tables are used for other purposes as well. Type definitions and constant declarations may be found in them, for example. The symbol table can also be used to communicate with the lexical analyzer. In the current compiler, a **typedef** creates a symbol-table entry for the new type, as if the type name were a variable name. A bit is set in the record to indicate that this is a **typedef**, however. The lexical analyzer then uses the symbol table to distinguish identifiers from type names. This approach has its drawbacks (discussed below), but can be quite useful.

Even though a symbol table is a database, it has special needs that must be met in specific ways. A symbol-table manager must have the following characteristics: Desirable symbol-table characteristics.

- Speed. Because the symbol table must be accessed every time an identifier or type is referenced, look-up time must be as fast as possible. Consequently, disk-based data-management systems are not appropriate here. The entire table should be in memory. On the down side, one of the main limitations on input-file size is often the maximum memory available for the symbol table.
- Ease of maintenance. The symbol table is probably the most complex data structure in the compiler. Its support functions must be organized so that someone other than the compiler writer can maintain them.
- Flexibility. A language like C does not limit the complexity of a variable declaration, so the symbol table must be able to represent variables of arbitrary type. This representation should be optimized for code-generation purposes. Similarly, the symbol table should be able to grow as symbols are added to it.
- Duplicate entries must be supported. Most programming languages allow a variable at an inner nesting level to have the same name as a variable at an outer nesting level. These are different variables, in spite of having the same name, and the scoping rules of the language determine which of these variables are active at a given moment. The active variable is said to *shadow* the inactive one. A distinct symbol Shadowing. table entry is required for each variable, and the database manager must be able to handle this situation.
- You must be able to quickly delete arbitrary elements and groups of elements from the table. For example, you should be able to delete all the local variables associated with a particular block level in an efficient manner, without having to look up each element separately.

The symbol table used here is organized in two layers. I'll call the innermost of Layers these the *database* layer. This layer takes care of physical table maintenance: inserting Database layer. new entries in the table, finding them, deleting them, and so forth. I'll call the outer layer the *maintenance* layer—it manages the table at a higher level, creating systems of Maintenance layer. data structures to represent specific symbols and inserting these structures into the table using the low-level insert function. Other subroutines at the maintenance level delete entire classes of symbols (variables declared at the same block level, for example), traverse all variables of a single class, and so forth.

6.3.2 Symbol-Table Data-Base Data Structures

Stack-based symbol
tables.

Several data structures can be used for the database layer of the symbol table, each appropriate in specific situations. The simplest possible structure is a linear array organized as a stack. New symbols are added to the end of the array with a push operation and the array is searched from top to bottom of stack. (The most recently added item is examined first.) This method, though crude, is quite workable provided that the table is small enough. The scope rules are handled by the back-to-front searching. Since variables declared at an inner nesting level are added to the table after those declared at a higher level, they are always found first. The database manager is trivial to implement.

One real advantage to a stack-based symbol table is that it's very easy to delete a block of declarations. Variable declarations are done in waves according to the current scoping level. For example, given input like this:

```
int    laurel, hardy;
{
    int        larry, curly, moe;
    {
        int house_of_representatives[ 435 ];
    }
}
```

`laurel` and `hardy` are inserted first as a block, then `larry`, `curly`, and `moe` are inserted, and then the `house_of_representatives` is inserted. The symbol-table stack looks like this when the innermost block is processed:

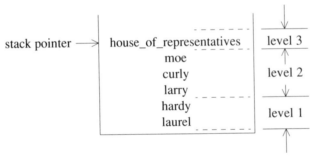

All variables associated with a block can be deleted at one time by adding a constant to the stack pointer.

Stack disadvantages.

The stack approach does have disadvantages other than the obvious one of the inefficient linear search required to find entries close to the beginning of the table. (This is not an insignificant problem—the compiler spends more time searching for symbol-table references than any other symbol-table operation. The time required for a linear search will be prohibitive if the table is large enough.) The maximum size of the stack-based table must be known at compile time, so the symbol table can't scale its size dynamically to fit the needs of the current input file. Consequently, the number of variables that can be handled by the system is limited. You have to allocate a worst-case table size to make sure that there is enough room.

Tree-based symbol
tables.

The search-time and limited-size problems can be solved, to some extent, by using a binary tree as the basic data structure. Average search times in a balanced binary tree are logarithmic, and the tree size can grow dynamically as necessary.

Tree deletions.

Deletion of an arbitrary node from a tree is difficult, but fortunately this is not an issue with most symbol-tables applications, because nodes for a given level are inserted into the tree as a block, and newer levels are deleted before the older ones. The most-recently inserted nodes tend to form leaves in the tree. If a variable at the most recent level is an interior node, then all its children will have been declared either at the same nesting level or in an inner block. The most recently added block of variables is always at the end of a branch, and all variables in that block can be removed by breaking the links to them without having to rearrange the tree. For example, a tree for the earlier code fragment is pictured in Figure 6.7. The dotted lines show the scoping levels. The `house_of_representatives` is deleted first by breaking a single link; `larry`, `curly`, and `moe` are deleted next, again by breaking single links; `laurel` and `hardy` are deleted by breaking the single link that points at `laurel`.

Figure 6.7. Symbol-Table Trees: Deletion

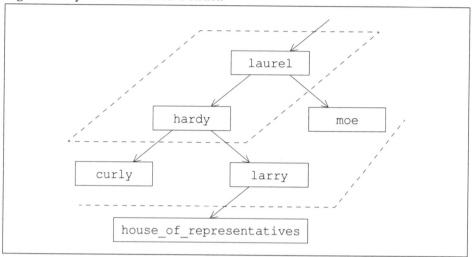

Binary trees do have disadvantages. First, it is a common practice for programmers to declare variables in alphabetical order. Since variables are added to the tree in the same order as the declarations, a simple binary tree degrades to a linked list in this situation, and the search times are linear rather than logarithmic. This problem can be solved at the cost of greater insert and delete times by using a height-balanced tree system such as an AVL tree,[11] but the shuffling around of nodes that's implicit in the rebalancing can destroy the ordering that made deletions easy to do. The other disadvantage of a tree-based symbol table is that *collisions*, situations where the same name is used for variables at different scope levels, are difficult to resolve. This problem, too, can be solved at the expense of lookup time. For example, you could have two key fields in the data structure used to represent a tree node, one for the name and one for the nesting level:

Tree disadvantages.

Collisions.

```
typedef struct tree_node
{
    char            name[ 32 ]; /* Variable name.        */
    int             level;      /* Nesting level.        */
    struct tree_node *right;    /* Right-child pointer.  */
    struct tree_node *left;     /* Left-child pointer.   */
    INFO_TYPE       info;       /* Other Information.    */
}
tree_node;
```

and then use both fields when comparing two nodes:

---

11. See: [Kruse] pp. 357–371 and [Tenenbaum] pp. 461–472 for a general discussion of AVL trees. [Holub1] contains a C implementation of an AVL-tree database manager.

```
compare( node1, node2 )
struct tree_node *node1, *node2;
{
    if( node1->level != node2->level )
        return(  node1->level - node2->level );
    else
        return( strcmp(node1->name, node2->name) );
}
```

You could also solve the collision problem by adding an additional field to the tree node—a pointer to the head of a linked list of conflicting nodes. Newly added entries would be put at the head of the list, and so would be found first when the list was searched. The system is pictured in Figure 6.8; it uses the following data structure:

```
typedef struct tree_node
{
    char              name[32];
    struct tree_node *right;     /* Right-child pointer.          */
    struct tree_node *left;      /* Left-child pointer.           */
    struct tree_node *conflicts; /* Conflicting-name-list head.   */
    INFO_TYPE         info;      /* Other information.            */
}
tree_node;
```

Figure 6.8. Using a Linked List to Resolve Collisions in a Tree-Based Table

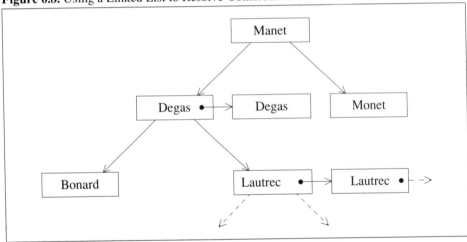

There is one final problem with a tree-based symbol table. The use of global variables is discouraged by most proponents of structured-programming because it's difficult to determine how global variables change value. As a consequence, a well-structured program accesses local variables more often than global ones. The local variables are added to the symbol table last, however, and these nodes tend to be farther away from the root in a tree-based table, so it takes longer to find them.

Hashed symbol tables.   It turns out that the the best data structure for most symbol-table applications is a *hash table*. An ideal hash table is an array that is indexed directly by the key field of the object in the table. For example, if the key field is a string made up of letters, digits, and underscores, the string could be treated as a base 63 number (26 lower-case letters + 26 upper-case letters + 10 digits + an underscore = 63 possible characters). Unfortunately, an array that could be indexed directly by a 16-character name would require $63^{16}-1$ or roughly 60,000,000,000,000,000,000,000,000,000 elements, most of which would be wasted because an average symbol table has only a few hundred objects in it.

The solution to this problem is to compress the array. A *hash table* is an array, indexed by key, that is compressed so that several elements of the uncompressed array can be found at a single location in the compressed array. To do this, you convert the key field that's used as the index in the uncompressed array into a pseudo-random number which is used as an index into the compressed array. This randomization process is called *hashing* and the number so generated is the key's *hash value*. The same key should always *hash* to the same pseudo-random number, but very similar keys should have very different hash values.

Collisions (situations where two keys hash to the same value) are resolved by making each array element the head of a linked list of table elements.[12] This method is appropriate in a symbol-table application because, if you always put the new node at the head of a chain rather than at the end, local variables automatically preempt global variables with the same name—they'll be found first when the list is searched. They are also found more quickly than they would be if stored in a binary tree.

A simple hash table of size three is pictured in Figure 6.9. The table has four members, with the keys `"a"`, `"b"`, `"c"`, and `"d"`. The hash values are computed by treating the name strings as numbers. An ASCII `'a'` has the decimal value 97, `'b'` is 98, and so on. These numbers are truncated down to an array index using a modulus division by the table size (3 in this case):

name	numeric value	value MOD table size
"a"	97	1
"b"	98	2
"c"	99	0
"d"	100	1

Figure 6.9. A Simple Hash Table

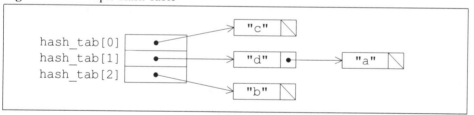

A simple hash function could just add together the characters in the name as if they were numbers, and then truncate the resulting sum to a valid array index with a modulus operation. An better function is *hashpjw*, shown in Listing 6.21.[13] *Hashpjw* uses an exclusive-or and shift strategy to randomize the hash value.

There has probably been more waste paper devoted to the subject of hash algorithms than any other topic in Computer Science. In general, the complex algorithms so described give very good theoretical results, but are so slow as to be impractical in a real application. An ideal hash function generates a minimum number of collisions, and the

12. The collision-resolution method used here is called "open" hashing. There are other ways of resolving collisions that won't be discussed because they are not much use in most practical applications. See [Tenenbaum] pp. 521–574 and [Kruse] pp. 112–135.

13. Hashpjw was developed by P.J. Weinberger and is described in [Aho], p. 436. The version in Listing 6.21 is optimized somewhat from the one in [Aho] and is tailored to a 16-bit **int**. There's a more general purpose version of the same function in Appendix A.

Listing 6.21. *hashpjw.c*— A 16-bit *hashpjw* Implementation

```
1    unsigned hash_pjw( name )
2    unsigned char    *name;
3    {
4        unsigned hash_val = 0;
5        unsigned i;
6
7        for(; *name ; ++name )
8        {
9            hash_val = (hash_val << 2) + *name ;
10           if( i = hash_val & 0x3fff )
11               hash_val = (hash_val ^ (i >> 12)) & ~0x3fff ;
12       }
13
14       return hash_val;
15   }
```

average search time (which is proportional to the mean chain length) should be roughly the same as an equivalent data structure such as a binary tree—it should be logarithmic. The maximum path length in a perfectly balanced tree with N elements is $\log_2 N$. A tree with 255 elements has a maximum chain length of 8 and an average chain length of roughly 7 $[(128{\times}8 + 64{\times}7 + 32{\times}6 +\ldots+ 2{\times}1)/255]$. You're okay as long as you can get a comparable average chain length in a hash table.

It's difficult to predict chain lengths from a given algorithm because the words found in the input control these lengths. An empirical analysis is quite workable, however, given a large enough data set. Table 6.10 shows the behavior of the hash_add() and hash_pjw() functions from Appendix A. The former just adds together the characters in the name; the latter is in Listing 6.21. 917 unique variable names gleaned from real C programs were used for the test input, and the table is 127 elements long.

The elapsed time is the amount of time used to run the test program. Since the only change was the choice of hash function, this number gives us a good indication of efficiency. You'll note that hash_pjw() is about 9% slower than hash_add(). The mean chain length for both algorithms is identical, and both algorithms use shorter average chain lengths than a binary tree of an equivalent size. Finally, the distribution of chain lengths is actually a little better with hash_add() than with hash_pjw()—there are more shorter chains generated by hash_add().

Addition as a hash function: advantages, disadvantages.

Weighing the foregoing, it seems as if simple addition is the preferable of the two algorithms because it yields somewhat shorter chains, executes marginally faster, and is smaller. Addition has two significant disadvantages, the main one being that characters are small numbers, so the hash values tend to pile up at one end of a large table. One of the reasons that addition performed well in the current example is the relatively small table size. hash_pjw() solves the bunching problem with the left shift on line nine of Listing 6.21, making it more appropriate for larger tables. Also, addition can't distinguish between identifiers that are permutations of the same name and *hashpjw* can, so the latter is a better choice if this situation comes up. Aho, using names gleaned from Pascal programs rather than C programs and a larger table size, got better results from *hashpjw* than I did.

Hash tables are almost ideal data structures for use in a symbol table. They are as efficient (if not more so) than binary trees, and are more appropriate for those applications in which several elements of the table might have the same key, as is the case when local and global variables share the same name.

Table 6.10. Performance of Two Hash Functions

Addition			Hashpjw		
Elapsed time		9.06 seconds	Elapsed time		9.61 seconds
Mean chain length:		7.22047	Mean chain length:		7.22047
Standard deviation:		2.37062	Standard deviation:		2.54901
Maximum chain length:		14	Maximum chain length:		13
Minimum chain length:		2	Minimum chain length:		1
0	chains of length	1	1	chain of length	1
1	chains of length	2	3	chains of length	2
8	chains of length	3	9	chains of length	3
7	chains of length	4	8	chains of length	4
18	chains of length	5	12	chains of length	5
13	chains of length	6	15	chains of length	6
22	chains of length	7	21	chains of length	7
22	chains of length	8	15	chains of length	8
16	chains of length	9	15	chains of length	9
8	chains of length	10	15	chains of length	10
7	chains of length	11	10	chains of length	11
2	chains of length	12	0	chains of length	12
2	chains of length	13	3	chains of length	13
1	chain of length	14	0	chains of length	14

6.3.3 Implementing the Symbol Table

I will use the hash functions described in Appendix A for the database layer of our symbol table. To summarize the appendix, the hash-table system described in Appendix A uses two data structures: the hash table itself is an array of pointers to "buckets", each bucket being a single data-base record. The buckets are organized as a linked list. When two keys hash to the same value, the conflicting node is inserted at the beginning of the list. This list of buckets is doubly linked—each bucket contains a pointer to both its predecessor and successor in the list. Arbitrary nodes can then be deleted from the middle of a chain without having to traverse the entire chain. You should review these functions now.

The basic hash functions are fine for simple symbol-table applications. They were used to good effect in **occs** and **LLama**, for example. Most programming languages require a little more complexity, however. First of all, many internal operations require the compiler to treat all variables declared at a common nesting level as a single block. For example, local variables in C can be declared at the beginning of any curly-brace delimited compound statement. A function body is not a special case, it's treated identically to a compound statement attached to a **while** statement, for example. The scope of any local variable is defined by the limits of the compound statement. For all practical purposes, a variable ceases to exist when the close curly-brace that ends that block in which it is declared is processed. The variable should be removed from the symbol table at that time. (Don't confuse compile and run time here. A **static** local variable continues to exist at run time, but it can be deleted from the symbol table because it can't be accessed at compile time once it is out of scope.)

Block deletions.

The compiler also has to be able to traverse the list of local variables in the order that they were declared. For example, when the compiler is setting up the stack frame, it has to traverse the list of arguments in the proper order to determine the correct offsets from the frame pointer. Both of those situations can be handled by providing a set of *cross links* that connect all variables at a particular nesting level. For example, there are three nesting levels in the following fragment:

```
int Godot;
waiting( vladimir, estragon )
{
    int pozzo ;
    while( condition )
    {
      int pozzo, lucky;
    }
}
```

Godot and waiting are at the outer level, the subroutine arguments and the first pozzo comprise the second block, and the third block has the second pozzo in it. Note that the arguments are grouped with the outer local variables and that the inner pozzo shadows the outer one while the inner block is active—the two pozzos are different variables, occupying different parts of the stack frame. Figure 6.10 shows how the symbol table looks when the innermost block is being processed. I'm assuming that vladimir hashes to the same value as pozzo. Note that the subroutine name [waiting()] is considered part of the outer block, but the arguments are part of the inner block. The hash table itself is at the left—the solid arrows are links used to resolve collisions within the table. Here, the array across the top holds the heads of the cross-link chains. This array could be eliminated by passing the head-of-chain pointers as attributes on the value stack, however. You can visit all symbol-table entries for variables at a given scoping level by traversing the cross links (the dashed lines). If the head-of-chain array was a stack, you could delete the nodes for a particular level by popping the head-of-list pointer and traversing the list, deleting nodes. The current C-compiler's symbol table is organized with cross links, as just described. A hash-table element is pictured in Figure 6.10.

The top two nodes (next and prev) are maintained by the hash-table functions described in depth in Appendix A. They point at the previous and next node in the collision chain. The double indirection lets you delete an arbitrary element from the table without having to traverse the collision chain to find the predecessor. The bottom fields are managed by the maintenance-layer, symbol-table functions and are declared as the symbol structure in Listing 6.22 along with the symbol table itself.

The name field in the symbol structure is the name as it appears in the input. The rname field is the symbol's name as it appears in the output. In the case of a global variable, rname holds the input name with a leading underscore appended. Local static variables are given arbitrary names by the compiler because local statics in two subroutines could have the same name. The names would conflict if both were used in the output, so an arbitrary name is used. Compiler-supplied names don't have leading underscores so can't conflict with user-supplied names. The rname field for automatic variables and subroutine arguments is a string, which when used in an operand, evaluates to the contents of the variable in question. For example, if an **int** variable is at offset −8 from the frame pointer, the rname will be "fp-8".

The level field holds the declaration level for the symbol (0 for global symbols, 1 if they're at the outermost block in a function, and so forth). level is used primarily for error checking. It helps detect a duplicate declaration.

The duplicate bit marks the extra symbols created by duplicate declarations like the following:

Figure 6.10. A Cross-linked Symbol Table

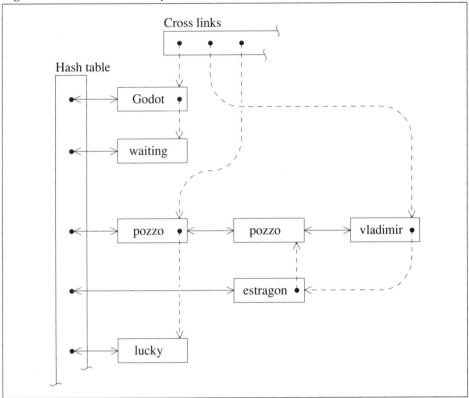

Figure 6.11. A Symbol-Table Element

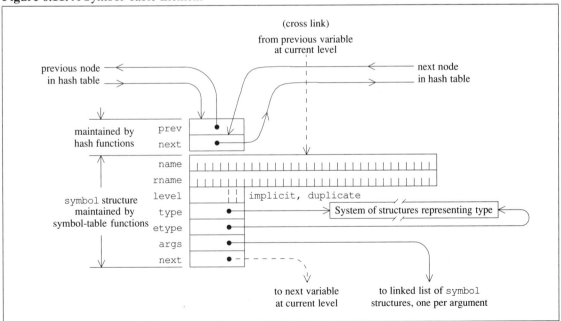

Listing 6.22. *symtab.h*— The Symbol Table

```
 1   /* SYMTAB.H:   Symbol-table definitions. Note that <tools/debug.h> and
 2    *             <tools/hash.h> must be #included (in that order) before the
 3    *             #include for the current file.
 4    */
 5
 6   #ifdef ALLOC                              /* Allocate variables if ALLOC defined. */
 7   #   define ALLOC_CLS /* empty */
 8   #else
 9   #   define ALLOC_CLS     extern
10   #endif
11
12   #define NAME_MAX   32                     /* Maximum identifier length.     */
13   #define LABEL_MAX 32                      /* Maximum output-label length.   */
14
15   typedef struct symbol                     /* Symbol-table entry.            */
16   {
17       unsigned char    name   [NAME_MAX+1];  /* Input variable name.           */
18       unsigned char    rname [NAME_MAX+1];   /* Actual variable name.          */
19
20       unsigned         level    : 13 ;      /* Declaration lev., field offset.*/
21       unsigned         implicit : 1  ;      /* Declaration created implicitly.*/
22       unsigned         duplicate : 1  ;     /* Duplicate declaration.         */
23
24       struct  link    *type;                /* First link in declarator chain.*/
25       struct  link    *etype;               /* Last  link in declarator chain.*/
26       struct  symbol *args;                 /* If a funct decl, the arg list. */
27                                             /* If a var, the initializer.     */
28       struct  symbol *next;                 /* Cross link to next variable at  */
29                                             /* current nesting level.         */
30   } symbol;
31
32   ALLOC_CLS   HASH_TAB  *Symbol_tab;         /* The actual table. */
```

>   **extern int** x;
>   ...
>   **int** x = 5;

It's convenient not to discard these symbols as soon as the duplication is found. The duplicate symbol is not put into the symbol table, however, and this bit lets you determine that the symbol has not been inserted into the table so you can delete it at a later time.

`symbol.implicit`

The `implicit` field is used to distinguish undeclared variables from implicit function declarations created when a subroutine is used before being defined. An implicit declaration of type **int** is created when an undeclared identifier is encountered by the compiler. If that identifier is subsequently used in a function call, its type is modified to "function returning **int**" and the `implicit` bit is cleared. If a symbol is still marked implicit when the compiler is done with the current block, then it is an undeclared variable and an appropriate error message is printed.

`symbol.type,`
`symbol.etype,`
`symbol.args.`

The `type` and `etype` fields in the `symbol` structure point to yet another data structure (discussed shortly) that describes the object's type. `args` keeps track of function arguments until they are added to the symbol table. It is the head of a linked list of `symbol` structures, one for each argument.

`symbol.next`

Finally, the `next` pointer is the cross link to the next variable at the same nesting level. Note that this field points at the `symbol` component of the combined structure, not at the header maintained by the hash functions.

6.3.4 Representing Types—Theory

The next issue is the representation of a variable's type. If a language is simple enough, types can be represented with a simple numeric coding in the `symbol` structure. For example, if a language had only two types, integer and floating point, you could define two constants like this:

Constrained types, numeric coding.

```
#define INTEGER 0
#define FLOAT   1
```

and add a field to the `symbol` structure that would be set to one or the other of these values. Pointers could be represented in a similar way, with a second variable keeping track of the levels of indirection For example, given a declaration like **int** `***p`, this second variable would hold 3. This sort of typing system is called a *constrained* system because there are only a limited number of possible types.

The situation is more complex in a language like C, which has an *unconstrained* typing system that permits virtually unlimited complexity in a variable declaration. A C variable's type must be represented by a system of data structures working in concert. You can see what's required by looking at how a C variable declaration is organized. Variable declarations have two parts: a *specifier* part which is a list of various keywords (**int**, **long**, **extern**, **struct**, and so forth) and a *declarator* part that is made up of the variable's name and an arbitrary number of stars, array-size specifiers (like `[10]`) and parentheses (used both for grouping and to indicate a function).

Unconstrained types.

Specifier.
Declarator.

The specifier is constrained—there are only a limited number of legal combinations of keywords that can be used here—so it can be represented by a single structure. The declarator is not constrained, however—any number of stars, brackets, or parentheses are permitted in any combination. Because of this organization, a type can be represented using two kinds of structures, one representing the specifier and another representing the declarator. The type definition is a linked list of these structures, and the `type` field in the `symbol` structure that we looked at earlier points at the head of the list (`etype` points at the end). All type representations have exactly one specifier structure, though there can be any number of declarators (including none), and it's convenient for the specifier to be at the end of the linked list—I'll explain why in a moment.

Let's look at some examples. A simple declaration of the form **short** `Quasimodo;` is represented like this:

Example type representations.

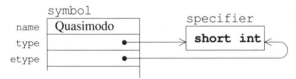

A pointer type, like **long** `*Gringoire;` adds a declarator structure, like this:

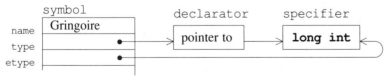

You read down the list just like you would parse the declaration in English. `Gringoire` is a pointer to a **long**. The `symbol` node holds the name, the second holds an indicator that the variable is a pointer, and the third node holds the **long**. An array of longs declared with **long** `Coppenole[10];` is represented as follows:

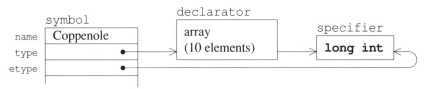

A pointer to an array of longs like **long** (*Frollo)[10]; has a *pointer* node inserted in between the symbol structure and the *array* declarator, like this:

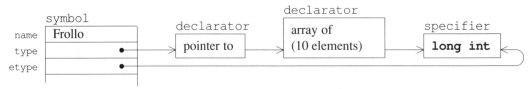

An array of pointers to longs such as **long** *Esmerelda[10] has the "pointer to" and "array of" nodes transposed, like this:

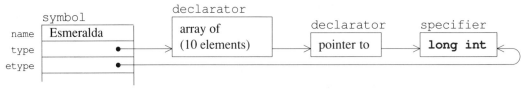

Derived types.

This system has an important characteristic that will be quite useful for generating code. The array-bracket, indirection, and structure-access operators generate temporary variables, just like the simple addition and multiplication operators discussed in earlier chapters. The types of these temporaries can be *derived* from the original type representation, often just by removing the first element in the chain. For example, in the earlier array-of-pointers-to-**long** example, an expression like Esmerelda[1] generates a temporary of type "pointer to long" that holds the referenced array element. The temporary's type is just the original chain, less the leading "array of" node. The address-of operator (&) is handled in much the same way by adding a "pointer to" node to the left of the chain.

6.3.5 Representing Types—Implementation

Implementing declarators.

The foregoing system of declarators and specifiers can be implemented with a system of several structures. A declarator is represented with the structure in Listing 6.23. There are two fields: dcl_type identifies the declarator as a pointer, array, or function, using the values defined on lines 33 to 35. If the declarator is an array, num_ele holds the number of elements. You'll need this number to increment a pointer to an array correctly, and to figure an array's size.

Implementing Specifiers.

Nouns.
Adjectives.

Specifiers are represented by the structure and macros in Listing 6.24. The situation is simplified here because the current C compiler ignores the **const** and **volatile** keywords. A C specifier consists of a basic type (call it a *noun*), and various modifiers (call them *adjectives*). C supports several nouns: **char**, **int**, **float**, **double**, **struct**, **union**, and **enum**. Only four of these are necessary in the current compiler, however: **char**, **int**, **void**, and **struct**. You would add **float** to this list if floating point were supported. A **double** could be treated as a **long float**. Enumerated types are treated as if they were **int**s. Unions are treated identically to structures—all the offsets to the fields are zero, however. An **int** is implied if a noun is missing from a declaration, as in **long** x. C also supports one implicit identifier that is declared just by using it: a label. The LABEL on line 46 takes care of this sort of identifier. The basic nouns are

Listing 6.23. *symtab.h*— A Declarator

```
33   #define POINTER        0              /* Values for declarator.type.    */
34   #define ARRAY          1
35   #define FUNCTION       2
36
37   typedef struct declarator
38   {
39       int dcl_type;                     /* POINTER, ARRAY, or FUNCTION    */
40       int num_ele;                      /* If class==ARRAY, # of elements */
41   } declarator;
```

represented by the noun field on line 64 of Listing 6.24, and the possible values for this field are defined on lines 42 to 46.

Next come the adjectives. These fall naturally into several categories that have mutually exclusive values. The most complex of these is the storage class represented by the sclass field on line 65 of Listing 6.24, which can hold one of the values defined on lines 47 to 52. These values are mutually exclusive—you can't have an **extern register**, for example. Note that the TYPEDEF class is used only to pass information around during the declaration. **typedef**s are also marked by a bit in the first element of the type chain—it's convenient to have this information duplicated while the declaration is being processed—we'll see why in a moment. Note that AUTO designates anything that can be on the run-time stack, and FIXED is anything at a fixed address in memory, whether or not it's declared **static**. The **static** keyword is used by the compiler to decide whether or not to make the variable public when it generates the code to allocate space for that variable.

The CONSTANT storage class is used for two purposes. First, when you declare an enumerated type like this:

CONSTANT **storage class.**

```
enum rabbits
{
    FLOPSY, MOPSEY, PETER, COTTONTAIL;
};
```

the compiler puts **int** entries for each of the elements of the enumerator list (FLOPSY, MOPSEY, PETER, and COTTONTAIL) into the symbol table and sets the CONSTANT attribute in the associated specifier. The const_val union on lines 72 to 82 of Listing 6.25-1 holds the value associated with the constant. A definition for FLOPSY is in Figure 6.12. The v_int field holds the numeric values of integer constants, but it's also used for string constants. When the compiler sees a string constant, it outputs a definition of the form

```
char S1[] = "contents of string" ;
```

and the numeric component of the label is stored in v_int—each string label has a unique numeric component. v_struct is used only if the current specifier describes a structure, in which case the noun field is set to STRUCTURE and v_struct points at yet another data structure (discussed momentarily) that describes the structure.

The oclass field on line 66 of Listing 6.24 remembers the C-code storage class that is actually output with the variable definition for a global variable. The contents of this field are undefined if the sclass field is not set to FIXED, and the possible values are defined on lines 54 to 59.

The _long field on line 67 selects either of two lengths for an integer variable. In the current application, the **long** keyword is ignored if the variable is of type **char**, and the **short** keyword is always ignored. All of this is summarized in Table 6.11. The

_long **and** _short.

Listing 6.24. *symtab.h*— A Specifier

```
42    #define INT        0      /* specifier.noun. INT has the value 0 so    */
43    #define CHAR       1      /* that an uninitialized structure defaults */
44    #define VOID       2      /* to int, same goes for EXTERN, below.      */
45    #define STRUCTURE  3
46    #define LABEL      4
47                              /* specifier.sclass                          */
48    #define FIXED      0      /*      At a fixed address.                  */
49    #define REGISTER   1      /*      In a register.                       */
50    #define AUTO       2      /*      On the run-time stack.               */
51    #define TYPEDEF    3      /*      Typedef.                             */
52    #define CONSTANT   4      /*      This is a constant.                  */
53
54                              /* Output (C-code) storage class             */
55    #define NO_OCLASS  0      /*      No output class (var is auto).       */
56    #define PUB        1      /*      public                              */
57    #define PRI        2      /*      private                             */
58    #define EXT        3      /*      extern                              */
59    #define COM        4      /*      common                              */
60
61
62    typedef struct specifier
63    {
64        unsigned noun        :3;   /* CHAR INT STRUCTURE LABEL              */
65        unsigned sclass      :3;   /* REGISTER AUTO FIXED CONSTANT TYPEDEF  */
66        unsigned oclass      :3;   /* Output storage class: PUB PRI COM EXT.*/
67        unsigned _long       :1;   /* 1=long.      0=short.                 */
68        unsigned _unsigned   :1;   /* 1=unsigned.  0=signed.                */
69        unsigned _static     :1;   /* 1=static keyword found in declarations.*/
70        unsigned _extern     :1;   /* 1=extern keyword found in declarations.*/
71
72        union
73        {                               /* Value if constant:               */
74            int          v_int;    /* Int & char values. If a string const.,*/
75                                   /* is numeric component of the label.    */
76            unsigned int v_uint;   /* Unsigned int constant value.          */
77            long         v_long;   /* Signed long constant value.           */
78            unsigned long v_ulong; /* Unsigned long constant value.         */
79
80            struct structdef *v_struct; /* If this is a struct, points at a */
81                                        /* structure-table element.         */
82        } const_val;
83
84    } specifier;
```

_unsigned bit on line 68 is used in much the same way as _long. The _extern and _static bits on the next two lines remember when the equivalent keyword is found in the input as the specifier list is parsed. They are needed by the compiler to figure the output storage class after the entire specifier has been processed.

There's one final problem. A declaration list can be made up of two types of structures: it can have zero or more declarators in it, and it always has exactly one specifier. You need some way to determine if a list element is a declarator or a specifier when all you have to work with is a pointer to an element. The problem is solved by *encapsulating* the two structures into a third structure that can be either a declarator or specifier. This is done with the link structure in Listing 6.25. The class field tells us what the following union contains. It's either a DECLARATOR or a

Encapsulation.
The link structure.

Figure 6.12. An Enumerator-List Element.

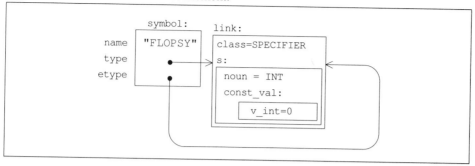

Table 6.11. Processing **long** and **short**.

input	noun	_long	length	notes
long int	INT	true	32 bits	
short int	INT	false	16 bits	same as **int**
int	INT	false	16 bits	
long char	CHAR	true	8 bits	same as **char**
short char	CHAR	false	8 bits	same as **char**
char	CHAR	false	8 bits	

SPECIFIER, as defined on lines 85 and 86. The next field points at the next element in the type chain. It's NULL if this is the specifier, which must come last in the chain. Finally, the tdef field is used when processing typedefs. It's used to distinguish whether a type chain was created by a **typedef** or by a normal declaration. You could treat **typedef** as a storage class, and mark it as such it in the sclass field of the specifier, but it's convenient not to have to chase down the length of the chain to the specifier to get this information.

Listing 6.25. *symtab.h*— A link in the Declaration Chain

```
85    #define DECLARATOR      0
86    #define SPECIFIER       1
87
88    typedef struct link
89    {
90        unsigned class   : 1;           /* DECLARATOR or SPECIFIER            */
91        unsigned tdef    : 1;           /* For typedefs. If set, current link */
92                                        /* chain was created by a typedef.    */
93        union
94        {
95            specifier    s;             /* If class == DECLARATOR             */
96            declarator   d;             /* If class == SPECIFIER              */
97        }
98        select ;
99        struct link  *next;             /* Next element of chain.             */
100
101   } link;
102
103   /*--------------------------------------------------------------------
104    * Use the following p->XXX where p is a pointer to a link structure.
105    */
106
```

→

Listing 6.25. continued...

```
107   #define NOUN          select.s.noun
108   #define SCLASS        select.s.sclass
109   #define LONG          select.s._long
110   #define UNSIGNED      select.s._unsigned
111   #define EXTERN        select.s._extern
112   #define STATIC        select.s._static
113   #define OCLASS        select.s.oclass
114
115   #define DCL_TYPE      select.d.dcl_type
116   #define NUM_ELE       select.d.num_ele
117
118   #define VALUE         select.s.const_val
119   #define V_INT         VALUE.v_int
120   #define V_UINT        VALUE.v_uint
121   #define V_LONG        VALUE.v_long
122   #define V_ULONG       VALUE.v_ulong
123   #define V_STRUCT      VALUE.v_struct
124
125   /*-------------------------------------------------------------------
126    * Use the following XXX(p) where p is a pointer to a link structure.
127    */
128
129   #define IS_SPECIFIER(p)   ( (p)->class == SPECIFIER )
130   #define IS_DECLARATOR(p)  ( (p)->class == DECLARATOR )
131   #define IS_ARRAY(p)       ( (p)->class == DECLARATOR && (p)->DCL_TYPE==ARRAY    )
132   #define IS_POINTER(p)     ( (p)->class == DECLARATOR && (p)->DCL_TYPE==POINTER )
133   #define IS_FUNCT(p)       ( (p)->class == DECLARATOR && (p)->DCL_TYPE==FUNCTION )
134   #define IS_STRUCT(p)      ( (p)->class == SPECIFIER  && (p)->NOUN == STRUCTURE )
135   #define IS_LABEL(p)       ( (p)->class == SPECIFIER  && (p)->NOUN == LABEL     )
136
137   #define IS_CHAR(p)        ( (p)->class == SPECIFIER  && (p)->NOUN == CHAR )
138   #define IS_INT(p)         ( (p)->class == SPECIFIER  && (p)->NOUN == INT  )
139   #define IS_UINT(p)        ( IS_INT(p) && (p)->UNSIGNED                     )
140   #define IS_LONG(p)        ( IS_INT(p) && (p)->LONG                         )
141   #define IS_ULONG(p)       ( IS_INT(p) && (p)->LONG && (p)->UNSIGNED        )
142   #define IS_UNSIGNED(p)    ( (p)->UNSIGNED                                  )
143
144
145   #define IS_AGGREGATE(p)   ( IS_ARRAY(p) || IS_STRUCT(p)      )
146   #define IS_PTR_TYPE(p)    ( IS_ARRAY(p) || IS_POINTER(p)     )
147
148   #define IS_CONSTANT(p)    (IS_SPECIFIER(p) && (p)->SCLASS == CONSTANT  )
149   #define IS_TYPEDEF(p)     (IS_SPECIFIER(p) && (p)->SCLASS == TYPEDEF   )
150   #define IS_INT_CONSTANT(p) (IS_CONSTANT(p) && (p)->NOUN   == INT       )
```

The macros on lines 107 to 123 of Listing 6.25 clean up the code a little by getting rid of some of the dots and field names. For example, if p is a pointer to a link, you can say p->V_INT rather than

```
p->select.d.const_val.v_int
```

to access that field.

Structures.

The foregoing system becomes even more complex when you introduce structures and unions into the picture. You need two more data structures for this purpose. First of all, the structure definitions are organized in an auxiliary symbol table called the *structure table*, declared on line 159 of Listing 6.26, below. The v_struct field of a

v_struct

specifier that describes a structure points at the structure-table element for that structure. The table is indexed by tag name if there is one—untagged structures are assigned arbitrary names. It contains `structdef` structures, defined on lines 151 to 157 of Listing 6.26. The `structdef` contains the tag name (`tag`), the nesting level at the point of declaration (`level`), and a pointer to a linked list of field definitions (`fields`), each of which is a `symbol` structure—one `symbol` for each field. The `level` field is here so that an error message can be printed when a duplicate declaration is found; it's recycled later to hold the offset to the field from the base address of the structure. These offsets are all zero in the case of a union; that's the only difference between a structure and a union, in fact. The `symbol`'s `next` field links together the field definitions. This organization means that you must use a linear search to find a field, but it lets you have an arbitrary number of fields.

`structdef`

Listing 6.26. *symtab.h*— Representing Structures

```
151    typedef struct structdef
152    {
153        char            tag[NAME_MAX+1];   /* Tag part of structure definition.      */
154        unsigned char   level;             /* Nesting level at which struct declared.*/
155        symbol          *fields;           /* Linked list of field declarations.     */
156        unsigned        size;              /* Size of the structure in bytes.        */
157    } structdef;
158
159    ALLOC_CLS HASH_TAB *Struct_tab;        /* The actual table.                      */
```

Figure 6.13 gives you an idea of how a reasonably complex declaration appears in the complete symbol-table system. I've left out irrelevant fields in the figure. The declaration that generated that table is as follows:

```
struct argotiers
{
    int             (* Clopin)();  /* Function pointer */
    double          Mathias[5];
    struct argotiers *Guillaume;
    struct pstruct { int a; } Pierre;
}
gipsy;
```

Note that isolating the `structdef` from the `field` lets you correctly process a declaration like the following:

```
struct one { struct two *p; };
struct two { struct one *p; };
```

because you can create a `struct_def` for **struct** two without having to know anything about this second structure's contents. The fields can be added to the `structdef` when you get to the **struct** two declaration.

The final part of *symtab.h*, in which various mappings from C types to C-code types are defined, is in Listing 6.27. Note that the various WIDTH macros from <*tools/c-code.h*> are used here, so you must include *c-code.h* before including *symtab.h* in your file.

C to C-code mappings.

Figure 6.13. Representing a Structure in the Symbol Table

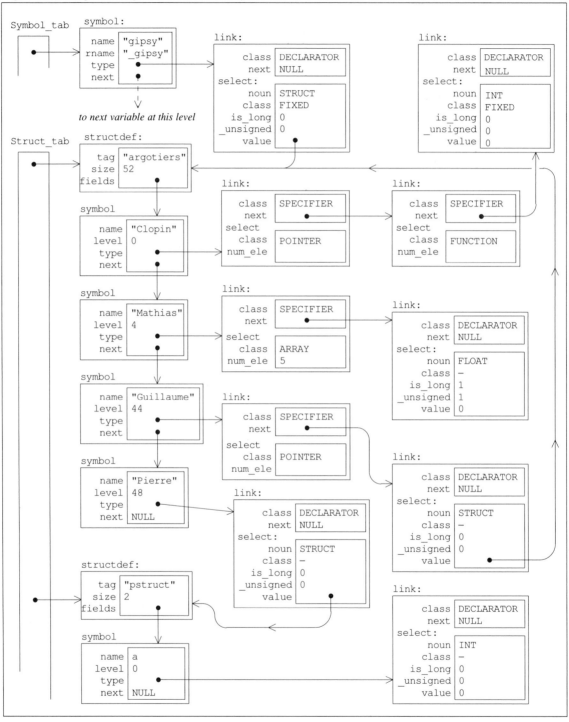

Listing 6.27. *symtab.h*— Sizes of Various Types

```
160   #define CSIZE      BYTE_WIDTH       /* char */
161   #define CTYPE      "byte"
162
163   #define ISIZE      WORD_WIDTH       /* int */
164   #define ITYPE      "word"
165
166   #define LSIZE      LWORD_WIDTH      /* long */
167   #define LTYPE      "lword"
168
169   #define PSIZE      PTR_WIDTH        /* pointer: 32-bit (8086 large model) */
170   #define PTYPE      "ptr"
171
172   #define STYPE      "record"         /* structure, size undefined */
173   #define ATYPE      "array"          /* array,     size undefined */
```

6.3.6 Implementing the Symbol-Table Maintenance Layer

Our next task is to build the symbol-table maintenance layer—the functions that manipulate the data structures described in the last section. The first set of functions, in Listing 6.28, take care of memory management. Three sets of similar routines are provided—they maintain the symbol, link, and structdef structure respectively. Taking the symbol-maintenance routines on lines 23 to 81 of Listing 6.28 as characteristic, the compiler creates and deletes symbols throughout the compilation process, so it's worthwhile to minimize the create-and-delete time for a node. discard_symbol() creates a linked list of freed nodes on line 63 rather than calling newsym() and freesym() [the hash-table-function versions of malloc() and free()] for every create and delete. Symbol_free points at the head of the free list; it is declared on line 15. new_symbol() calls newsym() on line 30 only if the free list is empty, otherwise it just unlinks a node from the list on line 33. The routines for the other structures work in much the same way. The only difference is that new_link(), since it's calling malloc() directly on line 96, can get nodes ten at a time to speed up the allocation process even further. LCHUNK—the number of nodes that are allocated at one time—is defined on line 19.

Listing 6.28. *symtab.c*— The Maintenance Layer: Memory-Management Functions

```
1    #include <stdio.h>
2    #include <stdlib.h>
3    #include <tools/debug.h>
4    #include <tools/hash.h>
5    #include <tools/l.h>
6    #include <tools/compiler.h>
7    #include <tools/c-code.h>
8    #include "symtab.h"          /* Symbol-table definitions.                 */
9    #include "value.h"           /* Value definitions.                        */
10   #include "proto.h"           /* Prototypes for all functions in this directory. */
11   #include "label.h"           /* Labels to use for compiler-generated symbols.   */
12
13   /*-------------------------------------------------------------------*/
14
15   PRIVATE symbol    *Symbol_free = NULL; /* Free-list of recycled symbols.    */
16   PRIVATE link      *Link_free   = NULL; /* Free-list of recycled links.      */
17   PRIVATE structdef *Struct_free = NULL; /* Free-list of recycled structdefs. */
18
```

➡️

Listing 6.28. continued. . .

```
19   #define LCHUNK   10           /* new_link() gets this many nodes at one shot.*/
20
21   /*-----------------------------------------------------------------------*/
22
23   PUBLIC   symbol   *new_symbol( name, scope )
24   char     *name;
25   int      scope;
26   {
27       symbol *sym_p;
28
29       if( !Symbol_free )                                    /* Free list is empty.*/
30           sym_p = (symbol *) newsym( sizeof(symbol) );
31       else                                                  /* Unlink node from   */
32       {                                                     /* the free list.     */
33           sym_p       = Symbol_free;
34           Symbol_free = Symbol_free->next ;
35           memset( sym_p, 0, sizeof(symbol) );
36       }
37
38       strncpy( sym_p->name, name, sizeof(sym_p->name) );
39       sym_p->level = scope;
40       return sym_p;
41   }
42
43   /* - - - - - - - - - - - - - - - - - - - - - - - - - - - - - - - - - - -*/
44
45   PUBLIC   void     discard_symbol( sym )
46   symbol  *sym;
47   {
48       /* Discard a single symbol structure and any attached links and args. Note
49        * that the args field is recycled for initializers, the process is
50        * described later on in the text (see value.c in the code), but you have to
51        * test for a different type here. Sorry about the forward reference.
52        */
53
54       if( sym )
55       {
56           if( IS_FUNCT( sym->type ) )
57               discard_symbol_chain( sym->args );           /* Function arguments. */
58           else
59               discard_value( (value *)sym->args );         /* If an initializer.  */
60
61           discard_link_chain( sym->type );                 /* Discard type chain. */
62
63           sym->next   = Symbol_free ;                      /* Put current symbol */
64           Symbol_free = sym;                               /* in the free list.  */
65       }
66   }
67
68   /* - - - - - - - - - - - - - - - - - - - - - - - - - - - - - - - - - - -*/
69
70   PUBLIC   void     discard_symbol_chain(sym)   /* Discard an entire cross-linked */
71   symbol  *sym;                                 /* chain of symbols.              */
72   {
73       symbol *p = sym;
74
75       while( sym )
76       {
77           p = sym->next;
78           discard_symbol( sym );
```

Listing 6.28. continued...

```
79              sym = p;
80          }
81  }
82
83  /*-------------------------------------------------------------------------*/
84
85  PUBLIC link     *new_link( )
86  {
87      /* Return a new link. It's initialized to zeros, so it's a declarator.
88       * LCHUNK nodes are allocated from malloc() at one time.
89       */
90
91      link *p;
92      int  i;
93
94      if( !Link_free )
95      {
96          if( !(Link_free = (link *) malloc( sizeof(link) * LCHUNK )) )
97          {
98              yyerror("INTERNAL, new_link: Out of memory\n");
99              exit( 1 );
100         }
101
102         for( p = Link_free, i = LCHUNK; --i > 0; ++p )    /* Executes LCHUNK-1 */
103             p->next = p + 1;                              /*          times. */
104
105         p->next = NULL ;
106     }
107
108     p         = Link_free;
109     Link_free = Link_free->next;
110     memset( p, 0, sizeof(link) );
111     return p;
112 }
113
114 /* - - - - - - - - - - - - - - - - - - - - - - - - - - - - - - - - - -*/
115
116 PUBLIC void     discard_link_chain( p )
117 link    *p;
118 {
119     /* Discard all links in the chain. Nothing is removed from the structure
120      * table, however. There's no point in discarding the nodes one at a time
121      * since they're already linked together, so find the first and last nodes
122      * in the input chain and link the whole list directly.
123      */
124
125     link *start ;
126
127     if( start = p )
128     {
129         while( p->next )          /* find last node */
130             p = p->next;
131
132         p->next   = Link_free;
133         Link_free = start;
134     }
135 }
136
```

➡

Listing 6.28. continued...

```
137     /*- - - - - - - - - - - - - - - - - - - - - - - - - - - - - - - */
138
139     PUBLIC  void    discard_link( p )                   /* Discard a single link. */
140     link    *p;
141     {
142         p->next    = Link_free;
143         Link_free  = p;
144     }
145
146     /*----------------------------------------------------------------------*/
147
148     PUBLIC  structdef *new_structdef( tag )              /* Allocate a new structdef. */
149     char    *tag;
150     {
151         structdef *sdef_p;
152
153         if( !Struct_free )
154             sdef_p = (structdef *) newsym( sizeof(structdef) );
155         else
156         {
157             sdef_p      = Struct_free;
158             Struct_free = (structdef *)(Struct_free->fields);
159             memset( sdef_p, 0, sizeof(structdef) );
160         }
161         strncpy( sdef_p->tag, tag, sizeof(sdef_p->tag) );
162         return sdef_p;
163     }
164
165     /* - - - - - - - - - - - - - - - - - - - - - - - - - - - - - - -*/
166
167     PUBLIC  void    discard_structdef( sdef_p )
168     structdef       *sdef_p;
169     {
170         /* Discard a structdef and any attached fields, but don't discard linked
171          * structure definitions.
172          */
173
174         if( sdef_p )
175         {
176             discard_symbol_chain( sdef_p->fields );
177
178             sdef_p->fields = (symbol *)Struct_free ;
179             Struct_free    = sdef_p;
180         }
181     }
```

Subroutines in Listing 6.29 manipulate declarators: add_declarator() adds declarator nodes to the end of the linked list pointed to by the type and etype fields in a symbol structure. The routine is passed a symbol pointer and the declarator type (ARRAY, POINTER, or FUNCTION—declared on line 33 of Listing 6.23, page 491). Subroutines in Listing 6.30 manipulate specifiers: they copy, create, and initialize specifier links.

Listing 6.31 contains routines that manipulate entire types and linked-lists of symbols. clone_type(), on line 226, copies an entire type chain. This routine is used in two places. First, when a variable that uses a **typedef** rather than a standard type is declared, the type chain is copied from the symbol representing the **typedef** to the

Listing 6.29. *symtab.c*— The Maintenance Layer: Declarator Manipulation

```
182    PUBLIC   void      add_declarator( sym, type )
183    symbol   *sym;
184    int      type;
185    {
186         /* Add a declarator link to the end of the chain, the head of which is
187          * pointed to by sym->type and the tail of which is pointed to by
188          * sym->etype. *head must be NULL when the chain is empty. Both pointers
189          * are modified as necessary.
190          */
191
192         link *link_p;
193
194         if( type == FUNCTION && IS_ARRAY(sym->etype) )
195         {
196             yyerror("Array of functions is illegal, assuming function pointer\n");
197             add_declarator( sym, POINTER );
198         }
199
200         link_p          = new_link();        /* The default class is DECLARATOR. */
201         link_p->DCL_TYPE = type;
202
203         if( !sym->type )
204             sym->type = sym->etype = link_p;
205         else
206         {
207             sym->etype->next = link_p;
208             sym->etype       = link_p;
209         }
210    }
```

Listing 6.30. *symtab.c*— The Maintenance Layer: Specifier Manipulation

```
211    PUBLIC   spec_cpy( dst, src )      /* Copy all initialized fields in src to dst.*/
212    link *dst, *src;
213    {
214
215         if( src->NOUN     ) dst->NOUN     = src->NOUN     ;
216         if( src->SCLASS   ) dst->SCLASS   = src->SCLASS   ;
217         if( src->LONG     ) dst->LONG     = src->LONG     ;
218         if( src->UNSIGNED ) dst->UNSIGNED = src->UNSIGNED ;
219         if( src->STATIC   ) dst->STATIC   = src->STATIC   ;
220         if( src->EXTERN   ) dst->EXTERN   = src->EXTERN   ;
221         if( src->tdef     ) dst->tdef     = src->tdef     ;
222
223         if( src->SCLASS == CONSTANT || src->NOUN == STRUCTURE)
224             memcpy( &dst->VALUE, &src->VALUE, sizeof(src->VALUE) );
225    }
```

symbol for the variable. You could keep around only one type chain in the **typedef** symbol, and make the new symbols type field point there, but this would complicate symbol deletion, because you'd have to keep track of the scope level of every link as you deleted nodes. Though this later method would be more conservative of memory, it complicates things enough so that I didn't want to use it. clone_type() is also used to create type chains for temporary variables, though here the copying is less defensible.

I'll discuss this second application when expression processing is discussed, below.

the_same_type, on line 258 of Listing 6.31, compares two type chains and returns true if they match. The storage class components of the specifier are ignored. When the third argument is true, a POINTER declarator is considered identical to a ARRAY declarator when they are found in the first positions of both type chains. This relaxation of strict type checking is necessary, again, for expression processing, because arrays are represented internally as a pointer to the first element. Strict checking is necessary when two declarations are compared for equivalence, however, so the third argument lets us disable this feature.

get_sizeof(), on line 302 of Listing 6.31, returns the size of an object of the type represented by its argument. Note that recursion is used on line 313 to process arrays. A declaration like this:

int a[10][20]

should return 400 (10 × 20 elements × 2 bytes per element). If the current declarator is an array, the size of the current dimension is remembered, and the the rest of the type chain is passed recursively to get_sizeof() to get the size of an array element. This could, of course, be done with a loop, but the recursion is more compact and arrays with more than three or four dimensions are rare. The other subroutines in the listing are self-explanatory.

The remainder of the maintenance layer, in Listing 6.32, is made up of subroutines that print symbols and convert fields to printable strings.

Listing 6.31. *symtab.c*— The Maintenance Layer: Type Manipulation

```
226    PUBLIC  link  *clone_type( tchain, endp )
227    link   *tchain;              /* input:  Type chain to duplicate.          */
228    link   **endp;               /* output: Pointer to last node in cloned chain.  */
229    {
230        /* Manufacture a clone of the type chain in the input symbol. Return a
231         * pointer to the cloned chain, NULL if there were no declarators to clone.
232         * The tdef bit in the copy is always cleared.
233         */
234
235        link  *last, *head = NULL;
236
237        for(; tchain ; tchain = tchain->next )
238        {
239            if( !head )                               /* 1st node in chain. */
240                head = last = new_link();
241            else                                      /* Subsequent node.   */
242            {
243                last->next = new_link();
244                last       = last->next;
245            }
246
247            memcpy( last, tchain, sizeof(*last) );
248            last->next = NULL;
249            last->tdef = 0;
250        }
251
252        *endp = last;
253        return head;
254    }
255
```

➡

```
Listing 6.31. continued...
256   /*-----------------------------------------------------------------------*/
257
258   PUBLIC  int      the_same_type( p1, p2, relax )
259   link    *p1, *p2;
260   int      relax;
261   {
262        /* Return 1 if the types match, 0 if they don't. Ignore the storage class.
263         * If "relax" is true and the array declarator is the first link in the
264         * chain, then a pointer is considered equivalent to an array.
265         */
266
267        if( relax && IS_PTR_TYPE(p1) && IS_PTR_TYPE(p2) )
268        {
269            p1 = p1->next;
270            p2 = p2->next;
271        }
272
273        for(; p1 && p2 ; p1 = p1->next, p2 = p2->next)
274        {
275            if( p1->class != p2->class )
276                return 0;
277
278            if( p1->class == DECLARATOR )
279            {
280                if( (p1->DCL_TYPE != p2->DCL_TYPE) ||
281                        (p1->DCL_TYPE==ARRAY && (p1->NUM_ELE != p1->NUM_ELE)) )
282                    return 0;
283            }
284            else                                            /* this is done last */
285            {
286                if( (p1->NOUN     == p2->NOUN     ) && (p1->LONG == p2->LONG ) &&
287                    (p1->UNSIGNED == p2->UNSIGNED ) )
288                {
289                    return ( p1->NOUN==STRUCTURE ) ? p1->V_STRUCT == p2->V_STRUCT
290                                                    : 1 ;
291                }
292                return 0;
293            }
294        }
295
296        yyerror("INTERNAL the_same_type: Unknown link class\n");
297        return 0;
298   }
299
300   /*-----------------------------------------------------------------------*/
301
302   PUBLIC  int      get_sizeof( p )
303   link    *p;
304   {
305        /* Return the size in bytes of an object of the the type pointed to by p.
306         * Functions are considered to be pointer sized because that's how they're
307         * represented internally.
308         */
309
310        int size;
311
312        if( p->class == DECLARATOR )
313            size = (p->DCL_TYPE==ARRAY) ? p->NUM_ELE * get_sizeof(p->next) : PSIZE;
```

➡

Listing 6.31. continued...

```
314        else
315        {
316            switch( p->NOUN )
317            {
318            case CHAR:      size = CSIZE;                    break;
319            case INT:       size = p->LONG ? LSIZE : ISIZE;  break;
320            case STRUCTURE: size = p->V_STRUCT->size;        break;
321            case VOID:      size = 0;                        break;
322            case LABEL:     size = 0;                        break;
323            }
324        }
325
326        return size;
327 }
328
329 /*------------------------------------------------------------------------*/
330
331 PUBLIC  symbol  *reverse_links( sym )
332 symbol  *sym;
333 {
334     /* Go through the cross-linked chain of "symbols", reversing the direction
335      * of the cross pointers. Return a pointer to the new head of chain
336      * (formerly the end of the chain) or NULL if the chain started out empty.
337      */
338
339     symbol *previous, *current, *next;
340
341     if( !sym )
342         return NULL;
343
344     previous = sym;
345     current  = sym->next;
346
347     while( current )
348     {
349         next            = current->next;
350         current->next   = previous;
351         previous        = current;
352         current         = next;
353     }
354
355     sym->next = NULL;
356     return previous;
357 }
```

Listing 6.32. *symtab.c*— The Maintenance Layer: Symbol-Printing Functions

```
358 PUBLIC  char     *sclass_str( class )     /* Return a string representing the */
359 int      class;                           /* indicated storage class.        */
360 {
361     return class==CONSTANT   ? "CON" :
362            class==REGISTER   ? "REG" :
363            class==TYPEDEF    ? "TYP" :
364            class==AUTO       ? "AUT" :
365            class==FIXED      ? "FIX" : "BAD SCLASS" ;
366 }
367
```

→

Listing 6.32. continued...

```
368    /*----------------------------------------------------------------*/
369
370    PUBLIC   char    *oclass_str( class )      /* Return a string representing the */
371    int      class;                            /* indicated output storage class.  */
372    {
373        return class==PUB ? "PUB"  :
374               class==PRI ? "PRI"  :
375               class==COM ? "COM"  :
376               class==EXT ? "EXT"  :   "(NO OCLS)" ;
377    }
378
379    /*----------------------------------------------------------------*/
380
381    PUBLIC   char    *noun_str( noun )         /* Return a string representing the */
382    int      noun;                             /* indicated noun.                  */
383    {
384        return noun==INT        ? "int"    :
385               noun==CHAR       ? "char"   :
386               noun==VOID       ? "void"   :
387               noun==LABEL      ? "label"  :
388               noun==STRUCTURE  ? "struct" : "BAD NOUN" ;
389    }
390
391    /*----------------------------------------------------------------*/
392
393    PUBLIC char   *attr_str( spec_p )          /* Return a string representing all */
394    specifier *spec_p;                         /* attributes in a specifier other  */
395    {                                          /* than the noun and storage class. */
396        static char str[5];
397
398        str[0] = ( spec_p->_unsigned ) ? 'u' : '.' ;
399        str[1] = ( spec_p->_static   ) ? 's' : '.' ;
400        str[2] = ( spec_p->_extern   ) ? 'e' : '.' ;
401        str[3] = ( spec_p->_long     ) ? 'l' : '.' ;
402        str[4] = '\0';
403
404        return str;
405    }
406
407    /*----------------------------------------------------------------*/
408
409    PUBLIC   char    *type_str ( link_p )
410    link    *link_p;                           /* Return a string representing the   */
411    {                                          /* type represented by the link chain. */
412        int        i;
413        static char target [ 80 ];
414        static char buf    [ 64 ];
415        int          available = sizeof(target) - 1;
416
417        *buf    = '\0';
418        *target = '\0';
419
420        if( !link_p )
421            return "(NULL)";
422
423        if( link_p->tdef )
424        {
425            strcpy( target, "tdef " );
426            available -= 5;
427        }
```

Listing 6.32. continued...

```
428
429          for(; link_p ; link_p = link_p->next )
430          {
431              if( IS_DECLARATOR(link_p) )
432              {
433                  switch( link_p->DCL_TYPE )
434                  {
435                  case POINTER:    i = sprintf(buf, "*" );                        break;
436                  case ARRAY:      i = sprintf(buf, "[%d]", link_p->NUM_ELE); break;
437                  case FUNCTION:   i = sprintf(buf, "()" );                       break;
438                  default:         i = sprintf(buf, "BAD DECL" );                 break;
439                  }
440              }
441              else  /* it's a specifier */
442              {
443                  i = sprintf( buf, "%s %s %s %s",    noun_str  ( link_p->NOUN    ),
444                                                      sclass_str( link_p->SCLASS  ),
445                                                      oclass_str( link_p->OCLASS  ),
446                                                      attr_str  ( &link_p->select.s));
447
448                  if( link_p->NOUN==STRUCTURE  || link_p->SCLASS==CONSTANT  )
449                  {
450                      strncat( target, buf, available );
451                      available -= i;
452
453                      if( link_p->NOUN != STRUCTURE )
454                          continue;
455                      else
456                          i = sprintf(buf, " %s", link_p->V_STRUCT->tag ?
457                                              link_p->V_STRUCT->tag : "untagged");
458                  }
459              }
460
461              strncat( target, buf, available );
462              available -= i;
463          }
464
465      return target;
466  }
467
468  /*----------------------------------------------------------------------*/
469
470  PUBLIC char *tconst_str( type )
471  link    *type;                      /* Return a string representing the value  */
472  {                                   /* field at the end of the specified type  */
473      static char buf[80];            /* (which must be char*, char, int, long,  */
474                                      /* unsigned int, or unsigned long). Return */
475      buf[0] = '?';                   /* "?" if the type isn't any of these.     */
476      buf[1] = '\0';
477
478      if( IS_POINTER(type)  &&  IS_CHAR(type->next) )
479      {
480          sprintf( buf, "%s%d", L_STRING, type->next->V_INT );
481      }
482      else if( !(IS_AGGREGATE(type) || IS_FUNCT(type)) )
483      {
484          switch( type->NOUN )
485          {
```

```
Listing 6.32. continued...
486             case CHAR:       sprintf( buf, "'%s' (%d)", bin_to_ascii(
487                                     type->UNSIGNED ? type->V_UINT
488                                                    : type->V_INT,1),
489                                     type->UNSIGNED ? type->V_UINT
490                                                    : type->V_INT,1    );
491                         break;
492
493             case INT:        if( type->LONG )
494                         {
495                             if( type->UNSIGNED )
496                                 sprintf(buf, "%luL", type->V_ULONG);
497                             else
498                                 sprintf(buf, "%ldL", type->V_LONG );
499                         }
500                         else
501                         {
502                             if( type->UNSIGNED )
503                                 sprintf( buf, "%u", type->V_UINT);
504                             else
505                                 sprintf( buf, "%d", type->V_INT );
506                         }
507                         break;
508         }
509     }
510
511     if( *buf == '?' )
512         yyerror("Internal, tconst_str: Can't make constant for type %s\n",
513                                             type_str( type ));
514     return buf;
515 }
516
517 /*-------------------------------------------------------------------*/
518
519 PUBLIC  char    *sym_chain_str( chain )
520 symbol  *chain;
521 {
522     /* Return a string listing the names of all symbols in the input chain (or
523      * a constant value if the symbol is a constant). Note that this routine
524      * can't call type_str() because the second-order recursion messes up the
525      * buffers. Since the routine is used only for occasional diagnostics, it's
526      * not worth fixing this problem.
527      */
528
529     int         i;
530     static char buf[80];
531     char        *p      = buf;
532     int         avail   = sizeof( buf ) - 1;
533
534     *buf = '\0';
535     while( chain && avail > 0 )
536     {
537         if( IS_CONSTANT(chain->etype) )
538             i = sprintf( p, "%0.*s", avail - 2, "const" );
539         else
540             i = sprintf( p, "%0.*s", avail - 2, chain->name );
541
542         p       += i;
543         avail   -= i;
544
```

→

Listing 6.32. continued...

```
545              if( chain = chain->next )
546              {
547                  *p++ = ',' ;
548                  i -= 2;
549              }
550          }
551
552      return buf;
553  }
554
555  /*---------------------------------------------------------------------*/
556
557  PRIVATE void psym( sym_p, fp )                    /* Print one symbol to fp. */
558  symbol  *sym_p;
559  FILE    *fp;
560  {
561      fprintf(fp, "%-18.18s %-18.18s %2d %p %s\n",
562                              sym_p->name,
563                              sym_p->type ? sym_p->rname : "------",
564                              sym_p->level,
565                              (void far *)sym_p->next,
566                              type_str( sym_p->type ) );
567  }
568
569  /*---------------------------------------------------------------------*/
570
571  PRIVATE void pstruct( sdef_p, fp )      /* Print a structure definition to fp */
572  structdef   *sdef_p;                    /* including all the fields & types.  */
573  FILE        *fp;
574  {
575      symbol      *field_p;
576
577      fprintf(fp, "struct <%s> (level %d, %d bytes):\n",
578                              sdef_p->tag,sdef_p->level,sdef_p->size);
579
580      for( field_p = sdef_p->fields; field_p; field_p=field_p->next )
581      {
582          fprintf(fp, "    %-20s (offset %d) %s\n",
583                      field_p->name, field_p->level, type_str(field_p->type));
584      }
585  }
586
587  /*---------------------------------------------------------------------*/
588
589  PUBLIC  print_syms( filename )          /* Print the entire symbol table to   */
590  char    *filename;                      /* the named file. Previous contents  */
591  {                                        /* of the file (if any) are destroyed.*/
592      FILE *fp;
593
594      if( !(fp = fopen(filename,"w")) )
595          yyerror("Can't open symbol-table file\n");
596      else
597      {
598          fprintf(fp, "Attributes in type field are:   upel\n"  );
599          fprintf(fp, "    unsigned (. for signed)-----+|||\n"  );
600          fprintf(fp, "    private  (. for public)------+||\n"  );
601          fprintf(fp, "    extern   (. for common)-------+|\n"  );
602          fprintf(fp, "    long     (. for short )--------+\n\n" );
603
```

Listing 6.32. continued...

```
604            fprintf(fp,"name                    rname            lev    next    type\n");
605            ptab( Symbol_tab, psym, fp, 1 );
606
607            fprintf(fp, "\nStructure table:\n\n");
608            ptab( Struct_tab, pstruct, fp, 1 );
609
610            fclose( fp );
611        }
612    }
```

6.4 The Parser: Configuration

I'll start looking at the compiler proper with the configuration parts of the **occs** input file. Listing 6.33 shows most of the header portion of the **occs** input file. The %union directive on lines 21 to 30 of Listing 6.33 types the value stack as a C union containing the indicated fields. Some of these fields are pointers to symbol-table structures, others to structures that are discussed below, and the last two fields are simple-variable attributes—num is for integer numbers, ascii for ASCII characters. Further down in the table, directives like <ascii> tell **occs** which fields to use for particular symbols. For example, an ASSIGNOP has an <ascii> attribute because the <ascii> directive precedes its definition on line 63. The ascii field of the union is used automatically if $N in a production corresponds to an ASSIGNOP. You don't have to say $N.ascii.

%union, used for C compiler's value stack.

Listing 6.33. *c.y*— **occs** Input File: Definitions Section

```
 1    %{
 2    #include <stdio.h>
 3    #include <stdlib.h>
 4    #include <signal.h>
 5    #include <tools/debug.h>        /* Misc. macros. (see Appendix A)          */
 6    #include <tools/hash.h>         /* Hash-table support. (see Appendix A)    */
 7    #include <tools/compiler.h>     /* Prototypes for comp.lib functions.      */
 8    #include <tools/l.h>            /* Prototypes for l.lib functions.         */
 9
10    #define ALLOC                   /* Define ALLOC to create symbol table in symtab.h. */
11    #include "symtab.h"             /* Definitions for the symbol-table.       */
12    #include "value.h"              /* Definitions used for expression processing. */
13    #include "label.h"              /* Prefixes used for compiler-generated labels. */
14    #include "switch.h"             /* Definitions used for switch processing. */
15    #include "proto.h"              /* Function prototypes for all .c files used by the */
16    %}                              /* parser. It is not printed anywhere in the book, */
17                                    /* but is included on the distribution disk. */
18
19    /*-----------------------------------------------------------------*/
20
21    %union {
22        char        *p_char;
23        symbol      *p_sym;
24        link        *p_link;
25        structdef   *p_sdef;
26        specifier   *p_spec;
27        value       *p_val;
28        int         num;            /* Make short if sizeof(int) > sizeof(int*) */
29        int         ascii;
```

Listing 6.33. continued. . .

```
30   }
31
32   /*-----------------------------------------------------------------------*/
33
34   %term    STRING          /* String constant.                             */
35   %term    ICON            /* Integer or long constant including '\t', etc. */
36   %term    FCON            /* Floating-point constant.                     */
37
38   %term    TYPE            /* int char long float double signed unsigned short */
39                           /* const volatile void                          */
40   %term    <ascii> STRUCT  /* struct union                                 */
41   %term    ENUM            /* enum                                         */
42
43   %term    RETURN GOTO
44   %term    IF ELSE
45   %term    SWITCH CASE DEFAULT
46   %term    BREAK CONTINUE
47   %term    WHILE DO FOR
48   %term    LC RC           /*        { }       */
49   %term    SEMI            /*         ;        */
50   %term    ELLIPSIS        /*        ...       */
51
52   /* The attributes used below tend to be the sensible thing. For example, the
53    * ASSIGNOP attribute is the operator component of the lexeme; most other
54    * attributes are the first character of the lexeme. Exceptions are as follows:
55    *       token       attribute
56    *       RELOP >        '>'
57    *       RELOP <        '<'
58    *       RELOP >=       'G'
59    *       RELOP <=       'L'
60    */
61
62   %left    COMMA                        /* ,                              */
63   %right   EQUAL <ascii> ASSIGNOP       /* =    *= /= %= += -= <<= >>= &= |= ^= */
64   %right   QUEST COLON                  /*             ? :                */
65   %left    OROR                         /* ||                             */
66   %left    ANDAND                       /* &&                             */
67   %left    OR                           /* |                              */
68   %left    XOR                          /* ^                              */
69   %left    AND                          /* &                              */
70   %left    <ascii> EQUOP                /* ==  !=                         */
71   %left    <ascii> RELOP                /* <=  >= <  >                    */
72   %left    <ascii> SHIFTOP              /* >> <<                          */
73   %left    PLUS  MINUS                  /* + -                            */
74   %left    STAR  <ascii> DIVOP          /* *  /   %                       */
75   %right   SIZEOF <ascii> UNOP INCOP    /*      sizeof    ! ~     ++ --    */
76   %left    LB RB LP RP <ascii> STRUCTOP /* [ ] ( )   . ->                 */
77
78
79                           /* These attributes are shifted by the scanner.   */
80   %term <p_sym> TTYPE     /* Name of a type created with a previous typedef.*/
81                           /* Attribute is a pointer to the symbol table     */
82                           /* entry for that typedef.                        */
83   %nonassoc <ascii> CLASS /* extern register auto static typedef. Attribute */
84                           /* is the first character of the lexeme.          */
85   %nonassoc <p_sym> NAME  /* Identifier or typedef name. Attribute is NULL  */
86                           /* if the symbol doesn't exist, a pointer to the  */
```

➡

```
Listing 6.33. continued...
87                              /* associated "symbol" structure, otherwise.     */
88
89   %nonassoc ELSE             /* This gives a high precedence to ELSE to suppress
90                               * the shift/reduce conflict error message in:
91                               *   s -> IF LP expr RP expr | IF LP expr RP s ELSE s
92                               * The precedence of the first production is the same
93                               * as RP. Making ELSE higher precedence forces
94                               * resolution in favor of the shift.
95                               */
96   %type <num> args const_expr test
97
98   %type <p_sym>   ext_decl_list ext_decl def_list def decl_list decl
99   %type <p_sym>   var_decl funct_decl local_defs new_name name enumerator
100  %type <p_sym>   name_list var_list param_declaration abs_decl abstract_decl
101  %type <p_val>   expr binary non_comma_expr unary initializer initializer_list
102  %type <p_val>   or_expr and_expr or_list and_list
103
104  %type <p_link>  type specifiers opt_specifiers type_or_class type_specifier
105  %type <p_sdef>  opt_tag tag struct_specifier
106  %type <p_char>  string_const target
107
108  /*-------------------------------------------------------------------
109   * Global and external variables. Initialization to zero for all globals is
110   * assumed. Since occs -a and -p is used, these variables may not be private.
111   */
112
113  %{
114  #ifdef YYACTION
115
116  extern char *yytext;                      /* generated by LeX */
117  extern const int yylineno, yyleng;
118  %}
```

**There are several other variables declared in this part of the
input file. I'll discuss these variables, below, as they are used.**

```
180  %{
181  #endif
182  %}
```

Lines 34 to 50 of Listing 6.33 contain definitions for those tokens that aren't used in expressions, so don't require precedence or associativity information. Lines 62 to 76 comprise a precedence chart in which the other tokens are defined. Lowest-precedence operators are at the top of the list, and tokens on the same line are at the same precedence level. Some of these tokens have the `<ascii>` attribute associated with them. These tokens all represent multiple input symbols. The attribute, created by the lexical analyzer and passed to the parser using the `yylval` mechanism described in Appendix E, serves to identify which input symbol has been scanned. You can access the attribute from within a production by using the normal $ mechanism—if a symbol with an `<ascii>` attribute is at $1 in the production, then that attribute can be referenced by using $1 in an action. Most `<ascii>` attributes are the first character of the lexeme—a few exceptions are listed in the comment on line 52 of Listing 6.33.

TYPE, CLASS, NAME, and ELSE are assigned precedence levels on lines 79 to 95 to eliminate various shift/reduce conflicts inherent in the grammar. (See Appendix E for a

Tokens not in expressions. Single tokens represent multiple symbols. Attributes differentiate them.

TYPE, CLASS, NAME, and ELSE have precedence.

description of what's going on.) The NAME and TTYPE tokens also have pointer-to-symbol-table-entry attributes associated with them. (A TTYPE is a type created by a previous **typedef**.) The lexical analyzer uses the symbol table to distinguish identifiers from user-defined types. It returns a NULL attribute if the input symbol isn't in the table, otherwise the attribute is a pointer to the appropriate symbol-table entry. I'll demonstrate how this is done in a moment.

%type

The %type directives on lines 96 to 106 of Listing 6.33 attach various attributes to nonterminal names. The abbreviations that are used in the names are defined in Table 6.12. The remainder of the header holds variable definitions, most of which aren't shown in Listing 6.33. They're discussed later along with the code that actually uses them.

Table 6.12. Abbreviations Used in Nonterminal Names

Abbreviation	Meaning	Abbreviation	Meaning
abs	abstract	expr	expression
arg	argument	ext	external
const	constant	opt	optional
decl	declarator	param	parameter
def	definition	struct	structure

SIGINT handling, cleanup.

Create temporary-files for code, data, and bss segments.

Skipping past the productions themselves for a moment, the end of the **occs** input file starts in Listing 6.34. This section contains various initialization and debugging routines that are used by the parser. The **occs** parser's initialization function starts on line 1306 of Listing 6.34. It creates temporary files and installs a signal handler that deletes the temporaries if SIGINT. is issued while the compiler is running. (SIGINT is issued when a Ctrl-C or Ctrl-Break is encountered under MS-DOS. Some UNIX systems also recognize DEL or Rubout.) init_output_streams(), starting on line 1251, creates three temporary files to hold output for the code, data, and bss segments. These files make it easier to keep the various segments straight as code is generated. The cleanup code that starts on line 1323 merges the three temporaries together at the end of the compilation process by renaming the data file and then appending the other two files.

Listing 6.34. *c.y*— **occs** Input File: Temporary-File Creation

```
1240   %%
1241   extern char *mktemp();
1242   extern FILE *yycodeout, *yydataout, *yybssout;  /* In occs output file. */
1243   extern yyprompt();                               /* In debugger.         */
1244
1245   #define OFILE_NAME "output.c"   /* Output file name.           */
1246   char    *Bss ;                 /* Name of BSS  temporary file. */
1247   char    *Code;                 /* Name of Code temporary file. */
1248   char    *Data;                 /* Name of Data temporary file. */
1249   /*-----------------------------------------------------------------*/
1250
1251   PRIVATE void init_output_streams( p_code, p_data, p_bss)
1252   char    **p_code, **p_data, **p_bss;
1253   {
1254       /* Initialize the output streams, making temporary files as necessary.
1255        * Note that the ANSI tmpfile() or the UNIX mkstmp() functions are both
1256        * better choices than the mktemp()/fopen() used here because another
1257        * process could, at least in theory, sneak in between the two calls.
1258        * Since mktemp uses the process id as part of the file name, this
1259        * is not much of a problem, and the current method is more portable
1260        * than tmpfile() or mkstmp(). Be careful in a network environment.
```
➡

Listing 6.34. continued...

```
1261        */
1262
1263       if( !(*p_code = mktemp("ccXXXXXX")) || !(*p_data = mktemp("cdXXXXXX")) ||
1264           !(*p_bss  = mktemp("cbXXXXXX"))
1265         )
1266       {
1267           yyerror("Can't create temporary-file names");
1268           exit( 1 );
1269       }
1270
1271       if( !(yycodeout=fopen(*p_code, "w")) || !(yydataout=fopen(*p_data, "w")) ||
1272           !(yybssout =fopen( *p_bss, "w"))
1273         )
1274       {
1275           perror("Can't open temporary files");
1276           exit( 1 );
1277       }
1278   }
1279
1280   /*------------------------------------------------------------------*/
1281   void      (*Osig)();  /* Previous SIGINT handler. Initialized in yy_init_occs().*/
1282
1283   PRIVATE sigint_handler()
1284   {
1285       /* Ctrl-C handler. Note that the debugger raises SIGINT on a 'q' command,
1286        * so this routine is executed when you exit the debugger. Also, the
1287        * debugger's own SIGINT handler, which cleans up windows and so forth, is
1288        * installed before yy_init_occs() is called. It's called here to clean up
1289        * the environment if necessary. If the debugger isn't installed, the call
1290        * is harmless.
1291        */
1292
1293       signal    ( SIGINT, SIG_IGN  );
1294       clean_up  (                  );
1295       unlink    ( OFILE_NAME       );
1296       (*Osig)();
1297       exit(1);                        /* Needed only if old signal handler returns. */
1298   }
1299
1300   /*------------------------------------------------------------------*/
1301   sym_cmp     (s1, s2) symbol   *s1, *s2; { return strcmp  (s1->name, s2->name);}
1302   struct_cmp  (s1, s2) structdef *s1, *s2; { return strcmp  (s1->tag,  s2->tag );}
1303   sym_hash    (s1)     symbol   *s1;      { return hash_add(s1->name ); }
1304   struct_hash (s1)     structdef *s1;      { return hash_add(s1->tag  ); }
1305
1306   PUBLIC  void    yy_init_occs( val )
1307   yystype *val;
1308   {
1309       yycomment("Initializing\n");
1310
1311       Osig = signal( SIGINT, SIG_IGN );
1312       init_output_streams( &Code, &Data, &Bss );
1313       signal( SIGINT, sigint_handler );
1314
1315       val->p_char = "---";          /* Provide attribute for the start symbol. */
1316
1317       Symbol_tab = maketab( 257, sym_hash,    sym_cmp    );
1318       Struct_tab = maketab( 127, struct_hash, struct_cmp );
1319   }
1320
```
➡

Listing 6.34. continued. . .

```
1321    /*-------------------------------------------------------------*/
1322
1323    PRIVATE void clean_up()
1324    {
1325        /* Cleanup actions. Mark the ends of the various segments, then merge the
1326         * three temporary files used for the code, data, and bss segments into a
1327         * single file called output.c. Delete the temporaries. Since some compilers
1328         * don't delete an existing file with a rename(), it's best to assume the
1329         * worst. It can't hurt to delete a nonexistent file, you'll just get an
1330         * error back from the operating system.
1331         */
1332
1333        extern FILE *yycodeout, *yydataout, *yybssout;
1334
1335        signal ( SIGINT, SIG_IGN );
1336        fclose ( yycodeout      );
1337        fclose ( yydataout      );
1338        fclose ( yybssout       );
1339        unlink ( OFILE_NAME     );  /* delete old output file (ignore EEXIST) */
1340
1341        if( rename( Data, OFILE_NAME ) )
1342            yyerror("Can't rename temporary (%s) to %s\n", Data, OFILE_NAME );
1343        else
1344        {                                           /* Append the other temporary  */
1345            movefile( OFILE_NAME, Bss , "a" );      /* files to the end of the      */
1346            movefile( OFILE_NAME, Code, "a" );      /* output file and delete the   */
1347        }                                           /* temporary files. movefile()  */
1348    }                                               /* is in appendix A.            */
```

Print the value stack,
`yypstk()`.

The remainder of the **occs** input file is in Listing 6.35. `yypstk()`, starting on line 1423, is used by the **occs** interactive debugger to print the value-stack contents. The routine is passed a pointer to the value stack item and a pointer to the equivalent string on the symbolic, debugging stack (the middle column in the stack window). It uses this string to identify which of the fields in the union are active, by searching the table on lines 1357 to 1415 with the `bsearch()` call on line 1432. The following switch then prints out stack item.

`main(),yyhook_a(),`
`yyhook_b()`

Listing 6.36 finishes up the start-up code with a `main()` function. The `yyhook_a()` routine is a debugger hook that prints the symbol table when a Ctrl-A is issued at the IDE's command prompt. The `yyhook_b()` lets you enable or disable the run-time trace feature discussed along with the `gen()` subroutine, below, from the debugger.

Listing 6.35. *c.y*— **occs** Input File: Initialization and Cleanup

```
1349   enum union_fields { NONE, P_SYM, P_LINK,    P_SDEF,    P_FIELD, P_SPEC,
1350                            P_CHAR, P_VALUE, SYM_CHAIN, ASCII, NUM         };
1351   typedef struct tabtype
1352   {
1353       char *sym;
1354       enum union_fields case_val;
1355   } tabtype;
1356
1357   tabtype Tab[] =
1358   {
1359           /*      nonterminal            field         */
1360           /*         name             in %union       */
1361
1362           { "ASSIGNOP",               ASCII           },
1363           { "CLASS",                  ASCII           },
1364           { "DIVOP",                  ASCII           },
1365           { "EQUOP",                  ASCII           },
1366           { "INCOP",                  ASCII           },
1367           { "NAME",                   P_SYM           },
1368           { "RELOP",                  ASCII           },
1369           { "SHIFTOP",                ASCII           },
1370           { "STRUCT",                 ASCII           },
1371           { "STRUCTOP",               ASCII           },
1372           { "TTYPE",                  P_SYM           },
1373           { "UNOP",                   ASCII           },
1374           { "abs_decl",               P_SYM           },
1375           { "abstract_decl",          P_SYM           },
1376           { "and_expr",               P_VALUE         },
1377           { "and_list",               P_VALUE         },
1378           { "args",                   NUM             },
1379           { "binary",                 P_VALUE         },
1380           { "const_expr",             NUM             },
1381           { "decl",                   P_SYM           },
1382           { "decl_list",              SYM_CHAIN       },
1383           { "def",                    SYM_CHAIN       },
1384           { "def_list",               SYM_CHAIN       },
1385           { "enumerator",             P_SYM           },
1386           { "expr",                   P_VALUE         },
1387           { "ext_decl",               P_SYM           },
1388           { "ext_decl_list",          SYM_CHAIN       },
1389           { "funct_decl",             P_SYM           },
1390           { "initializer",            P_VALUE         },
1391           { "initializer_list",       P_VALUE         },
1392           { "local_defs",             SYM_CHAIN       },
1393           { "name",                   P_SYM           },
1394           { "name_list",              SYM_CHAIN       },
1395           { "new_name",               P_SYM           },
1396           { "non_comma_expr",         P_VALUE         },
1397           { "opt_specifiers",         P_LINK          },
1398           { "opt_tag",                P_SDEF          },
1399           { "or_expr",                P_VALUE         },
1400           { "or_list",                P_VALUE         },
1401           { "param_declaration",      SYM_CHAIN       },
1402           { "specifiers",             P_LINK          },
1403           { "string_const",           P_CHAR          },
1404           { "struct_specifier",       P_SDEF          },
1405           { "tag",                    P_SDEF          },
1406           { "test",                   NUM             },
1407           { "type",                   P_LINK          },
```

➡

Listing 6.35. continued. . .

```
1408             { "type_or_class",        P_LINK             },
1409             { "type_specifier",       P_LINK             },
1410             { "unary",                P_VALUE            },
1411             { "var_decl",             P_SYM              },
1412             { "var_list",             SYM_CHAIN          },
1413             { "{72}",                 NUM                },
1414             { "{73}",                 P_VALUE            }
1415   };
1416
1417   tcmp( p1, p2 )
1418   tabtype *p1, *p2;
1419   {
1420        return( strcmp(p1->sym, p2->sym) );
1421   }
1422
1423   char    *yypstk( v, name )
1424   yystype *v;                       /* Pointer to value-stack item. */
1425   char    *name;                    /* Pointer to debug-stack item. */
1426   {
1427        static char buf[128];
1428        char           *text;
1429        tabtype        *tp, template;
1430
1431        template.sym = name;
1432        tp = (tabtype *) bsearch( &template, Tab, sizeof(Tab)/sizeof(*Tab),
1433                                                  sizeof(*Tab), tcmp);
1434
1435        sprintf( buf, "%04x ", v->num );      /* The first four characters in the */
1436        text = buf + 5;                       /* string are the numeric value of  */
1437                                              /* the current stack element.       */
1438                                              /* Other text is written at "text". */
1439        switch( tp ? tp->case_val : NONE )
1440        {
1441        case SYM_CHAIN:
1442                sprintf( text, "sym chain: %s",
1443                                v->p_sym ? sym_chain_str(v->p_sym) : "NULL" );
1444                break;
1445        case P_SYM:
1446                if( ! v->p_sym )
1447                    sprintf( text, "symbol: NULL" );
1448
1449                else if( IS_FUNCT(v->p_sym->type) )
1450                    sprintf( text, "symbol: %s(%s)=%s %1.40s",
1451                            v->p_sym->name,
1452                            sym_chain_str( v->p_sym->args ),
1453                            v->p_sym->type && *(v->p_sym->rname) ?
1454                                              v->p_sym->rname : "",
1455                            type_str(v->p_sym->type) );
1456                else
1457                    sprintf( text, "symbol: %s=%s %1.40s",
1458                            v->p_sym->name,
1459                            v->p_sym->type && *(v->p_sym->rname) ?
1460                                              v->p_sym->rname : "",
1461                            type_str(v->p_sym->type) );
1462                break;
1463        case P_SPEC:
1464                if( !v->p_spec )
1465                    sprintf( text, "specifier: NULL" );
```

```
Listing 6.35. continued...
1466                    else
1467                        sprintf( text, "specifier: %s %s", attr_str( v->p_spec ),
1468                                                    noun_str( v->p_spec->noun ) );
1469                    break;
1470        case P_LINK:
1471                    if( !v->p_link )
1472                        sprintf( text, "specifier: NULL" );
1473                    else
1474                        sprintf( text, "link: %1.50s", type_str(v->p_link) );
1475                    break;
1476        case P_VALUE:
1477                    if( !v->p_val )
1478                        sprintf( text, "_value: NULL" );
1479                    else
1480                    {
1481                        sprintf( text, "%cvalue: %s %c/%u %1.40s",
1482                                    v->p_val->lvalue    ? 'l'             : 'r' ,
1483                                    *(v->p_val->name)   ? v->p_val->name : "--",
1484                                    v->p_val->is_tmp    ? 't'             : 'v' ,
1485                                    v->p_val->offset,
1486                                    type_str( v->p_val->type ) );
1487                    }
1488                    break;
1489        case P_SDEF:
1490                    if( !v->p_sdef )
1491                        sprintf( text, "structdef: NULL" );
1492                    else
1493                        sprintf( text, "structdef: %s lev %d, size %d",
1494                                                    v->p_sdef->tag,
1495                                                    v->p_sdef->level,
1496                                                    v->p_sdef->size);
1497                    break;
1498        case P_CHAR:
1499                    if( !v->p_sdef )
1500                        sprintf( text, "string: NULL" );
1501                    else
1502                        sprintf( text, "<%s>", v->p_char );
1503                    break;
1504        case NUM:
1505                    sprintf( text, "num: %d", v->num );
1506                    break;
1507        case ASCII:
1508                    sprintf( text, "ascii: '%s'", bin_to_ascii(v->ascii, 1) );
1509                    break;
1510        }
1511        return buf;
1512    }
```

Listing 6.36. *main.c*— `main()` and a Symbol-Table-Printing Hook

```
 1    #include <tools/debug.h>
 2
 3    int      main( argc, argv )
 4    char     **argv;
 5    {
 6        UX( yy_init_occs(); )    /* Needed for yacc, called automatically by occs. */
 7
 8        argc = yy_get_args( argc, argv );
 9
10        if( argc > 2 )            /* Generate trace if anything follows file name on */
11            enable_trace();       /* command line.                                    */
12
13        yyparse();
14    }
15
16    /*--------------------------------------------------------------------*/
17    yyhook_a()                    /* Print symbol table from debugger with ctrl-A. */
18    {                             /* Not used in yacc-generated parser.            */
19        static int   x = 0;
20        char         buf[32];
21
22        sprintf    ( buf, "sym.%d", x++ );
23        yycomment  ( "Writing symbol table to %s\n", buf );
24        print_syms ( buf );
25    }
26
27    yyhook_b()                    /* Enable/disable run-time trace with Ctrl-b.       */
28    {                             /* Not used in yacc-generated parser.               */
29                                  /* enable_trace() and disable_trace() are discussed */
30                                  /* below, when the gen() call is discussed.         */
31        char buf[32];
32        if( yyprompt( "Enable or disable trace? (e/d): ", buf, 0 ) )
33        {
34            if( *buf == 'e' ) enable_trace();
35            else              disable_trace();
36        }
37    }
```

6.5 The Lexical Analyzer

Now that we've seen the tokens and the value-stack definition, we can look at the lexical analyzer specification (in Listing 6.37). This file is essentially the analyzer at the end of Appendix D, but it's been customized for the current parser by adding an attribute-passing mechanism. The **union** on lines 18 to 28, which reflects the %union definition in the **occs** input file, is used to pass attributes back to the parser. For example, when an ASSIGNOP is recognized on line 115, the first character of the lexeme is attached to the token by assigning a value to yylval, which is of the same type as a value-stack element. (The **union** definition on lines 18 to 28 doubles as an **extern** definition of yylval.) The parser pushes the contents of yylval onto the value stack when it shifts the state representing the token onto the state stack.

Also note that a newline is now recognized explicitly on line 132. The associated action prints a comment containing the input line number to the compiler's output file so that you can relate one to the other when you're debugging the output. You could also use this action to pass input-line-number information to a debugger.

Listing 6.37. *c.lex*— C Lexical Analyzer

```
 1    /* Lexical analyzer specification for C. This is a somewhat extended version
 2     * of the one in Appendix D. The main difference is that it passes attributes
 3     * for some tokens back to the parser, using the yylval mechanism to push
 4     * the attribute onto the value stack.
 5     */
 6
 7    %{
 8    #include <stdio.h>
 9    #include <search.h>         /* Function prototype for bsearch().   */
10    #include <tools/debug.h> /* Needed by symtab.h.               */
11    #include <tools/hash.h>  /* Needed by symtab.h.               */
12    #include <tools/l.h>
13    #include <tools/compiler.h>
14    #include "yyout.h"       /* Token defs. created by occs. Yacc uses y.tab.h. */
15    #include "symtab.h"      /* Needed to pass attributes to parser.       */
16    #include "value.h"       /* ditto                                      */
17
18    extern union {                      /* This definition must duplicate the %union */
19        char        *p_char;        /* in c.y.                                    */
20        symbol      *p_sym;
21        link        *p_link;
22        structdef   *p_sdef;
23        specifier   *p_spec;
24        value       *p_value;
25        int         integer;
26        int         ascii;
27    }
28    yylval;                             /* Declared by occs in yyout.c. */
29
30    extern FILE *yycodeout;             /* Declared by occs in yyout.c  */
31
32    /*--------------------------------------------------------------------*/
33
34    #define YYERROR(text)  yyerror("%s\n", text);  /* Does nothing in UNIX lex. */
35
36    /*--------------------------------------------------------------------*/
37    %}
38
39    let     [_a-zA-Z]          /* Letter                                  */
40    alnum   [_a-zA-Z0-9]       /* Alphanumeric character                  */
41    h       [0-9a-fA-F]        /* Hexadecimal digit                       */
42    o       [0-7]             /* Octal digit                             */
43    d       [0-9]             /* Decimal digit                           */
44    suffix  [UuLl]            /* Suffix in integral numeric constant     */
45    white   [\x00-\x09\x0b\s]     /* White space: all control chars but \n */
46
47    %%
48    "/*"                    {
49                                int i;
50
51                                while( i = ii_input() )
52                                {
53                                    if( i < 0 )
54                                        ii_flushbuf();                /* Discard lexeme. */
55
```

Listing 6.37. continued...

```
56                                       else if( i == '*'  &&  ii_lookahead(1) == '/' )
57                                       {
58                                           ii_input();
59                                           break;                      /* Recognized comment.*/
60                                       }
61                                   }
62
63                               if( i == 0 )
64                                   yyerror( "End of file in comment\n" );
65                           }
66
67  \"(\\.|[^\"])*\"      { return STRING; }
68
69  \"(\\.|[^\"])*\n     yyerror("Adding missing \" to string constant\n");
70                       yymore();
71
72  0{o}*{suffix}?                           |
73  0x{h}+{suffix}?                          |
74  [1-9]{d}*{suffix}?                 return ICON ;
75
76  ({d}+|{d}+\.{d}*|{d}*\.{d}+)([eE][-+]?{d}+)?[fF]?   return FCON ;
77
78  "("                  return LP;
79  ")"                  return RP;
80  "{"                  return LC;
81  "}"                  return RC;
82  "["                  return LB;
83  "]"                  return RB;
84
85  "->"                 |
86  "."                  yylval.ascii = *yytext;
87                       return STRUCTOP;
88
89  "++"                 |
90  "--"                 yylval.ascii = *yytext;
91                       return INCOP;
92
93  [~!]                 yylval.ascii = *yytext;
94                       return UNOP;
95
96  "*"                  return STAR;
97
98  [/%]                 yylval.ascii = *yytext;
99                       return DIVOP;
100
101 "+"                  return PLUS;
102 "-"                  return MINUS;
103
104 <<|>>                yylval.ascii = *yytext;
105                      return SHIFTOP;
106
107 [<>]=?               yylval.ascii = yytext[1] ? (yytext[0]=='>' ? 'G' : 'L')
108                                     : (yytext[0]                 );
109                      return RELOP;
110
111 [!=]=                yylval.ascii = *yytext;
112                      return EQUOP;
113
```

→

Listing 6.37. continued...

```
114   [*/%+\-&|^]=                  |
115   (<<|>>)=                       yylval.ascii = *yytext;
116                                  return ASSIGNOP;
117
118   "="                           return EQUAL;
119   "&"                           return AND;
120   "^"                           return XOR;
121   "|"                           return OR;
122   "&&"                          return ANDAND;
123   "||"                          return OROR;
124   "?"                           return QUEST;
125   ":"                           return COLON;
126   ","                           return COMMA;
127   ";"                           return SEMI;
128   "..."                         return ELLIPSIS;
129
130   {let}{alnum}*                 return id_or_keyword( yytext );
131
132   \n                            fprintf(yycodeout, "\t\t\t\t\t\t\t\t\t/*%d*/\n", yylineno);
133   {white}+                      ;  /* ignore other white space */
134   %%
135
136   /*----------------------------------------------------------------*/
137
138   typedef struct                 /* Routines to recognize keywords */
139   {
140       char   *name;
141       int    val;
142   }
143   KWORD;
144
145   KWORD  Ktab[] =                /* Alphabetic keywords   */
146   {
147       { "auto",     CLASS       },
148       { "break",    BREAK       },
149       { "case",     CASE        },
150       { "char",     TYPE        },
151       { "continue", CONTINUE    },
152       { "default",  DEFAULT     },
153       { "do",       DO          },
154       { "double",   TYPE        },
155       { "else",     ELSE        },
156       { "enum",     ENUM        },
157       { "extern",   CLASS       },
158       { "float",    TYPE        },
159       { "for",      FOR         },
160       { "goto",     GOTO        },
161       { "if",       IF          },
162       { "int",      TYPE        },
163       { "long",     TYPE        },
164       { "register", CLASS       },
165       { "return",   RETURN      },
166       { "short",    TYPE        },
167       { "sizeof",   SIZEOF      },
168       { "static",   CLASS       },
169       { "struct",   STRUCT      },
170       { "switch",   SWITCH      },
171       { "typedef",  CLASS       },
172       { "union",    STRUCT      },
173       { "unsigned", TYPE        },
```

➡

```
Listing 6.37. continued...
174        { "void",      TYPE            },
175        { "while",     WHILE           }
176    };
177
178    static  int     cmp( a, b )
179    KWORD   *a, *b;
180    {
181        return strcmp( a->name, b->name );
182    }
183
184    int     id_or_keyword( lex )      /* Do a binary search for a */
185    char    *lex;                     /* possible keyword in Ktab */
186    {                                 /* Return the token if it's */
187        KWORD       *p;               /* in the table, NAME       */
188        KWORD       dummy;            /* otherwise.               */
189
190        dummy.name = lex;
191        p = bsearch( &dummy, Ktab, sizeof(Ktab)/sizeof(KWORD), sizeof(KWORD), cmp);
192
193        if( p )                                           /* It's a keyword. */
194        {
195            yylval.ascii = *yytext;
196            return p->val;
197        }
198        else if( yylval.p_sym = (symbol *) findsym( Symbol_tab, yytext ) )
199            return (yylval.p_sym->type->tdef) ? TTYPE : NAME ;
200        else
201            return NAME;
202    }
```

6.6 Declarations

6.6.1 Simple Variable Declarations

This section moves from data structures to analyzing the code that manipulates those data structures. Declaration processing involves two main tasks: (1) you must assemble the linked lists that represent the types, attach them to symbols, and put the resulting structures into the symbol table, and (2) you must both generate C-code definitions for variables at fixed addresses and figure the frame-pointer-relative offsets for automatic variables. Many of the productions in the grammar work in concert to produce a single definition. Since these productions are discussed piecemeal, you should take a moment and look at the overall structure of the grammar in Appendix C. The declarations are all handled first, at the top of the grammar.

An example variable-declaration parse.

The best way to understand how the code generation works is to follow along as the parser works on an explicit example. (This is also a good approach for adding the code-generation actions in the first place: run a short sample through the parser observing the order in which reductions occur. Since actions at the far right of productions are executed in the same sequence as the reductions, you can see where the various actions need to be placed.) I'll use the following input to demonstrate simple declarations:

```
long int *x, y;
```

The parse of that input is shown, in symbolic form, in Table 6.13.[14]

Table 6.13. A Parse of `long int *x, y;`

	Stack	Next Action Taken by Parser
1	*(empty)*	Reduce by *ext_def_list* →ε
2	*ext_def_list*	Shift **TYPE** *(long)*
3	*ext_def_list* **TYPE**	Reduce by *type_specifier*→**TYPE**
4	*ext_def_list type_specifier*	Reduce by *type_or_class* →*type_specifier*
5	*ext_def_list type_or_class*	Reduce by *specifiers*→*type_or_class*
6	*ext_def_list specifiers*	Shift **TYPE** *(int)*
7	*ext_def_list specifiers* **TYPE**	Reduce by *type_specifier*→**TYPE**
8	*ext_def_list specifiers type_specifier*	Reduce by *type_or_class* →*type_specifier*
9	*ext_def_list specifiers type_or_class*	Reduce by *specifiers*→*specifiers type_or_class*
10	*ext_def_list specifiers*	Reduce by *opt_specifiers*→*specifiers*
11	*ext_def_list opt_specifiers*	Shift **STAR**
12	*ext_def_list opt_specifiers* **STAR**	Shift **NAME** *(x)*
13	*ext_def_list opt_specifiers* **STAR NAME**	Reduce by *new_name*→**NAME**
14	*ext_def_list opt_specifiers* **STAR** *new_name*	Reduce by *var_decl*→*new_name*
15	*ext_def_list opt_specifiers* **STAR** *var_decl*	Reduce by *var_decl*→**STAR** *var_decl*
16	*ext_def_list opt_specifiers var_decl*	Reduce by *ext_decl*→*var_decl*
17	*ext_def_list opt_specifiers ext_decl*	Reduce by *ext_decl_list* →*ext_decl*
18	*ext_def_list opt_specifiers ext_decl_list*	Shift **COMMA**
19	*ext_def_list opt_specifiers ext_decl_list* **COMMA**	Shift **NAME** *(y)*
20	*ext_def_list opt_specifiers ext_decl_list* **COMMA NAME**	Reduce by *new_name*→**NAME**
21	*ext_def_list opt_specifiers ext_decl_list* **COMMA** *new_name*	Reduce by *var_decl*→*new_name*
22	*ext_def_list opt_specifiers ext_decl_list* **COMMA** *var_decl*	Reduce by *ext_decl*→*var_decl*
23	*ext_def_list opt_specifiers ext_decl_list* **COMMA** *ext_decl*	Reduce by *ext_decl_list* →*ext_decl_list* **COMMA** *ext_decl*
24	*ext_def_list opt_specifiers ext_decl_list*	Reduce by {3}→ε
25	*ext_def_list opt_specifiers ext_decl_list* {3}	Shift **SEMI**
26	*ext_def_list opt_specifiers ext_decl_list* {3} **SEMI**	Reduce by *ext_def*→*opt_specifiers ext_decl_list* {3} **SEMI**
27	*ext_def_list ext_def*	Reduce by *ext_def_list* →*ext_def_list ext_def*
28	*ext_def_list*	Reduce by *program*→*ext_def_list* *(accept)*

Since all actions are performed as part of a reduction, the best way to see how the code works is to follow the order of reductions during the parse. First, notice how the ε production in

```
ext_def_list
      : ext_def_list ext_def
      | /* epsilon */
```

(on line 189 of Listing 6.38) is done first. This is always the case in left-recursive list productions: the nonrecursive component (whether or not it's ε) must be reduced first in order to put the recursive left-hand side onto the stack.[15] In the current example, the

---

14. If you have the distribution disk mentioned in the Preface, you can use the visible parser to see the parse process in action. The file *c.exe* is an executable version of the compiler described in this chapter. Get the parse started by creating a file called *test.c* containing the single line:

      `long int *x, y;`

Then invoke the parser with the command: `c test.c`. Use the space bar to singlestep through the parse.

15. The nonrecursive element of a <u>right</u>-recursive list production is always done <u>last</u>.

parser must get an *ext_def_list* onto the stack in order to be able to reduce by *ext_def_list→ext_def_list ext_def* at some later time, and the only way to get that initial *ext_def_list* onto the stack is to reduce by *ext_def_list→ε*.

Listing 6.38. *c.y*— Initialization and Cleanup Productions

```
183   %%
184   program : ext_def_list { clean_up(); }
185         ;
186
187   ext_def_list
188         : ext_def_list ext_def
189         | /* epsilon */
190         {
191                 yydata(   "#include <tools/virtual.h>\n" );
192                 yydata(   "#define  T(x)\n"               );
193                 yydata(   "SEG(data)\n"                   );
194                 yycode(   "\nSEG(code)\n"                 );
195                 yybss (   "\nSEG(bss)\n"                  );
196         }
197         ;
```

Initializations done in nonrecursive list element.

Syntactically, a program is a list of external definitions because of the productions on lines 187 to 189 of Listing 6.38. A reduction by the ε production on line 189 is always the first action taken by the parser, regardless of the input. This behavior is exploited in the current compiler to do various initializations on lines 189 to 196 of Listing 6.38. The

Generate SEG directives.

appropriate SEG directives are generated at the tops of the various segments, and a **#include** for *tools/virtual.h* is output at the top of the data segment, which is at the top of the output file after the three segments are combined at the end of the compilation. I'll discuss the empty T() macro on line 192 in a moment.

The associated cleanup actions are all done in the previous production:

```
program : ext_def_list { clean_up(); }
```

on line 184. Remember, this is a bottom-up parser, so the reduction to the goal symbol is the last action taken by the parser. The clean_up() action coalesces the output streams and deletes temporary files.

Specifier processing.

After initializing via the ε production, the parser starts processing the specifier component of the declaration. All of the specifier productions are shown together in Listing 6.39. Three types of specifier lists are supported:

opt_specifiers	Zero or more types and storage classes mixed together.
specifiers	One or more types and storage classes mixed together.
type	One or more types. (No storage classes are permitted.)

Note that the parser is not checking semantics here. It just recognizes collections of possible types and storage classes without testing for illegal combinations like a **short long**.

Pointer to link used as an attribute.

The parser starts by shifting the **TYPE** token (**long** in the current input) and then reduces *type_specifier→***TYPE**. (on line 229 of Listing 6.38). The associated action calls new_type_spec(), which gets a new link and initializes it to a specifier of the correct type. A pointer to the link structure is attached to the *type_specifier* by assigning it to $$. From here on out, that pointer is on the value stack at the position corresponding to the *type_specifier*. If a storage class is encountered instead of a **TYPE**, the action on line 226 of Listing 6.39 is executed instead of the action on line 189. This action modifies the storage-class component of the link rather than the type, but is

Listing 6.39. *c.y*— Specifiers

```
198   opt_specifiers
199         : CLASS TTYPE {     set_class_bit(  0, $2->etype ); /* Reset class.    */
200                             set_class_bit( $1, $2->etype ); /* Add new class. */
201                             $$ = $2->type ;
202                       }
203         | TTYPE       {     set_class_bit(0, $1->etype);  /* Reset class bits.*/
204                             $$ = $1->type ;
205                       }
206         | specifiers
207         | /* empty */                                             %prec COMMA
208                       {
209                             $$        = new_link();
210                             $$->class = SPECIFIER;
211                             $$->NOUN  = INT;
212                       }
213         ;
214   specifiers
215         : type_or_class
216         | specifiers type_or_class { spec_cpy( $$, $2 );
217                                   discard_link_chain( $2 ); }
218         ;
219   type
220         : type_specifier
221         | type type_specifier   {  spec_cpy( $$, $2 );
222                                   discard_link_chain( $2 ); }
223         ;
224   type_or_class
225         : type_specifier
226         | CLASS                 {  $$ = new_class_spec( $1 );   }
227         ;
228   type_specifier
229         : TYPE                  { $$ = new_type_spec( yytext );   }
230         | enum_specifier        { $$ = new_type_spec( "int"  );   }
231         | struct_specifier      { $$ = new_link();
232                                   $$->class    = SPECIFIER;
233                                   $$->NOUN     = STRUCTURE;
234                                   $$->V_STRUCT = $1;
235                                 }
236         ;
```

otherwise the same as the earlier one. Both `new_type_spec()` and `new_class_-spec()` are in Listing 6.40.

The next reductions are *type_or_class→ type_specifier* and *specifiers→ type_or_class*, neither of which has an associated action. The pointer-to-link attribute is carried along with each reduction because of the default `$$=$1` action that is supplied by the parser. The pointer to the `link` created in the initial reduction is still on the value stack, but now at the position corresponding to the *specifiers* nonterminal.

type_or_class→ type_specifier
specifiers→ type_or_class

The parser now processes the **int**. It performs the same set of reductions that we just looked at, but this time it reduces by

specifiers→specifiers type_or_class

rather than by

specifiers→type_or_class

as was done earlier. (We're on line nine of Table 6.13. The associated action is on lines

Listing 6.40. *decl.c*— Create and Initialize a `link`

```
1    #include <stdio.h>
2    #include <stdlib.h>
3    #include <tools/debug.h>
4    #include <tools/hash.h>
5    #include <tools/l.h>
6    #include <tools/compiler.h>
7    #include <tools/c-code.h>
8
9    #include "symtab.h"
10   #include "value.h"
11   #include "proto.h"
12
13   /* DECL.C       This file contains support subroutines for those actions in c.y
14    *              that deal with declarations.
15    */
16
17   extern void  yybss(), yydata();
18
19   /*-------------------------------------------------------------------------*/
20
21   PUBLIC   link      *new_class_spec( first_char_of_lexeme )
22   int      first_char_of_lexeme;
23   {
24       /* Return a new specifier link with the sclass field initialized to hold
25        * a storage class, the first character of which is passed in as an argument
26        * ('e' for extern, 's' for static, and so forth).
27        */
28
29       link *p  = new_link();
30       p->class = SPECIFIER;
31       set_class_bit( first_char_of_lexeme, p );
32       return p;
33   }
34
35   /*-------------------------------------------------------------------------*/
36
37   PUBLIC   void      set_class_bit( first_char_of_lexeme, p )
38   int      first_char_of_lexeme;
39   link     *p;
40   {
41       /* Change the class of the specifier pointed to by p as indicated by the
42        * first character in the lexeme. If it's 0, then the defaults are
43        * restored (fixed, nonstatic, nonexternal). Note that the TYPEDEF
44        * class is used here only to remember that the input storage class
45        * was a typedef, the tdef field in the link is set true (and the storage
46        * class is cleared) before the entry is added to the symbol table.
47        */
48
49       switch( first_char_of_lexeme )
50       {
51       case 0:   p->SCLASS = FIXED;
52                 p->STATIC = 0;
53                 p->EXTERN = 0;
54                 break;
55
56       case 't': p->SCLASS  = TYPEDEF   ; break;
57       case 'r': p->SCLASS  = REGISTER  ; break;
```

```
     Listing 6.40. continued. . .
 58            case 's': p->STATIC   = 1         ; break;
 59            case 'e': p->EXTERN   = 1         ; break;
 60
 61            default : yyerror("INTERNAL, set_class_bit: bad storage class '%c'\n",
 62                                                     first_char_of_lexeme);
 63                      exit( 1 );
 64                      break;
 65            }
 66      }
 67
 68      /*-------------------------------------------------------------------*/
 69
 70      PUBLIC  link     *new_type_spec( lexeme )
 71      char     *lexeme;
 72      {
 73          /* Create a new specifier and initialize the type according to the indicated
 74           * lexeme. Input lexemes are: char const double float int long short
 75           *                            signed unsigned void volatile
 76           */
 77
 78          link *p  = new_link();
 79          p->class = SPECIFIER;
 80
 81          switch( lexeme[0] )
 82          {
 83          case 'c':    if( lexeme[1]=='h' )               /* char | const   */
 84                           p->NOUN = CHAR ;               /* (Ignore const.) */
 85                       break;
 86          case 'd':                                       /* double         */
 87          case 'f':    yyerror("No floating point\n");    /* float          */
 88                       break;
 89
 90          case 'i':    p->NOUN    = INT;     break;       /* int            */
 91          case 'l':    p->LONG    = 1;       break;       /* long           */
 92          case 'u':    p->UNSIGNED = 1;      break;       /* unsigned       */
 93
 94          case 'v':    if( lexeme[2] == 'i' )             /* void | volatile */
 95                           p->NOUN = VOID;                /* ignore volatile */
 96                       break;
 97          case 's':    break;                             /* short | signed */
 98          }                                               /* ignore both    */
 99
100          return p;
101      }
```

216 to 217 of Listing 6.40.) There are currently three attributes of interest: $1 and $$ (which is initialized to $1 by the parser before executing the action) hold a pointer to the link structure that was assembled when the **long** was processed; $2 points at the link for the new list element—the **int**. The action code merges the two structures by copying all relevant fields from $2 to $$. The second link ($2) is then discarded. The action is illustrated in Figure 6.14.

If additional types or storage classes are present in the input, the parser loops some more, creating new links for each new list element and merging those new links into the existing one, discarding the new link after it's merged.

Having collected the entire specifier list, the parser now reduces by *opt_specifiers* *opt_specifiers→specifiers* on line 206 of Listing 6.40. There is no action. If the

Figure 6.14. Merging Links

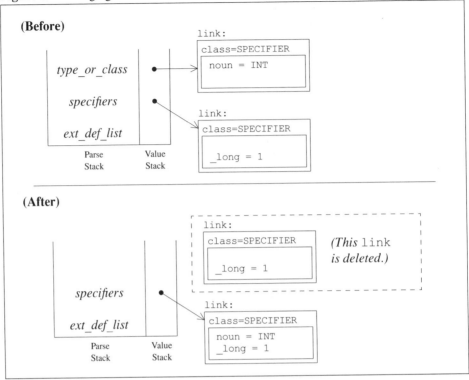

TTYPE, processing a **typedef**.

declaration were in terms of a **typedef**, *opt_specifiers*→**TTYPE** (just above the current production on line 203 of Listing 6.40) is executed instead of the list-collecting reductions we just looked at. The scanner attaches an attribute to the **TTYPE** token: a pointer to a `symbol` structure representing the **typedef**. The `name` field in the `symbol` is the type name rather than a variable name. The action on line 204 of Listing 6.40 passes the type string for this `symbol` back up the stack as *opt_specifiers'* attribute. This type chain differs from a normal one only in that the `tdef` bit is set in the leftmost `link` in the chain. The parser needs this information because a type that comes from a **typedef** could be an entire chain, including the declarators. A non-**typedef** declaration always yields a single specifier. If no specifier at all is present, then the action on lines 207 to 212 of Listing 6.40 is executed.[16] This action just sets up things as if an **int** had been found in the input.

The parser shelves the specifier on the value stack for a moment to move on to the declarator component of the declaration—it stores a pointer to the accumulated specifier `link` on the value stack as an attribute attached to the most recently pushed *specifier*

Declarator processing.

nonterminal. Declarator processing starts with a shift of the **STAR** and **NAME** tokens on lines 11 and 12 of Table 6.13 on page 523. The parser then starts reducing by the productions in Listing 6.41, below.

Identifier processing in declaration, *new_name*→**NAME**.

The first reduction is *new_name*→**NAME**. The action is on line 282 of Listing 6.41. There are two name productions to take care of two different situations in which names

---

16. `x;`, with no explicit type, is a perfectly legitimate declaration, the default **int** type and **extern** storage classes are used.

Listing 6.41. *c.y*— Variable Declarators

```
237   var_decl
238           : new_name                  %prec COMMA   /* This production is done first. */
239
240           | var_decl LP RP              {   add_declarator( $$, FUNCTION ); }
241           | var_decl LP var_list RP     {   add_declarator( $$, FUNCTION );
242                                             discard_symbol_chain( $3 );
243                                         }
244           | var_decl LB RB
245             {
246                     /* At the global level, this must be treated as an array of
247                      * indeterminate size; at the local level this is equivalent to
248                      * a pointer. The latter case is patched after the declaration
249                      * is assembled.
250                      */
251
252                     add_declarator( $$, ARRAY );
253                     $$->etype->NUM_ELE = 0;
254
255                     YYD( yycomment("Add POINTER specifier\n"); )
256             }
257
258           | var_decl LB const_expr RB
259             {
260                     add_declarator( $$, ARRAY );
261                     $$->etype->NUM_ELE = $3;
262
263                     YYD(yycomment("Add array[%d] spec.\n", $$->etype->NUM_ELE);)
264             }
265           | STAR var_decl                  %prec UNOP
266             {
267                     add_declarator( $$ = $2, POINTER );
268                     YYD( yycomment("Add POINTER specifier\n"); )
269             }
270
271           | LP var_decl RP { $$ = $2; }
272           ;
273
274   /*-------------------------------------------------------------------
275    * Name productions. new_name always creates a new symbol, initialized with the
276    * current lexeme. Name returns a preexisting symbol with the associated name
277    * (if there is one); otherwise, the symbol is allocated. The NAME token itself
278    * has a NULL attribute if the symbol doesn't exist, otherwise it returns a
279    * pointer to a "symbol" for the name.
280    */
281
282   new_name: NAME   {  $$ = new_symbol( yytext, Nest_lev );   }
283           ;
284
285   name    : NAME   {  if( !$1 || $1->level != Nest_lev )
286                           $$ = new_symbol( yytext, Nest_lev );
287                    }
288           ;
```

are used. Normally, the scanner looks up all identifiers in the symbol table to see whether or not they represent types so that it can return a **TTYPE** token when appropriate. In order to avoid unnecessary lookups, the scanner attaches a symbol-table pointer for an existing identifier to the **NAME** token if the identifier is in the table, otherwise the

Interaction between scanner and code generator via symbol table.

name→**NAME**.

attribute is NULL. This way the table lookup doesn't have to be done a second time in the code-generation action. The *new_name* takes care of newly-created identifiers. It ignores this passed-back symbol pointer, and allocates a new symbol structure, passing a pointer to the symbol back up the parse tree as an attribute attached to the *new_name* nonterminal. The *name*→**NAME** action (on lines 285 to 286, of Listing 6.41) uses the existing symbol. The test on line 285 identifies whether the returned symbol is at the current scoping level. If it is not, then the parser assumes that this is a new symbol (such as a local variable) that just happens to have the same name as an existing one, and allo-

Nest_lev.

cates a new symbol structure. Nest_lev keeps track of the current scope level; it is declared in Listing 6.42, which is part of the **occs**-input-file definitions section.

Listing 6.42. *c.y*— Identify Nesting Level (from **Occs** Definitions Section)

```
119    %{
120    int      Nest_lev;        /* Current block-nesting level.            */
121    %}
```

var_dcl→ *new_name*.

The next reduction, on line 15 of Table 6.13 on page 523), is *var_dcl*→*new_name*. The production is on line 238 of Listing 6.42. The only action is the implicit $$=$1, which causes the symbol pointer returned from *new_name* to be passed further up the tree, attached to the *var_dcl*. The %prec at the right of the line eliminates a shift/reduce conflict by assigning a very low precedence to the current production—the technique is discussed in Appendix E.

var_decl → **STAR** *var_decl*.

add_declarator().

The parser reduces by *var_decl*→**STAR** *var_decl* next. (We're moving from line 15 to line 16 of Table 6.13 on page 523—the action is on line 265 of Listing 6.42.) The action calls add_declarator() to add a pointer-declarator link to the type chain in the symbol that was created when the name was processed. The process is similar to that used to assemble an NFA in Chapter Two. Figure 6.15 shows the parse and value stacks both before and after this reduction is performed.

Note that the synthesized attribute for every right-hand side of this production is the same symbol structure that was allocated when the name was processed. The actions just add link structures to the symbol's type chain.

var_decl

If the declaration had been **int** **x, both stars would have been shifted initially, and the current reduction would have executed twice in succession, thereby adding a second pointer-declarator link to the end of the type chain in the symbol structure. The other productions that share the *var_decl* left-hand side do similar things, adding declarator links either for arrays or for functions, as appropriate, to the end of the type chain in the current symbol structure. Note that the actions on lines 240 to 243 handle the "function" component of a function-pointer declaration. I'll look at function declarations, including the *var_list* nonterminal, in a moment—briefly, the *var_list* takes care of function prototypes; the associated attribute is a pointer to the head of a linked list of symbol structures, one for each function argument. The action here just discards all the symbols in the list. Similarly, *const_expr* (on line 258) handles integer-constant expressions. This production is also discussed below, but the associated attribute is an integer. I'm using the <num> field in the value-stack union to hold the value.

Dummy *const_expr* pro- duction used for grammar development.

As an aside, a minor problem came up when adding the actions to the grammar—you can't do the expression-processing actions until the declarations are finished, but you need to use a constant expression to process an array declaration. I solved the problem by providing a dummy action of the form:

Figure 6.15. Adding Declarators to the Type Chain

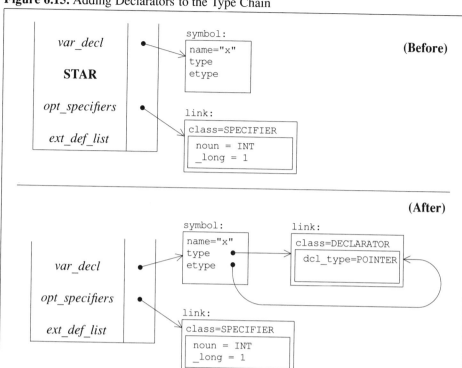

```
const_expr : expr { $$ = 10; }
           ;
```

until the declarations were working. The action was later replaced with something more reasonable.

When the parser finishes with the declarator elements (when the lookahead is a **COMMA**), the type chain in the `symbol` structure holds a linked list of declarator `links`, and the specifier is still on the value stack at a position corresponding to the *opt_specifiers* nonterminal. The comma is shifted, and the parser goes through the entire declarator-processing procedure again for the y (on lines 20 to 23 of Table 6.13 on page 523).

Now the parser starts to create the cross links for symbol-table entry—the links that join declarations for all variables at the current scoping level. It does this using the productions in Listing 6.43. The first reduction of interest is *ext_decl_list→ext_decl* executed on line 17 of Table 6.13. The associated action, on line 298 of Listing 6.43, puts a `NULL` pointer onto the value stack. This pointer marks the end of the linked list. The parse proceeds as just described, until the declaration for y has been processed, whereupon the parser links the two declarations together. The parse and value stacks, just before and just after the reduction by:

ext_decl_list→ext_decl_list **COMMA** *ext_decl*

are shown in Figure 6.16. and the code that does the linking is on lines 308 to 313 of Listing 6.43. If there were more comma-separated declarators in the input, the process would continue in this manner, each successive element being linked to the head of the list in turn.

Create cross links.
ext_decl_list → ext_decl.

ext_decl_list→
   ext_decl_list
   COMMA *ext_decl.*

Listing 6.43. *c.y*— Function Declarators

```
289    /*---------------------------------------------------------------
290     * Global declarations: take care of the declarator part of the declaration.
291     * (The specifiers are handled by specifiers).
292     * Assemble the declarators into a chain, using the cross links.
293     */
294
295    ext_decl_list
296            : ext_decl
297            {
298                    $$->next = NULL;                        /* First link in chain. */
299            }
300            | ext_decl_list COMMA ext_decl
301            {
302                    /* Initially, $1 and $$ point at the head of the chain.
303                     * $3 is a pointer to the new declarator.
304                     */
305
306                    $3->next = $1;
307                    $$      = $3;
308            }
309            ;
310
311    ext_decl
312            : var_decl
313            | var_decl EQUAL initializer { $$->args = (symbol *)$3; }
314            | funct_decl
315            ;
316
```

Initializers, symbol.args.

The only other issue of interest is the initializer, used on line 313 of Listing 6.43. I'll defer discussing the details of initializer processing until expressions are discussed, but the attribute associated with the initializer is a pointer to the head of a linked list of structures that represent the initial values. The `args` field of the `symbol` structure is used here to remember this pointer. You must use a cast to get the types to match.

Function declarators, *funct_decl*.

Before proceeding with the sample parse, it's useful to back up a notch and finish looking at the various declarator productions. There are two types of declarators not used in the current example, function declarators and abstract declarators. The function-processing productions start in Listing 6.44. First, notice the *funct_decl* productions are almost identical to the *var_decl* productions that were examined earlier. They both assemble linked lists of declarator `links` in a `symbol` structure that is passed around as an attribute. The only significant additions are the right-hand sides on lines 329 to 341, which handle function arguments.

Function-argument declarations.

The same *funct_decl* productions are used both for function declarations (**extern**s and prototypes) and function definitions (where a function body is present)—remember, these productions are handling only the declarator component of the declaration. The situation is simplified because prototypes are ignored. If they were supported, you'd have to detect semantic errors such as the following one in which the arguments don't have names. The parser accepts the following input without errors:

```
foo( int, long )
{
    /* body */
}
```

Figure 6.16. A Reduction by *ext_decl_list*→*ext_decl_list* **COMMA** *ext_decl*

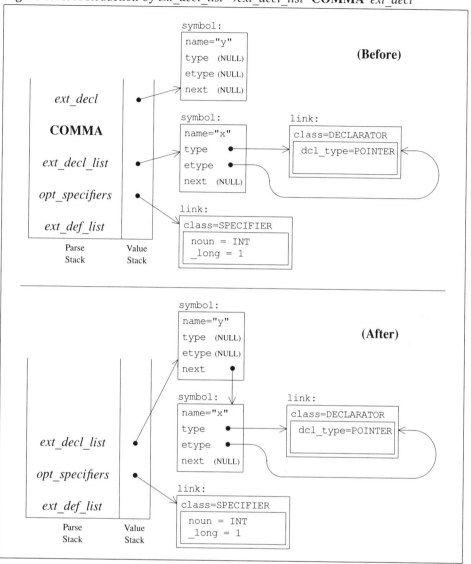

The `Nest_lev` variable is modified in the imbedded actions on lines 329 and 335 because function arguments are actually at the inner scoping level.

The function arguments can take two forms. A *name_list* is a simple list of names, as *name_list,* used for arguments in the older, K&R style, declaration syntax:

```
hobbit( frito, bilbo, spam )
short frito, bilbo;
```

A *var_list* takes care of both the new, C++-style syntax:

```
hobbit( short frito, short bilbo, int spam );
```

and function prototypes that use abstract declarators (declarations without names) such as the following:

```
hobbit( short, short, int );
```

All of these forms are recognized by the parser, but the last one is just ignored in the

Listing 6.44. *c.y*— Function Declarators

```
317   funct_decl
318         : STAR funct_decl              {   add_declarator( $$ = $2 , POINTER ); }
319         | funct_decl LB RB             {   add_declarator( $$, ARRAY );
320                                            $$->etype->NUM_ELE = 0;
321                                        }
322         | funct_decl LB const_expr RB {   add_declarator( $$, ARRAY );
323                                            $$->etype->NUM_ELE = $3;
324                                        }
325         | LP funct_decl RP             {   $$ = $2;                          }
326         | funct_decl LP RP             {   add_declarator( $$, FUNCTION ); }
327         | new_name LP RP               {   add_declarator( $$, FUNCTION ); }
328
329         | new_name LP { ++Nest_lev; } name_list { --Nest_lev; } RP
330           {
331                 add_declarator( $$, FUNCTION );
332
333                 $4        = reverse_links( $4 );
334                 $$->args = $4;
335           }
336         | new_name LP { ++Nest_lev; } var_list { --Nest_lev; } RP
337           {
338                 add_declarator( $$, FUNCTION );
339                 $$->args = $4;
340           }
341         ;
342   name_list
343         : new_name                     {
344                                            $$->next         = NULL;
345                                            $$->type         = new_link();
346                                            $$->type->class  = SPECIFIER;
347                                            $$->type->SCLASS = AUTO;
348                                        }
349         | name_list COMMA new_name {
350                                            $$            = $3;
351                                            $$->next      = $1;
352                                            $$->type      = new_link();
353                                            $$->type->class  = SPECIFIER;
354                                            $$->type->SCLASS = AUTO;
355                                        }
356         ;
357   var_list
358         : param_declaration                       { if($1) $$->next = NULL; }
359         | var_list COMMA param_declaration        { if($3)
360                                                      {
361                                                          $$       = $3;
362                                                          $3->next = $1;
363                                                      }
364                                                    }
365         ;
366   param_declaration
367         : type   var_decl          { add_spec_to_decl($1,  $$ = $2  ); }
368         | abstract_decl            { discard_symbol  ($1); $$ = NULL ; }
369         | ELLIPSIS                 {                       $$ = NULL ; }
370         ;
```

present application: The *abstract_decl* production used on line 368 of Listing 6.44 creates a `symbol` structure, just like the ones we've been discussing. There's no name, however. The action on line 368 just throws it away. Similarly, the **ELLIPSIS** that's used for ANSI variable-argument lists is just ignored on the next line.

The *name_list* and *var_list* productions are found on lines 342 to 365 of Listing 6.44. They differ from one another in only one significant way: A *name_list* creates a linked list of `symbols`, one for each name in the list, and the type chains for all these symbols are single specifier `links` representing **int**s. A *var_list* takes the types from the declarations rather than supplying an **int** type. By the time the parser gets back up to lines 329 or 336 of Listing 6.45-1 the argument list will have have been processed, and the attribute attached to the *name_list* or *var_list* will be a pointer to the head of a linked list of `symbol` structures. The `$$->args = $4` attaches this list to the `args` field of the `symbol` that represents the function itself. Figure 6.17 shows the way that

```
hobbit( short frito, short bilbo, int spam );
```

is represented once all the processing is finished.

Figure 6.17. Representing `hobbit(`**`short`**` frito, `**`short`**` bilbo, `**`int`**` spam)`

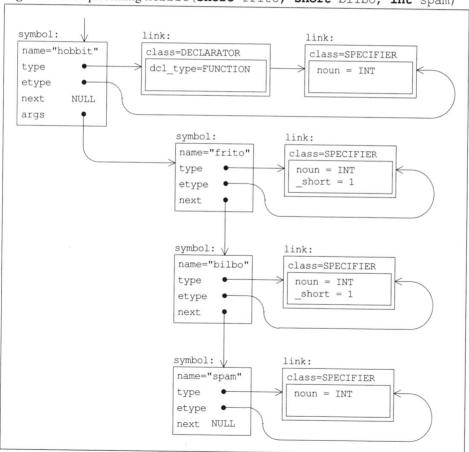

Note that the list of arguments is assembled in reverse order because, though the list is processed from left to right, each new element is added to the <u>head</u> of the list. The `reverse_links()` call on line 333 of Listing 6.44 goes through the linked list of `symbols` and reverses the direction of the `next` pointers. It returns a pointer to the new head of the chain (formerly the end of the chain).

Merge declarator and
specifier,
add_spec_to_decl().

One other subroutine is of particular interest: add_spec_to_decl(), called on
line 367 of Listing 6.44, merges together the specifier and declarator components of a
declaration. It's shown in Listing 6.45, below. Passed a pointer to a link that
represents the specifier, and a pointer symbol that contains a type chain representing the
declarator, it makes a copy of the specifier link [with the clone_type() call on line
132] and tacks the copy onto the end of the type chain.

Abstract declarators.

The last kind of declarator in the grammar is an abstract declarator, handled in Listing 6.46, below. If abstract declarators were used only for declarations, the productions
on lines 371 to 388 could be devoid of actions. You need abstract declarators for the cast
operator and **sizeof** statement, however. The actions here work just like all the other
declarator productions; the only difference is that the resulting symbol attribute has a
type but no name. The symbol structure is allocated on line 380—the ε production
takes the place of the identifier in the earlier declarator productions.

Returning to the parse in Table 6.13 on page 523, the parser has just finished with the
ext_decl_list and is about to reduce by {3}→ε. This production is supplied by **occs** to
process the imbedded action on lines 390 to 401 of Listing 6.47, below. **Occs** translates:

```
ext_def : opt_specifiers ext_decl_list { action... } SEMI
        ;
```

as follows:

```
ext_def : opt_specifiers ext_decl_list {3} SEMI
        ;
```

```
{3}     : /* empty */ { action... }
        ;
```

so that it can do the imbedded action as part of a reduction.

The action does three things: it merges the specifier and declarator components of
the declaration, puts the new declarations into the symbol table, and generates the actual
declarations in the output. The action must precede the **SEMI** because of a problem
caused by the way that the parser and lexical analyzer interact with one another. The
lexical analyzer uses the symbol table to distinguish identifiers from the synthetic types
created by a **typedef**, but symbol-table entries are also put into the symbol table by the
current production. The problem is that the input token is used as a lookahead symbol.
It can be read well in advance of the time when it is shifted, and several reductions can
occur between the read and the subsequent shift. In fact, the lookahead is required to
know which reductions to perform. So the next token is always read immediately after
shifting the previous token. Consider the following code:

Problems with scanner,
code-generator interac-
tion

```
typedef int itype;
itype      x;
```

If the action that adds the new type to the symbol table followed the SEMI in the grammar, the following sequence of actions would occur:

- Shift the SEMI, and read the lookahead symbol. itype has not been added to the
  symbol table yet, so the scanner returns a **NAME** token.
- Reduce by *ext_def*→{opt_specifiers ext_decl_list} **SEMI**, adding the itype to the
  symbol table.

The problem is solved by moving the action forward in the production, so that the parser
correctly acts as follows:

Listing 6.45. *decl.c*— Add a Specifier to a Declaration

```
102   void      add_spec_to_decl( p_spec, decl_chain )
103   link      *p_spec;
104   symbol    *decl_chain;
105   {
106       /* p_spec is a pointer either to a specifier/declarator chain created
107        * by a previous typedef or to a single specifier. It is cloned and then
108        * tacked onto the end of every declaration chain in the list pointed to by
109        * decl_chain. Note that the memory used for a single specifier, as compared
110        * to a typedef, may be freed after making this call because a COPY is put
111        * into the symbol's type chain.
112        *
113        * In theory, you could save space by modifying all declarators to point
114        * at a single specifier. This makes deletions much more difficult, because
115        * you can no longer just free every node in the chain as it's used. The
116        * problem is complicated further by typedefs, which may be declared at an
117        * outer level, but can't be deleted when an inner-level symbol is
118        * discarded. It's easiest to just make a copy.
119        *
120        * Typedefs are handled like this: If the incoming storage class is TYPEDEF,
121        * then the typedef appeared in the current declaration and the tdef bit is
122        * set at the head of the cloned type chain and the storage class in the
123        * clone is cleared; otherwise, the clone's tdef bit is cleared (it's just
124        * not copied by clone_type()).
125        */
126
127       link *clone_start, *clone_end ;
128       link **p;
129
130       for( ; decl_chain ; decl_chain = decl_chain->next )
131       {
132           if( !(clone_start = clone_type(p_spec, &clone_end)) )
133           {
134               yyerror("INTERNAL, add_typedef_: Malformed chain (no specifier)\n");
135               exit( 1 );
136           }
137           else
138           {
139               if( !decl_chain->type )                        /* No declarators. */
140                   decl_chain->type = clone_start ;
141               else
142                   decl_chain->etype->next = clone_start;
143
144               decl_chain->etype = clone_end;
145
146               if( IS_TYPEDEF(clone_end) )
147               {
148                   set_class_bit( 0, clone_end );
149                   decl_chain->type->tdef = 1;
150               }
151           }
152       }
153   }
```

Listing 6.46. *c.y*— Abstract Declarators

```
371    abstract_decl
372           : type   abs_decl    {      add_spec_to_decl   ( $1, $$ = $2 ); }
373           | TTYPE  abs_decl    {
374                                       $$ = $2;
375                                       add_spec_to_decl( $1->type, $2 );
376                               }
377           ;
378
379    abs_decl
380           : /* epsilon */              { $$ = new_symbol("",0);                  }
381           | LP abs_decl RP LP RP       { add_declarator( $$ = $2, FUNCTION ); }
382           | STAR abs_decl              { add_declarator( $$ = $2, POINTER  ); }
383           | abs_decl LB            RB { add_declarator( $$,       POINTER  ); }
384           | abs_decl LB const_expr RB { add_declarator( $$,       ARRAY    );
385                                         $$->etype->NUM_ELE = $3;
386                                       }
387           | LP abs_decl RP            { $$ = $2; }
388           ;
```

- Reduce by {3}→ε, adding the itype to the symbol table.
- Shift the SEMI, and read the lookahead symbol. itype is in the symbol table this time, so the scanner returns a **TTYPE** token.
- Reduce by *ext_def*→{opt_specifiers ext_decl_list} {3} **SEMI**.

Listing 6.47. *c.y*— High-Level, External Definitions (Part One)

```
389    ext_def : opt_specifiers ext_decl_list
390            {
391                   add_spec_to_decl( $1, $2 );
392
393                   if( !$1->tdef )
394                       discard_link_chain( $1 );
395
396                   add_symbols_to_table          ( $2 = reverse_links( $2 ) );
397                   figure_osclass                ( $2    );
398                   generate_defs_and_free_args   ( $2    );
399                   remove_duplicates             ( $2    );
400            }
401            SEMI
402
403            /* There are additional right-hand sides listed in subsequent listings.
404             */
```

The action on lines 390 to 401 of Listing 6.47 needs some discussion. The attribute associated with the *ext_decl_list* at $2 is a pointer to a linked list of symbol structures, one for each variable in the declarator list. The attribute associated with *opt_specifiers* at $1 is one of two things: either the specifier component of a declaration, or, if the declaration used a synthetic type, the complete type chain as was stored in the symbol-table entry for the **typedef**. In both cases, the add_spec_to_decl() call on line 391 modifies every type chain in the list of symbols by adding a copy of the type chain passed in as the first argument to the end of each symbol's type chain. Then, if the current specifier didn't come from a **typedef**, the extra copy is discarded on line 394. The symbols are added to symbol table on line 396. The figure_osclass() call on line 397 determines the output storage class of all symbols in the chain, `generate_defs_and_free_args()` outputs the actual C-code definitions, and `remove_duplicates()` destroys any duplicate declarations in case a declaration and definition of a global variable are both present. All of these subroutines are in Listings 6.48 and 6.49, below.

Listing 6.48. *decl.c*— Symbol-Table Manipulation and C-code Declarations

```
154   void      add_symbols_to_table( sym )
155   symbol   *sym;
156   {
157       /* Add declarations to the symbol table.
158        *
159        * Serious redefinitions (two publics, for example) generate an error
160        * message. Harmless redefinitions are processed silently. Bad code is
161        * generated when an error message is printed. The symbol table is modified
162        * in the case of a harmless duplicate to reflect the higher precedence
163        * storage class: (public == private) > common > extern.
164        *
165        * The sym->rname field is modified as if this were a global variable (an
166        * underscore is inserted in front of the name). You should add the symbol
167        * chains to the table before modifying this field to hold stack offsets
168        * in the case of local variables.
169        */
170
171       symbol *exists;                  /* Existing symbol if there's a conflict.    */
172       int      harmless;
173       symbol *new;
174
175       for(new = sym; new ; new = new->next )
176       {
177           exists = (symbol *) findsym(Symbol_tab, new->name);
178
179           if( !exists || exists->level != new->level )
180           {
181               sprintf ( new->rname, "_%1.*s", sizeof(new->rname)-2, new->name);
182               addsym  ( Symbol_tab, new );
183           }
184           else
185           {
186               harmless        = 0;
187               new->duplicate = 1;
188
189               if( the_same_type( exists->type, new->type, 0) )
190               {
191                   if( exists->etype->OCLASS==EXT || exists->etype->OCLASS==COM )
192                   {
193                       harmless = 1;
194
195                       if( new->etype->OCLASS != EXT )
196                       {
197                           exists->etype->OCLASS = new->etype->OCLASS;
198                           exists->etype->SCLASS = new->etype->SCLASS;
199                           exists->etype->EXTERN = new->etype->EXTERN;
200                           exists->etype->STATIC = new->etype->STATIC;
201                       }
202                   }
203               }
```

Listing 6.48. continued...

```
204                     if( !harmless )
205                         yyerror("Duplicate declaration of %s\n", new->name );
206                 }
207             }
208     }
209
210     /*----------------------------------------------------------------------*/
211
212     void      figure_osclass( sym )
213     symbol   *sym;
214     {
215         /* Go through the list figuring the output storage class of all variables.
216          * Note that if something is a variable, then the args, if any, are a list
217          * of initializers. I'm assuming that the sym has been initialized to zeros;
218          * at least the OSCLASS field remains unchanged for nonautomatic local
219          * variables, and a value of zero there indicates a nonexistent output class.
220          */
221
222         for( ; sym ; sym = sym->next )
223         {
224             if( sym->level == 0 )
225             {
226                 if( IS_FUNCT( sym->type ) )
227                 {
228                     if      ( sym->etype->EXTERN )  sym->etype->OCLASS = EXT;
229                     else if ( sym->etype->STATIC )  sym->etype->OCLASS = PRI;
230                     else                            sym->etype->OCLASS = PUB;
231                 }
232                 else
233                 {
234                     if      ( sym->etype->STATIC )  sym->etype->OCLASS = PRI;
235                     if      ( sym->args         )  sym->etype->OCLASS = PUB;
236                     else                            sym->etype->OCLASS = COM;
237                 }
238             }
239             else if( sym->type->SCLASS == FIXED )
240             {
241                 if      (  IS_FUNCT ( sym->type ))  sym->etype->OCLASS = EXT;
242                 else if (! IS_LABEL ( sym->type ))  sym->etype->OCLASS = PRI;
243             }
244         }
245     }
246
247     /*----------------------------------------------------------------------*/
248
249     void     generate_defs_and_free_args( sym )
250     symbol  *sym;
251     {
252         /* Generate global-variable definitions, including any necessary
253          * initializers. Free the memory used for the initializer (if a variable)
254          * or argument list (if a function).
255          */
256
257         for( ; sym ; sym = sym->next )
258         {
259             if( IS_FUNCT(sym->type) )
260             {
261                 /* Print a definition for the function and discard arguments
262                  * (you'd keep them if prototypes were supported).
263                  */
```

Listing 6.48. continued...

```
264
265                  yydata( "external\t%s();\n", sym->rname );
266                  discard_symbol_chain( sym->args );
267                  sym->args = NULL;
268          }
269      else if( IS_CONSTANT(sym->etype) || sym->type->tdef )
270      {
271          continue;
272      }
273      else if( !sym->args )                /* It's an uninitialized variable. */
274      {
275          print_bss_dcl( sym );            /* Print the declaration.          */
276      }
277      else                                 /* Deal with an initializer.       */
278      {
279          var_dcl( yydata, sym->etype->OCLASS, sym, "=" );
280
281          if( IS_AGGREGATE( sym->type ) )
282              yyerror("Initialization of aggregate types not supported\n");
283
284          else if( !IS_CONSTANT( ((value *)sym->args)->etype ) )
285              yyerror("Initializer must be a constant expression\n");
286
287          else if( !the_same_type(sym->type, ((value *) sym->args)->type, 0) )
288              yyerror("Initializer: type mismatch\n");
289
290          else
291              yydata( "%s;\n", CONST_STR( (value *) sym->args ) );
292
293          discard_value( (value *)(sym->args) );
294          sym->args = NULL;
295      }
296   }
297 }
298
299 /*-------------------------------------------------------------------*/
300
301 symbol  *remove_duplicates( sym )
302 symbol  *sym;
303 {
304     /* Remove all nodes marked as duplicates from the linked list and free the
305      * memory. These nodes should not be in the symbol table. Return the new
306      * head-of-list pointer (the first symbol may have been deleted).
307      */
308
309     symbol *prev  = NULL;
310     symbol *first = sym;
311
312     while( sym )
313     {
314         if( !sym->duplicate )                /* Not a duplicate, go to the      */
315         {                                    /* next list element.              */
316             prev = sym;
317             sym  = sym->next;
318         }
319         else if( prev == NULL )              /* Node is at start of the list.   */
320         {
321             first = sym->next;
322             discard_symbol( sym );
323             sym = first;
```

→

Listing 6.48. continued...

```
324              }
325          else                                  /* Node is in middle of the list. */
326          {
327              prev->next = sym->next;
328              discard_symbol( sym );
329              sym = prev->next;
330          }
331      }
332      return first;
333  }
```

Listing 6.49. *decl.c* — Generate C-Code Definitions

```
334  void     print_bss_dcl( sym )      /* Print a declaration to the bss segment. */
335  symbol   *sym;
336  {
337      if( sym->etype->SCLASS != FIXED )
338          yyerror( "Illegal storage class for %s", sym->name );
339      else
340      {
341          if( sym->etype->STATIC  &&  sym->etype->EXTERN )
342              yyerror("%s: Bad storage class\n", sym->name );
343
344          var_dcl( yybss, sym->etype->OCLASS, sym, ";\n" );
345      }
346  }
347
348  /*--------------------------------------------------------------------*/
349
350  PUBLIC  void var_dcl( ofunct, c_code_sclass, sym, terminator )
351
352  void    (* ofunct)();      /* Pointer to output function (yybss or yydata).  */
353  int     c_code_sclass;     /* C-code storage class of symbol.                */
354  symbol *sym;               /* Symbol itself.                                 */
355  char    *terminator;       /* Print this string at end of the declaration.   */
356  {
357      /* Kick out a variable declaration for the current symbol. */
358
359      char suffix[32];
360      char *type           = "" ;
361      int  size            = 1  ;
362      link *p              = sym->type;
363      char *storage_class  = (c_code_sclass == PUB) ?  "public"    :
364                             (c_code_sclass == PRI) ?  "private"   :
365                             (c_code_sclass == EXT) ?  "external"  :  "common" ;
366      *suffix = '\0';
367
368      if( IS_FUNCT(p) )
369      {
370          yyerror("INTERNAL, var_dcl: object not a variable\n");
371          exit( 1 );
372      }
373
374      if( IS_ARRAY(p) )
375      {
```

```
Listing 6.49. continued...
376              for(; IS_ARRAY(p) ; p = p->next )
377                  size *= p->NUM_ELE ;
378
379              sprintf( suffix, "[%d]", size );
380          }
381
382      if( IS_STRUCT(p) )
383      {
384          ( *ofunct )( "\nALIGN(lword)\n" );
385          sprintf( suffix, "[%d]", size * p->V_STRUCT->size );
386      }
387
388      if( IS_POINTER(p) )
389          type = PTYPE;
390      else                                    /* Must be a specifier. */
391          switch( p->NOUN )
392          {
393          case CHAR:      type = CTYPE;                       break;
394          case INT:       type = p->LONG ? LTYPE : ITYPE;    break;
395          case STRUCTURE: type = STYPE;                      break;
396          }
397
398      ( *ofunct )( "%s\t%s\t%s%s%s%s", storage_class, type,
399                                       sym->rname, suffix, terminator );
400  }
```

6.6.2 Structure and Union Declarations

Now, let's back up for a moment and look at more-complex types: structures and unions. These were handled at a high level on line 231 of Listing 6.39 on page 525, where a *struct_specifier* is recognized in place of a **TYPE** token. For example, everything from the **struct** up to the name is a *struct_specifier* in the following declaration:

struct_specifier.

```
struct tag
{
    int  tinker;
    long tailor;
    char soldier;
    struct tag *spy;
}
name;
```

A parse for this declaration is shown in Table 6.14. There are several points of interest here. First, the **STRUCT** token is returned by the scanner for both the **struct** and **union** lexemes. The associated <ascii> attribute is the first character of the lexeme. In practice, the only difference between a structure and a union is the way that the offsets to each field are computed—in a union the offsets are all zero. Since the two data types are syntactically identical, you need only one token with an attribute that allows the code-generation action to distinguish the two cases.

STRUCT recognized for both **struct** and **union**. <ascii> attribute.

The structure tag is handled in the parse on lines 4 to 6 of Table 6.14. The associated actions are on lines 426 to 444 of Listing 6.50, below. There are two actions of interest, *opt_tag*→ε on line 427 takes care of those situations where an explicit tag is not present. An arbitrary name is generated on line 430, and a new struct_def is allocated on the next line. Then the definition (with no fields as of yet) is added to the structure table on line 433. A pointer to the new structure-table element is passed up as an attribute.

Structure tags.

opt_tag→ε

Table 6.14. Parsing a Structure Definition

	Stack	Next Action
1	*(empty)*	Reduce: *ext_def_list*→ε **DATA:** `#include` `<tools/virtual.h>` **DATA:** `#define` `T(x)` **DATA:** `SEG(data)` **CODE:** `SEG(code)` **BSS:** `SEG(bss)`
2	*ext_def_list*	Shift: **STRUCT**
3	*ext_def_list* **STRUCT**	Shift: **NAME**
4	*ext_def_list* **STRUCT NAME**	Reduce: *tag*→**NAME**
5	*ext_def_list* **STRUCT** *tag*	Reduce: *opt_tag*→*tag*
6	*ext_def_list* **STRUCT** *opt_tag*	Shift: **LC**
7	*ext_def_list* **STRUCT** *opt_tag* **LC**	Reduce: *def_list*→ε
8	*ext_def_list* **STRUCT** *opt_tag* **LC** *def_list*	Shift: **TYPE**
9	*ext_def_list* **STRUCT** *opt_tag* **LC** *def_list* **TYPE**	Reduce: *type_specifier*→**TYPE**
10	*ext_def_list* **STRUCT** *opt_tag* **LC** *def_list* *type_specifier*	Reduce: *type_or_class*→*type_specifier*
11	*ext_def_list* **STRUCT** *opt_tag* **LC** *def_list* *type_or_class*	Reduce: *specifiers*→*type_or_class*
12	*ext_def_list* **STRUCT** *opt_tag* **LC** *def_list* *specifiers*	Shift: **NAME**
13	*ext_def_list* **STRUCT** *opt_tag* **LC** *def_list* *specifiers* **NAME**	Reduce: *new_name*→**NAME**
14	*ext_def_list* **STRUCT** *opt_tag* **LC** *def_list* *specifiers* *new_name*	Reduce: *var_decl*→*new_name*
15	*ext_def_list* **STRUCT** *opt_tag* **LC** *def_list* *specifiers* *var_decl*	Reduce: *decl*→*var_decl*
16	*ext_def_list* **STRUCT** *opt_tag* **LC** *def_list* *specifiers* *decl*	Reduce: *decl_list*→*decl*
17	*ext_def_list* **STRUCT** *opt_tag* **LC** *def_list* *specifiers* *decl_list*	Reduce: {65}→ε
18	*ext_def_list* **STRUCT** *opt_tag* **LC** *def_list* *specifiers* *decl_list* {65}	Shift: **SEMI**
19	*ext_def_list* **STRUCT** *opt_tag* **LC** *def_list* *specifiers* *decl_list* {65} **SEMI**	Reduce: *def*→*specifiers decl_list* {65} **SEMI**
20	*ext_def_list* **STRUCT** *opt_tag* **LC** *def_list* *def*	Reduce: *def_list*→*def_list def*
21	*ext_def_list* **STRUCT** *opt_tag* **LC** *def_list*	Shift: **TYPE**
22	*ext_def_list* **STRUCT** *opt_tag* **LC** *def_list* **TYPE**	Reduce: *type_specifier*→**TYPE**
23	*ext_def_list* **STRUCT** *opt_tag* **LC** *def_list* *type_specifier*	Reduce: *type_or_class*→*type_specifier*
24	*ext_def_list* **STRUCT** *opt_tag* **LC** *def_list* *type_or_class*	Reduce: *specifiers*→*type_or_class*
25	*ext_def_list* **STRUCT** *opt_tag* **LC** *def_list* *specifiers*	Shift: **NAME**
26	*ext_def_list* **STRUCT** *opt_tag* **LC** *def_list* *specifiers* **NAME**	Reduce: *new_name*→**NAME**
27	*ext_def_list* **STRUCT** *opt_tag* **LC** *def_list* *specifiers* *new_name*	Reduce: *var_decl*→*new_name*
28	*ext_def_list* **STRUCT** *opt_tag* **LC** *def_list* *specifiers* *var_decl*	Reduce: *decl*→*var_decl*
29	*ext_def_list* **STRUCT** *opt_tag* **LC** *def_list* *specifiers* *decl*	Reduce: *decl_list*→*decl*
30	*ext_def_list* **STRUCT** *opt_tag* **LC** *def_list* *specifiers* *decl_list*	Reduce: {65}→ε
31	*ext_def_list* **STRUCT** *opt_tag* **LC** *def_list* *specifiers* *decl_list* {65}	Shift: **SEMI**
32	*ext_def_list* **STRUCT** *opt_tag* **LC** *def_list* *specifiers* *decl_list* {65} **SEMI**	Reduce: *def*→*specifiers decl_list* {65} **SEMI**
33	*ext_def_list* **STRUCT** *opt_tag* **LC** *def_list* *def*	Reduce: *def_list*→*def_list def*
34	*ext_def_list* **STRUCT** *opt_tag* **LC** *def_list*	Shift: **TYPE**
35	*ext_def_list* **STRUCT** *opt_tag* **LC** *def_list* **TYPE**	Reduce: *type_specifier*→**TYPE**
36	*ext_def_list* **STRUCT** *opt_tag* **LC** *def_list* *type_specifier*	Reduce: *type_or_class*→*type_specifier*
37	*ext_def_list* **STRUCT** *opt_tag* **LC** *def_list* *type_or_class*	Reduce: *specifiers*→*type_or_class*
38	*ext_def_list* **STRUCT** *opt_tag* **LC** *def_list* *specifiers*	Shift: **NAME**
39	*ext_def_list* **STRUCT** *opt_tag* **LC** *def_list* *specifiers* **NAME**	Reduce: *new_name*→**NAME**
40	*ext_def_list* **STRUCT** *opt_tag* **LC** *def_list* *specifiers* *new_name*	Reduce: *var_decl*→*new_name*
41	*ext_def_list* **STRUCT** *opt_tag* **LC** *def_list* *specifiers* *var_decl*	Reduce: *decl*→*var_decl*
42	*ext_def_list* **STRUCT** *opt_tag* **LC** *def_list* *specifiers* *decl*	Reduce: *decl_list*→*decl*
43	*ext_def_list* **STRUCT** *opt_tag* **LC** *def_list* *specifiers* *decl_list*	Reduce: {65}→ε
44	*ext_def_list* **STRUCT** *opt_tag* **LC** *def_list* *specifiers* *decl_list* {65}	Shift: **SEMI**

continued...

The action on lines 437 to 444 is used when a tag is present in the definition, as is the case in the current example. The incoming attribute for the **NAME** token is useless here because this attribute is generated by a symbol-table lookup, not a structure-table lookup. The action code looks up the name in the structure table and returns a pointer to the entry if it's there. Otherwise, a new structure-table element is created and added to

Table 6.14. Continued. Parsing a Structure Definition

	Stack	Next Action
45	*ext_def_list* **STRUCT** *opt_tag* **LC** *def_list specifiers decl_list* {65} **SEMI**	Reduce: *def→specifiers decl_list* {65} **SEMI**
46	*ext_def_list* **STRUCT** *opt_tag* **LC** *def_list def*	Reduce: *def_list→def_list def*
47	*ext_def_list* **STRUCT** *opt_tag* **LC** *def_list*	Shift: **STRUCT**
48	*ext_def_list* **STRUCT** *opt_tag* **LC** *def_list* **STRUCT**	Shift: **NAME**
49	*ext_def_list* **STRUCT** *opt_tag* **LC** *def_list* **STRUCT NAME**	Reduce: *tag→***NAME**
50	*ext_def_list* **STRUCT** *opt_tag* **LC** *def_list* **STRUCT** *tag*	Reduce: *struct_specifier→***STRUCT** *tag*
51	*ext_def_list* **STRUCT** *opt_tag* **LC** *def_list struct_specifier*	Reduce: *type_specifier→struct_specifier*
52	*ext_def_list* **STRUCT** *opt_tag* **LC** *def_list type_specifier*	Reduce: *type_or_class→type_specifier*
53	*ext_def_list* **STRUCT** *opt_tag* **LC** *def_list type_or_class*	Reduce: *specifiers→type_or_class*
54	*ext_def_list* **STRUCT** *opt_tag* **LC** *def_list specifiers*	Shift: **STAR**
55	*ext_def_list* **STRUCT** *opt_tag* **LC** *def_list specifiers* **STAR**	Shift: **NAME**
56	*ext_def_list* **STRUCT** *opt_tag* **LC** *def_list specifiers* **STAR NAME**	Reduce: *new_name→***NAME**
57	*ext_def_list* **STRUCT** *opt_tag* **LC** *def_list specifiers* **STAR** *new_name*	Reduce: *var_decl→new_name*
58	*ext_def_list* **STRUCT** *opt_tag* **LC** *def_list specifiers* **STAR** *var_decl*	Reduce: *var_decl→***STAR** *var_decl*
59	*ext_def_list* **STRUCT** *opt_tag* **LC** *def_list specifiers var_decl*	Reduce: *decl→var_decl*
60	*ext_def_list* **STRUCT** *opt_tag* **LC** *def_list specifiers decl*	Reduce: *decl_list→decl*
61	*ext_def_list* **STRUCT** *opt_tag* **LC** *def_list specifiers decl_list*	Reduce: {65}→ε
62	*ext_def_list* **STRUCT** *opt_tag* **LC** *def_list specifiers decl_list* {65}	Shift: **SEMI**
63	*ext_def_list* **STRUCT** *opt_tag* **LC** *def_list specifiers decl_list* {65} **SEMI**	Reduce: *def→specifiers decl_list* {65} **SEMI**
64	*ext_def_list* **STRUCT** *opt_tag* **LC** *def_list def*	Reduce: *def_list→def_list def*
65	*ext_def_list* **STRUCT** *opt_tag* **LC** *def_list*	Shift: **RC**
66	*ext_def_list* **STRUCT** *opt_tag* **LC** *def_list* **RC**	Reduce: *struct_specifier→***STRUCT** *opt_tag* **LC** *def_list* **RC**
67	*ext_def_list struct_specifier*	Reduce: *type_specifier→struct_specifier*
68	*ext_def_list type_specifier*	Reduce: *type_or_class→type_specifier*
69	*ext_def_list type_or_class*	Reduce: *specifiers→type_or_class*
70	*ext_def_list specifiers*	Reduce: *opt_specifiers→specifiers*
71	*ext_def_list opt_specifiers*	Shift: **NAME**
72	*ext_def_list opt_specifiers* **NAME**	Reduce: *new_name→***NAME**
73	*ext_def_list opt_specifiers new_name*	Reduce: *var_decl→new_name*
74	*ext_def_list opt_specifiers var_decl*	Reduce: *ext_decl→var_decl*
75	*ext_def_list opt_specifiers ext_decl*	Reduce: *ext_decl_list→ext_decl*
76	*ext_def_list opt_specifiers ext_decl_list*	Reduce: {50}→ε **BSS:** ALIGN(lword) **BSS:** common record _name[16];
77	*ext_def_list opt_specifiers ext_decl_list* {50}	Shift: **SEMI**
78	*ext_def_list opt_specifiers ext_decl_list* {50} **SEMI**	Reduce: *ext_def→opt_specifiers ext_decl_list* {50} **SEMI**
79	*ext_def_list ext_def*	Reduce: *ext_def_list→ext_def_list ext_def*
80	*ext_def_list*	Reduce: *program→ext_def_list* *(Accept)*

the table, as before. This time the real tag is used rather than an arbitrary name, however.

The parser now moves on to process the field definitions, using the productions in Listing 6.51, below. These productions are effectively the same as the *ext_def_list* productions that handle global-variable definitions. In fact, most of the actions are identical. You need two sets of productions because function definitions (with bodies) are permitted only at the global level. As with an *ext_def,* the attribute associated with a *def* is a pointer to a cross-linked chain of symbols, one for each comma-separated declarator found in a definition, or NULL if no declarators were found. The *def_list* productions process a list of semicolon-terminated definitions, linking the cross-linked symbols

Structure-field definitions.

def_list

Listing 6.50. *c.y*— Structures

```
405     struct_specifier
406             : STRUCT opt_tag LC def_list RC
407                 {
408                         if( !$2->fields )
409                         {
410                                 $2->fields = reverse_links( $4 );
411
412                                 if( !illegal_struct_def( $2, $4 ) )
413                                         $2->size = figure_struct_offsets( $2->fields, $1=='s' );
414                         }
415                         else
416                         {
417                                 yyerror("Ignoring redefinition of %s", $2->tag );
418                                 discard_symbol_chain( $4 );
419                         }
420
421                         $$ = $2;
422                 }
423             | STRUCT tag                    { $$ = $2; }
424             ;
425
426     opt_tag : tag
427             | /* empty */    {
428                                     static unsigned label = 0;
429                                     static char      tag[16];
430                                     sprintf( tag, "%03d", label++ );
431
432                                     $$ = new_structdef( tag );
433                                     addsym( Struct_tab, $$ );
434                             }
435             ;
436
437     tag     : NAME          {
438                                     if( !($$=(structdef *) findsym(Struct_tab,yytext)))
439                                     {
440                                         $$          = new_structdef( yytext );
441                                         $$->level = Nest_lev;
442                                         addsym( Struct_tab, $$ );
443                                     }
444                             }
445             ;
```

from each individual definition together into a larger list. The new elements are added to the end of the list—the loop on line 450 finds the end. After the entire list is processed (on line 65 of the parse), the attribute associated with the *def_list* is a linked list of symbols, one for each field in the structure.

The parser now reduces by

struct_specifier→**STRUCT** *opt_tag* **LC** *def_list* **RC**

struct_specifier →
STRUCT *opt_tag* **LC**
def_list **RC**

Figuring offsets to fields.

The action is on lines 407 to 421 of Listing 6.50, and the subroutines that are used here are in Listing 6.52. The illegal_struct_def() call checks the field definitions to make sure that there's no recursion and that none of the fields are function definitions (as compared to function pointers, which are legal). The figure_struct_offsets() call on line 427 figures the offsets from the base address of the structure to the individual fields. The basic algorithm just traverses the linked list of symbols adding the

Listing 6.51. *c.y*— Local Variables and Function Arguments

```
446   def_list
447           : def_list def             {     symbol *p;
448                                             if( p = $2 )
449                                             {
450                                                 for(; p->next; p = p->next )
451                                                     ;
452                                                 p->next = $1;
453                                                 $$      = $2;
454                                             }
455                                       }
456           | /* epsilon */            {    $$ = NULL; }    /* Initialize end-of-list */
457           ;                                               /* pointer.              */
458
459   def
460           : specifiers decl_list { add_spec_to_decl( $1, $2 );     }
461                           SEMI    { $$ = $2;                        }
462
463           | specifiers SEMI       { $$ = NULL; }
464           ;
465
466   decl_list
467           : decl                     { $$->next = NULL;}
468           | decl_list COMMA decl
469           {
470               $3->next = $1;
471               $$       = $3;
472           }
473           ;
474
475   decl
476           : funct_decl
477           | var_decl
478           | var_decl EQUAL initializer {  yyerror( "Ignoring initializer.\n");
479                                           discard_value( $3 );
480                                       }
481           | var_decl COLON const_expr              %prec COMMA
482           | COLON const_expr                       %prec COMMA
483           ;
```

cumulative size of the preceding fields to the current offset. A minor problem is caused by alignment restrictions—padding may have to be added in the middle of the structure in order to get interior fields aligned properly. The structure is declared as a character array on line 76 of the parse (`record` is an alias for `byte`), and the individual fields are not declared explicitly—they are extracted from the proper location within the array when expressions are processed. As a consequence, the compiler has to worry about supplying padding that would normally be supplied by the assembler.

Structure-field alignment, padding.

This alignment problem actually arises in the current example. The first field is a two-byte int, but the second field requires four-byte alignment, so two spaces of padding have to be added to get the second field aligned properly. The situation is simplified, somewhat, by assuming that the first field is always aligned on a worst-case boundary. An `align(lword)` directive is generated by the compiler just above the actual variable definition for this purpose. Finally, note that the structure size is rounded up to be an even multiple of the worst-case alignment restriction on lines 464 and 465 of Listing 6.52 so that arrays of structures work correctly.

Structure size rounded up for arrays.

opt_specifier,   The structure definition is now reduced to an *opt_specifier*, and the parse continues just like a simple variable definition. One more right-hand side to *ext_def* is needed for structures. It is shown in Listing 6.53, and handles structure, union, and enumerated-type declarations that don't allocate space for a variable (such as a **struct** definition with a tag but no variable name). Note that the discard_link_chain() call on line 490 does not delete anything from the structure table.

Listing 6.52. *decl.c*— Structure-Processing Subroutines

```
401    int   illegal_struct_def( cur_struct, fields )
402    structdef *cur_struct;
403    symbol    *fields;
404    {
405        /* Return true if any of the fields are defined recursively or if a function
406         * definition (as compared to a function pointer) is found as a field.
407         */
408
409        for(; fields; fields = fields->next )
410        {
411            if( IS_FUNCT(fields->type) )
412            {
413                yyerror("struct/union member may not be a function");
414                return 1;
415            }
416            if( IS_STRUCT(fields->type) &&
417                            !strcmp( fields->type->V_STRUCT->tag, cur_struct->tag))
418            {
419                yyerror("Recursive struct/union definition\n");
420                return 1;
421            }
422        }
423        return 0;
424    }
425    /*------------------------------------------------------------------*/
426
427    int   figure_struct_offsets( p, is_struct )
428    symbol *p;                              /* Chain of symbols for fields. */
429    int     is_struct;                      /* 0 if a union.                */
430    {
431        /* Figure the field offsets and return the total structure size. Assume
432         * that the first element of the structure is aligned on a worst-case
433         * boundary. The returned size is always an even multiple of the worst-case
434         * alignment. The offset to each field is put into the "level" field of the
435         * associated symbol.
436         */
437
438        int   align_size, obj_size;
439        int   offset = 0;
440
441        for( ; p ; p = p->next )
442        {
443            if( !is_struct )                    /* It's a union. */
444            {
445                offset   = max( offset, get_sizeof( p->type ) );
446                p->level = 0;
447            }
448            else
449            {
450                obj_size  = get_sizeof    ( p->type );
451                align_size = get_alignment ( p->type );
```

```
Listing 6.52. continued...

452
453                  while( offset % align_size )
454                      ++offset;
455
456                  p->level  = offset;
457                  offset    += obj_size ;
458              }
459          }
460          /* Return the structure size: the current offset rounded up to the      */
461          /* worst-case alignment boundary. You need to waste space here in case   */
462          /* this is an array of structures.                                       */
463
464          while( offset % ALIGN_WORST )
465              ++offset ;
466          return offset;
467      }
468   /*-------------------------------------------------------------------------*/
469
470   int     get_alignment( p )
471   link    *p;
472   {
473      /* Returns the alignment--the number by which the base address of the object
474       * must be an even multiple. This number is the same one that is returned by
475       * get_sizeof(), except for structures which are worst-case aligned, and
476       * arrays, which are aligned according to the type of the first element.
477       */
478
479      int size;
480
481      if( !p )
482      {
483          yyerror("INTERNAL, get_alignment: NULL pointer\n");
484          exit( 1 );
485      }
486      if( IS_ARRAY( p )          ) return get_alignment( p->next );
487      if( IS_STRUCT( p )         ) return ALIGN_WORST;
488      if( size = get_sizeof( p ) ) return size;
489
490      yyerror("INTERNAL, get_alignment: Object aligned on zero boundary\n");
491      exit( 1 );
492   }
```

Listing 6.53. *c.y*— High-Level, External Definitions (Part Two)

```
484   /* ext_def :                                                        */
485          | opt_specifiers
486              {
487                  if( !($1->class == SPECIFIER && $1->NOUN == STRUCTURE) )
488                      yyerror("Useless definition (no identifier)\n");
489                  if( !$1->tdef )
490                      discard_link_chain( $1 );
491              }
492          SEMI
```

6.6.3 Enumerated-Type Declarations

The final definition recognized by the grammar is an enumerated type, handled at a high level on line 230 of Listing 6.39 (on page 525) where an *enum_specifier* is recognized in place of a **TYPE** token. An enumerated-type definition like this:

```
enum tag { rich_man, poor_man, beggar_man = 5, thief } x;
```

is treated as if the following had been used:

```
int x;
#define rich_man     0
#define poor_man     (rich_man + 1)
#define beggar_man   5
#define thief        (beggar_man + 1)
```

but the compiler recognizes the elements of the enumerated type directly rather than using a macro preprocessor. The high-level action in Listing 6.39 on page 525 just creates a specifier for an **int**, ignoring the tag component of the enumerated type.

Enumerated types are handled as integer constants.

The real work happens in the productions in Listing 6.54, which creates symbol-table entries for the symbolic constants (rich_man, and so forth). Internally, the compiler doesn't distinguish between an element of an enumerated type and any other integer constant. When an enumerated-type element is referenced, a symbol-table lookup is necessary to get the value; but thereafter, the value is handled just like any other integer constant. The Enum_val global variable keeps track of the current constant value. It is initialized to zero on line 507 of Listing 6.54, when the **enum** keyword is recognized. The enumerated-type elements are processed on lines 516 to 518. Enum_val is modified as necessary if an explicit value is given in the definition. In any event, do_enum(), in Listing 6.56, is called to create the symbol-table element, which is added to the table on the next line.

Enum_val, do_enum().

Listing 6.54. *c.y*— Enumerated Types

```
122  %{
123  int       Enum_val;        /* Current enumeration constant value  */
124  %}
```

```
493  enum_specifier
494          : enum name opt_enum_list      {  if( $2->type )
495                                                yyerror("%s: redefinition",$2->name);
496                                           else
497                                                discard_symbol($2);
498                                         }
499          | enum LC enumerator_list RC
500          ;
501
502  opt_enum_list
503          : LC enumerator_list RC
504          | /* empty */
505          ;
506
507  enum    : ENUM    { Enum_val = 0; }
508          ;
509
510  enumerator_list
511          : enumerator
512          | enumerator_list COMMA enumerator
513          ;
514
```

```
     Listing 6.54. continued...
515    enumerator
516              : name                       {    do_enum( $1, Enum_val++ );   }
517              | name EQUAL const_expr {     Enum_val = $3;
518                                            do_enum( $1, Enum_val++ );   }
519               ;
```

Listing 6.55. *decl.c*— Enumerated-Type Subroutines

```
493    PUBLIC void do_enum( sym, val )
494    symbol  *sym;
495    int     val;
496    {
497        if( conv_sym_to_int_const( sym, val ) )
498            addsym( Symbol_tab, sym );
499        else
500        {
501            yyerror( "%s: redefinition", sym->name );
502            discard_symbol( sym );
503        }
504    }
505    /*------------------------------------------------------------------*/
506    PUBLIC  int       conv_sym_to_int_const( sym, val )
507    symbol  *sym;
508    int     val;
509    {
510        /* Turn an empty symbol into an integer constant by adding a type chain
511         * and initializing the v_int field to val. Any existing type chain is
512         * destroyed. If a type chain is already in place, return 0 and do
513         * nothing, otherwise return 1. This function processes enum's.
514         */
515        link *lp;
516
517        if( sym->type )
518            return 0;
519        lp          = new_link();
520        lp->class   = SPECIFIER;
521        lp->NOUN    = INT;
522        lp->SCLASS  = CONSTANT;
523        lp->V_INT   = val ;
524        sym->type   = lp;
525        *sym->rname = '\0';
526        return 1;
527    }
```

6.6.4 Function Declarations

The next sort of declaration is a function declaration, handled, at the high level, by the remaining right-hand side to *ext_def*:

ext_def→opt_specifiers funct_decl { . . . } def_list { . . . } compound_stmt { . . . };

We'll look at the actual production in a moment. First, look at the parse of the following code in Table 6.15:

```
pooh(piglet, eeyore)
long eeyore;
{
}
```

This time I've shown the output as well as the parser actions; the three output streams are indicated by **CODE:**, **DATA:**, and **BSS:** in the table. The final compiler output (after the three streams have been merged) is in Listing 6.56.

Labels for `link`: generated after processing subroutine, printed above subroutine.

Output streams: code, data, bss.

Subroutine-prefix-and-suffix generation.

Prefix.

Suffix.

Arguments to `link` instruction.

Vspace, Tspace, Funct_name.

ext_def→opt_specifiers funct_decl {} *def_list* {} *compound_stmt* {}.

Note that the time at which the parser outputs something is not directly related to the position of that something in the output file. For example, the **#define**s for L0 and L1 at the <u>top</u> of the output file are not emitted by the parser until <u>after</u> the entire subroutine has been processed. This shuffling is accomplished by using two different output streams. The definitions are written to the *bss* stream; code is written to the *code* stream. The streams are merged in the following order: *data*, *bss*, and then *code*. So, all output to the *bss* stream appears <u>above</u> all *code*-stream output in the final program.

The code on lines nine to 14 of Listing 6.56 is generated at the top of every subroutine (with the obvious customizations). This block of instructions is called the subroutine *prefix*. The macro definitions on lines five and six of Listing 6.56 are also part of the prefix, even though these definitions end up at the top of the output file rather than immediately above the subroutine definition, because they are generated along with the rest of the prefix code. The code on lines 18 to 20 of Listing 6.56 is generated at the bottom of every subroutine and is called the subroutine *suffix*.

The L0 and L1 macros on lines five and six of Listing 6.56 are used as arguments in the `link` instruction at the top of the subroutine. The numeric component of the labels is unique—the next subroutine in the input file uses L2 and L3. In the current example, L0 holds the size, in bytes, of the local-variable region of the subroutine's stack frame; L1 holds the size of the temporary-variable region. Unfortunately, for reasons that I'll discuss in a moment, neither size is known until after the entire subroutine has been processed. The compiler solves the problems by generating the L0 and L1 labels at the same time that it outputs the `link` instruction. The label names are stored internally in the Vspace and Tspace arrays in Listing 6.57. The compiler puts the function name into Funct_name at the same time. Later on in the parse, after the subroutine has been processed and the sizes of the two regions are known, the compiler emits the **#define**s to the *data* segment, using the previously generated labels.[17]

The code to do all of the foregoing is in the first action of the following production:

ext_def→opt_specifiers funct_decl { . . . } def_list { . . . } compound_stmt { . . . };

found on lines 522 to 546 of Listing 6.58. The attribute attached to the *funct_decl* at $2

---

17. This technique is necessary only if you are generating code for a single-pass assembler. Two-pass assemblers let you define a label after it's used—the definition is picked up in the first pass and substitutions are made in the second. The two-pass VAX/UNIX assembler just generates the labels at the end of the subroutine code.

Table 6.15. A Parse of `pooh(piglet,eeyore)` **long** `eeyore;{}`

	Stack	Next Action
1	*(empty)*	Reduce: *ext_def_list* →ε **DATA: #include** `<tools/virtual.h>` **DATA: #define** `T(x)` **DATA:** `SEG(data)` **CODE:** `SEG(code)` **BSS:** `SEG(bss)`
2	*ext_def_list*	Reduce: *opt_specifiers*→ε
3	*ext_def_list opt_specifiers*	Shift: **NAME**
4	*ext_def_list opt_specifiers* **NAME**	Reduce: *new_name*→**NAME**
5	*ext_def_list opt_specifiers new_name*	Shift: **LP**
6	*ext_def_list opt_specifiers new_name* **LP**	Reduce: {28}→ε
7	*ext_def_list opt_specifiers new_name* **LP** {28}	Shift: **NAME**
8	*ext_def_list opt_specifiers new_name* **LP** {28} **NAME**	Reduce: *new_name*→**NAME**
9	*ext_def_list opt_specifiers new_name* **LP** {28} new_name	Reduce: *name_list*→*new_name*
10	*ext_def_list opt_specifiers new_name* **LP** {28} name_list	Shift: **COMMA**
11	*ext_def_list opt_specifiers new_name* **LP** {28} name_list **COMMA**	Shift: **NAME**
12	*ext_def_list opt_specifiers new_name* **LP** {28} name_list **COMMA NAME**	Reduce: *new_name*→**NAME**
13	*ext_def_list opt_specifiers new_name* **LP** {28} name_list **COMMA** new_name	Reduce: *name_list*→ *name_list* **COMMA** *new_name*
14	*ext_def_list opt_specifiers new_name* **LP** {28} name_list	Reduce: {29}→ε
15	*ext_def_list opt_specifiers new_name* **LP** {28} name_list {29}	*Shift:* **RP**

16	*ext_def_list opt_specifiers new_name* **LP** {28} name_list {29} **RP**	Reduce: *funct_decl*→
		    new_name **LP** {28} name_list {29}
		    RP

17	*ext_def_list opt_specifiers funct_decl*	Reduce: {51}→ε **CODE: #undef** T **CODE: #define** T(n) (fp-L0-(n*4)) **CODE:** PROC(_pooh,public) **CODE:** link(L0+L1);
18	*ext_def_list opt_specifiers funct_decl* {51}	Reduce: *def_list*→ε
19	*ext_def_list opt_specifiers funct_decl* {51} def_list	Shift: **TYPE**
20	*ext_def_list opt_specifiers funct_decl* {51} def_list **TYPE**	Reduce: *type_specifier*→**TYPE**
21	*ext_def_list opt_specifiers funct_decl* {51} def_list type_specifier	Reduce: *type_or_class*→*type_specifier*
22	*ext_def_list opt_specifiers funct_decl* {51} def_list type_or_class	Reduce: *specifiers*→*type_or_class*
23	*ext_def_list opt_specifiers funct_decl* {51} def_list specifiers	Shift: **NAME**
24	*ext_def_list opt_specifiers funct_decl* {51} def_list specifiers **NAME**	Reduce: *new_name*→**NAME**
25	*ext_def_list opt_specifiers funct_decl* {51} def_list specifiers new_name	Reduce: *var_decl*→*new_name*
26	*ext_def_list opt_specifiers funct_decl* {51} def_list specifiers var_decl	Reduce: *decl*→*var_decl*
27	*ext_def_list opt_specifiers funct_decl* {51} def_list specifiers decl	Reduce: *decl_list*→*decl*
28	*ext_def_list opt_specifiers funct_decl* {51} def_list specifiers decl_list	Reduce: {65}→ε
29	*ext_def_list opt_specifiers funct_decl* {51} def_list specifiers decl_list {65}	Shift: **SEMI**
30	*ext_def_list opt_specifiers funct_decl* {51} def_list specifiers decl_list {65} **SEMI**	Reduce: *def*→*specifiers decl_list* {65} **SEMI**
31	*ext_def_list opt_specifiers funct_decl* {51} def_list def	Reduce: *def_list*→*def_list def*
32	*ext_def_list opt_specifiers funct_decl* {51} def_list	Reduce: {52}→ε **CODE:** /* fp+4 = piglet [arg] */ **CODE:** /* fp+8 = eeyore [arg] */
33	*ext_def_list opt_specifiers funct_decl* {51} def_list {52}	Shift: **LC**
34	*ext_def_list opt_specifiers funct_decl* {51} def_list {52} **LC**	Reduce: {71}→ε

continued...

Table 6.15. Continued. A Parse of `pooh(piglet,eeyore) long eeyore;{}`

	Stack	Next Action
35	*ext_def_list opt_specifiers funct_decl* {51} def_list {52} **LC** {71}	Reduce: *def_list→ε*
36	*ext_def_list opt_specifiers funct_decl* {51} def_list {52} **LC** {71} def_list	Reduce: *local_defs→def_list*
37	*ext_def_list opt_specifiers funct_decl* {51} def_list {52} **LC** {71} local_defs	Reduce: *stmt_list→ε*
38	*ext_def_list opt_specifiers funct_decl* {51} def_list {52} **LC** {71} local_defs stmt_list	Shift: **RC**
39	*ext_def_list opt_specifiers funct_decl* {51} def_list {52} **LC** {71} local_defs stmt_list **RC**	Reduce: *compound_stmt→* **LC** {71} local_defs stmt_list **RC**
40	*ext_def_list opt_specifiers funct_decl* {51} def_list {52} compound_stmt	Reduce: *ext_def→opt_specifiers funct_decl* {51} def_list {52} compound_stmt **CODE:** `unlink();` **CODE:** `ret();` **CODE:** `ENDP(_pooh)` **BSS:** `#define L0 0 /* pooh loc. */` **BSS:** `#define L1 0 /* pooh tmp. */`
41	*ext_def_list ext_def*	Reduce: *ext_def_list→ext_def_list ext_def*
42	*ext_def_list*	Reduce: *program→ext_def_list* **Accept**

Listing 6.56. Compiler Output for Function Definition

```
 1   #include <tools/virtual.h>
 2   #define  T(x)
 3   SEG(data)
 4   SEG(bss)
 5   #define  L0 0    /* pooh: locals */
 6   #define  L1 0    /* pooh: temps. */
 7   SEG(code)
 8
 9   #undef   T
10   #define  T(n)  (fp-L0-(n*4))
11   PROC(_pooh,public)
12           link(L0+L1);
13                       /* fp+4 = piglet   [argument] */
14                       /* fp+8 = eeyore   [argument] */
15
16           /* Code from the body of the subroutine goes here. */
17
18           unlink();
19           ret();
20   ENDP(_pooh)
```

`symbol.args`, cross links.

Alphabetic componants of output labels, *label.h.*

is a pointer to a `symbol`, and the `args` field of that structure is itself a pointer to a linked list of additional `symbol` structures, one for each argument. The arguments, along with an entry for the function itself, are put into the symbol table on lines 530 to 532 of Listing 6.58. Putting the elements in the table does not affect the cross links. The arguments still form a linked list after the insertion. The `gen()` calls on line 540 and 541 actually emit the `PROC` and `link` directives—I'll come back to this subroutine later, when I discuss expression processing. The L prefix in the variable- and temporary-space labels, is put into the labels on lines 535 and 536 of Listing 6.58. `L_LINK` is defined along with several other label prefixes in *label.h*, Listing 6.59. These other label prefixes are used

Listing 6.57. *c.y*— Global Variables for Function-Declaration Processing (from **Occs** Definitions Section)

```
125   %{
126   char      Vspace[16];
127   char      Tspace[16];        /* The compiler doesn't know the stack-frame size
128                                  * when it creates a link() directive, so it outputs
129                                  * a link(VSPACE+TSPACE). Later on, it #defines VSPACE
130                                  * to the size of the local-variable space and TSPACE
131                                  * to the size of the temporary-variable space. Vspace
132                                  * holds the actual name of the VSPACE macro, and
133                                  * Tspace the TSPACE macro. (There's a different name
134                                  * for each subroutine.)
135                                  */
136
137   char      Funct_name[ NAME_MAX+1 ];       /* Name of the current function */
138   %}
```

for processing `if` statements, `while` loops, and so on. I'll discuss them further when the flow control statements are presented.

The parser now handles the K&R-style argument definitions. The new symbol-table entries are all of type **int**, because the *funct_decl* contains a *name_list*, not a *var_list*. Since no types are specified in the input argument list, **int** is supplied automatically. The parser processes the *def_list* next. When the *def_list*-processing is finished, the attribute at $4—the previous action was $3—will be a pointer to a linked list of symbols, one for each formal definition. The `fix_types_and_discard_syms()` call on line 549 of Listing 6.58 looks up each of the redefined symbols in the symbol table. If the symbol is there, the type is modified to reflect the redefinition; if it's not, an error message is generated. This subroutine also discards the `symbol` structures used for the redefinitions. The `figure_param_offsets()` call on line 550 traverses the argument list again because some elements of the list have just been modified to have new types. It patches the symbol structures so that the `rname` field holds an expression that can be used in a C-code instruction to access the variable. All these expressions are relative to the frame pointer (`WP(fp-8)` and so forth). The position in the argument list determines the value of the offset. The `print_offset_comment()` on line 551 prints the comment in the middle of the output that shows what all of these offsets are. All three subroutines are in Listing 6.60.

> K&R-style argument definitions.

Skipping past the function body and local-variable processing for a moment (all these are done in the *compound_stmt*), the end-of-function processing is all done in the third action in Listing 6.58, on lines 556 to 575. The `remove_symbols_from_-table()` call on line 560 deletes all the subroutine arguments from the symbol table. The subroutine itself stays in the table, however—it's a global-level symbol. The `discard_symbol_chain()` call on the next line frees the memory used for the associated `symbol` structures and associated type chains. The structure-table is not modified, so the structure definition persists even though the variable doesn't. Finally, the end-of-function code is output with the three `gen()` calls on the following lines, and the `link`-instruction labels are emitted on lines 568 to 571 of Listing 6.58.

> End-of-function processing.

> `link` labels emitted.

Listing 6.58. *c.y*— High-Level, External Definitions (Part Three)

```
520   /* ext_def :                                               */
521           | opt_specifiers funct_decl
522           {
523                   static unsigned link_val = 0;      /* Labels used for link args.*/
524
525                   add_spec_to_decl( $1, $2 );        /* Merge the specifier and   */
526                                                      /*              declarator.  */
527                   if( !$1->tdef )
528                       discard_link_chain( $1 );       /* Discard extra specifier.  */
529
530                   figure_osclass        ( $2 );          /* Update symbol table. */
531                   add_symbols_to_table ( $2 );          /* Add function itself. */
532                   add_symbols_to_table ( $2->args );     /* Add the arguments.   */
533
534                   strcpy ( Funct_name, $2->name            );
535                   sprintf( Vspace, "%s%d", L_LINK, link_val++ );
536                   sprintf( Tspace, "%s%d", L_LINK, link_val++ );
537
538                   yycode( "\n#undef   T\n" );
539                   yycode(   "#define   T(n) (fp-%s-(n*4))\n\n", Vspace );
540                   gen( "PROC", $2->rname, $2->etype->STATIC ? "private":"public");
541                   gen( "link", Vspace, Tspace );
542
543                   ++Nest_lev;       /* Make nesting level of definition_list
544                                      * match nesting level in the funct_decl
545                                      */
546           }
547           def_list
548           {
549                   fix_types_and_discard_syms ( $4                   );
550                   figure_param_offsets      ( $2->args            );
551                   print_offset_comment      ( $2->args, "argument" );
552
553                   --Nest_lev;      /* It's incremented again in the compound_stmt */
554           }
555           compound_stmt
556           {
557                   purge_undecl();                  /* Deal with implicit declarations */
558                                                    /* and undeclared symbols.         */
559
560                   remove_symbols_from_table ( $2->args );  /* Delete arguments. */
561                   discard_symbol_chain      ( $2->args );
562
563                   gen( ":%s%d", L_RET, rlabel(1) );      /* End-of-function */
564                   gen( "unlink"             );  /*            code. */
565                   gen( "ret"                );
566                   gen( "ENDP",  $2->rname    );
567
568                   yybss ( "\n#define  %s %d\t/* %s: locals */\n",
569                                   Vspace, loc_var_space(), $2->name );
570                   yybss (   "#define  %s %d\t/* %s: temps. */\n",
571                                   Tspace, tmp_var_space(), $2->name );
572
573                   tmp_reset();                     /* Reset temporary-variable system.*/
574                                                    /* (This is just insurance.)       */
575           }
576       ;
```

Listing 6.59. *label.h*— Output-label Definitions

```
 1    /* This file contains definitions for the various label prefixes. All labels
 2     * take the form: <prefix><number>, the <number> supplied by the code-generation
 3     * action. The prefixes are defined here.
 4     */
 5
 6    #define L_BODY           "BDY"    /* Top of the body of a for loop.           */
 7    #define L_COND_END       "QE"     /* End of conditional.                      */
 8    #define L_COND_FALSE     "QF"     /* True part of conditional (?:).           */
 9    #define L_DOEXIT         "DXIT"   /* Just after the end of the do/while.      */
10    #define L_DOTEST         "DTST"   /* Just above the test in a do/while.       */
11    #define L_DOTOP          "DTOP"   /* Top of do/while loop.                    */
12    #define L_ELSE           "EL"     /* Used by else processing.                 */
13    #define L_END            "E"      /* End of relational/logical op.            */
14    #define L_FALSE          "F"      /* False target of relational/logical op.   */
15    #define L_INCREMENT      "INC"    /* Just above the increment part of for loop. */
16    #define L_LINK           "L"      /* Offset passed to link instruction.       */
17    #define L_NEXT           "EXIT"   /* Outside of loop, end of if clause.       */
18    #define L_RET            "RET"    /* Above clean-up code at end of subroutine. */
19    #define L_STRING         "S"      /* Strings.                                 */
20    #define L_SWITCH         "SW"     /* Used for switches.                       */
21    #define L_TEST           "TST"    /* Above test in while/for/if.              */
22    #define L_TRUE           "T"      /* True target of relational/logical operator.*/
23    #define L_VAR            "V"      /* Local-static variables.                  */
```

Listing 6.60. *decl.c*— Process Subroutine Arguments

```
528   void      fix_types_and_discard_syms( sym )
529   symbol    *sym;
530   {
531       /* Patch up subroutine arguments to match formal declarations.
532        *
533        * Look up each symbol in the list. If it's in the table at the correct
534        * level, replace the type field with the type for the symbol in the list,
535        * then discard the redundant symbol structure. All symbols in the input
536        * list are discarded after they're processed.
537        *
538        * Type checking and automatic promotions are done here, too, as follows:
539        *          chars  are converted to int.
540        *          arrays are converted to pointers.
541        *          structures are not permitted.
542        *
543        * All new objects are converted to autos.
544        */
545
546       symbol *existing, *s;
547
548       while( sym )
549       {
550           if( !( existing = (symbol *)findsym( Symbol_tab,sym->name) )
551                                     || sym->level != existing->level )
552           {
553               yyerror("%s not in argument list\n", sym->name );
554               exit(1);
555           }
```

```
Listing 6.60. continued...
556        else if( !sym->type ||  !sym->etype )
557        {
558            yyerror("INTERNAL, fix_types: Missing type specification\n");
559            exit(1);
560        }
561        else if( IS_STRUCT(sym->type) )
562        {
563            yyerror("Structure passing not supported, use a pointer\n");
564            exit(1);
565        }
566        else if( !IS_CHAR(sym->type) )
567        {
568            /* The existing symbol is of the default int type, don't redefine
569             * chars because all chars are promoted to int as part of the call,
570             * so can be represented as an int inside the subroutine itself.
571             */
572
573            if( IS_ARRAY(sym->type) )               /* Make it a pointer to the */
574                sym->type->DCL_TYPE = POINTER;  /* first element.            */
575
576            sym->etype->SCLASS = AUTO;              /* Make it an automatic var.  */
577
578            discard_link_chain(existing->type); /* Replace existing type     */
579            existing->type    = sym->type;      /* chain with the current one.*/
580            sym->type         = NULL;           /* Must be NULL for discard_ - */
581                                                /* symbol() call, below.       */
582        }
583        s = sym->next;
584        discard_symbol( sym );
585        sym = s;
586    }
587 }
588
589 /*------------------------------------------------------------------*/
590
591 int     figure_param_offsets( sym )
592 symbol  *sym;
593 {
594    /* Traverse the chain of parameters, figuring the offsets and initializing
595     * the real name (in sym->rname) accordingly. Note that the name chain is
596     * assembled in reverse order, which is what you want here because the
597     * first argument will have been pushed first, and so will have the largest
598     * offset. The stack is 32 bits wide, so every legal type of object will
599     * require only one stack element. This would not be the case were floats
600     * or structure-passing supported. This also takes care of any alignment
601     * difficulties.
602     *
603     * Return the number of 32-bit stack words required for the parameters.
604     */
605
606    int  offset = 4;                /* First parameter is always at BP(fp+4). */
607    int  i;
608
609    for(; sym ; sym = sym->next )
610    {
611        if( IS_STRUCT(sym->type) )
612        {
613            yyerror("Structure passing not supported\n");
614            continue;
615        }
```

```
Listing 6.60. continued...
616
617                  sprintf( sym->rname, "fp+%d", offset );
618                  offset += SWIDTH ;
619          }
620
621          /* Return the offset in stack elements, rounded up if necessary.  */
622
623          return( (offset / SWIDTH) + (offset % SWIDTH != 0) );
624  }
625
626  /*---------------------------------------------------------------------*/
627
628  void     print_offset_comment( sym, label )
629  symbol   *sym;
630  char     *label;
631  {
632          /* Print a comment listing all the local variables. */
633
634          for(; sym ; sym = sym->next )
635              yycode( "\t/* %16s = %-16s [%s] */\n", sym->rname, sym->name, label );
636  }
```

6.6.5 Compound Statements and Local Variables

The next issue is the function body, which consists of a *compound_stmt*. As you can see from Listing 6.61, below, a compound statement is a list of statements (a *stmt_list*) surrounded by curly braces. Local-variable definitions (*local_defs*) can appear at the beginning of any compound statement, and since this same production is also used to process multiple-statement bodies of loops, and so forth, local variables can be defined at any nesting level.[18] The inner variables must shadow the outer ones until the compiler leaves its scoping level, however. The local version of the variable is used instead of another variable declared at a more outer level with an identical name.

Function bodies, compound_stmt.

Nested variable definitions.

It's difficult, though certainly possible, to modify the size of the stack frame every time that the compiler enters or leaves a scoping level. The main difficulty is temporary-variable management, which is much easier to do if the temporary variable space doesn't move around or change size during the life of a subroutine. My solution is to allocate space for all local variables, regardless of the scoping level, with the single link instruction at the top of the subroutine. From a space-allocation perspective, all variables are treated as if they were declared in the outermost scoping level at run time. At compile time, however, the symbol-table entry for an inner variable is created when that variable is declared, and it is deleted when the compiler leaves the scoping level for that variable. Even though an inner variable continues to exist at run time, that variable cannot be accessed from outside the compound statement because the symbol-table entry for the variable won't exist.

Handling scoping levels, memory allocation.

The obvious problem with this approach is that memory is wasted. In the following fragment, for example, the stack region used to store castor could be recycled for use by pollux; it isn't:

---

18. This is quite-legal C, though the practice is discouraged because it makes it difficult to find the variable definitions when they're buried in a subroutine.

Listing 6.61. *c.y*— Compound Statements

```
577    compound_stmt
578              : LC                                    {    ++Nest_lev;
579                                                            loc_reset();
580                                                       }
581              local_defs stmt_list RC   {    --Nest_lev;
582                                                            remove_symbols_from_table ( $3 );
583                                                            discard_symbol_chain        ( $3 );
584                                                       }
585              ;
586
587    local_defs
588              : def_list         {    add_symbols_to_table ( $$ = reverse_links( $1 ));
589                                       figure_local_offsets ( $$, Funct_name        );
590                                       create_static_locals ( $$, Funct_name        );
591                                       print_offset_comment ( $$, "variable"        );
592                                  }
593              ;
```

```
{
        {
            int castor;
        }
        {
            int pollux;
        }
}
```

Local-variable definitions are handled by the productions in Listing 6.61 and the subroutines in Listing 6.62. The *def_list* nonterminal on line 588 of Listing 6.61 is the same production that's used for structure fields. Its attribute is a pointer to the head of a linked list of symbols, one for each declaration. These symbols are added to the symbol table on line 588 in Listing 6.61.

Listing 6.62. *local.c*— Local-Variable Management

```
 1    #include <stdio.h>
 2    #include <stdlib.h>
 3    #include <tools/debug.h>
 4    #include <tools/hash.h>
 5    #include <tools/l.h>
 6    #include <tools/compiler.h>
 7    #include <tools/c-code.h>
 8    #include "symtab.h"
 9    #include "proto.h"
10    #include "label.h"
11
12    /* LOCAL.C Subroutines in this file take care of local-variable management.  */
13
14    PRIVATE int      Offset = 0 ;      /* Offset from the frame pointer (which also */
15                                       /* marks the base of the automatic-variable  */
16                                       /* region of the stack frame) to the most    */
17                                       /* recently allocated variable. Reset to 0   */
18                                       /* by loc_reset() at the head of every sub-  */
19                                       /* routine.                                  */
20
```
➡

Listing 6.62. continued...

```
21  extern void      yycode(), yydata(), yybss(), yycomment();
22  /*----------------------------------------------------------------------*/
23
24  void    loc_reset()
25  {
26      /* Reset everything back to the virgin state. Call this subroutine just */
27      /* before processing the outermost compound statement in a subroutine.  */
28
29      Offset = 0 ;
30  }
31  /*----------------------------------------------------------------------*/
32
33  int     loc_var_space()
34  {
35      /* Return the total cumulative size of the temporary-variable region in
36       * stack elements (not bytes). This call outputs the value of the macro
37       * that specifies the variable-space size in the link instruction. Calling
38       * loc_reset() also resets the return value of this subroutine to zero.
39       */
40
41      return( (Offset + (SWIDTH-1)) / SWIDTH );
42  }
43  /*----------------------------------------------------------------------*/
44
45  void    figure_local_offsets( sym, funct_name )
46  symbol  *sym;
47  char    *funct_name;
48  {
49      /* Add offsets for all local automatic variables in the sym list.  */
50
51      for(; sym ; sym = sym->next )
52          if( !IS_FUNCT( sym->type ) && !sym->etype->STATIC )
53              loc_auto_create( sym );
54  }
55  /* - - - - - - - - - - - - - - - - - - - - - - - - - - - - - - - -*/
56
57  void    loc_auto_create( sym )
58  symbol  *sym;
59  {
60      /* Create a local automatic variable, modifying the "rname" field of "sym"
61       * to hold a string that can be used as an operand to reference that
62       * variable. This name is a correctly aligned reference of the form:
63       *
64       *                  fp + offset
65       *
66       * Local variables are packed as well as possible into the stack frame,
67       * though, as was the case with structures, some padding may be necessary
68       * to get things aligned properly.
69       */
70
71      int align_size = get_alignment( sym->type );
72
73      Offset += get_sizeof( sym->type );          /* Offset from frame pointer */
74                                                  /* to variable.          */
75
76      while( Offset % align_size )                /* Add any necessary padding */
77          ++Offset;                               /* to guarantee alignment.   */
78
```

→

Listing 6.62. continued...

```
79          sprintf( sym->rname, "fp-%d", Offset );        /* Create the name.        */
80          sym->etype->SCLASS = AUTO;
81   }
82   /*----------------------------------------------------------------*/
83
84   void    create_static_locals( sym, funct_name )
85   symbol  *sym;
86   char    *funct_name;
87   {
88       /* Generate definitions for local, static variables in the sym list. */
89
90       for(; sym ; sym = sym->next )
91           if( !IS_FUNCT( sym->type ) && sym->etype->STATIC )
92               loc_static_create ( sym, funct_name );
93   }
94   /* - - - - - - - - - - - - - - - - - - - - - - - - - - - - - - -*/
95
96   void    loc_static_create( sym, funct_name )
97   symbol  *sym;
98   char    *funct_name;
99   {
100      static unsigned val;                    /* Numeric component of arbitrary name. */
101
102      sprintf( sym->rname, "%s%d", L_VAR, val++ );
103      sym->etype->SCLASS = FIXED ;
104      sym->etype->OCLASS = PRI   ;
105
106      var_dcl( yybss, PRI, sym, ";" );
107      yybss( "\t/* %s [%s(), static local] */\n", sym->name, funct_name );
108  }
109  /*----------------------------------------------------------------*/
110
111  void    remove_symbols_from_table( sym )
112  symbol  *sym;
113  {
114      /* Remove all symbols in the list from the table.  */
115
116      symbol *p;
117
118      for( p = sym; p ; p = p->next )
119          if( !p->duplicate )
120              delsym( Symbol_tab, p );
121          else
122          {
123              yyerror("INTERNAL, remove_symbol: duplicate sym. in cross-link\n");
124              exit( 1 );
125          }
126  }
```

Automatic variables:
figure_local_
    offsets().

The figure_local_offsets() call on line 589 of Listing 6.61 handles automatic variables. (The subroutine is on line 45 of Listing 6.62.) It goes through the list, adjusting the rnames to hold a string which, when used in an operand, references the variable. Ultimately, the reference will look something like this: WP(fp+6), but only the fp+6 is created here—the WP and parentheses are added later by the expression-processing code.

Offset.

The current offset from the base of the automatic-variable region is remembered in Offset, which is incremented by the size of each variable as space for it is allocated.

The variables are packed as closely as possible into the local-variable space. If alignment permits, they are placed in adjacent bytes. As with structures, padding is inserted if necessary to guarantee alignment. `figure_local_offsets()` is called at the top of every block, but `Offset` is reset to zero only at the top of the subroutine, so the size of the local-variable region continues to grow over the life of the subroutine as automatic variables are allocated. The final size of the region is determined once the entire subroutine has been processed by calling `loc_var_space()` on line 33 of Listing 6.62. This value is used at the end of the subroutine-processing code to define one of the macros that's passed to the `link` instruction.

`loc_var_space()`.

The `create_static_locals()` call on line 590 of Listing 6.61 handles **static** locals. The subroutine starts on line 84 of Listing 6.62. It goes through the list a second time, allocating space for the variable as if it were a **static** global variable. An arbitrary name is assigned instead of using the declared name, as was the case with true globals. This way, two subroutines can use the same name for a static variable without a conflict. All **static** locals are declared `private`, so conflicts with variables in other modules are not a problem. Symbols are removed from the table when the compiler leaves the scoping-level on lines 582 and 583 of Listing 6.61.

Static-local variables:
`create_static_locals()`

6.6.6 Front-End/Back-End Considerations

Packing variables onto the stack makes sense in a one-pass compiler, but it's contraindicated if the real code is going to be generated by a back end. The front end has no way of knowing what alignment restrictions apply to the target machine or the actual sizes of the various types. The back end's life can be made easier by assuming that all types are the same size and that there are no alignment restrictions. As it is, the back end might have to undo some of our work. If an **int** is 32 bits, it must unpack the variables. Similarly, if the worst-case alignment restriction is two rather than four, it must get rid of the extra padding.

Don't pack variables if back end is used.

If the front end is ignoring size and alignment, some mechanism is needed to pass the symbol-table information to the back end. Currently, the compiler's just throwing that information away when it leaves the scoping level. A better approach passes the symbol table to the back end as part of the intermediate code. For example, you can introduce a new, `local` storage class to C-code and generate definitions for all local symbols at the top of a block along with the **static**-variable definitions. A matching `delete(name)` directive can be generated at the end of the block to tell the back end that the symbol had gone out of scope.

Passing symbol table information to back end.

There's no need to worrying about the size at the intermediate-code level if all variables are the same size, The compiler's been keeping track of the size so that we can use `W()`,`L()` and so forth to access variables, but it wouldn't have to do so if everything was the same size. Consequently, both global and local variables can just be called out by name in the intermediate code. You can dispense with all the size-related, C-code addressing modes and register-access directives and just use the names: `_p`, rather than `WP(&_p)` or `WP(fp-16)`, `r0` rather than `r0.pp`. The back end can compute the offsets for local variables and make any necessary adjustments to the generated code, replacing the symbolic names with stack-relative access directives as necessary. This one change dramatically simplifies both the design of C-code and the complexity of the front end.

No need to keep track of sizes.

All of the foregoing applies to structures as well as simple variables—the fields should all be the same size and not be packed into the structure. Better yet, the front end could make no attempt to determine the offset to the field from the base of the structure. Structure members could be passed to the back end like this:

`member` *type structure_name.field_name*;

and the fields could be called out by name in the intermediate code rather than generating explicit offsets to them, using something like `struct_name.member_name`.

6.7 The `gen()` Subroutine

Reasons to use `gen()`.

The `gen()` subroutine was used in the last section to print out the few C-code instructions in the subroutine prefix and suffix. `gen()` is a general-purpose code-generation interface for the parser—all C-code instructions are emitted using `gen()` calls rather than `yycode()` calls. It seems reasonable to look at it now, before using it further. I've concentrated the code emission into a single subroutine for several reasons:

- Clarity in the source code. Once you've added leading tabs, trailing newlines, field widths, and so forth, direct `yycode()` calls are pretty hard to read. Since `gen()` takes care of all the formatting for you, the subroutine calls are more understandable, and the code more maintainable as a consequence. `gen()` also makes the output code more readable because the code is formatted consistently.

- Fewer C-code syntax errors. There are slight variations in syntax in the C-code instruction set. Some instructions must be followed by semicolons, others by colons, and still others by no punctuation at all. Some instructions take parenthesized arguments, others do not. `gen()` takes care of all these details for you, so the odds of a syntax error showing up in the output are much smaller.

- Portability. Since all the output is concentrated in one place, it's much easier to make changes to the intermediate language. You need only change a single subroutine instead of several `yycode()` calls scattered all over the parser. Similarly, it's easy to emit binary output rather than ASCII output—just change `gen()` to emit binary directly.[19]

- Debugging. The compiler takes a command line switch that causes it to generate a run-time trace. Instead of emitting a single C-code directive, the compiler emits the C-code directive surrounded by statements that print the directive itself, the contents of all the virtual registers, and the top few stack elements. This way, you can watch the effect of every output instruction as it's executed. It is much easier to emit these extra run-time-trace statements when all output is concentrated in one place.

The first argument to `gen()` is a string that specifies the instruction to emit—usually the op code. The number and type of any additional arguments are controlled by the first one—legal first arguments are summarized in Table 6.16. If an argument is a character-pointer, the string is printed; if it's an **int**, the number is converted to a string and printed, and so on. In addition, if the first character of an arithmetic instruction is an @, the @ is removed and a * is printed to the left of the destination string. This call:

@ as first character in format string.

```
gen( "@+=", "dst", "src" );
```

generates this code:

```
*dst += src;
```

Add comments to output code, `gen_comment()`.

The `gen()` subroutine is implemented in Listing 6.63 along with various support routines. `gen_comment()` (on line 81) puts comments in the output. It works like `printf()`, except that the output is printed to the right of the instruction emitted by the

---

19. This argument also holds for the code that creates declarations. I should have funneled all declarations through a single subroutine rather than using direct `yydata()` and `yybss()` calls. You may want to make that change to the earlier code as an exercise.

Table 6.16. The gen() Interface

First Argument	Second Argument	Third Argument	Output	Description
`"%="`	`char *dst;`	`char *src;`	`dst %= src;`	modulus
`"&="`	`char *dst;`	`char *src;`	`dst &= src;`	bitwise AND
`"*="`	`char *dst;`	`char *src;`	`dst *= src;`	multiply
`"*=%s%d"`	`char *dst;`	`int   src;`	`dst *= src;`	multiply dst by constant
`"+="`	`char *dst;`	`char *src;`	`dst += src;`	add
`"+=%s%d"`	`char *dst;`	`int   src;`	`dst += src;`	add constant to dst
`"-="`	`char *dst;`	`char *src;`	`dst -= src;`	subtract
`"-=%s%d"`	`char *dst;`	`int   src;`	`dst -= src;`	subtract constant from dst
`"/="`	`char *dst;`	`char *src;`	`dst /= src;`	divide
`"/=%s%d"`	`char *dst;`	`int src;`	`dst /= src;`	divide dst by constant
`"<<="`	`char *dst;`	`char *src;`	`dst <<= src;`	left shift dst by src bits
`">>="`	`char *dst;`	`char *src;`	`dst >>= src;`	right shift dst by src bits
`">L="`	`char *dst;`	`char *src;`	`lrs(dst,src);`	logical right shift dst by src bits
`"=-"`	`char *dst;`	`char *src;`	`dst =- src;`	two's complement
`"=~"`	`char *dst;`	`char *src;`	`dst =~ src;`	one's complement
`"|="`	`char *dst;`	`char *src;`	`dst |= src;`	bitwise OR
`"^="`	`char *dst;`	`char *src;`	`dst ^= src;`	bitwise XOR
`"="`	`char *dst;`	`char  *src;`	`dst = src;`	assign
`"=&"`	`char *dst;`	`char  *src;`	`dst = &src;`	load effective address
`"=*%s%v"`	`char *dst;`	`value *src;`	`dst = *name;` `dst = name;`	assign indirect. name is taken from src->name. If the name is of the form &name, then dst=name is output, otherwise dst=*name is output.
`":"`	`char *label;`	*(none)*	`label:`	label
`":%s%d"`	`char *alpha;`	`int num;`	`alphanum:`	label, but with the alphabetic and numeric components specified separately. gen(":%s%d", "P", 10) emits P10:.
`"BIT"`	`char *op1;`	`char *bit;`	`BIT(op1,bit)`	test bit
`"EQ"`	`char *op1;`	`char *op2;`	`EQ(op1,op2)`	equality
`"EQ%s%d"`	`char *op1;`	`int   op2;`	`EQ(op1,op2)`	equal to constant
`"GE"`	`char *op1;`	`char *op2;`	`EQ(op1,op2)`	greater than or equal
`"GT"`	`char *op1;`	`char *op2;`	`EQ(op1,op2)`	greater than
`"LE"`	`char *op1;`	`char *op2;`	`EQ(op1,op2)`	less than or equal
`"LT"`	`char *op1;`	`char *op2;`	`EQ(op1,op2)`	less than
`"NE"`	`char *op1;`	`char *op2;`	`EQ(op1,op2)`	not equal
`"U_GE"`	`char *op1;`	`char *op2;`	`EQ(op1,op2)`	greater than or equal, unsigned
`"U_GT"`	`char *op1;`	`char *op2;`	`EQ(op1,op2)`	greater than, unsigned
`"U_LE"`	`char *op1;`	`char *op2;`	`EQ(op1,op2)`	less than or equal, unsigned
`"U_LT"`	`char *op1;`	`char *op2;`	`EQ(op1,op2)`	less than, unsigned
`"PROC"`	`char *name;`	`char *cls;`	`PROC(name,cls)`	start procedure
`"ENDP"`	`char *name;`	*(none)*	`ENDP(name)`	end procedure
`"call"`	`char *label;`	*(none)*	`call(label);`	call procedure
`"ext_high"`	`char *dst;`	*(none)*	`ext_high(dst);`	sign extend
`"ext_low"`	`char *dst;`	*(none)*	`ext_low(dst);`	sign extend
`"ext_word"`	`char *dst;`	*(none)*	`ext_word(dst);`	sign extend
`"goto"`	`char *label;`	*(none)*	`goto label;`	unconditional jump
`"goto%s%d"`	`char *alpha;`	`int num;`	`goto alphanum;`	unconditional jump, but the alphabetic and numeric components of the target label are specified separately. gen("goto%s%d", "P", 10) emits goto P10;.
`"link"`	`char *loc;`	`char *tmp;`	`link(loc+tmp);`	link
`"pop"`	`char *dst;`	`char *type;`	`dst = pop(type);`	pop
`"push"`	`char *src;`	*(none)*	`push(src);`	push
`"ret"`	*(none)*	*(none)*	`ret();`	return
`"unlink"`	*(none)*	*(none)*	`ret();`	unlink

next gen() call. gen_comment() stores the comment text in Comment_buf (declared on line 77) so that it can be printed by a subsequent gen() call.

The enable_trace() and disable_trace() subroutines on lines 100 and 101 enable and disable the generation of run-time trace statements.

Run-time trace,
enable_trace(),
disable_trace().

gen() itself starts on line 113. It uses the lookup table on lines 21 to 74 to translate the first argument into one of the tokens defined on lines 13 to 19. The table lookup is done by the bsearch() call on line 132. Thereafter, the token determines the number and types of the arguments, which are pulled off the stack on lines 138 to 149. The ANSI variable-argument mechanism described in Appendix A is used. gen() does not emit anything itself—it assembles a string which is passed to a lower-level output routine. The switch starting on line 156 takes care of most of the formatting, using sprintf() calls to initialize the string. Note that a simple optimization, called *strength reduction* is done on lines 201 to 229 in the case of multiplication or division by a constant. If the constant is an even power of two, a shift is emitted instead of a multiply or divide directive. A multiply or divide by 1 generates no code at all. The comment, if any, is added to the right of the output string on line 236.

Strength reduction.

The actual output is done in print_instruction() on line 247 of Listing 6.63. This subroutine takes care of all the formatting details: labels are not indented, the statement following a test is indented by twice the normal amount, and so forth. print_instruction() also emits the run-time trace directives. These directives are written directly to yycodeout [with fprintf() calls rather than yycode() calls] so that they won't show up in the IDE output window. The trace is done using two macros: _P() prints the instruction, and _T() dumps the stack and registers. Definitions for these macros are written to the output file the first time that print_instruction() is called with tracing enabled (on Line 262 of Listing 6.63). The output definitions look like this:

Instruction output and formatting: print_instruction().

Run-time trace instructions: _P(), _T().

```
#define _P(s) printf( s )
#define _T()  pm(),printf(\"--------------------------------\\n\")
```

_P() just prints its argument, _T() prints the stack using a pm() call—pm() is declared in

Most statements are handled as follows:

```
                    _P( "a = b;" )
a = b;                   _T()
```

The trace directives are printed at the right of the page so that the instructions themselves will still be readable. The instruction is printed first, then executed, and then the stack and registers are printed. Exceptions to this order of events are as follows:

label:	_P("label:")
PROC(...)	_P("PROC(...)"); _T();
ret(...);	_P("ret(...)")
ENDP(...)	_P("ENDP(...)")

The trace for a logical test is tricky because both the test and the following instruction must be treated as a unit. They are handled as follows:

```
                    _P( "NE(a,b)" )
NE(a,b)                     {
                    _P( "goto x" );
    instruction;       _T(); }
```

Listing 6.63. *gen.c*— C-code Generation

```
1   #include <stdio.h>
2   #include <stdarg.h>
3   #include <tools/debug.h>
4   #include <tools/hash.h>
5   #include <tools/l.h>
6   #include <tools/compiler.h>
7   #include "symtab.h"
8   #include "value.h"
9   #include "proto.h"
10
11  PRIVATE int Trace = 0;              /* Generate run-time trace if true. */
12
13  typedef enum request
14  {
15      t_assign_addr, t_assign_ind, t_call, t_endp, t_ext, t_goto, t_goto_int,
16      t_label, t_label_int, t_link, t_logical, t_logical_int, t_lrs, t_math,
17      t_math_int, t_pop, t_proc, t_push, t_ret, t_unlink
18
19  } request;
20
21  struct ltab
22  {
23      char      *lexeme;
24      request   token;
25  }
26  Ltab[] =
27  {
28          {"%=",           t_math            },
29          {"&=",           t_math            },
30          {"*=",           t_math            },
31          {"*=%s%d",       t_math_int        }, /* Multiply var by constant. */
32          {"+=",           t_math            },
33          {"+=%s%d",       t_math_int        },
34          {"-=",           t_math            },
35          {"-=%s%d",       t_math_int        },
36          {"/=",           t_math            },
37          {"/=%s%d",       t_math_int        },
38          {":",            t_label           },
39          {":%s%d",        t_label_int       },
40          {"<<=",          t_math            },
41          {"=",            t_math            },
42          {"=&",           t_assign_addr     }, /* Get effective address. */
43          {"=*%s%v",       t_assign_ind      }, /* Assign indirect.       */
44          {"=-",           t_math            },
45          {">>=",          t_math            },
46          {">L=",          t_lrs             },
47          {"BIT",          t_logical         },
48          {"ENDP",         t_endp            },
49          {"EQ",           t_logical         },
50          {"EQ%s%d",       t_logical_int     },
51          {"GE",           t_logical         },
52          {"GT",           t_logical         },
53          {"LE",           t_logical         },
54          {"LT",           t_logical         },
55          {"NE",           t_logical         },
56          {"PROC",         t_proc            },
57          {"U_GE",         t_logical         },
58          {"U_GT",         t_logical         },
59          {"U_LE",         t_logical         },
```

→

Listing 6.63. continued...

```
60              {"U_LT",          t_logical     },
61              {"^=",            t_math        },
62              {"call",          t_call        },
63              {"ext_high",      t_ext         },
64              {"ext_low",       t_ext         },
65              {"ext_word",      t_ext         },
66              {"goto",          t_goto        },
67              {"goto%s%d",      t_goto_int    },
68              {"link",          t_link        },
69              {"pop",           t_pop         },
70              {"push",          t_push        },
71              {"ret",           t_ret         },
72              {"unlink",        t_unlink      },
73              {"|=",            t_math        }
74      };
75
76      #define NREQ ( sizeof(Ltab)/sizeof(*Ltab) )    /* Table size (in elements).   */
77      char Comment_buf[132];                         /* Remember comment text here. */
78
79      /*-----------------------------------------------------------------------*/
80
81      PUBLIC void gen_comment( format, ... )
82      char *format;
83      {
84          /* Works like printf(), but the string is appended as a comment to the end
85           * of the command generated by the next gen() call. There's no array-size
86           * checking---be careful. The maximum generated string length is 132
87           * characters. Overwrite any comments already in the buffer.
88           */
89
90          va_list    args;
91          va_start ( args, format              );
92          vsprintf ( Comment_buf, format, args );
93          va_end    ( args );
94      }
95
96      /*-----------------------------------------------------------------
97       * Enable/disable the generation of run-time trace output.
98       */
99
100     PUBLIC enable_trace()  { Trace = 1; }   /* Must call before parsing starts. */
101     PUBLIC disable_trace() { Trace = 0; }
102
103     /*-----------------------------------------------------------------------*/
104
105     PRIVATE int     cmp( a, b )      /* Compare two lexeme fields of an ltab. */
106     struct  ltab *a, *b;
107     {
108         return strcmp( a->lexeme, b->lexeme );
109     }
110
111     /*-----------------------------------------------------------------------*/
112
113     PUBLIC  gen( op ,... )                              /* emit code */
114     char    *op;
115     {
116         char        *dst_str, *src_str, b[80];
117         int         src_int, dst_int;
118         value       *src_val;
119         struct ltab *p, dummy;
```

Listing 6.63. continued...

```
120         request      tok;
121         va_list      args;
122         char         *prefix = " " ;
123         int          amt;
124
125         if( *op == '@' )
126         {
127             ++op;
128             prefix = "*" ;
129         }
130
131         dummy.lexeme = op;
132         if( !(p = (struct ltab *) bsearch(&dummy, Ltab, NREQ, sizeof(*Ltab), cmp)))
133         {
134             yyerror("INTERNAL gen: bad request <%s>, no code emitted.\n", op );
135             return;
136         }
137
138         va_start( args, op );                      /* Get the arguments. */
139         dst_str = va_arg( args, char* );
140         switch( tok = p->token )
141         {
142         case t_math_int:
143         case t_logical_int:
144         case t_goto_int:
145         case t_label_int:   src_int = va_arg( args, int    ); break;
146         case t_assign_ind:  src_val = va_arg( args, value* ); break;
147         default:            src_str = va_arg( args, char*  ); break;
148         }
149         va_end( args);
150
151         /* The following code just assembles the output string. It is printed with
152          * the print_instruction() call under the switch, which also takes care of
153          * inserting trace directives, inserting the proper indent, etc.
154          */
155
156         switch( tok )
157         {
158         case t_call:        sprintf(b," call(%s);",    dst_str          ); break;
159         case t_endp:        sprintf(b," ENDP(%s)",     dst_str, src_str ); break;
160         case t_ext:         sprintf(b," %s(%s);", op, dst_str           ); break;
161         case t_goto:        sprintf(b," goto %s;",     dst_str          ); break;
162         case t_goto_int:    sprintf(b," goto %s%d;",   dst_str, src_int ); break;
163         case t_label:       sprintf(b,"%s:",           dst_str          ); break;
164
165         case t_label_int:   sprintf(b,"%s%d:",         dst_str, src_int );
166                             tok = t_label;
167                             break;
168
169         case t_logical:     sprintf(b," %s(%s,%s)",   op, dst_str, src_str );
170                             break;
171
172         case t_logical_int: sprintf(b," %2.2s(%s,%d)", op, dst_str, src_int );
173                             tok = t_logical;
174                             break;
175
176         case t_link:        sprintf(b," link(%s+%s);",   dst_str, src_str ); break;
177         case t_pop:         sprintf(b," %-12s = pop(%s);",dst_str, src_str ); break;
```

Listing 6.63. continued...

```
178         case t_proc:        sprintf(b," PROC(%s,%s)",      dst_str, src_str ); break;
179         case t_push:        sprintf(b," push(%s);",        dst_str          ); break;
180         case t_ret:         sprintf(b," ret();"                              ); break;
181         case t_unlink:      sprintf(b," unlink();"                           ); break;
182
183         case t_lrs:         sprintf(b,"%slrs(%s,%s);",  prefix, dst_str, src_str);
184                     break;
185
186         case t_assign_addr: sprintf(b,"%s%-12s = &%s;", prefix, dst_str, src_str);
187                     break;
188         case t_assign_ind:
189                     if( src_val->name[0]=='&' )
190                         sprintf(b,"%s%-12s = %s;",prefix, dst_str, src_val->name+1);
191                     else
192                         sprintf(b,"%s%-12s = *%s;",prefix, dst_str, src_val->name);
193
194                     break;
195
196         case t_math:        sprintf(b,"%s%-12s %s %s;", prefix, dst_str, op, src_str);
197                     break;
198         case t_math_int:
199                     if( *op != '*'  &&  *op != '/' )
200                         sprintf(b,"%s%-12s %2.2s %d;", prefix, dst_str, op, src_int);
201                     else
202                     {
203                         switch( src_int )
204                         {
205                         case 1 :    amt = 0;       break;
206                         case 2 :    amt = 1;       break;
207                         case 4 :    amt = 2;       break;
208                         case 8 :    amt = 3;       break;
209                         case 16:    amt = 4;       break;
210                         case 32:    amt = 5;       break;
211                         case 64:    amt = 6;       break;
212                         case 128:   amt = 7;       break;
213                         case 256:   amt = 8;       break;
214                         case 512:   amt = 9;       break;
215                         case 1024:  amt = 10;      break;
216                         case 2048:  amt = 11;      break;
217                         case 4096:  amt = 12;      break;
218                         default:    amt = -1;      break;
219                         }
220
221                         if( !amt )
222                             sprintf(b, "/* %s%-12s %s 1; */", prefix, dst_str, op );
223
224                         else if( amt < 0 )
225                             sprintf(b, "%s%-12s %s %d;", prefix, dst_str, op, src_int);
226                         else
227                             sprintf(b, "%s%-12s %s %d;", prefix, dst_str,
228                                                 (*op == '*') ? "<<=" : ">>=" , amt);
229                     }
230                 break;
231         default:
232                 yyerror("INTERNAL, gen: bad token %s, no code emitted.\n", op );
233                 break;
234     }
235
```

Listing 6.63. continued...

```
236      if( *Comment_buf )              /* Add optional comment at end of line. */
237      {
238          concat( sizeof(b), b, b, (tok == t_label ? "\t\t\t\t" : "\t"),
239                                      "/* ",  Comment_buf, " */", NULL );
240          *Comment_buf = '\0';
241      }
242      print_instruction( b, tok );          /* Output the instruction. */
243  }
244
245  /*-----------------------------------------------------------------*/
246
247  PRIVATE void print_instruction( b, t )
248  char    *b;      /* Buffer containing the instruction.    */
249  request t;       /* Token representing instruction.        */
250  {
251      /* Print the instruction and, if trace is enabled (Trace is true), print
252       * code to generate a run-time trace.
253       */
254
255      extern FILE   *yycodeout, *yybssout;
256      static int    printed_defs = 0;
257      static int    last_stmt_was_test;
258
259      if( Trace && !printed_defs )
260      {
261          printed_defs = 1;
262          fprintf( yybssout,
263              "#define _P(s) printf( s )\n"                                      \
264              "#define _T()  pm(),printf(\"-------------------------------\\n\")"\
265              "\n\n" );
266      }
267
268      if( !Trace )                                /* just print the instruction */
269      {
270          yycode("%s%s%s\n", (t==t_label || t==t_endp || t==t_proc) ? ""    : "\t",
271                             (          last_stmt_was_test          ) ? " "  : ""   ,
272                             b );
273
274          last_stmt_was_test = (t==t_logical);
275      }
276      else if( t == t_logical )
277      {
278          fprintf( yycodeout, "\t\t\t\t\t" "_P(\"%s\\n\");\n", b);
279          yycode("\t%s\t\t{\n", b);                                          /*}*/
280          last_stmt_was_test = 1;
281      }
282      else
283      {
284          switch( t )
285          {
286          case t_label: yycode("%s", b);
287                        fprintf( yycodeout, "\t\t\t\t\t"  "_P(\"%s\\n\");",    b);
288                        break;
289
290          case t_proc:  yycode("%s", b);
291                        fprintf( yycodeout, "\t\t\t"      "_P(\"%s\\n\");",    b);
292                        fprintf( yycodeout,              "_T();"           );
293                        break;
294
```

```
Listing 6.63. continued...

295             case t_ret:
296             case t_endp: fprintf( yycodeout, "\t\t\t\t\t"  "_P(\"%s\\n\");" "\n",b);
297                          yycode("%s", b);
298                          break;
299
300             default:     fprintf( yycodeout, "\t\t\t\t\t"  "_P(\"%s\\n\");" "\n",b);
301                          yycode("\t%s%s",    last_stmt_was_test ? "     " : "",    b);
302                          fprintf( yycodeout, "\t\t\t"        "_T();"                 );
303             }
304
305             if( last_stmt_was_test )                                          /* { */
306             {
307                 putc( '}', yycodeout );
308                 last_stmt_was_test = 0;
309             }
310             putc( '\n', yycodeout );
311         }
312     }
```

6.8 Expressions

This section looks at how expressions are processed. Temporary-variable management is discussed as are lvalues and rvalues. The code-generation actions that handle
expression processing are covered as well. We've looked at expression parsing
sufficiently that there's no point in including extensive sample parses of every possible
production in the current section—I've included a few sample parses to explain the
harder-to-understand code-generation issues, but I expect you to be able to do the
simpler cases yourself. Just remember that order of precedence and evaluation controls
the order in which the productions that implement particular operators are executed.
Productions are reduced in the same order as the expression is evaluated.

The foregoing notwithstanding, if you have the distribution disk, you may want to
run simple expressions through the compiler (*c.exe*) as you read this and the following
sections. As you watch the parse, pay particular attention to the order in which reductions occur and the way that attributes are passed around as the parse progresses.

6.8.1 Temporary-Variable Allocation

All expressions in C are evaluated one operator at a time, with precedence and associativity determining the order of evaluation as much as is possible. It is conceptually
convenient to look at <u>every</u> operation as creating a temporary variable that somehow
references the result of that operation—our compiler does things somewhat more
efficiently, but it's best to think in terms of the stupidest possible code. This temporary,
which represents the evaluated subexpression, is then used as an operand at the next
expression-evaluation stage.

Our first task is to provide a mechanism for creating and deleting temporaries. One
common approach is to defer the temporary-variable management to the back end. The
compiler itself references the temporaries as if they existed somewhere as global variables, and the back end takes over the allocation details. The temporary variable's type
can be encoded in the name, using the same syntax that would be used to access the temporary from a C-code statement: `W(t0)` is a `word`, `L(t1)` is an `lword`, `WP(t2)` is a
`word` pointer, and so on. The advantage of this approach is that the back end is in a

*Defer temporary-variable
management to back
end.*

much better position than the compiler itself to understand the limitations and strengths of the target machine, and armed with this knowledge it can use registers effectively. I am not taking this approach here because it's pedagogically useful to look at a worst-case situation—where the compiler itself has to manage temporaries.

Temporary variables can be put in one of three places: in registers, in static memory, and on the stack. The obvious advantage of using registers is that they can be accessed quickly. The registers can be allocated using a stack of register names—essentially the method that is used in the examples in previous chapters. If there aren't enough registers in the machine, you can use a few run-time variables (called *pseudo registers*) as replacements, declaring them at the top of the output file and using them once the registers are exhausted. You could use two stacks for this purpose, one of register names and another of variable names, using the variable names only when there are no more registers available. Some sort of priority queue could also be used for allocation.

One real advantage to deferring temporary-variable allocation to the back end is that the register-versus-static-memory problem can be resolved in an efficient way. Many optimizers construct a syntax tree for the expression being processed, and analysis of this tree can be used to allocate temporaries efficiently (so that the registers are used more often than the static memory). This sort of optimization must be done by a postprocessor or postprocessing stage in the parser, however—the parser must create a physical syntax or parse tree that a second pass can analyze. Though it's easy for a simple one-pass compiler to use registers, it's difficult for such a compiler to use the registers effectively.

Another problem is function calls, which can be imbedded in the middle of expressions. Any registers or pseudo registers that are in use as temporaries must be pushed before calling the function and popped after the return. Alternately, code at the top of the called function could push only those registers that are used as temporaries in the function itself—there's a lot of pushing and popping in either case. This save-and-restore process adds a certain amount of overhead, at both compile time and run time.

The solution to the temporary-variable problem that's used here is a compromise between speed and efficiency. A region of the stack frame is used for temporaries.[20] This way, they don't have to be pushed because they're already on the stack.

Because the maximum size of the temporary-variable region needed by a subroutine varies (it is controlled by the worst-case expression in the subroutine), the size of the temporary-variable space changes from subroutine to subroutine. This problem is solved with the second macro that's used in the `link` instruction in the subroutine prefix. (L1 in the example in the previous section.) The macro is defined to the size of the temporary-variable region once the entire subroutine has been processed.

This approach—allocating a single, worst-case sized temporary-variable region—is generally better than a dynamic approach where the temporary-variable space is gradually expanded at run time by subtracting constants from the stack pointer as variables are needed The stack is shrunk with matching additions when the variable is no longer needed. This last approach can be more efficient of stack space, but it is both more difficult to do at compile time and is inefficient at run time because several subtractions and additions are needed rather than a single `link` instruction. Since most languages use very few, relatively small, temporaries as they evaluate expressions, this second

Registers as temporaries, pseudo registers.

Problems with function calls.

Temporaries on stack.

Dynamic temporary-variable creation.

---

20. In many machines, such as the Intel 8086 family, a stack-relative memory access is actually more efficient than a direct-mode memory access. It takes fewer clock cycles. Since none of the 8086-family machines have any general purpose registers to speak of, putting the temporaries on the stack is actually one of the most efficient solutions to the problem.

method is usually more trouble than its worth. Nonetheless, you may want to consider a dynamic approach if the source language has very large data types. For example, a special-purpose language that supported a `matrix` basic type and a matrix-multiplication operator would need a tremendous amount of temporary-variable space to process the following expression:

```
matrix a[100][100], b[100][100], c[100][100];
a = a * b * c;
```

It would be worthwhile not to waste this stack space except when the expression was actually being evaluated, so a dynamic approach makes sense here. If the stack just isn't large enough for temporaries such as the foregoing, the compiler could generate run-time calls to `malloc()` as part of the subroutine prefix, storing a pointer to the memory returned from `malloc()` on the stack. A run-time `free()` call would have to be generated as part of the subroutine suffix to delete the memory. Calling `malloc()` is a very-high-overhead operation, however, so it's best to use the stack if you can.

The next problem is the temporary variable's type, which varies with the operand types. The type of the larger operand is used for the temporary. The easiest solution (and the one used here) is to use the worst-case size for all temporaries, and align them all on a worst-case boundary. All temporaries take up one `lword`-sized stack element, which is guaranteed to be aligned properly because it's a stack word. Again, if the worst-case type was very large (if doubles were supported, for example), it would be worthwhile to go to the trouble to pack the temporaries into the stack region in a manner analogous to the local variables.

Figure 6.18 shows a stack frame with eight bytes of local-variable space and enough temporary space for two variables. The macro definitions at the top of the figure are generated at the same time as the subroutine prefix. The L0 macro evaluates to the size, in stack elements, of the local-variable region. (This is the same L0 that's passed to the `link` instruction.) The `T()` macro simplifies temporary-variable access in instructions. It is defined at the top of the file as an empty macro, and is then **#undef**ed and redefined to reference the current local-variable-space size at the top of every subroutine. The initial dummy definition is required because some compilers won't let you undefine a nonexistent macro. The following examples demonstrate how the macro is used:

`W(T(0))`   accesses the `word` in the bottom two bytes of the bottom temporary.

`L(T(1))`   accesses the `lword` that takes up the entire top temporary.

`*WP(T(0))`   accesses the `word` whose address is in the top temporary.

Figure 6.18. Storing Temporary Variables in the Stack Frame

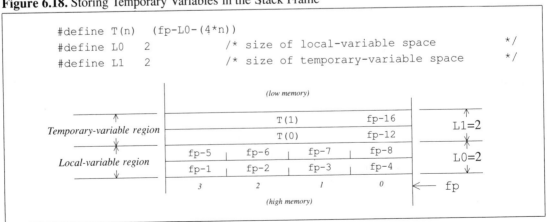

Though temporary variables are not packed into the stack frame, the temporary-variable space is used intelligently by the compiler—the same region of the stack is recycled as needed for temporaries. The strategy, implemented in Listing 6.64, is straightforward. (It's important not to confuse compile and run time, in the following discussion. It's easy to do. The temporary-variable allocator is part of the compiler, but it is keeping track of a condition of the stack at run time. All of the temporary-variable allocation and deallocation is done at compile time. A region of the stack is just used as a temporary at run time—the compiler determined that that region was available at compile time.)

Recycling temporaries.

Listing 6.64. *temp.c*— Temporary-Variable Management

```
 1   #include <stdio.h>
 2   #include <stdlib.h>
 3   #include <tools/debug.h>
 4   #include <tools/hash.h>
 5   #include <tools/l.h>
 6   #include <tools/compiler.h>
 7   #include <tools/c-code.h>
 8   #include "symtab.h"
 9   #include "value.h"
10   #include "proto.h"
11
12   /* Subroutines in this file take care of temporary-variable management.  */
13
14   #define REGION_MAX 128    /* Maximum number of stack elements that can be */
15                             /* used for temporaries.                        */
16   #define MARK      -1      /* Marks cells that are in use but are not the  */
17                             /* first cell of the region.                    */
18   typedef int CELL;         /* In-use (Region) map is an array of these.    */
19
20   PRIVATE CELL    Region[REGION_MAX];
21   PRIVATE CELL    *High_water_mark = Region;
22   /*----------------------------------------------------------------------*/
23
24   PUBLIC int tmp_alloc( size )
25   int     size;                          /* desired number of bytes */
26   {
27       /* Allocate a portion of the temporary-variable region of the required size,
28        * expanding the tmp-region size if necessary. Return the offset in bytes
29        * from the start of the rvalue region to the first cell of the temporary.
30        * 0 is returned if no space is available, and an error message is also
31        * printed in this situation. This way the code-generation can go on as if
32        * space had been found without having to worry about testing for errors.
33        * (Bad code is generated, but so what?)
34        */
35
36       CELL  *start, *p ;
37       int    i;
38
39       /* size = the number of stack cells required to hold "size" bytes.  */
40
41       size = ((size + SWIDTH) / SWIDTH)  -  (size % SWIDTH == 0);
42
43       if( !size )
44           yyerror("INTERNAL, tmp_alloc: zero-length region requested\n" );
45
46
```

→

```
Listing 6.64. continued...
47          /* Now look for a large-enough hole in the already-allocated cells.  */
48
49          for( start = Region; start < High_water_mark ;)
50          {
51              for( i = size, p = start;  --i >= 0  &&  !*p;  ++p )
52                      ;
53
54              if( i >= 0 )                                    /* Cell not found. */
55                  start = p + 1;
56              else                                           /* Found an area big enough. */
57                  break;
58          }
59
60          if( start < High_water_mark )                       /* Found a hole. */
61              p  = start;
62          else
63          {
64              if( (High_water_mark + size) > (Region + REGION_MAX) )    /* No room. */
65              {
66                  yyerror("Expression too complex, break into smaller pieces\n");
67                  return 0;
68              }
69              p = High_water_mark;
70              High_water_mark += size;
71          }
72
73          for( *p = size; --size > 0; *++p = MARK) /* 1st cell=size. Others=MARK */
74                  ;
75
76          return( start - Region );                          /* Return offset to start of region */
77                                                             /* converted to bytes.            */
78  }
79
80  /*------------------------------------------------------------------------*/
81
82  PUBLIC  void tmp_free( offset )
83  int   offset;                           /* Release a temporary var.; offset should */
84  {                                        /* have been returned from tmp_alloc().    */
85      CELL  *p = Region + offset;
86      int   size;
87
88      if( p < Region || p > High_water_mark || !*p || *p == MARK )
89          yyerror( "INTERNAL, tmp_free: Bad offset (%d)\n", offset );
90      else
91          for( size = *p; --size >= 0; *p++ = 0 )
92                  ;
93  }
94
95  /*------------------------------------------------------------------------*/
96
97  PUBLIC  void    tmp_reset()
98  {
99      /* Reset everything back to the virgin state, including the high-water mark.
100     * This routine should be called just before a subroutine body is processed,
101     * when the prefix is output. See also: tmp_freeall().
102     */
103     tmp_freeall();
104     High_water_mark = Region ;
105 }
106
```

```
Listing 6.64. continued...
107    /*----------------------------------------------------------------*/
108
109    PUBLIC  void     tmp_freeall()
110    {
111        /* Free all temporaries currently in use (without modifying the high-water
112         * mark). This subroutine should be called after processing arithmetic
113         * statements to clean up any temporaries still kicking around (there is
114         * usually at least one).
115         */
116        memset( Region, 0, sizeof(Region) );
117    }
118
119    /*----------------------------------------------------------------*/
120
121    PUBLIC  int      tmp_var_space()
122    {
123        /* Return the total cumulative size of the temporary-variable region in
124         * stack elements, not bytes. This number can be used as an argument to the
125         * link instruction.
126         */
127        return High_water_mark - Region;
128    }
```

The compiler keeps an internal array called `Region`—declared on line 20 of Listing 6.64—that tells it which stack elements in the temporary-variable space are in use at run time. The index of the cell in the array corresponds to the offset of the equivalent stack element. For example, `Region[N]` corresponds to the temporary variable at offset N (in stack elements) from the base of the temporary-variable region (not from the frame pointer). The array elements are zero if the corresponding stack element is available. For example, if `Region[4]` is zero, then the stack element at offset 4 from the base of the temporary space is available. The size of the array is controlled by `REGION_MAX`, declared on line 14 of Listing 6.64. This size limits the amount of temporary-variable space available to a subroutine. This size limits an expression's complexity because it limits the number of temporaries that can be used to evaluate the expression. The compiler prints an error message if the expression gets too complicated (if there aren't enough temporary variables to evaluate all the subexpressions).

The temporary-variable allocator, `tmp_alloc()`, starts on line 24 of Listing 6.64. It is passed the number of bytes required for the temporary, figures out how many stack elements are required for that temporary, and then allocates that many bytes from the temporary-variable region.[21] The allocation logic on lines 49 to 58 of Listing 6.64 searches the array from bottom to top looking for a free stack element. It allocates the first available stack element for the temporary. The `High_water_mark`, used here and declared on line 21 of Listing 6.64, keeps track of the size of the temporary-variable space. If the first available element is at a higher index than any previously allocated element, then `High_water_mark` is modified to point at the new element.

Compile-time map of run-time stack: `Region[]`.

Allocate temporary: `tmp_alloc()`.

`High_water_mark`.

---

21. The allocator I'm presenting here is actually more complex than necessary, because all temporary variables take up exactly one stack element in the current compiler. It seemed reasonable to demonstrate how to handle the more complex situation, where some temporaries can take up more than one stack element, however.

The cell is marked as "in use" on line 73. Marking a stack cell as 'in use'. The `Region` element corresponding to the first cell of the allocated space is set to the number of stack elements that are being allocated. If more than one stack element is required for the temporary, adjacent cells that are part of the temporary are filled with a place marker. Other subroutines in Listing 6.64 de-allocate a temporary variable by resetting the equivalent `Region` elements to zero, de-allocate all temporary variables currently in use, and provide access to the high-water mark. You should take a moment and review them now.

6.8.2 Lvalues and Rvalues

Expression evaluation, and the way that temporaries are used while doing the evaluation, is actually a more complex proposition than you would think, based on the examples in earlier chapters. Hitherto, we've used temporaries for one purpose only, to hold the value of a subexpression. We could do this because none of the grammars that we've seen are capable of modifying variables, only of using them. As soon as modification becomes a possibility, things start to get complicated—especially in a language like C that provides several ways to modify something (=, ++, --, and so forth).

Rvalues.

So far, the parsers that we've looked at always treated identifier references in the same way: They copied the contents of the referenced variable into a temporary and passed the name of that temporary back up as an attribute. The following grammar is a case in point:

```
e : e PLUS e   { yycode("%s += %s\n", $1, $3); free_name( $3 );  }
  | ID          { yycode("%s = _%s\n", $$ = new_name(), yytext ); }
  ;
```

The value stack is a stack of character pointers. The attribute is the name of the temporary that holds the partially-evaluated subexpression. Input like x+y generates the following code:

```
t0 = x;
t1 = y;
t1 += t0;
```

The kind of temporary that's used here—which holds something's value—is called an *rvalue*. In the current grammar, the y and z in x=y+z are said to *generate rvalues*—they create temporaries that hold a variable's value. (It's an rvalue because it can go to the right of the equals sign.) The + operator also generates an rvalue because the result of the operation is a run-time temporary holding the sum—the value of the subexpression.

Lvalues.

What happens when you introduce an assignment operator to the grammar? Our first, unsuccessful attempt at a solution treats the assignment operator just like the addition operator:

```
e : e PLUS  e {yycode("%s += %s\n", $1, $3); free_name( $3 );  }
  | e EQUAL e {yycode("%s  = %s\n", $1, $3); free_name( $3 );  }
  | ID         {yycode("%s  = _%s\n", $$ = new_name(), yytext ); }
  ;
```

The input x=y+z yields the following output:

```
t0  = x;
t1  = y;
t2  = z;
t1 += t2;
t0  = t1;
```

which doesn't do anything useful.

In order to do assignment correctly, you need to know the address of x (the memory location to modify), not its contents. To get this information you need to introduce a second type of temporary—one that holds an address. This kind of temporary is called an *lvalue* because it can be generated by subexpressions to the left of an equal sign. The grammar and code in Listing 6.65 supports both kinds of temporaries. They are distinguished from one another by the first character of the name. Rvalues start with R, lvalues with L. As was the case in earlier chapters, a simple stack strategy is used to allocate and free names. Error checking has been omitted to simplify things.

Listing 6.65. Expression Processing with Lvalues and Rvalues

```
1    %{
2        #define YYSTYPE char*
3    %}
4    %%
5    s       : e ;
6    e       : e PLUS e
7            {
8                char *target;
9
10               /* Convert $1 to an rvalue if necessary so that it can be used
11                * as the synthesized attribute.
12                */
13
14               if( *$1 != 'R' )
15               {
16                   yycode( "%s = %s\n", target = new_rvalue(), rvalue($1) );
17                   free_value($1);
18                   $1 = target;
19               }
20               $$ = $1;
21               yycode("%s += %s\n",  target, rvalue( $3 );
22               free_value( $3 );
23           }
24           | e EQUAL e
25           {
26               char *target;
27
28               if( *$1 != 'L' )
29                   yyerror("Lvalue required\n");
30               else
31               {
32                   if( *$3 != 'R' )              /* Convert $3 to an rvalue. */
33                   {
34                       yycode( "%s = %s\n", target = new_rvalue(), rvalue($3));
35                       free_value($3);
36                       $3 = target;
37                   }
38                   yycode( "*%s = %s", $1, $3 );
39                   free_value( $1 );
40                   $$ = $3;
41               }
42           }
43
44           | ID
45           {
46               yycode("%s  = &_%s\n", $$ = new_lvalue(), yytext );
47           }
48       ;
49   %%
```

Listing 6.65. continued...

```
50    char *Lvalues[4] = { "L0", "L1", "L2", "L3" };
51    char *Lp          = Lvalues;
52    char *Rvalues[4] = { "R0", "R1", "R2", "R3" };
53    char *Rp          = Rvalues;
54
55    char *new_lvalue() { return  *Lp++; }   /* Allocate a new lvalue.         */
56    char *new_rvalue() { return  *Rp++; }   /* Allocate a new rvalue.         */
57
58    void    free_value( val )                /* Free an lvalue or an rvalue. */
59    char    *val;
60    {
61        if( *val == 'L' ) *--Lp = val;
62        else              *--Rp = val;
63    }
64
65    char *rvalue( value )         /* If the argument is an lvalue, return a string  */
66    char *value;                  /* that can be used in an expression to reference */
67    {                             /* the lvalue's contents. (Add a * to the name.)  */
68        static char buf[16];
69
70        if( *lvalue == 'R' )                  /* it's already an rvalue */
71            return value;
72        sprintf( buf, "*%s", lvalue );
73        return buf;
74    }
```

Using the new grammar, the input x=y+z yields the following output:

```
L0   = &_x;
L1   = &_y;
L2   = &_z;
R0   = *L1;
R0   += *L2;
*L0  = R0;
```

which is awkward, but it works. The lvalues are converted to rvalues by preceding their names with a star. Note that the attribute synthesized in the assignment is the rvalue, not the lvalue. The assignment operator *requires* an lvalue to the left of the equals sign, but it *generates* an rvalue. That's why code like the following is illegal in C:

```
(x=y) = z;
```

even though

```
x = y = z;
```

is okay. (x=y) generates an rvalue—a temporary that holds the value of y—and explicit assignment to an rvalue is meaningless. In x=y=z, the operand to the right of the equal sign is always an rvalue and the operand to the left is always an lvalue. (Run it through the parser by hand if you don't believe me.)

Logical versus physical lvalues.
The code that the compiler just generated is pretty sorry. Fortunately, the compiler can do a simple optimization to fix things. Instead of passing around the name of a temporary variable as an attribute, it can pass a string which, when used as an operand in an instruction, evaluates correctly. This attribute is sometimes a temporary-variable name, but it can also take on other values. That is, instead of generating

```
L0 = &_x;
```

in the earlier example, and then passing around the string "L0" as an attribute, the

compiler can dispense with the assignment entirely and pass around "&_x" as an attribute. So you now have two types of lvalues: *physical* lvalues—temporary variables that
hold the address of something, and *logical* lvalues—expressions that evaluate to the
address of something when used as an operand. The compiler can distinguish between
the two by looking at the first character in the name; logical lvalues start with an ampersand.

Physical and logical lvalues.

Listing 6.66 shows the parser, modified to use logical lvalues. Changes are marked
with a ★. Very few changes have to be made. First, the code for assignment must be
modified on line 32 of Listing 6.66 to handle logical lvalues. The conditional just discards the leading ampersand if it's present, because the two operators in the expression
*&_x just cancel one another, yielding _x. Next, the **ID** action on lines 39 to 41 of Listing 6.66 must be changed to generate logical, rather than physical, lvalues. The name is
assembled into a string, and a copy of the string is passed as an attribute. (The copy is
freed on line 59.) Finally, the rvalue() subroutine is modified on lines 70 and 71 of
Listing 6.66 to recognize both kinds of lvalues.

Listing 6.66. Expression Processing with Logical Lvalues

```
 1   %{
 2        #define YYSTYPE char*
 3   %}
 4   %%
 5   s        : e ;
 6   e        : e PLUS e
 7            {
 8                    char *target;
 9
10                    if( *$1 != 'R' )
11                    {
12                        yycode( "%s = %s\n", target = new_rvalue(), rvalue($1) );
13                        free_value($1);
14                        $1 = target;
15                    }
16                    $$ = $1;
17                    yycode("%s += %s\n",  target, rvalue( $3 );
18                    free_value( $3 );
19            }
20            | e EQUAL e
21            {
22                    if( *$1 != 'L' )
23                        yyerror("Lvalue required\n");
24                    else
25                    {
26                        if( *$3 != 'R' )               /* Convert $3 to an rvalue. */
27                        {
28                            yycode( "%s = %s\n", target = new_rvalue(), rvalue($3));
29                            free_value($3);
30                            $1 = target;
31                        }
32                        yycode("*%s = %s", *$1=='&' ? ($1)+1 : $1, $3);  /* ★ */
33                        $$ = $3;
34                        free_value( $1 );
35                    }
36            }
37            | ID
38            {
39                    char buf[16];                                      /* ★ */
40                    sprintf( buf, "&%s", yytext );                     /* ★ */
```

→

Listing 6.66. continued...

```
41                     $$ = strdup( buf );                            /*   ★   */
42              }
43          ;
44  %%
45  char *Lvalues[4] = { "L0", "L1", "L2", "L3" };
46  char *Lp        = Lvalues;
47
48  char *Rvalues[4] = { "R0", "R1", "R2", "R3" };
49  char *Rp        = Rvalues;
50
51  char *new_lvalue() { return *Lp++; }    /* Allocate a new lvalue.       */
52  char *new_rvalue() { return *Rp++; }    /* Allocate a new lvalue.       */
53
54  free_value( val )                        /* Free an lvalue or an rvalue. */
55  char    *val;
56  {
57      if    ( *val == 'L' ) *--Lp = val;      /* Physical lvalue */
58      else if( *val == 'R' ) *--Rp = val;
59      else                    free( val );     /* Logical lvalue          ★   */
60  }
61
62  char *rvalue( value )         /* If the argument is an lvalue, return a string */
63  char *value;                  /* that can be used in an expression to reference */
64  {                             /* the lvalue's contents.                         */
65      static char buf[16];
66
67      if( *lvalue == 'R' )        /* It's already an rvalue. */
68          return value;
69
70      if( *lvalue == '&' )        /* Logical lvalue                         ★   */
71          return value + 1;       /* *&_x cancels. Just use the name.       ★   */
72
73      sprintf( buf, "*%s", lvalue );
74      return buf;
75  }
```

The new-and-improved code-generation actions translate the input x=y+z as follows:

```
R0  = _y ;
R0 += _z ;
_x  = R0;
```

Summary: lvalues and rvalues.

To summarize all of the foregoing and put it into the context of a real compiler: two types of temporaries can be created as an expression is evaluated: an *lvalue* which holds the address of the object that, in turn, holds the result of the previous operation, and an *rvalue* which holds the result itself. The terms come from an expression like:

```
x = y;
```

The rvalue, y (on the right of the equal sign), is treated differently from the lvalue, x (on the left). The y must evaluate to its contents, but the x must evaluate to an address—to the place where the y is to be stored.

An expression that is said to "generate an lvalue", can be seen as creating a temporary variable that holds an address of some sort, and the operator controls whether an lvalue or rvalue is generated. In the current C compiler, all identifier references generate lvalues—a temporary is created that holds the address of the referenced object. The following operators also generate lvalues:

```
 *      []     .       ->
```

Note that none of the foregoing operators do arithmetic—they all do a reference of some sort. Operators not in the foregoing list generate rvalues—a temporary is created that holds the result of the the operation. In addition, the following operators require their operands to be lvalues:

```
 ++  --   =   +=   -=   etc.
```

Other operators can handle both lvalue and rvalue operands, but to use them, they must convert the lvalues to rvalues by removing one level of indirection.

A quick way to determine whether an expression forms an lvalue or an rvalue is to put the expression to the left of an equals sign and see if it's legal. Given the following declarations:

```
int    x;
int    array[10];
int    *p = array;

struct  tag
{
    int          f1;
    int    f2[5];
}
structure;
```

the following expressions generate lvalues:

```
x
array          *array          array[n]
p              *p              *(p + n)
structure.f1   structure.f2[n]  *(structure.f2)
                                structure       (only if structure assignment is supported)
```

Note that both p and *p form lvalues, though the associated temporaries are of different types. The following are not lvalues because they can't appear to the left of an equal sign:

```
&x
array
structure.f2
structure      (only if structure assignment is not supported)
```

6.8.3 Implementing Values, Higher-Level Temporary-Variable Support

This section describes the current compiler's implementation of lvalues and rvalues. The value structure, in Listing 6.67, is used for both of them, and all of the expression-processing productions pass around pointers to value structures as attributes. The various fields are used as follows:

The value structure.

lvalue True if the structure represents an lvalue, false if it's an rvalue.

is_tmp True if the structure represents a real temporary variable (an rvalue or a physical lvalue), false otherwise.

offset Position of the temporary variable in the stack frame. This number is the absolute value of the offset, in stack elements, from the base address of the temporary-variable region to the variable itself [i.e. the number that is returned from tmp_alloc()].

name   If the current value is an rvalue, this field is a string which, when used as an operand, evaluates to the value of the previously computed subexpression. If it's an lvalue, this field is a string that evaluates to the address of the object generated from the previous subexpression.

type
etype   Points at the start and end of a type chain representing the value's type. If an rvalue, the name field references an object of the indicated type; if an lvalue, the name field evaluates to a pointer to an object of the indicated type. When an lvalue is created from a symbol (when an identifier is processed), a copy of the symbol's type chain is made and the copy is used in the value.

sym   When the lvalue is created from a symbol, this field points at that symbol. It's used only to print an occasional comment in the output, and is undefined if the lvalue was created by an operator like * or [].

Listing 6.67. *value.h*— Lvalues and Rvalues

```
1   /* VALUE.H:       Various definitions for (l|r)values. "symtab.h" must be
2    *                #included before #including this file.
3    */
4
5   #define VALNAME_MAX (NAME_MAX * 2)      /* Max. length of string in value.name */
6
7   typedef struct value
8   {
9       char      name[ VALNAME_MAX ]; /* Operand that accesses the value.      */
10      link      *type;               /* Variable's type (start of chain).     */
11      link      *etype;              /* Variable's type (end of chain).       */
12      symbol    *sym;                /* Original symbol.                      */
13      unsigned lvalue    :1;         /* 1 = lvalue, 0 = rvalue.               */
14      unsigned is_tmp    :1;         /* 1 if a temporary variable.            */
15      unsigned offset    :14;        /* Absolute value of offset from base of */
16                                     /* temporary region on stack to variable. */
17  } value;
18
19  #define LEFT  1                /* Second argument to shift_name() in value.c, */
20  #define RIGHT 0                /*                               discussed below. */
21
22  #define CONST_STR(p) tconst_str((p)->type)   /* Simplify tconst_str() calls */
23                                               /* with value arguments by      */
24                                               /* extracting the type field.   */
```

Constant value.   Note that values are used for constants as well as temporary variables. (There's a picture of one in Figure 6.19.) The attribute generated by *unop*→**ICON** is a pointer to a value structure for an rvalue. The type chain identifies the value as an **int** constant. [IS_CONSTANT(etype) in *symtab.h*, which examines the storage class of the right-most link in the chain, evaluates true.] Similarly, the numeric value of the constant is stored in the last link in the type chain (in the const_val union of the specifier substructure). The value structure's name field holds an ASCII string representing the number. The *unop*→**NAME** action that we'll look at momentarily creates an identical attribute if the identifier references an element of an enumerated type.

The advantage of this approach—using values for both constants and variables—is that all expression elements, regardless of what they are, synthesize value pointers as attributes.

Figure 6.19. A `value` that Represents an **int** Constant

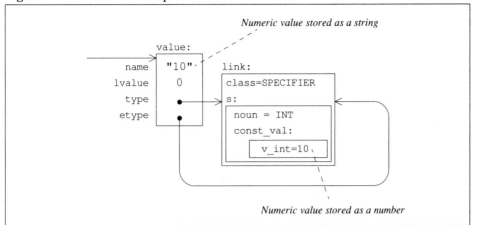

Listing 6.68 contains various subroutines that manipulate `value` structures. The low-level allocation and deletion routines (`discard_value()` on line 46 of Listing 6.68 and `new_value()` on line 84 of the same listing) work just like the link-management routines discussed earlier. The `values` are allocated from `malloc()`, but discarded by placing them on the linked free list pointed to by `Value_free`, declared on line 14. Several structures are allocated at once—the number of structures is controlled by `VCHUNK`, defined on line 19. The type chain associated with the `value` is discarded at the same time as the `value` itself.

`new_value()`,
`discard_value()`

Listing 6.68. *value.c*— Low-Level `value` Maintenance

```
1    #include <stdio.h>
2    #include <tools/debug.h>
3    #include <tools/hash.h>
4    #include <tools/l.h>
5    #include <tools/c-code.h>
6    #include <tools/compiler.h>
7    #include "symtab.h"
8    #include "value.h"
9    #include "proto.h"
10   #include "label.h"
11
12   /*  VALUE.C:    Routines to manipulate lvalues and rvalues. */
13
14   PRIVATE value *Value_free = NULL;
15   #define VCHUNK  8                /* Allocate this many structure at a time. */
16
17   /*-------------------------------------------------------------------*/
18
19   value   *new_value()
20   {
21       value *p;
22       int   i;
23
24       if( !Value_free )
25       {
26           if( !(Value_free = (value *) malloc( sizeof(value) * VCHUNK )) )
27           {
28               yyerror("INTERNAL, new_value: Out of memory\n");
29               exit( 1 );
```

Listing 6.68. continued...

```
30                  }
31
32              for( p = Value_free, i = VCHUNK; --i > 0; ++p )   /* Executes VCHUNK-1 */
33                  p->type = (link *)( p+1 );                    /*          times. */
34
35              p->type = NULL ;
36          }
37
38          p          = Value_free;
39          Value_free = (value *) Value_free->type;
40          memset( p, 0, sizeof(value) );
41          return p;
42      }
43
44      /*----------------------------------------------------------------------*/
45
46      void    discard_value( p )
47      value   *p;                                   /* Discard a value structure  */
48      {                                             /* and any associated links.  */
49          if( p )
50          {
51              if( p->type )
52                  discard_link_chain( p->type );
53
54              p->type = (link *)Value_free ;
55              Value_free = p;
56          }
57      }
58
59      /*----------------------------------------------------------------------*/
60
61      char    *shift_name( val, left )
62      value   *val;
63      int     left;
64      {
65          /* Shift the name one character to the left or right. The string might get
66           * truncated on a right shift. Returns pointer to shifted string.
67           * Shifts an & into the new slot on a right shift.
68           */
69
70          if( left )
71              memmove( val->name,   val->name+1, sizeof(val->name) - 1 );
72          else
73          {
74              memmove( val->name+1, val->name,   sizeof(val->name) - 1 );
75              val->name[ sizeof(val->name) - 1 ] = '\0' ;
76              val->name[0] = '&';
77          }
78
79          return val->name;
80      }
81
82      /*----------------------------------------------------------------------*/
83
84      char    *rvalue( val )
85      value   *val;
86      {
87          /* If val is an rvalue, do nothing and return val->name. If it's an lvalue,
88           * convert it to an rvalue and return the string necessary to access the
89           * rvalue. If it's an rvalue constant, return a string representing the
```

→

```
Listing 6.68. continued...
 90          * number (and also put that string into val->name).
 91          */
 92
 93          static char buf[ NAME_MAX + 2 ] = "*" ;
 94
 95          if( !val->lvalue )                              /* It's an rvalue already. */
 96          {
 97              if( IS_CONSTANT(val->etype) )
 98                  strcpy( val->name, CONST_STR(val) );
 99              return val->name;
100          }
101          else
102          {
103              val->lvalue = 0;
104              if( * val->name == '&' )                    /* *& cancels */
105              {
106                  shift_name(val, LEFT);
107                  return val->name;
108              }
109              else
110              {
111                  strncpy( &buf[1], val->name, NAME_MAX+1 );
112                  return buf;
113              }
114          }
115      }
116
117      char    *rvalue_name( val )
118      value   *val;
119      {
120          /* Returns a copy of the rvalue name without actually converting val to an
121           * rvalue. The copy remains valid only until the next rvalue_name call.
122           */
123
124          static char buf[ (NAME_MAX * 2) + 1 ];          /* sizeof(val->name) + 1 */
125
126          if( !val->lvalue )
127          {
128              if( IS_CONSTANT(val->etype) ) strcpy( buf, CONST_STR(val) );
129              else                          strcpy( buf, val->name      );
130          }
131          else
132          {
133              if( * val->name == '&' ) strcpy ( buf,        val->name + 1 );
134              else                     sprintf( buf, "*%s", val->name      );
135          }
136          return buf;
137      }
```

The `rvalue()` subroutine on line 84 of Listing 6.68 is used heavily in the expression-processing code. It is used to fetch the actual value associated with either an rvalue or lvalue. It is passed a `value` structure. If this `value` is an rvalue that represents a numeric constant, a string representing the constant's numeric value is returned. If it's a normal rvalue, the `name` field is returned.

      `rvalue()`

      `rvalue()` and rvalues.

If the argument is a pointer to an lvalue, the `value` is converted to an rvalue and a string that can be used to access the rvalue is returned. The conversion to rvalue involves modifying two fields. First, the `lvalue` field is set false. Then, if this is a

      `rvalue()` and logical lvalues.

logical lvalue, the name field is shifted one character to the left and the resulting string is returned.

If the incoming value represents a physical lvalue, a string containing the name preceded by a * is returned, but the name field isn't modified. This behavior is actually an anomaly because a physical rvalue is not created. That is, to be consistent with the logical lvalue case, the rvalue() subroutine should emit code to copy the object pointed to by the lvalue into a physical temporary variable. It should then modify the value structure to represent this new temporary rather than the original one. I haven't done this here because I wanted the code-generation actions to be able to control the target. For example, the following is taken from the code-generation action for a return statement. $2 is a pointer to a value for the object being returned. If the input takes the form **return** x, then $2 points at an lvalue. If the input takes the form **return** x+1, then $2 points at an rvalue:

```
gen( "=", IS_INT($2->type) ? "rF.w.low" : "rF.l", rvalue($2) );
```

The target (the physical rvalue) has to be one of two registers, not a temporary variable. Other situations arise where the target is a temporary, so I simplified the interface to rvalue() by requiring the caller to generate the physical rvalue if necessary. The string that's returned from rvalue() can always be used as the source operand in the assignment. The rvalue_name() subroutine on line 117 returns the same thing as rvalue(), but it doesn't modify the value structure at all, it just returns a string that you can use as a source operand.

The value-maintenance functions continue in Listing 6.69 with a second layer of higher-level functions. Temporary-variable values are also handled here. Two routines, starting on line 138, are provided for temporary-variable creation. tmp_create() is the lower-level routine. It is passed a type and creates an rvalue for that type using the low-level allocation routine discussed earlier [tmp_alloc()] to get space for the variable on the stack. A copy of the input type string is usually put into the value. An **int** rvalue is created from scratch if the type argument is NULL, however. If the second argument is true, a link for a pointer declarator is added to the left of the value's type chain. The value's name field is created by tmp_create(). It initialized to a string which is output as the operand of an instruction, and which accesses the temporary variable. The name is generated on line 175, and it looks something like this: WP(T(0)). The type component (WP) changes with the actual type of the temporary. It's created by get_prefix() on line 181. The 0 is the offset from the base of the temporary-variable region to the current variable. We saw the T() macro earlier. It translates the offset to a frame-pointer reference.

Listing 6.69. *value.c*— High-Level value Maintenance

```
138    value *tmp_create( type, add_pointer )
139    link   *type;              /* Type of temporary, NULL to create an int.      */
140    int    add_pointer;        /* If true, add pointer declarator to front of type */
141    {                          /* before creating the temporary.                 */
142
143         /* Create a temporary variable and return a pointer to it. It's an rvalue
144          * by default.
145          */
146
147        value *val;
148        link  *lp;
149
```

Listing 6.69. continued...

```
150         val         = new_value();
151         val->is_tmp = 1;
152
153         if( type )                                    /* Copy existing type. */
154             val->type  = clone_type( type, &lp );
155         else                                          /* Make an integer.    */
156         {
157             lp         = new_link();
158             lp->class  = SPECIFIER;
159             lp->NOUN   = INT;
160             val->type  = lp;
161         }
162
163         val->etype  = lp;
164         lp->SCLASS  = AUTO;                            /* It's an auto now, regardless */
165                                                       /* of the previous storage class. */
166         if( add_pointer )
167         {
168             lp          = new_link();
169             lp->DCL_TYPE = POINTER;
170             lp->next     = val->type;
171             val->type    = lp;
172         }
173
174         val->offset = tmp_alloc( get_size( val->type ) );
175         sprintf(val->name, "%s( T(%d) )", get_prefix(val->type), (val->offset + 1));
176         return( val );
177 }
178
179 /*------------------------------------------------------------------------*/
180
181 char    *get_prefix( type )
182 link    *type;
183 {
184     /* Return the first character of the LP(), BP(), WP(), etc., directive
185      * that accesses a variable of the given type. Note that an array or
186      * structure type is assumed to be a pointer to the first cell at run time.
187      */
188
189     int  c;
190
191     if( type )
192     {
193         if( type->class == DECLARATOR )
194         {
195             switch( type->DCL_TYPE )
196             {
197             case ARRAY:     return( get_prefix( type->next ) );
198             case FUNCTION:  return PTR_PREFIX;
199             case POINTER:
200                 c = *get_prefix( type->next );
201
202                 if    ( c == *BYTE_PREFIX  )  return BYTEPTR_PREFIX;
203                 else if( c == *WORD_PREFIX  )  return WORDPTR_PREFIX;
204                 else if( c == *LWORD_PREFIX )  return LWORDPTR_PREFIX;
205                                               return PTRPTR_PREFIX;
206                 break;
207             }
208         }
```

Listing 6.69. continued...

```
209          else
210          {
211              switch( type->NOUN )
212              {
213              case INT:          return (type->LONG) ?  LWORD_PREFIX : WORD_PREFIX;
214              case CHAR:
215              case STRUCTURE: return BYTEPTR_PREFIX ;
216              }
217          }
218      }
219      yyerror("INTERNAL, get_prefix: Can't process type %s.\n", type_str(type) );
220      exit( 1 );
221  }
222
223  /*-------------------------------------------------------------------*/
224
225  value   *tmp_gen( tmp_type, src )
226  link    *tmp_type;       /* type of temporary taken from here        */
227  value   *src;            /* source variable that is copied into temporary */
228  {
229      /* Create a temporary variable of the indicated type and then generate
230       * code to copy src into it. Return a pointer to a "value" for the temporary
231       * variable. Truncation is done silently; you may want to add a lint-style
232       * warning message in this situation, however. Src is converted to an
233       * rvalue if necessary, and is released after being copied. If tmp_type
234       * is NULL, an int is created.
235       */
236
237      value   *val;                              /* temporary variable         */
238      char    *reg;
239
240      if( !the_same_type( tmp_type, src->type, 1) )
241      {
242          /* convert_type() copies src to a register and does any necessary type
243           * conversion. It returns a string that can be used to access the
244           * register. Once the src has been copied, it can be released, and
245           * a new temporary (this time of the new type) is created and
246           * initialized from the register.
247           */
248
249          reg = convert_type( tmp_type, src );
250          release_value( src );
251          val = tmp_create( IS_CHAR(tmp_type) ? NULL : tmp_type, 0 );
252          gen( "=",  val->name, reg );
253      }
254      else
255      {
256          val = tmp_create( tmp_type, 0 );
257          gen( "=", val->name, rvalue(src) );
258          release_value( src );
259      }
260      return val;
261  }
262
263  /*-------------------------------------------------------------------*/
264
265  char    *convert_type( targ_type, src )
266  link    *targ_type;                    /* type of target object      */
267  value   *src;                          /* source to be converted     */
268  {
```

```
Listing 6.69. continued...
269        int    dsize;                        /* src size, dst size            */
270        static char reg[16];                 /* place to assemble register name */
271
272        /* This routine should only be called if the target type (in targ_type)
273         * and the source type (in src->type) disagree. It generates code to copy
274         * the source into a register and do any type conversion. It returns a
275         * string that references the register. This string should be used
276         * immediately as the source of an assignment instruction, like this:
277         *
278         *       gen( "=",  dst_name, convert_type( dst_type, src ); )
279         */
280
281        sprintf( reg, "r0.%s",  get_suffix(src->type) );         /* copy into */
282        gen    ( "=",  reg,      rvalue(src)          );         /* register. */
283
284        if( (dsize = get_size(targ_type)) > get_size(src->type) )
285        {
286            if( src->etype->UNSIGNED )                            /* zero fill */
287            {
288                if( dsize == 2 ) gen( "=", "r0.b.b1",   "0" );
289                if( dsize == 4 ) gen( "=", "r0.w.high", "0" );
290            }
291            else                                                 /* sign extend */
292            {
293                if( dsize == 2 ) gen( "ext_low",   "r0" );
294                if( dsize == 4 ) gen( "ext_word", "r0" );
295            }
296        }
297
298        sprintf( reg, "r0.%s",  get_suffix(targ_type) );
299        return reg;
300    }
301
302    /*----------------------------------------------------------------------*/
303
304    PUBLIC  int    get_size( type )
305    link    *type;
306    {
307        /* Return the number of bytes required to hold the thing referenced by
308         * get_prefix().
309         */
310
311        if( type )
312        {
313            if( type->class == DECLARATOR )
314                return (type->DCL_TYPE == ARRAY) ? get_size(type->next) : PSIZE ;
315            else
316            {
317                switch( type->NOUN )
318                {
319                case INT:       return (type->LONG) ?  LSIZE : ISIZE;
320                case CHAR:
321                case STRUCTURE: return CSIZE;
322                }
323            }
324        }
325        yyerror("INTERNAL, get_size: Can't size type: %s.\n", type_str(type));
326        exit(1);
327    }
328
```

```
      Listing 6.69. continued...
329     /*------------------------------------------------------------------*/
330
331     char    *get_suffix( type )
332     link    *type;
333     {
334         /* Returns the string for an operand that gets a number of the indicated
335          * type out of a register. (It returns the xx in : r0.xx). "pp" is returned
336          * for pointers, arrays, and structures--get_suffix() is used only for
337          * temporary-variable manipulation, not declarations. If an an array or
338          * structure declarator is a component of a temporary-variable's type chain,
339          * then that declarator actually represents a pointer at run time. The
340          * returned string is, at most, five characters long.
341          */
342
343         if( type )
344         {
345             if( type->class == DECLARATOR )
346                 return "pp";
347             else
348                 switch( type->NOUN )
349                 {
350                 case INT:        return (type->LONG) ?  "l" : "w.low";
351                 case CHAR:
352                 case STRUCTURE: return "b.b0";
353                 }
354         }
355         yyerror("INTERNAL, get_suffix: Can't process type %s.\n", type_str(type) );
356         exit( 1 );
357     }
358
359     /*------------------------------------------------------------------*/
360
361     void    release_value( val )
362     value   *val;                    /* Discard a value, first freeing any space   */
363     {                                /* used for an associated temporary variable. */
364         if( val )
365         {
366             if( val->is_tmp )
367                 tmp_free( val->offset );
368             discard_value( val );
369         }
370     }
```

Create and initialize temporary: `tmp_gen()`.

`tmp_gen()` on line 225 of Listing 6.69 both creates the temporary and emits the code necessary to initialize it. (`tmp_create()` doesn't initialize the temporary.) The subroutine is passed three arguments. The first is a pointer to a type chain representing the type of the temporary. An **int** is created if this argument is NULL. The second argument is a pointer to a `value` representing an object to be copied into the temporary. Code is generated to do the copying, and the source `value` is released after the code to do the copy is generated. If the source is an lvalue, it is converted to an rvalue first.

Type conversions.

`convert_type()`.

If the source variable and temporary variable's types don't match, code is generated to do any necessary type conversions. Type conversions are done in `convert_type()` on line 265 of Listing 6.69 by copying the original variable into a register; if the new variable is larger than the source, code to do sign extension or zero fill is emitted. The subroutine returns a string that holds the name of the target register. For example, the input code:

```
int  i;
long l;
foo(){ i=i+l; }
```

generates the following output:

```
r0.w.low  =  W(&_i);
ext_word(r0);
L( T(1) ) =  r0.l;

L( T(1) ) += L(&_l);

r0.l      =  L( T(1) );
W(&_i)    =  r0.w.low;
```

The first two lines, emitted by `convert_type()`, create a **long** temporary variable and initialize it from an **int**. The code copies i into a `word` register and then sign extends the register to form an `lword`. The string `"r0.l"` is passed back to `tmp_gen()`, which uses it to emit the assignment on the third line. The last two lines demonstrate how a truncation is done. `convert_type` emits code to copy `T(1)` into a register. It then passes the string `"r0.w.low"` back up to the calling routine, which uses it to generate the assignment.

The test on line 284 of Listing 6.69 checks to see if sign extension is necessary (by comparing the number of bytes used for both variables—`get_size()` starts on line 304 of Listing 6.69). Code to do the type conversion is done on lines 286 to 295 of Listing 6.69. `get_suffix`, used on line 298 to access the register, starts on 331 of listing 6.69.

The `release_value()` subroutine on line 361 of Listing 6.69 is a somewhat higher-level version of `discard_value()`. It's used for temporary variables and both discards the `value` structure and frees any stack space used for the temporary. Note that the original source `value` is discarded on line 250 of Listing 6.69 as soon as the variable is copied into a register, so the memory used by the original variable can be recycled for the new temporary.

`release_value()`.

6.8.4 Unary Operators

Armed with the foregoing, you can proceed to tackle expression processing, starting with the unary operators and working our way up the grammar to complete expressions. Because you're starting at the bottom, it is helpful to look at the overall structure of the expression productions in Appendix C before continuing. Start with the *expr* nonterminal and go to the end of the grammar.

The unary operators are handled by the right-hand sides of the *unary* nonterminal, which you get to like this:

compound_stmt	→	**LC** *local_defs stmt_list* **RC**
stmt_list	→	*stmt*
stmt	→	*expr* **SEMI**
expr	→	*binary* | *unary*

(I've both simplified and left out a few intermediate productions for clarity. See Appendix C for the actual productions.) The simplest of the *unary* productions are in Listing 6.70. The top production just handles parenthesized subexpressions, and the second right-hand side recognizes, but ignores, floating-point constants.

The right-hand side on line 597 handles integer constants, creating a `value` structure like the one examined earlier in Figure 6.19. `make_icon()`, in Listing 6.71, does the actual work, creating a `value` for the integer constant, which is then passed back up as an attribute. This subroutine is used in several other places so it does more than is

Integer constants, `make_icon()`.

Listing 6.70. *c.y*— Unary Operators (Part 1)—Constants and Identifiers

```
594    unary
595             : LP expr RP      { $$ = $2;                                        }
596             | FCON            { yyerror("Floating-point not supported\n");     }
597             | ICON            { $$ = make_icon ( yytext,  0 );                 }
598             | NAME            { $$ = do_name   ( yytext, $1 );                 }
```

required by the current production. In particular, the incoming parameter can represent the number either as an integer or as a string. Numeric input is used here by setting yytext to NULL.

Identifiers,
unary→**NAME**.

do_name().

Identifiers are handled by on line 598 of Listing 6.70, above. The attribute attached to the **NAME** at $1 is a pointer to the symbol table entry for the identifier or NULL if the identifier isn't in the table. The actual work is done by do_name(), in Listing 6.72, below.

Listing 6.71. *value.c*— Make Integer and Integer-Constant Rvalues

```
371    value   *make_icon( yytext, numeric_val )
372    char    *yytext;
373    int     numeric_val;
374    {
375        /* Make an integer-constant rvalue. If yytext is NULL, then numeric_val
376         * holds the numeric value, otherwise the second argument is not used and
377         * the string in yytext represents the constant.
378         */
379
380        value *vp;
381        link  *lp;
382        char  *p;
383
384        vp           = make_int();
385        lp           = vp->type;
386        lp->SCLASS   = CONSTANT;
387
388        if( !yytext )
389            lp->V_INT = numeric_val;
390
391        else if( *yytext == '\'' )
392        {
393            ++yytext;                          /* Skip the quote. */
394            lp->V_INT = esc( &yytext );
395        }
396        else                                   /* Initialize the const_val field    */
397        {                                      /* based on the input type. stoul()  */
398                                               /* converts a string to unsigned long.*/
399            for( p = yytext; *p ; ++p )
400            {
401                if     ( *p=='u' || *p=='U' ) { lp->UNSIGNED = 1; }
402                else if( *p=='l' || *p=='L' ) { lp->LONG     = 1; }
403            }
404            if( lp->LONG )
405                lp->V_ULONG = stoul( &yytext );
406            else
407                lp->V_UINT  = (unsigned int) stoul( &yytext );
408        }
409        return vp;
410    }
```

→

```
      Listing 6.71. continued...
411
412   /*---------------------------------------------------------------------*/
413
414   value   *make_int()
415   {                                            /* Make an unnamed integer rvalue. */
416       link  *lp;
417       value *vp;
418
419       lp          = new_link();
420       lp->class   = SPECIFIER;
421       lp->NOUN    = INT;
422       vp          = new_value();               /* It's an rvalue by default. */
423       vp->type    = vp->etype = lp;
424       return vp;
425   }
```

Listing 6.72. *op.c*— Identifier Processing

```
 1    #include <stdio.h>
 2    #include <stdlib.h>
 3    #include <tools/debug.h>
 4    #include <tools/hash.h>
 5    #include <tools/l.h>
 6    #include <tools/compiler.h>
 7    #include <tools/c-code.h>
 8    #include "symtab.h"
 9    #include "value.h"
10    #include "proto.h"
11    #include "label.h"
12
13    /* OP.C          This file contains support subroutines for the arithmetic */
14    /*               operations in c.y.                                        */
15
16    symbol  *Undecl = NULL; /* When an undeclared symbol is used in an expression,
17                             * it is added to the symbol table to suppress subse-
18                             * quent error messages. This is a pointer to the head
19                             * of a linked list of such undeclared symbols. It is
20                             * purged by purge_undecl() at the end of compound
21                             * statements, at which time error messages are also
22                             * generated.
23                             */
24
25    /*---------------------------------------------------------------------*/
26
27    value   *do_name( yytext, sym )
28    char    *yytext;                    /* Lexeme                                 */
29    symbol  *sym;                       /* Symbol-table entry for id, NULL if none. */
30    {
31        link   *chain_end, *lp ;
32        value  *synth;
33        char   buf[ VALNAME_MAX ];
34
35        /* This routine usually returns a logical lvalue for the referenced symbol.
36         * The symbol's type chain is copied into the value and value->name is a
37         * string, which when used as an operand, evaluates to the address of the
38         * object. Exceptions are aggregate types (arrays and structures), which
39         * generate pointer temporary variables, initialize the temporaries to point
```

➡

Listing 6.72. continued...

```
40              * at the first element of the aggregate, and return an rvalue that
41              * references that pointer. The type chain is still just copied from the
42              * source symbol, so a structure or pointer must be interpreted as a pointer
43              * to the first element/field by the other code-generation subroutines.
44              * It's also important that the indirection processing (* [] . ->) set up
45              * the same sort of object when the referenced object is an aggregate.
46              *
47              * Note that !sym must be checked twice, below. The problem is the same one
48              * we had earlier with typedefs. A statement like foo(){int x;x=1;} fails
49              * because the second x is read when the semicolon is shifted---before
50              * putting x into the symbol table. You can't use the trick used earlier
51              * because def_list is used all over the place, so the symbol table entries
52              * can't be made until local_defs->def_list is processed. The simplest
53              * solution is just to call findsym() if NULL was returned from the scanner.
54              *
55              * The second if(!sym) is needed when the symbol really isn't there.
56              */
57
58      if( !sym )
59          sym = (symbol *) findsym( Symbol_tab, yytext );
60
61      if( !sym )
62          sym = make_implicit_declaration( yytext, &Undecl );
63
64      if( IS_CONSTANT(sym->etype) )                                  /* it's an enum member */
65      {
66          if( IS_INT(sym->type) )
67              synth = make_icon( NULL, sym->type->V_INT );
68          else
69          {
70              yyerror("Unexpected noninteger constant\n");
71              synth = make_icon( NULL, 0 );
72          }
73      }
74      else
75      {
76          gen_comment("%s", sym->name);    /* Next instruction will have symbol */
77                                           /* name as a comment.                */
78
79          if( !(lp = clone_type( sym->type, &chain_end)) )
80          {
81              yyerror("INTERNAL do_name: Bad type chain\n" );
82              synth = make_icon( NULL, 0 );
83          }
84          else if( IS_AGGREGATE(sym->type) )
85          {
86              /* Manufacture pointer to first element */
87
88              sprintf(buf, "&%s(%s)",
89                              IS_ARRAY(sym->type) ? get_prefix(lp) : BYTE_PREFIX,
90                              sym->rname );
91
92              synth = tmp_create(sym->type, 0);
93              gen( "=", synth->name, buf );
94          }
95          else
96          {
97              synth           = new_value();
98              synth->lvalue = 1   ;
99              synth->type   = lp  ;
```

```
Listing 6.72. continued...
100                synth->etype   = chain_end;
101                synth->sym     = sym ;
102
103                if( sym->implicit || IS_FUNCT(lp) )
104                    strcpy( synth->name, sym->rname );
105                else
106                    sprintf(synth->name,
107                            (chain_end->SCLASS == FIXED) ? "&%s(&%s)" : "&%s(%s)",
108                                               get_prefix(lp), sym->rname);
109            }
110        }
111
112        return synth;
113    }
114
115    /*-------------------------------------------------------------------------*/
116
117    symbol   *make_implicit_declaration( name, undeclp )
118    char     *name;
119    symbol   **undeclp;
120    {
121        /* Create a symbol for the name, put it into the symbol table, and add it
122         * to the linked list pointed to by *undeclp. The symbol is an int. The
123         * level field is used for the line number.
124         */
125
126        symbol       *sym;
127        link         *lp;
128        extern int   yylineno;        /* created by LeX */
129        extern char  *yytext;
130
131        lp            = new_link();
132        lp->class     = SPECIFIER;
133        lp->NOUN      = INT;
134        sym           = new_symbol( name, 0 );
135        sym->implicit = 1;
136        sym->type     = sym->etype = lp;
137        sym->level    = yylineno;          /* Use the line number for the declaration */
138                                           /* level so that you can get at it later   */
139                                           /* if an error message is printed.         */
140
141        sprintf( sym->rname, "_%1.*s", sizeof(sym->rname)-2, yytext );
142        addsym ( Symbol_tab,        sym          );
143
144        sym->next  = *undeclp;                    /* Link into undeclared list. */
145        *undeclp   = sym;
146
147        return sym;
148    }
149
150    /*-------------------------------------------------------------------------*/
151
152    PUBLIC  void purge_undecl()
153    {
154        /* Go through the undeclared list. If something is a function, leave it in
155         * the symbol table as an implicit declaration, otherwise print an error
156         * message and remove it from the table. This routine is called at the
157         * end of every subroutine.
158         */
159
```

Listing 6.72. continued...

```
160        symbol *sym, *cur ;
161
162        for( sym = Undecl; sym; )
163        {
164            cur       = sym;              /* remove current symbol from list */
165            sym       = sym->next;
166            cur->next = NULL;
167
168            if( cur->implicit )
169            {
170                yyerror("%s (used on line %d) undeclared\n", cur->name, cur->level);
171                delsym( Symbol_tab, cur );
172                discard_symbol( cur );
173            }
174        }
175        Undecl = NULL;
176    }
```

The incoming `sym` argument is NULL when the scanner can't find the symbol in the table. The table lookup on line 58 of Listing 6.72 takes care of the time-delay problem discussed earlier when types were discussed. Code like this:

```
int x;
x = 1;
```

won't work because the symbol-table entry for `x` isn't created until after the second `x` is read. Remember, the action is performed after the **SEMI** is shifted, and the lookahead character is read as part of the shift operation.

Undeclared identifiers.   Undeclared identifiers pose a particular problem. The difficulty is function calls: an implicit declaration for the function must be created the first time the function is used. Undeclared variables are hard errors, though. Unfortunately, there's no way for the *unop*→**NAME** production to know how the name is being used. It doesn't know whether the name is part of a function call or not.

If the symbol really isn't in the table, `do_name()` creates an implicit declaration of type **int** for the undeclared identifier (on line 62 of Listing). -1 The `make_implicit_declaration()` subroutine is found on lines 117 to 148 of Listing 6.72. The new symbol is put into the symbol table, and the cross links form a linked list of undeclared symbols. The head-of-list pointer is `Undecl`, declared on line 16. The implicit `symbol` is marked as such by setting the `implicit` bit true on line 137 of Listing 6.72. The implicit symbol is modified when a function call is processed. A "function" declarator is added to the front of the type chain, and the `implicit` bit is turned off. I'll discuss this process in detail in a moment.

*make_implicit_-
declaration()*

After the entire subroutine is processed and the subroutine suffix is generated, `purge_undecl()` (on line 152 of Listing 6.72) is called to find and delete the undeclared symbols. This subroutine traverses the list of implicitly-generated symbols and prints "undeclared symbol" error messages for any of them that aren't functions. It also removes the undeclared variables from the symbol table and frees the memory.

purge_undecl()

One advantage of this approach is that the "undeclared symbol" error message is printed only once, regardless of the number of times that the symbol is used. The disadvantage is that the error message isn't printed until the entire subroutine has been processed.

Returning to the normal situation, by the time you get to line 64 of Listing 6.72, `sym` points at a `symbol` for the current identifier. If that symbol represents a constant, then it

Symbolic constants.

was created by a previous enumerated-type declaration. The action in this case (on lines 66 to 72) creates an rvalue for the constant, just as if the number, rather than the symbolic name, had been found.

If the current symbol is an identifier, a `value` is created on lines 74 to 110 of Listing 6.72. The type chain is cloned. Then, if the symbol represents an aggregate type such as an array, a temporary variable is generated and initialized to point at the first element of the aggregate. Note that this temporary is an rvalue, not an lvalue. (An array name without a star or brackets is illegal to the left of an equal sign.) It's also important to note that arrays and pointers can be treated identically by subsequent actions because a physical pointer to the first array element is generated—pointers and arrays are physically the same thing at run time. A `POINTER` declarator and an `ARRAY` declarator are treated identically by all of the code that follows. I'll explore this issue further, along with a few examples, in a moment.

If the current symbol is not an aggregate, a logical lvalue is created in the **else** clause on lines 95 to 109 of Listing 6.72. The `value`'s `name` field is initialized to a string that, when used as an operand in a C-code instruction, evaluates either to the address of the current object or to the address of the first element if it's an aggregate.

If the symbol is a function or if it was created with an implicit declaration, the name is used as is. (We're on lines 103 of Listing 6.72.) I'm assuming that an implicit symbol will eventually reference a function. The compiler generates bad code if the symbol doesn't, but so what? It's a hard error to use an undeclared variable.

All other symbols are handled by the `sprintf()` call on line 106 of Listing 6.72. The strategy is to represent all possible symbols in the same way, so that subsequent actions won't have to worry about how the name is specified. In other words, a subsequent action shouldn't have to know whether the referenced variable is on the stack, at a fixed memory address, or whatever. It should be able to use the name without thinking.

You can get this consistency with one of the stranger-looking, C-code storage classes. The one case that gives us no flexibility is a frame-pointer-relative variable, which must be accessed like this: `WP(fp+8)` . This string starts with a type indicator (`WP`), the variable reference itself is an address (`fp+8`), and an indirect addressing mode must be used to access the variable. To be consistent, variables at fixed addresses such as global variables are represented in a similar way—like this: `WP(&_p)`. The `fp+8` and `_p` are just taken from the `symbol`'s `name` field. The type (`WP`, here) is figured by `get_prefix()` by looking at the variable's actual type. Since we are forming lvalues, the names must evaluate to addresses, so we need one more ampersand in both cases. `&WP(fp+8)` and `&WP(&_p)` are actually put into the `name` array.

The next *unop* right-hand side, which handles string constants, is in Listing 6.73. The *string_const* productions in Listing 6.74 collect adjacent string constants and concatenate them into the `Str_buf` array, declared in the **occs** declarations section at the top of listing 6.74. The attribute attached to the *string_const* is a pointer to the assembled string, which is then turned into an rvalue by the `make_scon()` call on line 602 of Listing 6.73. The subroutine itself is in Listing 6.75. String constants are of type "pointer to **char**". The string itself is not stored internally by the compiler beyond the time necessary to parse it. When a string constant is recognized, a declaration like the following one is output to the *data* segment:

```
private   char   S156[]= "contents of string";
```

The numeric component of the label (156) is remembered in `v_int` field of the last `link` in the type chain, and the entire label is also loaded into the `value`'s `name` array.

The next operator, **sizeof**, is handled by the productions in Listing 6.76. Three cases have to be handled separately:

Creating identifier `values`.

Aggregate types represented by physical pointers at run time.

`value.name`

All symbols represented identically.

Using `&WP(&_p)` for lvalues

String constants.

*The **sizeof** operator.*

Listing 6.73. *c.y*— Unary Operators (Part 2)—String Constants

```
599   /* unop: */
600           | string_const  %prec COMMA
601                       {
602                           $$ = make_scon( $1 );
603                           yydata( "private\tchar\t%s[]=\"%s\";\n", $$->name,$1);
604                       }
```

Listing 6.74. *c.y*— Array in which String Constants are Assembled

```
139   %{
140   #define STR_MAX 512              /* Maximum size of a string constant.   */
141   char    Str_buf[STR_MAX];        /* Place to assemble string constants.  */
142   %}
```

```
605   string_const
606         : STRING
607             {
608                 $$       = Str_buf;
609                 *Str_buf = '\0';
610
611                 yytext[ strlen(yytext) - 1 ] = '\0' ;   /* Remove trailing " */
612
613                 if( concat(STR_MAX, Str_buf, Str_buf, yytext+1, NULL) < 0 )
614                     yyerror("String truncated at %d characters\n", STR_MAX );
615             }
616         | string_const STRING
617             {
618                 yytext[ strlen(yytext) - 1 ] = '\0' ;   /* Remove trailing " */
619
620                 if( concat(STR_MAX, Str_buf, Str_buf, yytext+1, NULL) < 0 )
621                     yyerror("String truncated at %d characters\n", STR_MAX );
622             }
623         ;
```

sizeof(`"string"`) evaluates to the number of characters in the string,
sizeof(*expression*) evaluates to the size of the temporary variable that holds the
result of the evaluation.

```
int  x;
long y;
sizeof( x );   /* = 2 (size of a  word ). */
sizeof( y );   /* = 4 (size of an lword). */
sizeof( x+y ); /* = 4 (size of an lword). */
```

sizeof(*type*)   evaluates to the number of bytes required by a variable of the
indicated type.

The returned attribute for all three cases is an integer-constant rvalue, the
`const_val` field of which holds the required size. The attribute attached to the *expr*
($3 in the second right-hand side in Listing 6.76) is a `value` for the temporary that holds
the result of the run-time expression evaluation. Its `type` field determines the size.
Similarly, the attribute attached to the *abstract_decl* ($3 in the third right-hand side in
Listing 6.76) is a nameless `symbol` that holds a type chain for the indicated type.

Listing 6.75. *value.c*— Make a String-Constant Rvalue

```
426    value    *make_scon( str )
427    char     *str;
428    {
429        link *p;
430        value *synth;
431        static unsigned label = 0;
432
433        synth          = new_value();
434        synth->type    = new_link();
435
436        p              = synth->type;
437        p->DCL_TYPE    = POINTER;
438        p->next        = new_link();
439
440        p              = p->next;
441        p->class       = SPECIFIER;
442        p->NOUN        = CHAR;
443        p->SCLASS      = CONSTANT;
444        p->V_INT       = ++label;
445
446        synth->etype   = p;
447        sprintf( synth->name, "%s%d", L_STRING, label );
448        return synth;
449    }
```

Listing 6.76. *c.y*— Unary Operators (Part 3)—`sizeof`

```
624    /* unop: */
625            | SIZEOF LP string_const RP                              %prec SIZEOF
626                                        { $$ = make_icon(NULL,strlen($3) + 1 ); }
627
628            | SIZEOF LP expr RP                                      %prec SIZEOF
629                                        { $$ = make_icon(NULL,get_sizeof($3->type));
630                                          release_value( $3 );
631                                        }
632            | SIZEOF LP abstract_decl RP                             %prec SIZEOF
633                                        {
634                                            $$ = make_icon( NULL,
635                                                    get_sizeof($3->type));
636                                            discard_symbol( $3 );
637                                        }
```

So far, none of the operators have generate code. With Listing 6.77, below, we move on to an operator that actually does something. The right-hand side in Listing 6.77 processes the cast operator. The test on line 641 checks to see if the cast is legal. If it is, and the source and destination types are both pointers, it just replaces the type chain in the operand with the one from the cast operator on lines 648 to 651. Note that this behavior, though common in C compilers, can cause problems because the contents of the pointer are not changed, only the type. A run-time alignment error occurs the first time you try to use the pointer if the alignment isn't correct.

Type-conversion operators.

Casts.

The third possibility, on line 655 of Listing 6.77, takes care of all other cases. The `tmp_gen()` call creates a temporary of the required type, copies the contents of the operand into the temporary (making any necessary type conversions and translating

Listing 6.77. *c.y*— Unary Operators (Part 4)—Casts and Address-of

```
638     /* unop: */
639             | LP abstract_decl RP unary                          %prec UNOP
640             {
641                     if( IS_AGGREGATE($2->type) )
642                     {
643                             yyerror( "Illegal cast to aggregate type\n" );
644                             $$ = $4;
645                     }
646                     else if( IS_POINTER($2->type) && IS_POINTER($4->type) )
647                     {
648                             discard_link_chain( $4->type );
649                             $4->type  = $2->type;
650                             $4->etype = $2->type;
651                             $$ = $4;
652                     }
653                     else
654                     {
655                             $$ = tmp_gen( $2->type, $4 );
656                     }
657             }
```

lvalues to rvalues as necessary), and finally, it deletes the value associated with the operand.

Unary minus, NOT, one's complement.

The next issue is the unary arithmetic operators, handled by the right-hand sides in Listing 6.78. The first one takes care of unary minus, the second handles the logical NOT and one's-complement operators (!, ˜). The attribute attached to the UNOP is the lexeme (passed in an **int** because it's only one character). Again, the work is done by a subroutine: do_unop(), at the top of Listing 6.79.

The ˜ and unary − operators.

The arithmetic operators are easy. The action (on lines 184 to 188 of Listing 6.79) just modifies the operand, passing the operator through to gen(). If the name field of the operand holds the string "W(fp+8)", then the following code is generated for unary minus and one's complement:

```
W(T(0)) =- W(fp+8);    /* -name */
W(T(0)) =˜ W(fp+8);    /* ˜name */
```

In the first case, the − is supplied in the production, in the second, the attribute is used.

The ! operator.

The logical NOT operator is a little harder to do because it must evaluate either to 1 or 0, depending on the truth or falsity of the operand. Assuming that x is at W(fp+6), the expression !x generates the following code:

```
        EQ( W(fp+6), 0 )                  /* if the operand if false */
                goto T0;
F0:         W( T(0) ) = 0;                        /* temp = 0 */
        goto E0;
T0:         W( T(0) ) = 1;                        /* temp = 1 */
E0:
```

tf_label()

The synthesized attribute is the temporary variable that holds the 1 or 0. All but the first two instructions are created by gen_false_true(), on line 206 of Listing 6.79. The T label takes care of the true situation, the F label with false, and the E (for *end*) lets the false case jump over the true one after making the assignment. The numeric component of all three labels is the same, and is generated by the tf_label() call on line 192 of Listing 6.79. (tf_label() is declared just a few lines down, on line 199.) This label is then passed to gen_false_true as an argument.

All but the first two lines of the output are emitted by `gen_false_true()`, starting   `gen_false_true()`
on line 206 of Listing 6.79. This subroutine is used by the actions for all of the logical
operators. It is passed the numeric component of the target labels and a pointer to the
operand's `value` structure. This second argument is used only to do a simple
optimization—if the operand is already a temporary variable of type **int**, then it is recycled to hold the result of the operation, otherwise a new temporary variable is created.
(The test is made on line 220 and the temporary is created on the next two lines.)
Remember, both the test and the jump to the true or false label are generated before
`gen_false_true()` is called, and once the jump has been created, the associated
`value` is no longer needed. The operand's `value` could be discarded by the calling routine if you didn't want to bother with the optimization.

Note that the low-level `tmp_create()` function, which creates but doesn't initialize the temporary, is used here. Also note that the `value` is discarded <u>before</u> the
`tmp_create()` call so that the same region of memory can be recycled for the result of
the operation.

Listing 6.78. *c.y*— Unary Operators (Part 5)—Unary Arithmetic Operators

```
658     /* unop: */
659             | MINUS    unary        { $$ = do_unop( '-', $2 );   }
660             | UNOP     unary        { $$ = do_unop( $1, $2 );   }    %prec UNOP
```

The pre and post, increment and decrement operators are processed by the produc-   `++` and `--`, `incop()`.
tions in Listing 6.80 and the `incop()` subroutine in Listing 6.81. The following input
file:

```
int x;
foo(){ ++x; }
```

generates the following code for the `++x`:

```
W(&_x)    += 1;         /* Increment x itself.              */
W( T(1) ) =  W(&_x);    /* Copy incremented value to temporary. */
```

The synthesized attribute is the temporary variable. A postincrement like `x++` works in a
similar manner, but the two instructions are transposed:

```
W( T(1) ) =  W(&_x);
W(&_x)    += 1;
```

Again, the synthesized attribute is the temporary—the value of the temporary is determined by whether a pre or post increment is used. The `++` and `--` operators require an
lvalue operand, but they both generate rvalue temporararies. Pre and postdecrements use
`-=` rather than `+=` but are otherwise the same as the increments.

Listing 6.82 contains various right-hand sides for the address-of operator (`&`) and the   Pointer and array dere-
dereference operators (`*`, `[]`, `.`, and `->`). The structure operators are grouped with the   ferencing.
rest of them because they all do essentially the same thing: add an offset to a pointer and
load the object at the indicated address into a temporary variable. All of these operators
generate rvalues. The all require either an lvalue operand, or an rvalue operand of type
"array", "structure", or "pointer". Remember that aggregate-type references generate a
temporary variable (an rvalue) holding the address of the object.

The first issue is getting an objects address. The address-of operator is processed by   Address-of operator (`&`)
unop→**AND** *unary* on line 665 of Listing 6.82. The `addr_of()` workhorse function is
in Listing 6.83, below. Only two kinds of incoming values are legal here: an lvalue or
an rvalue for an aggregate type such as a structure. In either case, the incoming value

Listing 6.79. *op.c*— Unary Minus and Ones-Complement Operator Processing

```
177   value *do_unop( op, val )
178   int     op;
179   value *val;
180   {
181       char    *op_buf = "=?" ;
182       int     i;
183
184       if( op != '!' )         /* ~ or unary - */
185       {
186           op_buf[1] = op;
187           gen( op_buf, val->name, val->name );
188       }
189       else                     /* ! */
190       {
191           gen( "EQ",         rvalue(val), "0"          ); /*    EQ(x, 0)        */
192           gen( "goto%s%d", L_TRUE,     i = tf_label() ); /*        goto T000; */
193           val = gen_false_true( i, val );                /* fall thru to F     */
194       }
195       return val;
196   }
197   /*-------------------------------------------------------------------*/
198
199   int     tf_label()
200   {                           /* Return the numeric component of a label for use as */
201       static int label;       /* a true/false target for one of the statements      */
202       return ++label;         /* processed by gen_false_true().                     */
203   }
204   /*-------------------------------------------------------------------*/
205
206   value   *gen_false_true( labelnum, val )
207   int     labelnum;
208   value   *val;
209   {
210       /* Generate code to assign true or false to the temporary represented by
211        * val. Also, create a temporary to hold the result, using val if it's
212        * already the correct type. Return a pointer to the target. The FALSE
213        * code is at the top. If val is NULL, create a temporary. Labelnum must
214        * have been returned from a previous tf_label() call.
215        */
216
217       if( !val )
218           val = tmp_create( NULL, 0 );
219
220       else if( !val->is_tmp || !IS_INT(val->type) )
221       {
222           release_value( val );
223           val = tmp_create( NULL, 0 );
224       }
225       gen( ":%s%d",    L_FALSE,   labelnum );  /* F000:                */
226       gen( "=",        val->name, "0" );       /*         t0 = 0       */
227       gen( "goto%s%d", L_END,     labelnum );  /*         goto E000;   */
228       gen( ":%s%d",    L_TRUE,    labelnum );  /* T000:                */
229       gen( "=",        val->name, "1" );       /*         t0 = 1;      */
230       gen( ":%s%d",    L_END,     labelnum );  /* E000:                */
231       return val;
232   }
```

Listing 6.80. *c.y*— Unary Operators (Part 6)—Pre and Postincrement

```
661   /* unop: */
662          | unary INCOP          { $$ = incop( 0, $2, $1 );    }
663          | INCOP unary          { $$ = incop( 1, $1, $2 );    }
```

Listing 6.81. *op.c*— Increment and Decrement Operators

```
233   value  *incop( is_preincrement, op, val )                 /* ++ or -- */
234   int    is_preincrement;            /* Is preincrement or predecrement.    */
235   int    op;                         /* '-' for decrement, '+' for increment */
236   value  *val;                       /* lvalue to modify.                   */
237   {
238       char  buf[ VALNAME_MAX ];
239       char  *name;
240       value *new;
241       char  *out_op  = (op == '+') ? "+=%s%d" : "-=%s%d" ;
242       int   inc_amt ;
243
244       /* You must use rvalue_name() in the following code because rvalue()
245        * modifies the val itself--the name field might change. Here, you must use
246        * the same name both to create the temporary and do the increment so you
247        * can't let the name be modified.
248        */
249
250       if( !val->lvalue )
251           yyerror("%c%c: lvalue required\n", op, op );
252       else
253       {
254           inc_amt = (IS_POINTER(val->type)) ? get_sizeof(val->type->next) : 1 ;
255           name    = rvalue_name( val );
256
257           if( is_preincrement )
258           {
259               gen( out_op, name, inc_amt );
260               val = tmp_gen( val->type, val );
261           }
262           else                                         /* Postincrement. */
263           {
264               val = tmp_gen( val->type, val );
265               gen( out_op, name, inc_amt );
266           }
267       }
268       return val;
269   }
```

Listing 6.82. *c.y*— Unary Operators (Part 7)—Indirection

```
664   /* unop: */
665          | AND     unary     { $$ = addr_of ( $2      );  }  %prec UNOP
666          | STAR unary        { $$ = indirect( NULL, $2 );  }  %prec UNOP
667          | unary LB expr RB  { $$ = indirect( $3,   $1 );  }  %prec UNOP
668          | unary STRUCTOP NAME { $$ = do_struct($1, $2, yytext); }  %prec STRUCTOP
```

already holds the desired address: The lvalue is an address by definition. An rvalue like the one created by *unop*→**NAME** for an aggregate object is a physical temporary variable that also holds the required address. So, all that the address-of action needs to do is modify the value's type chain by adding an explicit pointer declarator at the far left and change its value into an rvalue by clearing the lvalue bit. Keep this action in mind when you read about the * operator, below. I'll start with the pointer dereference (*) and the array dereference ([]), operators, handled by indirect() (in Listing 6.84, below).

* and []

Listing 6.83. *op.c*— Address-of Operator Processing

```
270   value *addr_of( val )
271   value *val;
272   {
273         /* Process the & operator. Since the incoming value already holds the
274          * desired address, all you need do is change the type (add an explicit
275          * pointer at the far left) and change it into an rvalue. The first argument
276          * is returned.
277          */
278
279         link  *p;
280
281         if( val->lvalue )
282         {
283             p          = new_link();
284             p->DCL_TYPE = POINTER;
285             p->next    = val->type;
286             val->type  = p;
287             val->lvalue = 0;
288         }
289         else if( !IS_AGGREGATE(val->type) )
290             yyerror( "(&) lvalue required\n" );
291
292         return val;
293   }
```

Listing 6.84. *op.c*— Array Access and Pointer Dereferencing

```
294   value *indirect( offset, ptr )
295   value *offset;                    /* Offset factor (NULL if it's a pointer). */
296   value *ptr;                       /* Pointer that holds base address.        */
297   {
298         /* Do the indirection, If no offset is given, we're doing a *, otherwise
299          * we're doing ptr[offset]. Note that, strictly speaking, you should create
300          * the following dumb code:
301          *
302          *             t0 = rvalue( ptr );     (if ptr isn't a temporary)
303          *             t0 += offset            (if doing [offset])
304          *             t1 = *t0;               (creates a rvalue)
305          *                                     lvalue attribute = &t1
306          *
307          * but the first instruction is necessary only if ptr is not already a
308          * temporary, the second only if we're processing square brackets.
309          *
310          * The last two operations cancel if the input is a pointer to a pointer. In
311          * this case all you need to do is remove one * declarator from the type
312          * chain. Otherwise, you have to create a temporary to take care of the type
313          * conversion.
314          */
```

Listing 6.84. continued...

```
315
316      link  *tmp      ;
317      value *synth    ;
318      int    objsize  ;      /* Size of object pointed to (in bytes)          */
319
320      if( !IS_PTR_TYPE(ptr->type) )
321          yyerror( "Operand for * or [N] Must be pointer type\n" );
322
323      rvalue( ptr );              /* Convert to rvalue internally. The "name" field  */
324                                  /* is modified by removing leading &'s from logical */
325                                  /* lvalues.                                         */
326      if( offset )                /* Process an array offset.                         */
327      {
328          if( !IS_INT(offset->type) || !IS_CHAR(offset->type) )
329              yyerror( "Array index must be an integral type\n" );
330
331          objsize = get_sizeof( ptr->type->next );      /* Size of dereferenced */
332                                                         /* object.              */
333
334          if( !ptr->is_tmp )                             /* Generate a physical  */
335              ptr = tmp_gen( ptr->type, ptr );           /* lvalue.              */
336
337          if( IS_CONSTANT( offset->type ) )             /* Offset is a constant.*/
338          {
339              gen("+=%s%d", ptr->name, offset->type->V_INT * objsize );
340          }
341          else                                           /* Offset is not a con- */
342          {                                              /* stant. Do the arith- */
343                                                         /* metic at run time.   */
344
345              if( objsize != 1 )                         /* Multiply offset by   */
346              {                                          /* size of one object.  */
347                  if( !offset->is_tmp )
348                      offset = tmp_gen( offset->type, offset );
349
350                  gen( "*=%s%d", offset->name, objsize );
351              }
352
353              gen( "+=",  ptr->name, offset->name );     /* Add offset to base. */
354          }
355
356          release_value( offset );
357      }
358
359      /* The temporary just generated (or the input variable if no temporary
360       * was generated) now holds the address of the desired cell. This command
361       * must generate an lvalue unless the object pointed to is an aggregate,
362       * whereupon it's n rvalue. In any event, you can just label the current
363       * cell as an lvalue or rvalue as appropriate and continue. The type must
364       * be advanced one notch to compensate for the indirection, however.
365       */
366
367      synth        = ptr;
368      tmp          = ptr->type;                           /* Advance type one notch. */
369      ptr->type    = ptr->type->next;
370      discard_link(tmp);
371
```

Listing 6.84. continued...

```
372         if( !IS_AGGREGATE(ptr->type->next) )
373             synth->lvalue = 1;                          /* Convert to lvalue.  */
374
375         return synth;
376     }
```

Operand to * or [] must
be array or pointer.
The best way to understand the code is to analyze what actually happens as the operator is processed. First of all, as was the case with the address-of operator, the operand must represent an address. It is one of two things: (1) **an array**, in which case the operand is an rvalue that holds the base address of the array, or (2) **a pointer**, in which case the operand is an lvalue for something of pointer type—the expression in the value's name field evaluates to the address of the pointer.

Attribute synthesized by
* and [] operators.
The next issue is the synthesized attribute, which is controlled by the type of the dereferenced object. The compiler needs to convert the incoming attribute to the synthesized attribute. If the dereferenced object is a nonaggregate, the synthesized attribute is an lvalue that holds the address of the dereferenced object. If the dereferenced object is an aggregate, then the attribute is an rvalue that holds the address of the first element of the object. In other words, the generated attribute must be the same thing that would be created by *unop*→**NAME** if it were given an identifier of the same type as the referenced object. Note that both the incoming and outgoing attributes are addresses.

Rules for forming lvalues
and rvalues when pro-
cessing * and [].
To summarize (if the following isn't clear, hold on for a second—several examples follow):

(1)   The dereferenced object is <u>not</u> an aggregate. The synthesized attribute is an <u>lvalue</u> that references that object, and:

    a.   if the incoming attribute is an <u>rvalue</u>, then it already contains the necessary address. That is, the incoming rvalue holds the address of the dereferenced object, and the outgoing lvalue must also hold the address of the dereferenced object. Consequently, no code needs to be generated in this case. The compiler does have to modify the value internally, however. First, by setting the lvalue bit true, and second, by removing the first link in the type chain. Remember, the generated lvalue is for the dereferenced object. If the incoming type is "pointer to **int**", the outgoing object is an lvalue that references the **int**.

       If the compiler's doing an array access rather than a pointer access, code must also be emitted to add an offset to the base address that's stored in the lvalue.

    b.   if the incoming attribute is a <u>logical</u> lvalue, then all the compiler needs to do is remove the leading ampersand and change the type as discussed earlier. The pointer variable is now treated as if it were a physical lvalue.

       If the compiler's processing an array access, it must create a physical lvalue in order to add an offset to it. It can't modify the declared variable to compute an array access.

    c.   if the incoming attribute is a <u>physical</u> lvalue, for a pointer, then you need to generate code to get rid of one level of indirection, and change the type as was discussed earlier. You can safely add an offset to the physical lvalue to do array access.

(2)   The dereferenced object <u>is</u> an aggregate. The synthesized attribute is an <u>rvalue</u> that points at the first element of the referenced array or structure, and:

    a.   if the incoming attribute is an <u>rvalue</u>, use it for the synthesized attribute, changing the type by removing the first declarator link and adding an offset as necessary.

b. if the incoming attribute is a <u>logical</u> lvalue, create a physical rvalue, with the type adjusted, as above.

c. if the incoming attribute is a <u>physical</u> lvalue, convert it to an rvalue by resetting the `lvalue` bit and adjust the type, as above.

Note that many of the foregoing operations generate no code at all—they just modify the way that something is represented internally. Code is generated only when an offset needs to be computed or an incoming lvalue references an aggregate object. Also, notice the similarities between processing a `&` and processing a `*`. The former adds a pointer declarator to the type chain and turns the incoming attribute into an rvalue; the latter does the exact opposite, removing a pointer declarator from the front of the type chain and turning the incoming attribute into an lvalue.

I'll demonstrate how indirection works with some examples. Parses of the following code is shown in Tables 6.17 to 6.23.

```
int *p, a[10];
foo()
{
    *p++;      *++p;      ++*p;      (*p)++;
    a[7];    ++p[3];    p++[3];
}
```

Table 6.17. Generate Code for `*p++;`

Parse and Value Stacks				Comments
stmt_list □				Shift **STAR**.
stmt_list □	**STAR** □			Shift **NAME**. The attribute for **NAME** is a pointer to the `symbol` for p.
stmt_list □	**STAR** □	**NAME** p		Reduce by *unary*→**NAME**. The action creates an lvalue that references the variable.
stmt_list □	**STAR** □	*unary* &WP(&_p)$_L$		Shift **INCOP**.

stmt_list □	**STAR** □	*unary* &WP(&_p)$_L$	**INCOP** '+'	Reduce by *unary*→*unary* **INCOP**. Emit code to increment p:
				    CODE: WP(T(1)) = WP(&_p);
				    CODE: WP(&_p) += 2;
				The synthesized attribute is an rvalue (of type "pointer to **int**") for the temporary variable.

stmt_list □	**STAR** □	*unary* WP(T(1))$_R$		Reduce by *unary*→**STAR** *unary*. $2 (under the *unary*) already contains the correct address and is of the correct type. Convert it to a physical lvalue that references *p (not p itself).
stmt_list □	*unary* WP(T(1))$_L$			Subsequent operations cannot access p; they can access *p with *WP(T(1)).

Neither the entire parse nor the entire parse stack is shown in the tables, but there's enough shown that you can see what's going on. The following symbols are on the stack to the left of the ones that are shown.

> *ext_def_list opt_specifiers funct_decl* {70} *def_list* {71} **LC** {65} *local_defs*

I've shown the value stacks under the parse stack. Attributes for most of the nonterminals are `value` structures—the `name` field is shown in the table. Subscripts indicate whether it's an lvalue (name) or rvalue (name). Logical lvalues start with an ampersand. A box (□) is used when there are no attributes. You should look at all these tables now, even though they're scattered over several pages.

I've used the ++ operators in these expressions because ++ requires an lvalue, but it generates an rvalue. The ++ is used to demonstrate how the indirection is handled with both kinds of incoming attributes. Other, more complex expressions [like `* (p+1)`] are

Table 6.18. Generate Code for `*++p;`

Parse and Value Stacks				Comments
stmt_list □				Shift **STAR**
stmt_list □	**STAR** □			Shift **INCOP**. The attribute for **INCOP** is the first character of the lexeme.
stmt_list □	**STAR** □	**INCOP** '+'		Shift **NAME**. The attribute for **NAME** is a pointer to the symbol for p.
stmt_list □	**STAR** □	**INCOP** '+'	**NAME** p	Reduce by *unary*→**NAME**. Create a logical lvalue that references p.
stmt_list □	**STAR** □	**INCOP** '+'	*unary* &WP(&_p)$_L$	Reduce by *unary*→**INCOP** *unary*. Emit code to increment p: **CODE:** WP(&_p) += 2; **CODE:** WP(T(1)) = WP(&_p); The synthesized attribute is an rvalue of type "pointer to **int**" that holds a copy of p. From this point on, the compiler has forgotten that p ever existed—at least for the purposes of processing the current expression.
stmt_list □	**STAR** □	*unary* WP(T(1))$_R$		Reduce by *unary*→**STAR** *unary*. The current reduction turns the attribute from the previous reduction it into a physical lvalue that references the dereferenced object (*p).
stmt_list □	*unary* WP(T(1))$_L$			

Table 6.19. Generate Code for `(*p)++;`

Parse and Value Stacks				Comments
stmt_list □				Shift **LP**
stmt_list □	**LP** □			Shift **STAR**
stmt_list □	**LP** □	**STAR** □		Shift **NAME**. The attribute is a pointer to a symbol structure for p.
stmt_list □	**LP** □	**STAR** □	**NAME** p	Reduce by *unary*→**NAME**. The synthesized attribute is a logical lvalue that references p.
stmt_list □	**LP** □	**STAR** □	*unary* &WP(&_p)$_L$	Reduce by *unary*→**STAR** *unary*. Convert the incoming logical lvalue for p to a physical lvalue that references *p.
stmt_list □	**LP** □	*unary* WP(&_p)$_L$		*unary* is now converted to *expr* by a series of reductions, not shown here. The initial attribute is passed through to the *expr*, however.
stmt_list □	**LP** □	*expr* WP(&_p)$_L$		Shift **RP**
stmt_list □	**LP** □	*expr* WP(&_p)$_L$	**RP**	Reduce by *unary*→**LP** *expr* **RP**. $$ = $2;
stmt_list □	*unary* WP(&_p)$_L$			Shift **INCOP**
stmt_list □	*unary* WP(&_p)$_L$	**INCOP** '+'		Reduce by *unary*→*unary***INCOP**. Emit code to increment *p: **CODE:** W(T(1)) = *WP(&_p); **CODE:** *WP(&_p) += 1; The synthesized attribute is an rvalue for the temporary that holds the incremented value of *p;
stmt_list □	*unary* W(T(1))$_R$			

handled in much the same way. (p+1, like ++p, generates an rvalue of type pointer.)

I suggest doing an exercise at this juncture. Parse the following code by hand, starting at the stmt_list, as in the previous examples, showing the generated code and the relevant parts of the parse and value stack at each step:

Table 6.20. Generate Code for `++*p;`

Parse and Value Stacks				Comments
stmt_list □				Shift **INCOP**
stmt_list □	**INCOP** `'+'`			Shift **STAR**
stmt_list □	**INCOP** `'+'`	**STAR** □		Shift **NAME**. The attribute for **NAME** is a pointer to the `symbol` structure for `p`.
stmt_list □	**INCOP** `'+'`	**STAR** □	**NAME** p	Reduce by *unary*→**NAME**. Create a logical lvalue for `p`.
stmt_list □	**INCOP** `'+'`	**STAR** □	*unary* `&WP(&_p)`$_L$	Reduce by *unary*→**STAR** *unary*. This reduction converts the logical lvalue that references `p` into a physical lvalue that references `*p`.
stmt_list □	**INCOP** `'+'`	*unary* □ `WP(&_p)`$_L$		Reduce by *unary*→**INCOP** *unary* Emit code to increment `*p`: **CODE:** `*WP(&_p) += 1;` **CODE:** `W(T(1))  = *WP(&_p);` The generated attribute is an rvalue that holds the contents of `*p` after the increment—this is a preincrement.
stmt_list □	*unary* `W(T(1))`$_R$			

Table 6.21. Generate Code for `a[7];`

Parse and Value Stacks				Comments
stmt_list □				Shift **NAME**. The attribute for **NAME** is a pointer to the `symbol` structure for `a`.
stmt_list □	*NAME* a			Reduce by *unary*→**NAME**. Since this is an array rather than a simple pointer variable, an rvalue is generated of type "pointer to first array element" (pointer to **int**, here): **CODE:** `W(T(1)) = &W(_a);`
stmt_list □	*unary* `W(T(1))`$_R$			Shift **LB**.
stmt_list □	*unary* `W(T(1))`$_R$	*LB* □		Shift **ICON**.
stmt_list □	*unary* `W(T(1))`$_R$	*LB* □	*ICON* "7"	Reduce by *unary*→**ICON**. The synthesized attribute is a `value` representing the constant 7.
stmt_list □	*unary* `W(T(1))`$_R$	*LB* □	*unary* 7$_R$	*unary* is reduced to *expr* by a series of reductions, not shown here. The attribute is passed through to the *expr*, however.
stmt_list □	*unary* `W(T(1))`$_R$	*LB* □	*expr* 7$_R$	Shift **RB**.
stmt_list □	*unary* `W(T(1))`$_R$	*LB* □ *expr* RB 7$_R$ □		Reduce by *unary*→**LB**expr**RB**. The incoming attribute is an rvalue of type "pointer to **int**." The following code is generated to compute the offset: **CODE:** `W(T(1)) += 14;` The synthesized attribute is an lvalue holding the address of the eighth array element.
stmt_list □	*unary* `W(T(1))`$_L$			The final attribute is an lvalue that references `a[7]`.

```
int *x[5];
**x;
*x[3];
x[1][2];
```

The other pointer-related operators are the structure-access operators: `.` and `->`. These are handled by the `do_struct()` subroutine in Listing 6.85. The basic logic is the same as that used for arrays and pointers. This time the offset is determined by the position of the field within the structure, however.

Structure access: `->` and `.`, `do_struct()`.

The final unary operator handles function calls. It's implemented by the *unop* right-hand sides in Listing 6.85 and the associated subroutines, `call()` and `ret_reg()`, in Listing 6.86. One of the more interesting design issues in C is that the argument list as a

Function calls.

Table 6.22. Generate Code for `p++[3];`

Parse and Value Stacks					Comments
stmt_list □					Shift **NAME**
stmt_list □	*NAME*				Reduce by *unary*→**NAME**.
stmt_list □	*unary* `&WP(&_p)`$_L$				Shift **INCOP**
stmt_list □	*unary* `&WP(&_p)`$_L$	**INCOP** `'+'`			Reduce by *unary*→*unary* **INCOP**. Emit code to increment the pointer. The synthesized attribute is an rvalue of type pointer to **int**. **CODE:** `WP(T(1)) = WP(&_p);` **CODE:** `WP(&_p) += 2;`
stmt_list □	*unary* `WP(T(1))`$_R$				Shift **LB**.
stmt_list □	*unary* `WP(T(1))`$_R$	**LB** □			Shift **ICON**.
stmt_list □	*unary* `WP(T(1))`$_R$	**LB** □	**ICON** `'3'`		Reduce by *unary*→**ICON**. The action creates an rvalue for an **int** constant. The numeric value is stored in `$$->etype->V_INT`.
stmt_list □	*unary* `WP(T(1))`$_R$	**LB** □	*unary* 3$_R$		Reduce *unary* to *expr* by a series of reductions, not shown. The original attribute is passed through to the *expr*.
stmt_list □	*unary* `WP(T(1))`$_R$	**LB** □	*expr* 3$_R$		Shift **RB**.
stmt_list □	*unary* `WP(T(1))`$_L$	**LB** □	*expr* 3$_R$	**RB** □	Reduce by *unary*→**ICON**. Code is generated to compute the address of the fourth cell: **CODE:** `WP(T(1)) += 6;` Since the incoming attribute is already a temporary variable of the correct type, there's no need to generate a second temporary here—the first one is recycled. Note that it is translated to an lvalue that references the fourth cell, however.
stmt_list □	*unary* `WP(T(1))`$_L$				

whole can be seen as a function-call operator which can be applied to any function pointer;[22] a function name evaluates to a pointer to a function, much like an array name evaluates to a pointer to the first array element. The code-generation action does four things: push the arguments in reverse order, call the function, copy the return value into an rvalue, discard the arguments by adding a constant to the stack pointer. For example, a call like the following:

```
doctor( lawyer, merchant, chief );
```

is translated to:

```
push( W(&_chief) );     /* push the arguments              */
push( W(&_merchant) );
push( W(&_lawyer) );
call( _doctor );        /* call the subroutine             */
W( T(1) ) = rF.w.low;   /* copy return value to rvalue     */
sp += 3;                /* discard arguments.              */
```

Function-argument processing, *non_comma_expr.*

The function arguments are processed by the *args* productions on lines 674 to 681 of Listing 6.86. A *non_comma_expr* recognizes all C expressions except those that use comma operators. You must do something like the following to get a comma operator into a function call:

---

22. This is actually a C++ism, but it's a handy way to look at it.

Table 6.23. Generate Code for `++p[3];`

Parse and Value Stacks					Comments
stmt_list □					Shift **INCOP**
stmt_list □	**INCOP** `'+'`				Shift **NAME**. The attribute is a `symbol` representing p.
stmt_list □	**INCOP** `'+'`	*NAME*			Reduce by *unary*→**NAME**. Convert `symbol` to an lvalue.
stmt_list □	**INCOP** `'+'`	*unary* `&WP(&_p)`ₗ			Shift **LB**
stmt_list □	**INCOP** `'+'`	*unary* `&WP(&_p)`ₗ	**LB** □		Shift **ICON**
stmt_list □	**INCOP** `'+'`	*unary* `&WP(&_p)`ₗ	**LB** □	**ICON** `'3'`	Reduce by *unary*→**ICON**. The synthesized attribute is a `value` structure representing an **int** constant. It's an rvalue. The actual value (3) is stored internally in that structure.
stmt_list □	**INCOP** `'+'`	*unary* `&WP(&_p)`ₗ	**LB** □	*unary* 3_R	Reduce *unary* to *expr* by a series of reductions, not shown. The original attribute is passed through to the *expr*.
stmt_list □	**INCOP** `'+'`	*unary* `&WP(&_p)`ₗ	**LB** □	*expr* 3_R	Shift **RB**.
stmt_list □	**INCOP** `'+'`	*unary* `&WP(&_p)`ₗ	**LB** □	*expr* 3_R **RB** □	Reduce by *unary*→*unary***LB** *expr* **RB**. Code is generated to compute the address of the fourth cell, using the offset in the value at $3 and the base address in the `value` at $1: **CODE:** `WP(T(1)) = WP(&_p);` **CODE:** `WP(T(1)) += 6;` You have to generate a physical lvalue because p itself may not be incremented. The synthesized attribute is an `lvalue` that holds the address of the fourth element.
stmt_list □	**INCOP** `'+'`	*unary* `WP(T(1))`ₗ			Reduce by *unary*→**INCOP** *unary*. Code is generated to increment the array element, the address of which is in the lvalue generated in the previous reduction. **CODE:** `*WP(T(1)) += 1;` **CODE:** `W(T(2)) = *WP(T(1));` The synthesized attribute is an rvalue that duplicates the contents of that cell.
stmt_list □	*unary* `W(T(2))`_R				

```
tinker( (tailor,cowboy), sailor );
```

This function call has two arguments, the first one is the expression (`tailor, cowboy`), which evaluates to `cowboy`. The second argument is `sailor`. The associated attribute is a `value` for that expression—an lvalue is used if the expression is a simple variable or pointer reference; an rvalue is used for most other expressions.

The *args* productions just traverse the list of arguments, printing the `push` instructions and keeping track of the number of arguments pushed. The argument count is returned back up the tree as the synthesized attribute. Note that the *args* productions form a <u>right</u>-recursive list. Right recursion is generally not a great idea in a bottom-up parser because all of the list elements pile up on the stack before any reductions occur. On the other hand, the list elements are processed in right to left order, which is convenient here because arguments have to be pushed from right to left. The recursion shouldn't cause problems unless the subroutine has an abnormally high number of arguments.

The `call()` subroutine at the top of Listing MN `"call()"` 6.85+2 generates both the `call` instruction and the code that handles return values and stack clean up. It also takes care of implicit subroutine declarations on lines 513 to 526. The action in *unary*→**NAME** creates a `symbol` of type **int** for an undeclared identifier, and this

args→... productions.
Right recursion gets arguments pushed in correct order.

unary→**NAME**

614

symbol eventually ends up here as the incoming attribute. The `call()` subroutine changes the type to "function returning int" by adding another `link` to the head of the type chain. It also clears the `implicit` bit to indicate that the symbol is a legal implicit declaration rather than an undeclared variable. Finally, a C-code **extern** statement is generated for the function.

Listing 6.85. *op.c*— Structure Access

```
377  value *do_struct( val, op, field_name )
378  value    *val;
379  int      op;                /* . or - (the last is for ->)  */
380  char     *field_name;
381  {
382      value        *new;
383      symbol       *field;
384      link         *lp;
385
386      /* Structure names generate rvalues of type structure. The associated  */
387      /* name evaluates to the structure's address, however. Pointers generate */
388      /* lvalues, but are otherwise the same.                                  */
389
390      if( IS_POINTER(val->type) )
391      {
392          if( op != '-' )
393          {
394              yyerror("Object to left of -> must be a pointer\n");
395              return val;
396          }
397          lp       = val->type;          /* Remove POINTER declarator from */
398          val->type = val->type->next;   /* the type chain and discard it. */
399          discard_link( lp );
400      }
401
402      if( !IS_STRUCT(val->type) )
403      {
404          yyerror("Not a structure.\n");
405          return val;
406      }                                   /* Look up the field in the structure table: */
407
408      if( !(field = find_field(val->type->V_STRUCT, field_name)) )
409      {
410          yyerror("%s not a field\n", field_name );
411          return val;
412      }
413
414      if( val->lvalue || !val->is_tmp )    /* Generate temporary for     */
415          val = tmp_gen( val->type, val );  /* base address if necessary; */
416                                            /* then add the offset to the */
417      if( field->level > 0 )               /* desired field.             */
418          gen( "+=%s%d", val->name, field->level );
419
420      if( !IS_AGGREGATE(field->type) )     /* If referenced object isn't */
421          val->lvalue = 1;                  /* an aggregate, use lvalue.  */
422
423                                            /* Replace value's type chain */
424                                            /* with type chain for the    */
425                                            /* referenced object:         */
426      lp = val->type;
```

```
Listing 6.85. continued...
427        if( !(val->type = clone_type( field->type, &val->etype)) )
428        {
429            yyerror("INTERNAL do_struct: Bad type chain\n" );
430            exit(1);
431        }
432        discard_link_chain( lp );
433        access_with( val );                              /* Change the value's name   */
434                                                         /* field to access an object */
435        return val;                                      /* of the new type.          */
436   }
437
438   /*----------------------------------------------------------------------*/
439
440   PRIVATE  symbol *find_field( s, field_name )
441   structdef        *s;
442   char             *field_name;
443   {
444        /* Search for "field_name" in the linked list of fields for the input
445         * structdef. Return a pointer to the associated "symbol" if the field
446         * is there, otherwise return NULL.
447         */
448
449        symbol    *sym;
450        for( sym = s->fields; sym; sym = sym->next )
451        {
452            if( !strcmp(field_name, sym->name) )
453                return sym;
454        }
455        return NULL;
456   }
457
458   /*----------------------------------------------------------------------*/
459
460   PRIVATE char    *access_with( val )
461   value   *val;
462   {
463        /* Modifies the name string in val so that it references the current type.
464         * Returns a pointer to the modified string. Only the type part of the
465         * name is changed. For example, if the input name is "WP(fp+4)", and the
466         * type chain is for an int, the name is be changed to "W(fp+4). If val is
467         * an lvalue, prefix an ampersand to the name as well.
468         */
469
470        char *p, buf[ VALNAME_MAX ] ;
471
472        strcpy( buf, val->name );
473        for( p = buf; *p && *p != '(' /*)*/ ; ++p )              /* find name */
474            ;
475
476        if( !*p )
477            yyerror( "INTERNAL, access_with: missing parenthesis\n" );
478        else
479            sprintf( val->name, "%s%s%s", val->lvalue ? "&" : "",
480                                          get_prefix(val->type), p);
481        return val->name;
482   }
```

Listing 6.86. *c.y*— Unary Operators (Part 8)—Function Calls

```
669     /* unop: */
670             | unary LP args RP        { $$ = call     ( $1,  $3 );    }
671             | unary LP       RP        { $$ = call     ( $1,  0 );    }
672             ;
673
674     args    : non_comma_expr  %prec COMMA    {   gen( "push", rvalue( $1 ) );
675                                                 release_value( $1 );
676                                                 $$ = 1;
677                                             }
678             | non_comma_expr COMMA args     {   gen( "push", rvalue( $1 ) );
679                                                 release_value( $1 );
680                                                 $$ = $3 + 1;
681                                             }
682             ;
```

Listing 6.87. *op.c*— Function-Call Processing

```
483     PUBLIC value *call( val, nargs )
484     value *val;
485     int    nargs;
486     {
487         link    *lp;
488         value   *synth;        /* synthesized attribute                  */
489
490         /* The incoming attribute is an lvalue for a function if
491          *          funct()
492          * or
493          *          int (*p)() = funct;
494          *          (*p)();
495          *
496          * is processed. It's a pointer to a function if p() is used directly.
497          * In the case of a logical lvalue (with a leading &), the name will be a
498          * function name, and the rvalue can be generated in the normal way by
499          * removing the &. In the case of a physical lvalue the name of a variable
500          * that holds the function's address is given. No star may be added.
501          * If val is an rvalue, then it will never have a leading &.
502          */
503
504         if( val->sym  &&  val->sym->implicit  &&  !IS_FUNCT(val->type) )
505         {
506             /* Implicit symbols are not declared. This must be an implicit function
507              * declaration, so pretend that it's explicit. You have to modify both
508              * the value structure and the original symbol because the type in the
509              * value structure is a copy of the original. Once the modification is
510              * made, the implicit bit can be turned off.
511              */
512
513             lp                  = new_link();
514             lp->DCL_TYPE        = FUNCTION;
515             lp->next            = val->type;
516             val->type           = lp;
517
518             lp                  = new_link();
519             lp->DCL_TYPE        = FUNCTION;
520             lp->next            = val->sym->type;
521             val->sym->type      = lp;
522
```

```
Listing 6.87. continued...
523              val->sym->implicit = 0;
524              val->sym->level    = 0;
525
526              yydata( "extern\t%s();\n", val->sym->rname );
527          }
528
529      if( !IS_FUNCT(val->type) )
530      {
531          yyerror( "%s not a function\n", val->name );
532          synth = val;
533      }
534      else
535      {
536          lp    = val->type->next;                    /* return-value type */
537          synth = tmp_create( lp, 0 );
538
539          gen( "call", *val->name == '&' ? &val->name[1] : val->name );
540          gen(  "=",    synth->name, ret_reg(lp) );
541
542          if( nargs )
543              gen( "+=%s%d" , "sp", nargs );
544
545          release_value( val );
546      }
547
548      return synth;
549  }
550
551  /*-------------------------------------------------------------------------*/
552
553  char     *ret_reg( p )
554  link     *p;
555  {
556      /* Return a string representing the register used for a return value of
557       * the given type.
558       */
559
560      if( IS_DECLARATOR( p ) )
561          return "rF.pp";
562      else
563          switch( p->NOUN )
564          {
565          case INT:      return (p->LONG) ?  "rF.l" : "rF.w.low" ;
566          case CHAR:     return "rF.w.low" ;
567          default:       yyerror("INTERNAL ERROR: ret_reg, bad noun\n");
568                         return "AAAAAAAAAAAAAAGH!";
569          }
570  }
```

6.8.5 Binary Operators

We can now breathe a collective sigh of relief. The declaration system and the unary operators are the hardest parts of the compiler and they're over with. We can now move on to the binary operators. Again, it's useful to look at the overall structure of the binary-operator productions before proceeding. These are summarized in Table 6.24.

Table 6.24. Summary of Binary-Operator Productions

expr	:	*expr*	**COMMA**	*non_comma_expr*		
	|	*non_comma_expr*				
non_comma_expr	→	*non_comma_expr*	**ASSIGNOP**	*non_comma_expr*		
	|	*non_comma_expr*	**EQUAL**	*non_comma_expr*		
	|	*non_comma_expr*	**QUEST**	*non_comma_expr*	**COLON**	*non_comma_expr*
	|	*or_expr*				
or_expr	→	*or_list*				
or_list	→	*or_list*	**OROR**	*and_expr*		
	|	*and_expr*				
and_expr	→	*and_list*				
and_list	→	*and_list*	**ANDAND**	*binary*		
	|	*binary*				
binary	→	*binary*	**PLUS**	*binary*		
	|	*binary*	**MINUS**	*binary*		
	|	*binary*	**STAR**	*binary*		
	|	*binary*	**DIVOP**	*binary*		
	|	*binary*	**SHIFTOP**	*binary*		
	|	*binary*	**AND**	*binary*		
	|	*binary*	**XOR**	*binary*		
	|	*binary*	**OR**	*binary*		
	|	*binary*	**RELOP**	*binary*		
	|	*binary*	**EQUOP**	*binary*		
	|	*unary*				

This grouping of the productions is a compromise between the strict grammatical approach in which the grammar alone determines precedence and associativity—all operators that share a precedence level are isolated into single productions—and the more flexible **yacc/occs** approach in which all binary operators are combined into a single production with many right-hand sides, associativity and precedence controlled by %left and %right directives. As you can see, the yacc approach has been used for most of the operators by putting them under the aegis of a single *binary* production. The %left and %right directives that control the precedence and associativity of these operators were discussed back towards the beginning of the current chapter. They're also at the top of Appendix C if you want to review them.

Several of the lower-precedence operators have been isolated from the rest of the binary operators for grammatical and code-generation reasons, however. The first issue is the *non_comma_expr* which recognizes all expressions except those that use the comma operator at the outermost parenthesis-nesting level. The following statement is not recognized by a *non_comma_expr*:

```
a = foo(), bar();
```

but this one is okay:

```
(a = foo(), bar());
```

because of the parenthesis. (Neither expression is a model of good programming style, but the language accepts them.) An *expr* accepts the comma operator at the outer level; both of the foregoing expressions are recognized. This isolation is required for grammatical reasons. Comma delimited lists of expressions are used in several places (for subroutine-argument lists, initializer lists, and so on). If an unparenthesised comma operator were permitted in any of these comma-delimited lists, the parser would not be able to distinguish between a comma that separated list elements and the comma operator. The practical consequence would be reduce/reduce conflicts all over the place. Isolating the comma operator lets you use a *non_comma_expr* in all of the comma-

Isolating the comma operator. Problems with comma-delimited lists.

delimited lists and an *expr* everywhere else.

The *expr* production, which handles the comma operator, is at the top of Listing 6.88. The imbedded action releases the `value` structure associated with the left element of the expression; the `value` for the right element is used as the synthesized attribute. The imbedded action is necessary to prevent the compiler from wasting a temporary variable. If $1 was released at the far right of the production, then both components of the list would be evaluated before the left one was discarded. (Run a parse of ++a, ++b by hand if you don't believe me.) Consequently, the temporary that holds the evaluated result of the *expr* would continue to exist while the *non_comma_expr* was being evaluated. Since the left term is going to be discarded anyway, there's no point in keeping it around longer than necessary.

The comma operator.

Listing 6.88. *c.y*— Binary Operators: Comma, Conditional, and Assignment

```
683   expr        : expr COMMA  {release_value($1);}  non_comma_expr  { $$=$4; }
684               | non_comma_expr
685               ;
686
687   non_comma_expr
688               : non_comma_expr QUEST  {  static int label = 0;
689
690
691                                          gen( "EQ",        rvalue( $1->name ), "0" );
692                                          gen( "goto%s%d", L_COND_FALSE,
693                                                             $<num>$ = ++label );
694                                          release_value( $1 );
695                                       }
696                 non_comma_expr COLON  {  $<p_val>$ = $4->is_tmp
697                                             ? $4
698                                             : tmp_gen($4->type, $4)
699                                             ;
700
701                                          gen( "goto%s%d", L_COND_END,   $<num>3 );
702                                          gen( ":%s%d",    L_COND_FALSE, $<num>3 );
703                                       }
704                 non_comma_expr        {  $$ = $<p_val>6;
705
706                                          if( !the_same_type($$->type, $7->type, 1) )
707                                             yyerror("Types on two sides of colon "\
708                                                     "must agree\n");
709
710                                          gen( "=",     $$->name,  $7->name   );
711                                          gen( ":%s%d", L_COND_END, $<num>3 );
712                                          release_value( $7 );
713                                       }
714               | non_comma_expr ASSIGNOP non_comma_expr {$$ = assignment($2, $1, $3);}
715               | non_comma_expr EQUAL    non_comma_expr {$$ = assignment( 0, $1, $3);}
716
717               | or_expr
718               ;
```

The *non_comma_expr* production, also in Listing 6.88, handles the conditional and assignment operators. A statement like this:

The conditional operator (a?b:c).

```
int mickey, minnie;
mickey = minnie ? pluto() : goofy() ;
```

generates the code in Listing 6.89.

Listing 6.89. Code Generated for the Conditional Operator.

```
1              EQ( W(&_minnie), 0 )    /* if( minnie == 0 )                 */
2                 goto QF1;            /*     branch around the first clause */
3
4              call(_pluto);           /* true part of the conditional:     */
5              W( T(1) ) = rF.w.low;   /*     rvalue = subroutine return value */
6              goto QE1;
7   QF1:
8              call(_goofy);           /* false part of the conditional */
9              W( T(2) ) = rF.w.low;   /*     rvalue = subroutine return value */
10
11             W( T(1) ) = W( T(2) );
12  QE1:
13             W(&_mickey) = W( T(1) );            /* final assignment */
```

The conditional is processed by the right-hand side on lines 688 to 712 of Listing 6.88. The only tricky issue here is the extra assignment just above the QE1 label in Listing 6.89. The problem, here, is inherent in the way a bottom-up parser works. It's very difficult for a bottom-up parser to tell the expression-processing code to put the result in a particular place; rather, the expression-processing code decides more or less arbitrarily where the final result of an expression evaluation will be found, and it passes that information back up the parse tree to the higher-level code. The difficulty with the conditional operator is the two action clauses (one for the true condition and a second for the false condition), both of which generate a temporary variable holding the result of the expression evaluation. Since the entire conditional must evaluate to only one temporary, code must be generated to copy the value returned from the false clause into the same temporary that was used for the true clause.

None of this would be a problem with a top-down parser, which can tell the subroutine that processes the action clause to put the final result in a particular place. For example, the high-level subroutine that processes the conditional in a recursive-descent parser can pass a `value` structure to the lower-level subroutines that generate the expression-processing code. These lower-level routines could then use that `value` for the final result of the expression-evaluation process.

Assignment operators.   The other two right-hand sides to *non_comma_expr* (on lines 714 and 715 of Listing 6.89) handle the assignment operators. The `assignment()` function in Listing 6.90 does all the work. The subroutine is passed three arguments: an operator (`op`) and `values` for the destination (`dst`) and source (`src`). The operator argument is zero for simple assignment, otherwise it's the first character of the lexeme: `'+'` for +=, `'<'` for <<=, and so on. This operator is, in turn, passed to `gen()` by adding it to the operator string on lines 588 and 589 of Listing 6.90.

The destination argument must be an lvalue. If it's a physical lvalue, `assignment()` tells `gen()` to add a star to the right of the destination name by adding an @ to the operator string on line 587 of Listing 6.90. The source operand is converted to an rvalue on line 593, then the assignment code is generated.

Implicit type conversion.   If the source and destination types don't match, an implicit type conversion must be performed as part of the assignment on line 616. The `convert_type()` subroutine is the same one that was used for temporary-variable initialization. (It's in Listing 6.69 on page 590.) `convert_type()` generates code to copy the source variable into a register and do any necessary sign extension or zero fill. It returns a string that can be used to reference the required register. As an example of the type-conversion process, given the following declarations:

Listing 6.90. *op.c*— Assignment Operators

```
571   value *assignment( op, dst, src )
572   int     op;
573   value *dst, *src;
574   {
575       char    *src_name;
576       char    op_str[8], *p = op_str ;
577       value   *val;
578
579       if( !dst->lvalue              ) yyerror    ( "(=) lvalue required\n" );
580       if( !dst->is_tmp && dst->sym ) gen_comment( "%s", dst->sym->name    );
581
582       /* Assemble the operator string for gen(). A leading @ is translated by
583        * gen() to a * at the far left of the output string. For example,
584        * ("@=",x,y) is output as "*x = y".
585        */
586
587       if(   *dst->name != '&'        ) *p++ =  '@' ;
588       if(   op                       ) *p++ =  op  ;
589       if(   op == '<' || op == '>'   ) *p++ =  op  ;              /* <<= or >>= */
590       /*  do always           */       *p++ =  '=' ;
591                                         *p++ =  '\0' ;
592
593       src_name = rvalue( src );
594
595       if( IS_POINTER(dst->type) && IS_PTR_TYPE(src->type) )
596       {
597           if( op )
598               yyerror("Illegal operation (%c= on two pointers);\n", op);
599
600           else if( !the_same_type( dst->type->next, src->type->next, 0) )
601               yyerror("Illegal pointer assignment (type mismatch)\n");
602
603           else
604               gen( "=", dst->name + (*dst->name=='&' ? 1 : 0), src_name );
605       }
606       else
607       {
608           /* If the destination type is larger than the source type, perform an
609            * implicit cast (create a temporary of the correct type, otherwise
610            * just copy into the destination. convert_type() releases the source
611            * value.
612            */
613
614           if( !the_same_type( dst->type, src->type, 1) )
615           {
616               gen( op_str, dst->name + (*dst->name == '&' ? 1 : 0),
617                                       convert_type( dst->type, src ) );
618           }
619           else
620           {
621               gen( op_str, dst->name + (*dst->name == '&' ? 1 : 0), src_name );
622               release_value( src );
623           }
624       }
625       return dst;
626   }
```

```
int   i, j, k ;
long  l ;
char  *p;
```

simple input like i=j=k; generates the following output:

```
W(&_j)  = W(&_k);
W(&_i)  = W(&_j);
```

A more complex assignment like *p=l=i generates:

```
r0.w.low = W(&_i);    /* convert i to long    */
ext_word(r0);
L(&_l)    = r0.l;     /* assign to l          */
r0.l      = L(&_l);   /* truncate l to char   */
*BP(&_p) = r0.b.b0;   /* assign to *p         */
```

The logical OR operator
(||).

The next level of *binary* operators handles the logical OR operator—the productions and related workhorse functions are in Listings 6.91, and 6.92.

Listing 6.91. *c.y*— Binary Operators: The Logical OR Operator and Auxillary Stack

```
143                               /* Stacks. The stack macros are all in  */
144                               /* <tools/stack.h>, included earlier     */
145   %{
146   #include <tools/stack.h>     /* Stack macros. (see Appendix A)        */
147
148   stk_err( o )
149   {
150       yyerror( o ? "Loop/switch nesting too deep or logical expr. too complex.\n"
151                  : "INTERNAL, label stack underflow.\n"  );
152       exit( 1 );
153   }
154
155   #undef  stack_err
156   #define stack_err(o)       stk_err(o)
157
158   stack_dcl (S_andor, int, 32);   /* This stack wouldn't be necessary if I were */
159                                   /* willing to put a structure onto the value  */
160                                   /* stack--or_list and and_list must both      */
161                                   /* return 2 attributes; this stack will hold   */
162                                   /* one of them.                                */
163   %}
```

```
719   or_expr : or_list          {    int label;
720                                    if( label = pop( S_andor ) )
721                                        $$ = gen_false_true( label, NULL );
722                               }
723           ;
724   or_list : or_list OROR      {    if( $1 )
725                                        or( $1, stack_item(S_andor,0) = tf_label());
726                               }
727             and_expr         {    or( $4, stack_item(S_andor,0) );
728                                    $$ = NULL;
729                               }
730           | and_expr         {    push( S_andor, 0 );
731                               }
732           ;
```

Listing 6.92. *op.c*— The Logical OR operator

```
627  void      or( val, label )
628  value    *val;
629  int       label;
630  {
631      val = gen_rvalue( val );
632
633      gen ( "NE",        val->name, "0"     );
634      gen ( "goto%s%d", L_TRUE,     label );
635      release_value( val );
636  }
637  /*--------------------------------------------------------------*/
638  value *gen_rvalue( val )
639  value *val;
640  {
641      /* This function is like rvalue(), except that emits code to generate a
642       * physical rvalue from a physical lvalue (instead of just messing with the
643       * name). It returns the 'value' structure for the new rvalue rather than a
644       * string.
645       */
646
647      if( !val->lvalue  || *(val->name) == '&' )  /* rvalue or logical lvalue */
648          rvalue( val );                          /* just change the name     */
649      else
650          val = tmp_gen( val->type, val );        /* actually do indirection  */
651
652      return val;
653  }
```

The only difficulty here is the requirement that run-time evaluation of expressions containing logical OR operators must terminate as soon as truth can be determined. Looking at some generated output shows you what's going on. The expression i||j||k creates the following output:

```
      NE(W(&_i),0)
          goto T1;
      NE(W(&_j),0)
          goto T1;
      NE(W(&_k),0)
          goto T1;
F1:
      W( T(1) ) = 0;
      goto E1;
T1:
      W( T(1) ) = 1;
E1:
```

The productions treat expressions involving || operators as an OR-operator-delimited list of subexpressions. The code that handles the individual list elements is on lines 724 to 730 of Listing 6.91. It uses the or() subroutine in Listing 6.92 to emit a test/branch instruction of the form:

```
NE(W(&_i),0)
    goto T1;
```

The code following the F1 label is emitted on line 721 of Listing 6.91 after all the list elements have been processed.

The main implementation-related difficulty is that the *or_list* productions really want to return two attributes: the `value` that represents the operand and the numeric component of the label used as the target of the output **goto** statement. You could do this, of course, by adding a two-element structure to the value-stack union, but I was reluctant to make the value stack wider than necessary because the parser would slow down as a consequence—it would have to copy twice as much stuff on every parse cycle. I solved the problem by introducing an auxiliary stack (S_andor), declared in the **occs** declaration section with the code on lines 146 to 163 of Listing 6.91. This extra stack holds the numeric component of the target label.

The best way to see what's going on is to follow the parse of i||j||k in Table 6.25. You should read the comments in that table now, looking at the source code where necessary to see what's going on.

Table 6.25. A Parse of i||j||k;

Parse Stack					S_andor	Comments
stmt_list □						Shift **NAME**. The shifted attribute is a pointer to the `symbol` that represents i.
stmt_list □	**NAME** i					Reduce by *unary*→**NAME**.
stmt_list □	*unary* W(&_i)$_L$					Reduce by *binary*→*unary*.
stmt_list □	*binary* W(&_i)$_L$					Reduce by *and_list*→*binary*.
stmt_list □	*and_list* W(&_i)$_L$					Reduce by *and_expr*→*and_list*.
stmt_list □	*and_expr* W(&_i)$_L$					Reduce by *or_list*→*and_list*. This is the first reduction in the list, so push 0 onto the S_andor stack. Note that, since this is the leftmost list element, the default $$=$1 is permitted to happen in order to tell the next reduction in the series what to do.
stmt_list □	*or_list* W(&_i)$_L$				0	Shift **OROR**.

stmt_list
□
	or_list
	W(&_i)$_L$
		OROR
		□
					0	Reduce by the imbedded production in *or_list*→*or_list* { } *and_expr*. This is the first expression in the list—the compiler knows that it's first because $1 isn't NULL. Call tf_label() to get the numeric component of the target label, and then replace the 0 at the top of the the S_andor stack with the the label number. This replacement tells the *or_expr*→*or_list* production that an ‖ has actually been processed—a reduction by *or_expr*→*or_list* occurs in every expression, even those that don't involve logical OR's. You can emit code only when the expression had an ‖ operator in it, however. The S_andor stack is empty if there wasn't one. The compiler emits the following code:
						    CODE: NE(W(&_i),0)
						    CODE: goto T1;

stmt_list □	*or_list* W(&_i)$_L$	**OROR** □	*{128}* □		1	Shift **NAME**. The shifted attribute is a pointer to the `symbol` that represents j.
stmt_list □	*or_list* W(&_i)$_L$	**OROR** □	*{128}* □	**NAME** j	1	Reduce by *unary*→**NAME**. The synthesized attribute is an lvalue for j.
stmt_list □	*or_list* W(&_i)$_L$	**OROR** □	*{128}* □	*unary* W(&_j)$_L$	1	Reduce by *binary*→*unary*.
stmt_list □	*or_list* W(&_i)$_L$	**OROR** □	*{128}* □	*binary* W(&_j)$_L$	1	Reduce by *and_list*→*binary*.
						continued...

The logical AND operator   The code to handle the logical AND operator (&&) is almost identical to that for the
(&&)   OR operator. It's shown in Listings 6.93 and 6.94. The expression i&&j&&k generates the following output:

Table 6.25. Continued. A Parse of `i||j||k;`

Parse Stack					S_andor	Comments
stmt_list ☐	*or_list* W(&_i)$_L$	**OROR** ☐	*{128}* ☐	*and_list* W(&_j)$_L$	1	Reduce by *and_expr*→*and_list*.
stmt_list ☐	*or_list*` W(&_i)$_L$	**OROR** ☐	*{128}* ☐	*and_expr* W(&_j)$_L$	1	Reduce by *or_list*→*or_list* **OROR** {128} *and_expr*. Emit code to handle the second list element: **CODE:** NE(W(&_j),0) **CODE:** **goto** T1; The numeric component of the label is at the top of the S_andor stack, and is examined with a `stack_item()` call. The post-reduction attribute attached to the *or_list* is NULL.
stmt_list ☐	*or_list* NULL				1	Shift **OROR**.
stmt_list ☐	*or_list* NULL	**OROR** ☐	☐		1	Reduce by imbedded production in *or_list*→*or_list* { } *and_expr*. This time, the attribute for $1 is NULL, so no code is generated.
stmt_list ☐	*or_list* NULL	**OROR** ☐	*{128}* ☐		1	Shift **NAME**. The shifted attribute is a pointer to the `symbol` that represents k.
stmt_list ☐	*or_list* NULL	**OROR** ☐	*{128}* ☐	**NAME** k	1	Reduce by *unary*→**NAME**. The synthesized attribute is an lvalue for k.
stmt_list ☐	*or_list* NULL	**OROR** ☐	*{128}* ☐	*unary* W(&_k)$_L$	1	Reduce by *binary*→*unary*.
stmt_list ☐	*or_list* NULL	**OROR** ☐	*{128}* ☐	*binary* W(&_k)$_L$	1	Reduce by *and_list*→*binary*.
stmt_list ☐	*or_list* NULL	**OROR** ☐	*{128}* ☐	*and_list* W(&_k)$_L$	1	Reduce by *and_expr*→*and_list*.
stmt_list ☐	*or_list* NULL	**OROR** ☐	*{128}* ☐	*and_expr* W(&_k)$_L$	1	Reduce by *or_list*→*or_list* **OROR** {128} *and_expr*. Emit code to process the third list element. The numeric component of the label is at the top of the S_andor stack. **CODE:** NE(W(&_k),0) **CODE:** **goto** T1; The synthesized attribute is also NULL, there.
stmt_list ☐	*or_list* NULL				1	Reduce by *or_expr*→*or_list*. The numeric component of the label is popped off the S_andor stack. If it's zero, then no `||` operators were processed. It's 1, however, so emit the targets for all the goto branches generated by the previous list elements. **CODE:** F1: **CODE:** W(T(1)) = 0; **CODE:** **goto** E1; **CODE:** T1: **CODE:** W(T(1)) = 1; **CODE:** E1: The synthesized attribute is an rvalue for the temporary that holds the result of the OR operation.
stmt_list ☐	*or_expr* W(T(1))$_R$					

```
        EQ(W(&_i),0)      /* i && j && k */
            goto F1;
        EQ(W(&_j),0)
            goto F1;
        EQ(W(&_k),0)
            goto F1;
            goto T1:
F1:
            W( T(1) ) = 0;
            goto E1;
T1:
            W( T(1) ) = 1;
E1:
```

Since the run-time processing has to terminate as soon as a false expression is found, the test instruction is now an EQ rather than an NE, and the target is the false label rather than the true one. The same S_andor stack is used both for the AND and OR operators. The **goto** T1 just above the F1 label is needed to prevent the last list element from falling through to the false assignment. Note that the logical AND and OR operators nest correctly. The expression

```
(i || j && k || l)
```

generates the output in Listing 6.95 (&& is higher precedence than ||). A blow-by-blow analysis of the parse of the previous expression is left as an exercise.

Listing 6.93. *c.y*— Binary Operators: The Logical AND Operator

```
733   and_expr: and_list          {   int label;
734                                    if( label = pop( S_andor ) )
735                                    {
736                                        gen( "goto%s%d", L_TRUE, label );
737                                        $$ = gen_false_true( label, NULL );
738                                    }
739                                }
740               ;
741   and_list: and_list ANDAND {   if( $1 )
742                                    and($1, stack_item(S_andor,0) = tf_label());
743                                }
744               binary          {   and( $4, stack_item(S_andor,0) );
745                                    $$ = NULL;
746                                }
747               | binary        {   push( S_andor, 0 );
748                                }
749               ;
```

Listing 6.94. *op.c*— The Logical AND Operator

```
654   void      and( val, label )
655   value     *val;
656   int       label;
657   {
658       val = gen_rvalue( val );
659
660       gen ( "EQ",        val->name, "0"    );
661       gen ( "goto%s%d",  L_FALSE,   label );
662       release_value( val );
663   }
```

Relational operators.

The remainder of the binary operators are handled by the *binary* productions, the first two right-hand sides of which are in Listing 6.96. The productions handle the relational operators, with the work done by the relop() subroutine in Listing 6.97. The **EQUOP** token matches either == or !=. A **RELOP** matches any of the following lexemes:

```
<=   >=   <   >
```

A single token can't be used for all six lexemes because the **EQUOP**s are higher precedence than the **RELOP**s. The associated, integer attributes are assigned as follows:

Listing 6.95. Output for `(i||j && k||l)`

```
 1                  NE(W(&_i),0)
 2                      goto T1;
 3                  EQ(W(&_j),0)
 4                      goto F2;
 5                  EQ(W(&_k),0)
 6                      goto F2;
 7   F2:
 8                  W( T(1) ) = 0;
 9                  goto E2;
10   T2:
11                  W( T(1) ) = 1;
12   E2:
13                  NE(W( T(1) ),0)
14                      goto T1;
15                  NE(W(&_l),0)
16                      goto T1;
17   F1:
18                  W( T(1) ) = 0;
19                  goto E1;
20   T1:
21                  W( T(1) ) = 1;
22   E1:
```

Token	Lexeme	Attribute
EQUOP	==	`'='`
EQUOP	!=	`'!'`
RELOP	>	`'>'`
RELOP	<	`'<'`
RELOP	>=	`'G'`
RELOP	<=	`'L'`

The `relop()` subroutine at the top of Listing 6.97 does all the work. It's passed the `relop()` operator's attribute and the two operands; `i<j` generates the following code:

```
    LT( W(&_i), W(&_j) )   /* compare i and j.                 */
        goto T1;           /* Jump to true case on success;    */
F1:                        /* otherwise, fall through to false.*/
    W( T(1) ) = 0;
    goto E1;
T1:
    W( T(1) ) = 1;
E1:
```

The comparison directive on the first line (`LT`) changes with the incoming operand: `LT` for `<`, `GT` for `>`, `EQ` for `==`, and so on. `relop()` generates the code in several steps. Both operands are converted to rvalues by the `gen_rvalue()` calls on lines 673 and 674 of Listing 6.96. The `make_types_match` call on the next line applies the standard C `make_types_match()` type-conversion rules to the two operands, generating code to promote the smaller of the two variables to the type of the larger one. The subroutine starts on line 712 of Listing 6.96. It's passed pointers to the two `values`, and it might modify those `values` because the conversion might create another, larger temporary. Normally, `make_types_match` returns 1. It returns 0 if it can't do the conversion, as is the case when one operand is an **int** and the other a pointer.

The **switch** on line 680 of Listing 6.96 translates the incoming attribute to an argument passed to the gen() call that generates the test on line 693. The **goto** is generated on the next line, and the numeric component of the target label is fetched from tf_label() at the same time. The code on lines 696 to 701 is doing a minor optimization. If the value passed into gen_false_true() is already a temporary of type **int**, then a second temporary is not created. If the original v1 isn't an **int** temporary, the code on lines 696 to 701 swaps the two values in the hope that v2 is a temporary.

Listing 6.96. *c.y*— Binary Operators: Relational Operators

```
750   binary
751           : binary RELOP      binary          { $$ = relop( $1, $2,  $3 ); }
752           | binary EQUOP      binary          { $$ = relop( $1, $2,  $3 ); }
```

Listing 6.97. *op.c*— Relational Operators

```
664   value   *relop( v1, op, v2 )
665   value   *v1;
666   int     op;
667   value   *v2;
668   {
669       char  *str_op ;
670       value *tmp;
671       int   label;
672
673       v1 = gen_rvalue( v1 );
674       v2 = gen_rvalue( v2 );
675
676       if( !make_types_match( &v1, &v2 ) )
677           yyerror( "Illegal comparison of dissimilar types\n" );
678       else
679       {
680           switch( op )
681           {
682           case '>': /* >  */   str_op = "GT";   break;
683           case '<': /* <  */   str_op = "LT";   break;
684           case 'G': /* >= */   str_op = "GE";   break;
685           case 'L': /* <= */   str_op = "LE";   break;
686           case '!': /* != */   str_op = "NE";   break;
687           case '=': /* == */   str_op = "EQ";   break;
688           default:
689               yyerror("INTERNAL, relop(): Bad request: %c\n", op );
690               goto abort;
691           }
692
693           gen    ( str_op,     v1->name, v2->name                  );
694           gen    ( "goto%s%d", L_TRUE,   label = tf_label()        );
695
696           if( !(v1->is_tmp && IS_INT( v1->type )) )
697           {
698               tmp = v1;                        /* try to make v1 an int temporary */
699               v1  = v2;
700               v2  = tmp;
701           }
702           v1 = gen_false_true( label, v1 );
703       }
704
```

Listing 6.97. continued...

```
705  abort:
706      release_value( v2 );                              /* discard the other value */
707      return v1;
708  }
709
710  /*---------------------------------------------------------------------*/
711
712  PRIVATE int make_types_match( v1p, v2p )
713  value   **v1p, **v2p;
714  {
715      /* Takes care of type conversion. If the types are the same, do nothing;
716       * otherwise, apply the standard type-conversion rules to the smaller
717       * of the two operands. Return 1 on success or if the objects started out
718       * the same type. Return 0 (and don't do any conversions) if either operand
719       * is a pointer and the operands aren't the same type.
720       */
721
722      value *v1 = *v1p;
723      value *v2 = *v2p;
724
725      link  *t1 = v1->type;
726      link  *t2 = v2->type;
727
728      if( the_same_type(t1, t2, 0)  &&  !IS_CHAR(t1) )
729          return 1;
730
731      if( IS_POINTER(t1) || IS_POINTER(t2) )
732          return 0;
733
734      if( IS_CHAR(t1) ) { v1 = tmp_gen(t1, v1);  t1 = v1->type; }
735      if( IS_CHAR(t2) ) { v2 = tmp_gen(t2, v2);  t2 = v2->type; }
736
737      if( IS_ULONG(t1) && !IS_ULONG(t2) )
738      {
739          if( IS_LONG(t2) )
740              v2->type->UNSIGNED = 1;
741          else
742              v2 = tmp_gen( t1, v2 );
743      }
744      else if( !IS_ULONG(t1) && IS_ULONG(t2) )
745      {
746          if( IS_LONG(t1) )
747              v1->type->UNSIGNED = 1;
748          else
749              v1 = tmp_gen( v2->type, v1 );
750      }
751      else if(  IS_LONG(t1) && !IS_LONG(t2) ) v2 = tmp_gen (t1, v2);
752      else if( !IS_LONG(t1) &&  IS_LONG(t2) ) v1 = tmp_gen (t2, v1);
753      else if(  IS_UINT(t1) && !IS_UINT(t2) ) v2->type->UNSIGNED = 1;
754      else if( !IS_UINT(t1) &&  IS_UINT(t2) ) v1->type->UNSIGNED = 1;
755
756      /* else they're both normal ints, do nothing */
757
758      *v1p = v1;
759      *v2p = v2;
760      return 1;
761  }
```

All other operators,
`binary_op()`

Most other binary operators are covered by the productions and code in Listings 6.98 and 6.99. Everything is covered but addition and subtraction, which require special handling because they can accept pointer operands. All the work is done in `binary_op()`, at the top of Listing 6.99. The routine is passed `values` for the two operands and an **int** that represents the operator. It generates the code that does the required operation, and returns a `value` that references the run-time result of the operation. This returned `value` is usually the incoming first argument, but it might not be if neither incoming `value` is a temporary. In addition, one or both of the incoming `values` is released.

Listing 6.98. *c.y*— Binary Operators: Other Arithmetic Operators

```
753   /* binary: */
754         | binary STAR     binary      { $$ = binary_op( $1, '*', $3 ); }
755         | binary DIVOP    binary      { $$ = binary_op( $1, $2,  $3 ); }
756         | binary SHIFTOP  binary      { $$ = binary_op( $1, $2,  $3 ); }
757         | binary AND      binary      { $$ = binary_op( $1, '&', $3 ); }
758         | binary XOR      binary      { $$ = binary_op( $1, '^', $3 ); }
759         | binary OR       binary      { $$ = binary_op( $1, '|', $3 ); }
```

Listing 6.99. *op.c*— Other Arithmetic Operators

```
762   value    *binary_op( v1, op, v2 )
763   value    *v1;
764   int      op;
765   value    *v2;
766   {
767       char *str_op ;
768       int  commutative = 0;         /* operator is commutative */
769
770       if( do_binary_const( &v1, op, &v2 ) )
771       {
772           release_value( v2 );
773           return v1;
774       }
775
776       v1 = gen_rvalue( v1 );
777       v2 = gen_rvalue( v2 );
778
779       if( !make_types_match( &v1, &v2 ) )
780           yyerror("%c%c: Illegal type conversion\n",
781                                      (op=='>' || op =='<') ? op : ' ', op);
782       else
783       {
784           switch( op )
785           {
786           case '*':
787           case '&':
788           case '|':
789           case '^':    commutative = 1;
790           case '/':
791           case '%':
792           case '<':                                    /* << */
793           case '>':                                    /* >> */
794                   dst_opt( &v1, &v2, commutative );
795
```

Listing 6.99. continued...

```
796                         if( op == '<' )
797                             str_op = "<<=" ;
798                         else if( op == '>' )
799                             str_op = IS_UNSIGNED(v1->type) ? ">L=" : ">>=" ;
800                         else
801                         {
802                             str_op = "X=";
803                             *str_op = op ;
804                         }
805
806                         gen( str_op, v1->name, v2->name );
807                         break;
808                 }
809         }
810     release_value( v2 );
811     return v1;
812 }
813
814 /*-------------------------------------------------------------------*/
815
816 PRIVATE int     do_binary_const( v1p, op, v2p )
817 value   **v1p;
818 int     op;
819 value   **v2p;
820 {
821     /* If both operands are constants, do the arithmetic. On exit, *v1p
822      * is modified to point at the longer of the two incoming types
823      * and the result will be in the last link of *v1p's type chain.
824      */
825
826     long  x;
827     link  *t1 = (*v1p)->type ;
828     link  *t2 = (*v2p)->type ;
829     value *tmp;
830
831     /* Note that this code assumes that all fields in the union start at the
832      * same address.
833      */
834
835     if( IS_CONSTANT(t1) && IS_CONSTANT(t2) )
836     {
837         if( IS_INT(t1) && IS_INT(t2) )
838         {
839             switch( op )
840             {
841             case '+':   t1->V_INT += t2->V_INT;        break;
842             case '-':   t1->V_INT -= t2->V_INT;        break;
843             case '*':   t1->V_INT *= t2->V_INT;        break;
844             case '&':   t1->V_INT &= t2->V_INT;        break;
845             case '|':   t1->V_INT |= t2->V_INT;        break;
846             case '^':   t1->V_INT ^= t2->V_INT;        break;
847             case '/':   t1->V_INT /= t2->V_INT;        break;
848             case '%':   t1->V_INT %= t2->V_INT;        break;
849             case '<':   t1->V_INT <<= t2->V_INT;       break;
850
851             case '>':   if( IS_UNSIGNED(t1) ) t1->V_UINT >>= t2->V_INT;
852                         else                  t1->V_INT  >>= t2->V_INT;
853                         break;
854             }
855             return 1;
```

```
Listing 6.99. continued...
856                     }
857                     else if( IS_LONG(t1) && IS_LONG(t2) )
858                     {
859                         switch( op )
860                         {
861                         case '+':   t1->V_LONG +=  t2->V_LONG;         break;
862                         case '-':   t1->V_LONG -=  t2->V_LONG;         break;
863                         case '*':   t1->V_LONG *=  t2->V_LONG;         break;
864                         case '&':   t1->V_LONG &=  t2->V_LONG;         break;
865                         case '|':   t1->V_LONG |=  t2->V_LONG;         break;
866                         case '^':   t1->V_LONG ^=  t2->V_LONG;         break;
867                         case '/':   t1->V_LONG /=  t2->V_LONG;         break;
868                         case '%':   t1->V_LONG %=  t2->V_LONG;         break;
869                         case '<':   t1->V_LONG <<= t2->V_LONG;         break;
870
871                         case '>':   if( IS_UNSIGNED(t1) ) t1->V_ULONG >>= t2->V_LONG;
872                                     else                  t1->V_LONG  >>= t2->V_LONG;
873                                     break;
874                         }
875                         return 1;
876                     }
877                     else if( IS_LONG(t1) && IS_INT(t2) )
878                     {
879                         switch( op )
880                         {
881                         case '+':   t1->V_LONG +=  t2->V_INT;          break;
882                         case '-':   t1->V_LONG -=  t2->V_INT;          break;
883                         case '*':   t1->V_LONG *=  t2->V_INT;          break;
884                         case '&':   t1->V_LONG &=  t2->V_INT;          break;
885                         case '|':   t1->V_LONG |=  t2->V_INT;          break;
886                         case '^':   t1->V_LONG ^=  t2->V_INT;          break;
887                         case '/':   t1->V_LONG /=  t2->V_INT;          break;
888                         case '%':   t1->V_LONG %=  t2->V_INT;          break;
889                         case '<':   t1->V_LONG <<= t2->V_INT;          break;
890
891                         case '>':   if( IS_UNSIGNED(t1) ) t1->V_ULONG >>= t2->V_INT;
892                                     else                  t1->V_LONG  >>= t2->V_INT;
893                                     break;
894                         }
895                         return 1;
896                     }
897                     else if( IS_INT(t1) && IS_LONG(t2) )
898                     {
899                         /* Avoid commutativity problems by doing the arithmetic first,
900                          * then swapping the operand values.
901                          */
902
903                         switch( op )
904                         {
905                         case '+':   x = t1->V_INT +  t2->V_LONG;
906                         case '-':   x = t1->V_INT -  t2->V_LONG;
907                         case '*':   x = t1->V_INT *  t2->V_LONG;
908                         case '&':   x = t1->V_INT &  t2->V_LONG;
909                         case '|':   x = t1->V_INT |  t2->V_LONG;
910                         case '^':   x = t1->V_INT ^  t2->V_LONG;
911                         case '/':   x = t1->V_INT /  t2->V_LONG;
912                         case '%':   x = t1->V_INT %  t2->V_LONG;
913                         case '<':   x = t1->V_INT << t2->V_LONG;
914
```

→

Listing 6.99. continued...

```
915                         case '>':   if( IS_UINT(t1) )  x = t1->V_UINT >> t2->V_LONG;
916                                     else               x = t1->V_INT  >> t2->V_LONG;
917                                     break;
918                 }
919
920                 t2->V_LONG = x;        /* Modify v1 to point at the larger   */
921                 tmp  = *v1p ;          /* operand by swapping *v1p and *v2p. */
922                 *v1p = *v2p ;
923                 *v2p = tmp  ;
924                 return 1;
925             }
926         }
927     return 0;
928 }
929 /*----------------------------------------------------------------------*/
930
931 PRIVATE void    dst_opt( leftp, rightp, commutative )
932 value   **leftp;
933 value   **rightp;
934 {
935     /* Optimizes various sources and destination as follows:
936      *
937      * operation is not commutative:
938      *          if *left is a temporary:  do nothing
939      *          else:                     create a temporary and
940      *                                    initialize it to *left,
941      *                                    freeing *left
942      *                                    *left = new temporary
943      * operation is commutative:
944      *          if *left is a temporary   do nothing
945      *      else if *right is a temporary swap *left and *right
946      *      else                          precede as if commutative.
947      */
948
949     value   *tmp;
950
951     if( ! (*leftp)->is_tmp )
952     {
953         if( commutative && (*rightp)->is_tmp )
954         {
955             tmp     = *leftp;
956             *leftp  = *rightp;
957             *rightp = tmp;
958         }
959         else
960             *leftp = tmp_gen( (*leftp)->type, *leftp );
961     }
962 }
```

binary_op() starts out by trying to perform a type of optimization called *constant folding*. If both of the incoming values represent constants, then the arithmetic is done internally at compile time rather than generating code. The result is put into the last link of whichever of the two incoming values was larger, and that value is also the synthesized attribute. The work is done by do_binary_constant() starting on line 816 of Listing 6.99. An **if** clause is provided for each of the possible incoming types. Note that do_binary_constant() is passed pointers to the value pointers. The extra indirection is necessary because, if the left operand is larger than the right operand,

Constant folding.

the two values are swapped (after doing the arithmetic, of course). The code to do the swapping starts on line 920.

If constant folding couldn't be performed, then `binary_op` must generate some code. It starts out on lines 776 and 777 of Listing 6.99 by converting the incoming `values` to rvalues. It then does any necessary type conversions with the `make_types_match()` call on line 779. The **switch** on line 784 figures out if the operation is commutative, and the `dst_opt()` on line 794 juggles around the operands to make the code more efficient.

`dst_opt()` starts on line 931 of Listing 6.99. It is also passed two pointers to `value` pointers, and it makes sure that the destination value is a temporary variable. If it's already a temporary, `dst_opt()` does nothing; otherwise, if the right operand is a temporary and the left one isn't, and if the operation is commutative, it swaps the two operands; otherwise, it generates a temporary to hold the result and copies the left operand into it.

Returning to `binary_op()`, the arithmetic instruction is finally generated on line 806 of Listing 6.99.

The last of the binary operators are the addition and subtraction operators, handled by the productions and code in Listings 6.100 and 6.101. The only real difference between the action here and the action for the operators we just looked at is that pointers are legal here. It's legal to subtract two pointers, subtract an integer from a pointer, or add an integer to a pointer. The extra code that handles pointers is on lines 1019 to 1057 of Listing 6.101.

The final group of expression productions are in Listing 6.102. They are pretty much self-explanatory.

`dst_opt()`

Addition and subtraction.

Listing 6.100. *c.y*— Binary Operator Productions: Addition and Subtraction

```
760    /* binary: */
761          | binary PLUS      binary      { $$ = plus_minus( $1, '+', $3 ); }
762          | binary MINUS     binary      { $$ = plus_minus( $1, '-', $3 ); }
763          | unary
764          ;
```

Listing 6.101. *op.c*— Addition and Subtraction Processing

```
963    value    *plus_minus( v1, op, v2 )
964    value    *v1;
965    int      op;
966    value    *v2;
967    {
968        value *tmp;
969        int    v1_is_ptr;
970        int    v2_is_ptr;
971        char   *scratch;
972        char   *gen_op;
973
974        gen_op    = (op == '+') ? "+=" : "-=";
975        v1        = gen_rvalue( v1 );
976        v2        = gen_rvalue( v2 );
977        v2_is_ptr = IS_POINTER(v2->type);
978        v1_is_ptr = IS_POINTER(v1->type);
979
```

Listing 6.101. continued...

```
980        /* First, get all the error checking out of the way and return if
981         * an error is detected.
982         */
983
984        if( v1_is_ptr && v2_is_ptr )
985        {
986            if( op == '+' || !the_same_type(v1->type, v2->type, 1) )
987            {
988                yyerror( "Illegal types (%c)\n", op );
989                release_value( v2 );
990                return v1;
991            }
992        }
993        else if( !v1_is_ptr && v2_is_ptr )
994        {
995            yyerror( "%c: left operand must be pointer", op );
996            release_value( v1 );
997            return v2;
998        }
999
1000       /* Now do the work. At this point one of the following cases exist:
1001        *
1002        *     v1:    op:    v2:
1003        *   number [+-] number
1004        *    ptr   [+-] number
1005        *    ptr    -    ptr                (types must match)
1006        */
1007
1008       if( !(v1_is_ptr || v2_is_ptr) )                /* normal arithmetic */
1009       {
1010           if( !do_binary_const( &v1, op, &v2 ) )
1011           {
1012               make_types_match( &v1, &v2 );
1013               dst_opt( &v1, &v2, op == '+' );
1014               gen( gen_op, v1->name, v2->name );
1015           }
1016           release_value( v2 );
1017           return v1;
1018       }
1019       else
1020       {
1021           if( v1_is_ptr && v2_is_ptr )                  /* ptr-ptr */
1022           {
1023               if( !v1->is_tmp )
1024                   v1 = tmp_gen( v1->type, v1 );
1025
1026               gen( gen_op, v1->name, v2->name );
1027
1028               if( IS_AGGREGATE( v1->type->next ) )
1029                   gen( "/=%s%d", v1->name, get_sizeof(v1->type->next) );
1030           }
1031           else if( !IS_AGGREGATE( v1->type->next ) )
1032           {
1033                                                          /* ptr_to_nonaggregate [+-] number */
1034               if( !v1->is_tmp )
1035                   v1 = tmp_gen( v1->type, v1 );
1036
1037               gen( gen_op, v1->name, v2->name );
1038           }
```

Listing 6.101. continued...

```
1039            else                                    /* ptr_to_aggregate [+-] number */
1040            {                                       /* do pointer arithmetic        */
1041
1042                scratch = IS_LONG(v2->type) ? "r0.l" : "r0.w.low" ;
1043
1044                gen( "=",         "r1.pp", v1->name                        );
1045                gen( "=",          scratch, v2->name                       );
1046                gen( "*=%s%d", scratch, get_sizeof(v1->type->next)   );
1047                gen( gen_op,      "r1.pp", scratch                        );
1048
1049                if( !v1->is_tmp )
1050                {
1051                    tmp = tmp_create( v1->type, 0 );
1052                    release_value( v1 );
1053                    v1 = tmp;
1054                }
1055
1056                gen( "=", v1->name, "r1.pp" );
1057            }
1058        }
1059        release_value( v2 );
1060        return v1;
1061    }
```

Listing 6.102. *c.y*— High-Level Expression Processing

```
765    opt_expr
766        : expr              { release_value( $1 ); tmp_freeall(); }
767        | /* epsilon */
768        ;
769
770    const_expr
771        : expr                          %prec COMMA
772                        {
773                            $$ = -1 ;
774
775                            if( !IS_CONSTANT( $1->type ) )
776                                yyerror("Constant required.");
777
778                            else if( !IS_INT( $1->type ) )
779                                yyerror("Constant expression must be int.");
780
781                            else
782                                $$ = $1->type->V_INT ;
783
784                            release_value($1);
785                            tmp_freeall();
786                        }
787        ;
788
789    initializer : expr                              %prec COMMA
790                | LC initializer_list RC    { $$ = $2; }
791                ;
792
793    initializer_list
794                : initializer
795                | initializer_list COMMA initializer
```

```
Listing 6.102. continued...
796                    {
797                            yyerror("Aggregate initializers are not supported\n");
798                            release_value( $3 );
799                    }
800            ;
```

6.9 Statements and Control Flow

The only part of the compiler we've yet to examine is the statement productions, discussed in this section.

6.9.1 Simple Statements and `if`/`else`

It's best to start by looking at some examples. Table 6.26 shows input and output for a few simple control-flow statements. Figure 6.20 shows a more complex example of nested `if`/`else` statements. (I've shown the complete compiler output in the Figure.)

The productions and subroutines that generate this code are in Listings 6.103 and 6.104. The *stmt_list* production at the top just assembles a list of zero or more statements. There are no attributes. The simplest statement is defined on line 801 as a single semicolon. There is no action. A statement can also comprise a curly-brace-delimited compound statement (on line 811).

Empty and compound statements.

The next line defines a statement as an expression followed by a semicolon. The associated action frees the value holding the result of the expression evaluation and releases any temporary variables. Note that many expressions create unnecessary final values because there's no way for the parser to know whether or not an expression is part of a larger expression. For example, an assignment to a temporary is emitted as part of processing the the ++ operator in the statement:

Expression statements.

    a++;

but that temporary is never used. It is an easy matter for an optimizer to remove this extra assignment, which is, in any event, harmless.

The two forms of **return** statement are handled on lines 814 and 816 of Listing 6.103. The first is a simple return, with no value. The second takes care of the value by copying it into the required return-value register and then releasing the associated `value` and temporaries. Because returning from a subroutine involves stack-cleanup actions, a jump to a label immediately above the end-of-subroutine code is generated here rather than an explicit `ret()` instruction. The numeric part of the label is generated by `rlabel()`, in Listing 6.104. The end-of-subroutine code is generated during the reduction by

`return` statements.

> *ext_def→opt_specifiers funct_decl def_list compound_stmt*

(on line 563 of Listing 6.58, page 556), which executes an `rlabel(1)` to increment the numeric part of the label for the next subroutine.

Table 6.26. Simple Control-Flow: **return** **goto** and **if**/**else**

Input	Output

return;	`goto RET0;` /* Generated by return statement */
	`...`
	`RET0:` /* Generated by end-of-subroutine */
	`unlink();` /* code. */
	`ret();`

return i+j;	`W( T(1) ) = W(&_i);` /* compute i + j */
	`W( T(1) ) += W(&_j);`
	`rF.w.low = W( T(1) );` /* return value in register */
	`goto RET0:`
	`...`
	`RET0:` /* Generated in end-of-subroutine processing */
	`unlink();`
	`ret();`

foo: ; **goto** foo;	`_foo:` `goto _foo;`

if(i < j)
    ++i;
	`TST1:`
	`LT(W(&_i),W(&_j))` /* evaluate (i < j) and put */
	`    goto T1;` /* the result into T(1) */
	`F1:`
	`W( T(1) ) = 0;`
	`goto E1;`
	`T1:`
	`W( T(1) ) = 1;`
	`E1:`
	`EQ(W( T(1) ),0)` /* this test does loop control */
	`    goto EXIT1;` /* don't execute body if false */
	`W(&_i)    += 1;` /* body of the if statement */
	`W( T(1) ) = W(&_i);`
	`EXIT1:`

if(i < j)
    ++i;
else
    ++j;
	`TST2:`
	`LT(W(&_i),W(&_j))` /* Evaluate (i < j) and put */
	`    goto T2;` /* the result into T(1). */
	`F2:`
	`W( T(1) ) = 0;`
	`goto E2;`
	`T2:`
	`W( T(1) ) = 1;`
	`E2:`
	`EQ(W( T(1) ),0)` /* This test does loop control. */
	`    goto EXIT2;` /* Jump to else clause if false.*/
	`W(&_i)    += 1;` /* Body of the if clause. */
	`W( T(1) ) = W(&_i);`
	`goto EL2;` /* Jump over the else. */
	`EXIT2:`
	`W(&_j)    += 1;` /* Body of the else clause. */
	`W( T(1) ) = W(&_j);`
	`EL2:`

Figure 6.20. Nested **if/else** Statements

Input		Output
| | ```
#include <tools/virtual.h>
#define  T(x)
SEG(data)
SEG(bss)
``` | |
| `int i, j;` | ```
common  word   _i;
common  word   _j;
``` | |
| ```
fred()
{
``` | ```
#define  L0 0   /* fred: locals */
#define  L1 0   /* fred: temps. */
SEG(code)
#undef   T
#define  T(n) (fp-L0-(n*4))
PROC(_fred,public)
        link(L0+L1);
``` | |
`int wilma;`	`/*        fp-2 = x        [variable] */`	
`if( i )` `{`	`TST1:`	
	` EQ(W(&_i),0)                /* i */` `       goto EXIT1;`	
`wilma=0;`	` W(fp-2)     = 0;          /* wilma */`	
`if( j )`	`TST2:`	
	` EQ(W(&_j),0)                /* j */` `       goto EXIT2;`	
`wilma=1;`	` W(fp-2)     = 1;          /* wilma */`	
`}`	`EXIT2:`	
`else`	`       goto EL1;`	
`{`	`EXIT1:`	
`if( j )`	`TST3:`	
	` EQ(W(&_j),0)                /* j */` `       goto EXIT3;`	
`wilma=2;`	` W(fp-2)     = 2;          /* wilma */`	
`else`	`       goto EL3;`	
	`EXIT3:`	
`wilma=3;`	` W(fp-2)     = 3;          /* wilma */`	
	`EL3:`	
`wilma=4;`	` W(fp-2)     = 4;          /* wilma */`	
`}`	`EL1:`	

`}`	`       unlink();`
	`       ret();`
	`       ENDP(_fred)`	

Listing 6.103. *c.y*— Statement Processing: **return**, **goto**, and **if/else**

```
801    stmt_list
802            : stmt_list statement
803            | /* epsilon */
804            ;
805
806    /*-------------------------------------------------------------
807     * Statements
808     */
809
810    statement
811            : SEMI
812            | compound_stmt
813            | expr SEMI            { release_value($1); tmp_freeall(); }
814            | RETURN        SEMI   { gen( "goto%s%d", L_RET, rlabel(0) ); }
815
816            | RETURN expr   SEMI   { gen("=", IS_INT     ($2->type) ? "rF.w.low" :
817                                            IS_POINTER($2->type) ? "rF.pp"    :
818                                                                   "rF.l",
819                                                                   rvalue($2) );
820                                     gen( "goto%s%d", L_RET, rlabel(0) );
821                                     release_value( $2 );
822                                     tmp_freeall();
823                                   }
824            | GOTO target SEMI     {  gen("goto",$2); }
825            | target COLON         {  gen(":",    $1); }
826                            statement
827
828            | IF LP test RP statement      {   gen( ":%s%d", L_NEXT, $3 );
829                                           }
830
831            | IF LP test RP statement ELSE {   gen( "goto%s%d", L_ELSE, $3 );
832                                               gen( ":%s%d",    L_NEXT, $3 );
833                                           }
834              statement            {   gen( ":%s%d",    L_ELSE, $3 );
835                                           }
836
```

Listing 6.104. *op.c*— Get Numeric Part of End-of-Subroutine Label

```
1062   rlabel( incr )                /* Return the numeric component of the next */
1063   {                             /* return label, postincrementing it by one */
1064       static int num;           /* if incr is true.                         */
1065       return incr ? num++ : num;
1066   }
```

goto statements and labels.

The **goto** processing on lines 824 and 825 of Listing 6.103. is similarly straightforward. The compiler just generates jump instructions and labels as needed. The *target*
nonterminal is at the top of Listing 6.105. It translates the label into a string which is
returned as an attribute. Note that the action is imbedded in the middle of the label-
processing production on line 825 of Listing 6.103. If the action were at the end, then
the label would be generated <u>after</u> the associated statement was processed.

The next two productions, on lines 828 and 831 of Listing 6.103, handle the **if** and
if/else statements. The best way to understand these actions is to compare the sample
input and output in Table 6.26 and Figure 6.20. The code for the test is generated by the

test nonterminal, on line 843 of Listing 6.105, which outputs a label over the test code, generates the test code via *expr*, and then generates the statement that branches out of the test on failure. The first label isn't used here, but the same *test* production is used by the loop-processing productions, below, and these productions need a way to jump back up to the test code from the bottom of the loop. The presence of an extra label in an **if** statement is harmless.

Listing 6.105. *c.y*— Statement Processing: Tests and **goto** Targets

```
837   target   : NAME                   {   static char buf[ NAME_MAX ];
838                                          sprintf(buf, "_%0.*s", NAME_MAX-2, yytext );
839                                          $$ = buf;
840                                      }
841            ;
842
843   test     :                        {   static int label = 0;
844                                          gen( ":%s%d", L_TEST, $<num>$ = ++label );
845                                      }
846            expr                      {
847
848                                          $$ = $<num>1;
849                                          if( IS_INT_CONSTANT($2->type) )
850                                          {
851                                              if( ! $2->type->V_INT )
852                                                  yyerror("Test is always false\n");
853                                          }
854                                          else  /* not an endless loop */
855                                          {
856                                              gen( "EQ",            rvalue($2), "0" );
857                                              gen( "goto%s%d", L_NEXT,      $$  );
858                                          }
859                                          release_value( $2 );
860                                          tmp_freeall();
861            | /* empty */             {   $$ = 0;  /* no test */
862                                      }
863            ;
```

The returned attribute is the numeric component of all labels that are associated with the current statement. You'll need this information here to generate the target label for the exit branch, and the same numeric component is used to process the **else**. For example, the inner **if/else** at the bottom if Figure 6.20 uses three labels: TST3:, EXIT3, and EL3. The outer **if/else** uses TST1:, EXIT1, and EL1. The numeric component is generated in the *test* production, and the various alphabetic prefixes are defined symbolically in *label.h*. (It's in Listing 6.59 on page 557.)

Numeric component of label.

Finally, note that if the *expr* is a constant expression, no test is printed. An error message is printed if the expression evaluates to zero because the code in the body of the loop or **if** statement is unreachable; otherwise, the label is generated, but no test code is needed because the body is always executed. This way, input like:

Constant expressions in tests.

```
while( 1 )
    ...
```

evaluates to:

```
label:
    ...
    goto label;
```

The alternative would be an explicit, run-time comparison of one to zero, but there's little point in that.

6.9.2 Loops, break, and continue

Loops.

Loops are handled by the productions in Listing 6.106; there's some sample input and output code in Table 6.27. The code generated for loops is very similar to that generated for an **if** statement. The main difference is a jump back up to the test at the bottom of the loop. The main difficulty with loops is **break** and **continue** statements, which are not syntactically attached to the loop-control productions. **break** and **continue** are treated just like labels by the productions on lines 915 and 923 of Listing 6.106. They can appear anywhere in a subroutine—there's nothing in the grammar that requires them to be inside a loop or **switch**. Nonetheless, you do need to know where to branch when a **break** or **continue** is encountered, and you need to detect a **break** or **continue** outside of a loop or **switch**.

The problem is solved with a few more auxiliary stacks, declared at the top of Listing 6.106. The top-of-stack item in S_brk is the numeric component of the target label for a **break** statement. The alphabetic component of the label is at the top of S_brk_label. I've used two stacks to save the trouble of calling sprintf() to assemble a physical label. The compiler pushes a label onto the stack as part of the initial loop-control processing (on line 866 of Listing 6.106, for example). It pops the label when the loop processing finishes on line 871 of Listing 6.106. S_con and S_con_label do the same thing for **continue** statements. If the stack is empty when a **break** or **continue** is encountered, the statement is outside of a loop, and a semantic error message is printed.

6.9.3 The switch Statement

The **switch** statement.

The final control-flow statement in the language is the **switch**. Switches can be processed in several different ways. First, bear in mind that a **switch** is really a vectored **goto** statement. Code like the following is legal, though it's bad style:

```
switch( i )
{
case 0: if( condition )
            donald();
        else
        {
case 1:     hewey();
            dewie();
            louie();
        }
        break;
}
```

You could do the same thing with **goto** statements as follows:

Table 6.27. Loops: **while**, **for**, and **do**/**while**

Input	Output

`while( i < 10 )`
`{`
   `break;`
   `continue;`
`}`
	`TST3:`
	    `LT(W(&_i),10)` `/* Evaluate (i<10) and put` `*/`
	      `goto T3;` `/* the result into T(1).` `*/`
	`F3:`
	    `W( T(1) ) = 0;`
	    `goto E3;`
	`T3:`
	    `W( T(1) ) = 1;`
	`E3:`
	    `EQ(W( T(1) ),0)` `/* Exit the loop if test fails.*/`
	      `goto EXIT3;`
	                  `/* Body of loop:` `*/`
	    `goto EXIT3;` `/*    break` `*/`
	    `goto TST3;` `/*    continue` `*/`
	
	    `goto TST3;` `/* jump back up to the test` `*/`
	`EXIT3:`

`do`
`{`
   `break;`
   `continue;`
`}`
`while( --i );`
	`DTOP1:` `/* Top-of-loop marker` `*/`
	                     `/* Body of loop:` `*/`
	    `goto DXIT1;` `/*    break` `*/`
	    `goto DTST1;` `/*    continue` `*/`
	`DTST1:`
	`TST1:`
	    `W(&_i)` `-= 1;` `/* Evaluate --i and put` `*/`
	    `W( T(1) )` `= W(&_i);` `/*    the result into T(1).*/`
	    `EQ(W( T(1) ),0)` `/* Exit loop if test fails.*/`
	      `goto EXIT1;`
	
	    `goto DTOP1;` `/* Jump back to top of loop */`
	`DXIT1:`
	`EXIT1:`

`for( i = 0; i < 10; ++i )`
`{`
   `break;`
   `continue;`
`}`
	`W(&_i)` `= 0;` `/* Initialization part of for.` `*/`
	`TST4:` `/* Top-of-loop marker` `*/`
	    `LT(W(&_i),10)` `/* Evaluate (i<10) and put` `*/`
	      `goto T4;` `/*        the result into T(1)` `*/`
	`F4:`
	    `W( T(1) ) = 0;`
	    `goto E4;`
	`T4:`
	    `W( T(1) ) = 1;`
	`E4:`
	    `EQ(W( T(1) ),0)` `/* Exit the loop if test fails.` `*/`
	      `goto EXIT4;`
	    `goto BDY4;` `/* Skip over the increment` `*/`
	`INC4:` `/* increment portion of for stmt.` `*/`
	    `W(&_i)` `+= 1;`
	    `W( T(1) ) = W(&_i);`
	    `goto TST4;` `/* Jump up to the test.` `*/`
	`BDY4:` `/* Body of the loop` `*/`
	    `goto EXIT4;` `/*    break` `*/`
	    `goto INC4;` `/*    continue (jump to increment).` `*/`
	
	    `goto INC4;` `/* Bottom of loop, jump to increment.*/`
	`EXIT4:`

Listing 6.106. *c.y*— Statement Processing: Loops, **break**, and **continue**

```
164   %{
165   /* These stacks are necessary because there's no syntactic connection break,
166    * continue, case, default and the affected loop-control statement.
167    */
168
169   stack_dcl (S_brk,        int,     32); /* number part of current break target  */
170   stack_dcl (S_brk_label, char *, 32); /* string part of current break target  */
171
172   stack_dcl (S_con,        int,     32); /* number part of current continue targ. */
173   stack_dcl (S_con_label, char *, 32); /* string part of current continue targ. */
174   %}
```

```
864   /* statement: */
865
866           | WHILE LP test RP        {  push(S_con, $3); push( S_con_label, L_TEST);
867                                         push(S_brk, $3); push( S_brk_label, L_NEXT);
868                                      }
869             statement               {  gen( "goto%s%d", L_TEST, $3 );
870                                         gen( ":%s%d",    L_NEXT, $3 );
871                                         pop( S_con ); pop( S_con_label );
872                                         pop( S_brk ); pop( S_brk_label );
873                                      }
874
875           | DO                      {  static int label;
876
877                                         gen(":%s%d", L_DOTOP, $<num>$ = ++label );
878                                         push( S_con,          label );
879                                         push( S_con_label,  L_DOTEST );
880                                         push( S_brk,          label );
881                                         push( S_brk_label,  L_DOEXIT );
882                                      }
883             statement WHILE         {  gen(":%s%d",    L_DOTEST,  $<num>2 ); }
884             LP test RP SEMI         {  gen("goto%s%d", L_DOTOP,   $<num>2 );
885                                         gen( ":%s%d",   L_DOEXIT,  $<num>2 );
886                                         gen( ":%s%d",   L_NEXT,    $7      );
887                                         pop( S_con );
888                                         pop( S_con_label );
889                                         pop( S_brk );
890                                         pop( S_brk_label );
891                                      }
892
893           | FOR LP opt_expr SEMI
894                   test     SEMI {
895                                         gen("goto%s%d, L_BODY,       $5 );
896                                         gen(":%s%d",  L_INCREMENT, $5 );
897
898                                         push(S_con, $5);
899                                         push(S_con_label,   L_INCREMENT );
900                                         push(S_brk, $5);
901                                         push(S_brk_label,   L_NEXT      );
902                                      }
903             opt_expr RP             {  gen("goto%s%d", L_TEST,       $5 );
904                                         gen(":%s%d",    L_BODY,       $5 );
905                                      }
906             statement               {  gen("goto%s%d", L_INCREMENT, $5 );
907                                         gen( ":%s%d",   L_NEXT,       $5 );
908
```

```
Listing 6.106. continued...
909                                        pop( S_con        );
910                                        pop( S_con_label );
911                                        pop( S_brk        );
912                                        pop( S_brk_label );
913                                   }
914
915        | BREAK SEMI              {    if( stack_empty(S_brk) )
916                                          yyerror("Nothing to break from\n");
917
918
919                                       gen_comment("break");
920                                       gen("goto%s%d", stack_item(S_brk_label,0),
921                                                       stack_item(S_brk,      0));
922                                   }
923        | CONTINUE SEMI           {    if( stack_empty(S_brk) )
924                                          yyerror("Continue not in loop\n");
925
926
927                                       gen_comment("continue");
928                                       gen("goto%s%d", stack_item(S_con_label,0),
929                                                       stack_item(S_con,0     ));
                                       }
```

```
if      ( i == 0 )  goto case0;
else if ( i == 2 )  goto case1;
else                goto end;

case0:  if( condition )
            donald();
        else
        {
case1:      hewey();
            dewie();
            louie();
        }
end:;
```

The simplest, and the least efficient, method of handling **switch** statements translates   Translation to **if/else**.
the **switch** and **case**s directly into a series of **if/else** statements. For example, code
like this:

```
switch( i )
{
case 0: /* code */
case 1: /* more code */
    ...
}
```

can be translated into the following C-code:

```
    EQ( i, 0 )              /* test for case 0: */
        goto SW1;
                            /* code */

    goto SW2:               /* Jump around test */
SW1:                        /* test for case 1: */
    EQ( i, 1 )
        goto SW3:

SW2:                        /* more code */

    ...
```

The main disadvantage of this method is run-time speed; a lot of unnecessary goto branches are needed to find the thing you're looking for. Moreover, you have to test every case explicitly to find the default one. In practice, translation to **if/else** is useful only if there are a very limited number of **case** statements.

One easy-to-do improvement eliminates the **goto** branches around the imbedded **case**-processing statements by moving all the tests to the bottom of the switch. This method is used by the current compiler, and is illustrated in Table 6.28. A jump at the top of the switch gets you to the test code, which then jumps back up to the correct place in the switch. A final **goto** branch jumps around the **case**-selection code if the last **case** doesn't have a **break** in it.

Table 6.28. Vectored Goto: **switch**

Input	Output

```switch(i)```
 ```{```
 ```case 0:```
 ```   i = 0;```
 ```   /* fall through */```
 ```case 1:```
 ```   i = 1;```
 ```   break;```
 ```default:```
 ```   i = 2;```
 ```   break;```
 ```}```
	``` goto SW1; /* Jump to case-processing code.*/```
	 ```SW3: /* Case 0 */```
	 ``` W(&_i) = 0; /* Fall through to next case. */```
	 ```SW4: /* Case 1 */```
	 ``` W(&_i) = 1;```
	 ``` goto SW2; /* break; */```
	 ```SW5: /* default: */```
	 ``` W(&_i) = 2;```
	 ``` goto SW2; /* break; */```
	
	 ``` goto SW2; /* Inserted by compiler in case */```
	 ``` /* last case has no break in it.*/```
	 ```SW1: /* Code to evaluate switch: */```
	 ``` EQ(W(&_i),0)```
	 ``` goto SW3; /* Jump to case 0. */```
	 ``` EQ(W(&_i),1)```
	 ``` goto SW4; /* Jump to case 1. */```
	 ``` goto SW5; /* Jump to default case. */```
	 ```SW2:```

Dispatch tables.

The main reason that I'm using this approach is that limitations in C-code won't let me use the more efficient methods. It's worthwhile discussing these other methods, however. All of the alternate **switch** strategies use a table to compute the **goto** branches. The first method uses a data structure called a *dispatch table*—an array of two-member structures. The first member is the argument to the **case** statement, the second is a **goto** instruction that branches to the required location in the code. The switch:

```
switch( i );
{
case 0: washington();
case 1: jefferson();
```

```
    case 3: adams();
    }
```

can be implemented with this table:

0	**goto** case0;
1	**goto** case1;
3	**goto** case3;

and this code:

```
    case0: washington();
    case1: jefferson();
    case3: adams();
```

The compiler generates code to look up the case value in the table, often using a run-time subroutine call. If the value is found, the matching **goto** statement is executed, otherwise a branch to the default case is used. The table can be sorted by case value at compile time so the compiler can use a binary search at run time to find the proper label.

An even more efficient method uses a data structure called a *jump table*. A jump table is an array of **goto** vectors, indexed by case value. The compiler can process the switch with a single test and an array lookup:

Jump tables.

if(argument to switch is in range)
       goto jump_table[argument_to_switch - value of smallest case];
else
       goto default case;

The table elements are adjusted so that `jump_table[0]` corresponds to the smallest number used as an argument to a **case** statement. Holes in the table—elements for which there are no corresponding **case**—are filled with jumps to the default case. Note that, if the range of case values is less than or equal to twice the total number of case values, the jump table will be no larger than an equivalent dispatch table.

Jump table vs. dispatch table size.

Though the current compiler can't use tables in the generated code, the method that it does use is easily adapted to this approach, because it assembles a compile-time model of the dispatch table. Listing 6.107 contains the data structures used for this purpose.

A dispatch-table element (`case_val`) is defined on lines three to seven. It contains two fields: `on_this` is the argument to the case statement, stored as an **int**, `go_here` is the numeric component of the label associated with this case; the alphabetic prefix is SW.

The `stab` structure, declared on line nine of Listing 6.107, is used to manage the table proper. It contains the following fields:

table	The dispatch table—an array of `case_val` structures.
cur	Points into `table` at the next available slot.
name	The `name` field of the `value` structure to which the expression argument of the **switch** statement evaluates. That is, a switch is recognized by the following production:

statement→**SWITCH LP** *expr* **RP** *compound_stmt*

The *expr* recognizes an entire expression—all code for evaluating the expression will have been generated when the *expr* is put onto the stack by the parser. This code creates a single `value` attribute that identifies the temporary variable that holds the run-time result of the expression evaluation; the `name` field from this `value` is copied to the `stab`'s name field.

<table>
<tr><td>def_label</td><td>The numeric component of the label associated with the default case. This number is 5 in the switch in Table 6.28.</td></tr>
<tr><td>stab_label</td><td>The numeric component of the labels that precede and follow the case-selection code. The label that follows the case-selection code has the value stab_label+1. This number is 1 in the switch in Table 6.28: SW1 precedes the selection code and SW2 follows it.</td></tr>
</table>

Listing 6.107. *switch.h*— Type Definitions for **switch** Processing

```
1    #define CASE_MAX 128            /* Maximum number of cases in a switch */
2
3    typedef struct case_val         /* a single dispatch-table element     */
4    {
5        int  on_this;               /* The N in a "case N:" statement      */
6        int  go_here;               /* Numeric component of label in output */
7    } case_val;                     /*                             code.   */
8
9    typedef struct stab             /* a switch table */
10   {
11       case_val *cur;                      /* pointer to next available slot in table */
12       case_val table[ CASE_MAX   ]; /* switch table itself.                    */
13       char     name [ VALNAME_MAX ]; /* switch on this rvalue                  */
14       int      def_label;            /* label associated with default case     */
15       int      stab_label;           /* label at top and bottom of selector    */
16                                       /* code. Bottom label is stab_label+1.    */
17   } stab;
```

The compiler keeps around a stack of pointers to stab structures, declared in Listing 6.108. The size of this stack limits the number of nested switch statements that are permitted in the input. A stab is allocated when the **switch** is processed, and a pointer to the stab is pushed. The pointer is popped after the entire switch has been processed. Every instance of a nested switch pushes a new stab pointer onto the stack, and that pointer is popped when the compiler is done with the nested switch.

Every **case** statement does two things: it emits a label of the form SW*n*, and it adds a new dispatch-table element for *n* to the stab structure at top of stack. (It modifies the entry pointed to by the cur field in the structure at top of stack, and then increments the cur field.) The numeric components of the label are just allocated sequentially by incrementing Case_label, also in Listing 6.108. The code that processes a **switch** is in Listings 6.108 and 6.109.

The only difficulty in the code is the point at which the value associated with the argument to the **switch** statement is released on line 945 of Listing 6.108. This is another compile-versus-run-time issue. The order of operations at run time is: (1) jump to the selector code at the bottom of the switch, (2) pick out the target label, (3) jump back up to that label. At run time, the value associated with the expr is used in step (2) to select the **goto** vector, and is not used further. Consequently, it can be recycled for use in the code that comprises the body of the switch. The selector code is not generated until after the body is processed, however. If the value was released after the selector code was printed, it could not be recycled in the **switch** body. Consequently, it's released at the top of the **switch**, before the body is processed. The value's name field is remembered in the stab structure so that the selector code can be generated later.

Listing 6.108. *c.y*— Statement Processing: The **switch** statement.

```
175   %{
176   int      Case_label = 0;                /* Label used to process case statements. */
177
178   stack_dcl (S_switch, stab *, 32); /* Switch table for current switch.          */
179   %}
```

```
930   /* statement: */
931         | SWITCH LP expr RP
932           {
933                  /* Note that the end-of-switch label is the 2nd argument to
934                   * new_stab + 1; This label should be used for breaks when in
935                   * the switch.
936                   */
937
938                  push( S_switch, new_stab($3, ++Case_label) );
939                  gen_comment("Jump to case-processing code" );
940                  gen("goto%s%d", L_SWITCH, Case_label );
941
942                  push( S_brk,        ++Case_label );
943                  push( S_brk_label, L_SWITCH      );
944
945                  release_value( $3 );
946                  tmp_freeall();
947           }
948         compound_stmt
949           {
950                  gen_stab_and_free_table( pop( S_switch ) );
951           }
952
953         | CASE const_expr COLON
954           {
955                  add_case     ( stack_item(S_switch,0), $2, ++Case_label );
956                  gen_comment ( "case %d:", $2                            );
957                  gen         ( ":%s%d"  , L_SWITCH, Case_label           );
958           }
959
960         | DEFAULT COLON
961           {
962                  add_default_case( stack_item(S_switch,0), ++Case_label );
963                  gen_comment("default:");
964                  gen(":%s%d", L_SWITCH, Case_label );
965           }
966         ;
```

Listing 6.109. *switch.c*— Switch Processing

```
1    #include <stdio.h>
2    #include <stdlib.h>
3    #include <tools/debug.h>
4    #include <tools/hash.h>
5    #include <tools/l.h>
6    #include <tools/compiler.h>
7    #include <tools/c-code.h>
8
9    #include "symtab.h"
10   #include "value.h"
11   #include "proto.h"
12   #include "label.h"
13   #include "switch.h"
14
15   /*------------------------------------------------------------------*/
16
17   PUBLIC   stab  *new_stab( val, label )
18   value    *val;
19   int      label;
20   {
21       /* Allocate a new switch table and return a pointer to it. Use free() to
22        * discard the table. Val is the value to switch on, it is converted to
23        * an rvalue, if necessary, and the name is stored.
24        */
25
26       stab *p;
27
28       if( !(p = (stab *) malloc(sizeof(stab)) ))
29       {
30           yyerror("No memory for switch\n");
31           exit( 1 );
32       }
33
34       p->cur        = p->table ;
35       p->stab_label = label;
36       p->def_label  = 0;
37       strncpy( p->name, rvalue(val), sizeof(p->name) );
38       return p;
39   }
40
41   /*------------------------------------------------------------------*/
42
43   PUBLIC   void    add_case( p, on_this, go_here )
44   stab     *p;
45   int      on_this;
46   int      go_here;
47   {
48       /* Add a new case to the stab at top of stack. The 'cur' field identifies
49        * the next available slot in the dispatch table.
50        */
51
52       if( p->cur  >  &(p->table[CASE_MAX-1]) )
53           yyerror("Too many cases in switch\n");
54       else
55       {
56           p->cur->on_this = on_this ;
57           p->cur->go_here = go_here;
58           ++( p->cur );
59       }
```

Listing 6.109. continued...

```
60      }
61
62      /* --------------------------------------------------------------------*/
63
64      PUBLIC   void     add_default_case( p, go_here )
65      stab     *p;
66      int      go_here;
67      {
68          /* Add the default case to the current switch by remembering its label */
69
70          if( p->def_label )
71              yyerror("Only one default case permitted in switch\n");
72
73          p->def_label = go_here;
74      }
75
76      /* --------------------------------------------------------------------*/
77
78      PUBLIC   void     gen_stab_and_free_table( p )
79      stab *p;
80      {
81          /* Generate the selector code at the bottom of the switch. This routine is
82           * emitting what amounts to a series of if/else statements. It could just
83           * as easily emit a dispatch or jump table and the code necessary to process
84           * that table at run time, however.
85           */
86
87          case_val   *cp;
88          char       nbuf[20];
89
90          gen( "goto%s%d", L_SWITCH, p->stab_label + 1 );
91          gen( ":%s%d",    L_SWITCH, p->stab_label     );
92
93          for( cp = p->table ; cp < p->cur ; ++cp )
94          {
95              gen( "EQ%s%d",   p->name,  cp->on_this );
96              gen( "goto%s%d", L_SWITCH, cp->go_here );
97          }
98
99          if( p->def_label )
100             gen( "goto%s%d", L_SWITCH, p->def_label );
101
102         gen( ":%s%d", L_SWITCH, p->stab_label + 1 );
103         free( p );
104     }
```

6.10 Exercises

6.1. What are the consequences of changing the initial productions in the current C
      grammar to the following:

> *program*   →   *ext_def_list*
> *ext_def_list*   →   *ext_def ext_def_list* | ε

Would the parser still work? For how long? This exercise points out the
differences between theoretical and practical grammars.

6.2.   Find all the bugs in the compiler presented in the current chapter and fix them.

6.3.   Draw a system of `symbol`, `link`, and `structdef` structures that represents the following global-variable definition:

```
struct Montague
{
      long   *(*Romeo[2])[5];
      short **Juliet[10];
      struct Montague *next;
}
*(* (* Capulet)[ 10 ])();
```

6.4.   Modify the compiler in the current chapter as follows:

   a. Add 4-byte **float**s to the compiler.

   b. Add 8-byte **double**s to the compiler.

   c. Add support for the **const**, **volatile**, and **register** storage classes.

   d. Make structures generate lvalues: Add structure assignment and add the ability to pass a structure to a subroutine (and to return it) by value.

   e. Add run-time initialization of automatic variables.

   f. Add compile-time initialization of static-local and global aggregates.

   g. Add support for signed and unsigned bit fields.

   h. Add support for function prototypes. A hard error should occur when the types in a definition disagree with a prototype. A warning should be printed (and any required type conversions be performed) when the arguments of a call differ from those in the prototype.

   You'll have to call run-time subroutines to do the floating-point operations because floating point is not supported in C-code.

6.5.   The scope of a structure in the current chapter's compiler is from the point of declaration to the end of the input file. This is incorrect—-structures should follow the same scoping rules as variables. Fix the problem.

6.6.   Though the compiler in the current chapter behaves reasonably well when it's given legal input, it has difficulty when presented with syntactically correct, but semantically incorrect input. Semantic errors, such as ++ being applied to a non-lvalue or an attempt to multiply two pointers, should be handled by printing an error message, and then pretending that legal input had been encountered by putting a legitimate attribute onto the value stack instead of garbage. Improve the semantic-error recovery in the current compiler.

6.7.   Most code generation has been concentrated into the `gen()` subroutine to facilitate portability to other target languages. Declarations are not handled by `gen`, however. Either modify `gen()` to handles declarations, or create a new `decl_gen()` subroutine that outputs all declarations. Modify the variable-declaration actions to use this subroutine.

6.8.   The compiler currently generates the following code for `i&&j&&k`:

```
                EQ(W(&_i),0)
                    goto F1;
                EQ(W(&_j),0)
                    goto F1;
                EQ(W(&_k),0)
                    goto F1;
                goto T1;
        F1:
                W( T(1) ) = 0;
                goto E1;
        T1:
                W( T(1) ) = 1;
        E1:
```

This code has an unreachable **goto** statement above the F1 label. Modify the compiler to generate the following code for the earlier input:

```
                EQ(W(&_i),0)
                    goto F1;
                EQ(W(&_j),0)
                    goto F1;
                NE(W(&_k),0)
                    goto T1;
        F1:
                W( T(1) ) = 0;
                goto E1;
        T1:
                W( T(1) ) = 1;
        E1:
```

6.9.   (a) Redesign C-code so that it is a more appropriate language for communication with a back end: the sizes of all objects should all be 1, and the stack should be 1 element wide; Space for local variables should not be allocated in the compiler (information about them should be passed to the back end to do the allocation), and so forth. Modify the compiler to emit your modified code.

(b) Write a back end that translates that code to a real assembly language.

6.10. The PostScript graphics-description language is a postfix assembly language used by many printers. It is described in Adobe System's *PostScript Language Reference Manual* (Reading, Mass.: Addison-Wesley, 1985). Write a C-to-PostScript Translator. You may define a subset of C for this purpose. All the standard PostScript functions should be supported as intrinsic functions (recognized as keywords by the compiler and processed directly).

6.11. The UNIX **troff** typesetting program is really an assembler. Its input is an assembly-language description of a document made up of interspersed text and "dot commands" (assembler directives). **Troff** translates that input into a typeset version of that document. Design a C-like language that can describe a document, and then implement a compiler that translates that language to **troff**. At minimum you must support **int**s, one-dimensional arrays, subroutines (which must be able to return **int** values), and **if/else**, **for**, and **while** statements. You should also support a basic `string` type, with operators for concatenation, comparison, and so forth. Finally, you should support an aliasing facility that lets you give reasonable names to built-in registers and special characters. You can use recursion to do the loops. For example, the following loop executes ten times:

```
.de Lp
.    if \\$1 \{\
.        executing iteration \\$1
.        nr x \\$1-1
.        Lp \\nx \}
..
.\"
.Lp 10        \" This call loops ten times
```

6.12. Write compilers that duplicate the UNIX **pic** and **eqn** preprocessors, translating descriptions of pictures and equations into **troff** commands.

6.13. Write an ANSI-C preprocessor. It must be able to handle the concatenation (**##**) and "stringizing" operator (**#**).

6.14. Write a program that reads a C input file and which outputs ANSI function prototypes for all functions in that file. Your program must be able to handle **#include** statements. Your output must be acceptable to a standard, ANSI compiler.

6.15. Write a program that reads a C file containing old-style function definitions like this:

```
apostles( mat, mark, luke, john, fred )
char *mat;
long  mark;
double luke;
{
}
```

and which outputs C++-style definitions like this:

```
apostles( char *mat, long mark, double luke, int john, int fred )
{
}
```

Note that the default **int** type must be supplied for john and fred.

6.16. Modify the solution to the previous exercise so that it goes in the other direction, translating C++ definitions to old-style C definitions.

6.17. Modify the solution to the previous exercise to translate an ANSI-C input file to pre-ANSI, K&R C. If several input files are listed on the program's command line, they should be translated individually. Output should be written to files with a *.k&r* extension. For example, *foo.c* should be translated, and the output placed in *foo.k&r*. (Use *.knr* on UNIX systems so that you don't have to quote the name.)

At very least, function definitions, string concatenation, and function-name mapping [such as remove() to unlink()], should be handled. If the first eight characters of an identifier are not unique, the identifier should be replaced with a unique 8-character name. These replacements should carry from one input file to another in the case of nonstatic global variables and subroutine names. That is, if several C input files are specified on your translator's command line, the files should be translated individually (not merged together), but the too-long global symbols that are translated in one file should be translated to the same arbitrary name in all files. Be careful to check that your arbitrary name is not already being used in the input file for some other purpose.

Structure assignment, passing structures to functions, and the returning of structures from a function should also be detected and translated into a form that can be handled by a compiler that supports none of these (you can use implicit memcpy() calls for this purpose).

6.18. Write a "beautifier" program that reads a randomly formatted C input file and which outputs the file with nice indenting showing the block level, lined up braces, and so forth. You should do intelligent things with comments, trying to line up the '/*' and '*/' tokens in end-of-line comments in neat columns, like this:

```
code            /* comment             */
more code       /* another comment     */
yet more code   /* yet another comment */
```

If a comment won't fit onto the end of a reformatted line, then it should be moved to the previous line. Multiple-line comments should be output as follows:

```
/* this is a
 * multiple-line
 * comment
 */
```

with the /* at the same indent level as the surrounding code.

6.19. One of the more useful features of C++ is "function overloading". You are permitted to declare several instances of the same function, each of which takes arguments of different types, like this:

```
overload Sophocles;
int    Sophocles( long   Jocasta, short Oedipus ){...}
double Sophocles( double Jocasta, char *Oedipus ){...}
```

The overload keyword tells the compiler that multiple definitions of a function are permitted. The compiler determines which version of the function to call by examining the types of the actual arguments in a given call. If the types in a call don't match the definition exactly, the standard type conversions are used to promote the argument to the correct type (a warning is printed if this is done). Do the following:

(a) Modify the C compiler in the current chapter to support function overloading.

(b) Write a preprocessor that translates overloaded functions to a form that can be handled by a standard ANSI compiler.

6.20. The Awk Programming Language is discussed in [Aho2]. Write a compiler that converts an awk input file to C.

6.21. (a) Write a C-to-Pascal converter.

(b) Write a Pascal-to-C converter. Your program must be able to handle nested subroutine declarations. The organization of the Pascal stack frame is discussed in Appendix B. This is a much harder problem than (a).

6.22. (a) Write a FORTRAN-to-C converter.

(b) Write a C-to-FORTRAN converter. All C data types must be handled properly, especially translation of C pointers to FORTRAN array indexes. This is a much harder problem than (a).

6.23. Modify *virtual.h* so that the registers and run-time stack are both 16 bits wide rather than 32 bits wide. Eliminate the lword basic type and .l register selector, and redefine the ptr type to be 16 bits wide. Finally, modify the compiler so that this new stack and register width is supported. The C word widths must remain unchanged—the compiler should still support a 32-bit **long int**, 16-bit **int**, and 8-bit **char**. How could you modify the compiler to make this translation easier?

6.24. Add an autodecrement and autoincrement addressing mode to C-code indirect modes [W(p++), WP(--p), and so forth], then modify the grammar and associated code-generation actions so that the following inputs generate a minimum number of C-code instructions:

```
*p++      *++p      *p--      *--p
```

6.25. Write a program that translates C-code into your favorite assembly language.

6.26. Write a C-code interpreter that takes a C-code program as input and executes that code directly. The following subroutines should be built into the interpreter (so that they can be called directly from a C-code program):

putb() Print the low byte of the top-of-stack item to standard output (in hex).

putw() Print the low word of the top-of-stack item to standard output (in hex).

putl() Print the long word at the top of stack to standard output (in hex).

puti() Print the long word at the top of stack to standard output (in decimal).

putc() Print the low byte of the top-of-stack item to standard output as an ASCII character.

puts() Print the string in the array whose address is at the top of stack to standard output.

getb() Input a hex byte from standard input and return it in rF.

getw() Input a hex word from standard input and return it in rF.w.low.

getl() Input a hex long word from standard input and return it in rF.

geti() Input a decimal long word and put it in rF.

getc() Input an ASCII character from standard input and return it in rF.b.b0.

dump() Print the contents of all registers to standard output.

dumps() Print the top 20 stack items to standard output.

Execution should begin with a subroutine called *main( )*, which must be supplied in the source file. You may require this function to be the first (or last) one in the file if you wish.

6.27. If you haven't done so already, make the interpreter in the previous exercise into a window-based system. One window displays the code as it's being executed, a second displays the register and stack contents, a third shows the contents of selected static variables (entered by you at a command prompt), and a fourth shows the C input line that corresponds to the output being executed. Use line numbers that are inserted into the output by the lexical analyzer for this last function.

6.28. If you haven't done so already, modify the interpreter to support the following breakpoint types:
   - Break when a specified source-code line is executed.
   - Break when a specified subroutine is called.
   - Break when a specified global variable is modified or takes on a specific value.
   - Break when a specified C-code instruction is executed.

6.29. If you haven't done so already, modify the interpreter to display the contents of both global and local variables by specifying their name at a command prompt. A local symbol should be displayed only when executing a subroutine that contains that symbol. You will need to pass symbol-table information between the compiler and interpreter to do this. Use an auxiliary file.

7

Optimization Strategies

This chapter looks at optimization strategies at a high level. It is not intended to be an in-depth discussion of the topic—something that would take a book of its own to cover adequately. The basic types of optimizations are described, however, and optimization techniques are discussed in a general way. The way that the choice of intermediate code affects optimization is also discussed.

Optimizations are easily divided into three categories: parser optimizations; linear, peephole optimizations; and structural optimizations. I'll look at these three categories one at a time.

7.1 Parser Optimizations

The first category includes all optimizations that can be done by the parser itself. The simplest of these really come under the category of generating good code to begin with: using logical lvalues rather than physical ones, minimizing the number of **goto** branches, and so forth. The other common parser optimization is *intrinsic-function generation*. Intrinsic function calls are translated directly by the compiler into code that does the action normally performed by the function. For example, `strcpy()` is often implemented as an intrinsic function. The lexeme `strcpy` is recognized by the compiler as a keyword, and there is a production of the form:

Intrinsic functions.

```
expr: STRCPY LP expr COMMA expr RP
```

in the grammar. The associated action generates code to copy one string to another rather than generating code to call the `strcpy()` function. Intrinsic functions are particularly useful with small workhorse functions, a call to which can often have a higher overhead than the code that does the work. Other common intrinsic functions are the math functions like `sin()`, `cos()`, and `sqrt()`.

Some of the optimizations discussed below can also be done directly by the parser (such as using a left shift to implement multiplication by a constant).

7.2 Linear (Peephole) Optimizations

The optimizations that can be done directly by the parser are, by necessity, limited in scope to single productions. It's difficult for the parser to optimize any code that takes more than one production to process. For example, the following compiler input:

```
int i;
    ...
i = 5;
++i;
return i + 1;
```

generates this output:

```
W(&_i)        =   5;
W(&_i)        +=  1;
W( T(1) )     =   W(&_i);
W( T(1) )     =   W(&_i);
W( T(1) )     +=  1;
rF.w.low      =   W( T(1) );
ret();
```

The two identical assignments on the third and fourth lines are unavoidable because they are generated by two separate statements—the first by the ++i and the second by the i+1. It's easy for a separate optimizer pass to recognize this situation, however, and eliminate the redundant assignment.

This section looks at various optimizations that cannot be done in the parser, but which can be done by an auxiliary optimizer pass that goes through the compiler's output in a linear fashion, from top to bottom. (It may have to go through the output several times, however.) This kind of optimizer is called a *peephole optimizer*—"peephole" because it examines small blocks of contiguous instructions, one block at a time, as if the code were being scrolled past a window and only the code visible in the window could be manipulated. The optimizer scans the code looking for patterns, and then makes simple replacements. Peephole optimizers are usually small, fast programs, needing little memory to operate.

The kind of optimizations that you intend to do is a major factor in deciding the type of intermediate language that the compiler should generate. A peephole optimizer is happiest working with triples or quads. I'll use the triples generated by the compiler in the last chapter for examples in the following discussion.

7.2.1 Strength Reduction

A *strength reduction* replaces an operation with a more efficient operation or series of operations that yield the same result in fewer machine clock cycles. For example, multiplication by a power of two can be replaced by a left shift which executes faster on most machines. (x*8 can be done with x<<3.) You can divide by a power of two with a right shift (x/8 is x>>3) and do a modulus division by a power of two with a bitwise AND (x%8 is x&7).

Other strength reductions are less obvious. For example, multiplication by small numbers can be replaced by multiple additions: t0*=3 can be replaced with

```
t1  = t0;
t0 += t1;
t0 += t1;
```

Combinations of shifts and additions can be used for multiplication by larger numbers: t0*=9 can be replaced by:

```
t1   = t0;
t1 <<= 3;
t0  += t1;
```

[That is, $t0 \times 9 \equiv (t0 \times 8) + t0 \equiv (t0 << 3) + t0$.] Larger numbers can also be handled this way: $t0*=27$ can be replaced by:

```
t1   = t0;
t1 <<= 1;
t0  += t1;
t1 <<= 2;
t0  += t1;
t1 <<= 1;
t0  += t1;
```

You can see what's going on by looking at how a binary arithmetic is performed. A binary multiplication is done just like a decimal multiplication. 27_{10} is 11011_2, so the multiplication is done like this:

```
            d d d d d d d d
        × 0 0 0 1 1 0 1 1
          ─────────────────
            d d d d d d d d
          d d d d d d d d
        0 0 0 0 0 0 0 0
      d d d d d d d d
      d d d d d d d d
    0 0 0 0 0 0 0 0
  0 0 0 0 0 0 0 0
+ 0 0 0 0 0 0 0 0
```

If there's a *1* in the multiplier, then the multiplicand, shifted left by a number of bits corresponding to the position of the *1* in the multiplier, is added to the product. At worst, you need as many shift/add steps as there are bits in the denominator. It's up to the optimizer to determine at what point it takes longer to do the shifts and additions than it does to use a multiplication instruction, but on many machines the shift/multiply strategy is faster for all but very large numbers. This last optimization is a classic example of a code-size-versus-execution-speed trade-off. The faster addition-and-shift code is much larger than the equivalent multiplication instruction.

There are also nonarithmetic strength reductions. For example, many machines have several different forms of jump or **goto** instruction, and the optimizer can sometimes modify the code so that the more efficient instruction can be used.

Instruction optimization.

7.2.2 Constant Folding and Constant Propagation

We've already seen constant folding at work in the last chapter, because the parser itself can do it in a limited way. Put simply, the compiler itself does any arithmetic that involves constants, if it can. An expression like $a+2*3$ is treated like $(a+6)$.

Order of evaluation can prevent the parser from doing constant folding. For example, the parser can't optimize the following input because of the left-to-right order of evaluation:

```
a + 1 + 3
```

The parser processes the $a+1$ first and puts the result into a temporary variable. The three is then added to the temporary. The following code is generated:

```
W( T(1) )    = W(&_i);
W( T(1) )   += 1;
W( T(1) )   += 3;
```

It's easy for an independent optimizer to see that $T(1)$ is modified twice in succession without being used between the modifications, however, and replace the foregoing with:

```
W( T(1) )      = W(& _i);
W( T(1) )      += 4;
```

Multiplication by one, addition and subtraction of zero, and shift by zero can be eliminated entirely.

Constant Propagation.

Constant folding is actually a simple case of a more general optimization called *constant propagation*. Many variables retain constant values over a large portion of their lifetimes. The compiler can note when a constant is assigned to a variable and use that constant rather than the variable when the variable is referenced in the code. The constant propagates until the variable is modified. For example, code like this:

```
_y = 5;
  ...
_x = _y;
```

can be replaced with

```
_y = 5;
  ...
_x = 5;
```

(Assignment of a constant to a variable is a more efficient operation than a memory-to-memory copy on most machines.) At a higher level, the loop in the following code:

```
int    i, j;

for( i = 5, j = 0; j < i ; ++j )
     foo( i );
```

can be treated as if the compiler had seen the following:

```
for( i = 5, j = 0; j < 5 ; ++j )
     foo( 5 );
```

The optimizer is, in effect, keeping track of the contents of all variables that contain constants. It keeps a local symbol table with an entry for each active variable, and that internal entry is modified to track modifications in the code. The internal value is modified every time the variable is modified. For example, this code:

```
t0   = 1;
t0 += 5;
t1   = t0;
```

is translated to this:

```
t0   = 1;
t1   = 6;
```

The compiler initializes an internal copy of t0 when the first line is encountered. It then modifies that internal copy by adding five to it when the t0+=5 is encountered and discards the t0+=5 instruction. Finally, the modified value is used when the substitution is made on the third input line.

7.2.3 Dead Variables and Dead Code

Dead variables.

One type of optimization often leads to another. In the previous example, t0 can be discarded after the constant propagation because it is not used anywhere. t0 is a *dead variable*—a variable that is initialized (and perhaps modified), but never referenced in a function call or to the right of an equals sign. The variable is considered dead from the last time it is used until it is reinitialized—like this:

```
t0 =   _a;
t0 += 5;
_x =   t0;
   ...              /* t0 is now dead                    */
t0 += 1;            /* This instruction can be eliminated. */
   ...
t0 = _b;            /* t0 is now resurrected.             */
```

At a higher level, the i in the following code is a dead variable—all references to it can be eliminated:

```
foo(x)
{
    int i;
    i = x;
    ++i;
}
```

A *dead assignment* is an extreme case of a dead variable. A dead assignment is an   Dead assignment.
assignment to a variable that is never used or modified. The initial assignment of t0= _a
in the earlier example is not a dead assignment because t0 is used later on in the code.
Nonetheless, dead assignments are very common in the output from the compiler in the
previous chapter because of the way that expressions are processed. All expressions
evaluate to something, and there is often a copy into an rvalue as the last step of the
expression evaluation. Code like this:

```
int x;
++x;
```

generates the following output:

```
W(fp-2)       += 1;            /* x */
W( T(1) )     = W(fp-2);
```

The final assignment to T(1) is a dead assignment because T(1) is never used. At a
higher level, the earlier constant propagation example translated this code:

```
for( i = 5, j = 0; j < i ; ++j )
    ...
```

into this:

```
for( i = 5, j = 0; j < 5 ; ++j )
    ...
```

The i=5 is now a dead assignment and can be eliminated.

Dead code is code that can't be reached or does nothing useful. For example, code   Dead code.
generated by the following input can be removed entirely:

```
if( 0 )
    do_something();
```

This input is translated to the following C-code:

```
    NE( 0, 0 )
      goto label;
    call( _do_something );
    W(T(1)) = rF.w.low;
label:
```

It is optimized in two steps. First, the dead assignment on the fourth line can be eliminated, yielding:

```
NE( 0, 0 )
    goto label;
call( _do_something );
label:
```

Since the NE always evaluates true, all code between the following **goto** and the label can be eliminated because it's unreachable. Similar optimizations involve the elimination of useless code (like the

```
goto F1;
F1:
```

which is generated at the end of a list of && operators). The following, more complex example takes two passes to optimize:

```
t0 = 0;
NE(t0,0)
    goto label;
  ...
label:
```

The first pass folds the constant 0 into t0, yielding this:

```
NE(0,0)
    goto label;
  ...
label:
```

The test now always fails, so it and the following **goto** instruction can both be eliminated.

Had we started with the following code:

```
t0 = 1;
NE(t0,0)
    goto label;
  ...
label:
```

the constant would fold to:

```
NE(1,0)
    goto label;
  ...
label:
```

which always tests true. Consequently the NE, the **goto**, and all code up to the label are dead and can be discarded. Note that the dead-code elimination is affected if there is a second entry point into the block. Input like the following:

```
switch( hitter )
{
case eddie_murray:  x = 1;
                    while( x )
                    {
case tony_phillips:     ...
                    }

}
```

(it's sick,[1] but it's legal) could generate output like this:

```
 x = 1;
NE(W(& x),0)
      goto label      Remove only this code.
 ...

label2:
 ...

label:
```

The constant 1 propagates into the test, resulting in dead code, but only the code up to `label2` can be eliminated because the **switch** could branch to the interior label. A region of code that has a single entry point and a single exit point (everything from a label or `PROC` directive up to the next **goto** or `ret()` instruction) is called a *basic block*, and some optimizations, such as the current one, can be performed only within the confines of a basic block.

Basic block.

As we just saw, dead variable and code elimination can interact with constant propagation in interesting ways. The `i` in the following code isn't a dead variable—at least initially:

Interaction between optimizations.

```
foo()
{
    int i, j, array[10];
    i = 5;
    ++i;
    j = array[i];
    ...
}
```

The compiler can propagate the constant 5 through to the array access, however:

```
foo()
{
    int i, j, array[10];
    i = 5;
    ++i;
    j = array[6];
    ...
}
```

Having done that, the `i` is now dead and can be eliminated:

```
foo()
{
    int j, array[10];
    j = array[6];
    ...
}
```

A form of dead-assignment elimination also applies to nonconstants. Code like the following, which is very common compiler output:

Nonconstant dead assignments.

---

1. That's a technical term.

```
t0 = _x;
   ...
_y = t0;
```

can be replaced by:

```
_y = _x;
```

unless _x is modified before t0 is used. For example, this code:

```
t0 = _x;
_y = t0;
t0 = _z;
```

can be optimized to:

```
_y = _x;
t0 = _z;
```

but the following cannot be optimized because _x is modified before t0 is used:

```
t0 = _x;
_x += 1;
_y = t0;
```

Hardware problems,
volatile.

All the foregoing optimizations can be a real headache when you're interfacing to hardware. For example, an 8-bit, memory-mapped I/O port at physical address 0x10 can be modeled as follows on many machines:[2]

```
char *port;
port = (char *)0x10;
```

Thereafter, you can access the port with *port. The following code, for example, is intended to pulse the low bit of the output port at periodic intervals:

```
*port = 0;       /* initialize output port to all zeros        */
while( *port )   /* read input port, terminate if data available */
{
    *port = 1;   /* pulse the low bit of the output port        */
    *port = 0;
    delay();
}
```

Unfortunately, many optimizers eliminate <u>all</u> of the previous code. The *port=1 is a dead assignment because *port is modified again before the value 1 is used, so the first optimization results in the following code:

```
*port = 0;
while( *port )
{
    *port = 0;
    delay();
}
```

Next, since the value of *port never changes (the same constant is always assigned to it), constant propagation takes over and the following code is produced:

---

2. or, better yet, with:

        `char *`**const** `port = 0x10;`

  The **const** says that port itself won't change value. You can also use a macro:

        `#define port ((char *)(0x10))`

```
*port = 0;
while( 0 )
    delay();
```

The initial assignment to `*port` can now be eliminated because `*port` isn't used anywhere, and the loop can be discarded because its body is unreachable.

The ANSI **volatile** keyword is used to suppress these optimizations. No assumptions are made as to the value of any variable that's declared volatile—the compiler assumes that the value can change at any time, even if no explicit code modifies it. You can suppress all optimizations in the previous example by declaring `port` as follows:

Suppress optimization with the **volatile** keyword.

```
volatile char *port;
```

or better yet:

```
volatile char *const port = 0x10;
```

This declaration says that the object at which `port` points is liable to change without notice, but that `port` itself is a constant whose value never changes.[3]

7.2.4 Peephole Optimization: An Example

I'll demonstrate the mechanics of peephole optimization with a simple example. The input:

```
i = 5;
++i;
return i + 1;
```

generates this output:

```
W(&_i)       = 5;
W(&_i)       += 1;
W( T(1) )    = W(&_i);
W( T(1) )    = W(&_i);
W( T(1) )    += 1;
rF.w.low     = W( T(1) );
ret();
```

This output has several inefficiencies built into it, all of which can be eliminated by a peephole optimizer. The optimizer must operate on a basic block: The current code has no labels into it, and a single exit point at the bottom, so it comprises a basic block.

The first optimizations to apply are constant folding and propagation. The approach is straightforward: Go through the compiler output performing those operations that you can. You'll need a symbol table, accessed by variable name, that holds the contents of that variable insofar as it can be determined.

The optimizer's first pass evaluates expressions, if possible, modifying the table's contents to reflect the computed value. It also substitutes any reference to a variable that holds a constant value with that constant. Here, the optimizer reads the first line, creates a symbol table entry for `_i` and initializes it to 5. It now reads the second line. There's already an entry for `i` in the table, and `_i` is being modified by a constant. Consequently, it increments the symbol-table entry from five to six, and modifies the code as follows:

---

3. The cast can be done like this:

```
#define port ((volatile char *)0x10)
```

```
        W(&_i)          = 5;
☞       W(&_i)          = 6;
        W( T(1) )       = W(&_i);
        W( T(1) )       = W(&_i);
        W( T(1) )       += 1;
        rF.w.low        = W( T(1) );
```

Now it reads the third and fourth lines. Seeing that _i holds a constant, it replaces the reference to _i with that constant as follows:

```
        W(&_i)          = 5;
        W(&_i)          = 6;
☞       W( T(1) )       = 6;
☞       W( T(1) )       = 6;
        W( T(1) )       += 1;
        rF.w.low        = W( T(1) );
```

It also makes a symbol-table entry for T(1), initializing it to 6. Reading the fifth line, it sees a variable that holds a constant (T(1)) being modified by a constant, so adjusts the internal symbol table and the output as before, yielding:

```
        W(&_i)          = 5;
        W(&_i)          = 6;
        W( T(1) )       = 6;
        W( T(1) )       = 6;
☞       W( T(1) )       = 7;
        rF.w.low        = W( T(1) );
```

Reading the final line, since T(1) holds a constant, it can be replaced with its value:

```
        W(&_i)          = 5;
        W(&_i)          = 6;
        W( T(1) )       = 6;
        W( T(1) )       = 6;
        W( T(1) )       = 7;
☞       rF.w.low        = 7;
```

Though there are still the same number of operations as before, they've all been translated to simple assignments.

The output from the first pass is now simplified further by going through it a second time, eliminating all dead variables—variables that aren't used in the current block. The strategy is, again, straightforward: Clear the symbol table, then go through the code, creating entries for all variables that appear as a source operand. Make a second pass eliminating all variables whose destination operand is not in the table. Since T(1) is not used in the source fields of any of the triples, all assignments to it are eliminated, yielding:

```
        W(&_i)          = 5;
        W(&_i)          = 6;
        rF.w.low        = 7;
```

The assignments to _i cannot be eliminated because the _i could be used later on in the code.

The final optimization eliminates dead assignments, starting with an empty symbol table and proceeding as follows:

(1) If a variable in the symbol table is modified by some instruction other than assignment, remove it from the table.

(2) When a variable appears as the destination in an assignment:

   a. If it's not in the table, add it, remembering the line number of the assignment instruction.

b. If the variable is in the table, discard the line referenced in the symbol-table entry, and then replace that symbol-table reference with one for the current line.

In the current example, the first assignment to `_i` is a dead assignment because `_i` is reinitialized before being used, so it is eliminated:

```
W(&_i)   = 6;
rF.w.low = 7;
```

7.3 Structural Optimizations

So far, all the optimizations that we've looked at can be performed by analyzing the linear output stream of the compiler. Some optimizations must analyze the overall structure of the code, however, and more sophisticated techniques must be used. All of these optimizations need to know something about the structure of the code being optimized. Consequently, they must work on a parse or syntax tree that represents the code, not on a series of instructions. One solution to this problem is for the parser to build a physical parse tree with structures and pointers rather than generating code; the parse tree can then be optimized, and finally traversed depth first to do the code generation. There are two difficulties with this approach. First, the optimizer can get pretty big, and there is often insufficient room in memory for it to be combined with the parser—two independent programs are needed. Similarly, the more code that you can get into memory at once, the more of the program's structure can be seen. There's no point in wasting memory for a parser. Finally, the entire parse tree isn't needed for optimization—a syntax tree representing the various statements and expressions is sufficient. The usual solution to the problem is for the parser to generate an intermediate language from which the syntax tree can be reconstructed, and that intermediate code is processed by the optimizer.

7.3.1 Postfix and Syntax Trees

The intermediate language most appropriate for this purpose is *postfix* or *Reverse-Polish Notation* (RPN). User's of Hewlett-Packard calculators and UNIX's **dc** desk-calculator program will already be familiar with this representation. In postfix notation, operands are pushed onto a stack without modification. Operators access the top few items on the stack, replacing them with the result of the operation. For example, the following C fragment

Postfix, Reverse-Polish Notation (RPN).

```
A * B + C * D
```

can be evaluated using the following postfix operations:

push A
push B
pop two items, multiply them, push the result
push C
push D
pop two items, multiply them, push the result
pop two items, add them, push the result

The result is on the top of the stack when the evaluation finishes. The two multiplications have to be done before the addition because * has higher precedence than +.

A postfix intermediate language is easy to generate because the compiler doesn't have to worry about assigning temporary variables—it just uses the run-time stack as its scratch space. Postfix is useful in interpreter implementations because postfix virtual machines are easy to implement. The interpreter can translate the source code into a postfix form, which is then executed in software on the virtual machine.

The main advantage of postfix, here, is that the optimizer can reconstruct the entire parse tree—or to be more exact, a compacted form of the parse tree called a *syntax tree*— from the list of instructions.

A common postfix representation uses one instruction per line. If that instruction is an rvalue reference, the contents of the variable are pushed onto the stack. If it's an lvalue reference, the address is pushed. If it's an arithmetic instruction, the top one or two stack elements are manipulated, and they are replaced by the result, which is either an lvalue or rvalue depending on the operator. The expression $A*B+A*B$ is represented as:

$$A_L$$
$$B_L$$
$$*$$
$$A_L$$
$$B_L$$
$$*$$
$$+$$

There's no need for an explicit "push" operator as long as the operators can be distinguished from variable names. Similarly, explicit parentheses are never necessary because the order of evaluation is determined by the sequence of operations, and all incoming variables are treated as lvalues because there's no need for explicit temporaries in the intermediate code. (Consequently, the subscripts in the earlier example are redundant and can be omitted.)

Generating postfix inter-mediate code.

The first order of business is making a parser that generates postfix intermediate code for expressions. I've done this in Listings 7.1 and 7.2. The code is simplified because no temporary variables are necessary.

Listing 7.1. *postfix.y*— Parser with Postfix Code Generation

```
 1   %term ICON   NAME
 2   %left PLUS   MINUS
 3   %left TIMES  DIVIDE
 4   %%
 5   s        : expr
 6            ;
 7
 8   expr     : NAME                      { yycode("%s\n", yytext ); }
 9            | ICON                      { yycode("%s\n", yytext ); }
10            | expr DIVIDE expr          { yycode("/\n"          ); }
11            | expr TIMES  expr          { yycode("*\n"          ); }
12            | expr PLUS   expr          { yycode("+\n"          ); }
13            | expr MINUS  expr          { yycode("-\n"          ); }
14            ;
15   %%
16   main(){ yyparse(); }
```

Converting the postfix in-termediate code to a syn-tax tree.

The next task is converting the intermediate code generated by our compiler back to a syntax tree. You can look at the generated intermediate code as a convenient way for the parser to pass the tree to the optimizer. The following syntax tree can be created when you run $A*B+A*B$ through the parser we just looked at:

Listing 7.2. *postfix.lex*— Lexical Analyzer for Postfix Code Generation

```
1   %{
2   #include "yyout.h"
3   %}
4   %%
5   [a-zA-Z_][a-zA-Z_0-9]*     return NAME;
6   [0-9]+                     return ICON;
7   "/"                        return DIVIDE;
8   "*"                        return TIMES;
9   "+"                        return PLUS;
10  "-"                        return MINUS;
11  .                          ; /* empty */
12  %%
```

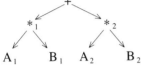

All internal nodes represent operators and all the leaves reference lvalues. Also, the grouping of operators and operands is as you would expect, given the operator precedence built into the grammar.

Before demonstrating how to do this reconstruction, we'll need a data structure to represent the nodes in the tree. Listing 7.3 shows this data structure (a node) and a constructor subroutine that makes new nodes [new()]. The node structure is a normal binary-tree node, having left and right children. In addition, the name field holds variable names (A and B in this case) or the operator if the node is an internal node. The contents of this field will be modified by the optimizer, however. The op field usually holds the operator (* or +), but it is set to 0 in leaf nodes.

Data structures to represent the syntax tree: node.

Listing 7.3. *optimize.c*— The node Data Structure, Used to Construct Syntax Trees

```
1    #include <stdlib.h>           /* <malloc.h> for UNIX */
2
3    typedef struct node
4    {
5        char          name[16];
6        int           op;
7        struct node   *left;
8        struct node   *right;
9    }
10   node;
11
12   node *new()
13   {
14       node *p;
15       if( !(p = (node *) calloc( 1, sizeof(node) ) ) )
16           exit(1);
17       return p;
18   }
```

Reconstructing the syntax tree. The build() subroutine in Listing 7.4 creates a syntax tree from a postfix input file. The input file must have one operand or operator per line and it must be perfect. That is, in order to simplify the code, I've dispensed with error detection. Input lines are read from standard input and the subroutine returns a pointer to the root node of the tree. The tree is built in a bottom-up fashion, using a local stack defined on line 22 to keep track of the partially-constructed tree. Figure 7.1 shows the syntax tree for the input discussed earlier as it is built—you'll notice the similarity between this process and the bottom-up parse process.

The **default** case on Line 30 is executed for variable names.[4] It allocates and initializes a new node, and then pushes a pointer to the new node onto the stack. The child pointers are initialized to NULL by new().

Operators are handled differently because they're internal nodes. A new node is allocated and initialized, then pointers to two existing nodes are popped and the child pointers of the new internal node are made to point at these. Finally, a pointer to the new node is pushed.

Listing 7.4. *optimize.c*— A Postfix to Syntax Tree Constructor

```
19    node      *build()
20    {
21        char    buf[80];
22        node    *stack[ 10 ];
23        node    **sp = stack - 1;
24        node    *p;
25
26        while( gets(buf) )
27        {
28            switch( *buf )
29            {
30            default:  p = new();
31                      strcpy( p->name, buf );
32                      *++sp = p;
33                      break;
34
35            case '*':
36            case '+':
37                      p            = new() ;
38                      p->right     = *sp-- ;
39                      p->left      = *sp-- ;
40                      p->op        = *buf  ;
41                      p->name[0]   = *buf  ;
42                      *++sp        = p      ;
43                      break;
44            }
45        }
46        return *sp--;
47    }
```

Generating code from the syntax tree. Code can be generated from this tree by doing a depth-first traversal (visit the children then the parent). At every lvalue (ie. variable reference), generate an instruction of the form temporary = variable. At every internal node, generate the code

---

4. The **default** case can go anywhere in the switch. It doesn't have to be at the end.

Figure 7.1. Building a Syntax Tree

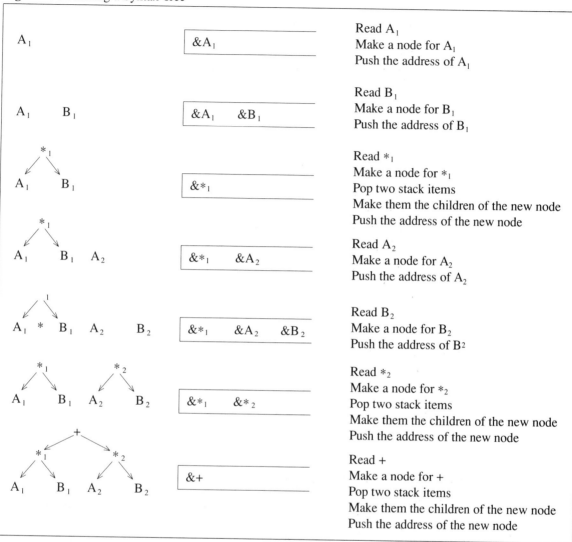

	Read A_1	
	Make a node for A_1	
	Push the address of A_1	

necessary to perform the operation on the temporaries that resulted from traversing the previous level, putting the result into a new temporary. The previously constructed tree generates the following output:

```
t0   =    A
t1   =    B
t1   *=   t0
t2   =    A
t3   =    B
t3   *=   t2
t3   +=   t1
```

The `trav()` subroutine in Listing 7.5 does the traversal. It takes the pointer returned from the previous `build()` call as its initial argument. If `root->op` is zero, then the current node is a leaf and you generate the code to move it to a temporary variable. The `sprintf()` call overwrites the `name` field with the name of the temporary variable. If the `op` field is nonnull, an interior node is being processed. In this case, `trav()` does an in-order traversal. The **if** statement is always true (for now—things will change momentarily). The following `printf()` call prints the instruction, using the `name` fields of the two children to find out what temporaries to use. The `strcpy()` call then overwrites the `name` field of the current node to reflect the temporary that got the result of the last operation.

Listing 7.5. *optimize.c*— A Syntax-Tree Traversing, Code-Generation Pass

```
48   trav( root )
49   struct node *root;
50   {
51       static int tnum = 0;
52
53       if( !root )
54           return;
55
56       if( !root->op )      /* leaf */
57       {
58           printf ( "t%d = %s\n", tnum, root->name );
59           sprintf( root->name , "t%d", tnum );
60           ++tnum;
61       }
62       else
63       {
64           trav( root->left  );
65
66           if( root->left != root->right )    /* Always true      */
67               trav( root->right );           /* unless optimized */
68
69           printf("%s %c= %s\n", root->right->name,
70                               root->op, root->left->name );
71           strcpy( root->name,   root->right->name );
72       }
73   }
```

7.3.2 Common-Subexpression Elimination

The code that `trav()` outputs isn't too great, because the subexpression A*B is evaluated twice. It would be better to perform the multiplication only once and use the generated rvalue twice. You'd like the following output:

```
t0   =    A
t1   =    B
t1   *=   t0
t1   +=   t1
```

This transformation is called *common subexpression elimination*, and is a good example of the type of optimization that you can do by analyzing, and then modifying, the syntax tree. Since both subtrees of the + node are identical, the optimizer can eliminate one subtree and make both pointers in the + node point at the remaining subtree. The new syntax tree looks like this:

Both pointers in the + node point at the * node. This modified data structure is called a *Directed Acyclic Graph* or *DAG*. The DAG is created from the syntax tree by the `opti-mize()` function in Listing 7.6. This routine traverses the interior nodes of the tree, comparing the two subtrees. If the subtrees are identical, the left and right pointers of the parent node are made to point at the same child, effectively removing the other child from the tree. The comparison is done using the `makesig()` function, which traverses an entire subtree, assembling a string that shows the pre-order traversal (visit the root, the left subtree, then the right subtree) of the subtree by concatenating all the name fields. For example, the original syntax tree, when traversed from the root, creates the following signature string:

> Directed acyclic graph (DAG).

```
+**<A><B><A><B>
```

If two subtrees generate the same signature, they're equivalent.

Brackets are placed around the identifiers because the left and right subtrees in the following expression would incorrectly generate the same signatures if they weren't there:

```
(A * ABB) + (AA * BB)
```

Finally, you traverse the DAG using the `trav()` function that was developed earlier. That **if** statement now comes into play, preventing us from traversing the common subtree twice.

7.3.3 Register Allocation

Syntax trees and DAG's are useful for other optimizations as well. The simplest of these is efficient register allocation. In general, it's better to use registers than memory for temporary variables. It's difficult for the front end to do register allocation efficiently, however, because it doesn't know how many registers the target machine has. There are two problems with translating temporary-variable references to register references. First, you might need more temporary variables than there are registers, and the register allocation should be done in such a way that the registers are used as efficiently as possible: The temporaries that are used most frequently should be put into registers. The second issue is subroutine calls imbedded in expressions. If registers are used as temporaries, then they have to be pushed before calling the function and restored afterwards.

Both of these problems are easily solved by analyzing the parse or syntax tree for an expression before generating code for that expression. For example, an expression like this:

```
carl / philip  + emanuel(a+b)  * bach
```

generates the syntax tree in Figure 7.2 Each interior node in the tree represents the generation or modification of a temporary variable, and the temporary can appear at several interior nodes. The register-versus-nonregister problem is solved by assigning registers to those temporaries generated along the longest paths in the tree. Similarly, the optimizer can examine that tree and, noticing the function call, can decide to use registers only for those temporaries generated after the function returns or, as is the case with the function's argument, are pushed as part of the call.

7.3.4 Lifetime Analysis

The next structure-related register optimization is *lifetime analysis*. This optimization takes care of a situation like the following:

Listing 7.6. *optimize.c*— A Subroutine for Common-Subexpression Elimination

```
 74    optimize( root )      /* Simplified optimizer--eliminates common subexpressions. */
 75    node    *root;
 76    {
 77          char sig1[ 32 ];
 78          char sig2[ 32 ];
 79
 80          if( root->right && root->left )
 81          {
 82                optimize( root->right );
 83                optimize( root->left  );
 84
 85                *sig1 = *sig2 = '\0';
 86                makesig( root->right, sig1 );
 87                makesig( root->left , sig2 );
 88
 89                if( strcmp( sig1, sig2 ) == 0 )    /* subtrees match */
 90                      root->right = root->left ;
 91          }
 92    }
 93
 94    makesig( root, str )
 95    node    *root;
 96    char    *str;
 97    {
 98          if( !root )
 99                return;
100
101          if( isdigit( *root->name )
102                strcat( str, root->name );
103          else
104          {
105                strcat( "<", root->name );
106                strcat( str, root->name );
107                strcat( ">", root->name );
108          }
109          makesig( root->left,  str );
110          makesig( root->right, str );
111    }
```

```
int i, j;

for( i = 10000; --i >= 0 ; )
   ...

for( j = 10000; --j >= 0 ; )
   ...
```

If the target machine has only a limited number of registers available for variables (say, one), then the **register** keyword can't be used effectively to improve the foregoing code. Ideally, because i is used only in the first loop and j only in the second, i should be placed in a register while the first loop is being executed, and j should be in a register while the second loop is executed. This determination can be made by analyzing the parse tree. In the simplest case, if a variable is found in only one subtree, then its life-time is restricted to the code represented by that subtree. More sophisticated analysis can handle the more complex cases. For example, variables used for loop control can be given precedence over the variables in the loop body, unless the ones in the body are

Figure 7.2. Using the Syntax Tree for Register Allocation

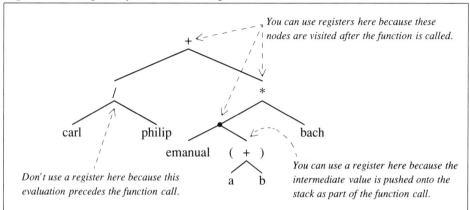

used more frequently than the control variables.

7.3.5 Loop Unwinding

Loop unwinding is a method of optimizing loop execution speed, usually at the cost of code size. Put simply, the optimizer replaces the entire loop with the code that comprises the loop body, duplicated the number of times that the loop would execute at run time. This optimization, clearly, can be done only when the loop-control criteria can be computed at compile time. A loop like this:

```
for( i = 3; --i > 0 ; )
    foo(i);
```

can be replaced with the following code:

```
foo(3);
foo(2);
foo(1);
i = 0;
```

Something like this:

```
int array[10];
for( p = array; p <= array + 2; ++p )
    foo( p );
```

can be translated as follows:

```
r0.pp = array;
foo( r0.pp )
r0.pp += sizeof(int);
foo( r0.pp )
r0.pp += sizeof(int);
foo( r0.pp )
r0.pp += sizeof(int);
_p = WP( r0.pp );
```

7.3.6 Replacing Indexes with Pointers

If the values of an array index can be computed at compile time, not only can the loop be unwound, but the inefficient array indexes can be replaced by direct pointer operations. For example, this loop:

```
for( i = 0; i <= 2 ; ++i )
    array[i] = 0xff ;
```

can be translated as follows:

```
r0.pp    = array;
W(r0.pp) = 0xff;
r0.pp    += sizeof(int);
W(r0.pp) = 0xff;
r0.pp    += sizeof(int);
W(r0.pp) = 0xff;
_i       = 3;
```

Note that the final assignment to _i is required in case _i is used further down in the code. Also, _i would have to be modified along with r0.pp if it were used in the loop body for something other than the array index.

7.3.7 Loop-Invariant Code Motion

Hoisting variables.

Loop-invariant optimizations analyze the body of a loop and *hoist* (move above the test portion of the loop) all of the code that doesn't change as the loop executes. For example, the division in the following loop is invariant:

```
for( i = 0; i < 10 ; ++i )
    array[i] += (numer/denom);
```

so you can modify the loop as follows:

```
r0.l = numer / denom ;

for( i = 0; i <= 2 ; ++i )
    array[i] += r0.l
```

The optimizations that we looked at earlier can also be applied here. Applying both array-index replacement and loop unwinding, you end up with the following C-code:

```
r0.l      =  numer ;
r0.l      /= denom;
r1.pp     =  array;
W(r1.pp)  =  r0.l ;
r1.pp     += sizeof(int);
W(r1.pp)  =  r0.l ;
r1.pp     += sizeof(int);
W(r1.pp)  =  r0.l ;
r1.pp     += sizeof(int);
i = 3;
```

Code-motion problems.

Note that hoisting division can cause problems if you're not careful. The following example bug is lifted from the Microsoft C (ver. 5.1) documentation. This loop:

```
for( i = 0; i <= 2 ; ++i )
    if( denom != 0 )
        array[i] += (numer/denom);
```

is optimized as follows:

```
r0.l = numer / denom ;

for( i = 0; i <= 2 ; ++i )
    if( denom != 0 )
        array[i] += r0.l ;
```

The division is moved outside the loop because it's invariant, but the preceding test is not moved with it. You'll now get a run-time divide-by-zero error if denom happens to be zero.

You, as a compiler writer, must decide if it's worth the risk of doing this kind of optimization. It's difficult for the compiler to distinguish between the safe and dangerous cases, here. For example, many C compilers perform risky optimizations because the compiler writer has assumed that a C programmer can understand the problems and take steps to remedy them at the source code level. It's better to provide the maximum optimization, even if it's dangerous, than to be conservative at the cost of less efficient code. A Pascal programmer may not have the same level of sophistication as a C programmer, however, so the better choice in this situation might be to avoid the risky optimization entirely or to require a special command-line switch to enable the optimization.

7.3.8 Loop Induction

Loop induction is a sort of strength reduction applied to loop-control statements. The optimizer tries to eliminate the multiplication implicit in array indexing by replacing it with the addition of a constant to a pointer. For example, a loop induction on a1 modifies this code

```
int a1[10][10], a2[10][10];

for( i = 0; i < 10; ++i )
    for( j = 0; j < 10; ++j )
        a1[i][j] = a2[i][j];
```

as follows:

```
t1 = array + 10;
for( t0 = a1; t0 < t1; t0 += 20 )      /* 20 == 10 * sizeof(int) */
{
    t3 = t0 + 20;                       /* 20 == 10 * sizeof(int) */

    for( t2 = t0; t2 < t3; t2 += sizeof(int) )
        *t2 = a2[i][j];

    j = 10;
}
i = 10;
```

7.4 Aliasing Problems

Many of the loop optimizations have problems with *pointer aliasing*—code in which a memory location can be accessed in more than one way (both by a pointer and directly, or by two pointers that contain the same address). For example, the following code creates an alias because both x and *p refer to the same memory location:

```
prometheus()
{
    int x, *p = &x;
}
```

Similarly, the following code creates less obvious aliases :

```
pyramus()
{
    int array[93];
    thisbe( array, array );
}

thisbe( p1,  p2 )
int *p1, *p2 ;
{
    /* *p1 and *p2 alias one another, here */
}

int x;
pandora()
{
    int *p = &x;

    /* *p is an alias for x, here */
}
```

The problem here is that the loop optimizations might modify one of the aliased variables without modifying the other one—the compiler has no way to know that the two variables reference the same object.

7.5 Exercises

7.1. Write a subroutine that multiplies two arbitrary **int**s using nothing but shift and multiply operations. The result should be returned in a **long**.

7.2. (a) Modify the compiler in the last chapter to replace all multiplication by constants with shift/add sequences and to replace all division by constants with shift/subtract sequences.

(b) Do the foregoing with a separate optimizer pass instead of modifying the compiler proper.

7.3. Write a peephole optimizer that works on the code generated by the compiler in the last chapter. At very least, it should do constant folding, dead-variable elimination, and dead assignment elimination.

7.4. Add an assignment operator (=) to the postfix tree constructor and optimizer presented earlier in this chapter. The input:

```
a
b
+
a
b
+
*
c
=
```

should generate the following:

```
t0 =   a
t1 =   b
t1 *= t0
t1 += t1
 c =   t1
```

Your program must be able to handle expressions like:

```
a = b = c
```

which should be translated to the following:

```
c
b
=
a
=
```

7.5. Modify your solution to the previous exercise to support the following C operators:

```
+    -    *    /    %    &    |    ~    (    )
=    ==   <    >    <=   >=   !    &&   ||
++   --
```

Standard associativity and precedence should be used.

7.6. (a) Modify the compiler in the previous chapter to generate a postfix intermediate language instead of C-code.

(b) Write an optimizer pass that does common-subexpression elimination on that postfix intermediate code.

(c) Write a back end that traverses the syntax tree created by the common-subexpression optimizer and generates C-code.

A

Support Functions

This appendix contains a myriad small subroutines that are used throughout the rest of the book. Collectively, they comprise a library called *comp.lib*. A few of the routines in this library are described elsewhere (the input and table-printing functions in Chapter Two, for example), but I've concentrated the other routines in one place so that the rest of the book won't be cluttered with distracting references to small subroutines whose function is not directly applicable to the matter at hand. It's important that you are familiar with the routines in this appendix, however—at least with the calling conventions, if not with the code itself.

Since straight code descriptions can be pretty deadly reading, I've organized each section to start with a description of subroutine-calling conventions and a discussion of how to use the routines in that section. This way, you can skip the blow-by-blow code descriptions if you're not interested. Most of the code is commented enough so that additional descriptive text isn't necessary. There's no point in making an overly long appendix even longer with descriptions of things that are obvious by reading the code.

Of the subroutines in this appendix, you should be particularly familiar with the <tools/debug.h> file described in the next section and with the set and hash-table functions described in the sections after that. It's worthwhile to thoroughly understand this code. You need to be familiar only with the calling conventions for the remainder of the functions in this appendix, however. The sources are presented, but they're not mandatory reading.

Directories used. The auxiliary files and subroutines described here are organized into several directories. Sources for subroutines of general utility are all in */src/tools*, those that are more directly compiler related are in */src/compiler/lib*. Most of the **#include** files used by the routines in this chapter are in */include/tools*, and they are included with a **#include** <tools/whatever.h> (I've set up */include* as my default library directory). The one exception is *curses.h*, which is in */include* itself, so that you can use a UNIX-compatible **#include** <curses.h>.

A.1 Miscellaneous Include Files

Many *.h* files are included at the tops of the various *.c* files presented in this book. With the exception of the files discussed in this chapter, all files included with angle brackets (*<stdio.h>*, *<signal.h>*, and so forth) are ANSI-compatible, standard-library files and should be supplied by your compiler vendor (in this case, Microsoft). If they aren't, then your compiler doesn't conform to ANSI and you'll have to work a little harder to port the code presented here. Most of these standard *.h* files are also supported by UNIX—those that aren't are supplied on the distribution disk so that you can port the code to UNIX without difficulty.

A.1.1 *debug.h*—Miscellaneous Macros

The *debug.h* file is **#include**d in virtually every *.c* file in this book. It contains several macro definitions that are of general utility, and sets up various definitions that are useful in debugging. It also contains several macros that take care of various 8086 portability issues. (It's useful, by the way, to look at the 8086-related macros even if you're not using an 8086—not only will you get a good idea of the things that you have to consider in order to make your code portable in general, but, since the 8086 is such a pervasive architecture, a specific knowledge of the machine lets you write your code so that it can be as portable as possible in any environment. It's a mistake to assume that your code will never have to move to the 8086 environment.)

Listing A.1. *debug.h*— Miscellaneous Macros of General Utility

```
 1  #ifdef   DEBUG
 2  #        define PRIVATE
 3  #        define D(x) x
 4  #else
 5  #        define PRIVATE static
 6  #        define D(x)
 7  #endif
 8  #define PUBLIC
 9
10  #ifdef MSDOS
11  #        define MS(x) x
12  #        define UX(x)
13  #        define ANSI
14  #        define _8086
15  #else
16  #        define MS(x)
17  #        define UX(x) x
18  #        define O_BINARY 0        /* no binary input mode in UNIX open()  */
19           typedef long time_t      /* for the VAX, may have to change this */
20           typedef unsigned size_t /* for the VAX, may have to change this */
21           extern char *strdup();   /* You need to supply one.             */
22  #endif
23
24  #ifdef   ANSI            /* If ANSI is defined, put arg lists into       */
25  #define P(x)    x        /* function prototypes.                         */
26  #define VA_LIST   ...    /* and use ellipsis if a variable number of args */
27  #else
28  #define P(x)   ()        /* Otherwise, discard argument lists and translate */
29  #define void   char      /* void keyword to int.                         */
30  #define VA_LIST _a_r_g_s /* don't use ellipsis                           */
31  #endif
32
```

→

Listing A.1. continued...

```
33   /* SEG(p)        Evaluates to the segment portion of an 8086 address.
34    * OFF(p)        Evaluates to the offset portion of an 8086 address.
35    * PHYS(p)       Evaluates to a long holding a physical address
36    */
37
38   #ifdef _8086
39   #define SEG(p)   ( ((unsigned *)&(p))[1] )
40   #define OFF(p)   ( ((unsigned *)&(p))[0] )
41   #define PHYS(p)  (((unsigned long)OFF(p)) + ((unsigned long)SEG(p) << 4))
42   #else
43   #define PHYS(p)   (p)
44   #endif
45
46   /* NUMELE(array)      Evaluates to the array size in elements
47    * LASTELE(array)     Evaluates to a pointer to the last element
48    * INBOUNDS(array,p)  Evaluates to true if p points into the array.
49    * RANGE(a,b,c)       Evaluates to true if a <= b <= c
50    * max(a,b)           Evaluates to a or b, whichever is larger
51    * min(a,b)           Evaluates to a or b, whichever is smaller
52    *                    associated with a pointer
53    * NBITS(type)        Returns number of bits in a variable of the indicated
54    *                    type;
55    * MAXINT             Evaluates to the value of the largest signed integer
56    */
57
58   #define NUMELE(a)       (sizeof(a)/sizeof(*(a)))
59   #define LASTELE(a)      ((a) + (NUMELE(a)-1))
60   #define TOOHIGH(a,p)    ((p) - (a) > (NUMELE(a) - 1))
61   #define TOOLOW(a,p)     ((p) - (a) < 0 )
62   #define INBOUNDS(a,p)   ( !(TOOHIGH(a,p) || TOOLOW(a,p)) )
63
64   #define _IS(t,x) (((t)1 << (x))!=0)  /* Evaluate true if the width of a     */
65                                        /* variable of type of t is < x. The !=0 */
66                                        /* assures that the answer is 1 or 0     */
67
68   #define NBITS(t) (4 * (1 + _IS(t, 4) + _IS(t, 8) + _IS(t,12) + _IS(t,16) \
69                            + _IS(t,20) + _IS(t,24) + _IS(t,28) + _IS(t,32) ) )
70
71   #define MAXINT (((unsigned)~0) >> 1)
72
73   #ifndef max
74   #    define max(a,b) ( ((a) > (b)) ? (a) : (b))
75   #endif
76   #ifndef min
77   #    define min(a,b) ( ((a) < (b)) ? (a) : (b))
78   #endif
79   #define RANGE(a,b,c)    ( (a) <= (b) && (b) <= (c) )
```

DEBUG

Local objects: PRIVATE.

The debugging versions of several macros are activated when DEBUG is **#define**d (either with an explicit **#define** or, more commonly, with a *-DDEBUG* on the compiler's command line) before *<tools/debug.h>* is included. The PRIVATE definition on line two expands to an empty string in this case—it effectively disappears from the input. When DEBUG is not defined, the alternative definition on line five is activated, so all PRIVATE variables become **static** variables when you're not debugging. This mechanism lets you put normally invisible variables and subroutines into the link map—so that you know where they are when you're debugging—and then limit their scope to the current file when debugging is completed. The complement to PRIVATE is

PUBLIC, defined on line eight. It is provided for documentation purposes only— PUBLIC variables and subroutines are those whose scope is not limited.

Global objects: PUBLIC.

The D(x) macro on lines three and six is used for printing debugging diagnostics. When DEBUG is defined, the macro expands to its argument, so

Debugging diagnostics, D().

```
D( printf("a diagnostic\n"); )
```

expands to

```
printf("a diagnostic\n");
```

Note that the semicolon is inside the parentheses. When DEBUG is not defined, the macro expands to an empty string and the argument is discarded. The earlier "printf( )" statement goes away. This method is preferable to the more usual

```
#ifdef DEBUG
printf("a diagnostic\n");
#endif
```

for several reasons: it's more readable; it requires only one line, rather than three; it doesn't mess up your indentation (many compilers require the **#** to be in the leftmost column). A multiple-line argument to D(x) must be done with backslashes, like this:

```
D(printf("%s in de %s wit' dinah, strumn' on de ol' %s",\
                    someone, "kitchen", "banjo" ); )
```

There's a potential problem here in that commas that are part of the argument to D() can be confused with the comma that separates macro arguments. ANSI says that commas enclosed by parentheses are not to be treated as argument separators (which is why the previous definition worked). Your compiler may not handle this case correctly, however. In any event, you'll have to parenthesize expressions that use the comma operator to pass them to D():

Commas in the D() macro argument.

```
D( (statement1,statement2); )
```

It's better style to use two D() invocations, however:

```
D( statement1; )
D( statement2; )
```

The macros on lines ten to 22 help you write portable code. The arguments to MS() are incorporated into the program only if MSDOS is **#define**d (it's defined automatically by the Microsoft compiler). Arguments to UX() (for UNIX) are active only if MSDOS is missing. I've also defined ANSI and _8086 macros that are active only if MSDOS is also active. Move the ANSI definition outside of the **#ifdef** if you're an ANSI-compatible UNIX compiler.

UNIX- and MS-DOS-specific code: MS(), UX().

ANSI, _8086.

The P macro on lines 25 and 28 handles another ANSI-related portability problem.[1] Many compilers (including many UNIX compilers) can't handle function prototypes. This macro uses a mechanism similar to the D() macro discussed earlier to translate prototypes into simple **extern** declarations if ANSI is not defined. For example, given the following input:

Transforming function prototypes to simple **extern**s, P().

```
int    dimitri P(( int x, long y ));
```

if ANSI is defined, the P(x) macro evaluates to its argument and the following

---

1. This macro is taken from [Jaeschke], p. 142, and is used in the Whitesmiths compiler.

translation results:

```
int    dimitri ( int x, long y );
```

otherwise, the macro discards its argument and evaluates to (), so the following will be created:

```
int    dimitri ();
```

Getting rid of the ellipsis
in the UNIX environment,
VA_LIST.

The ARGS macro on lines 26 and 30 takes care of yet another problem with non-ANSI compilers. An ANSI subroutine with a variable number of arguments is defined as follows:

```
printf( format, ... )
char *format;
```

The trailing ellipsis means "followed by any number of arguments of an arbitrary type." Earlier compilers don't support this mechanism. Consequently, you'd like to replace the ellipsis with a dummy argument name. You can do this with *debug.h* using the ARGS macro as follows:

```
printf( format, VA_LIST )
char *format;
```

VA_LIST expands to an ellipsis when ANSI is defined, otherwise it expands to the dummy argument name _a_r_g_s.

8086-related macros,
SEG(), OFF(), PHYS().

The macros on lines 39 to 41 of Listing A.1 handle portability problems inherent in the 8086 architecture. The SEG() and OFF() definition are ignored in other systems, and the PHYS() macro just evaluates to its argument in non-8086 environments. Before looking at the definitions for these macros, a short discussion of the 8086 internal architecture is necessary. The 8086 is really a 16-bit machine in that all internal registers are 16 bits wide. The machine has a 20-bit address space, however. The discrepancy is made up by using two registers to create a physical address. An address is formed from two 16-bit components representing the contents of the two registers: the *segment* and the *offset*. These are usually represented as two 4-digit hex numbers separated by a colon: 1234:5678. The segment portion is on the left, the offset on the right. A physical address is formed in the machine using the following formula:

Representing an address
in the 8086 architecture,
segment, offset.

```
physical_address == ( segment << 4 ) + offset;
```

Three special registers called CS, DS, SS hold the segment components of the addresses of objects in the code, data, and stack regions of your program. (A fourth segment register, called ES, is used if you need to access an object not in one of these segments).

Problems with
segment:offset address-
ing.

This architecture has several ramifications. First, there are two pointer sizes. If the segment component doesn't change over the life of the program, only the offset needs to be stored; pointers are 16 bits wide in this situation. For example, the DS register doesn't have to change if there's less then 64K of data and if the DS register is initialized to the base address of that 64K region. All cells within that region can be accessed using the fixed DS register by loading a 16-bit offset into the appropriate offset register—the segment portion of the address can be loaded once when the program loads. If the data area is larger than 64K, then 32-bit pointers composed of a 16-bit segment and a 16-bit offset componant must be used. You must load both the segment and offset componants into their respective registers to access the target variable. Typically, the segment is stored in the top 16 bits of the pointer and the offset is stored in the bottom 16 bits. The physical address is not stored. A 32-bit pointer that has both a segment and offset component is called a *far* pointer; a 16-bit pointer containing the offset component only is called a *near* pointer. Note that a program can have 16-bit data pointers and 32-bit function pointers and vice versa, depending on how much code or data there is.

Near and *far* pointers.

One of the other problems with the segmented architecture is that there are 4,096 ways to address every physical cell in memory. For example, the following all address physical address 0x10000: 1000:0000, 0FFF:0010, 0FFE:0020, 0FFD:0030, and so forth.

The PHYS(p) macro on line 41 of Listing A.1 evaluates to the physical address associated with an 8086 32-bit, far pointer—a pointer in which both the segment and offset components of the address are stored. It computes this address using the same procedure used by the 8086 itself, shifting the segment component left by four bits and adding it to the offset. The segment and offset portions are extracted by the SEG and OFF macros on the previous two lines, reproduced here:

Finding a physical address on an 8086, PHYS().

Isolating segment and offset components, SEG(), OFF().

```
#define SEG(p)  ( ((unsigned *)&(p))[1] )
#define OFF(p)  ( ((unsigned *)&(p))[0] )
```

Taking SEG() as characteristic, &(p) creates a temporary variable of type pointer-to-pointer which holds the address of that pointer in memory. &(p) can be treated as if it were the base address of an array of pointers—*(&p) and (&p)[0] both evaluate to p itself. The cast of (**unsigned** *) changes things, however. Now instead of being treated as an array of pointers, &p is treated as a two-element array of 16-bit **unsigned int**s, which are half the size of a pointer. The [1] picks up 16 bits of the 32-bit pointer, in this case the segment half. The [0] gets the offset half. These two macros are not at all portable, but they're more efficient than shift-and-mask operations, which are.

The NBITS(type) macro on line 68 of Listing A.1 evaluates to the number of bits in a variable of a particular integral type on the current machine. (NBITS(**int**) evaluates to the number of bits in an **int**.) It assumes that this number is 8, 16, 32, or 64, but the macro is easily modified to accept other values. The _IS macro on the previous line tests for one of these possibilities:

Number of bits required for a type, NBITS().

```
#define _IS(t,n)  (((t)1 << (n))!=0)
```

It is passed the type (t) and the current guess (n). It casts the number 1 into the correct type, and then shifts that number to the left by the required number of bits. The resulting binary number for several shift values and a 16-bit-wide type are shown below:

n	$1 << n$
0	0000000000000001
4	0000000000010000
8	0000000100000000
12	0001000000000000
16	0000000000000000
32	0000000000000000

The expression evaluates to 0 if a variable of type t contains fewer than n bits. The NBITS macro, adds together several terms, one for each group of four bits in the number. For example, when an **int** is 16 bits wide, _IS(int, 4), _IS(int, 8), and _IS(int,12) all evaluate to 1. The other terms evaluate to 0. Multiplying by four adjust the result to an actual bit count. I should point out that this macro, though huge, usually evaluates to a single constant at compile time. Since all the arguments are constants, none of the arithmetic needs to be done at run time. It's size might cause problems with your compiler's running out of macro-expansion space, however. Also, note that some compilers use greater precision for compile-time calculations than is available at run time—NBITS() won't work on these compilers.

MAXINT, on line 71, evaluates to the largest positive, two's-complement integer. (**unsigned**) 0 evaluates to an **unsigned int** with all bits set to 1. The left shift

Finding the largest integer, MAXINT.

puts a zero into the high bit—the cast to (**unsigned**) defeats any potential sign extension on the right shift.

Array-manipulation mac-
ros: NUMELE(),
LASTELE(), TOOHIGH(),
TOOLOW(), INBOUNDS().

The definitions on lines 58 to 62 of Listing A.1 are for array manipulations. NUMELE is passed an array name and evaluates to the number of elements in the array. LASTELE evaluates to the address of the last element in the array. TOOHIGH(array, p) evaluates to true only if the pointer p is above the array. TOOLOW(array, p) is true if p is beneath the start of the array.[2] INBOUNDS(array, p) is true if p is in bounds.

Maximum and minimum
values, max(), min(),
RANGE().

The macros on lines 73 to 79 of *debug.h* test for various ranges of integer values. max(a, b) evaluates to a or b, whichever is larger; min(a, b) evaluates to a or b, whichever is smaller; and RANGE(a, b, c) evaluates to true if a≤b≤c.

A.1.2 *stack.h* and *yystack.h*—Generic Stack Maintenance

Compilers tend to use stacks a lot. To simplify stack maintenance, a series of macros that declare and manipulate stacks of an arbitrary, nonaggregate type, are declared in *stack.h*. The macros are used as follows:

Create a stack.

```
stack_dcl(stack, type, size)
```

This macro creates a stack consisting of size objects of the given type. The type can be a simple type (like **int** and **long**) or a pointer (like **char***, **long****, and **struct** foo *). Stacks of aggregate objects like structures and arrays are not supported, however. Note that very complex types (like pointers to arrays) are best defined with a previous **typedef**, like this:

```
typedef int (*ptr_to_10_element_array)[10];
stack_dcl( stack, ptr_to_10_element_array, 128 );
```

otherwise they might not compile.

The stack_dcl macro declares three objects, the names of which are all derived from the stack argument as follows:

```
stack
p_stack
t_stack
```

If you put a definition of the form

```
#undef   stack_cls
#define  stack_cls  static
```

somewhere after the **#include** <tools/stack.h>, then the stack and stack pointer will have the indicated storage class (**static** here).

---

2. Though ANSI requires that a pointer be able to point just past the end of an array, it does not allow a pointer to go past the start of the array. This behavior has serious practical ramifications in the 8086 compact and large models, and you won't be able to use TOOLOW with these memory models. Most 8086 compilers assume that no data object in the compact or large model is larger than 64K. Consequently, once the initial segment-register load is performed, only the offset portion of the address needs to be checked or modified when a pointer is modified. This practice causes problems when the base address of the array is close to the bottom of a segment. If, for example, an integer array is based at 2000:0000, a pointer increment correctly yields the address 2000:0002, but a decrement will yield 2000:FFFE rather than 1000:FFFE because the segment portion of the address won't be modified. This incorrect pointer is treated as very large, rather than very small.

`stack_p(stack)`   *Access stack pointer directly.*

This macro evaluates to the name used internally for the stack pointer. (See also: `stack_ele()`, below.)

`push(stack, x)`   *Push an element.*

Push `x` onto the stack. The `stack` argument must have appeared in a previous `stack_dcl()` invocation. This macro checks for stack overflow and invokes the `stack_err()` macro, discussed below, if the stack is full. (The default action prints an error message and terminates the program.) The `push_(stack,x)` does no overflow checking, so it is faster.

`pop(stack)`   *Pop an element.*

Pop an item off the stack (like this: `x = pop(stack);`). The `stack` argument must have appeared in a previous `stack_dcl()` invocation. This macro checks for stack underflow and invokes the `stack_err` macro, discussed below, if the stack is empty. (The default action prints an error message and terminates the program.) The `pop_(stack)` macro does no underflow checking, so it is faster.

`popn(stack,amt)`   *Pop multiple elements.*

This macro pops `amt` elements from the indicated stack, and evaluates to the element that was at the top of stack before anything was popped. There's also a `popn_(stack,amt)` macro, which does no underflow checking, but is otherwise the same as `popn()`.

`stack_clear(stack)`   *Reinitialize stack.*

This macro sets the stack back to its initial, empty condition, discarding all stack elements.

`stack_ele(stack)`   *Get number of elements.*

This macro evaluates to the number of elements currently on the indicated stack.

`stack_empty(stack)`   *Test for stack empty.*

This macro evaluates to true if the stack is empty.

`stack_full(stack)`   *Test for stack full.*

This macro evaluates to true if the stack is full.

`stack_item(stack,offset)`   *Access arbitrary element.*

Evaluates to the item at the indicated offset from the top of the stack. Note that no range checking is done to see if `offset` is valid. Use `stack_ele()` to do this checking if you need it.

`stack_err(overflow)`   *Stack error handler.*

This macro is invoked to handle stack errors. The `overflow` argument is 1 if a stack overflow occurred (you tried to push an item onto a stack that was full). It's zero on an underflow (you tried to pop an item off an empty stack). The default action prints an error message and terminates the program, but you can **#undef** this macro and redefine it to do something more appropriate if you like. If this macro evaluates to something, that value will, in turn, come back from the `push` or `pop` macros when an error occurs. For example:

```
#undef  stack_err
#define stack_err(overflow)  0
```

will cause both `push` and `pop` to evaluate to 0 if an overflow or underflow occurs.

Stack-macro implementation.

The ANSI concatenation operator, ##.

The stack macros are implemented in *stack.h*, Listing A.2. These macros make heavy use of the ANSI concatenation operator, **##**. This operator is removed from a macro definition by the preprocessor, effectively concatenating the strings on either side of it. For example, given the invocation

```
stack_dcl(plates,int,128);
```

the typedef on line seven of Listing A.2 evaluates, first to

```
typedef int t_##plates;
```

(the **int** replaces `type` in the definition, the `plates` replaces `stack`) and then the **##** is removed, yielding:

```
typedef int t_plates;
```

Lines eight and nine will evaluate as follows:

```
t_plates plates[128];
t_plates *(p_plates) = plates + (128);
```

Downward-growing stacks are used for ANSI compatibility.

given the earlier `stack_dcl()` invocation. A downward-growing stack is created, so the stack pointer (`p_plates`) is initialized to just past the end of the stack. This initialization works correctly in ANSI C, which says that pointer can point one cell beyond the end of an array and still be valid, but a pointer is not permitted to go to the left of the array.

Pushing and popping, `push()`, `push_()`, `pop()`, `pop_()`, `popn()`, `popn_()`.

Since a downward-growing stack is implemented, a push is a predecrement (on line 23) and a pop is a postincrement (on line 31). This way the stack pointer always points at the top-of-stack item. The actual push and pop operations have been isolated into the `push_()` and `pop_()` macros because it's occasionally useful to do a push or pop without checking for stack overflow or underflow. Note that the `popn_()` macro on line 34 must evaluate to the top-of-stack element before anything is popped. A postincrement is simulated here by modifying the stack pointer by `amt` elements, and then reaching backwards with a `[-amt]` to get the previous top-of-stack element.

Stack-macro error processing, `stack_err()`.

The `stack_err()` macro on lines 39 and 40 use `ferr` to print an error message and then exits the program. (`ferr()` works like `printf()` except that it sends characters to `stderr` and calls `exit(1)` when it's done. It is discussed in depth below). In theory, the entire expression evaluates to `ferr()`'s return value, but since `ferr()` doesn't return, it's not really an issue here.

Double cast needed to convert int to pointer.

You need two casts on lines 27 and 31 where `stack_err()` is invoked because there's no telling what sort of value to which the macro will evaluate. The default `ferr()` call evaluates to an **int**, but since `stack_err()` can be redefined, you can't count on that. The stack type is also uncertain because it can be redefined. You can't just cast `stack_err()` to the same type as the stack because the stack might be an array of pointers—many compilers complain if you try to convert an **int** to a pointer. So you have to cast twice—first to **long** and then to the stack type—to suppress this error message. Though casting to **long** as an intermediate step fixes this problem, though it might introduce an unnecessary conversion if the stack type is an **int**, **short**, or **char**. These multiple type conversions will also cause portability problems if the `stack_err()` macro evaluates to something that won't fit into a **long** (like a **double**).

Stack macros for *occs*, *<yystack.h>*.

A second set of stack macros are in the file `<yystack.h>`, Listing A.3. These macros differ from the ones just described in three ways only: all the macro names are preceded by the characters `yy`, the generated names are prefaced by `yyt_` and `yyp_` rather

Listing A.2. *stack.h*— Stack-Maintenance Macros

```
 1    /* Stack.h        Stack-maintenance macros. Creates downward-growing stacks
 2     *                 (which should work in all six memory models).
 3     */
 4
 5    #define stack_cls       /* empty */
 6
 7    #define stack_dcl(stack,type,size)   typedef type t_##stack;                  \
 8                                         stack_cls t_##stack stack[size];         \
 9                                         stack_cls t_##stack (*p_##stack)         \
10                                                               = stack + (size)
11    #define stack_clear(stack) (  (p_##stack)  = (stack + \
12                                                      sizeof(stack)/sizeof(*stack)) )
13
14    #define stack_full(stack)  (  (p_##stack) <= stack )
15    #define stack_empty(stack) (  (p_##stack) >= (stack + \
16                                                      sizeof(stack)/sizeof(*stack)) )
17
18    #define stack_ele(stack)     ((sizeof(stack)/sizeof(*stack)) - (p_##stack-stack))
19
20    #define stack_item(stack,offset) ( *(p_##stack + (offset)) )
21    #define stack_p(stack)             p_##stack
22
23    #define push_(stack,x)   ( *--p_##stack = (x)    )
24    #define pop_(stack)      ( *p_##stack++          )
25
26    #define push(stack,x)    ( stack_full(stack)                                 \
27                                  ? ((t_##stack)(long)(stack_err(1)))            \
28                                  : push_(stack,x)                               \
29                                                                                 )
30    #define pop(stack)       ( stack_empty(stack)                                \
31                                  ? ((t_##stack)(long)(stack_err(0)))            \
32                                  : pop_(stack)                                  \
33                                                                                 )
34    #define popn_(stack,amt) ( (p_##stack += amt)[-amt]   )
35    #define popn( stack,amt) ( (stack_ele(stack) < amt)                          \
36                                  ? ((t_##stack)(long)(stack_err(0)))            \
37                                  : popn_(stack,amt)                             \
38                                                                                 )
39    #define stack_err(o)     ((o) ? ferr("Stack overflow\n" ) \
40                                   : ferr("Stack underflow\n") )
```

than `t_` and `p_`, and I've abbreviated `yystack` to `yystk`. The second set of macros are used only within the **LLama**- and **occs**-generated parsers. The extra `yy` avoids potential name conflicts with user-supplied names.

A.1.3 *l.h* and *compiler.h*

Two other include files are of interest: *l.h* contains prototypes for the routines in *l.lib*, (which contains run-time subroutines for LEX and **occs**-generated programs); *compiler.h* contains prototypes for the routines in *comp.lib* (which contains subroutines used by LEX and **occs** themselves). These files are not listed here because they are created automatically from within the makefile that creates the library. The Microsoft compiler's */Zg* switch—which outputs prototypes for all functions in the input file rather than compiling the file—is used. Copies of the prototype files are included on the distribution disk, however, and they are **#include**d by most of the source files in this book.

Listing A.3. *yystack.h*— Stack-Maintenance Macros: **LLama/Occs** Version

```
1    /* yystack.h     Stack-maintenance macros --- yacc and llama version.
2     */
3
4    #define yystk_cls      /* empty */
5
6    #define yystk_dcl(stack,type,size)    typedef type yyt_##stack;              \
7                                          yystk_cls yyt_##stack stack[size];     \
8                                          yystk_cls yyt_##stack (*yyp_##stack)   \
9                                                               = stack + (size)
10   #define yystk_clear(stack) (  (yyp_##stack) = (stack + \
11                                         sizeof(stack)/sizeof(*stack)) )
12
13   #define yystk_full(stack)  (  (yyp_##stack) <= stack )
14   #define yystk_empty(stack) (  (yyp_##stack) >= (stack + \
15                                         sizeof(stack)/sizeof(*stack)) )
16
17   #define yystk_ele(stack)     ((sizeof(stack)/sizeof(*stack)) - \
18                                                (yyp_##stack-stack))
19
20   #define yystk_item(stack,offset) ( *(yyp_##stack + (offset)) )
21   #define yystk_p(stack)           yyp_##stack
22
23   #define yypush_(stack,x) ( *--yyp_##stack = (x) )
24   #define yypop_(stack)    ( *yyp_##stack++        )
25
26   #define yypush(stack,x)    ( yystk_full(stack)                         \
27                                 ? ((yyt_##stack)(long)(yystk_err(1)))    \
28                                 : yypush_(stack,x)                       )
29
30   #define yypop(stack)       ( yystk_empty(stack)                        \
31                                 ? ((yyt_##stack)(long)(yystk_err(0)))    \
32                                 : yypop_(stack)                          )
33
34   #define yypopn_(stack,amt) ( (yyp_##stack += amt)[-amt]   )
35   #define yypopn( stack,amt) ( yystk_ele(stack) < amt)                   \
36                                 ? ((yyt_##stack)(long)(yystk_err(0)))    \
37                                 : yypopn_(stack,amt)                     )
38
39   #define yystk_err(o)       ((o) ? ferr("Stack overflow\n" ) \
40                                    : ferr("Stack underflow\n") )
```

A.2 Set Manipulation

Many of the operations involved in compiler writing—like creating state-machine tables from regular expressions and creating bottom-up parse tables from a grammar—involve operations on sets, and C, unlike Pascal, doesn't have a built-in set capability. Fortunately, it's not too hard to implement sets in C by means of bit maps—one-dimensional arrays of one-bit numbers. This section presents a package of bit-map-based, set-manipulation routines.

Bit maps.

A.2.1 Using the Set Functions and Macros

<tools/set.h>, SET.

To use the set routines, you must put a **#include** <tools/set.h> at the top of your file. The definitions for a SET are found there, and many of the set functions are actually macros defined in *<tools/set.h>*. The set routines are described in the following paragraphs. I'll give a few examples after the calling-conventions are described. If a name is in all caps in the following list, it's implemented as a macro, and most of these macros have side effects. Be careful.

`SET *newset(void)` | Create a set.

    Create a new set and return a pointer to it. Print an error message and raise SIGABRT if there's insufficient memory. Normally this signal terminates the program but you can use `signal()` to change the default action (the process is described in a moment). NULL is returned if `raise()` returns.

`void delset(SET *set)` | Delete a set.

    Delete a set created with a previous newset call and free the associated memory. The argument must have been returned from a previous `newset()` call.

`SET *dupset(SET *set)` | Duplicate a set.

    Create a new set that has the same members as the input `set`. This routine is more efficient than using `newset()` to create the set and then copying the members one at a time, but otherwise has the same effect.

`int _addset(SET *set, int bit)` | Internal set function: enlarge set.

    This is an internal function used by the ADD macro, and shouldn't be called by you.

`int num_ele(SET *set)` | Find number of elements in set.

    Return the number of elements in the input `set`. NULL sets (described below) are considered to be empty.

`int _set_test(SET *set1, SET *set2)` | Internal set function: test bits.

    This is another workhorse function used internally by the macros. Don't call it directly.

`int setcmp(SET *set1, SET *set2)` | Compare two sets.

    Compare two sets in a manner similar to `strcmp()` returning 0 if the sets are equivalent, <0 if set1<set2 and >0 if set1>set2. This routine lets you sort an array of SET's so that equivalent ones are adjacent. The determination of less than and greater than is pretty much arbitrary. (The routine just compares the bit maps as if you were doing a lexicographic ordering of an array of `int`s.)

`unsigned sethash(SET *set1)` | Compute hash value for set.

    This function is even more obscure than `setcmp()`. It is provided for those situations where a SET is used as the key in a hash table. It returns the sum of the individual words in the bit map.

`int subset(SET *set, SET *sub)` | Sub is subset of set.

    Return 1 if `sub` is a subset of `set`, 0 otherwise. Empty and null sets are subsets of everything, and 1 is returned if both sets are empty or null.

`void _set_op(int op, SET *dest, SET *src)` | Internal set function: binary operations.

    Another workhorse function used internally by the macros.

`void invert(SET *set)` | Complement set by inverting bits.

    Physically invert the bits in the set, setting 1's to 0 and vice versa. In effect, this operation removes all existing members from a set and adds all possible members that weren't there before. Note that the set must be expanded to the maximum possible size before calling `invert()`—ADD the largest element and then delete it. See also, `COMPLEMENT()`.

Clear set and make smaller.

void truncate(SET *set)

Clears the set and shrinks it back to the original, default size. Compare this routine to the `CLEAR()` macro, described below, which clears all the bits in the map but doesn't modify the size. This routine is really a more efficient replacement for `delset(s); s=newset();`. If the original set isn't very big, you're better off using `CLEAR()`.

Find next set element.

int next_member(SET *set)

When called several successive times with the same argument, returns the next element of the set each time it's called or −1 if there are no more elements. Every time the `set` argument changes, the search for elements starts back at the beginning of the set. A NULL argument also resets the search to the beginning of the set (and does nothing else). Strange things happen if you add members to the set between successive calls. If calls to `next_member()` are interspersed with calls to `pset()` (discussed below), `next_member()` won't work properly. Calls to `next_member()` on different sets cannot be interspersed.

Print set elements.

void pset(SET *set, **int** (*out)(), **void** *param)

Print the set. The output routine pointed to by `out` is called for each element of the set with the following arguments:

```
(*out)(param, "null",   -1);   Null set
(*out)(param, "empty",  -2);   Empty set
(*out)(param, "%d ",     N);   Set element N
```

This way you can use `fprintf()` as a default output routine.

dest = dest ∪ src.

UNION(SET *dest, SET *src)

Modify the `dest` set to hold the union of the `src` and `dest` sets.

dest = dest ∩ src.

INTERSECT(SET *dest, SET *src)

Modify the `dest` set to hold the intersection of the `src` and `dest` sets.

dest = symmetric difference.

DIFFERENCE(SET *dest, SET *src)

Modify the `dest` set to hold the symmetric difference of the `src` and `dest` sets. (An element is put into the target set if it is a member of `dest` but not of `src`, or vice versa.)

dest = src.

ASSIGN(SET *dest, SET *src)

Overwrite the `dest` with `src`.

Clear set.

CLEAR(SET *s)

Clear all bits in `s`, creating an empty set.

Add all elements to set.

FILL(SET *s)

Set all bits in `s` to 1, creating a set that holds every element in the input alphabet.

Complement set.

COMPLEMENT(SET *s)

Complement a set efficiently by modifying the set's `complement` bit. Sets complemented in this way can not be manipulated by `UNION()`, etc. See also, `invert()` and `INVERT()`.

`INVERT(SET *s)`   Invert all bits in bit map.

Complement a set by physically changing the bit map (see text).

`IS_DISJOINT(SET *s1, SET *s2)`   Test for disjoint.

Evaluate to true only if the two sets are disjoint (have no elements in common).

`IS_INTERSECTING (SET *s1, SET *s2)` Test for intersection.

Evaluate to true only if the two sets intersect (have at least one element in common).

`IS_EMPTY(SET *s)`   Test for empty set.

Evaluate to true only if set is empty (having no elements) or null (s is `NULL`)

`IS_EQUIVALENT(SET *s1, SET *s2)`   Text for equivalence.

Evaluate to true only if the two sets are equivalent (have the same elements).

`ADD(SET *s,` **`int`** `x)`   Add member to set.

Add the element `c` to set `s`. It is not an error to add an element to a set more than once.

`REMOVE(SET *s,` **`int`** `x)`   Remove member from set.

Remove the element `c` from set `s`. It is not an error to remove an element that is not in the set.

`TEST(SET *s,` **`int`** `x)`   Test for membership (all sets).

Evaluates to true if `x` is an element of set `s`.

`MEMBER(SET *s,` **`int`** `x)`   Test for membership (no complemented sets).

Evaluates to true if `x` is an element of set `s`. This macro doesn't work on `COMPLEMENT`ed sets, but it's both faster and smaller than `TEST`, which does. The distinction is described below.

The elements of sets must be numbers, though in many instances any arbitrary number will do. Enumerated types are almost ideal for this purpose, though **`#define`**s can be used too. For example: Sets, an example. Set elements are numbers.

```
typedef enum
{
    JAN, FEB, MAR,
    APR, MAY, JUN,
    JUL, AUG, SEP,
    OCT, NOV, DEC

} MONTHS;
```

creates 12 potential set elements. You can create two sets called `winter` and `spring` by using the following set operations:

```
#include <set.h>

SET   *winter, *spring;

winter = newset();
spring = newset();

ADD( JAN, winter );
ADD( FEB, winter );
ADD( MAR, winter );
ADD( APR, spring );
ADD( MAY, spring );
ADD( JUN, spring );
```

Set operations can now be performed using the other macros in *<tools/set.h>*. For example: IS_DISJOINT(winter,spring) evaluates to true because the sets have no elements in common; IS_EQUIVALENT(winter,spring) evaluates to false for the same reason. A third set that contains the union of spring and winter can be created with:

```
half_year = dupset( winter );
UNION( half_year, spring );
```

Something like:

```
half_year = dupset( winter );
INTERSECT(half_year, spring);
```

creates an empty set because there are no common elements.

Set implementation difficulties. Null and empty sets. There are two implementation difficulties with the set routines. The first is the difference between a null set and an empty set. (I'll bet that you thought that the difference was just one more obscure mathematical conundrum designed for no other purpose than to make undergraduates' heads swim). An empty set is a set that has no elements. In the case of the routines presented here, newset() and dupset() both create empty sets. They have allocated an internal data structure for representing the set, but that set doesn't have anything in it yet. A null set, however, is a SET pointer with nothing in it. For example:

```
SET *p = NULL;    /* p represents the null set     */
p = newset();     /* p now represents an empty set */
```

In practice, this difference means that the routines have to be a bit more careful with pointers than they would be otherwise, and are a little slower as a consequence.

Problems with complemented sets. Complimented sets present another problem. You'll notice that the eventual size of the set doesn't have to be known when the set is created by newset(). The set size is just expanded as elements are added to it. This can cause problems when you complement a set, because the complemented set should contain all possible elements of input alphabet except the ones that are in the equivalent, uncomplemented, set. For example, if you're working with a language that's comprised of the set of symbols {A, B, C, D, E, F, G} and you create a second set {A,C,E,G} from elements of the language, the complement of this second set should be {B,D,F}.

Complement by physically inverting bits. This ideal situation is difficult to do, however. Sets are represented internally as bit maps, and these maps are of finite size. Moreover, the actual size of the map grows as elements are added to the set. You can complement a set by inverting the sense of all the bits in the map, but then you can't expand the set's size dynamically—at least not without a lot of work. To guarantee that a complemented set contains all the potential elements, you first must expand the set size by adding an element that is one larger than any possible legitimate element, and then complement the expanded set. A second problem has to do with extra elements. The bit-map size is usually a little larger than the number of potential elements in the set, so you will effectively add members to the set if you just stupidly complement bits. On the plus side, set operations (union, intersection, etc.) are much easier to do on physically complemented sets.

An alternate method of complementing the set uses negative-true sets and positive-true sets. Here, you mark a set as negative or positive by setting a bit in the SET structure. You don't have to modify the bit map at all. If a set is marked negative-true when you test for membership, you can just reverse the sense of the test (evaluate to true if the requested bit is not false). Though this method solves the size problem, operations on negative-true sets are much harder to perform.

Complement by marking set as negative true.

Since the two representations are both useful, but in different applications, I've implemented both methods. The INVERT() macro performs a ones-complement on all bits currently in the bit map. Note that if new elements are added, the new bits won't be complemented. You should always expand a set out to the maximum number of elements (by adding and then removing the largest element) before inverting it. The COMPLEMENT() macro implements the second method. It doesn't modify the bit map at all; rather, it sets a flag in the SET structure to mark a set as negative true.

Physical complement, INVERT()

Logical complement, COMPLEMENT()

Because there are two different classes of sets (those that are complemented and those that are inverted), there are also two different macros for testing membership. MEMBER() evaluates to true only if the bit corresponding to the requested element is actually set to one. MEMBER() can't be used reliably on complemented sets, The TEST() macro can be used with complemented sets, but it's both larger and slower than MEMBER(). If a set is complemented, the sense of the individual bits is reversed as part of the testing process. If the set isn't complemented TEST() works just like MEMBER().

Testing for membership on complemented sets, MEMBER() vs. TEST().

The various set operations (UNION, INTERSECT, and so forth) are only valid on inverted sets. Use INVERT() if you're going to perform subsequent operations on the inverted set. I leave it as an exercise to the reader to make _set_op() work on complemented sets. The complement bit can represent all bits not in the bit map—if the complement bit is set, all bits not in the map are zero and vice versa. I've found these routines quite workable in their existing state—it seemed pointless to make the code both larger and slower to correct what has turned out not to be a problem.

Set operations work only on physically complemented sets.

A.2.2 Set Implementation

The set routines are implemented in two places, the first of which is the macro file <*tools/set.h*>, in Listing A.4. The file starts with various system-dependent definitions, concentrated in one place to make it easier to port the code. _SETTYPE (on line three) is used as the basic unit in a bit map. As I mentioned earlier, a bit map is a 1-dimensional array of 1-bit objects. In terms of set operations, a number is in the set if the array element at that position in the map is true (if bitmap[5] is true than 5 is in the set). The map is implemented using an array of _SETTYPEs as follows:

<tools/set.h>, _SETTYPE.

Implementing bit maps.

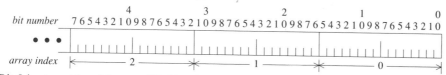

Bit 0 is at position 0 in array[0], bit 1 is at position 1 in array[0], bit 20 is at position 4 in array[1], and so forth. In order to make the array manipulation as efficient as possible, _SETTYPE should be the largest integral type that can be manipulated with a single instruction on the target machine. In an 8086, for example, the largest such type is a 16-bit word—larger numbers require several instructions to manipulate them—so I've used the 16-bit **short** as the _SETTYPE.

Listing A.4. *set.h*— Macro Definitions and Prototypes for Set Functions

```
1    /* SET.H:  Macros and function prototypes for the set functions */
2
3    typedef unsigned short    _SETTYPE ;              /* one cell in bit map    */
4    #define _BITS_IN_WORD       16
5    #define _BYTES_IN_ARRAY(x) (x << 1)               /* # of bytes in bit map */
6    #define _DIV_WSIZE(x)      ((unsigned)(x) >> 4)
7    #define _MOD_WSIZE(x)      ((x) & 0x0f    )
8    #define _DEFWORDS  8                              /* elements in default set */
9    #define _DEFBITS      (_DEFWORDS * _BITS_IN_WORD)  /* bits in default set    */
10   #define _ROUND(bit) (((_DIV_WSIZE(bit) + 8) >>3 ) <<3 )
11
12   typedef struct _set_
13   {
14       unsigned char nwords ;                  /* Number of words in map        */
15       unsigned char compl  ;                  /* is a negative true set if true */
16       unsigned      nbits  ;                  /* Number of bits in map          */
17       _SETTYPE      *map   ;                  /* Pointer to the map             */
18       _SETTYPE      defmap[ _DEFWORDS ];      /* The map itself                 */
19
20   } SET;
21
22   extern   int      _addset       P(( SET* , int                 ));;
23   extern   void     delset        P(( SET*                       ));;
24   extern   SET      *dupset       P(( SET*                       ));;
25   extern   void     invert        P(( SET*                       ));;
26   extern   SET      *newset       P(( void                       ));;
27   extern   int      next_member   P(( SET *                      ));;
28   extern   int      num_ele       P(( SET*                       ));;
29   extern   void     pset          P(( SET*, int (*)(), void*     ));;
30   extern   void     _set_op       P(( int,        SET*, SET*     ));;
31   extern   int      _set_test     P(( SET*, SET*                 ));;
32   extern   int      setcmp        P(( SET*, SET*                 ));;
33   extern   unsigned sethash       P(( SET*                       ));;
34   extern   int      subset        P(( SET*, SET*                 ));;
35   extern   void     truncate      P(( SET*                       ));;
36
37                                   /* Op argument passed to _set_op */
38   #define _UNION        0         /* x is in s1 or s2              */
39   #define _INTERSECT    1         /* x is in s1 and s2             */
40   #define _DIFFERENCE   2         /* (x in s1) && (s not in s2)    */
41   #define _ASSIGN       4         /* s1 = s2                       */
42
43   #define UNION(d,s)         _set_op( _UNION,      d, s )
44   #define INTERSECT(d,s)     _set_op( _INTERSECT,  d, s )
45   #define DIFFERENCE(d,s)    _set_op( _DIFFERENCE, d, s )
46   #define ASSIGN(d,s)        _set_op( _ASSIGN,     d, s )
47
48   #define CLEAR(s)       memset( (s)->map, 0, (s)->nwords * sizeof(_SETTYPE))
49   #define FILL(s)        memset( (s)->map, ~0, (s)->nwords * sizeof(_SETTYPE))
50   #define COMPLEMENT(s)  ( (s)->compl = ~(s)->compl )
51   #define INVERT(s)      invert(s)
52
53   #define _SET_EQUIV    0         /* Value returned from _set_test, equivalent */
54   #define _SET_DISJ     1         /*                                 disjoint  */
55   #define _SET_INTER    2         /*                              intersecting */
56
57   #define IS_DISJOINT(s1,s2)     ( _set_test(s1,s2) == _SET_DISJ  )
58   #define IS_INTERSECTING(s1,s2) ( _set_test(s1,s2) == _SET_INTER )
59   #define IS_EQUIVALENT(a,b)     ( setcmp((a),(b))  == 0          )
```

```
Listing A.4. continued...
60   #define IS_EMPTY(s)              ( num_ele(s)        == 0           )
61
62   /* All of the following have heavy-duty side-effects. Be careful. */
63
64   #define _GBIT(s,x,op) ( ((s)->map)[_DIV_WSIZE(x)] op (1 << _MOD_WSIZE(x)) )
65
66   #define REMOVE(s,x)   (((x) >= (s)->nbits) ? 0         : _GBIT(s,x,&= ~) )
67   #define ADD(s,x)      (((x) >= (s)->nbits) ? _addset(s,x) : _GBIT(s,x,|= ) )
68   #define MEMBER(s,x)   (((x) >= (s)->nbits) ? 0         : _GBIT(s,x,&  ) )
69   #define TEST(s,x)     (( MEMBER(s,x) )     ? !(s)->compl : (s)->compl    )
```

The macros on lines four to seven all reflect the size of the _SETTYPE and will have to be changed if _SETTYPE is changed. _BITS_IN_WORD is just that, the number of bits in a variable of type _SETTYPE. _BYTES_IN_ARRAY is passed a count, and it returns the number of bytes in an array of that many _SETTYPE-sized variables. In this case, I multiply the count by two using a left shift rather than doing something like s***sizeof**(_SETTYPE), which uses a multiply on my compiler — the shift is a more efficient operation than the multiply.

_BITS_IN_WORD, _BYTES_IN_ARRAY.

The _DIV_WSIZE(x) and _MOD_WSIZE(x) macros help determine the position of a particular bit in the map. The argument to both macros is the bit for which you want the position. The _DIV_WSIZE(x) macro evaluate to the array element that holds the bit. A _DIV_WSIZE(20) evaluates to 1 because bit 20 is in array[1]. It's just doing an integer divide by 16, though I'm using a left shift here for efficiency's sake. The _MOD_WSIZE(x) macro evaluate to the position of the bit within the word—the offset in bits from the least-significant bit in the word. A _MOD_WSIZE(20) evaluates to 4 because bit 20 is at offset 4 of array[1]. I'm doing an efficient modulus-16 operation by using a bitwise AND rather than a %.

Computing bit positions, _DIV_WSIZE(x), _MOD_WSIZE(x).

_DEFWORDS, on line eight of Listing A.4, determines the array size for a default bit map. Initially, all bit maps have this many elements. The size is expanded (in _DEFWORDS-sized chunks) if needed. _DEFWORDS is set to 8 here, so the default map can have 128 elements before it needs to be expanded. _DEFBITS, on the next line, is just the number of bits required for that many words.

_DEFWORDS, _DEFBITS, _ROUND.

The _ROUND macro is used to expand the size of the array. The array grows in _DEFWORDS-sized chunks. Say, for example, that the array starts out at the default size of 8 words, and you want to add the number 200 to the set. The array must be expanded to do so, and after the expansion, the array should have 16 elements in it (2 × _DEF-WORDS). In this situation the macro expands to:

    (((_DIV_WSIZE(200) + 8) >>3) <<3)

and one more level to:

    (((((**unsigned**) (200) >> 4) + 8) >>3) <<3)

The 200>>4 evaluates to 12, so bit 200 is in array[12]. 12 plus 8 is 20, and 20>>3 yields 2. (The >>3 is an integer divide by 8.) The final multiply by 8 (the <<3) yields 16, so the map array is expanded to 16 elements.

The SET itself is represented with the following structure, defined on lines 12 to 20 of Listing A.4.

Representing a set, SET.

```
typedef struct _set_
{
    unsigned char  nwords ;              /* Number of words in map */
    unsigned char  compl  ;              /* negative true if set   */
    unsigned       nbits  ;              /* Number of bits in map  */
    _SETTYPE       *map   ;              /* Pointer to the map     */
    _SETTYPE       defmap[_DEFWORDS]; /* The default map           */

} SET;
```

The number of bits in the map (`nbits`) could be computed from the number of words (`nwords`), but it's more efficient—of computation time, not space—to keep both numbers in the structure. The `compl` field is set to true if this is a negative-true set. The `defmap[]` array is the default bit map. Initially, `map` just points to it. When the map grows, however, a new array is allocated with `malloc()` and `map` is modified to point at the new array. This strategy is used rather than a `realloc()` call for run-time efficiency, at the cost of wasted memory—`realloc()` will generally have to copy the entire structure, but only the map needs to be copied if you do it yourself.

Set macros.

<set.h> continues on line 22 of Listing A.4 with function prototypes for the actual functions. The macros on lines 43 to 60 handle operations that actually modify a set (union, intersection, symmetric difference, and so forth). Most of them map to `set_op()` calls, passing in a constant to tell the subroutine which function is required. `CLEAR` and `FILL` modify the bit map directly, however, calling `memset()` to fill the bits with zeros or ones as appropriate.

CLEAR, FILL.

Adding and removing set members, ADD(), RE-MOVE(). Testing for membership, MEMBER().

The real heart of *<set.h>* are the set-manipulation macros at the end of the file, reproduced here:

```
#define _GBIT(s,x,op) (((s)->map)[_DIV_WSIZE(x)] op (1 << _MOD_WSIZE(x)))

#define REMOVE(s,x)  (((x) >= (s)->nbits) ? 0          : _GBIT(s,x,&= ~))
#define ADD(s,x)     (((x) >= (s)->nbits) ? _addset(s,x): _GBIT(s,x,|= ))
#define MEMBER(s,x)  (((x) >= (s)->nbits) ? 0          : _GBIT(s,x,&  ))
#define TEST(s,x)    (( MEMBER(s,x) )     ? !(s)->compl : (s)->compl   )
```

_GBIT.

The `REMOVE`, `ADD`, and `MEMBER` macros all evaluate to `_GBIT` invocations. The only difference is the operator (`op`) passed into the macro. The first part of `_GBIT` uses the following to select the array element in which the required bit is found:

```
( (s)->map )[ _DIV_WSIZE(x) ]
```

The second half of the macro shifts the number 1 to the left so that it will fall in the same position as the required bit, using

```
(1 << _MOD_WSIZE(x)) )
```

If you're accessing bit 5, the number 1 is shifted left 5 bits, yielding the following binary mask in a 16-bit word:

```
0000000000100000
```

The same shift happens when you access bit 20, but in this case the first half of the macro chooses `(s)->map[1]` rather than `(s)->map[0]`. The `op` argument now comes into play. The shifted mask is ORed with the existing array element to add it to the set. Similarly, the inverse of the mask is ANDed to the array element to clear a bit. OR is also used to test for membership, but since there's no = in `MEMBER`, the map is not modified.

Testing complemented sets for membership, TEST().

The `TEST` macro, which can handle complemented sets, works by first determining whether `x` is in the set, and then evaluating to the complement flag or its inverse, as appropriate. For example, the complemented flag will be 1 if `x` is in a negative true set, and MEMBER tests true if the bit is in the map. The inverse of the complement flag (0) is returned, however. I've used this somewhat convoluted approach because of the sheer size of the macro. TEST(s,x) expands to this monster:

```
((( ((x) >= (s)->nbits) ? 0 :
            (((s)->map)[((unsigned)(x)>>4)] & (1<<((x) & 0x0f))))) ?
            !(s)->compl : (s)->compl);
```

but the more obvious solution:

```
(s)->compl ? !MEMBER(s,x) : MEMBER(s,x)
```

turns into this:

```
(s)->compl
    ? !(((x) >= (s)->nbits) ? 0 :
                (((s)->map)[((unsigned)(x)>>4)] & (1<<((x) & 0x0f))))
    :  (((x) >= (s)->nbits) ? 0 :
                (((s)->map)[((unsigned)(x)>>4)] & (1<<((x) & 0x0f))))
```

which is even worse.

The functions needed for set manipulation are all in *set.c*, the first part of which is Listing A.5. The newset() function, which actually creates the new set, starts on line nine. Normally, a pointer to the newly allocated SET is returned. If insufficient memory is available, an error message is printed and the program is terminated by the raise(SIGABRT) call on line 21. raise() is an ANSI function which, in this case, causes the program to terminate. I've chosen to abort the program rather than return NULL (like malloc() does) because most applications will terminate the program anyway if memory isn't available. If you want NULL to be returned on an error rather than aborting the program, just disable the SIGABRT signal as follows:

> Creating sets, newset().

> raise().

```
#include <signal.h>
main()
{
    signal( SIGABRT, SIG_IGN );
}
```

Listing A.5. *set.c*— SET Creation and Destruction

```
1   #include  <stdio.h>
2   #include  <ctype.h>
3   #include  <signal.h>
4   #include  <stdlib.h>
5   #include  <string.h>
6   #include  <tools/debug.h>
7   #include  <tools/set.h>
8
9   PUBLIC SET      *newset()
10  {
11      /* Create a new set and return a pointer to it. Print an error message
12       * and raise SIGABRT if there's insufficient memory. NULL is returned
13       * if raise() returns.
14       */
15
16      SET *p;
17
18      if( !(p = (SET *) malloc( sizeof(SET) )) )
19      {
20          fprintf(stderr,"Can't get memory to create set\n");
21          raise( SIGABRT );
22          return NULL;              /* Usually won't get here */
```

→

Listing A.5. continued...

```
23          }
24          memset( p, 0, sizeof(SET) );
25          p->map    = p->defmap;
26          p->nwords = _DEFWORDS;
27          p->nbits  = _DEFBITS;
28          return p;
29      }
30
31      /*------------------------------------------------------------------*/
32
33      PUBLIC void    delset( set )
34      SET    *set;
35      {
36          /* Delete a set created with a previous newset() call. */
37
38          if( set->map != set->defmap )
39              free( set->map );
40          free( set );
41      }
42
43      /*------------------------------------------------------------------*/
44
45      PUBLIC SET     *dupset( set )
46      SET    *set;
47      {
48          /* Create a new set that has the same members as the input set */
49
50          SET    *new;
51
52          if( !(new = (SET *) malloc( sizeof(SET) )) )
53          {
54              fprintf(stderr,"Can't get memory to duplicate set\n");
55              exit(1);
56          }
57
58          memset( new, 0, sizeof(SET) );
59          new->compl  = set->compl;
60          new->nwords = set->nwords;
61          new->nbits  = set->nbits;
62
63          if( set->map == set->defmap )               /* default bit map in use */
64          {
65              new->map = new->defmap;
66              memcpy( new->defmap, set->defmap, _DEFWORDS * sizeof(_SETTYPE) );
67          }
68          else                                        /* bit map has been enlarged */
69          {
70              new->map = (_SETTYPE *) malloc( set->nwords * sizeof(_SETTYPE) );
71              if( !new->map )
72              {
73                  fprintf(stderr,"Can't get memory to duplicate set bit map\n");
74                  exit(1);
75              }
76              memcpy( new->map, set->map, set->nwords * sizeof(_SETTYPE) );
77          }
78          return new;
79      }
```

The `del_set()` function starting on line 33 is the `SET` destructor subroutine. It frees any memory used for an expanded bit map on line 38, and then frees the memory used for the `SET` itself.

`dupset()` (starting on line 45 of Listing A.5) duplicates an existing set. It's much more efficient than calling `new_set()` and then adding members to the new set one at a time.

The functions in Listing A.6 handle set enlargement: `_addset()` is called from the `ADD` macro when the bit map is not large enough to hold the requested bit. All it does is call `enlarge()` (which starts on line 95) to make the map larger, and then invokes `_GBIT` to set the bit. `_enlarge()` is passed the required number of words in the bit map (need). The test on line 106 causes the routine to return if no expansion is required. Note that `exit()` is called on line 114 if `enlarge()` can't get memory. I've done this rather than call `raise()` because I'm assuming that the value returned from `ADD` will not be tested. It would be risky to call `raise()` in this situation because the signal handler might have been reassigned to an empty function, as was discussed earlier.

The next part of *set.c* (in Listing A.7) consists of various testing functions. The `num_ele()` function, starting on line 126, determines the number of elements in the set. It does this by looking at the map array one byte at a time, using a table lookup to do the counting. The table in question is `nbits[]`, declared on lines 134 to 152. The table is indexed with a number in the range 0–255, and it evaluates to the number of bits set to 1 in that number. For example, the decimal number 93 is 01011101 in binary. This number has five ones in it, so `nbits[93]` holds 5. The loop on lines 162 and 163 just goes through the `map` array byte by byte, looking up each byte in `nbits[]` and accumulating the count in `count`.

The `_set_test()` function starting on line 170 of Listing A.7 compares two sets, returning `_SET_EQUIV` if the sets are equivalent (have the same elements), `_SET_INTER` if the sets intersect (have at least one element in common) but aren't equivalent, and `_SET_DISJ` if the sets are disjoint (have no elements in common). A bitwise AND is used to test for intersection on line 203—the test for equivalence was done on line 195 of Listing A.7. If the AND tests true, there must be at least one bit at the same relative position in both bit-map elements.

Note that the sets are made the same size with the `enlarge()` calls on lines 187 and 188 before they are compared, and this expansion can waste time if the sets are likely to be different sizes. For this reason, a second comparison function, `setcmp()`, is provided on line 215. This routine works like `strcmp()`, returning zero if the sets are equivalent, a negative number if `set1<set2`, and a positive number if `set1>set2`. Since `setcmp()` does not modify the set sizes, using it can be less time consuming than using `_set_test()`. The main purpose of this second comparison function is to let you sort an array of `SET` pointers so that the equivalent sets are adjacent. The determination of less than and greater than is pretty much arbitrary—the routine just compares the maps as if they were arrays of **int**s. `setcmp()` first compares the map elements that exist in both of the sets on lines 228 to 230. If there's a mismatch, the two bytes are subtracted to get a relative ordering. The code on lines 236 to 247 is executed only if the two sets are identical up to this point. The tail end of the larger set is then scanned to make sure that it's all zeros. If so, the two sets are equivalent. If not, the larger set is the greater.

The final comparison function is `subset()`, starting on line 275 of Listing A.7. `common` and `tail`, initialized on lines 289 to 298, are the number of words that exist in both sets, and the number of extra bytes that have to be tested in the potential subset. For example, if set A has 10 bytes and set B has 20, and if you're determining whether set A is a subset of set B, you need to look only at the first 10 bytes of both sets. It doesn't matter whether the last 10 bytes of set B have anything in them. If, however, you want

Listing A.6. *set.c*— Adding Members to and Enlarging a SET

```
80    PUBLIC int        _addset( set, bit )
81    SET      *set;
82    {
83        /* Addset is called by the ADD() macro when the set isn't big enough. It
84         * expands the set to the necessary size and sets the indicated bit.
85         */
86
87        void enlarge( int, SET* );                    /* immediately following */
88
89        enlarge( _ROUND(bit), set );
90        return _GBIT( set, bit, |= );
91    }
92
93    /* ------------------------------------------------------------------ */
94
95    PRIVATE void      enlarge( need, set )
96    SET      *set;
97    {
98        /* Enlarge the set to "need" words, filling in the extra words with zeros.
99         * Print an error message and abort by raising SIGABRT if there's not enough
100        * memory. NULL is returned if raise() returns. Since this routine calls
101        * malloc, it's rather slow and should be avoided if possible.
102        */
103
104       _SETTYPE  *new;
105
106       if( !set  ||  need <= set->nwords )
107           return;
108
109       D( printf("enlarging %d word map to %d words\n", set->nwords, need); )
110
111       if( !(new = (_SETTYPE *) malloc( need * sizeof(_SETTYPE)))  )
112       {
113           fprintf(stderr, "Can't get memory to expand set\n");
114           exit( 1 );
115       }
116       memcpy( new, set->map,        set->nwords * sizeof(_SETTYPE)          );
117       memset( new + set->nwords, 0, (need - set->nwords) * sizeof(_SETTYPE) );
118
119       if( set->map != set->defmap )
120           free( set->map );
121
122       set->map      = new  ;
123       set->nwords = (unsigned char) need ;
124       set->nbits   = need * _BITS_IN_WORD ;
125   }
```

to know whether the longer set (B) is a subset of the shorter one (A), all bytes that are not in set A (the extra 10 bytes in B) must be scanned to make sure they're all zeros. The common parts of the sets are scanned by the loop on line 303, and the tail of the larger set is scanned, if necessary, by the loop on line 307.

The next three functions, in Listing A.8, all modify a set one way or another. The _set_op() function on line 313 performs the union, intersection, symmetric difference, and assignment functions.

Set operations (union, intersection, symetric difference, assignment). _set_op().

I've used the same strategy here as I used earlier when the sets were different sizes. The common words are manipulated first, and the tail of the longer set is modified if

Listing A.7. *set.c*— Set-Testing Functions

```
126    PUBLIC int        num_ele( set )
127    SET     *set;
128    {
129        /* Return the number of elements (nonzero bits) in the set. NULL sets are
130         * considered empty. The table-lookup approach used here was suggested to
131         * me by Doug Merrit. Nbits[] is indexed by any number in the range 0-255,
132         * and it evaluates to the number of bits in the number.
133         */
134        static unsigned char nbits[] =
135        {
136            /*   0-15  */   0, 1, 1, 2, 1, 2, 2, 3, 1, 2, 2, 3, 2, 3, 3, 4,
137            /*  16-31  */   1, 2, 2, 3, 2, 3, 3, 4, 2, 3, 3, 4, 3, 4, 4, 5,
138            /*  32-47  */   1, 2, 2, 3, 2, 3, 3, 4, 2, 3, 3, 4, 3, 4, 4, 5,
139            /*  48-63  */   2, 3, 3, 4, 3, 4, 4, 5, 3, 4, 4, 5, 4, 5, 5, 6,
140            /*  64-79  */   1, 2, 2, 3, 2, 3, 3, 4, 2, 3, 3, 4, 3, 4, 4, 5,
141            /*  80-95  */   2, 3, 3, 4, 3, 4, 4, 5, 3, 4, 4, 5, 4, 5, 5, 6,
142            /*  96-111 */   2, 3, 3, 4, 3, 4, 4, 5, 3, 4, 4, 5, 4, 5, 5, 6,
143            /* 112-127 */   3, 4, 4, 5, 4, 5, 5, 6, 4, 5, 5, 6, 5, 6, 6, 7,
144            /* 128-143 */   1, 2, 2, 3, 2, 3, 3, 4, 2, 3, 3, 4, 3, 4, 4, 5,
145            /* 144-159 */   2, 3, 3, 4, 3, 4, 4, 5, 3, 4, 4, 5, 4, 5, 5, 6,
146            /* 160-175 */   2, 3, 3, 4, 3, 4, 4, 5, 3, 4, 4, 5, 4, 5, 5, 6,
147            /* 176-191 */   3, 4, 4, 5, 4, 5, 5, 6, 4, 5, 5, 6, 5, 6, 6, 7,
148            /* 192-207 */   2, 3, 3, 4, 3, 4, 4, 5, 3, 4, 4, 5, 4, 5, 5, 6,
149            /* 208-223 */   3, 4, 4, 5, 4, 5, 5, 6, 4, 5, 5, 6, 5, 6, 6, 7,
150            /* 224-239 */   3, 4, 4, 5, 4, 5, 5, 6, 4, 5, 5, 6, 5, 6, 6, 7,
151            /* 240-255 */   4, 5, 5, 6, 5, 6, 6, 7, 5, 6, 6, 7, 6, 7, 7, 8
152        };
153        int             i;
154        unsigned int    count = 0;
155        unsigned char   *p;
156
157        if( !set )
158            return 0;
159
160        p = (unsigned char *)set->map ;
161
162        for( i = _BYTES_IN_ARRAY(set->nwords) ; --i >= 0 ; )
163            count += nbits[ *p++ ] ;
164
165        return count;
166    }
167
168    /* ------------------------------------------------------------------ */
169
170    PUBLIC int    _set_test( set1, set2 )
171    SET     *set1, *set2;
172    {
173        /* Compares two sets. Returns as follows:
174         *
175         * _SET_EQUIV        Sets are equivalent
176         * _SET_INTER        Sets intersect but aren't equivalent
177         * _SET_DISJ         Sets are disjoint
178         *
179         * The smaller set is made larger if the two sets are different sizes.
180         */
181
182        int         i, rval = _SET_EQUIV ;
183        _SETTYPE    *p1, *p2;
184
```

Listing A.7. continued...

```
185        i = max( set1->nwords, set2->nwords);
186
187        enlarge( i, set1 );            /* Make the sets the same size  */
188        enlarge( i, set2 );
189
190        p1 = set1->map;
191        p2 = set2->map;
192
193        for(; --i >= 0 ; p1++, p2++ )
194        {
195            if( *p1 != *p2 )
196            {
197                /* You get here if the sets aren't equivalent. You can return
198                 * immediately if the sets intersect but have to keep going in the
199                 * case of disjoint sets (because the sets might actually intersect
200                 * at some byte, as yet unseen).
201                 */
202
203                if( *p1 & *p2 )
204                    return _SET_INTER ;
205                else
206                    rval = _SET_DISJ ;
207            }
208        }
209
210        return rval;                            /* They're equivalent   */
211    }
212
213    /* ------------------------------------------------------------------ */
214
215    PUBLIC setcmp( set1, set2 )
216    SET *set1, *set2;
217    {
218        /* Yet another comparison function. This one works like strcmp(),
219         * returning 0 if the sets are equivalent, <0 if set1<set2 and >0 if
220         * set1>set2.
221         */
222
223        int    i, j;
224        _SETTYPE    *p1, *p2;
225
226        i = j = min( set1->nwords, set2->nwords );
227
228        for( p1 = set1->map, p2 = set2->map ; --j >= 0 ;  p1++, p2++  )
229            if( *p1 != *p2 )
230                return *p1 - *p2;
231
232        /* You get here only if all words that exist in both sets are the same.
233         * Check the tail end of the larger array for all zeros.
234         */
235
236        if( (j = set1->nwords - i) > 0 )            /* Set 1 is the larger */
237        {
238            while( --j >= 0 )
239                if( *p1++ )
240                    return 1;
241        }
```

Listing A.7. continued...

```
242        else if( (j = set2->nwords - i) > 0)              /* Set 2 is the larger */
243        {
244            while( --j >= 0 )
245                if( *p2++ )
246                    return -1;
247        }
248
249        return 0;                                          /* They're equivalent  */
250   }
251
252   /* ------------------------------------------------------------------- */
253
254   PUBLIC unsigned sethash( set1 )
255   SET *set1;
256   {
257        /* hash the set by summing together the words in the bit map */
258
259        _SETTYPE     *p;
260        unsigned     total;
261        int          j;
262
263        total = 0;
264        j     = set1->nwords ;
265        p     = set1->map    ;
266
267        while( --j >= 0 )
268            total += *p++ ;
269
270        return total;
271   }
272
273   /* ------------------------------------------------------------------- */
274
275   PUBLIC int       subset( set, possible_subset )
276   SET     *set, *possible_subset;
277   {
278        /* Return 1 if "possible_subset" is a subset of "set". One is returned if
279         * it's a subset, zero otherwise. Empty sets are subsets of everything.
280         * The routine silently malfunctions if given a NULL set, however. If the
281         * "possible_subset" is larger than the "set", then the extra bytes must
282         * be all zeros.
283         */
284
285        _SETTYPE  *subsetp, *setp;
286        int    common;                  /* This many bytes in potential subset  */
287        int    tail;                    /* This many implied 0 bytes in b        */
288
289        if( possible_subset->nwords > set->nwords )
290        {
291            common = set->nwords ;
292            tail   = possible_subset->nwords - common ;
293        }
294        else
295        {
296            common = possible_subset->nwords;
297            tail   = 0;
298        }
299
```

Listing A.7. continued...

```
300        subsetp = possible_subset->map;
301        setp    = set->map;
302
303        for(; --common >= 0; subsetp++, setp++ )
304            if( (*subsetp & *setp) != *subsetp )
305                return 0;
306
307        while( --tail >= 0 )
308            if( *subsetp++ )
309                return 0;
310
311        return 1;
312    }
```

Listing A.8. *set.c*— Set Manipulation Functions

```
313    PUBLIC void      _set_op( op, dest, src )
314    int      op;
315    SET      *src, *dest;
316    {
317        /* Performs binary operations depending on op:
318         *
319         *  _UNION:        dest = union of src and dest
320         *  _INTERSECT:    dest = intersection of src and dest
321         *  _DIFFERENCE:   dest = symmetric difference of src and dest
322         *  _ASSIGN:       dest = src;
323         *
324         * The sizes of the destination set is adjusted so that it's the same size
325         * as the source set.
326         */
327
328        _SETTYPE    *d;      /* Pointer to destination map   */
329        _SETTYPE    *s;      /* Pointer to map in set1       */
330        unsigned    ssize;   /* # of words in src set        */
331        int         tail;    /* dest set is this much bigger */
332
333        ssize = src->nwords ;
334
335        if( (unsigned)dest->nwords < ssize ) /* Make sure dest set is at least */
336            enlarge( ssize, dest );              /* as big as the src set.        */
337
338        tail = dest->nwords - ssize ;
339        d    = dest->map ;
340        s    = src ->map ;
341
342        switch( op )
343        {
344        case _UNION:        while( --ssize >= 0 )
345                                *d++ |= *s++ ;
346                            break;
347        case _INTERSECT:    while( --ssize >= 0 )
348                                *d++ &= *s++ ;
349                            while( --tail >= 0 )
350                                *d++ = 0;
351                            break;
```

```
Listing A.8. continued...
352        case _DIFFERENCE: while( --ssize >= 0 )
353                              *d++ ^= *s++ ;
354                         break;
355        case _ASSIGN:     while( --ssize >= 0 )
356                              *d++  = *s++ ;
357                         while( --tail >= 0 )
358                              *d++ = 0;
359                         break;
360        }
361   }
362
363   /* ------------------------------------------------------------------ */
364
365   PUBLIC void     invert( set )
366   SET     *set;
367   {
368       /* Physically invert the bits in the set. Compare with the COMPLEMENT()
369        * macro, which just modifies the complement bit.
370        */
371
372       _SETTYPE *p, *end ;
373
374       for( p = set->map, end = p + set->nwords ; p < end ; p++ )
375           *p = ~*p;
376   }
377
378   /* ------------------------------------------------------------------ */
379
380   PUBLIC void     truncate( set )
381   SET     *set;
382   {
383       /* Clears the set but also set's it back to the original, default size.
384        * Compare this routine to the CLEAR() macro which clears all the bits in
385        * the map but doesn't modify the size.
386        */
387
388       if( set->map != set->defmap )
389       {
390           free( set->map );
391           set->map = set->defmap;
392       }
393       set->nwords = _DEFWORDS;
394       set->nbits  = _DEFBITS;
395       memset( set->defmap, 0, sizeof(set->defmap) );
396   }
```

necessary. The work is all done by the **while** loops in the **switch** on lines 342 to 360. It's probably better style to put one **while** statement outside the switch than to put several identical ones in the **case**s, but the latter is more efficient because the **switch** won't have to be re-evaluated on every iteration of the loop. The first **while** loop in every case takes care of all destination elements that correspond to source elements. The maps are processed one word at a time, ORing the words together for union, ANDing them for intersection, XORing them for symmetric difference, and just copying them for assignment. Note that the source set can not be larger than the destination set because of the earlier enlarge() call on line 336.

The second **while** loop in each **case** won't execute if the two sets are the same size, because the tail size will be zero. Otherwise, the destination set is larger and you must do different things to the tail, depending on the operation. Since the missing elements of the smaller set are all implied zeros, the following operations are performed:

union: Do nothing else to the destination because there are no more bits in the source set to add.

intersection: Clear all the bits in the tail of the destination because no bits are set in the source so there's no possibility of intersection.

difference: Do nothing because every bit that's set in the source set will not be set in the destination.

assignment: Set all bits in the tail of the destination to 0 (because the implied bits in the source are all 0).

The invert() subroutine starting on line 365 of Listing A.8 just goes through the map, reversing the sense of the bits. The truncate() function on line 380 restores a set to its initial, empty, condition. This last routine is really a more efficient replacement for:

```
delset( s );
s = newset();
```

You may be better off—in terms of speed—to clear the existing set with CLEAR rather than calling truncate(), because free() is pretty slow.

The final two set routines, which access and print entire sets, are in Listing A.9. The next_member() function on line 397 lets you access all elements of a set sequentially. When the function is called several successive times with the same argument, it returns the next element of the set with each call, or −1 if there are no more elements. Every time the set argument changes, the search for elements starts back at the beginning of the set. Similarly, next_member(NULL) resets the search to the beginning of the set (and does nothing else). You should not put any new elements in the set between a next_member(NULL) call and a subsequent next_member(set) call. Elements should not be added to the set between successive next_member() calls.

Accessing an entire set,
`next_member().`

Listing A.9. *set.c*— Getting Elements and Printing the Set

```
397    PUBLIC int        next_member( set )
398    SET      *set;
399    {
400        /* set == NULL                    Reset
401         * set changed from last call:    Reset and return first element
402         * otherwise                      return next element or -1 if none.
403         */
404
405        static SET    *oset          = NULL;   /* "set" arg in last call            */
406        static int    current_member = 0;      /* last-accessed member of cur. set */
407        _SETTYPE      *map;
408
409        if( !set )
410            return( (int)( oset = NULL ) );
411
412        if( oset != set )
413        {
414            oset              = set;
415            current_member = 0 ;
416
```

Listing A.9. continued...

```
417                for (map = set->map; *map == 0  &&  current_member < set->nbits; ++map)
418                    current_member += _BITS_IN_WORD;
419          }
420
421          /* The increment must be put into the test because, if the TEST() invocation
422           * evaluates true, then an increment on the right of a for() statement
423           * would never be executed.
424           */
425
426          while ( current_member++ < set->nbits )
427              if ( TEST(set, current_member-1) )
428                  return ( current_member-1 );
429          return ( -1 );
430      }
431
432  /* -------------------------------------------------------------------- */
433
434  PUBLIC void      pset ( set, output_routine, param )
435  SET      *set;
436  int      (*output_routine)();
437  void      *param;
438  {
439      /* Print the contents of the set bit map in human-readable form. The
440       * output routine is called for each element of the set with the following
441       * arguments:
442       *
443       * (*out)( param, "null",    -1);   Null set ("set" arg == NULL)
444       * (*out)( param, "empty",   -2);   Empty set (no elements)
445       * (*out)( param, "%d ",      N);   N is an element of the set
446       */
447
448      int i, did_something = 0;
449
450      if ( !set )
451          (*output_routine)( param, "null", -1 );
452      else
453      {
454          next_member( NULL );
455          while ( (i = next_member(set))  >= 0 )
456          {
457              did_something++;
458              ( *output_routine )( param, "%d ", i  );
459          }
460          next_member( NULL );
461
462          if ( !did_something )
463              ( *output_routine )(param, "empty",  -2 );
464      }
465  }
```

A major limitation to next_member() is that calls to next_member on different sets cannot be interspersed. This problem could be solved by putting the current_member counter (declared on line 406) into the SET structure rather than keeping it as a local **static** variable. Since I've never needed this functionality, I didn't want to add the extra overhead needed to support it. The loop on line 417 is skipping initial words in the bit map that are all zeros.

The `pset()` function on line 434 prints all the elements in a set. The standard call:

```
pset( set, fprintf, stdout );
```

prints the elements of the set, separated by space characters, and without a newline at the end of the list. The second argument can actually be a pointer to any function, however. The third argument is just passed to that function, along with a format string. The function is called indirectly through a pointer as follows:

```
(*out)( param, "null",  -1);      For null sets (set is NULL)
(*out)( param, "empty", -2);      For empty set (set has no elements)
(*out)( param, "%d ",    N);      Normally, N is an element of the set
```

Calls to `pset()` and `next_member()` should not be interspersed.

A.3 Database Maintenance—Hashing:

Compilers all need some sort of simple data-base management system. Typically the databases are small enough to fit into memory, so an elaborate file-based system is not only not required, but is contraindicated (because of the excessive access time). Of the various techniques that are available for data management, the most appropriate is the hash table.

The eight functions in this section implement a general-purpose, data-base manager that uses a hash strategy, but you can use these functions without any knowledge of the mechanics of manipulating a hash table. The hash functions are used in Chapter Two, but hashing isn't discussed until Chapter Six. You may want to read that discussion before proceeding. You can also just skim over the the function overviews that follow, skipping over the implementation details until you've read Chapter Six.

Listing A.10 shows a very simple application that creates a database that holds the `argv` entries, and then prints the entries. The details of all the function calls will be discussed in a moment, but to summarize: A single database record is defined with the **typedef** on line nine. An empty database is created on line 55 with a `maketab()` call, which is passed pointers to two auxiliary functions that control database manipulation: The hash function on line 17 translates the key field to a pseudo-random number, here using a shift and exclusive-OR strategy. The comparison function on line 31 does a lexicographic comparison of the key fields of two database records. The `newsym()` call on line 58 allocates space for a new database record, which is put into the database with the `addsym()` call on line 60.

Listing A.10. Program to Demonstrate Hash Functions

```
1   #include <stdio.h>
2   #include <tools/debug.h>
3   #include <tools/hash.h>
4
5   /* A application that demonstrates how to use the basic hash functions. Creates
6    * a database holding the argv strings and then prints the database.
7    */
8
9   typedef struct                    /* A database record */
10  {
11      char *key;
12      int  other_stuff;
13  } ENTRY;
14
```

➡

Listing A.10. continued...

```
15    /*-------------------------------------------------------------------*/
16
17    unsigned hash( sym )                          /* Hash function. Convert the key */
18    ENTRY   *sym;                                 /* to a number.                   */
19    {
20        char *p;
21        int  hash_value = 0;
22
23        for( p = sym->key; *p ; hash_value = (hash_value << 1) ^ *p++ )
24            ;
25
26        return hash_value;
27    }
28
29    /*-------------------------------------------------------------------*/
30
31    int cmp( sym1,  sym2 )                         /* Compare two database records. */
32    ENTRY   *sym1, *sym2;                          /* Works like strcmp().          */
33    {
34        return  strcmp( sym1->key, sym2->key );
35    }
36
37    /*-------------------------------------------------------------------*/
38
39    void print( sym, stream )          /* print a database record to the stream */
40    ENTRY   *sym;
41    FILE    *stream;
42    {
43        fprintf( stream, "%s\n", sym->key );
44    }
45
46    /*-------------------------------------------------------------------*/
47
48    main( argc, argv )
49    int     argc;
50    char    **argv;
51    {
52        HASH_TAB  *tab;
53        ENTRY     *p;
54
55        tab = maketab(31, hash, cmp);                /* make hash table        */
56        for( ++argv, --argc; --argc>=0; ++argv)      /* For each element of argv */
57        {
58            p = (ENTRY *) newsym(sizeof(ENTRY));     /* put it into the table    */
59            p->key = *argv;
60            addsym( tab, p );
61        }
62
63                                                     /* print the table. stdout is  */
64        ptab( tab, print, stdout, 1 );               /* passed through to print().  */
      }
```

Create hash table.

```
#include <tools/hash.h>
HASH_TAB *maketab        (unsigned maxsym, unsigned (*hash)(),
                          unsigned (*cmp)())
```

Make a hash table of the size specified in maxsym. The hash table is a data structure that the manager uses to organize the database entries. It contains a "hash table" array along with various other housekeeping variables. The maxsym argument controls the size of the array component of the data structure, but any number of entries can be put into the table, regardless of the table size. Different table sizes will affect the speed with which a record can be accessed, however. If the table is too small, the search time will be unnecessarily long. Ideally the table should be about the same size as the expected number of table entries. There is no benefit in making the table too large.[3] It's a good idea to make maxsym a prime number[4] Some useful sizes are: 47, 61, 89, 113, 127, 157, 193, 211, 257, 293, 337, 367, 401. If maxsym is zero, 127 is used.

The functions referenced by the two pointer arguments (hash and cmp) are used to manipulate the database. The hash function is called indirectly, like this:

```
(*hash)( sym );
```

where sym is a pointer to a region of memory allocated by newsym(), which is used like malloc() to allocate a new table element. The assumption is that newsym() is getting space for a structure, one field of which is the key. The hash function should return a pseudo-random number, the value of which is controlled by the key; the same key should always generate the same number, but different keys should generate different numbers. The simplest, but by no means the best, hash strategy just adds together the characters in the name. Better methods are discussed in Chapter Six. Two default hash functions are discussed below.

The comparison function (cmp) is passed two pointers to database records. It should compare the key fields and return a value representing the ordering of the keys in a manner analogous to strcmp(). A call to (*cmp)(p1, p2) should return a negative number if the key field in the structure pointed to by p1 is less than the one in *p2. It should return 0 if the two keys are identical, and it should return a positive number if the key in *p2 is greater.

maketab() prints an error message and raises SIGABRT if there's not enough memory. (It works the same way as newset() in this regard.)

Allocate memory for symbol.

```
void *newsym(int size)
```

This routine is used like malloc() to get space for a database record. The returned memory is initialized to zeros. Typically, you use newsym() to allocate a structure, one field of which is the key. The routine prints an error message and raises SIGABRT if there's not enough memory. The pointer returned from newsym() <u>may</u> <u>not</u> be passed to free(); use freesym(), below.

Free memory used by symbol.

```
void freesym(void *sym)
```

This routine frees the memory for a symbol created by a previous newsym()

---

3. You tend to get no fewer collisions in a too-long table. You just get holes.
4. The distribution of elements in the table tends to be better if the table size is prime.

call. You may not use `free()` for this purpose. Do not free symbols that are still in the table—remove them with a `delsym()` call first.

void *addsym(HASH_TAB *tabp, **void** *sym)

Add symbol to table.

Add a symbol to the hash table pointed to by `tabp`—a pointer returned from a previous `maketab()` call. The `sym` argument points at a database record, a pointer to which was returned from a previous `newsym()` call. You must initialize the key field of that record prior to the `addsym()` call.

void *findsym(HASH_TAB *tabp, **void** *sym)

Find symbol in table.

Return either a pointer to a previously-inserted database record or `NULL` if the record isn't in the database. If more than one entry for a given key is in the database, the most recently added one is found. The `sym` argument is used to identify the record for which you're searching. It is not used directly by `findsym()`, but is passed to the hash and comparison functions. The comparison function is called as follows:

```
(*cmp)(sym, item_in_table);
```

Here, `item_in_table` is a pointer to an arbitrary database element, and `sym` is just the second argument to `findsym()`.

Strictly speaking, `sym` should be a pointer to an initialized database record returned from `newsym()`. It's inconvenient, though, to allocate and initialize a structure just to pass it to `findsym()`. You can get around the problem in one common situation. If the `key` field is a character array, and that array is the first field in the structure, you can pass a character-string name to `findsym()` as the `key`. This is a hack, but is nonetheless useful. The technique is illustrated in Listing A.11. This technique works only if the key is a character array—the string must be physically present as the first few bytes of the structure. Character pointers won't work. Note that `strcmp()` is used as the comparison function. This works only because the array is at the top of the structure, so the structure pointer passed to `strcmp` is also the address of the key array.

Simplifying `findsym()` calls by subterfuge.

void delsym(HASH_TAB *tabp, **void** *sym)

Remove symbol from table.

Remove a symbol from the hash table, a pointer to which was returned by a previous `findsym()` call. `sym` is the pointer returned from `findsym()` and `tabp` is a pointer returned from `maketab()`. The record is removed from the table, but the associated memory is not freed, so you can recycle it—you can reinitialize the record and reinsert it into the table at a later time. Use `freesym()` to free the memory used by `sym`—you may not use `free()` for this purpose. It's a serious error to delete a symbol that isn't actually in the table—`addsym()` must have been called for a node before `delsym()` can be called.

void *nextsym(HASH_TAB *tabp, **void** *last)

Get next symbol.

This function finds all references to objects in a table that have the same name. The first such object is found by `find_sym()`. The second object is found by passing the pointer returned from `find_sym()` to nextsym(), which returns either a pointer to the next object or `NULL` if there are no such objects. Use it like this:

Listing A.11. Fooling `findsym()`

```
1    typedef struct
2    {
3        char   name[ SIZE ];          /* must be first, and must be an array */
4        int    other_stuff;
5    } ENTRY;
6
7    hash( key )
8    char *key;
9    {
10       int   i = 0;                   /* Add together characters in the name    */
11       while( *key )                  /* use a left shift to randomize the number */
12           i += *key++ << 1 ;
13   }
14
15   ignaz()
16   {
17       HASH_TAB    *tab;
18       extern      hash_add();       /* hash function */
19       extern      strcmp();
20       ENTRY       *p;
21       . . .
22       tab = maketab( 61, hash, strcmp );
23       . . .
24       p = findsym( Tab, "krazy" );
25   }
```

```
        p = findsym( Tab, "krazy" );    /* Get the first one. */
          ...
        if( !(p = nextsym(Tab, p)) )    /* Get the next  one. */
            /* no more symbols */
```

Third and subsequent objects are found by passing `nextsym()` the value returned from the previous `nextsym()` call.

Print entire database.

```
int ptab(HASH_TAB *tabp, void (*print)(), void *param,
         int sort)
```

Print all records in the database represented by the hash table pointed to by `tabp`. The function pointed to by `print` is called for every element of the table as follows:

```
    (*print)( sym, param )
```

If `sort` is false, the table elements are printed in random order and 1 is always returned. If `sort` is true, the table is printed only if the routine can get memory to sort the table. Zero is returned (and nothing is printed) if memory isn't available, otherwise 1 is returned and the table is printed in order controlled by the comparison function passed to `maketab()`. If this comparison function works as described earlier, the table is printed in ascending order. Reverse the sense of the return value to print in descending order. In the current example, you can change the comparison function as follows, reversing the arguments to `strcmp()`:

```
cmp( a, b )                        /* Print in descending order */
ENTRY *a, *b;
{
    return strcmp( b->key, a->key );
}
```

```
unsigned hash_add(char *name);
unsigned hash_pjw(char *name);
```

These two functions are hash functions that you can pass to maketab(). They are passed character strings and return a pseudo-random integer generated from that string. hash_add() just adds the character in the name—it's fast but doesn't work well if the table size is larger than 128 or if keys are likely to be permutations of each other. The hash_pjw() function uses a shift-and-exclusive-OR algorithm that yields better results at the cost of execution speed. As with findsym(), if the table entries have a character-array key at the top of the structure, these functions can be used directly by maketab(),

```
typedef struct
{
    char key[ 80 ];
    int stuff;
}
ENTRY;
...
    maketab(..., hash_pjw, ...);
```

Otherwise, you'll have to encapsulate the hash function inside a second function like this:

```
typedef struct
{
    int stuff;
    char *key;
}
ENTRY;

hash_funct( sym )
ENTRY         *sym;
{
    return hash_add( sym->key );
}
...
    maketab(..., hash_funct, ...);
```

A.3.1 Hashing—Implementation

I've used data abstraction extensively in the package presented here. That is, the mechanics of manipulating the database is hidden from the user of the routines. For example, the user calls one function to allocate a data-base block of an arbitrary size in a manner similar to malloc(). The block is then modified as necessary, and it's inserted into the database with a second function call. The mechanics of allocating space, of doing the insertion, and so forth, are hidden in the functions. Similarly, the internal data structures used for database maintenance are also hidden. This abstraction makes these routines quite flexible. Not only can you use them in disparate applications, but you can change the way that the database is maintained. As long as the subroutine-call interface is the same, you don't have to change anything in the application program.

The hash functions work with two data structures. I'll look at the C definitions and allocation functions first, and then describe how they work.

A hash-table element,
BUCKET, newsym().

The first structure is the BUCKET, declared in *hash.h*, (the start of which is in Listing A.12). The newsym() function, (in Listing A.12) allocates a BUCKET along with the memory requested by the user. newsym() simultaneously allocates enough memory for both the BUCKET header, and for a user space, the size of which is passed in as a parameter. It returns a pointer to the area just below the header, which can be used in any way by the application program:

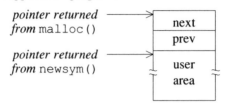

Listing A.12. *hash.h*— The BUCKET

```
1   typedef struct BUCKET
2   {
3       struct BUCKET           *next;
4       struct BUCKET           **prev;
5
6   } BUCKET;
```

Listing A.13. *hash.c*— BUCKET Allocation

```
9    PUBLIC void *newsym( size )
10   int      size;
11   {
12       /* Allocate space for a new symbol; return a pointer to the user space. */
13
14       BUCKET     *sym;
15
16       if( !(sym = (BUCKET *) calloc( size + sizeof(BUCKET), 1)) )
17       {
18           fprintf( stderr, "Can't get memory for BUCKET\n" );
19           raise( SIGABRT );
20           return NULL;
21       }
22       return (void *)( sym + 1 );              /* return pointer to user space */
23   }
24
25   /*-------------------------------------------------------------------*/
26
27   PUBLIC void freesym( sym )
28   void     *sym;
29   {
30       free( (BUCKET *)sym - 1 );
31   }
```

Freeing BUCKETs,
freesym().

The freesym() function, also in Listing A.13, frees the memory allocated by a previous newsym(). It just backs up the sym pointer to its original position and then calls free().

The hash table itself,
HASH_TAB.

The second data structure of interest is the HASH_TAB which holds the actual hash table itself. (It's declared in Listing A.14.) Like a BUCKET, it's a structure of variable length. The header contains the table size in elements (size), the number of entries currently in the table (numsyms), pointers to the hash and comparison functions (hash and cmp), and the table itself (table is the first element of the table). The numsyms field is used only for statistical purposes—it's not needed by any of the hash-table functions.

The maketab() function (in Listing A.15) allocates a single chunk of memory big enough to hold both the header and an additional area that will be used as the array. The table is declared as a one-element array, but the array can actually be any size, provided that there's enough available memory following the header. I'm taking advantage of the fact that C doesn't do array-boundary checking when the array is accessed.

Making a hash table, maketab().

Listing A.14. *hash.h—* HASH_TAB Definition

```
7    typedef struct  hash_tab_
8    {
9        int        size      ;      /* Max number of elements in table       */
10       int        numsyms  ;       /* number of elements currently in table */
11       unsigned (*hash)();          /* hash function                         */
12       int        (*cmp)()  ;      /* comparison funct, cmp(name,bucket_p); */
13       BUCKET    *table[1];          /* First element of actual hash table    */
14
15   } HASH_TAB;
```

Listing A.15. *hash.c—* HASH_TAB Allocation

```
32   PUBLIC HASH_TAB *maketab( maxsym, hash_function, cmp_function )
33   unsigned          maxsym;
34   unsigned          (*hash_function)();
35   int               (*cmp_function)();
36   {
37       /*  Make a hash table of the indicated size.  */
38
39       HASH_TAB  *p;
40
41       if( !maxsym )
42           maxsym = 127;
43                              /*   |<--- space for table ---->|<- and header -->| */
44       if( p=(HASH_TAB*) calloc(1,(maxsym * sizeof(BUCKET*)) + sizeof(HASH_TAB)) )
45       {
46           p->size    = maxsym     ;
47           p->numsyms = 0          ;
48           p->hash    = hash_function ;
49           p->cmp     = cmp_function  ;
50       }
51       else
52       {
53           fprintf(stderr, "Insufficient memory for symbol table\n");
54           raise( SIGABRT );
55           return NULL;
56       }
57       return p;
58   }
```

These two structures interact as shown in Figure A.1. The actual table is an array of BUCKET pointers. Empty table elements are set to NULL, and new BUCKETs are tacked onto the head of the list.

BUCKETs in a HASH_TAB.

Figure A.1. A Hash Table with Two Elements in It

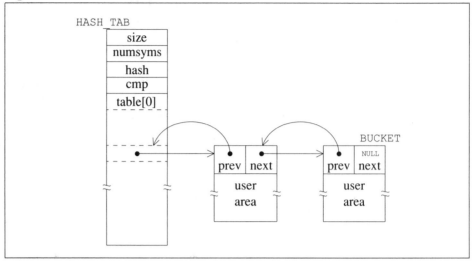

Adding symbols to the
table, addsym().

The addsym() function, which puts items into the table, is in Listing A.16. A pointer to the current hash-table element, p, is initialized on line 68 by calling the hash function indirectly through the hash pointer in the HASH_TAB header. Note that the BUCKET pointer (sym) comes into the routine pointing at the user area. It is decremented to point at the BUCKET header on line 68 after the hash function is called. The code on lines 70 to 73 link the new node to the head of a chain found at the previously computed array element.

Listing A.16. *hash.c*— Adding a Symbol to the Table

```
59   PUBLIC void *addsym( tabp, isym )
60   HASH_TAB *tabp;
61   void     *isym;
62   {
63       /* Add a symbol to the hash table.  */
64
65       BUCKET    **p, *tmp ;
66       BUCKET    *sym = (BUCKET *)isym;
67
68       p = & (tabp->table)[ (*tabp->hash)( sym-- ) % tabp->size ];
69
70       tmp       = *p  ;
71       *p        = sym ;
72       sym->prev = p   ;
73       sym->next = tmp ;
74
75       if( tmp )
76           tmp->prev = &sym->next ;
77
78       tabp->numsyms++;
79       return (void *)(sym + 1);
80   }
```

BUCKETs form a doubly
linked list, backwards
pointers.

Note that the chain of BUCKETs is a doubly-linked list. You need the backwards pointers to delete an arbitrary element in the table without having to search for that element. The only obscure point is the two stars in the definition of the backwards pointer—the forward pointer (next) is a pointer to a BUCKET, but the backwards pointer (prev) is a pointer to a BUCKET <u>pointer</u>. You need this extra level of indirection because the head of the chain is a simple pointer, not an entire BUCKET structure. The backwards pointer for the leftmost node in the chain points at the head-of-chain pointer. All other backwards pointers hold the address of the *next* field from the previous node.

You can see the utility of this system by looking at the code necessary to delete an arbitrary node. Say that you want to delete the node pointed to by p in the following picture:

Deleting a BUCKET from the table, delsym().

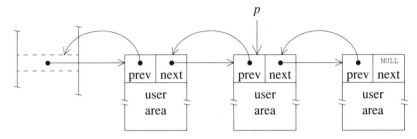

The removal can be accomplished with the following statement:

```
if(   *(p->prev) = p->next   )
     p->next->prev = p->prev ;
```

The pointer from the previous node (the one that points at the node to delete) is modified first so that it points around the deleted node. Then the backwards pointer from the next node is adjusted. The **if** is required because the next pointer is NULL on the last node in the chain. The double indirection on the backwards pointer makes this code work regardless of the position of the node in the chain—the first and last nodes are not special cases. The delsym() function, which removes an arbitrary node from the tree, is shown in Listing A.17.

Listing A.17. *hash.c*— Removing A Node From The Table

```
81   PUBLIC  void      delsym( tabp, isym )
82   HASH_TAB *tabp;
83   void      *isym;
84   {
85       /*  Remove a symbol from the hash table. "sym" is a pointer returned from
86        *  a previous findsym() call. It points initially at the user space, but
87        *  is decremented to get at the BUCKET header.
88        */
89
90       BUCKET   *sym = (BUCKET *)isym;
91
92       if( tabp && sym )
93       {
94           --tabp->numsyms;
95           --sym;
96
97           if(   *(sym->prev) = sym->next   )
98                sym->next->prev = sym->prev ;
99       }
100  }
```

Finding symbols,
findsym(), nextsym(). The two symbol-finding functions, findsym() and nextsym(), are in Listing A.18. findsym() just hashes to the correct place in the table and then chases down the chain, looking for the required node. It returns a pointer to the user area of the BUCKET (thus the +1 on line 119), or NULL if it can't find the required node. nextsym() just continues chasing down the same chain, starting where the last search left off.

Listing A.18. *hash.c*— Finding a Symbol

```
101    PUBLIC void      *findsym( tabp, sym )
102    HASH_TAB         *tabp;
103    void             *sym;
104    {
105        /*  Return a pointer to the hash table element having a particular name
106         *  or NULL if the name isn't in the table.
107         */
108
109        BUCKET      *p ;
110
111        if( !tabp )          /* Table empty */
112            return NULL;
113
114        p = (tabp->table)[ (*tabp->hash)(sym) % tabp->size ];
115
116        while(  p  &&  (*tabp->cmp)( sym, p+1 )  )
117                p = p->next;
118
119        return (void *)( p ? p + 1 : NULL );
120    }
121
122    /*-----------------------------------------------------------------------*/
123
124    PUBLIC void     *nextsym( tabp, i_last )
125    HASH_TAB *tabp;
126    void        *i_last;
127    {
128        /* Return a pointer the next node in the current chain that has the same
129         * key as the last node found (or NULL if there is no such node). "last"
130         * is a pointer returned from a previous findsym() of nextsym() call.
131         */
132
133        BUCKET *last = (BUCKET *)i_last;
134
135        for(--last; last->next ; last = last->next )
136                if( (tabp->cmp)(last+1, last->next +1) == 0 )    /* keys match */
137                        return (char *)( last->next + 1 );
138        return NULL;
139    }
```

Printing the entire data-
base: ptab(). The last of the support functions is ptab(), which prints the table. It starts on line 142 of Listing A.19. The loop on lines 166 to 173 prints the table in the most straightforward manner. The outer loop goes through the table from top to bottom looking for chains. The inner loop traverses the chain, calling the print function indirectly at each node.

The **else** clause on lines 177 to 214 handles sorted arrays. It allocates an array of BUCKET pointers on line 184 and initializes the array to point at every BUCKET in the table with the loop starting on line 189. (This is essentially the same loop that printed the unsorted array). The new array is sorted on line 208 using assort(), a variant of

Listing A.19. *hash.c*— Printing the Table

```
140    PRIVATE int        (*User_cmp)();
141
142    PUBLIC int ptab( tabp, print, param, sort )
143    HASH_TAB      *tabp;          /* Pointer to the table            */
144    void          (* print)();    /* Print function used for output  */
145    void          *param;         /* Parameter passed to print function */
146    int           sort;           /* Sort the table if true.         */
147    {
148        /* Return 0 if a sorted table can't be printed because of insufficient
149         * memory, else return 1 if the table was printed. The print function
150         * is called with two arguments:
151         *          (*print)( sym, param )
152         *
153         * Sym is a pointer to a BUCKET user area and param is the third
154         * argument to ptab.
155         */
156
157        BUCKET      **outtab, **outp, *sym, **symtab ;
158        int         internal_cmp();
159        int         i;
160
161        if( !tabp  ||  tabp->size == 0 )    /* Table is empty */
162            return 1;
163
164        if( !sort )
165        {
166            for( symtab = tabp->table, i = tabp->size ;  --i >= 0 ;  symtab++ )
167            {
168                /* Print all symbols in the current chain. The +1 in the print call
169                 * increments the pointer to the applications area of the bucket.
170                 */
171                for( sym = *symtab ; sym ; sym = sym->next )
172                    (*print)( sym+1, param );
173            }
174        }
175        else
176        {
177            /*      Allocate memory for the outtab, an array of pointers to
178             *      BUCKETs, and initialize it. The outtab is different from
179             *      the actual hash table in that every outtab element points
180             *      to a single BUCKET structure, rather than to a linked list
181             *      of them.
182             */
183
184            if( !( outtab = (BUCKET **) malloc(tabp->numsyms * sizeof(BUCKET*)) ))
185                return 0;
186
187            outp = outtab;
188
189            for( symtab = tabp->table, i = tabp->size ;  --i >= 0 ;  symtab++ )
190                for( sym = *symtab ; sym ; sym = sym->next )
191                {
192                    if( outp > outtab + tabp->numsyms )
193                    {
194                        fprintf(stderr,"Internal error [ptab], table overflow\n");
195                        exit(1);
196                    }
197
```

Listing A.19. continued...

```
198                      *outp++ = sym;
199                }
200
201           /*        Sort the outtab and then print it. The (*outp)+1 in the
202            *        print call increments the pointer past the header part
203            *        of the BUCKET structure. During sorting, the increment
204            *        is done in internal_cmp.
205            */
206
207           User_cmp = tabp->cmp;
208           assort( outtab, tabp->numsyms, sizeof( BUCKET* ), internal_cmp );
209
210           for( outp = outtab, i = tabp->numsyms; --i >= 0 ;  outp++ )
211                (*print)( (*outp)+1, param );
212
213           free( outtab );
214      }
215      return 1;
216 }
217
218 PRIVATE int internal_cmp( p1, p2 )
219 BUCKET **p1, **p2;
220 {
221      (*User_cmp)( *p1 + 1, *p2 + 1 );
222 }
```

the UNIX qsort() function that uses a Shell sort rather than a quicksort. (It's discussed later on in this appendix.) The sorted array is printed by the loop on line 210.

The sorting is complicated because, though the comparison function must be passed two pointers to the user areas of buckets, assort() passes the sort function two pointers to array elements. That is, assort() passes two pointers to BUCKET pointers to the comparison function. The problem is solved by putting a layer around the user-supplied comparison function. assort() calls internal_cmp(), declared on line 218, which strips off one level of indirection and adjusts the BUCKET pointer to point at the user space before calling the user-supplied function. The user's comparison functions must be passed by a global variable (User_cmp, declared on line 140).

Finishing up with the hash-table functions themselves, remainder of *hash.h* contains various function prototypes—it's shown in Listing A.20. Similarly, there are a bunch of **#include**s at the top of *hash.c*, shown in Listing A.21.

Listing A.20. *hash.h*— HASH_TAB Function Prototypes

```
16   extern HASH_TAB *maketab P(( unsigned maxsym, unsigned (*hash)(), int (*cmp)()));
17   extern void     *newsym  P(( int size ));
18   extern void     freesym  P(( void *sym ));
19   extern void     *addsym  P(( HASH_TAB *tabp, void *sym ));
20   extern void     *findsym P(( HASH_TAB *tabp, void *sym ));
21   extern void     *nextsym P(( HASH_TAB *tabp, void *last ));
22   extern void     delsym   P(( HASH_TAB *tabp, void *sym ));
23   extern int      ptab     P(( HASH_TAB *tabp, void(*prnt)(), void *par, int srt));
24   unsigned hash_add        P(( unsigned char *name ));      /* in hashadd.c */
25   unsigned hash_pjw        P(( unsigned char *name ));      /* in hashpjw.c */
```

Listing A.21. *hash.c*—**#include**s

```
1    #include <stdio.h>
2    #include <ctype.h>
3    #include <signal.h>
4    #include <stdlib.h>
5    #include <string.h>
6    #include <tools/debug.h>
7    #include <tools/hash.h>
```

A.3.2 Two Hash Functions

Implementations of the two default hash functions discussed in Chapter Six are shown in Listings A.22 and A.23.

Listing A.22. *hashadd.c*— An Addition-Based Hash Function

```
1    #include <tools/debug.h>
2    #include <tools/hash.h>
3    /*-------------------------------------------------------------------
4     * Hash function for use with the functions in hash.c. Just adds together
5     * characters in the name.
6     */
7
8    unsigned hash_add( name )
9    unsigned char   *name;
10   {
11       unsigned h ;
12
13       for( h = 0;   *name ;   h += *name++ )
14                ;
15       return h;
16   }
```

I've modified Aho's version of *hash_pjw* considerably in order to make it portable— the original version assumed that the target machine had a 32-bit **unsigned int**. All the macros on lines four to seven of Listing A.23 are for this purpose. NBITS_IN_UNSIGNED evaluates to the number of bits in an **unsigned int**, using the NBITS macro from *<tools/debug.h>*. You could also use the ANSI CHAR_BIT macro (defined in *limits.h*) and multiply it by eight, but that's risky because a **char** might not be eight bits wide. SEVENTY_FIVE_PERCENT evaluates to the number of bits required to isolate the bottom ¾ of the number. Given a 16-bit **int**, it will evaluate to 12. TWELVE_PERCENT works the same way, but it gets ⅛ of the number—2, given a 16-bit **int**. HIGH_BITS is a mask that isolates the bits in the top ⅛ of the number—it's 0x3fff for a 16-bit **int**.

Implementing hash_pjw().

Note that most of the computation in the macros is folded out of existence by the optimizer (because everything's a constant, so the arithmetic can be performed at compile time). For example:

```
h ^= g >> (int)((sizeof(unsigned) * CHAR_BIT) * .75 );
```

generates the following code with Microsoft C, version 5.0:

Listing A.23. *hashpjw.c*— The *hashpjw* Function

```
 1   #include <tools/debug.h>
 2   #include <tools/hash.h>          /* for prototypes only */
 3
 4   #define NBITS_IN_UNSIGNED        (        NBITS(unsigned int)        )
 5   #define SEVENTY_FIVE_PERCENT     ((int)( NBITS_IN_UNSIGNED * .75  ))
 6   #define TWELVE_PERCENT           ((int)( NBITS_IN_UNSIGNED * .125 ))
 7   #define HIGH_BITS                ( ~( (unsigned)(~0) >> TWELVE_PERCENT)   )
 8
 9   unsigned hash_pjw( name )
10   unsigned char    *name;
11   {
12       unsigned h = 0;                        /* Hash value */
13       unsigned g;
14
15       for(; *name ; ++name )
16       {
17           h = (h << TWELVE_PERCENT) + *name ;
18           if( g = h & HIGH_BITS )
19               h = (h ^ (g >> SEVENTY_FIVE_PERCENT)) & ~HIGH_BITS ;
20       }
21       return h;
22   }
```

```
    mov     cl,12
    shr     ax,cl
    xor     dx,ax
```

Similarly:

```
    g = h & ~( (unsigned)(~0) >> ((int)(NBITS_IN_UNSIGNED * .125)))
```

becomes:

```
    mov     dx,ax
    and     ax,-16384
```

If you modify these constants, don't convert the floating-point numbers to fractions, or else they'll end up as zero. For example, (NBITS_IN_UNSIGNED * (1/8)) won't work because the 1/8 will evaluate to 0 (integer arithmetic is used).

The algorithm uses a shift-and-XOR strategy to randomize the input key. The main iteration of the loop shifts the accumulated hash value to the left by a few bits and adds in the current character. When the number gets too large, it is randomized by XORing it with a shifted version of itself.

A.4 The ANSI Variable-Argument Mechanism

This book uses the ANSI-approved method of supporting subroutines with a variable number of arguments, which uses various macros declared in <*stdarg.h*>, for this purpose. Since not all C environments support <*stdarg.h*>, this section presents a version of the macros in this file. Before looking at <*stdarg.h*> itself, however, the following subroutine demonstrates how the macros are used. The print_int subroutine is passed an argument count followed by an arbitrary number of **int**-sized arguments, and it prints those arguments.[5]

Using the <stdarg.h> macros.

```
print_int( arg_count, ... )
int    arg_count;
{
    va_list args;

    va_start( args, arg_count );

    while( --arg_count >= 0 )
      printf( "%d ", va_arg(args, int) );

    va_end( args );
}
```

The args variable is a pointer to the argument list. It is initialized to point at the <u>second</u> argument in the list with the va_start() call, which is passed the argument pointer (args) and the name of the first argument (arg_count). This first argument can be accessed directly in the normal way—the va_arg() macro is used to get the others. This macro is passed the argument pointer, and the expected type of the argument. It evaluates to the current argument, and advances the argument pointer to the next one. In this case, the arguments are all **int**s, but they would be different types in an application like printf(). The va_end() macro tells the system that there are no more arguments to get (that the argument pointer has advanced to the end of the list).

> Start up variable-argument processing, va_start().

> Get arguments, va_arg().

> End variable-argument processing, va_end().

The foregoing is implemented in *<stdarg.h>*, shown in Listing A.24. The argument-pointer type, va_list, is a pointer to **char**. It's declared as such because pointer arithmetic on a character pointer is just plain arithmetic. When you add 1 to a character pointer, you actually add 1 to the physical pointer (because the size of a character is 1). The best way to understand the other two macros is to watch them work. A typical C compiler passes arguments to subroutines by pushing them onto the run-time stack in reverse order. A call like

> va_list, implemented as **char***.

```
int    me,
long   Ishmael;

call( me, Ishmael );
```

looks like this on the stack (assuming a 16-bit **int** and a 32-bit **long**):

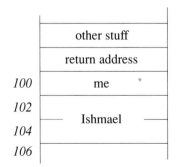

The va_start(me, arg_ptr); macro initializes arg_ptr to point at the second argument as follows: &first evaluates to the address of me—to 100—and 100+**sizeof**(first) yields 102, the base address of the next argument on the stack.

> Implementing va_start().

---

5. Note that the ellipsis in the print_int() argument list is not supported by UNIX C. The VA_LIST macro in *<debug.h>*, discussed on page 684, can be used to correct this deficiency. VA_LIST is used in various subroutines in subsequent sections.

Listing A.24. *stdarg.h*— Support for Variable-Argument Lists

```
1   typedef char *va_list;
2   #define va_start(arg_ptr,first)  arg_ptr = (va_list)&first + sizeof(first)
3   #define va_arg(arg_ptr,type)     ((type *)(arg_ptr += sizeof(type)))[-1]
4   #define va_end(arg_ptr)          /* empty */
```

Implementing va_arg().

The cast is required in front of &first in order to defeat pointer arithmetic; otherwise you'd get 104, because &first evaluates to an **int** pointer by default. A subsequent va_arg(arg_ptr,long) call will fetch Ishmael and advance the pointer. It expands to:

```
    ((long *)(arg_ptr += sizeof(long)))[-1]
```

The arg_ptr += **sizeof**(long) yields 106 in this example. That is, it yields a pointer just past the variable that you want. The (**long** *)(106) is treated as if it were a pointer to an array of longs that had been initialized to point at cell 106, and the [-1] gets the **long**-sized number in front of the pointer. You could think of the whole thing like this:

```
long      *p;

p = (long *)arg_ptr;        /* pointer to current argument  */
++p;                        /* skip past it                 */
target  = p[-1];            /* fetch it by backing up.      */
arg_ptr += sizeof(long);    /* skip to next argument        */
```

Note that some non-ANSI compilers can do the foregoing with:

```
    * ((long *)arg_ptr) ++
```

but this statement isn't acceptable to many compilers (because the cast forms an rvalue, and ++ must be applied to an lvalue).

A.5 Conversion Functions

This section contains descriptions of several small data-conversion subroutines:

Convert string to long.

```
long           stol (char **str)
unsigned long  stoul(char **str)
```

These routines are somewhat more powerful versions of the standard atoi(). stol() is passed the address of a character pointer (note the double indirection). It returns, in a long, the value of the number represented by the string, and updates the pointer to point past the number. If the string begins with a 0x, the number is assumed to be hex; otherwise, if it begins with a 0, the number is assumed to be octal; otherwise it is decimal. Conversion stops on encountering the first character that is not a digit in the indicated radix. Leading white space is ignored, and a leading minus sign is recognized. stoul() works much the same, except that it returns an **unsigned long**, and doesn't recognize a leading minus sign.

Translate escape sequences to binary.

```
int esc(char **s)
```

Returns the character associated with the "escape sequence" pointed to by *s and modifies *s to point past the sequence. The recognized strings are summarized in Table A.1.

Table A.1. Escape Sequences Recognized by `esc()`

Input string	Returned value	Notes
\b	0x08	Backspace.
\f	0x0c	Formfeed.
\n	0x0a	Newline.
\r	0x0d	Carriage return.
\s	0x20	Space.
\t	0x09	Horizontal tab.
\e	0x1b	ASCII ESC character.
DDD	0x??	Number formed of 1–3 octal digits.
\x*DD*	0x??	Number formed of 1–3 hex digits.
\^*C*	0x??	*C* is any letter. The equivalent control code is returned.
\c	c	a backslash followed by anything else returns the character following the backslash (and `*s` is advanced two characters).
c	c	Characters not preceded by a backslash are just returned (and `*s` is advanced 1 character).

`char` *bin_to_ascii(**int** c, **int** use_hex)

Convert binary to printing ASCII.

Return a pointer to a string that represents c in human-readable form. This string contains only the character itself for normal characters; it holds an escape sequence (\n, \t, \x00, and so forth) for others. A single quote (') is returned as the two-character string "\'". The returned string is destroyed the next time bin_to_ascii() is called, so don't call it twice in a single printf() statement. If use_hex is true then escape sequences of the form \xDD are used for nonstandard control characters (*D* is a hex digit); otherwise, sequences of the form \DDD are used (*D* is an octal digit).

stoul() and stol() are implemented in Listing A.25. The esc() subroutine is in Listing A.26, and bin_to_ascii() is in Listing A.26 All are commented sufficiently that no additional description is needed here.

Implementing esc().

Listing A.25. *stol.c*— Convert String-to-Long

```
 1    #include <ctype.h>
 2
 3    unsigned long    stoul(instr)
 4    char      **instr;
 5    {
 6        /*  Convert string to long. If string starts with 0x it is interpreted as
 7         *  a hex number, else if it starts with a 0 it is octal, else it is
 8         *  decimal. Conversion stops on encountering the first character which is
 9         *  not a digit in the indicated radix. *instr is updated to point past the
10         *  end of the number.
11         */
12
13        unsigned long num  = 0 ;
14        char             *str = *instr;
15
16        while( isspace(*str) )
17            ++*str ;
18
```

Listing A.25. continued...

```
19          if(*str != '0')
20          {
21              while( isdigit(*str) )
22                  num = (num * 10) + (*str++ - '0');
23          }
24          else
25          {
26              if (*++str == 'x'  ||  *str == 'X')                    /* hex  */
27              {
28                  for( ++str; isxdigit(*str); ++str )
29                      num = (num * 16) + ( isdigit(*str) ? *str - '0'
30                                                         : toupper(*str) - 'A' + 10 );
31              }
32              else
33              {
34                  while( '0' <= *str  &&  *str <= '7' )         /* octal */
35                  {
36                      num *= 8;
37                      num += *str++ - '0' ;
38                  }
39              }
40          }
41          *instr = str;
42          return( num );
43      }
44
45      /*----------------------------------------------------------------------*/
46
47      long    stol(instr)
48      char    **instr;
49      {
50          /* Like stoul(), but recognizes a leading minus sign and returns a signed
51           * long.
52           */
53
54          while( isspace(**instr) )
55              ++*instr ;
56
57          if( **instr != '-' )
58              return (long)( stoul(instr) );
59          else
60          {
61              ++*instr;                                    /* Skip the minus sign. */
62              return -(long)( stoul(instr) );
63          }
64      }
```

Listing A.26. *esc.c*— Map Escape Sequences to Binary

```
1      #include <stdio.h>
2      #include <ctype.h>
3      #include <tools/debug.h>
4
5      /* ESC.C          Map escape sequences to single characters */
6
```

Listing A.26. continued...

```
 7  PRIVATE int hex2bin P(( int c ));
 8  PRIVATE int oct2bin P(( int c ));
 9  /*------------------------------------------------------------*/
10
11  #define ISHEXDIGIT(x)  (isdigit(x)||('a'<=(x)&&(x)<='f')||('A'<=(x)&&(x)<='F'))
12  #define ISOCTDIGIT(x)  ('0'<=(x) && (x)<='7')
13
14  PRIVATE int hex2bin(c)
15  int     c;
16  {
17      /* Convert the hex digit represented by 'c' to an int. 'c' must be one of
18       * the following characters: 0123456789abcdefABCDEF
19       */
20      return (isdigit(c) ? (c)-'0': ((toupper(c))-'A')+10)  & 0xf;
21  }
22
23  PRIVATE int oct2bin(c)
24  int     c;
25  {
26      /* Convert the hex digit represented by 'c' to an int. 'c' must be a
27       * digit in the range '0'-'7'.
28       */
29      return ( ((c)-'0')  & 0x7 );
30  }
31
32  /*------------------------------------------------------------*/
33
34  PUBLIC  int     esc(s)
35  char    **s;
36  {
37      /* Map escape sequences into their equivalent symbols. Return the equivalent
38       * ASCII character. *s is advanced past the escape sequence. If no escape
39       * sequence is present, the current character is returned and the string
40       * is advanced by one. The following are recognized:
41       *
42       * \b       backspace
43       * \f       formfeed
44       * \n       newline
45       * \r       carriage return
46       * \s       space
47       * \t       tab
48       * \e       ASCII ESC character ('\033')
49       * \DDD     number formed of 1-3 octal digits
50       * \xDDD    number formed of 1-3 hex digits (two required)
51       * \^C      C = any letter. Control code
52       */
53
54      register int        rval;
55
56      if( **s != '\\' )
57          rval = *( (*s)++ );
58      else
59      {
60          ++(*s);                                     /* Skip the \ */
61          switch( toupper(**s) )
62          {
63          case '\0':  rval = '\\';                 break;
64          case 'B':   rval = '\b' ;                break;
```

```
Listing A.26. continued...
65              case 'F':    rval = '\f' ;                    break;
66              case 'N':    rval = '\n' ;                    break;
67              case 'R':    rval = '\r' ;                    break;
68              case 'S':    rval = ' ' ;                     break;
69              case 'T':    rval = '\t' ;                    break;
70              case 'E':    rval = '\033';                   break;
71
72              case '^':    rval = *++(*s) ;
73                           rval = toupper(rval) - '@' ;
74                           break;
75
76              case 'X':    rval = 0;
77                           ++(*s);
78                           if( ISHEXDIGIT(**s) )
79                           {
80                               rval  = hex2bin( *(*s)++ );
81                           }
82                           if( ISHEXDIGIT(**s) )
83                           {
84                               rval <<= 4;
85                               rval  |= hex2bin( *(*s)++ );
86                           }
87                           if( ISHEXDIGIT(**s) )
88                           {
89                               rval <<= 4;
90                               rval  |= hex2bin( *(*s)++ );
91                           }
92                           --(*s);
93                           break;
94
95              default:     if( !ISOCTDIGIT(**s) )
96                               rval = **s;
97                           else
98                           {
99                               ++(*s);
100                              rval = oct2bin( *(*s)++ );
101                              if( ISOCTDIGIT(**s) )
102                              {
103                                  rval <<= 3;
104                                  rval  |= oct2bin( *(*s)++ );
105                              }
106                              if( ISOCTDIGIT(**s) )
107                              {
108                                  rval <<= 3;
109                                  rval  |= oct2bin( *(*s)++ );
110                              }
111                              --(*s);
112                          }
113                          break;
114         }
115         ++(*s);
116     }
117     return rval;
118 }
```

Listing A.27. *bintoasc.c*— Convert Binary to Human-Readable String

```
 1   #include <stdio.h>
 2   #include <tools/debug.h>
 3   #include <tools/compiler.h>        /* for prototypes only */
 4
 5   char    *bin_to_ascii( c, use_hex )
 6   {
 7       /* Return a pointer to a string that represents c. This will be the
 8        * character itself for normal characters and an escape sequence (\n, \t,
 9        * \x00, etc., for most others). A ' is represented as \'. The string will
10        * be destroyed the next time bin_to_ascii() is called. If "use_hex" is true
11        * then \xDD escape sequences are used. Otherwise, octal sequences (\DDD)
12        * are used. (see also: pchar.c)
13        */
14
15       static unsigned char buf[8];
16
17       c &= 0xff ;
18       if( ' ' <= c  &&  c < 0x7f  &&  c != '\'' && c != '\\')
19       {
20           buf[0] = c;
21           buf[1] = '\0';
22       }
23       else
24       {
25           buf[0] = '\\' ;
26           buf[2] = '\0' ;
27
28           switch(c)
29           {
30           case '\\': buf[1] = '\\'; break;
31           case '\'': buf[1] = '\''; break;
32           case '\b': buf[1] = 'b' ; break;
33           case '\f': buf[1] = 'f' ; break;
34           case '\t': buf[1] = 't' ; break;
35           case '\r': buf[1] = 'r' ; break;
36           case '\n': buf[1] = 'n' ; break;
37           default  : sprintf( &buf[1], use_hex ? "x%03x" : "%03o", c );
38                       break;
39           }
40       }
41       return buf;
42   }
```

A.6 Print Functions

This section describes several output functions, many of which use the ANSI variable-argument mechanism and the conversion functions described in the last two sections. They are organized functionally.

void ferr(**char** *fmt,...)

Print error message and exit.

This routine is a version of printf() for fatal error messages. It sends output to stderr rather than stdout, and it doesn't return; rather, it terminates the program with the following call:

```
                    exit( on_ferr() );
```

(on_ferr() is described below). Normally, the routine works like printf()
in other respects. If, however, it is called with ferr(NULL, string), it works
like perror(string) in that it prints an error message associated with the most
recent I/O-system error. The program still terminates as described earlier, however. The source code for ferr() is in Listing A.28. The prnt() call on line
19 will be described in a moment.

Listing A.28. *ferr.c*— Fatal-Error Processing

```
 1   #include <stdio.h>
 2   #include <stdlib.h>       /* errno is declared here      */
 3   #include <stdarg.h>
 4   #include <tools/debug.h> /* VA_LIST definition is here  */
 5   #include <tools/l.h>      /* Needed only for prototype   */
 6
 7   /* Note that ferr() is typed as int, even though it usually doesn't return,
 8    * because it's occasionally useful to use it inside a conditional expression
 9    * where a type will be required. VA_LIST expands to ... if ANSI is #defined,
10    * otherwise it expands to _a_r_g_s_.
11    */
12
13   int     ferr( fmt, VA_LIST )
14   char    *fmt;
15   {
16           va_list           args;
17           va_start( args, fmt );
18
19           if( fmt ) prnt   ( fputc, stderr, fmt, args );
20           else      perror ( va_arg(args, char* )      );
21
22           va_end( args );
23           exit( on_ferr() );
24   }
```

Error handler for ferr().   **int** on_ferr(**void**)

This routine is the default error handler called by ferr() just before exiting. It
returns the current contents of the system errno variable, which is, in turn,
passed back up to the operating system as the process' exit status. You can provide your own on_ferr() to preempt the library version. The source code is in
Listing A.29.

Print human-readable   **void** fputstr(**char** *str, **int** maxlen, FILE *stream)
string.

This function writes a string (str) having at most maxlen characters to the indicated stream in human-readable form. All control characters, and so forth, are
mapped to printable strings using the bin_to_ascii() conversion function
described earlier (on page 727). The source code is in Listing A.30.

Print human-readable   **void** pchar(FILE *stream, **int** c)
character.

This function works like putc(), except that control characters are mapped to
human-readable strings using bin_to_ascii(). The source code is in Listing
A.31.

Listing A.29. *onferr.c*— Action Function for `ferr()`

```
1   #include <stdlib.h>
2   #include <tools/debug.h>
3   #include <tools/l.h>     /* Needed only for prototypes */
4
5   /* This is the default routine called by ferr when it exits. It should return
6    * the exit status. You can supply your own version of this routine if you like.
7    */
8   int     on_ferr()
9   {
10      extern int errno;
11      return errno;
12  }
```

Listing A.30. *fputstr.c*— Fatal-Error Processing—Service Routine

```
1   #include <stdio.h>
2   #include <tools/debug.h>
3   #include <tools/compiler.h>
4
5   /* FPUTSTR.C: Print a string with control characters mapped to readable strings.
6    */
7
8   void    fputstr( str, maxlen, stream )
9   char    *str;
10  FILE    *stream;
11  {
12      char *s;
13
14      while( *str  &&  maxlen >= 0 )
15      {
16          s = bin_to_ascii( *str++, 1 );
17          while( *s && --maxlen >= 0 )
18              putc( *s++ , stream );
19      }
20  }
```

Listing A.31. *pchar.c*— Print Character in Human-Readable Form

```
1   #include <stdio.h>
2   #include <tools/debug.h>
3   #include <tools/compiler.h>
4
5   void    pchar(c, stream)
6   FILE    *stream;
7   {
8       fputs( bin_to_ascii( c, 1 ), stream );
9   }
```

void printv(FILE *stream, **char** **argv)   Print vector array.

This function prints an `argv`-like array of pointers to strings to the indicated `stream`, one string per line (the `'\n'` is inserted automatically at the end of every string). The source code is in Listing A.32.

Listing A.32. *printv.c*— Print `argv`-like Vector Array

```
 1    #include <stdio.h>
 2
 3    void     printv( fp, argv )
 4    FILE     *fp;
 5    char     **argv;
 6    {
 7        /* Print an argv-like array of pointers to strings, one string per line.
 8         * The array must be NULL terminated.
 9         */
10        while( *argv )
11            fprintf( fp, "%s\n", *argv++ );
12    }
13
14    void     comment( fp, argv )
15    FILE     *fp;
16    char     **argv;
17    {
18        /* Works like printv except that the array is printed as a C comment. */
19
20        fprintf(fp, "\n/*-------------------------------------------------------\n");
21        while( *argv )
22                fprintf(fp, " * %s\n",  *argv++ );
23        fprintf(fp, " */\n\n");
24    }
```

Print multiple-line comment.

void comment(FILE *stream, **char** **argv)

This function also prints an `argv`-like array of pointers to strings to the indicated `stream`, one string per line. The output text is put into a C comment, however. Output takes the following form:

```
/*--------------------------------
 *  string in argv[0]
 *  string in argv[1]
 *  ....
 *  string in argv[N]
 */
```

The source code is also in Listing A.32.

A `printf()` workhorse function.

void prnt(**int** (*ofunct)(), **void** *ofunct_arg, **char** *format,
         va_list args)

`prnt()` is a variant on the UNIX `_doprnt()` and ANSI `vfprintf()` functions that lets you write `printf()`-like output routines in a portable way. It is passed a pointer to a single-character output function (`ofunct`), a parameter that is relayed to this output function (`ofunct_arg`), a pointer to a format string, and a pointer to the location on the run-time stack where the other arguments are found. This last parameter is usually derived using the `va_start()` macro in *<stdlib.h>*, described earlier.

To see how `prnt()` is used, `fprintf()` can be implemented as follows:

```
#include <stdio.h>
#include <stdarg.h>

fprintf( stream, format, ... );
FILE    *stream;
char    *format;
{
    extern int  fputc();
    va_list     args;
    va_start (args,  format );                      /* Get address of arguments. */
    prnt        (fputc, stream, format, args );
    va_end      (args);
}
```

sprintf() can be implemented as follows:

```
putstr(c, p)
int     c;
char    **p;
{
    *(*p)++ = c ;
}
sprintf(str, format, ...)
char    *str, *format;
{
    va_list   args;
    va_start (args,  format );
    prnt      (putstr, &str, format, args );
    *str = '\0' ;
    va_end    (args);
}
```

The prnt() subroutine is required by the curses implementation discussed below, which must be able to change the output subroutine at will. Neither the ANSI nor the UNIX function gives you this capability. The source code for prnt() is described in depth below.

void stop_prnt(**void**)   Clean up after prnt().

This routine must be called by all programs that use prnt() just before termination [after the last prnt() call].

The prnt(), subroutine is in Listing A.33. Two versions are presented, one for the ANSI environment and another for UNIX. The first version (on lines 19 to 31) produces an ANSI-compatible function. It uses vsprintf() to do the conversion into a buffer, and then prints the buffer. Though this version is desirable in that it supports all the printf() conversions, it has a drawback. The buffer requires a modicum of stack space, and the Microsoft implementation of vsprintf() also uses a lot of run-time stack. The second, UNIX compatible version of prnt() is on lines 37 to 65 of Listing A.33. There are two problems here: First, the UNIX variable-argument mechanism is different from the ANSI one, so slightly different procedures must be used to get arguments off the stack. Second, there is no UNIX equivalent to vsprintf(). The only available printf driver is _doprnt(), which works like the ANSI vprintf() function except that the arguments are in different positions. In order to use an arbitrary output function, you must format to a FILE, rewind the file, and then transfer characters one at a time to the desired output function. Ugh,[6] you may well say. This approach is

ANSI version of prnt().

UNIX version of prnt().

---

6. That's a technical term.

actually not as much of a kludge as it seems because the number of characters written and read is so small. More often than not, there's no disk activity at all because the reads and writes won't get past the I/O system's internal buffering.

Listing A.33. *prnt.c*— General-Purpose `printf()` Driver

```
 1    #include <stdio.h>
 2    #include <tools/debug.h>
 3    #include <tools/l.h>
 4
 5    /*--------------------------------------------------------------
 6     * Glue formatting workhorse functions to various environments. One of three
 7     * versions of the workhorse function is used, depending on various #defines:
 8     *
 9     * if ANSI is defined          vsprintf()   Standard ANSI function
10     * if ANSI is not defined    _doprnt()     Standard UNIX function
11     *
12     * The default with Microsoft C is MSDOS defined and ANSI not defined,
13     * so idoprnt() will be used unless you change things with explicit macro
14     * definitions.
15     */
16    #ifdef ANSI /*-----------------------------------------------------------*/
17    #include <stdarg.h>
18
19    PUBLIC void prnt( ofunct, funct_arg, format, args )
20    int      (*ofunct)();
21    void     *funct_arg;
22    char     *format;
23    va_list args;
24    {
25        char  buf[256], *p ;
26        int   vsprintf( char* buf, char* fmt, va_list args );
27
28        vsprintf(buf, format, args);
29
30        for( p = buf; *p ; p++ )
31            (*ofunct)( *p, funct_arg );
32    }
33
34    stop_prnt(){}
35
36    #else /* UNIX ------------------------------------------------------------*/
37    #include <varargs.h>
38
39    static FILE     *Tmp_file = NULL ;
40    static char     *Tmp_name ;
41
42    PUBLIC void prnt( ofunct, funct_arg, fmt, argp )
43    int      (*ofunct)();
44    void     *funct_arg;
45    char     *fmt;
46    int      *argp;
47    {
48        int   c;
49        char  *mktemp();
50
51        if( !Tmp_file )
52            if( !(Tmp_file = fopen( Tmp_name = mktemp("yyXXXXXX"), "w+") ))
53            {
54                fprintf(stderr,"Can't open temporary file %s\n", Tmp_name );
55                exit( 1 );
```

Listing A.33. continued...

```
56                }
57
58            _doprnt( fmt, argp,  Tmp_file );
59            putc   ( 0,          Tmp_file );
60            rewind (             Tmp_file );
61
62            while( (c = getc(Tmp_file)) != EOF && c )
63                (*ofunct)( c, funct_arg );
64            rewind( Tmp_file );
65        }
66
67    PUBLIC void  stop_prnt()
68    {
69        fclose( Tmp_file );              /* Remove prnt temporary file */
70        unlink( Tmp_name );
71        Tmp_file = NULL;
72    }
73
74    /*------------------------------------------------------------------------*/
75
76    PUBLIC void vfprintf( stream, fmt, argp )
77    FILE *stream;
78    char *fmt, *argp;
79    {
80        _doprnt( fmt, argp, stream );
81    }
82
83    PUBLIC void vprintf( fmt, argp )
84    char *fmt, *argp;
85    {
86        _doprnt( fmt, argp, stdout );
87    }
88
89    PRIVATE void putstr(c, p)
90    int      c;
91    char     **p;
92    {
93        *(*p)++ = c ;
94    }
95
96    PUBLIC void vsprintf( str, fmt, argp )
97    char *str, char *fmt, *argp;
98    {
99        prnt( putstr, &str, fmt, argp );
100       *str = '\0' ;
101   }
102   #endif
```

The temporary file is created automatically on lines 51 to 56 of Listing A.34 the first time prnt() is called. You must call stop_prnt() (on lines 67 to 72) to delete the file. You can do so after every prnt() call, but it's much more efficient to do it only once, just before the program terminates. You'll loose a FILE pointer in this case, but it saves a lot of time.

The final part of Listing A.33 (lines 76 to 101) contains UNIX versions of the ANSI vprintf(), vfprintf(), and vsprintf() functions.

A.7 Sorting

This sections describes two functions for sorting in-memory arrays: `ssort()` and `assort()`. Both are modeled after the UNIX `qsort()` function. I've provided alternate sorting functions because most `qsort()` implementations use a "quick sort", which does not behave particularly well with small arrays or arrays that might already be sorted. A Shell sort, which does not have these problems, is used here. Both sort functions are general-purpose functions that can be used on arrays of any type of object—the same sorting function can sort arrays of **int**s, arrays of character pointers, arrays of structures, and so forth. Taking `ssort()` as characteristic, `argv` is sorted as follows:

```
cmp( p1, p2 )
char **p1, **p2;
{
    return strcmp( *p1, *p2 );
}

main( argc, argv )
int   argc;
char  **argv;
{
    ssort( argv, argc, sizeof(*argv), cmp );
}
```

The sort function is passed the base address of the array to be sorted, the number of elements in the array, the size of one element, and a pointer to a comparison function. This comparison function is passed pointers to two array elements, and it should otherwise work like `strcmp()`, returning a negative number if the key associated with the first argument is less than the key associated with the second, zero if the two keys are equal, and a positive number if the second key is larger. You can use `ssort()` to sort an array of structures as follows:

```
typedef struct
{
    char  *key;
    int   other_stuff;
} record;

sort_cmp( p1, p2 )
record *p1, *p2;
{
    return( strcmp(p1->key, p2->key) );
}

plato()
{
    record field[ 10 ];
    ...
    ssort( field, 10, sizeof(record), sort_cmp );
}
```

Of course, it's usually better to sort arrays of pointers to structures rather than arrays of structures—there's a lot less to move when two array elements are swapped. The calling conventions for the two sort routines are as follows:

void ssort(**void** *base, **int** nel, **int** elesize, **int** (*cmp)())

Sort an array at base address `base`, having `nel` elements, each of `elesize` bytes. The comparison function, `cmp`, is passed pointers to two array elements and should return as follows:

cmp(p1, p2);	
*p1 < *p2	return a negative number
*p1 = *p2	return zero
*p1 > *p2	return a positive number

The ssort() function is identical in calling syntax to the standard qsort() function. A Shell sort is used by ssort(), however, rather than a quicksort. The Shell sort is more appropriate for use on arrays with a small number of elements and arrays that might already be sorted. Also, since Shell sort is nonrecursive, it is a safer function to use than quicksort, which can cause stack overflows at run time.

void assort(**void** **base, **int** nel, **int** elesize, **int** (*cmp)())   Sort array of pointers.

This routine is a version of ssort() optimized to sort arrays of pointers. It takes the same arguments as ssort() so that the routines can be used interchangeably on arrays of pointers. The base argument to assort() must reference an array of pointers, however, and the elesize argument is ignored.

A.7.1 Shell Sort—Theory

The sorting method used by ssort() is a Shell sort, named after its inventor, Donald Shell. It is essentially an improved bubble sort, so I'll digress for a moment and describe bubble sort. A bubble-sort that arranges an array of **int**s into ascending order   Bubble sort.
looks like this:

```
int array[ ASIZE ];
int i, j, temp ;

for( i = 1; i < ASIZE; ++i )
    for( j = i-1; j >= 0; --j )
        if( array[j] > array[j+1] )
            swap( array+i, array+j ); /* swap array[i] and array[j] */
```

The outer loop controls the effective array size. It starts out sorting a two-element array, then it sorts a three-element array, and so forth. The inner loop moves the new element (the one added when the effective array size was increased) to its correct place in the previously-sorted array. Consider a worst case sort (where the array is already sorted, but in reverse order):

5 4 3 2 1

In the first pass, the outer loop starts out with a two-element array:

5 **4**   3 2 1

And the inner loop swaps these two elements because they're out of place:

4 5   3 2 1

The next pass increases the effective array size to three elements:

4 5 **3**   2 1

And the 3 is moved into its proper place like this:

4 5 **3**   2 1
4 **3** 5   2 1
3 4 5   2 1

The rest of the sort looks like this:

```
3 4 5 2          1
3 4 2 5          1
3 2 4 5          1
2 3 4 5          1
2 3 4 5 1
2 3 4 1 5
2 3 1 4 5
2 1 3 4 5
1 2 3 4 5
```

As you can see, this worst-case sort is very inefficient. In an N-element array, roughly N^2 swaps (and as many comparisons) are required to get the array sorted. Even the average case requires N^2 comparisons, even though it will use fewer swaps. This behavior is quite measurable in most computer programs, and slows down the program unnecessarily.

Shell sort.

The Shell sort improves the bubble sort by trying to move the most out-of-place elements into the proper place as quickly as possible, instead of letting the out-of-place element percolate through the array one place at a time. Other sort strategies (such as the quicksort used for most `qsort()` implementations) are theoretically more efficient, but the overhead required by these other methods is often great enough that the theoretically less-efficient Shell sort is faster (at least with small arrays—less than a hundred elements or so).

The basic strategy of Shell sort is to partition the array into several smaller subarrays whose elements are spread out over the original array. The subarrays are sorted using a bubble sort, and then the array is repartitioned into a smaller number of subarrays, each having more elements. The process is continued until there's only one subarray comprising the entire array. For example, if the initial array looks like this:

```
6   5   4   3   2   1
```

You can partition it into three, two-element arrays like this:

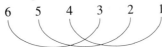

The first array is [6,3], the second is [5,2] and the third holds [4,1]. The distance between any two elements in the subarray is called the *gap* size. Here, the gap size is 3. The three subarrays are now sorted. The 6 and 3 will be swapped, as will the 5 and 2, and the 4 and 1, yielding the following:

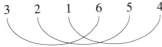

The array is repartitioned, this time with a gap size of two:

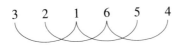

There are now two, three-element arrays having the members [3, 1, 5] and [2, 6, 4]. These are sorted, swapping the 1 and 3, and the 4 and 6, yielding.

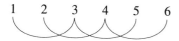

The gap size is now reduced to 1, yielding:

but, since this array is already sorted, nothing more needs to be done. Note that only 5 swaps were used here rather than the 15 swaps that would be required by the bubble sort. In the average case, roughly $N^{1.2}$ swaps are required to sort an array of size N.[7]

A.7.2 Shell Sort—Implementation

The ssort() function in Listing A.34 is a general-purpose Shell-sort function. The initial gap size is selected on line 16 from a number in the series: 1, 4, 13, 40, 121,...(3N+1). The largest number in this series that is less than or equal to the array size is used. (This is the series recommended by Knuth in *The Art of Computer Programming* as an optimal choice. Note that an even power of two, as is used in many Shell-sort implementations is among the worst choice of gap sizes.) The **for** statement on line 19 controls the size of the subarrays. The gap is divided by three on each pass, yielding the previous element in the foregoing series (40/3=13, 13/3=4, 4/3=1—I'm using integer division). The two loops on lines 20 to 33 are doing a bubble-sort pass on the partitioned subarray.

Choosing the gap size.

Since the compiler doesn't know the size of an array element at compile time, it can't do the pointer arithmetic; we have to do the pointer arithmetic ourselves by declaring the array to be a character array on line eight and then explicitly multiplying by the size of an array element every time a pointer is advanced (on lines 23 and 24). The array elements also have to be swapped one byte at a time. The swap time could be improved by passing a pointer to a swap function as well as a comparison function to ssort, but I wanted to maintain compatibility with the standard qsort(), and so didn't change any of the parameters.

Doing explicit pointer arithmetic.

One change that I did make is shown in Listing A.35. asort() is a version of ssort() that sorts only arrays of pointer-sized objects—the vast majority of cases. The routine takes the same arguments as ssort(), but it ignores elsize.

Implementing asort().

A.8 Miscellaneous Functions

This section discusses six routines that don't fit nicely into any of the other categories:

```
int copyfile(char *dst, char *src, char *mode)
int movefile(char *dst, char *src, char *mode)
```

Copy entire file.
Move entire file.

copyfile() copies the contents of the file named in src to the file named in

---

7. See [Knuth], vol. 3, pp. 84f.

Listing A.34. *ssort.c*— General-Purpose Shell Sort

```
1   /* SSORT.C              Works just like qsort() except that a shell sort, rather
2    *                      than a quick sort, is used. This is more efficient than
3    * quicksort for small numbers of elements, and it's not recursive (so will use
4    * much less stack space).
5    */
6
7   void    ssort( base, nel, elsize, cmp )
8   char    *base;
9   int     nel, elsize;
10  int     (*cmp)();
11  {
12      int     i, j;
13      int     gap, k, tmp ;
14      char    *p1, *p2;
15
16      for( gap=1; gap <= nel; gap = 3*gap + 1 )
17          ;
18
19      for( gap /= 3;  gap > 0  ; gap /= 3 )
20          for( i = gap; i < nel; i++ )
21              for( j = i-gap; j >= 0 ; j -= gap )
22              {
23                  p1 = base + ( j      * elsize);
24                  p2 = base + ((j+gap) * elsize);
25
26                  if( (*cmp)( p1, p2 ) <= 0 )          /* Compare two elements    */
27                      break;
28
29                  for( k = elsize; --k >= 0 ;)         /* Swap two elements, one */
30                  {                                     /* byte at a time.        */
31                      tmp    = *p1;
32                      *p1++ = *p2;
33                      *p2++ = tmp;
34                  }
35              }
36  }
```

dst. If the mode argument is `"w"`, the destination is overwritten when it already exists; otherwise, the contents of the source file are appended to the end of the destination. The return values are as follows:

   0   Copy was successful.

 −1   Destination file couldn't be opened.

 −2   Source file couldn't be opened.

 −3   Read error while copying.

 −4   Write error while copying.

`movefile()` works like `copyfile()`, except that the source file is deleted if the copy is successful. `movefile()` differs from the standard `rename()` function in that it allows a move across devices (from one disk to another), and it supports an append mode—`rename()` is faster if you're moving a file somewhere else on the same device, and `rename()` can be used on directory names, however. The sources for `copyfile()` and `movefile()` are in Listings A.36 and A.37.

Listing A.35. *assort.c*— `ssort()` Optimized for Arrays of Pointers

```
1   /* ASSORT.C              A version of ssort optimized for arrays of pointers. */
2
3   void     assort( base, nel, elsize, cmp )
4   void     **base;
5   int      nel;
6   int      elsize;           /* ignored */
7   int      (*cmp)();
8   {
9       int      i, j, gap;
10      void     *tmp, **p1, **p2;
11
12      for( gap=1; gap <= nel; gap = 3*gap + 1 )
13          ;
14
15      for( gap /= 3;  gap > 0  ; gap /= 3 )
16          for( i = gap; i < nel; i++ )
17              for( j = i-gap; j >= 0 ; j -= gap )
18              {
19                  p1 = base + ( j      );
20                  p2 = base + ((j+gap) );
21
22                  if( (*cmp)( p1, p2 ) <= 0 )
23                      break;
24
25                  tmp = *p1;
26                  *p1 = *p2;
27                  *p2 = tmp;
28              }
29  }
```

Listing A.36. *copyfile.c*— Copy Contents of File

```
1   #include <stdio.h>
2   #include <stdlib.h>
3   #include <errno.h>
4   #include <fcntl.h>
5   #include <sys/types.h>
6   #include <sys/stat.h>
7   #include <io.h>
8
9   #define ERR_NONE          0
10  #define ERR_DST_OPEN     -1
11  #define ERR_SRC_OPEN     -2
12  #define ERR_READ         -3
13  #define ERR_WRITE        -4
14
15  copyfile( dst, src, mode )
16  char    *dst, *src;
17  char    *mode;             /* "w" or "a" */
18  {
19      /* Copy the src to the destination file, opening the destination in the
20       * indicated mode. Note that the buffer size used on the first call is
21       * used on subsequent calls as well. Return values are defined, above.
22       * errno will hold the appropriate error code if the return value is <0.
23       */
24
```

→

Listing A.36. continued...

```
25          int              fd_dst, fd_src;
26          char             *buf;
27          int              got;
28          int              werror;
29          int              ret_val = ERR_NONE  ;
30          static unsigned size     = 31 * 1024 ;
31
32          while( size > 0  &&  !(buf = malloc(size)) )
33              size -= 1024;
34
35          if( !size )            /* couldn't get a buffer, do it one byte at a time */
36          {
37              size = 1;
38              buf  = "xx";      /* allocate a buffer implicitly */
39          }
40
41          fd_src = open(src, O_RDONLY | O_BINARY );
42          fd_dst = open(dst, O_WRONLY | O_BINARY | O_CREAT |
43                                          (*mode=='w' ? O_TRUNC : O_APPEND),
44                                          S_IREAD|S_IWRITE);
45
46          if      ( fd_src == -1 ){ ret_val = ERR_SRC_OPEN; }
47          else if( fd_dst == -1 ){ ret_val = ERR_DST_OPEN; }
48          else
49          {
50              while( (got = read(fd_src, buf, size))  >  0 )
51                  if( (werror = write(fd_dst, buf, got)) == -1 )
52                  {
53                      ret_val = ERR_WRITE;
54                      break;
55                  }
56
57              if( got == -1 )
58                  ret_val = ERR_READ;
59          }
60
61          if( fd_dst != -1 ) close ( fd_dst );
62          if( fd_src != -1 ) close ( fd_src );
63          if( size   > 1   ) free ( buf     );
64
65          return ret_val;
66  }
```

Listing A.37. *movefile.c*— Move File to Different Device

```
1   movefile( dst, src, mode )      /* Works like copyfile() (see copyfile.c)     */
2   char     *dst, *src;            /* but deletes src if the copy is successful */
3   char     *mode;
4   {
5       int  rval;
6       if( (rval = copyfile(dst, src, mode)) == 0 )
7           unlink( src );
8       return rval;
9   }
```

`int *memiset(int *dst, int with_what, int count)`   Fill memory with integer values.

This function is a version of the standard `memset()` function but it works on integer-sized objects rather than bytes. It fills `count` `int`s, based at `dst`, with the pattern in `with_what` and returns `dst`. The source code is in Listing A.38.

Listing A.38. *Array*— Initialize

```
 1   /* Works like memset but fills integer arrays with an integer value    */
 2   /* The count is the number of ints (not the number of bytes).          */
 3
 4   int      *memiset( dst, with_what, count )
 5   int      *dst, with_what, count;
 6   {
 7       int *targ;
 8       for( targ = dst; --count >= 0 ; *targ++ = with_what )
 9           ;
10       return dst;
11   }
```

`int concat(int size, char *dst, ...)`   Concatenate strings.

The `concat()` function concatenates an arbitrary number of strings into a single destination array (`dst`) of the indicated `size`. At most `size-1` characters are copied. All arguments following the `dst` argument are the source strings to be concatenated, and the list should end with a `NULL`. For example, the following code loads the `english` array with the string `angles, saxons, jutes`:

```
#include <stdio.h>    /* For NULL definition */

char   target[ SIZE ];

concat( SIZE, target, "angles, ", "saxons, ",  " jutes", NULL );
```

The second and third arguments can be the same, but the target-string pointer cannot appear in any of the other arguments. The following concatenates `new_string` to the end of `target`. This usage is easier to use than the standard `strncat()` function in many situations because it doesn't require you to keep a tally of the unused space in the target array.

```
concat( SIZE, target, target, new_string );
```

The source code is in Listing A.39. The amount of available space is returned, or −1 if the string was truncated.

`void searchenv(char *filename, char *env_name, char *pathname)`   Search for file along directory path listed in an environment string.

This function searches for a specific file (`filename`), first in the current directory, and then along a path specified in the environment variable whose name is in `env_name`. The variable should hold a semicolon or space-delimited list of directory names. If the file is found, the full path name (including the file-name component) is put into `pathname`; otherwise, `pathname` will contain an empty, null-terminated string. The source code is in Listing A.40.

`FILE *driver_1(FILE *output, int lines, char *fname)`   Copy driver-template file.
`int  driver_2(FILE *output, lines)`

These routines work together to transfer a template file to a L^{E}X or **occs** output file. `driver_1()` must be called first. It searches for the file named in `fname`

Listing A.39. *concat.c*— Concatenate Strings

```
1   #include <stdio.h>
2   #include <stdarg.h>
3   #include <debug.h>        /* VA_LIST definition */
4
5   int      concat( size, dst, VA_LIST )
6   int      size;
7   char     *dst;
8   {
9       /* This subroutine concatenates an arbitrary number of strings into a single
10      * destination array (dst) of size "size." At most size-1 characters are
11      * copied. Use it like this:
12      *            char target[SIZE];
13      *            concat( SIZE, target, "first ", "second ",..., "last", NULL);
14      */
15
16      char     *src;
17      va_list  args;
18      va_start( args, dst );
19
20      while( (src = va_arg(args,char *)) && size > 1 )
21          while( *src && size-- > 1 )
22              *dst++ = *src++ ;
23
24      *dst++ = '\0';
25      va_end( args );
26      return (size <= 1 && src && *src) ? -1 : size ;
27  }
```

Ctrl-L delimits parts of driver-template file.

by looking first in the current directory and then in any directory on the path specified by the LIB environment. This environment can list several, semicolon-delimited directory names.

The file should contain one or more Ctrl-L-delimited parts. The first part is copied by driver_1() to the stream indicated by output. If lines is true, then a **#line** directive that references the template file's current line number is output just before the block is output. NULL is returned if the template file can't be opened, otherwise the FILE pointer for the template file is returned. You can use this pointer to close the file after it has been copied.

All other Ctrl-L-delimited parts of the template file are printed by successive calls to driver_2(). One part is printed every time it's called. 1 is returned normally, 0 at end of file (if there are no more parts to print).

Use @ to mark comments in driver-template file.

Lines that begin with an @ sign are ignored by both subroutines. It's a fatal error to call driver_2() without a previously successful driver_1() call.

The source code for both routines is in Listing A.41.

A.9 Low-Level Video I/O Functions for the IBM PC

This section presents a set of very low-level terminal I/O functions for the IBM PC. They are used by the *curses* implementation presented in the next section. The routines in this section are the only ones in the *curses* package that are system dependent. As a consequence, I've not bothered to make them portable, because they'll always have to be rewritten if you port the code to another compiler.

Listing A.40. *searchen.c*— Search for File Along Path Specified in Environment

```
1    #include <stdio.h>
2
3    #define PBUF_SIZE 129              /* Maximum length of a path name - 1 */
4
5    void    searchenv( filename, envname, pathname )
6    char    *filename;      /* file name to search for                  */
7    char    *envname;       /* environment name to use as PATH          */
8    char    *pathname;      /* Place to put full path name when found   */
9    {
10       /* Search for file by looking in the directories listed in the envname
11        * environment. Put the full path name (if you find it) into pathname.
12        * Otherwise set *pathname to 0. Unlike the DOS PATH command (and the
13        * microsoft _searchenv), you can use either a space or semicolon
14        * to separate directory names. The pathname array must be at least
15        * 128 characters.
16        */
17
18       char  pbuf[PBUF_SIZE];
19       char  *p ;
20       char  *strpbrk(), *strtok(), *getenv();
21
22       strcpy( pathname, filename );
23       if( access( pathname, 0 ) != -1 )            /* check current directory */
24           return;                                  /* ...it's there.          */
25
26       /* The file doesn't exist in the current directory. If a specific path was
27        * requested (ie. file contains \ or /) or if the environment isn't set,
28        * return a NULL, else search for the file on the path.
29        */
30
31       if( strpbrk(filename,"\\/")  ||  !(p = getenv(envname)) )
32       {
33           *pathname = '\0';
34           return;
35       }
36
37       strncpy( pbuf, p, PBUF_SIZE );
38       if( p = strtok( pbuf, "; " ) )
39       {
40           do
41           {
42               sprintf( pathname, "%0.90s\\%0.20s", p, filename );
43
44               if( access( pathname, 0 ) >= 0 )
45                   return;                          /* found it */
46           }
47           while( p = strtok( NULL, "; ") );
48       }
49       *pathname = '\0' ;
50   }
```

Two sets of complementary routines are presented here: a set of direct-video functions that write directly into the IBM's display memory (they are MGA and CGA compatible), and a set of similar routines that use the video functions built into the IBM-PC ROM-BIOS to do the I/O. The direct-video routines are faster, the BIOS routines are, at least in theory, more portable. (The direct-video functions work better than the BIOS ones in clones that have nonstandard BIOS implementations.)

Listing A.41. *driver.c*— Copy Driver Template to Output File

```
1    #include <stdio.h>
2    #include <ctype.h>
3    #include <stdlib.h>
4    #include <tools/debug.h>
5    #include <tools/compiler.h>      /* for prototypes */
6
7    /*------------------------------------------------------------*/
8
9    PUBLIC FILE *driver_1  P(( FILE *output, int line,  char *file_name    ));
10   PUBLIC int    driver_2 P(( FILE *output, int line                      ));
11
12   PRIVATE FILE *Input_file = NULL ;
13   PRIVATE int   Input_line;            /* line number of most-recently read line */
14   PRIVATE char File_name[80];          /* template-file name                     */
15
16   /*------------------------------------------------------------*/
17
18   PUBLIC FILE *driver_1( output, lines, file_name )
19   FILE     *output;
20   char     *file_name;
21   {
22       char path[80];
23
24       if( !(Input_file = fopen( file_name, "r" )) )
25       {
26           searchenv( file_name, "LIB", path );
27           if( !*path || !(Input_file = fopen( path, "r")) )
28               return NULL;
29       }
30
31       strncpy( File_name, file_name, sizeof(File_name) );
32       Input_line = 0;
33       driver_2( output, lines );
34       return Input_file;
35   }
36
37   /*------------------------------------------------------------*/
38
39   PUBLIC int driver_2( output, lines )
40   FILE     *output;
41   {
42       static char buf[ 256 ];
43       char         *p;
44       int           processing_comment = 0;
45
46       if( !Input_file )
47           ferr( "INTERNAL ERROR [driver_2], Template file not open.\n");
48
49       if( lines )
50           fprintf( output, "\n#line %d \"%s\"\n", Input_line + 1, File_name );
51
52       while( fgets(buf, sizeof(buf), Input_file) )
53       {
54           ++Input_line;
55           if( *buf == '\f' )
56               break;
57
```

→

Listing A.41. continued...

```
58              for( p = buf; isspace(*p); ++p )
59                      ;
60              if( *p == '@' )
61              {
62                  processing_comment = 1;
63                  continue;
64              }
65              else if( processing_comment )          /* Previous line was a comment, */
66              {                                       /* but current line is not.     */
67                  processing_comment = 0;
68                  if( lines )
69                      fprintf( output, "\n#line %d \"%s\"\n", Input_line, File_name );
70              }
71              fputs( buf, output );
72          }
73      return( feof(Input_file) );
74  }
```

A.9.1 IBM Video I/O—Overview

You need to know a little about low-level I/O to understand the function descriptions that follow. The IBM PC uses several different hardware adapters for video output. The most common are the Color Graphics Adapter (CGA) and Monochrome Graphics Adapter (MGA). Most other interface cards can emulate one or the other of these. Both the MGA and CGA use a block of memory to represent the screen—a two-dimensional array in high memory holds the characters that are currently being displayed. The position of the character in the array determines the position of the character on the screen. Several such arrays, called *video display pages*, are available, but only one page can be displayed at a time. Both systems use a 25×80 array, but the MGA bases the default video page at absolute memory location 0xb0000 (B000:0000), and the CGA puts it at 0xb8000. The other pages are at proportionally higher addresses. *[margin: Memory-mapped screens, MGA, CGA.]* *[margin: Video display pages.]*

Both cards use a 16-bit word to represent each character. The low byte is an extended ASCII code for the character. (All 255 codes are used, the extra ones are for funny characters like smiley faces and hearts.) The high byte is used for *attributes*. This *attribute byte* is pictured in Figure A.2. The high bit of the attribute byte controls character blinking (it's blinking if the bit is set). The next three bits determine the background color. The next bit controls the intensity of the foreground color—of the character itself. If it's set, the character is displayed in high intensity. The bottom three bits determine the foreground color (the color of the character itself). The only difference between the color and monochrome adapters is the way that the colors are interpreted. The monochrome adapter recognizes only black and white; the code for blue, when used as a foreground color, causes the MGA to print the character underlined. *[margin: Characters and attributes.]* *[margin: Blinking, intensity, color.]*

Note that the foregoing applies only to the CGA and MGA, other adapters do things slightly differently, and the situation is actually more complex for the CGA. If you have a CGA and want more details, video interfacing is covered in depth in Chapter 4 of Peter Norton's book: *The Peter Norton Programmer's Guide to the IBM PC* (Bellevue, Wash.: Microsoft Press, 1985).

The following functions use direct-video access to address the screen: *[margin: Direct-video functions.]*

int dv_init(**void**) *[margin: Initialize direct-video functions.]*

Initialize the direct-video functions. At present this routine just checks to see if a color card is installed and changes the internal base address of the video memory.

Figure A.2. Attribute Bits

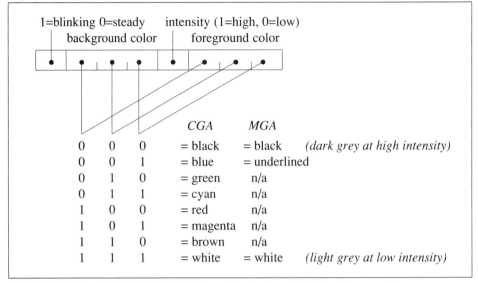

(The monochrome and color cards map video memory to different base addresses.) It returns zero if an 80-column text mode is not available (the direct-video functions will not work in this case), or 1 if everything's okay.

Clear region of screen.

```
void dv_clr_region(int left, int right, int top,
                int bottom, int attrib)
```

Clear the region of screen defined by a box with the upper-left corner at (left,top) and the lower-right corner at (right,bottom). The region is cleared by filling the area with space characters having the indicated attribute. Symbolic defines for the attributes are in <tools/termlib.h>, discussed below. The cursor position is not modified.

Clear screen.

```
void dv_clrs(attrib)
```

Clear the entire screen by filling it with space characters having the indicated attribute. The cursor position is not modified.

Direct-video `printf()`.

```
void dv_printf(int attrib, char *fmt,...)
```

A printf() that uses direct-video writes. Output characters all have the indicated attribute. The prnt() function described earlier does the actual printing.

Display character and attribute.

```
void dv_putc(int c,int attrib)
```

Write a single character to the screen at the current cursor position, and with the indicated attribute. The following characters are special:

\0	ignored
\f	clear screen and home cursor
\n	send cursor to left edge of next line
\r	send cursor to left edge of current line
\b	back up cursor one character (non-destructive backspace)

The screen scrolls up if you go past the bottom line. Characters that go beyond the end of the current line wrap around to the next line.

void dv_ctoyx(**int** y, **int** x)   Change cursor position.

> Position the cursor at the indicated row (y) and column (x). The top-left corner of the screen is (0,0), the bottom-right corner is (24,79).

void dv_getyx(**int** *rowp, **int** *colp)   Get cursor position.

> Modify *rowp and *colp to hold the current cursor position. The top-left corner of the screen is (0,0), the bottom-right corner is (24,79).

dv_incha(**void**)   Input character from
                                                                           screen.

> Return the character and attribute at current cursor position. The character is in the low byte of the returned value and the attribute is in the high byte.

void dv_outcha(**int** c)   Display character and at-
                                                                           tribute without moving
                                                                           cursor.

> Write character and attribute to screen without moving the cursor. The character is in the low byte of c and the attribute is in the high byte. Note that the special characters supported by dv_putc() are not supported here. They will print as funny-looking IBM graphics characters.

void dv_replace(**int** c)   Display character without
                                                                           moving cursor.

> Like dv_outcha(), this function writes the character to the screen without moving the cursor, but the attribute is not modified by dv_replace().

void dv_putchar(**int** c)   Display normal character.

> Write a character to the screen with normal attributes (black background, white foreground, not blinking, normal-intensity, not underlined). This function uses dv_putc() for its output, so it supports the same special characters, scrolling, line wrap, and so forth.

dv_puts(**char** *str, **int** move)   Display string.

> Write a string to screen. If move is true, the cursor is positioned at the end of the string, otherwise the cursor is not moved. Normal attributes, as described in earlier dv_putchar(), are used. This function uses dv_putc() for its output.

void dv_putsa(**char** *str, **int** attrib)   Display string with attri-
                                                                           butes.

> Write string to screen, giving characters the indicated attributes. The cursor is positioned just after the rightmost character. This function uses dv_putc() for its output.

#include <tools/termlib.h>

```
SBUF *dv_save      (int left, int right, int top, int bottom)
SBUF *dv_restore (SBUF *sbuf)
SBUF *dv_freesbuf(SBUF *sbuf)
```
Save and restore region of screen. Discard save buffer.

> These three functions work together to save and restore the characters in a specified region of the screen. dv_save saves all characters in the box with corners at (top,left) and (bottom,right). It returns a pointer that can be passed to a subsequent dv_restore() call to restore that region to its original condition. dv_save terminates the program with an error message if it can't get memory. The cursor is not modified by either function. The SBUF structure, used for this purpose, is defined in <tools/termlib.h> Note that the memory used for this structure is not freed, you must do that yourself with a df_freesbuf(sbuf) call after the dv_restore() call. For convenience,

dv_restore() returns its own argument, so you can say:

```
dv_freesbuf( dv_restore( sbuf) );
```

if you like.

Scroll region arbitrary direction.

void dv_scroll_line(**int** left, **int** right, **int** top, **int** bottom,
                        int dir, **int** attrib)

Scroll the indicated region of the screen by one line or column. The dir argument must be one of the characters: ʹuʹ, ʹdʹ, ʹlʹ, or ʹrʹ for up, down, left, or right. The cursor is not moved. The opened line or column is filled with space characters having the indicated attribute.

Scroll region up or down.

void dv_scroll(**int** left, **int** right, **int** top, **int** bottom, **int** amt,
                 int attrib)

Scroll the indicated region of the screen up or down by the indicated number of lines (amt), filling the new lines with space characters having the indicated attribute. Negative amounts scroll down, positive amounts scroll up.

Video-BIOS functions that mimic direct-video functions.

There are two sets of I/O routines that use the video-BIOS rather than direct-video reads and writes. The routines in Table A.2 behave exactly like the dv_ routines that were discussed earlier. For example, vb_getyx() works exactly like dv_getyx(), but it uses the video BIOS. Names that are in all caps are implemented as macros.

Table A.2. Video-BIOS Macros and Functions That Work Like Direct-Video Functions

Function or macro.†			Has side effects?
void	VB_CLRS	(attrib)	no
void	VB_CLR_REGION	(left, right, top, bottom, attrib)	yes
void	VB_CTOYX	(y, x)	no
void	vb_freesbuf	(sbuf)	–
void	vb_getyx	(yp, xp)	–
int	VB_INCHA	( )	no
void	VB_OUTCHA	(c)	yes
void	VB_PUTCHAR	(c)	no
void	vb_putc	(c, attrib)	–
void	vb_puts	(str, move_cur)	–
void	VB_REPLACE	(c)	yes
SBUF	*vb_restore	(sbuf)	–
SBUF	*vb_save	(left, right, top, bottom)	–
void	VB_SCROLL	(left, right, top, bottom, amt, attrib)	yes
† Names in all caps are macros.			

Other video-BIOS functions.

The second set of BIOS routines gives you access to features that are not easy to implement directly. Of these, the cursor-movement functions are used by the direct-video routines to move the physical cursor. As with the earlier group, names in all caps represent macros, but none of these macros have side effects.

Create block cursor.

void VB_BLOCKCUR(**void**)

Make the cursor a block cursor rather than the normal underline.

Create underline cursor.

void VB_NORMALCUR(**void**)

Make the cursor a normal, underline, cursor.

void VB_CURSIZE(**int** top, **int** bottom)

(right margin: Change cursor size.)

Change the cursor size by making it extend from the indicated top scan line to the bottom one. The line numbers refer to the box in which the character is drawn. A character on the CGA is 8 scan lines (dots) high, and the line numbers go from 0 to 7. They go from 0 to 12 on the MGA. A normal, underline cursor can be created with VB_CURSIZE(6,7) on the CGA, and VB_CURSIZE(11,12) on the MGA. VB_CURSIZE(0,7) creates a block cursor on the CGA, filling the entire area occupied by a character. VB_CURSIZE(0,1) puts a line over the character rather than under it. VB_CURSIZE(13,13) makes the cursor disappear entirely. If the top line is larger than the bottom, you'll get a two-part cursor, so VB_CURSIZE(11,1) creates a cursor with lines both above and below the character on the MGA.

int vb_getchar(**void**)

(right margin: Get character from keyboard.)

Get a character directly from the keyboard. The typed character is returned in the low byte of the returned integer, the high byte holds the auxiliary byte that marks ALT keys and such. See the *IBM Technical Reference* for more information. You can use this function to read key codes that can't be accessed by some compilers' standard I/O system. Similarly, vb_getchar() gets characters from the keyboard, even if input is redirected, though it's more portable to open the console directly for this purpose.

int VB_GETCUR(**void**)

(right margin: Get cursor position.)

Return the current cursor position. The top byte of the return value holds the row, the bottom byte the column.

int VB_GETPAGE(**void**)

(right margin: Get video page number.)

Return a unique number identifying the currently active video-display page.

int vb_iscolor(**void**)

(right margin: Determine display adapter.)

Returns one of the following values:

1	CGA is installed an it's in an 80-column text mode
0	MGA is installed
−1	CGA is installed and it's not in an 80-column text mode

The return value is controlled by the current video mode as follows:

Mode	Return value
2 or 3	1
7	0
anything else	−1

void VB_SETCUR(posn)

(right margin: Move physical cursor.)

Modify current cursor position. The top byte of posn holds the row (y), the bottom byte, the column (x). The top-left corner of the screen is (0,0).

A.9.2 Video I/O—Implementation

This section presents the code that implements the foregoing functions. Most of the actual code is pretty boring, and it's presented with no additional comment in the text. A high-level discussion of the data structures and techniques used is discussed however.

I'm assuming, in this section, that you're familiar to some extent with the IBM
ROM-BIOS interface. If you need this information, read Peter Norton's book: *The Peter
Norton Programmer's Guide to the IBM PC* (Bellevue, Wash.: Microsoft Press, 1985),
which covers all this material. I'm also assuming that your compiler has a mechanism
for generating a software interrupt—most do. I'm using the Microsoft `int86()`
because it's portable—newer versions of the compiler have more efficient BIOS-access
functions in the library, and you may want to modify the code to use these functions.

The `int86()` function.

Attribute definitions,
`SBUF`, `WORD`, `IMALLOC`,
`IFREE`: *<tools/termlib.h>*

The *<tools/termlib.h>* file is used both by application programs and by the I/O functions themselves. It's shown in Listing A.42. The macros on lines five to 12 are the
codes for the basic colors described earlier. The `FGND()` and `BGND()` macros on lines
14 and 15 put the color code into the foreground or background position within the attribute byte. (`FGND` is just for documentation, it doesn't do anything. `BGND` shifts the color
four bits to the left.) The `NORMAL`, `UNDERLINED`, and `REVERSE` definitions on lines 17
to 19 of Listing A.42 define all legal color combinations for the monochrome card: a normal character, an underlined character, and a reverse-video character. Finally, `BLINK-
ING` and `BOLD` (on lines 21 and 22 of Listing A.42) can be ORed with the colors to make
the character blink or be displayed at high intensity.

Listing A.42. *termlib.h*— Video-I/O Definitions

```
1    /* Various definitions for the termlib. Note that if your program includes both
2     * termlib.h and vbios.h, termlib.h must be included FIRST.
3     */
4
5    #define BLACK              0x00      /* Color Card.      */
6    #define BLUE               0x01
7    #define GREEN              0x02
8    #define CYAN               0x03
9    #define RED                0x04
10   #define MAGENTA            0x05
11   #define BROWN              0x06
12   #define WHITE              0x07
13
14   #define FGND(color)        (color)
15   #define BGND(color)        ((color) <<4)
16
17   #define NORMAL             (FGND(WHITE)  | BGND(BLACK))     /* Monochrome card */
18   #define UNDERLINED         (FGND(BLUE)   | BGND(BLACK))
19   #define REVERSE            (FGND(BLACK)  | BGND(WHITE))
20
21   #define BLINKING           0x80      /* May be ORed with the above    */
22   #define BOLD               0x08      /* and with each other           */
23
24   /*-------------------------------------------------------------------
25    * If USE_FAR_HEAP is true then use the far heap to save screen images in the
26    * small model. You must recompile the termlib if you change this #define.
27    */
28
29   typedef unsigned int WORD;
30
31   #if( USE_FAR_HEAP )
32           typedef WORD far *IMAGEP;
33           #define IMALLOC  _fmalloc
34           #define IFREE    _ffree
35   #else
36           typedef WORD    *IMAGEP;
37           #define IMALLOC  malloc
38           #define IFREE    free
```

Listing A.42. continued...

```
39    #endif
40
41    typedef struct  SBUF /* used by vb_save, vb_restore, dv_save, and dv_restore */
42    {
43            unsigned int  top, bottom, left, right;
44            IMAGEP        image;
45    } SBUF;
46
47    /*--------------------------------------------------------------------
48     *      Prototypes for the video-BIOS access routines.
49     */
50
51    extern   int  vb_iscolor       ( void                                    );
52    extern   void vb_getyx         ( int *yp,int *xp                         );
53    extern   void vb_putc          ( int c, int attrib                       );
54    extern   void vb_puts          ( char *str,int move_cur                  );
55    extern   int  vb_getchar       ( void                                    );
56    extern   SBUF *vb_save         ( int l,int r,int t,int b                 );
57    extern   SBUF *vb_restore      ( SBUF *sbuf                              );
58    extern   void vb_freesbuf      ( SBUF *sbuf                              );
59
60    /*--------------------------------------------------------------------
61     *      Prototypes for the equivalent direct video functions.
62     */
63
64    extern   int  dv_init          ( void                                    );
65    extern   void dv_scroll_line   ( int x_left,int x_right,int y_top,       \
66                                        int y_bottom, int dir,int attrib );
67    extern   void dv_scroll        ( int x_left,int x_right,int y_top,       \
68                                        int y_bottom, int amt,int attrib );
69    extern   void dv_clrs          ( int attrib                             );
70    extern   void dv_clr_region    ( int l,int r,int t,int b,int attrib     );
71    extern   void dv_ctoyx         ( int y,int x                            );
72    extern   void dv_getyx         ( int *rowp,int *colp                    );
73    extern   void dv_putc          ( int c,int attrib                       );
74    extern   void dv_putchar       ( int c                                  );
75    extern   int  dv_puts          ( char *str,int move_cur                 );
76    extern   void dv_putsa         ( char *str,int attrib                   );
77    extern   int  dv_incha         ( void                                   );
78    extern   void dv_outcha        ( int c                                  );
79    extern   void dv_replace       ( int c                                  );
80    extern   void dv_printf        ( int attribute,char *fmt,...            );
81    extern   SBUF *dv_save         ( int l,int r,int t,int b                );
82    extern   SBUF *dv_restore      ( SBUF *sbuf                             );
83    extern   void dv_freesbuf      ( SBUF *sbuf                             );
```

The WORD **typedef** on line 29 of Listing A.42 is an attempt to get a portable definition for a 16-bit unsigned quantity. It's used later to access a single 16-bit, character/attribute pair from the video page.

Portable 16-bit data type, WORD.

The definitions on lines 31 to 39 of Listing A.42 are compiler dependent. They control from where, in real memory, the buffers used for an SBUF will be allocated. In an average window application, where you need to save the area under a new window before creating it, a considerable amount of memory can be used to store these old images (25×80×!2=4,000 bytes for the whole screen), and that much memory may not be available in an 8086 small-model program. You don't want to convert the entire program to the medium or compact model because this conversion will slow down all the

Screen-save buffer, SBUF.

The 'far heap,'
USE_FAR_HEAP,
_fmalloc(),
_ffree().

The **far** keyword.

Video-BIOS definitions,
vbios.h.

pointer accesses. It's possible, however, for a small-model program to allocate and use a region of memory outside of the normal 64K data area (called the *far heap*). The Microsoft _fmalloc() function gets memory from the far heap, and returns a 32-bit far pointer. The _ffree() function puts memory back into the far heap. The far heap is used for window images if USE_FAR_HEAP is defined above line 31 of Listing A.42 (or with a *-DUSE_FAR_HEAP* command-line switch). The far keyword on line 32 tells the Microsoft compiler to use a 32-bit pointer that holds both the segment and offset components of the address when _fmalloc() is used to allocate memory.

The next *.h* file of interest is *vbios.h*, which is used locally by the video-BIOS functions. It's in Listing A.43. Two interrupts are of interest here: the video interrupt, whose number is defined on line five, and the keyboard interrupt defined on the next line. The definitions on lines seven to 15 let you select a specific function—each interrupt can do several things, and the function-number determines which of these functions are performed. All of the foregoing is described in great depth in Peter Norton's book if you need more background information.

Listing A.43. *vbios.h*— Video-BIOS Service Definitions

```
 1   #ifndef NORMAL
 2   #include <tools/termlib.h>
 3   #endif
 4
 5   #define VIDEO_INT      0x10    /* Video interrupt            */
 6   #define KB_INT         0x16    /* Keyboard interrupt         */
 7   #define CUR_SIZE       0x1     /* Set cursor size            */
 8   #define SET_POSN       0x2     /* Modify cursor posn         */
 9   #define READ_POSN      0x3     /* Read current cursor posn   */
10   #define SCROLL_UP      0x6     /* scroll region of screen up */
11   #define SCROLL_DOWN    0x7     /*   " down                   */
12   #define READ_CHAR      0x8     /* Read character from screen */
13   #define WRITE          0x9     /* Write character            */
14   #define WRITE_TTY      0xe     /* Write char & move cursor   */
15   #define GET_VMODE      0xf     /* Get video mode & disp pg   */
```

Accessing the video
BIOS, _Vbios().

Most video-BIOS functions implemented as macros.

Direct-video definitions, *video.h*. Video-memory base addresses, MONBASE, COLBASE.

Screen dimensions, NUMROWS, NUMCOLS.

Accessing characters and attributes, CHARACTER. Representing entire screen, DISPLAY.

The video BIOS is accessed by _Vbios() in Listing A.44. The Microsoft *int86( )* function, a prototype for which is in *<dos.h>*, communicates with the BIOS using the normal interrupt mechanism. It is passed an interrupt number and pointers to two REGS structures that represent the 8086 register set. The first of these holds the desired contents of the registers before the interrupt is executed, the second holds the values of the registers after the interrupt returns. Most of the video-BIOS functions are actually macros that evaluate to _Vbios() calls. These are also defined in *<tools/vbios.h>* and are shown in Listing A.45.

The third *.h* file, *video.h* in Listing A.46, is used locally by the direct-video functions. MONBASE and COLBASE (defined on lines one and two of Listing A.46) are the base addresses of page 0 of the monochrome and color adapters. The addresses are in the canonical segment/offset form used by most 8086 compilers, the high 16 bits are the segment and the low 16 bits are the offset. The dimensions of the screen (in characters) are controlled by NUMROWS and NUMCOLS on the lines three and four of Listing A.46.

The CHARACTER structure defined on lines six to 11 of Listing A.46 describes a single character/attribute pair. Using a structure to access the high byte is a better strategy than a shift because it's more efficient in most compilers. A DISPLAY, defined on the next line, is a 25×80 array of these character/attribute pairs.

Listing A.44. _vbios.c_— Video-BIOS Interface Function

```
 1   #include <dos.h>
 2   #include <tools/vbios.h>
 3   #include "video.h"
 4
 5   /* This file contains a workhorse function used by the other video I/O  */
 6   /* functions to talk to the BIOS. It executes the video interrupt.      */
 7
 8   int     _Vbios( service, al, bx, cx, dx, return_this )
 9   int     service;               /* Service code, put into ah.            */
10   int     al, bx, cx, dx;        /* Other input registers.                */
11   char    *return_this;          /* Register to return, "ax", "bh", "dx" only. */
12   {
13       union REGS  regs;
14
15       regs.h.ah = service;
16       regs.h.al = al;
17       regs.x.bx = bx;
18       regs.x.cx = cx;
19       regs.x.dx = dx;
20       int86( VIDEO_INT, &regs, &regs);
21       return ( *return_this == 'a' ) ?  regs.x.ax :
22              ( *return_this == 'b' ) ?  regs.h.bh : regs.x.dx ;
23   }
```

The dv_Screen pointer declared on line 16 of Listing A.46 points at the base address of the video memory for the current adapter (it's initialized for the monochrome card but it can be changed at run time). The SCREEN macro on line 21 of Listing A.46 uses dv_Screen to randomly access a specific character or attribute on the screen. For example, the following puts a high-intensity *X* in the lower-right corner of the screen:

Accessing video memory directly, dv_Screen, SCREEN

```
#include <termlib.h>
#include <video.h>
SCREEN[ 25 ][ 79 ].character = 'X' ;
SCREEN[ 25 ][ 79 ].attribute = NORMAL | BOLD ;
```

The elaborate casts are needed because you can't cast a pointer into an array, but you can cast it to an array pointer. Since dv_Screen is a pointer to an entire two-dimensional array as compared to a pointer to the first element, the star in SCREEN gets you the array itself. Looked at another way, a pointer to an entire array is special in two ways. First, if you increment it, you'll skip past the entire array, not just one element. Second, the pointer is treated internally as if it were a pointer to a pointer. That is, the array pointer is treated internally as if it points at an array of pointers to rows, similar to argv. An extra star is needed to select the correct row. This star doesn't change the value of the pointer, only its type—dv_Screen and *dv_Screen both evaluate to the same number, but the types are different. dv_Screen (without the star) is of type *pointer to two-dimensional array*, the first element of which is one-dimensional array of CHARACTERs. *dv_Screen (with the star) is of type *pointer to one-dimensional array* (*pointer to row*), the first element of which is a single CHARACTER. All this is discussed in greater depth in Chapter 6.

The definitions on lines 23 to 25 of Listing A.46 work just like the foregoing, except that the screen is treated as an array of 16-bit numbers rather than as an array of CHAR-ACTERs. The dv_ functions are in Listings A.47 to A.67.

Listing A.45. *vbios.h*— Macros That Implement Video-BIOS Functions

```
16   /* These video-BIOS functions are implemented as macros.
17    *
18    * VB_INCHA      Returns the character and attribute ORed together.  Character in
19    *               the low byte and attribute in the high byte.
20    * VB_GETPAGE    Return the currently active display page number
21    * VB_GETCUR     Get current cursor position. The top byte of the return value
22    *               holds the row, the bottom by the column. Pagenum is the video
23    *               page number. Note that VB_GETPAGE() will mess up the fields in
24    *               the Regs structure so it must be called first.
25    * VB_CURSIZE    Change the cursor shape to go from the top to the bottom scan
26    *               line.
27    * VB_OUTCHA     Write a character and attribute without moving the cursor. The
28    *               attribute is in c's high byte, the character is the low byte.
29    * VB_REPLACE    Same as VB_OUTCHA but uses the existing attribute byte.
30    * VB_SETCUR     Modify current cursor position. The top byte of "posn" value
31    *               holds the row (y), the bottom byte, the column (x). The top-left
32    *               corner of the screen is (0,0). Pagenum is the video-display-page
33    *               number.
34    * VB_CTOYX(y,x) Like VB_SETCUR but y and x coordinates are used.
35    * VB_SCROLL     Scroll the indicated region on the screen. If amt is <0,
36    *               scroll down; otherwise, scroll up.
37    * VB_CLRS       Clear the entire screen
38    * VB_CLR_REGION Clear a region of the screen
39    * VB_BLOCKCUR   Change to a block cursor.
40    * VB_NORMALCUR  Change to an underline cursor.
41    * VB_PUTCHAR    like vb_putc, but uses white on black for the attribute.
42    */
43
44   #define VB_GETPAGE()      _Vbios( GET_VMODE, 0, 0, 0, 0,                      "bh")
45   #define VB_INCHA()        _Vbios( READ_CHAR, 0, VB_GETPAGE(), 0, 0,          "ax")
46   #define VB_GETCUR()       _Vbios( READ_POSN, 0, VB_GETPAGE(), 0, 0,          "dx")
47   #define VB_CURSIZE(t,b)   _Vbios( CUR_SIZE,  0,0,((t)<<8)|(b),0,             "ax")
48   #define VB_OUTCHA(c)      _Vbios( WRITE,      (c)&0xff,((c)>>8)&0xff, 1, 0,  "ax")
49   #define VB_REPLACE(c)     VB_OUTCHA( (c & 0xff) | (VB_INCHA() & ~0xff) );
50   #define VB_SETCUR(posn)   _Vbios( SET_POSN,  0, VB_GETPAGE() << 8, 0,(posn), "ax")
51   #define VB_CTOYX(y,x)     VB_SETCUR( ((y) << 8) | ((x) & 0xff) )
52   #define VB_SCROLL(xl, xr, yt, yb, amt, attr) _Vbios( \
53                             ((amt) < 0) ? SCROLL_DOWN : SCROLL_UP, \
54                             abs(amt), (attr) << 8, ((yt) << 8) | (xl), \
55                                              ((yb) << 8) | (xr), "ax"\
56                                     )
57
58   #define VB_CLRS(at)             VB_SCROLL( 0,  79,  0, 24, 25,        (at))
59   #define VB_CLR_REGION(l,r,t,b,at) VB_SCROLL( (l),(r),(t),(b),((b)-(t))+1,(at))
60
61   #define VB_BLOCKCUR()     VB_CURSIZE( 0, vb_iscolor() ? 7 : 12 )
62   #define VB_NORMALCUR()    ( vb_iscolor() ? VB_CURSIZE(6,7) : VB_CURSIZE(11,12) )
63   #define VB_PUTCHAR(c)     vb_putc( (c), NORMAL )
```

Listing A.46. *video.h*— Definitions for Direct-Video Functions

```
1    #define MONBASE           (DISPLAY far *) 0xb0000000
2    #define COLBASE           (DISPLAY far *) 0xb8000000
3    #define NUMROWS           25
4    #define NUMCOLS           80
5
6    typedef struct
7    {
8        unsigned char letter;
9        unsigned char attribute;
10
11   } CHARACTER;
12
13   typedef CHARACTER        DISPLAY[ NUMROWS ][ NUMCOLS ];
14
15   #ifdef ALLOC
16       DISPLAY far *dv_Screen = (DISPLAY far *) MONBASE ;
17   #else
18       extern  DISPLAY far *dv_Screen;
19   #endif
20
21   #define SCREEN            (* dv_Screen)
22
23   typedef short            CHAR_ATTRIB;
24   typedef CHAR_ATTRIB      VDISPLAY[ NUMROWS ][ NUMCOLS ];
25   #define VSCREEN           (* (VDISPLAY far *)dv_Screen )
```

Listing A.47. *dv_clr_r.c*— Clear Region of Screen (Direct Video)

```
1    #include "video.h"
2
3    void    dv_clr_region( l, r, t, b, attrib )
4    {
5        int   ysize, xsize, x, y ;
6
7        xsize = (r - l) + 1;                /* horizontal size of region */
8        ysize = (b - t) + 1;                /* vertical size of region   */
9
10       for( y = ysize; --y >= 0 ;)
11           for( x = xsize; --x >= 0 ; )
12           {
13               SCREEN[ y + t ][ x + l ].letter    = ' ';
14               SCREEN[ y + t ][ x + l ].attribute = attrib ;
15           }
16   }
```

Listing A.48. *dv_clrs.c*— Clear Entire Screen (Direct Video)

```
1    #include "video.h"
2
3    void    dv_clrs( attrib )
4    {
5        /*  Clear the screen. The cursor is not moved.  */
6
```

→

Listing A.48. continued...

```
 7        CHARACTER far        *p = (CHARACTER far *) ( dv_Screen );
 8        register int         i ;
 9
10        for( i = NUMROWS * NUMCOLS;  --i >= 0 ; )
11        {
12            (p  )->letter    = ' ';
13            (p++)->attribute = attrib ;
14        }
15    }
```

Listing A.49. *dv_frees.c*— Free an SBUF (Direct Video)

```
 1    #include <stdlib.h>
 2    #include <tools/termlib.h>
 3    #include "video.h"
 4                                       /* Free an SBUF as is allocated by vb_save(). */
 5    void      dv_freesbuf( p )
 6    SBUF      *p;
 7    {
 8        IFREE( p->image );
 9        free ( p );
10    }
```

Listing A.50. *dv_init.c*— Initialize Direct-Video Functions

```
 1    #include "video.h"
 2
 3    int       dv_init()
 4    {
 5        int i;
 6        if( (i = vb_iscolor()) >= 0 )
 7            dv_Screen = i ? COLBASE : MONBASE ;
 8        return( i != -1 );
 9    }
```

Listing A.51. *dv_print.c*— A Direct-Video `printf()`

```
 1    #include <stdio.h>
 2    #include <stdarg.h>
 3    #include <tools/debug.h>        /* For VA_LIST definition */
 4    #include "video.h"
 5
 6    void      dv_printf( attrib, fmt, VA_LIST )
 7    int       attrib;
 8    char      *fmt;
 9    {
10        /* Direct-video printf, characters will have the indicated attributes.  */
11        /* prnt() is in curses.lib, which must be linked to your program if you */
12        /* use the current function.                                           */
13
```

→

Listing A.51. continued...

```
14        extern dv_putc();
15        va_list args;
16
17        va_start( args, fmt );
18        prnt     ( dv_putc, attrib, fmt, args );
19        va_end  ( args );
20    }
```

Listing A.52. *dv_putc.c*— Write Character to Screen with Attribute (Direct Video)

```
1    #include "video.h"
2    #include <tools/vbios.h>
3
4    static int      Row = 0;        /* Cursor Row    */
5    static int      Col = 0;        /* Cursor Column */
6
7    /*----------------------------------------------------------------*/
8    /* Move cursor to (Row, Col)                                      */
9
10   #define fix_cur() _Vbios( SET_POSN, 0, 0, 0, (Row << 8) | Col , "ax" )
11
12   /*----------------------------------------------------------------*/
13
14   void     dv_putc( c, attrib )
15   {
16       /* Write a single character to the screen with the indicated  attribute.
17        * The following are special:
18        *
19        * \0      ignored
20        * \f      clear screen and home cursor
21        * \n      to left edge of next line
22        * \r      to left edge of current line
23        * \b      one character to left (non-destructive)
24        *
25        * The screen will scroll up if you go past the bottom line. Characters
26        * that go beyond the end of the current line wrap around to the next line.
27        */
28
29       switch( c )
30       {
31       case 0:     break;                           /* Ignore ASCII NULL's */
32
33       case '\f':  dv_clrs( attrib );
34                   Row = Col = 0;
35                   break;
36
37       case '\n':  if( ++Row >= NUMROWS )
38                   {
39                       dv_scroll_line(0,79,0,24, 'u', NORMAL );
40                       Row = NUMROWS-1 ;
41                   }
42                                                   /* Fall through to '\r' */
43       case '\r':  Col = 0;
44                   break;
45
```

→

```
Listing A.52. continued...
46        case '\b':  if( --Col < 0 )
47                        Col = 0;
48                    break;
49
50        default :    SCREEN[ Row ][ Col ].letter    = c       ;
51                     SCREEN[ Row ][ Col ].attribute = attrib ;
52                     if( ++Col >= NUMCOLS )
53                     {
54                         Col = 0;
55                         if( ++Row >= NUMROWS )
56                         {
57                             dv_scroll_line(0,79,0,24, 'u', NORMAL );
58                             Row = NUMROWS-1 ;
59                         }
60                     }
61                     break;
62        }
63        fix_cur();
64  }
65
66  /*------------------------------------------------------------------*/
67
68  void dv_ctoyx( y, x )
69  {                        /* Position the cursor at the indicated row and column */
70        Row = y;
71        Col = x;
72        fix_cur();
73  }
74
75  /*------------------------------------------------------------------*/
76
77  void    dv_getyx( rowp, colp )
78  int     *rowp, *colp;
79  {                        /* Modify *rowp and *colp to hold the cursor position. */
80        *rowp = Row;
81        *colp = Col;
82  }
83
84  /*------------------------------------------------------------------*/
85
86  int     dv_incha()              /* Get character & attribute from screen. */
87  {
88        return  (int) VSCREEN[ Row ][ Col ];
89  }
90
91  void dv_outcha(c)               /* Write char. & attrib. w/o moving cursor. */
92  {
93        VSCREEN[ Row ][ Col ] = c ;
94  }
95
96  void  dv_replace(c)             /* Write char. only w/o moving cursor */
97  {
98        SCREEN[ Row ][ Col ].letter = c ;
99  }
```

Listing A.53. *dv_putch.c*— Write Character to Screen, Normal Attribute (Direct Video)

```
1    #include "video.h"
2    #include <tools/termlib.h>
3
4    void    dv_putchar( c )
5    {
6        dv_putc( c & 0xff, NORMAL );
7    }
```

Listing A.54. *dv_puts.c*— Write String to Screen, Normal Attribute (Direct Video)

```
1    #include "video.h"
2    #include <tools/termlib.h>
3
4    dv_puts( str, move )
5    char     *str;
6    {
7        /* Write string to screen, moving cursor to end of string only if move is
8         * true. Use normal attributes.
9         */
10
11       int orow, ocol;
12
13       dv_getyx( &orow, &ocol );
14
15       while( *str )
16           dv_putc( *str++, NORMAL );
17
18       if( !move )
19           dv_ctoyx( orow, ocol );
20   }
```

Listing A.55. *dv_putsa.c*— Write String to Screen, with Attribute (Direct Video)

```
1    #include "video.h"
2
3    void    dv_putsa( str, attrib )
4    register char    *str;
5    register int     attrib;
6    {
7        /* Write string to screen, giving characters the indicated attributes. */
8
9        while( *str )
10           dv_putc( *str++, attrib );
11   }
```

Listing A.56. *dv_resto.c*— Restore Saved Region (Direct Video)

```
1    #include <stdio.h>
2    #include <tools/termlib.h>
3    #include "video.h"
4
5    SBUF    *dv_restore( sbuf )
6    SBUF    *sbuf;
7    {
8        /* Restore a region saved with a previous dv_save() call. The cursor is
9         * not modified. Note that the memory used by sbuf is not freed, you must
10        * do that yourself with a dv_freesbuf(sbuf) call.
11        */
12
13       int      ysize, xsize, x, y ;
14       IMAGEP   p;
15
16       xsize = ( sbuf->right  - sbuf->left ) + 1 ;
17       ysize = ( sbuf->bottom - sbuf->top  ) + 1 ;
18       p     = sbuf->image;
19
20       for( y = 0; y < ysize ; ++y )
21           for( x = 0; x < xsize ; ++x )
22               VSCREEN[ y + sbuf->top ][ x + sbuf->left ] = *p++;
23
24       return sbuf;
25   }
```

Listing A.57. *dv_save.c*— Save Region (Direct Video)

```
1    #include <stdio.h>
2    #include <stdlib.h>
3    #include "video.h"
4    #include <tools/termlib.h>
5
6    SBUF *dv_save( l, r, t, b )
7    {
8        /* Save all characters and attributes in indicated region. Return a
9         * pointer to a save buffer. The cursor is not modified. Note that the
10        * save buffer can be allocated from the far heap, but the SBUF itself is
11        * not. See also, dv_restore() and dv_freesbuf();
12        */
13
14       int        ysize, xsize, x, y ;
15       IMAGEP     p;
16       SBUF       *sbuf;
17
18       xsize = (r - l) + 1;
19       ysize = (b - t) + 1;
20
21       if( !(sbuf = (SBUF *) malloc(sizeof(SBUF)) ))
22       {
23           fprintf(stderr, "Internal error (dv_save): No memory for SBUF.");
24           exit( 1 );
25       }
26       if( !(p = (IMAGEP) IMALLOC(xsize * ysize * sizeof(WORD))))
27       {
28           fprintf(stderr, "Internal error (dv_save): No memory for image");
29           exit( 2 );
```

Listing A.57. continued...

```
30          }
31
32          sbuf->left    = l;
33          sbuf->right   = r;
34          sbuf->top     = t;
35          sbuf->bottom  = b;
36          sbuf->image   = p;
37
38          for( y = 0; y < ysize ; ++y )
39              for( x = 0; x < xsize ; ++x )
40                  *p++ = VSCREEN[ y + t ][ x + l ];
41
42          return sbuf;
43      }
```

Listing A.58. *dv_scree.c*— Direct-Video Variable Allocation

```
1   #define ALLOC
2   #include "video.h"
3
4   /* This file has no code in it. It just allocates space for the variables
5    * defined in video.h
6    */
```

Listing A.59. *dv_scrol.c*— Scroll Region of Screen (Direct Video)

```
1   #include "video.h"
2
3   static  void cpy_row( dest_row, src_row, left_col, right_col )
4   {
5       /* Copy all characters between left_col and right_col (inclusive)
6        * from src_row to the equivalent position in dest_row.
7        */
8
9       CHARACTER far  *s ;
10      CHARACTER far  *d ;
11
12      d = & SCREEN[ dest_row ][ left_col ];
13      s = & SCREEN[ src_row  ][ left_col ];
14
15      while( left_col++ <= right_col )
16          *d++ = *s++;
17  }
18
19  /*-------------------------------------------------------------------*/
20
21  static  void cpy_col( dest_col, src_col, top_row, bot_row )
22  {
23      /* Copy all characters between top_row and bot_row (inclusive)
24       * from src_col to the equivalent position in dest_col.
25       */
26
27      CHARACTER far *s = & SCREEN[ top_row ][ src_col  ];
28      CHARACTER far *d = & SCREEN[ top_row ][ dest_col ];
29
```
→

Listing A.59. continued...

```
30          while( top_row++ <= bot_row )
31          {
32              *d = *s;
33              d += NUMCOLS;
34              s += NUMCOLS;
35          }
36      }
37
38      /*----------------------------------------------------------------------*/
39
40      static  void clr_row( row, attrib, left_col, right_col )
41      {
42          /* Clear all characters in the indicated row that are between left_col and
43           * right_col (inclusive).
44           */
45
46          CHARACTER far *p = & SCREEN[ row ][ left_col ];
47
48          while( left_col++ <= right_col )
49          {
50              (p  )->letter    = ' ';
51              (p++)->attribute = attrib ;
52          }
53      }
54
55      /*----------------------------------------------------------------------*/
56
57      static  void clr_col( col, attrib, top_row, bot_row )
58      {
59          /* Clear all characters in the indicated column that are between top_row
60           * and bot_row (inclusive).
61           */
62
63          CHARACTER far *p = & SCREEN[ top_row ][ col ];
64
65          while( top_row++ <= bot_row )
66          {
67              p->letter    = ' ';
68              p->attribute = attrib ;
69              p += NUMCOLS ;
70          }
71      }
72
73      /*======================================================================*
74       *                      Externally accessible functions:               *
75       *======================================================================*
76       */
77
78      void dv_scroll_line ( x_left, x_right, y_top, y_bottom, dir, attrib )
79      {
80          /* Scroll the window located at:
81           *
82           * (y_top, x_left)
83           *                      +---------+
84           *                      |         |
85           *                      |         |
86           *                      +---------+
87           *                                      (y_bottom, x_right)
88           *
89           * Dir is one of:  'u', 'd', 'l', or 'r' for up, down, left, or right.
```

→

Listing A.59. continued...

```
90          * The cursor is not moved. The opened line is filled with space characters
91          * having the indicated attribute.
92          */
93
94         int         i;
95         CHARACTER far *p;
96
97         if( dir == 'u' )
98         {
99             for( i = y_top; i < y_bottom ; i++ )
100                cpy_row( i, i+1, x_left, x_right );
101            clr_row( y_bottom, attrib, x_left, x_right );
102        }
103        else if( dir == 'd' )
104        {
105            for( i = y_bottom; --i >= y_top ; )
106                cpy_row( i+1, i, x_left, x_right );
107            clr_row( y_top, attrib, x_left, x_right );
108        }
109        else if( dir == 'l' )
110        {
111            for( i = x_left; i < x_right; i++ )
112                cpy_col( i, i+1, y_top, y_bottom );
113            clr_col( x_right, attrib, y_top, y_bottom );
114        }
115        else /* dir == 'r' */
116        {
117            for( i = x_right; --i >= x_left ; )
118                cpy_col( i+1, i, y_top, y_bottom );
119            clr_col( x_left, attrib, y_top, y_bottom );
120        }
121    }
122
123    /*----------------------------------------------------------------------*/
124
125    void dv_scroll( x_left, x_right, y_top, y_bottom, amt, attrib )
126    {
127        /* Scroll the screen up or down by the indicated amount. Negative
128         * amounts scroll down.
129         */
130
131        int dir = 'u';
132
133        if( amt < 0 )
134        {
135            amt = -amt;
136            dir = 'd' ;
137        }
138        while( --amt >= 0 )
139            dv_scroll_line( x_left, x_right, y_top, y_bottom, dir, attrib );
140    }
```

Listing A.60. *vb_frees.c*— Free Save Buffer (Video BIOS)

```
 1   #include "video.h"
 2   #include <tools/termlib.h>
 3   #include <stdlib.h>
 4
 5   void      vb_freesbuf( p )
 6   SBUF      *p;
 7   {                                      /* Free an SBUF as is allocated by vb_save(). */
 8       IFREE( p->image );
 9       free ( p );
10   }
```

Listing A.61. *vb_getch.c*— Get Character from Keyboard (Keyboard!BIOS)

```
 1   #include <dos.h>
 2   #include <tools/vbios.h>
 3
 4   int       vb_getchar()
 5   {
 6       /* Get a character directly from the keyboard */
 7
 8       union REGS  regs;
 9       regs.h.ah = 0 ;
10       int86( KB_INT, &regs, &regs );
11       return( (int)regs.x.ax );
12   }
```

Listing A.62. *vb_getyx.c*— Get Cursor Position (Video BIOS)

```
 1   #include <tools/vbios.h>
 2
 3   void      vb_getyx( yp, xp )
 4   int       *yp, *xp;
 5   {
 6       register int        posn;
 7
 8       posn = VB_GETCUR();
 9       *xp  = posn     & 0xff ;
10       *yp  = (posn >> 8) & 0xff ;
11   }
```

Listing A.63. *vb_iscol.c*— Test for Color Card (Video BIOS)

```
 1   #include <tools/vbios.h>
 2
 3   int vb_iscolor()                    /* Returns true if a color card is active */
 4   {
 5       int mode = _Vbios( GET_VMODE, 0, 0, 0, 0, "ax" ) & 0xff ;
 6       return( (mode == 7          ) ? 0  :
 7               (mode == 2 || mode == 3) ? 1  :  -1 );
 8   }
```

Listing A.64. *vb_putc.c*— Write Character in TTY Mode (Video BIOS)

```
 1    #include <tools/termlib.h>
 2    #include <tools/vbios.h>
 3
 4    void vb_putc( c, attrib )
 5    {
 6        /* Write a character to the screen in TTY mode. Only normal printing
 7         * characters, BS, BEL, CR and LF are recognized. The cursor is automatic-
 8         * ally advanced and lines will wrap. The WRITE_TTY BIOS service doesn't
 9         * handle attributes correctly, so printing characters have to be output
10         * twice---once by VB_OUTCHA to set the attribute bit, and atain using
11         * WRITE_TTY to move the cursor. WRITE_TTY picks up the existing attribute.
12         */
13
14        if( c != '\b' && c != '\007' && c != '\r' && c != '\n' )
15            VB_OUTCHA( (c & 0xff) | (attrib << 8) );
16
17        _Vbios( WRITE_TTY, c, attrib & 0xff, 0, 0, "ax" );
18    }
```

Listing A.65. *vb_puts.c*— Write String in TTY Mode (Video BIOS)

```
 1    #include <tools/vbios.h>
 2
 3    void        vb_puts( str, move_cur )
 4    register char    *str;
 5    {
 6        /* Write a string to the screen in TTY mode. If move_cur is true the cursor
 7         * is left at the end of string. If not the cursor will be restored to its
 8         * original position (before the write).
 9         */
10
11        int posn;
12
13        if( !move_cur )
14            posn = VB_GETCUR();
15
16        while( *str )
17            VB_PUTCHAR( *str++ );
18
19        if( !move_cur )
20            VB_SETCUR( posn );
21    }
```

Listing A.66. *vb_resto.c*— Restore Saved Region (Video BIOS)

```
 1    #include "video.h"
 2    #include <tools/vbios.h>
 3    #include <stdlib.h>
 4
 5    SBUF    *vb_restore( sbuf )
 6    SBUF    *sbuf;
 7    {
```

→

Listing A.66. continued...

```
 8          /* Restore a region saved with a previous vb_save() call. The cursor is
 9           * not modified. Note that the memory used by sbuf is not freed, you must
10           * do that yourself with a vb_freesbuf(sbuf) call.
11           */
12
13          int       ysize, xsize, x, y ;
14          IMAGEP    p;
15
16          xsize = ( sbuf->right  - sbuf->left ) + 1 ;
17          ysize = ( sbuf->bottom - sbuf->top  ) + 1 ;
18          p     = sbuf->image;
19
20          for( y = 0; y < ysize ; ++y )
21              for( x = 0; x < xsize ; ++x )
22              {
23                  VB_CTOYX( y + sbuf->top, x + sbuf->left );
24                  VB_OUTCHA( *p );
25                  ++p;                 /* VB_OUTCHA has side effects so can't use *p++ */
26              }
27          return sbuf;
28      }
```

Listing A.67. *vb_save.c*— Save Region (Video BIOS)

```
 1      #include <stdio.h>
 2      #include <stdlib.h>
 3      #include <tools/termlib.h>   /* must be included first */
 4      #include <tools/vbios.h>
 5
 6      SBUF *vb_save( l, r, t, b )
 7      {
 8          /* Save all characters and attributes in indicated region. Return a pointer
 9           * to a save buffer. The cursor is not modified. Note that the save buffer
10           * is allocated from the far heap but the sbuf itself is not. See also,
11           * dv_restore() and dv_freesbuf();
12           */
13
14          int         ysize, xsize, x, y ;
15          IMAGEP      p;
16          SBUF        *sbuf;
17
18          xsize = (r - l) + 1;
19          ysize = (b - t) + 1;
20
21          if( !(sbuf = (SBUF *) malloc(sizeof(SBUF)) ))
22          {
23              fprintf(stderr, "Internal error (vb_save): No memory for SBUF.");
24              exit( 1 );
25          }
26
27          if( !(p = (IMAGEP) IMALLOC(xsize * ysize * sizeof(WORD))))
28          {
29              fprintf(stderr, "Internal error (vb_save): No memory for image.");
30              exit( 2 );
31          }
32
```

➡

Listing A.67. continued...

```
33          sbuf->left   = l;
34          sbuf->right  = r;
35          sbuf->top    = t;
36          sbuf->bottom = b;
37          sbuf->image  = p;
38
39          for( y = 0; y < ysize ; ++y )
40              for( x = 0; x < xsize ; ++x )
41              {
42                  VB_CTOYX( y + t , x + l );
43                  *p++ = VB_INCHA();
44              }
45
46          return sbuf;
47      }
```

A.10 Low-level-I/O, Glue Functions

"Glue" functions are intermediate-level functions that allow your program to access low-level functions in a portable way. In the current context, the glue functions let you access either the direct-video or video-BIOS low-level-I/O functions without having to change the function calls in the program itself. If your program uses these glue functions instead of the actual I/O subroutines, you can choose which set of functions to use by linking either direct-video or BIOS libraries to your final program, without having to change the program itself. The glue-to-I/O-function mapping is summarized in Table A.3.

Table A.3. Mapping Glue Routines to I/O Functions

Glue Function†		Mapped to This Function	
		Direct-video mode	**BIOS mode**
void clr_region	(l,r,t,b,attrib)	dv_clr_region	VB_CLR_REGION
void cmove	(y,x)	dv_ctoyx	VB_CTOYX
void curpos	(**int** *yp, **int** *xp);	dv_getyx	vb_getyx
void doscroll	(l,r,t,b,a,at)	dv_scroll	VB_SCROLL
void freescr	(SBUF *p);	dv_freesbuf	vb_freesbuf
int incha	()	dv_incha	VB_INCHA
int inchar	()	dv_incha	VB_INCHA
void outc	(c, attrib)	dv_putc	vb_putc
void replace	(c);	dv_replace	VB_REPLACE
SBUF *restore	(SBUF *b);	dv_restore	vb_restore
SBUF *savescr	(l,r,t,b)	dv_save	vb_save
† Unspecified argument types are **int**.			

The glue functions are declared in *glue.c*, Listing A.68. One of three sets of functions are compiled depending on the existence of various macros as follows:

One of three sets of glue functions can be compiled, R, V, A.

If this macro is **#define**d	Use this interface
R	Video-BIOS.
V	Direct-video.
A	Select automatically at run time (autoselect).

Select between direct video and video BIOS at run time, autoselect mode.

Initializing the low-level I/O functions, init().

The VIDEO environment.

You can compile *glue.c* three times, once with R defined, once with V defined, and once with neither defined. The version of *glue.obj* that you link then determines which set of I/O functions are called into the final program.

In "autoselect" mode, the glue functions select one or the other of the sets of I/O functions at run time. The init() function is used for this purpose. Normally, when R or V are #defined at compile time, init() just initializes for the required mode, returning zero if the BIOS is used (if R is defined) or 1 if direct-video functions are used.

If A is **#define**d at compile time, the init() function selects either the BIOS or direct-video routines at run time. An init(0) call forces use of the BIOS, init(1) forces use of direct-video functions, init(-1) causes init() to examine the *VIDEO* environment variable and chose according to its contents—if *VIDEO* is set to "DIRECT" or "direct", the direct-video functions are used, otherwise the video-BIOS is used. init() returns 0 if the BIOS is selected, 1 if the direct-video functions are selected. The one disadvantage to autoselect mode is that both libraries must be in memory at run time, even though you're using only one of them.

Listing A.68. *glue.c*— Glue Functions for Low-Level I/O

```
 1   #include <stdio.h>
 2   #include <stdlib.h>
 3   #include <tools/debug.h>
 4   #include <tools/termlib.h>
 5   #include <tools/vbios.h>
 6
 7   /* GLUE.C        This file glues the curses package to either the video-
 8    *               BIOS functions or to the direct-video functions.
 9    */
10
11   #if (!defined(R) && !defined(V))
12   #       define AUTOSELECT
13   #endif
14
15   /*-------------------------------------------------------------------*/
16   #ifdef R
17
18   init(how)                     { return 0;                              }
19   cmove(y,x)                    { return VB_CTOYX   (y,x);               }
20   curpos(yp,xp) int *yp,*xp;    { return vb_getyx   (yp,xp);             }
21   replace(c)                    { return VB_REPLACE (c);                 }
22   doscroll(l,r,t,b,a,at)        { return VB_SCROLL  (l,r,t,b,a, at );    }
23   inchar()                      { return VB_INCHA   ( )  & 0xff ;        }
24   incha()                       { return VB_INCHA   ( );                 }
25   outc(c, attrib)               { return vb_putc    (c, attrib);         }
26   SBUF *savescr(l,r,t,b)        { return vb_save    (l,r,t,b);           }
27   SBUF *restore(b)   SBUF *b;   { return vb_restore (b);                 }
28   freescr(p)         SBUF *p;   { return vb_freesbuf(p);                 }
29   clr_region(l,r,t,b,attrib)    { return VB_CLR_REGION(l,r,t,b,attrib);  }
30
31   int is_direct(){ return 0; };
32   #endif
33
```

Listing A.68. continued...

```
34    /*-----------------------------------------------------------------------*/
35    #ifdef V
36
37    cmove(y,x)                    { return dv_ctoyx     (y,x);                    }
38    curpos(yp,xp) int *yp,*xp; { return dv_getyx       (yp,xp);                  }
39    replace(c)                    { return dv_replace   (c);                     }
40    doscroll(l,r,t,b,a,at)        { return dv_scroll    (l,r,t,b,a,at);          }
41    inchar()                      { return dv_incha     ( ) & 0xff;              }
42    incha()                       { return dv_incha     ( );                     }
43    outc(c,attrib)                { return dv_putc      (c, attrib);             }
44    SBUF *savescr(l,r,t,b)        { return dv_save      (l,r,t,b);               }
45    SBUF *restore(b)   SBUF *b; { return dv_restore     (b);                     }
46    freescr(p)          SBUF *p; { return dv_freesbuf   (p);                     }
47    clr_region(l,r,t,b,attrib) { return dv_clr_region  (l,r,t,b,attrib);        }
48
49    init( how )                                              /* Initialize */
50    {
51        if( !dv_init() )
52        {
53            fprintf(stderr, "MGA or CGA in 80-column text mode required\n");
54            exit( 1 );
55        }
56        return 1;
57    }
58
59    int is_direct(){ return 1; };
60    #endif
61
62    /*-----------------------------------------------------------------------*/
63    #ifdef A
64
65    static int Dv = 0 ;
66
67    init( how )
68    int how;          /* 0=BIOS, 1=direct video, -1=autoselect */
69    {
70        char *p;
71
72        if( Dv = how )
73        {
74            if( how < 0 )
75            {
76                p  = getenv( "VIDEO" );
77                Dv = p && ((strcmp(p,"DIRECT")==0 || strcmp(p,"direct")==0));
78            }
79
80            if( Dv && !dv_init() )
81            {
82                fprintf(stderr, "MGA or CGA in 80-column text mode required\n");
83                exit( 1 );
84            }
85        }
86
87        return Dv;
88    }
89
90    /* The following statements all depend on the fact that a subroutine name
91     * (without the trailing argument list and parentheses) evaluates to a temporary
92     * variable of type pointer-to-function. Therefore, function names can be treated
93     * as a pointer to a function in the conditionals, below. For example, curpos()
```

➡

Listing A.68. continued...

```
 94     * calls dv_getyx if Dv is true, otherwise vb_getyx is called. ANSI actually
 95     * says that the star isn't necessary. The following should be legal:
 96     *
 97     *       return (Dv ? dv_ctyx : VB_CTOYX)( y, x );
 98     *
 99     * but many compilers (including Microsoft) don't accept it. Macros, clearly,
100     * must be treated in a more standard fashion.
101     */
102
103     curpos(yp,xp) int *yp,*xp; {return(Dv? *dv_getyx    :*vb_getyx    )(yp,xp);        }
104     SBUF *savescr(l,r,t,b)     {return(Dv? *dv_save     :*vb_save     )(l,r,t,b);      }
105     SBUF *restore(b) SBUF *b;  {return(Dv? *dv_restore  :*vb_restore  )(b);            }
106     freescr(p)       SBUF *p;  {return(Dv? *dv_freesbuf:*vb_freesbuf)(p);             }
107     outc(c, attrib)            {return(Dv? *dv_putc     :*vb_putc     )(c, attrib);    }
108
109     replace(c)                 { if(Dv) dv_replace(c); else VB_REPLACE(c);            }
110     cmove(y,x)                 { if(Dv) dv_ctoyx(y,x); else VB_CTOYX(y,x);            }
111     inchar()                   { return( Dv? dv_incha()  : VB_INCHA()     ) & 0xff;   }
112     incha()                    { return( Dv? dv_incha()  : VB_INCHA()     );          }
113
114     doscroll(l,r,t,b,a,at)
115     {
116         if( Dv ) dv_scroll(l,r,t,b,a,at);
117         else     VB_SCROLL(l,r,t,b,a,at);
118     }
119
120     clr_region(l,r,t,b,attrib)
121     {
122         if( Dv ) dv_clr_region(l,r,t,b,attrib);
123         else     VB_CLR_REGION(l,r,t,b,attrib);
124     }
125
126     int is_direct(){ return Dv; };
127     #endif
```

A.11 Window Management: Curses

The low-level I/O functions are really too low level to be useful—higher-level functions are needed. Since I write a lot of code that has to work in both the MS-DOS and UNIX environments, it seemed sensible to mimic a set of UNIX functions under MS-DOS. Among other things, this approach solves various incompatibility problems between the two systems. For example, the Microsoft, MS-DOS C compiler doesn't have UNIX-compatible fcntl() or ioctl() functions, it doesn't support the /dev/tty device for the console (you have to use /dev/con or CON), and it doesn't provide any sort of termcap or curses-compatible function library. Consequently, it's difficult to port code that does low-level I/O from the Microsoft compiler to UNIX.

Curses.

The most serious omission in the earlier list is the lack of a curses library. For the uninitiated, *curses* is a collection of terminal-independent, low-level I/O functions. The package was written by Ken Arnold, then at U.C. Berkeley. These routines let you do things like move the cursor around on the screen, create and delete windows, write text and seek to specific window-relative cursor positions and so forth. The windows can be overlapping and they support individual wrap-around, scrolling, and so forth. The curses

Termcap database.

functions can talk to virtually any terminal. They accomplish this feat by using the *termcap* terminal database and interface library developed by Bill Joy. The database is an ASCII file that contains definitions for the various escape sequences needed to get around on specific terminals, and the interface library lets you access these machine-specific escape sequences in a portable and transparent way.

The real curses routines talk to the terminals efficiently over a serial line. They always send the minimum number of characters necessary to modify the current screen. Curses keeps two internal images of the screen. One of these reflects what's actually on the screen, and the other is a scratch space that you modify using the various curses functions. When you tell curses to do a refresh, it compares the scratch buffer with the actual screen image and then sends out the minimum number of characters necessary to get these images to match. This behavior is especially important when you're running a program via a modem and characters are coming at 1200 baud. Redrawing the entire screen every time you scroll a four-line by 10-character window is just unacceptable behavior. It takes too long. Curses solves the problem by redrawing only those parts of the screen that have actually changed.

Curses is designed for efficient serial communication.

The UNIX curses functions are described in depth in [Arnold] and also in [Haviland]. Since the implementation details can vary somewhat from installation to installation, I strongly recommend that you read your own system documentation as well.

The current section describes the behavior of my own curses implementation, which **occs** uses for window management in interactive debugging environment. My system models Berkeley curses—there are a few minor differences between it and System V versions. I've written several quite complex programs using these functions, programs that maintain several windows on the screen simultaneously, all of which are being updated at different rates. Moreover, the finished programs have ported to UNIX (BSD 4.3) with literally no modification. I have not implemented the entire curses library, however, and I've added a few features to my own package that are not supported by the real curses. You can write a UNIX-compatible program using my functions, but there are minor (but documented) differences that can cause problems if you're not careful. For example, support for overlapping windows is limited (you can't write reliably to a window that has a second window on top of it). Subwindows aren't supported. This last problem means that you can't move a window along with the associated subwindows. Similarly, you have to delete or update the subwindows explicitly, one at a time. Pseudo-subwindows can be used, but only if you don't move them. My package does implement a few handy features not found in the UNIX version, however. You can hide a window without deleting it, and there is a provision for making boxed windows.

Curses portability issues.

This section just describes my own functions. Though I point out the important differences from UNIX, you'll have to read the UNIX documentation too if you intend to write portable code. The two systems do behave differently in many ways. Note that, since these routines are not intended to port to UNIX, I haven't done things like use the UX() and VA_LIST macros in <*debug.h*> to make them portable.

A.11.1 Configuration and Compiling

The curses functions talk to the screen using the low-level I/O functions described in the previous section. Curses automatically selects between the CGA and MGA adapters by using the autoselect version of the glue functions. (The CGA must be running in an 80-column mode, though.) Curses normally uses the ROM-BIOS routines, which are slow but portable. If, however, a VIDEO environment variable exists, and that variable is set to the string DIRECT, the direct-video functions will be used. (Do this with a set VIDEO=DIRECT from the DOS prompt.) The BIOS functions are noticeably slower than the direct-video functions. The speed problem is most evident when you are saving and restoring the area under a window. Moving a visible window in an incremental fashion (one space or line at a time) is a particularly painful process when you're using the BIOS. It's better, in this instance, to hide the window, move it where you want it, and then redisplay it.

curses.lib, termlib.lib.

The curses functions are all in a library called *curses.lib*, and the I/O routines are in *termlib.lib.* Both of these must be linked to the final program.

A.11.2 Using Curses

<curses.h>

Curses itself is part macro and part subroutine. The file *<curses.h>* should be **#include**d at the top of every file that uses the curses functions. Supported functions are described in this section, grouped functionally.

A.11.2.1 Initialization Functions.

Initialize,
terminate curses.

```
void initscr(void);
void endwin (void);
```

initscr() initializes the curses package. It should be called at the head of your main() subroutine, before any other curses functions are called. endwin() cleans up. It should always be called before your program exits.

In UNIX programs, the terminal can be left in an unknown state if you abort your program with a BREAK. If you exit abnormally from a program that uses curses, only to find your terminal acting funny (not echoing, not handling tabs or newlines properly, and so forth), you can usually correct the problem by typing *tset* with no arguments. If that doesn't work, try <NL>*reset*<NL> where *<NL>* is a newline or Ctrl-J. If that doesn't work try *stty cooked echo nl*, and if that doesn't work, hang up and log on again. To avoid this sort of flailing around, it's much better for your program to trap SIGINT and call endwin() from within the service routine. Use the following:

```
#include <signal.h>
#include <curses.h>

onintr()
{
    endwin();
    exit( STATUS );
}
main()
{
    signal  ( SIGINT, onintr );
    initscr ( void );
}
```

A.11.2.2 Configuration Functions.
Once the curses package is initialized, you should determine how your terminal is going to respond to typed characters. Six routines are provided for this purpose:

Set unbuffered,
buffered input.

```
int crmode   (void);
int nocrmode(void);
```

These routines control input buffering; crmode() disables buffering—characters will be available as soon as they're typed. A nocrmode() call cancels a previous crmode(). In *nocr* mode, an entire line is read before the first character is returned. The only editing character available in nocrmode() is a backspace, which deletes the character to the left of the cursor. Many curses programs use crmode(), but some implementations won't work properly unless nocrmode() is active.

```
int echo   (void);                                                              Echo characters.
int noecho(void);                                                               Do not echo.
```

If `echo()` is called, characters are echoed as they're typed; `noecho()` suppresses the echoing—you'll have to echo the character yourself every time you read a character. The real curses gets very confused when `echo()` is enabled. The problem here is that curses doesn't know about any character that it has not itself written to the screen. Since characters are echoed by the operating system rather than curses, the package doesn't know that they're there. As a consequence, when curses does a screen refresh, it won't delete the characters that it doesn't know about and the screen rapidly fills with unwanted and unerasable characters. It's best always to call `noecho()` at the top of your program. Another echo-related problem found in the MS-DOS versions of curses. Character echo cannot be suppressed with the MS-DOS buffered-input function. So `echo()` and `noecho()` have no effect on a program if `nocrmode()` is active.

```
int nl   (void);                                                                Map newlines.
int nonl(void);                                                                 Do not map newlines.
```

A `nl()` call causes a newlines (`'\n'`) to be converted to a carriage-return, line-feed sequence on output; an input carriage return (`'\r'`) is also mapped to a newline. If `nonl()` is called, no mapping is done. It's usually convenient to call `nl()` at the top of your program, but again, many UNIX curses packages fail to work properly unless `nonl()` is specified. You have to do all the `'\n'` to `\r\n` mapping yourself in *nonl* mode, of course.

A.11.2.3 Creating and Deleting Windows.
This section describes the functions that create and delete windows. There are two kinds of windows. A normal window and a *subwindow*. In UNIX curses, a subwindow is affected by all commands that also affect the parent. When a parent window is refreshed by curses, all subwindows are refreshed too. Similarly, when you delete or move a parent window, all the subwindows are deleted or moved. This feature is not supported in the current implementation, though you can pretend that subwindows exist if you don't move them. The mechanics of this process are discussed below.   Subwindows.

A default window, called `stdscr`, which occupies the entire screen, is created automatically by `initscr()`, and several functions are provided to modify this window. A `stdscr` variable is defined in `<curses.h>`, and it can be passed as a WINDOW pointer to any of the curses functions in a manner analogous to `stdout`. You shouldn't declare `stdscr` explicitly in your program, just use it. For convenience, most functions have a version that uses `stdscr`, rather than an explicit window, in a manner analogous to `putchar()`. If you are using curses only for cursor movement and are not creating additional windows, you can use `stdscr` directly and don't need to use any of the functions described in this section.   The *stdscr* window.

The `stdscr` variable in *<curses.h>*.

In UNIX applications, it's often convenient to declare all windows as subwindows to `stdscr`. For example, the save-screen mechanism used in yydebug.c won't work unless all the windows are subwindows of `stdscr` because it reads characters from `stdscr` itself.

```
WINDOW *newwin(int lines, int cols, int begin_y, int begin_x);                  Create window, subwin-
WINDOW *subwin(WINDOW *win, int lines, int cols, int begin_y,                   dow.
            int begin_x);
```

This function creates a new window, `lines` rows high and `cols` columns wide with the upper-left corner at (`begin_y`, `begin_x`). [All coordinates here are (*y,x*), where *y* is the row number and *x* is the column number. The upper-left   Coordinates are (y,x), y=row, x=column. Upper left corner is (0,0).

corner of the screen is (0,0).] A pointer to a WINDOW structure, declared in *<curses.h>*, is returned in a manner analogous to fopen() returning a FILE.

Windows are created as visible, unboxed, with scrolling disabled, and with line wrap enabled. Characters that go past the end of line show up at the left edge of the next line, but the window won't scroll when you get to the bottom. The text under the window is saved by default and is restored when the window is moved or deleted. The window is automatically cleared as part of the creation process and there's no way to disable this clearing. All of these defaults can be changed with subroutine calls discussed below.

The subwin() call is provided for UNIX compatibility. It is mapped to a newwin() call (the first argument is ignored).

Enable or disable scrolling.

```
scrollok(WINDOW *win, int flag);
```

This macro is passed a WINDOW pointer and a flag. If flag is true, the indicated window is allowed to scroll. Otherwise the window does not scroll and characters that go off the bottom of the window are discarded. Scrolling is always enabled on the stdscr window.

Nonstandard: enable or disable line wrap.

```
wrapok(WINDOW *win, int flag);
```

This macro enables or disables line wrap if flag is false, enables it otherwise. Line wrap is enabled by default. When wrapping is disabled, characters written past the edge of the window are discarded rather than appearing on the next line.

Nonstandard:

Box windows.
No boxes.

```
void boxed   (void);
void unboxed(void);
```

The lack of support for subwindows complicates management of windows with boxes around them considerably. A UNIX-compatible method for creating boxed windows is described below in the discussion of the box() function. It's not practical to use this function if windows will be moved, however. I've solved the problem to some extent by adding a mechanism for creating boxed windows in which the box is an integral part of the window and cannot be overwritten by the text. All windows created with newwin() after boxed() has been called will have an integral box as part of the window. You can go back to normal, unboxed windows by calling unboxed(). IBM box-drawing characters are used for the border.

Nonstandard: change colors.

```
void ground    (WINDOW *win, int fore, int back);
void def_ground(int fore, int back);
```

ground() lets you change foreground (fore) and background (back) colors on the IBM/PC. The color codes are defined symbolically in *<tools/termlib.h>*. def_ground() changes the default foreground and background colors. All windows created after a def_ground() call have the indicated colors. Use ground() to selectively change the attribute associated with specific characters written to a window; only those characters written to the window after the ground() call are affected. If you want to change an existing window's color without modifying the window's contents, you must change the color with ground() and then read each character individually and write it back using winch() and addch().

BUGS: delwin() doesn't know about color changes, you must set the ground back to NORMAL and call wclear() before deleting the window.

```
void save   (void);
void nosave(void);
```

Normally, when you create a window, the text under that window is saved so that it can be replaced when the window is moved or deleted. This is a needless waste of memory if you're not going to delete or move the window. Once `nosave()` has been called, the underlying text is not saved by subsequent `newwin()` calls. Saving can be reenabled by calling `save()`. Text under `stdscr` is never saved.

```
delwin(WINDOW *win);
```

This function removes a window from the screen, usually restoring the text that was underneath the window. If `nosave()` was active when the window was created, however, an empty box is left on the screen when the window is deleted. Overlapping windows must be deleted in the opposite order from which they were created. Similarly, if you move one window on top of a second one, you must delete the top window first. I'd suggest keeping a stack of active windows so that you know the order in which they are created.

A.11.2.4 Subroutines That Affect Entire Windows.

```
WINDOW *hidewin(WINDOW *win);
WINDOW *showwin(WINDOW *win);
```

The only way to get rid of a UNIX-curses window is to delete it. This is inconvenient when you really just want to make it invisible for a while and then redisplay it later. The nonstandard `hidewin()` function hides the window (makes it disappear but does not delete it). It returns NULL if the window can't be hidden for some reason (usually not enough memory is available to save the image), or the `win` pointer on success. The window can be resurrected sometime later with a `showwin()` call. `showwin()` returns NULL (and does nothing) if the window wasn't hidden, otherwise the `win` argument is returned. `hidewin()` always returns its argument—it terminates the program with an error message if it can't get memory to hide the window.

It's okay to move a hidden window, it will just reappear at the new location when you call `showwin()`. You cannot, however, write to a hidden window or the written characters will be lost. Similarly, the restrictions of deleting windows in the opposite order from which they were created also applies to hiding and redisplaying them. When windows can overlap, you must always hide the most-recently displayed window first.

```
int mvwin(WINDOW *win, int y, int x);
```

This function moves a window to an absolute location on the screen. The area under the window is restored, the window is moved to the indicated location, and it is then redisplayed, saving the text that is now under the window first. You should move only the topmost of several overlapping windows. The normal UNIX `mvwin()` returns ERR and does nothing if the new coordinates would have moved any part of the window off the screen. I've changed this behavior somewhat by always moving the window as far as I can. The window still won't move off the screen, but it may move a little if it wasn't already at the screen's edge. If you prefer UNIX compatibility, change the 0 in **#define** LIKE_UNIX 0 in mvwin.c (below) to 1 and recompile.

```
mvwinr(WINDOW *win, int y, int x);
```

This nonstandard macro lets you move a window relative to the current window position. Positive values of y move down, negative values move up. Similarly, positive values of x move right and negative values go left. For example,

```
mvwinr( win, -5, 10 );
```

moves the window pointed to by win five spaces up from, and 10 spaces to the right of its current position. Like mvwin(), you can't move the window off the screen.

Refresh stdscr.

Refresh window.

void refresh (**void**);
void wrefresh(WINDOW *win);

These macros are used by the real curses to do a screen refresh. They force the screen to coincide with the internal representation of the screen. No characters are actually written out to the terminal until a refresh occurs. My own curses writes to the screen immediately, so both of these macros expand to null strings—they are ignored. You'll need them to be able to port code to UNIX, however. refresh() refreshes the whole screen (the stdscr window and all subwindows of stdscr); wrefresh(win) is passed a WINDOW pointer and refreshes only the indicated window.

Draw box in window.

int box(WINDOW *win, **int** vert, **int** horiz);

This subroutine draws a box in the outermost characters of the window using vert for the vertical characters and horiz for the horizontal ones. I've extended this function to support the IBM box-drawing characters. If IBM box-drawing characters are specified for vert and horiz, box() will use the correct box-drawing characters for the corners. The box-drawing characters are defined in *<tools/box.h>* as follows:

symbolic value	numeric value	description
HORIZ	0xc4	Single horizontal line.
D_HORIZ	0xcd	Double horizontal line.
VERT	0xb3	Single vertical line.
D_VERT	0xba	Double vertical line.

Boxes may have double horizontal lines and single vertical ones, or vice versa. The UNIX box() function uses the vertical character for the corners.

Note that box() doesn't draw a box around the window; rather, it draws the box in the outermost characters of the window itself. This means that you can overwrite the border if your output lines are too wide. When you scroll the window, the box scrolls too. Normally, this problem is avoided by using the subwindow mechanism. A large outer window is created and boxed, a smaller subwindow is then created for the text region.

Creating a boxed window with box().

A function that creates a bordered window in this way is shown in Listing A.69. The outer window is created on line 14, the inner, nested one on line 22. The outer window just holds the box and the inner window is used for characters. This way, you can overflow the inner window and not affect the outer one (that holds the border). The function returns a pointer to the text window. If you plan to move or delete the window, you'll need the pointer to the outer window too, and will have to modify the subroutine accordingly.

Listing A.69. Creating a Boxed Window

```
 1  WINDOW  *boxwin( lines, cols, y_start, x_start, title )
 2  char    *title;
 3  {
 4      /* This routine works much like the newwin() except that the window has a
 5       * box around it that won't be destroyed by writes to the window. It
 6       * accomplishes this feat by creating two windows, one inside the other,
 7       * with a box drawn in the outer one. It prints the title centered on the
 8       * top line of the box. Note that I'm making all windows subwindows of the
 9       * stdscr to facilitate the print-screen command.
10       */
11
12      WINDOW *outer, *inner;
13
14      outer = subwin(stdscr, lines, cols, y_start, x_start);
15
16      box( outer, '|', '-' );
17
18      wmove  ( outer, 0, (cols - strlen(title))/2 );
19      wprintw( outer, "%s", title );
20
21      wrefresh( outer );
22      return subwin( stdscr, lines-2, cols-2, y_start+1, x_start+1 );
23  }
```

A.11.2.5 Cursor Movement and Character I/O.

```
int  move (y, x);
int  wmove(WINDOW *win, y, x);
void getyx(WINDOW *win, y, x);
```

Move cursor.

Get cursor position (MACRO).

These functions support cursor movement. move() moves the cursor to the indicated absolute position on the screen. The upper-left corner of the screen is (0,0). wmove() moves the cursor to the relative position within a specific window (pointed to by win). The upper-left corner of the window is (0,0). If you try to move past the edge of the window, the cursor will be positioned at the closest edge. The getyx() macro loads the current cursor position for a specific window into y and x. Note that this is a macro, not a subroutine, so you should not precede y or x with an address-of operator (&). A getyx(stdscr,y,x) call loads the current absolute cursor position into y and x.

```
int getch (void);
int wgetch(WINDOW *win);
```

Get character and echo to window

These functions are used for direct keyboard input. getch() gets a character from the keyboard and echoes it to stdscr, wgetch() echoes the character to the indicated window (if echo() is enabled, that is). Note that crmode() has to be enabled to get the character as soon as it's typed. Otherwise the entire line will be buffered. It's unfortunate that many compiler manufactures, Microsoft included, have chosen to use getch() as the name of their standard direct keyboard-input function. You'll need to specify a /NOE switch to Microsoft link to prevent the linker from attempting to call in both versions of the subroutine.

Use Microsoft Link's /NOE switch to avoid name conflicts.

Read functions.

```
inch    (void);
winch   (WINDOW *win);
mvinch (int y, int x);
mvwinch(WINDOW *win, int y, int x);
```

These functions let you read back characters that are displayed on the screen. `inch()` returns the character at the current cursor position (that is, from `stdscr`). `mvinch(y,x)` moves the cursor to the indicated position and then returns the character at that position; the `winch()` and `mvwinch(win,y,x)` versions do the same, but the cursor position is relative to the origin of the specified window. Note that the `y` and `x` coordinates are relative to the origin of the indicated window, not to the entire screen. (0,0) is the top left corner of the window. Some older versions of curses don't support the `mv` versions of this command. Note that all four functions work as if all windows were declared as subwindows to `stdscr`. This is not the case in UNIX systems, in which a read from `stdscr` can get a character from the standard screen that is currently obscured by an overlapping window.

`printf()` to `stdscr`.
`printf()` to window.

```
void printw(char *fmt,...);
int wprintw(WINDOW *win, char *fmt,...);
```

These functions are used for formatted output. `printw()` works just like `printf()`; `wprintw()` is the same but it prints to the indicated window, moving the cursor to the correct position in the new window if necessary. (The cursor is moved to the position immediately following the character most recently written to the indicated window.) `printw()` pays no attention to window boundaries, but `wprintw()` wraps when you get to the right edge of the window and the window scrolls when you go past the bottom line (provided that `scrollok()` has been called for the current window).

Character-output functions.

```
void addch  (int c);
int  waddch (WINDOW *win, int c);
void addstr (char *str);
int  waddstr(WINDOW *win, char *str);
```

These functions are the curses equivalents of `putc()`, `putchar()`, `puts()`, and `fputs()`: `addch()` works like `putchar()`; `waddch()` writes a character to the indicated window (and advances the cursor); `addstr()` and `waddstr()` work like `fputs()`, writing a string to `stdscr` or the indicated window. Neither `addstr()` nor `waddstr()` add a newline at the end of the string. `addch()` and `waddch()` treat several characters specially:

'\n' Clear the line from the current cursor position to the right edge of the window. If `nl()` is active go to the left edge of the next line, otherwise go to the current column on the next line. In addition, if scrolling is enabled, the window scrolls if you're on the bottom line.

'\t' is expanded into an 8-space field. If the tab goes past the right edge of the window, the cursor wraps to the next line.

'\r' gets you to the left edge of the window, on the current line.

'\b' backs up one space but may not back up past the left edge of the window. A nondestructive backspace is used (the character on which the initial cursor sits is not erased). The curses documentation doesn't say that '\b' is handled specially but it does indeed work.

ESC The ESC character is not handled specially by UNIX but my `waddch()` does do so. Don't use explicit escape sequences if portability is a consideration. All characters between an ASCII ESC and an alphabetic character (inclusive) are sent to the output but are otherwise ignored. This behavior let's you send escape sequences directly to the terminal to change character attributes and so forth. I'm assuming here that you won't change windows in the middle of an escape sequence.

`waddch()` returns `ERR` (defined in `<curses.h>`) if the character had caused the window to scroll illegally or if you attempt to write to a hidden window.

```
void werase    (WINDOW *win);
void erase     (void);
void wclear    (WINDOW *win);
void clear     (void);
void wclrtoeol (WINDOW *win);
void clrtoeol  (void);
```

Erase window, entire screen, to end of line.

These functions all erase one or more characters. `clear()` and `erase()` both clear the entire screen, `wclear()` and `werase()` both clear only the indicated window, `wclrtoeol()` clears the line from the current cursor position in the indicated window to the right edge of the indicated window, and `clrtoeol()` clears from the current cursor position to the right edge of the screen.

```
int scroll (WINDOW *win);
int wscroll(WINDOW *win, int amt);
```

Scroll window.

These two functions scroll the window: `scroll()` scrolls the indicated window up one line, `wscroll()` scrolls by the indicated amount—up if `amt` is positive, down if it's negative. `wscroll()` is not supported by the UNIX curses. Both functions return 1 if the window scrolled, 0 if not.

There's one caveat about scrolling. The UNIX functions have a bug in them: when a window scrolls, the bottom line is not cleared, leaving a mess on the screen. This problem is not restricted to the `scroll()` subroutine but occurs any time that the window scrolls (as when you write a newline on the bottom line of the window or when a character wraps, causing a scroll. As a consequence, if you're porting to UNIX, you should always do a `clrtoeol()` immediately after either scrolling or printing a newline. Unfortunately, there's no easy way to tell if a window has scrolled because of a character wrap. My curses package doesn't have this problem—the bottom line of the window is always cleared on a scroll.

A.11.3 Curses—Implementation

This section discusses my curses implementation. Note that I haven't bothered to make this code UNIX compatible—I'm assuming that you're going to use the native UNIX curses in that environment. For the most part, the code is straightforward and needs little comment. The `WINDOW` structure is declared on lines one to 17 of *<tools/curses.h>* (Listing A.70). The macros for `bool`, `reg`, `TRUE`, `FALSE`, `ERR`, and `OK` are defined in the UNIX *<curses.h>* file so I've put them here too, though they're not particularly useful. Be careful of:

The `WINDOW` structure.

Problems with `if(foo()==TRUE)`.

```
if( foo() == TRUE )
```

`TRUE` is **#define**d to 1 but, in fact, any nonzero value is true. As a consequence, `foo()` could return a perfectly legitimate true value that didn't happen to be 1, and the test would fail. The test:

```
                if( foo() != FALSE )
```

ERR returned by curses
output functions.

is safer. Most of the output functions return ERR if a write would normally have caused
a scroll but scrolling is disabled.

Listing A.70. *curses.h*— WINDOW Definitions and Macros

```
 1   typedef struct _window_
 2   {
 3       int  x_org;               /* X coordinate of upper-left corner    */
 4       int  y_org;               /* Y coordinate of upper-left corner    */
 5       int  x_size;              /* Horizontal size of text area.        */
 6       int  y_size;              /* Vertical  size of text area.         */
 7       int  row;                 /* Current cursor row    (0 to y_size-1) */
 8       int  col;                 /* Current cursor column (0 to x_size-1) */
 9       void *image;              /* Image buffer. Holds what used to be  */
10                                 /* under the window.                    */
11       unsigned wrap_ok    :1 ;  /* Line wrap is enabled in this win.    */
12       unsigned scroll_ok  :1 ;  /* Scrolling permitted in this window   */
13       unsigned hidden     :1 ;  /* Window is hidden (nonstandard)       */
14       unsigned boxed      :1 ;  /* Window is boxed  (nonstandard)       */
15       unsigned attrib     :8 ;  /* attribute used for character writes  */
16
17   } WINDOW;
18
19   #define bool     unsigned int
20   #define reg      register
21   #define TRUE     (1)
22   #define FALSE    (0)
23   #define ERR      (0)
24   #define OK       (1)
25
26   /*------------------------------------------------------------
27    * The following macros implement many of the curses functions.
28    */
29
30   #define getyx( win, y, x )  \
31                       ((x) = ((WINDOW*)(win))->col, (y) = ((WINDOW*)(win))->row)
32
33   #define refresh()
34   #define scrollok(win,flag) ((win)->scroll_ok = (flag))
35   #define wrapok(win,flag)   ((win)->wrap_ok   = (flag))
36   #define wrefresh(win)        /* empty */
37
38   /*------------------------------------------------------------
39    * Nonstandard Macros: movewin() moves the window relative to the current
40    *                     position. Negative is left or up, positive is right or
41    * down. ground() changes the fore and background colors for subsequent writes
42    * to the window.
43    */
44
45   #define mvwinr(w,dy,dx) mvwin((w),((w)->y_org - (w)->boxed) + (dy), \
46                                      ((w)->x_org - (w)->boxed) + (dx) )
47
48   #define ground(win,f,b)     ( win->attrib = ((f) & 0x7f) | ((b) & 0x7f) << 4)
49
50   /*------------------------------------------------------------
51    * Externs for the window functions and #defines to map the standard screen
52    * functions to the stdscr versions. There are a few idiosyncrasies here.
53    * In particular, mvcur() just ignores it's first two arguments and maps to a
54    * move() call. Similarly, subwin() just maps to a newwin() call, and clearok()
```

→

Listing A.70. continued...

```
55      * isn't supported. You must clear the window explicitly before writing to it.
56      */
57
58      extern   WINDOW            *stdscr;
59      extern   void endwin       (void);
60      extern   void initscr      (void);
61      extern   int waddch        (WINDOW *, int);
62
63      #define addch(c)           waddch(stdscr, c)
64
65      extern   int waddstr       (WINDOW *, char *);
66      #define addstr(s)          waddstr(stdscr,s)
67
68      extern   int wclrtoeol     (WINDOW *        );
69      #define clrtoeol()         wclrtoeol(stdscr)
70
71      extern   int werase        (WINDOW *        );
72      #define erase              werase(stdscr)
73
74      #define wclear(w)          werase(w)
75      #define clear()            werase(stdscr)
76
77      extern   int wgetch        (WINDOW *);
78      #define getch()            wgetch( stdscr )
79
80      extern   int wmove         (WINDOW *, int, int );
81      #define move(y,x)          wmove( stdscr,(y),(x)   )
82      #define mvcur(oy,ox,y,x)   move((y),(x))
83
84      extern   int wprintw       (WINDOW *, char *, ... );
85      extern   int printw        (          char *, ... );
86
87      extern   int wscroll       (WINDOW *, int            );
88      #define scroll(win)        wscroll(win,1)
89
90      extern   int winch         (WINDOW *);
91      #define inch()             winch(stdscr)
92      #define mvinch(y,x)        ( wmove(stdscr,y,x), winch(stdscr) )
93      #define mvwinch(w,y,x)     ( wmove(w,      y,x), winch(w)      )
94
95      extern   WINDOW *newwin    (int ,int ,int ,int );
96      #define subwin(w,a,b,c,d)  newwin(a,b,c,d)
97
98      /*--------------------------------------------------------
99       * Externs for functions that don't have stdscr versions
100      */
101
102     extern   int box           (WINDOW *,int ,int );              /* UNIX functions */
103     extern   int crmode        (void);
104     extern   int delwin        (WINDOW *);
105     extern   int echo          (void);
106     extern   int mvwin         (WINDOW *win, int y, int x);
107     extern   int nl            (void);
108     extern   int nocrmode      (void);
109     extern   int noecho        (void);
110     extern   int nonl          (void);
111     extern void boxed          ( void );                          /* Nonstandard functions */
112     extern void unboxed        ( void );
113     extern void save           ( void );
114     extern void nosave         ( void );
```

➡

Listing A.70. continued...

```
115    extern void def_ground ( int, int );
```

The comma operator in `mvinch()` and `mvwinch()`. Writing multiple-statement macros.

The `mvinch()` and `mvwinch()` macros on lines 92 and 93 of Listing A.70 use the comma, or *sequence*, operator. The comma operator evaluates from left to right, and the entire expression evaluates to the rightmost object in the list. For example, the `mvinch()` looks like:

```
#define mvinch(y,x)  (move(y,x), inch())
```

An equivalent subroutine is:

```
mvinch(y,x)
{
    move(y,x);
    return inch();
}
```

The comma operator is used because there are two statements that have to be executed, the `move()` call and the `inch()` call. Were you to define the macro as:

```
#define mvinch(y,x) move(y,x); inch()
```

the following code wouldn't work:

```
if( condition )
      mvinch(y,x);
```

because it would expand to:

```
if( condition )
      move(y,x);
inch();
```

Putting curly braces around the statements doesn't help. For example:

```
#define mvinch(y,x) {move(y,x); inch();}
```

```
if( condition )
      mvinch(y, x);
else
      something();
```

expands to

```
if( condition )
{
    move(y,x);
    inch();
}
;
else
      something();
```

Here the `else` will try to bind with the semicolon, which is a perfectly legitimate statement in C, causing a *No matching if for else* error message. Though the comma operator solves both of these problems, it isn't very readable. I don't recommend using it unless you must. Never use it if curly braces will work in a particular application. The remainder of curses is in Listings A.71 to A.87.

Listing A.71. *box.h*— IBM/PC Box-Drawing Characters

```
 1    /*---------------------------------------------------------
 2     * BOX.H:   #defines for the box-drawing characters
 3     *---------------------------------------------------------
 4     *       The names are:
 5     *
 6     *       UL      Upper left corner
 7     *       UR      Upper right corner
 8     *       LL      lower left corner
 9     *       LR      lower right corner
10     *       CEN     Center (intersection of two lines)
11     *       TOP     Tee with the flat piece on top
12     *       BOT     Bottom tee
13     *       LEFT    Left tee
14     *       RIGHT   Right tee
15     *       HORIZ   Horizontal line
16     *       VERT    Vertical line.
17     *
18     *                       UL    -TOP-     UR              HORIZ
19     *                              |
20     *                       L              R               V
21     *                       E      |       I               E
22     *                       F--   -CEN-   --G              R
23     *                       T      |       H               T
24     *                       |              T
25     *                              |
26     *                       LL    -BOT-    LR
27     *
28     * The D_XXX  defines have double horizontal and vertical lines.
29     * The HD_XXX defines have double horizontal lines and single  vertical  lines.
30     * The VD_XXX defines have double  vertical  lines and single horizontal lines.
31     *
32     * If your terminal is not IBM compatible, #define all of these as '+' (except
33     * for the VERT #defines, which should be a |, and the HORIZ #defines,  which
34     * should be a -) by #defining NOT_IBM_PC before including this file.
35     */
36
37    #ifdef NOT_IBM_PC
38    #    define IBM_BOX(x)
39    #    define OTHER_BOX(x) x
40    #else
41    #    define IBM_BOX(x)    x
42    #    define OTHER_BOX(x)
43    #endif
44
45    #define VERT            IBM_BOX( 179 )  OTHER_BOX( '|' )
46    #define RIGHT           IBM_BOX( 180 )  OTHER_BOX( '+' )
47    #define UR              IBM_BOX( 191 )  OTHER_BOX( '+' )
48    #define LL              IBM_BOX( 192 )  OTHER_BOX( '+' )
49    #define BOT             IBM_BOX( 193 )  OTHER_BOX( '+' )
50    #define TOP             IBM_BOX( 194 )  OTHER_BOX( '+' )
51    #define LEFT            IBM_BOX( 195 )  OTHER_BOX( '+' )
52    #define HORIZ           IBM_BOX( 196 )  OTHER_BOX( '-' )
53    #define CEN             IBM_BOX( 197 )  OTHER_BOX( '+' )
54    #define LR              IBM_BOX( 217 )  OTHER_BOX( '+' )
55    #define UL              IBM_BOX( 218 )  OTHER_BOX( '+' )
56    #define D_VERT          IBM_BOX( 186 )  OTHER_BOX( '|' )
57    #define D_RIGHT         IBM_BOX( 185 )  OTHER_BOX( '+' )
58    #define D_UR            IBM_BOX( 187 )  OTHER_BOX( '+' )
59    #define D_LL            IBM_BOX( 200 )  OTHER_BOX( '+' )
```

➡

Listing A.71. continued...

```
60   #define D_BOT              IBM_BOX( 202 )   OTHER_BOX( '+' )
61   #define D_TOP              IBM_BOX( 203 )   OTHER_BOX( '+' )
62   #define D_LEFT             IBM_BOX( 204 )   OTHER_BOX( '+' )
63   #define D_HORIZ            IBM_BOX( 205 )   OTHER_BOX( '-' )
64   #define D_CEN              IBM_BOX( 206 )   OTHER_BOX( '+' )
65   #define D_LR               IBM_BOX( 188 )   OTHER_BOX( '+' )
66   #define D_UL               IBM_BOX( 201 )   OTHER_BOX( '+' )
67   #define HD_VERT            IBM_BOX( 179 )   OTHER_BOX( '|' )
68   #define HD_RIGHT           IBM_BOX( 181 )   OTHER_BOX( '+' )
69   #define HD_UR              IBM_BOX( 184 )   OTHER_BOX( '+' )
70   #define HD_LL              IBM_BOX( 212 )   OTHER_BOX( '+' )
71   #define HD_BOT             IBM_BOX( 207 )   OTHER_BOX( '+' )
72   #define HD_TOP             IBM_BOX( 209 )   OTHER_BOX( '+' )
73   #define HD_LEFT            IBM_BOX( 198 )   OTHER_BOX( '+' )
74   #define HD_HORIZ           IBM_BOX( 205 )   OTHER_BOX( '-' )
75   #define HD_CEN             IBM_BOX( 216 )   OTHER_BOX( '+' )
76   #define HD_LR              IBM_BOX( 190 )   OTHER_BOX( '+' )
77   #define HD_UL              IBM_BOX( 213 )   OTHER_BOX( '+' )
78   #define VD_VERT            IBM_BOX( 186 )   OTHER_BOX( '|' )
79   #define VD_RIGHT           IBM_BOX( 182 )   OTHER_BOX( '+' )
80   #define VD_UR              IBM_BOX( 183 )   OTHER_BOX( '+' )
81   #define VD_LL              IBM_BOX( 211 )   OTHER_BOX( '+' )
82   #define VD_BOT             IBM_BOX( 208 )   OTHER_BOX( '+' )
83   #define VD_TOP             IBM_BOX( 210 )   OTHER_BOX( '+' )
84   #define VD_LEFT            IBM_BOX( 199 )   OTHER_BOX( '+' )
85   #define VD_HORIZ           IBM_BOX( 196 )   OTHER_BOX( '-' )
86   #define VD_CEN             IBM_BOX( 215 )   OTHER_BOX( '+' )
87   #define VD_LR              IBM_BOX( 189 )   OTHER_BOX( '+' )
88   #define VD_UL              IBM_BOX( 214 )   OTHER_BOX( '+' )
```

Listing A.72. *cur.h*— Curses Fuctions **#include**s

```
1    #include <stdio.h>
2    #include <stdlib.h>
3    #include <ctype.h>
4    #include <curses.h>            /* routines in the library.        */
5    #include <stdarg.h>            /* va_list and va_start (ANSI)     */
6    #include <tools/debug.h>
7    #include <tools/termlib.h>
8    #include <tools/box.h>         /* of IBM box-drawing characters            */
9    #include "proto.h"             /* function prototypes for curses functions */
10                                  /* (distributed on disk but not printed here */
```

Listing A.73. *box.c*— Draw Box in Window

```
1    #include "cur.h"
2
3    box( win, vert, horiz )
4    WINDOW  *win;
5    {
6        /* Draws a box in the outermost characters of the window using vert for
7         * the vertical characters and horiz for the horizontal ones. I've
8         * extended this function to support the IBM box-drawing characters. That
9         * is, if IBM box-drawing characters are specified for vert and horiz,
10        * box() will use the correct box-drawing characters in the corners. These
```

→

Listing A.73. continued...

```
11          * are defined in * box.h as:
12          *
13          *      HORIZ    (0xc4)   single horizontal line
14          *      D_HORIZ  (0xcd)   double horizontal line.
15          *      VERT     (0xb3)   single vertical line
16          *      D_VERT   (0xba)   double vertical line.
17          */
18
19      int      i, nrows;
20      int      ul, ur, ll, lr;
21      int      oscroll, owrap, oy, ox;
22
23      getyx( win, oy, ox );
24      oscroll      = win->scroll_ok;  /* Disable scrolling and line wrap    */
25      owrap        = win->wrap_ok;    /* in case window uses the whole screen */
26      win->scroll_ok = 0;
27      win->wrap_ok  = 0;
28
29      if( !((horiz==HORIZ || horiz==D_HORIZ) && (vert ==VERT || vert ==D_VERT)) )
30              ul = ur = ll = lr = vert ;
31      else
32      {
33          if( vert == VERT )
34          {
35              if(horiz==HORIZ)
36                  ul=UL,     ur=UR,     ll=LL,     lr=LR;
37              else
38                  ul=HD_UL, ur=HD_UR, ll=HD_LL, lr=HD_LR;
39          }
40          else
41          {
42              if( horiz == HORIZ )
43                  ul=VD_UL, ur=VD_UR, ll=VD_LL, lr=VD_LR;
44              else
45                  ul=D_UL,  ur=D_UR,  ll=D_LL,  lr=D_LR;
46          }
47      }
48
49      wmove ( win, 0, 0 );
50      waddch( win, ul   );                        /* Draw the top line */
51
52      for( i = win->x_size-2; --i >= 0 ; )
53          waddch( win, horiz );
54
55      waddch( win, ur );
56      nrows = win->y_size - 2 ;                    /* Draw the two sides */
57
58      i = 1 ;
59      while( --nrows >= 0 )
60      {
61              wmove ( win, i, 0 );
62              waddch( win, vert );
63              wmove ( win, i++, win->x_size - 1 );
64              waddch( win, vert );
65      }
66
67      wmove ( win, i, 0 );                         /* Draw the bottom line */
68      waddch( win, ll   );
69
```

➡

Listing A.73. continued...

```
70          for( i = win->x_size-2; --i >= 0 ; )
71                  waddch( win, horiz );
72
73          waddch( win, lr );
74          wmove ( win, oy, ox );
75          win->scroll_ok = oscroll ;
76          win->wrap_ok   = owrap ;
77  }
```

Listing A.74. *delwin.c*— Delete Window

```
1   #include "cur.h"
2
3   delwin( win )
4   WINDOW  *win;
5   {
6       /* Copy the saved image back onto the screen and free the memory used for
7        * the buffer.
8        */
9
10      if( win->image )
11      {
12          restore ( (SBUF *) win->image );
13          freescr ( (SBUF *) win->image );
14      }
15      free( win );
16  }
```

Listing A.75. *hidewin.c*— Hide a Window

```
1   #include "cur.h"
2
3   WINDOW  *hidewin( win )
4   WINDOW  *win;
5   {
6       /* Hide a window. Return NULL and do nothing if the image wasn't saved
7        * originally or if it's already hidden, otherwise hide the window and
8        * return the win argument. You may not write to a hidden window.
9        */
10
11      SBUF *image;
12
13      if( !win->image || win->hidden )
14          return NULL;
15
16      image = savescr(((SBUF*)(win->image))->left, ((SBUF*)(win->image))->right,
17                      ((SBUF*)(win->image))->top, ((SBUF*)(win->image))->bottom );
18
19      restore( (SBUF *) win->image );
20      freescr( (SBUF *) win->image );
21      win->image  = image;
22      win->hidden = 1;
23      return( win );
24  }
```

Listing A.76. *initscr.c*— Initialize Curses

```
1    #include "cur.h"
2
3    WINDOW  *stdscr;
4
5    void    endwin()                            /* Clean up as required */
6    {
7        cmove( 24,0 );
8    }
9
10   void    initscr()
11   {
12       /* Creates stdscr. If you want a boxed screen, call boxed() before this
13        * routine. The underlying text is NOT saved. Note that the atexit call
14        * insures a clean up on normal exit, but not with a Ctrl-Break, you'll
15        * have to call signal() to do that.
16        */
17
18       nosave();
19       init(-1);
20       stdscr = newwin( 25, 80, 0, 0 );
21       save();
22       atexit( endwin );
23   }
```

Listing A.77. *mvwin.c*— Move a Window

```
1    #include "cur.h"
2
3    /* Move a window to new absolute position. This routine will behave in one of
4     * two ways, depending on the value of LIKE_UNIX when the file was compiled.
5     * If the #define has a true value, then mvwin() returns ERR and does nothing
6     * if the new coordinates would move the window past the edge of the screen.
7     * If LIKE_UNIX is false, ERR is still returned but the window is moved flush
8     * with the right edge if it's not already there. ERR says that the window is
9     * now flush with the edge of the screen. In both instances, negative
10    * coordinates are silently set to 0.
11    */
12
13   #define LIKE_UNIX 0
14
15   #if ( LIKE_UNIX )
16   #       define UNIX(x) x
17   #       define DOS(x)
18   #else
19   #       define UNIX(x)
20   #       define DOS(x) x
21   #endif
22
23   mvwin( win, y, x )
24   WINDOW  *win;
25   {
26       int old_x, old_y, xsize, ysize, delta_x, delta_y, visible;
27       SBUF *image;
28
29       if( win == stdscr )            /* Can't move stdscr without it going  */
30           return ERR;                /* off the screen.                     */
31
```

→

Listing A.77. continued...

```
32          /* Get the actual dimensions of the window: compensate for a border if the
33           * window is boxed.
34           */
35
36          old_x = win->x_org   -  win->boxed ;
37          old_y = win->y_org   -  win->boxed ;
38          xsize = win->x_size + (win->boxed * 2);
39          ysize = win->y_size + (win->boxed * 2);
40
41          /* Constrain x and y so that the window can't go off the screen */
42
43          x = max( 0, x );
44          y = max( 0, y );
45          if( x + xsize > 80 )
46          {
47              UNIX( return ERR;        )
48              DOS ( x = 80 - xsize;    )
49          }
50          if( y + ysize > 25 )
51          {
52              UNIX( return ERR;        )
53              DOS ( y = 25 - ysize;    )
54          }
55
56          delta_x = x - old_x;                        /* Adjust coordinates. */
57          delta_y = y - old_y;
58
59          if( delta_y == 0 && delta_x == 0 )
60                  return ERR;
61
62          if( visible = !win->hidden )
63                  hidewin( win );
64
65          win->y_org      += delta_y;
66          win->x_org      += delta_x;
67          image           = (SBUF *) win->image;
68          image->top      += delta_y;
69          image->bottom   += delta_y;
70          image->left     += delta_x;
71          image->right    += delta_x;
72
73          if( visible )
74              showwin( win );
75          return( OK );
76      }
```

Listing A.78. *showwin.c*— Display a Previously Hidden Window

```
1   #include "cur.h"
2
3   WINDOW  *showwin( win )
4   WINDOW  *win;
5   {
6       /* Make a previously hidden window visible again. Return NULL and do
7        * nothing if the window wasn't hidden, otherwise return the win argument.
8        */
9
```

Listing A.78. continued...

```
10          SBUF  *image;
11
12          if( !win->hidden )
13              return( NULL );
14
15          image = savescr(((SBUF*)(win->image))->left, ((SBUF*)(win->image))->right,
16                          ((SBUF*)(win->image))->top,  ((SBUF*)(win->image))->bottom);
17
18          restore( (SBUF *) win->image );
19          freescr( (SBUF *) win->image );
20          win->image  = image;
21          win->hidden = 0;
22
23          /* Move the cursor to compensate for windows that were moved while they
24           * were hidden.
25           */
26          cmove( win->y_org + win->row, win->x_org + win->col );
27          return( win );
28      }
```

Listing A.79. *waddstr.c*— Write String to Window

```
1   #include "cur.h"
2
3   waddstr( win, str )
4   WINDOW  *win;
5   char    *str;
6   {
7       while( *str )
8           waddch( win, *str++ );
9   }
```

Listing A.80. *wclrtoeo.c*— Clear from Cursor to Edge of Window

```
1   #include "cur.h"
2
3   wclrtoeol( win )
4   WINDOW  *win;
5   {
6       /* Clear from cursor to end of line, the cursor isn't moved. The main
7        * reason that this is included here is because you have to call it after
8        * printing every newline in order to compensate for a bug in the real
9        * curses. This bug has been corrected in my curses, so you don't have to
10       * use this routine if you're not interested in portability.
11       */
12
13      clr_region( win->x_org +  win->col , win->x_org + (win->x_size - 1),
14                  win->y_org +  win->row , win->y_org +  win->row,
15                  win->attrib                                          );
16  }
```

Listing A.81. *werase.c*— Erase Entire Window

```
1    #include "cur.h"
2
3    werase( win )
4    WINDOW  *win;
5    {
6        clr_region( win->x_org, win->x_org + (win->x_size - 1),
7                    win->y_org, win->y_org + (win->y_size - 1),
8                    win->attrib                                 );
9
10       cmove( win->y_org, win->x_org );
11       win->row = 0;
12       win->col = 0;
13   }
```

Listing A.82. *winch.c*— Move Window-Relative Cursor and Read Character

```
1    #include "cur.h"
2
3    int     winch( win )
4    WINDOW  *win;
5    {
6        int y, x, c;
7
8        curpos( &y, &x );
9        cmove( win->y_org + win->row, win->x_org + win->col );
10       c = inchar();
11       cmove( y, x );
12       return c;
13   }
```

Listing A.83. *wincreat.c*— Create a Window

```
1    #include "cur.h"
2    #include <tools/box.h>
3
4    /*-------------------------------------------------------
5     * Window creation functions.
6     * Standard Functions:
7     *
8     *    WINDOW    *newwin( lines, cols, begin_y, begin_x )
9     *              creates a window
10    *
11    * Nonstandard Functions:
12    *
13    *    save()   Area under all new windows is saved (default)
14    *  nosave()   Area under all new windows is not saved
15    *
16    *  boxed()            Window is boxed automatically.
17    * unboxed()           Window is not boxed (default)
18    * def_ground(f,b)     Set default foreground color to f, and background color
19    *                     to b.
20    *-------------------------------------------------------
21    */
22
```

```
     Listing A.83. continued...
23   PRIVATE int Save  = 1;          /* Save image when window created      */
24   PRIVATE int Box   = 0;          /* Windows are boxed                   */
25   PRIVATE int Attrib = NORMAL;    /* Default character attribute byte    */
26
27   void save    () { Save = 1;    }
28   void nosave  () { Save = 0;    }
29   void boxed   () { Box  = 1;    }
30   void unboxed () { Box  = 0;    }
31
32   void def_ground( f, b ) { Attrib = (f & 0x7f) | ((b & 0x7f) << 4); }
33
34   /*-----------------------------------------------------------*/
35
36   WINDOW  *newwin( lines, cols, begin_y, begin_x )
37
38   int     cols;      /* Horizontal size (including border)   */
39   int     lines;     /* Vertical size   (including border)   */
40   int     begin_y;   /* X coordinate of upper-left corner    */
41   int     begin_x;   /* Y coordinate of upper-left corner    */
42   {
43       WINDOW       *win;
44
45       if( !(win = (WINDOW *) malloc( sizeof(WINDOW) )) )
46       {
47           fprintf(stderr,"Internal error (newwin): Out of memory\n");
48           exit(1);
49       }
50
51       if( cols > 80 )
52       {
53           cols   = 80;
54           begin_x = 0;
55       }
56       else if( begin_x + cols > 80 )
57           begin_x = 80 - cols;
58
59       if( lines > 25 )
60       {
61           lines   = 25;
62           begin_y = 0;
63       }
64       else if( begin_y + lines > 25 )
65           begin_x = 25 - cols;
66
67       win->x_org       = begin_x ;
68       win->y_org       = begin_y ;
69       win->x_size      = cols    ;
70       win->y_size      = lines   ;
71       win->row         = 0 ;
72       win->col         = 0 ;
73       win->scroll_ok   = 0 ;
74       win->wrap_ok     = 1 ;
75       win->boxed       = 0 ;
76       win->hidden      = 0 ;
77       win->attrib      = Attrib ;
78       win->image       = !Save ? NULL : savescr( begin_x, begin_x + (cols  - 1) ,
79                                                  begin_y, begin_y + (lines - 1) );
80       werase(win);
81
```

Listing A.83. continued...

```
82        if( Box )                              /* Must be done last */
83        {
84            box( win, VERT, HORIZ );           /* Box it first          */
85            win->boxed   = 1;
86            win->x_size -= 2;                   /* Then reduce window size */
87            win->y_size -= 2;                   /* so that the box won't   */
88            win->x_org  += 1;                   /* be overwritten.         */
89            win->y_org  += 1;
90
91            cmove( win->y_org, win->x_org );
92        }
93        return win;
94    }
```

Listing A.84. *winio.c*— Miscellaneous Window I/O Functions

```
1    #include "cur.h"
2
3    /*-------------------------------------------------------
4     * WINIO.C      Lowest level I/O routines:
5     *        waddch(win,c)            wgetch(win)
6     *        echo()                  noecho()
7     *        nl()                    nonl()
8     *        crmode()                nocrmode()
9     *-------------------------------------------------------
10    */
11
12   PRIVATE int Echo   = 1;          /* Echo enabled                    */
13   PRIVATE int Crmode = 0;          /* If 1, use buffered input        */
14   PRIVATE int Nl     = 1;          /* If 1, map \r to \n on input     */
15                                    /* and map both to \n\r on output  */
16   echo    () {  Echo = 1; }
17   noecho  () {  Echo = 0; }
18   nl      () {  Nl   = 1; }
19   nonl    () {  Nl   = 0; }
20
21   crmode()
22   {
23       Crmode = 1;
24   }
25
26   nocrmode()
27   {
28       Crmode = 0;
29   }
30
31   /*-----------------------------------------------------------*/
32
33   static   char     *getbuf(win, buf)
34   WINDOW   *win;
35   char     *buf;
36   {
37       /* Get a buffer interactively. ^H is a destructive backspace. This routine
38        * is mildly recursive (it's called from wgetch() when Crmode is false.
39        * The newline is put into the buffer. Returns it's second argument.
40        */
41
```

Listing A.84. continued...

```
42          register int c;
43          char            *sbuf = buf;
44
45          Crmode = 1;
46          while( (c = wgetch(win)) != '\n' && c != '\r' )
47          {
48              switch( c )
49              {
50              case '\b':   if( --buf >= sbuf )
51                              wprintw( win, " \b" );
52                          else
53                          {
54                              wprintw( win, " " );
55                              putchar('\007');
56                              buf = sbuf;
57                          }
58                          break;
59
60              default:     *buf++ = c;
61                          break;
62              }
63          }
64          *buf++ = c    ;        /* Add line terminator (\n or \r) */
65          *buf   = '\0';
66          Crmode = 0    ;
67          return sbuf   ;
68      }
69
70  /*-----------------------------------------------------------*/
71
72  int     wgetch( win )
73  WINDOW  *win;
74  {
75      /* Get a character from DOS without echoing. We need to do this in order
76       * to support (echo/noecho). We'll also do noncrmode input buffering here.
77       * Maximum input line length is 132 columns.
78       *
79       * In nocrmode(), DOS functions are used to get a line and all the normal
80       * command-line editing functions are available. Since there's no way to
81       * turn off echo in this case, characters are echoed to the screen
82       * regardless of the status of echo(). In order to retain control of the
83       * window, input fetched for wgetch() is always done in crmode, even if
84       * Crmode isn't set. If nl() mode is enabled, carriage return (Enter, ^M)
85       * and linefeed (^J) are both mapped to '\n', otherwise they are not mapped.
86       *
87       * Characters are returned in an int. The high byte is 0 for normal
88       * characters. Extended characters (like the function keys) are returned
89       * with the high byte set to 0xff and the character code in the low byte.
90       * Extended characters are not echoed.
91       */
92
93      static unsigned char buf[ 133 ] = { 0 };
94      static unsigned char *p        = buf;
95      static          int  numchars  = -1;
96      register        int  c;
97
98      if( !Crmode )
99      {
```

Listing A.84. continued...

```
100          if( !*p )
101               p = getbuf( win, buf );
102          return( Nl && *p == '\r' ) ? '\n' : *p++ ;
103      }
104    else
105    {
106          if( (c = bdos(8,0,0) & 0xff) == ('Z'-'@') )        /* Ctrl-Z */
107               return EOF ;
108          else if( !c )                                       /* Extended char */
109               c = ~0xff | bdos(8,0,0) ;
110          else
111          {
112              if( c == '\r' &&  Nl )
113                   c = '\n' ;
114
115              if( Echo )
116                   waddch( win, c );
117          }
118          return c;
119      }
120 }
121
122 /*------------------------------------------------------------*/
123
124 int     waddch( win, c )
125 WINDOW  *win;
126 int     c;
127 {
128      /*  Print a character to an active (not hidden) window:
129       *  The following are handled specially:
130     /  *
131       *  \n  Clear the line from the current cursor position  to the right edge
132       *      of the window. Then:
133       *          if nl() is active:
134       *              go to the left edge of the next line
135       *          else
136       *              go to the current column on the next line
137       *      In addition, if scrolling is enabled, the window scrolls if you're
138       *      on the bottom line.
139       *  \t  is expanded into an 8-space field. If the tab goes past the right
140       *      edge of the window, the cursor wraps to the next line.
141       *  \r  gets you to the beginning of the current line.
142       *  \b  backs up one space but may not back up past the left edge of the
143       *      window. Nondestructive. The curses documentation doesn't say that
144       *      \b is handled explicitly but it does indeed work.
145       *  ESC This is not standard curses but is useful. It is valid only if
146       *      DOESC was true during the compile. All characters between an ASCII
147       *      ESC and an alphabetic character are sent to the output but are other
148       *      wise ignored. This let's you send escape sequences directly to the
149       *      terminal if you like. I'm assuming here that you won't change
150       *      windows in the middle of an escape sequence.
151       *
152       * Return ERR if the character would have caused the window to scroll
153       * illegally, or if you attempt to write to a hidden window.
154       */
155
156      static  int     saw_esc = 0;
157      int             rval    = OK;
158
```

Listing A.84. continued...

```
159         if( win->hidden )
160             return ERR;
161
162         cmove(win->y_org + win->row, win->x_org + win->col);
163
164     #ifdef DOESC
165         if( saw_esc )
166         {
167             if( isalpha( c ) )
168                 saw_esc = 0;
169             outc(c, win->attrib );
170         }
171         else
172     #endif
173         {
174             switch( c )
175             {
176     #ifdef DOESC
177             case '\033': if( saw_esc )
178                             saw_esc = 0;
179                          else
180                          {
181                              saw_esc = 1;
182                              outc('\033', win->attrib );
183                          }
184                          break;
185     #endif
186             case '\b':   if( win->col > 0 )
187                          {
188                              outc( '\b', win->attrib  );
189                              --( win->col );
190                          }
191                          break;
192
193             case '\t':   do {
194                              waddch( win, ' ' );
195                          } while( win->col % 8 );
196                          break;
197
198             case '\r':   win->col = 0;
199                          cmove(win->y_org + win->row, win->x_org);
200                          break;
201
202             default:     if( (win->col + 1) < win->x_size )
203                          {
204                              /* If you're not at the right edge of the window, */
205                              /* print the character and advance.               */
206
207                              ++win->col;
208                              outc(c, win->attrib );
209                              break;
210                          }
211                          replace(c);          /* At right edge, don't advance */
212                          if( !win->wrap_ok )
213                              break;
214
215                          /* otherwise wrap around by falling through to newline */
216
```

➡

Listing A.84. continued...

```
217              case '\n': if( c == '\n' )          /* Don't erase character at far */
218                             wclrtoeol( win );  /* right of the screen.         */
219
220                         if( Nl )
221                             win->col = 0;
222
223                         if( ++(win->row) >= win->y_size )
224                         {
225                             rval = wscroll( win, 1 );
226                             --( win->row );
227                         }
228                         cmove( win->y_org + win->row, win->x_org + win->col);
229                         break;
230              }
231         }
232     return rval;
233 }
```

Listing A.85. *wmove.c*— Move Window-Relative Cursor

```
1   #include "cur.h"
2
3   wmove( win, y, x )
4   WINDOW  *win;
5   {
6       /* Go to window-relative position. You can't go outside the window. */
7
8       cmove( win->y_org + (win->row = min(y,win->y_size-1)) ,
9               win->x_org + (win->col = min(x,win->x_size-1)) );
10  }
```

Listing A.86. *wprintw.c*— Formated Print to Window

```
1   #include "cur.h"
2
3   PRIVATE int Errcode = OK;
4
5   PRIVATE wputc(c, win)
6   int     c;
7   WINDOW *win;
8   {
9       Errcode |= waddch( win, c );
10  }
11
12  wprintw( win, fmt, ... )
13  WINDOW  *win;
14  char    *fmt;
15  {
16      va_list args;
17      va_start( args, fmt );
18
19      Errcode = OK;
20      prnt( wputc, win, fmt, args );
21      va_end( args );
22      return Errcode;
```

➡

Listing A.86. continued...

```
23    }
24
25    printw( fmt, ... )
26    char    *fmt;
27    {
28        va_list args;
29        va_start( args, fmt );
30
31        Errcode = OK;
32        prnt( wputc, stdscr, fmt, args );
33        va_end( args );
34        return Errcode;
35    }
```

Listing A.87. *wscroll.c—* Scroll Window

```
1     #include "cur.h"
2
3     /*------------------------------------------------------------
4      * Scroll the window if scrolling is enabled. Return 1 if we scrolled. (I'm
5      * not sure if the UNIX function returns 1 on a scroll but it's convenient to
6      * do it here. Don't assume anything about the return value if you're porting
7      * to UNIX. Wscroll() is not a curses function. It lets you specify a scroll
8      * amount and direction (scroll down by -amt if amt is negative); scroll()
9      * is a macro that evaluates to a wscroll call with an amt of 1. Note that the
10     * UNIX curses gets very confused when you scroll explicitly (using scroll()).
11     * In particular, it doesn't clear the bottom line after a scroll but it thinks
12     * that it has. Therefore, when you try to clear the bottom line, it thinks that
13     * there's nothing there to clear and ignores your wclrtoeol() commands. Same
14     * thing happens when you try to print spaces to the bottom line; it thinks
15     * that spaces are already there and does nothing. You have to fill the bottom
16     * line with non-space characters of some sort, and then erase it.
17     */
18
19    wscroll(win, amt)
20    WINDOW  *win;
21    {
22        if( win->scroll_ok )
23            doscroll( win->x_org, win->x_org + (win->x_size-1),
24                      win->y_org, win->y_org + (win->y_size-1), amt, win->attrib );
25
26        return win->scroll_ok ;
27    }
```

B

Notes on Pascal Compilers

Though the material covered in Chapter Six applies to most compilers, languages such as Pascal, which support nested subroutine declarations, arguments passed by reference, and so forth, have their own set of problems.

B.1 Subroutine Arguments

Passing by value.

The first issue is differentiating between arguments passed by value and arguments passed by reference. With the exception of arrays, all arguments in C are passed by value—the argument's value (the contents of a variable, for example) is passed to the subroutine rather than the argument itself. Pascal doesn't differentiate between arrays and other types, however. Unless you tell the compiler to do otherwise, everything is passed by value, so the entire array must be copied onto the stack as part of the subroutine call. Similarly, records must be copied to the stack to pass them to a subroutine (as must structures in ANSI C).

Passing by reference.

In a call by reference, the called subroutine can modify the contents of a variable local to the calling subroutine. A reference to the variable is passed, not its contents. In C, you'd do this by passing a pointer to the variable, and this approach works in Pascal as well, except that the compiler takes care of the details. If a subroutine argument is declared using the **var** keyword, then the address of the object is passed to the subroutine. The subroutine itself must access that object indirectly through the pointer.

An alternative approach is not practical in most languages, but should be mentioned primarily so that you don't use it. You can pass all arguments to the subroutine by value, just as if they were arguments to a C subroutine. Rather than discarding the arguments after the subroutine returns, however, you can pop their modified values from the stack back into the original variables. This approach has the advantage of simplifying the called subroutine's life considerably because it doesn't have to keep track of the extra level of indirection. The obvious disadvantage is that large objects, such as arrays, require a lot of stack space if passed by value. A less obvious, but more serious, disadvantage is illustrated by the following subroutine:

```
function tweedle( var dum: integer; var dee: integer ): integer;
begin
    dum = 1;
    return dum + dee;
end
```

`tweedle()`'s return value is undefined when a copy-in/copy-out strategy is used and the arguments are identical, as follows:

```
var
    arg:    integer;
    result: integer;
begin
    arg    := 100;
    result := tweedle( arg, arg );
end
```

The assignment `dum=1` should modify both `dum` and `dee` and the function should return 2. If the arguments are copied onto the stack, however, `dum` alone is modified, so `101` is returned. The other problem is the undefined order of evaluation in the arguments. There's no way to tell which of the two arguments will be popped first when the subroutine returns. If the left argument, which corresponds to `dum`, is popped first, then `arg` is set to `100`; otherwise, `arg` is be set to `1`.

B.2 Return Values

The next issue is a function's return value. Aggregate objects, such as arrays and records, can't be returned in registers because they're too big. The usual approach is to allocate an area of static memory using `malloc()` or some similar memory allocator, copy the aggregate object into this memory, and return a pointer to the region in a register. You can also reserve a fixed region of static memory for this purpose—all functions copy the aggregate object to the same fixed region of memory. A pointer doesn't have to be returned in this case because everybody knows where the returned object can be found. On the other hand, the size of the fixed region will limit the size of the returned object.

Returning aggregate objects.

B.3 Stack Frames

The next issue is the stack frame. Pascal supports nested subroutine definitions. A child subroutine (declared inside the parent subroutine) must be able to access all variables that are local to the parent in addition to its own local variables. In general, all variables declared at more outer scoping levels must be accessible to the inner subroutine. The subroutines in Figure B.1 illustrate the problems. `clio` can be accessed from inside all three subroutines. Other local variables can be accessed only from within the subroutines where they are declared, however. Similarly, `calliope` can't access `terpsichore` or `melpomene`. The situation is complicated, somewhat, by `erato` containing a recursive call to itself.

The stack frame, when the recursive call to `erato` is active, is shown in Figure B.3. There is one major difference between these stack frames and the C stack frame: the introduction of a second pointer called the *dynamic link*. The *static link* is the old frame pointer, just as in C. The dynamic link points, not at the previously active subroutine, but at the parent subroutine in the nesting sequence—in the declaration. Since `erato` and `thalia` are both nested inside `calliope`, their static links point at `calliope`'s stack frame. You can chase down the dynamic links to access the local variables in the

Static and dynamic links.

Figure B.1. Pascal Nested Subroutines

```
                procedure calliope( polyhymnia: integer);
                var
                     clio: integer;
                begin
                     procedure erato( urania: integer );
                     var
                          terpsichore: integer;
                     begin
                          ...
                          erato(3);
                     end

                     procedure thalia( euterpe: integer );
                     var
                          melpomene: integer;
                     begin
                          ...
                          erato(2);
                     end
                     ...
                     thalia(1);
                end
```

Figure B.2. Pascal Stack Frames

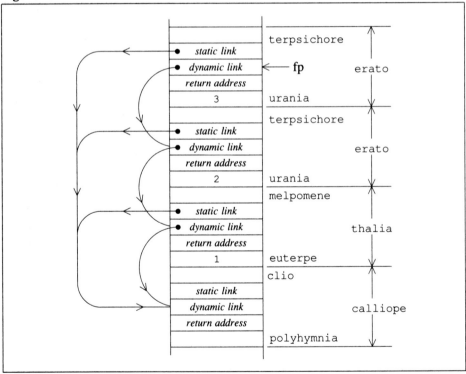

outer routine's stack frame. For example, `clio` can be accessed from `erato` with the following C-code:

```
r0.pp = WP(fp - 4);     /* r0 = static link */
_x    = W(r0.pp - 8);   /* x  = cleo        */
```

You can access `polyhymnia` from `erato` with:

```
r0.pp = WP(fp - 4);     /* r0 = static link */
_x    = W(r0.pp + 8);   /* x  = cleo        */
```

This organization can cause problems with **goto** statements. It's possible for a **goto** statement in `erato` to reference a label in `calliope`, for example. You can't just jump to the label in this case because the stack will be left with inactive stack frames on it, so you must treat the **goto** something like a **return**, adjusting the frame and stack pointers before making the jump—you must simulate return statements until the stack frame for the subroutine that contains the target label is active.

In order to make this simulation easier, Pascal delegates the responsibility of cleaning up the stack somewhat differently than C: it's the responsibility of the called function to delete the entire stack frame—both local variables and arguments—before returning. As an added advantage, the Pascal calling conventions tend to make somewhat smaller programs because the compiler doesn't have to generate an add-constant-to-stack-pointer directive after every subroutine call—programs usually have more subroutine calls than definitions. Finally, as a matter of convention rather than necessity, arguments to Pascal subroutines are pushed by the calling function in forward rather than reverse order. The leftmost argument is pushed first. This convention makes it difficult to write a Pascal function that takes a variable number of arguments unless the compiler provides some run-time mechanism for finding and identifying the type of the leftmost argument.

The Pascal `goto`*.*

Called subroutine cleans up stack. Less code is generated.

Arguments pushed in forward order.

C

A Grammar for C

This appendix summarizes the grammar used in Chapter Six. The organization here is different from that in Chapter Six in that it's more hierarchical. Line numbers in the following listing don't match the ones in Chapter 6. End-of-production actions are not shown, though imbedded actions are indicated with a {}. I've replaced the semicolon required at the end of a **yacc** or **occs** production with a blank line. The following abbreviations are used in the nonterminal names:

abs	abstract
arg(s)	argument(s)
const	constant
decl	declarator
def	definition
expr	expression
ext	external
opt	optional
param	parameter
struct	structure

Listing C.1. *c.y*— A C Grammar

```
 1    %union {                          /* The value stack. */
 2        char        *p_char;
 3        symbol      *p_sym;
 4        link        *p_link;
 5        structdef   *p_sdef;
 6        specifier   *p_spec;
 7        value       *p_val;
 8        int         num;             /* Make short if sizeof(int) > sizeof(int*). */
 9        int         ascii;
10    }
11
12    %term   STRING        /* String constant.                              */
13    %term   ICON          /* Integer or long constant including '\t', etc. */
14    %term   FCON          /* Floating-point constant.                      */
```

Listing C.1. continued...

```
15   %term     TYPE                 /* int char long float double signed unsigned short */
16                                  /* const volatile void                             */
17   %term     <ascii> STRUCT       /* struct union                                    */
18   %term            ENUM          /* enum                                            */
19
20   %term      <p_sym> TTYPE             /* type created with typedef            */
21   %nonassoc <ascii> CLASS              /* auto extern register static typedef */
22   %nonassoc <p_sym> NAME
23   %nonassoc        ELSE
24
25   %term     RETURN GOTO
26   %term     IF ELSE
27   %term     SWITCH CASE DEFAULT
28   %term     BREAK CONTINUE
29   %term     WHILE DO FOR
30   %term     LC RC                /*          { }       */
31   %term     SEMI                 /*           ;        */
32   %term     ELLIPSIS             /*          ...       */
33
34   %left     COMMA                /* ,                                                */
35   %right    EQUAL <ascii> ASSIGNOP  /* =    *= /= %= += -= <<= >>= &= |= ^= */
36   %right    QUEST COLON          /*          ? :                                     */
37   %left     OROR                 /* ||                                               */
38   %left     ANDAND               /* &&                                               */
39   %left     OR                   /* |                                                */
40   %left     XOR                  /* ^                                                */
41   %left     AND                  /* &                                                */
42   %left     <ascii> EQUOP        /* ==  !=                                           */
43   %left     <ascii> RELOP        /* <= >= < >                                        */
44   %left     <ascii> SHIFTOP      /* >> <<                                            */
45   %left     PLUS  MINUS          /* + -                                              */
46   %left     STAR  <ascii> DIVOP  /* * / %                                            */
47   %right    SIZEOF <ascii> UNOP INCOP  /*      sizeof   ! ~      ++ --    */
48   %left     LB RB LP RP <ascii> STRUCTOP /* [ ] ( ) . ->                     */
```

                                                            High-Level Definitions

```
49   program : ext_def_list { clean_up(); }
50
51   ext_def_list
52           : ext_def_list ext_def
53           | /* epsilon */
54
55   ext_def : opt_specifiers ext_decl_list {} SEMI
56           | opt_specifiers {} SEMI
57           | opt_specifiers funct_decl {} def_list {} compound_stmt
58
59   ext_decl_list
60           :   ext_decl
61           |   ext_decl_list COMMA ext_decl
62
63   ext_decl: var_decl
64           | var_decl EQUAL initializer
65           | funct_decl
```

                                                                       Specifiers

```
66   opt_specifiers
67           : CLASS TTYPE
68           | TTYPE
69           | specifiers
70           | /* empty */
```

→

Listing C.1. continued…

```
71
72   specifiers
73           : type_or_class
74           | specifiers type_or_class
75
76   type    : type_specifier
77           | type type_specifier
78
79   type_or_class
80           : type_specifier
81           | CLASS
82
83   type_specifier
84           : TYPE
85           | enum_specifier
86           | struct_specifier
```

Enumerated Constants

```
87   enum_specifier
88           : enum name opt_enum_list
89           | enum LC enumerator_list RC
90
91   opt_enum_list
92           : LC enumerator_list RC
93           | /* empty */
94
95   enum    : ENUM
96
97   enumerator_list
98           : enumerator
99           | enumerator_list COMMA enumerator
100
101  enumerator
102          : name
103          | name EQUAL const_expr
```

Variable Declarators

```
104  var_decl: new_name                        %prec COMMA
105          | var_decl LP RP
106          | var_decl LP var_list RP
107          | var_decl LB RB
108          | var_decl LB const_expr RB
109          | STAR var_decl                    %prec UNOP
110          | LP var_decl RP
111
112  new_name: NAME
113  name    : NAME
```

Function Declarators

```
114  funct_decl
115          : STAR funct_decl
116          | funct_decl LB RB
117          | funct_decl LB const_expr RB
118          | LP funct_decl RP
119          | funct_decl LP RP
120          | new_name LP RP
121          | new_name LP {} name_list {} RP
122          | new_name LP {} var_list  {} RP
123
```

➡

Listing C.1. continued...

```
124   name_list
125          : new_name
126          | name_list COMMA new_name
127
128   var_list: param_declaration
129          | var_list COMMA param_declaration
130
131   param_declaration
132          : type  var_decl
133          | abstract_decl
134          | ELLIPSIS
```

Abstract Declarators

```
135   abstract_decl
136          : type  abs_decl
137          | TTYPE abs_decl
138
139   abs_decl: /* epsilon */
140          | LP abs_decl RP LP RP
141          | STAR abs_decl
142          | abs_decl LB            RB
143          | abs_decl LB const_expr RB
144          | LP abs_decl RP
145
```

Structures

```
146   struct_specifier
147          : STRUCT opt_tag LC def_list RC
148          | STRUCT tag
149
150   opt_tag : tag
151          | /* empty */
152
153   tag     : NAME
```

Local Variables and Function Arguments

```
154   def_list: def_list def
155          | /* epsilon */
156
157   def     : specifiers decl_list {} SEMI
158          | specifiers SEMI
159
160   decl_list
161          : decl
162          | decl_list COMMA decl
163
164   decl    : funct_decl
165          | var_decl
166          | var_decl EQUAL initializer
167          | var_decl COLON const_expr       %prec COMMA
168          | COLON const_expr                %prec COMMA
169
170   initializer
171          : expr                            %prec COMMA
172          | LC initializer_list RC
173
174   initializer_list
175          : initializer
176          | initializer_list COMMA initializer
177
```

➡

Listing C.1. continued...

Statements

```
178   compound_stmt
179         : LC {} local_defs stmt_list RC {}
180
181   local_defs
182         : def_list
183
184   stmt_list
185         : stmt_list statement
186         | /* epsilon */
187
188   statement
189         : expr SEMI
190         | compound_stmt
191         | RETURN          SEMI
192         | RETURN expr     SEMI
193         | SEMI
194         | GOTO target SEMI
195         | target COLON {} statement
196         | SWITCH LP expr RP {} compound_stmt
197         | CASE const_expr COLON
198         | DEFAULT COLON
199         | IF LP test RP statement
200         | IF LP test RP statement ELSE {} statement
201         | WHILE LP test RP {} statement
202         | FOR LP opt_expr SEMI test  SEMI {} opt_expr RP {} statement
203         | DO {} statement WHILE {} LP test RP SEMI
204         | BREAK SEMI
205         | CONTINUE SEMI
206
207   test    : {} expr
208         | /* empty */
209
210   target  : NAME
```

Expressions

```
211   opt_expr: expr
212         | /* epsilon */
213
214   const_expr
215         : expr                           %prec COMMA
216
217   expr    : expr COMMA  {}  non_comma_expr
218         | non_comma_expr
219
220   non_comma_expr
221         : non_comma_expr QUEST {} non_comma_expr COLON {} non_comma_expr
222         | non_comma_expr ASSIGNOP non_comma_expr
223         | non_comma_expr EQUAL    non_comma_expr
224         | or_expr
225
226   or_expr : or_list
227   or_list : or_list OROR {} and_expr
228         | and_expr
229
230   and_expr: and_list
231   and_list: and_list ANDAND {} binary
232         | binary
233
```

Listing C.1. continued…

```
234   binary   : binary RELOP      binary
235            | binary EQUOP      binary
236            | binary STAR       binary
237            | binary DIVOP      binary
238            | binary SHIFTOP    binary
239            | binary AND        binary
240            | binary XOR        binary
241            | binary OR         binary
242            | binary PLUS       binary
243            | binary MINUS      binary
244            | unary
245
246   unary    : LP expr RP
247            | FCON
248            | ICON
249            | NAME
250            | string_const  %prec COMMA
251            | SIZEOF LP string_const RP              %prec SIZEOF
252            | SIZEOF LP expr RP                      %prec SIZEOF
253            | SIZEOF LP abstract_decl RP             %prec SIZEOF
254            | LP abstract_decl RP unary              %prec UNOP
255            | MINUS    unary                         %prec UNOP
256            | UNOP     unary
257            | unary    INCOP
258            | INCOP    unary
259            | AND      unary                         %prec UNOP
260            | STAR     unary                         %prec UNOP
261            | unary LB expr RB                       %prec UNOP
262            | unary STRUCTOP NAME                    %prec STRUCTOP
263            | unary LP args RP
264            | unary LP      RP
265
266   string_const
267            : STRING
268            | string_const STRING
269
270   args     : non_comma_expr                         %prec COMMA
271            | non_comma_expr COMMA args
```

=========== D ===========

L^EX

This appendix is a user's manual for L^EX,[1] a program that translates an input file made up of intermixed regular expressions and C source code into a lexical analyzer. Appendix E contains a user's manual for **occs**, a compiler-compiler modeled after the UNIX **yacc** utility that translates an augmented, attributed grammar into a bottom-up parser.

This (and the next) appendix describe L^EX and **occs** in depth. L^EX and **occs** are both very similar to the equivalent UNIX utilities, and you can use the UNIX **lex** and **yacc** rather than L^EX and **occs** to implement the compiler in Chapter Six, though you should read the UNIX documentation for these programs rather than this (and the next) appendix if you do. Footnotes are used to point out differences between L^EX and **occs** and their UNIX counterparts—you can ignore them if you're not interested in using the UNIX programs. In general, you should have little difficulty going from one system to the other.

D.1 Using L^EX and Occs Together

L^EX and **occs** work together in an integrated fashion, though L^EX can be used without **occs** for many noncompiler applications. Both utilities can be viewed as C preprocessors. L^EX takes as input files made up of interspersed L^EX directives and C source code and outputs a table-driven lexical analyzer. **Occs** outputs a parser. The interaction between L^EX and **occs** is pictured in Figure D.1.

The L^EX output file is called *lexyy.c*, and this file contains a tokenizer function called yylex().[2] This function reads characters from the input stream, returning a token (and the associated lexeme) on every call. It is called by the **occs**-generated parser every time a token is required. Similarly, **occs** creates a file called *yyout.c*, which includes a parser subroutine called yyparse().[3] Somewhere in your program, there must be a call to

---

1. I'm calling it L^EX to differentiate it from the UNIX program of the same name, which will be called **lex** throughout this manual. You can pronounce it as "leck" if you want to, but I wouldn't advise it.

2. UNIX lex creates a file called *lex.yy.c*; the lexical analyzer function is still called yylex(), however.

3. The **yacc** equivalent to *yyout.c* is *y.tab.c*; yyparse() is used by both programs.

Figure D.1. Creating a Compiler with LᴱX and **occs**

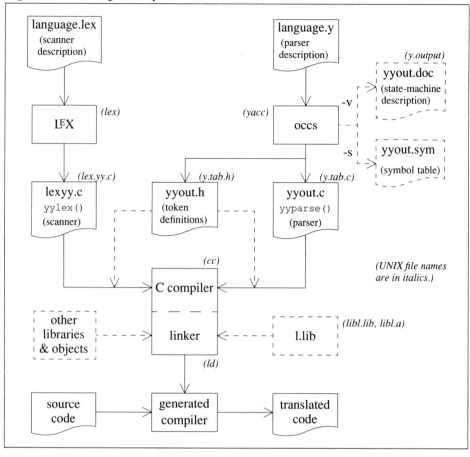

yyparse() to start up the parser.

The *l.lib* library contains various subroutines that are used by the lexical analyzer and should be linked into the final program.[4] Note that *l.lib* includes a main() subroutine which loops, calling yylex() repetitively until yylex() returns zero. You can, of course, provide your own main(), and the one in the library will not be linked. [You must do this in the final compiler or else the parser will never be called. It's a common mistake to forget to provide a main().]

There are several steps in creating a workable compiler using LᴱX and **occs**. The first step is to write a lexical-analyzer specification as a LᴱX input file, and to define a grammar in a way acceptable to **occs** (all this is discussed below and in Appendix E). You then run the input files through the appropriate programs, generating several *.c* and *.h* files.

LᴱX creates *lexyy.c*, as was discussed earlier. **Occs** actually creates two source files: *yyout.c* contains source code for the parser and tables; *yyout.h* contains **#define**s for all the tokens.[5]

---

4. The UNIX programs use */usr/lib/libl.lib* (alternately named */usr/lib/libl.a* in some systems). Incorporate this library into your program with a *cc files...-ll* directive when you link.

5. **yacc** calls the file *y.tab.h* and generates the file only if you specify -d on the command line. **Occs** always generates yyout.h, however.

One of these token values (and only these values) must be returned by your lexical analyzer for each input symbol.[6] The special symbol `_EOI_`, always `#define`d as zero in *yyout.h*, is returned by the LEX-generated analyzer at end of input. You should not return this value yourself as a token value, or **occs** (and **yacc**) will get confused.[7] A typical development cycle with Microsoft C looks something like this:[8]

```
vi compiler.lex        Create LEX input specification.
vi compiler.y          Create occs input specification.
lex compiler.lex       Create lexyy.c from LEX input specification.
occs -vD compiler.y    Create yyout.c and yyout.h from occs input specification.
cl -c lexyy.c          Compile everything and link.
cl -c yyout.c
cl lexyy.obj yyout.obj -link l.lib
```

The various files generated by LEX and **occs** are summarized in Table D.1. The *yyout.h* file is generally `#include`d in the LEX input specification, so you shouldn't compile *lexyy.c* until you've run **occs**.

D.2 The LEX Input File: Organization

The remainder of this appendix describes the lexical-analyzer generator, LEX. My implementation of LEX is a proper subset of the similarly named UNIX utility.[9] The input file is divided into three parts, separated from one another by `%%` directives:

```
definitions
%%
rules
%%
code
```

The *%%* must be the leftmost two characters on the line. The *definitions* section contains two things: macro definitions and user-supplied code. All code must be delimited

---

6. **yacc** also lets you use literal characters as tokens. If you put a `%term '+'.` into the **yacc** input file, you can return an ASCII '+' from the lexical analyzer. **Occs** doesn't support this mechanism. You'd have to put a `%term PLUS` in the **occs** input file and a `return PLUS;` statement in the lexical analyzer.

7. **yacc** doesn't define `_EOI_` for you—it nonetheless treats 0 as an end-of-input marker.

8. The UNIX development cycle looks like this:
   ```
   vi compiler.lex
   vi compiler.y
   lex compiler.lex
   yacc -vd compiler.y
   cc -c lex.yy.c
   cc -c y.tab.c
   cc -o compiler y.tab.o lex.yy.o -ll
   ```

9. For those of you who are familiar with the UNIX program, the following features are not supported by LEX:
   - The / lookahead operator is not supported.
   - The `%START` directive and the `<name>` context mechanism are not supported.
   - The `{N,M}` operator (repeat the previous regular expression *N* to *M* times) is not supported.
   - The `REJECT` mechanism is not supported (but `yymore()` is).
   - The `%S`, `%T`, `%C`, and `%R` directives are not supported. Similarly, the internal-array-size modification directives `%p`, `%n`, `%e`, `%a`, `%k`, and `%o`) aren't supported.
   - The internal workings of the output lexical analyzer (especially the input mechanism) bear virtually no relation to the UNIX program. You won't be able to hack the LEX output in the same ways that you're used to.

Table D.1. LEX and **Occs** Output Files

Generated by	**Occs/LEX** name	UNIX name	Command-line Switches	Description
LEX/**lex**	lexyy.c	lex.yy.c	none needed	C source code for lexical analyzer function, `yylex()`.
occs/yacc	yyout.c	y.tab.c	none needed	C Source code for parser subroutine, `yyparse()`
	yyout.h	y.tab.h	**occs**: none needed **yacc**: -d	**#define**s for the tokens.
	yyout.sym	not available	-s -S -D	Symbol-table showing various internal values used by the parser, including production numbers, TOKEN values, and so forth. This table is useful primarily for debugging.
	yyout.doc	y.output	**occs**: -v -V **yacc**: -v	A human-readable description of the LALR state machine used by the parser. The file also contains copies of all the error and warning messages that are sent to the screen as the input is processed. It's useful for debugging the grammar. The −V version of the table holds LALR(1) lookaheads for all the items, and FIRST sets for all the nonterminals. The −v version contains lookaheads only for those items that trigger reductions, and does not contain FIRST sets.

with `%{` and `%}` directives like this:

```
%{
#include <stdio.h>
extern int something; /* This code is passed to the output */
%}
%%
```

The percent sign must be the leftmost character on the line.[10] Code blocks in the definitions section should contain **#include**s, external definitions, global-variable definitions, and so forth. In general, everything that would go at the top of a C program should also go at the top of the LEX input file.

Anything outside of a `%{ %}` block is taken to be a macro definition. These consist of a name followed by white space (blanks or tabs), followed in turn by the macro's contents. For example:

---

10. UNIX **lex** supports directives like this:

```
%{ #include <stdio.h> %}
```

   LEX requires you to use the following, however:

```
%{          #include <stdio.h>      %}
```

```
digit      [0-9]           /* decimal digit         */
hexdigit   [0-9a-fA-f]     /* hexadecimal digit     */
alpha      [a-zA-Z]        /* alphabetic character */
```

Comments.

Macro expansion is discussed further, below. C-style comments are permitted anywhere in the definitions section—they are ignored along with any preceding white space. C comments in a `%{...%}` block are passed to the output, however.

Skipping the middle, *rules*, section for a moment, the third, *code* section is just passed to the output file verbatim. Generally, the initial definitions section should contain only code that is used in the rules section; moreover, it should contain only variable definitions, **extern** statements, and the like. All other code, including the subroutines that are called from the rules section, should be defined in the last, code section.

D.3 The LᴱX Rules Section

The *rules* in the middle part of the LᴱX input specification have two components: a regular expression like the ones described both in Chapter Two and below, and C-source-code fragments that are executed when input that matches the regular expression is found. The regular expressions must start in the leftmost column, and they are

Whitespace.

separated from the code by white space (spaces or tabs). This means that you can't put a literal space character or tab into a regular expression. Use the `\s` or `\t` escape sequence for this purpose. You can also use double quotes—a `" "` matches a space—but the escape sequences are preferable because you can see them. The code part of the rule may take up several lines, provided that the lines begin with white space. That is, all lines that start with white space are assumed to be part of the code associated with the previous regular expression. A possible rule section looks like this:

```
%%
lama      printf("Priest\n");  /* A one-ell lama            */
llama     printf("Beast \n");  /* A two-ell llama           */
lll+ama   printf("Fire! \n");  /* A three-ell lllama, four */
                               /* alarmer, and so forth.    */
%%
```

which, when given the input:

```
lama
llama
lllama
```

recognizes the various kinds of lamas.[11]

D.3.1 LᴱX Regular Expressions

The LᴱX regular-expression syntax is essentially the one described in Chapter Two. It is summarized below, along with discussions of LᴱX's peculiarities. Regular expressions are formed of a combination of normal characters and "metacharacters", which

Metacharacters.

have special meanings. The following characters are used as metacharacters—they are described in depth below:

```
*  +  ?  {  }  [  ]  (  )  .  ^  $  "  \
```

---

11. See [Nash].

Note that the term "newline" is used in a nonstandard way in the following definitions. A *newline* here, is either an ASCII carriage return <u>or</u> a linefeed character (`'\r'` or `'\n'`). This usage is consistent with most MS-DOS applications because the input characters are read in binary, not translated mode, so all input lines are terminated with a `\r\n` pair. By recognizing either `'\n'` or `'\r'` as a newline, L^EX-generated code work can work in the UNIX environment, in MS-DOS translated, and in MS-DOS binary modes as well. If you want strict UNIX compatibility, you can use the *−u* command line switch discussed below to redefine newline to be a single linefeed character.

Newline, nonstandard definition.

c   A single character that is not used as a metacharacter forms a regular expression. The multiple-character sequences shown in Table D.2 also match single characters. These are known as *escape sequences*. Note that in MS-DOS, binary-mode input is used by L^EX. This means that all lines are terminated with the two-character sequence `\r\n`. A `\n` matches the linefeed, but not the carriage return. It can be risky to test for an explicit `\r` or `\n` in the MS-DOS environment (but see ^ and $, below). Double quotes can also be used to take away the meaning of metacharacters: `"*?"` matches an asterisk followed by a question mark.

Matching normal characters, escape sequences.

Table D.2. L^EX Escape Sequences

Escape sequence	Matches	Recognized by UNIX
\b	backspace	yes
\f	formfeed	yes
\n	linefeed (end of line character)	yes
\r	carriage return	yes
\s	space	yes
\t	tab	yes
\e	ASCII ESC character (`'\033'`)	no
ddd	number formed of three the octal digits *ddd*	yes
\x*dd*	A number formed of the two hex digits *dd*. Two digits must be present—use `\x02` for small numbers.	no
\^*C*	(backslash, followed by an up arrow, followed by a letter) matches a control character. This example matches Ctrl-C.	no
c	\ followed by anything else matches that character; so, \. matches a dot, * matches an asterisk, and so forth.	yes

cc	Two regular expressions concatenated form a regular expression.	Concatenation.
e|*e*	Two regular expressions separated by a vertical bar recognize either the expression to the left of the bar or the expression to the right of the bar.	OR operator.
(*e*)	Parentheses are used for grouping.	Grouping.
^	An up arrow anchors the pattern to beginning of line. If the first character in the expression is a ^, then the expression is recognized only if it is at the far left of a line.	Beginning-of-line anchor.
$	A dollar sign anchors the pattern to end of line. If the last character in the expression is a $, then the expression is recognized only if it is at the far right of a line.	End-of-line anchor.
.	A period (pronounced dot) matches any character except the newline (`'\r'` or `'\n'` normally, `'\n'` if *−u* is specified).	Match any character.

Character classes. [...] Brackets match any of the characters enclosed in the brackets. If the first character following the bracket is an up arrow (^), any character except the ones specified is matched. Only six characters have special meaning inside a character class:

    {   Start of macro name
    }   End of macro name
    ]   End of character class
    −   Range of characters
    ^   Indicates negative character class
    "   Takes away special meaning of characters up to next quote mark
    \   Takes away special meaning of next character

Use \], \-, \\, and so forth, to put these into a class. Since other metacharacters such as *, ?, and + are not special here, the expression [*?+] matches a star, question mark, or plus sign. Also, a negative character class doesn't match a newline character—[^a-z] actually matches anything except a lower-case character or a newline. Use ([^a-z]|[\r\n]) to match the newline, too. Note that a negative character class must match a character—^[^a-z]$ does not match an empty line. The line must have at least one character on it, but that character may not be a lower-case letter.

Empty character classes.   LEX supports two special character classes not supported by the UNIX **lex**. An empty character class ([]) matches all white space, with white space defined liberally as any character whose ASCII value is less than or equal to a space (all control characters and a space). An empty negative character class ([^]) matches anything but white space.

Closure operators. * + ? A regular expression followed by a * (pronounced star) matches that expression repeated zero or more times; a + matches one or more repetitions; a ? matches zero or one repetitions.

Greedy algorithm.   Note that LEX uses a *greedy* algorithm to match a pattern. It matches the longest possible string that can satisfy the regular expression. Consequently, something like .* is dangerous (it absorbs all the characters on the line). The expression (.|\n)* tries to absorb an entire input file, but will probably cause an input-buffer overflow.

Macro expansion. {*name*} Braces are used to expand a macro name. (The {m,n} notation described in Chapter 2 is not supported by LEX.) The *name* must be part of a macro definition in the first of the input file.

You can use the macros as an element of a regular expression by surrounding the name with curly braces. Given the earlier macro definitions:

```
digit     [0-9]        /* decimal digit      */
hexdigit  [0-9a-fA-f]  /* hexadecimal digit  */
alpha     [a-zA-Z]     /* alphabetic character */
%%
```

a hex number in C can be recognized with 0x{hexdigit}+. An alphanumeric character can be recognized with the following expression:

```
({alpha}|{digit})
```

Macros nest, so you could do the following.

```
digit [0-9]
alpha [a-zA-Z]
alnum ({alpha}|{digit})
```

You could do the same with:

```
digit 0-9
alpha a-zA-Z
alnum [{digit}{alpha}]
```

The ^ and $ metacharacters work properly in all MS-DOS input modes, regardless of whether lines end with \r\n or a single \n. Note that the newline is not part of the lexeme, even though it must be present for the associated expression to be recognized. Use and\r\n to put the the end of line characters into the lexeme. (The \r is not required in UNIX applications, in fact it's an error under UNIX.) Note that, unlike the vi editor ^$ does not match a blank line. You'll have to use an explicit search such as \r\n\r\n to find empty lines.

The operator precedence is summarized in the Table D.3. All operators associate left to right.

Table D.3. Regular-Expression Operator Precedence

operator	description	level
( )	parentheses for grouping	1 (highest)
[ ]	character classes	2
* + ?	closure: 0 or more, 1 or more, 0 or 1	3
cc	concatenation	4
|	OR	5
^ $	anchors to beginning and end of line	6 (lowest)

By default, input that doesn't match a regular expression is silently absorbed. You can cause an error message to be printed when bad input is encountered by putting the following into the definitions section:[12]

```
%{
    #define YYBADINP
%}
```

In general, it's a good idea to put one rule of the form

```
    .    ;
```

at the very end of the rules section. This default rule matches all characters not recognized by a previous expression, and does nothing as its action.

When two conflicting regular expressions are found in the input file, the one that comes first is recognized. The expression that matches the longest input string always takes precedence, however, regardless of the ordering of expressions in the file. Consider the following input file:

```
a.      return DOO;
aa+     return WHA;
```

Given the input aa, DOO will be returned because a. comes first in the file. Given the input aaa, the second expression is active because the longer string is matched.

---

12. UNIX **lex** behaves differently. It prints the unrecognized string to standard output and doesn't support YYBADINP.

D.3.2 The Code Part of the Rule

The code portion of the rule can be any legal C-code. It ends up in the output as part of a **switch** statement, so be careful with **break**s. yylex() does not return unless an explicit **return** statement is included in one of the actions associated with a regular expression. On the other hand, a legal C statement must be attached to every regular expression, even if that statement is only a single semicolon.

Using local variables in actions.

The action code does not have to be surrounded with curly braces, but if you do so, you can use local variables in the code, as in:

```
expression    {
                      int i;
                      ...
              }
```

The scope of the local variable is limited by the curly braces, as in normal C. Global variables must be defined in a %{...%} block in the definitions section.

If a vertical bar is used in place of an action, the action associated with the next rule is used. For example:

```
0x[0-9a-fA-F]+          |
0[0-7]+                 |
[1-9][0-9]*    return( NUMERIC_CONSTANT );
```

causes the **return** statement to be executed if any of the three expressions are matched.

Subroutines for use in actions.

Several subroutines, variables, and macros are available for use inside any of your actions (in either the rules or code section, but not in a %{...%} block in the definitions section). The subroutines are all in *l.lib*, which must be linked to your program. You can provide your own versions of all of them, however, in which case the ones in the library are not linked. The macros definitions are all imbedded in the LᴱX output file itself, and their definitions are discussed in depth in Chapter Two. LᴱX supports the following subroutines and macros:

Default main().

void main()

The short main() subroutine shown in Listing D.1 is provided in *l.lib* as a convenience in testing lex-generated recognizers. It just loops, calling yylex() until yylex() returns zero. It's linked automatically if you don't provide a main() of your own. This default main() can cause problems if you forget to put a main() in an **occs**-generated compiler. In this case, main() is fetched from the library, and the parser is never activated.

Current lexeme.

char *yytext

This variable points at the lexeme that matches the current regular expression. The string is '\0' terminated.

Lexeme length.

int yyleng

The number of characters in yytext, excluding the final '\0'.

Input line number.

int yylineno

The current input line number. If the lexeme spans multiple lines, it is the number of the last line of the lexeme.

Input a character to the current lexeme.

int input()

Read (and return) the next input character—the one following the last character in the lexeme. The new character is added to the end of the lexeme (yytext) by

Listing D.1. *yymain.c*— The `main()` Subroutine in *l.lib*

```
1   #include <stdlib.h>
2   #include <tools/debug.h>
3   #include <tools/l.h>
4
5   void    main( argc, argv )
6   char    **argv;
7   int     argc;
8   {
9       /* A default main module to test the lexical analyzer.
10      */
11
12      if( argc == 2 )
13          ii_newfile( argv[1] );
14
15      yylex();
16      exit( 0 );
17  }
```

L^EX and `yyleng` is adjusted accordingly.[13] EOF (as defined in *<stdio.h>*) is returned at end of file.

ECHO

Echo current lexeme to the screen.

Print the current lexeme to a stream named `yyout`, which is initialized to `stdout`. This is just an alias for `fprintf(yyout,"%s",yytext)`. Do not use this macro if you intend to use the **occs** interactive debugging environment described in Appendix E—it messes up the windows.

void output(**int** c)

Output a character.

Print *c* to the output stream. The FILE pointer used for this stream is called `yyout` and is initialized to `stdout`. You can change the file with `fopen()` if you like. Do not use this function if you intend to use the **occs** interactive-debugging environment described in Appendix E—it messes up the windows.

void unput(**int** c)

Push back one character.

Pushes the indicated character back into the input stream. Note that *c* effectively overwrites `yytext[yyleng-1]` and then makes the lexeme one character smaller. Both `yyleng` and `yytext` are modified; c will be read as the next input character.[14]

YYERROR(**char** *s)

Print internal error message.

This macro is not supported by the UNIX **lex.** It is used to print internal error messages generated by the lexical analyzer itself. The default macro prints the string, *s*, to `stderr`. You will probably want to redefine this macro for **occs**—put the following into the L^EX input file's definition section:

---

13. UNIX **lex** doesn't modify the `yytext` or `yyleng`; it just returns the next input character.

14. UNIX **lex** does not modify `yytext` or `yyleng`. It just pushes back the character.

```
%{
    #define YYERROR(str) yyerror("%s\n", str);
%}
```

Push back multiple input characters.

void yyless(**int** n)

Push *n* characters back into the input stream. Again, yytext and yyleng are adjusted to reflect the pushed back characters.[15] You cannot push back more than yyleng characters.

Initialize LEX parser.

void yy_init_lex()

This subroutine is called by yylex() before it reads any input. You can use it to do any run-time initializations that are required before the lexical analyzer starts up. It's particularly handy if you want to initialize variables that are declared **static** in the definitions part of the LEX input file. You can define a yy_init_lex() that does the initializations at the bottom of the input file, and this function is called automatically. The default routine, in *l.lib*, does nothing. It's in Listing D.2.[16]

Listing D.2. *yyinitlx.c*— Initialize LEX

```
1   void yy_init_lex( ) {}   /* Default initialization routine--does nothing. */
```

Keep processing after expression is recognized.

void yymore()

Invoking this macro causes yylex() to continue as if the regular expression had not been recognized. Consider the following regular expression and action (which recognizes a subset of the legitimate string constants in C):

```
\"[^\"]*\"   {    if( yytext[yyleng-2] == '\\' )
                      yymore();
             else
                 return STRING;
         }
```

The regular expression recognizes a double quote (") followed by anything except a second double quote repeated zero or more times. The quotes have to be escaped with a backslash because they're special characters to LEX. The problem here is escaped double quotes within strings, as in

```
"string with a \" in it"
```

The regular expression is satisfied when the first double quote is encountered. The action code looks at the character preceding the ending quote mark (yytext[yyleng-2]). If that character is a backslash, yymore() is called, and more input will be processed as if the offending double quote had not been seen. The same code is executed a second time when the third double quote is found; but here, there's no preceding backslash so the **return** STRING is executed.

---

15. UNIX **lex** does not modify yytext or yyleng; it just pushes back the characters.

16. UNIX **lex** does not support this mechanism. You're on your own when it comes to initializations.

int yywrap()

This subroutine is called by the lexical analyzer at end of file. The name stands for "go ahead and wrap up the processing", so yywrap() returns true if processing should terminate [in which case yylex() returns zero.] The default routine, in *l.lib*, just returns 1. It's in Listing D.3. You can provide your own yywrap() however, and yours will be linked instead of the library routine. Typically, you'd use yywrap() to handle a series of input files. It would open the next input file in the series with each call, returning zero until there were no more files to open, whereupon it would return one. There's an example in Listing D.4.

Listing D.3. *yywrap.c*— Library Version

```
1   int       yywrap()          /* yylex() halts if 1 is returned */
2   {
3       return( 1 );
4   }
```

Listing D.4. A User-Defined yywrap()

```
1   int  Argc;                    /* Copy of argc as passed to main(). */
2   char **Argv;                  /* Copy of argv as passed to main(). */
3
4   yywrap()
5   {
6       if( --Argc >= 0 )
7       {
8           if( ii_newfile( *Argv ) != -1 )
9           {
10              ++Argv;
11              return 0;                /* New file opened successfully. */
12          }
13          fprintf(stderr, "Can't open %s\n", *Argv );
14      }
15      return 1;
16  }
17
18  main( argc, argv )
19  int     argc;
20  char    **argv;
21  {
22      Argc = argc - 1;
23      Argv = argv + 1;
24      ii_newfile( *argv )
25      while( yylex() )
26          ;                            /* Discard all input tokens. */
27  }
```

YYBADINP

If this macro is **#define**d in a %{...%} block in the definitions section, an error message is printed when an input sequence that's not recognized by any regular expression is encountered at run time. Otherwise, the unrecognized input is silently ignored at run time.[17]

Low-level input functions.

The longest permissible lexeme is 1024 bytes.[18] An error message is printed if you try to read more characters. If a lexeme is likely to exceed this length, you'll have to work with one of the low-level input functions that LEX itself uses, synopsized below, and described in depth in Chapter Two. None of these functions are supported by UNIX **lex**.

Low-level input routine.

`int ii_input()`

This is a somewhat more flexible input function than `input()`. Normally, it returns the next input character (and stretches the lexeme one character). It returns zero on end of file and −1 if it can't read a character because the input buffer is full [see `ii_flushbuf()`]. Note that `yyleng` is not modified by `ii_input()`.

Low-level lookahead.

`int ii_lookahead(int n)`

You can use this routine to look ahead in the input without actually reading a character. `ii_lookahead(0)` returns the last character in the lexeme. `ii_lookahead(1)` returns the next character that will be read. `ii_lookahead(-1)` returns the penultimate character in the lexeme. The maximum forward lookahead is 32 characters, and you can look back only as far as the beginning of the current lexeme.

Open new input file.

`int ii_newfile(char *name)`

Use this routine to open a new input file. The *name* is the file name. The routine returns a file descriptor for the open file or −1 if it can't open the file. As is the case with normal input functions, the global variable `yyerror` will hold an error code identifying the problem. This routine automatically closes the current input file before opening the new one, so it's actually an error if you close the current input file explicitly before calling `ii_newfile()`.[19]

Flush low-level input buffers.

`int ii_flushbuf()`

This routine flushes the input buffer, discarding all characters currently in it and destroying the current lexeme. It can be used to continue reading when `ii_input()` returns −1. Note that `yylex`, `yyleng`, and `yylineno` are all invalid after this routine is called. It's usually used only when you're doing something like absorbing a long comment—when the contents of the lexeme are immaterial. It returns 1 if everything's okay, 0 at end of file.

Change system-level input functions.

`int ii_io(int (*open)(), int (*close)(), int (*read)())`

You can use this routine to change the low-level, unbuffered I/O functions used by the input routines. It takes three function pointers as arguments, the first is a pointer to an open function, the second to a close function, and the third to a read function. These should work just like the standard UNIX I/O functions with the same name, at least in terms of the external interface. The open function is called

---

17. UNIX **lex** does not support this mechanism. It just writes the unrecognized characters to standard output.

18. 128 bytes is typical in UNIX **lex**.

19. UNIX **lex** does not use this input mechanism; rather, it uses the buffered I/O system for its input and gets input from a stream called `yyin`. This stream is initialized to `stdin`, but you can modify it using `fopen()`. You must use `ii_input()` to change the LEX input stream, however.

as follows:

```
#include <fcntl.h>
#ifdef MSDOS
#       define O_MODE (O_RDONLY|O_BINARY)
#else
#       define O_MODE (O_RDONLY)
#endif
 ...
int fd;
 ...
if( (fd = (*open)(name, O_MODE)) != -1 )
{
    /* file open was successful */
}
return fd;
```

It should return an **int**-sized number that can't be confused with standard input (anything but zero), and that same number will be passed to the read and close functions as follows:

```
int   got;
char  *load_characters_here; /* base address of the buffer      */
int   read_this_many_bytes;  /* number of characters requested  */
int   got;                   /* number of characters actually read */
int   fd;                    /* value returned from previous open */
 ...
if((got=(*read)(fd, load_characters_here, read_this_many_bytes))==-1)
    process_end_of_file();
 ...
(*close)( fd );
```

All variables and subroutines used both by LEX and its input functions start with one of the following character sequences:[20]

Names start with yy Yy YY ii_.

```
yy  Yy  YY  ii_
```

Don't start any of your own symbols with these characters.

D.4 LEX Command-Line Switches

LEX takes various command-line switches that modify its behavior. These are summarized in Table D.4[21]

LEX automatically compresses the tables that it generates so that they'll take up less room in the output. A ten-to-one compression rate is typical. The default compression method eliminates equivalent rows and columns from the tables and is best for most practical applications. The −c and −f switches can be used to control the table-compression, however. The −f (for fast) switch eliminates compression entirely, yielding much larger tables, but also giving a faster lexical analyzer. The −c switch changes the compression algorithm to one in which each character/next-state pair is stored as a two-byte object. This method typically (though not always) gives you smaller tables and a

Controlling table compression, −c, −f.

---

20. You have to worry only about the yy prefix with **lex**.

21. Of these, only −t and −f are supported by UNIX **lex**. The **lex** −v switch prints a one-line summary of internal statistics only—the LEX −v is more verbose. The lex −n switch suppress the verbose-mode output, and is not supported by LEX.

Table D.4. LEX Command-Line Switches

Switch	Description
−c*N*	Use pair compression, *N* is the threshold. The default *N* is 4.
−f	For fast. Don't compress tables.
−h	Suppress header comment that describes state machine.
−H	Print the header only.
−l	Suppress **#line** directives in the output.
−m*name*	Use *name* as template-file name rather than lex.par.
−t	Send output to standard output instead of lexyy.c
−u	UNIX mode (. is everything but \n)
−v	Verbose mode, print various statistics.
−V	More verbose, print internal diagnostics as lex runs.

slower lexical analyzer than the default method. The -c switch takes an optional numeric argument (-c5) that specifies the threshold above which the pair compression kicks in for a given row of the table. If the row has more than the indicated number of nonerror transitions, it is not compressed. The default threshold, if no number is specified, is four. In any event, the −v switch can be used to see the actual table size, so you can decide which method is most appropriate in a particular situation.

Header comment, −h, −H.

The −h and −H switches are used to control the presence of a larger header comment that is output at the top of lexyy.c. This comment describes the state machine that LEX uses to recognize the regular expressions. A lower-case *h* suppresses this comment. An upper-case *H* suppresses all output except the comment.

Suppressing #line directives, −l.

LEX automatically generates **#line** directives in the output file. These cause the compiler to print error messages that reference lines in the the original LEX input file rather than the output file. They are quite useful when you're trying to track down syntax errors. The **#line** can confuse source-level debuggers, however, so −l (that's an ell) is provided to eliminate them.

Choose an alternate driver file, −m.

The LIB environment.

LEX itself creates only a small part of the output file. The majority is stored in a *template file* called *lex.par*, discussed in depth in Chapter 2. LEX searches for this file, first in the current directory and then along a path specified by semicolon-delimited directory names in the *LIB* environment. The −m*name* switch can be used to specify an explicit file name to use as the template. There's no space between the *m* and the name.

Use standard output, −t.

UNIX-compatible newline, −u.

The −t switch causes LEX to send output to standard output rather than *lexyy.c*.

The −u switch changes the definition of a "newline" to be consistent with UNIX rather than MS-DOS. Normally a newline is either a carriage return or linefeed (′\r′ or ′\n′). In UNIX mode, however, a newline is a single linefeed. This definition affects the . operator, which matches anything except a newline, and a negative character class, which matches anything except a newline or one of the specified characters.

Verbose-mode output, −v, −V.

The −v switch causes LEX to print various statistics, such as the output table sizes, to standard output. −V forces more-verbose output, which describes the internal workings of the program as it runs. This last switch is useful primarily for debugging LEX itself; it's also handy if you want to see a running commentary of the subset construction used to create a DFA from an NFA, described in Chapter Two.

D.5 Limits and Bugs

Table-size limits.

Several limits are imposed on the LEX input file. In addition, several internal limits will affect the workings of LEX. These are summarized in Table D.5. There are two limits on the action components to the rules. No single rule (including the action) can be longer than 2,048 bytes, and the space used by all the actions combined cannot exceed 20,480 bytes. If either of these limits are exceeded, fix the problem by moving some of the imbedded code into subroutines declared in the third part of the LEX input specification.

Table D.5. LEX Limits

Maximum space available for all actions combined	20,480	bytes
Maximum characters in a single rule (including the action)	2,048	bytes
Maximum number of NFA states	512	states
Maximum number of DFA states	254	states

The limits on NFA and DFA states refer to the maximum size of internal tables used by LEX (see Chapter Two). There are always fewer DFA than NFA states. If you exceed either of these limits, you'll either have to reduce the number of regular expressions in the input file or simplify the expressions. Two simplification techniques can be used with little difficulty:

Simplifying expressions to get smaller internal table size.

(1) Character classes take up less room than the | operator so they should be used whenever possible; [012] is preferable to (0|1|2). The character class uses two states; the expression with | operator uses ten.

Use character classes, not |.

(2) Use multiple rules with shared actions rather than the OR operator if possible. This rule:

Use shared actions, not |.

```
abc         |
def         printf("abc or def");
```

requires one fewer NFA state than this one:

```
abc|def  printf("abc or def");
```

(3) One of the least efficient ways to use LEX is to recognize long strings that do not contain metacharacters. A simple string uses roughly as many NFA states as it has characters—"0123456789" requires 11 states, but a closure operator or character class uses only a few states. These sorts of strings can cause problems when you try to do something like this:

Don't use long literal matches.

```
<Ctrl-A>        printf("<Ctrl-A>\n");
<Ctrl-B>        printf("<Ctrl-B>\n");
<Ctrl-C>        printf("<Ctrl-C>\n");
<Ctrl-D>        printf("<Ctrl-D>\n");
<Ctrl-E>        printf("<Ctrl-E>\n");
<Ctrl-F>        printf("<Ctrl-F>\n");
<Ctrl-G>        printf("<Ctrl-G>\n");
<Ctrl-H>        printf("<Ctrl-H>\n");
<Ctrl-I>        printf("<Ctrl-I>\n");
<Ctrl-J>        printf("<Ctrl-J>\n");
<Ctrl-K>        printf("<Ctrl-K>\n");
<Ctrl-L>        printf("<Ctrl-L>\n");
```

Though the final state machine uses only 31 DFA states, 121 NFA states are required to produce this machine. A better solution is:

```
%%
<Ctrl-[A-L]>    switch( yytext[6] )
                {
                case 'A':     printf("<Ctrl-A>\n");        break;
                case 'B':     printf("<Ctrl-B>\n");        break;
                case 'C':     printf("<Ctrl-C>\n");        break;
                case 'D':     printf("<Ctrl-D>\n");        break;
                case 'E':     printf("<Ctrl-E>\n");        break;
                case 'F':     printf("<Ctrl-F>\n");        break;
                case 'G':     printf("<Ctrl-G>\n");        break;
                case 'H':     printf("<Ctrl-H>\n");        break;
                case 'I':     printf("<Ctrl-I>\n");        break;
                case 'J':     printf("<Ctrl-J>\n");        break;
                case 'K':     printf("<Ctrl-K>\n");        break;
                case 'L':     printf("<Ctrl-L>\n");        break;
                }
%%
```

which requires only 11 NFA states.

Use lookup tables to disambiguate lexemes.

Keyword recognition presents a similar problem that can be solved in much the same way. A single expression can be used to recognize several similar lexemes, which can then be differentiated with a table lookup or calls to `strcmp()`. For example, all keywords in most languages can be recognized by the single expression `[a-zA-Z_]+`. Thereafter, the keywords can be differentiated from one another with a table look up. There's an example of this process below.

Problems with anchors.

A bug in LEX affects the way that the default . action is handled if the beginning-of-line anchor (^) is also used in the same input specification. The problem is that an explicit match of \n is added to the beginning of all patterns that are anchored to the start of line (in order to differentiate ^x from x$ from ^x$ from x—it should be possible to have all four patterns in the input file, each with a different accepting action). The difficulty here is that an input file like this:

```
%%
^ab     return AB;
.       return NOT_AB;
%%
```

generates a machine like this:

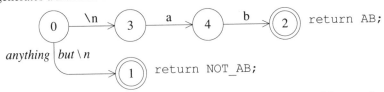

The problem lies in the way that the LEX-generated state machine works. When it fails out of a nonaccepting state, the machine backs up to the most-recently-seen accepting state. If there is no such state, the input lexeme is discarded. Looking at the previous machine, if you are in State 4, the machine fails if a character other than b is in the input. Not having seen an accepting state, the machine discards the newline and the a rather than performing the default **return** NOT_AB action. You can correct the problem by making State 3 an accepting state that also executes the **return** NOT_AB action. Do this by modifying the input file as follows:

```
%%
^ab     return AB;
\n      |
.       return NOT_AB;
%%
```

D.6 Example: A Lexical Analyzer for C

Listing D.5. shows a sample LEX input file for a C lexical analyzer. Listing D.6, *yyout.h*, contains the token definitions. Various macros are defined on lines 11 to 17 of Listing D.5. The `suffix` macro is for recognizing characters that can be appended to the end of a numeric constant, such as `0x1234L`. Note that all characters from an ASCII NUL up to a space (that is, all control characters) are recognized as white space.

Listing D.5. *c.lex—* LEX Input File for a C Lexical Analyzer

```
 1   %{
 2   /* Lexical analyzer specification for C. Note that CONSTANTS are
 3    * all positive in order to avoid confusions (to prevent a-1 from
 4    * being interpreted as NAME CONSTANT rather than NAME MINUS CONSTANT).
 5    */
 6
 7   #include "yyout.h"
 8   #include <search.h>        /* Function prototype for bsearch() */
 9   %}
10
11   let      [_a-zA-Z]         /* Letter                                        */
12   alnum    [_a-zA-Z0-9]      /* Alphanumeric character                        */
13   h        [0-9a-fA-F]       /* Hexadecimal digit                             */
14   o        [0-7]             /* Octal digit                                   */
15   d        [0-9]             /* Decimal digit                                 */
16   suffix   [UuLl]            /* Suffix in integral numeric constant           */
17   white    [\x00-\s]         /* White space                                   */
18
19   %%
20   "/*"                  {
21                              int i;
22
23                              while( i = ii_input() )
24                              {
25                                  if( i < 0 )
26                                      ii_flushbuf();    /* Discard Lexeme */
27
28                                  else if( i == '*'  &&  ii_lookahead(1) == '/' )
29                                  {
30                                      ii_input();
31                                      break;            /* Recognized comment */
32                                  }
33                              }
34
35                              if( i == 0 )
36                                  yyerror( "End of file in comment\n" );
37                          }
38
39   \"(\\.|[^\"])*\"      return STRING;
40   \"(\\.|[^\"])*[\r\n]  yyerror("Adding missing \" to string constant\n");
41                          return STRING;
42
```

➡

Listing D.5. continued. . .

```
43   '.'                              |              /* 'a', 'b', etc.           */
44   '\\.'                            |              /* '\t', '\f', etc.          */
45   '\\{o}({o}{o}?)?'                |              /* '\123', '\12', '\1'        */
46   '\\x{h}({h}{h}?)?'               |              /* '\x123', '\x12', '\x1'     */
47   0{o}*{suffix}?                   |              /* 0, 01, 012, 012L, etc.     */
48   0x{h}+{suffix}?                  |              /* 0x1, 0x12, 0x12L, etc.     */
49   [1-9]{d}*{suffix}?       return ICON;   /* 123, 123L, etc.            */
50
51   ({d}+|{d}+\.{d}*|{d}*\.{d}+)([eE][-+]?{d}+)?[fF]?   return FCON ;
52
53   "("                     return LP;
54   ")"                     return RP;
55   "{"                     return LC;
56   "}"                     return RC;
57   "["                     return LB;
58   "]"                     return RB;
59
60   "->"                    |
61   "."                     return STRUCTOP;
62   "++"                    |
63   "--"                    return INCOP;
64   [~!]                    return UNOP;
65
66   "*"                     return STAR;
67   [/%]                    return DIVOP;
68   "+"                     return PLUS;
69   "-"                     return MINUS;
70   <<|>>                   return SHIFTOP;        /* <<   >>         */
71   [<>]=?                  return RELOP;          /* >  <  >=  <=   */
72   [!=]=                   return EQUOP;          /* !=  ==          */
73   [*/%+-&|^]=             |                      /* += -= *=, etc  */
74   (<<|>>)=                return ASSIGNOP;       /* >>=  <<=        */
75   "="                     return EQUAL;
76   "&"                     return AND;
77   "^"                     return XOR;
78   "|"                     return OR;
79   "&&"                    return ANDAND;
80   "||"                    return OROR;
81   "?"                     return QUEST;
82   ":"                     return COLON;
83   ","                     return COMMA;
84   ";"                     return SEMI;
85   {let}{alnum}*           return id_or_keyword( yytext );
86   {white}+               /* ignore white space */
87   .                      yyerror( "Illegal character <%s>\n", yytext );
88   %%
89
90   /*---------------------------------------------------------------*/
91
92   typedef struct                   /* Routines to recognize keywords */
93   {
94       char  *name;
95       int   val;
96   }
97   KWORD;
98
99   KWORD  Ktab[] =                   /* Alphabetic keywords  */
100  {
101      { "auto",    CLASS       },
102      { "break",   BREAK       },
```

```
Listing D.5. continued...

103         { "case",      CASE          },
104         { "char",      TYPE          },
105         { "continue",  CONTINUE      },
106         { "default",   DEFAULT       },
107         { "do",        DO            },
108         { "double",    TYPE          },
109         { "else",      ELSE          },
110         { "extern",    CLASS         },
111         { "float",     TYPE          },
112         { "for",       FOR           },
113         { "goto",      GOTO          },
114         { "if",        IF            },
115         { "int",       TYPE          },
116         { "long",      TYPE          },
117         { "register",  CLASS         },
118         { "return",    RETURN        },
119         { "short",     TYPE          },
120         { "sizeof",    SIZEOF        },
121         { "static",    CLASS         },
122         { "struct",    STRUCT        },
123         { "switch",    SWITCH        },
124         { "typedef",   CLASS         },
125         { "union",     STRUCT        },
126         { "unsigned",  TYPE          },
127         { "void",      TYPE          },
128         { "while",     WHILE         }
129     };
130
131     int     cmp( a, b )
132     KWORD   *a, *b;
133     {
134         return strcmp( a->name, b->name );
135     }
136
137     int     id_or_keyword( lex )    /* Do a binary search for a  */
138     char    *lex;                   /* possible keyword in Ktab  */
139     {                               /* Return the token if it's  */
140         KWORD       *p;             /* in the table, NAME        */
141         KWORD       dummy;          /* otherwise.                */
142
143         dummy.name = lex;
144         p = bsearch( &dummy, Ktab, sizeof(Ktab)/sizeof(KWORD),
145                                             sizeof(KWORD), cmp);
146         return( p ? p->val : NAME );
147     }
```

The rule on lines 20 to 37 of Listing D.5 handles a comment. The main problem here   Comments.
is the potential comment length. A single regular expression can't be used to recognize a
comment because various internal limits on lexeme length will be exceeded by long
comments. So, the code looks for the beginning-of-comment symbol, and then sits in a
while loop sucking up characters until an end-of-comment is encountered. The
ii_flushbuf( ) call on line 26 forces an internal buffer flush (discarding the partially-
collected lexeme) if the input buffer overflows. Note that this comment processing isn't
portable to UNIX **lex**. An alternate strategy is shown in Listing D.7. This second method
works fine under UNIX, but disallows comments longer than 1024 bytes if used with my
LEX.

Listing D.6. *yyout.h*— C Token Definitions

```
 1   /*        token     value     lexeme                           */
 2
 3   #define _EOI       0      /* end-of-input symbol                */
 4   #define NAME       1      /* identifier                         */
 5   #define STRING     2      /* "string constant"                  */
 6   #define ICON       3      /* integer constant or character constant */
 7   #define FCON       4      /* floating-point constant            */
 8   #define PLUS       5      /* +                                  */
 9   #define MINUS      6      /* -                                  */
10   #define STAR       7      /* *                                  */
11   #define AND        8      /* &                                  */
12   #define QUEST      9      /* ?                                  */
13   #define COLON      10     /* :                                  */
14   #define ANDAND     11     /* &&                                 */
15   #define OROR       12     /* ||                                 */
16   #define RELOP      13     /*  > >= < <=                         */
17   #define EQUOP      14     /*  == !=                             */
18   #define DIVOP      15     /* /   %                              */
19   #define OR         16     /* |                                  */
20   #define XOR        17     /* ^                                  */
21   #define SHIFTOP    18     /* >> <<                              */
22   #define INCOP      19     /* ++ --                              */
23   #define UNOP       20     /* ! ~                                */
24   #define STRUCTOP   21     /* . ->                               */
25   #define TYPE       22     /* int, long, etc.                    */
26   #define CLASS      23     /* extern, static, typedef, etc.      */
27   #define STRUCT     24     /* struct union                       */
28   #define RETURN     25     /* return                             */
29   #define GOTO       26     /* goto                               */
30   #define IF         27     /* if                                 */
31   #define ELSE       28     /* else                               */
32   #define SWITCH     29     /* switch                             */
33   #define BREAK      30     /* break                              */
34   #define CONTINUE   31     /* continue                           */
35   #define WHILE      32     /* while                              */
36   #define DO         33     /* do                                 */
37   #define FOR        34     /* for                                */
38   #define DEFAULT    35     /* default                            */
39   #define CASE       36     /* case                               */
40   #define SIZEOF     37     /* sizeof                             */
41   #define LP         38     /* (   (left parenthesis)             */
42   #define RP         39     /* )                                  */
43   #define LC         40     /* {   (left curly)                   */
44   #define RC         41     /* }                                  */
45   #define LB         42     /* [   (left bracket)                 */
46   #define RB         43     /* ]                                  */
47   #define COMMA      44     /* ,                                  */
48   #define SEMI       45     /* ;                                  */
49   #define EQUAL      46     /* =                                  */
50   #define ASSIGNOP   47     /* += -=, etc.                        */
```

String constants.

The next two rules, on lines 39 to 41 handle string constants. The rules assume that a string constant cannot span a line, so the first rule handles legal constants, the second rule handles illegal constants that contain a newline rather than a terminating close quote. (ANSI is unclear about whether newlines are permitted in string constants. I'm assuming that they are not permitted because string concatenation makes them unnecessary. Consequently, a hard error is printed here rather than a warning.)

Listing D.7. A UNIX Comment-Processing Mechanism

```
 1  %%
 2  "/*"            {
 3                      int i, lasti = 0;
 4
 5                      while( (i = input())  &&  i != EOF )
 6                      {
 7                          if( i == '/'  &&  last_i == '*' );
 8                              break;
 9                      }
10
11                      if( i == 0 || i == EOF )
12                          yyerror( "End of file in comment\n" );
13                  }
14  %%
```

Most of the complexity comes from handling backslashes in the string correctly. The strategy that I used earlier:

```
\"[^\"]*\"    if( yytext[yyleng-2] == '\\' )
                  yymore();
              else
                  return STRING;
```

doesn't work in a real situation because this expression can't handle strings in which the last character is a literal backslash, like "\\". It also can't handle newlines in string constants, for which an error should be printed. The situation is rectified on line 39 of Listing D.5 by replacing the character class in the middle of \"[^\"]*\" with the following subexpression (I've added some spaces for clarity):

```
( \\.  |  [^\"] )*
```

This subexpression recognizes two things: two-character sequences where the first character is a backslash, and single characters other than double quotes. The expression on line 40 handles the situation where the closing quote is missing. It prints an error message and returns a STRING, as if the close quote had been found.

All the rules on lines 43 to 49 recognize integer constants of some sort. The first five are for the various character constants and the last four are for numeric constants. Floating-point constants are recognized on line 51.

The rule on line 85 recognizes both identifiers and keywords. I've done this to minimize the table sizes used by the LᴱX-generated analyzer. The id_or_keyword() subroutine is used to distinguish the two. It does a binary search in the table declared on lines 99 to 129, returning the appropriate token if the current lexeme is in the table, otherwise it returns NAME. The bsearch() function on line 144 does the actual search. It is a standard ANSI function that's passed a key, a pointer to a table, the number of elements in the table, the size of one element (in bytes), and a pointer to a comparison function. This last function is called from bsearch(), being passed the original key and a pointer to one array element. It must compare these, but otherwise work like strcmp(). The comparison function used here is declared on lines 131 to 135. The remainder of the rules are straightforward.

Using lookup table to differentiate identifiers from keywords.

D.7 Exercises

D.1. Newlines in string constants are not handled particularly well by the LᴇX input file presented in the previous section. The current file assumes that newlines are not permitted in constants, so it inserts a close quote when a newline is encountered. Rewrite the regular expressions for string constants so that they will do the following:

- Print a warning if a newline is found in a constant, and then take the next line as a continuation of the previous line. That is, the close quote should not be inserted by the lexical analyzer; rather, it should recognize multiple-line strings.
- If the newline in the string constant is preceded by a backslash, however, the warning message is suppressed.

D.2. The UNIX **vi** editor supports a *tags* feature. When the cursor is positioned on a subroutine name, typing a Ctrl-] causes the current file to be saved, the file that contains the indicated subroutine is then read into the editor, and the cursor is positioned at the first line of the subroutine. **Vi** accomplishes this feat with the aid of supplemental file called *tags*, which is created by a utility called *ctags*. The tags file consists of several lines, each having the following fields:

    subroutine_name   file_name   search_pattern

The three fields are separated by tabs, and the search pattern consists of the actual first line of the subroutine, surrounded by /ˆ and $/. For example:

```
main    main.c  /ˆmain( argc, argv )$/
```

Using LᴇX, write a version of **ctags** that recognizes all subroutine declarations and all subroutine-like macro definitions in a C program. It should not recognize external declarations. That is, none of the following should generate an entry in the output file:

```
extern      larry ();
char        *curly( int x );
PRIVATE double  moe   ( void );
```

You can assume that subroutine declarations will follow a standard formatting convention. Hand in both the program and documentation describing what the input must look like for a declaration to be recognized.

D.3. Write a version of **ctags** for Pascal programs.

D.4. Using LᴇX, write a version of the UNIX `calendar` utility. Your program should read in a file called *calendar* and print all lines from that file that contain today's date somewhere on the line. All the following forms of dates should be recognized:

        7/4/1776
        7/4/76   Assume 20th century, so this entry is for 1976.
        7/4   Assume the current year.
        7-4-1776
        7-4-76
        7-4
        1776-7-4   Since 1776 can't be a month, assume European ordering.
        July 4, 1776

July 4 1776
July 4
Jul 4   Three-character abbreviations for all month names are supported.
Jul. 4   The abbreviation can be followed by an optional period.
4 July
4 July, 1776
4 July, 76
4 July, '76
4 Jul. '76

E

LLama and Occs

LLama and **occs** are compiler-generation tools that translate an augmented, attributed grammar into a parser. They are essentially C preprocessors, taking as input a file containing intermixed C source code, grammatical rules, and compiler directives, and outputting the C source code for a parser subroutine.

This appendix is a user's manual for both **LLama** and **occs**, the two compiler compilers developed in Chapters Four and Five. (**Occs** stands for "the Other Compiler-Compiler System". It's pronounced "ox.") An understanding of the theoretical parts of these chapters (sections marked with asterisks in the table of contents) will be helpful in reading the current Appendix. Similarly, a discussion of how to use **occs** and **LLama** in conjunction with LEX is found at the beginning of Appendix D, which you should read before continuing.

Both **LLama** and **occs** are modeled after the UNIX **yacc** utility, though **LLama** builds a top-down, LL(1) parser while **occs** builds a bottom-up, LALR(1) parser. The compiler in Chapter Six can be constructed both with **occs** or with **yacc**. If you intend to use the UNIX utility, your time will be better spent reading the UNIX documentation than the current appendix.

LLama and **occs** are both discussed in one appendix because they are very similar at the user level. I will discuss the common parts of both systems first, and then describe the individual characteristics of **occs** and **LLama** in separate sections. Both programs are *compiler compilers*, because they are themselves compilers which translate a very-high-level-language description of a compiler to a high-level-language source code for a compiler. I will use the term *compiler compiler* when I'm talking about characteristics shared by both systems.

E.1 Using The Compiler Compiler

Like LEX, **occs** and **LLama** are C preprocessors. They take as input a file that contains an augmented, attributed grammar that describes a programming language, and they create the C source code for a parser for that language. C source-code fragments that specify code-generation actions in the input are passed to the output with various translations made in that source code to give you access to the parser's value stack. **Occs** outputs the source for a bottom-up parser (both the tables and the parser itself);

LLama outputs a top-down parser. The generated parser subroutine is called `yyparse()`—just call this subroutine to get the parsing started. The subroutine returns zero if it parses the input successfully, −1 if an unrecoverable error in the input is encountered. A mechanism is provided for you to return other values as well. `yyparse()` expects to get input tokens from a scanner subroutine generated by LEX, the interaction was discussed at the beginning of Appendix D.

The parser subroutine, `yyparse()`.

Occs, despite superficial similarities, is not **yacc**—I've made no attempt to perpetuate existing deficiencies in the UNIX program in order to get compatibility with UNIX. **Occs** has a better error-recovery mechanism than **yacc** (though it's still not ideal), the output code is more maintainable, and it provides you with a considerably improved debugging environment. This last change, activated when you compile with YYDEBUG defined, gives you a window-oriented debugging system that lets you actually watch the parse process in action. You can watch the parse stack change, see attributes as they're inherited, set breakpoints on various stack conditions and on reading specified symbols, and so forth. I've documented differences between **occs** and **yacc** in footnotes; these are of interest only if you're already familiar with **yacc**. **LLama**, of course, is radically different from **yacc** in that it uses a completely different parsing technique. Don't be misled by the superficial similarities in the input formats.

Unfortunately, it's difficult to present either compiler compiler in a hierarchical fashion—you may have to read this Appendix twice. Similarly, the description of the attribute-passing mechanism will make more sense after you've seen it used to build the C compiler in Chapter Six.

E.2 The Input File

The **LLama** and **occs** input files, like LEX input files, are split up into three sections, separated from one another with `%%` directives:

Input-file organization.

definitions
`%%`
rules
`%%`
code

Both the definitions and code sections can be empty.

E.3 The Definitions Section

The first part of the input file contains both directives to the compiler compiler itself and C source code that is used later on in the rules section. As with the LEX input format, the code must be surrounded by `%{` and `%}` directives.[1] All the directives start with a percent sign, which must be in the leftmost column. Those directives that are unique to one or the other of the programs are discussed later, but those directives that are shared by both **LLama** and **occs** are summarized in Table E.1.

Code in the definitions section.

The `%token` and `%term` directives are used to declare nonterminal symbols in the grammar. The directive is followed by the name of the symbol, which can then be used

Defining tokens: `%token`, `%term`.

---

1. **Yacc** passes lines that start with white space through to the output without modification, as if they were part of a `%{...%}` delimited code block. **Occs** does not support this mechanism.

Table E.1. Occs and **LLama** % Directives

Directive	Description
%%	Separates the three sections of the input file.
%{	Starts a code block in the definitions section. All lines that follow, up to a line that starts with a %} directive, are written to the output file unmodified.
%}	Ends a code block.
%token	Defines a token.
%term	A synonym for %token.
/* */	C-like comments are recognized—and ignored—by **occs**, when found outside of a %{...%}-delimited code block. They are passed to the output if found inside a code block.

later in a production in the rules section. For example:

```
%term  LP RP     /*  ( and )          */
%term  ID        /*  an identifier     */
%term  NUM       /*  a number          */
%token PLUS STAR /*  +  *              */
```

yyout.h: Token definitions

Several names can be listed on a single line. **Occs** creates an output file called *yyout.h* which holds symbolic values for all these tokens, and these values must be returned from the lexical analyzer when the equivalent string is recognized.[2] For example, the previous declarations produce the following *yyout.h* file:

```
#define _EOI_ 0
#define LP    1
#define RP    2
#define ID    3
#define NUM   4
#define PLUS    5
#define STAR    6
```

Token names.

The arguments to %term are used verbatim for the macro names in *yyout.h*. Consequently, they must obey the normal C naming conventions: The token names must be made up of letters, numbers, and underscores, and the first symbol in the name cannot be a number.[3] The definitions in *yyout.h* can then be used from within a LEX input file to build a lexical analyzer. A sample LEX file is in Listing E.1.

Code Blocks %{...%}

Code blocks, delimited by %{ and %} directives, are also found in the definitions section. These blocks should contain the normal things that would be found at the top of a C file: macro definitions, **typedef**s, global-variable declarations, function prototypes, and so forth. Certain macro names are reserved for use by the compiler compiler, however, and these are summarized in Table E.2.[4] You can modify the parser's behavior by defining these macros yourself in a code block in the definitions section (there's no need to **#undef** them first).

---

2. **Yacc** creates a file called *y.tab.h*, and the file is created only if *–d* is specified on the command line.

3. **Yacc** doesn't impose these restrictions. Also, **yacc** (but not **occs**) accepts a definition of the form %token NAME *number*, in which case it uses the indicated number for the token value rather than assigning an arbitrary value.

4. Of these, YYABORT, YYACCEPT, YYDEBUG YYMAXDEPTH, and YYSTYPE are supported by **yacc**. The YYDEBUG flag just activates a running log of shift and reduce actions to the screen—there is no interactive debugging environment.

Listing E.1. *expr.lex*— LᴱX Input Specification for Simple Expressions

```
 1    %{
 2        #include   "yyout.h"
 3    %}
 4    %%
 5    "+"      return  PLUS;
 6    "*"      return  STAR;
 7    "("      return  LP;
 8    ")"      return  RP;
 9    [0-9]+   return  NUM;
10    [a-z]+   return  ID;
11    %%
```

In addition to the foregoing, the file *<stdio.h>* is automatically **#include**d at the top of the parser file before any code that you specify in the definitions section is output. It's harmless, though unnecessary, for you to **#include** it explicitly. Similarly, *"yyout.h"* and the ᴀɴsɪ variable-argument-list-definitions file, *<stdarg.h>*, is also **#include**d automatically.[5] Finally, the **yacc** version of the stack macros are included (*<tools/yystack.h>*). These are described in Appendix A.

Note that all the symbols that **occs** uses start with YY, yy, or Yy. You should not start any of your own names with these characters to avoid possible name conflicts.

Internal names: yy, Yy, YY

E.4 The Rules Section

The rules section of the input file comprises all lines between an initial %% directive and a second %% directive or end of file. Rules are made up of augmented, attributed productions: grammatical rules and code to be executed. A rules section for an **occs** input file is shown in Listing E.2 along with the necessary definitions section. (I'll discuss this file in greater depth in a moment; it's presented here only so that you can see the structure of an input file.)

Productions take the form:

left-hand_side **:** *right-hand_side* **|** *rhs_2* **|**...**|** *rhs_N* **;**

Occs' modified BNF: representing productions.

A colon is used to separate the left- from the right-hand side instead of the → that we've used hitherto. A vertical bar (|) is used to separate right-hand-sides that share a single left-hand side. A semicolon terminates the whole collection of right-hand sides. Terminal symbols in the grammar must have been declared with a previous %term or %token, and their names must obey the C naming conventions.

Nonterminal names can be made up of any collection of printing nonwhite characters except for the following:

Nonterminal names.

% { } [ ] ( ) < > * : | ; ,

There can't be any imbedded spaces or tabs. Imbedded underscores are permitted. Imbedded dots can be used as well, but I don't suggest doing so because dots make the *yyout.doc* file somewhat confusing.[6] I'd suggest using lower-case letters and underscores

---

5. **Yacc** actually puts the token definitions in the output file. **Occs** puts the definitions in *yyout.h* and **#include**s it in the output file.

6. Exactly the opposite situation applies to **yacc**. An imbedded underscore should be avoided because an underscore is used to mark the current input position in *yyout.doc*.

Table E.2. Macros that Modify the Parser

YYABORT	This macro determines the action taken by the parser when an unrecoverable error is encountered or when too many errors are found in the input. The default macro is: **#define** YYABORT **return**(1) but you can redefine it to something else in a code block at the top of the **occs** input file if you prefer. Note that there are no parentheses attached to the macro-name component of the definition.
YYACCEPT	This macro is like YYABORT, except that it determines the accepting action of the parser. The standard action is **return** 0, but you can redefine it to something else if you prefer.
YYCASCADE	(**Occs** only.) This constant controls the number of parser operations that have to follow an error before another error message is printed. It prevents cascading error messages. It's initialized to five. **#define** it to a larger number if too many error messages are printed, a smaller number if too many legitimate error messages suppressed.
YYD(x)	If the –D switch is specified, then all text in a YYD macro is expanded, otherwise it's ignored. For example, the following printf() statement is executed only if –D is present on the **occs** command line. YYD(printf("hi there");)
YYDEBUG	Set automatically by the –D command-line switch to enable the interactive debugging environment, but you can define it explicitly if you like. The contents are unimportant.
YYMAXDEPTH	This macro determines the size of the state and value stacks. It's 128 by default, but you may have to enlarge it if you get a "Parse stack overflow" error message at run time. You can also make it smaller for some grammars.
YYMAXERR	(**Occs** only.) Initially defined to 25, the value of this macro determines when the parser will quit because of too many syntax errors in the input.
YYPRIVATE	Defining this macro as an empty macro makes various global-variable declarations public so that you can see them in a link map. Use the following: **#define** YYPRIVATE /*nothing*/
YYSHIFTACT(tos)	(**Occs** only.) This macro determines the default shift action taken by the parser. That is, it controls what gets put onto the value stack when an input symbol is shifted onto the stack. It is passed a pointer to the top of the value stack after the push (tos). The default definition looks like this: **#define** YYSHIFTACT(tos) ((tos)[0]=yylval) (yylval is used by the lexical analyzer to shift an attribute associated with the current token. It is discussed below.) You can redefine YYSHIFTACT as an empty macro if none of the tokens have attributes.
YYSTYPE	This macro determines the typing of the value stack. It's discussed at length in the text.
YYVERBOSE	If this macro exists, the parser uses more verbose diagnostic messages when YYDEBUG is also defined.

Listing E.2. *expr.y*— **Occs** Rules Section for the Expression Compiler

```
 1    %term LP RP      /* ( and )                  */
 2    %term ID         /* an identifier            */
 3    %term NUM        /* a number                 */
 4    %term PLUS       /* +                        */
 5    %term STAR       /* *                        */
 6    %%
 7    /* A small expression grammar that recognizes numbers, names, addition (+),
 8     * multiplication (*), and parentheses. Expressions associate left to right
 9     * unless parentheses force it to go otherwise. * is higher precedence than +.
10     * Note that an underscore is appended to identifiers so that they won't be
11     * confused with rvalues.
12     */
13
14    s        : e ;
15
16    e        : e PLUS e    { yycode("%s += %s\n", $1, $3); free_name( $3 );  }
17             | e STAR e    { yycode("%s *= %s\n", $1, $3); free_name( $3 );  }
18             | LP e RP     { $$ = $2;                                        }
19             | NUM         { yycode("%s  = %s\n",  $$ = new_name(), yytext ); }
20             | ID          { yycode("%s = _%s\n",  $$ = new_name(), yytext ); }
21             ;
22    %%
```

for nonterminal names and upper-case letters for tokens, as in Listing E.2. This way you can tell what something is by looking at its name. It's a hard error to use a nonterminal that is not found somewhere to the left of a colon.

Text surrounded by curly braces is code that is executed as a parse progress. In a top-down **LLama** parser, the code is executed when it appears at the top of the parse stack. In the bottom-up **occs** parser, the code is executed when a reduction by the associated production is performed.

Augmentations: putting code in a production.

ε productions are represented with an empty right-hand side (and an optional action). It's best to comment the fact that the production has been left empty on purpose. All the following are legitimate ε productions:

ε productions.

```
a :   /* empty */
    ;

b :   /* epsilon */ { an_action(); }
    ;

c :   normal_rhs    { an_action();      }
    | /* epsilon */ { another_action(); }
    ;
```

I'd suggest using the formatting style shown in Listing E.2. The colons, bars, and semicolons should all line up. The nonterminal name should start at the left column and the body of a production should be indented. The curly braces for the actions all line up in a nice column. If a name is too long, use the following:

Formatting.

```
very_long_left_hand_side_name
      : right_hand_side     { action(1); }
      | another             { action(2); }
      ;
```

Any valid C statement that's permitted inside a C subroutine is allowed in an action, with the following caveats:

return and **break** statements in actions.

(1) A **break** statement at the outermost level terminates processing of the current action but not the parser itself.

(2) All **return** statements must have an associated value. A simple **return** is not permitted.

(3) A **return** statement causes the parser to return only if it takes a nonzero argument. That is, **return** 0 causes processing of the current action to stop, but the parsing continues; **return** 1 forces the parser to return to the calling routine, because the argument is nonzero. The argument to **return** is returned from yyparse().

(4) The YYACCEPT and YYABORT macros determine what happens when the parser terminates successfully (accepts the input sentence) or fails (rejects the input sentence). The default actions return 0 and 1 respectively, so you should not return either of these values from within an action.

Local variables in actions.

You can't declare subroutines in an action because the actions themselves are inside a subroutine. You can, however, declare local variables after any open brace, and you can use an action that's several lines long. The following is okay:

```
left_hand_side : right_hand_side
                {
                    int i, monster;
                    for( i = 10; --i >= 0 ;)
                        bug( i, monster );
                }
            ;
```

Of course, you can't declare a local variable in one action and access that variable from another. True global variables that are declared in a %{...%} block in the definitions sections can be accessed everywhere.

The start production.

The first production in the rules section is taken as the start production and is treated specially: Its left-hand side is the goal symbol and it can have only one right-hand side.[7]

E.5 The Code Section

The third part of the input file, the *code section,* comprises all text after the second %% directive. This entire section is written to the output file verbatim. It is used the same way as the L^EX code section—it should contain subroutines that are called from the actions. Note that the **occs** code section differs from both the L^EX and **LLama** sections in that dollar attributes (discussed below) can be used in the code found there.[8]

E.6 Output Files

LLama and **occs** create several output files—their interaction with L^EX is discussed at the beginning of Appendix D. The two programs use different names for these files, however, and these are summarized in Table E.3.

---

7. Some versions of **yacc** support a **%start** directive that lets you define an arbitrary production as the start production. This mechanism isn't supported by **occs**.

8. **Yacc** doesn't permit this: dollar attributes may be used only in the rules sections.

Table E.3. Files Generated by **Occs** and **LLama**

Occs Name	**LLama** Name	Command-line Switches	Contains
yyout.c	llout.c	*none*, −p	Normally contains parser and action code taken from original grammar. If −p is specified to **occs**, this file contains the parser only. (**LLama** doesn't support a −p switch.)
yyact.c		−a	If −a is specified to **occs**, this file contains code for the action components of the productions and all of the code portion of input file (but not the parser). **LLama** doesn't support −a.
yyout.h	llout.h	*none*	Contains **#define**s for the tokens.
yyout.sym	llout.sym	−s, −S, −D	The symbol table. The −S version contains more information than the −s version. Specifying −D implies −s—you can get more-verbose tables with −DS.
yyout.doc		−v, −V	Used only by **occs**, contains the LALR(1) state-machine description along with any warning messages that are sent to the screen.

E.7 Command-Line Switches

The basic command-line usage for both programs is the same:

```
occs  [-switches] file
llama [-switches] file
```

where the *file* is an input specification file, as just discussed. The programs take the following command-line switches:[9]

−a   (**occs** only.) Rather than creating a combined parser-and-action file, the action subroutine only is output to the file *yyact.c*. The parser component of the output file can be created using the *-p* switch, described below.

Generate Action Subroutine.

−c*[N]*   (**LLama** only.) This switch controls the parse-table compression method; it works just like the L^{E}X switche with the same name. It changes the compression algorithm to one in which each character/next-state pair is stored as a two-byte object. This method typically (though not always) gives you smaller tables and a slower parser than the default method. The −c switch takes an optional numeric argument (−c5, for example) that specifies the threshold above which the pair compression kicks in for a given row of the table. If the row has more than the indicated number of nonerror transitions, it is not compressed. The default threshold, if no number is specified, is four.

*Pair compress **LLama** parse tables.*

−D   Enables the interactive debugging environment in the generated parser. All that this switch really does is insert a **#define** YYDEBUG into the output file. You can do the same thing yourself by putting an explicit **#define** in the input specification. Specifying −D also causes −s to be set.

Activating the interactive debugging environment.

−f   (**LLama** only.) This switch causes the output tables to be uncompressed, thereby speeding up the parser a little at the cost of program size.

Uncompressed tables.

---

9. Of these, only −v is supported by **yacc**, though **yacc** is considerably less verbose than **occs**. **occs**' −D switch is nothing like **yacc**'s −d switch.

Making private variables public.	−g	Several global variables and subroutines are used in the output parser. These are declared `static` by default, so their scope is limited to *yyout.c* (or *llout.c*). The −*g* switch causes the compiler compiler to make these variables global to the entire program. You can achieve the same effect by putting the following in the first section of the input specification:

```
%{ #define YYPRIVATE %}
```

Suppress `#line` directives.	−l	(l is an ell.) **Occs** and **LLama** usually generate `#line` directives that cause the C compiler's error messages to reflect line numbers in the original input file rather than the output file. (A preprocessor directive of the form `#line` *N* `"file"` tells the compiler to pretend that it's on line *N* of the indicated `file`.) These directives can cause problems with source-level debuggers, however, and the −*l* switch gives you a way to turn them off. Generally you should not use −*l* until you've eliminated all the syntax errors from the input file. Resist the temptation to modify the output file in order to fix a syntax error. It's too easy to forget to modify the input too, and the output file is destroyed the next time you use the compiler compiler.

Alternative parser templates. The LIB environment variable.	−m	**Occs** and **LLama** both generate only part of the parser. They create the parse tables and a few macros and typedefs needed to compile those tables. The remainder of the parser is read from a template file, called *occs.par* (in the case of **occs**) and *llama.par* (in the case of **LLama**). The programs look for these files, first in the current directory, and then along all directories specified in the LIB environment variable. LIB should contain a semicolon-delimited list of directories. The −*m* command-line switch is used to specify an alternate template file. For example:

```
occs -m/usr/allen/template/template.par
```

tells **occs** to read a file called template.par from the /usr/allen/template directory rather than using the default template. The template files are discussed in depth in Chapters Four and Five. Note that there's no space between the *m* and the first character of the path name.

Create parser only.	−p	(**occs** only.) Rather than creating a combined parser-and-action file, the parser component of the file is output to the file *yyout.c*. No actions are put into *yyout.c*—the action component of the output file can be created using the -*a* switch, described earlier.
Symbol Tables.	−S −s	These switches causes the symbol-table file (*yyout.sym* for **occs** and *llout.sym* for **LLama**) to be generated. A capital S causes the symbol-table file to contain more information—the FIRST( ) sets for each nonterminal are printed in the **occs** table, and both FIRST and FOLLOW sets are printed in **LLama**'s.
Use stdout.	−t	Causes **occs** to output the parser to standard output rather than to the *yyout.c* file.
Send large tables to *yyoutab.c*.	−T	The table-compression method used by **occs** can create several hundred small arrays, and some compilers can't handle that many declarations in a single file. The -*T* switch splits the parser file up into two portions, one containing the parser and most of the tables, the other containing the two biggest tables—the ones most likely to give the compiler problems. These parser is put into *yyout.c* as usual. The two parse tables are put into *yyoutab.c*. The two files can then be compiled independently and linked together. You can use this switch in conjunction to the -*a* and -*p* switches to split the parser into three parts. Use:

```
occs -pT input.y    Create yyout.c and yyparse.c
occs -a  input.y    Create actions file
```

−V
−v

The −v switch puts **occs** and **LLama** into verbose mode. **Occs** generates a file called *yyout.doc* which contains a human-readable description of the LALR(1) state machine. There is no equivalent file from **LLama**. Both programs send progress reports to the screen as they work and they print various statistics describing table sizes, and so forth, when done. −V works like −v except that more information about the internal workings of **occs** and **LLama** than you're interested in seeing is printed on the screen. It's used primarily for debugging **occs** itself or for seeing how the LALR(1) state machine is put together. −V. also puts the LALR(1) lookaheads for every kernel item (rather than just for the items that cause reductions) into *yyout.doc*.

Verbose-mode. LALR(1) state-machine description.

−w

Suppress all warning messages. These warnings announce the presence of shift/reduce and reduce/reduce conflicts found when the state machine is constructed. Once you've ascertained that these warnings are harmless, you can use −w to clean up the screen. Warnings are printed to yyout.doc, even if −w is specified, and the number of warnings is always printed at the end of an **occs** run, even if the warnings themselves aren't printed.

Suppress warning messages.

−W

Normally, the number of hard errors is returned to the operating system as the exit status. If −W is specified, the exit status is the sum of the number of hard errors and warning messages. This switch is handy if you want the UNIX **make** utility (or equivalent) to terminate on warnings as well as errors.

E.8 The Visible Parser[10]

An **occs**- and **LLama**-generated parser can function in one of two ways. In *production mode*, it just parses the input and generates code, as you would expect. In *debug mode*, however, a multiple-window interactive debugging environment (or IDE) is made available to you. Debug mode is enabled in one of two ways, either specify −D on the **occs** command-line, or put the following in the rules section of your input file:

Production and debug mode.

IDE (interactive debugging environment).

```
%{ #define YYDEBUG %}
```

The resulting file should be compiled and linked to three libraries: *l.lib*, *curses.lib*, and *termlib.lib*.[11] Only the first of these libraries is necessary if you're not compiling for debugging. The **occs** source file for a small expression compiler is on the software-distribution disk mentioned in the preface, along with the curses and termlib libraries. You may need to recompile the libraries to get them to work properly if you're not using Microsoft C (or QuickC). An executable version of the compiler (*expr.exe*) is also on the disk, however, so you don't have to recompile right now. Make the expression compiler with Microsoft C as follows:

Compiling for Debugging.

---

10. This section describes how to use the interactive debugging environment. If at all possible, you should have an **occs** output file, compiled for interactive debugging, running in front of you as you read. An executable version of the expression compiler described below is provided on the software distribution disk in the file *expr.exe*.

11. Use `cc files... -ll -lcurses -ltermlib` in UNIX.

```
occs -vD expr.y
lex  -v  expr.lex
cl -o expr.exe yyout.c lexyy.c -link l.lib curses.lib termlib.lib
```

Then run it with:

```
expr test
```

where *test* is an input file containing a simple expression composed of numbers, variable names, plus signs, asterisks, and parentheses. The expression must be the first and only line in the file.

Direct-video output.

The VIDEO environment variable.

In the MS-DOS environment, the debugger uses the ROM-BIOS for its output. It can also use direct-video writes, however, and on some clones this approach is more reliable than using the BIOS. To activate the direct-video routines, set the VIDEO environment to DIRECT with the following command to COMMAND.COM:

```
set VIDEO=DIRECT
```

The direct-video routines assume that either an MGA, or a CGA running in high resolution, 25×80 text mode is present (it automatically selects between these two display adapters). Most other video adapters can simulate one or the other of these modes. The program will not work with a CGA running in one of the other text modes (25×20 or 25×40), however. Issue a MODE BW80 request at the DOS prompt to get the CGA into high-resolution, text mode.

Window names.

The program comes up with several empty windows, as shown in Figure E.1. The *stack* window is used to show the state and value-stack contents; the *comments* window holds a running description of the parse process; generated code is displayed in the *output* window, the *lookahead* window displays the most-recently read token and lexeme— the current lookahead symbol, and the *prompts* window is used to communicate with the debugger. The size of the stack window can be changed by specifying an optional *-sN* command-line switch when you invoke the program, as in *expr -s15 test*. In this case the stack window occupies 15 lines. The other windows scale themselves to take up what's left of the screen.

Changing stack-window size from the command line.

Several commands are supported by the debugger; you can see a list by typing a question mark, which prints the list shown in Figure E.2. The easiest command to use is the *g* command (for go) which just starts up the parsing. Figure E.3 shows the various windows several stages into parsing the expression a*(b+c). The parsing can be stopped at any time by pressing any key.

In Figure E.3, the parser has just read the *c* (but it has not yet been shifted onto the parse stack). The ID c in the *lookahead* window is the most recently read token and lexeme. The *output* window shows code that has been output so far, and the current parse stack is shown in the *stack* window.

The output window shows output sent to all three segment streams. The leftmost column identifies the segment—it holds a C for code, D for data, or B for bss. Because the window is so narrow, sequences of white-space characters (tabs, spaces, and so forth) are all replaced with a single space character in this window.

The stack window always displays the topmost stack elements. If the stack grows larger than the window, the stack window scrolls so that the top few stack elements are displayed. The three columns in the *stack* window are (from left to right): the parse stack, the parse stack represented in symbolic form rather than numbers, and the value stack. Several commands other than *g* are recognized at the "Enter command" prompt in the *prompts* window:

Figure E.1. The Initial Debug Screen

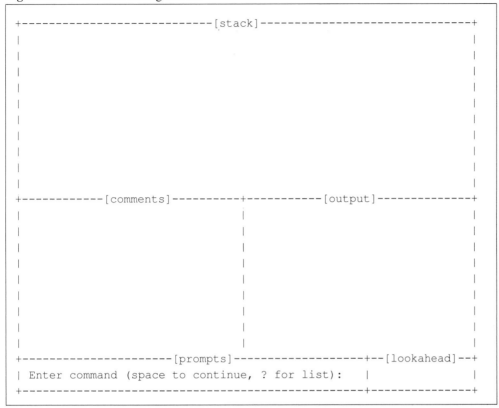

Figure E.2. Debug-Mode Commands

```
a   (A)bort parser by reading EOI     l    (L)og output to file
b   modify or examine (B)reakpoint    n/N  (N)oninteractive mode
d   set (D)elay time for go mode      q    (Q)uit (exit to dos)
f   read (F)ile                       r    (R)efresh stack window
g   (G)o (any key stops parse)        w    (W)rite screen to file or device
i   change (I)nput file               x    Show current and prev. le(X)eme

                Space or Enter to single step
```

space, You can single step through the parse by repetitively pressing the space bar or   Single step.
enter   the Enter key. In practice, this is usually more useful than *g* which can go by
            faster than you can see.

Ctrl-A, These two commands are deliberately not printed on the help screen. They are   Debugger hooks.
Ctrl-B debugger hooks. Ctrl-A causes the debugger to call the subroutine
            yyhook_a(), and Ctrl-B calls yyhook_b(). The default versions of these
            routines do nothing. You can use these commands for two things. First, its
            often useful to run the IDE under a compiler debugger like **sdb** or CodeView,
            and you can use a hook as an entry point to the debugger: Set a breakpoint at
            yyhook_a() and then start the parser running; issuing a Ctrl-A then returns
            you to the debugger.

Figure E.3. The Windows Several Steps into a Parse

```
+-------------------------------[stack]--------------------------------+
|                                                                      |
|                                                                      |
|                                                                      |
|                                                                      |
|                                                                      |
|                                                                      |
|   6|                  PLUS | _t1                                      |
|   5|                    e | _t1                                       |
|   3|                   LP | _t0                                       |
|   7|                 STAR | _t0                                       |
|   4|                    e | _t0                                       |
|   0|                    S | <empty>                                   |
+------------[comments]------------+-------------[output]--------------+
|Shift <LP> (goto 3)               |B| public word _t0,_t1,_t2,_t3;    |
|Advance past ID <b>               |B| public word _t4,_t5,_t6,_t7;    |
|Shift <ID> (goto 1)               |C| _t0 = a                         |
|Advance past PLUS <+>             |C| _t1 = b                         |
|Reduce by (5) e->ID               |                                   |
|    (goto 5)                      |                                   |
|Shift <PLUS> (goto 6)             |                                   |
|Advance past <PLUS>               |                                   |
|Read ID <c>                       |                                   |
+--------------------------[prompts]-------------------+---[lookahead]---+
| Enter command (space to continue, ? for list):      |ID c             |
+-----------------------------------------------------+-----------------+
```

The two hook subroutines are in modules by themselves, so you can use them to add capabilities to the IDE by linking your own versions rather than the library versions. For example, its occasionally useful to print the symbol table when you are debugging the parts of the compiler that are processing declarations. This capability can't be built into the IDE because there's no way of knowing what the data structures will look like. The problem is solved by supplying a subroutine called yyhook_a() which prints the symbol table. Your version is linked rather than the default library version, so a Ctrl-A command now prints the symbol table.

a This command aborts the parse process by forcing the lexical analyzer to return the end-of-input marker on all subsequent calls. Compare it with the **q** command, which exits immediately to the operating system without returning to the parser itself.

Breakpoints.

b The *b* command is used to set, clear, or examine breakpoints. Four types of breakpoints are supported:

input (i) breaks when a specified symbol is input.

input line (l) breaks when the input sweeps past the specified input line. This breakpoint is activated only when the lexical analyzer returns a token, and it's possible to specify an input line that doesn't have any tokens on it. (In this case, the break occurs when the first token on a line following the indicated one is read.)

Note that this breakpoint, unlike any of the others, is automatically cleared as soon as it is triggered.

stack (s) breaks as soon as a specified symbol appears at the top of the parse stack. In a **LLama** parser, parsing stops before any action code is executed.

production (p) breaks just before the parser applies a specific production. In **occs**, it breaks just before the reduction. In **LLama**, it breaks just before replacing a nonterminal with its right-hand side.

When you enter *b,* you are prompted for one of these types (enter an *i, l, s,* or *p* for "input,", "line", "stack," or "production"). You are then prompted for a symbol. The different kinds of breakpoints can take different inputs in response to this prompt:

input (1) A decimal number is assumed to be a token value, as defined in *yyout.h* or *yyout.sym* (*llout.h* or *llout.sym* if **LLama**). Parsing stops when that token is read. (2) A string that matches a token name (as it appears in a `%term` or `%token` directive) behaves like a number—parsing stops when that token is read. (3) Any other string causes a break when the current lexeme matches the indicated string. For example, if you have a `%term` NAME in the input file and the compiler compiler puts a **#define** NAME 1 in *yyout.h* or *llout.h*, then entering either the string 1 or the string NAME causes a break the next time a **NAME** token is read. You can also enter the string Illiavitch, whereupon a break occurs the next time *Illiavitch* shows up as a lexeme, regardless of the token value.

input line Enter the input line number.

stack (1) If you enter a number, parsing stops the next time that number appears at the top of the real parse stack (the leftmost column in the *stack* window). (2) Any other string is treated as a symbolic name, and parsing stops the next time that name appears at the top of the symbol stack (the middle column in the window).

production You must enter a number for this kind of breakpoint. Parsing stops just before the particular production is applied (when it's replaced in a **LLama** parser and when a reduction by that production occurs in an **occs** parser). Production numbers can be found in the *yyout.sym* or *llout.sym* file, generated with a *−s* or *−S* command-line switch.

There's no error checking to see if the string entered for a stack breakpoint actually matches a real symbol. The breakpoint-processing routines just check the input string against the symbol displayed in the symbolic portion of the stack window. If the two strings match, the parsing stops. The same technique is used for input breakpoints. If the symbol isn't a digit, then the breakpoint string is compared, first against the input lexeme, and then by looking up the name of the current lexeme. If either string matches, then parsing stops.

Three other breakpoint commands are provided: *c* clears all existing breakpoints, *d* displays all existing breakpoints, and *?* prints the help screen shown in Figure E.4.

d The *d* command is used to slow down the parse. The parsing process, when started with a *g* command, nips along at a pretty good clip, often too fast for you to see what's going on. The *d* command is used to insert a delay between

Adding a delay in go mode.

Figure E.4. Breakpoint Help Screen

```
Select a breakpoint type (i,p,or s) or command (c or l)

Type: Description:              Enter breakpoint as follows:
  i     input...................number for token value
                                or string for lexeme or token name
  l     input line..............input line number
  p     reduce by production......number for production number
  s     top-of-stack symbol.......number for state-stack item
                                or string for symbol-stack item
  s = clear all breakpoints
  l = list  all breakpoints
```

every parse step. Setting the delay to 0 puts it back to its original blinding speed. Delay times are entered in seconds, and you can use decimal fractions (1, 2.5, .5, and so forth) if you like.

Examine file.   **f**   The *f* command lets you examine a file without leaving the debugger. You are prompted for a file name, and the file is then displayed in the stack window, one screenfull at a time.

Go!   **g**   The *g* command starts the parse going.

Specify input file.   **i**   The *i* command lets you change the input file from the one specified on the command line. It prompts you for a file name.

Log all output to file.   **l**   This command causes the entire parse to be logged to a specified file, so that you can look at it later. If you're running under MS-DOS, you can log to the printer by specifying *prn:* instead of a file name. Some sample output is shown in Figures E.5 and E.6. Output to the CODE window is all preceded by CODE–>. Most other text was COMMENT-window output. The parse stack is drawn after every modification in one of two ways (you'll be prompted for a method when you open the log file). Listing E.3 shows vertical stacks and Listing E.4 shows horizontal stacks. The latter is useful if you have relatively

Specifying horizontal stacks.   small stacks or relatively wide paper—it generates more-compact log files in these situations. The horizontal stacks are printed so that items at equivalent positions on the different stacks (parse/state, symbol, and value) are printed one atop the other, so the column width is controlled by the stack that requires the widest string to print its contents—usually the value stack. If you specify horizontal stacks at the prompt, you will be asked which of the three stacks to print. You can use this mechanism to leave out one or more of the three stacks.

Noninteractive mode: **n,**   These commands put the parser into noninteractive mode. The **n** command
Create log without win-   **N**   generates a log file quickly, without having to watch the whole parse happen
dow updates   before your eyes. All screen updating is suppressed and the parse goes on at much higher speed than normal. A log file must be active when you use this command. If one isn't, you'll be prompted for a file name. You can't get back into normal mode once this process is started. The **N** command runs in noninteractive mode without logging anything. It's handy if you just want to run the
Run parser without log-   parser to get an output file and aren't interested in looking at the parse process.
ging or window updates.

Listing E.3. Logged Output—Vertical Stacks

```
 1   CODE->public word _t0, _t1, _t2, _t3;
 2   CODE->public word _t4, _t5, _t6, _t7;
 3
 4   Shift start state
 5       +---+------------------+
 6     0|   0|                 S | -
 7       +---+------------------+
 8   Advance past NUM <1>
 9   Shift <NUM> (goto 2)
10       +---+------------------+
11     0|   2|               NUM | -
12     1|   0|                 S | -
13       +---+------------------+
14   Advance past PLUS <+>
15   CODE-> _t0 = 1
16
17   Reduce by (4) e->NUM
18       +---+------------------+
19     0|   0|                 S | -
20       +---+------------------+
21       (goto 4)
22       +---+------------------+
23     0|   4|                 e | _t0
24     1|   0|                 S | -
25       +---+------------------+
26   Shift <PLUS> (goto 6)
27       +---+------------------+
28     0|   6|              PLUS | _t0
29     1|   4|                 e | _t0
30     2|   0|                 S | -
31       +---+------------------+
32   Advance past NUM <2>
33   Shift <NUM> (goto 2)
34       +---+------------------+
35     0|   2|               NUM | _t0
36     1|   6|              PLUS | _t0
37     2|   4|                 e | _t0
38     3|   0|                 S | -
39       +---+------------------+
40   Advance past STAR <*>
41   CODE-> _t1 = 2
```

q   returns you to the operating system.   Quit.

r   An *r* forces a STACK-window refresh. The screen-update logic normally   Redraw stack window.
changes only those parts of the STACK window that it thinks should be
modified. For example, when you do a push, the parser writes a new line into
the stack window, but it doesn't redraw the already existing lines that
represent items already on the stack. Occasionally, your value stack can
become corrupted by a bug in your own code, however, and the default update
strategy won't show you this problem because it might not update the
incorrectly modified value stack item. The *r* command forces a redraw so that
you can see what's really on the stack.

w   (for write) dumps the screen to an indicated file or device, in a manner analo-   Save screen to file.
gous to the Shift-PrtSc key on an IBM PC. This way you can save a snapshot

Listing E.4. `Logged Output—Horizontal Stacks`

```
 1   CODE->public word _t0, _t1, _t2, _t3;
 2   CODE->public word _t4, _t5, _t6, _t7;
 3
 4   Shift start state
 5      PARSE   0
 6      SYMBOL  S
 7      ATTRIB  -
 8   Advance past NUM <1>
 9   Shift <NUM> (goto 2)
10      PARSE   0    2
11      SYMBOL  S    NUM
12      ATTRIB  -    -
13   Advance past PLUS <+>
14   CODE-> _t0 = 1
15
16   Reduce by (4) e->NUM
17      PARSE   0
18      SYMBOL  S
19      ATTRIB  -
20      (goto 4)
21      PARSE   0    4
22      SYMBOL  S    e
23      ATTRIB  -    _t0 (e)
24   Shift <PLUS> (goto 6)
25      PARSE   0    4         6
26      SYMBOL  S    e         PLUS
27      ATTRIB  -    _t0 (e) _t0 (PLUS)
28   Advance past NUM <2>
29   Shift <NUM> (goto 2)
30      PARSE   0    4    6       2
31      SYMBOL  S    e    PLUS    NUM
32      ATTRIB  -    _t0  _t0     _t0
33   Advance past STAR <*>
34   CODE->_t1 = 2
```

of the current screen without having to enable logging. Any IBM box-drawing characters used for the window borders are mapped to dashes and vertical bars. I used the *w* command to output the earlier figures. Note that the output screen is truncated to 79 characters because some printers automatically print a linefeed after the 80th character. This means that the right edge of the box will be missing (I put it back in with my editor when I made the figures).

Display lexeme.   **x**   Display both the current and previous lexeme in the comments window. The token associated with the current lexeme is always displayed in the *tokens* window.

E.9 Useful Subroutines and Variables

There are several useful subroutines and variables available in an **occs**- or **LLama**-generated parser. These are summarized in Table E.4 and are discussed in this section.

void yyparse()

This subroutine is the parser generated by both **occs** and **LLama**. Just call it to get the parse started.

char *yypstk(YYSTYPE *val, **char** *sym)

This subroutine is called from the debugging environment and is used to print the value stack. It's passed two pointers. The first is a pointer to a stack item. So, if your value stack is a stack of character pointers, the first argument will be a pointer to a character pointer. The second argument is always a pointer to a string holding the symbol name. That is, it contains the symbol stack item that corresponds to the value stack item. The returned string is truncated to 50 characters, and it should not contain any newline characters. The default routine in *l.lib* assumes that the value stack is the default **int** type. It's shown in Listing E.5. This subroutine is used in slightly different ways by **occs** and **LLama**, so is discussed further, below.

int yy_get_args(**int** argc, **char** **argv)

This routine can be used to modify the size of the *stack* window and to open an input file for debugging. The other windows automatically scale as appropriate, and the stack window is not allowed to get so large that the other windows disappear. Typically, yy_get_args() is called at the top of your main() routine, before yyparse() is called. The subroutine is passed argv and argc and it scans through the former looking for an argument of the form *-sN*, where N is the desired stack-window size. The first argument that doesn't begin with a minus sign is taken to be the input file name. That name is not removed from argv. All other arguments are ignored and are not removed from argv, so you can process them in your own program. The routine prints an error message and terminates the program if it can't open the specified input file. Command-line processing stops immediately after the input file name is processed. So, given the line:

```
program -x -s15 -y foo -s1 bar
```

argv is modified to:

```
program -x -y foo -s1 bar
```

the file *foo* is opened for input, and the stack window will be 15 lines high. A new value of argc that reflects the removed argument is returned.

This routine can also be used directly, rather than as a command-line processor. For example, the following sets up a 17-line stack window and opens *testfile* as the input file:

```
char *vects[] = {"", "-s17", "testfile"};
yy_get_args( 3, vects );
```

void yy_init_occs (YYSTYPE *tos)

These routines are called by yyparse() after it has initialized the various stacks, but before it has read the first input token. That is, the initial start symbol has been pushed onto the state stack, and garbage has been pushed onto the corresponding entry on the value stack, but no tokens have been read. The subroutine is passed a pointer to the (only) item on the value stack. You can use yy_init_occs() to provide a valid attribute for this first value-stack element. A user-supplied version of both functions is also useful when main() isn't in the **occs** input file, because it can be used to initialize **static** global variables in the

Table E.4. Useful Subroutines and Variables

```
int      yyparse          ( void );
int      yylex            ( void );

char     *yypstk          ( void *value_stack_item, char *symbol_stack_item );

void     yycomment        ( char *fmt, ... );
void     yycode           ( char *fmt, ... );
void     yydata           ( char *fmt, ... );
void     yybss            ( char *fmt, ... );

int      yy_get_args      ( int argc, char **argv );

void     yy_init_occs     ( void );
void     yy_init_llama    ( void );
void     yy_init_lex      ( void );

void     yyerror          ( char *fmt, ... );

FILE     *yyout           = stdout;  /* output stream for code */
FILE     *yybssout        = stdout;  /* output stream for bss  */
FILE     *yydataout       = stdout;  /* output stream for data */
```

Listing E.5. *yypstk.c*— Print Default Value Stack

```
1   /* Default routine to print user-supplied portion of the value stack.  */
2
3   char      *yypstk(val,sym)
4   void      *val;
5   char      *sym;
6   {
7       static char buf[32];
8       sprintf( buf, "%d", *(int *)val );
9       return buf;
10  }
```

parser file. It's easy to forget to call an initialization routine if it has to be called from a second file. The default subroutines, in *l.lib*, do nothing. (They are shown in Listings E.6 and E.7.)

Listing E.6. *yyinitox.c*— **Occs** User-Initialization Subroutine

```
1   void yy_init_ox( tos ) void *tos; { }
```

Print parser error messages.

void yyerror(**char** *fmt,...)

This routine is called from *yyparse( )* when it encounters an error, and you should use it yourself for error messages. It works like `printf( )`, but it sends output to `stderr` and it adds the current input line number and token name to the front of the message, like this:

Listing E.7. *yyinitll.c*— Default **LLama** Initialization Function

```
1   void yy_init_llama( tos ) void *tos; { }
```

> ERROR (line 00 near TOK): *your message goes here.*

The *00* is replaced by the current line number and *TOK* is replaced by the symbolic name of the current token (as defined in the **occs** input file). The routine adds a newline at the end of the line for you.

```
void yycomment(char *fmt,...)
void yycode    (char *fmt,...)
void yydata    (char *fmt,...)
void yybss     (char *fmt,...)
```
Output functions.

These four subroutines should be used for all your output. They work like printf(), but write to appropriate windows when the debugging environment is enabled. When the IDE is not active, yycomment writes to standard output and is used for comments to the user, yycode() writes to a stream called yycodeout and should be used for all code, yydata() writes to a stream called yydataout and should be used for all initialized data, yybss() writes to a stream called yybssout and should be used for uninitialized data.

All of these streams are initialized to stdout, but you may change them at any time with an fopen() call. Don't use freopen() for this purpose, or you'll close stdout. If any of these streams are changed to reference a file the debugger sends output both to the file and to the appropriate window. If you forget and use one of the normal output routines like puts() or printf(), the windows will get messed up, but nothing serious will happen. printf() is automatically mapped to yycode if debugging is enabled, so you can use printf() calls in the **occs** input file without difficulty. Using it elsewhere in your program causes problems, however.

```
void yyprompt(char *prompt, char *buf, int get_str)
```
Print a message to the prompt window.

This subroutine is actually part of the debugger itself, but is occasionally useful when implementing a debugger hook, described earlier. It prints the prompt string in the IDE's *prompts* window, and then reads a string from the keyboard into buf. (there's no boundary checking so be careful about the array size). If get_str is true, an entire string is read in a manner similar to gets(), otherwise only one character is read. If an ESC is encountered, the routine returns 0 immediately, otherwise 1 is returned.

E.10 Using Your Own Lexical Analyzer

Occs and **LLama** are designed to work with a L^{E}X-generated lexical analyzer. You can build a lexical analyzer by hand, however, provided that it duplicates L^{E}X's interface to the parser.

You must provide the following subroutines and variables to use the interactive debugging environment without a lex-generated lexical analyzer:

```
char  *yytext;                    current lexeme
int   yylineno;                   current input line number
int   yyleng;                     number of characters in yytext[]
int   yylex(void);                return next token and advance input
char  *ii_ptext(void);            return pointer to previous lexeme
int   ii_plength(void);           return length of previous lexeme
int   ii_mark_prev(void);         copy current lexeme to previous lexeme
int   ii_newfile(char *name);     open new input file
```

The scanner must be called `yylex()`. It must return either a token defined in *yyout.h* or zero at end of file. You'll also need to provide a pointer to the current lexeme called `yytext` and the current input line number in an `int` called `yylineno`. The `ii_ptext()` subroutine must return a pointer to the lexeme that was read immediately before the current one—the current one is in `yytext` so no special routine is needed to get at it. The string returned from `ii_ptext()` does not have to be `'\0'` terminated. Like `yyleng`, `ii_plength()` should evaluate the the number of valid characters in the string returned from `ii_ptext()`. `ii_mark_prev()` should copy the current lexeme into the previous one. `ii_newfile()` is called when the program starts to open the input file. It is passed the file name. The real `ii_newfile()` returns a file handle that is used by `yylex()` in turn. Your version of `ii_newfile()` need only do whatever is necessary to open a new input file. It should return a number other than −1 on success, −1 on error. Note that input must come from a file. The debugging routines will get very confused if you try to use `stdin`.

E.11 Occs

This section describes **occs**-specific parts of the compiler compiler. A discussion of the **LLama**-specific functions starts in Section E.12

E.11.1 Using Ambiguous Grammars

The **occs** input file supports several `%` directives in addition to the ones discussed earlier. (All **occs** directives are summarized in Table E.5. They will be described in this and subsequent sections.)

A definitions section for a small expression compiler is shown in Listing. E.8. The analyzer will recognize expressions made up of numbers, identifiers, parentheses, and addition and multiplication operators (+ and *). Addition is lower precedence than multiplication and both operators associate left to right. The compiler outputs code that evaluates the expression. The entire file, from which the definitions section was extracted, appears at the end of the **occs** part of this appendix.

Specifying precedence and associativity, `%term`, `%left`, `%right`, `%nonassoc`.

Terminal symbols are defined on lines one to six. Here, the `%term` is used for those terminal symbols that aren't used in expressions. `%left` is used to define left-associative operators, and `%right` is used for right-associative operators. (A `%nonassoc` directive is also supplied for declaring nonassociative operators.) The higher a `%left`, `%right`, or `%nonassoc` is in the input file, the lower its precedence. So, `PLUS` is lower precedence than `STAR`, and both are lower precedence than parentheses. A `%term` or `%token` is not needed if a symbol is used in a `%left`, `%right`, or `%nonassoc`. The precedence and associativity information is used by **occs** to patch the parse tables created by an ambiguous input grammar so that the input grammar will be parsed correctly.

Table E.5. Occs % Directives and Comments

Directive	Description
%%	Delimits the three sections of the input file.
%{	Starts a code block. All lines that follow, up to a %} are written to the output file unchanged.
%}	Ends a code block.
%token	Defines a token.
%term	A synonym for %token.
/* */	C-like comments are recognized—and ignored—by **occs**, even if they're outside of a %{ %} delimited code block.
%left	Specifies a left-associative operator.
%right	Specifies a right-associative operator.
%nonassoc	Specifies a nonassociative operator.
%prec	Use in rules section only. Modifies the precedence of an entire production to resolve a shift/reduce conflict caused by an ambiguous grammar.
%union	Used for typing the value stack.
%type	Attaches %union fields to nonterminals.

Listing E.8. *expr.y*— **occs** Definitions Section for a Small Expression Compiler

```
 1   %term   ID          /*  a string of lower-case characters    */
 2   %term   NUM         /*  a number                             */
 3
 4   %left   PLUS        /*  +                                    */
 5   %left   STAR        /*  *                                    */
 6   %left   LP RP       /*  (  )                                 */
 7
 8   %{
 9   #include <stdio.h>
10   #include <ctype.h>
11   #include <stdlib.h>
12
13   extern char         *yytext;       /* In yylex(), holds lexeme */
14   extern char         *new_name();   /* declared at bottom of this file */
15
16   typedef char        *stype;        /* Value stack */
17   #define YYSTYPE      stype
18
19   #define YYMAXDEPTH   64
20   #define YYMAXERR     10
21   #define YYVERBOSE
22   %}
```

Most of the grammars in this book use recursion and the ordering of productions to get proper associativity and precedence. Operators handled by productions that occur earlier in the grammar are of lower precedence; left recursion gives left associativity; right recursion gives right associativity. This approach has its drawbacks, the main one being a proliferation of productions and a correspondingly larger (and slower) state machine. Also, in a grammar like the following one, productions like 2 and 4 have no purpose other than establishing precedence—these productions generate single-reduction states, described in Chapter Five.

```
0.  s   →   e
1.  e   →   e + t
2.      |   t
3.  t   →   t * f
4.      |   f
5.  f   →   ( e )
6.      |   NUM
7.      |   ID
```

Occs lets you redefine the foregoing grammar as follows:

```
%term NUM   ID

%left PLUS      /*  +  */
%left STAR      /*  *  */
%left LP RP     /*  ( )  */
%%

s     :         e ;

e     :         e PLUS e
      |         e STAR e
      |         LP e RP
      |         NUM
      |         ID
      ;
%%
```

The ambiguous grammar is both easier to read and smaller. It also generates smaller parse tables and a somewhat faster parser. Though the grammar is not LALR(1), parse tables can be built for it by using the disambiguation rules discussed in Chapter Five and below. If there are no ambiguities in a grammar, `%left` and `%right` need not be used—you can use `%term` or `%token` to declare all the terminals.

E.11.2 Attributes and the Occs Value Stack

Accessing bottom-up attributes, `$$`, `$1`, etc.

The **occs** parser automatically maintains a value stack for you as it parses. Moreover, it keeps track of the various offsets from the top of stack and provides a simple mechanism for accessing attributes. The mechanism is best illustrated with an example. In S→A B C, the attributes can be accessed as follows:

```
S  :   A    B    C  ;
$$     $1   $2   $3
```

That is, `$$` is the value that is inherited by the left-hand side after the reduce is performed. Attributes on the right-hand side are numbered from left to right, starting with the leftmost symbol on the right-hand side. The attributes can be used anywhere in a curly-brace-delimited code block. The parser provides a default action of `$$=$1` which

Default action: $$=$1.

can be overridden by an explicit assignment in an action. (Put a `$$` to the left of an equals sign [just like a variable name] anywhere in the code part of a rule.)

Attributes and ε productions.

The one exception to the `$$=$1` rule is an ε production (one with an empty right-hand side)—there's no `$1` in an ε production. A reduce by an ε production pops nothing (because there's nothing on the right-hand side) and pushes the left-hand side. Rather than push garbage in this situation, **occs** duplicates the previous top-of-stack item in the push. **Yacc** pushes garbage.

Typing the value stack.

By default, the value stack is of type **int**. Fortunately, it's easy to change this type. Just redefine `YYSTYPE` in the definitions section of the input file. For example, the expression compiler makes the value stack a stack of character pointers instead of **int**s with the following definitions:

```
%{
    typedef char    *stype;
    #define YYSTYPE stype
%}
```

The `typedef` isn't needed if the stack is redefined to a simple type (**int**, **long**, **float**, **double**, and so forth). Given this definition, you could use `$1` to modify the pointer itself and `*$1` to modify the object pointed to. (In this case, `*$1` modifies the first character of the string.) A stack of structures could be defined the same way:

```
%{
    typedef struct
    {
        int     harpo;
        long    groucho;
        double  chico;
        char    zeppo[10];
    }
    stype;

    #define YYSTYPE stype
%}
```

You can use `$1.harpo`, `$2.zeppo[3]`, and so forth, to access a field. You can also use the following syntax: `$<harpo>$`, `$<chico>1`, and so forth—`$<chico>1` is identical to `$1.chico`. following statements:

Input	Expanded to
$$	`Yy_val`
$N in the rules section	`yysp[ `*constant*` ]`
$N in the code section	`yysp[ (Yy_rhslen - `*constant*`) ]`

`yysp` is the value-stack pointer. `Yy_rhslen` is the number of symbols on the right-hand side of the production being reduced. The *constant* is derived from N, by adjusting for the size of the right-hand side of the current production. For example, in a production like

```
S : A B C ;
```

`$1`, `$2`, and `$3` evaluate to the following:

```
Yy_vsp[ -2 ]  /* $1 */
Yy_vsp[ -1 ]  /* $2 */
Yy_vsp[ -0 ]  /* $3 */
```

Be careful of saying something like `$$=$2` if you've defined `YYSTYPE` as a structure. The whole structure is copied in this situation. (Of course, if you want the whole structure to be copied…) Note that the default action (`$$=$1`) is always performed before any of the actions are executed, and it affects the entire structure. Any specific action modifies the default action. This means that you can let some fields of a structure be inherited in the normal way and modify others explicitly. For example, using our earlier structure, the following:

Copying Structures.

```
{ $$.harpo = 5; }
```

modifies the `harpo` field, but not the `groucho`, `chico`, or `zeppo` fields, which are inherited from `$1` in the normal way.

The entire 24-byte structure is copied at every shift or reduce. Consequently, it's worth your effort to minimize the size of the value-stack elements. Note that the parser is built assuming that your compiler supports structure assignment. If this isn't the case, you'll have to modify the parser to use `memcpy()` to do assignments.

Occs' attribute support is extended from that of **yacc** in that dollar attributes can be used in both the rules and code sections of the input specification (**yacc** permits them only in the rules section). **Occs** treats `$0` as a synonym for `$$`. Finally, **occs** permits negative attributes. Consider the following:

```
s   : X A B C
b   : E                         { $$ = $-1 + $-2 };
```

Negative attributes ($-1). The `$-1` evaluates to the attributes for the symbol immediately below the E on the value stack. To see what the negative attributes are doing, consider the condition of the stack just before the reduce by $b{\to}$E:

`$1` references the attributes associated with E in the normal way; `$-1` references A's attributes, and `$-2` references X's attributes. **Occs** normally prints an error message if you try to reference an attribute that's outside the production (if you tried to use `$3` on a right-hand side that had only two elements, for example). It's possible to reference off the end of the stack if the numbers get too negative, however—no error message is printed in this case. For example, a `$-3` in the earlier example just silently evaluates to garbage (the start symbol doesn't have any attributes).

Now, look closely at the attribute-passing mechanism for the expression compiler, reproduced below:

```
e   : e PLUS e { gen("%s += %s;", $1, $3); free_name( $3 ); }
    | e STAR e { gen("%s *= %s;", $1, $3); free_name( $3 ); }
    | LP e RP  { $$ = $2;                                     }
    | NUM      { gen("%s = %s;", $$ = new_name(), yytext ); }
    | ID       { gen("%s = %s;", $$ = new_name(), yytext ); }
    ;
```

The $e{\to}$**NUM** and $e{\to}$**ID** actions on lines four and five are identical. They output a move instruction and then put the target of the move (the name of the rvalue) onto the value stack as an attribute. The `$$=$2` in the $e{\to}$**LP** e **RP** action on the third line just moves the attribute from the e that's buried in the parentheses to the one on the left-hand side of the production. The top two productions are doing the real work. To see how they function, consider the sample parse of A+2 in Figure E.5. The transition of interest is from stack picture six to seven. `_t0` and `_t1` were put onto the stack when the rvalues were created (and they're still there). So, we can find the temporaries used for the rvalues by looking at `$1` and `$2`. The inherited attribute is the name of the temporary that holds the result of the addition.

%union—Automatic field-name generation. Because the value stack is more often then not typed as a `union`, a mechanism is provided to keep track of the various fields and the way that they attach to individual symbols. This mechanism assumes a common practice, that specific fields within a union are used only by specific symbols. For example, in a production like this:

```
e : e divop e
```

where `divop` could be either a / or % (as in C), you would need to store one of two attributes on the value stack. The attribute attached to the `e` would be a pointer to a string holding the name of a temporary variable; the attribute attached to the `divop` would be '/' for divide and '%' for a modulus operation. To do the foregoing, the value stack must be typed to be a union of two fields, one a character pointer and the other an `int`. You could do this using an explicit redefinition of `YYSTYPE`, as discussed earlier:

Figure E.5. A Parse of A*2

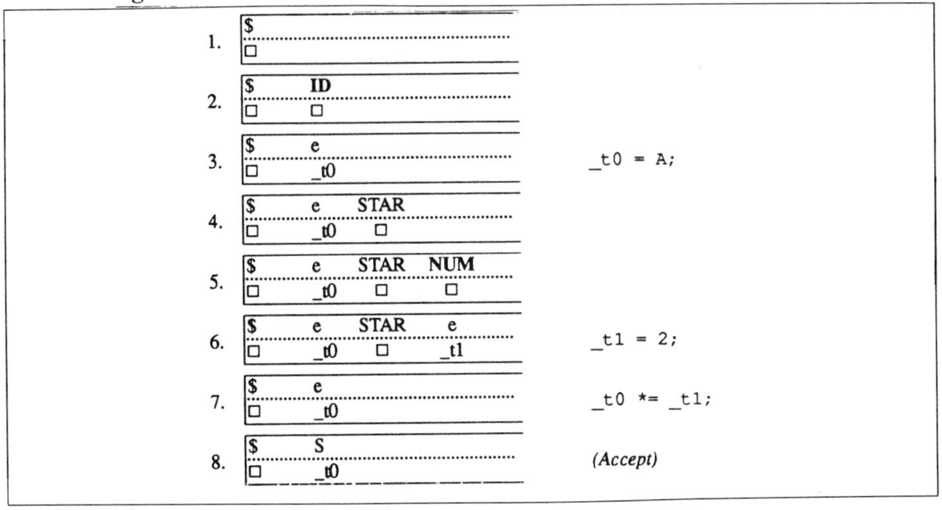

```
typedef union
{
    char   *var_name ;
    int    op_type ;
}
yystype;

#define YYSTYPE yystype
```

but the %union directive is a better choice. Do it as follows:

```
%union {
    char   *var_name ;
    int    op_type ;
}
```

A %union activates an automatic field-name generation feature that is not available if you just redefine YYSTYPE. Given the earlier production (e : e DIVOP e), we'd like to be able to say $$, $1, and so forth, without having to remember the names of the fields. That is, you want to say

```
$1 = new_name();
```

rather than

```
$1.var_name = new_name();
```

Do this, first by using the %union, and then attaching the field names to the individual terminal and nonterminal symbols with a *<name>* operator in token-definition directive (%term, %left, etc.) or a %type directive. The *name* can be any field name in the %union. For example:

<name> and %type

```
%term <op_type> DIVOP
%type <var_name> e
```

attaches the op_type field to all *DIVOP*s and the var_name field to all *e*'s. That is, if a <name> is found in a %term, %token, %left, %right, or %nonassoc directive, the indicated field name is automatically attached to the specified token. The angle brackets are part of the directive. They must be present, and there may not be any white space between them and the actual field name. The %type directive is used to attach a field name to a nonterminal.

Listing E.9. *union.y*— Using %union: An Example

```
 1   %union {
 2     int    op_type;
 3     char   *var_name;
 4   }
 5
 6   %term  DIVOP                                    /*  / or %  */
 7   %type <var_name> e statement
 8   %type <op_type>  divop
 9
10   %%
11   goal      : statement
12             ;
13
14   statement : e divop e
15             {
16                     if( $2 == '/' )
17                        gen( "%s /= %s;", $1, $3 )
18                     else
19                        gen( "%s %= %s;", $1, $3 )
20
21                     free_name( $3 );
22                     $$ = $1
23             }
24             ;
25   divop     : DIVOP  { $$ = *yytext; }
26             ;
27   %%
```

A real example of all the foregoing is in Listing E.9. The grammar recognizes a single statement made up of two numbers separated by a DIVOP, which can be a / or %. The $$ in the divop rule on line 25 references the op_type field of the union because divop is attached to that field on line eight. Similarly, the $2 on line 16 references the op_type field because $2 corresponds to a divop in this production, and divop was attached to op_type on line eight. The $1 and $3 on lines 17, 19, 21, and 22 reference the var_name field because they correspond to an e in the production and were attached to e on line seven. Similarly the $$ on line 22 references var_name because it corresponds to a statement, which was also attached to a var_name on line seven.

The field stays active from the point where it's declared to the end of the current directive. For example, in

```
%token ONE <field1> TWO THREE <field2> FOUR
```

<field1> is attached to TWO and THREE, and <field2> is attached to FOUR. ONE has no field attached to it. If a $$ or $N corresponds to a symbol that has no explicit %union field attached to it, a default **int**-sized field is used and a warning message is printed.[12] Also, note that the nonterminal name on the left-hand side of a production must be found in a previous %type in order to use $$ in the corresponding right-hand side. The %type directive can have more than one nonterminal symbol listed in it, but it may have only one *<name>* and the name must be the first thing in the list. Similarly, the *<name>* in a %left and so forth applies only to those terminals that follow it in the list.[13]

$<field>N

The *$<field>N* syntax described earlier can also be used to access a field of a %union. This syntax takes precedence over the default mechanism, so you can use it

---

12. **Yacc** doesn't print the warning.

13. **Yacc** is very picky about type matching when you use this mechanism. Since this pickyness is now supported by most compilers, I've not put any type checking into **occs**. It just stupidly makes the substitutions discussed earlier.

when you want to override the default field for a particular symbol. It's also useful in imbedded actions where there's no mechanism for supplying a field name to $$. For example, in:

```
%union { integer }
    ...
%%
x  :  a  { $<integer>$ = 1; }  b  { foo( $<integer>2 );  }
   ;
```

The $<integer>$ is used to put 1 into the integer field of the synthesized attribute. That number is later referenced using the $<integer>2 in the second action. Since the field type is an integer, you could also use the default field as follows:

```
x  :  a  { $$ = 1: }  b  {  foo($2);  }
   ;
```

but **occs** prints a warning message when no field is specified, as is the case here. (**Yacc** doesn't print the warning).

Occs translates all %unions into a **typedef** and redefinition of YYSTYPE. The foregoing example is output as follows:

typedef for %union: yystype.

```
typedef union
{
    int    yy_def;
    char   *var_name ;
    int         op_type ;
}
yystype;

#define YYSTYPE yystype
```

The YYSTYPE definition is generated automatically. Both it and the yystype type name will be useful later on. The yy_def field is used for the default situation, where the symbol specified in a dollar attribute has not been attached to an explicit symbol. For example, if the following production is found <u>without</u> a preceding %type <field> e t:

```
t : e PLUS e { $$ = $1 + $3; } ;
```

the yy_def field will be used for both $$ (because there's no field attached to the t) and for $1 and $2 (because there's no field attached to the e either).

E.11.3 Printing the Value Stack

If you're using the default stack type of **int** you don't have to do anything special to print the value stack in the debugging environment because the default stack-printing routine, yypstk( ), will be called in from the library. The library version of this routine assumes a stack of integers.

Printing an **int** value stack.

If you've changed the stack type, either by redefining the YYSTYPE or macro or by using a %union, you'll need to provide a version of the yypstk() function for the debugger to use. The function is passed a pointer to a value-stack element and a second pointer to the equivalent symbol-stack element. It must return a pointer to a string that represents the value-stack element.

Printing a non-**int** value stack.

If the value stack is a simple type, such as a stack of character pointers, then printing the stack contents is easy:

```
typedef char *stack_type ;
#define YYSTYPE stack_type ;
%%
    ...                                              /* productions go here */
%%
char   *yypstk( value, symbol )
YYSTYPE *value;                                      /* pointer to a character pointer */
char     *symbol;
{
    return *value;

}
```

When the value stack is typed with a %union, things are a little more complicated. Listing E.10 shows how the value stack for the earlier example would be printed. The %union forces the value stack to be an array of yystypes, and a pointer to one element of this array is passed to yypstk(). The second, symbol argument to yypstk() is used to select the correct field of the **union**.

Listing E.10. *yypstk2.c*— Printing Attributes for a %union

```
1    %union {
2        int    op_type;
3        char   *var_name;
4    }
5
6    %term  DIVOP                                         /*  / or %  */
7    %type <var_name> e statement
8    %type <op_type>  divop
9    %%
10           ...
11   %%
12   yypstk( value, symbol )
13   yystype *value;
14   char    *symbol;
15   {
16       static char buf[80];
17
18       if( !strcmp(symbol,"e") || !strcmp(symbol,"statement") )
19           return value->var_name ;
20
21       if( !strcmp(symbol,"divop") )
22       {
23           sprintf( buf, "%c", value->op_type );
24           return buf;
25       }
26       else
27           return "---";    /* other symbols don't have attributes in this  */
28                            /* application.                                 */
29   }
```

If you were using the default, **int** attribute field in the union, the **return "---"** statement on line 27 would be replaced with the following:

```
sprintf( buf, "%d", value->yy_def );
return buf;
```

E.11.4 Grammatical Transformations

Imbedded actions (ones that are in the middle of a production) can be used in an **occs** grammar, but you have to be careful with them. The problem is that actions can be executed only during a reduction. Consequently, if you put one in the middle of a production, **occs** has to shuffle the grammar by adding an ε production. For example:

Imbedded actions.

```
s   :   a { action(1); } b c { action(2); }
    ;
```

is modified by **occs** as follows:

```
s    :   a 0001 b c { action(2); } ;
0001 : { action(1); }                              ;
```

Unfortunately, that extra ε production can introduce shift/reduce conflicts into the state machine. It's best, if possible, to rewrite your grammar so that the imbedded production isn't necessary:

```
s        : prefix b c { action(2); };
prefix : a               { action(1); };
```

Using the attribute mechanism is also a little tricky if you imbed an action in a production. Even though imbedded actions are put in their own production, the $1, $2, and so forth reference the parent production. That is, in:

```
s : a b { $$ = $1 + $2 } c  {$$ = $1 + $2 + $3 + $4} ;
```

the $1 and $2 in both actions access the attributes associated with a and b. $$ in the left action is accessed by $3 in the right action. (That is, this $$ is actually referencing the 0001 left-hand side inserted by **occs**.) The $$ in the right action is attached to s in the normal way. $4 accesses c. Note that $3 and $4 are illegal in the left action because they won't be on the parse stack when the action is performed. An error message is generated in this case, but only if the reference is in the actual grammar section of the **yacc** specification. Illegal stack references are silently accepted in the final code section of the input file.

Occs supports the two non-**yacc** transformations. Brackets are used to designate optional parts of a production. The following input:

Optional subexpressions, [...].

```
s : a [ b ] c ;
```

is translated internally to:

```
s    : a 001 c
     ;

001  : b
     | /* epsilon */
     ;
```

Note that attributes in optional productions can be handled in unexpected ways (which actually make sense if you consider the translation involved). For example, in:

```
s -> a  [b c {$$ = $1 + $2;}]   d   {$$ = $1 + $2 + $3;}
```

The $$=$1+$2 in the optional production adds the attributes associated with *b* and *c* and attaches the result to the entire optional production. The action on the right adds together the attributes associated with *a*, the entire optional production *bc* and *d*. That is, $2 in the right production is picking up the $$ from the optional production. Note that the $2 used in the right action is garbage if the ε production was taken in the optional part of the production. As a consequence, optional productions are typically not used when attributes need to be passed.

Optional productions nest. The following is legal:

```
s -> a [ b [c] [d [e]] ] f
```

though almost incomprehensible—I wouldn't recommend using it. The maximum nesting level is 8. Note that optional subexpressions can introduce duplicate productions. That is:

```
s : b [c] d
  | e [c]
  ;
```

creates:

```
s    : b 001 d
     | e 002
     ;
001 : c
     | /* epsilon */
     ;
002 : c
     | /* epsilon */
     ;
```

It's better to use the following in the original grammar:

```
s     : b opt_c d
      | e opt_c
      ;
opt_c : c
      | /* empty */
      ;
```

Also note that

```
s : [x] ;
```

is acceptable but needlessly introduces an extra production:

```
s   : 001 ;
001 : x | /* empty */ ;
```

It's better to use:

```
s : x | /* empty */ ;
```

Repeating subexpressions. [...]*.

Adding a star after the right bracket causes the enclosed expression to repeat zero or more times. A left-associative list is used by **occs**; a right-associative list is used by **LLama**. The internal mappings for all kinds of brackets are shown in the Table E.6. You can't use this mechanism if you need to pass attributes from *b* back up to the parent, primarily because you can't attach an action to the added ε production. The extra ε production may also add shift/reduce or reduce/reduce conflicts to the grammar. Be careful.

Some examples—a comma-separated list that has at least one element is:

```
s : a [ COMMA a ]* ;
```

A dot-separated list with either one or two elements is:

```
s : a [DOT a] ;
```

One or more repetitions of *b* is:

```
s : a b [b]* c ;
```

Table E.6. Occs Grammatical Transformations

Input	Output	
`s : a [b] c ;`	`s   : a 001 c` `001 : b | /* epsilon */ ;`	
`s : a [b]* c ;`	`s   : a 001 c` `001 : 001 b | /* epsilon */ ;`	*(occs version)*
`s : a [b]* c ;`	`s   : a 001 c` `001 : b 001 | /* epsilon */ ;`	*(llama version)*

E.11.5 The *yyout.sym* File

You can see the transformations made to the grammar, both by adding imbedded actions and by using the bracket notation for optional and repeating sub-productions, by looking in the symbol-table file, *yyout.sym,* which will show the transformed grammar, not the input grammar. The symbol-table file is generated if –*D*, –*S*, or –*s* is specified on the command line. A *yyout.sym* for the grammar in Listing E.2 on page 841 is in Listing E.11. (It was generated with `occs -S expr.y`.)

Generating the symbol table, *yyout.sym*, –D, –S, –s.

Listing E.11. *yyout.sym*— Occs Symbol-Table Output

```
 1    --------------- Symbol table ------------------
 2
 3   NONTERMINAL SYMBOLS:
 4
 5   e (257)   <>
 6      FIRST : ID NUM LP
 7        5: e -> ID
 8        4: e -> NUM
 9        3: e -> LP e RP ............................................PREC 3
10        2: e -> e STAR e ...........................................PREC 2
11        1: e -> e PLUS e ...........................................PREC 1
12
13   s (256)  (goal symbol) <>
14      FIRST : ID NUM LP
15        0: s -> e
16
17   TERMINAL SYMBOLS:
18
19   name            value   prec   assoc   field
20   STAR              4      2       1      <>
21   RP                6      3       1      <>
22   PLUS              3      1       1      <>
23   NUM               2      0       -      <>
24   ID                1      0       -      <>
25   LP                5      3       1      <>
```

Taking a few lines as a representative sample:

```
e (257)   <>
   FIRST : ID NUM LP
     5: e -> ID
     4: e -> NUM
     3: e -> LP e RP ................................PREC 3
```

the top line is the name and internal, tokenized value for the left-hand side. The <> on the right contains the field name assigned with a %type directive. Since there was none in this example, the field is empty. Had the following appeared in the input:

```
%type <field> e
```

the <field> would be on the corresponding line in the symbol table. The next line is the symbol's FIRST set. (The list of terminal symbols that can appear at the far left of a parse tree derived from the nonterminal.) That is, it's the set of tokens which can legitimately be next in the input when we're looking for a given symbol in the grammar. Here, we're looking for an *e*, and an **ID**, **NUM**, or **LP**. can all start an *e*. The FIRST sets are output only if the symbol table is created with −*S*.

Right-hand sides in
yyout.sym, production
numbers.

The next few lines are the right-hand sides for all productions that share the single left-hand side. The number to the left of the colon is the production number. These are assigned in the order that the productions were declared in the source file. The first production is 0, the second is 1, and so forth. Note that the production that has the goal symbol on its left-hand side is always Production 0. Production numbers are useful for setting breakpoints in the interactive debugging environment. (You can set a breakpoint on reduction by a specific production, provided that you know its number.) The PREC

field gives the relative precedence of the entire production. This level is used for resolving shift/reduce conflicts, also discussed below. Note that the productions shown in this

table are the ones actually used by **occs**—any transformations caused by imbedded actions or the [] operator are reflected in the table. Productions are sorted alphabetically by left-hand side.

The second part of the table gives information about the terminal symbols. For example:

```
name              value  prec  assoc   field
PLUS                3      1     l      <>
NUM                 2      0     -      <>
```

Here, 3 is the internal value used to represent the PLUS token. It is also the value assigned to a PLUS in *yyout.h*. The prec field gives the relative precedence of this symbol, as assigned with a %left, %right, or %nonassoc directive. The higher the number, the higher the precedence. Similarly, the assoc is the associativity. It will have one of the following values:

l	left associative
r	right associative
n	nonassociative
-	Associativity is not specified. The token was declared with a %term or %token rather than a %left, %right, or %nonassoc directive.

Finally, the field column lists any %union fields assigned with a <name> in the %left, %right, and %nonassoc directives. A <> is printed if there is no such assignment.

E.11.6 The *yyout.doc* File

The *yyout.doc* file holds a description of the LALR(1) state machine used by the **occs**-generated parser. It is created if −*v* or −*V* is present on the command line. The *yyout.doc* file for the grammar in Listing E.2 on page 841 is shown in Table E.7. Figure E.6 shows the state machine in graphic form.

This machine has ten states, each with a unique number (running from 0 to 9). The top few lines in each state represent the LALR(1) kernel items. You can use them to see the condition of parse stack when the current state is reached. For example, the header from State 9 looks like this:

```
State 9:
    e->e .PLUS e
    e->e PLUS e .   [$ PLUS STAR RP]
    e->e .STAR e
```

The dot is used to mark the current top of stack, so everything to the left of the dot will be on the stack. The top-of-stack item in State 9 is an *e* because there's an *e* immediately to the left of the dot. The middle line is telling us that there may also be a PLUS and another *e* under the *e* at top of stack.

If the dot is at the far right (as it is on the middle line), then a handle is on the stack and the parser will want to reduce. The symbols in brackets to the right of the production are a list of those symbols that (at least potentially) cause a reduction if they're the next input symbol and we are in State 9. (This list is the LALR(1) lookahead set for the indicated LR item, as discussed in Chapter Five.) The lookahead set is printed for every kernel item (as compared to only those items with the dot at the far right) if −*V* is used rather than −*v*. Note that these are just potential reductions, we won't necessarily do the reduction on every symbol in the list if there's a conflict between the reduction and a potential shift. A $ is used in the lookahead list to represent the end-of-input marker.

The next lines show the possible transitions that can be made from the current state. There are four possibilities, which will look something like the following:

```
Reduce by 3 on PLUS
```

says that a reduction by Production 3 occurs if the next input symbol is a PLUS.

```
Shift to 7 on STAR
```

says that a 7 is shifted onto the stack (and the input advanced) if the next input symbol is a STAR.

```
Goto 4 on e
```

takes care of the push part of a reduction. For example, starting in State 0, a **NUM** in the input causes a shift to State 2, so a 2 is pushed onto the stack. In State 2, a PLUS in the input causes a reduce by Production 4 (*e*→**NUM**), which does two things. First, the 2 is popped, returning us to State 0. Next, the parser looks for a goto transition (in State 0) that is associated with the left-hand side of the production by which we just reduced. In this case, the left-hand side is an ε, and the parser finds a Goto 4 on e in State 0, so a 4 is pushed onto the stack as the push part of the reduction. The final possibility,

```
Accept on end of input
```

says that if the end-of-input marker is found in this state, the parse is successfully terminated.

Symbols that cause reductions in *yyout.doc* state.

Transitions in *yyout.doc*, shift, reduce, accept.

Table E.7. *yyout.doc* (Generated from Listing E.2)

```
State 0:                                  State 6:
    s->.e                                     e->e PLUS .e

    Shift to 1 on ID                          Shift to 1 on ID
    Shift to 2 on NUM                         Shift to 2 on NUM
    Shift to 3 on LP                          Shift to 3 on LP
    Goto 4 on e                               Goto 9 on e

State 1:                                  State 7:
    e->ID .  [$ PLUS STAR RP ]                e->e STAR .e

    Reduce by 5 on End of Input               Shift to 1 on ID
    Reduce by 5 on PLUS                       Shift to 2 on NUM
    Reduce by 5 on STAR                       Shift to 3 on LP
    Reduce by 5 on RP                         Goto 10 on e

State 2:                                  State 8:
    e->NUM .  [$ PLUS STAR RP ]               e->LP e RP .  [$ PLUS STAR RP ]

    Reduce by 4 on End of Input               Reduce by 3 on End of Input
    Reduce by 4 on PLUS                       Reduce by 3 on PLUS
    Reduce by 4 on STAR                       Reduce by 3 on STAR
    Reduce by 4 on RP                         Reduce by 3 on RP

State 3:                                  State 9:
    e->LP .e RP                               e->e .PLUS e
                                              e->e PLUS e .  [$ PLUS STAR RP]
    Shift to 1 on ID                          e->e .STAR e
    Shift to 2 on NUM
    Shift to 3 on LP                          Reduce by 1 on End of Input
    Goto 5 on e                               Reduce by 1 on PLUS
                                              Shift to 7 on STAR
State 4:                                      Reduce by 1 on RP
    s->e .  [$ ]
    e->e .PLUS e                          State 10:
    e->e .STAR e                              e->e .PLUS e
                                              e->e .STAR e
    Accept on end of input                    e->e STAR e .  [$ PLUS STAR RP]
    Shift to 6 on PLUS
    Shift to 7 on STAR                        Reduce by 2 on End of Input
                                              Reduce by 2 on PLUS
State 5:                                      Reduce by 2 on STAR
    e->e .PLUS e                              Reduce by 2 on RP
    e->e .STAR e
    e->LP e .RP                               6/254  terminals
                                              2/256  nonterminals
    Shift to 6 on PLUS                        6/512  productions
    Shift to 7 on STAR                        11     states
    Shift to 8 on RP
```

Figure E.6. State Machine Represented by the *yyout.doc* File in Listing E.11

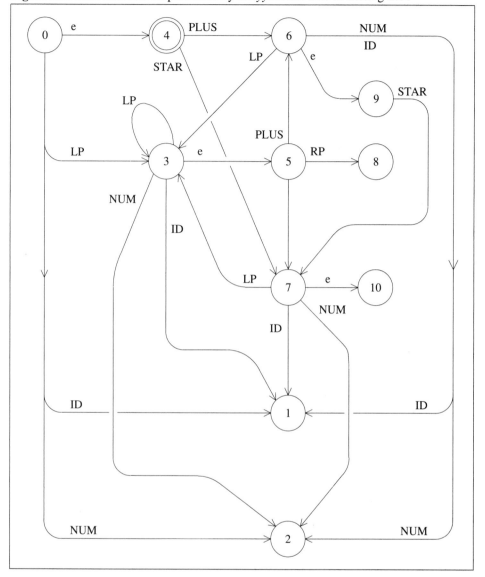

E.11.7 Shift/Reduce and Reduce/Reduce Conflicts

One of the main uses of the *yyout.doc* file is to see how shift/reduce and reduce/reduce conflicts are solved by **occs**. You should never let a WARNING about an inadequate state go by without looking in *yyout.doc* to see what's really going on.

Occs uses the disambiguating rules discussed in Chapter Five to resolve conflicts. Reduce/reduce conflicts are always resolved in favor of the production that occurred earlier in the grammar. Shift/reduce conflicts are resolved as follows:

Resolving shift/reduce and reduce/reduce conflicts.

(1) Precedence and associativity information is assigned to all terminal symbols using `%left`, `%right`, and `%nonassoc` directives in the definitions part of the input file. The directives might look like this:

```
%left   PLUS MINUS
%left TIMES DIVIDE
%right  ASSIGN
```

The higher a directive is in the list, the <u>lower</u> the precedence. If no precedence or associativity is assigned, a terminal symbol will have a precedence level of zero (very low) and be nonassociative.

Using %prec.

Productions are assigned the same precedence level as the rightmost terminal symbol in the production. You can override this default with a `%prec TOKEN` directive to the right of the production. (It must be between the rightmost symbol in the production and the semicolon or vertical bar that terminates the production). `TOKEN` is a terminal symbol that was declared with a previous `%left`, `%right`, or `%nonassoc`, and the production is assigned the same precedence level as the indicated token. **Occs**, but not **yacc**, also allows statements of the form

   %prec *number*

where the *number* is the desired precedence level (the higher the number, the higher the precedence). The *number* should be greater than zero.

(2) When a shift/reduce conflict is encountered, the precedence of the terminal symbol to be shifted is compared with the precedence of the production by which you want to reduce. If the terminal or production is of precedence zero, then resolve in favor of the shift.

(3) Otherwise, if the precedences are equal, resolve using the following table:

associativity of lookahead symbol	*resolve in favor of*
left	reduce
right	shift
nonassociative	shift

(4) Otherwise, if the precedences are not equal, use the following table:

precedence	*resolve in favor of*
lookahead symbol < production	reduce
lookahead symbol > production	shift

The `%prec` directive can be used both to assign a precedence level to productions that don't contain any terminals, and to modify the precedences of productions in which the rightmost nonterminal isn't what we want. A good example is the unary minus operator, used in the following grammar:

```
%term       NUM
%left       MINUS PLUS
%left       TIMES
%nonassoc VERY_HIGH
%%

s : e ;
e : e PLUS  e
  | e MINUS e
  | e TIMES e
  | MINUS e    %prec VERY_HIGH
  | NUM
  ;
%%
```

Here, the `%prec` is used to force unary minus to be higher precedence than both binary minus and multiplication. VERY_HIGH is declared only to get another precedence level for this purpose. **Occs** also lets you assign a precedence level directly. For example,

```
| MINUS e       %prec 4
```

could have been used in the previous example.[14] C's **sizeof** operator provides another example of how to use `%prec`. The precedence of **sizeof** must be defined as follows:

```
expression : SIZEOF LP type_name RP       %prec SIZEOF
           ;
```

in order to avoid incorrectly assigning a **sizeof** the same precedence level as a right parenthesis.

The precedence level and `%prec` operator can also be used to resolve shift/reduce conflicts in a grammar. The first technique puts tokens other than operators into the precedence table. Consider the following state (taken from yyout.doc).

Using `%prec` to resolve shift/reduce conflicts.

```
WARNING: State  5: shift/reduce conflict ELSE/40 (choose shift)

State 5:
    stmt-> IF LP expr RP stmt.
       |   IF LP expr RP stmt. ELSE stmt
```

The default resolution (in favor of the shift) is correct, but it's a good idea to eliminate the warning message (because you don't want to clutter up the screen with harmless warning messages that will obscure the presence of real ones). You can resolve the shift/reduce conflict as follows. The conflict exists because **ELSE**, not being an operator, is probably declared with a `%term` rather than a `%left` or `%right`. Consequently, it has no precedence level. The precedence of the first production is taken from the **RP** (the rightmost terminal in the production), so to resolve in favor of the shift, all you need do is assign a precedence level to ELSE, making it higher than **RP**. Do it like this:

```
%left     LP RP /* existing precedence of LP               */
%nonassoc ELSE  /* higher precedence because it follows LP */
```

Though you don't want to do it in the current situation, you *could* resolve in favor of the reduce by reversing the two precedence levels. (Make **ELSE** lower precedence than **LP**).

The second common situation is illustrated by the following simplification of the C grammar used in Chapter Six. (I've left out some of the operators, but you get the idea.)

```
function_argument
        : expr
        | function_argument COMMA expr  /* comma separates arguments */
        ;
expr
        : expr STAR     expr
        | expr COMMA    expr             /* comma operator */
        | expr DIVOP    expr
          ...
        | term
        ;
```

A shift/reduce conflict is created here because of the COMMA operator (the parser

---

14. Yacc doesn't permit this. You have to use a bogus token.

doesn't know if a comma is an operator or a list-element separator), and this conflict is displayed in *yyout.doc* as follows:

```
WARNING: State 170: shift/reduce conflict COMMA/102 (choose shift)
State 170:
    function_argument-> expr. (prod. 102, prec. 0)
            [COMMA RP ]
    expr-> expr. STAR expr
    expr-> expr. COMMA expr
    expr-> expr. DIVOP expr
```

The problem can be solved by assigning a precedence level to production 102: *function_argument→expr*. (It doesn't have one because there are no terminal symbols in it). You can resolve in favor of the reduce (the correct decision, here) by giving the production a precedence level greater than or equal to that of the comma. Do this in the input file as follows:

```
expr_list
    : expr                              %prec COMMA
    | expr_list COMMA expr
    ;
```

Similarly, you could resolve in favor of the shift by making the production lower precedence than the COMMA (by replacing the COMMA in the %prec with the name of a lower-precedence operator). Since the comma is the lowest-precedence operator in C, you'd have to do it here by creating a bogus token that has an even lower precedence, like this:

```
%nonassoc VERY_LOW      /* bogus token (not used in the grammar) */
%left     COMMA
    ...
%%
    ...
expr_list
    : expr                              %prec VERY_LOW
    | expr_list COMMA expr
    ;
```

Shift/reduce and reduce/reduce conflicts are often caused by the implicit ε productions that are created by actions imbedded in the middle of a production (rather than at the far right), and the previous techniques can not be used to resolve these conflicts because there is no explicit production to which a precedence level can be assigned. For this reason, it's best to use explicit ε productions rather than imbedded actions. Translate:

```
x : a {action();} b ;
```

to this:

```
x       : a action b ;
action  : /* empty */ {action();} ;
```

or to this:

```
x       : a' b
a'      : a {action();}
```

These translations probably won't eliminate the conflict, but you can now use %prec to resolve the conflict explicitly.

It's not always possible to do a translation like the foregoing, because the action may have to access the attributes of symbols to its left in the parent production. You can sometimes eliminate the conflict just by changing the position of the action in the production, however. For example, actions that follow tokens are less likely to introduce conflicts than actions that precede them. Taking an example from the C grammar used in Chapter Six, the following production generated 40-odd conflicts:

```
and_list
        : and_list {and($1);} ANDAND binary  { and($4); $$=NULL; }
        | binary
        ;
```

but this variant generated no conflicts and does the same thing:

```
and_list
        : and_list ANDAND  {and($1);}  binary  { and($4); $$=NULL; }
        | binary
        ;
```

E.11.8 Error Recovery

One of the ways that **occs** differs considerably from **yacc** is the error-recovery mechanism.[15] **Occs** parsers do error recovery automatically, without you having to do anything special. The *panic-mode* recovery technique that was discussed in Chapter 5 is used. It works as follows:

Panic-mode error recovery.

(0) An error is triggered when an error transition is read from the parse table entry for the current input and top-of-stack symbols (that is, when there's no legal outgoing transition from a state on the current input symbol).
(1) Discard the state at the top of stack.
(2) Look in the parse table and see if there's a legal transition on the current input symbol and the uncovered stack item. If so, we've recovered and the parse is allowed to progress, using the modified stack. If there's no legal transition, and the stack is not empty, go to 1.
(3) If all items on the stack are discarded, restore the stack to its original condition, discard an input symbol, and go to 1.

The algorithm continues either until it can start parsing again or the entire input file is absorbed. In order to avoid cascading error messages, messages are suppressed if a second error happens right on the tail of the first one. To be more exact, no messages are printed if an error happens within five parse cycles (five shift or reduce operations) of the previous error. The number of parse cycles can be changed with a

Avoiding cascading error messages, YYCASCADE.

```
%{ #define YYCASCADE desired_value %}
```

in the specifications section. Note that errors that are ignored because they happen too soon aren't counted against the total defined by YYMAXERR.

E.11.9 Putting the Parser and Actions in Different Files

Unfortunately, **occs** can take a long time to generate the parse tables required for a largish grammar. (Though it usually takes less time for **occs** to generate *yyout.c* than it does for Microsoft C to compile it.) To make program development a little easier, a mechanism is provided to separate the table-making functions from the code-generation

---

15. **Yacc** uses a special error token, which the parser shifts onto the stack when an error occurs. You must provide special error-recovery productions that have error tokens on the right-hand sides. The mechanism is notoriously inadequate, but it's the only one available if you're using **yacc**. See [Schreiner] pp. 65–82 for more information.

Using the –p and –a
command-line switches.

functions. The *-p* command-line switch causes **occs** to output the tables and parser only (in a file called *yyout.c*). Actions that are part of a rule are not output, and the third part of the **occs** input file is ignored. When *-a* is specified, only the actions are processed, and tables are not generated. A file called *yyact.c* is created in this case.

Once the grammar is stable you can run **occs** once with *-p* to create the tables. Thereafter, you can run the same file through **occs** with *-a* to get the actions. You now have two files, *yyout.c* and *yyact.c*. Compile these separately, and then link them together. If you change the actions (but not the grammar), you can recreate *yyact.c* using **occs** −a without having to remake the tables. Remember that actions that are imbedded in the <u>middle</u> of a production will effectively modify the grammar. If you modify the position of an action in the grammar, you'll have to remake the tables (but not if you modify only the action code). On the other hand, actions added to or removed from the far right of a production will not affect the tables at all, so can be modified, removed, or added without needing to remake the tables.

YYACTION, YYPARSER.

The first, definitions part of the **occs** input file is always output, regardless of the presence of *−a* or *−p*. The special macro YYPARSER is generated if a parser is present in the current file, YYACTION is generated if the actions are present. (Both are defined when neither switch is specified.) You can use these in conjunction with **#ifdef**s in the definitions section to control the declaration of variables, and so forth (to avoid duplicate declarations). It's particularly important to define YYSTYPE, or put a %union, in both files—if you're not using the default int type, that is—otherwise, attributes won't be

Yy_val, Yy_vsp, and
Yy_rhslen made public
by –p or –a.

accessed correctly. Also note that three global variables whose scope is normally limited to *yyout.c*—Yy_val, Yy_vsp, and Yy_rhslen— are made public if either switch is present. They hold the value of $$, the value-stack pointer, and the right-hand side length.

Listing E.12 shows the definitions section of an input file that's designed to be split up in this way.

Listing E.12. Definitions Section for *−a/−p*

```
 1   %{
 2   #ifdef YYPARSER       /* If parser is present, declare variables.     */
 3   #    define CLASS
 4   #    define _(x) x
 5   #else                 /* If parser is not present, make them externs. */
 6   #    define CLASS extern
 7   #    define _(x)
 8   #endif
 9
10   CLASS int x _( = 5 );  /* Evaluates to "int x = 5;" in yyparse.c and to */
11                          /* "extern int x;" in yyacts.c.                 */
12   %}
13
14   %union {               /* Either a %union or a redefinition of YYSTYPE  */
15       ...                /* should go here.                              */
16   }
17
18   %term ...              /* Token definitions go here.                   */
19   %left ...
20   %%
```

E.11.10 Shifting a Token's Attributes

It is sometimes necessary to attach an attribute to a token that has been shifted onto the value stack. For example, when the lexical analyzer reads a **NUMBER** token, it would be nice to shift the numeric value of that number onto the value stack. One way to do this is demonstrated by the small desk-calculator program shown in the the **occs** input file in Listing E.13. The L&X lexical analyzer is in Listing E.14. This program sums together a series of numbers separated by plus signs and prints the result. The input numbers are converted from strings to binary by the `atoi()` call on line 12 and the numeric value is also pushed onto the stack here. The numeric values are summed on line eight, and the result is printed on line four. The difficulty, here, is that you need to introduce an extra production on line 12 so that you can shift the value associated with the input number, making the parser both larger and slower as a consequence.

Using an extra production to shift attribute for a token.

Listing E.13. Putting Token Attributes onto the Value Stack—Using A Reduction

```
1   %term NUMBER      /* a collection of one or more digits   */
2   %term PLUS        /* a + sign                             */
3   %%
4   statement : expr statement       { printf("The sum is %d\n", $1); }
5             | /* empty */
6             ;
7
8   expr      : expr PLUS number     { $$ = $1 + $3;           }
9             | /* empty */
10            ;
11
12  number    : NUMBER               { $$ = atoi(yytext);     }
13            ;
14  %%
```

Listing E.14. Lexical Analyzer for Listing E.13

```
1   #include "yyout.h"      /* token definitions */
2   %%
3   [0-9]+      return NUMBER;
4   \+          return PLUS;
5   .      ;                /* ignore everything else */
6   %%
```

An alternate solution to the problem is possible by making the lexical analyzer and parser work together in a more integrated fashion. The default action in a shift (as controlled by the `YYSHIFTACT` macro described earlier) is to push the contents of a variable called `yylval` onto the value stack. The lexical analyzer can use this variable to cause a token's attribute to be pushed as part of the shift action (provided that you haven't modified `YYSHIFTACT` anywhere).[16] The procedure is demonstrated in Listings E.15 and E.16, which show an alternate version of the desk calculator. Here, the lexical analyzer assigns the numeric value (the attribute of the **NUMBER** token) to `yylval` before

Using `yylval` to pass attributes from scanner to parser.

---

16. Note that **yacc** (but not **occs**) also uses `yylval` to hold $$, so it should never be modified in a **yacc** application, except as described below (or you'll mess up the value stack).

returning the token. That value is shifted onto the value stack when the token is shifted, and is available to the parser on line eight.

Listing E.15. Passing Attributes from the Lexical Analyzer to the Parser

```
1   %term NUMBER      /* a collection of one or more digits   */
2   %term PLUS        /* a + sign                             */
3   %%
4   statement : expr statement        { printf("The sum is %d\n", $1); }
5             | /* empty */
6             ;
7
8   expr      : expr PLUS NUMBER      { $$ = $1 + $3; }
9             | /* empty */
10            ;
11  %%
```

Listing E.16. Lexical Analyzer for Listing E.15

```
1   %{
2   #include "yyout.h"      /* token definitions                    */
3   extern int yylval;      /* declared by parser in occs output file */
4   %}
5   %%
6   [0-9]+  yylval = atoi(yytext);  /* numeric value is synthesized in shift */
7           return NUMBER;
8
9   \+      return PLUS;
10  .       ;                       /* ignore everything else */
11  %%
```

yylval is of type YYSTYPE—**int** by default, but you can change YYSTYPE explicitly by redefining it or implicitly by using the %union mechanism described earlier. If you do change the type, be careful to also change any matching **extern** statement in the LEX input file as well.

Note that this mechanism is risky if the lexical analyzer is depending on the parser to have taken some action before a symbol is read. The problem is that the lookahead symbol can be read well in advance of the time that it's shifted—several reductions can occur after reading the symbol but before shifting it. The problem is best illustrated with an example. Say that a grammar for C has two tokens, a **NAME** token that's used for identifiers, and a **TYPE** token that is used for types. A **typedef** statement can cause a string that was formerly treated as a **NAME** to be treated as a **TYPE**. That is, the **typedef** effectively adds a new keyword to the language, because subsequent references to the associated identifier must be treated as if they were **TYPE** tokens.

It is tempting to try to use the symbol table to resolve the problem. When a **typedef** is encountered, the parser creates a symbol-table entry for the new type. The lexical analyzer could then use the symbol table to distinguish **NAME**s from **TYPE**s. The difficulty here lies in input such as the following:

```
typedef int itype;
itype x;
```

In a bottom-up parser such as the current one, the symbol-table entry for the **typedef** will, typically, not be created until the entire declaration is encountered—and the parser can't know that it's at the end of the declaration until it finds the trailing semicolon. So, the semicolon is read and shifted on the stack, and the next lookahead (the second `itype`) is read, <u>before</u> doing the reduction that puts the first `itype` into the symbol table—the reduction that adds the table entry happens after the second `itype` is read because the lookahead character must be read to decide to do the reduction. When the scanner looks up the second `itype`, it won't be there yet, so it will assume incorrectly that the second `itype` is a **NAME** token. The moral is that attributes are best put onto the stack during a reduction, rather than trying to put them onto the stack from the lexical analyzer.

E.11.11 Sample Occs Input File

For convenience, the **occs** input file for the expression compiler we've been discussing is shown in Listing E.17.

Listing E.17. *expr.y*— An Expression Compiler (Occs Version)

```
 1   %term   ID          /*  a string of lower-case characters   */
 2   %term   NUM         /*  a number                            */
 3
 4   %left   PLUS        /*  +                                   */
 5   %left   STAR        /*  *                                   */
 6   %left   LP RP       /*  (  )                                */
 7
 8   %{
 9   #include <stdio.h>
10   #include <ctype.h>
11   #include <malloc.h>
12
13   extern char         *yytext;        /* In yylex(), holds lexeme       */
14   extern char         *new_name();    /* declared at bottom of this file */
15
16   typedef char        *stype;         /* Value stack */
17   #define YYSTYPE      stype
18
19   #define YYMAXDEPTH   64
20   #define YYMAXERR     10
21   #define YYVERBOSE
22   %}
23
24   %%
25   /* A small expression grammar that recognizes numbers, names, addition (+),
26    * multiplication (*), and parentheses. Expressions associate left to right
27    * unless parentheses force it to go otherwise. * is higher precedence than +.
28    * Note that an underscore is appended to identifiers so that they won't be
29    * confused with rvalues.
30    */
31
32   s       : e ;
33
34   e       : e PLUS e    { yycode("%s += %s\n", $1, $3); free_name( $3 ); }
35           | e STAR e    { yycode("%s *= %s\n", $1, $3); free_name( $3 ); }
36           | LP e RP     { $$ = $2;                                       }
37           | NUM         { yycode("%s = %s\n",  $$ = new_name(), yytext ); }
38           | ID          { yycode("%s = _%s\n", $$ = new_name(), yytext ); }
39           ;
40   %%
41
```

Listing E.17. continued. . .

```
42    /*-------------------------------------------------------------------*/
43    char    *yypstk( ptr )
44    char    **ptr;
45    {
46        /* Yypstk is used by the debugging routines. It is passed a pointer to a
47         * value-stack item and should return a string representing that item. In
48         * this case, all it has to do is dereference one level of indirection.
49         */
50
51        return *ptr ? *ptr : "<empty>" ;
52    }
53
54    /*-------------------------------------------------------------------*/
55
56    char   *Names[] = { "t0", "t1", "t2", "t3", "t4", "t5", "t6", "t7" };
57    char   **Namep  = Names;
58
59    char    *new_name()
60    {
61        /* Return a temporary-variable name by popping one off the name stack.  */
62
63        if( Namep >= &Names[ sizeof(Names)/sizeof(*Names) ] )
64        {
65            yyerror("Expression too complex\n");
66            exit( 1 );
67        }
68
69        return( *Namep++ );
70    }
71
72    free_name(s)
73    char    *s;
74    {                              /* Free up a previously allocated name */
75        *--Namep = s;
76    }
77
78    /*-------------------------------------------------------------------*/
79
80    yy_init_occs()
81    {
82        /* Generate declarations for the rvalues */
83
84        yycode("public word _t0,_t1,_t2,_t3;\n");
85        yycode("public word _t4,_t5,_t6,_t7;\n");
86    }
87
88    main( argc, argv )
89    char    **argv;
90    {
91        /* Open the input file, using yy_get_args() if we're debugging or
92         * ii_newfile() if not.
93         */
94
95    #ifdef YYDEBUG
96        yy_get_args( argc, argv );
97    #else
98        if( argc < 2 )
99        {
100           fprintf( stderr, "Need file name\n");
101           exit(1);
```

➡

Listing E.17. continued...

```
102          }
103          else if( ii_newfile(argv[1]) < 0 )
104          {
105              fprintf( stderr, "Can't open %s\n", argv[1] );
106              exit(2);
107          }
108      #endif
109          yyparse();
110          exit( 0 );
111      }
```

Listing E.18. *expr.lex*— LᴱX Input File for Expression Compiler

```
 1   %{
 2   #include "yyout.h"
 3   %}
 4   %%
 5   "+"       return PLUS;
 6   "*"       return STAR;
 7   "("       return LP;
 8   ")"       return RP;
 9   [0-9]+    return NUM;
10   [a-z]+    return ID;
11   %%
```

E.11.12 Hints and Warnings

- Though input defaults to standard input in production mode (as compared to debug mode), the input routines really expect to be working with a file. The default, standard-input mode is intended for use in pipes, not for interactive input with a human being. This expectation can produce unexpected consequences in an interactive situation. Since the input is always one token ahead of the parser, the parser's actions can appear to be delayed by one token. This delay is most noticeable at end of file, because the last token in the input stream isn't processed until an explicit end-of-file marker is read. If you're typing the input at the keyboard, you'll have to supply this marker yourself. (Use *Ctrl-D* with UNIX; the two-character sequence *Ctrl-Z Enter* under MS-DOS).

- Though you can redefine YYPRIVATE to make various global **static** variables public for the purpose of debugging, you should never modify any of these global variables directly.

- Once the grammar is working properly, make changes very carefully. Very small changes in a grammar can introduce masses of shift/reduce and reduce/reduce conflicts. You should always change only one production at a time and then remake the tables. Always back up the current input file before modifying it so that you can return to a working grammar if you mess up (or use a version-control system like SCCS).

- Avoid ε productions and imbedded actions—they tend to introduce shift/reduce conflicts into a grammar. If you must introduce an imbedded production, try to put it immediately to the right of a terminal symbol.

- Avoid global variables in the code-generation actions. The attribute mechanism should be used to pass all information between productions if at all possible (sometimes it's not). Grammars are almost always recursive. Consequently, you'll find that global variables tend to be modified at unexpected times, often destroying information that you need for some subsequent action. Avoiding global variables can seem difficult. You have to work harder to figure out how to do things—it's like writing a program that uses subroutine return values only, without global variables or subroutine arguments. Nonetheless, it's worth the effort in terms of reduced development time. All of the global-variable-use issues that apply to recursive subroutines apply to the action code in a production.

- The assignment in the default action ($$=$1) is made <u>before</u> the action code is executed. Modifying $1 inside one of your own actions will have no effect on the value of $$. You should modify $$ itself.

- If you are using the *-a* and *-p* switches to split the parser into two files, remember that actions imbedded in a production actually modify the grammar. If you add or move such an action, you must remake the tables. You can add or remove actions at the far right of a production without affecting the tables, however.

Occs is not **yacc**, and as a consequence, many hacks found in various books that discuss the UNIX utilities must be avoided when using **occs**:

- Because of the way that the input is processed, it's not safe to modify the lexeme from the parser or to do any direct input from the parser. All tokens should be returned from LEX in an orderly fashion. You must use yytext, yylineno, and yyleng to examine the lexeme. It's risky for code in the parser to modify these variables or to call any of the ii_ input routines used by LEX. The problem here is that **occs** and **LLama** both read one token ahead—a second, lookahead token will already have been read <u>before</u> any action code is processed. The token in yytext is the current token, not the lookahead token.

- By the same token (so to speak) you should never modify the **occs** or **LLama** value stack directly, always use the dollar-attribute mechanism—$$, $1, and so on—to do so. The contents of the yylval, which has the same type as a stack element, is shifted onto the value stack when a state representing a token is shifted onto the state stack, and you can use this variable to shift an attribute for a token. (Just assign a value to yylval before returning the token). It is not possible for code in a LEX-generated lexical analyzer to modify the value stack directly, as is done in some published examples of how to use the UNIX utilities. Use yylval.

- The **occs** error-recovery mechanism is completely automatic. Neither the **yacc** error token, nor the yyerrok action is supported by **occs**. The error token can be removed from all **yacc** grammars. Similarly, all yyerrok actions can be deleted. If a **yacc** production contains nothing but an error token and optional action on it's right-hand side, the entire production should be removed (don't just delete the right-hand side, because you'll introduce a hitherto nonexistent ε production into the grammar).

- The **occs** start production may have only one right-hand side. If a **yacc** grammar starts like this:

```
baggins : frodo
        | bilbo
        ;
```

add an extra production at the very top of the **occs** grammar (just after the %%):

```
start : baggins ;
```

E.12 LLama

The remainder of this appendix describes the **LLama**-specific parts of the compiler compiler. The main restriction in using **LLama** is that the input grammar must be LL(1). **LLama** grammars are, as a consequence, harder to write than **occs** grammars. On the other hand, a **LLama**-generated parser will be both smaller and faster than an **occs** parser for an equivalent grammar.

E.12.1 Percent Directives and Error Recovery

The % directives supported by **LLama** are summarized in Table E.8. **LLama** supports one % directive over and above the standard directives. The %synch is placed in the definitions section of the input file—use it to specify a set of *synchronization tokens* for error recovery. A syntax error is detected when the top-of-stack symbol is a terminal symbol, and that symbol is not also the current lookahead symbol. The error-recovery code does two things: it pops items off the stack until the top-of-stack symbol is a token in the synchronization set, and it reads tokens from input until it finds the same token that it just found on the stack, at which point it has recovered from the error. If the parser can't find the desired token, or if no token in the synchronization set is also on the stack, then the error is unrecoverable and the parse is terminated with an error flag. yyparse() usually returns 1 in this case, but this action can be changed by redefining YYABORT. (See table E.2 on page 840).

The %synch directive, synchronization tokens.

Changing the action taken by the parser on an error.

Table E.8. LLama % Directives and Comments

Directive	Description
%%	Delimits the three sections of the input file.
%{	Starts a code block. All lines that follow, up to a %} are written to the output file unchanged.
%}	Ends a code block.
%token	Defines a token.
%term	A synonym for %token.
/* */	C-like comments are recognized—and ignored—by **occs**, even if they're outside of a %{ %} delimited code block.
%synch	Define set of synchronization tokens.

Several tokens can be listed in the %synch directive. Good choices for synchronization symbols are tokens that end something. In C, for example, semicolons, close parentheses, and close braces are reasonable selections. You'd do this with:

```
%term  SEMI CLOSE_PAREN CLOSE_CURLY
  . . .
%synch SEMI CLOSE_PAREN CLOSE_CURLY
```

E.12.2 Top-Down Attributes

The **LLama** value stack and the $ attribute mechanism are considerably different from the one used by **occs**. **LLama** uses the top-down attribute-processing described in Chapter Four. Attributes are referenced from within an action using the notation $$, $1, $2, and so forth. $$ is used in an action to reference the attribute that was attached to the nonterminal on the left-hand side before it was replaced. The numbers can be used to reference attributes attached to symbols to the right of the current action in the grammar. The number indicates the distance from the action to the desired symbol. ($0 references

LLama attributes, $$, $1, etc.

the current action's own attributes.) For example, in

```
stmt :            {$1=$2=new_name();} expr {free_name($0);} SEMI stmt ;
```

the $1 in the left action modifies the attribute attached to expr, the $2 references the attribute attached to the second action, which uses $0 to get that attribute. $$ references the attribute attached to the left-hand side in the normal way. Attributes flow across the grammar from left to right.

E.12.3 The LLama Value Stack

Typing LLama's value stack.

The **LLama** value stack is a stack of structures, as was described in Chapter Four. The structure has two fields, defined in the **LLama**-generated parser as follows:

```
typedef struct      /* Typedef for value-stack elements.       */
{
    YYSTYPE left;   /* Holds value of left-hand side attribute. */
    YYSTYPE right;  /* Holds value of current-symbol's attribute.*/
}
yyvstype;
```

The YYSTYPE structure is defined as an **int** by default, but you can redefine it in the definitions section of the input file as follows:

```
%{
typedef char *stack_type;   /* Use stack of character pointers. */
#define YYSTYPE stack_type
%}
%%
```

In this case, the dollar attribute will be of the same type as YYSTYPE. That is $$, $1, and so forth, reference the character pointer. You can use *$1 or $1[2] to access individual characters in the string. If the stack is a stack of structures or unions, as in:

```
%{
typedef union
{
    int        integer;
    char *string;
}
stack_type;    /* Use stack of character pointers */
#define YYSTYPE stack_type
%}
%%
```

You can access individual fields like this: $$.integer or $1.string.

Initializing the value stack with yy_init_llama().

The initialization subroutine for the **LLama**-generated parser, yy_init_llama(), is called after the stack is initialized but before the first lexeme is input—the start symbol will have been pushed onto the parse stack, and garbage onto the value stack. The initialization routine is passed a pointer to the garbage entry for the pushed start symbol. The default routine in *l.lib* does nothing, but you can use your own yy_init_llama(p) to provide an attribute for the goal symbol so that subsequent replacements won't inherit garbage. Your replacement should be put at the bottom of the **LLama** input file and should look something like this:

```
yy_init_llama( p )
yyvstype *p;
{
    p->left = p->right = initial attribute value for goal symbol;
}
```

The `yyvstype` type is a two-part structure used for the value-stack items described earlier.

The `yypstk()` routine used to print value-stack items in the debugging environment is passed a pointer to a value-stack item of type (a pointer to a `yyvstype` structure) and a string representing the symbol. You could print character-pointer attributes like this:

Printing the value-stack, `yypstk()`, `yyvstype`.

```
%{
typedef char *stack_type;    /* Use stack of character pointers.*/
#define YYSTYPE stack_type
%}
%%
    ...
%%
char *yypstk(tovs, tods)    /* Print attribute stack contents.*/
yyvstype *tovs;
char    *symbol;
{
    static char buf[64];
    sprintf(buf,"[%0.30s,%0.30s]", tovs->left, tovs->right);
    return buf;
}
```

E.12.4 The *llout.sym* File

LLama produces a symbol table file if the $-s$ or $-S$ switch is specified on the command line. Listing E.19 shows the symbol table produced by the input file at the end of this appendix.

Generating the symbol-table file, –s –S.

The first part of the file is the nonterminal symbols. Taking expr as characteristic, the entry looks like this:

```
expr (257)
    FIRST : NUM_OR_ID LP
    FOLLOW: RP SEMI
      2: expr -> term expr' ..................SELECT: NUM_OR_ID LP
```

The 257 is the symbol used to represent an expr on the parse stack, the next two lines are the FIRST and FOLLOW sets for expr. (These are present only if $-S$ was used to generate the table.) The next lines are all productions that have an expr on their left-hand side. The number (2, here) is the production number, and the list to the right is the LL(1) selection set for this production. The production number is useful for setting breakpoint on application of that production in the debugging environment.

If the production contains an action, a marker of the form { N } is put into the production in place of the action. All these action symbols are defined at the bottom of *llout.sym* (on lines 51 to 57 of the current file). Taking {0} as characteristic:

```
{0}   512, line 42 : {$1=$2=newname();}
```

The 512 is the number used to represent the action on the parse stack, the action was found on line 42 of the input file, and the remainder of the line is the first few characters of the action itself.

The middle part of the symbol table just defines tokens. The numbers here are the same numbers that are in *llout.h*, and these same values will be used to represent a token on the parse stack.

E.12.5 Sample **LLama** Input File

Listing E.20 is a small expression compiler in **LLama** format.

Listing E.19. A **LLama** Symbol Table

```
 1    --------------- Symbol table ------------------
 2
 3    NONTERMINAL SYMBOLS:
 4
 5    expr (257)
 6       FIRST : NUM_OR_ID LP
 7       FOLLOW: RP SEMI
 8         2: expr -> term expr' ..................SELECT: NUM_OR_ID LP
 9
10    expr' (259)
11       FIRST : PLUS <epsilon>
12       FOLLOW: RP SEMI
13         3: expr' -> PLUS {2} term {3} expr' .....SELECT: PLUS
14         4: expr' -> ...........................SELECT: RP SEMI
15
16    factor (260)
17       FIRST : NUM_OR_ID LP
18       FOLLOW: PLUS TIMES RP SEMI
19         8: factor -> NUM_OR_ID {6} ..............SELECT: NUM_OR_ID
20         9: factor -> LP expr RP .................SELECT: LP
21
22    stmt (256)   (goal symbol)
23       FIRST : NUM_OR_ID LP <epsilon>
24       FOLLOW: $
25         0: stmt -> ............................SELECT: $
26         1: stmt -> {0} expr {1} SEMI stmt .......SELECT: NUM_OR_ID LP
27
28    term (258)
29       FIRST : NUM_OR_ID LP
30       FOLLOW: PLUS RP SEMI
31         5: term -> factor term' .................SELECT: NUM_OR_ID LP
32
33    term' (261)
34       FIRST : TIMES <epsilon>
35       FOLLOW: PLUS RP SEMI
36         6: term' -> TIMES {4} factor {5} term' ..SELECT: TIMES
37         7: term' -> ...........................SELECT: PLUS RP SEMI
38
39    TERMINAL SYMBOLS:
40
41    name               value
42    LP                   4
43    NUM_OR_ID            3
44    PLUS                 1
45    RP                   5
46    SEMI                 6
47    TIMES                2
48
49    ACTION SYMBOLS:
50
51    {0}     512, line 42 : {$1=$2=newname();}
52    {1}     513, line 42 : {freename($0);}
53    {2}     514, line 48 : {$1=$2=newname();}
54    {3}     515, line 49 : { yy_code("%s+=%s\\n",$$,$0); freename($0); }
55    {4}     516, line 56 : {$1=$2=newname();}
56    {5}     517, line 57 : {yy_code("%s*=%s\\n",$$,$0); freename($0);}
57    {6}     518, line 61 : { yy_code("%s=%0.*s\\n",$$,yyleng,yytext); }
```

Listing E.20. *expr.lma*— An Expression Compiler (Llama Version)

```
 1  %term  PLUS              /*  +                                    */
 2         TIMES             /*  *                                    */
 3  %term  NUM_OR_ID         /*  a number or identifier              */
 4  %term  LP                /*  (                                    */
 5  %term  RP                /*  )                                    */
 6  %term  SEMI              /*  ;                                    */
 7
 8  %{
 9      /*------------------------------------------------------------
10       * Rvalue names are stored on a stack. name() pops a name off the stack and
11       * freename(x) puts it back. A real compiler would do some checking for
12       * stack overflow here but there's no point in cluttering the code for now.
13       */
14
15      char *Namepool[] =
16      {
17          "t0", "t1", "t2", "t3", "t4", "t5", "t6", "t7", "t8", "t9"
18      };
19      char **Namep = Namepool ;
20
21      char *newname()          { return(*Namep++);      }
22      char *freename( char *x) { return(*--Namep = x); }
23
24      extern char *yytext;
25      extern int  yyleng;
26
27      #define YYSTYPE char*
28  %}
29
30  %synch SEMI RP
31
32  %%
33  /* A small expression grammar that recognizes numbers, names, addition (+),
34   * multiplication (*), and parentheses. Expressions associate left to right
35   * unless parentheses force it to go otherwise. * is higher precedence than +
36   */
37
38  stmt    :          /* eps */
39          |          {$1=$2=newname();} expr {freename($0);} SEMI stmt
40          ;
41
42  expr    :          term expr'
43          ;
44
45  expr'   :          PLUS {$1=$2=newname();} term
46                        { yy_code("%s+=%s\n",$$,$0); freename($0); } expr'
47          |          /* epsilon */
48          ;
49
50  term    :          factor term'
51          ;
52
53  term'   :          TIMES {$1=$2=newname();} factor
54                        {yy_code("%s*=%s\n",$$,$0); freename($0);} term'
55          |          /* epsilon */
56          ;
57
```

```
58    factor  :         NUM_OR_ID { yy_code("%s=%0.*s\n",$$,yyleng,yytext); }
59            |         LP expr RP
60            ;
61    %%
62    /*----------------------------------------------------------*/
63
64    yy_init_llama( p )
65    yyvstype *p;
66    {
67        p->left = p->right = "-" ;
68    }
69
70    char *yypstk(tovs, tods)
71    yyvstype *tovs;
72    char      *tods;
73    {
74        static char buf[128];
75        sprintf(buf,"[%s,%s]", tovs->left, tovs->right);
76        return buf;
77    }
78
79    main( argc, argv )
80    char      **argv;
81    {
82        yy_get_args( argc, argv );
83        yyparse();
84        exit( 0 );
85    }
```

F

A C-code Summary

This appendix summarizes all the C-code directives described in depth in Chapter Six. Many of the tables in that chapter are also found here.

Figure F.1. The C-code Virtual Machine

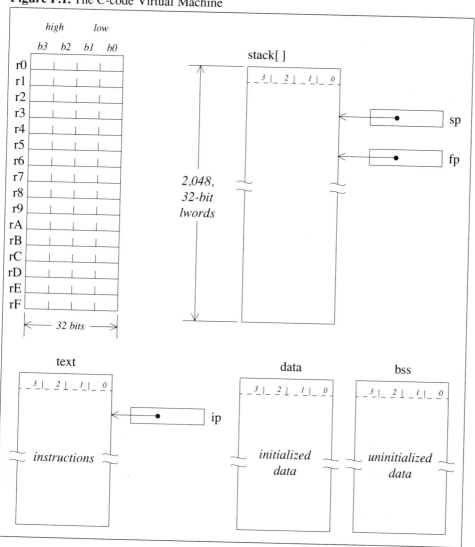

Table F.1. Registers

r*N*	General-purpose register (r0, r1,..., r9, rA, ..., rF).
sp	Stack pointer.
fp	Frame pointer.
ip	Instruction pointer.
r*N*.pp	Access 32-bit register as pointer to something. Must use an addressing mode to specify type of object pointed to.
r*N*.w.high	Access word in high 16-bits of register.
r*N*.w.low	Access word in low 16-bits of register.
r*N*.b.b3	Access most significant byte of register (MSB).
r*N*.b.b2	Access low byte of high word.
r*N*.b.b1	Access high byte of low word.
r*N*.b.b0	Access least significant byte of register (LSB).

Table F.2. Types, Storage Classes, and Declarations

Types	
byte	8-bit
array	(alias for byte—used to declare pointers to arrays)
record	(alias for byte—used to declare structures)
word	16-bit
lword	32-bit
ptr	generic pointer
Storage classes	
private	Space is allocated for the variable, but the variable can not be accessed from outside the current file.
public	Space is allocated for the variable, and the variable can be accessed from any file in the current program. It is illegal for two public variables to have the same name, even if they are declared in separate files.
external	Space for this variable is allocated elsewhere. There must be a public or common definition for the variable in some other file.
common	Space for this variable is allocated by the linker. If a variable with a given name is declared common in one module and public in another, then the public definition takes precedence. If there are nothing but common definitions for a variable, then the linker allocates space for that variable in the bss segment.
Declarations	
class type name;	Variable of indicated *type* and storage *class*.
class type name [*size*];	Array of indicated *type* and storage *class*; *size* is optional if initialized with C-style initializer.
All declarations in the *data* segment <u>must</u> be initialized using a C-style initializer. Nonetheless, pointers may not be initialized with string constants, only with the address of a previously-declared variable. Declarations in the *bss* segment <u>may</u> <u>not</u> be initialized.	

Index

Cross Reference by Symbol

All entries take the following form:

`symbol_name`   listing(line) *file*, page

The page number is the page on which the listing starts, not the one on which the specified line is found.

_8086	A.1(14) *debug.h*, 681	ALLOC_CLS	6.22(7,9) *symtab.h*, 488
Abort	4.8(102) *yydebug.c*, 243	alnum	D.5(12) *c.lex*, 829
ACCEPT	2.39(31) *dfa.h*, 125	alnum	6.37(40) *c.lex*, 519
access_with()	6.85(460) *op.c*, 614	alnum	5.6(6) *expr.lex*, 384
ACT	5.22(62) *yystate.c*, 413	alnum	5.6(5) *expr.lex*, 384
ACT_FILE	4.20(100) *parser.h*, 277	alpha	D.6(11) *yyout.h*, 832
ACTION	4.18(2) *llout.h*, 276	AND	6.94(654) *op.c*, 626
Actions	5.22(64) *yystate.c*, 413	and()	D.6(14) *yyout.h*, 832
ACT_TEMPL	4.20(106) *parser.h*, 277	ANDAND	A.1(13) *debug.h*, 681
Actual_lineno	2.22(16) *globals.h*, 87	ANSI	6.23(34) *symtab.h*, 491
ADD()	A.4(67) *set.h*, 696	ARRAY	A.4(41) *set.h*, 696
add_action()	5.23(113) *yystate.c*, 413	_ASSIGN	A.4(46) *set.h*, 696
add_case()	6.109(43) *switch.c*, 650	ASSIGN()	6.90(571) *op.c*, 621
addch()	A.70(63) *curses.h*, 784	assignment()	D.6(50) *yyout.h*, 832
add_declarator()	6.29(182) *symtab.c*, 501	ASSIGNOP	4.26(49) *acts.c*, 290
add_default_case()	6.109(64) *switch.c*, 650	Associativity	A.35(3) *assort.c*, 743
add_goto()	5.23(157) *yystate.c*, 413	assort()	A.83(25) *wincreat.c*, 794
add_lookahead()	5.29(928) *yystate.c*, 425	Attrib	4.8(138) *yydebug.c*, 243
addreductions()	5.30(958) *yystate.c*, 431	Attr_pix	6.32(393) *symtab.c*, 504
addr_of()	6.83(270) *op.c*, 606	attr_str()	6.27(173) *symtab.h*, 497
_addset()	A.6(80) *set.c*, 702	ATYPE	2.48(21) *pairs.c*, 143
add_spec_to_decl()	6.45(102) *decl.c*, 537	ATYPE	2.47(8) *print_ar.c*, 142
addstr()	A.70(66) *curses.h*, 784	ATYPE	6.24(50) *symtab.h*, 492
addsym()	A.16(59) *hash.c*, 718	AUTO	A.68(12) *glue.c*, 772
add_symbols_to_table()	6.48(154) *decl.c*, 539	AUTOSELECT	5.24(197) *yystate.c*, 416
add_synch()	4.26(628) *acts.c*, 290	Available	6.9(46) *virtual.h*, 465
add_synch()	4.26(690) *acts.c*, 290	B	A.42(15) *termlib.h*, 754
add_to_dstates()	2.41(119) *dfa.c*, 129	BGND()	6.99(762) *op.c*, 630
add_to_rhs()	4.26(488) *acts.c*, 290	binary_op()	A.27(5) *bintoasc.c*, 731
add_unfinished()	5.25(267) *yystate.c*, 418	bin_to_ascii()	6.19(80) *virtual.h*, 475
ADJ_VAL()	4.20(74) *parser.h*, 277	BIT()	A.4(4) *set.h*, 696
advance()	1.3(87) *lex.c*, 17	_BITS_IN_WORD	A.42(5) *termlib.h*, 754
advance()	4.25(38) *llpar.c*, 285	BLACK	A.42(21) *termlib.h*, 754
advance()	2.28(392) *nfa.c*, 97	BLINKING	A.42(6) *termlib.h*, 754
ALIGN()	6.7(44) *virtual.h*, 462	BLUE	4.25(124) *llpar.c*, 285
ALIGN_WORST	6.8(11) *c-code.h*, 462	body()	A.42(22) *termlib.h*, 754
ALLOC	6.33(10) *c.y*, 509	BOLD	A.70(19) *curses.h*, 784
ALLOC	A.58(1) *dv_scree.c*, 765	bool	A.71(49) *box.h*, 787
ALLOCATE	2.52(10) *lex.c*, 155	BOT	2.20(27) *nfa.h*, 85
ALLOCATE	2.38(147) *terp.c*, 120	BOTH	A.73(3) *box.c*, 788
		box()	

Tear out this card and fill
in all necessary information.
Then enclose this card with
your check or money order
only in an envelope and
mail to:

Software Engineering Consultants
Compiler Design in C
P.O.Box 5679
Berkeley, California 94705

Please send the following. PAYMENT ENCLOSED
(check or money order drawn on a U.S. bank only):

Software for *Compiler Design in C*, including binaries
and sources. Requires an IBM-PC or compatible with 640K
RAM; hard disk suggested. Sources are UNIX compatible.

_____ copies, 5-1/4" disk, at $60.00 _____

_____ copies, 3-1/2" disk, at $60.00 _____

Total for software _____

Local sales tax (California residents only) _____

Total enclosed _____

☐ Check here for information about site licenses for educational institutions only.

This is your shipping label. Please print or type.

Ship to: _____

_____

_____

_____

_____